Urbanisation and State Formation in the Ancient Sahara and Beyond

The themes of sedentarisation, urbanisation and state formation are fundamental ones in the archaeology of many diverse parts of the world. Hitherto these concepts have been little explored in relation to early societies of the Saharan zone. Discussion of these issues in relation to the precocious civilisations that bordered the vast North African desert has rarely considered the possibility that they were interconnected by long-range contacts and knowledge networks. The orthodox opinion of many of the key oasis zones within the Sahara is that they were not created before the early Medieval period and the Islamic conquest of Mediterranean North Africa. Major claims of this volume are that the ultimate origins of oasis settlements in many parts of the Sahara were considerably earlier, that by the first millennium AD some of these oasis settlements were of a size and complexity to merit the categorisation 'towns' and that a few exceptional examples were focal centres within proto-states or early state-level societies.

MARTIN STERRY is Honorary Research Fellow at Durham University. His research on the archaeology of the Sahara and North Africa makes particular use of GIS and remote sensing. He has undertaken fieldwork on various projects in Italy, Britain, Libya and most recently southern Morocco, where he is co-director of the Middle Draa Project. He has published many articles on the Libyan Fazzan, Saharan trade, urbanisation and oasis settlements.

DAVID J. MATTINGLY is Professor of Roman Archaeology at the University of Leicester. He has worked in the Sahara for forty years and is the author of many books and articles related to Saharan archaeology, such as *Farming the Desert* (2 vols, 1996), which won the James R. Wiseman book award of the American Institute of Archaeology, and *The Archaeology of Fazzan* series (4 vols, 2003–2013). He was the principal investigator of the European Research Council-funded Trans-SAHARA Project (2011–2017) which created the groundwork for this volume, and he is the overall series editor of *Trans-Saharan Archaeology*, in which this is the third of four projected volumes.

THE TRANS-SAHARAN ARCHAEOLOGY SERIES

Series Editor
D. J. Mattingly

Trade in the Ancient Sahara and Beyond
Edited by D. J. Mattingly, V. Leitch, C. N. Duckworth, A. Cuénod, M. Sterry and F. Cole

Burials, Migration and Identity in the Ancient Sahara and Beyond
Edited by M. C. Gatto, D. J. Mattingly, N. Ray and M. Sterry

Urbanisation and State Formation in the Ancient Sahara and Beyond
Edited by M. Sterry and D. J. Mattingly

Forthcoming:
Mobile Technologies in the Ancient Sahara and Beyond
Edited by C. N. Duckworth, A. Cuénod and D. J. Mattingly

Urbanisation and State Formation in the Ancient Sahara and Beyond

Edited by

MARTIN STERRY
Durham University

DAVID J. MATTINGLY
University of Leicester

Trans-Saharan Archaeology Volume 3
Series Editor:
David J. Mattingly

European Research Council
Established by the European Commission

The Society for Libyan Studies

CAMBRIDGE
UNIVERSITY PRESS

CAMBRIDGE
UNIVERSITY PRESS

University Printing House, Cambridge CB2 8BS, United Kingdom

One Liberty Plaza, 20th Floor, New York, NY 10006, USA

477 Williamstown Road, Port Melbourne, VIC 3207, Australia

314–321, 3rd Floor, Plot 3, Splendor Forum, Jasola District Centre,
New Delhi – 110025, India

79 Anson Road, #06–04/06, Singapore 079906

Cambridge University Press is part of the University of Cambridge.

It furthers the University's mission by disseminating knowledge in the pursuit of education, learning, and research at the highest international levels of excellence.

www.cambridge.org
Information on this title: www.cambridge.org/9781108494441
DOI: 10.1017/9781108637978

First published 2020

Printed in the United Kingdom by TJ International Ltd. Padstow Cornwall

A catalogue record for this publication is available from the British Library.

Library of Congress Cataloging-in-Publication Data
Names: Sterry, Martin, editor. | Mattingly, D. J., editor.
Title: Urbanisation and state formation in the ancient Sahara and beyond / edited by M. Sterry, Durham University, D.J. Mattingly, University of Leicester.
Description: Cambridge, United Kingdom ; New York, NY : Cambridge University Press, 2020. | Series: Trans-Saharan archaeology ; volume 3 | Includes bibliographical references.
Identifiers: LCCN 2019039763 (print) | LCCN 2019039764 (ebook) | ISBN 9781108494441 (hardback) | ISBN 9781108637978 (ebook)
Subjects: LCSH: Cities and towns – Africa, Sub-Saharan – History – To 1500. | Human settlements – Africa, Sub-Saharan – History – To 1500. | City-states – Africa, Sub-Saharan – History – To 1500. | Africa, Sub-Saharan – History. | Africa, North – History.
Classification: LCC HT114 .U728 2020 (print) | LCC HT114 (ebook) | DDC 307.760967–dc23
LC record available at https://lccn.loc.gov/2019039763
LC ebook record available at https://lccn.loc.gov/2019039764

ISBN 978-1-108-49444-1 Hardback

Contents

Figures

Tables

Contributors

Muftah al-Haddad is Professor at the University of Azzaytuna, Tarhuna, Libya.

Youssef Bokbot is Professor at the National Institute for Archaeological Sciences and Heritage (INSAP), Morocco.

Anna Lucille Boozer is Associate Professor at Baruch College, New York.

Maria Carme Belarte is Research Professor at ICREA, Barcelona (Spain), and researcher at the Catalan Institute of Classical Archaeology (ICAC), Tarragona (Spain).

Chloé Capel is Post-Doctoral Researcher at the Université Paris I.

David N. Edwards is Lecturer in the School of Archaeology and Ancient History, University of Leicester.

Francisco José Cantero is Research Associate at the University of Barcelona.

Nabil Kallala is Emeritus Professor at the University of Tunis and the former President of the Institut national du patrimoine (INP), Tunisia.

Dani López is a carpologist at ArqueoVitis SCCL and Research Associate at the University of Barcelona.

Kevin C. MacDonald is Professor of African Archaeology at the Institute of Archaeology, London.

Susan Keech McIntosh is Herbert S. Autrey Professor of Anthropology at Rice University, Houston, Texas.

Carlos Magnavita is Research Fellow in the Frobenius Institute, Goethe-University Frankfurt.

David J. Mattingly is Professor in the School of Archaeology and Ancient History, University of Leicester.

Stefania Merlo is Senior Lecturer at Witwatersrand University, South Africa.

Lucia Mori is Assistant Professor in the Department of Classics, Sapienza University of Rome.

Sam Nixon is Curator and Head of Africa Section at the British Museum.

Marta Portillo is EU Horizon 2020 Marie Sklodowska-Curie Fellow, Department of Archaeology, University of Reading.

Joan Ramon is Research Associate at the University of Barcelona.

Louise Rayne is Research Associate on the Endangered Archaeology Project in the School of Archaeology and Ancient History, University of Leicester.

Joan Sanmartí is Professor in the Department of History and Archaeology, University of Barcelona.

Judith Scheele is Director of Studies at the École des hautes études en sciences sociales (EHESS), Marseille.

Martin Sterry is Honorary Research Fellow in the Department of Archaeology, Durham University.

Pol Trousset is Emeritus Researcher of the Centre Camille Julian, Aix-en-Provence.

Sílvia Valenzuela is Principal Researcher ERC-StG ZooMWest, Consejo Superior de Investigaciones Científicas (CSIC), Barcelona.

Andrew Wilson is Professor of Archaeology of the Roman Empire, University of Oxford.

Preface

When I was working on my PhD thesis on the Roman province of Tripolitania (north-west Libya) in the early 1980s, I became intrigued by a desert people who inhabited Fazzan, the area of the Central Sahara to the south of Tripolitania. This was my first introduction to the Garamantes. They were regularly mentioned in the ancient Greek and Roman sources, though seldom in complimentary terms – for the most part being depicted as nomadic and uncouth barbarians.[1] However, some pioneering archaeological work in the 1930s and then again in the 1960s–1970s had revealed their physical traces to be considerably more sophisticated than would be assumed on the basis of the literary stereotypes.[2]

This volume arises out of my subsequent direct engagement across more than 20 years now with the archaeology of Fazzan. In 1996, I was given the chance to renew field research in what were effectively the Garamantian heartlands. Following an initial scoping visit that year, I directed the Fazzan Project across six years, carrying out excavations and survey around the capital of the Garamantes at Garama (Old Jarma), with an emphasis on tracing evidence for their settlements, but also mapping other archaeological features including cemeteries and irrigation systems.[3] A notable result of this work was the clear demonstration of the sophisticated and substantial network of oasis farming settlements that lay at the heart of the Garamantian territory. Rather than being 'nomadic barbarians', the Garamantes now appear to have been predominantly sedentary oasis farmers, living in substantial permanent and complex settlements of mudbrick buildings. That is not to say that the Garamantes did not also incorporate pastoral elements, as will be further discussed at various points below, but simply to highlight the unexpected density and sophistication of sedentary oasis settlements. There

[1] See in particular, Mattingly 2003, 79–81; 2011, 34–37 on the concept of 'progressive barbarisation' imposed by ancient authors as a factor of distance from the Mediterranean.

[2] Ayoub 1967; Daniels 1968; 1970; 1971; 1989; Pace *et al.* 1951.

[3] There were five seasons of fieldwork (1997–2001) and a finds study season (2002). The results are now fully published as Mattingly 2003; 2007; 2010; 2013 (now free to download from the Society for Libyan Studies website). Funding for the Fazzan Project came primarily from the Society for Libyan Studies, the Leverhulme Trust, the British Academy and the Arts and Humanities Research Council.

is strong evidence to identify the top level of their settlement hierarchy as 'urban' in character and their overall society as an early Saharan state.[4] The prime aim of this volume is to evaluate those claims in a broader geographical and chronological framework.

My work on the Garamantes has subsequently evolved through a series of further projects. Between 2007 and 2011, I directed the Desert Migrations Project, with a particular focus on Garamantian burials and funerary traditions.[5] The increasing availability of high resolution satellite imagery opened a new avenue of research in 2011, the Peopling the Desert project, which extended research on the Garamantes to another of the major oasis bands in Fazzan, the Murzuq depression.[6] Another survey on the oasis of Ghadamis in Western Libya was cut short by the Libyan civil war in 2011 and it has so far been impossible to complete that work. The Trans-SAHARA Project (2011–2017) marked a further evolution of this body of work, seeking to place the Garamantes in their Saharan context and to address the wider implications of the results obtained in the earlier work.[7] As part of the Trans-SAHARA project, although unable to return to Libya for fieldwork, we continued to work closely with Libyan colleagues – who followed up with ground visits to sites we identified through satellite image analysis. This has contributed to a number of specific studies of historic oasis clusters that are reported on below. We also commenced a new phase of work on early oases in the Wadi Draa area of southern Morocco (see below, Chapter 6). The widening of our field of investigation has been hugely beneficial to our thinking about the Garamantes.

One of the major obstacles hindering understanding of the Sahara through history is that the study of the desert and the neighbouring zones of North Africa, the Nile Valley, Sudan and West Africa has tended to be compartmentalised into chronologically or regionally specific investigations. Broader synthesis across the vast Trans-Saharan zone has been lacking. The term 'Trans-Saharan' should be understood in the context of this book as referring to the connected spaces of the Sahara and its eastern, northern and southern peripheries. The Sahara has often been likened to a great sea and no sea can be understood without reference to its adjacent

[4] Mattingly 2013, 530–34; Mattingly and Sterry 2013.

[5] Five planned seasons of fieldwork were completed by 2011, but the scheduled study season could not take place in 2012 because of the Libyan civil war. Interim reports have been published in *Libyan Studies* from 2007 to 2011, Mattingly *et al.* 2007; 2008; 2009; 2010a; 2010b; 2011a. Funding for the Desert Migrations Project came primarily from the Society for Libyan Studies.

[6] Sterry and Mattingly 2011; 2013; Sterry *et al.* 2012. The Peopling the Desert Project was funded by the Leverhulme Trust.

[7] The Trans-SAHARA project was funded by the European Research Council (grant no. 269418).

shore-lands. The idea of Trans-Saharan perspectives on historical developments thus shares much in common with recent studies of the Mediterranean, which have stressed the importance of connectivity and supra-regional influences.[8]

The work of the Trans-SAHARA project was organised around a series of four workgroups, each one supported by early career post-doctoral research associates and each dealing with a discrete group of themes: trade; migration, burial practice and identity; mobile technologies; urbanisation and state formation. As a key element of the work programme, a workshop was held at Leicester for each of the workgroups, to which international scholars working on neighbouring areas of the Trans-Saharan zone were invited. From the outset, these workshops were conceived as offering a chance to engage a group of leading experts in the field in a high-level debate about the implications of the new information on the Garamantes for studies of the wider Trans-Saharan world. Papers were commissioned for an intended series of agenda-setting volumes on Trans-Saharan Archaeology and pre-circulated so that the workshop sessions focused entirely on discussion of their content. The volumes in this series are thus unusual edited books in that each one has at its core an extended and detailed presentation of the key results of the Trans-SAHARA research team's work, combined with the comparative perspectives of invited external experts. As the Cambridge University Press reviewers of the volumes have noted, in the interests of promoting debate we also invited critique and contradiction from these external specialists. We think that adds to the special character of the resulting books, integrating new evidence with a broad overview of the state of the field and combining agenda-setting ideas with different perspectives.

This third volume in the resulting series of four, thus presents some of the key work of the Trans-SAHARA team and an international pool of collaborators on the themes of urbanisation and state formation. The territorial expanse of the Trans-Saharan zone is vast and, given the hostile climate and environment of the Sahara across the last 5,000 years, it is perhaps unsurprising that scholarly research has become regionally segmented. Archaeologists have most commonly self-identified with one of the great civilisations bordering the Sahara: the Classical or Medieval Maghrib, the Nilotic civilisations or the precocious polities of West Africa. Saharan historical archaeologists have been fewer in number, vastly outnumbered by prehistorians (and especially the

[8] Abulafia 2011; Broodbank 2013; Horden and Purcell 2000. See Lichtenberger 2016 for the explicit comparison of Mediterranean and Sahara.

devotees of rock art). The Trans-Saharan archaeology series seeks to explore the interconnections across this zone in new ways, bringing together archaeologists, anthropologists and historians from different regions, varied academic traditions and multiple time periods and cultural phases.[9] The volumes are designed to reassess traditional assumptions about the history and archaeology of the zone, to present and assess alternative hypotheses and to set a fresh agenda for future studies. The Sahara has for too long been seen as a vast empty space, separating and keeping apart areas of precocious state formation and urbanisation along the Nile valley, in the Mediterranean zone of Libya and the Maghrib, in Sub-Saharan territories around Lake Chad and the West African Niger Bend area. Recent archaeological studies have started to cast doubt on this for certain parts of the Sahara and it seems an appropriate time to review the larger picture of pre-Islamic and early Islamic developments across this entire zone.

As we are asking our readers to often step outside their core areas of knowledge and expertise to engage with material from other parts of the Trans-Saharan zone, place names and their mapping have exercised us all. Systems of transliteration and spelling of place names across the Trans-Saharan region vary enormously and the same site can be presented in several distinct ways. We have tried to impose a measure of consistency in the transliteration of names, following the practice I adopted for the *Archaeology of Fazzan* series. However, for ease of recognition some exceptions have been allowed for sites whose canonical spelling is so well established in the literature. We trust that the maps provided will prove helpful with the identification of places named in the text, but hope that readers will share our sense of being on a journey of discovery as they read the following contributions. Most of the site mapping on satellite imagery is the work of Martin Sterry. Thanks are also due to Mike Hawkes for the production or revision of many other line drawings in the volume.

David Mattingly

References

Abulafia, D. 2011. *The Great Sea: A Human History of the Mediterranean*. London: Allen Lane.

[9] This book is a prime output of an Advanced Grant (269418) awarded by the European Research Council, the Trans-SAHARA Project (principal investigator David Mattingly at the University of Leicester) 2011–2017.

Ayoub, M.S. 1967. *Excavations in Germa between 1962 and 1966*. Tripoli: Ministry of Education.

Broodbank, C. 2013. *The Making of the Middle Sea. A History of the Mediterranean from the Beginning to the Emergence of the Classical World*. London: Thames and Hudson.

Daniels, C.M. 1968. Garamantian excavations: Zinchecra 1965–67. *Libya Antiqua* 5: 113–94.

Daniels, C.M. 1970. *The Garamantes of Southern Libya*. London: Oleander.

Daniels, C.M. 1971. The Garamantes of Fezzan. In F.F. Gadallah (ed.), *Libya in History*. Benghazi: University of Libya, 261–87.

Daniels, C.M. 1989. Excavation and fieldwork amongst the Garamantes. *Libyan Studies* 20: 45–61.

Horden, P. and Purcell, N. 2000. *The Corrupting Sea: A Study of Mediterranean History*. Oxford: Blackwell.

Lichtenberger, A. 2016. 'Sea without water' – Conceptualising the Sahara and the Mediterranean. In M. Dabag, D. Haller, N. Jaspert and A. Lichtenberger (eds), *New Horizons. Mediterranean Research in the 21st Century*. Paderborn: Ferdinand Schoningh, 267–83.

Mattingly, D.J. (ed.). 2003. *The Archaeology of Fazzan. Volume 1, Synthesis*. London: Society for Libyan Studies, Department of Antiquities.

Mattingly, D.J. (ed.). 2007. *The Archaeology of Fazzan. Volume 2, Site Gazetteer, Pottery and Other Survey Finds*. London: Society for Libyan Studies, Department of Antiquities.

Mattingly, D.J. (ed.). 2010. *The Archaeology of Fazzan. Volume 3, Excavations Carried out by C.M. Daniels*. London: Society for Libyan Studies, Department of Antiquities.

Mattingly, D.J., 2011. *Imperialism, Power and Identity Experiencing the Roman Empire*. Princeton: Princeton University Press.

Mattingly, D.J. (ed.). 2013. *The Archaeology of Fazzan. Volume 4, Survey and Excavations at Old Jarma (Ancient Garama) Carried out by C.M. Daniels (1962–69) and the Fazzan Project (1997–2001)*. London: Society for Libyan Studies, Department of Antiquities.

Mattingly, D.J. and Sterry, M. 2013. The first towns in the Central Sahara. *Antiquity* 87.366: 503–18.

Mattingly, D.J., Lahr, M., Armitage, S., Barton, H., Dore, J., Drake, N., Foley, R., Merlo, S., Salem, M., Stock, J. and White, K. 2007. Desert Migrations: People, environment and culture in the Libyan Sahara. *Libyan Studies* 38: 115–56.

Mattingly, D.J., Dore, J. and Lahr, M. (with contributions by others) 2008. DMP II: 2008 fieldwork on burials and identity in the Wadi al-Ajal. *Libyan Studies* 39: 223–62.

Mattingly, D.J., Lahr, M. and Wilson, A. 2009. DMP V: Investigations in 2009 of cemeteries and related sites on the west side of the Taqallit promontory. *Libyan Studies* 40: 95–131.

Mattingly, D.J., Abduli, H., Aburgheba, H., Ahmed, M., Ali Ahmed Esmaia, M., Baker, S., Cole, F., Fenwick, C., Gonzalez Rodriguez, M., Hobson, M., Khalaf, N., Lahr, M., Leitch, V., Moussa, F., Nikita, E., Parker, D., Radini, A., Ray, N., Savage, T., Sterry, M. and Schörle, K. 2010a. DMP IX: Summary report on the fourth season of excavations of the Burials and Identity team. *Libyan Studies* 41: 89–104.

Mattingly, D.J., Al-Aghab, S., Ahmed, M., Moussa, F., Sterry, M. and Wilson, A.I. 2010b. DMP X: Survey and landscape conservation issues around the Taqallit headland. *Libyan Studies* 41: 105–32.

Mattingly, D.J., Abduli, H., Ahmed, M., Cole, F., Fenwick, C., Gonzalez Rodriguez, M., Fothergill, B.T., Hobson, M., Khalaf, N., Lahr, M., Moussa, F., Nikita, E., Nikolaus, J., Radini, A., Ray, N., Savage, T., Sterry, M. and Wilson, A.I. 2011. DMP XII: Excavations and survey of the so-called Garamantian Royal Cemetery (GSC030–031). *Libyan Studies* 42: 89–102.

Pace, B., Sergi, S. and Caputo, G. 1951. Scavi sahariani. *Monumenti Antichi* 41: 150–549.

Sterry, M. and Mattingly, D.J. 2011. DMP XIII: Reconnaissance survey of archaeological sites in the Murzuq area. *Libyan Studies* 42: 103–16.

Sterry, M. and Mattingly, D.J. 2013. Desert Migrations Project XVII: Further AMS dates for historic settlements from Fazzan, South-West Libya. *Libyan Studies* 44: 127–40.

Sterry, M., Mattingly, D.J. and Higham, T. 2012. Desert Migrations Project XVI: Radiocarbon dates from the Murzuq region, Southern Libya. *Libyan Studies* 43: 137–47.

PART I

Introduction

1 Introduction to the Themes of Sedentarisation, Urbanisation and State Formation in the Ancient Sahara and Beyond

DAVID J. MATTINGLY AND MARTIN STERRY

Introduction

This volume explores a series of linked themes that have wide relevance in world archaeology: sedentarisation, urbanisation and state formation. In this opening chapter we review some of the key background to recent debate on these themes and identify some of the Saharan particularities which complicate the application of models developed elsewhere.

A dominant discourse on the Sahara throughout history has been the idea of a 'nomad menace', coupled with a persistent emphasis on the Sahara as largely uninhabited and uninhabitable.[1] It is true that pastoralism has at all times been a key mode of life and mobile populations have underpinned the development of networks variously used for trade and raiding.[2] Yet the lifestyle and inter-relations of mobile peoples of the historic Sahara, such as the Tuareg, have always been contingent to a greater or lesser extent on the existence of sedentary communities, both within the Sahara and at its fringes. A second dominant discourse of the modern era has been the assumption of dependence of African societies on exogenous contact and colonisation in order to achieve social evolution.[3] Both of these discourses need to be challenged and re-evaluated in the light of recent advances in archaeological knowledge.

A third key issue concerns the chronology of key developments within the historic Saharan world – the emergence of trade and networks of

[1] Rachet 1970 for an extreme example of the tendency.

[2] Cf. *inter alia*, Nicolaisen and Nicolaisen 1997; Shaw 1983.

[3] Gsell 1972a; 1972b, 1–11 for a classic characterisation of North Africa and the impact of Phoenician colonisation. Even in more recent appraisals, there remains a reluctance among modern scholars to recognise the degree of sedentarism present in Maghrib and Sahara prior to the coming of Carthage and Rome, Desanges 1980. See also Mattingly 2011a; 2016, for a fuller analysis.

connectivity, the movements of people and the cultural connections between them (including shared elements of a common Saharan cultural *koine*), the technological inventions and transfers within the zone and the emergence of sedentary oasis communities. These have commonly been viewed as only really taking off after the Islamic conquest of northern Africa. A prime contention of the Trans-SAHARA project is that the ultimate origins must be sought much earlier in the Protohistoric period. This volume follows already published monographs dealing with early trade in the Sahara[4] and burials, migration and identity.[5] The trade volume highlighted a much greater level of Saharan connectivity and inter-regional contacts in the pre-Islamic era. While incontrovertible evidence for commerce remains elusive (and impossible to quantify), this is not least because so much Saharan trade has involved organic items or high value commodities like gold and ivory that are under-represented in the archaeological record. However, archaeometrical analyses now provide us with a 'smoking gun' effect, connecting, for example, some Sub-Saharan metal artefacts with Mediterranean metal sources. Similarly, the review of burial practices and the isotopic signatures obtained from human remains highlighted a high degree of mobility and motion in the pre-Islamic Sahara. The final Trans-Saharan Archaeology volume covers questions relating to mobile technologies and likewise supports the conclusion of the other volumes that the Sahara was a much more populated and developed space in the Protohistoric period.[6] This volume completes the thematic review, by focusing on settlements and what they contribute to our understanding of Saharan societies. Each volume stands on its own, of course, but they are also part of an interlocking meta-analysis and frequent reference will be made in the following pages to contributions to the other volumes in the series.

The first part of this book focuses on the evidence for the early development of oases in different parts of the Sahara, as well as considering to what extent the largest or most complex oasis settlements merit identification as 'urban'. In this volume we talk of a Protohistoric period of Saharan history and archaeology with proposed dates of *c.*1000 BC–650 AD.[7]

[4] Mattingly *et al.* 2017a. [5] Gatto *et al.* 2019. [6] Duckworth *et al.* Forthcoming.

[7] We prefer a more defined Protohistoric period which sits between the Pastoral/Late Neolithic periods and the Medieval period. It is characterised by a range of societal and technological changes (e.g. metalworking, cereal agriculture and sedentary settlements). We generally avoid pre-Islamic as the uncritical use of this term ignores the varied and important processes by which different communities chose to convert (or not) to Islam during the Medieval period. We acknowledge, however, the longstanding use of the terms 'pre-Islamic' and 'Islamic' which many of our authors choose to keep. These can be helpful for distinguishing specific practices that are

In a concluding discussion at the end of the first section (Chapter 8), we draw together some ideas about what sort of models of urbanism are applicable to the ancient Saharan context.

The second section of the book then turns to a series of regional case studies from lands bordering the Sahara to look at the urban development of neighbouring societies and evidence of early state formation. The evidence of early Islamic urbanisation and oasis formation is also reviewed in detail, not least because much previous work on Saharan oases has focused on sites of this period.[8] A final concluding chapter returns to the nature of political and social complexity in desert environments and the vexed question of whether it is justifiable to identify states in the Sahara itself in antiquity. As a result of our detailed work on their heartlands in southern Libya, the Garamantes are a prime subject of interest, but the contributors to this volume also consider evidence from other times or places for complex levels of social organisation.

Sedentarisation and the Creation of Oases

In the Sahara proper, sedentarisation is synonymous with the emergence of oases (Fig. 1.1). The oasis is a fundamental aspect of the Sahara, engrained in public perceptions of the desert.[9] One of the most enduring popular perceptions of the oasis is the perennial lake in the midst of sand dunes ringed by a thin band of vegetation – the equivalent of small uninhabited islands for ship-wrecked mariners. Though such extraordinary locations do exist outside mirages (Fig. 1.2), they are rare and exotic exceptions. Oases are more commonly well frequented places with more vegetation and accessible water, if often less available as surface lakes and streams than the archetypal image.[10] The derivation of the term 'oasis' (*ouhat*) is very ancient, going back to Pharaonic times and seeming to denote the specific location of the closest oases to the Nile. The term in ancient Egyptian also meant a 'large open cauldron', which correlates with the typical physical setting of those

antithetical to Muslim practices such as the construction of burial cairns (although even here the division is perhaps not as binary as is often suggested).

[8] See in particular, Capel, Chapter 16; MacDonald, Chapter 13; McIntosh, Chapter 14; Nixon, Chapter 17, this volume. Also recent publications by Aillet *et al.* 2017 (Sedrata); Messier and Miller 2015 (Sijilmasa).

[9] For conventional accounts of the Sahara and its oases, see *inter alia*, Gautier 1970; Laureano 1991; Sèbe 1989; Sèbe and Sèbe 2003; Villiers and Hirtle 2002.

[10] On the definition of oases, see now Purdue *et al.* 2018b, especially 12–13.

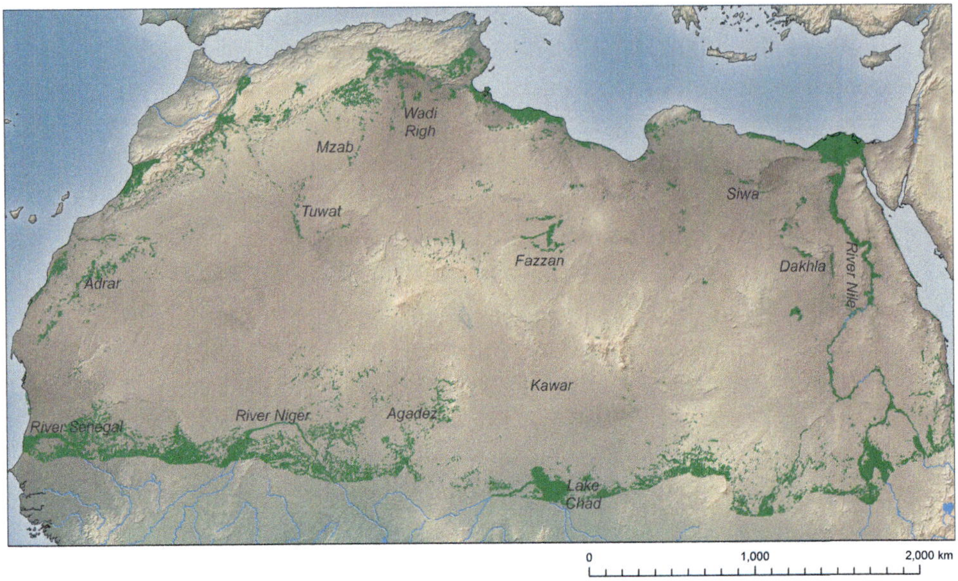

Figure 1.1. Map of the principal oasis groups and areas of modern vegetation (as identified from a MODIS NDVI) in hyper-arid and arid areas of the Sahara.

oases within depressions.[11] Despite, or perhaps because of, the early origin of the term, oases have no universal agreed definition. This is not normally a problem, they are so distinct from surrounding desert that a 'know it when you see it' attitude works for almost all case studies. However, when encompassing a view across the whole of the Sahara and ranging into areas of pre-desert, Sahel and river valleys we require something more robust if we are to achieve consistency. Published definitions include 'a fertile green spot in a desert waste, especially a sandy desert',[12] 'an area in the midst of a desert which is made fertile by the presence of water',[13] and 'an area within a desert region where there is sufficient water to sustain animal and plant life throughout the year'.[14] Although fairly vague, these definitions share in common an interest in the potential for fertile plant growth and a corresponding availability of water, but there is no attempt to distinguish between naturally occurring and man-made phenomena. The definition of desert is also problematic as this is a botanical term suggesting therefore that oases are defined by pockets of non-desert plants (of which the most recognisable is undoubtedly the date palm). Biomes combining similar plants, animals and climates provide one route to distinguishing desert and oasis, so, for example, we can identify Saharan montane xeric

[11] Vallogia 2004, 25. [12] Stone 1967, 211–68. [13] Perrin and Mitchell 1967.
[14] Goudie *et al.* 1994.

Figure 1.2. The 'archetypal' oasis? Lake Umm al-Ma in the Ubari Sand Sea, Libya.

woodlands, but it is hard to gather a satisfactory level of data for the entirety of the Sahara and this broad brush approach passes over many of the locally specific oasis environments that may be a square kilometre or less in area. Nor does this approach encompass the subtleties and connections that make up an oasis. Instead we prefer a multi-dimensional approach that identifies different types of oases through a number of factors.

Oasis Vegetation

In keeping with botanical definitions the first factor in an oasis is fertile vegetation. In the classic form, oases have dense groves of date palms which provide the shade for fruit trees, cereals and other crops. These palmeries have such a dramatic effect that a climatic 'oasis effect' has been noted wherein the overall temperature of the oasis is lower during the day and higher at night and there is a higher humidity around the palms.[15] While palms can naturally wind pollinate and propagate there are distinct advantages to human cultivation: higher numbers of fruit bearing female plants and faster growing cuttings instead of seedlings. Oases in which date palms form the keystone species are therefore almost all anthropic to greater or lesser degree. Other vegetation forms are possible, particularly in the mountains where pools of standing water (*guelta*) or seasonal streams and rivers can form. These can have quite different combinations of tamarisk, shrubs and grasses to palm oasis and are far more reliant on the slightly higher, but less predictable rainfall that affects Saharan highlands – a wadi that turns green with vegetation for one month in an exceptional year may be dry for several years after. Recently, the development of centre pivot ('crop circle') irrigation wherein vegetation is watered with sprinklers on a rotating boom has created a new form of oasis based on monoculture or a limited range of crops.

Moreover, vegetation cannot be the only determinant as examples exist of oases with little or no cultivation such as modern al-Khalil on the Malian-Algerian frontier or the salt mines of Tawdenni and Taghaza also in Mali.[16] In these cases food and sometimes fresh water were imported to feed the inhabitants. While this is extreme, even for the Sahara, the movement of food to support oasis populations is common and probably has a long history.[17] This is a theme to which we return below.

Saharan Climate

The lack of water is a key determinant of deserts. The 200 mm isohyet has long been used as a crude indicator between desert and non-desert (Fig. 1.3), but this is a highly mobile boundary and the vegetation it supports can expand or shrink hundreds of kilometres in a few years, for instance encompassing or excluding the major oases of Mauritania and Mali. The northern border is less mobile due to the rain shadow caused by the Atlas mountains that distinguishes well the start of oases in the Maghrib. The United Nations Environment Programme definition of desert relies on aridity rather than just precipitation. The centre

[15] For example, Potchter *et al.* 2008.

[16] Scheele 2012; see Sterry and Mattingly, Chapter 7, this volume.

[17] Scheele 2012; Wilson 2012.

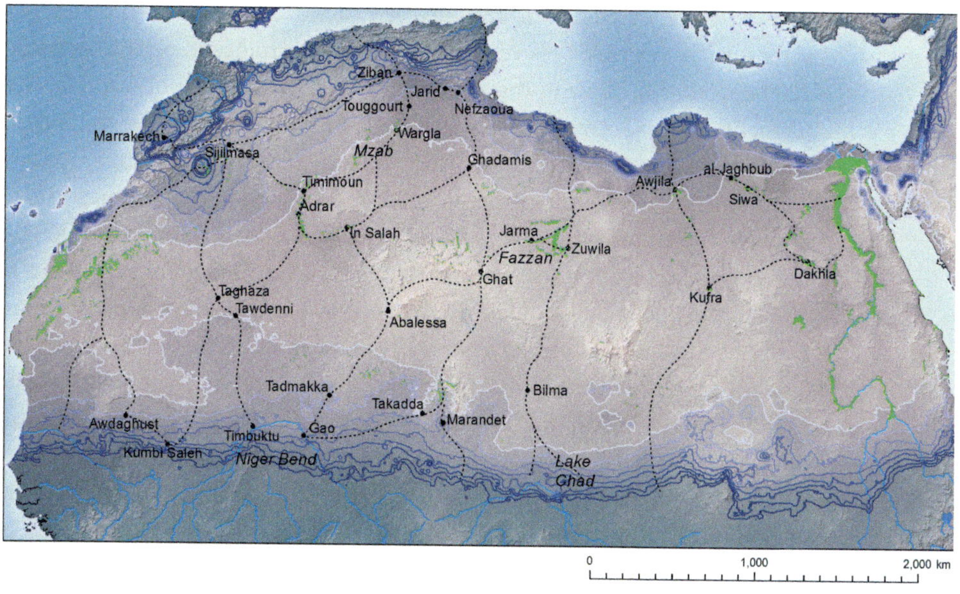

Figure 1.3. Major routes across the Sahara in relation to rainfall data.

of the Sahara can be classified as hyperarid and the northern and southern borders as arid. While the hyperarid zone is a good descriptor for the location of oases in the south, the northern oases sit fully within the arid zone which stretches into and over the Atlas and Aures mountains. The difference between the measures of precipitation and aridity is partly a reflection of the much higher winter temperatures that are experienced closer to the equator and the nature of the very different weather patterns between the southern fringe of the Mediterranean and the northern fringe of the tropics.

While it remains difficult to find a suitable climatic description for the present, the problems are even greater in the past. Localised studies in Fazzan, the Niger Bend and Ennedi have allowed the construction of detailed climate histories showing that the changing nature of these biomes with types and extent of vegetation directly linked to the water histories of these places.[18]

A few words are necessary at the outset concerning changes to the climate and environment of the Sahara in the past.[19] At various times in prehistory the Sahara has oscillated between wet and arid phases. The concept of a green Sahara is now well appreciated in relation to the pluvial

[18] Cremaschi 1998; Lutz and Lutz 1995.

[19] For some of the most recent syntheses on the subject, see: Brooks *et al.* 2005; Cremaschi and Zerboni 2011; Kuper and Kröpelin 2006; Leveau 2018, especially 19–43; Mattingly 2003, 37–74, 327–46 with reviews of earlier literature.

phases, which created substantial river systems and vast lakes.[20] The last significant wet phase was in the Early-Middle Holocene period, broadly 10,000–3500 BC. During this period, the wide availability of water in the form of seasonal rivers, small lakes and a high water table supported Saharan connectivity and mobility.[21] As a general trend, mobile human communities of hunter-gatherers adapted to herding of domesticated animals – primarily cattle.[22] Although there is evidence for periodic climatic oscillations already within the Early-Mid Holocene phase, with a major abrupt arid spell recorded at around 6200 BC, it is apparent that with the Late Holocene, at *c.*3500 BC, there was a significant step in climatic change, which marked the start of the modern hyper-arid phase in the Sahara. Minor climatic oscillations are still recorded in some parts of the Sahara, such as certain of the mountain massifs, which received somewhat higher rainfall than the region as a whole, but the human experience of, and interaction with, the Sahara over the last 5,000 years has concerned a harsh desert environment that imposes limitations on settlement, movement and lifestyles. That is not to say, of course, that the desert denies long-range movements and contacts, but that these have necessarily become more focused along axes where water is more readily available in the form of springs and a high water table. There has been progressive decline in water availability in the Sahara as non-renewable sub-surface water sources have been diminished by natural and anthropogenic action and this has had implications for both Saharan populations and the ease of movement.[23]

Interpolating the climatic data is not straightforward. In the north, the climate of the Neolithic humid phase or the 'Green Sahara' became progressively drier from 7000 BP/5000 BC with areas of desert expanding from the north-east. Palaeolakes in the Nubian Sahara appear to have dried up by around 3500 BP/2000 BC, marking the end of transhumant cattle herding in the Wadi Howar.[24] The palaeo-oasis of the Wadi Tanzzuft gradually contracted from 5000 BP/3000 BC until reaching something close to its current form around 2000 BP (first century AD), before contracting again in the last 25 years as a result of demographic pressure.[25] The drying of the Sahara has been heterogeneous, and in the case of West Africa may have occurred through two abrupt phases of desiccation at

[20] deMenocal and Tierney 2012; Larrasoaña *et al.* 2013; see also www.greensahara-leverhulme.com/ [last accessed 2 September 2019].

[21] Drake *et al.* 2011; Manning and Timpson 2014.

[22] di Lernia 2013.

[23] Cremaschi and Zerboni 2009; Drake *et al.* 2004.

[24] Kuper and Kröpelin 2006.

[25] Cremaschi 2006.

*c.*4000–3500 BP/2000–1500 BC and *c.*2500 BP/500 BC.[26] While the limits of the Sahara may have been more stable over the last 2,000 years there have been oscillations that affected all or parts of the region. In the Middle Niger, precipitation has oscillated between dry and wet phases with numerous severe droughts interspersed with floods.[27] The Middle Niger dry phase of 300 BC–AD 300 coincides with a slight increase in rainfall in Fazzan between 400 BC and AD 250.[28] But it must be emphasised that after 3000 BC, the minor fluctuations in rainfall have not changed the fundamental reality of the Sahara as a desert environment in which cultivation has generally been dependent on subterranean water sources or by stream flow from (sometimes distant) rainfall zones.[29]

The oases of the Sahara must be recognised as an artificial phenomenon, created in the context of this Holocene aridification phase that extends down to present times. After the climate changed decisively around 5,000 years ago, we should first consider the significance of refugia, select environments within the desert that offered enhanced possibilities of supporting human or animal life and vegetation.[30] Examples of refugia in a drying out Sahara include the relict lakes of once larger bodies of water (gradually declining in size) or mountain massifs that received slightly higher rainfall, feeding water holes and providing seasonal vegetation. It is perfectly logical that people and animals will have congregated around such locations as the climate became more hostile. But as Purdue *et al.* recognise there are important distinctions between refugia and oases:

> In anthropology, refugia are commonly regarded as isolated ecological niches where past populations retracted (allopatry) during hyperarid periods, while oases are commonly regarded as water-rich spaces in arid landscapes modified by humans (typically through cultivation and irrigation) in the form of artificial niches.[31]

The importance of human actions in transforming refugia into oases is important, while, equally, it must be stressed that many refugia did not become oases. For example, most of the relict lakes of the third millennium BC eventually dried up and people were obliged to move on.[32] In recent years

26 Kuhlmann *et al.* 2004; Shanahan *et al.* 2006. 27 Nicholson 1979.

28 Compare McIntosh, S. 1995, 9–11 with Cremaschi 2003, 11–12.

29 Leveau 2018, demonstrates that even minor fluctuations for the desert margins and the Maghrib proper during Classical antiquity had potentially more profound implications for those zones.

30 Purdue *et al.* 2018b, 9–12. 31 Purdue *et al.* 2018b, 9.

32 See Gauthier and Gauthier Forthcoming for an important study that tracks human activity following shrinking lake margins in Chad.

some scholars have used Niche Construction Theory (NCT) as a conceptual framework that bridges between deterministic environmental and anthropocentric explanations.[33] It is also very obviously suited to the fact that oases are essentially constructed niches within constrained environmental settings and this closely correlates with our approach in this volume.

Oasis Water-Sources

Just as the form of vegetation is variable, so too is the water that makes up the other component of an oasis. Several principal forms of hydraulic regime can be identified (Fig. 1.4):[34]

Perennial Rivers

Active rivers with year-round flow are extremely rare in the Sahara. The exceptional instances are the two great rivers, the Nile and the Niger, with the Nile running right across the Sahara, while the Niger penetrates and runs along its southern margin before turning south again. Less celebrated is the Wadi Draa in Morocco, which is the only perennial river to flow into the Sahara from the north. It runs south-east for 200 km out of the High Atlas ranges, before turning abruptly westwards towards the Atlantic, though only in years of exceptional flood does water penetrate all the way to the Ocean. The Senegal is also worth noting as it currently delimitates the southern extent of the Sahara on the Atlantic coast. The exploitation of rivers for irrigation relies on the ability to divert or lift water from the main channel onto adjacent land (Fig. 1.4a). This may take the form of casual exploitation of periodic flood events or to engineered systems of barrages and diversion canals, linked to networks of channels (Fig. 1.4b) to distribute water in a controlled manner.

Seasonal Wadis

There are a number of important rivers that flow only seasonally or on an exceptional basis dependent on sporadic rainfall, sometimes resulting in spectacular flash floods. Some of the most important of these are wadi systems that flow from the Atlas ranges of Morocco and western Algeria, fed by seasonal rains and snow melt. The most celebrated examples are the Wadi Ziz (Sis) and the Wadi Rheris (Gheris) that feed the south-eastern

[33] Purdue *et al.* 2018a, various papers and Purdue *et al.* 2018b, 17–19.

[34] For an overview, see also Wilson *et al.* Forthcoming. The analysis here builds on classic geographical studies of Saharan hydrology, Capot-Rey 1953; Gautier 1970.

Figure 1.4. Examples of irrigation regimes: a) diversion dam in the Wadi Draa; b) Medieval irrigation canal Wadi Draa; c) seasonal runoff irrigation, Bani Walid, Libyan pre-desert; d) conical mounds marking vertical shafts of multiple foggaras, Tafilalat, Morocco; e) ancient artesian spring header basin, Ghadamis; f) animal driven well (dalw), Fazzan; g) oasis gardens and distribution channels, Wadi Draa (photos a-e), g): D. Mattingly; photo f): C. Daniels.

Moroccan oasis of Tafilalat, of which Sijilmasa was the celebrated early Medieval capital. Another important seasonal wadi system *c.*150 km east of Sijilmasa comprised the Wadi Gir/Saoura, which in exceptional years carries floodwaters deep into the Sahara to augment the aquifer that feeds the Tuwat oases. In eastern Algeria there are numerous small wadi systems on the south side of Aurés Mountains. Beyond the Jabal in Tripolitania are the seasonal wadis of the Libyan Valleys with the

Zemzem and the Sofeggin the largest (Fig. 1.4c). The exploitation methods for non-perennial streams include diversion of floodwaters onto adjacent terraces as with perennial rivers, though also commonly extend to cultivation of the dry river beds once the floodwaters have subsided. Floodwater or runoff farming varies in intensity, depending on the relative predictability or regularity of rain. At one extreme it is marked by adventitious scratch cultivation of wadis where floods have occurred, at the other it involves the construction of a complex infrastructure of walls to control the flow of water, limit erosion and gullying, along with water-storage features, like cisterns.[35] The former may relate to transhumant pastoral populations, the latter normally indicate sedentary farmers. Sedentary floodwater farming represents a fundamentally different hydrological approach to irrigation compared to oases that are dependent on groundwater sources.[36]

Springs

After perennial rivers, the most valuable water resource in a desert environment is a perennial spring. Two major types of spring need to be differentiated, artesian and non-artesian sources. Artesian springs are those that reach the surface from deep water deposits under pressure. These can be prolific and long-lasting water sources and, once the springhead is contained and linked to a network of distribution channels, can potentially irrigate large areas (Fig. 1.4e). Non-artesian springs generally extract from higher perched water tables, have a less abundant flow and because of the non-renewable nature of the groundwater in much of the Sahara tend to have a more limited life span. There is a particularly important group of artesian springs in the northern Algerian/Tunisian Sahara (oases of the Wadi Rhir, Jarid, Nefzaoua). Artesian springs have often been improved by human enterprise, not only in constructing header tanks and canals, but also in digging additional deep shafts to tap the artesian waters (though such work is extremely hazardous and difficult). Spring-fed lakes exist in some sand seas, but the nature of such interdune depressions constrains the ability to use the water to irrigate wide areas.

Wells

Groundwater in areas lacking springs is most commonly tapped by the construction of wells. Where the water table lay close to the surface

[35] See Barker *et al.* 1996a; 1996b for the classic investigation of Saharan floodwater farming. Also in Cyrenaica, on the north-eastern edge of the Sahara there are many seasonal wadis.

[36] Mattingly 2004b.

(at a depth of at most a few metres) the most common traditional water lifting device is the *shaduf* or balance beam well, in which a counterbalanced beam allows a bucket to be repeatedly dipped into the well and emptied into a distribution channel. Where water lies at greater depth, the mechanical effort of raising it is commensurately higher, involving either human or animal power (*dalw* wells) to draw up the water (Fig. 1.4f).[37] Irrigation that depends on wells and buckets tends to have a lower yield in water than that relating to systems exploiting flowing water and require far more labour on a day to day basis.

Groundwater Catchments

In the Suf oasis of the Great Eastern Erg a high water table beneath dunes has been exploited by the laborious mechanism of digging down in the interdune depressions to create micro-catchments where palms and other crops are irrigated by the groundwater.[38] This exploits in an extreme way a key characteristic of many oases. It is an underappreciated fact that in many oases the date palms are not watered directly, but rather, with their deeper root systems, are sustained by the generally higher groundwater level of the oasis. The main irrigation efforts are directed towards watering small garden plots where cereals and legumes are intensively cultivated. A serious decline in the level of the water table is often advertised by a catastrophic decline in the health of the date palms, as we witnessed first hand in Fazzan between 1996 and 2011.[39]

Foggaras

The foggara is the Saharan variant of a technology known in Iran as the *qanat*. This is a distinctive form of irrigation, with high initial costs (and recurrent maintenance demands). It exploits a difference in level that is sometimes found between the water table beneath a valley or basin floor and surrounding hills or escarpments. Where the water table at the side of a valley is at a higher absolute level above the sea than the centre of the valley, a low gradient underground channel can be dug to carry water from a mother well to a point towards the centre of the valley where the channel breaks the surface, effectively forming an artificial spring. Foggara construction involves the digging of long lines of shafts (which can be spotted by distinctive donut-shaped rings of spoil at the surface) to allow regular

[37] See Wilson and Mattingly 2003, 266–70 for a discussion of the main well types.
[38] Battailon 1955. [39] Mattingly 2013, 31, with figure 2.6.

access to the subterranean channel for the purposes of initial tunnelling and recurrent maintenance (Fig. 1.4d). The earliest foggaras in the Eastern Sahara can be dated to the mid first millennium BC, with the Garamantian heartlands of the Central Sahara containing some of best-documented and most extensive evidence for Protohistoric foggara construction.[40] They are also attested in many other parts of the Sahara, though the chronology of introduction of the technology within different regions is not generally closely dated. Foggaras were particularly important as a means of overcoming a shortage of local springs.

The scarce water generated by the different forms of irrigation described above is generally distributed by carefully measured volume or time allocation along minor channels into small garden plots, where cereals and other annual crops are cultivated shaded by palms and other fruit trees (Fig. 1.4g).

Distribution of Different Irrigation Techniques

As the detailed case studies that are presented in Chapters 2–7 show, Saharan regions made use of the different hydraulic resources available

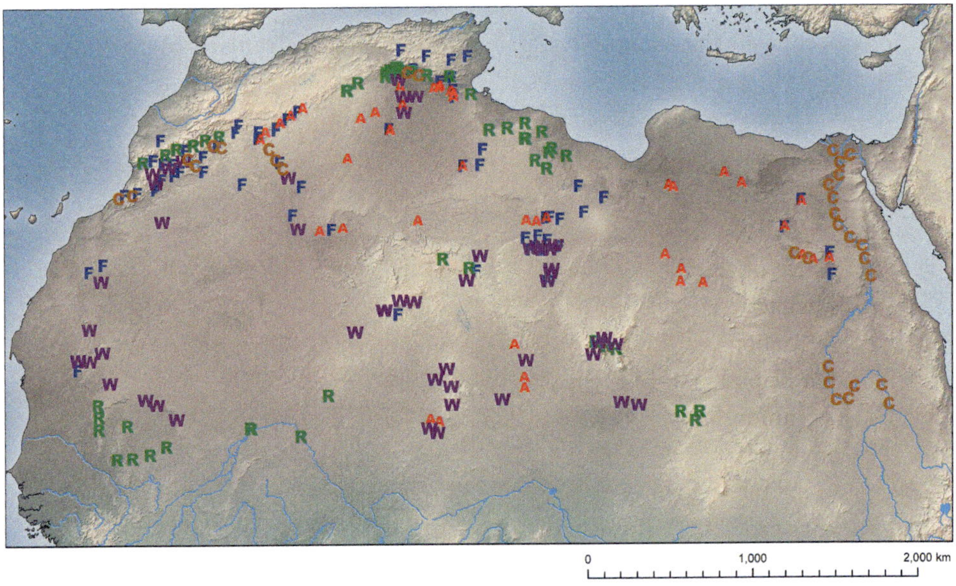

Figure 1.5. Distribution of different irrigation technologies across the Sahara: rainfall runoff (R), springs (A), wells (W), underground irrigation channels/foggaras (F), canals (C).

[40] Wilson 2005; Wilson and Mattingly 2003.

or suitable to the local topography and used a range of technologies for exploiting them. The overall distribution pattern of irrigation technologies in the Sahara is a complex mosaic, dependent on local hydrological resources, topography and social factors (Fig. 1.5). There was thus no uniform blueprint for creating oases in the Sahara, as the background hydraulic conditions varied so much. While the most abundant and most accessible sources of water (like rivers and springs) were favoured locations for early oasis development, every locality and each water source presented its own challenges and the costs of oasis agriculture were always high, both at start up and recurrently. Simple diffusionist models cannot explain the spread of the oasis, but at the same time the importance of the acquisition of the technological know-how that underpinned oasis farming should not be underestimated. This issue of mobile technologies is the focus of a separate volume in this series.[41] The important point for us here is that Saharan oases were enormously varied in their evolution, with many showing evidence of the addition of secondary irrigation works to supplement the primary hydraulic regime at some point. Such diversification could have been driven by population growth and a need to expand the cultivated area, or equally may have been a response to a declining water table impacting the primary irrigation system.

Oasis Networks

So far we have considered oases as zones of fertile vegetation within arid environments, with variability in the nature of both parts. However, one of the key differences between an oasis and an isolated well could be considered to be the presence of people on a permanent, semi-permanent or seasonal basis at oases, while wells sometimes receive only periodic visits. If we see oases as concentrations of people within a desert this opens up different dimensions that help to explain the variability we see archaeologically.

There is a common idea that oases were miraculously productive locations. The Roman writer Pliny the Elder is typical in his laudatory account of the fecundity of the oasis of Tacape on the Tunisian coast – extolling the multiple harvests produced by several layers of crops from palms, to grapes to cereals) grown in gardens with a premium price tag attached to such plots of land.[42] However, an important aspect of oasis agriculture is that its high capital investment and running costs were often not economically

[41] Duckworth *et al.* Forthcoming. [42] Pliny, *Natural History* 18.188.

sustainable solely from the products of the land. Oases were 'miraculous' in that they represented humanly created or humanly enhanced vegetated niches within the desert wastes, but they were expensive to create and run. As Scheele has argued persuasively, oases were uneconomic without reference to other activities and networks in the desert environment – including symbiotic relations with pastoral groups and trade, creating value systems that could subsidise and sustain the elevated costs of oasis farming.[43]

Scheele thus conceives oases as networks. Many, perhaps most, oases make little economic sense, as the costs of developing and maintaining hyper-intensive agriculture are not met by the potential crop returns.[44] This is certainly true of the early modern period as has been demonstrated with the malnutrition and starvation caused by the blocking of trade, and hence food to the Tuwat oases in the early twentieth century.[45] Mid-twentieth-century records of Ghadamis demonstrate that the town's gardens could barely produce half the food needed for its small population (the rest had to be imported from Tripoli) and poverty was a commonplace of other oases under Italian colonial rule.[46] It is an open question to what extent this was true of earlier periods, but in any case, high investment costs for the development and maintenance of oases should be considered the rule in all oases.

There are three key points arising from this. Firstly, as we shall see also with cities, oases must always have existed as networks, rather than as isolated individual sites. The linkages to other points in the network were needed in order to cover initial outlay and growth and when necessary also to provide support for a struggling community. The domestication of key pack animals like donkeys, horses, mules and camels has been another crucial factor in facilitating the navigation of the arid spaces of the Sahara.[47] All the beasts of burden mentioned above were present in the Sahara by the later first millennium BC, though the importance of the camel increased over time with the progressive drop in water tables increasing the distance between and the delivery capacity of wells on Saharan trails.[48] It is precisely because of such constraints on movement and habitation that the Sahara is such an interesting theatre in which to explore themes related to human connectivity across space.

Secondly, the creation of new oases should be viewed as a conscious expansion of that network, with commercial contacts being a driving force.

[43] Scheele 2010. [44] Scheele 2012, 28–36; see also Pascon 1984, 9. [45] Scheele 2010.
[46] Eldblom 1968; Scarin 1934. [47] Lichtenberger 2016, 269. [48] Mattingly *et al.* Forthcoming.

Here of course there is a strong convergence with the conclusions of the Trans-Saharan trade volume.[49]

Thirdly, the rationale for creating oases was not solely dependent on fertile potential (that is, linked to the main botanical and climatic definition of oases), but rather reflected wider social and economic benefits perceived for the network. Thus, a number of oases are linked to salt-mining and others have a crucial role as staging posts along trade routes. In extreme cases this can lead to oasis settlements without an oasis, or rather with the oasis cultivation lying tens or even hundreds of kilometres distant.

As oases are intertwined between climatic, hydrological, botanical, technological, economic and social histories, it is perhaps no surprise that archaeological coverage is so patchy by region and period. Research into Saharan prehistory has tended to concentrate on studying the decline of pastoral communities in a drying environment, but while shrinking grasslands may in some cases have had the potential to become oases, in most cases the long-term water sources were lacking. The evidence of Late Neolithic communities (*c.*3000–1000 BC) tends to be best preserved precisely in the locations least suited for continuing human activity. Hence these studies have tended to paint a picture of decline into oblivion rather than evolution towards oasis landscapes. Meanwhile, studies that have looked at the recent and Medieval history of specific oases, may struggle to understand the nature of Protohistoric oases as the earliest activity is masked by later palimpsest oasis infrastructure and the logic of the modern oasis is sometimes distant from ancient climates, economies and communities. The Protohistoric period is thus often obscured, with important consequences for our understanding of the beginnings of Saharan agriculture, the evolution of oasis communities and the uptake of mobile technologies such as metallurgy and irrigation strategies.[50]

Past Oases and Their Populations

As we shall see, the earliest oases in the Eastern Sahara date back to the third millennium BC. Yet the ultimate origins of the vast majority of Saharan oases and the identity of their first populations are unknown, or assumed but unproven. The default verdict, sometimes with the supporting 'evidence' of foundation myths, for many oases in the Sahara is that they were created no earlier than the Medieval period.[51] However, there is

[49] Mattingly *et al.* 2017a, 433–40. [50] Haour 2003, 224.

[51] On foundation legends in Tidikelt and Tuwat, see Lehuraux 1943. For the Medieval emphasis in general accounts of Saharan oases and trade, see *inter alia* Austen 2010; Lydon 2009; Thiry 1995.

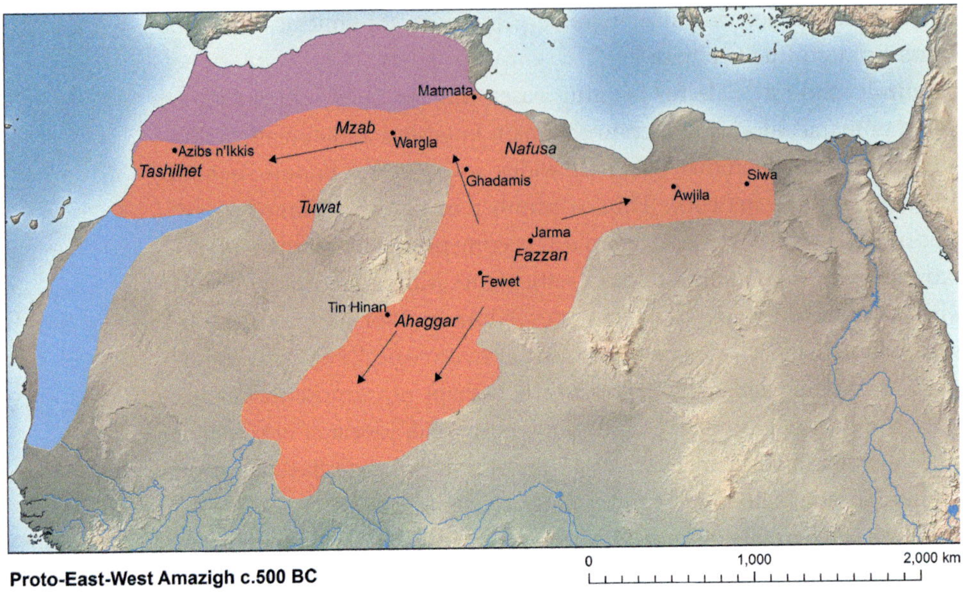

Figure 1.6. The distribution of Proto-East-West Amazigh language (orange) *c*.500 BC. The blue and purple colour zones represent earlier expansions of Proto-Amazigh and related languages (after Fentress 2019).

also an interesting persistence of legends of Jewish or Christian groups being responsible for the first irrigation works and fortified villages (*qsur*).[52] The linguistic evidence suggests that between the third millennium BC and the seventh century AD, many parts of the Sahara became dominated by Berber speaking groups (Amazigh), though there is considerable complexity and divergence concerning the links between the various Berber language branches.[53] The best fit interpretation of the data by Fentress notes a close correlation between major extension of Berber speaking zones and some of the dating of oasis foundations and expansions that are discussed in this volume (Fig. 1.6).[54] To the north and west of the Garamantes this relates to the territories traditionally ascribed to the peoples known collectively as the Gaetuli in the ancient sources. The Amazigh are often presented as the indigenous population of Mediterranean North Africa – that is, phenotypically white, but things appear to have been more complicated in the Saharan Berber-speaking

[52] Gautier 1905, 24–28, concerning a strong tradition recording Jewish migration to Tuwat (Algeria) in the late Roman period; Jacques-Meunié 1982, 173–85, on local tradition in the Draa (Morocco) of Jewish and Christian groups established there before the arrival of Islam.

[53] See in particular the different reconstructions proposed by Blench 2019 and Ehret 2019.

[54] Fentress 2019.

zones. The skeletal evidence suggests these were ethnically very mixed communities of people with Mediterranean, Sub-Saharan and intermediate ethnic markers.[55] There were also areas of the Sahara, where non Berber populations held sway, most notably the Tubu/Teda of the Tibesti region on the Libyan/Chad border.[56]

As this volume will demonstrate, there is now increasing archaeological evidence of Protohistoric establishment of oasis communities – notably focused on the Garamantes. The heyday of the Garamantes coincided with the Roman Empire, but their heartlands in the Libyan Sahara lay far to the south of the Roman frontier.

Even if the Garamantes are now recognised as an important exception, Protohistoric development of oases elsewhere in the Sahara remains underappreciated. One of the reasons for the historiographical blindspot concerning precocious oasis development relates to the persistent belief in the modern colonial era that the desert was occupied in Roman times only by nomads.[57] This was sometimes presented as a reason why the Roman Empire chose not to conquer the desert regions – ignoring the evidence that significant sectors of the desert were actually incorporated into the frontier zone. Overall, there has been a general failure to consider either the possibility that oases already existed in these areas before contact with the Roman Empire or the implications of this.[58] Pastoralists there certainly were, but they were not alone and, in concert, pastoral and sedentary groups represented a much more significant scale of Saharan population than has traditionally been recognised. As we shall see there are plenty of indicators that oases existed in the Protohistoric period and in fact pre-Roman origins of many oases are indicated by among other factors the prominence of date palm iconography in Carthaginian artworks or the appearance of the date palm on Cyrenaican coinage.[59] Pliny's famous

[55] Gatto *et al.* 2019, especially Chapters 4 and 5.

[56] Beltrami 2007; Chapelle 1957; Cline 1950; Nachtigal 1974; Rohlfs 2003.

[57] Two paired papers in the very first volume of the *Travaux de l'institut de recherché sahariennes* provide a perfect illustration of this, Leschi 1942, writing about Rome's relationship with Saharan nomads and the companion paper by Capot-Rey 1942 focusing on nomads in the French Sahara. This has had important implications for the interpretation of the Roman frontier, Cagnat 1914; Gsell 1933; Guey 1939. See Shaw 1981; 1983; Trousset 1982; 2012 for important historiographical discussions of 'nomads'. See now also the important overview article of Leveau 2018 on the social implications of the environmental and climatic conditions of the Roman frontier in the desert margins.

[58] See, for example, Toutain 1896.

[59] Cherif 2006, 74–75 palms on stelae, on razors 75–76, 76 on coins; Quinn 2018, 86–122. Though the popularity of palm imagery at Carthage played on the similarity of the Greek terms for the tree and the 'Phoenicians', the allusion only really works in a region where date palms (and knowledge of them) were well established. Roman iconography of Africa frequently depicts her

account of the oasis of Tacape (Gabes) leaves no doubt about its pre-Roman origins.[60]

Certain characteristics of the Garamantian oases, which have been conclusively dated to Protohistoric periods, are helpful in framing an agenda for tracing early sedentarism in other parts of the Sahara.[61] These include:

- a concentration of population around water sources or potential hydraulic resources, evidenced by the appearance of new settlement forms such as hillforts or dense funerary landscapes;
- the adoption of a developed agricultural package, with obvious affinities with the oases of the Western Egyptian Desert;
- the association with people riding horses and driving chariots and slightly later also the camel, as evidenced in rock art studies;[62]
- the movement of ideas and competencies (pyrotechnologies, irrigation works including the foggara, spinning and weaving, a written Libyan script);
- the construction of distinctive styles of fortified structures (*qsur*);
- evidence of trade contacts.

In the following chapters, we focus primarily on the physical traces and chronology of settlements, but in some cases we shall make reference to wider sources of evidence, including some proxy markers. There are various strands of evidence that can be called on as indicative proxies of early origins for the oases. These include a number of sites where there was a Roman military presence, often supported by epigraphic finds and some investigation of the forts themselves.[63] Even without explicit demonstration that the adjacent oasis was already developed prior to the arrival of the army, the existence of an oasis would seem to be a *sine qua non* for the support of units posted to remote desert locations. Literary evidence also provides compelling evidence for Roman or pre-Roman era activity at a number of centres that can be identified with later oasis sites. Early European travellers in the Sahara, colonial administrators and mappers also reported on Protohistoric or Roman ruins and antiquities in many oasis clusters. Finds of Latin inscriptions, dressed stone blocks (including

personified with an elephant trunk headrest associated with palms, as on a ceramic plate illustrated by Laporte 2011, 147. For pre-Roman Cyrenaican coinage featuring palms, see Robinson 1965.

60 Pliny, *Natural History* 18.188.

61 The work here builds on the *Archaeology of Fazzan* reports, Mattingly 2003; 2007; 2010; 2013.

62 Now superbly illustrated by Barnett 2019a; 2019b.

63 See Mattingly *et al.* 2013 for a short summary on the Roman frontier in Africa, taking account of the new data on oasis development.

architectural elements such as bases, columns and capitals) are strong indicators at oases in the Roman frontier zone, but these probably only represent the tip of the iceberg, as mudbrick architecture was the norm in the oases and stone architecture the exception. Villages built entirely in mudbrick and which did not gain access to large quantities of imported Mediterranean goods like pottery will be difficult to place chronologically without radiocarbon dating. Nonetheless, all finds of Roman material in the Sahara merit careful consideration as potential markers of Protohistoric development.[64]

Pre-Islamic burial monuments are an important category of evidence. Primarily cairns and drum-shaped tombs, these are typically dated to *c*.500 BC–AD 650, but earlier and later examples are known.[65] Especially when concentrated in dense cemeteries around oases, these are a potential indicator of early origins.[66] The organisation of these cairns and drum shaped tombs into regular and dense cemeteries, as opposed to more dispersed funerary zones, may be an indication of locations with permanent settlements.

Dating the irrigation technology used in the oases is incredibly difficult, but one particularly distinctive type of feature can be shown to have Protohistoric origins and to have played an important part in the early establishment of oases. This was the foggara, essentially a Saharan variant of the Persian *qanat*, which was introduced to Egypt by the Persians. Foggaras have had a long life in many oases down to the present and have regularly been assumed to be Medieval in date, but the possibility of a Protohistoric spread of the technology can no longer be ignored.[67]

Finally, the abundant rock art of the Sahara includes a number of depictions of actual oases associated with images of people riding horses, driving chariots and sometimes also featuring camels.[68] There are also images of what appear to be schematic representations of fortified sites similar to the *qsur* of the Garamantes (on which see below). Detailed study of the Garamantian heartlands has demonstrated that there were dense concentrations of horse and camel imagery alongside the oasis, indicating

64 For summary accounts of finds of Roman material culture in the Sahara, see Mauny 1956; 1978; Salama 1981.

65 Gatto *et al.* 2019.

66 Camps 1961; Gauthier 2015; Grébénart 1985; Paris 1984; 1996; Reygasse 1950.

67 See Wilson *et al.* Forthcoming.

68 Camps and Gast 1982; Gauthier and Gauthier 2011; Hachid 2000, 136–72; Lhote 1982; Mauny 1978, 277–92 (map 282); Muzzolini 1990. For the depictions of oases and palms, see di Lernia and Zampetti 2008, 90–97, 127–29; Hachid 2000, 207–14.

a close social relationship between the two.[69] However, some of the rock art clusters occur far from oasis centres, showing that it was also produced by people living in remote locations and more mobile lifestyles.[70] In such cases, it may be that the imagery reflects more on the inter-relationships between pastoralists and oasis communities in terms of trade, raiding and other cultural aspects. The extensive distribution (reaching the Western Sahara) of this sort of historic era rock art (first millennium BC and later), associated with both pastoral groups and oasis locations, is another possible marker of more extensive oasis networks that underpinned successive phases of development. Since oasis networks were highly dependent on communication across the desert, the spread of horse and camel breeding was essential to their maintenance.

Libyan inscriptions in early variants of the Tuareg *tifinagh* script may be another sign of the emergence of complex societies and is a further behavioural trait that could be linked to early oasis cultivating and trading societies.[71] Whatever the specific meaning of inscriptions and rock art images, the commonalities between widely separated material within the Sahara indicates an already connected space in the Protohistoric period.[72]

Urbanism

Towns are the second theme of this volume and are a defining characteristic of complex polities,[73] though with a multiplicity of definitions having been put forward. These include those built round checklists of urban traits,[74] those that emphasise the roles of towns within landscapes and people's lives,[75] those that contrast rural and urban identities[76] and those that dismiss the idea that there are defining features.[77]

Homogenising models, such as the consumer city that was once favoured by ancient historians for the Mediterranean in antiquity, have been increasingly abandoned in favour of comparative or particularist

[69] See Barnett 2019a, 230–45 and 258–77, for locational and social analysis of horse/camel period rock engravings in te Wadi al-Ajal.

[70] di Lernia and Zampetti 2008; Hachid 1998; Mori, F. 1998.

[71] Barnett 2019a, 161–69; Brogan 1975; Daniels 1975; Hachid 2000, 173–90; Mattingly 2003, 317–24; Rebuffat 1975.

[72] Cf. Ennabli 2004, for a fairly recent restatement of the view that the Sahara was impassable ('infranchisable') in the Roman era.

[73] Throughout this paper we use towns/cities interchangeably to describe ancient urban settlements of varied types. On towns in global history, see Clark 2013; Renfrew 2008.

[74] See *inter alia*, Childe 1950; cf. Talbert 2000; Smith, M. 2003; Smith, M.E. 2009.

[75] Yoffee 2005; 2009. [76] Cowgill 2004; Reader 2004. [77] Smith, A.T. 2003.

approaches.[78] The role of towns as centres or agglomerations remains important: whether of size and population density;[79] of particular functions and craft specialisations;[80] of economic networks and development;[81] of farming hinterlands or zones of raw material exploitation;[82] of social complexity and authority.[83] However, there is increasing interest in the cost of towns as a form of complexity,[84] the relationship between size and communication,[85] their legitimacy and resiliency within different social strategies[86] and spatial forms such as clusters of settlements or low density settlement.[87] Above all, there is awareness that urban societies are not an inevitability, but one of many variations, with versions distinct to their ecologies. Cities and systems of cities are multi-scalar, often transformed by cross-scale interactions and sustained by urban innovation.[88] To investigate these requires substantial exploration and most likely excavation of both the urban centre and its hinterland.

New additions are still being made to the list of societies identified as urbanised, especially in regions of the world where archaeological data have been hitherto limited or under-explored. In such cases, it may be helpful to look on cities as 'supernova' that re-routed and transformed patterns of everyday life, changing the landscape of country-city interactions.[89] In archaeologically blank parts of the world, the search for cities should focus on settlements that are very distinct from other settlement types, promoting new forms of social life and changes in interactions with a hinterland zone.

Urban centres, even of small size, placed increased stress on their inhabitants' ability to feed themselves and therefore had to be sustained or supplemented through other means. Such sites can quickly hit a limit and become what Fletcher describes as 'stasis settlements' – rare, very large settlements for the region that maintain their size for long periods of time.[90]

This model is reminiscent of dendritic settlement systems in which flows of goods and information branch outward from a single large centre, but this 'town' monopolises economic development at the expense of its hinterland.[91] Junker has recently reformulated the model describing it as a concentration of political and economic power within primate centres

[78] Bowman and Wilson 2011; Marcus and Sabloff 2008; Nijman 2007; Osborne and Cunliffe 2005; York *et al.* 2011.
[79] Marzano 2011. [80] McIntosh, R. 2005. [81] Wilson 2011. [82] Cowgill 2004.
[83] Smith, A.T. 2003; cf. McIntosh, S. 1999. [84] Tainter 2000. [85] Fletcher 1995.
[86] Cf. Crumley 2005. [87] McIntosh, R. 2005 . [88] Ernstson *et al.* 2010.
[89] Yoffee 2005, 61–62; *contra* Morley 2011, 151. [90] Fletcher 1995, 115–17.
[91] Johnson 1970; Kelley 1976; Smith, C.A. 1976.

that exert weakening authority over a series of linearly radiating settlements.[92] Most often they occurred because of the dominant role that long-distance trade played in the local economy. Finally, environmental and/or cultural constraints on transport can result in a linear convergence of trade networks on a single strategically located centre.

Saharan Urbanism and Urban Networks

There is a growing body of work questioning the applicability of European or Western models of urbanisation to the realities of Africa and to African societies.[93] What we hope to demonstrate in this book is that the Sahara not only underwent a process of localised sedentarisation in the first millennia BC/AD, but that some of the key oases that emerged merit consideration as urban centres. In the same way that oases have tended to belong to networks, rather than exist in splendid isolation, so it is plausible that nodal centres within those networks fulfilled roles that may be considered urban. The extent to which these urban centres were influenced by other urban societies in the Trans-Saharan zone is a more complicated issue. A feature of the debate among contributors to this book concerns the interplay of exogenous and endogenous factors. Other factors that are discussed by various contributors include an increase in social hierarchisation and inequality, issues of security, and the importance of trade in the emergence of Saharan urbanism. Slave-trading is an important and controversial aspect of early Saharan trading and urban systems – the possibility that the Garamantes were an early example of the sort of slaving state that later dominated the Sub-Saharan zone certainly merits consideration.[94]

Trade network models also fit well with oasis centres, like the Garamantian capital Jarma.[95] Jarma was located in an area with accessible groundwater that could have supplied caravans as well as residents and was situated on a potential intersection of east-west and north-south communication routes through Fazzan. Comparative cases in the Hellenistic world suggest that these centres often underwent rapid population growth because they were connected to the outside world through trade or as colonial points of entry.[96]

[92] Junker 2006, 213–14.

[93] See MacDonald 2013; Mattingly and MacDonald 2013; McIntosh, R. 2015; McIntosh and McIntosh 1993; Sinclair 2013.

[94] Fentress 2011. [95] Mattingly and Sterry 2013. [96] Morris 2006.

State Formation

It is a logical corollary to the identification of urbanisation in the Sahara and its neighbouring lands, to ask whether these urban societies merit recognition as early polities. The third big theme in this book is thus state formation. Much depends of course on what one means by this and how exactly we choose to define states.

What Do We Mean by 'State'?

The debate about what constitutes a state is as heated as that concerning what defines a town. In the past, the tendency was to link state formation to an evolutionary vision of human societies moving from simple and scattered bands, to tribes, to chiefdoms, to polities.[97] More recently there has been a reaction against such evolutionary or neo-evolutionary models, at least when they are broadly drawn and crudely applied.[98] Nonetheless, it is hard to escape entirely from evolutionary judgements in assessing what marks early states and civilisations out from other ancient societies and a possible way to mitigate some of the issues with the western bias of evolutionary theory is to attempt to combine emic and etic perspectives.[99] Just as towns often stand out as different from other sorts of settlement, so early states may also have been differentiated from other contemporary communities. What is clear from the best recent work is that hierarchy, agriculture and urbanisation are key social components in defining the primitive state.[100] Much debate still focuses on two categories of state: the city state and the territorial state. The former relates to the formation of networks of self-governing polities based on a single main centre, while the latter concerns the emergence of more hierarchical urban structures and the coalescence of centralised nodes of power and authority. Territorial states could evolve out of networks of city states or independently of the prior existence of such smaller states.[101] Most city states tended to remain relatively small-scale societies (though with some notable exceptions) and were often parts of cultural *koine* with wider parameters. Territorial states

97 For classic statements of this kind see Sahlins and Service 1960; Service 1975.

98 See *inter alia* Trigger 2003, 40–52; Yoffee 2005, 4–21 attack socio-evolutionary theory from different perspectives, but both ultimately retain the concept of evolution in analysing early cities and states.

99 Trigger 2003, 62–65.

100 Trigger 2003, highlights kingship, class, urbanism, food production and land ownership, trade and craft production.

101 Trigger 2003, 92–109.

could be very extensive and be responsible for significant cultural changes within their territories, leading to their recognition as civilisations.[102] Some states might thus be identified as civilisations, but not all. So an important supplementary question to the basic one about whether the Garamantes constituted a state concerns what sort of state model the evidence suits best and whether this also equates with recognition of a distinctive civilisation.

In their influential recent book, Flannery and Marcus have made a good case for the underpinning significance of the emergence and reinforcement of social inequality in the creation of kingdoms and empires.[103] Drawing on a wide array of examples from different parts of the world and varied periods, they demonstrate many commonalities in the formation of early states, and the human behaviour and physical structures that underpinned them.[104] A key point they make is that once a kingdom existed in a region, it provided a model for future kingdoms – the social knowledge could not be uninvented.[105] The Garamantes bear comparison with many of the examples of early kingdoms described by Flannery and Marcus, especially in the manner in which their society developed out of a base shared in common with contemporary groupings into something manifestly different and distinctive.[106]

Examples of States

Mario Liverani, who has studied early state formation across a wide range of contexts from the Near East to North Africa, has been in no doubt about the recognition of the Garamantes as an early state.[107] He suggests that the concept of 'mirror state' may be useful in considering the Garamantian case.[108] This idea, developed specifically in the context of nomadic empires of the Asian steppe, saw them as examples of societies adapting ideas and structures of state organisation from neighbouring states/empires – not so much in terms of simple diffusionist emulation, but as a practical means of dealing effectively with such neighbouring powers. In organising things like tribute extraction from agriculture, livestock raising and commerce, military organisation and levying of troops, labour needs for the construction of monumental buildings and major irrigation works, religious foci,

[102] Trigger 2003, 40–52. [103] Flannery and Marcus 2012, especially 547–64.
[104] Flannery and Marcus 2012, 341–471. [105] Flannery and Marcus 2012, 422.
[106] For previous claims of Garamantian state formation, see Liverani 2006, 431–44; Mattingly 2003, 346–62; 2004a; 2006; 2011b; 2013, 530–34.
[107] Liverani 2006, 431–44; 2007. [108] Liverani 2006, 439–40, following Barfield 1989; 2001.

long-range communications, specialist craft production and markets, the Garamantes could have drawn on observations of a range of peoples they had contact with. In a connected Trans-Saharan world, they did not have to invent everything for themselves.

The Sahara was bordered by a variety of early states by the late first millennium BC: to east (Egypt),[109] south-east (Meroe/Kush),[110] south (Lake Chad area),[111] south-west (Niger Bend area)[112] and north (kingdoms of Cyrene; Numidia, Mauretania; empires of Carthage and Rome).[113] The histories, semantics and physical characteristics of these states vary considerably one from another. Given the central position of the Garamantes within the Trans-Saharan world, we should be careful neither to privilege nor to exclude any one of these from consideration. The key point we would make is that the Garamantes developed their society within a Trans-Saharan world of states and proto-states. Obviously, the lack of detailed historical documentation on their administrative organisation, legal provisions and so on, makes the assessment of the Garamantian state much more difficult than say the Roman one. However, we would argue that there are important markers that identify the Garamantes as certainly possessing some characteristics of early states and evidence hinting at the likely presence of other aspects.

A long standing view is the idea that segmented Berber societies have been antithetical to state formation. In part this has been a consequence of the modern colonial era's attitude to indigenous North Africans, denying them an active role in history in favour of an emphasis on the creative contributions of incomers and colonists.[114] Brett and Fentress typify such views:

> There is no evident progression from the relatively anarchic tribal structures to the Hellenistic state: nor, indeed, is there any reason to expect it. From what we have seen, the development of the Hellenistic monarchies in North Africa between the fourth and first centuries BC occurred in emulation of the major polities and was in no way a spontaneous occurrence.[115]

[109] Flannery and Marcus 2012, 394–421 for a detailed study of the rise of the kingdom of Egypt in the fourth millennium BC, which had profound regional implications.

[110] Edwards 1996; 1998; Chapter 9, this volume; Welsby 1996; 2013.

[111] Magnavita, Chapter 14, this volume.

[112] McIntosh, R. 2005; McIntosh, S. 1999; Chapter 15, this volume.

[113] Cyrene: Chamoux 1953; Numidia: Camps 1960; Kallala and Sanmartí 2011; Sanmartí *et al.* 2012; Sanmartí *et al.*, Chapter 11, this volume; Mauretania: Bokbot, Chapter 12, this volume; Carthage: Fantar 1993; Rome: Desanges *et al.* 2010; Mattingly and Hitchner 1995; Quinn 2009, Wilson, Chapter 10, this volume.

[114] Mattingly 2011a, 43–72. A similar point is made by Monroe 2013, 704–5 regarding modern colonial myths inhibiting study of early states across Africa.

[115] Brett and Fentress 1996, 34, but see also Fantar 1993; Laronde and Golvin 2001.

In view of the new evidence of precocious agriculture, technological advances and proto-urbanism in Numidia, initially independent of Phoenician influence, it is a moot point whether such dismissive views of an African component in urbanisation and state formation are still sustainable.[116]

The Structure of the Volume

In the next part of the volume, mostly written by the co-editors with contributions from a number of others, we offer an overall review of the evidence for early development of Saharan oases, starting in Chapter 2 with the heartlands of the Garamantes in the Central Sahara (Fig. 1.7). From there we move back in time and eastwards (Chapters 3–4), to review the evidence from the oases of the Western Desert of Egypt and eastern Libya. As well as an overall survey chapter by the editors, we include a more focused study by Anna Boozer of the important data from the highly developed Roman-era urban centres of the Western Egyptian oases. These represent outstanding, but in some ways atypical, examples of urban development in the Sahara, due to the close links between the Egyptian oases and the Nile Valley. Chapter 5 explores the northern oases that formed the Roman frontier from north-western Libya to central Algeria. Chapter 6 continues further west again to the oases of western Algeria and southern Morocco. Chapter 7 concludes our survey with a study of the Southern Sahara to the north of Chad, Niger, Mali and Mauritania, regions which were at various times dominated by the empires of Kanim and Songhay as well as the Tubu and Tuareg peoples (including the sultanate of Agadez).

The first half of this volume thus pulls together a vast dossier of information and bibliography relating to the main oases groups in the Sahara. We have also exploited the increasing availability of high resolution satellite imagery to make assessments of the archaeology, both where sites have been previously reported and frequently where there has been no systematic archaeological research of Protohistoric and early Medieval sites. We believe that these two aspects alone can provide a new starting point for future work.

One of the major problems with demonstrating Protohistoric origins is the lack of systematic archaeological investigation and scientific dating for

[116] Sanmartí, Chapter 11, this volume; Mattingly 2016.

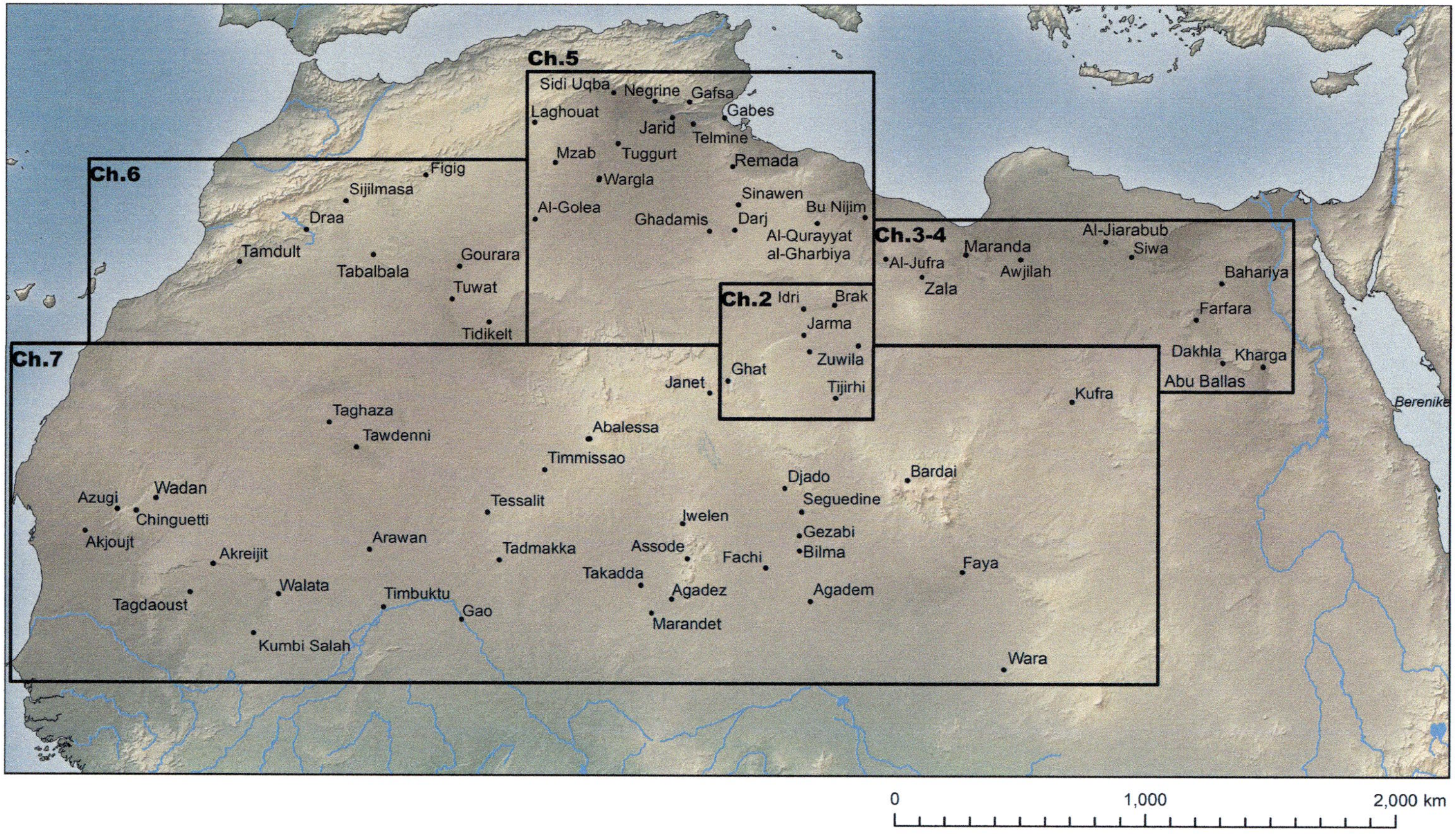

Figure 1.7. Places discussed in Chapters 2–8.

the vast majority of these oasis groups, the notable exceptions being the Libyan Central Sahara and the Western Egyptian Desert. The dating of most sites is very crude and for many locations the best we can say is that there was activity at some point in the Roman period. As we shall see, the available evidence suggests that there was a broad chronological shift from east to west, with the earliest oases in the Western Egyptian Desert dated to the third and second millennium BC, the earliest indications from the Central Sahara dated to the end of the second millennium BC and more extensive development in the first millennium BC. A plausible working hypothesis might be that the initial development in the Algerian and Moroccan Sahara occurred in the late first millennium BC and early first millennium AD, but that remains to be verified.[117] It is also possible that the Western Sahara followed its own distinctive trajectory given the vast distances involved. For instance, the role of Tichitt culture in the wider Trans-Saharan sphere is still poorly understood.

Further discussion of the motivations and processes of oasis creation is the subject of Chapter 8.[118] Many uncertainties remain and particularly as our study progressed further to the west we have had to rely on hints and suggestions more than hard evidence. The picture is currently hypothetical in places, but at the same time we believe that the sheer volume of oasis sites for which Protohistoric development can be demonstrated (or plausibly argued) means that we must view the alternative picture of an underdeveloped and barren Saharan world prior to the Medieval period as equally unproven at present. What is needed is more work on Saharan oases – however remote a possibility that may seem at the present time – and especially a concerted approach to radiocarbon dating of sites (see below).

As well as examining other case studies of urbanisation in the Trans-Saharan world, the second half of this book explores the theme of state formation, again with a particular focus on African specificities and contexts. A series of case studies focusing on the lands bordering the Sahara and spanning the Protohistoric and Medieval eras is presented (Fig. 1.8).

117 New radiocarbon datings from Wadi Draa in Morocco on settlements associated with cereal cultivation and early metallurgy, suggest development in the early centuries AD, but some of the tombs in the associated cemeteries certainly date back to the first millennium BC. See Mattingly *et al.* 2017b and unpublished data.

118 Building on previous discussions of the evolution of social and settlement hierarchy in desert areas, see *inter alia* Barker and Gilbertson 2000; Liverani 2006. The relation between oasis settlement and trade will be further considered there, see Mattingly *et al.* 2017a; Mitchell 2005; Wilson 2012.

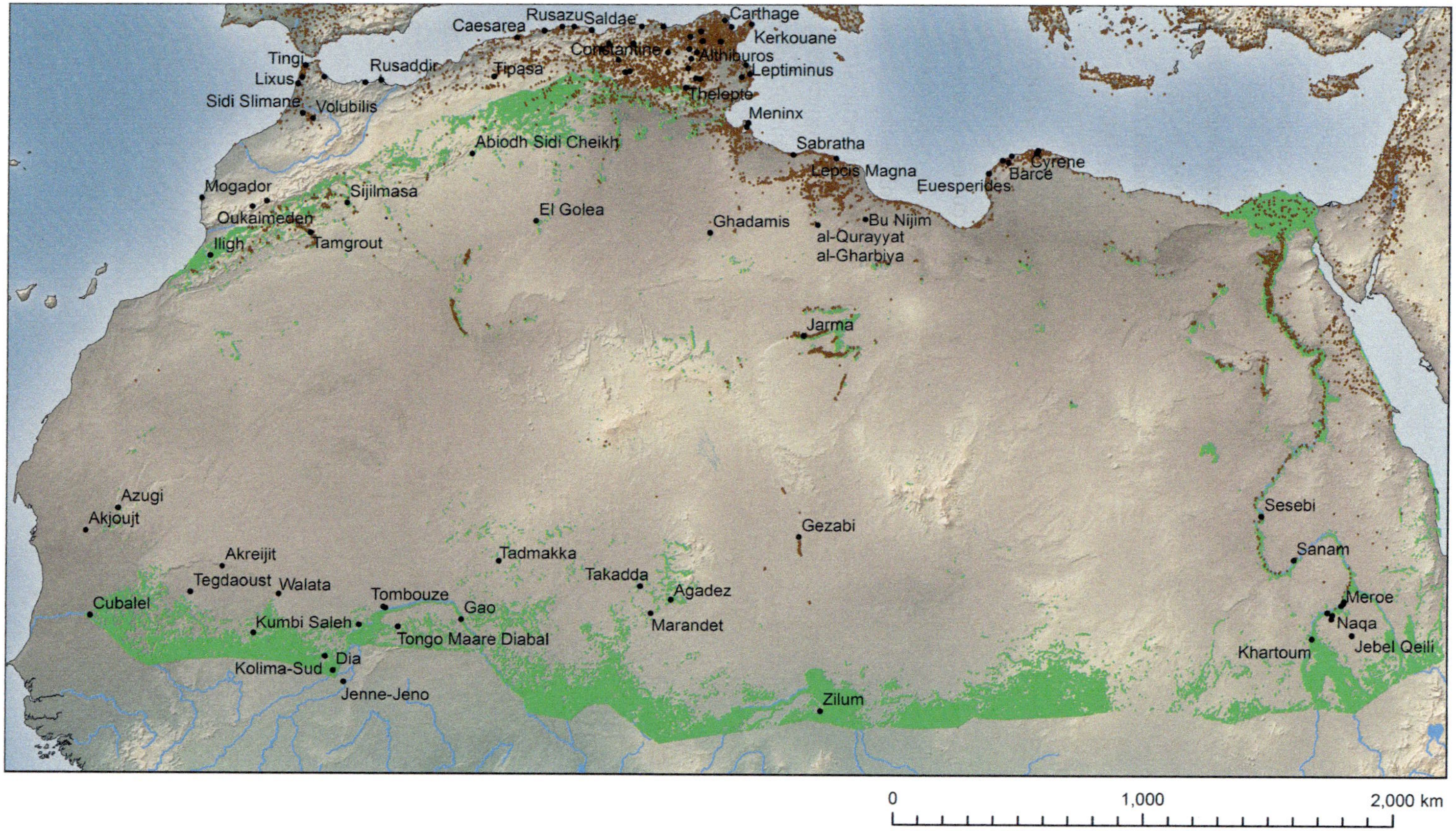

Figure 1.8. Places discussed in Chapters 9–18.

In looking at the neighbouring zones in Part III, we have chosen to follow a broadly anticlockwise tour around the Sahara, starting from the Nile Valley. In Chapter 9, David Edwards presents a case study focused on the Nubian kingdom of Meroe, asking interesting questions about the nature of royal power and its manifestation in architecture and settlement organisation.

The next group of chapters have a focus on the Mediterranean hinterland of North Africa, once seen as a zone dependent on external influences and colonisation for its socio-economic evolution. However, it can now be argued that both exogenous and endogenous factors contributed to the emergence of urbanisation and state formation. Andrew Wilson in Chapter 10 presents an important new survey of the Greek, Phoenician and especially Roman influences in the development of the Classical cities of the Maghrib. He shows an awareness of the significance of the important work of Joan Sanmartí at the site of Althiburos, which is summarised in Chapter 11. Excavations beneath a small Roman town in western Tunisia have revealed a deeply stratified and complex settlement dating back to almost 1000 BC and associated from the outset with sedentary agriculture. The point at which this settlement might be deemed urban cannot be settled on current evidence, but the significance of the long endogenous proto-urban sequence is clear and establishes a very different sort of analysis. It invites us to explore what an African model of urbanism may have contributed to the Roman-era cities described by Wilson.[119] Althiburos is important not just as a type site for pre-Roman urbanism in the Maghrib, but also for the window it opens on the nature and early formation process of the Numidian kingdom that had emerged as a political force by the third century BC. Similar issues are raised in Chapter 12 by Youssef Bokbot, discussing the nature of first millennium BC settlement in Morocco and its relation to the emergence of social complexity there. The narrative is clearly intertwined with that of Phoenician entrepôts along the North African coast, but again he argues persuasively that in the past we have too much emphasised the contributions of external groups and underestimated the role of indigenous society in early urbanism. Here too, an early state, the Mauretanian kingdom, had appeared by the later centuries BC.

The following three chapters all deal with aspects of urbanisation in and bordering the Southern Sahara. In Chapter 13, Kevin MacDonald reviews the evidence for the emergence of complex settlements in the Southern

[119] See Mattingly 2016, for an extended discussion about this new paradigm.

Sahara and the Niger Bend area, starting with the precocious Tichitt settlement sequence from the second millennium BC. A complementary view is offered by Susan McIntosh in Chapter 14, though with a greater focus on the early Medieval developments in the Niger Bend area and Senegal Valley. She also highlights the long distance trading contacts of the early centres as being important in their development. Although neither MacDonald nor McIntosh can identify precise evidence of direct contacts between the early West African polities and the Garamantes, in general they are supportive of the view that there were significant contacts with the Saharan world in this period that need further evaluation in future work. In Chapter 15, Carlos Magnavita provides an overview of the emergence of large fortified sites in the Lake Chad basin in the first millennia BC/AD. Again, there is a lack of direct evidence of contact with the Garamantes, though one of the possible explanations of the fortified sites is that they were a response to slave raiding from the north, whether direct by Garamantian expeditions or sub-contracted by them to the people of the Kawar oases. It must be recognised, however, that a key problem in evaluating the trade contacts between the Sub-Saharan zone and the Sahara is that so much of Saharan trade is in archaeologically invisible or vestigial materials (slaves, salt, gold, other metals, textiles, leather goods, etc.).[120]

The next pair of chapters has a focus on the Medieval Sahara. We noted already how interpretation of town formation in Phoenician/Roman Africa has been skewed hitherto by a dominant colonialist discourse that has obscured or marginalised indigenous developments. New evidence is prompting a reappraisal of the role of local actors. Similar themes of competing narratives of endogenous and exogenous urban foundation and state formation are explored for the late first millennium AD in Morocco by Chloé Capel in Chapter 16. The town of Sijilmasa was one of the key northern portal cities of Medieval Trans-Saharan trade and attracted alternative foundation myths. There has been a general consensus that this was an *ex novo* creation of town and oasis landscape in the mid-eighth century. While Capel's analysis offers an important reinterpretation of different elements of the historiography, she highlights important evidence hinting at Protohistoric activity in the vicinity of Sijilmasa. The recent work in Wadi Draa, reported in Chapter 6, offers further support for the view that the early Medieval golden age of Sijilmasa built on an already established sedentary community in the Tafilalat oasis.

[120] Mattingly *et al.* 2017a.

Chapter 17 by Sam Nixon provides a detailed review of the evidence of the early Medieval/Islamic trading towns in the Southern Sahara and on its edge, serving as portals into West Africa. He illustrates the distinctive features of such sites and how they differed from contemporary West African centres.

While we must be explicit at the outset in saying that we believe the sum of the evidence supports the idea that the Garamantian kingdom was a state, we have deliberately sought to consider and to engage with a diverse array of views in this volume. Judith Scheele makes a strong case in Chapter 18 for considering such an alternative viewpoint – arguing that the Sahara has for most of its history been essentially stateless and dominated by pastoral groups with shifting power structures and attachments, where control of people has tended to be more important than formal delimitation of territory. Her chapter serves as an important reminder that our goal is ultimately not to simply divide between state and non-state entities and confine activities to one or other of these, but rather to look at the full range of how power was held and used.

The concluding discussion by the editors in Chapter 19, attempts to pull together some of the key discussions about the potential linkages between urbanism and state formation in early historical settings in Africa. This volume is by no means intended as a comprehensive review of the many varieties of African urbanism and early polities, but we hope to have demonstrated the importance of enlarging the sphere of such debates, to take account of contemporary developments across the Trans-Sahara zone. We argue strongly that more attention needs to be given to local influences and models for the institutions that evolved in the Sahara, while also recognising the inherent connectedness of the Saharan world from the first millennium BC. The issue of state formation in the Trans-Saharan world, especially in the Protohistoric period and within the Sahara itself is controversial. We shall argue that some Protohistoric Saharan societies are better understood as states or polities, though again this seems to have been a rare development (Meroe, Siwa and the Garamantes are the outstanding early cases).

While the authors of the chapters in this book are not in entire agreement about the definitions of state that suit these African polities, there is a strong consensus that the conventional models of state formation developed in the context of Europe and Western civilisation are ill-suited to the African examples. As with urbanisation, we need to be more open to the importance of 'African' ways of defining and enshrining power within societies. 'State' and 'state formation' have to be reconceptualised to make sense of the Trans-Saharan world. To follow Lekson's corollary – if we are arguing over whether the Garamantes or similar groups were or were not states, then they must be really interesting.[121]

The Dating of Protohistoric and Historic Sites in the Saharan Zone

A crucial problem concerning the issues that this volume seeks to address is the lack of absolute dates from many of the oasis regions of the Sahara, bearing on their origins and evolution. Most application of radiocarbon dating in the Sahara has related to prehistory, with relatively little attempt to date Protohistoric and historic sites. It is not just the early chronology that is obscure, the Medieval phases of many key sites are equally poorly understood, with folklore outweighing scientific dating criteria. However, our investigations have revealed that there is more evidence now available than is perhaps currently appreciated. Since the late 1990s, our work in the Central Saharan heartlands of the Garamantes has involved a major programme of scientific dating of such sites, with 177 radiocarbon dates in total.[122] The Italian mission in the same broad region has published a further 85 relevant dates.[123] We have now initiated a similar programme of AMS dating in relation to our survey in the Moroccan Wadi Draa, with 77 dates already available.[124] These dating programmes have demonstrated the potential to differentiate between Protohistoric and Medieval settlements and underpin our new appreciation of the scale and complexity of Protohistoric Saharan sedentarism.[125]

In the absence of diagnostic pottery and well dated excavated sequences in many areas of the Sahara, the close dating of sites and monuments is fraught with difficulties. Traditional radiocarbon dating, involving substantial amounts of material for analysis often suffered from the effects of mixed samples or 'old wood' charcoal. However, high precision AMS dates, often obtained from an individual seed or small amounts of grass temper and chaff used in the manufacture of mudbrick, offer much greater certainty that samples are not mixed and relate to annual or short-lived

121 Lekson 2009.

122 Mattingly 2007; 2010; Mattingly *et al.* 2015; Sterry and Mattingly 2011; 2013; Sterry *et al.* 2012.

123 Liverani 2006; Mori, L. 2013.

124 Mattingly *et al.* 2017b.

125 See now Mattingly *et al.* 2018, for a first overall presentation of the AMS dating programme of the Trans-SAHARA project.

materials.[126] While a few anomalous dates have still been delivered, our experience is that a very high percentage of samples submitted (especially from temper included in mudbrick and pisé construction) have provided reliable dates for the construction. There are also plateaux effects in the radiocarbon calibration curve that extend the range in certain periods, but it is broadly possible to recognise activity phases and to distinguish between the early first millennium BC, the later first millennium BC, the early centuries of the first millennium AD, the later first millennium AD and the earlier centuries of the second millennium AD. Where sufficient dates are obtained, and especially where they come from an established stratigraphic sequence, it is possible to narrow the range through Bayesian modelling, as we did for phasing activity at the Garamantian capital of Old Jarma.[127]

A supplementary, but highly important, contribution of this book is thus that we have systematically gathered all the available radiocarbon dates for the Sahara from *c.*1000 BC onwards and present them together here in a standardised and consistent manner.[128] All dates (both older radiometric and AMS) have been recalibrated using Oxcal 4.3 and calibration curve IntCal13 to two standard deviations (95.4 per cent confidence interval).[129] Dates are presented in a series of tables related to each region as described in Chapters 2–7. It is hoped that this will also encourage the spread of scientific dating and reporting to other Saharan sites. The contextual detail of some samples is lacking and a few samples yielded modern dates, a reminder that sites are constantly being reworked and modified down to the present. We hope that this resource of more than 1,000 absolute dates will be of value to the scholarly community and regional heritage organisations and that it will stimulate further attempts to date key sites and monuments of the historic Sahara. While our main focus in this book has been with the potential Protohistoric origins of urbanisation and state formation, it is self-evident from a glance at the tables of dates that the Medieval history of the Saharan oases can also be brought into much closer focus through improved dating. If there is an overriding conclusion of this

[126] For an explanation of sampling methods, see Sterry *et al.* 2012, 138–39.

[127] For the Bayesian modelling of the Jarma sequence see, Mattingly 2013, 125–34.

[128] Two major sources of dates are Vernet and Aumassip 1992 and Manning and Timpson 2014. We have additionally conducted a review of the journals *Radiocarbon* and *Archaeometry* as well as a systematic oasis by oasis search. Where possible we present the site name, explanation of site type/context, material dated, Laboratory reference, uncalibrated range and calibrated date. We shall be grateful to receive additional information on any dates listed as well as additional dates, so that we can maintain and update this date list in future.

[129] Bronk Ramsey 2009; Reimer *et al.* 2013.

volume, it is that urbanisation and state formation in the Trans-Saharan zone are themes that need to be studied in a diachronic and spatially extensive framework.

References

Aillet, C., Cressier, P. and Gilotte, S. (ed.). 2017. *Sedrata. Histoire et archéologie d'un carrefour du Sahara médiéval à la lumière des archives inédites de Marguerite van Berchem*. Madrid: Casa de Velázquez.

Austen, R.A. 2010. *Trans-Saharan Africa in World History*. Oxford: Oxford University Press.

Barfield, T. 1989. *The Perilous Frontier*. Oxford: Blackwell.

Barfield, T. 2001. The shadow empires: Imperial state formation along the Chinese-nomad frontier. In S. Alcock, T. D'Altroy, K. Morrison and C. Sinopoli (eds), *Empires. Perspectives from Archaeology and History*. Cambridge: Cambridge University Press, 10–41.

Barker, G. and Gilbertson, G. (eds). 2000. *The Archaeology of Drylands: Living at the Margin*. London: Routledge.

Barker, G., Gilbertson, D., Jones, B. and Mattingly, D.J. 1996a. *Farming the Desert. The UNESCO Libyan Valleys Archaeological Survey. Volume 1, Synthesis*. (Principal editor, G. Barker). Paris/London: UNESCO, Society for Libyan Studies.

Barker, G., Gilbertson, D., Jones, B. and Mattingly, D.J. 1996b. *Farming the Desert. The UNESCO Libyan Valleys Archaeological Survey. Volume 2, Gazetteer and Pottery*. (Principal editor, D.J. Mattingly). Paris/London: UNESCO, Society for Libyan Studies.

Barnett, T. 2019a. *An Engraved Landscape. Rock Carvings in the Wadi al-Ajal, Libya. Volume 1: Synthesis*. London: Society for Libyan Studies.

Barnett, T. 2019b. *An Engraved Landscape. Rock Carvings in the Wadi al-Ajal, Libya. Volume 2: Gazetteer*. London: Society for Libyan Studies.

Battailon, G. 1955. *Le Souf. Etude de géographie humaine*. Alger: Institut de Recherches Sahariennes, mémoire n° 2.

Beltrami, V. 2007. *Il Sahara Centro-Orientale Dalla Preistoria Ai Tempi Dei Nomadi Tubu: The Central-Oriental Sahara from Prehistory to the Times of the Nomadic Tubus*. Oxford: BARS.

Blench, R. 2019. The linguistic prehistory of the Sahara. In Gatto *et al.* 2019, 431–63.

Bowman, A. and Wilson, A. (eds). 2011. *Settlement, Urbanization, and Population*. Oxford: Oxford University Press.

Brett, M. and Fentress, E. 1996. *The Berbers*. Oxford: Blackwell.

Brogan, O. 1975. Inscriptions in the Libyan alphabet from Tripolitania and some notes on the tribes of the region. In Bynon and Bynon 1975, 267–89.

Bronk Ramsey, C. 2009. Bayesian analysis of radiocarbon date. *Radiocarbon* 51.1: 337–60.

Brooks, N., di Lernia, S., Drake, N., Chiapello, I., Legrand, M., Moulin, C. and Prospero, J. 2005. The environment-society nexus in the Sahara from prehistoric times to the present day. *The Journal of North African Studies* 304: 253–92.

Bynon, J. and Bynon, T. (eds). 1975. *Hamito-Semitica*. The Hague: Mouston.

Cagnat, R. 1914. La frontière militaire de la Tripolitaine à l'époque romaine. *Mémoires de l'Académie des Inscriptions et Belles Lettres* 39: 77–109.

Camps, G. 1960. Massinissa ou les débuts de l'histoire. *Libyca* 8.1: 1–320.

Camps, G. 1961. *Aux origines de la Berbérie. Monuments et rites funéraires protohistoriques*. Paris: Arts et Metiers Graphiques.

Camps, G. and Gast, M. (eds). 1982. *Les chars préhistoriques du Sahara*. Aix en Provence: Institut de Recherches Méditerranéennes.

Capot-Rey, R. 1942. Le nomadisme pastoral dans le Sahara français. *Travaux de l'Institut de Recherches Sahariennes* 1: 63–86.

Capot-Rey, R. 1953. *Le Sahara Français* (L'Afrique Blanche Francaise II). Paris: Presses universitaires.

Chamoux, F. 1953. *Cyrène sous la monarchie des Battiades*. Paris: BEFAR.

Chapelle, J. 1957. *Black Nomads of the Sahara* (Translated by F. Schütze). Paris: Librairie Plon.

Cherif, Z. 2006. Le palmier dattier et son image dans l'iconographie cartaginoise. In M.H. Fantar (ed.), *Le Sahara et l'homme. Un savoir pour un savoir faire*. Tunis: Université de Tunis, 67–84.

Childe, V.G. 1950. The urban revolution. *Town Planning Review* 21.1: 3–17.

Clark, P. (ed.). 2013. *The Oxford Handbook of Cities in World History*. Oxford: Oxford University Press.

Cline, W. 1950. *The Teda of Tibesti, Borkou and Kawar*. Mwenasha: General Series in Anthropology.

Cowgill, G.L. 2004. Origins and development of urbanism: Archaeological perspectives. *Annual Review of Anthropology* 33: 525–49.

Cremaschi, M. 1998. Late Quaternary geological evidence for environmental changes in Western Fazzan (Libyan Sahara). In M. Cremaschi and S. di Lernia (eds), *Wadi Teshuinat, Palaeoenvironment and Prehistory in South-Western Fezzan*. Milan: CNR, 13–48.

Cremaschi M. 2003. Steps and timing of the desertification during the Late Antiquity. The case study of the Tanzzuft oasis (Libyan Sahara). In M. Liverani (ed.), *Arid Lands in Roman Times*, AZA 4. Firenze: Edizioni All'Insegna del Giglio, 1–14.

Cremaschi M. 2006. The Barkat oasis in the changing landscape of Wadi Tannezzuft during the Holocene. In: Liverani 2006, 13–24.

Cremaschi, M. and Zerboni, A. 2009. Early to Middle Holocene landscape exploitation in a drying environment: Two case studies compared from the Central Sahara (SW Fezzan, Libya). *Comptes Rendus Geoscience* 341: 689–702.

Cremaschi, M. and Zerboni, A. 2011. Human communities in a drying landscape. Holocene climate change and cultural response in the Central Sahara. In I.P. Martini and W. Chesworth (eds), *Landscape and Societies, Selected Cases*. London: Springer, 67–89.

Crumley, C. 2005. Remember how to organize: Heterarchy across disciplines. In C. S. Beekman and W. Baden (eds), *Nonlinear Models for Archaeology and Anthropology: Continuing the Revolution*. Aldershot: Ashgate, 35–50.

Daniels, C.M. 1975. An ancient people of the Libyan Sahara. In Bynon and Bynon 1975, 249–65.

deMenocal, P.B. and Tierney, J.E. 2012. Green Sahara: African humid periods paced by Earth's orbital changes. *Nature Education Knowledge* 3.10: 12.

Desanges, J. 1980. *(Pline l'ancien) Histoire naturelle Livre V.1–46 (L'Afrique du nord)*. Paris: Collection Budé.

Desanges, J., Duval, N., Lepelley, C. and Daint-Amans, S. 2010. *Carte des routes et des cités de l'est de l'Africa à la fin de l'antiquité*. Turnhout (BE): Biblio de l'Antiquité Tardive, Brepols.

di Lernia, S. 2013. The emergence and spread of herding in northern Africa: A critical reappraisal. In Mitchell and Lane 2013, 527–40.

di Lernia, S. and Zampetti, D. 2008. *Le pitture rupestri dell'Acacus tra passato e futuro*. Firenze: All'Insegna del Giglio.

Dowler, A. and Galvin, E.R. (eds). 2011. *Money, Trade and Trade Routes in Pre-Islamic North Africa*. London: British Museum Press.

Drake, N., Wilson, A., Pelling, R., White, K., Mattingly, D.J. and Black, S. 2004. Water table decline, springline desiccation and the early development of irrigated agriculture in the Wadi al-Ajal, Libyan Fazzan. *Libyan Studies* 35: 95–112.

Drake, N.A., Blench, R.M., Armitage, S.J., Bristow, C.S., White K.H. 2011. Ancient watercourses and biogeography of the Sahara explain the peopling of the desert. *Proceedings of the National Academy of Sciences of America* 108: 458–62.

Duckworth, C., Cuénod, A. and Mattingly, D.J. (eds). Forthcoming. *Mobile Technologies in the Ancient Sahara and Beyond*. Trans-Saharan Archaeology Volume 4. Cambridge: Cambridge University Press and The Society for Libyan Studies.

Edwards, D.N. 1996. *The Archaeology of the Meroitic State: New Perspectives on Its Social and Political Organisation*. Oxford: Archaeopress.

Edwards, D.N. 1998. Meroe and the Sudanic kingdoms. *Journal of African History* 39.2: 175–93.

Ehret, C. 2019. Berber peoples in the Sahara and North Africa: Linguistic historical proposals. In Gatto *et al.* 2019, 464–94.

Eldblom, L. 1968. *Structure foncière, organisation et structure sociale. Une étude sur la vie socio-économique dans les trois oasis libyennes de Ghat, Mourzouk et particulièrement Ghadamès*. Lund: Uniskol.

Ennabli, A. 2004. Entre Afrique du nord antique et Afrique sub-saharienne: un obstacle infranchisable. In A. Bazzana and H. Bocoum (eds), *Du nord au sud du*

Sahara. Cinquante ans d'archéologie française en Afrique du ouest et au Maghreb. Bilan et perspectives. Paris: Editions Sepia, 23–24.

Ernstson, H., van der Leeuw, S.E., Redman, C.L., Meffert, D.J., Davis, G., Alfsen, C., and Elmqvist, T. 2010. Urban transitions: On urban resilience and human-dominated ecosystems. *Ambio* 39.8: 531–45.

Fantar, M. 1993. *Carthage. Approche d'une civilisation*, 2 vols. Tunis: Les Éditions de la Méditerranée.

Fentress, E. 2011. Slavers on chariots. In Dowler and Galvin 2011, 64–71.

Fentress, E. 2019. The archaeological and genetic correlates of Amazigh linguistics. In Gatto *et al.* 2019, 495–524.

Flannery, K. and Marcus, J. 2012. *The Creation of Inequality. How Our Prehistoric Ancestors Set the Stage for Monarchy, Slavery and Empire*. Cambridge (Mass): Harvard University Press.

Fletcher, R. 1995 *The Limits of Settlement Growth. A Theoretical Outline*. Cambridge: Cambridge University Press.

Gatto, M.C., Mattingly, D.J., Ray, N. and Sterry, M. (eds). 2019. *Burials, Migration and Identity in the Ancient Sahara and Beyond*. Trans-Saharan Archaeology Volume 2. Series editor D.J. Mattingly. Cambridge: Cambridge University Press.

Gautier, E.-F. 1905. *Les oasis sahariennes*. Algérie: Imp Fontana.

Gautier, E.-F. 1970. *Sahara. The Great Desert* (translated from the French by D.F. Mayhew). London: Octagon.

Gauthier, Y. 2015. Pre-Islamic dry-stone monuments of the central and Western Sahara. In C. Ruggles (ed.), *Handbook of Archaeoastronomy and Ethnoastronomy*. New York: Springer Science, 1059–77.

Gauthier, Y. and Gauthier, C. 2011. Des chars et des Tifinagh: étude aréale et corrélations. *Les Cahiers de l'AARS* 15: 91–118.

Gauthier, Y. and Gauthier, C. Forthcoming. L'impact du climat sur le peuplement des zones lacustres sahariennes du Tchad septentrional (Borkou, Ennedi, Tibesti) à l'Holocène. In *Recherches croisées sur les écosystèmes lacustres tchadiens* (coll. intern., N'Djamena, 25–27 avril 2017).

Goudie, A.S., Atkinson, B.W., Gregory, K.J., Simmons, I.G., Stoddart, D.R. and Sugden, D. (eds). 1994. *Encyclopedic Dictionary of Physical Geography*. Second Edition. Oxford: Blackwell.

Grébénart, D. 1985. *Le néolithique final et les débuts de la métallurgie. La région d'In Gall – Tegidda N Tesemt (Niger)*. Etudes Nigeriennes no. 49. Niamey: Institut de Recherches en Sciences Humaines.

Gsell, S. 1972a. *Histoire ancienne de l'Afrique du nord. Tome I Les conditions de développement historique. Les temps primitifs, la colonisation phénicienne et l'empire de Carthage*. Osnabrück: Otto Zeller Verlag.

Gsell, S. 1972b. *Histoire ancienne de l'Afrique du nord. Tome V Les royaumes indigènes, orientation sociale, politique et économique*. Osnabrück: Otto Zeller Verlag.

Gsell, S. 1933. La Tripolitaine et le Sahara au III siècle de notre ère. *Mémoires de l'Académie des Inscriptions et Belles Lettres* 43.1: 149–66.

Guey, J. 1939. Note sur le 'limes' romain de Numidie et le Sahara au IVe siècle. *Mélanges de l'Ecole Française de Rome* 56: 178–248.

Hachid, M. 1998. *Le Tassili des Ajjer. Aux sources de l'Afrique, 50 siècles avant les pyramides.* Paris: Paris-Méditerranée.

Hachid, M. 2000. *Les premiertes berbères. Entre Méditerranée, Tassili et Nil.* Aix-en-Provence: Edisud.

Haour, A. 2003. One hundred years of archaeology in Niger. *Journal of World Prehistory* 17.2: 181–234.

Jacques-Meunié, D. 1982. *Le Maroc saharien des origins à 1670*, 2 vols. Paris: Klincksieck.

Johnson, E.A.J. 1970. *The Organization of Space in Developing Countries.* Cambridge (Mass): Harvard University Press.

Junker, L.L. 2006. Population dynamics and urbanism in premodern island south-east Asia. In G.R. Storey (ed.), *Urbanism in the Preindustrial World: Cross-Cultural Approaches.* Tuscaloosa: The University of Alabama Press, 203–30.

Kallala, N. and Sanmartí, J. 2011. *Althiburos I. La fouille dans l'aire du capitole et la nécropole méridionale.* Tarragona: Institut Català d'Arqueologia Clàssica.

Kelley, K.B. 1976. Dendritic central-place systems and the regional organization of Navajo trading posts. In C.A. Smith (ed.), *Regional Analysis. Volume 1: Economic Systems.* New York: Academic Press, 219–54.

Kuhlmann, H., Meggers, H., Freudenthal, T. and Wefer, G. 2004. The transition of the monsoonal and the N Atlantic climate system off NW Africa during the Holocene. *Geophysical Research Letters* 31.22.

Kuper, R. and Kröpelin, S. 2006. Climate-controlled Holocene occupation in the Sahara: motor of Africa's evolution. *Science* 313: 803–87.

Laporte, J.-P. 2011. Particularités de la province de Maurétanie Césarienne (Algerie central et occidentale). In Briand-Ponsart, C. and Modéran, Y. (eds), *Provinces et identités provinciales dans l'Afrique romaine.* Caen: Université de Caen, 111–50.

Larrasoaña J.C., Roberts A.P. and Rohling E.J. 2013. Dynamics of Green Sahara periods and their role in hominin evolution. *PLoS ONE* 8.10: e76514.

Laronde, A. and Golvin, J.-C. 2001. *L'Afrique antique. Histoire et monuments.* Paris: Tallader.

Laureano, P. 1991. *Sahara. Jardin méconnu.* Paris: Larousse.

Lehuraux, L. 1943. Les origines des oasis du Tidikelt et du Bas-Touat. *Travaux de l'Institut de Recherches Sahariennes* 2: 105–20.

Lekson, S.H. 2009. *A History of the Ancient Southwest.* Santa Fe: School for American Research Press.

Leschi, L. 1942. Rome et les nomades du Sahara central. *Travaux de l'Institut de Recherches Sahariennes* 1: 47–62.

Leveau, P. 2018. Climat, sociétés et environment aux marges sahariennes du Maghreb: Une approche historiographique. In S. Guédon (ed.), *La frontière méridionale du Maghreb. Approches croisées (Antiquité-Moyen Âge).* Bordeaux: Ausonius, 19–106.

Lhote, H. 1982. *Les chars rupestres sahariennes des Syrtes au Niger, par le pays des Garamantes et des Atalantes*. Toulouse: Editions des Hespérides.

Lichtenberger, A. 2016. 'Sea without water' – conceptualising the Sahara and the Mediterranean. In M. Dabag, D. Haller, N. Jaspert and A. Lichtenberger (eds), *New Horizons. Mediterranean Research in the 21st Century*. Paderborn: Ferdinand Schoningh, 267–83.

Liverani, M. (ed.). 2006. *Aghram Nadharif. The Barkat Oasis (Sha'abiya of Ghat, Libyan Sahara) in Garamantian Times*. Firenze: All'Insegna del Giglio.

Liverani, M. 2007. La struttura sociale dei Garamanti in base alle recenti scoperte archeologiche. *Rendiconti dell'Accademia Nazionale dei Lincei* Ser 9, 18: 155–204.

Lutz, R. and Lutz, G. 1995. *The Secret of the Desert. The Rock Art of the Messak Settafet and Messak Mellet, Libya*. Innsbruck: Golf Verlag.

Lydon, G. 2009. *On Trans-Saharan Trails: Islamic Law, Trade Networks and Cross-cultural Exchange in Nineteenth-Century Western Africa*. Cambridge: Cambridge University Press.

MacDonald, K. 2013. Complex societies, urbanism and trade in the western Sahel. In Mitchell and Lane 2013, 829–44.

McIntosh, R. 2005. *Ancient Middle Niger: Urbanism and the Self-Organizing Landscape*. Cambridge: Cambridge University Press.

McIntosh, R. 2015. Different cities: Jenne-jeno and African urbanism. In *The Cambridge World History: Volume 3, Early Cities in Comparative Perspective, 4000 BCE–1200 CE*. Cambridge: Cambridge University Press, 364–80.

McIntosh, S.K. (ed.). 1995. *Excavations at Jenne-jeno, Hambarketolo and Kaniana (Inland Niger Delta, Mali): The 1981 Season*. University of California Monographs in Anthropology. Berkeley: University of California Press.

McIntosh, S.K. 1999. *Beyond Chiefdoms: Pathways to Complexity in Africa*. Cambridge: Cambridge University Press.

McIntosh, S.K. and McIntosh, R.J. 1993. Cities without citadels: Understanding urban origins along the Middle Niger. In T. Shaw, P. Sinclair, B. Andah, and A. Okpoku (eds), *The Archaeology of Africa: Food, Metals and Towns*. London: Routledge, 622–41.

Manning, K. and Timpson, A. 2014. The demographic response to Holocene climate change in the Sahara. *Quaternary Science Reviews* 101: 28–35.

Marcus, J. and Sabloff, J.A. (eds). 2008. *The Ancient City: New Perspectives on Urbanism in the Old and New World*. Santa Fe: School for Advanced Research Press.

Marzano, A. 2011. Rank-size analysis and the Roman cities of the Iberian Peninsula and Britain: some considerations. In Bowman and Wilson 2011, 196–228.

Mattingly, D.J. 2003. *The Archaeology of Fazzan, Volume 1 Synthesis*. London: Society for Libyan Studies.

Mattingly, D.J. 2004a. Nouveaux aperçus sur les Garamantes: Un état saharien? *Antiquités africaines* 37 (2001) [2004]: 45–61.

Mattingly, D.J. 2004b. Surveying the desert: From the Libyan Valleys to Saharan oases. In M. Iacovou (ed.), *Archaeological Field Survey in Cyprus. Past History, Future Potentials. Proceedings of a Conference Held at the University of Cyprus, 1–2 December 2000*. London: BSA monograph 11, 163–76.

Mattingly, D.J. 2006. The Garamantes: The first Libyan state. In D. Mattingly, S. McLaren, E. Savage, Y. al-Fasatwi and K. Gadgood (eds), *The Libyan Desert. Natural Resources and Cultural Heritage*. London: Society for Libyan Studies, 189–204.

Mattingly, D.J. 2007. *The Archaeology of Fazzan. Volume 2, Site Gazetteer, Pottery and other Survey Finds*. London: Society for Libyan Studies, Department of Antiquities.

Mattingly, D.J. 2010. The *Archaeology of Fazzan. Volume 3, Excavations Carried out by C.M. Daniels*. London: Society for Libyan Studies.

Mattingly, D.J. 2011a. *Imperialism, Power and Identity: Experiencing the Roman Empire*. Princeton: Princeton University Press.

Mattingly, D.J. 2011b. The Garamantes of Fazzan: An early Libyan state with Trans-Saharan connections. In Dowler and Galvin 2011, 49–60.

Mattingly, D.J. 2013. *The Archaeology of Fazzan, Volume 4. Survey and Excavations at Old Jarma (Ancient Garama) Carried out by C. M. Daniels (1962–69) and the Fazzan Project (1997–2001)*. London: Society for Libyan Studies.

Mattingly, D.J. 2016. Who shaped Africa? The origins of agriculture and urbanism in Maghreb and Sahara. In N. Mugnai, J. Nikolaus and N. Ray (eds), *De Africa Romaque. Merging Cultures across North Africa*. London: Society for Libyan Studies, 11–25.

Mattingly, D.J. and Hitchner, R.B. 1995. Roman Africa: An archaeological review. *Journal of Roman Studies* 85: 165–213.

Mattingly, D.J. and MacDonald, K. 2013. Early cities: Africa. In P. Clark (ed.), *The Oxford Handbook of Cities in World History*. Oxford: Oxford University Press, 66–82.

Mattingly, D.J. and Sterry, M. 2013. The first towns in the Central Sahara. *Antiquity* 87.366: 503–18.

Mattingly, D.J., Rushworth, A., Sterry, M. and Leitch, V. 2013. *The African Frontiers*. Frontiers of the Roman Empire series, general editor, D. Breeze. Edinburgh: Hussar.

Mattingly, D.J., Sterry, M. and Edwards, D. 2015. The origins and development of Zuwīla, Libyan Sahara: An archaeological and historical overview. *Azania* 50.1: 27–75.

Mattingly, D.J., Leitch, V., Duckworth, C.N., Cuénod, A., Sterry, M. and Cole, F. (eds). 2017a. *Trade in the Ancient Sahara and Beyond*. Trans-Saharan Archaeology Volume 1. Series editor D.J. Mattingly. Cambridge: Cambridge University Press.

Mattingly, D.J., Bokbot, Y., Sterry, M., Cuénod, A., Fenwick, C., Gatto, M., Ray, N., Rayne, L., Janin, K., Lamb, A., Mugnai, N. and Nikolaus, J. 2017b. Long-term history in a Moroccan oasis zone: The Middle Draa Project 2015. *Journal of African Archaeology*, 15: 141–72.

Mattingly, D.J., Sterry, M., al-Haddad, M. and Bokbot, Y. 2018. Beyond the Garamantes: The early development of Saharan oases. In Purdue *et al.* 2018a, 205–28.

Mattingly, D.J., Sterry, M. and Fothergill, B.T. Forthcoming. Animal traffic in the Sahara. In V. Blanc-Bijon (ed.), *XIe Colloque international Histoire et Archéologie de l'Afrique du Nord.* Marseille: Presses universitaires de Provence.

Mauny, R. 1956. Monnaies antiques trouvées en Afrique au sud du 'limes' romain. *Libyca* 4: 249–61.

Mauny, R. 1978. Trans-Saharan contacts and the Iron Age in West Africa. In J.D. Fage (ed.), *The Cambridge History of Africa, Volume 2.* Cambridge: Cambridge University Press, 272–341.

Messier, R. and Miller, J. 2015. *The Last Civilized Place. Sijilmasa and Its Saharan Destiny.* Austin: University of Texas Press.

Mitchell, P.J. 2005. *African Connections: Archaeological Perspectives on Africa and the Wider World.* Walnut Creek: Altamira Press.

Mitchell, P. and Lane, P. 2013. *The Oxford Handbook of African Archaeology.* Oxford: Oxford University Press.

Monroe, J.C. 2013. The archaeology of the precolonial state in Africa. In Mitchell and Lane 2013, 702–22.

Mori, F. 1998. *The Great Civilization of the Ancient Sahara.* Rome: L'Erma di Bretschneider.

Mori, L. (ed.). 2013. *Life and Death of a Rural Village in Garamantian Times. The Archaeological Research in the Oasis of Fewet (Libyan Sahara).* Firenze: All'Insegna del Giglio.

Morley, N. 2011. Cities and economic development in the Roman Empire. In Bowman and Wilson 2011, 143–60.

Morris, I. 2006. The growth of Greek cities in the first millennium BC. In G. R. Storey (ed.), *Urbanism in the Preindustrial World: Cross-Cultural Approaches.* Tuscaloosa: The University of Alabama Press, 27–51.

Muzzolini, A. 1990. Au sujet de la datation des chars au gallop volant. *Sahara* 2: 115–18.

Nachtigal G. 1974. *Sahara and Sudan, vol I, Tripoli and Fezzan, Tibesti or Tu.* Translated by A.G.B. and H.J. Fisher. London: C. Martin.

Nicholson, S.E. 1979. The methodology of historical climate reconstruction and its application to Africa. *Journal of African History* 20.1: 31–49.

Nicolaisen, J. and Nicolaisen, I. 1997. *The Pastoral Touareg, Ecology, Culture and Society*, 2 vols. London: Thames and Hudson.

Nijman, J. 2007. Introduction – comparative urbanism. *Urban Geography* 28.1: 1–6.

Osborne, R. and Cunliffe, B. (eds). 2005. *Mediterranean Urbanization 800–600 BC.* Oxford: Oxford University Press.

Paris, F. 1984. *La région d'In Gall - Tegidda-n Tesemt (Niger). Programme archéologique d'urgence 1977–1981. III. Les sépultures du néolithique final à l'Islam.* Niamey: Institut de Recherches en Sciences Humaines.

Paris, F. 1996. *Les sépultures du Sahara nigérian, du Néolithique à l'Islamisation*, 2 vols. Paris: Bondy.

Pascon, P. 1984. *La Maison d'Iligh et l'histoire sociale du Tazerwalt.* Rabat: Société Marocaine des Editeurs Réunis.

Perrin, R.M.S. and Mitchell, C.W. 1967. *Glossary of Local Physiographic and Hydrogeological Terms about World Hot Deserts.* Military Engineering Experimental Establishment, Christchurch. Report No. 1124.

Potchter, O., Goldman, D., Kadish, D. and Iluz, D. 2008. The oasis effect in an extremely hot and arid climate: The case of southern Israel. *Journal of Arid Environments* 72.9: 1721–33.

Purdue, L., Charbonnier, J. and Khalidi, L. (eds). 2018a. *Des refuges aux oasis: Vivre en milieu aride de la Préhistoire à aujourd'hui. XXXVIIIe rencontres internationales d'archéologie et d'histoire d'Antibes.* Antibes: Éditions APDCA.

Purdue, L., Charbonnier, J. and Khalidi, L. 2018b. Introduction. Living in arid environments from prehistoric times to the present day: Approaches to the study of refugia and oases. In Purdue *et al.* 2018a, 9–32.

Quinn, J.C. 2009. North Africa. In A. Erskine (ed.), *A Companion to Ancient History.* Oxford: Blackwell, 260–72.

Quinn, J.C. 2018. *In Search of the Phoenicians.* Princeton: Princeton University Press.

Rachet, M. 1970. *Rome et les Berbères. Un probleme militaire d'Auguste à Diocletian.* Brussels: Collection Latomus.

Reader, J. 2004. *Cities.* London: William Heinemann.

Rebuffat, R. 1975. Graffiti en libyque de Bu Njem. *Libya Antiqua* 11–12: 165–87.

Reimer, P.J., Bard, E., Bayliss, A., Beck, J.W., Blackwell, P.G., Bronk Ramsey, C., Grootes, P.M., Guilderson, T.P., Haflidason, H., Hajdas, I., Hatté, C., Heaton, T. J., Hoffmann, D.L., Hogg, A.G., Hughen, K.A., Kaiser, K.F., Kromer, B., Manning, S.W., Niu, M., Reimer, R.W., Richards, D.A., Scott, E.M., Southon, J.R., Staff, R.A., Turney, C.S.M. and van der Plicht, J. 2013. IntCal13 and Marine13 radiocarbon age calibration curves 0–50,000 years cal BP. *Radiocarbon* 55.4: 1869–87.

Renfrew, C. 2008. The city through time and space. In J. Marcus and J.A. Sabloff (ed.), *The Ancient City: New Perspectives on Urbanism in the Old and New World.* Santa Fe: School for advanced Research Press, 29–52.

Reygasse, M. 1950. *Monuments funéraires préislamiques de l'Afrique du Nord.* Paris: Arts et Métiers Graphiques.

Robinson, E.S.G. 1965. *Catalogue of the Greek Coins of Cyrenaica.* Vol. 29. Bologna: A. Forni.

Rohlfs, G. 2003. *Voyages et explorations au Sahara. Tome V, Koufra - les oasis de Djofra et de Djalo 1878–1879* (translated by J. Debetz). Paris: Karthala.

Sahlins, M. and Service, E. (eds). 1960. *Evolution and Culture*. Ann Arbor: University of Michigan Press.

Salama, P. 1981. The Sahara in classical antiquity. In G. Mokhtar (ed.), *UNESCO General History of Africa, II Ancient Civilisations of Africa*. Paris: UNESCO, 513–32.

Sanmartí, J., Kallala, N., Belarte. M.C., Ramon, J., Telmini, B.M., Jornet, R. and Miniaoui, S. 2012. Filling gaps in the protohistory of the eastern Maghreb: The Althiburos Archaeological Project (el Kef, Tunisia). *Journal of African Archaeology* 10.1: 21–44.

Scarin, E. 1934. *Le oasi del Fezzan*. Bologna: Nicola Zanichelli.

Scheele, J. 2010. Traders, saints, and irrigation: Reflections on Saharan connectivity. *The Journal of African History* 51.3: 281–300.

Scheele, J. 2012. *Smugglers and Saints of the Sahara: Regional Connectivity in the Twentieth Century*. Cambridge: Cambridge University Press.

Sèbe, A. 1989. *Moula-Moula. Le Sahara à vol d'oiseau*. Vidauban: Collection Tagoulmoust.

Sèbe, A. and Sèbe, T. 2003. *Sahara: The Atlantic to the Nile*. London: Hachette.

Service, E. 1975. *Origins of the State and Civilization: The process of cultural evolution*. New York: Norton.

Shanahan, T.M., Overpeck, J.T., Wheeler, C.W., Beck, J.W., Pigati, J.S., Talbot, M. R., Scholz, C.A., Peck, J. and King, J.W. 2006. Paleoclimatic variations in West Africa from a record of late Pleistocene and Holocene lake level stands of Lake Bosumtwi, Ghana. *Palaeogeography, Palaeoclimatology, Palaeoecology 242*.3: 287–302.

Shaw, B.D. 1981. Fear and loathing: The nomad menace in Roman Africa. In C. M. Wells (ed.), *Roman Africa/L'Afrique Romaine. The 1980 Vanier lectures*. Ottowa: Les Presses de L'Université d'Ottawa, 29–50.

Shaw, B.D. 1983. 'Eaters of flesh, drinkers of milk': The ancient ideology of the pastoral nomad. *Ancient Society* 13–14 (1982–1983): 5–31.

Sinclair, P. 2013. The archaeology of African urbanism. In Mitchell and Lane 2013, 689–702.

Smith, A.T. 2003. *The Political Landscape: Constellations of Authority in Early Complex Polities*. Los Angeles: University of California Press.

Smith, C.A. 1976. Exchange systems and the spatial distribution of elites: The organization of stratification in agrarian societies. In C.A. Smith (ed.), *Regional Analysis. Volume 2: Social Systems*. New York: Academic Press, 309–74.

Smith, M. (ed.). 2003. *The Social Construction of Ancient Cities*. Washington, DC: Smithsonian Books.

Smith, M.E. 2009. V. Gordon Childe and the urban revolution: an historical perspective on a revolution in urban studies. *Town Planning Review* 80: 2–29.

Sterry, M. and Mattingly, D.J. 2011. DMP XIII: Reconnaissance survey of archaeological sites in the Murzuq area. *Libyan Studies* 42: 89–116.

Sterry, M, and Mattingly, D.J. 2013. Desert Migrations Project XVII: Further AMS dates for historic settlements from Fazzan, south-west Libya. *Libyan Studies* 44: 127–40.

Sterry, M, Mattingly, D.J. and Higham, T. 2012. Desert Migrations Project XVI: Radiocarbon dates from the Murzuq region, southern Libya. *Libyan Studies* 43: 137–47.

Stone, R.G. 1967. A desert glossary. *Earth Science Reviews* 3: 211–68.

Tainter, J.A. 2000. Problem solving: complexity, history, sustainability. *Population and Environment* 22.1: 3–41.

Talbert, R.J.A. (ed.). 2000. *Barrington Atlas of the Greek and Roman World.* Princeton: Princeton University Press.

Thiry, J. 1995. *Le Sahara libyen dans l'Afrique du nord médiéval.* Leuven: Orientalia Lovaniensia Analecta, 72.

Toutain, J. 1896. Les Romains dans le Sahara. *Mélanges de L'Ecole Française de Rome* 16: 63–77.

Trigger, B. 2003. *Understanding Early Civilizations: A Comparative Study.* Cambridge: Cambridge University Press.

Trousset, P. 1982. L'image du nomade saharien dans l'historiographie antique. *Production pastorale et sociéte* 10: 97–105.

Trousset, P. 2012. Nomadisme (Saharien en Afrique du nord dans l'antiquité). *Encyclopedie berbère* fasc 34. Aix-en-Provence: Edisud, 5578–89.

Valloggia, M. 2004. *Les oasis d'Egypte dans l'antiquité. Des origins au deuxième millénaire avant J.-C.* Bischheim: Infolio.

Vernet, R. and Aumassip, G. 1992. *Le Sahara et ses marges: Paléoenvironnements et occupation humaine à l'Holocène: Inventaire des datations 14C.* Meudon: CNRS.

Villiers, M. de and Hirtle, S. 2002. *Sahara. A Natural History.* New York: Walker and Company.

Welsby, D. 1996. *The Kingdom of Kush.* London: British Museum.

Welsby, D. 2013. Kerma and Kush and their neighbours. In Mitchell and Lane 2013, 751–64.

Wilson, A.I. 2005. Foggara irrigation, early state formation and Saharan trade: The Garamantes of Fazzan. *Schriftenreihe der Frontinus-Gesellschaft* 26: 223–34.

Wilson, A.I. 2011. City sizes and urbanization in the Roman Empire. In Bowman and Wilson 2011, 161–95.

Wilson, A.I. 2012. Saharan trade: Short-, medium- and long-distance trade networks in the Roman period. *Azania: Archaeological Research in Africa* 47.4: 409–49.

Wilson, A.I. and Mattingly, D.J. 2003. Irrigation technologies: Foggaras, wells and field systems. In Mattingly 2003, 235–78.

Wilson, A.I., Mattingly, D.J. and Sterry, M. Forthcoming. The diffusion of irrigation technologies in the Sahara in antiquity: Settlement, trade and migration. In Duckworth *et al.* Forthcoming.

Yoffee, N. 2005. *Myths of the Archaic State: Evolution of the Earliest Cities, States and Civilizations*. Cambridge: Cambridge University Press.

Yoffee, N. 2009. Making ancient cities plausible. *Reviews in Anthropology* 38: 264–89.

York, A.M., Smith, M.E. Stanley, B.W., Stark, B.L., Novic, J., Harlan, S.L., Cowgill, G.L. and Boone, C.G. 2011. Ethnic and class clustering through the ages: A transdisciplinary approach to urban neighbourhood social patterns. *Urban Studies* 48.11: 2399–415.

PART II

Oasis Origins in the Sahara: A Region-by-Region Survey

2 Garamantian Oasis Settlements in Fazzan

DAVID J. MATTINGLY, STEFANIA MERLO, LUCIA MORI AND MARTIN STERRY

Introduction

In this chapter we present a case study of early oasis development relating to the area of south-west Libya known as Fazzan and the ancient people known as the Garamantes. The Garamantes were first firmly identified with this area by Duveyrier in the mid-nineteenth century.[1] As will be explained in more detail below, the archaeological rediscovery of the Garamantes properly commenced with a pioneering Italian mission in 1933.[2] There were some large-scale excavations in the 1960s by Mohammed Ayoub and importantly this included work at the Garamantian capital of Old Jarma (ancient Garama), but the poor quality of the work limited the value of the published outputs.[3] More reliable results were achieved by the team led by Charles Daniels between 1959 and 1977, excavating and surveying a number of sites in the area close to Jarma.[4] But, crucially, some of his most important results were not published at the time and this allowed misnomers about the Garamantes to persist well into the 1990s.[5] Far from being a predominantly pastoral, tribal

1 Duveyrier 1864, 275–79. Barth 1857 had wanted to identify Jarma with Garama, but was not convinced by what he saw, seeing the mausoleum as a southern outlier of the Roman dominínion.

2 Pace *et al.* 1951.

3 Ayoub 1967; 1968. For a review of the issues with his excavations see Mattingly 2010, 214–21; 2013, 67–71.

4 For some of his key summary publications, see Daniels 1969; 1970; 1971a; 1989.

5 To give a few examples, Connah 2004, a book on 'Forgotten Africa', does not mention the Garamantes or the early emergence of oasis agriculture; Ehret 2002, 221–22 discusses the Berber migration in the Sahara of the last two millennia BC in terms of scattered groups, without the rise of any polity level units, emphasising trade and warfare as key factors and ignoring the potential importance of oasis agriculture; Lassère 2015, 61, while acknowledging the possible importance of the Garamantes, specifically denies that other Saharan peoples (Gaetules and Aethiopes) were oasis cultivators.

society, the Garamantian kingdom needs reassessing as being founded on multiple oasis communities (some of urban character) and arguably being identifiable as an early state.[6]

Several distinct projects involving the authors of this chapter over the last 20 years have contributed to this dramatic new assessment of the Garamantes. With the exception of the Western Desert of Egypt, this is archaeologically the most intensively investigated area of the Sahara. While the proximity of the Western Desert to the Nile Valley can account for the precocious development there, the implications of the work on the Garamantes are paradigm changing precisely because Fazzan is a remote Central Saharan location, at least 1,000 km from the nearest contemporary urban polities.

Fazzan comprises three main east-west bands of oases, the Wadi ash-Shati to the north, the Wadi al-Ajal in the centre and the Murzuq/Hufra depression (ending in the ash-Sharqiyat area) to the south.[7] There are two outlying clusters of oases in north-south aligned depressions to the south-west (Wadi Tanzzuft) and south-east (Wadi Hikma) that have also been associated with the Garamantes.

The Garamantes first appear in history in Herodotus' account of the Libyan desert, but can be traced archaeologically to populations who were already sedentary and practising agriculture by the early first millennium BC.[8] The earliest, and overall by far the most characteristic archaeological evidence for the Garamantes comes from the Wadi al-Ajal, close to Jarma. While there are cultural links with the other areas of Fazzan, there are also differences. It is thus likely that the term 'Garamantes' evolved over time to accommodate the spread of the power of the group based in the Wadi al-Ajal over neighbouring oases and Saharan communities. The development of oasis communities did not follow exactly the same path or same chronology in Fazzan and, below, we review the principal evidence for each of the zones defined above.

In the Neolithic period, much of Fazzan comprised a savannah landscape in between more verdant sand sea landforms, punctuated by many small lakes, and with some notable upland features (mountains and

[6] For developing argument about the Garamantes as a state, see Mattingly 2003, 346–62; 2004; 2006; 2013, 530–34. Hachid 2000, 92–194, despite being unaware of the latest archaeological evidence, makes a good attempt to contextualise the Garamantes in Saharan and Berber long-term history and to bring out their distinctiveness.

[7] Key studies on the oases of Fazzan include Despois 1946; Gigliarelli 1932; Lethielleux 1948; Sahara Italiano 1937; Scarin 1934. For a useful summary of Medieval sources on these sites, see Thiry 1995.

[8] Mattingly 2003, 76–90, for the literary sources,

plateaux) supplied by springs. Following major climatic change *c.*5000 years ago, hyper-arid desert conditions became established and over time the lakes and springs diminished and dried up.[9] Population groups that had at one time been fairly mobile became tied to the remaining water sources and congregated more and more in the lowest lying areas of the landscape where water was still available at (or easily reachable from) the surface. The later phases of rock art in Fazzan feature horses, chariots, images of palm trees and finally camels, providing strong proxy evidence for the emergence of oasis communities.[10]

Hydraulic conditions varied considerably across Fazzan. Artesian springs are relatively uncommon apart from in the Wadi ash-Shati and the Ghat/Tanzzuft area. However, the difficulty of enhancing the flow of the natural springs in ash-Shati and Ghat with dug artesian wells may have limited the scale of oasis development in these artesian areas for a considerable time. The parts of Fazzan that show the most significant evidence of early oasis development were those that have depended to a greater extent on an elevated water table below the floor of the depression, which could be tapped by means of shallow balance wells, or more elaborately by underground irrigation channels (foggaras). Deeper animal powered wells (*dalw*) appear to be a development of the Medieval period, by which time the level of the groundwater appears to have fallen in some areas to a depth beyond the reach of the balance wells.

History of Research

A number of early European travellers passed through Fazzan in the nineteenth century describing various features of historical interest and remaining a valuable source, especially for the early modern period. The first formal archaeological investigations in Fazzan took place in the winter of 1933–1934 during the Italian colonial period as part of scientific missions into all aspects of life in Fazzan.[11] The majority of the archaeological work was in the Wadi al-Ajal where *c.*100 tombs were excavated in the cemeteries close to Jarma.[12] The mission also conducted a lightning tour of the major centres to the south – Murzuq, Traghan and Zuwila,[13] and concluded their work with a short expedition to Ghat where they excavated four tombs on the Quqaman hill overlooking the old caravan town

[9] Cremaschi 2003.

[10] Barnett 2019a; 2019b; Barnett and Mattingly 2003, 283–88, 301–17; di Lernia and Zampetti 2008.

[11] Pace *et al.* 1951; for a summary see Mattingly 2003, 16–18.

[12] Pace *et al.* 1951, 211–386.

[13] Pace *et al.* 1951, 416–19.

(*medina*).[14] They also identified the first evidence of stone-footed and mudbrick buildings at Jarma, Zinkekra and Qasr Larku (though were not able to demonstrate conclusively the Garamantian date). A French expedition was carried out in the area of Ghat from 1944 to 1945, and Leschi undertook a systematic excavation of the cemeteries at Barkat (related to the fortified citadel of Aghram Nadharif) and Tin Alkum (now in Algeria), whose results were mostly unpublished.[15] The French geographers Despois and Letheilleux surveyed some of the ruined villages and fortifications in Fazzan.[16] These include the first serious reports from the Wadi ash-Shati, where Despois described Qasr Bin Aghenneb, north of Winzrik, comparing it with the Tripolitanian *qsur* of Roman date.[17] Despois suggested a connection between a group of large rectangular *qsur* with projecting angle towers and the foggara irrigation systems: 'il est intéressant de constater que presque partout, les vestiges de foggara voisinent avec les ruines des enceintes fortifiées ou des forts'.[18] Another French expedition led by Pauphillet in 1949 excavated tombs in the eastern Wadi al-Ajal and at Tajirhi in the Wadi Hikma.[19]

In 1961, Mohammed S. Ayoub, the controller of Antiquities in Fazzan, started a series of excavations at cemeteries and settlements in the Wadi al-Ajal, most notably Jarma itself between 1962 and 1967. Research into the Garamantes was also conducted by Charles Daniels from 1958 to 1977. Drawing on aerial photographs of the region, Daniels conducted the first systematic surveys of the Wadi al-Ajal and Murzuq-Hufra depression and also excavated at Zinkekra, Jarma, Saniat Jibril and a number of escarpment settlements.[20] Daniels also made a short visit to DabDab in the ash-Shati where he recorded a cemetery, a foggara and a settlement. Daniels' research established that, from the early first millennium BC, there were permanent settlements whose inhabitants were practising oasis agriculture. Between the 1960s and 1990s, Helmut Ziegert carried out a number of excavations at settlements in Fazzan including Budrinna, Jarma, Zuwila and at a suspected Garamantian settlement at Idri in the Wadi ash-Shati.[21]

14 Pace *et al.* 1951, 386–91; De Agostini 1934.

15 Leschi 1945. For an overview of the history of research on the Garamantes in the Wadi Tanzzuft, see Gatto 2006; Mori 2013.

16 Despois 1946; Lethielleux 1948.

17 Despois 1946, 223.

18 Despois 1946, 57–61, quote at p. 57.

19 Bellair *et al.* 1953, 71–98; Bellair and Pauphillet 1959.

20 Daniels 1968; 1969; 1970; 1971a; 1971b; 1973; 1975; 1977; 1989; the final publication of Daniels work took place after his death and can be found in Mattingly 2007; 2010; 2013.

21 Most of this research remains unpublished: Mattingly 2003, 20; Ziegert 1969. Note also the summary account of the Garamantes in German, Ruprechtsberger 1997.

The most recent phase of archaeological research into historic period Fazzan began in 1997 with the renewal of the Italian-Libyan Archaeological Mission in Messak and Akakus of Sapienza University of Rome under Mario Liverani and the British-Libyan Fazzan Project under David Mattingly. The Italian-Libyan Archaeological Mission, based in Ghat, excavated two major sites at Aghram Nadharif and Fewet as well as several smaller explorations of outlying sites in the Wadi Tanzzuft.[22] The Fazzan project excavated at Jarma and conducted systematic surveys in the Wadi al-Ajal and in the western part of the Murzuq/Hufra depression.[23]

From 2007 to 2011, the Desert Migrations Project (DMP) followed up the British-Libyan work, with a particular emphasis on burials, but also with some exploratory survey in other areas of the main oasis sectors in Fazzan. In 2007–2008, Merlo conducted a first systematic survey of the Wadi ash-Shati as part of the DMP, confirming a long-term chronology of occupation and a substantial Garamantian presence.[24] In 2011, just prior to the Libyan Civil War, Mattingly and Sterry led a short survey of the central Murzuq/Hufra depression, again with important results.[25]

In the synthesis that follows, we present data from each of the main oases zones of Fazzan in turn and draw attention both to similarities and contrasts in the sort of oasis landscapes and settlement histories that have been recorded (Fig. 2.1). Cumulatively, the evidence from Fazzan makes an incontestable case for large-scale pre-Islamic development of sedentary oasis societies alongside Saharan pastoral groupings. Coupled with some explicit historical source information, there is a wide range of archaeological evidence (settlements, burials, irrigation technologies, material culture, rock art imagery, botanical remains) and above all scientific dating. A total of >270 radiocarbon (mostly AMS) dates are now available from Protohistoric and historic sites in several areas of Fazzan and these demonstrate the scale and spread of oasis settlement in this region, as well as providing a level of chronological detail that is unparalleled for this period elsewhere in the Sahara (Table 2.1 summarises the data).[26] Although, this chapter will focus primarily on the Garamantian period, the list also includes some relevant Medieval and early modern dates, as well as a few from the late Pastoral phase.

[22] Liverani 2006; Mori 2013. [23] Mattingly 2003; 2007; 2010; 2013.

[24] Mattingly *et al.* 2007, Merlo *et al.* 2008, Merlo *et al.* 2013.

[25] Sterry and Mattingly 2011; 2013; Sterry *et al.* 2012.

[26] For previous overview of the dates, see Mattingly *et al.* 2018 and for subsets of the dates, see Liverani 2006, 363–74; Mattingly 2007, 294–302; 2010, 78–82; 2013, 43–63, 125–34, 525–29; Mori 2013, 66–69; Sterry and Mattingly 2013; Sterry *et al.* 2012.

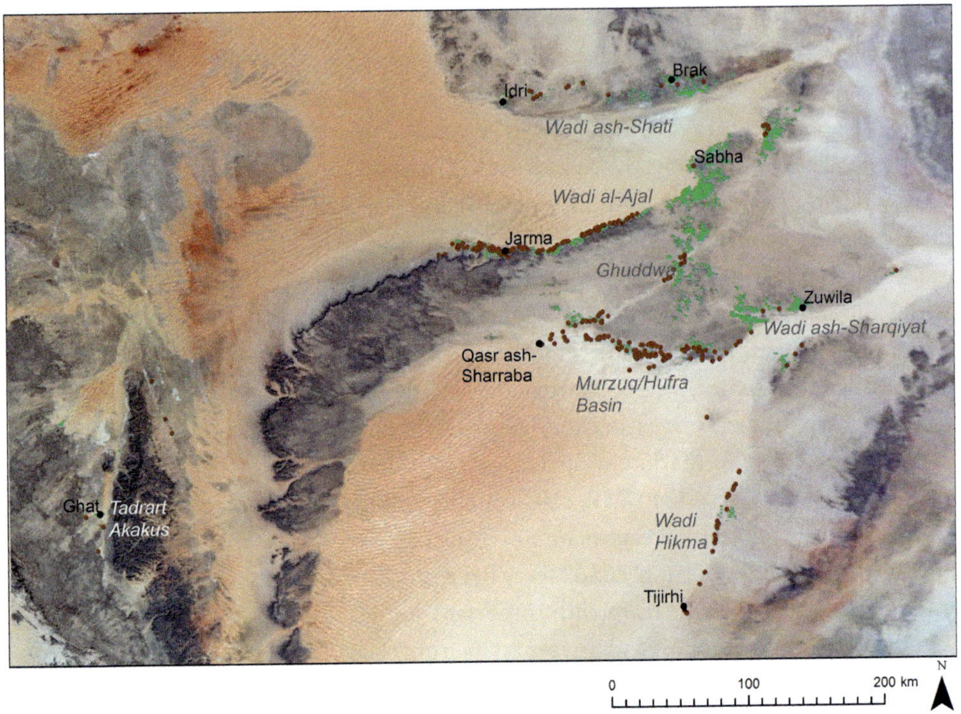

Figure 2.1. Fazzan showing main regions and sites discussed in the text. The brown dots are certain or probable Garamantian oasis settlements.

The evidence reviewed here highlights four major stages of settlement development in Fazzan that correlate with the Early Garamantian period (1000–500 BC), the Proto-Garamantian period (500–1 BC), the Classic Garamantian period (AD 1–300) and the Late Garamantian period (AD 300–700).

Wadi al-Ajal and Jarma (Ancient Garama)

The Wadi al-Ajal comprised the heartlands of the Garamantes (Fig. 2.2). It is not a natural water course, but a 150-km-long, narrow depression, mostly only a few kilometres wide, between the Ubari sand sea to the north and a steep cliff-like sandstone escarpment of Massak Sattafat to the south. There are no artesian spring sources in Wadi al-Ajal, but a high water table, perhaps adventitiously still accessible at some points in the form of phreatic springs in the first millennium BC, will have supported palms and encouraged the development of additional irrigation measures.

Table 2.1 *Protohistoric and historic radiocarbon dates from the Central Sahara (Fazzan)*

Area/Site	Context	Material	Reference	Date	Calibrated
Wadi al-Ajal					
TIN001	Hillfort, Area A2, building by gate	Sorghum	Beta-194236	2180±40 BP	371–113 calBC
TIN001	Area A2, building by gate	Pearl millet	Beta-194237	2130±40 BP	355–46 calBC
TIN001	Area A2, building by gate	Barley	OxA-9573	2117±37 BP	351–43 calBC
TIN001	Area A2, building by gate	Barley	OxA-9574	2074±40 BP	198 calBC–calAD 5
EDS010	Within amphora at *qasr*	Grape	OxA-X-2632-15	1536±25 BP	calAD 427–586
EDS027	*Qasr*	Wood	OxA-X-2632-23	1260±25 BP	calAD 670–860
TAG001	Cemetery, Area 3	Date stone	OxA-X-2632-20	1592±26 BP	calAD 408–539
TAG001	Cemetery, Area 3	Date stone	OxA-29179	1106±23 BP	calAD 890–989
TAG001	Cemetery, Area 3	Date stone	OxA-29244	364±25 BP	calAD 1451–1633
TAG001	Cemetery, Area 3	Date stone	OxA-X-2632-21	309±25 BP	calAD 1492–1648
TAG001	Cemetery, Area 5	Date wood?	OxA-X-2555-52	1830±80 BP	calAD 24–385
TAG001	Cemetery, Area 5	Date stone	OxA-29180	1144±25 BP	calAD 777–975
TAG006	Cemetery	Wood	OxA-X-2554-7	2366±27 BP	533–389 calBC
TAG006	Cemetery	Date stone	OxA-29245	2228±29 BP	382–204 calBC
TAG006	Cemetery	Date stone	OxA-29246	138±25 BP	calAD 1671–1943
TAG006	Cemetery	Date stone	OxA-29247	141±28 BP	calAD 1669–1945
TAG011	*Qasr*	Wood	OxA-9935	2055±70 BP	352 calBC–calAD 83
TAG021	Cemetery	Date wood	OxA-32219	1527±26 BP	calAD 428–600
TAG063	Cemetery	Human tissue	OxA-32321	2283±33 BP	405–210 calBC
TAG063	Cemetery	Date stone	OxA-29248	2153±28 BP	356–94 calBC
ELH013	Mudbrick lining of foggara	Unknown	OxA-26746	2243±26 BP	391–206 calBC
ZIN003.5	Hillfort	Unknown	OxA-X-2632-27	2281±27 BP	402–231 calBC
ZIN013	Hillfort, context 10	Date stone	OxA-3072	2620±70 BP	927–540 calBC

Table 2.1 (*cont.*)

Area/Site	Context	Material	Reference	Date	Calibrated
ZIN013	Hillfort, context 155 hearth	Charcoal	I-6323	2695±100 BP	1127–543 calBC
ZIN013	Hillfort, context 33	Date stone	OxA-3073	2530±70 BP	807–430 calBC
ZIN013	Hillfort, context 51 hearth	Charcoal	I-6321	2595±90 BP	918–430 calBC
ZIN013	Hillfort, apsed room	Charcoal	OxA-6322	2560±110 BP	905–405 calBC
ZIN062	Hillfort, context 1 within building	Wheat	OxA-3070	2560±70 BP	835–430 calBC
ZIN071	Hillfort, accumulation within building	Wheat	OxA-3071	2670±70 BP	1010–591 calBC
ZIN071	Hillfort, mixed debris	Charcoal,	I-6341	2560±110 BP	905–405 calBC
ZIN105	Below hillfort, predates mudbrick building	Charcoal	I-6324	2410±120 BP	803–209 calBC
ZIN105	W area in mudbrick building	Barley	OxA-3075	2490±70 BP	790–416 calBC
ZIN218	Occupation levels	Date stone	OxA-X-2632–19	2515±27 BP	792–542 calBC
ZIN218	Occupation levels	Date stone	OxA-29242	2510±30 BP	791–540 calBC
ZIN218	Occupation levels	Date stone	OxA-X-2633–16	2328±28 BP	474–262 calBC
ZIN220	Cemetery	plant remains	OxA-X-2635–54	2567±27 BP	806–570 calBC
ZIN220	Cemetery	Textile	OxA-X-2557–9	2067±26 BP	171–1 calBC
ZIN337	Hearth in building	Barley	OxA-3074	2620±70 BP	927–540 calBC
ZIN700	Beneath large cairn	Date stone	OxA-29243	2295±28 BP	405–234 calBC
UAT004	Burial cairn	Seeds celtis sp.	OxA-29241	2173±30 BP	361–119 calBC
UAT008	Cemetery	Human tissue	OxA-32324	2242±30 BP	391–206 calBC
UAT008	Cemetery	Date stone	OxA-X-2632–24	1948±27 BP	20 calBC–calAD 126
UAT008	Cemetery	Human tissue	OxA-32223	1917±26 BP	calAD 23–133
UAT008	Cemetery	Textile	OxA-X-2635–52	1913±27 BP	calAD 20–206
UAT008	Cemetery	Unknown	OxA-32322	1886±30 BP	calAD 60–218
UAT008	Cemetery	Human tissue	OxA-32222	1867±28 BP	calAD 76–227
UAT008	Cemetery	other unknown	OxA-32323	1852±29 BP	calAD 85–234
UAT050	Cemetery	Date stone	OxA-32214	1719±27 BP	calAD 250–390

UAT050	Cemetery	Date stone	OxA-32213	1716±28 BP	calAD 251–392
UAT050	Cemetery	Charcoal	OxA-32215	1279±26 BP	calAD 671–771
UAT051	Cemetery	Charcoal	OxA-32293	1425±26 BP	calAD 585–658
UAT056	Cemetery	Charcoal	OxA-32294	1006±25 BP	calAD 985–1147
UAT056	Cemetery	Charcoal	OxA-32295	966±27 BP	calAD 1018–1155
GER001	Old Jarma, Garamantian capital	Charcoal	Hv-4805	2700±100 BP	
GER001	G1	Date wood	OxA-32292	2112±29 BP	204–48 calBC
GER001	G1 (542) 5-late	Barley	OxA-26708	1837±28 BP	calAD 86–244
GER001	G1 (469) 4-mid	Barley	OxA-26749	1774±25 BP	calAD 142–338
GER001	G1 (468) 4-early	Barley	OxA-27254	1685±24 BP	calAD 260–415
GER001	G1 (391) 4-late	Grape	OxA-26748	1576±24 BP	calAD 420–543
GER001	G1 (389) 3-mid	Barley	OxA-27005	1542±25 BP	calAD 427–575
GER001	G1 (283) 3-early	Barley	OxA-26747	1274±25 BP	calAD 673–772
GER001	G1 (1009) 10-early	Date stone	OxA-12707	2247±31 BP	394–206 calBC
GER001	G1 (358) 3-late	Date stone	OxA-10340	122±35 BP	calAD 1677–1941
GER001	G1 (375) 2-early	Cucurbitaceae	OxA-10341	812±35 BP	calAD 1165–1271
GER001	G1 (376) 4-late	Date stone	OxA-10342	204±34 BP	calAD 1643–. . .
GER001	G1 (391) 4-late	Barley	OxA-10343	1657±39 BP	calAD 257–535
GER001	G1 (402) 3-mid	Date stone	OxA-12701	1584±28 BP	calAD 411–543
GER001	G1 (4031) 8-late	Date stone	OxA-12705	2224±28 BP	379–204 calBC
GER001	G1 (468) 4-early	Barley	OxA-10344	1730±37 BP	calAD 231–398
GER001	G1 (535) 5-late	Cotton	Beta-194241	1600±40 BP	calAD 383–557
GER001	G1 (542) 5-late	Barley grain	OxA-10347	1776±37 BP	calAD 133–345
GER001	G1 (572) 5-late	Date stone	OxA-10345	1661±35 BP	calAD 257–532
GER001	G1 (586) 3-early	Wheat	OxA-10346	1554±36 BP	calAD 417–582
GER001	G1 (607) 5-mid	Pearl millet	OxA-10290	1930±80 BP	160 calBC–calAD 314
GER001	G1 (61) 1-early	Pumpkin or squash	OxA-10288	220±55 BP	calAD 1518–. . .
GER001	G1 (611) 5-early	Date stone	OxA-10352	1690±38 BP	calAD 252–420

Table 2.1 (*cont.*)

Area/Site	Context	Material	Reference	Date	Calibrated
GER001	G1 (65) 1 to 2	Maize	OxA-10339	95±37 BP	calAD 1681–1938
GER001	G1 (652) 5-late	Date stone	OxA-10349	1269±35 BP	calAD 663–865
GER001	G1 (655) 5-late	Date stone	OxA-10350	1285±36 BP	calAD 656–857
GER001	G1 (661) 6-late	Cotton	Beta-194240	1770±40 BP	calAD 135–379
GER001	G1 (661) 6-late	Barley	OxA-10351	1727±36 BP	calAD 236–396
GER001	G1 (665) 6-early	Barley	OxA-10289	1670±55 BP	calAD 243–535
GER001	G1 (678) 6-mid	Date stone	OxA-10353	1764±37 BP	calAD 141–381
GER001	G1 (686) 6-late	Date stone	OxA-10354	1657±37 BP	calAD 257–534
GER001	G1 (753) 4-late	Charcoal	OxA-12709	950±26 BP	calAD 1025–1154
GER001	G1 (82) 1 to 2	Maize	OxA-10338	161±35 BP	calAD 1663–. . .
GER001	G1 (824) 6-early	Date stone	OxA-12702	1817±30 BP	calAD 125–322
GER001	G1 (864) 8-late	Pearl millet	Beta-194239	1930±40 BP	40 calBC–calAD 209
GER001	G1 (925) 7-late	Date stone	OxA-12703	1856±29 BP	calAD 83–232
GER001	G1 (951) 9-early	Date stone	OxA-12706	2219±29 BP	373–203 calBC
GER001	G1 (951) 9-early	Pearl millet	Beta-194242	2160±40 BP	361–92 calBC
GER001	G1 (955) 10-late	Date stone	OxA-12713	2246±27 BP	391–207 calBC
GER001	G1 (962) 9-early	Date stone	OxA-12712	2133±28 BP	350–54 calBC
GER001	G1 (963) 7-late	Date stone	OxA-12704	1960±30 BP	40 calBC–calAD 121
GER001	G1 (978) 8-early	Charcoal	OxA-12708	2123±28 BP	346–52 calBC
GER001	G2 section (cf. 2057) 5-late	Unknown	unknown	1285±95 BP	calAD 598–970
GER001	G2 section (2057) 5-late	Date stone	OxA-12710	1303±26 BP	calAD 660–769
GER001	G2 section (2057) 5-late	Grape	OxA-12711	1322±26 BP	calAD 653–766
GER001	G3 (3014) 1 to 2	Pearl millet	OxA-10348	170±34 BP	calAD 1656–. . .
GER001.4	(219)	Date stone	OxA-9575	2260±34 BP	399–207 calBC
GER001.5	Below wall	Charcoal	OxA-9576	1928±34 BP	37 calBC–calAD 138
GER001.5	Below wall	Charcoal	OxA-9820	1901±38 BP	calAD 24–219

GER001.6	In mosque foundations	Charcoal	OxA-9632	921±36 BP	calAD 1026–1203
GER001.9	City wall	plant remains tamarisk?	OxA-26494	972±29 BP	calAD 1016–1155
GER001.9	City wall	Charcoal	OxA-9933	1135±45 BP	calAD 774–990
GER001.13	D-shaped tower	Charcoal	OxA-9934	270±40 BP	calAD 1486–. . .
GER001.15	Below pier of mosque	Date stone	OxA-9577	1062±34 BP	calAD 895–1025
GER001.15	Below pier of mosque	Date stone	OxA-9578	716±35 BP	calAD 1225–1386
GER001.34	NW gate	Date stone	OxA-26739	194±23 BP	calAD 1657–. . .
GER001.65	*Qasaba* tower	Twigs	OxA-9769	492±34 BP	calAD 1330–1454
GER001.65	*Qasaba* wall	Date stone	OxA-9579	532±32 BP	calAD 1318–1440
GSC030	Royal Cemetery, tomb 8 (original burial)	Date stone	OxA-29181	1555±29 BP	calAD 422–567
GSC030	Royal Cemetery, tomb 8 (possible robbing)	Date stone	OxA-29249	206±27 BP	calAD 1648–. . .
GSC031	Royal Cemetery, XX	Date stone	OxA-29250	1747±27 BP	calAD 235–381
Tuwash area	Burial from wadi collected by Ulrich Hallier, university Bonn	Unknown	Bonn-145	1950±60 BP	92 calBC–calAD 220
Wadi al-Ajal	Ziegert – unknown context	Unknown	Hv-5479	2115±130 BP	415 calBC–calAD 214
Wadi al-Ajal	Ziegert – unknown context	Unknown	Hv-6980	1965±420 BP	1018 calBC–calAD 889
Wadi al-Ajal	Ziegert – unknown context	Unknown	Hv-5487	1830±85 BP	
Wadi al-Ajal	Ziegert – unknown context	Unknown	Hv-5486	660±165 BP	calAD 1020–1632
FUG022	*Qasr*	Date stone	OxA-26737	399±23 BP	calAD 1440–1619
FUG022	*Qasr*	Date stone	OxA-26738	374±23 BP	calAD 1448–1630
CHA031	Infill of foggara channel	Charcoal	OxA-9581	modern± BP	calAD 1896–1904
TEK010	*Qasr* (medieval type)	Charcoal	OxA-10100	1110±40 BP	calAD 778–1018
FJJ013	*Qasr*	Unknown	OxA-26493	1645±31 BP	calAD 267–535
FJJ056	*Qasr*	Date stone	OxA-26736	1687±25 BP	calAD 258–415
GRE015	*Qasr*	Date stone	OxA-26751	1581±25 BP	calAD 417–541
GRE015	*Qasr*	Date stone	OxA-26750	1542±25 BP	calAD 427–575

Table 2.1 (*cont.*)

Area/Site	Context	Material	Reference	Date	Calibrated
LEK018	*Qasr* (medieval type)	Date stone	OxA-9821	404±32 BP	calAD 1434–1625
LEK021	*Qasr*	Charcoal	OxA-9823	1632±35 BP	calAD 342–536
Budrinna	Child (mummified)?	Human tissue	KI-394	1470±110 BP	calAD 340–770
Budrinna	Child (mummified)?	Human tissue	KI-396	1330±40 BP	calAD 643–770
Budrinna	Child (mummified)	Human tissue	KI-392	1360±60 BP	calAD 563–774
ZOU015	Fortified stone village	Twigs	OxA-9822	279±32 BP	calAD 1496–1796
GBD001	*Qasr*	Charcoal	OxA-9853	1560±45 BP	calAD 405–595
GBD001	Enceinte	Date stone	OxA-9580	1614±35 BP	calAD 356–543
GBD002	*Qasr*	Charcoal	OxA-9941	1654±35 BP	calAD 259–534
GBD007	*Qasr*	Charcoal	OxA-9825	1684±35 BP	calAD 255–423
BNH005	*Qasr* (medieval)	preserved timber	OxA-9824	582±35 BP	calAD 1298–1419
Massak Sattafat	Unknown context	Charcoal	UGAMS-5854	2980±25 BP	1277–1121 calBC
Massak Sattafat	Unknown context	Charcoal	UGAMS-5857	1790±25 BP	calAD 136–326
Wadi Barjuj/Wadi Utba					
MAR001	*Qasr*	Tamarisk	OxA-9940	1600±40 BP	calAD 383–557
SCH020	Qasr ah-Sharraba, *qasr* B	Date stone	OxA-26740	1687±24 BP	calAD 259–413
SCH020	Qasr ah-Sharraba, *qasr* A	Date stone	OxA-26742	1509±24 BP	calAD 432–615
SCH020	Qasr ah-Sharraba, NW tower of fort	Plant remains	OxA-26741	795±23 BP	calAD 1210–1274
SCH020	Qasr ah-Sharraba, build-up within qasr A	Charcoal	OxA-9826	918±32 BP	calAD 1029–1187
SCH020	Qasr ah-Sharraba, *qasr* A	Charcoal	OxA-9631	1721±39 BP	calAD 235–405
SCH020	Qasr ah-Sharraba, *qasr* A	Charcoal	OxA-9942	1431±33 BP	calAD 569–659

Murzuq Basin					
MZQ001	Old Murzuq, S side town wall	Cereal	OxA-26492	415±31 BP	calAD 1427–1620
MZQ001	Old Murzuq, house in abandoned S area	Unknown	OxA-26735	380±23 BP	calAD 1446–1626
MZQ001	Old Murzuq, SW city wall	Date stone	OxA-26733	1.04707±0.00289 BP	calAD 1896–1904
MZQ001	Old Murzuq, SW city wall	Date stone	OxA-25826	1.06715±0.00272 BP	calAD 1896–1904
MZQ001	Old Murzuq, D-shaped tower, S town wall	Unknown	OxA-26734	71±22 BP	calAD 1695–1919
MZQ001	Old Murzuq, D-shaped tower, town wall	Date stone	OxA-25827	98±21 BP	calAD 1691–1925
MZQ001	Old Murzuq, late buttress, *qasaba*	Date stone	OxA-25828	143±22 BP	calAD 1669–1945
MZQ007	*Qasr*	Wood	OxA-26725	1621±23 BP	calAD 386–535
MZQ007	*Qasr* (medieval phase)	Acacia	OxA-25825	572±24 BP	calAD 1308–1418
MZQ021	*Qasaba* in fortified village	Unknown	OxA-25796	477±26 BP	calAD 1411–1450
MZQ021	Enceinte of fortified village	Rodent bone	OxA-X-2475-37	97±26 BP	calAD 1687–1927
MZQ031	Dispersed village	Tamarisk	OxA-25797	270±28 BP	calAD 1520–1798
HHG001	Gate of central *qasr*	Unknown	OxA-26726	1578±24 BP	calAD 420–541
HHG001	SW corner of central *qasr*	Date stone	OxA-25821	1577±23 BP	calAD 421–541
HHG001	SW corner outer enceinte	Unknown	OxA-26487	1581±30 BP	calAD 410–545
HHG006	*Qasr*	Unknown	OxA-26490	1840±38 BP	calAD 76–314
HHG007	*Qasr*	Date stone	OxA-25829	1772±26 BP	calAD 142–340
HHG008	*Qasr*	Unknown	OxA-26728	1614±24 BP	calAD 392–536
HHG012	*Qasaba* of fortified village	Date stone	OxA-25831	543±21 BP	calAD 1321–1431
HHG012	Mosque in fortified village	Date wood	OxA-25830	530±22 BP	calAD 1327–1436
HHG013	*Qasr*	Cereal	OxA-26488	1714±31 BP	calAD 249–395
HHG014	*Qasr*	Date wood	OxA-26727	1630±24 BP	calAD 348–535
HHG014	*Qasr*	Date wood	OxA-25832	1585±23 BP	calAD 416–540
HHG014	Late disturbance/fire on *qasr*	Unknown	OxA-26489	1.36896±0.00437 BP	calAD 1896–1904
GAT001	*Qasr*	Unknown	OxA-25833	1582±22 BP	calAD 419–539
GAT007	*Qasr*	Date stone	OxA-25834	117±21 BP	calAD 1682–1936
GAT010	*Qasr*, buttressing NE tower	Date stone	OxA-25823	1580±24 BP	calAD 420–540
GAT010	*Qasr*, E wall	Olive?	OxA-25822	1577±22 BP	calAD 421–541

Table 2.1 (*cont.*)

Area/Site	Context	Material	Reference	Date	Calibrated
GAT012	*Qasr*	Cereal	OxA-26491	1783±29 BP	calAD 136–333
ZZW013	SE tower secondary *qasr*	Date stone	OxA-25824	1644±26 BP	calAD 337–532
ZZW013	SE tower secondary *qasr*	Cereal	OxA-26729	1589±23 BP	calAD 414–539
ZZW014	*Qasr*	Unknown	OxA-26731	1587±24 BP	calAD 414–540
ZZW016	*Qasr*	Unknown	OxA-25869	1662±25 BP	calAD 266–426
ZZW018	SE tower *qasr*	Date stone	OxA-25870	1730±25 BP	calAD 247–383
ZZW018	SE corner of *qasr*	Unknown	OxA-26732	1552±24 BP	calAD 426–563
ZZW101	*Qasr*	Unknown	OxA-26730	1507±25 BP	calAD 432–619
Zuwila					
ZUL001	Zuwila, pisé wall of citadel	Date stone	OxA-26743	1065±23 BP	calAD 900–1020
ZUL002	Zuwila, 'White mosque'	Date stone	OxA-26744	1260±24 BP	calAD 670–857
ZUL003	Zuwila, tombs of Banu Khattab	Unknown	OxA-26745	1029±24 BP	calAD 976–1031
ZUL003	Zuwila, tombs of Banu Khattab	Unknown	OxA-26495	1038±27 BP	calAD 904–1032
Wadi Tanzzuft					
Wadi Tanzzuft	Burial 00/195		Gx-28482	3530±40 BP	1971–1745 calBC
Wadi Tanzzuft	Burial 00/195bis		Gx-28483	3030±40 BP	1407–1131 calBC
Wadi Tanzzuft	Burial 00/98 T4		Gx-28440	2310±40 BP	482–209 calBC
Wadi Tanzzuft	Burial 96/129 S2		Gx-28441	3370±40 BP	1752–1533 calBC
Wadi Tanzzuft	Burial 96/129 T1		Gx-28476	3850±40 BP	2461–2204 calBC
Wadi Tanzzuft	Burial 96/129 T1		Gx-26255	3080±40 BP	1431–1231 calBC
Wadi Tanzzuft	Burial 96/129 T10		Gx-28479	2720±190 BP	1386–406 calBC
Wadi Tanzzuft	Burial 96/129 T2		Gx-26256	2910±40 BP	1224–980 calBC
Wadi Tanzzuft	Burial 96/129 T3		Gx-27386	3760±40 BP	2293–2036 calBC
Wadi Tanzzuft	Burial 96/129 T3bis		Gx-28477	2930±40 BP	1258–1011 calBC
Wadi Tanzzuft	Burial 96/129 T4		Gx-28478	2550±30 BP	801–551 calBC
Wadi Tanzzuft	Burial 97/5 RT	Date stone	Gx-27385	1700±40 BP	calAD 246–416

Wadi Tanzzuft	Burial 97/5 SF 25	Charcoal	Gx-27383	1850±80 BP	18 calBC–calAD 380
Wadi Tanzzuft	Burial 97/5 SF 7	Charcoal	Gx-27384	1740±40 BP	calAD 174–400
Wadi Tanzzuft	Burial 97/5 T1		Gx-28450	4280±100 BP	3326–2580 calBC
Wadi Tanzzuft	Burial T43		Gx-28481	3310±40 BP	1687–1503 calBC
Wadi Tanzzuft	Burial T6		Gx-28480	3330±40 BP	1731–1511 calBC
Wadi Tanzzuft	THA4	Charcoal	GX-20011-AMS	3890±60 BP	2564–2155 calBC
Fewet	Settlement Fw1		Gx-28452	2950±70 BP	1390–943 calBC
Fewet	Settlement Fws1b3		Gx-30340-AMS	2230±50 BP	396–186 calBC
Fewet	Settlement Fw23		Gx-30339	2260±70 BP	507–114 calBC
Fewet	Settlement FwS1b2		Gx-30335-AMS	2070±40 BP	195 calBC–calAD 16
Fewet	Settlement Fw5		UGAMS-13136	2020±20 BP	88 calBC–calAD 50
Fewet	Settlement Fw6		UGAMS-13137	1990±25 BP	44 calBC–calAD 63
Fewet	Settlement Fw4		Gx-30341-ext	2060±70 BP	353 calBC–calAD 79
Fewet	Settlement Fw13		Gx-30337-AMS	2000±40 BP	111 calBC–calAD 83
Fewet	Settlement Fw16		Gx-30343-AMS	1980±40 BP	88 calBC–calAD 124
Fewet	Settlement Fw9		Gx-30342-AMS	1970±40 BP	50 calBC–calAD 125
Fewet	Settlement Fw14		Gx-30338-AMS	1940±40 BP	45 calBC–calAD 136
Fewet	Settlement Fw28		Gx-31078-AMS	1950±70 BP	151 calBC–calAD 233
Fewet	Settlement FW11		Gx-30336-AMS	1890±60 BP	38 calBC–calAD 252
Fewet	Settlement kiln		Gx-31081	710±60 BP	calAD 1210–1400
Fewet necropolis	T1287 H4		UGAMS-02205	3590±40 BP	2117–1779 calBC
Fewet necropolis	T669 H1		UGAMS-02203	2520±40 BP	798–521 calBC
Fewet necropolis	T41 H1		UGAMS-02204	2390±40 BP	747–389 calBC
Fewet necropolis	T1210 H1		UGAMS-08704a	2320±25 BP	411–361 calBC
Fewet necropolis	T719 H1		UGAMS-02200	2360±70 BP	760–231 calBC
Fewet necropolis	T1226 H1		UGAMS-02209	2290±40 BP	408–208 calBC
Fewet necropolis	T1197 H1		UGAMS-02201	2230±40 BP	388–202 calBC
Fewet necropolis	T1191		UGAMS-02210	2220±40 BP	387–197 calBC

Table 2.1 (*cont.*)

Area/Site	Context	Material	Reference	Date	Calibrated
Fewet necropolis	T669 H1		LTL-13707A	2220±45 BP	391–184 calBC
Fewet necropolis	T1261 H1		UGAMS-02206	2160±40 BP	361–92 calBC
Fewet necropolis	T1223 H1		UGAMS-8705a	2120±25 BP	334–53 calBC
Fewet necropolis	T1223 H1		UGAMS-8705	2060±25 BP	166 calBC–calAD 1
Fewet necropolis	T715 H1		LTL-13441A	1962±40 BP	45 calBC–calAD 125
Fewet necropolis	T976 H1		UGAMS-02208	1960±40 BP	43 calBC–calAD 125
Fewet necropolis	T914 H1		UGAMS-08703	1940±25 BP	calAD 7–126
Fewet necropolis	T1210 H1		UGAMS-08704	1900±25 BP	calAD 32–210
Fewet necropolis	T954 H1		UGAMS-02202	1920±40 BP	19 calBC–calAD 214
Fewet necropolis	T716 H1		UGAMS-08702a	1840±25 BP	calAD 88–240
Fewet necropolis	T914 H1		UGAMS-08703a	1810±25 BP	calAD 130–317
Fewet necropolis	T716 H1		UGAMS-08702	1740±25 BP	calAD 240–381
Aghram Nadharif	Citadel		Gx-27380	2380±50 BP	751–377 calBC
Aghram Nadharif	Citadel		Gx-28443-AMS	2250±40 BP	397–204 calBC
Aghram Nadharif	Citadel		Gx-27379	2290±90 BP	750–109 calBC
Aghram Nadharif	Citadel		GX-2090-AMS	2090±30 BP	195–42 calBC
Aghram Nadharif	Citadel		Gx-28453	1980±60 BP	166 calBC–calAD 134
Aghram Nadharif	Citadel		Gx-27382	1990±70 BP	194 calBC–calAD 208
Aghram Nadharif	Citadel		Gx-28444-AMS	1930±40 BP	40 calBC–calAD 209
Aghram Nadharif	Citadel		Gx-28445-AMS	1920±40 BP	19 calBC–calAD 214
Aghram Nadharif	Citadel		Gx-24267	1880±75 BP	42 calBC–calAD 329
Aghram Nadharif	Citadel		Gx-24268	1760±70 BP	calAD 87–416
Aghram Nadharif	Citadel		Gx-28442	1590±40 BP	calAD 391–560
Aghram Nadharif	Citadel		Gx-27920-AMS	1580±40 BP	calAD 397–565
Aghram Nadharif	Citadel		Gx-27029	1610±90 BP	calAD 241–630
Aghram Nadharif	Citadel		Gx-31080	770±70 BP	calAD 1046–1390

Aghram Nadharif	Citadel		Gx-27381	670±60 BP	calAD 1251–1411
el-Barkat I	Burial		Sa-92	1330±120 BP	calAD 431–975
el-Barkat II	Burial		Sa-93	1680±150 BP	calAD 29–649
Tadrart Akakus					
Adad	*Qasr*	Unknown	Gx-30334-AMS	2090±40 BP	333 calBC–calAD 2
Adad	*Qasr*	Unknown	Gx-30329-AMS	2040±40 BP	167 calBC–calAD 51
Imessarajen	*Qasr*	Unknown	Gx-30331-AMS	2060±30 BP	170 calBC–calAD 4
Imessarajen	*Qasr*	Unknown	Gx-30334-AMS	2050±40 BP	174 calBC–calAD 49
Imessarajen	*Qasr*	Unknown	Gx-30332-AMS	1950±40 BP	41 calBC–calAD 129
Imessarajen	*Qasr*	Unknown	Gx-30328-ext	2020±100 BP	356 calBC–calAD 220
Imessarajen	*Qasr*	Unknown	Gx-30330-AMS	1550±40 BP	calAD 418–594
Erg Uan Kasa	94/106	Wood	Gx-20710	2375±110 BP	791–206 calBC
Uan Amil	Rock shelter	Dung	Bo-341	1260±60 BP	calAD 655–891
Uan Muhuggiag	Rock shelter deposit B/1	Date stone	OxA-4389	2130±70 BP	
Uan Muhuggiag	Rock shelter deposit B/1	citrullus colocynthis	Gd-4290	2220±220 BP	807 calBC–calAD225
Uan Muhuggiag	Rock shelter deposit B/1	Coprolite	Gd-4288	2770±80 BP	1127–798 calBC
Uan Muhuggiag	Rock shelter wall	Dung	Enea	3195±70 BP	1627–1292 calBC
Uan Muhuggiag	Rock shelter Tr 1A Level 2	Animal bone	OxA-17909	2925±27 BP	1214–1030 calBC
Uan Muhuggiag	Rock shelter Tr 1A Level 2	Animal bone	OxA-17960	2915±28 BP	1209–1017 calBC
Wadi Hikma					
Tajirhi	Burial	Leather	Sa-78	1190±120 BP	calAD 615–1118

Figure 2.2. Garamantian settlement (and probable Garamantian settlement) in the Wadi al-Ajal.

Jarma itself sits adjacent to a spring which in Medieval times still served to fill the moat around its walls. However, mechanical exploitation of groundwater has always been the predominant irrigation strategy here. In the nineteenth century water was still to be found in places at a depth of only a few metres, easily reachable with simple balance wells (the *shaduf*). The most remarkable aspect of Garamantian irrigation in the Wadi al-Ajal (and to a lesser extent in other areas) was its strong reliance on more advanced technology, the foggara irrigation systems. These are underground water channels similar to the Near Eastern *qanat* and the technology was almost certainly transferred from Persia to Egypt in the sixth–fifth centuries BC and from there along the oasis chain that links the Western Desert with Fazzan.[27] Examples in the Western Desert oases have been dated to the fifth century BC and, as we shall see, one example in Fazzan has now been dated scientifically to the fourth–third century BC.[28]

Along the southern escarpment of the Wadi al-Ajal there are notable concentrations of pre-Islamic burial monuments – variously estimated at 60,000–120,000 or even 250,000.[29] Although the Garamantian dates of the

[27] Wilson 2006; 2009; Wilson and Mattingly 2003.

[28] See Wilson *et al.* Forthcoming, for full presentation of the date.

[29] These comprise a mixture of circular shafts, cairns, drum tombs and mudbrick constructions, Pace *et al.* 1951, 210–12; Daniels 1989, 49. Recent surveys in some of these cemeteries suggest that the older estimates of numbers were significantly undercounted, Mattingly *et al.* 2008; 2009; 2010a; 2010b; 2011. For a summary account, Mattingly *et al.* 2019.

settlements at Zinkekra, Jarma and Saniat Jibril were first demonstrated in the 1960s–1970s, until recently almost no other habitation sites had been conclusively assigned to the Garamantian era. Based largely on Daniels' work, the Barrington Atlas sheet compiled by Mattingly in the late 1990s showed only 10 settlements and 32 major cemeteries in the Wadi al-Ajal.[30] Subsequent fieldwalking in the oasis has identified the existence of many sites, though surface traces are not always distinct enough to clarify whether we are dealing with settlements or cemeteries. However, many sites have some upstanding remains, in particular of fortified square buildings (*qsur*), and surface pottery and AMS dates have revealed a surprising number of these to predate the Medieval period. We can now recognise *c.*100 Garamantian villages and hamlets in the Wadi al-Ajal, with very high densities in two areas where our survey work has been more intensive (the Taqallit to al-Hatiya sector of the wadi, *c.*30 km west of Jarma, and the immediate environs of Jarma).[31] There was a complex chronological sequence of development here, from a relatively small number of sites that appear to have originated in the early first millennium BC, to a major phase of expansion in the latter centuries BC, consolidation in the early centuries AD and apparently some contraction and concentration on fortified oasis villages in late antiquity.

There was an initial (Early Garamantian) phase of hillfort activity at suitable sites along the escarpment edge (Fig. 2.3).[32] The type site is Zinkekra,[33] where a settlement was established by the early first millennium BC, associated from the beginning with an agricultural package including wheat, barley and the grape vine alongside the date palm.[34] The early buildings at the site were oval and sub-rectangular huts with one to three rooms, but by the later centuries BC, the site took on a more proto-urban character with mudbrick construction of complex multi-roomed rectilinear buildings and surrounding walls and embankments.[35]

30 Mattingly 2000 for the Barrington Atlas map. The total number of cemetery sites is actually much larger than portrayed there (Mattingly 2007, includes >300 cemeteries of Garamantian, or probable Garamantian, date from the Wadi al-Ajal alone) and this always made it probable that significant numbers of contemporary settlements would be found when searched for. The Fazzan Project work (1997–2001) and subsequent work as part of the Desert Migrations Project and the Trans-SAHARA Project has dramatically added to this total, see Mattingly 2013, 525–34.

31 Mattingly 2007, 64–167; 2013, 525–29; Mattingly *et al.* 2010b, 117–31 (Taqallit).

32 About 20 such sites are now known, though not all can be closely dated, Mattingly 2003, 136–42; 2010, 19–119.

33 Daniels 1968; Hawthorne *et al.* 2010, 19–84.

34 Van der Veen 1992; Van der Veen and Westley 2010.

35 Mattingly 2010, 22–26, on the walls.

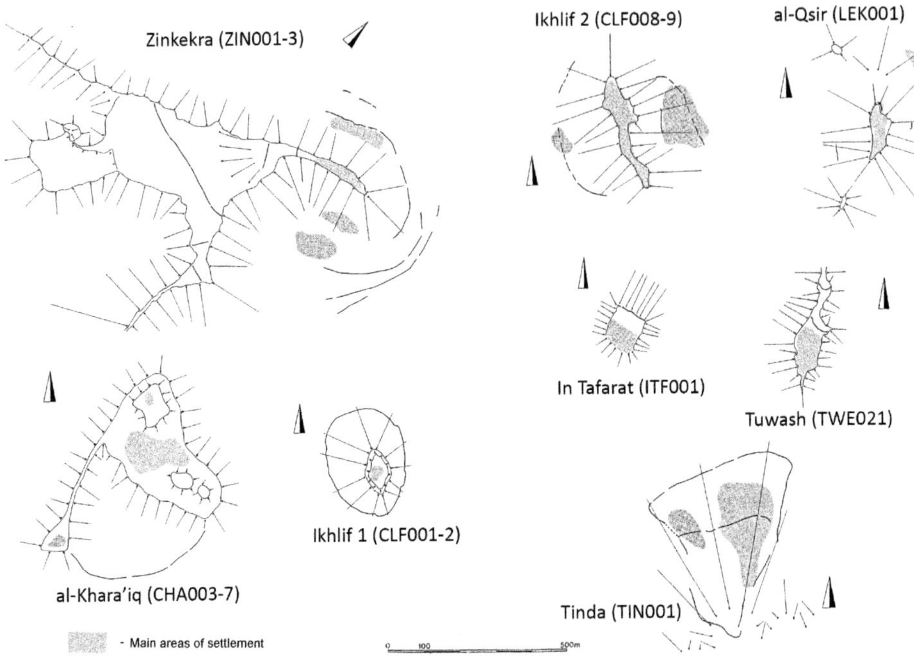

Figure 2.3. Comparative plans of Garamantian hillfort sites in Wadi al-Ajal (see Mattingly 2007; 2010 for details of these sites).

The later phases at Zinkekra overlapped with the earliest evidence for the construction of new mudbrick settlements in the centre of the depression, a kilometre or more away from the escarpment and now more closely connected with the probable location of the irrigated gardens. The occupation sequence at Zinkekra is well-dated by a sequence of AMS and Radiometric radiocarbon dates to the first millennium BC, with an earlier group and a later group indicating prolonged habitation (see Table 2.1).[36]

The long-term capital of the Garamantes was one of these new oasis settlements, established at Old Jarma (ancient Garama) from *c.*400 BC.[37] As the Garamantian capital (described as a *metropolis* by the ancient sources), it is perhaps unsurprising to find some unusual features, as yet unparalleled at other Garamantian sites.[38] This site was *c.*9 ha in area and from the first century BC featured buildings utilising dressed stone masonry alongside regular mudbrick construction (Fig. 2.7a). In the first and second centuries AD, some buildings were erected in ashlar quality

[36] Mattingly 2007, 294–95; 2010, 78–82.

[37] Mattingly 2013; 2016; cf. also the publications of Ayoub 1967; 1968.

[38] Pliny, *Natural History* 5.35–38, Ptolemy, *Geography* 4.6.30, on Jarma; cf. Mattingly 2013, 9–10, 530–34, for discussion.

masonry and utilising Mediterranean influenced architectural features (columns, capitals and architrave, etc.).[39] One of these was almost certainly a Garamantian temple.[40]

Botanical remains attest to the oasis agricultural economy, which seems to have become more intensive by the Classic Garamantian period with the introduction of summer crops like sorghum and pearl millet, as well as cotton.[41] An extensive series of AMS dates allow us to trace occupation at the site from *c.*400 BC until its final abandonment in 1935.[42] Garama merits recognition as a true urban settlement and it may have had defences from an early date, though evidence is inconclusive. In late antiquity it appears to have had a central fortified compound (*qasr*), a feature now widely recognised at other Late Garamantian sites.[43]

Close by was a *c.*3.5 ha undefended village settlement, Saniat Jibril (Fig. 2.5 – GER002).[44] The site is dated by imported ceramics to the first to fourth centuries AD, though there are some hints of earlier and later activity. Of particular interest is the recognition of extensive manufacturing activity (metallurgy, bead making, weaving and glass working).[45] Similar evidence was also noted at Jarma and indicates that Garamantian society was not wholly dependent on oasis agriculture.[46]

A particularly instructive example of the pattern of development of oasis centre settlement relates to the area around the Taqallit headland, *c.*30 km west of Jarma. Here there are very limited traces of Early Garamantian activity, but there was a dramatic transformation of the landscape in the Proto-Urban phase, with the creation of at least 11 main settlements linked to major cemeteries of drum and corbelled cairns along the escarpment by the lines of shafts of foggara irrigation systems. Dating evidence links the initial development of all of these elements in the oasis landscape to the latter centuries BC, although the scale and complexity of the archaeology certainly represents a great deal of subsequent consolidation. The lack of evidence for a substantial localised population prior to this point, supports the identification of this as pioneer farming development, with settlers expanding into this area from parts of the wadi where oasis farming was already established (Fig. 2.4). The firm dating of new crops and of the construction of a foggara to this phase suggests that the expansion was also enabled by technological developments. The settlement pattern in this area suggests a very dense

[39] Mattingly 2013, 67–115. [40] Mattingly 2013, 93–100, 203–25, 291–92.
[41] Pelling 2005; 2008; 2013a; 2013b. [42] Mattingly 2007, 294–302; 2013, 125–34.
[43] Mattingly 2013, 90–92, 513, 532; Mattingly and Sterry 2013.
[44] Mattingly *et al.* 2010c, 123–204. [45] Mattingly 2007, 448–62; 2010, 126–30.
[46] Mattingly 2013, 511–12, 515–17.

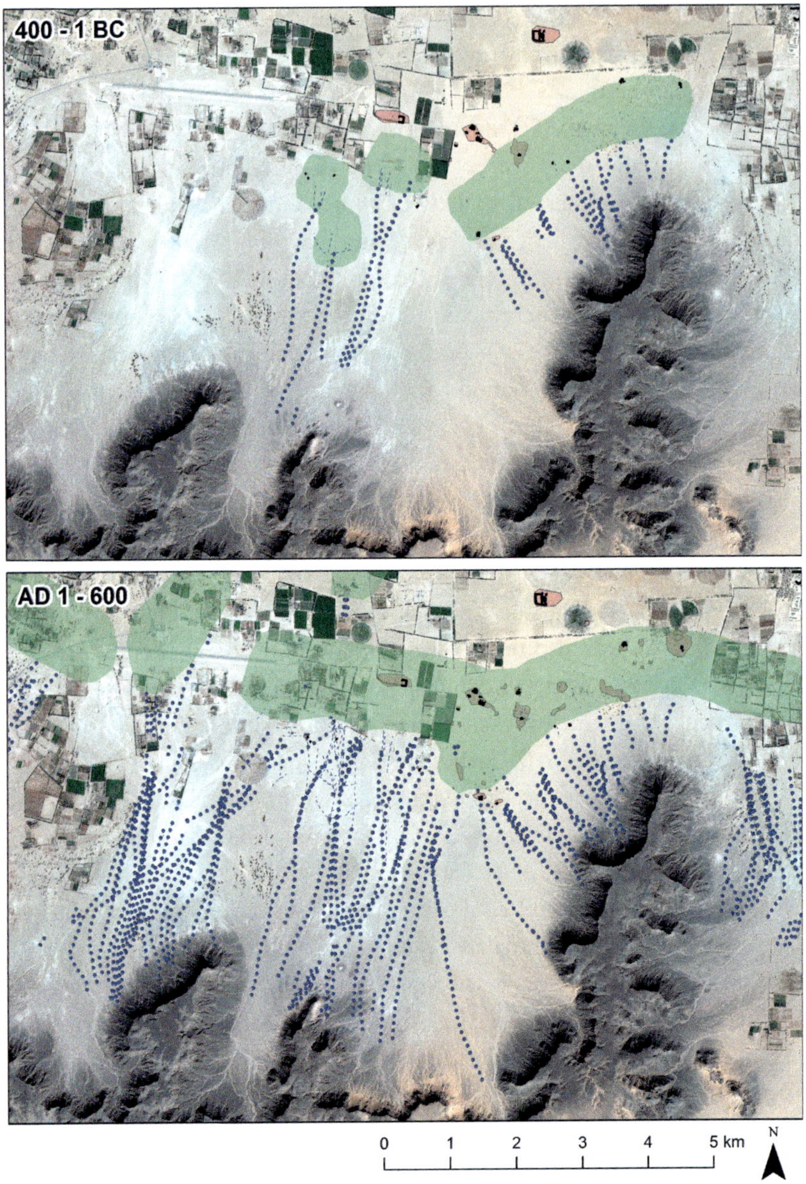

Figure 2.4. Hypothetical development sequence in the Taqallit landscape (WorldView-2 image, 14 January 2013, copyright DigitalGlobe)

network of oasis villages, mostly of a few hectares in size, lying at the delivery end of foggaras that originated at the escarpment, where substantial drum cairns and corbel cairns close to the mother-wells made a statement about communal rights to the precious water that was mined at great cost by construction of the foggaras. That implies a link between the village

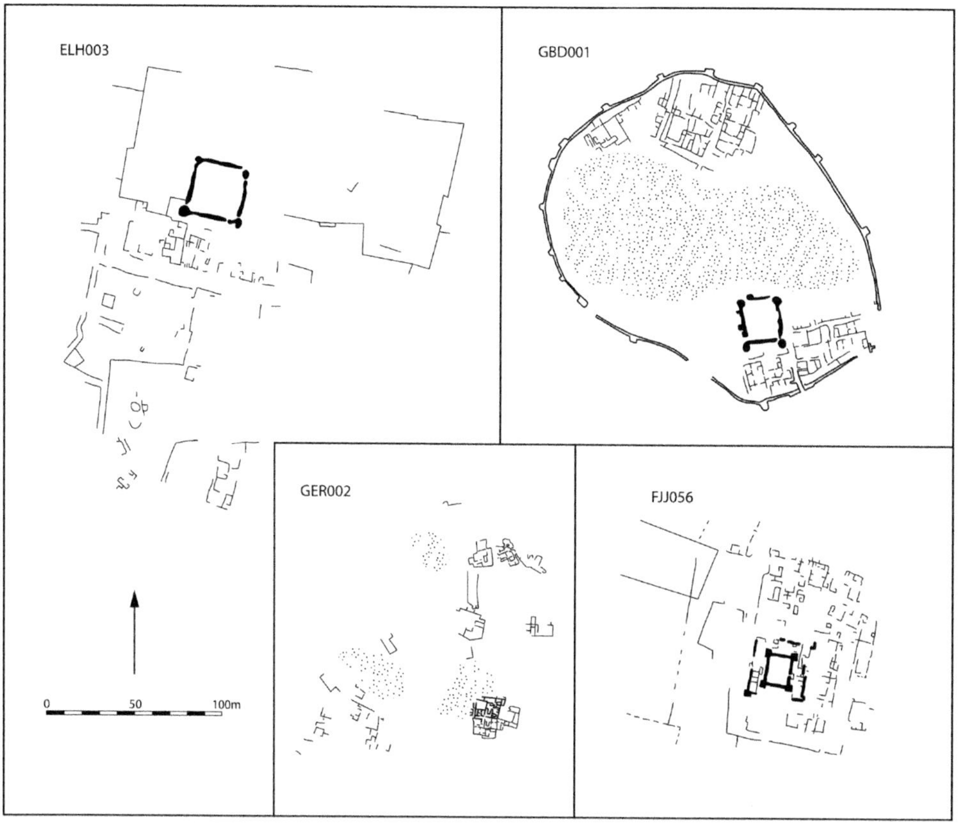

Figure 2.5. Examples of Garamantian village settlements from the Wadi al-Ajal: a) ELH003; b) GBD001; c) GER002; d) FJJ056.

communities and the construction and enjoyment of the advantages of foggara systems, with each settlement having control of at least one or a small group of foggaras. It is notable that in this detailed case study, fortified structures (*qsur*) were eventually constructed at the 11 main settlement locations, though only two sites show strong indications of continuity into the Medieval period.

An AMS dating programme, focused on *qsur* in the eastern Wadi al-Ajal, has established a Late Garamantian date for many fortified sites in the wadi, a conclusion supported by surface finds of Roman pottery at many sites when visited (Fig. 2.5). This trend towards construction of fortified buildings within previously open settlements or to construct fortified village-size compounds appears to be a general characteristic of Late Garamantian settlement. The numbers, and close proximity of many of these sites, strongly suggest that most of these sites were not military outposts, but part of a changing settlement hierarchy.

The revised picture of settlement in the Wadi al-Ajal thus reveals an initial phase of oasis cultivation associated with hillfort sites, beginning in the early first millennium BC (or perhaps a little earlier).[47] The initial settlement appears to have been fairly sparse, but by the latter centuries BC there was evidently a significant increase in the numbers of villages and these now spread onto low-lying locations immediately adjacent to the cultivated area in the wadi.[48] This was accompanied by the construction of major irrigation works (foggaras). The foggaras and the new low-lying villages evidently appeared in the Wadi al-Ajal landscape at the same time as a number of new crops from Sub-Saharan Africa (pearl millet, sorghum and cotton) and this can hardly be coincidental. The Proto-Urban phase was a time of dramatically increasing population and expanding pioneer cultivation within the valley.

Many of the villages of the Proto-Urban and Classic Garamantian periods appear to have been open undefended settlements, but in the Late Garamantian era there was an increasing emphasis on fortified settlements, contained within walls with projecting towers, or fortified buildings (*qsur*) at the hearts of settlements.

Barnett's recently published survey of the rock art of the Wadi al-Ajal has revealed a wealth of material that is contemporary with or later than the Garamantes, including significant clusters of images of horses, horsemen, chariots and ancient Libyan inscriptions at key entry points into the valley and at prominent promontory locations.[49] The imagery is normally associated with natural features, rather than Garamantian settlements and burials.

A final point of distinction to be made about the Wadi al-Ajal is that the funerary archaeology of this oasis belt was significantly more complex and varied than that of many of the other areas identified as 'Garamantian'.[50] In addition to standard Saharan styles of cairn burial, drum tombs and shaft burials, the population of the Garamantian heartlands close to Jarma also experimented with a wide range of novel tomb types, especially rectangular and stepped monuments, but also pyramids and even Roman style

[47] di Lernia and Manzi 2002, 179, for a date stone with an AMS date of 1200 calBC from a late Pastoral burial in the Wadi Tanzzuft, *c.*400 km south-west of Jarma. This possibly indicates the existence of some pioneer cultivation of the date palm in the central Sahara by that date.

[48] For possible traces of Garamantian gardens in Wadi al-Ajal, see Mattingly 2007, 157–58, 196–98.

[49] Barnett 2019a, 113 (59 horse representations and 157 camels), 149 (nine chariot representations), 267–76 (for clustering of such imagery along main routeways along and out of Wadi al-Ajal).

[50] See now Gatto *et al.* 2019a, for the Trans-Saharan Archaeology volume focused on burial rites.

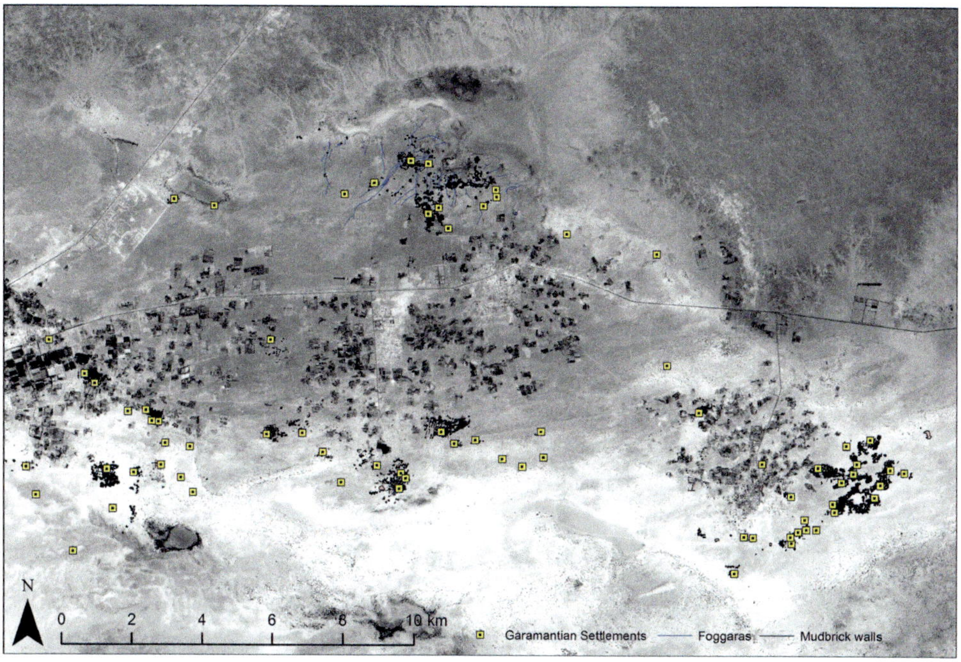

Figure 2.6. Distribution of Garamantian oasis sites in the Murzuq depressions.

mausolea.[51] The heartland cemeteries and settlements also reveal much more extensive evidence of trade contacts between the Garamantes and the Mediterranean world.[52] The fact that there was significant divergence in trade contacts, funerary and settlement archaeology between the Garamantian heartlands and the other oasis clusters within Fazzan may indicate some social distinctions between the peoples of these discrete oases. At the same time, there is also sufficient shared in common between different oasis groups to suggest that there were overarching factors that bound these disparate oases together with the Garamantes.

The Murzuq/Hufra Basin and ash-Sharqiyat

The southern oasis band in Fazzan, comprising a series of contiguous depressions (the Wadi Barjuj, Wadi Utba, the Murzuq depression, the Hufra and ash-Sharqiyat), runs for over 200 km east to west along the

[51] See the complementary overview study of Garamantian burials, Mattingly *et al.* 2019; also Mattingly and Edwards 2003.

[52] Leitch *et al.* 2017, 323–33.

northern edge of the Murzuq sand sea. Until recently no certain Garamantian era sites were known in this area, though some reconnaissance survey work by Daniels in 1968 had hinted at it.[53] There are numerous abandoned mudbrick *qsur* and settlements in this zone, though the general assumption previously has been that they were of Medieval or early modern construction.[54] Although the Fazzan Project work initially highlighted the possibility of an early date for some of these sites,[55] the more recent availability of high resolution satellite imagery has transformed the picture. Satellite remote-sensing has identified a large dossier of abandoned settlement sites and, with the benefit of some limited ground visits, we can divide these into three broad categories:

1. Mudbrick rectilinear arrangements around *qsur*, often with fortified enceintes and in close association with rectilinear field systems and cairn cemeteries.
2. Mudlump nucleated sites with irregular shapes and arrangements.
3. Stone, mudlump and *zariba* (palm front huts) dispersed settlements with a mixture of rectilinear and curvilinear structures.

Field survey of 79 sites in 2011, from which ceramics and AMS dating samples were obtained, have demonstrated that the first group date to *c.* AD 100–700 with the more heavily fortified examples in the latter half of this range. Conversely, the second group were of late Medieval date and the final group were of more recent date implying that there was a radical change in settlement forms in the Medieval period.[56] We have demonstrated the Garamantian nature of many of the fortified settlements identified on the satellite imagery and there are clear links between these settlements and irrigation works and pre-Islamic cemetery types.[57] Figure 2.6 shows dense settlement clusters of suspected or proven Garamantian date.

Qasr ash-Sharraba

A particularly important site is Qasr ash-Sharraba, located towards the western limits of oasis cultivation and which we have identified as an

[53] Daniels 1968; 1989; cf. also Boxhall 1968.
[54] Despois 1946, 59–60; Lethielleux 1948, 13, 48–50; Mattingly 2003, 146–54; Sterry *et al.* 2012.
[55] Edwards 2001; Mattingly 2007, 254–88.
[56] Mattingly and Sterry 2013; Sterry and Mattingly 2011; 2013; Sterry *et al.* 2012.
[57] The dating of a substantial number of *qsur* to the Late Garamantian era is particularly significant as previously these mudbrick castles had been uniformly assumed to be Medieval in date, see Sterry and Mattingly 2013; Sterry *et al.* 2012.

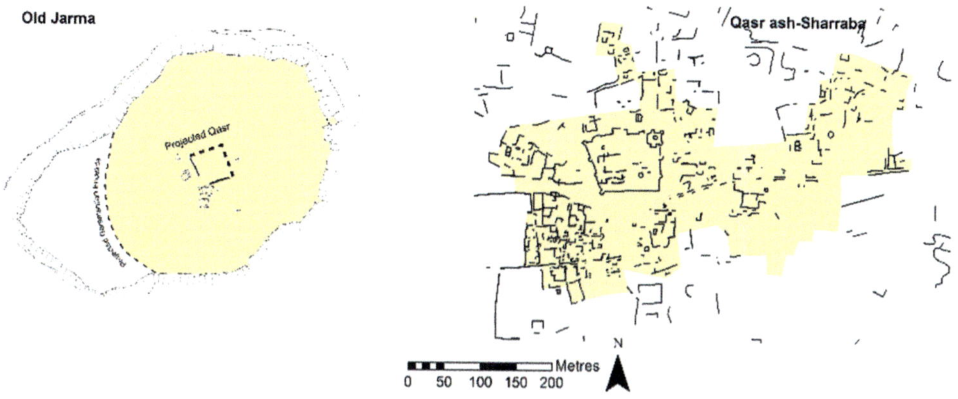

Figure 2.7. Possible Garamantian urban centres: a) Old Jarma; b) Qasr ash-Sharraba.

urban centre (Fig. 2.7b).[58] This is very similar in form to the settlements described above, but on a much larger scale. The site comprises an unwalled settlement of *c.*15–18 ha, at the heart of which lay a large fort-like compound (0.7 ha) with external towers. In the north-east corner of the fort was a tower-like *qasr* and a second *qasr* stood independently in the settlement to the west of the fort. A very extensive field system (556 ha) is preserved around the town which contains two further *qsur* and some isolated buildings. On the surrounding hills, especially to the south, there were at least 24 drum cairn and shaft cemeteries containing thousands of tombs. The earliest surface pottery from the cemeteries dates to the second century AD, perhaps indicating the initial growth of the site, but six AMS dates from the fortified citadel and *qsur* suggest that construction and occupation of these continued through Late Garamantian times into the early Islamic era. The nature of the twelfth-century activity is currently unclear. To the west of Qasr ash-Sharraba, the Wadi Barjuj is uncultivated today, but there are some additional traces of Garamantian cemeteries, settlements and hydraulic systems (wells and a variant on the foggara), associated with Roman pottery.[59]

The Murzuq Basin

The area east of the early modern capital Murzuq has been investigated in detail, following the release of high resolution satellite imagery. Because modern oasis cultivation has retreated from parts of this area, ancient sites

[58] Mattingly 2003, 149–50; 2007, 261–65; Mattingly and MacDonald 2013; Mattingly and Sterry 2013, 506–10.

[59] Mattingly *et al.* 2008, 250–51.

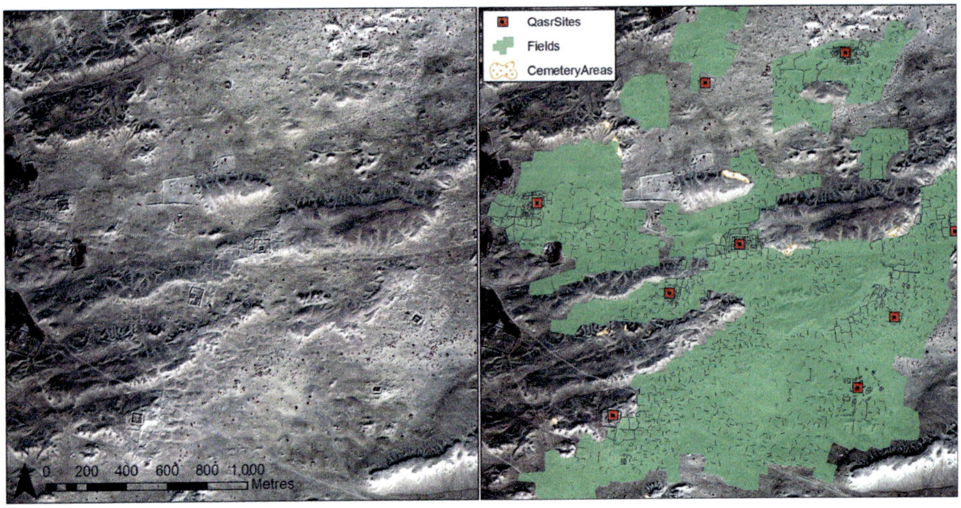

Figure 2.8. Detailed mapping of the Garamantian fortified settlements and their associated gardens in the Zizaw area (WorldView-2 image, 23 November 2002, copyright DigitalGlobe).

and abandoned gardens are particularly well preserved. Four main areas of sites were visited on the ground in 2011: Murzuq (MZQ), Gawat (GWT), Hij Hijayl (HHG) and Zizaw (ZZW), including a total of 33 *qsur* from many of which Roman-era pottery was recovered, subsequently confirmed by AMS dates from 15 sites. A particularly striking cluster of sites was recorded in a 6 km^2 area at Zizaw. Here no less than 11 fortified settlements can be identified, each located at the centre of a set of gardens and with each village only a few hundred metres from the next one (Fig. 2.8). Garamantian style burials are identifiable close to several of the sites (comprising shaft burials and drum cairns). The irrigation here was by means of shallow *shaduf* wells dug in the centre of many of the gardens. A variant form of shallow foggara has been identified in one part of this area (HHG), but never seems to have supplanted the use of shallow wells.

The architecture of these fortified sites is strikingly similar to that of late Roman military outposts, which may have provided remote inspiration, though here the interpretation of the complex as a group of fortified oasis villages seems inescapable, given the density of these sites and their clear agricultural associations.[60] The Garamantian origin of this type of rectangular fortified site, with external bastion towers, is now firmly established

[60] Mattingly *et al.* 2013b, for a contextual study of the Garamantian *qsur* in relation to similar fortified sites in the Roman frontier zones of North Africa. Cf. also Mattingly *et al.* 2013a, for Roman military architecture.

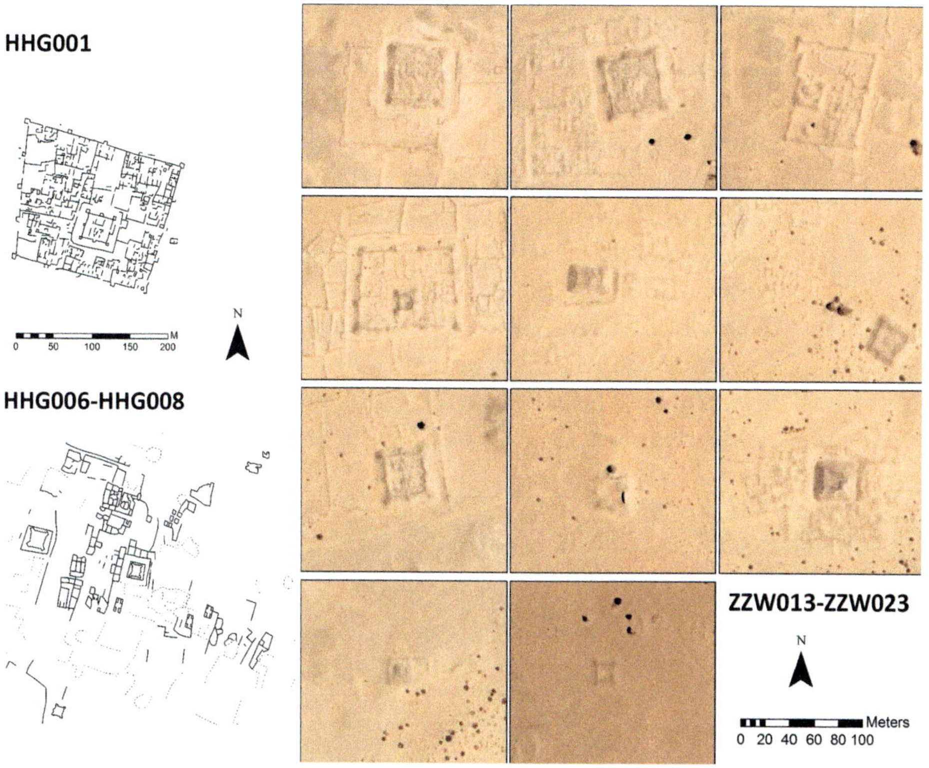

Figure 2.9. Comparative plans of fortified sites (*qsur*) in the Murzuq depression (imagery: Google, DigitalGlobe).

and a number of representative plans of examples (for many of which we have secure AMS dates in the range calAD 300–600) are shown in Figure 2.9.

Our investigation of the settlement pattern has been led by the visibility of substantial fortified structures on the satellite imagery and, as stated, the date of the *qsur* is predominantly Late Garamantian (late antique). The ultimate origins of oasis cultivation in the Murzuq depression thus remain uncertain, as the apparent lack of first millennium BC settlement here could be due to the greatly reduced susceptibility of undefended settlements to identification in satellite remote sensing. Nonetheless, in the Murzuq area the fortified buildings and fortified settlements sit at the centre of clusters of gardens in a way that suggests they were laid out together. Although there were some foggara channels here, the more common irrigation method seems to have involved centrally placed *shaduf* wells within fields/gardens. Therefore, while there may have been some earlier sites, our preliminary reading of the evidence is that the extensive development of the southern oasis zone occurred at a later date than the Wadi al-Ajal – specifically in the Classic and Late Garamantian period.

Zuwila

Another important centre in eastern Fazzan was Zuwila, long recognised as the pre-eminent site in the Early Islamic period.[61] Survey has identified the existence of a significant Garamantian settlement at this location. The early Medieval site was embellished with a 4.5 ha fortified enclosure to the north of a 20 ha open settlement. The larger settlement area appears to have originated in the Garamantian period and seems to have related to both gardens with well irrigation and a zone of foggara-fed irrigation (Fig. 2.10). There are also several cemeteries that have yielded Roman material. Towards the centre of the unenclosed settlement there was a (now destroyed) large *qasr* with projecting towers (60 × 70 m, ZUL004 on Fig. 2.10). Roman imports have been found close to this structure, which we believe to be Late Garamantian in date. The

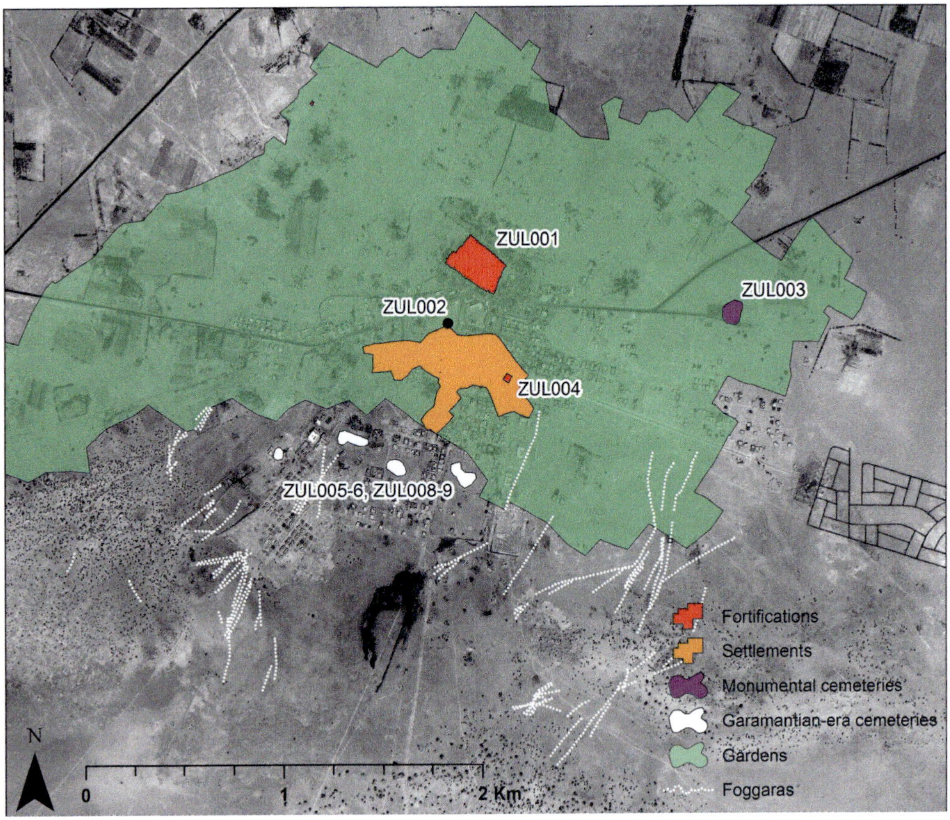

Figure 2.10. Detail of possible Garamantian centre at Zuwila (Worldview-2 image, 30 October 2011, copyright DigitalGlobe).

[61] Mattingly *et al.* 2015; Mattingly and Sterry 2018 on Zuwila; see also Ziegert 1969, on Garamantian rock-cut burials.

earliest origins of Zuwila are unknown, though Daniels reported seeing an eye-bead there, which is a hint of trade connections by the latter centuries BC. It is possible that Zuwila had already become an urban-scale centre in the Late Garamantian period (compare the size of the possible settlement area around the central *qasr* on Fig. 2.10 with Jarma and ash-Sharraba, as shown in Fig. 2.7) and that this might have played a part in its supplanting Jarma as the pre-eminent early Islamic centre in Fazzan.

Umm al-Aranib, al-Bdayir, Humera, Misqwin, Tmissa

At Umm al-Aranib there is a group of *c.*10 foggaras that run south-north into a small depression (Fig. 2.11). At least 15 foggaras run north-south at al-Bdayir and feed into an extensive area of field-systems on the edge of a playa.[62] There are several thin scatters of cairns and possible hut clearings on the plateaux to the north. South of al-Bdayir another foggara group (about five in number) run south to north into the same depression. At the southern end of these there is a badly preserved mudbrick settlement of *c.*0.5 ha that may contain a fortification. It looks similar to Garamantian settlements in the Murzuq region and 500 m to the north-west of the settlement there is a nucleated shaft cemetery (*c.*6 ha) that is almost certainly of Classic Garamantian date. Another foggara group of *c.*20 channels runs into the oasis of Misqwin. Two square *qsur* with corner towers are visible (*c.*15 × 15 m and *c.*28 × 28 m), both very similar morphologically to Late Garamantian examples.

To the east of Zuwila, on a secondary route towards Zala (and onwards towards Egypt), Tmissa is a large multi-phase settlement on the edge of

Figure 2.11. Garamantian sites in eastern Fazzan.

62 An unusual 0.8 ha sub-circular fortification with ten evenly spaced towers may be dated to the period of Kanimi dominance in the thirteenth–fifteenth centuries.

a large playa. At the centre of the settlement there appears to have been a square *qasaba*, which was later heavily modified and incorporated into the fabric of the town's housing. There is also a sub-oval enclosure *c.*5.5 ha with the *qasaba* built into the south-east side.[63] Around 1.8 km to the west are the remains of a large field system with numerous wells on the western side of which is a possible Late Garamantian *qasr*.

Some 30 km to the south of Zuwila, across an intervening area of sand dunes, around Tirbu there are a few further sites with suspected Garamantian origins, again associated with *qsur* and foggaras.[64]

Wadi ash-Shati

The Wadi ash-Shati is a topographic depression that runs east-west, between the southern flanks of the al-Qarqaf arch to the north and the Ramlat Zellaf to the south (*c.*160 km long and 40–60 km wide). Unlike the majority of oases in Fazzan, those of ash-Shati are not positioned in the lowest portion of the depression. Instead, they are located in the northern part of the depression, on a sandstone piedmont. The sandstone stratum appears as a sequence of small sterile mesas and stepped profiles, resulting in a landscape of mounds and spurs, which stand out from the slight depressions covered by alluvial sands.

Wadi ash-Shati is unusual in Fazzan in deriving its water from both a confined aquifer, located under a roof of compact crystalline sandstone, and from phreatic surface water.[65] As a consequence, humans exploited both the numerous artesian springs and the shallow ground water which was easy to reach by means of dug wells. In the 1930s Scarin documented 277 natural springs and 612 wells in the wadi. Some of the artesian springs were natural (for example, the six small springs aligned along a natural fissure in Maharuqa), but the majority were artificial.[66] This aspect has made ash-Shati the most agriculturally developed and populated region of Fazzan in the Medieval and early modern periods.[67] The region is also known for its iron ore deposits.[68]

[63] This was in disrepair by the time the site was visited by Hornemann 1802, 53–55, though he mentions that there were reputedly inscriptions among the ruins. See also Despois 1946, 95, for a plan and description of these features.

[64] Mattingly 2007, 282, Tirbu. [65] Despois 1946; Dubay 1980.

[66] Scarin 1937a; 1937b; cf. also Despois 1946.

[67] The colonial Italian census of 1936 (Scarin 1937b) reported 13,769 inhabitants as opposed to 6,398 in the Wadi al-Ajal and 5,504 in the Southern oases, see also Mattingly 2013, 537.

[68] These were described by Desio 1937 and then further studied by Goudarzi 1970; 1971 and Turk *et al.* 1980.

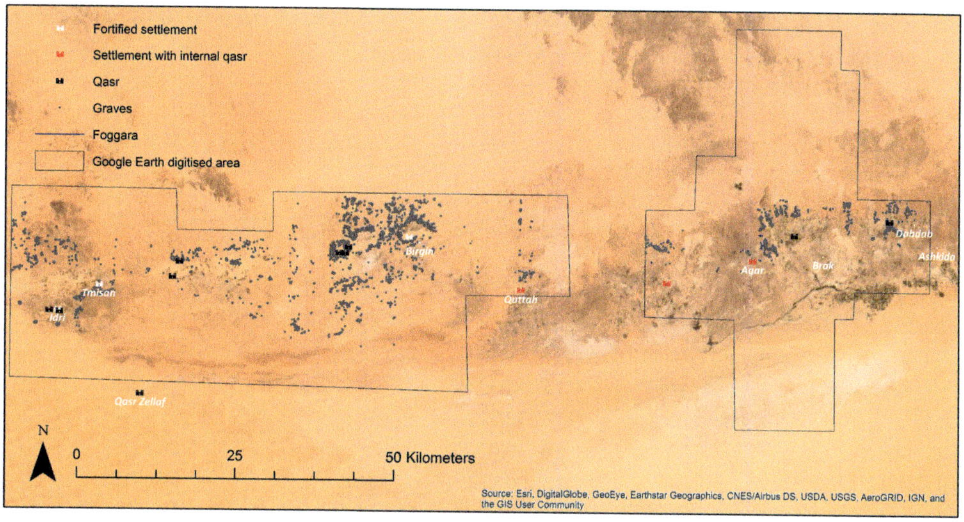

Figure 2.12. Garamantian sites recorded in the Wadi ash-Shati.

Despite being the most populated part of Fazzan in the early twentieth century, the Wadi ash-Shati has been little explored archaeologically.[69] Barth recorded the existence at Idri, of rock-cut chambers, possibly originally intended for burial.[70] Better explored for its rock art panels,[71] the wadi was visited by Daniels, recording several sites in the area of Dabdab, including a cemetery, a settlement and a foggara.[72] A first systematic survey from 2007 to 2008,[73] and ongoing intensive remote sensing based mapping, has now confirmed a long-term chronology of occupation and a substantial Garamantian presence (Fig. 2.12).

The particularly favourable hydrological conditions made the wadi one of the prime targets of government-funded agricultural schemes in the early 1970s. Land reclamation at that time coupled with massive infrastructural development,[74] has had a significant effect on the preservation of the archaeological record, with sites much altered or destroyed.

So far 12 *qsur* of probable Garamantian origins have been identified, and three fortified villages of the same period (Table 2.2). This does not exclude possible Garamantian origins of other settlements, which are characterised by the presence of inner walls and fortified structures and which were occupied until the colonial periods (for example Quttah). Both these

[69] Barich and Baistrocchi 1987; Biagetti and di Lernia 2008; Cremaschi and di Lernia 1998; 2001; di Lernia and Manzi 2002; di Lernia *et al.* 2001; Liverani 2006.

[70] Barth 1857, 154. [71] Graziosi 1942; Le Quellec 1987.

[72] The sites with associated photographs have been published in Mattingly 2007.

[73] Merlo *et al.* 2008; 2013. [74] Pliez 2004.

Table 2.2 *List of* qsur *and fortified settlements surveyed in the Wadi ash-Shati. The site of Bir al-Qasr was reported by the local informant Mustafa Habib*

Code	Locality *(local name of structure)*	Long. E (deg/min)	Lat. N (deg/min)	Altitude (m asl)	Size (m)
Qsur					
ADW001	Adwesa *(Qasr Bin Maherik)*	12° 35.455'	27° 44.489'	409	50 × 20
IDR002	Idri	13° 3.327'	27° 26.579'	383	Not ascertainable
IDR023	Idri	13° 2.352'	27° 26.634'	373	30 × 20
IDR025	Ramlat Zellaf	13° 11.144'	27° 19.888'	402	20 × 16
IDR030	*(Bir al-Qasr)**	13° 0.987'	27° 30.924'		11 × 10
ABY001	*(Qasr Abyad)*	13° 30.919'	27° 32.396'	383	22 × 18
ABY006		13° 30.614'	27° 31.905'	367	20 × 14
ABY007		13° 30.022'	27° 31.925'	378	20 × 15
WIN001	Hatiya Winzrik *Qasr Ain Omar*	13° 14.061'	27° 29.680'	373	30 × 25
WIN002	Hatiya Winzrik *Qasr Bin Aghenneb*	13° 14.721'	27° 30.918'	390	50 × 35
DBD002	Dabdab	14° 22.534'	27° 35.289'	390	56 × 40
BRK010	Tamzawa	14° 13.379'	27° 34.022'	380	25 × 26 (remains of two walls only)
Other Fortified Sites					
IDR001	Idri	13° 03.165'	27° 26.707'	406	100 × 90
TIM001	Tmisan	13° 07.030'	27° 28.849'	394	70 × 20
BRG001	Birgin	13° 36.676'	27° 33.388'	372	190 × 23/70

settlement forms are characterised by a building technique that was based on stone. It was used either for the entirety of the structure or at least for its base, on which a mudbrick superstructure was built. Two isolated and very poorly preserved *qsur* – IDR002 and ABD006 – form the only exceptions to this, since they consist of a small mound of decaying mudbricks. The arrangement of the stone blocks, although varied both in type of shape, material and pattern, tends to be very regular. This is a distinctive character that differentiates the *qsur* and fortified settlements from other stone-built structures in the wadi (isolated houses, dispersed and nucleated settlements), which are rather irregular in arrangement and varied in the type of construction material. Further, it suggests a broad chronological commonality.

Surface pottery (including Roman imports) collected from around a number of the isolated *qsur* can be ascribed to the Classic and Late Garamantian periods. Amongst the isolated *qsur*, only one was located in the southern part of the depression, Qasr Zellaf (IDR025) a well-defined stone and mudbrick structure with an internal partition. The others lay near the northern edge of the depression and were all located above 360 masl.

The *qsur* were located on eroded relicts of Pliocene sedimentary sequences, which serve as upstanding topographical features in the surrounding landscape. No ditches were noted surrounding the *qsur* and in general, their plans were irregular since they followed the shape of these natural spurs/hills and they lack evidence of towers. However, Qasr Abyad (ABY001), although on a natural spur, was rectangular in plan and possessed two towers. Frequently the *qsur* were either in proximity to an extended cemetery or had a limited number of cairns (generally quite large in size) in their vicinity. In some cases additional structures were noted in the vicinity of the *qsur*, generally a rectangular building with at least one or two internal partitions. Qasr Bin Maherik (ADW001) and Qasr Zellaf (IDR025) were more isolated, lacking surrounding traces of cemeteries or field systems (either ancient or modern). These *qsur* were located respectively to the north-west and south of the depression, on the line of previously hypothesised routes from Ghadamis to Idri and from Idri to Jarma. Most *qsur* in the wadi occurred in groups of two or three within a radius of less than 5 km rather than being isolated.

Three fortified settlements of a different type were identified, at Idri, Tmisan and to the west of Birgin. The first two occupy the flat top of a substantial isolated hill (and have evident similarities with the Zinkekra-type hillforts of the Wadi al-Ajal), whilst the Birgin site is at an elevation of only 6 m above the present day surrounding sand dune surface. The three sites had outer walls that followed the profile of the natural relief on which they are located. This determined their shape, which is irregular in nature and size. Idri and Birigin were built with a mix of stone and mudbrick both for the external wall and internal partitions; Tmisan is characterised by the exclusive use of cut stone for the entire settlement. Surface material culture points to a Garamantian origin for these sites. Whilst Birgin was eventually abandoned and the settlement moved *c.*1 km east, Idri and Tmisan experienced a different pattern during later times. The nucleated village settlements were both moved down to the foot of the elevated area. The non-contemporaneity of the top and bottom settlements in both instances is demonstrated by the substantially different building techniques used, with the introduction of mudbrick and irregular stone built structures.

Substantial nucleated cemeteries characterised the area surrounding both the *qsur* (with the exception of the isolated examples) and fortified sites.[75] Their morphology and spatial distribution is clearly connected with the settlements, confirming the probable Classic Garamantian age of the overall system. The organisation of settlements analysed thus far presents a concentric configuration, with the *qasr* or fortified village in the middle, a first circle of sparse graves or small nucleated cemeteries in close proximity to the settlement, a circle where modern (and presumably ancient) wells and field systems are located, and finally a number of longitudinal and/or nucleated cemeteries that radiated in all directions from the cultivated areas. It therefore seems that the particular topography of the northern part of the depression was used to create a distinctive spatial pattern, probably reflecting the chronology, but possibly also the social stratification of occupation in the Garamantian period.

There is limited evidence as yet for a pre-Garamantian funerary landscape and, with caution, it is therefore suggested that the early oasis occupation of the wadi is to be linked with the expansion of the Garamantian kingdom, most probably during the Classic Garamantian period. On the other hand, there is some rock art imagery of chariots in the ash-Shati and two of the places named in Pliny's account of the campaign of Balbus in 20 BC chime with Wadi ash-Shati toponyms: Dedris with modern Idri and Baracum with modern Brak. Idri as noted was a hillfort site, which again might suggest a first millennium BC origin. Pliny also mentions a location called Thelgae or Matelge with a hot spring, which would suit the Wadi ash-Shati hydrology.[76] This might suggest that some initial development had begun around the main natural springs in the first millennium, but that settlement expansion occurred later. The continuity of exploitation of the northern oases during the Late Garamantian period is also highly probable, with a possible abandonment of some of the isolated outposts but a continuous occupation of the majority of the settlements. As in the Murzuq area we need to note that research has been focused on the more upstanding fortified sites, which were mainly of Late Garamantian date. We cannot exclude that there were undefended settlements that have so far escaped detection on the satellite images. However, the overall number of Garamantian burials identified in the ash-Shati is consistent with

[75] So far over 12,000 single cairn and drum graves have been plotted in the wadi thanks to the increasing availability of high resolution satellite imagery through Google Earth. It is expected that the total number will be in the region of 20–30,000, once the systematic study of the imagery is completed.

[76] On the rock art, see Le Quellec 1987. Pliny, *Natural History* 5.35–37; Desanges 1980, for commentary.

the relatively less dense settlement distribution observed here when compared with the Wadi al-Ajal.

Some Outlying Oases in Eastern and Northern Fazzan

Ghuddwa

Located mid-way between the Wadi al-Ajal, Murzuq/Hufra basin and ash-Sharqiyat, Ghuddwa is a small, but strategic oasis in Fazzan (Fig. 2.1). Several Garamantian cemeteries with very characteristic Garamantian funerary furniture and imported Roman pottery have been identified here, as well as the remains of five or six *qsur*, two of which have yielded some imported Roman pottery. No AMS dates have been obtained here, but the morphology of some of the *qsur* is also consistent with a Late Garamantian date.[77] There is a string of Garamantian cemeteries and possible settlements along the line of the Wadi an-Nashwa that connects Ghuddwa with the Wadi Utba and Qasr ash-Sharraba area to the south-west, a few of the former were visited by Daniels in 1968.[78]

The Ubari Sand Sea Lake Villages

A number of salty lakes are located in the Ubari sand sea between the Wadi al-Ajal and Wadi ash-Shati. A brief survey of the village of Mandara,[79] on the shores of the homonymous salty lake in the Ubari sand sea has identified a mudbrick *qasr* (30 × 20 m), which, according to local informants, has been in ruins in living memory. The site yielded Roman pottery, brought to light during the excavation of deep wells. This is testimony of early oasis occupation in the Ubari sand sea of at least one of its oasis villages by the well-known lakes of that area.[80] Survey connected with oil prospection in this area also revealed a number of concentrations of Roman pottery, possibly linked to exploitation of mineral salt deposits in and around these lakes.[81]

[77] Mattingly 2007, 267–70. [78] Mattingly 2007, 271–72.

[79] Part of a survey of the recently abandoned lake villages of Gabroun, Trouna and Mandara conducted in 2007 and 2008 (Mattingly *et al.* 2007 and Merlo *et al.* 2008).

[80] On the lakes of the Ubari sand sea and the Dawada people in general, see Bellair 1951; Bruce-Lockhart and Wright 2000.

[81] Unpublished work involving Mattingly, see Lahr *et al.* 2009.

Sabha, Samnu and al-Abid

There is no certain archaeological evidence of ancient origins of Sabha (Fig. 2.1). However, there has not been any archaeological investigation of the several villages that housed the Early Modern population of the oasis and it is possible that these overlay earlier settlements. The name Sabai appears linked with Garama in Ptolemy and is a suggestive hint that there was a settlement of some sort in the Sabha oasis by the second century AD.[82] Some 3 km to the west of modern Sabha there is a recently bulldozed mudbrick mound that was likely a *qasr*, if so this would suggest some form of Garamantian settlement.

A number of hills in the Sabha area have evidence of scattered cairns. A range of hills 45 km to the east of Sabha features a group of hilltop settlements with small enclosures similar to those found in the Wadi al-Ajal and are likely Proto-Urban Garamantian or earlier in date. At Samnu there are the remains of two or perhaps three small *qsur* isolated amongst the modern gardens. On the edge of the cultivated area there is a low hill on the south-east spur of which is a small settlement (45 × 15 m). Also on this hill are *c.*200 shaft and drum tombs clustered into five groups and a building aligned east-west 20 × 10 m that is similar to the buildings sometimes found on the east side of *qsur* and the burial structure UAT003.[83]

An extensive network of foggaras is known in relation to the al-Abid oasis north-east of Sabha and although conclusive evidence is lacking this could indicate an early development on the routes between Fazzan and al-Jufra oases to the north and Zala in the east (see Chapter 3).[84] The main foggara group led into a system of gardens of *c.*200 ha extent. Further foggaras fed gardens to the north-east and north-west. Settlement remains are few, but include at least two *qsur* and a large hilltop enclosure (with only a few internal features). The largest area of settlement appears to underlie a colonial era fort and the remains are much disturbed. Several of the hills on either side have rings of drum cairns encircling them, though there are no visible shaft cemeteries.

Wadi Tanzzuft and the Tadrart Akakus

Wadi Tanzzuft is a 200 km long, north-south oriented valley with an ephemeral stream, that runs along a *cuesta*, whose western side is formed

[82] Ptolemy, *Geography* 4.6.12. [83] Mattingly 2007, 107–09. [84] Nachtigal 1974, 61.

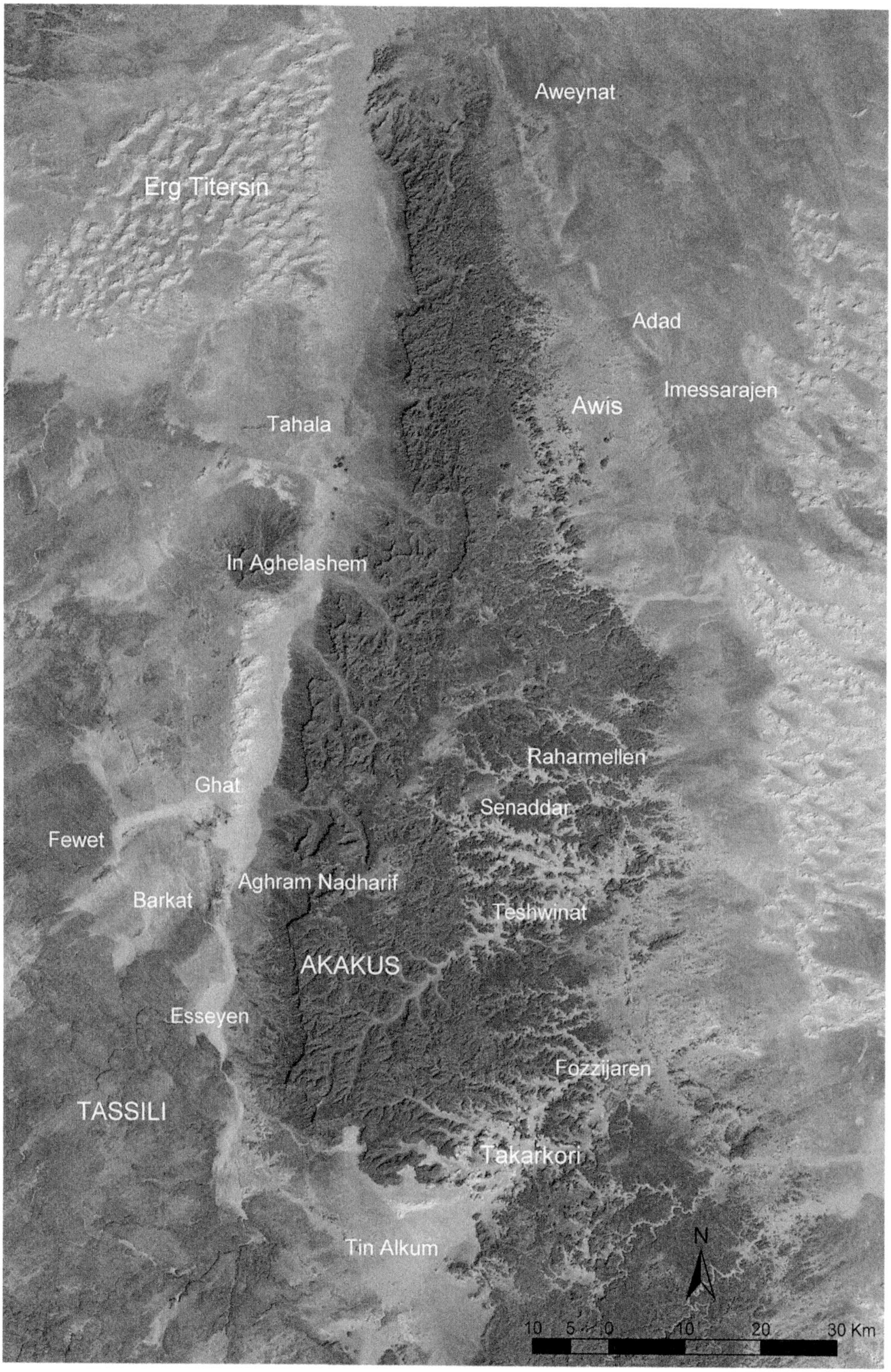

Figure 2.13. Garamantian sites recorded in the Wadi Tanzzuft and Wadi Awis.

by the edge of the Tassili range, while the eastern side in marked by the steep cliff of the Tadrart Akakus mountain. Garamantian-era activity has been traced in the main valley and in the mountain and desert landscapes adjoining it.

Wadi Tanzzuft

The source of the wadi is located in the Takarkori area (southern Tadrart Akakus), and its northern reach has been identified in a wide endorheic depression at the western fringe of the Edeyen of Ubari.[85] The main course of the wadi is surrounded by lowlands with inselberg/pediment type relief, alluvial fans, dried lakes, and small sand seas. Radiocarbon dates on archaeological sites buried inside the alluvial plain indicate that the northern part of Wadi Tanzzuft was still fed by the river in the second and first millennia BC, while a prominent contraction of the oasis followed a dramatic drop in precipitation and subsequent unsteady climatic phase in the first half of the first millennium AD. The presence of artesian springs in several parts of the valley is an important aspect of the hydrology. This resulted in the formation of three separate oases (Ghat, al-Barkat and Fewet) in the southern part of the wadi (Fig. 2.13).[86] The existence of another natural artesian spring at al-Uwaynat (Sardalas) at the northern end of the Tanzzuft valley may have supported an oasis settlement there too, but no conclusive evidence has been found beneath the modern small town.

An incipient sedentism has been hypothesised for the Ghat oasis from the beginning of the first millennium BC by the finding of an open-air site with evidence of irrigation devices and a hybrid ceramic production, combining decorative patterns typical of the late Pastoral culture (simple impressions and rocker impression) with the Garamantian ones (twisted cord simple or roulette impressions).[87] But settlements dated to the Garamantian period have not been identified at Ghat, probably because they are deeply buried under the Medieval and modern town.[88] There are major Garamantian cemeteries adjacent to Ghat that were excavated by Pace *et al.* – these surely attest to a major settlement close by.[89] The cemeteries recorded in the al-Barkat and Fewet oases, by their scale and locations, also strongly suggest the presence of additional undiscovered Garamantian settlement sites in the other Tanzzuft oasis areas.[90] In addition, a number of fortified *qsur* have been recorded, some on the edge of the oasis zone, others along the approach routes, like the Wadi Awis.

85 Cremaschi and Zerboni 2009; 2013. 86 Cremaschi and Zerboni 2011; 2013.
87 Mori *et al.* 2013. 88 Liverani 2000; Scarin 1937c. 89 Pace *et al.* 1951; Gatto *et al.* 2019a.
90 For the funerary remains in Wadi Tanzzuft, see the overview study by Gatto *et al.* 2019b.

Fewet

The emergence of domestic architecture in the form of small compounds made of mudbricks is dated to the third century BC, as illustrated by research on the oasis of Fewet. However, radiocarbon dates from a large cemetery in the same area suggest an earlier occupation of the oasis, from at least the sixth century BC.[91] At the edge of the modern village of Tan Afella, the remains of a small village covering an area of *c.*850 m^2 were brought to light, though only its south-east corner was well preserved (Fig. 2.14b). The site remained in use until the beginning of the first century AD. It was planned and built as a single structure, for the dwelling of a small clan with an egalitarian socio-economic base.[92] The settlement had a defensive character, with a single gate and a communal well, which ensured water availability also in the event of an external danger. A large central courtyard facilitated interior circulation and most probably provided a protected space for working activities, such as threshing, grinding of cereals, pottery, basketry and leather production. The dwelling rooms were built against the inner face of the perimeter, and were generally arranged in units composed of two rooms: a larger square room flanked by a smaller rectangular one. The surface of the five preserved dwelling units ranged from 10 to 28 m^2, with an average of *c.*18.5 m^2.[93] Building techniques and materials were rather homogeneous: roughly dressed sandstone slabs were used almost exclusively for the mudbrick wall foundations and for the footing of the village wall. Mudbrick was the main building material and bricks were highly standardised both in size (50 × 35 × 8 cm, implying the use of moulds of the same shape) and in composition. The Fewet compound was the earliest structure excavated in the Tanzzuft region built in mudbricks, but the craft and standardisation of the mudbrick work implies an introduction and experimentation prior to the third century BC.[94] Local hand-made pottery, grinding stones, polishers, bone tools, vesicular basalt lamps and iron tools were found inside the rooms, together with faunal and botanical remains showing a community with a fully developed irrigated agriculture, based on Near-Eastern crops,[95] and

[91] Mori and Ricci 2013.

[92] A total number of 13 residential units for the excavated compound has been supposed, with about 40 individuals. See Castelli *et al.* 2005 especially section by Mori, 73–84; Liverani 2006; Mori 2010; 2013.

[93] The two-roomed unit is an architectural pattern which is attested in other settlements of the Fazzan, in Garamantian times. In the Wadi al-Ajal it was found at Zinkekra from the Early Garamantian phase (Daniels 1968; Mattingly 2010, 83), and was still in use up to the second century AD in the first phase of Saniat Jibril (Daniels 1971b, 6–7; Mattingly 2010, 155).

[94] Mori 2013, 63–66. [95] Mercuri *et al.* 2013.

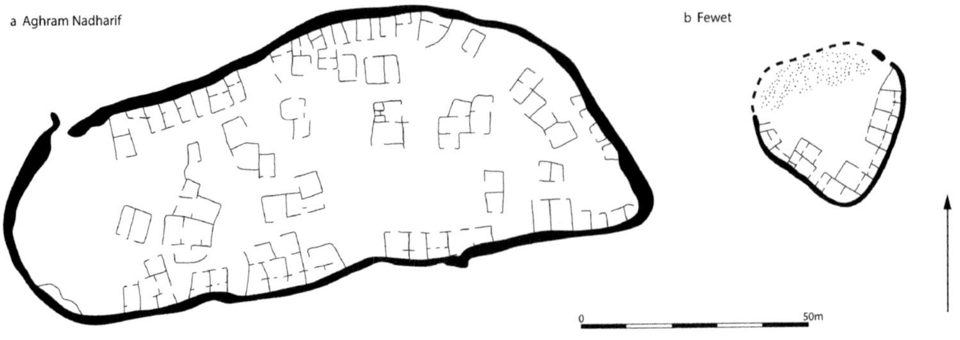

Figure 2.14. Comparative plans of Garamantian sites in the Tanzzuft area.

the herding of livestock together with the hunting of wild animals like Barbary sheep, hares and gazelles.[96]

A cemetery composed of 1,329 stone tumuli, already in use during the late Pastoral period, developed as the burial ground of the entire community of the oasis from the sixth century BC to the third century AD.[97]

Aghram Nadharif

The oases of Garamantian Fazzan reached their peak in the first centuries AD.[98] In Wadi Tanzzuft this meant the building of larger fortified citadels protecting the oases villages and the construction of a series of forts/castles at strategic points in the open desert in order to control the main passageways of the caravan routes.[99] On the eastern fringe of the Barkat oasis, the stone citadel of Aghram Nadharif, 'the city of alum', was built on a low sandstone terrace, overlooking a long stretch of the Wadi Tanzzuft. The settlement was built in the first half of the first century BC and was used till the fourth century AD.[100] The fortified citadel has an irregular oblong shape, following the morphology of the rock spur on which it was built, with an inner surface area, excluding the city-wall of approximately 0.6 ha (Fig. 2.14a).[101] The outer enceinte was a 2-m-thick stone wall, reaching *c*.2.5 m in height. The city wall was provided with two towers on the east side, still standing to a maximum height of 4.5 m, possibly duplicated by two more

[96] Alhaique 2013. [97] Liverani *et al.* 2013; Mori *et al.* 2013.
[98] Liverani 2006, 2007a/b; Mattingly 2013, 530–34.
[99] Liverani 2006, 363–74; Biagetti and di Lernia 2008.
[100] For the sequence of the ^{14}C datings upon which this reconstruction was proposed see Liverani 2006, 363–74 and in particular tables 30.I and II.
[101] Putzolu 2006.

whose remains are too poorly preserved to be interpreted with certainty. Four gates gave access to the citadel. Three areas of the interior were excavated, mainly uncovering residential houses with storage facilities – pits dug in the bedrock and bins built above the floor, with thin partition walls – and small working areas, together with lanes and open courtyards. Once again, the houses had a two-roomed standard plan, similar to the ones in the Fewet compound, but here entirely built in stone. The layout of dwelling modules was much more articulated and the layout more complex than that of the Fewet compound and built to host a larger part of the sedentary oasis community.[102] Clusters of fireplaces in the area surrounding the citadel testify to the contemporary presence of ephemeral settlements; a scattered population living in pastoral encampments has also been identified throughout the southern Tanzzuft valley.[103] The settlement seems entirely built up of domestic units and no 'public' building has been identified, a situation which seems again to reflect the presence of an 'egalitarian' community, based on the local kin structure. This social structure is also reflected in the nearby cemetery, located just on the opposite bank of the wadi, on a rocky terrace. Approximately 590 tumuli were identified on the basis of a satellite Ikonos image,[104] and from this preliminary observation they show rather uniform typologies, with conical and drum-shaped tumuli. The greater richness and volume of Mediterranean imports in the burials close to Ghat hints that the region's political elite, which probably promoted the building of similar citadels like Aghram Nadharif, was located there.[105] Two of the burials excavated by Leschi have dates that are broadly contemporary with Aghram Nadharif.[106]

In Wadi Tanzzuft this settlement system was apparently strongly related to the development of the caravan trade and it seems to have collapsed by the Late Garamantian phase, as suggested by the abandonment of the stone citadels and forts. As far as settlements are concerned, from the fourth century AD this region underwent a shift from an oasis-based territorial society to the probable hegemony of pastoral tribes.[107]

[102] See Liverani 2006, 395–409; 2007b: 165–68 for spatial analysis and demographic calculations. According to his reconstruction the site could include a maximum of 65 houses hosting an estimated population of approximately 260 inhabitants, at its peak.

[103] Cremaschi 2006, 18–19. [104] Castelli and Liverani 2006, Table 4.1.

[105] Liverani 2006, 416–17.

[106] Leschi 1945. The dates are reported in Fagan 1965, 115: Sa-92, 1330±120, calAD 431–975; Sa-93, 1680±150, calAD 29–649.

[107] Liverani 2006, 461–62.

Tadrart Akakus

The deeply incised valleys on the east side of the Akakus range and the main passes across the mountains have also yielded traces of Garamantian era activity. Rock art in many of the rock shelters of the Akakus wadis extends to horse period imagery, assumed to be contemporary with the Garamantes and featuring depictions of chariots, biconical figures and palm trees. Radiocarbon dates from some of the rock shelters confirm the intensity of occupation at this time (Table 2.1). Such sites provide tantalising glimpses of the relationships between pastoral groups and the oasis dwellers. The building of the Aghram Nadharif citadel adjacent to the oasis of Barkat was undertaken contemporary to the construction of a network of fortified sites in the Akakus region. Three isolated *qsur* have been identified and preliminary investigation showed a foundation date which ranges from the end of the first century BC to the first century AD (Figs 2.13–2.14).[108] The best preserved structures were found along the eastern fringes of the Akakus mountain, facing the Wadi Awiss where two forts/castles have been identified that strongly resemble Aghram Nadharif both in building techniques and in dating. The forts/castles of Imassarajen and Adad were located far from the oasis of Wadi Tanzzuft, but lie along one of the caravan routes connecting that valley with Wadi Barjuj and the Murzuq region through the *aqba* (pass) of Aghelachem, which crosses the Akakus.[109] A unique funerary monument, the so-called 'Royal tumulus' of In-Aghelachem, was built in Wadi Tanzzuft, close to this *aqba*. It was composed of a huge stepped tomb enriched by a considerable number of small features, heaps of stones and U-shaped structures which do not have parallels in our area.[110] It was probably the burial of a chieftain, controlling the important mountain pass, and testifies to the presence of autonomous pastoral groups contemporary to the occupation phase of Aghram Nadharif and the desert *qsur*.

The castles/forts of Adad and Imassarajen were protected by a massive stone wall and were surrounded by complex open-air sites, formed by a number of stone structures of different shape and nature and fire places. Small test trenches showed the use of mudbricks with painted plaster for the inner partition walls. Both structures, did not survive the collapse of the Garamantian kingdom, just like Aghram Nadharif.

No detail of the inner planning was readable from the extant structures but some information on demography and population came from the cemeteries related to each site, which were located a few hundred metres from the living

[108] Mori 2012. [109] Biagetti and di Lernia 2008. [110] di Lernia and Manzi 2002, 102–16.

areas. A total of 325 tumuli were mapped for Imassarajen, and 156 for Adad; the most recurrent type was the drum-shaped tomb followed by the conical cairn.[111] The itineraries of caravan routes on the western side of the Akakus were conditioned by water availability and by the possibility of crossing the mountain through the *aqbas*. Two main mountain passes in the northernmost part of the Akakus mountain were probably in use in Garamantian times, demonstrated by the presence of rock inscriptions and engravings attributable to that period. At the *aqba* Irlarlaren, the longest inscription in Old Libyan characters known in Fazzan up to now has been recorded.[112] The concentrations of the rock art sites featuring Horse and Camel styles, traditionally dated to the Protohistorical and historical periods, seems to partially replicate the distribution of Tifinagh scripts.[113]

Wadi Hikma

Al-Qatrun and Tajirhi are the largest of a number of minor oasis settlements along the Wadi Hikma, a linear depression running from north to south parallel to the eastern edge of the Murzuq sand sea. A series of *qsur* have been reported down this corridor that links Fazzan with Tibesti and Lake Chad, though hitherto these have generally been assumed to be Medieval in date (Fig. 2.1).[114] Many of these are large and sit within extensive garden systems that are far from any of the known early modern and Medieval villages (Fig. 2.15). At Tajirhi, a foggara has been identified and a burial in the pre-Islamic tradition has been radiocarbon dated to the second half of the first millennium AD.[115] Given the close similarity in the architecture and layout of the Wadi Hikma *qsur* and those of the Murzuq depression to the north, early origins for some elements of this line of oases seem highly probable.

Comparing Settlement Trajectories and Concluding Discussion

Fazzan now provides ample evidence for the origins of oasis cultivation in the first millennium BC in the central Sahara. The data available indicate

[111] Biagetti and di Lernia 2008. [112] Liverani 2006, 437–39; Ait Kaci 2007.
[113] Biagetti *et al.* 2012. [114] Despois 1946, 57–61; cf. also Bruce-Lockhart and Wright 2000.
[115] Bellair and Pauphillet 1959; Bellair *et al.* 1953; Fagan 1965, 115, Sa-78 1190±120, calAD 615–1118.

Figure 2.15. Detail of abandoned oasis settlement and gardens in the Wadi Hikma area, *c.*5 km south-east of Tajirhi (WorldView-2 image, 29 April 2012, copyright DigitalGlobe).

that all the main oasis areas of Fazzan were developed to a greater or lesser extent during the Garamantian period and that the total number of oasis settlements numbered in the hundreds, including many substantial villages and a few sites of urban scale. This seems to have begun in different sub-regions at different moments in time and with varying intensity of development. Currently, the earliest evidence relates to the Wadi al-Ajal, with precocious agriculture in the first half of the first millennium BC and more intensive expansion in the latter centuries BC. There is also strong evidence for late first millennium BC development in the Ghat area of the Wadi Tanzzuft. On the other hand, the evidence from the Murzuq depression and the Wadi ash-Shati seems at present to point to somewhat later development, mainly focused on the first half of the first millennium AD, though as noted Pliny's account of the campaign of Balbus suggests that some of the natural springs of the Wadi ash-Shati were already exploited by the late first millennium BC.

The Early Garamantian period (1000–500 BC) is quite distinct from the later phases and is firmly associated with promontories and high ground. These hilltop and escarpment sites are predominantly found in the Wadi al-Ajal and around Sabha, but with examples known from the Wadi ash-Shati, Wadi Tanzzuft and Wadi Hikma. They are extremely heterogeneous in size, form and layout, but there are some commonalities in features. The occupied area on top of hilltops was generally very small and only in one example did it exceed 1 ha, although where there were additional enclosing walls at the scarp base much larger areas were enclosed. A majority of examples have occupation on the slopes of the hills although again most of these were fairly small in size and some lacked significant fortifications. A subset of these sites had large complexes of walls on and at the base of slopes and enclosing large areas (these reached 10 ha and more, for example: Zinkekra, Tinda, al-Khara'iq and Ikhlif 2) in some cases this also includes some evidence of terracing.[116] These encircling embankments are thought to be a development of the Proto-Urban Garamantian phase (500–1 BC).

The hilltops were generally difficult to access and, while ideal as refuges and for storage, they were somewhat impractical for daily use by farming communities. The slope settlements were better suited for occupation by these farmers, while still remaining relatively secure. The larger complexes combined elements of refuge with occupation on the low slopes. The archaeobotanical remains leave no doubt that the inhabitants practised oasis agriculture and Van der Veen's analysis of the botanical samples from the site has indicated that much of the basic processing work, especially of grain was carried out on top of the plateau, with more fruits and less processing waste found in the terraced housing on the scarps of the hillfort.[117] The development of the large complexes seems to have been a relatively late phenomenon, perhaps as late as the third to first centuries BC and linked to a widespread expansion of agriculture and population in Fazzan.

It was also in the Proto-Urban period that we have the earliest evidence of settlement within oases, notably the walled Tin Afella compound at Fewet in the Ghat region, but also at Jarma and at multiple sites close to the Taqallit peninsular in the Wadi al-Ajal.[118] At this date we can also demonstrate the introduction of foggara irrigation technology, the development of dense cairn cemeteries on the slopes of the Hamada in the Wadi al-Ajal and around the Ghat oasis and the first indications of trade with the Mediterranean in the form of imported ceramics.

In these early periods we can question to what extent we have evidence of either state formation or urbanisation. During the period 1000–500 BC

[116] Mattingly 2003, 139–41. [117] Van der Veen and Westley 2010, 517–18.

[118] Note AMS dates in Table 2.1. Also Mattingly *et al.* 2010b, 117–25 for the settlements near Taqallit and notes on possible Punic and Garamantian Proto Urban pottery.

the number of permanent settlements and their scale appears small, quite unlike those found in parts of the south-Western Sahara at this time.[119] In the period 500–1 BC, it has been argued that the one- and two-roomed buildings of Fewet (up to 28 m^2 in size) provide evidence of an egalitarian society.[120] This basic form of structure is found amongst all the hilltop sites but in the more densely occupied sites (such as Tinda) they are commonly arranged into compounds (not dissimilar to the Fewet compound itself). While the cairn cemeteries contemporary to these sites do show signs of diverse identities, the lack of excavated settlements apart from Fewet means that we are still some way off from being able to distinguish evidence of social differentiation, especially between compounds, from the material culture. While they vary in size and complexity (no doubt in part from their varied histories), the only evidence of more substantial constructions are the enclosing walls and terraces. The wider arrangement would suggest clumps of oasis cultivation that developed around natural springs or in places where there were other accessible water sources. Settlement in the Proto-Urban phase appears to have been based around numerous smaller and quite egalitarian settlements, with not much sense of an emerging social or settlement hierarchy at this date.

At the start of the Classic Garamantian phase, around the start of the first century AD, there are the earliest indications of more substantial buildings and more complex architecture focused on sites round Jarma. At Jarma itself a stone-footed temple was constructed in the centre of the settlement, on the slopes of Zinkekra a series of multiple-roomed rectilinear structures were built with ashlar footings, at Uatuat (UAT003) a tomb was elaborated with a large mudbrick enclosure. Elsewhere, the compound architecture continued at Aghram Nadharif, Ghat and at a number of sites in Wadi ash-Shati (such as ADW001) in which small low hills were enclosed and filled with structures on a rectilinear arrangement (these are smaller and denser than the hilltop examples described above, but they represent a persistent settlement form that continued on into the Medieval period). The most important development in the settlement record in the early first millennium AD concerns large nucleated sites with evidence of monumental buildings, craft specialisation and in particular control of Trans-Saharan trade. The two prime examples are Jarma in the Wadi al Ajal and Qasr ash-Sharraba in the Murzuq/Hufra depression. Another possible urban site, Zuwila, in the ash-Sharqiyat region, was potentially larger than both, but the lack of

[119] Those found in the Dhars of Mauritania, see MacDonald, Chapter 13, this volume.
[120] Mori 2013, 63–66; Mori *et al.* 2013.

structured survey on the now destroyed site makes it impossible to distinguish between the Medieval and Garamantian remains (Fig. 2.10). In the Wadi al-Ajal and Murzuq/Hufra basin there were large numbers of smaller sites consisting of rectilinear mudbrick buildings, square *qsur* or both. Outside these regions there were also *qsur* in Wadi ash-Shati and Hikma, but only a few with associated settlement and a few of somewhat irregular shape in the Tanzzuft. The Saniat Jibril type of open site seems largely confined to the area around Jarma and Taqallit in the Wadi al-Ajal, but this may be due in part to the lack of intensive survey in other regions.[121] The largest number of settlements can be attributed to this period, especially in the Wadi al-Ajal and Wadi Tanzzuft although this is partly due to the widespread distribution of distinctive Mediterranean imports that make identifying settlements easier than in other periods.

In the Late Garamantian period (AD 300–700) there was an increasing emphasis on fortification throughout the Wadi al-Ajal and the Murzuq/Hufra basin with all known settlements from this period featuring central *qsur* and many further fortified with enceintes and protruding towers. There are signs of a general shift in settlement towards central and eastern Fazzan with no known Late Garamantian settlements in the Wadi Tanzzuft. The many fortified sites in the Murzuq-Hufra basin and Wadi Hikma (paralleled by some indications of a shift in wealth and importance of villages from west to east within the Wadi al-Ajal)[122] foreshadow the eclipse of Jarma and the further development of Zuwila as the chief centre in Fazzan in the early Medieval period.

Table 2.3 summarises the distribution of different types of settlement sites within the various regions of Fazzan. These differences in part relate to topographical variability, but do suggest that there were some underlying regional preferences, chronological factors and localised trends at play. Perhaps this is one of the most interesting conclusions to emerge from this overview. The label 'Garamantian' covers a wide range of settlement forms within Fazzan, yet it is only through intensive survey work and direct scientific dating that many of these sites have been finally recognised as Garamantian. Similar work is needed in other Saharan regions where the same sort of architectural forms occur to see whether some of those settlements may also be of pre-Islamic date.

[121] Only the Tanzzuft area has seen any substantial pedestrian survey, but this seems to have focused mainly on burials.

[122] This is evident in terms of the numbers of Garamantian *qsur*, the distribution of late Roman pottery and more elite burial monuments/cemeteries. Nonetheless, Jarma seems to have remained the Garamantian capital at this date.

Table 2.3 *The distribution of site types between the different regions of Fazzan.*

Region	Hilltop Refuge	Slope Settlement	Hilltop and slope complex	Mudbrick compound/ settlement (w/o *qasr*)	Fortified low hilltop (rectilinear arrangement)	Urban site	Isolated *Qasr*	Village with *qsur*	Fortified settlement with *qsur*
Wadi ash-Shati	X?				X	X?	X	X	
Wadi al-Ajal	X	X	X	X		X	X	X	X
Murzuq/Hufra Basin				X?	X	X	X	X	X
Wadi Tanzzuft	X			X	X			X	
Wadi Hikma	X?						X	X	X

Tracing early oasis settlements in the Sahara is not straightforward as they are often buried and masked beneath later settlements and gardens. The Garamantian sites are to some extent unusual for their visibility due to the intensity of trade with the Roman empire, but it is salutary to observe that it is only in the last 20 years that fieldwork and AMS dating has allowed us to demonstrate in Fazzan the occupation of the hundreds of early first millennium AD oasis settlements. Even in the absence of ground truthing and direct dating at many other locations, defensive features such as the *qsur* and dense cairn and shaft cemeteries help us highlight areas for consideration. Other characteristics of the Garamantian oases which may be helpful for tracing early sedentarism in other parts of the Sahara include:

- the adoption of a developed agricultural package, with obvious affinities with the oases of the Western Egyptian Desert;
- the association with rock art images of people riding horses, driving chariots and the first images of camels;
- the movement of ideas and competencies (pyrotechnologies, irrigation works including the foggara, spinning and weaving, written script);
- the evidence of trade contacts.[123]

A final observation of the Garamantian settlement pattern is that it did not follow the same distribution found in later periods. In the 1930s the Wadi ash-Shati accounted for more than a third of the *c.*33,500 inhabitants of Fazzan, whilst the Wadi al-Ajal had only *c.*6,500. In the Wadi al-Ajal there are 125 identified Garamantian settlements compared to just 29 villages or hamlets still occupied in 1931, whereas in the Wadi ash-Shati there are just 15 known Garamantian settlements – less than half the 1931 total. While varying levels of archaeological preservation and visibility are factors, the consecutive capitals of Fazzan: Jarma, Zuwila, Traghan, Murzuq and Sabha should make clear that oases are not static environments and that where we find settlement today is not where we should necessarily expect it to have been located in the past.

References

Ait Kaci, A. 2007. Recherche sur l'ancêtre des alphabets libyco-berbères. *Libyan Studies* 38: 13–37.

Alhaique, F. 2013. The faunal remains. In Mori 2013, 191–98.

[123] Mattingly 2017, for an overview of Garamantian and Saharan trade.

Ayoub, M.S. 1967. *Excavations in Germa between 1962 and 1966*. Tripoli: Ministry of Education.

Ayoub, M.S. 1968. *Excavations in Germa (Fezzan). Cemetery of Saniat Ben-Howidy*. Tripoli: Ministry of Education.

Barich, B.E. and Baistrocchi, M. 1987. *Archaeology and Environment in the Libyan Sahara: The Excavations in the Tadrart Acacus, 1978–1983* (Cambridge Monographs in African Archaeology 23/ BAR International Series 369). Oxford: British Archaeological Reports.

Barnett, T. 2019a. *An Engraved Landscape. Rock Carvings in the Wadi al-Ajal, Libya. Volume 1: Synthesis*. London: Society for Libyan Studies.

Barnett, T. 2019b. *An Engraved Landscape. Rock Carvings in the Wadi al-Ajal, Libya. Volume 2: Gazetteer*. London: Society for Libyan Studies.

Barnett, T. and Mattingly, D.J. 2003. The engraved heritage: Rock art and inscriptions. In Mattingly 2003, 279–326.

Barth, H. 1857. *Travels and Discoveries in North and Central Africa* (reprint 1965). London: Frank Cass.

Bellair, P. 1951. La ramla des Daouada (Fezzan). *Travaux de l'Institut de Recherches Sahariennes* 7: 69–86.

Bellair, P. and Pauphillet, D. 1959. L'âge des tombes préislamiques de Tejerhi (Fezzan). *Travaux de l'Institut de Recherches Sahariennes* 18: 183–85.

Bellair, P., Gobert, E.-G., Jodot, P. and Pauphilet, D. 1953. *Mission au Fezzan*. Tunis: Institut Hautes Etat Tunis.

Biagetti, S. and di Lernia, S. 2008. Combining intensive field survey and digital technologies: New data on the Garamantian castles of Wadi Awiss, Acacus Mts, Libyan Sahara. *Journal of African Archaeology* 6.1: 57–85.

Biagetti, S., Ait Kaci, A., Mori, L. and di Lernia, S. 2012. Writing the desert. The 'Tifinagh' rock inscriptions of the Tadrart Acacus (south-west Libya). *Azania* 47: 153–74.

Boxhall, P. 1968. *Near East Land Forces Expedition to Murzuk, Libya. Expedition Report*. Nicosia: Nicolaou and Sons Ltd.

Bruce-Lockhart, J. and Wright, J. 2000. *Difficult and Dangerous Roads. Hugh Clapperton's Travels in Sahara and Fezzan*. London: Sickle Moon.

Castelli, R. and Liverani, M. 2006. Cemeteries around the Barkat oasis. In Liverani 2006, 25–28.

Castelli, R., Cremaschi, M., Gatto, M.C., Liverani, M. and Mori, L. 2005. A preliminary report of excavations in Fewet, Libyan Sahara. *Journal of African Archaeology* 3.1: 69–102.

Connah, G. 2004. *Forgotten Africa. An Introduction to its Archaeology*. London: Routledge.

Cremaschi M. 2003. Steps and timing of the desertification during the Late Antiquity. The case study of the Tanzzuft oasis (Libyan Sahara). In M. Liverani (ed.), *Arid Lands in Roman Times*, AZA 4. Firenze: Edizioni All'Insegna del Giglio, 1–14.

Cremaschi M. 2006. The Barkat oasis in the changing landscape of Wadi Tannezzuft during the Holocene. In Liverani 2006, 13–24.

Cremaschi, M. and di Lernia, S. (eds). 1998. *Wadi Teshuinat. Palaeoenvironment and Prehistory in South-Western Fezzan (Libyan Sahara). Survey and Excavations in the Tadrart Acacus, Erg Uan Kasa, Messak Sattafet and Edeyen of Murzuq, 1990–1995*. Milan: All'Insegna del Giglio.

Cremaschi, M. and di Lernia, S. 2001. Environment and settlements in the Mid-Holocene palaeo-oasis of Wadi Tanzzuft (Libyan Sahara). *Antiquity* 75: 815–25.

Cremaschi M. and Zerboni A. 2009. Early to middle Holocene landscape exploitation in a drying environment: two case studies compared from the Central Sahara (SW Fezzan, Libya). *Comptes Rendus Géoscience* 341: 689–702.

Cremaschi M. and Zerboni A. 2011. Human communities in a drying landscape. Holocene climate change and cultural response in the Central Sahara. In I. P. Martini and W. Chesworth (eds), *Landscape and Societies, Selected cases*. New York: Springer Science, 67–89.

Cremaschi M. and Zerboni A. 2013. Fewet: an oasis at the margin of Wadi Tanezzuft. In Mori 2013, 7–15.

Daniels, C.M. 1968. Garamantian excavations: Zinchecra 1965–1967. *Libya Antiqua* 5: 113–94.

Daniels, C.M. 1969. The Garamantes. In W.H. Kanes (ed.), *Geology, Archaeology and Prehistory of the Fezzan, Libya*. Tripoli: Petroleum Exploration Society of Libya, Eleventh Annual Field Conference, 31–52.

Daniels, C.M. 1970. *The Garamantes of Southern Libya*. London: Oleander.

Daniels, C.M. 1971a. The Garamantes of Fezzan. In F.F. Gadallah (ed.), *Libya in History. Proceedings of a Conference Held at the Faculty of Arts, University of Libya 1968*. Benghazi: University of Benghazi, 261–85.

Daniels C.M. 1971b. Excavations at Saniat Gebril, Wadi el-Agial, Fezzan. *Libyan Studies* 2: 6–7.

Daniels, C.M. 1973. The Garamantes of Fezzan – an interim report of research, 1965–1973. *Libyan Studies* 4: 35–40.

Daniels, C.M. 1975. An ancient people of the Libyan Sahara. In J. Bynon and T. Bynon (eds), *Hamito-Semitrica*. The Hague: Mouston, 249–65.

Daniels, C.M. 1977. Garamantian excavations (Germa) 1977. *Libyan Studies* 8: 5–7.

Daniels, C.M. 1989. Excavation and fieldwork amongst the Garamantes. *Libyan Studies* 20: 45–61.

De Agostini E. 1934. La conca di Gat. In *Governo della Tripolitania e della Cirenaica, Servizio di studi, Bollettino Geografico* 5–6: 14–27.

Desanges, J. 1980. *(Pline l'ancien) Histoire naturelle Livre V.1–46 (L'Afrique du nord)*. Paris: Collection Budé.

Desio, A. 1937. Geologia e morfologia. In *Sahara Italiano* 1937, 39–94.

Despois, J. 1946. *Mission scientifique du Fezzan (1944–1945) III Géographie humaine*. Algiers: Université d'Alger.

di Lernia, S. and Manzi, G. (eds). 2002. *Sand, Stones and Bones. The Archaeology of Death in the Wadi Tanzzuft Valley* (5000–2000 BP). Firenze: All'Insegna dell Giglio.

di Lernia, S. and Zampetti, D. (eds). 2008. *La memoria dell'arte. Le pitture rupestri dell'Acacus tra passato e futuro*. Firenze: All'Insegna dell Giglio.

di Lernia, S., Bertolani, G.B., Merighi, F., Ricci, F.R., Manzi, G. and Cremaschi M. 2001. Megalithic architecture and funerary practices in the late prehistory of Wadi Tenezzuft (Libyan Sahara). *Libyan Studies* 32: 29–48.

Dubay, L. 1980. Ground water in Wadi Ash Shati, Fazzan – a case history of resource development. In M.J. Salem and M.T. Busrewil (eds), *The Geology of Libya* II. London: Academic Press, 611–26.

Duveyrier, H. 1864. *Les Touareg du nord. Exploration du Sahara*. Paris: Challamel Ainé.

Edwards, D. 2001. Archaeology in the southern Fazzan and prospects for future research. *Libyan Studies* 32: 49–66.

Ehret, C. 2002. *The Civilizations of Africa. A History to 1800*. Oxford: James Currey.

Fagan, B.M. 1965. Radiocarbon dates for Sub-Saharan Africa (from *c*.1000 B.C.). *Journal of African History* 6.1: 107–16.

Gatto, M. 2006. The Garamantes in the Ghat-Barkat area: previous research. In Liverani 2006, 21–24.

Gatto, M., Mattingly, D.J., Ray, N. and Sterry, M. (eds). 2019a. *Burials, Migration and Identity in the Ancient Sahara and Beyond*. Trans-Saharan Archaeology Volume 2. Series editor D.J. Mattingly. Cambridge: Cambridge University Press and The Society for Libyan Studies.

Gatto, M.C. Mori, L. and Zerboni, A. 2019b. Identity markers in south-western Fazzan. Were the people of the Wadi Tanzzuft/Tadrart Akakus region Garamantes? In Gatto *et al.* 2019a, 108–33.

Gigliarelli, U. 1932. *Il Fezzan*. Tripoli: Governo della Tripolitania.

Goudarzi, G.H. 1970. *Geology and Mineral Resources of Libya – a Reconnaissance*. Washington, DC: US Geological Survey Prof Paper 660.

Goudarzi, G.H. 1971. Geology of the Shati valley area iron deposit, Fezzan, Libyan Arab Republic. In C. Gray (ed.), *First Symposium on the Geology of Libya*. Tripoli: Faculty of Science, University of Libya, 489–500.

Graziosi, P. 1942. *L'arte rupestre della Libia*. Napoli: Edizioni della Mostra d'Oltremare.

Hachid, M. 2000. *Les premiers Berbères. Entre Méditerannée, Tassili et Nil*. Aix-en-Provence: Edisud.

Hawthorne J, Mattingly D.J. and Daniels C.M. 2010. Zinkekra: An Early Garamantian escarpment settlement and associated sites. In Mattingly 2010: 19–84.

Hornemann, F. 1802. *The Journal of Frederick Hornemann's Travels from Cairo to Mourzouk the Capital of the Kingdom of Fezzan in Africa in the Years 1797–9*. London: G. and W. Nichol.

Lahr, M.M., Foley, R.F., Mattingly, D.J. and Le Quesne, C. 2009. *Area 131, Jarma, Fazzan: Archaeological Mitigation of Seismic Acquisition 2006–2008 – Final Report.* Unpublished Consultancy report for Occidental Libya Oil and Gas BV and Libyan Department of Antiquities.

Lassère, J.-M. 2015. *Africa, quasi Roma (256 av. J.-C. – 711 apr. J.-C.).* Paris: CNRS editions.

Leitch, V., Duckworth, C., Cuénod, A., Mattingly, D.J., Sterry, M. and Cole, F. 2017. Early Saharan trade: The inorganic evidence. In Mattingly *et al.* 2017, 287–340.

Leschi, L. 1945. La mission scientifique au Fezzan. Archéologie. *Travaux de l'Institut de Recherches Sahariennes* 3: 183–86.

Le Quellec, J.-L. 1987. *L'art rupestre du Fezzan septentrional (Libye): Widyan Zreda et Tarut* (Wâdi esh-Shâti) (BAR International Series 365). Oxford: British Archaeological Reports.

Lethielleux, J. 1948. *Le Fezzan. Ses jardins, ses palmiers. Notes d'ethnologie et d'histoire.* Tunis: Imp. Bascone et Muscat.

Liverani, M. 2000. The Libyan caravan road in Herodotus IV.181–184. *Journal of the Economic and Social History of the Orient* 43.4: 496–520.

Liverani, M. (ed.). 2006. *Aghram Nadharif. The Barkat Oasis (Sha'abiya of Ghat, Libyan Sahara) in Garamantian Times.* Firenze: All'Insegna del Giglio.

Liverani, M. 2007a. Cronologia e periodizzazione dei Garamanti. Acquisizioni e prospettive. *Athenaeum* 95: 633–62.

Liverani, M. 2007b. La struttura sociale dei Garamanti in base alle recenti scoperte archaelogiche. *Rendiconti dell'Accademia Nazionale dei Lincei Ser* 9.18: 155–204.

Liverani, M., Barbato, L., Cancellieri, E., Castelli, R. and Putzolu, C. 2013. The survey of the Fewet necropolis. In Mori 2013, 199–252.

Mattingly, D.J. 2000. Garama. In R. Talbert (ed.), *Barrington Atlas of the Greek and Roman World.* Princeton: Princeton University Press, map 36 and Map-by-Map Directory pp. 545–51.

Mattingly, D.J. 2003. *The Archaeology of Fazzan. Volume 1, Synthesis.* London: Society for Libyan Studies, Department of Antiquities.

Mattingly, D.J. 2004. Nouveaux aperçus sur les Garamantes: Un état saharien? *Antiquités africaines* 37 (2001) [2004]: 45–61.

Mattingly, D.J. 2006. The Garamantes: The first Libyan state. In Mattingly *et al.* 2006, 189–204.

Mattingly, D.J. 2007. *The Archaeology of Fazzan. Volume 2, Site Gazetteer, Pottery and other Survey Finds.* London: Society for Libyan Studies, Department of Antiquities.

Mattingly, D.J. 2010. *The Archaeology of Fazzan. Volume 3, Excavations Carried out by C.M. Daniels.* London: Society for Libyan Studies, Department of Antiquities.

Mattingly, D.J. 2013. *The Archaeology of Fazzan. Volume 4, Survey and Excavations at Old Jarma (Ancient Garama) Carried out by C. M. Daniels (1962–69) and the*

Fazzan Project (1997–2001). London: Society for Libyan Studies, Department of Antiquities.

Mattingly, D.J. 2016. The Garamantes and after: The biography of a Central Saharan oasis 400 BC – AD 1900. In G. Bartoloni and M.G. Biga (eds), *Not Only History: Proceedings of the Conference in Honor of Mario Liverani Held in Sapienza-Università di Roma, Dipartimento di Scienza dell'Antichità, 20–21 April 2009*. Winina Lake, Indiana: Eisenbrauns, 147–69.

Mattingly, D.J. 2017. The Garamantes and the origins of Saharan trade: State of the field and future agendas. In Mattingly *et al.* 2017, 1–52.

Mattingly D.J. and Edwards D. 2003. Religious and funerary structures. In Mattingly 2003, 177–234.

Mattingly, D.J. and MacDonald, K.C. 2013. Africa. In P. Clark (ed.), *Oxford Handbook of Cities in World History*. Oxford: Oxford University Press, 66–82.

Mattingly, D.J. and Sterry, M. 2013. The first towns in the Central Sahara. *Antiquity* 87.366: 503–18.

Mattingly, D.J. and Sterry, M. 2018. Zuwila and Fazzan in the 7th–10th centuries AD. In G. Anderson, C. Fenwick and M. Rosser-Owen (eds), *The Aghlabids and Their Neighbours: An Interdisclipinary Workshop on Art & Material Culture in Ninth-Century North Africa*. Leuven: Brill, 551–72.

Mattingly, D.J., McLaren, S., Savage, E. al-Fasatwi, Y. and Gadgood, K. (eds). 2006. *The Libyan Desert. Natural Resources and Cultural Heritage*. London: Society for Libyan Studies.

Mattingly, D.J., Lahr, M., Armitage, S., Barton, H., Dore, J., Drake, N., Foley, R., Merlo, S., Salem, M., Stock, J. and White, K. 2007. Desert Migrations: People, environment and culture in the Libyan Sahara. *Libyan Studies* 38: 115–56.

Mattingly, D.J., Dore, J. and Lahr, M. (with contributions by others). 2008. DMP II: 2008 fieldwork on burials and identity in the Wadi al-Ajal. *Libyan Studies* 39: 223–62.

Mattingly, D.J., Lahr, M. and Wilson, A. 2009. DMP V: Investigations in 2009 of cemeteries and related sites on the west side of the Taqallit promontory. *Libyan Studies* 40: 95–131.

Mattingly, D.J., Abduli, H., Aburgheba, H., Ahmed, M., Ali Ahmed Esmaia, M., Baker, S., Cole, F., Fenwick, C., Gonzalez Rodriguez, M., Hobson, M., Khalaf, N., Lahr, M., Leitch, V., Moussa, F., Nikita, E., Parker, D., Radini, A., Ray, N., Savage, T., Sterry, M. and Schörle, K. 2010a. DMP IX: Summary report on the fourth season of excavations of the Burials and Identity team. *Libyan Studies* 41: 89–104.

Mattingly, D.J., al-Aghab, S., Ahmed, A., Moussa, F., Sterry, M and Wilson, A.I. 2010b. DMP X: Survey and landscape conservation issues around the Taqallit headland. *Libyan Studies* 41: 105–32.

Mattingly D.J., Hawthorne J. and Daniels C.M. 2010c. Excavations at the Classic Garamantian settlement of Saniat Jibril. In Mattingly 2010, 123–204.

Mattingly, D.J., Abduli, H., Ahmed, M., Cole, F., Fenwick, C., Fothergill, B.T., Gonzalez Rodriguez, M., Hobson, M., Khalaf, N., Lahr, M., Moussa, F.,

Nikita, E., Nikolaus, J., Radini, A., Ray, N., Savage, T., Sterry, M. and Wilson, A.I. 2011. DMP XII: Excavations and survey of the so-called Garamantian Royal Cemetery (GSC030-031). *Libyan Studies* 42: 89–102.

Mattingly, D.J., Rushworth, A., Sterry, M. and Leitch, V. 2013a. *The African Frontiers*. Frontiers of the Roman Empire series, general editor, D. Breeze. Edinburgh: Hussar.

Mattingly, D.J., Sterry, M. and Leitch, V. 2013b, Fortified farms and defended villages of Late Roman and Late Antique Africa. *Antiquité Tardive* 21: 167–88.

Mattingly, D.J., Sterry, M. and Edwards, D. 2015. The origins and development of Zuwila, Libyan Sahara: An archaeological and historical overview of an ancient oasis town and caravan centre. *Azania* 50.1: 27–75. Available at: http://dx.doi.org/10.1080/0067270X.2014.980126 [last accessed 4 September 2019].

Mattingly, D.J., Leitch, V., Duckworth, C.N., Cuénod, A., Sterry, M. and Cole, F. (eds). 2017. *Trade in the Ancient Sahara and Beyond*. Trans-Saharan Archaeology Volume 1. Series editor D.J. Mattingly. Cambridge: Cambridge University Press and The Society for Libyan Studies.

Mattingly, D.J., Sterry, M., al-Haddad, M. and Bokbot, Y. 2018. Beyond the Garamantes: The early development of Saharan oases. In Purdue *et al.* 2018a, 205–28.

Mattingly, D.J., Gatto, M., Ray, N. and Sterry, M. 2019. Dying to be Garamantian: Burial and migration in Fazzan. In Gatto *et al.* 2019a, 51–107.

Mercuri, A.M., Bosi, G. and Buldini, F. 2013. Seeds, fruit and charcoal from the Fewet compound. In Mori 2013, 177–90.

Merlo, S., Hakenbeck, S.E. and Balbo, A. 2008. DMP IV: 2008 fieldwork on historic settlement in the Wadi ash-Shati and the Dawada lake villages. *Libyan Studies* 39: 295–98.

Merlo, S., Hakenbeck, S. and Balbo, A.L. 2013. Desert Migrations Project XVIII: The archaeology of the northern Fazzan: A preliminary report. *Libyan Studies* 44: 141–61.

Mori, L. 2010. Between the Sahara and the Mediterranean coast: The archaeological research in the oasis of Fewet (Fazzan, Libyan Sahara) and the rediscovery of the Garamantes. In M. Dalla Riva (ed.), *Meetings between Cultures in the Ancient Mediterranean, XVII Congresso Internazionale di Archeologia Classica, Roma 22–26 settembre 2008*. Rome: Bollettino di Archeologia, volume speciale, 17–29.

Mori, L. 2012. Fortified citadels and castles in southern Fazzan (Libyan Sahara) in Garamantia times. In F. Jesse and C. Vogel (eds), *The Power of Walls. Fortifications in Ancient Northeastern Africa*. Cologne: Heinrich-Barth-Institut of Cologne, 195–216.

Mori, L. (ed.). 2013. *Life and Death of a Rural Village in Garamantian Times. The Archaeological Research in the Oasis of Fewet (Libyan Sahara)*, AZA Monographs 6. Firenze: All'Insegna del Giglio.

Mori, L. and Ricci, F. 2013. The excavation of the Fewet necropolis. In Mori 2013, 253–317.

Mori, L., Gatto M.C., Zerboni A. and Ricci F. 2013. Life and death at Fewet. In Mori 2013, 375–87.

Nachtigal G. 1974. *Sahara and Sudan, vol I, Tripoli and Fezzan, Tibesti or Tu.* Translated from the German by A.G.B. and H.J. Fisher. London: C. Hurst and Co.

Pace, B., Sergi, S. and Caputo, G. 1951. Scavi sahariani. *Monumenti Antichi* 41: 150–549.

Pelling, R. 2005. Garamantian agriculture and its significance in a wider North African context: The evidence of the plant remains from the Fazzan Project. *The Journal of North African Studies* 10.3–4: 397–411.

Pelling, R. 2008. Garamantian agriculture: The plant remains from Jarma, Fazzan. *Libyan Studies* 39: 41–71.

Pelling, R. 2013a. The archaeobotanical remains. In Mattingly 2013, 473–94.

Pelling, R. 2013b. Botanical data appendices. In Mattingly 2013, 841–52.

Pliez, O. 2004. La fin de l'état demiurge? Les nouvelles facettes de l'urbain dans le Sahara libyen. *Autrepart* 31: 59–74.

Putzolu, C. 2006. The topography of the site. In Liverani 2006, 29–40.

Ruprechtsberger, E.M. 1997. *Die Garamanten, Geschichte und Kultur eines Libyschen Volkes in der Sahara.* Mainz: Verlag Philipp von Zabern.

Sahara Italiano 1937 = *Il Sahara Italiano, I. Fezzan e oasi di Gat.* Rome: Società Italiana arto grafiche.

Scarin, E. 1934. *Le oasi del Fezzan*, 2 vols. Bologna: Nicola Zanichelli.

Scarin, E. 1937a. Insediamenti e tipi di dimore. In *Sahara Italiano* 1937, 515–60.

Scarin, E. 1937b. Descrizione delle oasi e gruppi di oasi. In *Sahara Italiano* 1937, 603–44.

Scarin, E. 1937c. *L'insediamento umano della zona Fezzanese di Gat.* Firenze: Centro di studi coloniali.

Sterry, M. and Mattingly, D.J. 2011. DMP XIII: Reconnaissance survey of archaeological sites in the Murzuq area. *Libyan Studies* 42: 103–16.

Sterry, M, and Mattingly, D.J. 2013. Desert Migrations Project XVII: Further AMS dates for historic settlements from Fazzan, south-west Libya. *Libyan Studies* 44: 127–40.

Sterry, M, Mattingly, D.J. and Higham, T. 2012. Desert Migrations Project XVI: Radiocarbon dates from the Murzuq region, southern Libya. *Libyan Studies* 43: 137–47.

Thiry, J. 1995. *Le Sahara Libyen dans l'Afrique du Nord Medievale.* Leuven: Orientalia Lovaniensia Analecta, 72.

Turk, T.M., Doughri, A.K. and Banerjee, S. 1980. A review of the recent investigation on the Wadi ash-Shati iron ore deposits, Northern Fazzan, Libya. In M.J. Salem and M.T. Busrewil (eds), *The Geology of Libya III.* London: Academic Press, 1019–43.

Van der Veen, M. 1992. Garamantian agriculture: The plant remains from Zinchecra, Fezzan. *Libyan Studies* 23: 7–39.

Van der Veen, M. and Westley, B. 2010. Palaeoeconomic studies. In Mattingly 2010, 488–522.

Wilson, A.I. 2006. The spread of foggara-based irrigation in the ancient Sahara. In Mattingly *et al.* 2006, 205–16.

Wilson, A.I. 2009. Foggaras in ancient North Africa or how to marry a Berber princess. In *Contrôle et distribution de l'eau dans le Maghreb antique et medieval.* Rome: CEFR, 19–39.

Wilson, A.I. and Mattingly, D.J. 2003. Irrigation technologies: Foggaras, wells and field systems. In Mattingly 2003, 234–78.

Wilson, A.I., Mattingly, D.J. and Sterry, M.S. Forthcoming. The diffusion of irrigation technologies in the Sahara in antiquity: Settlement, trade and migration. In C. Duckworth, A. Cuénod and D.J. Mattingly (eds), *Mobile Technologies in the Sahara and Beyond.* Cambridge: Cambridge University Press.

Ziegert, H. 1969. Überblick zur jüngeren Besiedlungsgeschichte des Fezzan. *Berliner Geographischen Abhandlungen* 8: 49–58.

3 | Pre-Islamic Oasis Settlements in the Eastern Sahara

DAVID J. MATTINGLY, MARTIN STERRY, LOUISE RAYNE AND MUFTAH AL-HADDAD

Introduction

This chapter will review the evidence of early oasis development in Western Egypt and Eastern Libya, broadly following the course of the 'route of the oases', running west from the Nile to Siwa, then onwards to Awjila and al-Jufra in Libya, where it met the major north-south route from the Mediterranean to Garamantian Fazzan and beyond to Chad.[1] The evidence presented for pre-Islamic oasis development is particularly strong in this part of the Sahara; indeed the origins of agriculture at some of the Egyptian oases went back to the third millennium BC and the route as a whole seems to have been well-developed by the fifth century BC.

We suggest that the ultimate origins of oasis agriculture in the Western Desert are to be sought in the Nile Valley and the Fayum, with a package of plants and irrigation techniques first developed there, then adopted in the oasis depressions of the Western Desert – notably Kharga, Dakhla, Farfara, Bahariya and Siwa (Fig. 3.1). From Siwa the line of oases was extended along the northern edge of the great Libyan sand sea, to al-Jiarabub and the Awjila group to the south of Cyrenaica (Fig. 3.2). Beyond Awjila, the Syrtic desert crossing was facilitated by the existence of a number of small oases, Marada, Zala, Tagrifet. The al-Jufra group at the south-western boundary of Syrtica has been little explored hitherto, but new satellite image analysis and some ground visits allow a new appreciation of the importance of this cluster.[2]

[1] On the oasis route, see Herodotus 4.181–184; Liverani 2000; 2006, 445–56; Rebuffat 1970b.

[2] The account below summarises past publication and new work carried out as part of the Trans-SAHARA project.

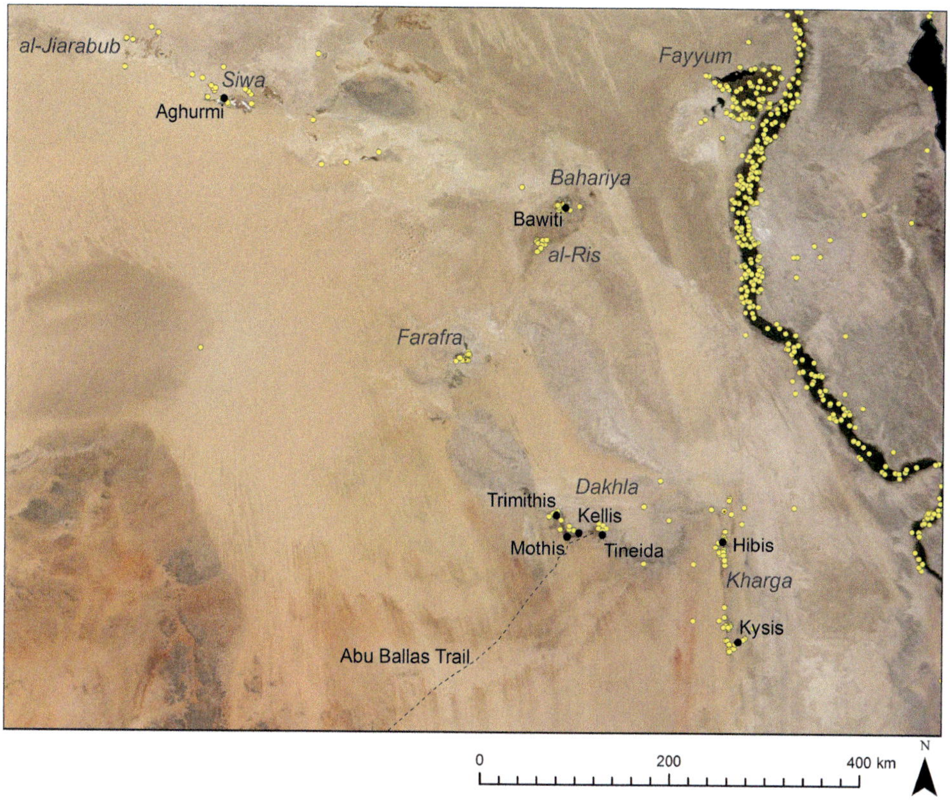

Figure 3.1. Western Desert showing main regions and sites discussed in the text.

Western Desert of Egypt

The next chapter by Boozer presents a more detailed picture of the Roman era settlement in the Western Desert oases and in consequence we only highlight some of the main bibliography and provide a concise outline for that area here. The quantity of archaeological research conducted in the Western Desert is disproportionately large in comparison to the rest of the Sahara, with a bibliography now running to hundreds of items, reflecting the work of a number of large international and Egyptian teams working in the oases over many years.[3] However, the orientation of research is to a large extent Egyptological, with the gaze primarily directed east to the Nile, rather than further west along the Saharan trails.[4] To the extent that

[3] See for instance, the excellent online bibliography of the Dakhla oasis project, available at: www.amheida.org/inc/pdf/amheida_bibliography.pdf [last accessed 4 September 2019].

[4] See Kuhlmann 2013 for a rare exception.

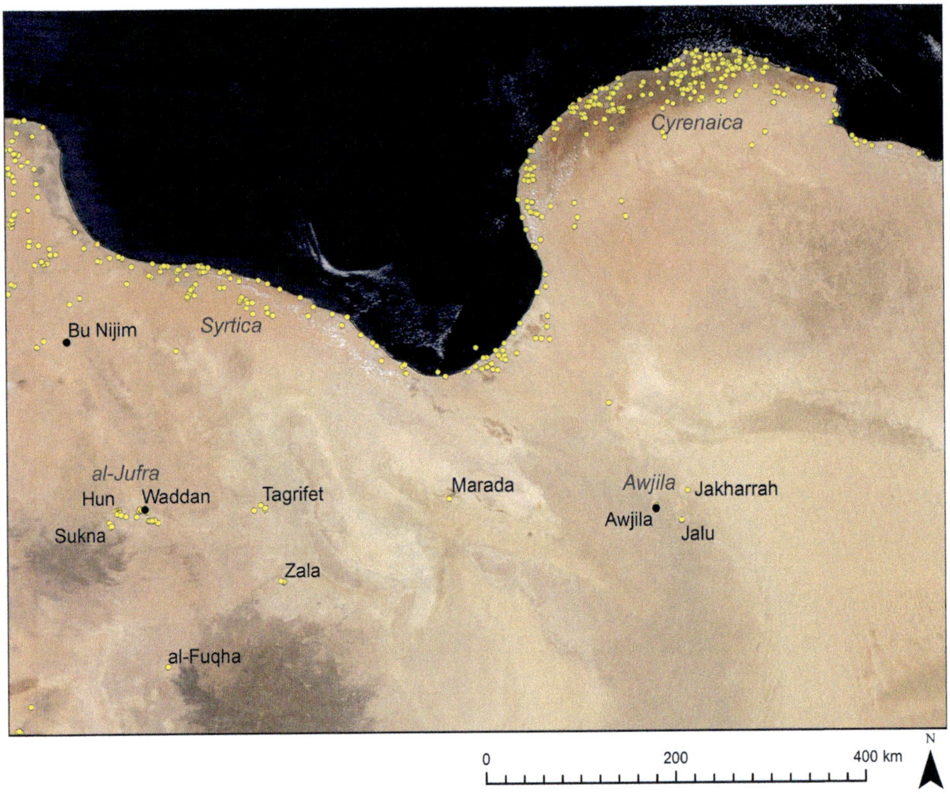

Figure 3.2. Eastern Libya showing main regions and sites discussed in the text.

the Libyan population of the desert are considered, it is mainly as pastoral and warlike people who needed to be pacified and controlled by the ruling power of Egypt.[5] This is, of course, a reflection of the influence and impact of Pharaonic and later Hellenistic and Roman overlordship of these oases, backed up by some profound shared cultural preferences (temple architecture, hieroglyphs, mummies, etc.). In Classical writings, the perspective of the nature of desert peoples became even more based around crude stereotypes.[6] Approaches that stress the external interventions of the

5 Bates 1914; Leahy 1990; Midant-Reynes and Tristant 2008; O'Connor and Reid 2003. Cf. Bowman 1989, 12: 'To the east and west . . . lay inhospitable or mountainous desert. The western desert was punctuated by a series of oases, supporting a small population . . . their secure occupation was an important factor in controlling incursion or potential disruption by bands of desert nomads.'

6 Colin 2000 provides a particularly uncritical perspective on the Libyan peoples between Cyrenaica and Egypt in the Classical sources, taking at face value the emphasis on pastoralism (40–86), with only limited mention of oasis cultivation (115–19) and a complete denial of the existence of long-range trade in the Sahara (45–57). Cf. Mattingly 2003, 76–90.

Pharaonic state of Egypt or its Hellenistic and Roman successors in the development of the oases miss an important element of the story, not just in the opening chapters of oasis formation, but in relation to the Sahara overall. The Sahara was not empty space when oases were established and some of the pre-existing populations were important agents in the process.

The later prehistory of the Eastern Sahara has revealed the existence there of wide-ranging pastoral peoples, whose lives were transformed following climatic change around 5,000 years ago.[7] Some of these Libyan peoples no doubt sought refuge within the Nile Valley and played a part in the transformation of Nilotic society at that time, but others seem to have remained in the desert regions, now focused increasingly on the springs and relict lakes of the depressions, where oases were later to appear. The communications between the Nilotic peoples and the Libyans of the Western Desert were important and these groups had symbiotic reasons as well as issues of neighbourly competition and warfare. Though the Egyptian sources emphasise the pastoral and barbaric character of the Libyan peoples, the representations of them show them when in battle having access to the high technology of warfare – metal swords, chariots – and being able to deliver significant levels of tribute. Although many accounts of the Libyan peoples (variously called Meshwesh, Libu and Tehenu) still emphasise that these were nomadic peoples, it seems more plausible to consider that by the first millennium BC (and perhaps considerably earlier) these were societies comprising both pastoral and oasis cultivating elements. In addition, trade between the Nile and the desert regions seems to have been initiated early in the Old Kingdom.[8]

The peculiar hydrology of the River Nile, with its annual floods, created what was in effect an immense linear oasis of cultivated land along its course. From there, irrigation techniques and a package of cultivated crops spread into surrounding desert areas. The earliest oases in the Sahara are plausibly to be sought in the Western Egyptian Desert, where there are certain traces of Old Kingdom (third millennium BC) activity at several locations (see below). Although the settlement trajectory was not always consistent, by the Roman era there was very extensive settlement within these oasis zones, which fall into several main groups.[9] An important

[7] Jennerstrasse 8 2002; cf. Barich and Hassan 1990; McDonald 2003; Wendorf and Schild 1980; Wendorf *et al.* 1984.

[8] See the important article by Kuhlman 2002, arguing for its existence by the III or IV Dynasty (mid-third millennium BC). Also now, Morkot 2016.

[9] See Mattingly 2000a, map 73; Müller-Wollermann 2000, map 75; Wagner 2000, map 79, for the Oasis Magna, Oasis Parva and Siwa.

recent overview of Ptolemaic activity in the oases has shown that pre-Roman activity was much more extensive and well developed than sometimes imagined.[10] The oases of the Western Desert as a group were well connected with the Nile Valley from early times and were frequently mentioned in historical sources both of the Pharaonic periods and in later Classical times.[11] Nonetheless, the oases were distinctively different hydrologically compared with the Nile Valley in that water, though a scarce resource, was available all year round. The water also emerged naturally from artesian thermal springs in these depressions, obviating the need to search for it.[12] Both these aspects favoured early development of oasis agriculture as a complement to the lands irrigated annually by the Nile flood. Table 3.1 presents the relevant radiocarbon dates for sites discussed in this chapter.

The Fayyum

Arguably, the earliest oases of the Western Desert were those of the Fayyum.[13] The Fayyum is a triangular depression, *c.*100 × 90 km, with a 40 km long lake along its northern edge that was sacred to the crocodile god.[14] Sedentary settlement and agriculture in the depression around the Fayyum lake began during the Old Kingdom (2686–2181 BC). However, the major expansion of agriculture and population in Fayyum began during the Middle Kingdom (2055–1650 BC) when Nile floodwaters were diverted into the depression to enhance irrigation there. There were 114 villages in Fayyum in Hellenistic times and this intensity of activity continued into Roman times, with well-developed towns such as Boubastis, Dionysias, Karanis, Philadelphia, Theadelphia and many villages.[15] Detailed plans of a number of the Fayyum cities have been established and their overall location is very interesting within the depression, in that many of them were established around the margins of the lakes and the fringes of the cultivated zone.[16] Although the Fayyum is highly atypical of the other Saharan oases, because of the augmentation of the irrigation

[10] Gill 2016.
[11] Abboudy Ibrahim 1992; Abd el-Ghany 1992; Bagnall 1997; Ball 1942; Giddy 1987; Reddé 1989; Wagner 1987.
[12] Gautier 1970, 139–59, for a general overview of hydrology of the Egyptian oases.
[13] Vivian 2000, 211–17. [14] Müller-Wollermann 2000, 1125–26.
[15] Many toponyms mentioned in papyri cannot be located precisely, as is evident from Müller-Wollermann 2000; Rathbone 1996. It is clear, however, that the Fayyum was very densely inhabited by the Roman period and a highly productive agricultural region.
[16] Davoli 1998; 2012. See also Carpentiero 2016 for discussion of town planning in Fayyum.

Table 3.1 *Protohistoric and historic radiocarbon dates from the Eastern Sahara*

Area/Site	Context	Material	Reference	Date (BP)	Calibrated
Kharga					
Abu Ziyar	Cooking remains	Charcoal	Not given	3605±48	2134–1781 calBC
Kysis	Mudbrick (temple)	Charcoal	Gif?	2260±60	415–166 calBC
Al-Deir	Irrigation canal	Charcoal	CEDAD-LTL-13096A	2138±40	356–49 calBC
Al-Deir	Irrigation canal	Charcoal	UCIAM-76668/ULA-1623	1770±15	calAD 226–331
Al-Deir	Palaeosoil	Charcoal	UGAMS-1124/ULA-3179	2810±25	1025–901 calBC
Al-Deir	Palaeosoil	Charcoal	UGAMS-11244/ULA-3180	2210±25	364–202 calBC
Al-Deir	Palaeosoil	Charcoal	UCIAM-76668/ULA-1625	2130±15	204–96 calBC
Al-Deir	Palaeosoil	Charcoal	Poz-56029	1850±15	calAD 91–231
Dakhla					
Yardang AM66	Palaeosoil	Charcoal	LTL-8373	2805±34	1049–848 calBC
Yardang GS001	Palaeosoil	Charcoal	LTL-8364	2710±55	980–797 calBC
Yardang GS001	Palaeosoil	Charcoal	LTL-8369	2599±36	835–590 calBC
Yardang GS001	Palaeosoil	Charcoal	LTL-8366	2527±40	799–540 calBC
Spring GS022	Palaeosoil	Charcoal	LTL-8368	2315±42	510–210 calBC
Yardang AM72	Palaeosoil	Charcoal	LTL-8375	2220±33	379–202 calBC
Yardang GS001	Palaeosoil	Charcoal	LTL-8365	2186±40	377–118 calBC
Spring GS022	Palaeosoil	Charcoal	LTL-8367	2101±35	342–40 calBC
Yardang AM70	Palaeosoil	Charcoal	LTL-8374	2062±35	176 calBC–calAD 17
Yardang GS011	Palaeosoil	Charcoal	LTL-8372	1935±33	21 calBC–calAD 133
Yardang GS011	Palaeosoil	Charcoal	LTL-8370	1933±33	21 calBC–calAD 134
Ein Tirghi cemetery	Burial E31 Sk25	Human remains	TO-4476	2745±70	1071–796 calBC
Ein Tirghi cemetery	Burial E31 Sk36	Human remains	TO-4476	2750±60	1030–803 calBC
Kellis 1 cemetery	Mummy 1	Human tissue	GX-19942	2130±75	374 calBC–calAD 4

Table 3.1 (*cont.*)

Area/Site	Context	Material	Reference	Date (BP)	Calibrated
Kellis 1 cemetery	Mummy 1	Human tissue	Beta-119805	1940±60	88 calBC–calAD 230
Kellis 1 cemetery	Mummy 1	Textile	Beta-119803	1960±40	43 calBC–calAD 125
Kellis 1 cemetery	Mummy 2	Textile	Beta-119811	1860±60	calAD 23–326
Kellis 1 cemetery	Mummy 3	Human tissue	GX-20367	2075±60	351 calBC–calAD 58
Kellis 1 cemetery	Mummy 4	Human tissue	Beta-119806	2210±50	395–164 calBC
Kellis 1 cemetery	Mummy 4	Human tissue	Beta-170565	2010±40	156 calBC–calAD 75
Kellis 1 cemetery	Mummy 4	Human tissue	Gx-19943	2280±75	730–116 calBC
Kellis 1 cemetery	Mummy 4	Human tissue	Beta-119810	2280±70	703–164 calBC
Kellis 1 cemetery	Mummy 5	Human tissue	Gx-20366	1830±60	calAD 57–341
Kellis 1 cemetery	Mummy 5	Human tissue	Beta-119809	3070±70	1496–1126 calBC
Kellis 1 cemetery	Mummy 5	Resin	Gx-19941	2225±105	728 calBC–calAD 4
Kellis 1 cemetery	Mummy 5	Resin	Beta-119802	2320±40	511–214 calBC
Kellis 1 cemetery	Mummy 6	Human tissue	Gx-19944	2020±75	347calBC–calAD 133
Kellis 1 cemetery	Mummy 7	Human tissue	Gx-19945	2335±155	800–55 calBC
Kellis 1 cemetery	Mummy 7	Human tissue	Gx-19946	2005±105	356 calBC–calAD 238
Kellis 1 cemetery	Mummy 7	Resin	Beta-120426	2580±50	836–541 calBC
Kellis 1 cemetery	Mummy 7	Resin	Beta-170566	2660±40	901–792 calBC
Kellis 1 cemetery	Mummy 7	Resin	Beta-172212	2660±40	901–792 calBC
Kellis 1 cemetery	Mummy 7	Textile	Gx-19947	2695±75	1051–760 calBC
Kellis 1 cemetery	Mummy 7	Textile	Beta-119804	1950±40	41 calBC–calAD 129
Kellis 1 cemetery	Mummy 8	Human tissue	Beta-143632	1890±40	calAD 28–230
Kellis 1 cemetery	Mummy 8	Human tissue	Beta-143633	1870±30	calAD 73–226
Kellis 1 cemetery	Mummy 8	Human tissue	Beta-119807	1800±60	calAD 82–380
Kellis 1 cemetery	Mummy 9	Human tissue	GX-20368	2245±60	406–167 calBC
Kellis 1 cemetery	Mummy 9	Human tissue	Beta-170567	2240±40	393–204 calBC
Kellis 1 cemetery	Mummy 9	Human tissue	Beta-172213	2160±40	361–92 calBC

Kellis 1 cemetery	Mummy 10	Human tissue	Beta-119807	1800±60	calAD 82–380
Kellis 1 cemetery	Mummy 15	Human tissue	Gx-19938	1880±95	91 calBC–calAD 383
Kellis 1 cemetery	Mummy 15	Human tissue	Gx-19937	2205±90	416 calBC–calAD 3
Kellis 1 cemetery	Mummy 15	Textile	Gx-19939	2515±375	1607 BC–calAD 233
Kellis 1 cemetery	Mummy 15	Wood	Gx-19940	2005±115	358 calBC–calAD 240
Kellis 2 Cemetery	Burial	Human bone	TO-5475	1840±60	calAD 52–355
Kellis 2 Cemetery	Burial K2-B6	Human bone	TO-5476	1670±50	calAD 244–535
Kellis 2 Cemetery	Burial K2-B6	Human bone	TO-6104	1600±50	calAD 344–569
Kellis 2 Cemetery	Burial	Human bone	TO-6256	1720±50	calAD 145–423
Kellis 2 Cemetery	Burial	Human bone	TO-6257	1920±50	38 calBC–calAD 219
Kellis 2 Cemetery	Burial	Human bone	TO-6013	1590±50	calAD 352–580
Kellis 2 Cemetery	Burial	Human bone	TO-10274	1800±50	calAD 85–345
Kellis 2 Cemetery	Burial	Human bone	TO-10275	1840±50	calAD 65–326
Kellis 2 Cemetery	Burial	Human bone	TO-10276	1850±50	calAD 56–322
Kellis 2 Cemetery	Burial	Human bone	TO-10277	1780±40	calAD 131–377
Kellis 2 Cemetery	Burial	Human bone	TO-10278	1880±40	calAD 53–236
Bahariya					
Qasr Allam	Mudbrick structure	Not given	Not given	2402±50	753–394 calBC
Qasr Allam	Mudbrick structure	Not given	Not given	2410±53	756–396 calBC
Qasr Allam	Level above child inhumations	Date stone	Not given	1585±45	calAD 386–575
Abu Ballas trail					
Staging post	From underneath stashed pots	Basket	UtC-8868	3226±88	1732–1290 calBC
Abu Ballas 85/55–2	With cups and bowls	Charcoal	KIA-20684	3785±25	2289–2140 calBC
Abu Ballas 85/55–2	Hearth	Charcoal	KIA-20682	3675±35	2192–1952 calBC
Abu Ballas 85/55–2	Donkey droppings	Barley	KIA-23062	3095±30	1429–1280 calBC
Jaqub 00/20	Storage Jar	Barley	Poz-23221	3520±35	1939–1749 calBC
Jaqub 99/30–1	Hearth	Charcoal	Erl-2876	3232±53	1627–1412 calBC
Jaqub 99/30–1	Hearth	Charcoal	Erl-2877	2963±52	1377–1015 calBC

Table 3.1 *(cont.)*

Area/Site	Context	Material	Reference	Date (BP)	Calibrated
Jaqub 99/30–1	Hearth	Charcoal	KN-5359	2895±40	1211–946 calBC
Jaqub 99/30–1	Hearth	Date stone	KIA-12423	2880±35	1194–936 calBC
Jaqub 99/31–3	With cups and bowls	Charcoal	KIA-20683	3755±30	2284–2041 calBC
Jaqub 99/31–3		Charcoal	KIA-21008	3240±20	1607–1446 calBC
Al-Jiarabub					
Site not clear	Funerary bed within tomb	Wood	GX-30372	1980±70	173 calBC–calAD 210
Awjila					
Al-Darb al-Kabir	Rock-cut burial	Textile	OxA-33721	2177±31	362–164 calBC
Al-Jufra					
Delbak (WDN001)	From mudbrick wall of settlement	Charcoal	OxA-33869	1281±32	calAD 659–776
Delbak (WDN001)	From mudbrick wall of settlement	Seeds	OxA-33964	7590±40*	Date rejected
HUN006	From mudbrick wall of settlement	Charcoal	OxA-33870	996±27	calAD 987–1151
HUN006	From mudbrick wall of settlement	Plant remains	OxA-33871	1257±25	calAD 672–862
HUN003	From mudbrick wall of settlement	Charred seeds	OxA-33872	97±27	calAD 1685–1928
HUN003	From mudbrick wall of settlement	Plant remains	OxA-33873	79±25	calAD 1692–1920
South-east Libya					
No data	No data	Tamarisk	Hv-3761	2300±145	780–51 calBC
No data	No data	Wood	Hv-3762	1625±145	calAD 85–659

system by canalised Nile floodwaters, the region was probably of crucial importance for the evolution of irrigation and cultivation technologies in a fundamentally desert landscape.

Kharga

Kharga (*c.*200 km west of the Nile to the south of Fayyum) was known with neighbouring Dakhla in Roman times as Oasis Magna (Great Oasis). The depression, bordered by escarpments to the east and north, is 220 km long north-south, but only 15–40 km wide east-west. There are two discrete zones of oasis settlement within the basin, towards its northern and southern ends, each dominated by a major town – Hibis in the north and Kysis (Dush) in the south.[17] The archaeology has been examined by a number of projects in recent decades.[18] There is textual and archaeological evidence of Pharaonic activity here and, though not proven archaeologically as yet, this must extend back here (as at Dakhla further west, see below) to the Old Kingdom. There were three major sites in the Roman period,[19] but numerous other villages (some fortified) and traces of ancient activity, including important temple complexes at both major centres and some smaller settlements. The Christian cemetery at Bagawat close by Hibis is notable for its domed and painted mausolea.[20]

An important aspect of recent work has been the thorough investigation of extensive oasis garden areas irrigated by foggaras. Some of the foggaras have been dated to the fifth and fourth centuries BC and seem to link also to documentary records post-dating the Persian take-over of Egypt, which probably marked the introduction of this technology from the Persian heartlands.[21] The documentary evidence relating to the irrigation regime in the Kharga oasis during the Persian period provides confirmation of the importance and sophistication of oasis agriculture by this date.[22]

The many fortified sites in the oasis have traditionally been interpreted as Roman military garrison points. While some undoubtedly were Roman military bases, others were potentially of more local origin, especially

[17] Jackson 2002, 163–97; Reddé *et al.* 2004; Vivian 2000, 52–105; Wagner 2000.

[18] See *inter alia*, Bravard *et al.* 2016b; Dunand *et al.* 2010; 2012; 2013; Fakhry 1942; Gill 2016, 130–34; Ibrahim 2013; Tallet *et al.* 2013.

[19] In addition to Hibis and Kysis, there was another extensive settlement in the northern area known today as Ain Umm Dabadib, Jackson 2002, 190–91; Rossi 2000.

[20] Jackson 2002, 180–83.

[21] Agut-Labordère 2018; Bousquet 1996; Gonon 2018; Wuttman *et al.* 2000; cf. Wilson 2006.

[22] Chaveau 2001; 2005; Newton *et al.* 2013.

bearing in mind the parallels of late antique fortified settlements in Fazzan (described in the previous chapter).[23]

An important aspect of Kharga is that it was the point of departure of important overland routes to Nubia and to the Chad/Darfur region, the so-called 40-day route, along which a number of minor oases developed (such as Selima).[24] The route that followed a desert detour to the Nubian centres on the Upper Nile was in many ways more practicable than following the course of the river south. We need more information on the oases of northern Sudan, but it is a reasonable assumption that their origins were also early.

Dakhla

The Dakhla oasis group (*c.*150 km west of Kharga) has also been the focus of intensive archaeological research for many years.[25] The oasis depression measures *c.*70 km east-west and 30 km north-south, with steep escarpments marking the north and east limits.[26] Roman era settlement and oasis cultivation fell into three main areas: an eastern area with a main site near Tineida, a central area with two main towns, Kellis and Mothis, and a western area with a main urban site called Trimithis.[27] There is now good excavated evidence of Old Kingdom activity, notably at Ain Asil (Balat), evidently the Old Kingdom capital.[28] The fortified town of Ain Asil was the base for the pharaoh's governors in the oasis, as several burial monuments and important epigraphic finds attest. Some accounts are cautious regarding the development of the oasis at this early date, seeing Ain Asil as a control fort, from which trading parties could be sent towards Nubia.[29] However, the accumulating archaeological evidence of other Old Kingdom sites calls this into question. There was another 5-ha mudbrick settlement called Ain al-Gazzareen, and around 30 other locations have produced evidence of Pharaonic activity.[30] The documentation from Ain

23 Jackson 2002, 166–67, 176–77, 183–89; Reddé 1999; Rossi 2013; Vivian 2000, 65–66; Wagner 1987.

24 Kirkwan 1971; Förster and Riemer 2013; Morkot 1996; 2016; Welsby 1996.

25 See *inter alia*, the Dakhla oasis Project monograph series (15 volumes), notably Bagnall *et al.* 2013; Bowen and Hope 2003; Hope and Bowen 2002; Hope and Mills 1999; Wiseman 2008.

26 Jackson 2002, 197–227; Vivian 2000, 106–42.

27 Davoli 2012; 2013; Warner 2013, for a good summary study of the towns.

28 Valloggia 2004, for an overview account of excavations at the Old Kingdom site of Balat/Ain Aseel/Ayn Asil.

29 Boozer 2015b, 7–10.

30 Mills 2002; 2013; Mills and Kaper 2003; Pettman 2013; Smekalova *et al.* 2003. See also Hope and Pettman 2013; Mills 1999a for a summary of evidence of Pharaonic activity in Dakhla.

Asil indicates the collection of agricultural produce among other things, presumably from oasis farmers within the depression. There are also references to goods that appear to be traded (including commodities like salt, carnelian, ochre) and possible stockpiling of goods for carriage on Saharan trails.[31] From the earliest times, therefore, Dakhla oasis appears to have had a double focus on agriculture and trade.

Ptolemaic activity in the oasis is now known to have been far more extensive than at one time believed.[32] By Hellenistic and Roman times the main centres were at Ismant al-Kharab (Kellis)[33] and Amheida (Trimithis) and another substantial site existed at Mut al-Kharab.[34] The extensive excavations at Kellis have revealed a complex Roman town, where substantial temple complexes, some decorated with elaborate wall paintings, later gave way to Christian churches, and where bath-houses and wealthy houses, lay alongside extensive zones of manufacturing activity (furnaces and kilns).[35] Trimithis was a particularly large urban site at *c.*100 ha, though excavation there has mainly focused on domestic housing of Roman date, with important results.[36] Geoarchaeological survey around Trimithis has identified the formation of irrigation soils from the Late Pharaonic period and degradation of the soils in the third and fourth centuries AD.[37] Cemeteries have been identified close to many of the main settlements.[38] A notable feature of the Dakhla oasis is the relative lack of fortified settlements there (only two compared with ten or more at Kharga), perhaps related to the fact that west of Dakhla extends a great sand sea and security may have been less of an issue than in Kharga which could be accessed by a multiplicity of routes.[39]

Abu Ballas

At 200 km from Dakhla on the trail towards Gilf Kebir lies Abu Ballas (literally ‘pottery hill’), one of a string of archaeological sites.[40] Here there is a scatter of late Old Kingdom or early First Intermediate Period ceramics (*c.*2200–2100 BC) making it the earliest evidence of incipient Trans-Saharan networks. This and the other sites have no suitable water sources

[31] Valloggia 2004, 99–102, 144–49. [32] Gill 2016, especially 97–127 for the sites.
[33] Hope and Bowen 2002 (168–69 for the overall plan); Knudstad and Frey 1999.
[34] Boozer 2013a; 2013b; Jackson 2002, 213–16. For Mut al-Kharab, see Gill 2016, 19–41.
[35] See in particular, various papers in Hope and Bowen 2002. Also Mills 1999b on pottery production in the oasis.
[36] Boozer 2010; 2011; 2012; 2015a. [37] Bravard *et al.* 2016a.
[38] Aufderheide *et al.* 2004; Bashendi 2013; Stewart *et al.* 2003. [39] Kucera 2013.
[40] Förster 2013; 2015.

nearby and all food and water appears to have been carried in by donkey to create a supply depot. The trail was in use through the second millennium BC, but there is very little evidence of use in more recent periods. Of particular significance are plant remains of dates and barley from 1194–936 calBC to 1429–1280 calBC, respectively.[41] This is the earliest evidence of these important crops west of the Egyptian oases.

Farfara

Some 310 km north of Dakhla and 175 km south-west of Bahariya is the small depression of Farfara (or Farafra).[42] Only a couple of relatively small settlements and three cemeteries are known in the oasis, all evidently of Roman date, though textual sources seem to indicate Pharaonic origins here.[43] There are indications in recent work that the ancient activity in the oasis was in fact more extensive.[44] Libyan inscriptions are known from the Farfara basin, but have not been transcribed.[45]

Bahariya

Bahariya is a substantial oasis depression 350 km west of Cairo (94 km north-south and 42 km east-west maximum). Together with the outlying oasis depression of Farfara to the south, Barhariya was known as Oasis Parva (Lesser Oasis) in antiquity. The Barhariya oasis group lies *c.*500 km north of the Great Oasis and 240 km west of Fayyum. Pharaonic (Middle Kingdom) and Roman activity have long been known here.[46] Bahariya consists of two separate areas of oasis, separated by *c.*40 km of desert: a northern area around al-Qasr/Bawiti (ancient Psobthis) and a southern area sometimes referred to as al-Hayz oasis. Around Bawiti there is a standing Roman triumphal arch and Fakhry uncovered a temple dedicated to Alexander the Great,[47] while there has been an important discovery of unrobbed Roman era mummified burials at Bawiti in the 1990s.[48] More recent work has also focused on sites in the southern parts of the

[41] Förster 2015.

[42] Barich and Hassan 1990; Beadnell 1901, Gallinaro 2018, for topographical setting and prehistoric evidence.

[43] Fakhry 1974; Jackson 2002, 230–32; Mattingly 2000a; Vivian 2000, 143–73.

[44] Gill 2016, 134–35. [45] Jackson 2002, 297, n. 5.

[46] Ball and Beadnell 1903; Fakhry 1942; 1942/1950; 1974; Gill 2016, 135–37; Gosline 1990; Jackson 2002, 233–39; Vivian 2000, 174–212. For the latest dating evidence of Pharaonic activity, see Dospěl and Suková 2013, 185–67.

[47] Fakhry 1942; 1942/1950. [48] Hawas 2000.

basin.[49] Here again irrigation seems to have been improved at some point by the introduction of foggara technology.[50] In the al-Hayz cluster 11 settlements of Pharaonic or Hellenistic or Roman/Byzantine date have been identified and there were at least nine settlements in the northern oasis.[51] Some of the largest settlements like al-Ris are urban in scale.[52] There were at least two major fortresses in the Bahariya depression, at al-Hayz in the south and Qasr Muharib in the north.

Siwa

Since the first reports of lost Persian armies and the pilgrimage of Alexander the Great, the oasis of Ammon (Siwa) has always been the most celebrated spot in the Eastern Sahara. There was a hot spring here that reputedly (though inaccurately) varied in temperature between night and day, but its greater fame was due to its status as the great oracular centre of the desert god Ammon.[53] The relative difficulty of access has merely deepened Siwa's mystique.[54] The Siwa depression is *c.*80 km long east-west with a series of spring-fed lakes between the north side of the great Libyan Sand Sea and south-west of the Qattara depression. There are a few indications of outlying settlements and cemeteries in the direction of Barhariya to the south-east and al-Jiarabub *c.*50 km to the north-west is arguably an associated secondary depression of the Siwa group.[55] There are at least 14 known ancient cemeteries spaced out along the depression, implying at least an equivalent number of settlements, of which eight can be demonstrated archaeologically and several of which were ornamented by temples using ashlar masonry.[56] The main temple of the oracle can be identified with a substantial structure of the sixth century BC at Aghurmi, 4 km from modern Siwa at the heart of the oasis. Many of the rock-cut tombs of the ancient cemeteries contained mummified bodies.

Al-Jiarabub

As noted, the oasis cluster of al-Jiarabub is really a north-western outlier of the Siwa group, lying only 50 km from the north-western edge of the Siwa depression. However, today it is located mainly on the Libyan side of the

[49] Dospěl and Suková 2013. [50] Dospěl and Suková 2013, 271–85.
[51] Dospěl and Suková 2013, 6–7. [52] Dospěl and Suková 2013, 32.
[53] Ball 1942 for the sources. See also Fakhry 1944; 1950; 1973.
[54] Belgrave 1923; Hornemann 1802, 14–29; Prorok 2001; Rohlfs 2002a/b.
[55] Herschend 2009, 298–321 for an unexpectedly detailed study of Siwa in a book on the Swedish Iron Age; Mattingly 2000a.
[56] Gill 2016, 137–40; Jackson 2002, 240–60; Kuhlmann 1998; 2013.

Egyptian border. There are still a few lakes within the depression (the depression is generally below sea level), reminiscent of the Siwa lakes. The water resources are rather saline and there are few palms here today.[57] Yet despite this unpropitious appearance, the oasis has had strategic importance as a cross-road location between the main east to west route and routes running south to Kufra and north towards Cyrenaica. The four main archaeological sites lie at spring sites close to the edge of the basin, controlling the main approach routes from the east, west, north and south. Most of the evidence recorded to date relates to several cemeteries of rock-cut tombs (Ain Melfa – with hundreds of burials, Abbiar Zergum, Ain Abu Zaid, ad-Fregia – the last two with smaller numbers of tombs), from which mummified bodies and a range of Roman artefacts have been retrieved.[58] The tombs are rock cut chamber tombs, generally square and with multiple loculi or at any rate used for multiple burials. The dead appear in general to have been properly mummified in the Egyptian fashion, with linen or cotton wrappings and removal of vital organs.[59] The bodies were buried in extended supine position on rock-cut loculi shelves or on wooden beds. One mummy of second-century AD date has been analysed in Italy and is now in the Tripoli museum.[60] Further mummies, retrieved during work in the 1990s by the Libyan Department of Antiquities, are stored in the museum stores at Cyrene and have been partly studied by an Italian team.[61] The tombs have been heavily pillaged over the years, but from the better preserved examples that have been excavated, it is clear that they were often equipped with wooden doors and accompanied by a wide range of grave goods (coloured textiles, wheel-made pottery, glass, combs, metal jewellery, glass and stone beads, spindle whorls etc.). A Roman date is indicated by the finds and radiocarbon dates have confirmed this, including a date on a wooden bed of 170 calBC to calAD 180.[62] The burials have many similarities with those of the Siwa oasis to the south-east and the burial rite especially emphasises the connections with the Egyptian oases. Oases to the west of al-Jiarabub have not produced evidence of deliberately mummified burials and in those western locations the body was normally laid on the side in a flexed position, more typical of the Saharan tradition.[63] Al-Jiarabub, thus seems to mark a point of division in funerary

[57] Lloyd-Owen 2009, 42: 'The area of Giarabub at the best of times is not very attractive and its water supply was always brackish and unpleasant.'

[58] D'Ercole and Martellone 2006; 2009; Saraullo 2009; Wright 1997.

[59] D'Ercole and Martellone 2009, 57–59. [60] Kenrick 2013, 329–30.

[61] D'Anastasio 2009; d'Anastasio *et al.* 2009.

[62] D'Ercole and Martellone 2009, 66 (GX-30372, 1980±70 BP).

[63] Two mummified bodies found in the Garamantian heartlands appear to be the result of natural desiccation, rather than deliberate treatment of the body and both were covered with simple shrouds, rather than being systematically wrapped in cloth bandages, Mattingly *et al.* 2008, 233–39.

practices at Saharan oasis.[64] On the other hand, Libyan inscriptions in a primitive script have been reported from the Ain Melfa cemetery, demonstrating some cultural connection of the people buried here with the Libyan Saharan peoples further west.[65]

The lack of settlement evidence reported is almost certainly a factor of the state of modern research here, which has focused almost exclusively on the visible (and threatened) tombs. In fact, the most recent Italian work has identified at least two settlement sites. The first is a hilltop site immediately above the Ain Melfa tombs, with a second settlement site, including a tower built of well-dressed stone blocks reported by the smaller cemetery of Sand Hill (ad-Fregia).[66] The modern town of al-Jiarabub, at the extreme western edge of the depression, also looks to have traces of earlier settlement below the modern one. Though it is 20–30 km away from the three main cemeteries, which strongly suggests that there are additional settlements to be discovered, there are reported burials from just north of al-Jiarabub.[67] Ain Melfa and Abbiar Zergum are located close to the extant lake in the far north-eastern part of the basin and could plausibly relate to a single settlement. Ad-Fregia lies in a subsidiary basin, to the south-west of the main depression and about 15 km south of al-Jiarabub.[68]

Awjila and Syrtica

There are a number of important oases along the main Saharan route running to the north of the great Libyan sand sea and south of Cyrenaica and Syrtica.[69] In this section we discuss the Awjila group, Marada, Tagrifet and Zala, while the next section will deal with the al-Jufra oases, which marked the western terminus of this route. The oasis of Kufra, which lies to the south of the main east-west route is discussed in Chapter 7, in relation to the Tibesti and the southern Libyan desert.[70]

Awjila

One of the most celebrated Libyan oases in the ancient sources after Ammon (Siwa) and Garama (Jarma), this was evidently another oracular

[64] Gatto *et al.* 2019, 528–29. [65] Saraullo 2009, 55. [66] D'Ercole and Martellone 2009, 59–60.
[67] D'Ercole and Martellone 2009. [68] Mattingly 2000b; Mohamed 1998; 2007; Wright 1997.
[69] For cartography see Goodchild 1954a; 1954b; Mattingly 2000b; 2000c. On the desert route from Egypt into Libya, see Guédon 2010; Liverani 2000; 2006; Rebuffat 1970a; 1970b; 2004.
[70] Sterry and Mattingly, Chapter 7, this volume.

centre of Ammon[71] and the principal centre of the Libyan people known as the Nasamones. The encounter of the Nasamones with Rome followed a similar path to that of the Garamantes. There were early hostile encounters, with Roman campaigns launched against them in both the Augustan and Flavian periods.[72] There has been comparatively little archaeological investigation of Awjila; the massive scale of modern oil exploration in the desert to west of here has led to much redevelopment over recent decades and the near total obliteration of the traditional oasis settlements, though a few distinctive Medieval mosques survive at Awjila itself.[73] There are two mosques in the oasis attributed to the seventh century, one associated with the reputed tomb of Sidi Abdallah ibn Sa'ad ibn Abi-Sarh (died AD 656).

The Awjila group actually comprises three distinct clusters of oasis, arranged in a triangular pattern and separated one from the other by *c.*25–30 km. Awjila is the most westerly of these and surely coincides with the ancient site of Augila, mentioned by Herodotus and others.[74] A Libyan colleague, Fuaad Bentaher, sent us news of the discovery of three Classical period rock-cut tombs at al-Darb al-Kabir, Awjila, to the north of the historic core. A sample of textiles from the burial has now been radiocarbon dated to 362–164 calBC confirming the first millennium BC activity at this oasis.[75] The early Arab military conquest of Awjila clearly attests to its importance as a population centre at that time. To the north-east (Gicherra/Jakharrad) and south-east (Jialo) are two additional foci, at both of which Pacho noted traces of ruins and ancient habitations in the 1820s.[76] While it cannot be demonstrated that these go back to pre-Islamic times, on the balance of probability it must be likely that all three of the Awjila oases were developed in pre-Islamic times.

Marada

Marada is a small oasis between Awjila and the al-Jufra group, marking an important watering point along the east to west route running south of Syrtica, along with Zelden and Zala. There were evidently abandoned structures seen by Pacho, but no archaeological research has ever been

[71] Mattingly 1995, 39, 168. [72] Mattingly 1995, 70–75. [73] Kenrick 2013, 25–28.
[74] Pacho 1827; Scarin 1937, 13–44. [75] OxA 33721, 2177±31 BP.
[76] Pacho 1827, map (inset detail). Cf. also Rohlfs 2002a, 156–68; 2003, 152–67 for two dismal stays in Awjila and Djalo; Hornemann 1802, 37–39 also gives a brief account, but makes no specific reference to ancient remains.

carried out here and the area lies at the heart of the modern oil fields. Its antiquity is thus unproven, but likely.[77]

Zala

Zala is a small oasis at a key location south of the Syrtic coast and just east of the forbidding basalt plateau lands of the Jabal bin Ghanima. This was an important stage between Awjila and Fazzan, from where trails diverge towards Sirte, al-Jufra and Zuwila. The early accounts of Rohlfs and Scarin highlight an important water source in the 12 × 5 km depression supporting 100,000 palms.[78] The old village at Zala was originally a fortified site on top of a flat-topped hill (rather reminiscent of Waddan, see below), but this was entirely demolished to make way for an Italian colonial era fort, with the settlement then displaced to around the foot of the hill.[79] There was certainly pre-Islamic activity in the oasis, as Rebuffat recorded two additional stone fortified structures (28 × 23 m and 18 × 18 m), both evidently associated with some Roman pottery, which he interpreted as Roman outposts.[80] These are to be found in the south-western part of the modern oasis, close to the modern fort. There is no evidence in fact to suggest that either were Roman forts rather than examples of indigenous fortifications (*qsur*) found throughout Fazzan and Tripolitania. Ward and Scarin both mention a foggara in this oasis, although this has not been relocated.[81] At *c.*10 km to the north of the main oasis is a small abandoned oasis (Tirsa) that is bypassed by the modern road over the Jabal. There are two small clusters of buildings of unknown date on the east side of the palms and a few scattered cairns on the surrounding hills.[82]

Tagrifet

This small oasis lies east of Waddan and directly north of Zala towards the Syrtic coast, with a route running up to the Sirte/Madina Sultan area. Di Vita recorded a fortified site 200 m in circumference in a dominant

77 Mattingly 2000c; Rebuffat 1970a.
78 Scarin 1938, 75–83; Rohlfs 2003, 136–39 for general description.
79 Scarin 1938, TAV XIX for air-photograph and ground shot.
80 Rebuffat 1970a, 17–18; 1970b. For the Roman pottery, see Rebuffat *et al.* 1970, 64, 80, 83 (sherds C102, A90, A120).
81 Scarin 1938, 81–82; Ward 1968, 35.
82 Nachtigal 1974, 167 indicates that this Tirsa was still occupied in the nineteenth century.

position overlooking an area of ancient cultivation.[83] There is also an intriguing report of Roman coins found here in 1964.[84] Inspection of available satellite imagery shows that there are at least three large ruined settlements in this oasis. The first is a fortification on a hilltop spur with two enclosures (almost certainly di Vita's fortified site). It has signs of internal stone buildings, but these are in a poor state of repair. On a slight rise 1.8 km to the north is a 3.5 ha settlement within an enceinte. There are at least two major phases to this settlement visible from its plan and a large rectangular building at its core. This site has some morphological similarities with the al-Jufra settlements with associated Roman pottery (see below).[85] An abandoned field system 1 km to the west is probably associated with this settlement. Further areas of gardens are visible around the same playa, but with no obvious settlement remains. The third settlement is 10 km to the west and consists of a large rectilinear enclosure within a small area of abandoned gardens. To the north, close to the standing remains of a colonial era fort are two lines of mounds that may be foggaras, although there are no other visible traces that can be linked with them. There is very little funerary evidence in this oasis, but a small cluster of mounds, at least some of which are cairns, are located to the south.

Al-Fuqha

A tiny oasis and also one of the most isolated, al-Fuqha was mentioned by al-Bakri as on the subsidiary route between Zala and Zuwila, via Tmissa.[86] The oasis consists of a small mudbrick village and a few scattered gardens. Notable archaeological remains include a hilltop settlement, probably walled, that sits on a small plateau and a handful of small foggaras that feed the gardens just to the south of the hilltop.

The Oases of al-Jufra

The oases of al-Jufra are an important cluster lying between Fazzan and the Syrtic coast and the evidence from Fazzan creates a strong presumption

[83] See also di Vita 1964, 94; Rebuffat 1970b, 181–83.

[84] See also di Vita 1964, 94 n. 158 on the unpublished find of second-century bronze coins reported in *Sunday Ghibli* 9/2/1964. See also Rebuffat 1970b, 183.

[85] This is also possibly the site of Tagrifet mentioned by al-Bakri, de Slane 1859, 30–31.

[86] Thiry 1995, 435 see also Scarin 1938, 54–57, and TAV IX. al-Bakri, de Slane 1859, 31.

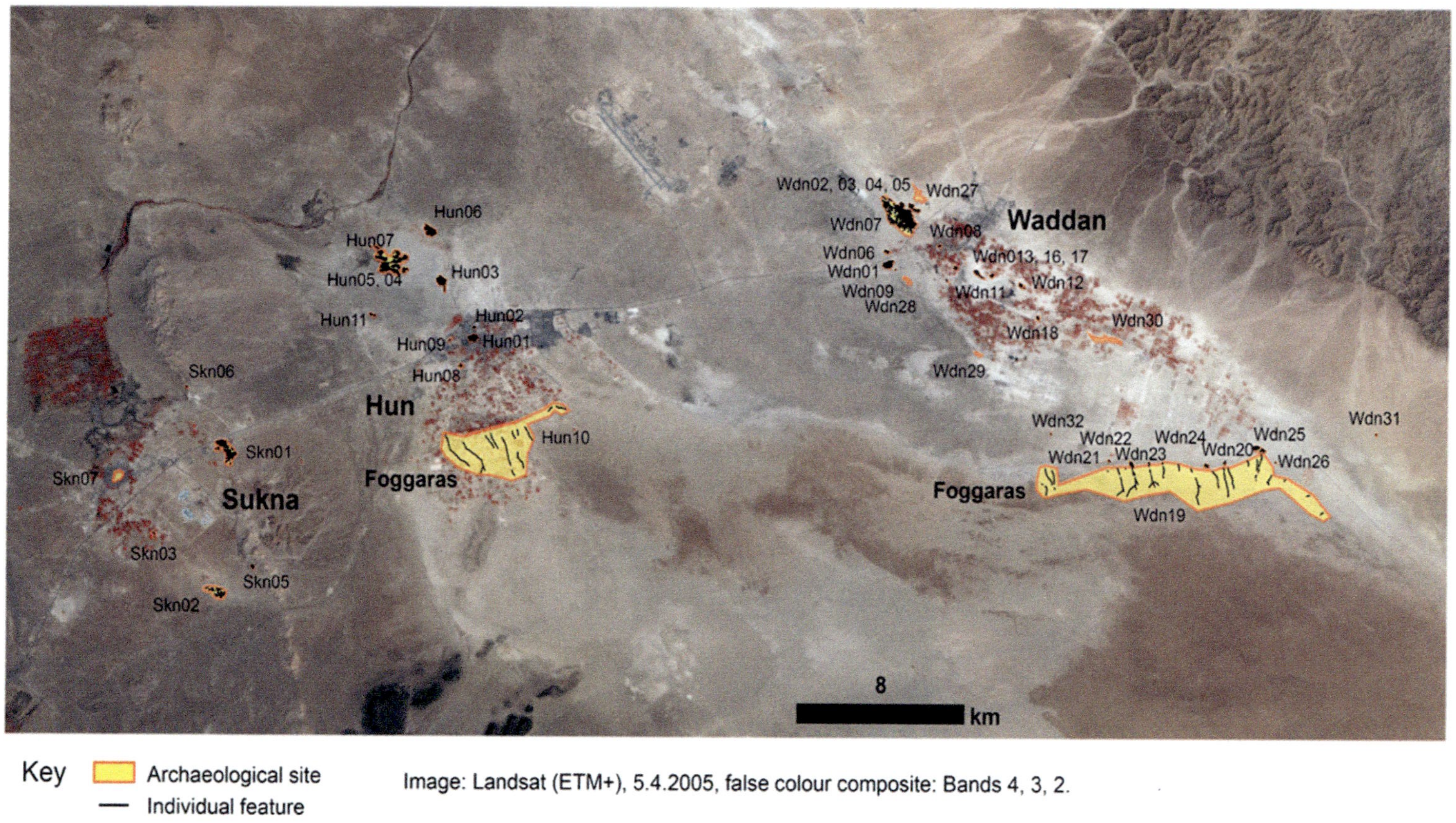

Figure 3.3. Sites in al-Jufra oasis.

that this oasis zone was also active in pre-Islamic times.[87] The three main oasis settlements of Waddan, Hun and Sukna are 16–20 km apart in an east-west line (Fig. 3.3). The early modern fortified towns were described in detail by nineteenth-century travellers[88] and there is a good overall study of the oases from the 1930s.[89] However, there has been little archaeological work in the al-Jufra area. The oases were still Berber speaking in the nineteenth century.

Our remote-sensing investigation of the overall al-Jufra area has revealed the presence of a sequence of urban-scale settlements and old irrigation systems that clearly predate the modern period. Subsequently, a team of Libyan archaeologists led by Muftah al-Haddad conducted a short survey of the region and obtained samples for radiocarbon dating (see below). An interesting aspect of al-Jufra is its intermediate position between Mediterranean and Fazzan, where as Nachtigal put it, 'stone is still a commoner building material than it is farther south, but poorly constructed bricks of sun-dried clay, used instead of stone, appear more frequently than they do near the north coast'.[90] This hybridity in construction materials is also evident in the archaeology recorded.[91]

Waddan

Waddan was evidently the dominant oasis in the al-Jufra group at the time of the Arab conquest in the AD 640s, though in more recent times it seems that Sukna has been the regional centre.[92] The early Arab sources identify Waddan as the capital of a kingdom and a key site that the Arab authorities established treaty relations with.[93] There is some archaeological evidence from the immediate environs of the early modern town. Rebuffat evidently found a Roman amphora fragment 6 km to the north (about twice as far from Waddan as the site of Busi, WDN002/4/5, see below) and also recovered third-century Roman pottery from the castle at the centre of

[87] Mattingly 1995, 7, 48.

[88] Rohlfs 2003, 93–131 for a general account of the al-Jufra. See also, Denham and Clapperton 1826, xxv–xxvii; Lyon 1821, 70–80; Nachtigal 1974, 50–55.

[89] Scarin 1938.

[90] Nachtigal 1974, 52.

[91] Following initial reconnaissance work by Martin Sterry, Libyan colleagues led by Muftah al-Haddad visited a number of the sites on the ground in early 2014, taking photographs, recording structural detail and obtaining material for dating. Further mapping has been carried out in 2015 by Louise Rayne and Martin Sterry as a joint undertaking of the Trans-SAHARA and EAMENA projects.

[92] Nachtigal 1974, 50–53 on the predominance of early modern Sukna.

[93] De Slane 1859, 30–31; Levtzion and Hopkins 1981, 12–13 and 63; Thiry 1995, 76–109.

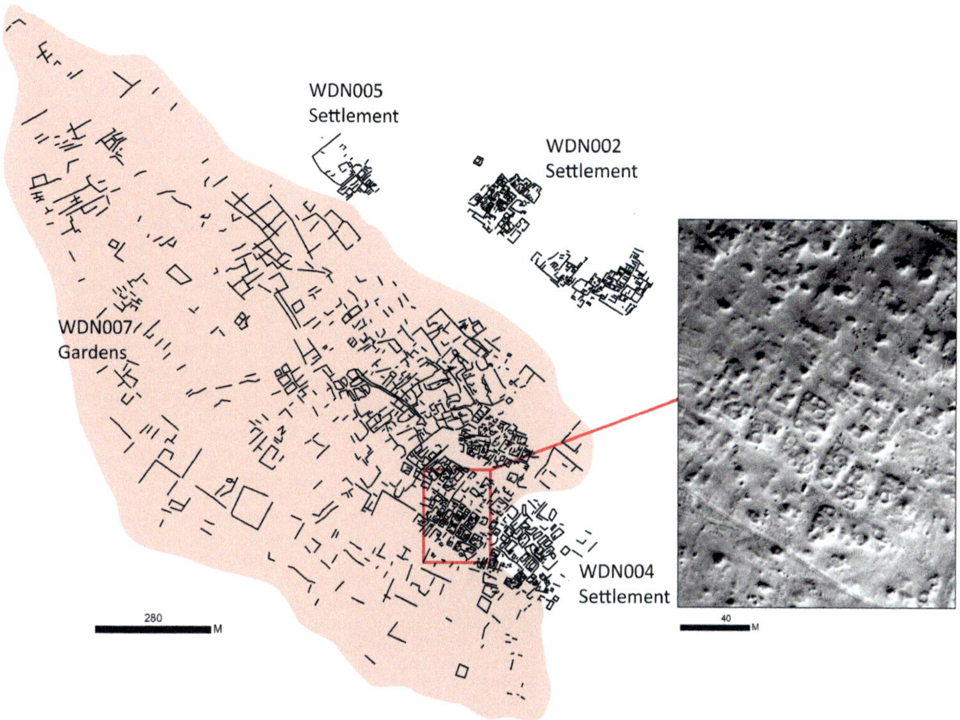

Figure 3.4. The settlement and associated field-system of Busi (WDN002, 004–005, 007).

the modern town.[94] This castle comprised an irregular fortified enceinte on an elevated rocky outcrop and has long been recognised as of likely pre-Islamic date.[95]

Our analysis of satellite imagery has now identified several additional population centres in this oasis. To the north-west of the modern town are a group of three settlements collectively known as Busi (WDN002, WDN004 and WDN005), covering at least 8.5 ha on the edge of a large (116 ha) area of abandoned gardens (WDN007) (Fig. 3.4).[96] Just 2.5 km to the south-west (west of modern Waddan) are two further settlements of 8.5 ha (Delbak, WDN001) and 1.6 ha (WDN006) (Fig. 3.5). Material from the northern group is consistent with Rebuffat's amphora fragment and of likely Roman date. Finds from the south-west group include glass and ceramics that appear to be of Roman date, as well as some probable Islamic

[94] Rebuffat 1969, 181, 187; 1970b, 187; Rebuffat *et al.* 1970, 121. See also Pace 1951, 425–29 for a gold treasure found there of unusual representational style (Saharan?) and of possible pre-Islamic type.

[95] Scarin 1938, 50–52 (with plan); Tav. X for air-photographs.

[96] Substantial bulldozing of these settlements hides their true extent.

Figure 3.5. Comparative plans of larger settlements in al-Jufra oasis.

material. A sample obtained from the exposed mudbrick wall of an otherwise buried structure at WDN001 returned a date of calAD 659–776.[97]

All five of these settlements were probably occupied into the Medieval period and their names recall the descriptions by al-Bakri and al-Idrisi of two centres called Tum (possibly abandoned at this time) and Dilbak. However, the nearby hills also have cemeteries of several hundred clustered cairns, suggesting that these centres were occupied at least in late antiquity if not earlier. Elsewhere, between the modern gardens to the south-east of Waddan, there is a rectangular fortification (60 × 36 m) that sits within

[97] The site numbering in this section and in Table 3.1 is revised from the initial publication, Mattingly *et al.* 2018. Future reference should be to the dates and site numbers given here.

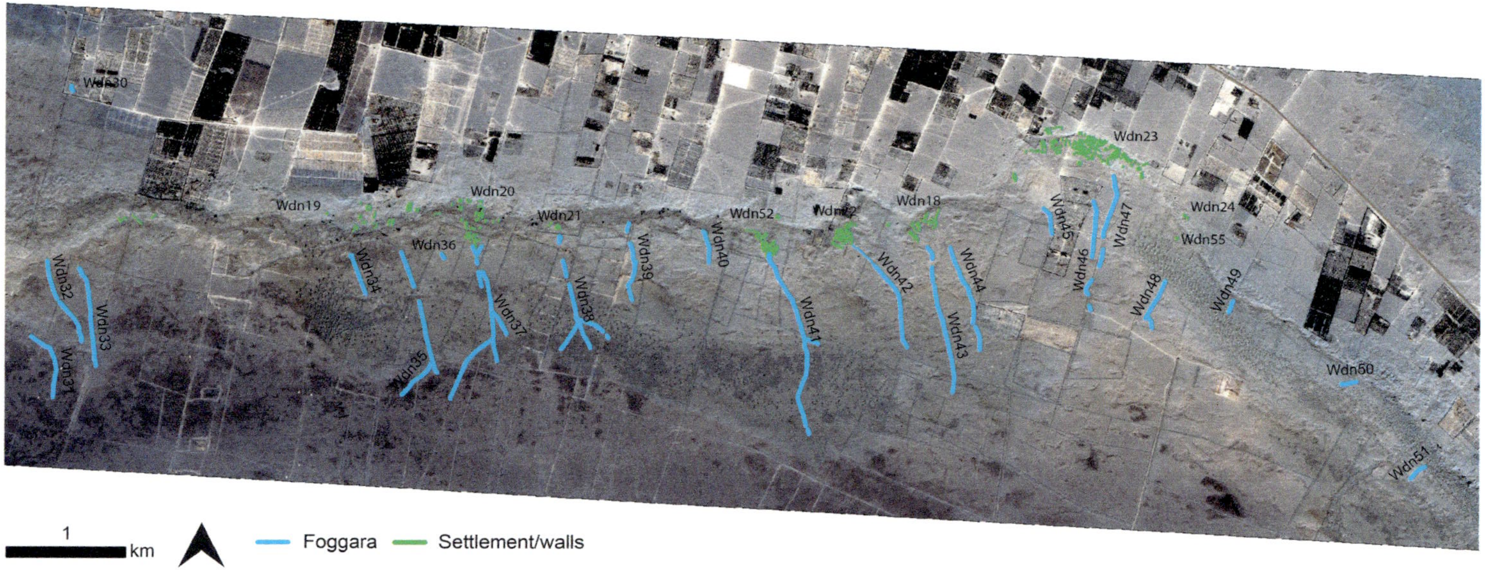

Figure 3.6. Foggaras and settlements in al-Jufra oasis.

a small area of heavily eroded settlement. Patches of abandoned gardens are visible to the east and a group of three heavily truncated foggaras (visible in two areas 2 km apart) may have irrigated these. Moving further to the south-west there are more cairns on small hills, but the most remarkable archaeological remains are found along a 13-km stretch of escarpment edge. Here there are 23 foggaras leading to at least 14 small settlements and gardens clusters (Fig. 3.6). Only one of these was surveyed on the ground and it was not possible to obtain suitable material for radiocarbon dating, but ceramics from the site were from fabric groups that are indicative of a Roman date. Both the settlements and the irrigation works are partly truncated and at imminent risk of destruction from modern agricultural developments.

Hun

Although truncated by the modern town, Hun is the only one of the three oases to still retain a sizeable portion of its early modern buildings. Clapperton described this as 'recently built' when he visited in the 1820s and commented that the community had moved from a nearby settlement *c.*4 km to the north.[98] In fact, there are two abandoned settlements in that direction (see Fig. 3.5). The first (HUN003) is a walled settlement, much enveloped by sand dunes, but still visible just under 3 km to the north. This was certainly occupied in the post-Medieval period as demonstrated by two dated samples from the enclosing wall of calAD 1685–1928 and calAD 1692–1920.[99] Yellow and dark green glazed ceramics along with a mosque, marabout and cemetery further demonstrate the Medieval and later date of this site. The second (HUN006), a further 2 km to the north, is another much larger settlement, badly damaged by modern bulldozing. It is undoubtedly of greater antiquity, the ceramics appear to include Roman coarsewares, amphorae and a pale cream-coloured pottery that is possibly early Islamic in date. Two radiocarbon samples have been dated to calAD 672–862 and calAD 987–1151.[100] However, despite its large size (15.5 ha), the only possible mention of the site is al-Bakri who describes a town near Waddan called Holl as having a large population and many date palms and springs. A fourth town-sized unwalled settlement (HUN004) has been located 4 km to the north-west of the modern town, beyond the sand dunes that cover HUN003. This lies on the edge of a large playa, the remains of irrigation works and gardens are found across its entirety. Garden walls can also be found in the area of dunes between the large settlements. There is very little

[98] Scarin 1938, 47. [99] OxA-33872 and OxA-33873. [100] OxA-33870 and OxA-33871.

archaeology visible to the south of the town, but a group of foggaras (now largely destroyed by modern developments, but detected on 1970s Corona imagery) fed a depression 4 km to the south of Hun, the date of these is unknown but most likely of similar age as those to the south-east of Waddan.

Sukna

The Sukna oasis has seen the most modern development, leaving little visible or known archaeologically about its deeper history.[101] Lyon thought about 2,000 people still dwelt within the early modern walled town, noting its seven gates (only one being wide enough to admit a loaded camel), its projecting towers, the narrow streets and two storey houses constructed in stone and mud.[102] According to the informants of Nachtigal, this walled town was only 300 years old and in full decline by the 1860s:

> The town forms an elongated heptagon . . . there are seven gates and thirty-two bastions in the surrounding walls, which are made from limestone and cement, but failed to make any impression of security . . . the wooden supports of the gates . . . seemed to be the most solid element in the enclosing wall . . . The gigantic castle, completely ruined and no longer serving any useful purpose, towers above everything else.[103]

Walls, *qasbah* and domestic quarters of the Medieval/early modern town have all been swept away in modern redevelopment across the last 20 years.[104] However, 6 km to the south we have identified another large unwalled settlement of 5 ha with distinctive long rectangular houses and several hectares of abandoned gardens. Another notable site is a hilltop settlement, almost certainly of the first millennium BC, indicating a possible early occupation of this oasis group.

Conclusion

The archaeological evidence demonstrates quite clearly the early development of oasis settlements and trading contacts in the Egyptian Western Desert by the mid-third millennium BC. Although we only have *termini ante quem* for the oases extending further west into the Eastern Sahara, Siwa and Awjila were certainly in existence by the mid first millennium BC (with archaeological evidence and the textual attestation of Herodotus for both). For the oases of Syrtica and al-Jufra at present we can only affirm the

[101] Scarin 1938, 41–50, TAV VII–VIII for air-photos. [102] Lyon 1821, 72.
[103] Nachtigal 1974, 52. [104] Nachtigal 1974, 150–52.

evidence of Roman period activity. In all probability, however, we can use the evidence for very early first millennium BC agriculture in Fazzan to cross-date the initial evolution of the oases between Bahariya and the Garamantian heartlands to the late second or early first millennia BC. Only detailed fieldwork at some of these intermediate points will allow that to be demonstrated explicitly, but this should be the default hypothesis.

It is no surprise to encounter urban-scale oasis centres in the Western Desert, where the journey from Fayum and Nile was only a few days' travel. But it is less expected to see urbanisation in less accessible early oases. A second really important observation of this chapter concerns the scale and sophisticated plans of a number of the sites identified among the Libyan oases, in particular in al-Jufra. As noted, several of these appear to be pre-Islamic in origin and match the evidence already presented from the Garamantian heartlands for possible urban sites there.

The third, key conclusion is that many of these Eastern Saharan oases share elements in common with each other: an agricultural package (involving dates, cereals, figs, grapes, even olives), access to Roman pottery and other material culture, knowledge of the foggara irrigation system. There are also some important differences. Among the Egyptian oases, the influence of Nilotic civilisation is strong in all periods from the Old Kingdom to the Byzantine era. The burial rite involving mummified supine bodies, often laid in rock-cut chamber tombs, can be traced as far as al-Jirabub, but no further. The other Libyan oases seem to adhere most closely to a Saharan tradition of crouched burials under circular cairns (though the Garamantes also had a significant engagement with rectangular burial monuments, mastaba-style stepped tombs and even small pyramids. In the Egyptian oases there is much evidence of external writing systems (hieroglyphs, demotic Egyptian, Greek), with occasional but rare examples of Libyan scripts. From al-Jiarabub westwards, the primary written language appears to have been Libyan, with virtually no evidence of Latin or Greek beyond the frontiers of the Mediterranean states.

References

Abboudy Ibrahim, M. 1992. The western desert of Egypt in the classical writings. In Carratelli 1992, 209–17.

Abd el-Ghany, M. 1992. The oases in Roman Egypt in the light of papyri. In Carratelli 1992, 3–12.

Agut-Labordère, D. 2018. The agricultural landscape of Ayn Manawir (Kharga oasis, Egypt) through the Persian period ostraca (Vth–IVth century BC). In Purdue *et al.* 2018, 359–77.

Aufderheide, A.C., Nissenbaum, A. and Cartmell, L. 2004. Radiocarbon date recovery from bitumen-containing Egyptian embalming resins. *Journal of the Society for the Study of Egyptian Antiquities* 31: 87–96.

Bagnall, R.S. 1997. *The Kellis Agricultural Account Book (P. Kell. IV Gr. 96)* Dakhleh Oasis Project: Monograph 7. Oxford: Oxbow Books (Oxbow Monograph 92).

Bagnall, R.S., Davoli, P. and Hope, C.A. (eds). 2013. *The Oasis Papers 6: Proceedings of the Sixth International Conference of the Dakhleh Oasis Project.* Oxford: Oxbow Books.

Ball, J. 1942. *Egypt in the Classical Geographers.* Cairo: Government Press.

Ball, J. and Beadnell, H.J.L. 1903. *Baharia Oasis: Its topography and geology.* Cairo: Survey Department, Public Works Ministry.

Barich, B.E. and Hassan, F.A. 1990. Il Sahara e le oasi: Farafra nel deserto occidentale egiziano. *Sahara* 3: 53–62.

Bashendi, M. 2013. Cemeteries in Dakhleh. In Bagnall *et al.* 2013, 249–62.

Bates, O. 1914. *The Eastern Libyans.* London: MacMillan (reprint 1970).

Beadnell, H.J.L. 1901. *Farafra Oasis: Its Topography and Geology.* Cairo: National Printing Department.

Belgrave, C.D. 1923. *Siwa: The Oasis of Jupiter Ammon.* London: John Lane, The Bodley Head Ltd.

Boozer, A. 2010. Memory and microhistory of an Empire: domestic contexts in Roman Amheida, Egypt. In D. Borić (ed.), *Archaeology and Memory.* Oxford: Oxbow Books, 138–57.

Boozer, A. 2011. Forgetting to remember in the Dakhleh Oasis, Egypt. In M. Bommas (ed.), *Cultural Memory and Identity in Ancient Societies.* London and New York: Continuum Publishers, 109–26.

Boozer, A. 2012. Globalizing Mediterranean identities: The overlapping spheres of Egyptian, Greek, and Roman worlds at Trimithis. *Journal of Mediterranean Archaeology* 25.2: 93–116.

Boozer, A. 2013a. Archaeology on Egypt's edge: Archaeological research in the Dakhleh Oasis, 1819–1977. *Ancient West and East* 12: 117–56.

Boozer, A. 2013b. Frontiers and borderlands in imperial perspectives: Exploring Rome's Egyptian frontier. *American Journal of Archaeology* 117.2: 275–92.

Boozer, A. 2015a. *A Late Roman-Egyptian House in the Dakhla Oasis: Amheida House B2.* New York: Institute for the Study of the Ancient World, New York University Press.

Boozer, A. 2015b. The social impact of trade and migration: The Western Desert in Pharaonic and post-Pharaonic times. In C. Riggs (ed.), *Oxford Handbooks Online in Archaeology.* Oxford: Oxford University Press. DOI:10.1093/oxfordhb/9780199935413.013.37.

Bousquet, B. 1996. *Tell-Douch et sa région. Géographie d'une limite de milieu à une frontière d'empire*. Cairo: IFAO.

Bowen, G.E. and Hope, C.A. 2003. *The Oasis Papers 3: Proceedings of the Third International Conference of the Dakhleh Oasis Project*. Oxford: Oxbow Books.

Bowman, A. 1989. *Egypt after the Pharaohs*. Berkeley: California University Press.

Bravard, J.-P., Mostafa, A., Davoli, P., Adelsberger, K.A., Ballet, P., Garcier, R., Calcagnile, L. and Quarta, G. 2016a. Construction and deflation of irrigation soils from the Pharaonic to the Roman period at Amheida (Trimithis), Dakhla Depression, Egyptian Western Desert. *Géomorphologie* 22.3: 305–24.

Bravard, J.-P., Mostafa, A., Garcier, R., Tallet, G., Ballet, P, Chevalier, Y. and Tronchère H. 2016b. Rise and fall of an Egyptian oasis: artesian flow, irrigation soils, and historical agricultural development in El-Deir, Kharga depression, Western Desert of Egypt. *Geoarchaeolgy* 31.6: 467–86.

Carpentiero, G. 2016. Continuity and change in Hellenistic town planning in Fayum (Egypt). Between tradition and innovation. In Mugnai *et al.* 2016, 73–100.

Carratelli, G. (ed.). 1992. *Roma et l'Egitto nell'antichità classica. Cairo 6–9 Febbraio 1989*. Rome: Istituto poligrafico e Zecca dello Stato.

Chaveau, M. 2001. Les qanâts dans les ostraca de Manawir. In P. Briant (ed.), *Irrigation et drainage dans l'antiquité, qanâts et canalisations souterraines en Iran, Egypte et en Grèce*. Paris: Thotm editions, 137–42.

Chaveau, M. 2005. Irrigation et exploitation de la terre dans l'oasis de Kharga à l'époque perse. *Les cahiers de recherches de l'institut de papyrologie et égyptologie de Lille* 25: 157–63.

Churcher, C.S. and Mills, A.J. 1999. *Reports from the Survey of Dakhleh Oasis 1977–87*. Dakhleh Oasis Project Monograph 2. Oxford: Oxbow Books.

Colin, F. 2000. *Les peuples Libyens de la Cyrénaique à l'Egypte d'après les sources de l'antiquité classique*. Louvain: Académie Royale de Belgique.

D'Anastasio, R. 2009. Proposal for a project on the anthropological and paleopathological study and preservation of the human mummies from Jarabub (Lybia). In Menozzi 2009, 51–52.

D'Anastasio, R., Vitullo, G. and Urso, M. 2009. Studio preliminare antropometrico e paleopatologico delle mummie e dei reperti ossei da Giarabub e ora al magazzino di Cirene. In Menozzi 2009, 45–51.

D'Ercole, V. and Martellone, A. 2006. Ricognizione preliminare nell'oasi di Giarabub. In Fabricotti and Menozzi 2006, 457–66.

D'Ercole, V. and Martellone, A. 2009. Ricognizione preliminare nell'oasi di Giarabub. In Menozzi 2009, 57–67.

De Slane, M.G. 1859. *Description de l'Afrique septentrionale par el-Bekri*. Paris: Imprimerie impériale.

Davoli, P. 1998: *L'archeologia urbana nel Fayyum di età ellenistica e romana*. Napoli: G. Procaccini.

Davoli, P. 2012. Reflections on urbanism in Graeco-Roman Egypt: A historical and regional perspective. In E. Subías, P. Azara, J. Carruesco, I. Fiz and R. Cuesta (eds), *The Space of the City in Graeco-Roman Egypt: Image and Reality*. Tarragona: Institut Català d'Arqueologia Clàssica, 69–92.

Davoli, P. 2013. Amheida 2007–2009: New results from the excavations. In Bagnall *et al.* 2013, 263–78.

Denham, D. and Clapperton, H. 1826. *Narration of Travels and Discoveries in Northern and Central Africa in the Years 1822–1824*. London: John Murray.

Di Vita, A. 1964. Il 'limes' Romano di Tripolitania nella sua concretezza archaeologica e nella sua realtà storica. *Libya Antiqua* 1: 65–98.

Dospěl, M. and Suková, L. 2013. *Bahriya Oasis. Recent Research into the Past of an Egyptian Oasis*. Prague: Charles University.

Dunand, F., Heim, J.-L. and Lichtenberg, R. 2010. *El-Deir. Nécropoles* I. *La nécropole Sud*. Paris: Cybèle.

Dunand, F., Heim, J.-L. and Lichtenberg, R. 2012. *El-Deir. Nécropoles* II. *Les nécropoles Nord et Nord-Est*. Paris: Cybèle.

Dunand, F., Heim, J.-L. and Lichtenberg, R. 2013. Les nécropoles d'el-Deir (Oasis de Kharga). In Bagnall *et al.* 2013, 279–96.

Fabricotti, E. and Menozzi, O. 2006. *Cirenaica: Studi, scavi e scoperte. Atti del X Convegno di Archeologia Cirenaica Chieti 24–26 Novembre 2003 Nuovi dati da città e territorio*. Oxford: BAR S1488.

Fakhry, A. 1942. *Recent Explorations in the Oases of the Western Desert*. Cairo: French Institute of Oriental Archaeology.

Fakhry, A. 1942/1950. *Bahria Oasis*, 2 vols. Cairo: Service des antiquités de l'Egypte.

Fakhry, A. 1944. *Siwa Oasis. Its History and Antiquities*. Cairo: Government Press.

Fakhry, A. 1950. *The Oasis of Siwa. Its Customs, History and Monuments*. Cairo: Wadi El-Nil Press.

Fakhry, A. 1973. *The Oases of Egypt. I, Siwa*. Cairo: American University in Cairo Press.

Fakhry, A. 1974. *The Oases of Egypt. II, Bahariyah and Farfara Oases*. Cairo: American University in Cairo Press.

Förster, F. 2013. Beyond Dakhla: The Abu Ballas trail in the Libyan Desert (SW Egypt). In Förster and Reimer 2013, 297–337.

Förster, F. 2015. *Der Abu Ballas Weg. Eine pharanische Karawanenroute durch die Libysche Wüste*. Africa Praehistorica 28. Cologne: Heinrich-Barth Institut.

Förster, F. and Reimer, H. 2013. *Desert Road Archaeology in Ancient Egypt and Beyond*. Cologne: Heinrich-Barth Institut.

Gallinaro, M. 2018. *Mobility and Pastoralism in the Egyptian Western Desert. Steinplätze in the Holocene Regional Settlement Patterns*. Firenze: All'Insegna del Giglio.

Gatto, M.C., Mattingly, D.J., Ray, N. and Sterry, M. (eds). 2019. *Burials, Migration and Identity in the Ancient Sahara and Beyond*. Trans-Saharan Archaeology Volume 2. Series editor D.J. Mattingly. Cambridge: Cambridge University Press.

Gautier, E.-F. 1970. *Sahara. The Great Desert* (translated from the French by D.F. Mayhew). London: Octagon.

Giddy, L.L. 1987. *Egyptian Oases. Bahariya, Dakhla, Farafra and Kharga during Pharonic Times*. Warminster: Aris & Phillips Ltd.

Gill, J.C.R. 2016. *Dakhleh Oasis and the Western Desert of Egypt under the Ptolemies*. Oxford: Oxbow Books.

Gonon, T. 2018. La gestion de l'eau dans le désert oriental égyptien durant les temps historiques, de l'époque perse à nos jours: Le site de ʿAyn Manâwîr et la prospection du bassin sud de l'oasis de Kharga. In Purdue *et al.* 2018, 269–90.

Goodchild, R.G. 1954a. *Tabula Imperii Romani: Lepcis Magna (Sheets H.33 1.33)*. Oxford: Society of Antiquaries of London.

Goodchild, R.G. 1954b. *Tabula Imperii Romani: Cyrene (Sheets H.34 I.34)*. Oxford: Society of Antiquaries of London.

Gosline, S.L. 1990. *Bahariya Oasis Expedition. Season Report for 1988 Part I Survey of Qarat Hilwah*. San Antonio: Van Siclen Books.

Guédon, S. 2010. *Le voyage dans l'Afrique romaine*. Bordeaux: Ausonius.

Hawas, Z. 2000. *Valley of the Golden Mummies*. Cairo: AUC Press.

Herschend, F. 2009. *The Early Iron Age in South Scandinavia. Social Order in Settlement and Landscape*. Uppsala: Uppsala University Press.

Hope, C.A. and Bowen, G.E. 2002. *Dakhleh Oasis Project: Preliminary Reports on the 1994–1995 to 1998–1999 Field Seasons*. Oxford: Oxbow Books.

Hope, C.A. and Mills, A.J. 1999. *Dakhleh Oasis Project: Preliminary Reports on the 1992–1993 and 1993–1994 Field Seasons*. Oxford: Oxbow Books.

Hope, C.A. and Pettman, A.J. 2013. Egyptian connections with Dakhleh oasis in the Early Dynastic period to Dynasty IV: New data from Mut al-Kharab. In Bagnall *et al.* 2013, 147–66.

Hornemann, F. 1802. *The Journal of Frederick Hornemann's Travels from Cairo to Mourzouk the Capital of the Kingdom of Fezzan in Africa in the Years 1797–9*. London: G. and W. Nichol.

Ibrahim, A.I. 2013. Major archaeological sites in Kharga Oasis and some recent discoveries by the Supreme Council of Antiquities. In Bagnall *et al.* 2013, 1–8.

Jackson, R.B. 2002. *At Empire's Edge. Exploring Rome's Egyptian Frontier*. New Haven: Yale University Press.

Jennerstrasse 8. 2002. *Tides of the Desert. Contribution to the Archaeology and Environmental History of Africa in Honour of Rudolph Kuper*. Cologne: Heinrich Barth Institut.

Kenrick, P. 2013. *Archaeological Guides: Cyrenaica*. London: Society for Libyan Studies.

Kirkwan, L.P. 1971. Roman expeditions to the Upper Nile and the Chad-Darfur region. In F.F. Gadallah (ed.), *Libya in History. Proceedings of a Conference Held at the Faculty of Arts, University of Libya 1968*. Benghazi: University of Benghazi, 253–61.

Knudstad, J.E. and Frey, R.A. 1999. Kellis, the architectural survey of the Romano-Byzantine town at Ismant el-Kharab. In Churcher and Mills 1999, 189–214.

Kucera, P. 2013. Al-Qasr: the Roman castrum of Dakhleh Oasis. In Bagnall *et al.* 2013, 205–16.

Kuhlmann, K.P. 1998. Roman and Byzantine Siwa: Developing a latent picture. In O.E. Kaper (ed.), *Life on the Fringe: Living in the Southern Egyptian Deserts during the Roman and Early Byzantine Periods*. Leiden: Research School CNWS, 159–80.

Kuhlmann, K.P. 2002. The 'oasis bypath' or the issue of desert trade in Pharaonic times. In Jennerstrasse 8 2002, 125–70.

Kuhlmann, K.P. 2013. The realm of two deserts: Siwa oasis between east and west. In Förster and Reimer 2013, 133–66.

Leahy, A. 1990. *Libya and Egypt c1300–750 BC*. London: Society for Libyan Studies.

Levtzion, N. and Hopkins, J.F.P. (eds). 1981. *Corpus of Early Arabic Sources for West African History*. Cambridge: Cambridge University Press.

Liverani, M. 2000. The Libyan caravan road in Herodotus IV.181–184. *Journal of the Economic and Social History of the Orient* 43.4: 496–520.

Liverani, M. (ed.). 2006. *Aghram Nadharif. The Barkat Oasis (Sha'abiya of Ghat, Libyan Sahara) in Garamantian Times*. Firenze: All'Insegna del Giglio.

Lloyd-Owen, D. 2009. *The Long Range Desert Group 1940–1945: Providence Their Guide*. Barnsley: Pen and Sword.

Lyon, G.F. 1821. *A Narrative of Travels in Northern Africa in the Years 1818–1819 and 1820*. London: John Murray.

McDonald, M.M.A. 2003. The early Holocene Masara A and Masara C cultural sub-units of Dakhleh Oasis, within a wider cultural setting. In Bowen and Hope 2003, 43–70.

Mattingly, D.J. 1995. *Tripolitania*. London: Batsford.

Mattingly, D.J. 2000a. Ammon. In R. Talbert (ed.), *Barrington Atlas of the Greek and Roman World*. Princeton: map 73 and Map-by-Map Directory pp. 1108–16.

Mattingly, D.J. 2000b. Cyrene. In R. Talbert (ed.), *Barrington Atlas of the Greek and Roman World*. Princeton: map 38 and Map-by-Map Directory pp. 558–69.

Mattingly, D.J. 2000c. Syrtica. In R. Talbert (ed.), *Barrington Atlas of the Greek and Roman World*. Princeton: map 37 and Map-by-Map Directory pp. 552–57.

Mattingly, D.J. 2003. *The Archaeology of Fazzan. Volume 1, Synthesis*. London: Society for Libyan Studies, Department of Antiquities.

Mattingly, D.J., Dore, J. and Lahr, M. (with contributions by others). 2008. DMP II: 2008 fieldwork on burials and identity in the Wadi al-Ajal. *Libyan Studies* 39: 223–62.

Mattingly, D.J., Sterry, M., al-Haddad, M. and Bokbot, Y. 2018. Beyond the Garamantes: The early development of Saharan oases. In L. Purdue, J. Charbonnier and L. Khalidi (eds), *Des refuges aux oasis: Vivre en milieu aride de la Préhistoire à aujourd'hui. XXXVIIIe rencontres internationales d'archéologie et d'histoire d'Antibes*. Antibes: Éditions APDCA, 205–28.

Menozzi, O. (ed.). 2009. *Chieti University Cyrene Season June 2009. Preliminary Report*. Privately circulated report.

Midant-Reynes, B. and Tristant, Y. (eds). 2008. *Egypt at Its Origins 2*. Dudley, MA: Uitgeverij Peeters en Departement Oosterse Studies.

Mills, A.J. 1999a. Pharaonic Egyptians in the Dakhleh oasis. In Churcher and Mills 1999, 171–78.

Mills, A.J. 1999b. Pottery manufacture in the Dakhleh oasis. In Churcher and Mills 1999, 215–43.

Mills, A.J. 2002. Deir el-Hagar, Ain Birbiyeh, Ain el-Gazzareen and el-Muzawwaqa. In Hope and Bowen 2002, 25–30.

Mills, A.J. 2013. An Old Kingdom trading post at ʻAin el-Gazzareen, Dakhleh Oasis. In Bagnall *et al.* 2013, 177–80.

Mills, A.J. and Kaper, O.E. 2003. ʻAin el-Gazzareen: Developments in the Old Kingdom settlement. In Bowen and Hope 2003, 123–29.

Mohamed, F.A. 1998. El Jaghbub. In E. Catani and S. Maria Marengo (eds), *La Cirenaica in età antica*. Macerata: Istituti editoriali e poligrafici internazionali, 263–73.

Mohamed, F.A. 2007. Trial excavations at el-Jaghbub. In L. Gasperini and S. M. Marengo (eds), *Cirene e la Cirenaica nell'antichità: atti del convegno internazionale di studi: Roma-Frascati, 18–21 dicembre 1996*. Tivoli: Edizioni Tored, 1–16.

Morkot, R. 1996. The Darb el-Arbain, the Kharga oasis and its forts and other desert routes. In D.M. Bailey (ed.), *Archaeological Research in Ancient Egypt*. Ann Arbor: JRA supplementary volume, 82–94.

Morkot, R. 2016. Before Greeks and Romans: Eastern Libya and the oases, a brief review of interconnections in the Eastern Sahara. In Mugnai *et al.* 2016, 27–38.

Mugnai, N., Nikolaus, J. and Ray, N. (eds). 2016. *De Africa Romaque. Merging Cultures Across North Africa*. London: Society for Libyan Studies, 27–38.

Müller-Wollermann, R. 2000. Memphis-Oxyrhynchus. In R. Talbert (ed.), *Barrington Atlas of the Greek and Roman World*. Princeton: map 75 and Map-by-Map Directory pp. 1125–39.

Nachtigal G. 1974. *Sahara and Sudan, Vol I, Tripoli and Fezzan, Tibesti or Tu*. Translated from the German by A.G.B. and H.J. Fisher. London: C. Hurst.

Newton, C., Whitbread, T., Agut-Labordere, D. and Wuttman, M. 2013. L'agriculture oasienne à l'époque perse dans le sud de l'oasis de Kharga (Egypte, Ve–IVe s. AEC). *Revue d'ethnoécologie* 4: 2–18.

O'Connor, D. and Reid, A. (eds). 2003. *Ancient Egypt in Africa*. London: UCL Press.

Pace, B. 1951. Parte I. In B. Pace, S. Sergi and G. Caputo, Scavi sahariani. *Monumenti Antichi* 41: 151–200.

Pacho, J.R. 1827. *Relation d'un voyage dans la Marmarique, la Cyrénaique et les oasis d'Audjelah et de Maradeh*. Paris: Lib. Firmin Didot.

Pettman, A. 2013. The date of the occupation of ʻAin el-Gazzareen based on ceramic evidence. In Bagnall *et al.* 2013: 181–208.

Prorok, B.K. de. 2001. *In Quest of Lost Worlds: Five Archaeological Expeditions 1925–1934*. Santa Barbara: Narrative Press (reprint of 1935 book).

Purdue, L., Charbonnier, J. and Khalidi, L. (eds). 2018a. *Des refuges aux oasis: Vivre en milieu aride de la Préhistoire à aujourd'hui. XXXVIIIe rencontres internationales d'archéologie et d'histoire d'Antibes*. Antibes: Éditions APDCA.

Rathbone, D. 1996. Towards a historical topography of the Fayyum. In D.M. Bailey (ed.), *Archaeological Research in Roman Egypt*. Ann Arbor: JRA Supplement 19, 50–56.

Rebuffat, R. 1969. Deux ans de recherches dans le sud de la Tripolitaine. *Comptes rendus de l'académie des inscriptions et belles lettres* 1969: 189–212.

Rebuffat, R. 1970a. Routes d'Egypte de la Libya Interieure. *Studi Magrebini* 3: 1–20.

Rebuffat, R. 1970b. Zella et les routes d'Egypte. *Libya Antiqua* 6–7: 181–87.

Rebuffat, R. 2004. Les romains et les routes caravanieres africaines. In M. Fantar (ed.), *Le Sahara. Lien entre les peuples et les cultures*. Tunis: Université de Tunis, 221–60.

Rebuffat, R., Gassend, J.M., Guery, R. and Hallier, G. 1970. Bu Njem 1968. *Libya Antiqua* 6–7: 9–105.

Reddé, M. 1989. Les oasis d'Egypte. *Journal of Roman Archaeology* 2: 281–90.

Reddé, M. 1999. Sites militaires romains de l'oasis de Kharga. *Bulletin de l'Institut Française d'Archéologie Orientale* 99: 377–96.

Reddé, M., Ballet, P., Barbet, A. and Bonnet, C. 2004. *Kysis: fouilles de l'Ifao à Douch, oasis de Kharga, 1985–1990*. Cairo: Institut Français d'Archéologie Orientale.

Rohlfs, G. 2002a. *Voyages et explorations au Sahara. Tome III, Tripolitaine - Cyrenaique - Siwah 1868–1869* (translated by J. Debetz). Paris: Karthala.

Rohlfs, G. 2002b. *Voyages et explorations au Sahara. Tome IV, Désert Libyque. Siwah et les oasis d'Egypte 1873–1874* (translated by J. Debetz). Paris: Karthala.

Rohlfs, G. 2003. *Voyages et explorations au Sahara. Tome V, Koufra - les oasis de Djofra et de Djalo 1878–1879* (translated by J. Debetz). Paris: Karthala.

Rossi, C. 2000. Umm el-Dabadib, Roman settlement in the Kharga oasis: Description of the visible remains, with a note on Ayn Amur. *Mitteilungen des Deutschen Archäologischen Instituts Abteilung Kairo* 56: 235–52.

Rossi, C. 2013. Controlling the borders of the Empire: The distribution of Late-Roman 'forts' in the Kharga Oasis. In Bagnall *et al.* 2013, 331–36.

Saraullo, L. 2009. L'oasi di el-Jaghbub. In Menozzi 2009, 52–57.

Scarin, E. 1937. *Le oasi cirenaiche del 29° parallelo*. Firenze: Sansoni.

Scarin, E. 1938. *La Giofra e Zella (le oasi del 29 parallelo della Libia occidentale)*. Firenze: Sansoni.

Smekalova, T.N., Mills, A.J. and Herbich, T. 2003. Magnetic survey at 'Ain el-Gazzareen. In Bowen and Hope 2003, 131–35.

Stewart, J.D., Molto, J.E. and Reimer, P. 2003. The chronology of Kellis 2: The interpretive significance of radiocarbon dating of human remains. In Bowen and Hope 2003, 345–64.

Tallet, G., Bravard, J.-P., Garcier, R., Guédon, S. and Mostapha, A. 2013. The survey project at el-Deir, Kharga Oasis: First results, new hypotheses. In Bagnall *et al.* 2013, 349–61.

Thiry, J. 1995. *Le Sahara Libyen dans l'Afrique du nord medievale*. Leuven: Orientalia Lovaniensia Analecta, 72.

Valloggia, M. 2004. *Les oasis d'Egypte dans l'Antiquité. Des origins au deuxiène millénaire avant J.-C.* Bischhelm: Infolio.

Vivian, C. 2000. *The Western Desert of Egypt. An Explorer's Handbook*. Cairo: American University in Cairo Press.

Wagner, G. 1987. *Les Oasis d'Egypte*. Cairo: Institut Français d'Archéologie Orientale du Caire.

Wagner, G. 2000. Oasis Magna. In R. Talbert (ed.), *Barrington Atlas of the Greek and Roman World*. Princeton: map 79 and Map-by-Map Directory pp. 1164–69.

Ward, P. 1968. *Touring Libya. The Southern Provinces*. London: Faber.

Warner, N. 2013. Amheida: Architectural conservation and site development, 2004–2009. In Bagnall *et al.* 2013, 363–79.

Welsby, D. 1996. *The Kingdom of Kush*. London: British Museum.

Wendorf, F. and Schild, R. 1980. *Prehistory of the Eastern Sahara*. New York: Academic.

Wendorf, F., Schild, R. and Close, A.E. (eds). 1984. *Cattle-Keepers of the Eastern Sahara: The Neolithic of Bir Kiseiba*. Dallas: Southern Methodist University.

Wilson, A.I. 2006. The spread of foggara-based irrigation in the ancient Sahara. In D.J. Mattingly, S. McLaren, E. Savage, Y. al-Fasatwi and K.Gadgood (eds), *The Libyan Desert. Natural Resources and Cultural Heritage*. London: Society for Libyan Studies, 205–16.

Wiseman, M.F. 2008. *The Oasis Papers 2: Proceedings of the Second International Conference of the Dakhleh Oasis Project*. Oxford: Oxbow Books.

Wright, G.R.H. 1997. Tombs at the oasis of Jeghbub: An exploration in 1955. *Libyan Studies* 28: 29–41.

Wuttmann, M., Gonon, T. and Thiers, C. 2000. The qanats of ʿAyn-Manâwîr (Kharga Oasis, Egypt). *Journal of Achaemenid Studies and Researches* 1: 1–11. www.achemenet.com

4 The Urbanisation of Egypt's Western Desert under Roman Rule

ANNA LUCILLE BOOZER

Introduction

The oases of Egypt's Western Desert had long been a focus of Egyptian, Persian, and Ptolemaic exploitation and investment by the time they were incorporated into the Roman Empire.[1] Despite this long history of intervention, it is clear that the oases of antiquity reached their greatest occupational density under Roman rule. Along with this population increase came substantial investment in cities. Several of these centres acquired formal urban status within the Empire, signalling their importance in the Roman political, social, and economic organisation of their Empire.

As systematic research in the Western Desert began in the 1970s, we can make only tentative suggestions about diachronic change, the morphology of urban sites, and the causes of these developments.[2] Despite the many *lacunae* in what follows, it is important to explore the urbanisation of the Western Desert now in order to guide future research in this remarkable region. In particular, this chapter examines the relationship between urbanisation and phases of colonialism and imperialism, which brought these oases into new social, economic and political relationships.

My starting point for these queries focuses upon diachronic change in the Western Desert, with the caveat that we still have much to learn about the development of this region. One of the hindrances to learning more about the changes in this region is that settlement appears to have been continuous in many areas, resulting in tells.[3] Roman ruins are typically the

[1] As discussed more fully by Mattingly *et al.*, Chapter 3, this volume.

[2] For a historiography of archaeological research in the Dakhla oasis, see Boozer 2013a.

[3] *Contra* Giddy 1987, who argued that the oases had single-phase settlements. This problem of later settlements masking earlier ones is common among early oasis settlements across the Sahara, see discussion by Mattingly and Sterry, Chapter 1, this volume.

only visible remains on these sites, which prevents us from describing accurately what pre-Roman settlement forms looked like.[4] Despite this paucity of data, keyhole excavations, documentary sources, and the occasional accessible remains of earlier phases can shape hypotheses about the developmental trajectory of urbanism in this region. A sub-set of this first query is an in-depth analysis of Roman urbanism in this region. While under Roman rule, the Western Desert reached its greatest occupational density from antiquity until the modern era.[5] There are only two well-mapped and well-preserved settlement sites to discuss: Ismant al-Kharab/Kellis and Amheida/Trimithis. Mut el Kharab/Mothis, Kysis and Kharga City were also important sites, but their urban form is less clear due to modern occupation. Amheida (known as Trimithis in Roman times) was occupied over thousands of years and ultimately achieved city status. It is relatively unencumbered with later settlement, modern architecture and agricultural intrusions. Trimithis will be discussed in more detail here as a key case study of urbanism in the Western Desert.

The second line of enquiry draws together evidence from the previous section to explore the potential economic links between the Western Desert and the Nile Valley, as well as Nubia and other areas of the Sahara. These economic links probably hold the answer as to how the region was developed and why it eventually collapsed. The question of urban collapse in the Western Desert will be the final theme explored below. It appears that the Western Desert experienced a significant population reduction in the late fourth century AD. Major sites such as Amheida, Kellis, and Kysis were abandoned at this time. Habitation seems to have re-focused on fortresses, some of which were continuously occupied from approximately the fifth century AD through to the recent past (with some in continuing occupation).[6] In the absence of destructive layers or any documentary 'explanation' for this significant change, we must explore comparisons and logical hypotheses. Despite all of this uncertainty, it is essential to explore these three questions relating to the urbanisation of the Western Desert now, rather than at a later phase of research, so we can plan our research strategies.

[4] The Roman development of the Western Desert finds comparisons in other areas of the Sahara, see Mattingly *et al.*, Chapter 5, this volume.

[5] Although, see Gill 2015, who argues that the Romans built upon Ptolemaic developments. The imprint of Ptolemaic activity is less visible than Roman activity due to tells.

[6] On the Roman castrum, al-Qasr, see Kucera 2013.

Geography of the Western Desert

From the Pharaonic to Roman Periods, the basic geographic compass constituting Egypt was the Nile Valley, which terminates in the Delta, and the Fayum (Fig. 4.1). Beyond this core area lay: the Eastern Desert; the oases of the Western Desert; further out to the west the Libyan Desert beyond the oases; to the south, Nubia. Egypt proper incorporated these marginal zones during times of prosperity, but often lost control of them during periods of insecurity. The Western Desert comprises two-thirds of the land within the current boundaries of Egypt. The primary ecological niches within an otherwise harsh environment are the five oases – Siwa, Bahariya, Farafra, Dakhla, and Kharga. Bahariya and Farafra together were known as the Oasis Parva (Lesser Oasis) in antiquity. The Dakhla oasis and

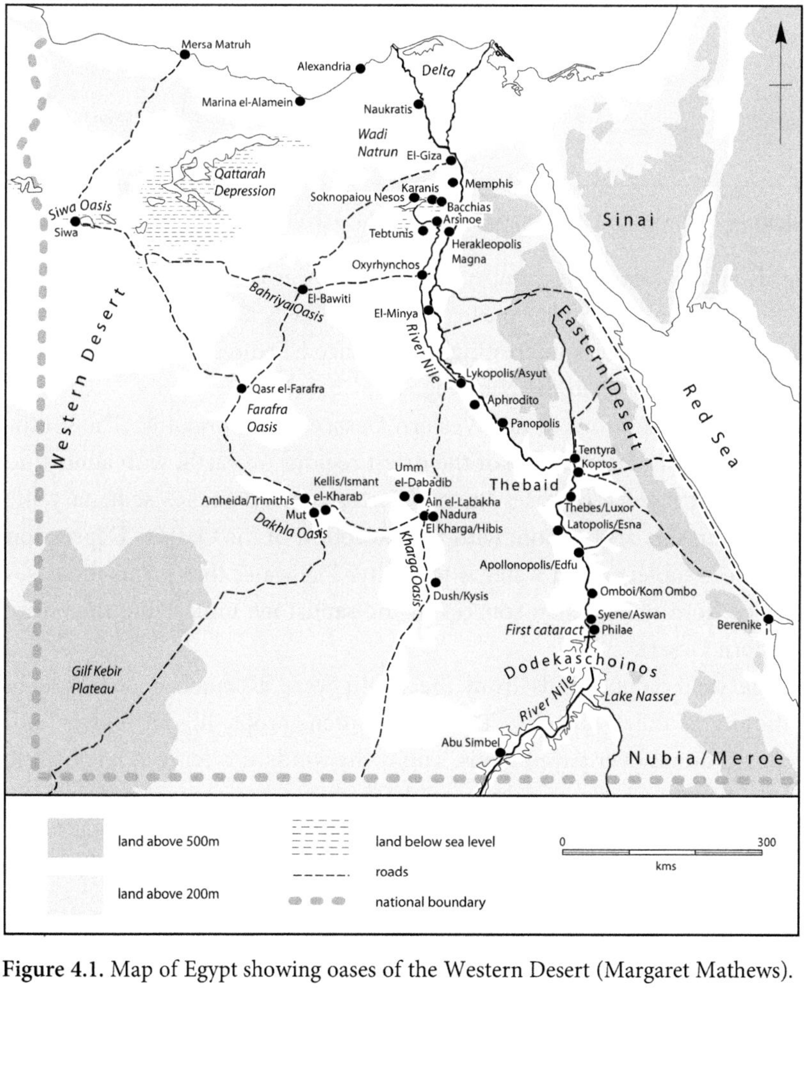

Figure 4.1. Map of Egypt showing oases of the Western Desert (Margaret Mathews).

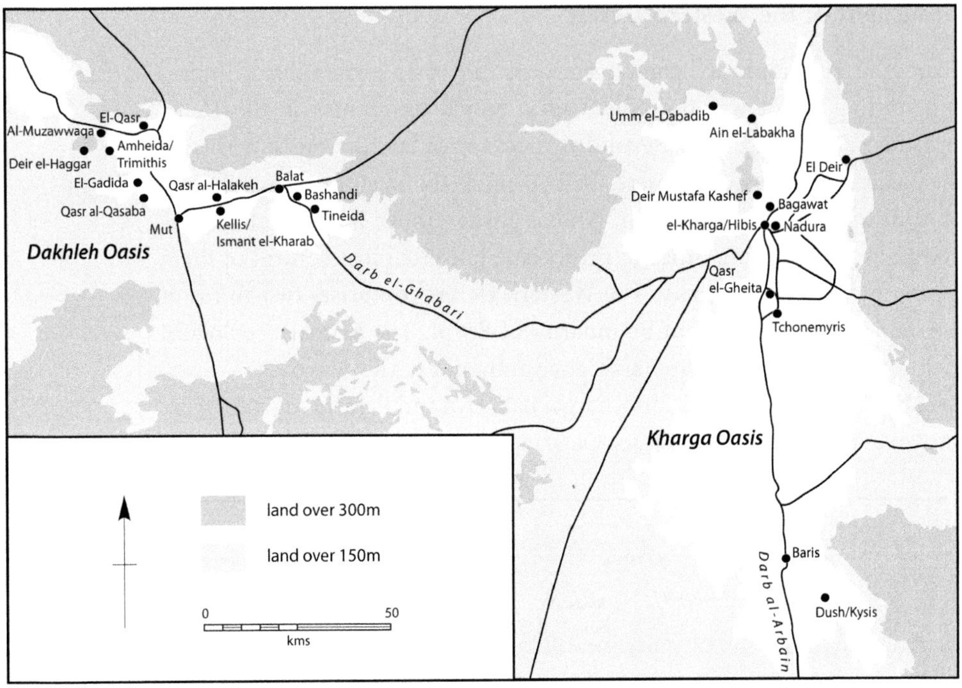

Figure 4.2. The Great Oasis, map of Kharga and Dakhla (Margaret Mathews).

the Kharga oasis were grouped together as the Oasis Major (the Great Oasis). In Arabic, *Dakhla* means the *Inner* Oasis and *Kharga* means the *Outer* Oasis, which is interesting, as distance is expressed with respect to the desert, rather than the Nile (Fig. 4.2).[7]

Climatic conditions in the Western Desert are unforgiving. The southern half of this desert is one of the driest regions on earth, with almost no rain. The presence of oases in the Western Desert makes sedentary life possible in this arid region, with the exception of the Qattara Depression where the subterranean water is too salty. The water that forms the oases derives from the artesian sources in the sandstone underlying the entire Western Desert.[8]

The sand-laden winds from the north were as much an obstacle in antiquity as they are today. The wind flattens crops, fills in houses, and deposits dunes over paved roads. Today the winds also serve as an obstacle to fieldwork, which is only possible in the winter months (October–March), and even then formidable sandstorms are not uncommon. The extreme temperatures also make life and fieldwork difficult. They range

[7] For the Oasis Magna, Oasis Parva, and Siwa, see Wagner 2000, map 79.
[8] Schild and Wendorf 1977, 10.

from 0–2° C just before sunrise to 20–25° C by midday; in summer maximums reach at least 40° C for extended periods.[9]

Egyptians considered 'oasis country' to be the desert region west of the Nile, extending until 'nearly' [*haud procul*] the Fayyum (*T3 wḥ3tjw*; Arabic: *Bilad al-Wahat*).[10] Regionally, locals were called *wḥ3tw* or *oasites*, but the term also applied to oases west of Egyptian-held territory, according to a list from Edfu.[11] Egypt's rulers incorporated these peripheral areas into Egypt proper during times of prosperity, but these regions often slipped into self-rule during periods of greater uncertainty. Although peoples of the Eastern and Western Deserts of Egypt were connected to Egypt proper throughout Egyptian history they remained peripheral to mainstream Egyptian culture and world-views.

Diachronic Change: Pre-Roman Settlement Patterns and Urbanism

The starting point for this chapter is an examination of diachronic change in the Western Desert. The oases were occupied from prehistoric to Roman times, but our ability to accurately locate sites and interpret the site morphology is difficult before the Roman Period.[12] There appears to have been continuous occupation at many sites (for example, Mut, Amheida, Balat), which created tells of material. Archaeological material deriving from desert roads peripheral to the oases themselves fills in some of the knowledge gaps created by these tells. From these roads, we see clear evidence of prehistoric and Protohistoric long-distance travel involving the oases and there are signs of old connections between Sudan and the oases.[13]

These desert roads mostly appeared during a time when the Saharan environment had begun to shift into a fully arid landscape due to climactic drying, beginning in about 5000 BC.[14] A consequence of this aridification of the Western Desert was the movement into the oases and the Nile Valley of hunter-gatherers and pastoral nomads. They established more sedentary communities clustered around these more fertile regions.[15] These sedentary communities were then compelled to find the most favourable networks of transportation between the oases and areas further afield to reduce the

[9] Giddy 1987, 3. [10] Kamal 1935, vol. 1, 395. [11] Aufrère 2000.

[12] See Mattingly and Sterry, Chapters 2–3, 5–8, this volume, who argue that pre-Islamic sedentary oasis settlements can be found across the Sahara, contrary to past expectations.

[13] Gatto 2002; Kröpelin and Kuper 2007; Riemer 2004; 2009; Riemer and Kuper 2000.

[14] Kuper and Kröpelin 2006. [15] Kuper 2002.

impact of the harshness of the desiccated environment.[16] Under the Fourth Dynasty (*c.*2613–2494 BC), the Egyptian Pharaoh, Khufu (2589–2566 BC) sent expeditions to the oases to seek a mysterious item called 'mefat'.[17] Egyptian control over the 'inner' oases was established shortly thereafter.

Settlement data within the oases also first appears during the Old Kingdom (*c.*2649–2150 BC). At the juncture of two major roads in the east of Dakhla, the Darb el-Tawil and another road that leads to the Darb el-Arbain, there is a large multi-phase settlement at Ain Asyl/Balat and a cemetery at Qila el-Dabba. The dates of these sites range from the Old Kingdom (late Fifth/early Sixth Dynasties, *c.*2400 BC) to the Second Intermediate Period (*c.*1650–1550 BC), with a late reoccupation in the Roman Period. Ain Asyl/Balat seems to have been the site of the Old Kingdom capital in Dakhla. The settlement was once surrounded by a large mud-brick enclosure wall, which subsided towards the east in antiquity and was later built on top of. The interior of this urban complex was well-built and planned. The funerary chapels of three governors of the oasis were located at this site. A stele was found in one of these buildings, which contains a copy of a royal decree of Pepi II that mentions establishing a 'dwelling of vital strength'.[18] Initially, Ain Asyl may have been an outpost in a 'foreign' territory, but it seems that the *oasites* and those manning the outpost integrated over time. Epigraphic material excavated at Balat/Ain Asyl strongly suggests that Egyptian expeditions to the far west, as well as to other desert regions, operated from the Dakhla oasis.[19] In recent years, evidence has shown that Pharaonic Egypt attempted to explore the desert west of the oases, from at least the Old Kingdom.[20] Since the Late Old Kingdom or the First Intermediate Period (*c.*2200/2100 BC), Egyptians were able to traverse the nearly 400 km stretch from Dakhla to the Gilf Kebir, and potentially even further.[21] Dakhla's governors were called 'admirals' and subsequent Egyptian expedition leaders carried nautical titles underscoring the explorative nature of their roles.[22] There may have been raids into Upper Nubia at this time, which were part of the same Egyptian expansion of exploration, trade, and extraction.[23]

Additionally, more than 20 potential Old Kingdom 'satellite sites' in the Dakhla oasis attest to the increasing importance of the oasis from the Old Kingdom onward.[24] Excavations at Mut el-Kharab, a significant locale

[16] Riemer and Förster 2013, 33. [17] Kuhlmann 2005. [18] Pantalacci 1985.
[19] Pantalacci 2013. [20] Kuhlmann 2002; Kröpelin and Kuper 2007.
[21] Riemer and Förster 2013, 48. [22] Helk 1975, 127–32; Valloggia 1985. [23] Török 2009, 56.
[24] Giddy and Grimal 1979; Osing 1982, 1; Soukiassian *et al.* 1990. On pharaonic Dakhla, see also Hope and Pettman 2013; Mills 1999b; 2002; 2013; Mills and Kaper 2004.

from at least as early as the Old Kingdom until today, have revealed ceramics and architectural features dating to the Old Kingdom.[25] The western portion of Dakhla, near the village of al-Qasr, has revealed a larger cluster of Old Kingdom settlements. None of these sites is fully excavated and they are only partially published.[26]

There is only sparse archaeological data relating to the Middle Kingdom (*c.*2055–1650 BC), although evidence of outposts along desert roads suggest that there were once Middle Kingdom settlements, as well as trade links, in Dakhla and Kharga.[27] Similarly, little is known about New Kingdom (*c.*1550–1070 BC) occupation. This *lacuna* is largely because oasis sites were continuously occupied and the older remains are covered by subsequent occupation. A few stone blocks from Kharga's Hibis Temple indicate that there was once a New Kingdom temple in the same location, but nothing is known of its form.[28] There is some ceramic and documentary evidence of the Third Intermediate Period (*c.*1069–664 BC) from Mut el-Kharab, suggesting continued occupation from the Old Kingdom.[29]

Under the Persians (525–402; 343–332 BC), the oasis region seems to have become an important strategic area since there are growing signs of an imperial presence in the form of temples and waterworks. Settlements, if not cities, must have accompanied this investment. It is unclear why the Persians devoted such time and energy to this region. Agricultural goods from the area may have been attractive as may have been the trade links that the oases provided to the south. Kuhlmann suggests that gold may have been the primary incentive. Gold was the chief Nubian commodity and the oases and Nubia were closely interconnected. Over the course of the fifth century BC, signs of activity along the roads connecting the Great Oasis to the Nile Valley increased.[30] New technologies for water management, such as *qanats*, also appear to have been developed during the

25 Some Sheikh Muftah handmade wares, taken as the work of indigenous Dakhla inhabitants, were found alongside a smaller number of Nile Valley wares, including some identifiable carinated Meidum bowl fragments, Hope 2005, 50–53. These Meidum bowl fragments were made of Nile Valley marl fabric and were certainly imported. Hope suggests that these ceramics may date to Dynasties IV and V and therefore to the initial phases of Egyptian annexation and colonisation of Dakhla, Hope *et al.* 2009; see also Kuhlmann 2002.

26 Kilns for ceramics production were found at one site, Mills 1999a; 1999b.

27 Castel and Tallet 2001; Darnell 2002a, 172–73; 2007b, 38, figure 3; 2013b, 22, 25, 257.

28 Cruz-Uribe 1999.

29 Hope 2004; 2005. Attempts to make general statements about the Third Intermediate Period in Dakhla have been forced to grasp at evidence dating to many hundreds of years after the Third Intermediate Period, Hubschmann 2012.

30 Kuhlmann 2013, 159–60. This is attested by graffiti naming Darius I and by the presence of *sigha*-pots (a variety of flask), datable to the fifth century BC, which have been found along these same roads, Darnell 2000; Di Cerbo and Jasnow 1996).

Persian Period.[31] This technology almost certainly passed further west across the Sahara along the chain of oases that links the Western Desert with Fazzan.[32]

Although the Kharga oasis has some evidence for Pharaonic activity, significantly more material survives from the Late Period onward. The Persians were active in the Kharga area and the sites around Kharga rose in importance at this time.[33] At least four temples were constructed in Kharga, along with an increased number of structures.

The temple of Amun at Hibis, located just north of the modern town, Kharga city, is the best known of Kharga's Persian temples.[34] Qasr el-Ghuieta, 17 km south of Hibis, also has a temple (ancient Perwesekh).[35] Ain Manawir, in the southern reaches of the oasis, has an agricultural settlement on a small hill, which includes a mud-brick temple dedicated to Osiris, as well as two groups of houses.[36] At least 22 *qanats* fed the agricultural fields below this site.[37] Several hundred ostraka, written in Demotic (a script form of writing derived from a northern form of Hieratic in a late phase of the Egyptian language), attest to the Persian period occupation of this site.[38] French archaeologists working at Dush/Kysis found a temple in the southernmost edge of the oasis and dating to the Persian period.[39] A settlement dating from the Persian period has revealed a temple, some important documents written in Demotic script and traces of the irrigation system dating to about 500 BC.[40] This building activity and

[31] *Qanat* (plural *qanatha, qanawat*; Anglicised as 'qanats'; also known as foggaras) is an Arabic term for an underground gallery connecting a water source with a cistern some distance away from it. On qanats, see Newton 2013. For qanats in Kharga, see Bousquet 1996; Chauveau 2005; Schacht 2003; Wuttman 2001; Youssef 2012. See also the fuller discussion of foggaras by Mattingly *et al.*, Chapters 2 and 3, this volume.

[32] Mattingly *et al.*, Chapter 2, this volume; Wilson 2002; 2006; 2009; Wilson and Mattingly 2003.

[33] Cruz-Uribe 1999.

[34] Temple construction began in the Saite Period, likely during the reign of Psametik II, with additions by Darius I, Hakor, Nectanebo I and II, and possibly Ptolemy IV, Davies 1953; Winlock 1941; for an alternative dating interpretation, see Cruz-Uribe 1988.

[35] Approximately 19 × 10 m with some early portions that appear to date to the 25th or 26th Dynasties. It contains additional contributions by Darius I, and Ptolemies III, IV, and X. The Theban triad is depicted in relief decoration, suggesting connections with both Hibis and Thebes. This temple is surrounded by a fortress considered to be of Roman date, but this dating conjecture has not been verified, Cruz-Uribe 1999; Darnell 2007a; 2013a.

[36] Grimal 1997, 340–42; Wuttman 1996, 393–40.

[37] Wuttmann *et al.* 1998; 2000; Wuttman 2001.

[38] These *ostraka* also provide details concerning water rights and land management, Chauveau 1996; 2001; 2005; 2008.

[39] Conceptually, the south of Kharga seems to have been considered to be 'Kush'. Dush<Greek: Kysis<Old Persian: Kusiya, Mitchell 1992.

[40] Bousquet 1996, 195–202.

the Kharga qanats attest to a growing population, but urban sites are unknown from the Kharga oasis during the Late Period.

The Dakhla oasis provides a patchy, but growing, corpus of data on Persian Period occupation. The epigraphic material from Amheida's temple has provided an important collection of cartouches with Late Period names that indicate governmental investment in the oases.[41] Mut el-Kharab has revealed substantial quantities of Late Period ceramics in the vicinity of the Seth Temple, which require further study, but once again suggest the continuing significance of Mut.[42] At some time before this period, the centre of power in Dakhla seems to have shifted from further east in Balat/Ain Asil to Mut, where it still remains.[43] Qanats have also been identified in Dakhla, although they have not been thoroughly researched yet.

Until recently, evidence for Ptolemaic (305–30 BC) activity was thought to be limited in comparison to the Roman activity in the Western Desert. Recent research on Dakhla ceramics revises this assumption and suggests that substantial settlement and agricultural activities occurred in Dakhla during this period.[44] These results suggest that ceramics that were often lumped into Roman temporal brackets ought to be re-examined. Architectural remains are fragmentary during this period, based upon our current understanding, but may be hidden beneath Roman ruins. It is equally possible that some ruins categorised as Roman during initial surveys may be re-attributed as Ptolemaic upon further examination.[45]

One of the largest ancient towns of Dakhla lay in the eastern part of the oasis at the site of Ain Birbiya, although it is the temple that has been the focus of the excavations.[46] Modern-day Mut (ancient Mothis) seems to have been the capital of Dakhla during the Ptolemaic and Roman Periods. The ancient town is only preserved in small islands of tell formations within the modern city. Among these disturbed urban remnants is a large Ptolemaic and Roman era temple dedicated to Seth, the patron deity of the oasis.[47]

Once again, the Kharga oasis provides obscure evidence of settlement data. Qasr Zaiyan (ancient Tchonemuris), 27 km south of Hibis, appears to date from the Ptolemaic era, although the only dated inscription is Roman

41 Kaper 2009; Kaper and Davoli 2006; Kaper and Demarée 2006. 42 Hope *et al.* 2009.

43 Sterry and Mattingly, Chapter 8, this volume, argue that Saharan towns frequently experience power shifts and relocations over time, rather than remaining fixed on single sites.

44 Gill 2012a; 2012b. 45 For a summary of the initial survey, see Churcher and Mills 1995.

46 Mills 1999b. It was called *'Imret* in Egyptian and perhaps *Mesobe* in Greek (*P Kellis* IV 74–75). On the temple, see Kaper 2010.

47 Hope *et al.* 2009. Much of Gill's ceramics data derives from Mut, Gill 2012a; 2012b.

and dates from the reign of Antoninus Pius (AD 140). Egyptian archaeologists working at the site cleared much of the temple precinct, exposing a substantial granary and associated administrative quarters.[48] Other areas of the site remain unexcavated and the finds are unpublished.

Roman Urbanisation of the Western Desert

The Western Desert experienced a large population increase under Roman rule, which appears to have developed and expanded upon pre-existing settlement patterns. This expansion can be characterised as urbanisation in the case of some oases, namely Kharga and Dakhla, but potentially others as well. This pattern of urbanisation complements the broad trend of urbanisation found across Roman North Africa, which became one of the most densely urbanised regions of the Empire.[49]

Kharga

Under Roman rule (30 BC–AD 641), Kharga experienced its greatest prosperity and took shape with new fortresses.[50] The location of these forts suggests that Roman administrators were concerned with internal security as well as trade routes, but it is uncertain if they represent a response to changing circumstances or were part of an overarching strategy, because dating remains uncertain.[51]

Hibis was the ancient capital of the Kharga oasis during the Roman Period. Little is known of this settlement's form beyond the Metropolitan Museum of Art excavations 1909–1910, which uncovered a few houses with vaulted ceilings and frescoed paintings. It appears to have been garrisoned and the Temple to Amun-Re stood at the centre of town.[52] The towns of Kysis, Ain Manawir and Shams el-Din/Mounesis, appear to

[48] Cruz-Uribe 1999. [49] See Wilson, Chapter 10, this volume.

[50] Reddé 1999. The character of the fortresses themselves signifies that they were primarily residential since the walls were not nearly wide enough to sustain an earnest attack, Ikram and Rossi 2004; Rossi 2000.

[51] Morkot 1996, 87.

[52] Winlock 1941. The Metropolitan Museum of Art (New York, NY, USA) had an exhibition that focused on objects from Kharga in 2013, see: www.metmuseum.org/exhibitions/listings/2012/kharga-oasis [last accessed 4 September 2019]. They have also digitised many of Herbert E. Winlock's notes and journals from his excavations: http://libmma.contentdm.oclc.org/cdm/landingpage/collection/p16028coll10 [last accessed 4 September 2019].

have had populations engaged in trade and cultivation, both important practices on the trade route that the fortress guarded.[53]

In southern Kharga, the Institut Français d'Archéologie Orientale have been excavating at Qasr Dush (ancient Kysis) from 1976 onwards.[54] It is the best-documented site in this oasis and, although the Roman occupation is best-known, it may have had occupation, at least temporarily, since the Fourth Dynasty. In the Roman Period, Dush was a garrisoned fortress with a settlement and temple to Sarapis (originally Osiris). Cemeteries lie to the north and west of the town itself, with the Roman cemeteries being the largest and located to the south-east.[55] Inscriptions dating to the reigns of Roman emperors Domitian (AD 51–96), Hadrian (AD 76–138), and Antoninus Pius (AD 86–161) have been exposed.[56]

Siwa

The Siwa oasis was far removed from the rest of the oases in the Western Desert. There is little evidence of prehistoric occupation at Siwa.[57] No ancient Egyptian sources concerning the oases mention Siwa.[58] Egypt seems to have found few appealing luxury goods or specialty items in Siwa and so the oasis connected more to eastern Libya for most of its history. The development of Siwa seems to have taken off particularly once the Greeks began to immigrate into Cyrenaica from the seventh century BC onwards.[59] These Greeks may have been interested in Siwa as a connection point to Nubian gold.[60] There is no evidence of Carthaginians exchanging goods with or engaging with Siwa or areas east of Siwa.[61] The Siwa oasis remains a mystery in the Roman Period, although markedly less so than in earlier periods. Siwa lost its political sovereignty and became a province of the Roman Empire (*nomus hamoniacus*) in *c.*74 BC when the Pentapolis came under Roman Rule (*c.*96 BC). The oasis only became part of Egypt after Muhammad ʻAli forcibly incorporated it into Egypt proper (AD 1819–1820).[62]

[53] Wagner 1987, 182–83.

[54] Dunand *et al.* 1992; 2005; Harrison 2007; Reddé *et al.* 2004. On the ceramics from Douch/Kysis, see Ballet 1990; 2000; 2004.

[55] Dunand *et al.* 1992; Reddé *et al.* 2004. [56] Reddé 1990.

[57] On the available evidence of prehistoric habitation, see Hassan 1976; 1978.

[58] Kuhlmann 2013, 144. The only possible reference is from the Edfu topographical list, dating to Hellenistic times, Aufrère 2000.

[59] Kuhlmann 2013, 147. [60] Kuhlmann 2013, 160. [61] Kuhlmann 1988, 97–101.

[62] Kuhlmann 2013, 146.

At Siwa the Supreme Council of Antiquities has carried out excavations at Bilad el-Rum, a cemetery with elaborate rock-cut tombs replete with entrance doorways and exterior chambers constructed in limestone. The results of the excavation have not been published yet. Tombs in Siwa suggest a moderate resident population in the Ptolemaic and Roman Periods. Although these tombs have been scavenged over the years, it is clear that they follow mortuary patterns common to the Nile Valley.[63] Siwan settlement sites, such as Ain el-Qurayshat and Abu Shuruf, have been under exploration only recently. Ain el-Qurayshat has many olive oil presses concentrated together, an adjacent residential zone, and a temple. The houses were mud-brick and built around large courtyards, reflecting a more Romanised plan than traditional Egyptian practices.[64] These houses somewhat resemble those from Kellis in the Dakhla oasis. Industrial oil production can also be found in other areas in eastern Siwa, such as Abu Shuruf, Timeira, and al-Ma'asir.[65] Under the reign of Trajan (AD 98–117), it seems that wide-scale olive cultivation was introduced. At Siwa, the olive became the oasis' foremost crop, above even the date palm.[66] Oil from Siwa, known as the 'oil from Ammon', fetched a higher price than 'oasis oil'.[67]

Bahariya

Bahariya oasis shows signs of occupation throughout antiquity and particularly in the Roman Period.[68] The oasis is divided into two regions: the north clustered around al-Qasr/Bawiti (ancient Psobthis) and the southern area, known as al-Hayz. There appears to have been heavy occupation in the northern part of the oasis, but the ruins (east of Bawiti) have not been excavated. Ahmed Fakhry uncovered a temple dedicated to Alexander the Great at Bawiti and there is a Roman triumphal arch nearby.[69] Qusur Muharib consists of a Roman Period village with buildings of two storeys and some very large houses as well as a mud brick fortress.[70] Little is known

[63] Fakhry 1990, 173–74.

[64] Kuhlmann 1998. Egyptian houses typically had a courtyard off to one side or behind houses.

[65] Kuhlmann 1988, 167–73.

[66] Kuhlmann 2013, 140. Siwa was also a source for fossilised ammonites, which resembled the ram horns, and were considered to be a sacred gemstone, Rohlfs 1875, 169–70, Kuhlmann 2013, 154. See also Pliny, *Natural History* 37.60.167.

[67] Kuhlmann 2013, 150.

[68] Ball and Beadnell 1903; Fakhry 1974; Gosline 1990; Thissen 2013. For popular accounts of Bahariya, see Jackson 2002, 233–39; Vivian 2002, 174–212.

[69] Fakhry 1974. [70] Fakhry 1974, 106, 108.

about the individual houses or their contents. Among the most spectacular finds of the Roman Period are the remains of 'golden mummies' at Bawiti.[71] The settlement to which this cemetery belongs has not been identified yet, but they derive from a necropolis associated with the capital of Bahariya and give some indication as to the wealth and importance of this oasis during the Roman Period. The gold used to make these masks indicates links with Nubia, which was the closest source for this precious metal. The only known mine of iron ore in the Western Desert can be found on the edge of the escarpment north of Bahariya, which seems to have been exploited in antiquity.[72] To the south of this oasis, in the area of el-Haiz, scant evidence of occupation can be found that dates to prehistoric, Old Kingdom, Second Intermediate Period and the New Kingdom.[73] By contrast, Roman occupation can be found at 10 out of the 13 surveyed sites.[74] Two small churches and a late Roman cemetery also have been found in this area.[75] Recently, excavation has begun at a late Roman settlement, known as Bir el-Showish.[76] Military architecture as well as oil and wine presses have been found elsewhere at el-Haiz, again attesting to the introduction of crops prized by the Roman Empire as well as a resident population about which little is known.[77] Qanat irrigation technologies were also introduced in Bahariya to enable this agricultural exploitation.[78]

Farafra

Most of the antiquities found in Farafra oasis date to Roman times, but these are relatively insignificant. The visible Roman ruins consist of Ain Della (north of Farafra) and Ain Besay to the south. Ain Besay consists of an ancient cemetery, two mud brick buildings, rock-cut tombs, and a chapel.[79] Qanats have also been identified in Farafra.[80]

Dakhla

The Dakhla oasis was profoundly impacted by Roman rule, as shown by the Dakhla Oasis Project (DOP) archaeological survey of the oasis between 1977 and 1983, which revealed over 200 Roman Period sites in the oasis.[81] This survey was the first broad scale research conducted in the oases. Since

[71] Hawass 2000. [72] Kuhlmann 2013, 147. [73] Dospěl and Suková 2013, 6–7.
[74] Dospěl and Suková 2013, 7. [75] Mullins 2011. [76] Verner and Benesovska 2008, 54.
[77] Hawass 2000, 148–67. [78] de Angeli 2013, 276–79.
[79] Barich and Hassan 1990; Fakhry 1974. See also, Jackson 2002, 230–32; Vivian 2002, 143–73.
[80] de Angeli 2013, 279–80. [81] Churcher and Mills 1995.

1986, Colin A. Hope of Monash University has conducted excavations at Ismant al-Kharab/Kellis, which appears to have been occupied during the first to fourth centuries AD. It had a monumental temple to the local god, Tutu.[82] Two monumental, classical style tombs dating to the third century AD were found in the north of Kellis. According to Hope, these tombs find parallels only in Libya; they also resemble depictions of buildings on coins from North Africa (first century BC) and Alexandria (second century AD), signalling potential connections to these regions.[83] Small houses, wealthy houses, cemeteries, and other tombs have also been excavated. Of particular interest are economic and literary texts that place Kellis at the centre of a regional economy during the fourth century AD.[84] Importantly, these excavations have revealed architectural and decorative motifs, as well as portable objects, that suggest Roman Mediterranean influences and interaction.[85] The settlement form shows clusters of structure types and organisation but little formal planning. Excavations at Mut el-Kharab, like those from Trimithis, point towards a wealthy local population. The Temple of Seth and its associated structures, which originated (as noted earlier) in the Late Period demonstrate significant activity throughout the Roman period.[86]

Trimithis: A Roman Period City in the Western Desert

Trimithis offers an ideal case study for Roman urbanism in Egypt's Western Desert since it had city status and sufficient visible architecture for mapping its urban layout. The lack of other demonstrable urban sites within the oases, despite their many villages, follows the pattern Mattingly and Sterry describe for pre-Islamic Sahara oasis settlements.[87]

Excavations at Amheida/Trimithis since 2004, led by Roger S. Bagnall, have contributed valuable information on Roman Dakhla urbanism. However, despite active research at Amheida, there are, as elsewhere in Dakhla, hindrances to exploring diachronic change. Most of the visible architectural remains at Amheida relate to Trimithis, the Roman city and it is the best-understood phase of the site. Earlier phases of occupation have been recovered, particularly in the area of the temple mound, where excavation has revealed a great depth to the tell formation that underlies

[82] On Tutu, see Kaper 2003. [83] Hope 1999. [84] Bagnall 1997; 2008.
[85] Hope and Whitehouse 2004; 2006; Kaper 2012. [86] Hope *et al.* 2009.
[87] Sterry and Mattingly, Chapter 8, this volume.

the many phases to the destroyed temple.[88] Despite these keyholes into earlier phases of occupation at Amheida, a secure timeline of activity is not possible at this time.

Topographical survey of visible remains continues to define the extent and form of Trimithis's urban fabric, although preliminary conjectures regarding the layout can be made at this time (Fig. 4.3).[89] Trimithis is a large urban site that may be as large as 100 ha, although the core occupied area was much smaller. Defining the perimeter of the site is difficult because it is surrounded by ancient farmhouses and villages, as well as modern agricultural fields, roads, and Bedouin villages that overlie parts of the site.[90] Trimithis manifests a diversity of structure types within its urban core, as can be expected for a major regional centre. This diversity attests to the multi-purpose function of the city for such likely roles as administration, tax collection, law, governance, craft production, and trade. This range in functions relates to political and cultural reference points of Western Desert cities being focused upon the Nile Valley and Egypt.

The Trimithis houses seem to be single- or, in some cases, possibly two-storey mudbrick structures with mainly barrel-vaulted roofs and some palm reed and mud flat roofs. Industrial areas can be found distributed among the domestic structures, but primarily along what we currently understand to be the edges of the city. A temple mound on the west side, around which the Roman settlement curves, and mortuary structures along the southern side are also clearly evident among the surface remains. Agricultural fields occupied the low-lying surrounding landscape. Governmental, administrative, or so-called 'public buildings' have not yet been identified securely.

There are two major streets currently identifiable at Trimithis. First, a broad east-west oriented road (S1) provided access into the city from the east. It leads from the industrial and domestic area on the north-eastern portion of the site towards an area north of the temple mound, but it turns

88 Hypotheses regarding diachronic change and urban development can be found in Boozer 2014. For a more thorough discussion of changes in the temple area, and particularly from Egyptian religion to Christianity, see Bagnall and Cribiore 2012. Temples, as spiritual centres, could offer an additional reason for urbanism in a particular locale. See Scheele, Chapter 18, this volume.

89 See Amheida.org. On diachronic change within Trimithis' urban form, see Boozer 2014. Geophysics was employed for several seasons at Trimithis, but the results did not yield significant new data, except upon the temple mound, Smekalova and Smekalov 2005; 2006. Instead, most of the observations are based upon mapping completed using a standard Total Station.

90 On the so-called columbarium farmhouses of Dakhla, which cluster around Trimithis, see Mills 1993; also Boozer 2019.

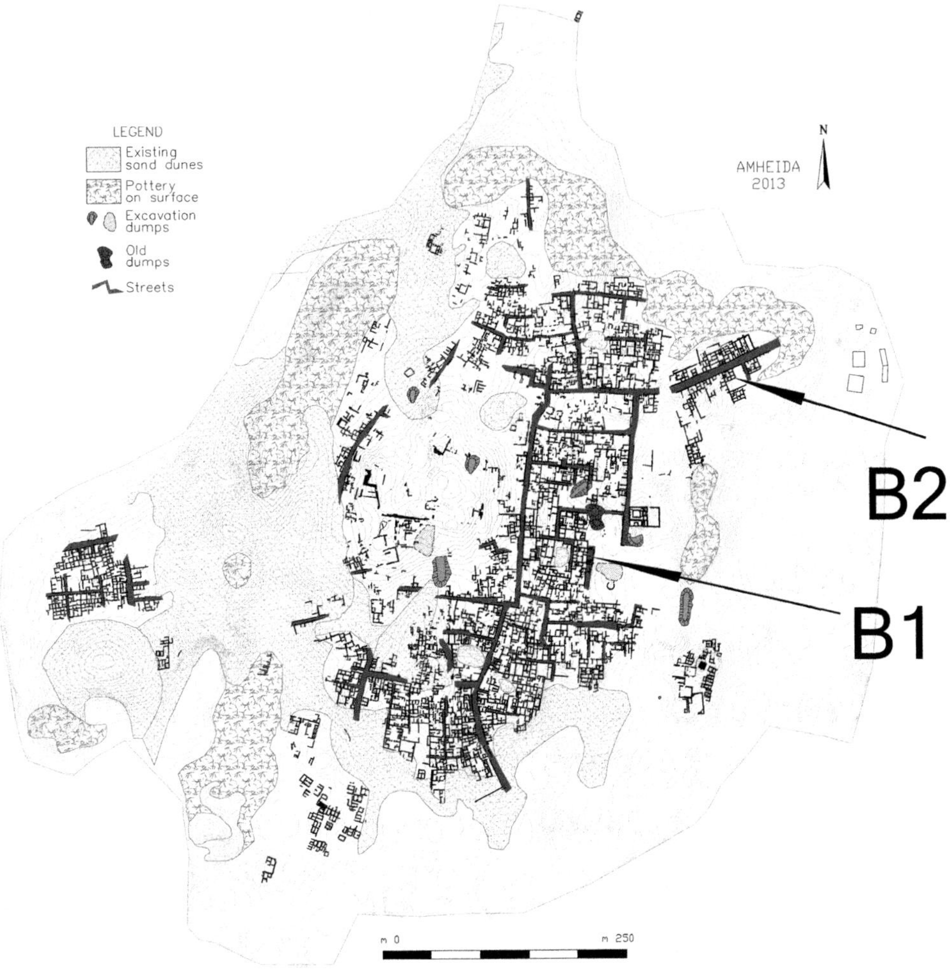

Figure 4.3. Plan of Trimithis (Amheida) (Courtesy of the Amheida Project).

sharply off axis and then stops abruptly before reaching the temple mound itself. At 6.82 m across, it is the widest identified road at Trimithis. It appears that this road and the structures along its east side may have been built during a single phase of construction. Area 1, which clusters around this street, appears to have been occupied from the early-mid third to early fourth century AD (on the basis of surface ceramics) and seems to have been constructed at the same time as the street itself.

The only modifications to the Area 1 street are small features constructed just outside doorways that may have served as windbreaks, refuse breaks, or bollards to protect house fronts from traffic (or all three). This situation can be found just west of House B2, and comparanda to this situation can be found at Kellis, Karanis and Dimé/Soknopaiou Nesos.[91] The maintenance of a road without blockages suggests that there may have been institutional involvement in maintaining the road.[92] By contrast, blockages often signify lack of civic control, as can be seen elsewhere at Trimithis (for example, streets S2 and S3, see below).

The second major street is a north-south oriented road that extends from the mortuary area in the south-eastern portion of the city (Area 3) to the north (Area 1). The major north-south oriented road is approximately 5.73 m wide, at its greatest extent, although the width varies considerably depending upon the location. This road is the only clear north-south artery across the city. The road shifts and winds along its passage and this road appears to be less planned than the Area 1 road. This road appears to have had structures built into it over time, which made it less effective as a major conduit across the city. Nonetheless, it was probably an important road as it linked up the northern and southern zones of Trimithis. It meets up with the main road in Area 1 after a sharp turn to the north-east. Smaller east-west throughways and alleys intersect with the road. This street might well have served a performative function, since it is likely that it was used for public funeral – among other – processions down to the tomb area (Area 3) from the rest of the city. Such processions of honour and acclaim were common throughout Roman Egypt as well as the Roman Empire more broadly.[93]

In addition to these major roads there are some less-fully traced out streets and alleys. One street runs roughly parallel to the major north-south road and is located between this road and the temple mound. Some additional east-west aligned streets also occur. Curiously, the project has not yet identified any streets connecting the eastern settlement area with the temple mound, nor have we found any trace of the temple *dromos* (entrance passage).[94]

The buildings at Trimithis are preserved up to 3 m in height above the site surface, although most of the visible architecture peeks up above the sand by only 0.5 m or so. From these visible remains, some structures appear to be laid out in an orderly plan of large blocks (*insulae*), such as in Area 1, the immediate vicinity around House B1, and south of Area 4. The north-eastern part of the site (Area 1) appears to have been laid out in a single phase and the structures in this area share similar plans. The Area 1 layout – along with structures to the south-west – is oriented north/north-

[91] Hope *et al.* 1989; 1992, 41–42. For a summary, see Boozer 2015. [92] Keith 2003, 63.
[93] Haas 1993; MacCormack 1981. [94] Congedo and De Santis 2006, 20.

west, south/south-east. The centre of the Roman site (Area 2) also contains several houses that, from the surface, appear to share similar layouts. Area 2 structures have a general north-south orientation. This area contains mostly fourth-century ceramics on the surface. Likewise, in an area just south of the temple (Area 4), a series of roads delineate the eastern boundary of a housing block where at least one significant, decorated house is identifiable on the basis of surface architecture and pigmented plaster.[95] South of Area 4 the layout follows a similar north-south orientation. It is unclear when Trimithis took on this urban form, although it is evident that some form of urban planning led to its present shape.

Other areas of the site seem to have grown up much more organically, perhaps filling in spaces between planned areas. These areas can be found north and west of House B1 and west of House B2. Area 4 is architecturally complex and highly deteriorated so its overall plan remains unclear. It is likely that the temple of Area 4 resembled other Roman Period Egyptian temples,[96] and the temples of Roman Dakhla in particular.[97] Like the temple itself, the area surrounding the temple is complex and largely destroyed so it will require substantial research before the layout and phasing are understood.

Trimithis Comparanda

Documentary research has shown that Trimithis continued to grow in size into the fourth century and it officially achieved city status by AD 304, when it was described as 'Trimithis *polis*' in a papyrus.[98] Although population estimates for Trimithis cannot be given accurately at this time, we do have several cities we can use for comparison. Bagnall estimates the population of Hermopolis to be between 25,000 and 50,000, on the basis of the list of *oikia* houses (*SPV* V. 101) and the average Egyptian metropolis to be at 25,000 (although we may consider Trimithis to be on the smaller side).[99] With these estimates in mind, it would not be unreasonable to suggest a population of approximately 10,000–15,000 or so in late Roman Trimithis, but such conjectures probably will change as we gain more data.[100]

95 Congedo and De Santis 2006, 20.

96 Kaper and Davoli 2006. On late phases of the temple mound, see also Bagnall and Cribiore 2012.

97 Kaper 1997, 1998b.

98 *P.Kell.* I G.49.1–2; Bagnall and Ruffini 2004, 143–44, for the latest discussion of the urban status.

99 Bagnall 1993, 53; Bagnall and Frier 1994, 55.

100 This number corrects an earlier estimate (Boozer 2014), thanks to critiques provided by A. Wilson that a density of 250 people per ha would be more likely. For a discussion of the size

The urban status of Trimithis gives us some sense of civic governance at this oasis city. The political constitutions of cities required the elite to serve as local councillors (*decuriones*) and to hold a sequence of magistracies and priesthoods that required them to exercise their political, judicial, and religious authority on a regular basis. The size of each local council varied according to the city's population. It is likely that individual towns had fixed sizes for their town councils and that council size was subject to official regulation.[101]

By the early fourth century, the top echelons of the provincial aristocracy made their careers in state service and as councillors. Typically the heads of wealthier families took collective responsibility for city finances.[102] Such magistrates and councillors dominated the public life of late Roman cities.[103] At Trimithis, we excavated the house (B1) of a city councillor named Serenos, who was identified from a substantial corpus of *ostraka* recovered from this house.[104] The structure (B1) that housed Serenos was emblematic of his prestigious civic role and the wall paintings in one of the rooms underscored Trimithis's city status.[105]

Promotions to city status often led to significant expansion and development of the urban form. Upon acquisition of city status, the foundation of a city might involve building operations, particularly in the erection of public buildings.[106] Scholars have identified the development of monumental civic structures as a key component of the Roman redesign of cities such as Carthage/Colonia Concordia Iulia (Tunisia), Lepcis Magna (Libya), Italica (Spain), Colchester (Britain) and other cities across the empire.[107] Sometimes these urban redesigns involved the substantial clearance of private houses for the emplacement of new civic buildings that were emblematic of the empire. This clearance, in turn, created the opportunity to design Roman-style houses in place of local styles.[108]

On the other hand, some cities experienced difficulties following upon the acquisition of city status, as at Oxyrhynchus (Egypt). By AD 235 many houses in the city were abandoned (*P.Oslo* 3.111). At some time between AD 232 and 247 the Oxyrhynchites lamented their own ruin, although the city continued to be occupied well beyond this period.[109]

and population of other North African Roman urban sites, see Wilson, Chapter 10, this volume.

101 Tacoma 2006, 126. 102 Mitchell 2007, 180–81. 103 Edmondson 2006.

104 Bagnall and Ruffini 2004; 2012. 105 Boozer 2010; 2012. 106 Jones 1964, 720.

107 Edmondson 2006, especially 251, 268–69.

108 For example, Julio-Claudian Mérida (Lusitania), Alba Calzado 2004; Edmondson 2006, 561.

109 On the inhabitants of Oxyrhynchus lamenting their ruin, see Parsons 2007, 58–59.

Comparisons across Roman North Africa suggest that urban expansion took place primarily between the late first through the early third centuries AD. There was a notable decline in public construction by the late third century, but individuals maintained a high standard of living until at least the later fourth or early fifth century AD.[110] In most cases, excavation and survey have shown that the area of urban settlement in the early Imperial period remained fully occupied under the Late Empire. In some cities (for example, Cuicul/Djemila, Sitifis/Setif and Thamugadi/Timgad), new built-up areas were constructed in the fourth century, attesting to population increases.[111]

There has been remarkably little research on diachronic urban development in Roman North Africa, although there have been some recent developments on this front for Late Antiquity.[112] For example, Wilson suggests that a typical feature of revitalised Roman North African cities may have been densely packed urban areas of mixed usage, containing houses and workshops.[113] In particular, Wilson cites Sabratha (Libya) as an example of a city that experienced this form of development in the late second or early third century AD. These dates are slightly earlier (*c.*50 years) than we find in Area 1 at Trimithis, but the type of urban space that Wilson describes is reminiscent of the Dakhla case study.

It is crucial to question the origins of town planning traditions in the Western Desert.[114] The impact of Roman rule on cities has received much attention by scholars.[115] Often, scholars have argued that a Roman influence can be seen clearly through formal urban planning. In particular, orthogonal or Hippodamean planning has been considered a signature attribute of Roman urban planning. Yet, cities with regular layouts occur in many different regions and historic periods for pragmatic reasons. Rather than simply betraying cultural roots, regularity may simply indicate the new foundation of a site or neighbourhood as well as a centralised authority guiding development. We should remain mindful that Greek models of urbanism often overshadow the equally legitimate urbanisms found in the

110 Lepelley 1992; Mattingly and Hitchner 1995, 185.

111 Duval 1982a; 1982b; Février 1964; Lassus 1969.

112 For critiques, see Mattingly 1994, 11; Mattingly and Hitchner 1995, 186. On Late Antique developments, see Leone 2007.

113 Wilson 2002, 258–59.

114 For similar queries into the cultural roots of urban design, see Wilson, Chapter 10, Bokbot, Chapter 12, and Nixon, Chapter 17, this volume.

115 For example, Alston 2002; Fentress 2000; Goodman 2007; Laurence *et al.* 2011; Liebeschuetz 2000; Lomas 1989.

Near East and Africa. 'Grid-plans' and urban planning more broadly were neither exclusive to the Greek and Roman worlds, nor universal within them.

With this disclaimer in mind, caution must be exercised when attributing elements of planning to any cultural group at Trimithis given that Egyptians, Greeks, and Romans had strong traditions of urban planning. The town plans of Ptolemaic and Roman settlements in Egypt are often more regularly laid out than Trimithis, following north-south/east-west orientations across the entire site or, sometimes, other orientations related to the placement of a central temple or the geographical terrain. This regularity may be due, in part, to the more rigid grid-planning that occurred during Ptolemaic Egypt for the foundation of new cities, as can be expected for new design projects. The potential Ptolemaic impact upon Trimithis's form is not visible at this time, but must be considered to be possible.

Pragmatism seems to have been the major factor influencing the orchestration of city plans and it is not necessary to interpret planning as the victory of Egyptian, Greek, or Roman factors in the final choice of design. A settlement's layout (regular versus irregular) is often an index of the circumstances of urban growth, and particularly the presence of a centralised authority overseeing urban development.[116]

Parallels for portions of Trimithis can be found in the array of Roman Period settlement types in Egypt, rather than elsewhere in the Sahara since the Western Desert was oriented primarily towards the Nile Valley. Geography served as a determining factor for a range of both planned and organic cities of Roman Egypt. For example, parts of Alexandria follow the Hippodamean system – a rectangular grid divided into regular blocks.[117] Even so, the natural topography was exploited in the construction of public architecture; a great theatre and the Serapeum were built on the limestone ridge that overlooked the entire city. Streets and canals leading from the Great Harbour to Lake Mareotis emphasised the north-south axis of Alexandria. Alexandria contained typical Greek elements such as an agora,[118] a theatre, a bouleuterion (council hall),[119] law courts, a gymnasium, a hippodrome, temples to Greek gods,[120] and an armoury.[121] On the domestic level, the housing complex at Kom el-Dikka in Alexandria resembles a hybrid between the large *insulae* of late antique Ostia and Rome and the multi-storey houses from Egyptian towns

[116] Joshi 2000, 34. [117] Empereur 1998, 56. [118] Arrian, *Anabasis*. 3.1.5.
[119] Delia 1991, 15. [120] Strabo 17.1.9–10. [121] Philo, *In Flaccus* 92.

such as Karanis and Bacchias.[122] Excavations at Kom el-Dikka by Polish archaeologists have provided critical information about both public and private facilities in Alexandria for the late Roman and Byzantine centuries.[123]

Likewise, geography seems to have determined planning at smaller sites, such as Berenike, on the Red Sea.[124] Berenike covered approximately 7 ha, and was a major Red Sea port with extensive commercial contacts locally, regionally, and in the greater world context.[125] It was occupied from *c*.300 BC to early AD 600 and its peak periods were in the early (first–second centuries AD) and late (fourth–fifth centuries AD) Roman Periods. Berenike also seems to have been laid out in a rough pattern of blocks and streets and did not have an enclosure wall. Over time the town shifted slowly to the east.[126] As with these sites, the layout of Trimithis exploited the natural topography for promoting religious spaces and organising the location of domestic structures. Geography also determined the fertile areas around Trimithis, necessitating that elevated areas be devoted to construction and lower areas to agriculture.

Other settlements show a sense of spatial organisation rather than concerted planning, with houses arranged in single rows or built back-to-back in double rows that roughly formed rectangular blocks.[127] For example, Karanis, in the Fayum, was built following two major north-south thoroughfares, with no clear east-west through streets. The life span of Karanis extended from *c*.300 BC to AD 600. It was an enormous settlement, covering 60 ha including areas of occupational debris. The town had an irregular street layout and appears to have expanded organically from its Ptolemaic centre, first to the east and west, and then to the north. As population levels receded, the occupied area shrank back from the north and returned to its central core.[128] It is evident from the plans that there was a rough system of grouping houses into *insulae*, particularly during the later periods.[129]

Likewise, the Ptolemaic through early Islamic structures at Syene/Aswan are oriented on narrow streets running north-south, intersected by smaller lanes.[130] Various teams excavated a portion of Syene/Aswan, which the Swiss Institute for Archaeological Research in Ancient Egypt (Cairo, Egypt) eventually surveyed and published.[131] The exposed area is quite modest (40 × 100 m) and includes the Ptolemaic Temple of Isis and

[122] Haas 1997, 195. [123] Rodziewicz 1984; 1991. [124] Sidebotham and Wendrich 1998, 87.
[125] Whitcomb and Johnson 1979, 5. [126] Wendrich 1998, 246. [127] Badawy 1978, 33.
[128] Boak and Peterson 1931, 3–9. [129] Boak and Peterson 1931, 40.
[130] Jaritz and Rodziewicz 1994, 119. [131] Jaritz and Rodziewicz 1994; 1996.

a residential area to the north that consists of approximately 23 houses. An enclosure wall, possibly constructed in the third century BC, seems to have ordered the orientation of the streets and structures.[132] Although Karanis and Syene do not exhibit clear planning, they show a preference, like Trimithis, for major north-south streets. Likewise, the situation of consistently oriented housing can be found in Area 1 at Trimithis and in discrete patches across the site. Indeed, I suggest that there are several formally planned *insulae* at Trimithis.

Economic Links with the Western Desert

The economic links between the Western Desert and the Nile Valley, Nubia, and Libya may provide some explanation for Roman urbanisation in the Western Desert. In particular, trade and resource extraction/exploitation can be linked to imperial exploitation of the region.[133]

Three themes emerge from analysis of Roman Period economic links: (1) the agricultural goods that were suitable to *oasite* conditions and that seem to have spread west across the Sahara, (2) the technologies used to provide water that were essential to managing these goods and which also spread west, and (3) the evidence of trade contacts found through road networks and material indices, although the latter are more difficult to trace.

First, the Roman Empire exploited the Western Desert oases for their agricultural potential, as it did with other parts of Roman North Africa.[134] There was change over time and summer crops, such as sorghum, pearl millet, and cotton appear to have become more common during the Roman Period. Such crops were particularly suited to the oases because of the perennial water supply, unlike the Nile River.[135] It is not clear exactly how these crops reached Egypt, as currently they are known at earlier dates in the Central Sahara.[136] The particular environmental conditions for cultivating these agricultural goods created a clear motivation for developing the Western Desert. Unfortunately the ultimate destinations of these agricultural goods are difficult to trace, even in the desiccated conditions of

[132] Jaritz and Rodziewicz 1994, 11; 1996.

[133] Evidence of development within desert oases under the Garamantian Kingdom and the Roman Empire can be found elsewhere in the Sahara, see Mattingly *et al.*, Chapter 3, this volume. The Roman exploitation of Trans-Saharan caravan routes has been demonstrated in the Sahara, Liverani 2006; Mattingly 2013, 530–34; see now, Mattingly *et al.* 2017.

[134] See Wilson, Chapter 10, this volume.

[135] Bagnall 1997; 2008.

[136] Mattingly *et al.*, Chapter 2, this volume.

the Sahara, because the botanical remains do not survive well and/or archaeologists did not sample for them.

Second, irrigation technologies including qanats/foggaras were essential to the development of urban and smaller-scale sites in the Western Desert from the Persian Period onward. These technologies seem to have moved westward across the Sahara, also enabling population growth and urbanisation.[137] In the Western Desert, it is clear that this technology allowed oasite farmers to move into new and more difficult hydrological zones to grow agricultural products that are particularly suited to oasis environments.

Third, the oases had well-developed trade contacts from the earliest stages of their sedentary occupational history. Trade contacts with the Nile Valley are visible from at least as early as the Old Kingdom, but it is not clear that the Nile Valley inhabitants only sought oasite products. Exotic goods west and south of the oases may have been their primary interest, along with the control of trade routes that led south. Although it would be tempting to argue for Trans-Saharan trade, evidence currently supports only local-level trade within a network that consisted of the Western Desert oases, the Nile Valley, and regions to the south.[138]

Archaeological research on the roads connecting the oases to the Nile Valley is still in its infancy.[139] Even so, we can recognise signs of trade through the spread of objects and materials, technical knowledge, and other cultural traits.[140] There is evidence of trade centres, caravanserais, trading depots, and checkpoints along the evident major road systems. Giddy compiled data on old roads and tracks to produce an outline of Western Desert oasis routes that is currently being investigated archaeologically.[141]

[137] Mattingly and Sterry, Chapter 8, this volume.

[138] There is much debate about the possibility of Trans-Saharan trade with the inner oases (namely Dakhla and Kharga). On the 'myth' of Trans-Saharan trade, see Swanson 1975. Those who support such trade rely upon new evidence from the 'Abu Ballas Trail', which has ceramic assemblages dating from the late Old Kingdom/early First Intermediate Period and a hieroglyphic graffito, Clayton *et al.* 2008; Kröpelin and Kuper 2007. Those who find such claims of a trade network dubious include Bagnall 2012; Kuhlmann 2013; O'Connor and Reid 2003.

[139] For an overview of the paucity of research on roads, with particular reference to Ancient Egypt and the Sahara, see Riemer and Förster 2013. On Saharan networks in Roman times, see Wilson 2012. For a road map of the historical Trans-Saharan trade network, see Ross 2011, XV.

[140] See above discussion for imports to the oases. It is difficult to identify oasis goods in the Nile Valley (and elsewhere). For a discussion of the spread of objects, ideas, and language across the Sahara, see Masonen 2012.

[141] Giddy 1987, 5–27. For a review of Giddy, with a comment on the road networks in Dakhla, see Mills 1991. See also the Theban Desert Road Survey, directed by John and Deborah Darnell since 1993 (for example, Darnell 2002b). For the impact of the Theban Desert Road Survey on perceptions of the desert, see Friedman 2002b.

The North Kharga oasis survey project has demonstrated that there was a major expansion of road traffic during late Roman times.[142] Oil, wine, and cotton were the major commodities shipped from Kharga to the Nile Valley during this period. Kuhlmann argues that gold and, to a lesser extent, salt, may have played a major role in trade in pre-Islamic times.[143]

An important aspect of Kharga is that it was the point of departure of a number of overland trade routes to Nubia and the Chad/Darfur region, the so-called Forty Days Road, along which a number of minor oases developed (such as Selima).[144]

Until recently, material evidence of trade connections and goods has not been easy to trace because of both preservation and recognition issues. Ceramics and other goods from the oasis have only been recognised and seriated in the past few decades.[145] As a result, it is likely that there are additional oasite goods that have been overlooked in the analyses of material beyond the oases. Growing comparisons of the pottery fabrics of New Kingdom amphorae from both the Nile Valley and the Egyptian oases already are beginning to shed light on over-land connections in Egypt's Western Desert.[146]

Various types of salt (alum; rock- or table salt; also vitriol) exist in the oases themselves and were mined there throughout history.[147] Dates were another significant commodity. These two products, dates and salt, were attractive beyond the fringes of the oases. Accounts from Herodotus (4.172), as well as much later writers describe travellers, marauders, and raiders journeying great distances to loot date plantations.[148]

Another debatable, and often invisible, commodity is a human one: slaves. We know little about the ancient slave trade in Africa, but modern comparisons can be informative. Slaves were sold and traded at Siwa from early Muslim times until fairly recently.[149] Kuhlman suggests that the history of slavery in Siwa may extend back even further.[150] Kulhman adds that the introduction of the camel might have aided the importation of slaves from greater distances, including locales in Sudan.[151] There is

[142] Rossi and Ikram 2013. [143] Kuhlmann 2013.
[144] Kirkwan 1971; Rossi and Ikram 2013; Welsby 1996.
[145] Research by Pascale Ballet, Deborah Darnell, Colin Hope, and James C.R. Gill, among others, have made crucial advances in Western Desert Ceramics. See bibliography for citations elsewhere to their works.
[146] Hope 2002. [147] Kuhlmann 2013, 140.
[148] On the Awjila from Kufra, see Hamilton 1856, 181, 191, 197. On marauders from Kufra/Tubu and regions south of Dakhla (Bidayat from Ennedi or Mergah) who raided Siwa and Dakhla, see Nachtigal 1974, vol. 2, 36; Stanley 1912, 32; Rohlfs 1875, 250.
[149] Belgrave 1923, 96, 150. [150] Kuhlmann 2013, 156. [151] Kuhlmann 2013, 157.

little published about the slave trade in Egypt, Fazzan, and elsewhere for the pre-Islamic era, but the potential for the movement of peoples to provide labour for new agricultural investments created by reclaimed land through qanat technologies should not be overlooked.[152]

The Collapse of Urbanism in the Western Desert

By the fifth century there is evidence of a significant reduction in occupation at major sites such as Dush/Kysis in Kharga and Ismant al-Kharab/Kellis in Dakhla.[153] Amheida/Trimithis in Dakhla, with its lack of clear evidence of any fifth century activity, likely shared the same destiny. This collapse mirrors a pattern of shrinking urban sites and populations across Roman North Africa.[154] This regional collapse is reminiscent of a broader Roman imperial collapse that is theorised, but rightly queried, for this time period.[155]

It is unclear what factors catalysed urban collapse in the Western Desert. Saharan comparanda suggest that the disruption of trade routes detrimentally impacted cities, which stagnated and experienced massive population declines.[156] Within the local economy consisting of the Western Desert, the Nile Valley and Upper Nubia, the often-blamed Blemmyes and other nomadic groups of the area may have had a hand in disrupting trade. Raids upon caravans may have made the already-expensive overland trade less desirable. It is also possible that the *oasite* agricultural package (wine, dates, cotton, and other summer crops) could be accessed more easily elsewhere after the fourth century, thereby rendering Western Desert trade routes less attractive. Equally, it is possible that the protection of trade routes in the Western Desert was de-prioritised. All of these possibilities may have worked in concert to disrupt trade and, in turn, urbanism in the Western Desert.[157]

[152] However, see Fentress 2011; Wilson 2012. There are more published accounts beginning with the nineteenth-century slave trade, during a period when it was in decline and European abolitionist governments took an active interest in its cessation, Lane and MacDonald 2011; Savage 1992; Wright 1988.

[153] On Dush, see Wagner 1987. On Ismant al-Kharab, see Marlow and Mills 2001.

[154] Wilson, Chapter 10, this volume.

[155] Jones 1964, 1025–68; Liebeschuetz 2000, 29–32.

[156] Erdblom 1968, 305–14; Sterry and Mattingly, Chapter 8, this volume.

[157] See Fenwick, forthcoming for a discussion of 'boom-and-bust' cycles in pre-Islamic and Islamic North Africa.

Discussion

I return to the questions posed at the beginning of this chapter regarding (1) diachronic change, and, particularly, the character of the Romano-Egyptian urbanisation, (2) economic links, and (3) the causes of abandonment in order to draw together these queries to see if we can sketch out testable hypotheses for understanding the development and collapse of urbanism in Egypt's Western Desert.

(1) *Diachronic change*: it appears that the Old Kingdom was a significant phase of Nile Valley Egyptian colonisation. Following this intervention, it appears that the Persian Period involved the next most visible imprint upon the landscape of the Western Desert with the introduction of qanat technology. The Roman Period was the most heavily occupied phase for the oases until the modern era.

Given the tell formation of sites, it is difficult to deduce the impact of Persian and subsequent Ptolemaic urban development on the later Roman urbanisation of the Western Desert. Even so, it seems that there are some Roman North African patterns of urban development evident at least at Amheida, if not other sites in the oasis. Large-scale urbanisation of the Western Desert occurred along with Roman rule. This urbanisation may be different in scale but not necessarily in kind (at least in all respects) in comparison to earlier phases, about which we know frustratingly little. This Roman investment may have been due to the economic potential of the oases themselves.[158] There also were imperial benefits to creating a buffer zone around the Nile Valley and in securing trade routes.[159] In sum, it seems that Roman investments in the region built upon and intensified settlement at important pre-existing locales in the oases, but we cannot yet define the attributes of these pre-existing settlements.[160]

(2) *Economy*: it is clear that goods intrinsic to the oases were of interest to various large state systems, but the links to further exotica may have been even more attractive. The long-term, if episodic, use of these trade routes may be the reason for the development of urbanism in particular locales within the oases as well as their eventual decline.

[158] For example, Mills 1993 argues that the Romans created a 'New Valley' scheme, much like the modern Egyptian government did, to increase agricultural land and outputs.

[159] Boozer 2013b.

[160] Compare to Nixon, Chapter 17, this volume, who detects a pre-existing, if poorly understood, settlement at Essouk, which later became an early Islamic entrepôt.

(3) *Abandonment*: The oases continued to be occupied after Roman rule, but the population density declined substantially. Decreases in trade may be the cause. As Kuhlmann observes, 'trade is like water; it will flow either along the easiest or the only possible way, and it abides by its course unless extraordinary circumstances force a change'.[161] When trade became too difficult in the Western Desert, or when other options became viable, it took another course. From the seventh century AD, it seems that Siwa was the starting point for journeys leading into the Bilad al-Sudan (Takrur, Ghana, Mali, Gao, Bilma [Kawar] or Chad) from Fazzan or Tibesti.[162] Dakhla appears to have been forgotten as a connection to the south, at least from what is known from Classical Arab Sources.[163]

Marauders are another possibility that could have made Western Desert trade less attractive and economically viable. The introduction of the camel would have made the oases more accessible to nomads and other groups that would have found them out of range for foot travel. These marauders may have targeted caravans or simply crops themselves, such as dates (as described above), which made oasis goods too costly and troublesome to continue to import.

Despite the abandonment of major cities in the Western Desert, the subsequent shape of settlement life in Dakhla rested on many old foundations. The refocus of settlement to smaller villages and fortresses shows continuity in location, if not form.[164] Moreover, some cities, such as Mut in Dakhla and Kharga City in Kharga, appear to have had continual occupation through to the present day. A narrative for the next phase of settlement life in the Western Desert remains to be told. Perhaps the patterns we might find are not nearly as different as it appears from our current vantage.

References

Alba Calzado, M. 2004. Arquitectura doméstica. In X. Dupré Raventós (ed.), *Mérida. Colonia Augusta Emerita (Las capitales provinciales de Hispania 2)*. Rome: L'Erma di Bretschneider, 67–83.

[161] Kuhlmann 2013, 133. [162] Kuhlmann 2013, 134.

[163] Kuhlmann 2013, 135. Under Arab rule, it was Siwa's extreme western position among the oases along with its role as a gateway to Egypt for Maghribinian and African pilgrims that made this oasis, rather than Dakhla, the starting point for Trans-Saharan camel caravans to the south and south-west, Kuhlmann 2013, 161.

[164] Kucera 2013.

Alston, R. 2002. *The City in Roman and Byzantine Egypt*. London and New York: Routledge.

Aufrère, S. 2000. La liste des sept oasis d'Edfou. *Bulletin de l'Institut Français d'Archeologie Orientale* 100: 79–127.

Badawy, A. 1978. *Coptic Art and Archaeology: The Art of the Christian Egyptians from the Late Antique to the Middle Ages*. Cambridge, MA: MIT Press.

Bagnall, R.S. 1993. *Egypt in Late Antiquity*. Princeton: Princeton University Press.

Bagnall, R.S. (ed.). 1997. *The Kellis Agricultural Account Book (P.Kell. IV Gr. 96)*. Oxford: Oxbow Monograph 92.

Bagnall, R.S. 2008. Economy and ecology in the Kellis agricultural account book. In M.F. Wiseman (ed.), *The Oasis Papers 2: Proceedings of the Second International Conference of the Dakhleh Oasis Project*. Oxford: Oxbow Books, 115–18.

Bagnall, R.S. 2012. Dakhla and the West in late antiquity: framing the problem. In S. Guédon (ed.), *Entre Afrique et Égypte: relations et échanges entre les espaces au sud de la Méditerranée à l'époque romaine*. Paris: Editions Ausonius, 39–44.

Bagnall, R.S. and Cribiore, R. 2012. Christianity on Thoth's Hill. In Bagnall *et al.* 2012, 409–15.

Bagnall, R.S. and Frier, B.W. 1994. *The Demography of Roman Egypt*. Cambridge and New York: Cambridge University Press.

Bagnall, R.S. and Ruffini, G.R. 2004. Civic life in fourth-century Trimithis: two ostraka from the 2004 excavations. *Zeitschrift fur Papyrologie und Epigraphik* 149: 143–52.

Bagnall, R.S. and Ruffini, G.R. 2012. *Ostraka from Trimithis Volume 1: Texts from the 2004–2007 Seasons*. New York: Institute for the Study of the Ancient World and New York University Press.

Bagnall, R.S., Davoli, P. and Hope, C.A. (eds). 2012. *The Oasis Papers 6: Proceedings of the Sixth International Conference of the Dakhleh Oasis Project*. Oxford: Oxbow Books.

Ball, J. and Beadnell, H.J.L. 1903. *Bahariya Oasis: Its Topography and Geology*. Cairo: Survey Department, Public Works Ministry.

Ballet, P. 1990. Annexe II. La céramique du site urbain de Douch/Kysis. *Bulletin de l'Institut Français d'Archeologie Orientale* 90: 298–301.

Ballet, P. 2000. La céramique. Notes et remarques. In A. Hussein (ed.), *Le sanctuaire rupestre de Piyris à Ayn al-Labakha*. Cairo: Institut Français d'Archéologie Orientale, 91–105.

Ballet, P. 2004. Jalons pour une histoire de la céramique romaine au sud de Kharga, Douch 1985–1990. In Reddé 2004, 209–240.

Bard, K.A. (ed.). 1999. *Encyclopaedia of the Archaeology of Ancient Egypt*. London: Routledge.

Barich, B.E. and Hassan, F.A. 1990. Il Sahara e le oasi: Farafra nel deserto occidentale egiziano. *Sahara* 3: 53–62.

Belgrave, C.D. 1923. *Siwa: The Oasis of Jupiter Amman*. London: William Brendon and Son, Ltd.

Boak, A.E.R. and Peterson, E.E. 1931. *Karanis: Topographical and Architectural Report of Excavations during the Seasons 1924–28*. Ann Arbor: University of Michigan.

Boozer, A.L. 2010. Memory and microhistory of an empire: domestic contexts in Roman Amheida, Egypt. In D. Borić (ed.), *Archaeology and Memory*. Oxford: Oxbow Books, 138–57.

Boozer, A.L. 2012. Globalizing Mediterranean identities: the overlapping spheres of Egyptian, Greek and Roman worlds at Trimithis. *Journal of Mediterranean Archaeology* 25.2: 93–116.

Boozer, A.L. 2013a. Archaeology on Egypt's edge: archaeological research in the Dakhleh oasis, 1819–1977. *Ancient West & East* 12: 117–56.

Boozer, A.L. 2013b. Frontiers and borderlands in imperial perspectives: exploring Rome's Egyptian frontier. *American Journal of Archaeology* 117.2: 275–92.

Boozer, A.L. 2014. Adapting urban space in late Roman Trimithis (Dakhleh oasis, Egypt). In E. O'Connell (ed.), *Egypt in the First Millennium AD: Perspectives from New Fieldwork*. Leuven: Peeters, Orientalia Lovaniensia Analecta, 23–42, plates 1–3.

Boozer, A.L. 2015. Inside and out: Romano-Egyptian housing from the Fayyum and the Dakhleh Oasis. In C. Hope and A. Di Castro (eds), *Housing and Habitat in the Mediterranean World: Responses to Different Climates*. Leuven: Peeters, 187–200.

Boozer, A.L. 2019. Looking for singles in the archaeological record of Roman Egypt. In S.R. Huebner and C. Laes (eds), *The Single Life in the Roman and Later Roman Worlds*. Cambridge: Cambridge University Press.

Bousquet, B. 1996. *Tell-Douch et sa région : géographie d'une limite de milieu à une frontière d'Empire*. Cairo: Institut français d'archéologie orientale.

Bowen, G.E. and Hope, C. (eds). 2004. *The Oasis Papers 3, Proceeding of the Third International Conference of the Dakhleh Oasis Project, Dakhleh Oasis Project: Monograph 14*. Oxford: Oxbow Books.

Castel, G. and Tallet, P. 2001. Les inscriptions d'El-Harra, oasis de Bahareya. *Bulletin de l'Institut Français d'Archeologie Orientale* 101: 99–136.

Chauveau, M. 1996. Les archives d'un temple des oasis au temps des Perses. *Bulletin de l'Institut Français d'Archeologie Orientale* 137: 32–47.

Chauveau, M. 2001. Les qanâts dans les ostraca de Manâwir. In P. Briant (ed.), *Irrigation et drainage dans l'Antiquité, qanâts et canalisations souterraines en Iran, en Égypte et en Grèce*. Paris: Thotm Éditions, 137–42.

Chauveau, M. 2005. Irrigation et exploitation de la terre dans l'oasis de Kharga à l'époque perse. *Les Cahiers de Recherches de l'Institut de Papyrologie et d'Égyptologie de Lille* 25: 157–63.

Chauveau, M. 2008. Les archives démotiques d'époque perse: À propos des archives démotiques d'Ayn-Manawîr. In P. Briant, W.F.M. Henkelman and M.W. Stolper (eds), *Les archives des fortifications de Persépolis dans le monde acheménide*. Paris: De Boccard, 517–24.

Churcher, C.S. and Mills, A.J. 1995. *Reports from the Survey of the Dakhleh Oasis: 1977–1987*. Oxford: Oxbow Books.

Clayton, J., de Trafford, A. and Borda, M. 2008. A hieroglyphic inscription found at Jebel Uweinat mentioning Yam and Tekhebet. *Sahara* 19: 129–34.

Congedo, F. and De Santis, V. 2006. *Topographical Survey*. New York: Columbia University.

Cruz-Uribe, E. 1988. *Hibis Temple Project, Vol. 1: Translations, Commentary, Discussions and Sign List*. San Antonio: Van Siclen Books.

Cruz-Uribe, E. 1999. Kharga oasis, Late Period and Graeco-Roman sites. In Bard 1999, 406–08.

Darnell, D. 2000. Oasis ware flasks and kegs from the Theban desert. *Cahier de la céramique égyptienne* 6: 227–33.

Darnell, J.C. 2002a. The narrow doors of the desert: discoveries of the Theban desert road survey. In B. David and M. Wilson (eds), *Inscribed Landscapes*. Honolulu: University of Hawaii Press, 104–21.

Darnell, J.C. 2002b. Opening the narrow doors of the desert: discoveries of the Theban desert road survey. In Friedman 2002a, 132–55.

Darnell, J.C. 2007a. The antiquity of the Ghueita temple. *Göttinger Miszellen* 212: 29–40.

Darnell, J.C. 2007b. The deserts. In T. Wilkinson (ed.), *The Egyptian World*. London and New York: Routledge, 29–48.

Darnell, J.C. 2013a. A bureaucratic challenge? Archaeology and administration in a desert environment (second millennium B.C.E.). In J.C.M. Garcia (ed.), *Ancient Egyptian Administration*. Leiden: Brill, 785–830.

Darnell, J.C. 2013b. The Girga road: Abu Ziyâr, Tundaba, and the integration of the southern oases into the Pharaonic state. In Förster and Riemer 2013, 221–63.

Davies, N.D.G. 1953. *The Temple of Hibis in El Khargeh Oasis III: The Decorations*. New York: Metropolitan Museum of Art.

de Angeli, S. 2013. Qanat landscapes in the oases of the Western Desert of Egypt: the cases of the Bahariya and Farafra oases. In Dospěl and Suková 2013, 271–85.

Delia, D. 1991. *Alexandrian Citizenship during the Roman Principate*. Atlanta: Scholars Press.

Di Cerbo, C., and Jasnow, R. 1996. Five Persian period demotic and hieroglyphic graffiti from the site of Apa Tyrannos at Armant. *Enchoria* 23: 32–38.

Dospěl, M. and Suková, L. 2013. Explorations of the El-Hayz oasis: issues, approaches, challenges. In Dospěl and Suková 2013, 3–18.

Dunand, F. Heim, J.-L. and Henein, N. 1992. *Douch I: La nécropole. Exploration archéologique, Monographie des tombes 1 à 72: structures sociales, économiques, religieuses de l'Égypte Romaine*. Cairo: Institut Français d'Archéologie Orientale du Caire.

Dunand, F., Heim, J.-L. Henein, N. and Lichtenberg, R. 2005. *Douch V. La nécropole de Douch. Exploration archéologique vol. 2. Monographie des tombes 73 à 92*. Cairo: Institut Français d'Archéologie Orientale du Caire.

Duval, N. 1982a. L'urbanisme de Sufetula (Sbeitla). *Aufstieg und Niedergang der römischen Welt* 2 (10.2): 596–632.

Duval, N. 1982b. Topographie et urbanisme d'Ammaedara. *Aufstieg und Niedergang der römischen Welt* 2 (10.2): 633–71.

Edmondson, J. 2006. Cities and urban life in the western provinces of the Roman Empire, 30 BCE–250 CE. In D. Potter (ed.), *Companion to the Roman Empire*. Oxford: Blackwell, 250–80.

Empereur, J.-Y. 1998. *Alexandria Rediscovered*. New York: G. Braziller.

Erdblom, L. 1968. *Structure foncière: organisation et structure sociale*. Lund: Uniskol.

Fakhry, A. 1974. *Bahriyah and Farafra* (2003 reprint). Cairo and New York: American University in Cairo Press.

Fakhry, A. 1990. *Siwa Oasis*. Cairo: American University in Cairo Press.

Fenwick, C. Forthcoming. Archaeology, empire and the Arab conquest of North Africa. *Past and Present*.

Fentress, E. (ed.). 2000. *Romanization and the City: Creation, Transformations, and Failures*. Portsmouth: Journal of Roman Archaeology Supplement.

Fentress, E. 2011. Slavers on chariots. In A. Dowler and E.R. Galvin (eds), *Money, Trade and Trade Routes in Pre-Islamic North Africa*. London: British Museum Press, 65–71.

Février, P.A. 1964. Notes sur le développement urbain en Afrique du Nord: les examples comparés de Djémila et de Sétif. *Cahiers Archeologiques* 14: 1–26.

Förster, F. and Riemer, H. (eds). 2013. *Desert Road Archaeology in Ancient Egypt and Beyond*. Köln: Heinrich-Barth-Institut.

Friedman, R. 2002a. *Egypt and Nubia: Gifts of the Desert*. London: British Museum Press.

Friedman, R. 2002b. Foreword. In Friedman 2002a, xiii–xv.

Gatto, M.C. 2002. Two Predynastic pottery caches at Bir Sahara (Egyptian Western Desert). *Sahara* 13: 51–60.

Giddy, L.L. 1987. *Egyptian Oases: Baḥariya, Dakhla, Farafra, and Kharga during Pharaonic Times*. Warminster: Aris & Phillips Ltd.

Giddy, L.L., and Grimal, N. 1979. Balat: sondage sur le site de Ain Aseel, rapport préliminaire. *Bulletin de l'Institut Français d'Archeologie Orientale* 79: 21–30.

Gill, J.C.R. 2012a. Ptolemaic activity in Dakhleh oasis. In *The 7th International Conference of the Dakhleh Oasis Project: New Developments in the Archaeology of the Egyptian Western Desert and Its Oases*. Leiden: Leiden University.

Gill, J.C.R. 2012b. Ptolemaic Period pottery from Mut al-Kharab, Dakhleh oasis. In Bagnall *et al.* 2012, 231–41.

Gill, J.C.R. 2015. *Dakhleh Oasis and the Western Desert in Egypt under the Ptolemies*. Oxford: Oxbow Books.

Goodman, P. 2007. *The Roman City and Its Periphery from Rome to Gaul*. New York: Routledge.

Gosline, S.L. 1990. *Bahariya Oasis Expedition Season Report for 1988: Part 1, Survey of Qarat Hilwah.* San Antonio, Texas: Van Siclen Books.

Grimal, N. 1997. Travaux de l'institut français d'archéologie orientale en 1996–1997. *Bulletin de l'Institut Français d'Archeologie Orientale* 97: 313–429.

Haas, C. 1993. Alexandria's *Via Canopica*: political expression and urban topography from Augustus to ᶜAmr Ibn al-ᶜAs. In N. Swelim (ed.), *Alexandrian Studies in Memoriam Daoud Abdu Daoud.* Alexandria: Société Archéologique d'Alexandrie, 123–38.

Haas, C. 1997. *Alexandria in Late Antiquity: Topography and Social Conflict.* Baltimore: The Johns Hopkins University Press.

Hamilton, J. 1856. *Wanderings in North Africa* (1985 reprint). London: John Murray.

Harrison, R. 2007. Materiality, ambiguity and the unfamiliar in the archaeology of inter-societal confrontations: a case study from northwest Australia. In P. Cornell and F. Fahlander (eds), *Encounters, Materialities, Confrontations: Archaeologies of Social Space and Interaction.* Newcastle: Cambridge Scholars Publishing.

Hassan, F. 1976. Prehistoric studies of the Siwa oasis region, northwestern Egypt (1975 field season). *Nyame Akuma* 9: 18–34.

Hassan, F. 1978. Archaeological exploration of the Siwa region. *Current Anthropology* 19: 146–48.

Hawass, Z. 2000. *Valley of the Golden Mummies.* New York: Harry N. Abrams.

Helk, W. 1975. *Wirtschaftsgeschichte des Alten Ägypten im 3. und 2. Jahrtausend vor Chr.* Leiden/Cologne: Brill.

Hope, C.A. 1999. Dakhla oasis, Ismant el-Kharab. In Bard 1999, 222–26.

Hope, C.A. 2002. Oases amphorae of the New Kingdom. In Friedman 2002a, 95–131.

Hope, C.A. 2004. The excavations at Ismant el-Kharab and Mut el-Kharab in 2004. *Bulletin of the Australian Centre for Egyptology* 15: 19–49.

Hope, C.A. 2005. Report on the excavations at Ismant el-Kharab and Mut el-Kharab in 2005. *Bulletin of the Australian Centre for Egyptology* 16: 35–83.

Hope, C.A. and Pettman, A.J. 2013. Egyptian connections with Dakhleh oasis in the Early Dynastic period to Dynasty IV: new data from Mut el-Kharab. In Bagnall *et al.* 2012, 147–66.

Hope, C.A. and Whitehouse, H. 2004. The gladiator jug from Ismant el-Kharab. In Bowen and Hope 2004, 291–310.

Hope, C.A. and Whitehouse, H. 2006. A painted residence at Ismant el-Kharab (Kellis) in the Dakhleh oasis. *Journal of Roman Archaeology* 19: 312–28, colour plates 1–10.

Hope, C.A., Kaper, O.E., Bowen, G.E. and Patten, S.F. 1989. Dakhleh Oasis Project: Ismant el-Kharab 1991–92. *Journal of the Society for the Study of Egyptian Antiquities* 19: 1–26.

Hope, C.A., Kaper, O.E. and Bowen, G.E. 1992. Excavations at Ismant el-Kharab – 1992. *The Bulletin of the Australian Centre for Egyptology* 3: 41–49.

Hope, C.A., Bowen, G.E., Cox, J., Dolling, W., Milner, J. and Pettmen, A. 2009. Report on the 2009 season of excavations at Mut el Kharab, Dakheh oasis. *Bulletin of the Australian Centre for Egyptology* 20: 47–86.

Hubschmann, C. 2012. Searching for an oasis identity: Dakhleh oasis in the Third Intermediate period. In C.M. Knoblauch and J.C Gill (eds), *Egyptology in Australia and New Zealand 2009.* Oxford: Archaeopress, 61–70.

Ikram, S. and Rossi, C. 2004. North Kharga Oasis Survey 2001–2002 preliminary report: Ain Gib and Qasr el-Sumayra. *Mitteilungen des Deutschen Archäologischen Institutes, Abteilung Kairo* 60: 69–92, Tafel 8–9.

Jackson, R.B. 2002. *At Empire's Edge: Exploring Rome's Egyptian Frontier.* New Haven: Yale University Press.

Jaritz, H. and Rodziewicz, M. 1994. Syene – review of the urban remains and its pottery. *Mitteilungen des Deutschen Archäologischen Institutes Abteilung Kairo* 50: 115–41.

Jaritz, H. and Rodziewicz, M. 1996. Syene – investigation of the urban remains in the vicinity of the temple of Isis (II). *Mitteilungen des Deutschen Archäologischen Institutes Abteilung Kairo* 52: 233–49.

Jones, A.H.M. 1964. *The Later Roman Empire, 284–602: A Social, Economic and Administrative survey* III (1986 reprint). Baltimore: Johns Hopkins.

Joshi, M.C. 2000. Application of geometry in the planning of an ancient settlement: Sisupalgarh, a case study. In J.M. Malville and L.M. Gujral (eds), *Ancient Cities, Sacred Skies: Cosmic Geometries and City Planning in Ancient India.* New Delhi: Aryan Books International, 34–39.

Kamal, Y. 1935. *Monumenta Cartographica Africae et Aegypti [6 vols]* (1987 reprint). Cairo: Le Caire.

Kaper, O.E. 1997. *Temples and Gods in Roman Dakhleh: Studies in the Indigenous Cults of an Egyptian Oasis.* PhD, Rijksuniversiteit te Groningen.

Kaper, O.E. (ed.). 1998a. *Life on the Fringe: Living in the Southern Egyptian Deserts during the Roman and Early-Byzantine Periods.* Leiden: Research School CNWS.

Kaper, O.E. 1998b. Temple building in the Egyptian deserts during the Roman period. In Kaper 1998a, 139–58.

Kaper, O.E. 2003. *The Egyptian God Tutu: A Study of the Sphinx-God and Master of Demons with a Corpus of Monuments.* Leuven: Peeters.

Kaper, O.E. 2009. Epigraphic evidence from the Dakhleh oasis in the Libyan period. In G.P.F. Broekman, R.J. Demarée and O.E. Kaper (eds), *The Libyan Period in Egypt, Historical and Cultural Studies into the 21st–24th Dynasties: Proceedings of a Conference at Leiden University, 25–27 October 2007.* Leiden: Netherlands Institute for the Near East, 149–59.

Kaper, O.E. 2010. Galba's cartouches at Ain Birbiyeh. In K. Lembke, M. Minas-Nerpel and S. Pfeiffer (eds), *Transition and Transformation: Egypt under Roman Rule.* Leiden: Brill, 181–201.

Kaper, O.E. 2012. The western oases. In C. Riggs (ed.), *The Oxford Handbook of Roman Egypt*. Oxford: Oxford University Press, 717–35.

Kaper, O.E. and Davoli, P. 2006. A new temple for Thoth in the Dakhleh oasis. *Egyptian Archaeology* 28: 12–14.

Kaper, O.E. and Demarée, R.J. 2006. A donation stela in the name of Takeloth III from Amheida, Dakhleh oasis. *Jaarbericht Ex Oriente Lux* 39: 19–37.

Keith, K. 2003. The spatial patterns of everyday life in Old Babylonian neighborhoods. In M.L. Smith (ed.), *The Social Construction of Ancient Cities*. Washington and London: Smithsonian Books, 56–80.

Kirkwan, L.P. 1971. Roman expeditions to the Upper Nile and the Chad-Darfur region. In F. Gadallah (ed.), *Libya in History. Proceedings of a Conference Held at the Faculty of Arts, University of Libya 1968*. Benghazi: University of Libya, 253–61.

Kröpelin, S. and Kuper, R. 2007. More corridors to Africa. *Cahiers de recherches de l'Institut de Papyrologie et d'Égyptologie de Lille* 26: 219–29.

Kucera, P. 2013. Al-Qasr: the Roman castrum of Dakhleh oasis. In Bagnall *et al.* 2012, 205–16.

Kuhlmann, K.P. 1988. *Das Ammoneion: Archäologie, Geschichte und Kultpraxis des Orakels von Siwa*. Mainz: Von Zabern.

Kuhlmann, K.P. 1998. Roman and Byzantine Siwa: developing a latent picture. In Kaper 1998a, 159–80.

Kuhlmann, K.P. 2002. The 'oasis bypath' or the issue of desert trade in Pharaonic times. In Jennerstrasse 8 (eds), *Tides of the Desert: Contributions to the Archaeology and Environmental History of Africa in Honour of Rudolph Kuper*. Köln: Heinrich-Barth-Institut, Africa praehistorica 14, 125–70.

Kuhlmann, K.P. 2005. Der Wasserberg des Djedefre (Chufu 01/1). Ein Lagerplatz mit Expeditionsinschriften der 4. Dynastie im Raum der Oase Dachla. *Mitteilungen des Deutschen Archäologischen Institutes, Abteilung Kairo* 61: 243–89.

Kuhlmann, K.P. 2013. The realm of two deserts: Siwa oasis between East and West. In Förster and Riemer 2013, 133–66.

Kuper, R. 2002. Routes and roots in Egypt's Western Desert: the Early Holocene resettlement of the Eastern Sahara. In Friedman 2002a, 1–12.

Kuper, R. and Kröpelin, S. 2006. Climate-controlled Holocene occupation in the Sahara: motor of Africa's evolution. *Science* 313: 803–87.

Lane, P., and MacDonald, K. (eds). 2011. *Slavery in Africa: Archaeology and Memory*. Oxford: Proceedings of the British Academy.

Lassus, J. 1969. *Visite à Timgad*. Algiers: Ministère de l'Education Nationale.

Laurence, R., Esmonde-Cleary, S. and Sears, G. 2011. *The City in the Roman West, c.250 BC–c.AD 250*. Cambridge: Cambridge University Press.

Leone, A. 2007. *Changing Townscapes in North Africa from Late Antiquity to the Arab Conquest*. Bari: Epipuglia.

Lepelley, C. 1992. The survival and fall of the Classical city in Late Roman Africa. In J. Rich (ed.), *The City in Late Antiquity*. London and New York: Routledge, 50–76.

Liebeschuetz, J.H.W.G. 2000. *The Decline and Fall of the Roman City*. Oxford and New York: Oxford University Press.

Liverani, M. (ed.). 2006. *Aghram Nadharif. A Garamantian Citadel in the Wadi Tannezzuft*. Firenze: All'Insegna del Giglio.

Lomas, K. 1989. Roman imperialism and the city in Italy. In R. Laurence and J. Berry (eds), *Cultural Identity in the Roman Empire*. London and New York: Routledge, 64–78.

MacCormack, S. 1981. *Art and Ceremony in Late Antiquity*. Berkeley: University of California Press.

Marlow, C.A. and Mills, A.J. (eds). 2001. *The Oasis Papers. Proceedings of the First International Symposium of the Dakhleh Oasis Project*. Oxford: Oxbow Books.

Masonen, P. 2012. The Sahara as highway for trade and knowledge. In S.E. Alcock, J. Bodel and R.J.A. Talbert (eds). *Highways, Byways, and Road Systems in the Pre-Modern World*. Malden/Oxford: John Wiley & Sons, 168–75.

Mattingly, D.J. 1994. *Tripolitania*. Ann Arbor: University of Michigan Press.

Mattingly, D.J. 2013. *The Archaeology of Fazzan. Volume 4, Survey and Excavations at Old Jarma (Ancient Garama) Carried out by C.M. Daniels (1962–69) and the Fazzan Project (1997–2001)*. London: Society for Libyan Studies, Department of Antiquities.

Mattingly, D.J. and Hitchner, R.B. 1995. Roman Africa: an archaeological review. *The Journal of Roman Studies* 85: 165–213.

Mattingly, D.J., Leitch, V., Duckworth, C.N., Cuénod, A., Sterry, M. and Cole, F. (eds). 2017. *Trade in the Ancient Sahara and Beyond*. Trans-Saharan Archaeology Volume 1. Series editor D.J. Mattingly. Cambridge: Cambridge University Press.

Mills, A.J. 1991. [Review of] Lisa L. Giddy, 'Egyptian Oases: Bahariya, Dakhla, Farafra and Kharga during Pharaonic Times'. *Bibliotheca Orientalia* 48: 132–35.

Mills, A.J. 1993. The Dakhleh oasis columbarium farmhouse. *Bulletin de la societé archéologique d'Alexandrie* 45: 192–98.

Mills, A.J. 1999a. Dakhleh oasis: dynastic and Roman sites. In Bard 1999, 220–22.

Mills, A.J. 1999b. Pharaonic Egyptians in the Dakhleh oasis. In C.S. Churcher and A.J. Mills (eds), *Reports from the Survey of the Dakhleh Oasis, Western Desert of Egypt: 1977–1987*, (Dakhleh Oasis Project: Monograph 2). Oxford: Oxbow Monograph 99, 171–78.

Mills, A.J. 2002. Deir el-Hagar, Ain Birbiyeh, Ain el-Gazzareen and el-Muzawwaqa. In C.A. Hope and G.E. Bowen (eds), *Dakhleh Oasis Project: Preliminary Reports on the 1994–95 to 1998–99 Field Season*. Oxford: Oxbow Books, 25–30.

Mills, A.J. 2013. An Old Kingdom trading post at 'Ain el-Gazzareen, Dakhleh oasis. In Bagnall *et al.* 2012, 177–80.

Mills, A.J. and Kaper, O.E. 2004. Ain el-Gazzareen: developments in the Old Kingdom settlement. In Bowen and Hope 2004, 123–29.

Mitchell, F.C. 1992. Where was Putu-Iaman? *Proceedings of the Seminar for Arabian Studies* 22: 69–80.

Mitchell, S. 2007. *A History of the Later Roman Empire, AD 284-641: The Transformation of the Ancient World.* Malden, MA; Blackwell.

Morkot, R.G. 1996. The Darb el-Arbain, the Kharga oasis and its forts, and other desert routes. In D.M. Bailey (ed.), *Archaeological Research in Roman Egypt.* Ann Arbor, MI: Journal of Roman Archaeology Supplement, 82–94.

Mullins, P.R. 2011. The archaeology of consumption. *Annual Review of Anthropology* 40: 133–44.

Nachtigal, G. 1974. *Sahara and Sudan* (translated by A.G.B. Fisher and H.J. Fisher). London: Hurst & Co.

Newton, C., Whitbread, T., Agut-Labordière, D. and Wuttmann, M. 2013. L'agriculture oasienne à l'époque perse dans le sud de l'oasis de Kharga (Égypte, Ve-IVe s. AJC). *Revue d'Ethnoécologie* 4: 2–18.

O'Connor, D. and Reid, A. (eds). 2003. *Ancient Egypt in Africa.* London: UCL Press.

Osing, J.R. (ed.). 1982. *Denkmäler der Oase Dachla: aus dem Nachlass von Ahmed Fakhry.* Mainz am Rhein: Philipp von Zabern.

Pantalacci, L. 1985. Un décret de Pépi II en faveur des gouverneurs de l'oasis de Dakhla. *Bulletin de l'Institut Français d'Archeologie Orientale* 85: 245–54.

Pantalacci, L. 2013. Broadening horizons: distant places and travels in Dakhla and the Western Desert at the end of the 3rd millennium. In Förster and Riemer 2013, 283–96.

Parsons, P. 2007. *City of the Sharp-Nosed Fish: Greek Papyri Beneath the Egyptian Sand Reveal a Long-Lost World.* London: Phoenix.

Reddé, M. 1990. Quinze années de recherches françaises à Douch. Vers un premier bilan. *Bulletin de l'Institut Français d'Archeologie Orientale* 90: 281–301.

Reddé, M. 1999. Sites militaires romains de l'oasis de Kharga. *Bulletin de l'Institut Francais d'Archeologie Orientale* 99: 377–96.

Reddé, M., Ballet, P., Barbet, A. and Bonnet, C. 2004. *Kysis: fouilles de l'Ifao à Douch, oasis de Kharga, 1985–1990.* Cairo: Institut Français d'Archéologie Orientale.

Riemer, H. 2004. News about the Clayton rings: long distance desert travellers during Egypt's Predynastic. In S. Hendrickx, T. Friedman, K. Cialowicz and M. Chlodnicki (eds), *Egypt at Its Origins. Studies in Memory of Barbara Adams.* Orientalia Lovaniensia Analecta 138. Leuven/Paris: Peeters, 971–89.

Riemer, H. 2009. A potsherd from northwest of Abu Minqar and the dispersal of Sheikh Muftah pottery in the Western Desert of Egypt. *Sahara* 20: 57–62.

Riemer, H. and Förster, F. 2013. Ancient desert roads: towards establishing a new field of archaeological research. In Förster and Riemer 2013, 19–58.

Riemer, H. and Kuper, R. 2000. 'Clayton rings': enigmatic ancient pottery in the Eastern Sahara. *Sahara* 12: 91–100.

Rodziewicz, M. 1984. *Les habitations romaines tardives d'Alexandrie et la lumiere des fouilles polonaises à Kom el-Dikka*. Warsaw: ánstwowe Wydawnictwo Naukowe.

Rodziewicz, M. 1991. A brief record of the excavations at Kom el-Dikka in Alexandria (1960–1980). *Bulletin de la societé archéologique d'Alexandrie* 44: 1–70.

Rohlfs, G. 1875. *Drei Monate in der Libyschen Wüste. Von Gerhard Rohlfs. Mit Beiträgen von P. Ascherson, W. Jordan und K. Zittel, sowie einer Originalkarte von W. Jordan, 16 Photographien nach Ph. Remelâe, 11 Steindruck-Tafeln und 18 Holzschnitten*. Cassel: T. Fischer.

Ross, E. 2011. A historical geography of the trans-Saharan trade. In G. Krätli and G. Lydon (eds), *The Trans-Saharan Book Trade. Manuscript Culture, Arabic Literacy and Intellectual History in Muslim America*. Leiden/Boston: Brill, 1–34; map on p. xv.

Rossi, C. 2000. Umm el-Dabadib, Roman settlement in the Kharga oasis: description of the visible remains with a note on 'Ain Amur. *Mitteilungen des Deutschen Archäologischen Instituts, Abteilung Kairo* 56: 335–52, Tafel 35–39.

Rossi, C. and Ikram, S. 2013. Evidence of desert routes across northern Kharga (Egypt's Western Desert). In Riemer and Förster 2013, 265–82.

Savage, E. (ed.). 1992. *The Human Commodity: Perspectives on the Trans-Saharan Slave Trade*. London: Frank Cass.

Schacht, I. 2003. A preliminary survey of the ancient *qanat* system of the Northern Kharga oasis. *Mitteilungen des Deutschen Archäologischen Institutes, Abteilung Kairo* 59: 279–306.

Schild, R. and Wendorf, F. 1977. *The Prehistory of the Dakhleh Oasis and Adjacent Desert*. Warsaw: Zaklad narodowy imienia ossolinskich wydawnictwo polskiej akademii nauk.

Sidebotham, S.E., and Wendrich, W.Z. 1998. Berenike: archaeological fieldwork at a Ptolemaic-Roman port on the Red Sea coast of Egypt: 1994–1998. *Sahara* 10: 85–96.

Smekalova, T.N., and Smekalov, S. 2005. *Magnetic Survey*. New York: Columbia University.

Smekalova, T.N., and Smekalov, S. 2006. *Geophysical Survey*. New York: Columbia University.

Soukiassian, G., Wuttman, M. and Schaad, D. 1990. La ville d''Ayn-Asil à Dakhla. État des recherches. *Bulletin de l'Institut Français d'Archeologie Orientale* 90: 347–58.

Stanley, C.V.B. 1912. The oasis of Siwah. *Journal of African Society* 11: 290–324.

Swanson, J.T. 1975. The myth of trans-Saharan trade during the Roman era. *International Journal of African Historical Studies* 8: 582–600.

Tacoma, L.E. 2006. *Fragile Hierarchies. The Urban Elites of Third-Century Roman Egypt*. Leiden: Brill.

Thissen, H.-J. 2013. Donkeys and water: demotic ostraca in Cologne as evidence for desert travel between Oxyrhynchos and the Bahariya oasis in the 2nd Century BC. In Förster and Riemer 2013, 391–97.

Török, L. 2009. *Between Two Worlds: the Frontier Region between Ancient Nubia and Egypt, 3700 BC–500 AD*. Leiden: Brill.

Valloggia, M. 1985. Les amiraux de l'oasis de Dakhleh. In *Mélanges offerts à Jean Vercoutter*. Paris: Éditions recherche sur les civilisations, 355–64.

Verner, M. and Benesovska, H. 2008. *Unearthing Ancient Egypt: Fifty Years of the Czech Archaeological Exploration in Egypt*. Prague: Charles University.

Vivian, C. 2002. *The Western Desert of Egypt: An Explorer's Handbook*. Cairo: American University in Cairo Press.

Wagner, G. 1987. *Les Oasis d'Égypte à l'époque grecque, romaine et byzantine d'après les documents grecs*. Cairo: Institut Français d'Archéologie Orientale du Caire.

Wagner, G. 2000. Oasis Magna. In R.J.A. Talbert (ed.), *Barrington Atlas of the Greek and Roman World*. Princeton: Princeton University Press, map 79.

Welsby, D. 1996. *The Kingdom of Kush: The Napatan and Meroitic Empires*. London: British Museum Press.

Wendrich, W.Z. 1998. Fringes are anchored in warp and weft: the relations between Berenike, Shenshef and the Nile Valley. In Kaper 1998a, 243–51.

Whitcomb, D.S. and Johnson, J.H. 1979. *Quseir Al-Qadim 1978: Preliminary Report*. Cairo: American Research Center in Egypt, Inc.

Wilson, A.I. 2002. Urban production in the Roman world: the view from North Africa. *Papers of the British School at Rome* 70: 231–73.

Wilson, A.I. 2006. The spread of foggara-based irrigation in the ancient Sahara. In D.J. Mattingly, S. McLaren, E. Savage, Y. al-Fasatwi, and K. Gadgood (eds), *The Libyan Desert. Natural Resources and Cultural Heritage*. London: Society for Libyan Studies, 205–16.

Wilson, A.I. 2009. Foggaras in ancient North Africa or how to marry a Berber princess. In *Contrôle et distribution de l'eau dans le Maghreb antique et médiéval*. Rome: École française de Rome, 19–39.

Wilson, A.I. 2012. Saharan trade in the Roman period: short-, medium- and long-distance trade networks. *Azania: Archaeological Research in Africa* 47.4: 409–49.

Wilson, A.I. and Mattingly, D.J. 2003. Irrigation technologies: foggaras, wells and field systems. In D.J. Mattingly (ed.), *The Archaeology of Fazzan. Volume 1, Synthesis*. London: Society for Libyan Studies, Department of Antiquities, 234–78.

Winlock, H.E. 1941. *The Temple of Hibis in El Khargeh Oasis*. III. New York: Metropolitan Museum of Art.

Wright, J. 1988. Murzuk and the Saharan slave trade in the 19th century. *Libyan Studies* 29: 89–96.

Wuttman, M. 1996. Premier rapport préliminaire des travaux sur le site de ʻAyn-Manâwîr (oasis de Kharga). *Bulletin de l'Institut Français d'Archeologie Orientale* 96: 385–451.

Wuttman, M. 2001. Les qanats de ʻAyn manāwīr. In P. Briant (ed.), *Irrigation et drainage dans l'Antiquité. Qanâts et canalisations souterraines en Iran, en Égypte et en Grèce*. Paris: Thotm Éditions (Persika 2), 109–36.

Wuttman, M., Barakat, H., Bousquet, B., Chauveau, M., Gonon, T., Marchand, S., Robin M. and Schweitzer, A. 1998. 'Ayn Manawir (oasis de Kharga). Deuxième rapport préliminaire. *Bulletin de l'Institut Français d'Archeologie Orientale* 98: 367–462.

Wuttman, M., Gonon, T. and Thiers, C. 2000. The qanats of 'Ayn-Manâwîr (Kharga oasis, Egypt). *Journal of Achaemenid Studies and Researches* 1: 1–11.

Youssef, S. 2012. Qanats in the Dakhleh oasis. In *7th International Conference of the Dakhleh Oasis Project: New Developments in the Archaeology of the Egyptian Western Desert and Its Oases, 20–24 June 2012*. Netherlands: Leiden University.

5 Pre-Islamic Oasis Settlements in the Northern Sahara

DAVID J. MATTINGLY, MARTIN STERRY,
MUFTAH AL-HADDAD AND POL TROUSSET

Introduction

This chapter focuses on the oases of the northern Sahara, both those close to and in some cases incorporated within the frontiers of the Roman provinces of Africa. With the exception of some outstanding contributions from our co-author Pol Trousset, there has been little consideration of the potential scale or on the ground reality of oasis development in the Roman frontier region.[1] This is only partly explicable in terms of the lack of detailed archaeological work at these sites – as we shall demonstrate there is quite a lot of fragmentary evidence to support the case for widespread oasis development in pre-Islamic times. In large measure the lack of recognition of the importance of oases here relates to the long-prevailing myth that Rome was confronted in this frontier zone by nomadic (or at best transhumant) peoples.[2] It is hoped that what follows will provoke a full re-evaluation of Rome's African frontiers and what they were designed to deal with. There are clearly major implications if, in place of a few scattered bands of pastoralists, Rome was confronted by *both* pastoralists and settled and populous oasis communities. The descriptive survey will pick up from Chapter 3 by starting at Bu Nijim, the main oasis to the north of al-Jufra on the main route to the Mediterranean, where a Roman fort was established in AD 201. It will then proceed more or less westwards along the frontier zone, finishing in the Ouled Nail mountains and the oases directly south of there in the Mzab and Wargla groups.[3] The very far western Algerian oases

[1] Trousset 1986a; 1987a; 1987b; 1995; 2012a. The chapter is mainly written by the first two named authors, but we worked with the third author on the section on Ghadames and have made use of unpublished notes provided by the fourth author.

[2] Trousset 1982b; 2012b. See also, Leveau 2018, for a sweeping historiographical overview.

[3] For the geography of the Tunisian and Algerian oasis zones, see Despois and Raynal 1967, 421–49.

will be considered in the next chapter in its overview of the western Sahara.[4] Available radiocarbon dates are presented in Table 5.1.

The Tripolitanian Pre-Desert and the Hamada al-Hamra

The region (and later Roman province) of Tripolitana comprised western Libya and southern Tunisia, covering a linear distance of over 1,000 km from the Syrtic desert to the Chott Jarid (Fig. 5.1). For much of this distance, the Roman provincial territory ran through, or was closely bordered by, pre-desert or desert landscapes. The Hamada al-Hamra is a massive and largely waterless rocky plateau area between the Tripolitanian pre-desert and Fazzan.[5] The two major Trans-Saharan routes in Libya have traditionally skirted this hostile environment, one running some way to the east of the Hamada through al-Jufra and on to Fazzan, the other skirting its west flank through Ghadamis and Ghat.

However, despite the difficulties of travel at the hotter periods of the year, the Hamada is not impassable. The campaign of Cornelius Balbus *c.*20 BC appears to have traversed part of it in passing from Ghadamis to Garamantian lands. In AD 70 the Roman army reduced the time required to reach the Garamantian heartlands by using the 'head of the rock road' (*iter praeter caput saxi*), almost certainly to be identified with the direct route from Tripoli via Gharyan, Mizda, al-Qurayyat al-Gharbia, Shwerif, to Brak in the Wadi ash-Shati.[6] From Mizda to Brak the route runs partly over and partly along the eastern edge of the Hamada.

The first site we shall examine is Bu Nijim on the eastern route, which continued south to al-Jufra.[7] The second part of this section will look at the sites associated with the 'central' route via the Hamada al-Hamra, specifically Mizda and al-Qurayyat al-Gharbia. The third section will look at sites on the western route north from Ghadamis to the Nefzaoua oases.

The Eastern Route

Bu Nijim

The Roman fort and garrison settlement at Bu Nijim is one of the best explored locations of the Roman frontier in Africa, lying between the

[4] See Sterry *et al.*, Chapter 6, this volume. [5] Mattingly 1995, 6–7.
[6] Pliny, *Natural History*, 5.38; Desanges 1980, 411–14, for discussion.
[7] See Mattingly *et al.*, Chapter 3, this volume.

Table 5.1 *Protohistoric and historic radiocarbon dates from the Northern Sahara*

Area/Site	Context	Material	Reference	Date	Calibrated
Tripolitanian Pre-Desert					
Wadi Ganima	Alluvial terrace	Charcoal	Q-656	614±100 BP	calAD 1207–1470
Adzam (village)	Midden	Charcoal	GrN-13539	435±20 BP	calAD 1430–1472
Adzam (village)	Midden	Charcoal	GrN-13538	405±25 BP	calAD 1437–1618
Adzam (village)	Midden	Charcoal	GrN-13540	390±20 BP	calAD 1445–1618
Ben Telis (village)	Midden	Charcoal	GrN-13526	555±30 BP	calAD 1310–1431
Ben Telis (village)	Midden	Charcoal	GrN-13525	390±30 BP	calAD 1441–1631
Gh75 (qasr)	Midden	Charcoal	GrN-13536	1770±25 BP	calAD 143–342
Gh75 (qasr)	Midden	Charcoal	GrN-13537	1765±25 BP	calAD 145–378
Kh41 (qasr)	Midden	Charcoal	GrN-13524	1510±70 BP	calAD 412–652
Kh41 (qasr)	Midden	Charcoal	GrN-13523	1380±90 BP	calAD 430–875
Lm3 (qasr)	Timber	Wood	HAR-5838	1840±70 BP	calAD 23–376
Lm3 (qasr)	Same sample as above	Wood	HAR-5689	1710±70 BP	calAD 132–533
Lm3 (qasr)	Same sample as above	Wood	HAR-5840	1720±80 BP	calAD 126–535
Lm4 (farm)	Occupation layer	Charcoal	GrN-13531	2075±35 BP	189 calBC–calAD 2
Lm4 (farm)	Construction material	Charcoal	GrN-13533	1975±25 BP	41 calBC–calAD 74
Lm4 (farm)	Abandonment layer	Charcoal	GrN-13535	1910±60 BP	41 calBC–calAD 237
Lm4 (farm)	Occupation layer	Charcoal	GrN-13532	1835±30 BP	calAD 86–246
Lm4 (farm)	Destruction layer	Charcoal	GrN-13530	1770±30 BP	calAD 138–345
Lm4 (farm)	Destruction layer	Charcoal	GrN-13529	1710±25 BP	calAD 253–395
Lm4 (farm)	Abandonment layer	Charcoal	GrN-13534	615±45 BP	calAD 1287–1410
Nf82 (farm)	Midden	Charcoal	GrN-13527	1790±50 BP	calAD 92–381
Nf82 (farm)	Midden	Charcoal	GrN-13528	1750±50 BP	calAD 138–394
Al-Qurayyat al-Gharbia	Mortar floor	Charcoal	Erl-16639	1595±38 BP	calAD 390–551
Al-Qurayyat al-Gharbia	Buttress wall (mortar)	Charcoal	Erl-16637	1551±43 BP	calAD 415–598
Al-Qurayyat al-Gharbia	Column base (mortar)	Charcoal	Erl-16638	1538±42 BP	calAD 420–605

Table 5.1 (*cont.*)

Area/Site	Context	Material	Reference	Date	Calibrated
Ghadamis					
Ghadamis	Not given	Charcoal	Gif-4581	2600±50 BP	
Qasr Ghlul	Occupation layer	Charcoal	OxA-34787	1501±23 BP	calAD 435–625
Qasr Ghlul	Occupation layer	Plant remains	OxA-34790	992±22 BP	calAD 991–1150
Qasr Ghlul	Occupation layer	Plant remains	OxA-34985	946±30 BP	calAD 1025–1156
Qasr Ghlul	Occupation layer	Date stone	OxA-34788	914±22 BP	calAD 1034–1168
Qasr Ghlul	Same sample as above	Date stone	OxA-34789	909±23 BP	calAD 1037–1186
Southern Tunisia					
El Menaguib	Tumulus 1	Charcoal	Pa-2352	4520±150 BP	
El Menaguib	Bazina 24	Human bone	Pa-2368	1845±30 BP	calAD 85–239
El Menaguib	Tumulus 4	Human bone	Pa-2352	1970±45 BP	88 calBC–calAD 130
Djebel Aziza	Berber retreat	Charcoal	Hv-6979	415±130 BP	calAD 1286– . . .
Djebel Aziza	Berber retreat	Charcoal	Hv-6977	250±50 BP	calAD 1483– . . .
Oued el Akarit	Lithic scatter	Shells	Orsay	3100±190 BP	1869–850 calBC
Oued el Akarit	Lithic scatter	Shells	GaK-3454	1470±190 BP	calAD 135–963
Kebili Km 97			Hv-6976	295±40 BP	calAD 1477–1791
Smidet Zine			Hv-6974	130±120 BP	calAD 1517– . . .
Les Perles		Ostrich egg shell	Mc-723	2400±100	795–232 calBC
Er Regaa		Ostrich egg shell	Hv-7974	2440±100	802–370 calBC
Southern Algeria					
El Golea			Hv-5620	3345±140 BP	2022–1302 calBC
El Golea			Hv-9699	1930±260 BP	729 calBC–calAD 636
Ben Dahi		Ostrich egg shell	HV-7975	3435±100	2016–1505 calBC
Hassi el-Mejna		Lac. shells	Orsay	3380±150	2131–1305 calBC
Hassi Cheikh C		Diat	Orsay	3330±70	1862–1446 calBC
Hassi Cheikh C		Diat	Orsay	3230±200	2026–1001 calBC
Hassi Cheikh A		Diat	Orsay	3230±200	2026–1001 calBC
Hassi Cheikh B		Diat	Orsay	3220±200	2018–980 calBC
Hassi Cheikh		Diat	Orsay	3080±255	2016–788 calBC

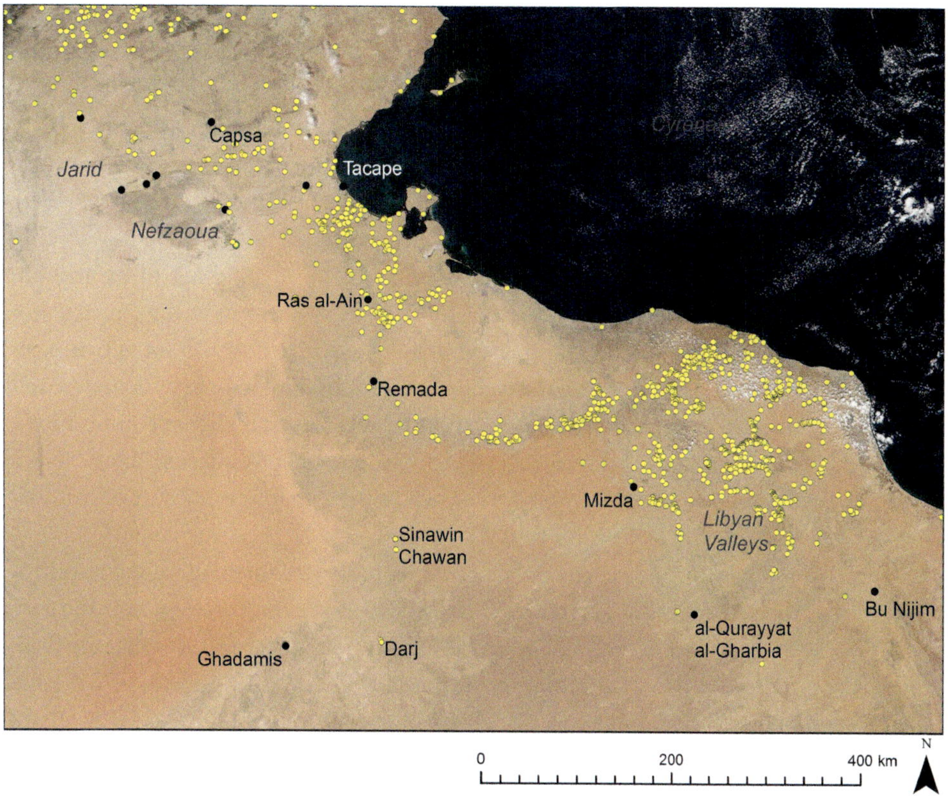

Figure 5.1. South Tunisia and Tripolitania, main regions and sites discussed in the text.

Greater Syrtes embayment and the al-Jufra oases along a natural seismic corridor known as the Hun Graben. The fort is often starkly depicted in relation to its desert environment, whether in Lyon's famous painting of its north gate or the aerial view of its buildings engulfed by sand dunes.[8] The fort is situated on the south-east side of a small L-shaped oasis. The modern village lies on the west side of the oasis *c.*1.5 km from the fort, a loose straggle of houses. The location is in a rather waterless area and despite its small size the wells and oasis at Bu Nijim has been historically important. For instance, it was the point on the nineteenth-century slave route from Bornu where responsibility for the security of caravans passed from Fazzan to Tripoli jurisdiction.[9]

[8] Lyon 1821, f. p. 67; Mattingly *et al.* 2013, 86–89.

[9] Mattingly 1995, 156. Nachtigal 1974, 47, gives a concise account of the depressed state of this small oasis, reputedly the most northerly in the province of Fazzan in the late nineteenth century.

The excavations by Rebuffat in the 1960s–1970s provide a particularly detailed record for the fort and garrison settlement, as well as establishing the location of outlying temples and nearby outposts on the desert routes.[10] Epigraphic evidence dates the foundation of the fort very precisely, to 24 January AD 201 and there is an abundance of documentation on the activities of the garrison down to *c.*AD 263. The 1.28 ha fort was surrounded by a substantial walled garrison settlement (*c.*14 ha) recently truncated by an agricultural development.[11] The buildings of the fort and garrison settlement made extensive use of palm wood in the construction of roofs and vaults, emphasising the site's proximity to an active oasis. Libyan inscriptions on the walls of a house in the garrison settlement could relate to passing traders, or alternatively to the local Libyan community of the oasis.[12] Roman ostraca (texts written on pot sherds) attest to the existence of a *statio cameliorum* here – presumably some sort of caravanserai attached to either the oasis or fort.[13]

There is no direct evidence of earlier oasis settlement at this location and the nearest hillfort sites are 35–50 km to the north. However, near the oasis there are two clusters of poorly preserved rectilinear features that are likely the remains of oasis gardens and/or buildings. There are also a small number of Roman period farms and cisterns around the wells in the Wadi Bai al-Kabir (which eventually connects to al-Qurayyat ash-Sharqiya.[14]

The Central Route

Al-Qurayyat al-Gharbia

The two small oases of al-Qurayyat al-Gharbia and al-Qurayyat ash-Sharqiya are *c.*20 km apart, but are equally significant as rare spring-fed oases in otherwise very inhospitable wadis. The fact that both were marked by Roman military installations is a strong indication that the oases pre-dated the frontier here. Had the oases been deliberately created by the Roman army to serve the needs of its advanced garrison post, you would imagine that resources would have been focused on a single site, rather than on creating two distinct loci requiring surveillance. Neither oasis is large, but the western oasis (al-Gharbia) covers

[10] Rebuffat 1967; 1970a; 1970b; 1971; 1975b; 1975c; 1977a; 1980; 1982; 1989; 2004. Compare, Goodchild 1954a; Mattingly 1995, 95–97.

[11] Mattingly 1995, 134–35. [12] Rebuffat 1975a.

[13] Marichal 1992, 100–6, 122, no. 5; compare, Guédon 2010, 83–85. [14] Rebuffat 1982.

*c.*1,000 × 200 m and was the site of the major fort. The UNESCO Libyan Valleys survey and more recently a team led by Michael Mackensen have studied the Roman fort which dominates the oasis from a rocky terrace above its eastern edge.[15] There are indications of a civil settlement around the fort and a trace on an early air-photograph of a possible fortified enclosure on a spur overlooking the western side of the oasis.[16] A second rectangular enclosure with playing card corners lies 700 m to the north-east of the fort and settlement and is potentially the remains of an earlier fortlet. There are also small patches of oasis cultivation in the parallel wadis 2.5 km to the east and 1 km north-west of al-Qurayyat al-Gharbia. In both cases there are traces of wadi cultivation and abandoned one- or two-room houses along the flanks of the wadi as well as a scatter of burial cairns on the plateaux above. Although these features cannot be dated, it is further evidence of human investment at some point in time in developing the cultivated landscape. Like Bu Nijim, the fort was an early third century addition to the frontier deployment, presumably implanted at an already existing oasis site. Radiocarbon, ceramic and coin evidence from the most recent excavations suggests that occupation continued within the fort (with an 80-year hiatus) until the mid-sixth century AD.[17]

Al-Qurayyat ash-Sharqiya

The Roman fortlet sits on a prominent spur well above the small oasis (*c.*400 × 250 m) and although no inscription has been found, a military interpretation seems certain.[18] It is undoubtedly of Roman era construction and is associated with Roman pottery. There has been limited investigation of the oasis, though a decorated architrave near the fortlet may relate to a mausoleum. There are some rock-cut houses and mudbrick houses on the fringe of the cultivated area and this would be the area to look for evidence of the suspected civilian population. Around 7 km to the north-east of the oasis, the spur on the east side of the wadi is divided by a wall (similar to hillforts like Zinkekra). There are a few possible buildings 500 m further north, but little evidence to suggest that this defended outcrop ever developed into something more substantial.

[15] Barker *et al.* 1996a, 114–16; 1996b, 98–103; Goodchild 1954a; Mackensen 2010; 2011; 2012; Mattingly 1995, 92–95; Welsby 1988.

[16] Barker *et al.* 1996b, 104–5. [17] Mackensen 2010; 2011; 2012.

[18] Barker *et al.* 1996b, 125; Mattingly 1995, 104–5.

Mizda

Mizda was an important staging point on the route north from the two Qurayyat outposts. It lay at an important strategic location, just north of the Hamada al-Hamra at the crossing of the plain of the Wadi Soffegin close to the effective western limit of the zone of intensive floodwater farming of the pre-desert wadis. Two Roman roads marked with milestones converge on the location, surely indicating that Mizda was an important centre, most likely at some point a frontier fort.[19] The early European travellers reported on a double oasis community, divided between a north-western and a south-eastern village, separated by a short distance.[20] The Italian fort built here in the early twentieth century incorporated quite a lot of Roman stonework as well as inscriptions, some brought in from nearby sites, but some almost certainly gathered in the immediate vicinity.[21] The architecture of the ruins of the Medieval/early modern oasis villages has many similarities with the post-Roman Berber village that was built over the ruins of al-Qurayyat al-Gharbia. Recent survey has recovered second–third century Roman pottery sherds from the oasis around the old town and adds weight to the suggestion that there was a Roman fort and civil settlement here.[22] As with other oasis forts, the likelihood is that the oasis predated the installation of the garrison.

The Libyan Valleys

Between the main routes running north from al-Qurayyat al-Gharbia and Bu Nijim lay the Tripolitanian pre-desert zone, where a distinctive pattern of sedentary settlement developed in the early centuries AD, based on floodwater farming in the bottom of wadis (see Fig. 1.4c). This has been one of the best studied examples of run-off farming in North Africa.[23] Although the hydrological aspect of desert farming was very different here to the groundwater dependent oases of Fazzan,[24] there are nonetheless some striking similarities in settlement types, especially the nature of hillforts, villages and late Roman fortified sites (*qsur*) and those we have seen in the Garamantian lands 500 km to the south.[25]

[19] Mattingly 1995, 97 for the argument.
[20] Barth 1857, 99–103, who reported extensive ruins extending into the plain; Rohlfs 2001, 102–5.
[21] *IRT* p. 215 and numbers 883–84. [22] Schimmer 2012. [23] Barker *et al.* 1996a; 1996b.
[24] Mattingly 2004; 2014. [25] Barker *et al.* 1996a, 116–18, 127–34.

Ghadamis and Associated Oases

Ghadamis and Its environs

On the north-western side of the Hamada al-Hamra and close up against the eastern limit of the Great Eastern Erg, is the remarkable and isolated oasis of Ghadamis,[26] another site for which we have ancient literary evidence of pre-Roman origins. The site is dependent on a natural artesian spring, though there is some evidence that this was enhanced through exploitation of additional water sources at certain points. Pliny's account of the campaign of Cornelius Balbus in 20 BC mentioned a region known as Phazania.[27] In spite of the apparent similarity of name, Phazania does not correspond with modern Fazzan, but appears to have related to the desert zone around Ghadamis, separated from modern Fazzan by the Ubari Sand Sea and the Hamada al-Hamra.[28] The names of three *urbes* of the Phazanii – Alele, Cilliba and Cidamus – were also recorded by Pliny and the latter can be identified with the oasis settlement of Ghadamis. The western and northern limits of Phazania were probably defined by the Grand Erg Oriental and by the identification of Alele and Cilliba with the names of Roman frontier forts at the small oases of Talalati (Ras al-Ain) and Tillibari (Remada) in southern Tunisia.[29]

The epigraphic evidence for ancient Cidamus includes a series of Latin inscriptions that indicate a Roman military presence in the third century AD. There are also funerary texts in Latin and Latino-Punic relating to civilians and several examples of Libyan inscriptions.[30]

The archaeological evidence for early Ghadamis is less abundant than one might expect of a UNESCO World Heritage site, though the standing buildings of the marvellously atmospheric early modern town are an understandable distraction.[31] Archaeological survey that we initiated in 2011 to investigate the broader archaeological context of the oasis was prematurely interrupted by the Libyan Revolution of that year.[32] The most famous pre-Islamic remains are a group of late Roman era funerary monuments (*asnam*) that stood just south of the oasis on the flanking

26 For the classic early modern accounts of Ghadamis, see Duveyrier 1864; Richardson 1848. For medieval accounts, Thiry 1995.

27 Pliny, *Natural History* 5.35–38.

28 The best discussion of Pliny's account of the campaign of Balbus is Desanges 1980; see also Desanges 1957; 1978; Mattingly 1995; 2003.

29 Mattingly 1995, 25–30.

30 Mattingly and Sterry 2010, Appendix 1, 106–13 lists 20 inscriptions from Ghadames including Latin, probable Latino-Punic and Libyan texts; *IRT* 907–9; Reynolds 1958.

31 Aymo 1958 for the famous Ghadamensi houses.

32 Mattingly and Sterry 2010.

low rocky plateau.[33] The *asnam* can be identified as of the same type as the late Roman colonnaded tombs from the pre-desert site of Ghirza.[34] In addition to many architectural fragments and relief sculptures relating to these tombs, the town has also yielded numerous other columns and architectural elements demonstrating that there were major stone-built buildings of Mediterranean inspiration there.[35] There is certainly some Roman imported pottery reported within the oasis gardens to confirm the antiquity of the oasis cultivation, even if it is not possible to isolate the footprint of the ancient site.[36] It is most likely to have been built up close to the spring. The spring basin at Ghadamis and the associated canal network is evidently of long antiquity and is located *c.*100 m outside the central square of the Early Modern town (Fig. 5.2; cf. also Fig. 1.4e).[37]

A number of other structures around the oasis are also suspected to indicate pre-Islamic activity. Qasr Mqdul is a circular tower-like building on the west side of the oasis gardens.[38] There appears to be Roman tile built into it and some associated ceramic finds again appeared Roman. Given that the monument lies within the pre-Islamic cemetery zone, it may have had a funerary function – it is certainly difficult to make sense of as a dwelling. An isolated 'tower' structure on the north-east side of the oasis gardens turned out on close inspection to be a small stone-built mausoleum. Its location away from the Islamic cemetery areas strongly suggests a pre-Islamic date.[39] Slightly further out from the main oasis are two satellite settlements associated with foggaras, at Tunin *c.*3 km west of Ghadamis and at Qasr Glul, 6.5 km to the north.[40] Qasr Glul is a rocky fortress site, with complex defences and a deep well that had been bored down through the centre of the outcrop it sits on. It is associated with a now abandoned oasis area fed by the foggaras. Recently obtained radiocarbon dates identify two possible phases of occupation with a sample from the mortar of a defensive wall of calAD 435–625, suggesting the site was established in late antiquity, and three further samples from the late tenth

[33] Corò 1956; Mercier 1953; Mattingly and Sterry 2010, 62–79.

[34] Brogan and Smith, 1984, 121–47.

[35] Corò 1956, 23; Duveyrier 1864, 250 and Planche X, figure 1; Mattingly and Sterry 2010, 87–91; Richardson 1848, I, 210.

[36] Rebuffat 1969, 194–95; 1972, 322–23.

[37] The most detailed study of the spring system is Eldblom 1968.

[38] Corò 1956, 10–12; Mattingly and Sterry 2010, 83–84.

[39] Mircher *et al.* 1863, illustrated on fold-out map, pl.3. Relocated by Ghadames Archaeological Survey in 2011, Mattingly *et al.* 2011.

[40] Mattingly and Sterry 2010, 91–101.

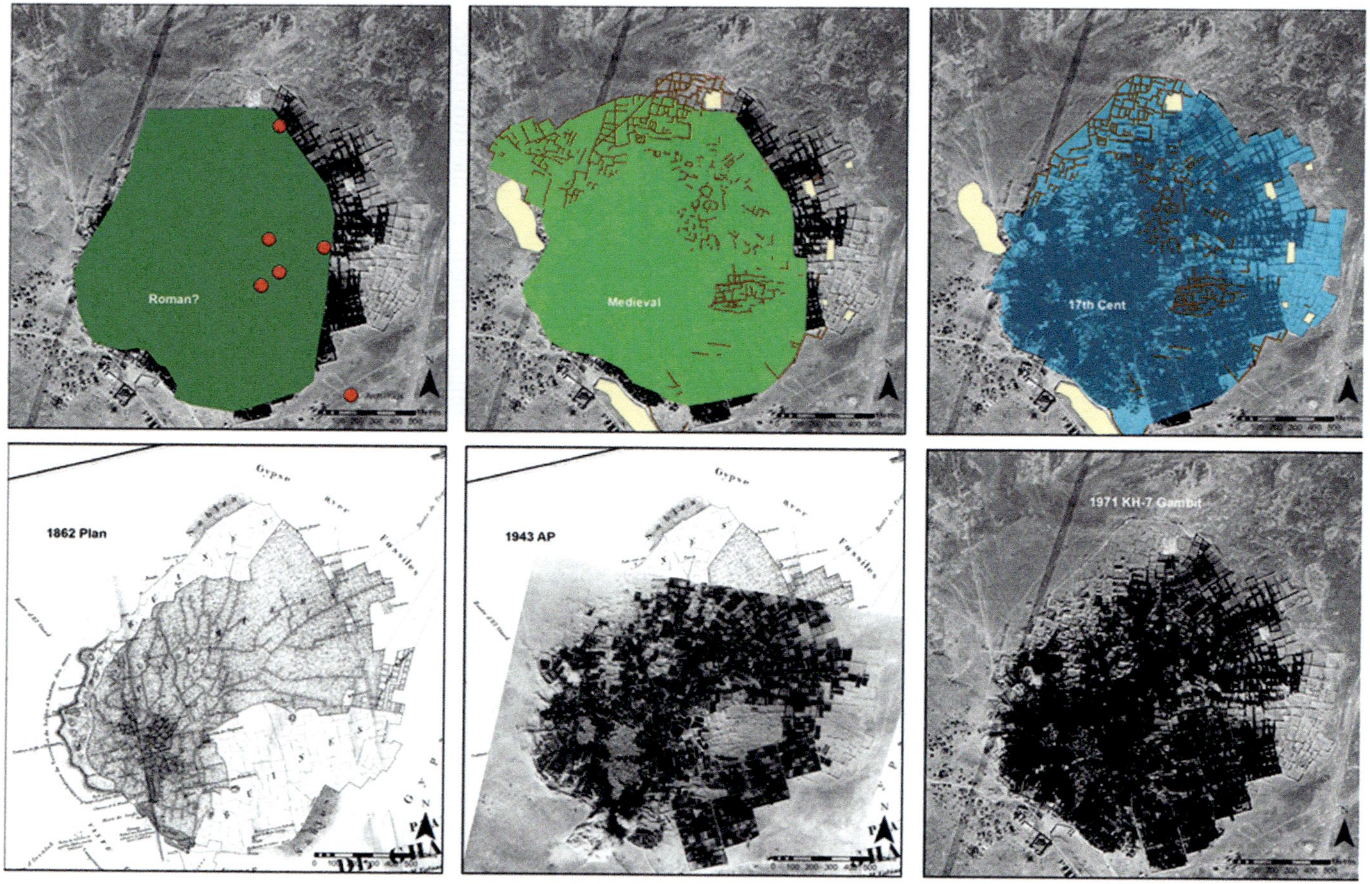

Figure 5.2. Proposed development of the Ghadamis oasis from Roman to Present (red circles - architectural fragments, brown lines - surveyed garden walls, yellow polygons - Medieval to modern cemeteries).

to mid-twelfth centuries.[41] There are a foggara, abandoned fields and Moslem burials associated with the site.

Darj

Located 92 km to the east of Ghadamis, Darj is a small collection of oases that is an important stopping point on the trade routes. Although the oasis is now greatly expanded by modern development, early writers recorded four separate small oases here.[42] Darj – with gardens totalling *c.*150 ha, Terguddah – 2.2 km to the north, Madress – 9 km to the west and Fiffelt – comprising 4–5 houses between Madress and Darj.[43] Perugini described Darj as measuring 1,500 × 400 m with 11,000 palms, 7 springs, 30 wells and many distribution channels at the centre of which is a clustered village 230 × 230 m similar to that at the centre of Tunin. Prospection by Rebuffat identified a polygonal fortified structure at Fiffelt and at Madress a circular fort and a 'Roman fortlet'.[44] It is difficult to reconcile these observations with sites noted from satellite imagery. An enigmatic circular feature is visible 650 m north-west of Madress while the village itself is clustered on a spur with the remains of further buildings on its east side. To the north of Madress where the road crosses a line of hills there is a large cairn field that winds along the edge for 2.5 km with *c.*500–1,000 cairns. The hill to the west of Terguddah has a small outpost on its southern tip of unknown date and there is a sizable area of disturbed ground that seems likely to have been hut clearings and animal enclosures. To the north-west, on another spur, there is a large polygonal enclosure, but with no signs of settlement, just to the north of this is a small group of square huts. To the north and in the wadi there is a square fortification 30 × 30 m, probably built of stone that may be linked to the Roman military judging by the two-towered gatehouse on its southern side. Like Ghadamis, Darj appears to have a natural artesian spring; however, the strip of cultivation north of Terguddah was originally fed by at least 20 foggara channels. None are very long, but they range from very small to large shafts, perhaps suggesting that they tap water reservoirs at different depths.

41 OxA-34787, 1501±23 BP, calAD 435–625; OxA-34790, 992±22 BP, calAD 991–1150; OxA-34985, 946±30 BP, calAD 1025–1156; OxA-34988 and OxA-34989 R_Combine 912±16 BP, X^2 test: df=1 T=0.0(5% 3.8) calAD 1039–1165.

42 See Richardson 1848, I, 255–56; Perugini 1929, 97.

43 Largeau 1881, 234 calls these Degoutta, Materes and Tfelfet. Rebuffat 1977b, 418 offers a slightly different position for Fiffelt to the north-east of Madress.

44 Rebuffat 1972, 323–24.

Chawan and Sinawin

Some 90 km north of Darj (140 km north-east of Ghadamis) are the small oases of Chawan and Sinawin. At Chawan, Rebuffat recorded three fortifications: an oval fort on a hill and two rectangular 'fortlets' of third and fourth century date.[45] The old centre of Chawan is 140 × 115 m and surrounded by sparse and scattered gardens, although modern construction has destroyed much of the area of the spring-fed oasis. Richardson described Chawan as a small place sharing a population of 60 with Sinawin.[46] Most of the archaeological evidence is to the north of Chawan. There are at least 12 small foggaras leading into the gardens that stretch 1.5 km to the north-east and 500 m further north is a small hilltop fortification that must be Rebuffat's oval fort. It is not clear where the fortlets were located, however 3.5 km to the north-east there is a small scarp, below which there are four rectangular structures, three are very similar to the open farms found in the Libyan Valleys to the east, the final one is possibly a *qasr*; a Roman date for all four is likely. On top of the scarp is a cairnfield of *c.*100 tombs.

Sinawin, 7 km to the north-east of Chawan, is a fortified village on top of a small hill on the edge of a small oasis and area of sabkha. The oldest part measures 126 × 85 m, but there has been significant modern building on all sides across the whole of the oasis. When Richardson visited he described 30 to 40 inhabitants living in 'half a dozen or more mud hovels' (mudbrick houses). The oasis consisted of four or five patches of cultivation protected by two or three mud and stone round towers called *burges*.[47]

The Tripolitanian Jabal

The Tripolitanian Jabal is relatively well-watered at its eastern end, progressively less so as one travels west towards the Tunisian border and then north to the Nefzaoua.[48] Although technically dry farming is possible in part of the Jabal, the irregular pattern of rainfall favours floodwater farming and the exploitation of springs that support a number of small oases. The early Roman frontier seems to have been organised in relation to a road that ran along the crest of the Jabal or just behind it. A number of Roman military outposts along the *limes* road that followed the Jabal plateau were established

[45] Rebuffat 1972, 323. [46] Richardson 1848, I, 80–81.

[47] Richardson 1848, I, 79. In 2005 Mattingly noted some Roman pottery imports in and around the old settlement.

[48] For cartography, see Goodchild 1954b; Mattingly 2000a.

alongside springs and oases: Ain Wif (Thenadassa)[49] and Ain al-Auenia (Auru).[50]

An interesting aspect of the *limes Tripolitanus* is that the hill range of the Jabal marks a fairly sharp division between desert and the cultivated zone with many of the passes through the mountain marked by short linear barriers (conventionally referred to as *clausurae*) as far east as Madina Ragda and with notable concentrations south of Remada and north of Tatahouine. While these were accompanied by watch-towers and manned gates through the barriers, supporting their identification as Roman frontier works, some are adjacent to hillforts that may indicate an earlier period of control of these *passages obligés*.[51]

There are many cairns in the Tunisian half of the Tripolitanian Jabal recorded in the *Atlas préhistorique de le Tunisie*. The cairn cemetery of El Menaguib has been excavated by Paris and Ghaki, who indicated that some (perhaps the majority?) should be placed in the late first/early first millennium BC/AD on the basis of radiocarbon dates and ceramic spot-dates.[52]

Remada and Ras al-Ain

Remada is an oasis near the Tunisian/Libyan border on the main route south towards Ghadamis. A Roman fort (Tillibari) was built here in the second century AD (probably under Hadrian), with major renovation being carried out in the Severan period.[53] The fort was destroyed during French colonial development, but Euzennat and Trousset were able to reconstruct some key details.[54] It is clear that there was also a civil settlement and an oasis here. The closest range of hills, 7 km to the south-east contains a small hillfort with a second 17 km from Remada, both lie close to the modern road through the Jabal. Again, it is reasonable to question whether the sequence was fort then oasis, or more likely that the oasis already existed when the fort was constructed at this location.

A short distance to the south-east, Dehibat is on the site of a presumed Roman road station and Roman ruins have been reported from the vicinity of the modern oasis village.[55] To the north of Remada in the edge of the

[49] Mattingly 1982; 1995, 81, 99–102. [50] Mattingly 1995, 102; Reynolds and Simpson 1967.

[51] Mattingly 1995, 106–15; Trousset 1984b; cf Mattingly *et al.* 2013, 70–80.

[52] Paris and Ghaki 2010.

[53] Desanges *et al.* 2010, 266–67 for the literary and epigraphic evidence.

[54] See Euzennat 1973; Euzennat and Trousset 1975; Mattingly 1995, 90–92; Trousset 1974, 116–18.

[55] Trousset 1974, 123–26.

Great Eastern Erg along the Dahar lay the fortlet of Tisavar (Ksar Rhilane). This well-preserved fortlet, often depicted in splendid isolation among the dunes, was in fact located 3.3 km west of the small oasis of Bou Flidja, though no certain evidence of ancient occupation has been reported there.[56]

There are also several smaller oases in the Tunisian sector of the Jabal to the north of Remada that were marked by Roman military outposts.[57] The fort and associated garrison settlement at Ras al-Ain (Talalati) sits alongside a small oasis *c.*10 km north-east of Foum Tatahouine.[58]

The Nefzaoua Oases

The Nefzaoua oases lie on the south-east side of the Chott Jarid and the south side of the Chott Fjaj (Fig. 5.3).[59] The salt flats are seasonal and so are the direct routes from the north and north-west across them, making the alternative approach to the oases from the east either side of the Tebaga range very important. To the south, the oases are screened by the Grand Erg Oriental, but passage is possible from the direction of Ghadamis along the pre-desert corridor known as the Dahar. In the early twentieth century there were *c.*40 small oases in Nefzaoua, based around numerous artesian wells and groves containing *c.*500,000 palms,[60] though the 200 active springs were many fewer and less productive than those of the Jarid.[61] There were also 57 identifiable foggaras, known locally as *khraig* (sing. *khariga*), although more than half have been destroyed by the modern expansion of the oases.[62] Given the many signs of activity in the Roman period, there is a very strong presumption in this case that there was already pre-Roman occupation and cultivation. The oases were a main centre of the people known as the Nybgenii and is a strong candidate to have been part of the *regio Arzugitana* in late antiquity.[63] The Nybgenii were probably implicated in the Tacfarinan revolt (a major rebellion of Gaetulian peoples in AD 17–23) and subsequently their territory was subject to Roman land survey (delimitation) in AD 29. Their principal centre

56 Desanges *et al.* 2010, 268–69.

57 Donau 1906; Gauckler 1900; Heron de Villefosse 1894; Hilaire 1901; Lecoy de la Marche 1894.

58 Desanges *et al.* 2010, 225–26; Mattingly 1995, 98; Trousset 1974, 98–102.

59 On the Nefzaoua, see Mattingly 1995, 15–16, 30–31, 131–32; Mattingly 2000a; Moreau 1947, 53–111; Trousset 1974, 41–50, 143–48; 2012a, 5382–89.

60 Gendre 1908; Heywood 1926, 330; Moreau 1947, 13–42.

61 Martel 1965, I, 33. See also Baduel and Baduel 1980; Carton 1896/1897; Gauckler 1900/1912; Trousset 1986a; 1986b; 1987a for general considerations of the importance of different hydrological regimes in southern Tunisia.

62 Suter 1962 recorded 57 foggaras from maps and aerial photographs.

63 Ellefi 2015 has many interesting observations, though he does not fully appreciate the scale and significance of the ancient oasis population here.

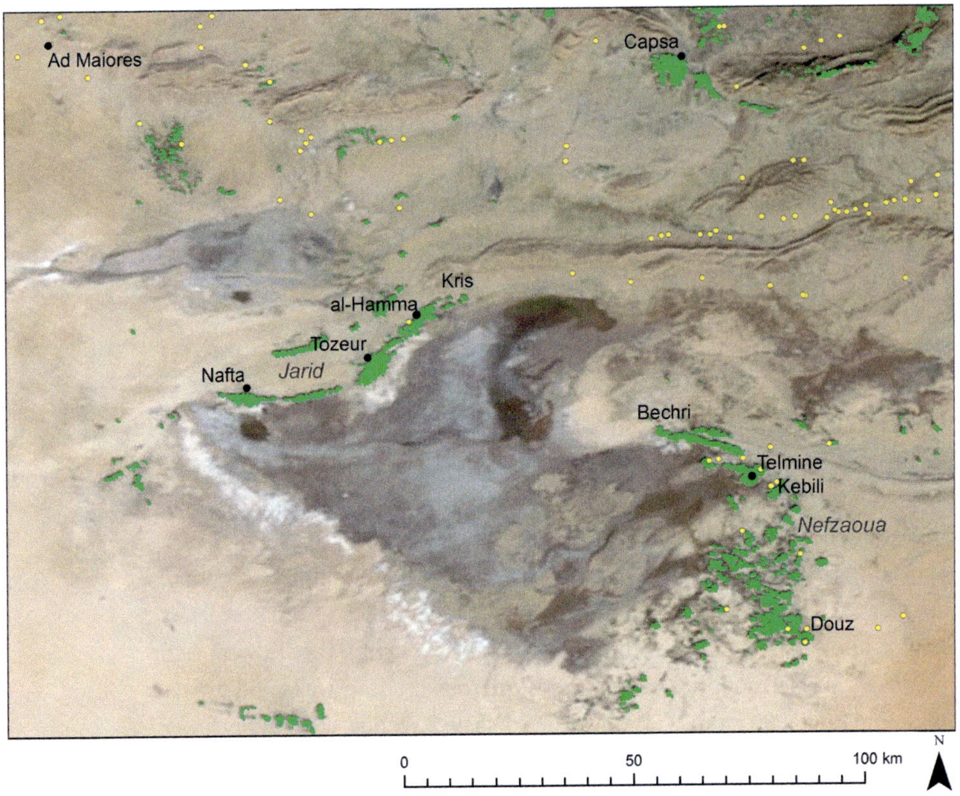

Figure 5.3. Nefzaoua and surrounding oases: main regions and sites discussed in the text.

was recognised as a *civitas* town by Rome in the Flavian period, becoming a *municipium* under Hadrian. This site, known as Turris Tamalleni, has been identified with the oasis village of Telmine.[64]

The Telmine Oasis

Modern Telmine is a small village, sitting on a low hill at the heart of dense palm groves. The hill is today surrounded by a ring road and seems plausibly identifiable as a large artesian spring mound on which the settlement grew up. Although enclosing a small area (7–8 ha), it seems probable that the annular road marks the limits of the original settlement (which perhaps was demarcated by a wall or ditch). Two inscriptions referring to the *municipium*

[64] Trousset 1974, 43–46; cf. Gascou 1972, 134–35. Desanges *et al.* 2010, 274–75 summarise main literary, epigraphic and archaeological discoveries at Telmine and other main Nafzaoua oases. On the Chott Jarid in antiquity, see Peyras and Trousset 1988.

Figure 5.4. Photograph of Roman remains at the main spring of Telmine/Turris Tamelleni.

were found at Telmine and it is generally agreed to have been the site of Turris Tamalleni. The evidence for Roman construction at Telmine has come from the area of the mound, with finds of numerous classical capitals and columns from several ancient buildings, including 20 column shafts, 21 capitals and five bases relating to at least five or six different architectural schema (Fig. 5.4).[65] In the same palm grove as Telmine are two further villages with significant ancient remains. Rabta has produced a column base and two fragmentary Latin inscriptions among other traces of Roman occupation.[66] Manssoura had access to its own spring and there are again ashlar blocks and architectural elements indicating Roman construction. Numerous inscription fragments were found built into a 'native fortification' on a hill known as Torra above Manssourra.[67] There are thus three or four separate locations within the Telmine oasis where we have evidence of Roman stone architecture being employed, but given the physical distance between these locations (>1.5 km) it is implausible that these are all parts of a single very large urban centre (Fig. 5.5). Rather, we seem to witness the monumentalising of typical small oasis villages within different parts of the palm grove, supplied by different springs, in much the same way that

[65] Trousset 1974, 45; Toutain 1903, 289–303. [66] Trousset 1974, 43; Toutain 1903, 297, 301.
[67] Trousset 1974, 42–43; Toutain 1903, 297–303.

Figure 5.5. Areas of Roman materials in the vicinity of Telmine/Turris Tamelleni (imagery: Google, GigitalGlobe).

the modern villages exist alongside each other. On the epigraphic evidence, Telmine appears to equate to the municipal centre, but it is plausible that its population subsumed the inhabitants of these neighbouring villages.

North of Telmine there is a group of ten foggaras along a 3.5 km front that stop some 2 km short of the modern oasis.[68] Their presence implies that the palm groves of the Telmine oasis group originally had a major extension on or close to its northern edge. Presumably this would have had its own small settlement cluster(s) although these are not visible on satellite imagery today.

[68] Today their remnants flow into a system of floodwater barrages, but this seems to be a later adaption of a presumably failing system.

The Western Nefzaoua

To the west of Telmine, a narrow ridge of higher ground projects out into the Chott Jarid, with a line of villages along it and their palm groves and gardens laid out predominantly on the ground sloping away to both the south and north. Two villages in this part of the Nefzaoua have produced traces of Roman buildings or activity. At the far west end of this linear group of oases, the village of Bechri has yielded abundant dressed stone blocks, as well as elements of columns and sculptural fragments. The site marked the south-east end of the trans-Chott route to the Jarid (Kriz in the Jarid was at the north-west end), so the presence here of a significant settlement and monuments is not surprising.[69] Traces of further structures and columns have been noted at Oum Semaa a few kilometres to the east.[70] Between Djezira and Zaoura the oasis gardens were fed by 43 foggara systems which ran north and south between the peaks of the western spur of the Tebaga range.

Kebili

Moving east from Telmine, the modern major town of Kebili contains significant numbers of *spolia* from Roman buildings and fragments of inscriptions. Although the provenance of some of this material is not certain, the fact that early travellers accounts noted that Roman stonework was built into house foundations in the old village of Kebili and in other places on the fringe of the palm grove (Kasr Tebal, Dar al-Kaid) strongly suggests Roman era settlement.[71] Just to the east at Kedouat Johala, a Roman era cremation cemetery was identified.[72]

Douz and Other Outlying Oases of Southern and South-Western Nefzaoua

To the south of Kebili, further oases around Douz have also yielded Roman material: Bechilli (walls), Jamna (column fragments and stone blocks), Douz (coins) and Nouail (columns and mills).[73] Other ruins noted by early travellers are less certainly Roman, but a pre-Islamic origin cannot be excluded: al-Qalaa, Ghidema, Sabria.[74]

The Roman land survey of AD 29 and the Flavian recognition of a native *civitas* centre[75] surely implies that oases were established here prior to the

69 Toutain 1903, 393–94; Trousset 1974, 42.
70 Trousset 1974, 42.
71 Toutain 1903, 394; Trousset 1974, 46–47.
72 Trousset 1974, 47–48.
73 Trousset 1974, 48–50; compare, Toutain 1903, 324, 335.
74 Trousset 1974, 49–50; compare, Toutain 1903, 49–50.
75 Trousset 1978b.

Roman conquest, though it is certainly possible that the number and scale of oasis settlements increased substantially in subsequent centuries. It is also noteworthy that foggara irrigation, as at Ghadamis, al-Jufra and Fazzan, was used in the Nefzaoua along with the canalisation of a number of important artesian springs.[76] The diversification of hydraulic techniques suggests a growth in cultivated area and population at some point.

A number of Libyan inscriptions have been found in Nefzaoua, including at Negga, Henchir Krannfir and Henchir al-Agareb, and these provide strong proxy evidence for pre-Roman origins and complex societies among the Libyan population.[77] There are also some isolated mudbrick structures on the edges of the oases. Morphologically these are not too dissimilar to Roman-era farms and hint that there were rural establishments along with the oasis centres.[78]

The Tripolitanian Coastal Oases

Oases appear to have been a common factor in the establishment of towns and other settlements along the arid coastline of Syrtica and Tripolitania.[79] Even today, driving along the coastal road, one is struck by the recurrence of palm groves alongside many of the famous sites. In western Tripolitania, the oases link to the same aquifers that feed the Jarid and Nefzaoua oases, though with weaker flow rates as one moves eastwards. The springs tend to occur close to the coast in the wadi beds, creating localised oases at sites such as Gabes (see below), Terboubou, Kettana, Mareth, Zarat.[80] In eastern Tripolitania, the ancient towns of Sabratha and Oea (Tripoli) both had significant oases adjacent, this was particularly extensive in the case of the latter's gardens (known as the *menscia*).[81] Roman activity is attested at many of these locations and references to two separate Roman road stations called 'ad Palmam' on the Tripolitanian coastal road implies the existence of several more.[82] The pre-Roman origins of oasis agriculture at many of these sites seems assured by the prime example of Tacapae.

[76] Capot Rey 1953, 327. [77] Chabot 1940; Trousset 1974, 42, 73, 79. [78] Guery 1986.

[79] See Mattingly 1995, 6, 12–13; Mattingly 2000a; 2000b (Syrtica). On oasis cultivation in medieval and more recent times, see Beechey and Beechey 1828, 33–112; Brett 1976; de Mathuisieulx 1912, 196–200; Franchi 1912.

[80] Martel 1965, I, 30–33.

[81] Mattingly 1995, 122; on the *menscia*, see Laing in Bovill 1964; Tully 1817, 51–54.

[82] Mattingly 1995, 62–64; *Tabula Peutingeriana* VII.4, VIII.1.

Tacapae

The Tunisian harbour city of Gabes (ancient Tacapae or Tacape) controlled a *passage obligé* along the coastal plain. The oasis of Gabes is fed by a series of springs located 10 km inland in the Wadi Gabes, creating a long linear palm grove containing 200,000 palms and running *c.*6 km long and 1–2 km broad. There is no suggestion in the sources that the creation of Tacapae was due to Roman initiative, rather Pliny marvelled at the extraordinary productivity of the alien oasis agriculture, where palms, fruit trees and cereals/legumes formed several distinct layers of cultivation.[83] The exact location of the ancient town here is not clearcut, somewhat surprising for a town that achieved *colonia* status by the early third century, but not that dissimilar in fact to some of the other oases towns in Roman Africa.[84] The early modern oasis at Gabes comprised a series of ten villages spread across the oasis, of which the two largest (Menzel and Jara) lay on the south bank of the wadi close to the sea and the presumed ancient harbour. The concentration of ancient stonework in Menzel and Jara seem to ensure early origins, as also at two other sites (Chenini and the hill of Boulbaba).[85] The seemingly multiple traces of settlement within the oasis again does not accord with our expectation of a Roman *municipium* or *colonia*, but is a recurrent feature of these oasis centres.

Other South Tunisian Oases

Having described the important oasis cluster of the Nefzaoua and the coastal site of Tacapae above, in this section we discuss the other oasis clusters of southern Tunisia.

From Tacapae to Capsa

Aquae Tacapitanae

Inland from Tacapae there was a Roman spa site on a hot spring at al-Hamma (Aquae Tacapitanae) that again fed an important oasis cluster.[86] The Roman road of AD 14 was driven straight from Tacapae to Aquae Tacapitanae, strongly suggesting that the oasis already existed at this date.[87] In the early twentieth century there were two oasis villages in the al-

[83] Pliny, *Natural History* 18.188; Trousset 1986a, 173–76; 1987a.
[84] Desanges *et al.* 2010, 224 for the sources and epigraphic data.
[85] Trousset 1986a, 167–68; cf Babelon *et al.* 1893/1913, feuille 147; Hilaire 1900; Monlezun 1885.
[86] Heywood 1926, 330; Trousset 1974, 17–18. [87] Donau 1907.

Hamma (al-Qasr and Debdaba) and the measured distance from Tacapae confirms that the remains of a Roman bath complex exploiting the thermal spring at al-Qasr correspond with Aquae Tacapitanae. There are also other traces of Roman period remains adjacent to a secondary oasis to the west.

Capsa

Gafsa (ancient Capsa) depends on a spring at a prominent gap in the mountain chain that forms the southern border of the Tunisian tell in a region of generally scarce water resources. From this gap, two major desert roads run respectively south-west to the Jarid oases and south-east to the Nefzaoua. In more recent times Gafsa has been described as the 'key to the Jarid'.[88] The oasis fans out to the south of the town, mainly on the west side of a prominent wadi channel. There is a subsidiary oasis on the east side of the wadi, corresponding to two villages (al-Ksar and Lalla), suggesting the possibility of a secondary early oasis settlement also, though no specific traces have been reported.[89] Capsa corresponds with the centre of the modern town on the west side of the wadi, where Roman baths are known, and architectural fragments of Roman date were visible in the mosques and private houses in the early twentieth century.[90] In Roman times the location was a low mound in the centre of the gap in the mountain range. The clearest evidence for the antiquity of the oasis is the testimony of Sallust and his account of the surprise attack on the town by Marius in 107 BC.[91] The town was described by Sallust as walled at this date, but by making a forced march at night Marius arrived undetected and successfully stormed the settlement when the gates were opened at daybreak to allow the population to access their gardens. Although according to Sallust, the population was killed or enslaved and the town burnt, the revival of such an important oasis was probably not long delayed. The town remained under Numidian control until 46 BC, but was almost certainly assigned a garrison in the early first century AD as it was a key location on the AD 14 road from Tacapae to the main base of the *legio III Augusta* at Ammaedara (Haidra). The site became a *municipium* and later an

[88] Borderaux 1907, 177.

[89] Lahbib 2010 links the presence of springs here to a fault that runs from Lalla westwards, which suggests that the origin of the Lalla oasis, fed by a famous spring, ought to also be ancient, see Douglas 1912, 42–43.

[90] Borderaux 1907, 57–58; Douglas 1912, 12 noted the thousands of Roman blocks built into later walls and that the two main springs rose in the Kasbah and in the Roman baths, known locally as the *termid*; Heywood 1926, 324; Mrabet 2004, 20–24; Saumagne 1962, 519–23.

[91] Sallust, *Bellum Jugurthinum* 89–91. See Berthier 1981, 71; Borderaux 1907, 181–82.

honorary colony under Rome. At 17 km to the east of Gafsa there is a line of foggaras that underlies the modern villages of Lortess and El Guettar – 12 are still visible and some of them appear to be of substantial size.

Minor Oases between Capsa and Nafzaoua (Seftimi and Limagues)

Seftimi and Limagues are very small oases on the northern flank of the Jabal Tabaga, close to the southern shore of the Chott Fajaj at the end of crossing points of the Chott. Both these oases have yielded traces of Roman activity.[92]

The Jarid

Located *c.*60–100 km south-west of Gafsa, the oases of the Jarid were known in the Islamic era as Kastiliya, after their fortified character, perhaps ultimately derived from the Latin term *castella*.[93] There is certainly ample evidence to attest pre-Islamic origins for all four of the main oasis clusters in the Jarid (al-Wadian, al-Hamma, Tozeur and Nafta), situated along a narrow and low-lying isthmus between two great chotts (Jarid and Rharsa).[94] The term 'Jarid' means 'branch of the palm' or region of the palm.[95] The palms of the Jarid have a high reputation in Tunisia and there are numerous artesian springs (some thermal) that feed the complex irrigation regime, which is evidently of considerable antiquity.[96] Both Tozeur and Nafta, the two biggest oases in the early twentieth century, possessed about 200,000 palms.[97] Many local customs and festivals also evoke pre-Islamic origins, as is the case in the 'Festival of Spring'.[98]

Roman activity in the Jarid is attested from the Flavian period, with a boundary stone of the governor Javolenus Priscus (AD 83) indicating the north-eastern limits of the lands of the *civitas Thigensium*.[99] In the reign of Nerva, a fort (*castellum Thigensium*) was built at Gouifla on the Capsa-Thiges road close to the northern entry point to the oasis proper.[100]

The literary and epigraphic evidence strongly suggests that three of the oasis settlements here were eventually accorded full urban status (Thiges,

92 Trousset 1974, 50. 93 *Encyclopedia Islam*, sv Kastiliya; Trousset 1986a. Cf. Euzennat 1972.
94 Heywood 1926, 325–26. 95 Guerin 1862, 250.
96 Douglas 1912, 83; Gendre 1908; Martel 1965, I, 30–33; Trousset 1986a; 1986b; 1987a; Vuillot 1893, 89–113. An interesting feature of the system of water division at Tozeur is that one of the main dividers of an important branch was known as 'Garahman', Trousset 1986a, 183, figure 8.
97 Heywood 1926, 326. 98 Payre 1942a; 1942b; Trousset 1995.
99 Trousset 1978a, 28; *CIL* 8.23165.
100 *CIL* 8.23166; Euzennat 1971; Trousset 1978a, 28–29, for the localisation of the inscription.

Thusuros and Nepte). Thiges was named on an inscription as a *civitas*.[101] The names of Thiges, Thusuros and Nepte also featured in the ancient itineraries.[102] Bishops of Thusuros and Nepta were included in the episcopal list for Byzacena.[103]

Kriz and the al-Wadian oasis

Thiges is now generally equated with the oasis of al-Wadian and in particular with the vicinity of Kriz, where there are extensive ancient ruins at al-Guebba and an inscription of Silvanus Mercury on a neighbouring hill, close to the north-western terminus of an important seasonal crossing route of the Chott that provided a link between the Jarid and the Nefzaoua.[104] Toussaint described extensive traces of ancient settlement and noted much ancient pottery at al-Guebba.[105] There was also a hot spring at Kriz and the villages of Cededa and Oulad Majed within the Kriz oasis were also locations with signs of ancient activity.[106]

Al-Hamma

On the northern flank of the Kriz oasis group, al-Hamma of the Jarid has numerous traces of ancient activity including a pool and irrigation channel.[107]

Tozeur

Thusuros is the ancient name for Tozeur and early travellers noted extensive reuse of ancient stonework in more recent houses.[108] Dressed stone of Roman date was visible in the foundations of many houses in the south-west quarter of Tozeur in the early twentieth century.[109] In addition, reconstruction of the main mosque in a southern suburb at Blad al-Hadar, near

101 *CIL* 8.23165; Trousset 1990. 102 *Tabula Peutingeriana* V.4–5.

103 Lancel 1972/1991, I, 140; Lepelley 1979 ; 1981. 104 Trousset 1982a.

105 Toussaint 1907, 310.

106 Duveyrier 1915, 53; Guérin 1862, 252–54; Toussaint 1907, 310; Trousset 1978a, 29–31; 1986a, 170–72. See also Desanges *et al.* 2010, 246, for a summary of literary and epigraphic evidence.

107 Toussaint 1907, 309; Vuillot 1893, 89–95.

108 Duveyrier 1915, 86 (stones and columns in gardens round Tozeur); Guérin 1862, 258; Toussaint 1907, 310 (noted particular concentration of ancient materials in the south-west quarter of the town). See also Vuillot 1893, 95–106.

109 Douglas 1912, 89 reports seeing Roman stonework, fragments of cipollino columns reused as door sills and a gold coin of Gordian.

the centre of the oasis, revealed Roman period remains. This includes a substantial foundation in ashlar blocks reused as the foundation of the mudbrick minaret.[110] There are additional traces of Roman ruins at Bir Kastilia and at Draa al-Barhla (Henchir Helbla) on the north-east side of the oasis.[111]

Nafta

Ancient Nepte or Agarsel Nepte is equated with the oasis town of Nafta, where early travellers again noted ancient stonework and capitals reused, though in lesser quantity than at Tozeur.[112] There are traces of Roman columns and other stonework at Garat bel-Adda, midway between Nafta and Tozeur.[113] The oasis of Nafta centres on a north-south ravine, where numerous artesian springs well up.[114] The abundance and power of the springs of Nafta and Tozeur made these ideal locations for precocious oasis development.

Oases along the Roman Frontier in Eastern Algeria

The next group of oases straddles the modern Tunisian-Algerian border, but are best treated as a group.

Oases of the Nemencha

Chebika and Tamerza

To the west of the Jarid oases, the Chott al-Rharsa deflects the Roman frontier road towards the north-west, where it runs along the southern flank of an east-west range, with relatively few south-north access routes. Several small oases associated with Roman ruins or placenames exist along this Nemencha range, often at points where seasonal wadis issue from the mountain front, most notably at (or near) Chebika (Speculum), Tamerza (ad Turres) and Mides along the major route north towards Tebessa.[115]

[110] Mrabet 2004, 33–34, photo of Bled el-Hachem minaret; Trousset 1995.
[111] Desanges *et al.* 2010, 275; Toussaint 1907, 310; Trousset 1978a, 29; 1986a, 184.
[112] Desanges *et al.* 2010, 187; Toussaint 1907, 310. [113] Toussaint 1907, 310.
[114] Douglas 1912, 94 provides a vivid description; Heywood 1926, 326.
[115] Desanges *et al.* 2010, 215; Trousset 1978a, 26–28; 1980b.

Negrine

At *c.*45 km west of Chebika across the Algerian border, the Roman fort at Besseriani (Nigrenses Maiores)[116] lies 5 km south of the oasis of Negrine, which is tucked back into the mountain valley.[117] Immediately to the west of the fort are extensive traces of ancient irrigation systems, while a substantial palm grove still exists in the valley in which Negrine is located.[118] The fort was surrounded by a large civil settlement of *c.*20 ha, eventually walled and promoted at some point to *municipium* status. That is, this was a properly constituted Roman town, notwithstanding the fact that it retained a garrison post at its centre until late Roman times.[119] However, ancient activity here was not limited to the immediate vicinity of the fort. The name Nigrenses Maiores implies a connection with a people called the Nigrenses and the modern settlement of Negrine and an older abandoned settlement called Negrine el-Khadim (*c.*3 km north-west of Negrine) clearly evoke the same name. At both of these locations significant evidence has been found of pre-Islamic activity. At the abandoned mudbrick site of Negrine al-Khadim, both Roman and Islamic era pottery has been noted and excavations in 1960 uncovered a Roman mosaic.[120] There are also a number of suggestive traces from around the village of Negrine itself, including a fortified promontory site (undated), a reported find of coins and another of a Byzantine ostracon mentioning olive oil production.[121]

Other Sites South of the Aures Mountains

There were further Roman military stations to the west of Nigrenses Maiores, occupying similar topographic positions at the outlet of mountain passes, where oases now exist. Mdlia, noted by Baradez, sits within an extensive area of abandoned fields, settlements and *qsur* reminiscent of the Garamantian landscapes of Fazzan.[122] Ad Medias is generally identified

116 The site was recorded as Ad Maiores in the *Tabula Peutingeriana*, but the name has recently been plausibly expanded and restored as Nigrenses Maiores, see Laporte and Dupuis 2009, 57–58. The important thing to note is that this name indicates that the settlement combined a fort and a chief settlement of an indigenous people, the Nigrenses.

117 See now Laporte and Dupuis 2009, for a detailed recapitulation of all the evidence from the group of sites here. Also Desanges *et al.* 2010, 96.

118 Birebent 1962, 118, 121 for the ancient irrigation systems; Gueneau 1907 for an early report.

119 Laporte and Dupuis 2009, 58–62, 68–74; Mattingly 1986.

120 Laporte and Dupuis 2009, 74–75.

121 Laporte and Dupuis 2009, 75, 90–91; cf. Fentress 1979, 97; Ragot 1874, 298.

122 Baradez 1949a, 147–48; see also Baradez 1957; Birebent 1962 on the field systems and irrigation works.

with an undated fortified site 'en berbere' at Henchir Taddert.[123] Roman Badias, possibly to be identified with a rectangular tell-like mound on the edge of the modern settlement of Bades, also sat on an irrigated fan just south of the Aures. The irrigation here seems to have in part exploited seasonal runoff from the mountain valley. There are epigraphic and written records indicating that this was a Roman frontier post, but modern buildings cover the site.[124]

Wadi Jedi and the Ziban

The region to the south-west of the Aures mountains comprises another concentrated area of oases in close connection with the Roman frontier (Fig. 5.6).[125] The pre-Roman origins of some at least

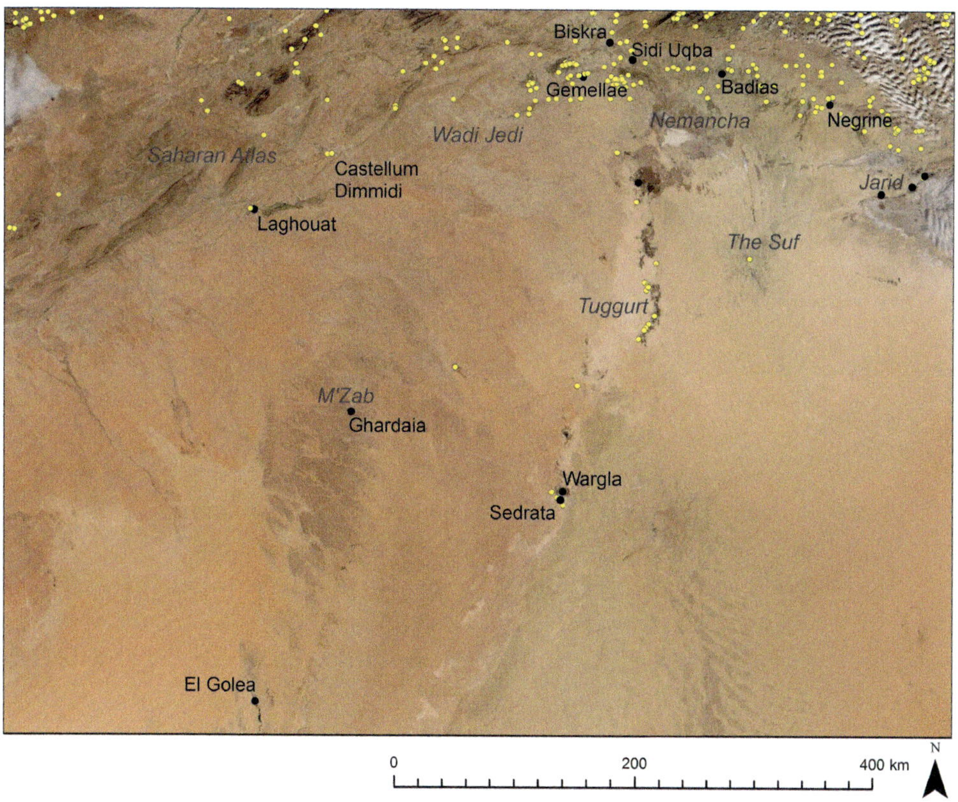

Figure 5.6. Eastern Algeria, main regions and sites discussed in the text.

[123] Desanges *et al.* 2010, 96–97. [124] Fentress 1979, 98; Ragot 1874, 294.

[125] Meouak 2018, for a wide-ranging review of the Medieval sources, the potential pre-Islamic origins and the environmental setting of the Ziban.

of these oases can be argued by a plausible interpretation of Pliny's account of the African campaign of Cornelius Balbus in 20 BC. Among the list of sites that Pliny states were paraded on placards at the triumphal procession in Rome relating to the Garamantian campaign, there was a group of names that seem to relate to a different theatre of war (*Tabudium oppidum, Milgis Gemella oppidum, Thuben oppidum, Viscera*).[126] These names appear remarkably similar to the later Roman placenames from the Algerian frontier/Ziban oasis zone (Thabudeos, Gemellae, Tubnae and Vescera).

Sidi Uqba

Thabudeos has for long been identified with the oasis of Sidi Uqba, *c.*15 km south-east of Biskra, where Uqba bin Nafi was buried after his death in battle in AD 683. Two possible Roman fortifications have been recognised *c.*6 km north of the modern settlement of Sidi Uqba, a trapezoidal late Roman enceinte with projecting towers and a rectangular tell-like mound that probably represents successive villages built up over a second-century Roman fort platform.[127] Roman pottery was also noted at the site in 1980.[128] In the irrigated fan around the site are numerous remains of *qsur* and field systems.

Biskra

Biskra is the capital of the Ziban district and the largest of the oases (150,000 palms in 1926) stretching for 5 km along the Wadi Biskra. Traces of ancient Vescera have been obliterated in modern times as the town has grown extensively. However, traces of a fort on the west bank and a civil settlement on the east bank of the Wadi Biskra are indicated in nineteenth-century reports.[129] The oasis developed on both sides of the Wadi Biskra, fed by canals carrying water from two groups of springs located a short distance north, with the larger palm groves on the west bank including several old villages and smaller palmeries on the east bank at Lahlia and Filiach.[130] The Ziban (the name means the 'area of villages') is in

[126] Pliny, *Natural History* 5.37; Desanges 1980, 400–10.

[127] Baradez 1949a, 279–87; Benseddik 2018; Fentress 1979, 88.

[128] The site was visited along with others in the Wadi Jedi, Ziban and Ouled Nail districts by the lead author with Barri Jones, Charles Daniels and Rob Burns in December 1980.

[129] Fentress 1979, 88; Meouak 2018, 216–21; Ragot 1874, 278.

[130] Vuillot 1893, map as frontispiece; Daumas 1845, 103–5 described Biskra as less a town, more a reunion of seven villages in the palm groves. He also confirms the presence of Roman structures at Filiach.

itself highly suggestive of the oasis character of most of the main settlements. The oases benefit both from springs and from the seasonal floodwaters carried down from the Zab and Ouled Nail mountains into the Wadi Jedi and its tributaries.

Wadi Jedi Area

Exploring the Ziban region south-west of Biskra, Hamy reported a number of sites with a Roman appearance (including ashlar stone, columns etc.), as well as circular drum cairns and megalith burials of Protohistoric tradition.[131] A more detailed study of the Protohistoric burials of this region was carried out by Roffo, confirming a Roman date, but profoundly Saharan burial traditions.[132] Daumas reported Roman remains in at least 14 oasis villages of the Ziban.[133]

The Roman fort of Gemellae and the nearby oasis of Mlili provide more conclusive evidence of impressive Roman era activity (Fig. 5.7). The fort is located on the south side of the Wadi Jedi, while the oasis of Mlili lies over 1 km away on the north bank and seems to divide into two main zones (which may account for the 'twin name' = Gemellae). Mlili presumably is derived from the original Libyan name for the pre-Roman oasis, which was rendered as Milgis by Pliny. As at Nigrenses Maiores, the fort is surrounded by a substantial walled garrison settlement, which gained *municipium* status.[134] The greatest density of Roman elements seen by Hamy were around the Roman forts of Gemellae and Doucen, but he also noted the remains of a stone building in Mlili oasis itself, reused as the foundations of a modern house.[135]

Doucen is another oasis location with evidence for a sequence of Roman forts identified by Baradez, which indicate an early origin of the oasis prior to its nineteenth-century refoundation.[136] Satellite remote-sensing has identified another probable fort, 17 km to the south-east of Doucen on the north bank of the Wadi Jedi. Also on the north bank, a major fortified settlement, with several additional rectangular fortified compounds, was located a few kilometres to the south-west towards Ouled Jellal.[137] It is highly likely that there were further early settlements associated with the

131 Hamy 1896. 132 Roffo 1938. 133 Daumas 1845, 105, 148.

134 On the fort, see Baradez 1948; 1949a; 1949b; 1966a; 1966b; 1967; Fentress 1979; Trousset 1977.

135 Hamy 1896.

136 Capot-Rey 1953, 237. On the Roman forts, see Baradez 1949a, 116, 123; Fentress 1979, 85.

137 The site is difficult to locate today and is probably destroyed. Based on a photo reprinted in Baradez 1949a, 124, the site lay adjacent to a stretch of the wadi that supported substantial oasis gardens and the morphology suggests pre-Islamic origins.

Figure 5.7. The headquarters building in the centre of the fort and vicus of Gemellae.

dense oasis zone that stretches along this part of the Wadi Jedi, encompassing Ouled Jellal and Sidi Khaled, *c.*7 km to its west.

Another intriguing aspect of the Roman frontier disposition in the Wadi Jedi area is that a linear barrier (*fossatum*) was constructed to the south of the wadi, running east-west for *c.*50 km and equipped with watch towers, gates and supporting small outposts and fortlets.[138] The positioning of the fort of Gemellae south of the wadi placed it in a good position to co-ordinate this frontier sector. But what was the purpose of this complex arrangement? The French colonial view interpreted it as an attempt by the Roman authorities to protect new agricultural investments to the north from pastoral movements and nomadic attacks from the south. An alternative proposition is that it created a line of Roman control between the densely populated oasis settlements of the Zab and Ziban, and other oases and potential population centres further to the south (see below, Southern Algerian Oases Beyond the Frontier).

Hodna and the Saharan Atlas

From Viscera, the Roman frontier continued as a line of forts and outposts running north towards the Chott al-Hodna. Along part of this sector there

[138] Baradez 1949a; 1967; Daniels 1987; Mattingly *et al.* 2013. For some insightful discussions of the nature of the African frontier, see Trousset 1980a; 1984a; 1984b.

was another sector of linear barrier (the Mesarfelta *fossatum* sector) and there were a number of forts and minor military outposts at the small oases that controlled the main western passes through the Aures mountains to the north-east, such as Ad Calceum Herculis and Burgus Speculatorum (al-Kantara).[139] The *fossatum* appears to have terminated close to the Chott al-Hodna at the substantial fortified town of Tubna (Tobna), where the Roman fort is overlain by Byzantine and Islamic era fortifications.[140] The plain is irrigated by seasonal wadis and its development may be considered as a quasi-oasis. Slightly to the north-east lay the site of Zarai, where a Roman fort was placed on a route leading towards Cirta and where a famous customs edict has been found.[141]

The Saharan Atlas forms an imposing salient to the south-west of the Chott al-Hodna. It is made up of several main blocks (the Zab, the Ouled Nail and the Jabal Amour). The heart of the Saharan Atlas comprises linear ranges aligned south-west to north-east, rising to over 1,500 m in places, with high plateau plain lands in between. The major wadis issuing from the mountains flow into the areas of Chotts to the north-east (Hodna) and the south-east (Melrhir). At the fringes of the mountains there are a number of substantial oases in these wadis, notably Bou Saada in the north-east and the line of sites along the Wadi Jedi from Laghouat to Gemellae, including Messaad (site of the Roman fort of Castellum Dimmidi),[142] Sidi Khaled, Ouled Jellal. No certain traces of Roman settlement have been found at Laghouat, but this oasis sits at a key junction point between Saharan routes that run east-west (connecting the Biskra area with southern Morocco) and north-south via Ghardaia.[143] It would be surprising in light of the other regional oasis developments if this was not also a precocious development. The Roman frontier disposition in the Saharan Atlas has long been remarked on as unusual. The frontier of the province of Mauretanian Caesarensis lies well to the north and the Numidian frontier well to the east, running from Biskra up to Zarai on the east side of the Chott al-Hodna. However, from the second century onwards it is clear that there

[139] Baradez 1949a, 229–42. Though Baradez was sceptical that the fort of Ad Calceum Herculis was to be sought in the oasis of al-Kantara itself, he does note the substantial collection of Roman dressed stone from the three villages of the al-Kantara oasis (331–32). Material from al-Kantara includes inscriptions, architectural elements, altars, sculpted stone, tombstones, etc. and the largest concentration was from a spot on the right bank of the wadi just south of the oasis.

[140] Baradez 1949a, 293; Fentress 1979, 92.

[141] For the Zarai tariff, see France 2014; Guédon 2014; Trousset 2003.

[142] Fentress 1979, 87–88; Picard 1944. See also the sites identified by Morizot 1999.

[143] Heywood 1926, 172–74. There is a tradition of textile working in the oasis, based on wool production in the Saharan Atlas.

was a substantial investment made in garrisoning the Saharan Atlas, with many of these forts placed at springs at the key access/egress points: Ausum (Sadouri), al-Ghara, Ain Rich.[144]

Southern Algerian Oases Beyond the Frontier

The oases in this section (Mzab, Tuggurt, Wargla, Suf) have not yet produced direct evidence of Protohistoric activity and clearly lay well outside the Roman frontier. The lack of recognisable Roman structures is not surprising if we accept that the first French investigators associated Rome with cut-stone buildings.[145] However, a number of finds of Roman artefacts have been reported from the general area of the Mzab, Tuggurt and Wargla oases by Mauny and Salama, including coins and Roman pottery.[146] A number of authors have picked up on the possibility that these oases could be the location from where the Pharusii (mentioned by Strabo) set off across the desert on horseback (with waterskins slung below their mounts) passing the area of the 'lakes' (chotts?) to reach the high plains around Cirta.[147] The case for pre-Islamic origins is suggestive, if unproven at present. Given the demonstrable extent of oasis development in the Jarid, Wadi Jedi and Ziban zones along the Roman frontier to the north of them it is a moot point whether these rare locations of springs and a high water table were entirely neglected until the Islamic era. These oases should be a priority for future investigation.

Tuggurt and the Wadi Rhir

The Tuggurt oasis is the major centre in a line of *c.*25 oases that follow the north-south line of the Wadi Rhir, demarcating the western edge of the Great Eastern Erg.[148] In the early colonial period it was seen as the start of the pestilential desert, because of the prevalence of malaria there.[149] This is an area

[144] Fentress 1979, 114; Faure and Leveau 2015; Laporte 2004. [145] Berbrugger 1862, 31.

[146] Mauny 1956; 1978; Salama 1981, 514–15, sites 7–9 (Ghourd el-Oucif, Hassi el-Hadjar and Fort Miribel).

[147] Strabo, *Geography* 17.3.7; Romey 1992, 20; Rouvillois-Brigol 1975, 9–10.

[148] For the hydrology see Berbrugger 1862; Durand and Guyot 1955; Savornin 1947; 1950. For summary descriptions of oases, see Berbugger 1862, 36–43; Heywood 1926, 254–57; Nesson in Nesson *et al.* 1973.

[149] Berbrugger 1862, 30–31; compare, de Villiers and Hirtle 2002, 115–16 for the observation that at many of the south Algerian oases the additional artesian wells dug by the French increased the pools of surface water for mosquitoes to breed in, greatly increasing the prevalence of malaria.

of artesian hydrology and the first springs must have come to the surface naturally – almost certainly still feeding the 16 small lakes/pools (*bahar*) that lie at the centre of some of the palmeries. These seem to have been the focal points around which the local people have tried to dig further artesian wells to augment the supply.[150] Some unusual circular or radiating palmeries can be recognised on air-photographs and satellite imagery and these seem to represent the traditional layout of gardens around the major or primary springs.[151] The artesian water lies at considerable depth (average 45 m), sometimes beneath clay, which has a tendency to subside after a few years, and sometimes beneath many metres of impermeable rock. A special class of well diggers existed among these oasis communities in more recent times, capable of undertaking the difficult and dangerous work.[152] Prior to the French colonial administration making substantial additions to the number of artesian wells with modern drilling equipment, the oases were much smaller.[153] Nevertheless, there were still 340,000 palms prior to the establishment of the new wells. Little is known about the archaeology of any of the oases here and the history has been somewhat romanticised.[154]

Tuggurt is *c.*200 km south of Biskra, but the northernmost outposts of this oasis chain are only about 50 km from Biskra and 20–30 km south of the *fossatum*. Uqba ibn Nafi evidently initiated a campaign against the people of the Wadi Rhir, but, having reached the hills of ad-Dour that mark the northern limits of the valley, he turned back instead.[155] If there was well-established oasis agriculture to the north and naturally occurring artesian springs in the Wadi Rhir, it seems implausible that some oasis development was not underway here at an early date.

Between Tuggurt and Sidi Amrane, a small number of settlements are visible along a now unused part of the wadi. At least one of these has a square *qasr* similar to those found further north in the Roman period. To the immediate north-west of Tuggurt are a cluster of large abandoned settlements and oasis gardens, though these seem likely to be Medieval in date. The circumstantial

150 Berbrugger 1862, 20–27 lists the following bahar springs: ʻel-Salehin and Merzioui [Merdjadja], Tebaiche, el-Ourir, Nsir'a, Bakhbakha, Oriana [x 2], Djama, Ain Zerga [Tineguidin], Sidi Amran, Sidi Yahya, Orlan and el-Arais [Tamerna-Djedida], Tattouin [x 2].

151 Nesson 1965, 92–104.

152 Berbrugger 1862, 44–83, for a detailed account of the digging of a traditional artesian well. Due to the tendency for intervening perched water tables to flood the shafts, the task of releasing the artesian layer of pressurised water involves the diggers working under water for prolonged periods, with exceptional danger at the moment of breaking through into the artesian layer.

153 For early accounts of the Tuggurt oasis villages, see Daumas 1845, 121–42; Hurabeille 1899.

154 Fontaine 1952. Féraud 2012, 8–125 is a more useful if disjointed compendium of information on the history of the oases.

155 Berbrugger 1862, 28–31.

case for Roman era activity in this oasis group is particularly strong. If oasis cultivation was well established at Biskra and other oases of the Ziban in the pre-Roman era it would be surprising if the similar potential of the artesian springs of the Wadi Rhir and Tuggurt area had not also been developed. Likewise, the elaborate *fossatum* control line makes much more sense if it was designed to regulate contact with both pastoral groups and substantial oasis communities south of the Roman frontier.

The Suf

To the north-east of Tuggurt in the direction of the Jarid are the challenging dunes of the Great Eastern Erg. However, midway along this difficult route lies the extraordinary group of oases known as the Suf, with al-Wad the largest among them.[156] Unlike most of the sand seas, which support only limited oasis development at their heart, due to a very high water table, the Suf communities have established gardens and micro-catchments in the interdune basins (supporting 290,000 palms). Textile production has been a feature of these oases in the past.[157] The domed architecture and overall character of these villages and the associated cultivation practices is very distinctive and seemingly entirely Islamic in character. However, it is worth bearing in mind that if the Tuggurt area did see some pre-Islamic development, this could also be a possibility for the Suf, given its geographical position between other oases. There have been a number of Roman coin finds reported in the Great Eastern Erg, including some from the Suf itself.[158] Routes lead out of the sands to the Jarid *c.*100 km to the north-east, towards Negrine *c.*130 km to the north, towards Biskra *c.*230 km to the north-west and to Tuggurt at 95 km to the south-west.

Wargla

Wargla is a separate cluster of oases *c.*160 km south-west of Tuggurt.[159] The oasis has long had a reputation as being among the earliest of Algerian

[156] Battailon 1955, especially 27–32 for history and 33–46 for recorded settlements, though these are evidently of Medieval or early modern date. See also Daumas 1845, 189–94, for names of villages and modern population groups; Féraud 2012, 126–44.

[157] Heywood 1926, 258–60.

[158] Féraud 2012, 369; Mauny 1956, 252 specifies a cache of 60 silver coins from *c.*40 km south-west of al-Wad; Salama 1981, 514–15.

[159] See Rouvillois-Brigol 1975; also her section in Nesson *et al.* 1973; Lethielleux 1983; Romey 1992. The detailed study of the most famous Medieval site, Sedrata, also contains much information on the wider zone of Wargla, Aillet *et al.* 2017.

oases.[160] Ibn Khaldun implied its first occupation dated back to the ninth century and it was certainly an early centre of Ibadite resistance in the tenth century AD. There are also oral traditions that it was involved in the seventh-century resistance to Uqba ibn Nafi,[161] and that it had associations with Jewish Berbers. Numerous 'Berber ruins' are reported, but are mostly undated.[162] In fact numerous Roman coin finds have been reported from the Wargla area,[163] as well as Carthaginian gold coins from Hassi al-Hajira between Wargla and al-Golea in 1920,[164] suggesting that some activity could date considerably earlier than the Islamic tradition. The palm groves (500,000 palms in the early twentieth century) are sustained by the subterranean waters of the Wadi Mya and *c.*200 artesian wells/springs.[165] The remains of a small number of foggaras are also to be found on the west side of the oasis. From Wargla routes run south across hostile terrain towards the Ahaggar and Tamanrasset (1,500 km) and west to the Mzab.[166]

Sedrata

Largely buried below the dunes immediately to the south of Wargla, the abandoned early Islamic town (tenth century) of Sedrata is exceptionally large for an oasis settlement (*c.*30 ha, Fig. 5.8). There are also visible traces of an extensive area of gardens.[167] There is no evidence of pre-Islamic origins of settlement of the Ibadite town, though some Protohistric activity in the vicinity is possible.[168] Beyond them there are ruins of a number of rectangular buildings of unknown date on top of the isolated flat-topped

[160] Daumas 1845, 72–79; Lethielleux 1983, 5.20; Rouvillois-Brigol 1975, 9–12.

[161] Rouvillois-Brigol 1975, 12.

[162] Bensaad 2013; Tarry 1884 (though most of the published site plans seem to have Islamic elements like mosques). On the other hand, Rouvillois-Brigol 1975, 65 notes the lack of certainty over dating: 'le problème de la foundation des ksar et donc leur age reste toujours posé'. As we have seen in Chapter 2, these types of fortified sites are well attested in the Garamantian kingdom and Wargla is about the same distance from Gabes as Ghadamis. Romey 1992, 22–23 concludes that pre-Islamic origins for the Wargla group are probable.

[163] Rouvillois-Brigol 1975, 11, following Féraud 2012, 369, mentions 'nombreuses monnaies romaines' found in the region south of the Roman frontier and bought by French officers, including 12 late Roman coins of Constantine and Maximian. There must have been at least 15 coins in total as Féraud says he bought 12 and other officers in the 1871 military column with him also bought some. This contradicts Mauny's assertion (1956, 251) that Roman coins have never been found in Wargla, al-Golea etc.

[164] Lethielleux 1983, 9. [165] Féraud 2012, 358–67. [166] Heywood 1926, 257–58.

[167] Van Berchem 1953a; 1953b. See now Aillet *et al.* 2017, for a detailed volume on the site and its environs (fig. 1b between pages 4 and 5 is the best plan of the urban site/palace complex and the related gardens).

[168] Aillet *et al.* 2017, 39–41, review the evidence for the 'black hole' of the pre-Islamic era, but are ultimately pessimistic that earlier oasis foundation can be corroborated at present.

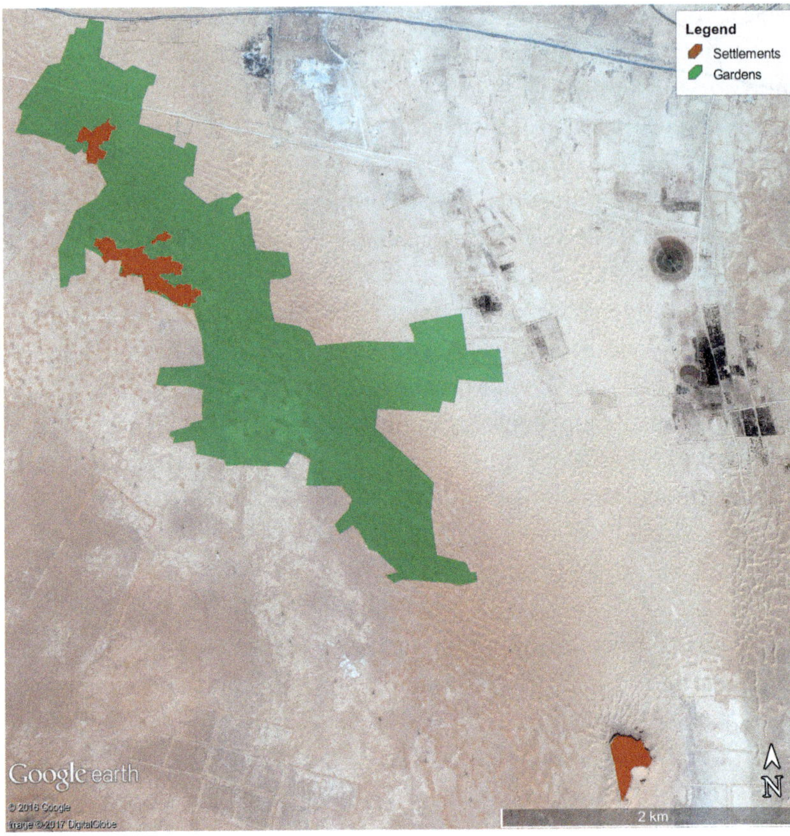

Figure 5.8. Satellite image of Sedrata (imagery: Google, DigitalGlobe).

hillfort of Gara Krima (5.2 ha), with an 80 m+ deep well dug through solid rock to reach the water table.[169] The visible elements at Gara Krima may be Medieval and early modern, but earlier origins of the site seem probable.

Ghardaia and the Mzab

Ghardaia is the main centre of the Mzab,[170] a small cluster of unusual oases, located to the west of the main north-south depression of the Wadi Righ and Wargla oases. These are located not in a large depression, but in the upper reaches of a series of deep gorge-like valleys. Ghardaia lies *c.*170 km south-east of Laghouat and 180 km south of Ouled Jellal. It is also accessible via the Wargla oases *c.*190 km to the east along the Wadi

[169] Aillet *et al.* 2017, 345–56, for various observations of Gara Krima.

[170] Amat 1888; Doumone 2010; cf. d'Armagnac 1934; Roche 1970.

Mzab. The main oasis group in the Mzab comprises five towns (Ghardaia, Melika, Bou Noura, Beni Izguen and al-Atteuf) in a *c.*7 km stretch of the Wadi Mzab, where a high water table is augmented by periodic flash floods in the dry river bed.[171] The irrigation is mainly from shallow wells, but the irregular wadi floods are exploited by means of a series of four barrages in the wadi.[172] At least one foggara is reported here, but none have been located on satellite imagery. Foggaras are also known in the Wargla, at In Salah (and the Tidikelt and Tuwat oases to its west).[173] The Wadi Mzab terminates in a chott on the north side of Wargla. The history of the Mzab oases is built around the usual foundation myths, but limited archaeological investigation has taken place, mainly focused on the Medieval and early modern architecture – which is quite distinctive. In the early modern era, the Mzab population had a reputation for being nonconformist (Ibadite Berbers), with a sizeable Jewish minority. The morphology of the various settlements is somewhat varied and their enceintes as reported in the nineteenth century comprised multiple phases of differing construction, pisé, mudbrick and stone. The core areas of the towns are built up, with a generally oval shape, potentially representing a long urban history. No obvious pre-Islamic tombs have been recorded, but given the constraints of the narrow valley this is a location where successive phases of settlement and cemeteries are likely to have occupied the same physical space.

A route leads from Ghardaia down the east edge of the Great Western Erg to al-Golea *c.*270 km to the south. Beyond al-Golea, the route continues south to In Salah (400 km) and then Tamanrasset and the Ahaggar (650 km).

Conclusions

This section of our survey has demonstrated that there is compelling and widespread evidence for Protohistoric oasis development in north-western Libya and southern Tunisia and Algeria in and close to the Roman frontier zone. In desert areas, the placement of Roman forts and minor installations often corresponded with water sources. In the past, this has been portrayed as an attempt primarily to supervise the movement of pastoral groups by controlling access to the major wells. Yet, the fact that many military

[171] Amat 1888, pl. II and Roche 1970, for maps showing the wadi and its five distinct centres, now totally transformed into a single urban sprawl. Sèbe 1989 includes some spectacular aerial views of the Ghardaia oasis towns.

[172] Amat 1888, 52–63 on the hydrology.

[173] Capot-Rey 1953, 320 Carte VII; Cornet 1952.

installations were placed at, or in close proximity to, oasis locations suggests that there were other concerns. A significant proportion of forts along this stretch of desert frontier were situated at oases: Bu Nijim, al-Qurayyat al-Gharbia, Mizda, Ghadamis, Remada, Ras al-Ain, Bezeroes, Besseriani, Biska, Sidi Okba, Gemellae, Doucen, Castellum Dimmidi, as were many of the smaller fortlets like al-Qurayyat ash-Sharqiya, Ain Wif, Ain al-Avenia, Tisavar (Qasr Rhilane), etc. (Fig. 5.9). This is a clear and hitherto underappreciated pattern and it raises the chicken and egg question of which came first, fort or oasis? These Northern Saharan locations, including pre-desert margins, correspond with the areas where our ancient sources recurrently referred to peoples known as Gaetuli, conventionally interpreted in modern times as scattered pastoral groups.[174] The identification of a strong association between the Gaetuli and early oases is thus of considerable significance.

The archaeological evidence is too unrefined to offer a clear guide on the foundation dates of these oases, though finds of Roman material culture, including stone architectural elements, sometimes Latin inscriptions, etc., confirm the activity in the early centuries AD at many sites, including numerous oases where no military installations have been recorded.[175] There are compelling reasons to argue that many of these oases originated in the first millennium BC and were thus already established centres of the Gaetulian peoples at the time of first contact with the Roman army. When the Roman Empire extended its direct control into these desert regions, it placed its garrisons at locations where water and food supplies were readily available and close to the major population centres of the region. The campaign of Caius Marius against Capsa in 110 BC was explicitly made against an oasis town, while the famous coastal oasis of Tacapae has yielded evidence of Libyphoenician stelae. When Cornelius Balbus made his celebrated campaign against a series of desert peoples in 20 BC, the list of locations captured (as displayed at his triumph in Rome and reported by Pliny), plainly extended well beyond the Libyan oasis sites of Ghadamis and Jarma. A significant group of names correspond to the Algerian oases centres around Biskra and Gemellae, as noted above. The importance of the palm iconography in Punic artworks and coins is a further demonstration that the oasis was a well-established part of the landscape by the last centuries BC. It is of course

[174] The Gaetuli are long overdue a thorough review in light of the sort of evidence gathered in this and the next chapter. For a range of views, see Desanges 1962; 1980, 342–46; Hamdoune 2018, 63–64; 69–70; Leveau 2018, 91–93; Mattingly 1995, 26, 29–32.

[175] The systematic collation of evidence here allows us to go a lot further than previous speculations, see for instance Marouf 1980.

conceivable that there was significant growth in the numbers of oasis settlements in the Roman era beyond the number that existed at first contact. Nonetheless, the conclusion that the oases of the Roman frontier zone were starting to be developed from the later first millennium BC (if not earlier) seems inescapable.

As concerns the oases beyond the frontier in southern Algeria, the current state of knowledge reflects more an absence of evidence than evidence of absence. Apart from a few isolated finds of Roman material culture (mainly coins), there is little hard information. Oases that were throughout the Roman period outside the frontier were less likely to receive an abundance of Roman material culture or to adopt monumental stone architecture on the Roman model. The Garamantes and Cidamensi are the main exceptions to this rule. Yet, if oases were well established in the frontier zone itself, it is entirely plausible that they were also developed at some of the key locations beyond the frontier where hydraulic conditions were favourable. The Roman frontier deployment in the Gemellae/Biskra sector, fronted by a long linear earthwork (*fossatum*) looks to be designed to manage contact with people coming from the direction of the Wadi Rhir and Tuggurt. A recent study of the customs tariff of Zarai from the Algerian sector of this frontier by Guédon has identified that part of the text seems to concern textiles traded across the frontier.[176] Textile production has been a traditional mainstay of oasis communities in this region, one that emphasises the essential links between oasis cultivators and pastoral groups of the desert. More intensive work on the Garamantes has identified significant textile production and has highlighted this and other manufacturing activity in the oases as a key element of ancient Saharan trade.[177] For these reasons, we suggest that the default assumption in future work should be that some of the initial oasis development in the Wadi Rhir, Wargla, Ghardaia, Mzab and perhaps the Suf must have occurred by the early first millennium AD at the latest.

The sort of oasis sites that developed in the Roman frontier zone are distinctive from those of the Western Egyptian Desert, or the Garamantian heartlands.[178] They also differ from the normal patterns of urban development in Roman Africa.[179] There are probably two main reasons for this, one relating to the nature of Roman garrison settlements, the other to the adaptation of a Roman Mediterranean urban model by oasis societies. The nature of the military-focused communities that coalesced around army

[176] Guédon 2014. [177] Guédon 2017; Mattingly 2010, 523–30; Mattingly and Cole 2017.
[178] See Chapters 2–4, this volume. [179] Wilson, Chapter 10, this volume.

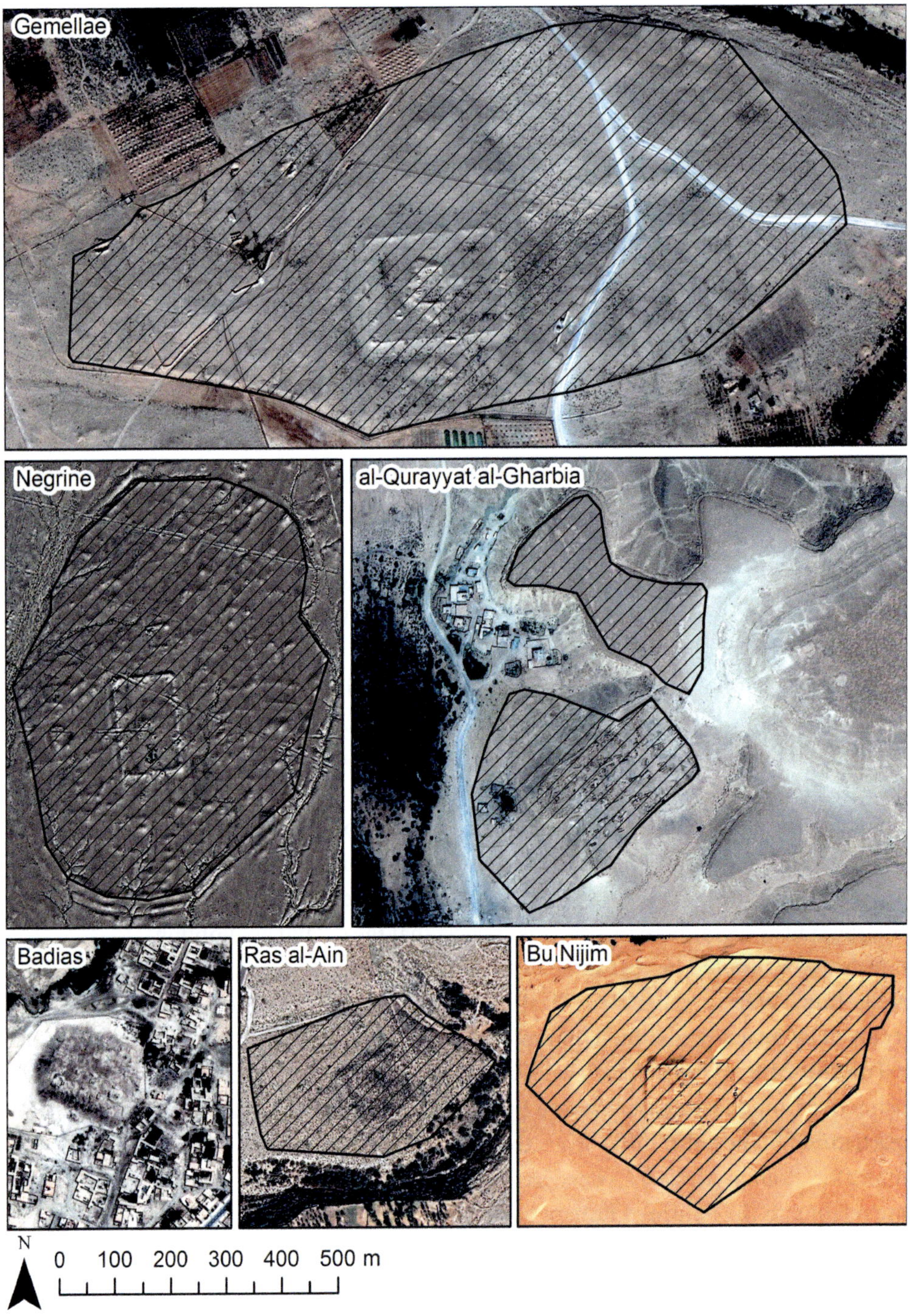

Figure 5.9. Comparative plans of Oasis forts and settlements (Bu Nijim, al-Qurayyat al-Gharbia, Ras al-Ain, Negrine, Badias, Gemellae) (imagery: Google, DigitalGlobe).

bases was likely to differentiate such locations from neighbouring oases. Garrison towns in many ages have a certain character that sets them apart from civilian towns. In the case of the African frontier, there are indications that the major military bases were built on the fringe of established oases, with the fort centrally positioned within a defined garrison settlement (*vicus*), as illustrated by the case studies of Bu Nijim, Nigrenses Maiores and Gemellae (Fig. 5.9). The second and third named sites both went on to acquire full urban status as *municipia*, but lack many of the standard amenities of Roman towns in Africa, while long retaining the central focus of a garrison post.

The *civitas* of the Nybgenii at Telmine in the Nefzaoua (and perhaps also the major centres in the Jarid) reveals another type of urban development. The apparently small size of the core urban settlement reflects what may be a normative pattern in oasis societies in Roman Africa, with the population split between multiple villages and small towns, each with associated gardens, rather than to coalesce into a single large centre. It is a moot point whether the Roman *municipium* (as Telmine became under Hadrian) actually designated a single location or rather encompassed a number of villages in the immediate area of Telmine. The major city at Tacapae (Gabes) has proved elusive to trace on the ground, perhaps because in reality it too was formed of several adjacent nuclei within the oasis. Although there is evidence of an engagement with Classical architecture and institutions at the urban oases of the frontier zone – as illustrated by finds at Ghadamis, Telmine, Tozeur, Besseriani, Gemellae, for instance – it seems inherently unlikely in terms of what survives and what is currently known of these sites that they were miniature versions of the typical urban centres of northern Tunisia, Libya or Algeria. Again, future work is needed to shed more light on the typical amenities and layout of such oasis towns. This pattern stands in contrast to the larger size of some of the major towns in the Egyptian oases, though there also we may note the presence in some districts of multiple village scale settlements.[180]

The wider implications of the existence of a world of oases in the African frontier zone lie beyond the scope of this volume and will be developed elsewhere.[181] The negative stereotyping of the peoples of the northern

180 See Boozer Chapter 4; Mattingly *et al.* Chapter 3, this volume.

181 On the Roman frontier in Africa, see now the recent reviews of Guédon 2018a; 2018b. Further work is needed to take full account of the different model proposed here for the partial sedentarisation of Saharan populations in and beyond the frontier zone.

Sahara in Roman sources also needs more critical analysis.[182] So too does the pernicious afterlife of a deeply prejudiced modern colonial discourse on Saharan populations and the recognition that oasis communities had the capacity to develop into urban societies is an important step in this regard.[183] However, it is apparent that traditional models that focus either on ideas of warlike nomadic people[184] or assimilatable transhumant pastoralists[185] both require revision to take account of the new reality of the substantial population bodies and productive capacities of the many oases that existed alongside pastoral groups in the northern Sahara.

References

Aillet, C., Cressier, P. and Gilotte, S. (ed.). 2017. *Sedrata. Histoire et archéologie d'un carrefour du Sahara médiéval à la lumière des archives inédites de Marguerite van Berchem.* Madrid: Casa de Velázquez.

Amat, C. 1888. *Le M'zab et les M'zabites.* Paris: Challamel editions.

Aroca, A. 1942. *Uau el-Chebir. L'oasi della redenzione.* Milan: Ministero Dell'Africa Italiana.

Aymo, J. 1958. La maison ghadamsie. *Travaux de l'institut de recherches Sahariennes de l'Université d'Alger* 17: 157–94.

Babelon, E, Cagnat, R and Reinach, S. 1893/1913. *Atlas archéologique de la Tunisie.* Paris: Ministère de la guerre.

Baduel, A. and Baduel, P. 1980. Le pouvoir de l'eau dans le sud-Tunisien. *Revue de l'Occident Musulman et de la Méditerranée* 30.2: 101–34.

Baradez, J. 1948. Gemellae, un camp d'Hadrien et une ville des confins sahariens aujord'hui ensélevis sous les sables. *Comptes Rendues à l'Académie des Inscriptions et Belles Lettres* 1948: 390–95.

Baradez, J. 1949a. *Vue aérienne de l'organisation romaine dans le sud Algérienne. Fossatum Africae.* Paris: Éd. arts et métiers graphiques.

Baradez, J. 1949b. Gemellae un camp d'Hadrien et une ville des confins sahariens aujord'hui ensélevis sous les sables. *Revue Africaine* 93: 5–24.

Baradez, J. 1957. Travaux hydrauliques romaines révéles par photographies aériennes dans un région aujord'hui steppienne. In *Actes du 79th Congrès National des Societés Savants, Alger 1954.* Paris: 273–75.

182 Desanges 1962, for the best collation of the source material. While there is an entry on a people referred to in the Classical sources as Oasitae and many entries on key oasis groups in the *Encyclopédie berbère*, there is tellingly no entry for 'oasis'.

183 See, for example, Aroca 1942, 217–25 on the 'etno criminalità libica' and 281–90 'la criminalità dei nomadi'. For an analysis of such crude models, see Leveau 2018; Mattingly 2011, 43–72.

184 Cagnat 1914; Guey 1939; Leschi 1942; Toutain 1896.

185 Trousset 1984a; 1986b; Whittaker 1978.

Baradez, J. 1966a. Deux amphithéatres inédits du 'limes' de Numidie: Gemellae et Mesarfelta. In *Mélanges d'archéologie, d'épigraphie et d'histoire, offerts à Jerome Carcopino*. Paris: Hachette, 55–63.

Baradez, J. 1966b. Les thermes légionnaires de Gemellae. In *Corolla Memoriae Erich Swoboda Dedicata*. Köln: Böhlau Verlag, 14–22.

Baradez, J. 1967. Compléments inédits au 'Fossatum Africae'. In *Studien zu den Militargrenzen Roms: Vortrage des 6. Internationalen Limes Kongresses in Süddeutschland*. Köln: Böhlau Verlag, 200–10.

Barker, G.W., Gilbertson, D, Jones, B. and Mattingly, D. 1996a. *Farming the Desert. The UNESCO Libyan Valleys Archaeological Survey, vol. 1 Synthesis* (editor G. Barker). Paris: UNESCO.

Barker, G.W., Gilbertson, D, Jones, B. and Mattingly, D. 1996b. *Farming the Desert. The UNESCO Libyan Valleys Archaeological Survey, vol. 2 Gazetteer and Pottery* (editor D. Mattingly). Paris: UNESCO.

Barth, H. 1857. *Travels and Discoveries in North and Central Africa* (reprint 1965). London: Ward Lock and Co.

Battailon, G. 1955. *Le Souf. Etude de geographie humaine*. Alger: Memoires de l'Institut de recherches sahariennes 2.

Beechey, F.W. and Beechey, H.W. 1828. *Proceedings of the Expedition to Explore the North Coast of Africa from Tripoly Eastward*. London: John Murray.

Bensaad, A. 2013. Ouargla. *Encyclopédie berbère* fasc. 36. Aix-en-Provence: Edisud, 5899–910.

Benseddik, N. 2018. Sidi Okba ou Thouda-Thabudeos: Un nouveau milliaire. In Guédon 2018, 207–14.

Berbrugger, A. 1862. *Les puits artesiens des oasis meridionales de l'Algerie*. Paris: Hachette.

Berthier, A. 1981. *La Numidie. Rome et la Maghreb*. Paris: Picard.

Birebent, J. 1962. *Aquae Romanae*. Algiers: Bacournies

Bisson, J. 1957. *Le Gourara. Etude de géographie humaine*. Alger: Memoires de l'Institut de recherches sahariennes 3.

Borderaux, P. 1907. *La Capsa ancienne. La Gafsa moderne*. Paris: Challamel.

Bovill, E.W. (ed.). 1964. *Missions to the Niger Vol. I The Journal of F. Hornemann's travels from Cairo to Murzuk in the years 1799–1798. The Letters of Alexander Gordon Laing 1824–26*. Cambridge: Hakluyt Society.

Brett, M. 1976. The journey of al-Tijani to Tripoli at the beginning of the fourteenth century A.D./eighth century AH. *Libyan Studies* 7: 41–51.

Brogan, O. and Smith, D.J. 1984. *Ghirza: A Romano-Libyan Settlement in Tripolitania*. Tripoli: Department of Antiquities, Libyan Antiquities Series 1.

Cagnat, R. 1914. La frontière militaire de la Tripolitaine à l'époque romaine. *Mémoires de l'Institut National de France, Académie des Inscriptions et Belles Lettres* 39: 77–109.

Capot-Rey, R. 1953. *Le Sahara Français* (L'Afrique Blanche Française II). Paris: Presses universitaires.

Carton, L. 1896/1897. Etudes sur les travaux hydrauliques des romains en Tunise. *Revue Tunisienne* 3: 373–85, 530–564; *Revue Tunisienne* 4: 27–85.
Chabot, J.B. 1940. *Recueil des inscriptions libyque*. Paris: Imprimerie nationale.
Cornet, A. 1952. Essai sur l'hydrogéologie du Grand Erg Oriental et des régions limitrophes (les foggaras). *Travaux de l'Institut de Recherches Sahariennes* 8: 71–122.
Corò, F. 1956. Ghadames archeologica. Storia degli studi delle esplorazioni e dei risultati su alcuni fra i più tipici antichi monumenti dell'oasi famosa, Libia. *Rivista trimestriale di studi Libici* 4.34: 3–26.
Daniels, C.M. 1987. Africa. In J. Wacher (ed.), *The Roman World*, vol. 1. London: Routledge, 223–65.
D'Armagnac, Lt. 1934. *Le Mzab et les pays Chamba*. Alger: Editions Baconnier.
Daumas, E. 1845. *Le Sahara algerien. Etudes geographiques, statistiques et historiques sur la region au sud des etablissments français en Algerie*. Paris: Langlois et Leclerc.
De Mathuisieulx, H.M. 1912. *La Tripolitaine d'hier et de demain*. Paris: Hachette.
Desanges, J. 1957. Le triomphe de Cornelius Balbus (19 B.C.). *Revue Africaine* 101: 5–43.
Desanges, J. 1962. *Catalogue des tribus africaines de l'antiquité classique à l'ouest du Nil*. Dakar: Université de Dakar.
Desanges, J. 1978. *Recherches sur l'activité des Méditerranéens aux confins de l'Afrique*. Rome: Collection *de l'École française de Rome* 38.
Desanges, J. 1980. *(Pline l'ancien) Histoire naturelle Livre V.1–46 (L'Afrique du nord)*. Paris: Les Belles Lettres.
Desanges, J., Duval, N. and Lepelley, C. 2010. *Carte des routes et des cités de l'est de l'Africa à la fin de l'antiquité*. Paris: Bibl. Antiquité tardive 17.
Despois, J. and Raynal, R. 1967. *Géographie de l'Afrique du Nord-Ouest*. Paris: Payot.
Donau, R. 1906. Notes sur des ruines du sud-Tunisien. *Bullétin archéologique du comité des travaux historiques et scientifiques* 1906: 113–22.
Donau, R. 1907. Etude sur la voie romaine de Tacapae à Turris Tamalleni. *Bulletin de la Societé archéologique de Sousse* 1907: 52–67; 173–90.
Douglas, N. 1912. *Fountains in the Sand*. London: Secker.
Doumane, S. 2010. Mzab. *Encyclopédie berbère* fasc. 32. Aix-en-Provence: Edisud, 5173–81.
Durand, J.H. and Guyot, J. 1955. L'irrigation des cultures dans l'oued Righ. *Travaux de l'Institut de Recherches Sahariennes* 13: 75–130.
Duveyrier, H. 1864. *Les Touareg du nord. Exploration du Sahara*. Paris: Challamel.
Duveyrier, H. 1915. *Sahara algérien et tunisien. Journal de route de Henri Duveyrier* (edited by C. Mannoir and H. Schizner). Paris: Challamel.
Eldblom, L. 1968. *Structure foncière. Organisation et structure sociale. Une étude comparative sur la vie socio-économique dans les trois oasis libyennes de Ghat, Mourzouk et particulièrement Ghadamès*. Lund: Uniksol.

Ellefi, M. 2015. *L'Arzugitana: Recherches d'histoire et d'archéologie sur une entité africaine de l'antiquité tardive*. Unpublished PhD thesis, University of Sousse.

Euzennat, M. 1971. Le castellum Thigensium (région de Metlaoui, Tunisie). *Bullétin archéologique du comité des travaux historiques et scientifiques* ns 7B: 229–39.

Euzennat, M. 1972. Quatre années de recherches sur la frontière romaine en tunisie Méridionale. *Comptes Rendues à l'Académie des Inscriptions et Belles Lettres* 1972: 7–27.

Euzennat, M. 1973. Tillibari, forteresse du 'limes Tripolitanus'. *Bullétin archéologique du comité des travaux historiques et scientifiques* 1973: 143–44.

Euzennat, M. and Trousset, P. 1975. *Le camp de Remada, fouilles inédites du commandant R. Donau*. Aix-en-Provence (privately circulated) = *Africa* 5–6, 1978: 111–89.

Faure, P. and Leveau, P. 2015. Une nouvelle inscription séverienne du Djebel Bou Kahil (Ouled Naïl, Djelfa, Algérie) et son apport à la connaissance des confins de la Numidie. *Antiquités africaines* 51: 119–42.

Fentress, E.W.B. 1979. Numidia and the Roman army. Social, military and economic aspects of the frontier zone. Oxford: BAR S53.

Féraud, L.-C. 2012. *Les Ben-Djellab, sultans et Touggourt: Notes historiques sur le sud-Constantinois Ued Righ. Souf, Ziban*. Alger: Livres editions.

Fontaine, P. 1952. *Touggourt, capitale des oasis*. Paris: Eds Dervy.

France, J. 2014. Normes douanières et réglementation des échanges, trois questions simples sur le tarif de Zaraï (Numidie). *Antiquités Africaines* 50: 93–110.

Franchi, S. 1912. *Richerche e studi agrologici sulla Libia. I, La zona di Tripoli*. Bergamo: Istituto italiano d'arti grafiche.

Gascou, J. 1972. *La politique municipale de l'Empire romain en Afrique Proconsulaire de Trajan é Septime Sévère*. Paris: *Publications de l'École française de Rome*.

Gauckler, P. 1900/1912. *Enquête sur les installations hydrauliques romaines en Tunisie*, 2 vols. Paris: Imprimerie rapide.

Gauckler, P. 1900. Notes sur les fouilles executées dans le Sahara tunisien. *Comptes Rendues à l'Académie des Inscriptions et Belles Lettres* 1900: 541–47.

Gendre, F. 1908. De Gabes à Nefta (Le Nefzaoua et le Djerid). *Revue Tunisienne* 15: 383–411, 499–520.

Goodchild, R.G. 1954a. Oasis forts of 'legio III Augusta' on the routes to the Fezzan. *Papers of the British School at Rome* 22: 56–68.

Goodchild, R.G. 1954b. *Tabula Imperii Romani: Lepcis Magna (Sheets H.33 1.33)*. Oxford: Society for Antiquaries.

Guédon, S. 2010. *Le voyage dans l'Afrique romaine*. Bordeaux: Ausonius.

Guédon, S. 2014. La 'lex uestis peregrinae' dans le tarif de Zaraï. *Antiquités Africaines* 50: 105–17.

Guédon, S. 2017. Circulation and trade in textiles in the southern borders of Roman Africa. In Mattingly *et al.* 2017, 259–84.

Guédon, S. 2018a. *La frontière romaine de l'Africa sous le Haut-Empire*. Madrid: Casa de Velazquez.

Guédon, S. (ed.). 2018b. *La frontière méridionale du Maghreb. Approches croisées (Antiquité-Moyen Âge)*. Bordeaux: Ausonius.

Gueneau, Capt. 1907. Ruines de la région de Negrine. *Bullétin archéologique du comité des travaux historiques et scientifiques* 1907: 314–35.

Guérin, V. 1862. *Voyages archéologiques dans la Regence de Tunis*. Paris: Plon.

Guery, R. 1986. Chronologie de quelques établisements de la frontière romaine du sud tunisien, à partir de la céramique collectée sur les sites. In *Akten des 13 Internationalen Limeskongresses Aalen, Sept. 1983*. Stuttgart: Theiss Verlag, 600–4.

Guey, J. 1939. Note sur le 'limes' romain de Numidie et le Sahara au IVe siècle. *Mélanges de l'école française de Rome* 56: 178–248.

Hamdoune, C. 2018. *Ad fines Africae Romanae. Les mondes tribaux dans les provinces maurétaniennes*. Bordeaux: Ausonius.

Hamy, E.-T. 1896. Note sur de nouvelles observations archéologiques recueillies entre El-Alia et Biskra. *Comptes rendus des séances de l'Académie des Inscriptions et Belles-Lettres* 40.1: 10–15.

Heron de Villefosse, 1894. Rapport sur la mission du Lieutenant d'artillerie, H. Lecoy de la Marche, dans le sud Tunisien. *Comptes Rendues à l'Académie des Inscriptions et Belles Lettres* 1894: 469–81.

Heywood, C. 1926. *Algeria and Tunisia*. Paris and London: Librarie Hachette.

Hilaire, Capt. 1900. L'emplacement de Tacape. *Bullétin archéologique du comité des travaux historiques et scientifiques* 1900: 115–25.

Hilaire, Capt. 1901. Note sur la voie stratégique romaine qui longeait la frontière militaire de la Tripolitaine. Essai d'identification des gîtes d'étapes de la portion de cette voie comprise entre ad Templum et Tabuinati. *Bullétin archéologique du comité des travaux historiques et scientifiques* 1901: 95–105.

Hurabeille, J. 1899. *Au pays du bleu. Biskra et les oasis environnants*. Paris: Challamel.

Lahbib, B.A.M. 2010. *Etude de rationalisation d'eau de l' oasis historique de Gafsa*. ASM/GIAHS. Rome: FAO.

Lancel, S. 1972/1991. Actes de la conférence de Carthage en 411. Paris: Ed du Cerf: SC 194, 195, 224, 383.

Laporte, J.-P. 2004. Trois sites militaires sévériens en Algérie moyenne: Grimidi, Tarmount (*Aras*), El Gahra. *L'Africa romana* 15: 439–77.

Laporte, J.-P. and Dupuis, X. 2009. De Nigrenses Maiores à Négrine. *Antiquités africaines* 45: 51–102.

Largeau, V. 1881. *Le Sahara Algerien. Les deserts de l'Erg*. Paris: Libraire Hachette.

Lecoy de la Marche, H. 1894. Recherche d'une voie romaine du Golfe de Gabes vers Rhadames. *Bullétin archéologique du comité des travaux historiques et scientifiques* 1894: 389–413.

Lepelley, C. 1979. *Les cités de l'Afrique romaine au Bas-Empire. I, La permanence municipal*. Paris: Etudes augustiniennes.

Lepelley, C. 1981. *Les cités de l'Afrique romaine au Bas-Empire. II, Notices d'histoire municipal.* Paris: Etudes augustiniennes.

Leschi, L. 1942. Rome et les nomades du Sahara central. *Travaux de l'Institut de Recherches Sahariennes I*: 47–62.

Lethielleux, J. 1983. *Ouargla. Cité saharienne des origines au début du XXe siècle.* Paris: Paul Geuthner.

Leveau, P. 2018. Climat, sociétés et environment aux marges sahariennes du Maghreb: Une approche historiographique. In Guédon 2018b, 19–106.

Lyon, G.F. 1821. *A Narrative of Travels in Northern Africa in the Years 1818–1819 and 1820.* London: John Murray.

Mackensen, M. 2010. Das severische Vexillationskastell Myd(–)/Gheriat el-Garbia am limes Tripolitanus (Libyen) – Bericht über die Kampagne 2009. *Mitteilungen des Deutschen Archäologischen Instituts, Römische Abteilung* 116: 363–458.

Mackensen, M. 2011. Das severische Vexillationskastell Myd(–) und die spätantike Besiedlung in Gheriat el-Garbia (Libyen). Bericht über die Kampagne im Frühjahr 2010. *Mitteilungen des Deutschen Archäologischen Instituts, Römische Abteilung* 117: 247–375.

Mackensen, M. 2012. New fieldwork at the Severan fort of Myd(–)/Gheriat el-Garbia on the limes Tripolitanus. *Libyan Studies* 43: 41–60.

Marichal, R. 1992. *Les ostraca du Bu Njem.* Tripoli: Department of Antiquities.

Marouf, N. 1980. *Lecture de l'espace oasien.* Paris: Sinbad.

Martel, A. 1965. *Les confins Saharo-tripolitains de la Tunisie (1881–1911)*, 2 vols. Paris: Presses universitaires de France.

Mattingly, D.J. 1982. The Roman road-station at Thenadassa (Ain Wif). *Libyan Studies* 13: 73–80.

Mattingly, D.J. 1986. Soldier or civilian? Urbanisation on the frontiers of Roman Africa. *Popular Archaeology* Dec 1985/Jan 1986: 61–66.

Mattingly, D.J. 1995. *Tripolitania.* London: Batsford.

Mattingly, D.J. 2000a. Tripolitana. In R. Talbert (ed.), *Barrington Atlas of the Greek and Roman World.* Princeton: map 35 and Map-by-Map Directory pp. 529–44.

Mattingly, D.J. 2000b. Syrtica. In R. Talbert (ed.), *Barrington Atlas of the Greek and Roman World.* Princeton: map 37 and Map-by-Map Directory pp. 552–57.

Mattingly, D.J. (ed.). 2003. *The Archaeology of Fazzan. Volume 1, Synthesis.* London: Society for Libyan Studies, Department of Antiquities.

Mattingly, D.J. 2004. Surveying the desert: From the Libyan Valleys to Saharan oases. In M. Iacovou (ed.), *Archaeological Field Survey in Cyprus. Past History, Future Potentials. Proceedings of a Conference Held at the University of Cyprus, 1–2 December 2000.* London: BSA monograph 11, 163–76.

Mattingly, D.J. (ed.). 2010. *The Archaeology of Fazzān. Volume 3, Excavations Carried out by C.M. Daniels.* London: Society for Libyan Studies, Department of Antiquities.

Mattingly, D.J. 2011. *Imperialism, Power and Identity. Experiencing the Roman Empire.* Princeton: Princeton University Press.

Mattingly, D.J. 2014. Castles in the desert: Living in Libyan landscapes. In K. Boyle, R. Rabett and C. Hunt (eds), *Living in the Landscape. Essays in Honour of Graeme Barker*. Cambridge: McDonald Institute Monographs, 299–311.

Mattingly, D.J. and Cole, F. 2017. Visible and invisible commodities of trade: The significance of organic materials in Saharan trade. In Mattingly *et al.* 2017, 211–30.

Mattingly, D.J. and Sterry, M.S. 2010. *Ghadames Archaeological Survey. Phase 1 Desk-top Report*. Unpublished consultancy report produced for Libyan Department of Antiquities, Ghadames Development Authority and BP.

Mattingly D.J., Ahmed, M., Sterry, M., Fenwick, C. and Moussa, F. 2011. *The Ghadames Archaeological Survey Phase 2 Work February 2011. Preliminary Report on Work Accomplished Prior to Suspension of Project*. Unpublished consultancy report produced for Libyan Department of Antiquities, Ghadames Development Authority and BP.

Mattingly, D.J., Rushworth, A., Sterry, M. and Leitch, V. 2013. *The African Frontiers*. Frontiers of the Roman Empire series, general editor, D. Breeze. Edinburgh: Hussar.

Mattingly, D.J., Leitch, V., Duckworth, C.N., Cuénod, A., Sterry, M. and Cole, F. (eds). 2017. *Trade in the Ancient Sahara and Beyond*. Trans-Saharan Archaeology Volume 1. Series editor D.J. Mattingly. Cambridge: Cambridge University Press.

Mauny, R. 1956. Monnaies antiques trouvées en Afrique au sud du limes romain. *Libyca* 4: 249–61.

Mauny, R. 1978. Trans-Saharan contacts and the Iron Age in West Africa. In J. D. Fage (ed.), *The Cambridge History of Africa*, vol. 2. Cambridge: Cambridge University Press, 272–341.

Mercier, R. 1953. Les idoles de Ghadames. *Revue Africaine* 97: 17–47.

Meouak, M. 2018. Biskra et ses oasis au Moyen Âge, marge aurésienne, marge saharienne? Notes préliminaires. In Guédon 2018b, 215–42.

Mircher, H., Polignac, L. de, Vatonne, F. and Hoffman. 1863. *Mission de Ghadames (septembre, octobre, novembre et décembre 1862). Rapports officiels et documents à l'appui*. Alger: Typographie Duclaux.

Monlezun, Capt. 1885. Les ruines de Tacape (Gabes). *Bullétin archéologique du comité des travaux historiques et scientifiques* 1885: 126–31.

Moreau, P. 1947. *Des lacs du sel aux chaos de sable. Le pays de nefzaouas*. Tunis: Bascone & Muscat.

Morizot, P. 1999. La présence romaine dans le Djebel Amour (Algérie): Apport des images Spot et de la photographie aérienne. In *Frontières et limites géographiques de l'Afrique du Nord antique, Hommage à Pierre Salama, Actes de la Table ronde réunie à Paris les 2 et 3 mai 1997*. Paris: Publications de la Sorbonne, 185–94.

Mrabet, A. 2004. *La Tunisie du sud. Sites et monuments*. Tunis: Simpact.

Nachtigal G. 1974. *Sahara and Sudan, vol I, Tripoli and Fezzan, Tibesti or Tu*, translated by A.G.B. and H.J. Fisher. London: C. Martin.

Nesson, C. 1965. Structure agraire et evolution sociale dans les oasis de l'oued Righ. *Travaux de l'Institut de Recherches Sahariennes* 24: 85–127.

Nesson, C., Rouvillois-Brigol, M., and Vallet, J. 1973. *Oasis du sahara algérien.* Paris: Institut géographique national.

Paris, F. and Ghaki, M. 2010. Les monuments mégalithiques du sud tunisien: État de la question. *Les nouvelles de l'archéologie* 120–121: 71–74.

Payre, G. 1942a. Une fete du printemps au Djerid. *Revue Tunisienne* 1942: 171–77.

Payre, G. 1942b. Amines d'oasis au Djerid. *Revue Tunisienne* 1942: 335–39.

Perugini, Ilo. 1929. *Gadames. Monografia del teritorio.* Tripoli: Comando R.C.T. C. della Tripolitania.

Peyras, J. and Trousset, P. 1988. Le 'lac Tritonis' et les noms antiques du Chott el Jerid. *Antiquités africaines* 24: 149–204.

Picard, G.C. 1944. *Castellum Dimmidi.* Algiers: de Boccard.

Ragot, W.R. 1874. Le Sahara de la Province de Constantine. *Récueil des notices et mémoires de la société archéologique de Constantine* 16: 91–299.

Rebuffat, R. 1967. Bu Njem 1967. *Libya Antiqua* 3–4:49–137.

Rebuffat, R. 1969. Deux ans de recherches dans le sud de la Tripolitaine. *Comptes Rendues à l'Académie des Inscriptions et Belles Lettres* 1969: 189–212.

Rebuffat, R. (with contributions by others) 1970a. Bu Njem 1968. *Libya Antiqua* 6–7: 9–105.

Rebuffat, R. 1970b. Bu Njem 1970. *Libya Antiqua* 6–7: 107–65.

Rebuffat, R. 1971. Recherches en Tripolitaine du sud. *Revue Archéologique* 1971 ns2: 177–84.

Rebuffat, R. 1972. Nouvelles recherches dans le sud de la Tripolitaine. *Comptes Rendues à l'Académie des Inscriptions et Belles Lettres* 1972: 319–39.

Rebuffat, R. 1975a. Graffiti en Libyque de Bu Njem. *Libya Antiqua* 11–12: 165–87.

Rebuffat, R. 1975b. Bu Njem 1971. *Libya Antiqua* 11–12: 189–242.

Rebuffat, R. 1975c. Trois nouvelles campagnes dans le sud de la Tripolitaine. *Comptes Rendues à l'Académie des Inscriptions et Belles Lettres* 1975: 495–505.

Rebuffat, R. 1977a. Bu Njem 1972. *Libya Antiqua* 13–14: 37–77.

Rebuffat, R. 1977b. Dix ans de recherches dans le prédesert de Tripolitaine. *Libya Antiqua* 13–14: 79–91.

Rebuffat, R. 1980. A propos du 'limes Tripolitanus'. *Revue Archéologique* 1980.1: 105–24.

Rebuffat, R. 1982. Recherches dans le désert de Libye. *Comptes Rendues à l'Académie des Inscriptions et Belles Lettres* 1982: 188–99.

Rebuffat, R. 1989. Le camp romain de Gholaia (Bu Njem). *Libyan Studies* 20: 155–67.

Rebuffat, R. 2004. Les romains et les routes caravanieres africaines. In M. Fantar (ed.), *Le Sahara. Lien entre les peuples et les cultures.* Tunis: Université de Tunis, 221–60.

Reynolds, J.M. 1958. Three inscriptions from Ghadames in Tripolitania. *Papers of the British School at Rome* 26: 135–36.

Reynolds, J.M. and Simpson, W.G. 1967. Some inscriptions from el-Auenia, near Yefren in Tripolitania. *Libya Antiqua* 3–4: 45–47.

Richardson, J. 1848. *Travels in the Great Desert of Sahara in 1845–46*, 2 vols. London: R. Bentley.

Roche, M. 1970. *Le Mzab: Architecture ibadite en Algérie*. Bellegarde: Antaud.

Roffo, P. 1938. Sépultures indigènes antéislamiques en pierres sèches, étude sur trois nécropoles de l'Algérie centrale. *Revue Africaine* 82: 197–242.

Rohlfs, G. 2001. *Voyages et explorations au Sahara. Tome II, Tripoli - Rhadamès - Fezzan - Kaouar - Bornou 1865–1867* (translated by J. Debetz). Paris: Karthala.

Romey, A. 1992. *Histoire, mémoire et sociétés: l'exemple de N'Gouss, oasis berbèréphone du Sahara (Ouagla)*. Paris: Awal/l'Harmattin.

Rouvillois-Brigol, M. 1975. *Le pays de Ouargla (Sahara algérien). Variations et organisation d'un espace rural en milieu désertique*. Paris: Université Paris-Sorbonne.

Salama, P. 1981. The Sahara in classical antiquity. In G. Mokhtar (ed.), *UNESCO General History of Africa, II Ancient Civilisations of Africa*. Paris: UNESCO, 513–32.

Saumagne, C. 1962. Capsa, les vestiges de la cite latine de Gafsa. *Cahiers de Tunisie* 37–40: 519–23.

Savornin, J. 1947. Le plus grand appareil hyrdraulique du Sahara (nappe artésienne dite de l'Albia). *Travaux de l'Institut de Recherches Sahariennes* 4: 25–66.

Savornin, J. 1950. Le Bas-Sahara (appareil artésienne le plus simple du Sahara). *Travaux de l'Institut de Recherches Sahariennes* 6: 45–62.

Schimmer, F. 2012. New evidence for a Roman fort and vicus at Mizda (Tripolitania). *Libyan Studies* 43: 33–39.

Sèbe, A. 1989. *Moula-Moula. Le Sahara à vol d'oiseau*. Vidauban: Collection Tagoulmoust.

Suter, K. 1962. Über Quelltöpfe, Quellhügel und Wasserstollen des Nefzaoua (Südtunesien). *Vierteljahrsschr. Nat. Ges. Zürich, Jg.* 107.2: 49–64.

Tarry, H. 1884. Les villes berberès de la vallée de l'oued Mya. *Revue d'ethnographie* 3: 1–44.

Thiry, J. 1995. *Le Sahara Libyen dans l'Afrique du Nord Medievale*. Leuven: Orientalia Lovaniensia Analecta, 72.

Toussaint, P-M. 1907. Résumé des reconnaisances archéologiques exécutées par les officiers des Brigade Topographiques d'Algérie et de Tunisie. Campagne de 1905–1906. *Bullétin archéologique du comité des travaux historiques et scientifiques* 1907: 308–14.

Toutain, J. 1896. Les Romains dans le Sahara. *Mélanges de l'école française de Rome* 16: 63–77.

Toutain, J. 1903. Notes et documents sur les voies stratégiques et sur l'occupation militaire du sud Tunisien à l'époque romaine. *Bullétin archéologique du comité des travaux historiques et scientifiques* 1903: 272–409.

Trousset, P. 1974. *Recherches sur le 'limes Tripolitanus' du chott el-Djerid à la frontière tuniso-libyenne*. Paris: Editions CNRS.

Trousset, P. 1977. Le camp de Gemellae sur le 'limes' de Numidie d'après les fouilles de Colonel Baradez (1947–50). In J. Fitz (ed.), *Akten des Internationalen Limeskongresses*, 1976. Budapest: Akadémiai Kiadó, 559–76.

Trousset, P. 1978a. Reconnaisances archéologiques sur la frontière saharienne de l'Empire romain dans le sud-ouest de la Tunisie. *Actes 101e Congrès National des Societés Savantes, Lille. Archéologie*. Paris: Bibliothèque national, 21–33.

Trousset, P. 1978b. Les bornes du Bled Segui. Nouveaux aperçus sur la centuriation romaine du sud Tunisie. *Antiquités africaines* 12: 125–78.

Trousset, P. 1980a. Signification d'une frontière: nomades et sédentaires dans la zone du 'limes' d'Afrique. In W.S. Hanson and L.J.F. Keppie (eds), *Roman Frontier Studies 1979. Papers Presented to the 12th International Congress of Roman Frontier Studies*. Oxford: BAR S71, 931–43.

Trousset, P. 1980b. Les milliaires de Chebika (sud Tunisien). *Antiquités africaines* 15: 135–54.

Trousset, P. 1982a. Le franchissement des chotts du sud Tunisien dans l'antiquité. *Antiquités africaines* 18: 45–59.

Trousset, P. 1982b. L'image du nomade saharien dans l'historiographie antique. *Production pastorale et sociéte* 10: 97–105.

Trousset, P. 1984a. L'idée de frontière au Sahara d'après les données archéologiques. In P. Baduel (ed.), *Enjeux Sahariens*. Paris: CNRS, 47–78.

Trousset, P. 1984b. Note sur un type d'ouvrage linéaire du 'limes' d'Afrique. *Bullétin archéologique du comité des travaux historiques et scientifiques* ns 17B: 383–98.

Trousset, P. 1986a. Les oasis présahariennes dans l'antiquité: partage de l'eau et division du temps. *Antiquités africaines* 22: 161–91.

Trousset, P. 1986b. Limes et 'frontière climatique'. In *Histoire et archéologie de l'Afrique du Nord, 3e Colloque International Montpellier, 1985*. Paris: CNRS, 55–84.

Trousset, P. 1987a. L'organisation de l'oasis dans l'antiquité (exemples de Gabés et du Jérid). In A. de Réparaz (ed.), *L'eau et les hommes en Méditerranée*. Paris: CNRS, 25–41.

Trousset, P. 1987b. De la montagne au désert: Limes et maitrise de l'eau. *Revue de l'Occident Musulman et de la Méditerranée* 41–42: 90–115.

Trousset, P. 1990. Thiges et la civitas Thigensium. In *L'Afrique dans l'occident romain (Ier siècle av. J. -C.-IVe siècle ap. J.-C)*. Rome: Publications de l'École française de Rome, 143–67.

Trousset, P. 1995. Djerid. *Encyclopédie berbère*, fasc 16. Aix-en-Provence, Edisud: 2461–65.

Trousset, P. 2003. Le tarif de Zaraï: Essai sur les circuits commerciaux dans la zone présaharienne. *Antiquités Africaines* 38–39: 355–73.

Trousset, P. 2012a. Nefzaoua. *Encyclopédie berbère*, fasc 33. Aix-en-Provence, Edisud: 5382–89.

Trousset, P. 2012b. Nomadisme (Saharien en Afrique du nord dans l'antiquité. *Encyclopedie berbère*, fasc 34. Aix-en-Provence, Edisud: 5578–89.

Tully, R. 1817. *Narrative of a Ten Years' Residence at Tripoli in Africa*. London: H. Colburn.

Van Berchem, M. 1953a. Deux campagnes de fouilles à Sedrata 1951–52. *Travaux de l'Institut de Recherches sahariennes* 10: 123–38.

Van Berchem, M. 1953b. *Sedrata, une ville au moyen âge ensevelie dans les sables du Sahara algérien*. Alger: Documents algériens, série monographie 11.

Villiers, M. de and Hirtle, S. 2002. *Sahara. A Natural History*. New York: Walker and Company.

Vuillot, P. 1893. *Des Zibans au Djerid par les Chotts Algériens*. Paris: Oberthus.

Welsby, D. 1988. The defences of the Roman forts at Bu Ngem and Gheriat el-Garbia. In P. Bidwell, R. Miket and B. Ford (eds), *Portae Cum Turribus. Studies of Roman Fort Gates*. Oxford: BAR S206, 63–82.

Whittaker, C.R. 1978. Land and labour in North Africa. *Klio* 60.2: 331–62.

6 Pre-Islamic Oasis Settlements in the North-Western Sahara

MARTIN STERRY, DAVID J. MATTINGLY
AND YOUSSEF BOKBOT

Introduction

This chapter focuses on the northern oases of the Western Sahara (Fig. 6.1). As with the Northern Sahara, the North-western Sahara has also too often been dismissed as wholly nomadic before the development of Arab trading networks. There have been only limited attempts to view the region as a whole, as opposed to restricted studies of the different oasis groups. In this chapter we start with the western end of the Saharan Atlas and move west towards the Atlantic through the Wadi Gir, Wadi Saoura, Tafilalat, Wadi Draa and Wadi Noun. We conclude with a diversion to some outlying oases to the south, Gourara and Tuwat at the southern end of the Wadi Gir and Tabalbala *c.*300 km to the west of Tuwat. This broad zone also needs to be considered in relation to the south-western Saharan sites that are presented in Chapter 7. The Western Sahara as a whole has been structured around several extended north to south trading routes and is known for its famous trading towns. The rich mineral resources, especially silver and copper in the High Atlas, Anti-Atlas mountain ranges and the Adrar Plateau were another distinctive aspect of the human exploitation of the Western Sahara. The Protohistoric archaeology of the region has been somewhat underexplored, though as we shall see has great potential.[1] In the Medieval and early modern periods the kingdoms of the Almoravids and Saadi in Morocco and the kingdoms of Ghana, Mali and Songhay in the Sahel repeatedly made efforts to extend their control over the region and its lucrative trade.

The Roman sources mention a number of indigenous peoples lying to the south of the Roman provincial territory of Mauretania Tingitana in northern Morocco and these were evidently considered to be distinct from

[1] Bokbot 2015.

the Maures of the north.[2] The population of the Wadi Draa are specifically referred to as Gaetuli.[3] As we noted in the previous chapter, references to Gaetuli elsewhere along the frontier zone correlate broadly with groups who we suggest combined pastoral activity and sedentary oasis farming.

While early oasis settlements have hitherto been elusive archaeologically, there are some important proxy elements of Protohistoric activity in the area, notably large funerary landscapes of pre-Islamic burials[4] and rock art featuring horsemen, chariots and camels.[5] There are some dense concentrations of this sort of evidence either adjacent to oasis zones, or marking the close approach routes to the oasis. We shall allude to this evidence where relevant below, but want to stress at the outset that whether these related to sedentary or pastoral groups, we suspect that their dense clustering close to oasis locations suggests a connection with the initial stages of sedentarisation and oasis creation.[6]

Available radiocarbon dates are presented in Table 6.1.

Oases of North-Western Algeria and Southern Morocco

The development of oases in southern Morocco and the extreme west of Algeria has been of a rare and distinctive type compared to much of the rest of the Sahara. The key hydrological feature in this region is several significant wadi systems with available 'surface water' as a result of snow melt and rainfall on the High Atlas and Anti-Atlas ranges. These run far out into the desert to the south: the Wadi Gir/Saoura, the Wadi Ziz and the Wadi Draa, as well as the Wadi Noun which flows into the Atlantic.[7] The distribution of date palms in Morocco highlights the existence of two predominant oasis zones: the Wadi Draa and the Erfoud/Rissani area (Tafilalat) on the Wadi Ziz. There are in addition numerous much smaller palmeries in the Wadi Gir, the Wadi Noun and in other wadis on the southern and south-eastern sides of the Atlas ranges fed from run-off from the mountain face.[8] There are no significant stands of palms in the mountains or to their north side. The greater size of the palmeries in the Draa and

[2] See now Hamdoune 2018, for a detailed overview of the ancient indigenous peoples of the Western Maghrib and the Saharan margins.

[3] Pliny, *Natural History* 5.9–10 (Gaetulos Daras), though there were evidently also black Africans nearby (Aethiopas Darathitas).

[4] Bokbot 2019. [5] Gauthier and Gauthier 2011; 2015; Simoneau 1977.

[6] As also argued in other volumes of this series, see Mattingly 2017, 22–24; Mattingly *et al.* 2019, 6–17.

[7] For the geographical setting, see Despois and Raynal 1967, 458–73; Gautier 1970, 76–87.

[8] Joly 1948, 204, 209 for maps.

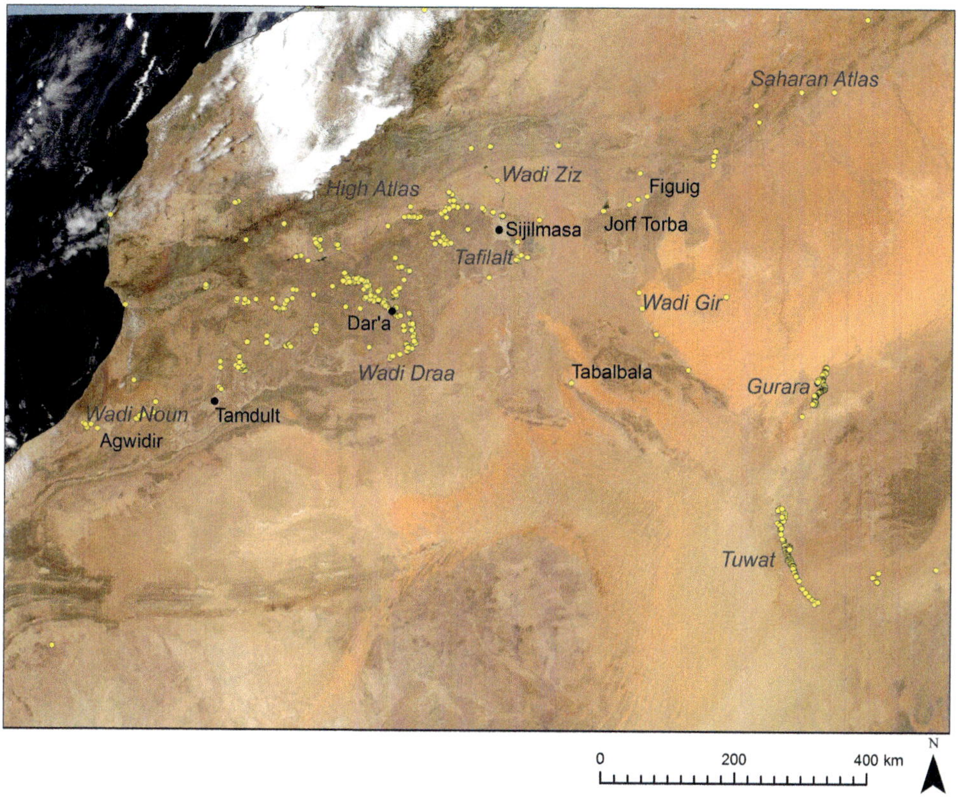

Figure 6.1. North-west Sahara, main regions and sites discussed in the text.

the Ziz indicates the perennial or near perennial nature and greater flow of these wadis, a unique occurrence in the Sahara, where the only other permanent rivers relate to Sub-Saharan catchments (Niger and Nile). The Gir/Saoura is notable on the other hand for the depth of penetration of its more seasonal floodwaters, extending as far south as Tuwat.

While the historical data on the Moroccan oases mostly dates to the Islamic era, there are a number of significant hints at pre-Islamic origins.[9] A most compelling argument for an early date of the first activity in the two major oases is that they are fed by perennial rivers and are thus among the most obvious and simplest of hydrological situations to exploit.[10]

The first Roman encounter with the people of the zone to the south of the Atlas can be precisely dated to the early AD 40s, when two generals

[9] Jacques-Meunié 1982 (especially 159–89 for discussion of pre-Islamic evidence).

[10] Rohlfs 2001, for a mid-nineteenth-century account of both the major Moroccan oases. See also Capel, Chapter 16, this volume for discussion of the difficulties of irrigation in the Tafilalat.

Table 6.1 *Protohistoric and historic radiocarbon dates from the Western Sahara*

Area/Site	Context	Material	Reference	Date	Calibrated
Wadi Gir					
Jorf Torba	Tomb 19	Human bone	Pa-1252	2230±60 BP	403–120 calBC
Jorf Torba	Tomb 28	Human bone	Pa-1257	1760±60 BP	calAD 128–402
Jorf Torba	Tomb 27	Human bone	Pa-1260	1700±60 BP	calAD 143–534
Tafilalat					
Ahshilifa Barrage	Dam #5	Charcoal	Not given	350±70 BP	calAD 1432–1664
Ziz Barrage	At head of Ziz	Charcoal	Not given	650±35 BP	calAD 1279–1396
Sijilmasa	T41.D014	Wood	Not given	1360±70 BP	calAD 545–863
Sijilmasa	T21A.D035	Charcoal	Not given	990±90 BP	calAD 780–1252
Sijilmasa	T28.D155	Charcoal	Not given	710±90 BP	calAD 1058–1421
Sijilmasa	T50.D014 Phase 0/I	Charcoal	Not given	1270±50 BP	calAD 660–876
Sijilmasa	T52.D019 Phase I	Wood	Not given	1700±60 BP	calAD 138–527
Sijilmasa	T42.D096 Phase I	Charcoal	Not given	1480±70 BP	calAD 424–660
Sijilmasa	T21A.D059 Phase I	Charcoal	Not given	1350±180 BP	calAD 258–1030
Sijilmasa	T41.D013 Phase I	Wood	Not given	1280±40 BP	calAD 657–864
Sijilmasa	T52.D017 Phase I	Charcoal	Not given	1230±40 BP	calAD 683–887
Sijilmasa	T21A.D055 Phase IA	Charcoal	Not given	1260±70 BP	calAD 648–947
Sijilmasa	T21A.D062 Phase IB	Charcoal	Not given	1410±100 BP	calAD 413–863
Sijilmasa	T52.D012 Phase I/II	Wood	Not given	1430±40 BP	calAD 558–663
Sijilmasa	T21A.D042 Phase I/II	Charcoal	Not given	1260±120 BP	calAD 576–1016
Sijilmasa	T40.D018 Phase I/II	Charcoal	Not given	1210±50 BP	calAD 678–952
Sijilmasa	T21A.D038 Phase I/II	Charcoal	Not given	1010±80 BP	calAD 779–1217
Sijilmasa	T32.D091 Phase II	Charcoal	Not given	1240±80 BP	calAD 654–986
Sijilmasa	T32.D104 Phase II	Charcoal	Not given	1010±60 BP	calAD 894–1162
Sijilmasa	T21A.D040 Phase IIA	Charcoal	Not given	1140±90 BP	calAD 675–1030
Sijilmasa	T21.D066 Phase IIA	Charcoal	Not given	910±60 BP	calAD 1019–1245
Sijilmasa	T38.D017 Phase IIB	Charcoal	Not given	1190±70 BP	calAD 682–981

Sijilmasa	T21.D029 Phase IIB	Charcoal	Not given	1080±120 BP	calAD 681–1184
Sijilmasa	T21.D047 Phase IIB	Charcoal	Not given	1020±90 BP	calAD 777–1212
Sijilmasa	T32.D083 Phase II/III	Charcoal	Not given	1210±60 BP	calAD 675–966
Sijilmasa	T40.D016 Phase II/III	Charcoal	Not given	1090±130 BP	calAD 670–1185
Sijilmasa	T32.D061 Phase III	Charcoal	Not given	1000±80 BP	calAD 782–1220
Sijilmasa	T31.D009 Phase III/IV	Charcoal	Not given	1250±60 BP	calAD 657–939
Sijilmasa	T54.D005 Phase III/IV	Wood	Not given	480±50 BP	calAD 1315–1616
Sijilmasa	T54.D005 Phase III/IV	Wood	Not given	450±50 BP	calAD 1398–1630
Sijilmasa	T54.D005 Phase III/IV	Wood	Not given	410±40 BP	calAD 1427–1632
Sijilmasa	T34.D012 Phase IV	Wood	Not given	970±80 BP	calAD 894–1224
Sijilmasa	T32.D053 Phase IV	Charcoal	Not given	360±100 BP	calAD 1328–1950
Sijilmasa	T34.D012 Phase IV/V	Charcoal	Not given	1220±130 BP	calAD 566–1117
Sijilmasa	Bab al-Monsouria	Not given	Beta-431101	390±30 BP	calAD 1441–1631
Sijilmasa	Bab al-Monsouria	Not given	Beta-431103	390±30 BP	calAD 1441–1631
Sijilmasa	Bab al-Monsouria	Not given	Beta-431102	340±30 BP	calAD 1470–1640
Tafilalat	P08-03	Charcoal	Not given	1123±23 BP	calAD 880–987
Tafilalat	P08-02	Charcoal	Not given	964±27 BP	calAD 1019–1155
Wadi Draa					
BOU001	From mudbrick wall of building	Plant remains (grass)	OxA-33783	933±31 BP	calAD 1025–1164
BOU002	From SE wall of *qasr*	Charcoal (cf. tamarix sp.)	OxA-33784	1196±32 BP	calAD 713–945
BOU003	From SE wall of *qasr*	Charcoal (cf. tamarix sp.)	OxA-33823	870±26 BP	calAD 1046–1244
BOU009	From mudbrick wall of building	Plant remains	OxA-33824	810±27 BP	calAD 1170–1270
BOU022	From mudbrick wall of building	Plant remains (grass)	OxA-33718	969±37 BP	calAD 997–1159
BOU033	Outer wall of *qasr*	Charcoal (cf. tamarix sp.)	OxA-35336	1050±25 BP	calAD 901–1025
BOU036	From mudbrick wall of building	Charcoal (cf. tamarix sp.)	OxA-35361	899±28 BP	calAD 1040–1211

Table 6.1 (*cont.*)

Area/Site	Context	Material	Reference	Date	Calibrated
BOU038	From mudbrick wall of building	Charcoal (cf. tamarix sp.)	OxA-35362	894±26 BP	calAD 1042–1214
BOU051	From mudbrick wall of building	Wood	OxA-35447	331±25 BP	calAD 1482–1642
BOU051	From mudbrick wall of possible mosque	Charcoal	OxA-35363	287±29 BP	calAD 1493–1664
BOU051	From mudbrick wall of building	Plant remains (grass)	OxA-35647	174±23 BP	calAD 1662–present
BOU053	From mudbrick wall of *qasr*	Date stone	OxA-35364	535±27 BP	calAD 1320–1438
BOU053	From mud bonding of stone wall	Charcoal (cf. tamarix sp.)	OxA-35365	450±26 BP	calAD 1418–1469
BOU054	From clay-lined pit T3 (3111)	Barley grain	OxA-35367	1338±28 BP	calAD 646–767
BOU054	From clay-lined pit T1 (3104)	Charcoal (cf. tamarix sp.)	OxA-35366	1318±27 BP	calAD 655–767
BOU057	Hearth within chapel-tomb	Charcoal	OxA-35303	2710±80 BP	1107–768 calBC
BOU057	Floor of chapel-tomb	Charcoal	OxA-35403	1820±29 BP	calAD 92–320
BOU057	Above floor of chapel-tomb	Charcoal (cf. tamarix sp.)	OxA-35185	1751±27 BP	calAD 230–381
BOU064	Burnt clay feature	Charcoal	OxA-35368	890±40 BP	calAD 1034–1220
BOU071	From mudbrick wall of building	Charcoal	OxA-35369	802±27 BP	calAD 1186–1274
BOU073	From mudbrick wall of building	Charcoal (cf. tamarix sp.)	OxA-35370	874±26 BP	calAD 1045–1224
BOU076	From mudbrick wall of building	Charcoal	OxA-35371	874±26 BP	calAD 1045–1224
BOU092	Burnt clay feature	Wood	OxA-35603	833±26 BP	calAD 1163–1258
BOU105	From mudbrick wall of building	Charcoal (cf. tamarix sp.)	OxA-35372	957±26 BP	calAD 1022–1155
BOU110	From mudbrick wall of building	Charcoal (cf. tamarix sp.)	OxA-35373	971±27 BP	calAD 1016–1155
BOU117	Neolithic pottery scatter	Ostrich Egg Shell	OxA-35225	8147±39 BP	7302–7057 calBC

BSM001	Mortar from mosque	Charcoal	OxA-35375	988±26 BP	calAD 991–1152
BSM001	Mortar from qasba	Charcoal (cf. tamarix sp.)	OxA-35374	900±26 BP	calAD 1039–1210
BSM002	Pisé wall	Charcoal	OxA-35376	472±26 BP	calAD 1414–1451
LAR001	Cemetery	Human bone	OxA-33338	2649±28 BP	894–791 calBC
LAR001?	Cemetery	Bone	Gif-2912	2369±250 BP	1082–129 calBC
LAR002	Trench 1, context 1015	Charcoal	OxA-32373	1504±28 BP	calAD 432–633
LAR002	Same sample as above	Charcoal (cf. tamarix sp.)	OxA-33825	1616±27 BP	calAD 389–536
LAR002	(same sample as above)	(same sample as above)	OxA-33826	1676±28 BP	calAD 260–422
LAR002	Trench 1, context 1019	Charcoal	OxA-33827	1638±27 BP	calAD 339–534
LAR002	Trench 2, context 1021	Charcoal (cf. tamarix sp.)	OxA-33828	1121±28 BP	calAD 778–994
LAR002	Trench 2, context 1021	Barley grain	OxA-33829	1377±27 BP	calAD 612–679
LAR003	Trench 1, context 2006	Charcoal	OxA-33719	823±28 BP	calAD 1166–1263
LAR004	From pisé of S enclosing wall	Charcoal	OxA-32374	878±25 BP	calAD 1046–1221
LAR005	Trench 1, context 1014	Charcoal (cf. tamarix sp.)	OxA-33720	1589±30 BP	calAD 406–542
LAR006	From external wall (intrusive)	Plant remains	OxA-33898	104±28 BP	calAD 1682–1935
LAR031	Surface of offering structure	Calcined bone	OxA-33899	1344±30 BP	calAD 641–765
TAG008	Mortar from tower of enceinte	Charcoal (cf. tamarix sp.)	OxA-35378	1082±27 BP	calAD 895–1017
TAG008	Mortar from tower of enceinte	Charcoal (cf. tamarix sp.)	OxA-35377	1057±27 BP	calAD 900–1024
TAG009	From pisé wall	Textile	OxA-35604	993±24 BP	calAD 990–1150
TAG010	From mudbrick wall of building	Plant remains	OxA-35448	409±21 BP	calAD 1437–1615
TAG014	Occupation layer Tr1 (2033)	Charcoal (cf. tamarix sp.)	OxA-35187	1658±28 BP	calAD 263–526
TAG014	Occupation layer Trench 1 (2032)	Charcoal (cf. tamarix sp.)	OxA-35186	1544±27 BP	calAD 426–577

Table 6.1 (*cont.*)

Area/Site	Context	Material	Reference	Date	Calibrated
TAK001	From a mudbrick wall	Plant remains	OxA-33900	129±29 BP	calAD 1675–1942
TAK004	From mortar of outer wall	Charred seeds	OxA-35652	943±26 BP	calAD 1028–1155
TAK004	From S boundary wall (intrusive)	Sheep/goat pellet	OxA-33850	Modern± BP	0
TAK006	Trench 1 (2010)	Charcoal (cf. Tamarix sp.)	OxA-33851	1560±26 BP	calAD 423–557
TAK006	Trench 2 (2012)	Charcoal	OxA-33852	1586±28 BP	calAD 411–542
TAK013	From mortar of outside wall	Plant remains	OxA-33853	365±26 BP	calAD 1450–1634
TAK016	From pisé wall	Charcoal	OxA-33854	243±24 BP	calAD 1528– . . .
TAM001	Trench 1 (3028)	Charcoal	OxA-33966	1512±27 BP	calAD 430–615
TIN001	Trench 4 (3030)	Charcoal	OxA-35188	1490±27 BP	calAD 475–643
TIN005	From pisé wall	Wood	OxA-35449	768±22 BP	calAD 1222–1279
TIN015	Occupation layer, Trench 2 (1054)	Wheat grain	OxA-35192	1631±27 BP	calAD 345–535
TIN015	Fill layer Trench 2 (1028)	Charcoal	OxA-33855	1624±25 BP	calAD 382–536
TIN015	Occupation layer Trench 2 (1053)	Barley grain	OxA-35190	1607±29 BP	calAD 396–538
TIN015	Occupation layer Trench 4 (1051)	Barley grain	OxA-35189	1601±26 BP	calAD 402–537
TIN015	Fill layer Trench 2 (1028)	Wheat grain	OxA-35191	1594±27 BP	calAD 405–539
TIN033	From pisé wall	Date stone	OxA-35648	633±24 BP	calAD 1287–1396
TIR006	From wall of *qasr*	Plant remains	OxA-32432	919±25 BP	calAD 1030–1169
TIR008	Occupation layer Trench 1 (3116)	Charcoal (cf. Tamarix sp.)	OxA-35649	1500±24 BP	calAD 437–631
TIR013	Occupation layer Trench 1 (3119)	Wheat grain	OxA-35194	1604±28 BP	calAD 399–537
TIR013	Occupation layer Trench 1 (3118)	Wheat grain	OxA-35193	1588±29 BP	calAD 408–542
TIS007	Occupation layer Trench 1 (2067)	Charcoal	OxA-35650	911±23 BP	calAD 1035–1184
TIS008	Metalworking debris Trench 1 (2068)	Charcoal (cf. Tamarix sp.)	OxA-35196	1812±27 BP	calAD 128–320
TIS008	Same sample as above	Same sample as above	OxA-35195	1795±29 BP	calAD 133–326
ZAG001	Trench 2, context 3021	Date stone	OxA-32372	792±25 BP	calAD 1210–1275
ZAG001	Trench 1, context 3004	Date stone	OxA-33856	688±26 BP	calAD 1269–1387

ZAG001	Same sample as above	Charcoal	OxA-33857	946±26 BP	calAD 1026–1155
ZAG001	From mortar of S enclosing wall	Charcoal	OxA-33858	974±25 BP	calAD 1015–1155
ZAG001	From mortar of citadel	Date stone	OxA-35651	908±26 BP	calAD 1035–1203
ZAG002	From mortar of S enclosing wall	Charcoal	OxA-32521	989±26 BP	calAD 991–1152
ZAG002	Trench 1, context 1007 (fabric of mudbrick wall)	Charcoal	OxA-33859	1113±27 BP	calAD 878–995
ZAG002	From mortar in W enclosing wall	Charcoal (cf. palm)	OxA-33860	975±26 BP	calAD 1014–1155
ZAG002	From mortar of W wall of tomb	Charcoal	OxA-33861	992±26 BP	calAD 989–1151
ZAG002	From secondary phase of S enclosing wall	Charcoal (cf. tamarix sp.)	OxA-33862	972±25 BP	calAD 1016–1155
ZAG002	From mortar of E gate	Charcoal (cf. palm)	OxA-33863	1023±26 BP	calAD 971–1115
ZAG002	From tower in E wall	Charcoal (cf. tamarix sp.)	OxA-33864	983±26 BP	calAD 995–1153
ZAG022	Trench 1 (intrusive)	Seeds (geraniaceae family)	OxA-33865	Modern± BP	-
ZAG040	From pisé wall	Charcoal	OxA-33866	307±24 BP	calAD 1493–1649
ZAG042	From pisé wall	Date stone	OxA-33867	205±24 BP	calAD 1649– . . .
ZAG046	From pisé wall	Plant remains (grass)	OxA-33967	234±25 BP	calAD 1639– . . .
ZAG048	From pisé wall	Plant remains	OxA-33868	128±24 BP	calAD 1678–1940
ZAG048	From pisé wall	Charcoal (palm)	OxA-33901	195±29 BP	calAD 1648– . . .
Wadi Noun					
Adrar Zerzem	Tumulus 2, burial	Human bone	Hela-14884	1430±35 BP	calAD 565–660
Agwidir	From underneath the building, layer 21, STC 35	Charcoal	Beta-259285	Data missing	calAD 900–1030
Agwidir	From underneath the building, layer 21, STC 35	Wood	Beta-259286	Data missing	calAD 1000–1160
Agwidir	From wall construction, STC 35	Wood	Beta-259287	Data missing	calAD 1020–1200
Agwidir	End of occupation, layer 71, STC 35	Charcoal	Beta-259282	Data missing	calAD 1030–1220
Agwidir	Wall of the tabiya	Charcoal	Beta-259290	Data missing	calAD 1040–1260

Table 6.1 (*cont.*)

Area/Site	Context	Material	Reference	Date	Calibrated
Agwidir	North-west tower	Charcoal	Beta-259284	Data missing	calAD 1160–1280
Agwidir	Roof of the stable, layer 59, STC 35	Charcoal	Beta-259281	Data missing	calAD 1170–1280
Agwidir	Occupation of house, layer 43, STC 35	Charcoal	Beta-259283	Data missing	calAD 1280–1410
Agwidir	From foundation trench of wall	Charcoal	Beta-259289	Data missing	calAD 1440–1640
Agwidir	Sondage A, layer 5	Charcoal	Beta-259288	Data missing	calAD 1480–1660
Foum Asca	Layer at base of trench 1	Shell	Beta-295799	2880±40 BP	1207–931 calBC
Foum Asca	Layer at base of trench 3	Shell	Beta-295800	1950±40 BP	41 calBC – calAD 129
Tuflit el-Harratin	Well, STC41, sondage 1, silo 1, context 2	Charcoal	Beta-259291	Data missing	calAD 690–980
Tuflit el-Harratin	Furnace, next to copper ore, slag and glazed lamp, STC41, sondage 2, context 15	Charcoal	Beta-259291	Data missing	calAD 710–980
Tuwat					
Between Tamentit and Adrar, Complex 1	Wall of *qasr*	Wood	Hv-9702	600±55 BP	calAD 1286–1421
Between Tamentit and Adrar, Complex 2	Wall of mosque	Wood	Hv-9703	470±65 BP	calAD 1310–1632

were sent in succession over the Atlas.[11] These expeditions took place 60 years after the famous campaigns of Balbus against the oases of the Ziban, Ghadamis and Fazzan, but seem to conform to a similar pattern. Although some commentators have argued that the Roman troops were pursuing rebels from north of the Atlas southwards, Dio's comments indicate that their opponents were familiar with the desert environment and conditions. Although they have generally been assumed to have been nomads,[12] just as has proved the case with the peoples of the Ziban and Fazzan, it is plausible that they included oasis dwellers. The corollary of the campaigns is that the account in Ptolemy's *Geography* relating to interior Africa south of the Atlas contains reference to numerous settlements, some of which are specifically designated as 'towns'.[13] It would be hazardous to attempt to reconstruct the Saharan world in detail from Ptolemy's lists of names and co-ordinates; indeed the geographical errors and imprecisions are well established.[14] Ptolemy's account of the Sahara, although clearly geographically flawed by a tendency to join the dots between widely separated phenomena, nonetheless indicates that Rome had acquired knowledge of a large number of peoples, rivers, lakes and significant settlements deep in the Sahara. In particular, he mentions two 'great rivers of the interior' the Gir and the Niger and it is clear from the text that these were at least seasonally active streams. These major wadis were evidently a focus of population including 'urban-scale' settlements at some locations. The logical conclusion is that this refers to some of our major oases zones – and indeed the Garamantian capital Garama (Jarma) is listed as a *metropolis* along with two other locations: Nigira, on the north bank of the Niger (probably the Algerian Wadi Jedi in this context) and Gira, below the Gir river (Wadi Gir/Saouara).[15]

In the Medieval and Early Modern world, the oases of the Western Sahara were among the most prominent, populous and influential, with a profound importance for Saharan trade and for the security of the Muslim states of the Maghrib.[16] The *Bilad as-Siba*, land of disorder, as

[11] Pliny, *Natural History* 5.14–16; Dio, *Histories* 60.9; de la Chappelle 1934, for general discussion.

[12] De la Chappelle 1934, 110.

[13] Ptolemy, *Geography* 4.6; cf. Martin 1908, 30–31 who identifies 17 names in Ptolemy's account with modern Berber toponyms. The plausibility of specific name suggestions seems less significant than the overall observation that Ptolemy's account reproduces Berber toponyms and attributes them to a Saharan locale, where the only urban-scale sites must have been oases.

[14] On the toponyms, population groups and Roman knowledge of the western Sahara, see especially Desanges 1962; 1978; 1980.

[15] Ptolemy, *Geography* 4.6.

[16] On the rising importance of the trade connections of the Western Sahara in the Medieval era, see *inter alia*, Lydon 2009; MacDonald 2011; Mauny 1978; Vanacker 1973.

the mountainous and desert south of Morocco was known, was a recurrent source of insurrection against the *Bilad al-Mahkzan*, land of order, comprising the northern plains of Morocco.[17] Yet it was from the *Bilad as-Siba* and 'especially the land of desert and palm oasis lying to the east of the Atlas that almost every dynasty of Sultans rose to conquer and replace the last'.[18] Several factors help explain how the Western Sahara could be such a potent threat to successive states in the Western Maghrib. Firstly, the desert settlements were shielded to the north by the imposing Atlas ranges, with limited passes over which armies could be taken and which are closed at times in winter – making continuous control of the south by the powers in the north extremely difficult. Even the French colonial regime in the twentieth century chose to operate hegemonically through the intermediary 'lords' of the Atlas passes.[19] The second factor is that the oases, especially of the Draa and Tafilalat, are among the largest and most productive in the Sahara and have supported substantial populations.[20] Rohlfs reported hundreds of fortified villages in the Draa and Tafilalat oases, with an alleged combined population of 350,000 in the mid-nineteenth century, likewise Ibn Khaldun describes these regions along with Figuig, the Gourara and Tuwat as each having hundreds of *qsur* or villages.[21] Even if a little inflated, this was a very large manpower reserve and in combination with additional pastoral groups of the desert, could pose a potent military threat, albeit that they were as often engaged in internecine warfare with each other.[22] The Almoravid, Almohad, Merinid, Saadian and Alouite dynasties all originated, or gained critical strength, in the oases of Draa and Tafilalat.[23]

Transposing this sort of pattern into the remoter past represents another thing altogether, of course. However, if pre-Islamic oasis settlement and Saharan trade can be demonstrated, it is plausible that the same combination of their relative isolation, the mass of the oasis populations and the development of trade in the Moroccan Sahara had an influence on the pattern of Roman provincial government in Mauretania Caesariensis and Tingitana. We have already noted the evidence of Roman campaigns beyond the Atlas as a sequel to the annexation of the Mauretanian kingdom in the AD 40s. Yet most commentators on Roman Morocco have concluded that the mountains

[17] For the best and most detailed account of the history of the Moroccan Sahara, see Jacques-Meunié 1982. For the explanation of the *Bilad as-Siba*, see Maxwell 2004, 29–31; Dunn 1977.

[18] Maxwell 2004, 30. [19] Maxwell 2004. [20] Joly 1948.

[21] Levtzion and Hopkins 2000, 325; Rohlfs 2001, 56, 174.

[22] On the inter-oasis raiding between Draa, Tafilalat and Guir, see Landau 1969, 92; Rolhfs 2001, 168–69, 178.

[23] Jacques-Meunié 1982; Lugan 2000.

were essentially a barrier to the south and, if Rome had occasional problems with indigenous peoples thereafter, it is commonly assumed that these were montane groups.[24] On the other hand, it is striking how the geography of Roman Tingitana reflects some key aspects of the later Islamic territory. The triangular northern tip of the country is defined by two main routes running south and south-east from Tingi/Tangiers. In the Roman period, the western coastal route ended at Sala/modern Rabat, while the eastern inland route led to Volubilis at the foot of the Middle Atlas, in relatively close proximity to successive Islamic cities of Moulay Idris, Meknes and Fez. All of these south-eastern sites are located in a position to serve as a western terminus of a land route from the rest of the Maghrib to the east of the Mouloya river, but they were also the northern end points of routes across the High Atlas to the Tafilalat. The most notable difference between the Roman and Medieval periods is that in the latter era further large cities were established to the south, such as Marrakech and Sijilmasa.

To approach this from another direction, the town of Volubilis was an extraordinary urban creation, and one already well established under the Mauretanian kingdom that preceded the Roman province. Traditional accounts have not satisfactorily explained the reasons for its prominence in this inland location. The possibility that this was a centre from which connections were maintained with both mountain and desert peoples to the south and south-east bears serious consideration.[25] As we shall see, the current evidence for oasis development in this part of the Sahara suggests it may have begun a little later than the central Saharan zone dominated by the Garamantes.

The prime aim of this chapter is to assess whether any evidence exists to demonstrate early oasis development in the Western Sahara. There has been little archaeological research on these oases hitherto, but we present below some significant pointers to their initial development by the early first millennium AD. The order of discussion below will start in the north-east and move gradually south-west along the southern flank of the Atlas mountains. The following sections will then turn to other oases of the western Algerian Sahara, the far south of Morocco and Mauritania. Although the arguments we adduce for development of these oases suggest

[24] For traditional accounts of Mauretania, see Carcopino 1943; Châtelain 1944. On the frontier, see Euzennat 1989; Mattingly *et al.* 2013, 40–62; Rebuffat 1999.

[25] The famous altars of peace erected at Volubilis, celebrating treaty relations between Rome and a people known as the Baquates has led to much speculation, but no great clarity, as to the whereabouts of the lands of the Baquates. See Rebuffat 1999, 276–82; Shaw 1987. The possibility that the geo-political context of these treaties spread beyond the Atlas mountains has not been seriously considered.

a somewhat later date than is supported by the evidence presented above for oases further east in the Sahara, we would emphasise that the hydrological conditions in the Moroccan Sahara were well suited for an early evolution of oasis farming. The volume of water running off the High Atlas mountains into the desert lands bordering their southern and eastern flanks not only directly supports oasis cultivation, but also recharges the water table in these areas.

Wadi Gir/Wadi Saoura

To the west of Laghouat, at the west end of the Saharan Atlas, there is a group of oases that lie *c.*250 km south of the Roman frontier forts of Mauretania Caesariensis. These are Moghrar, Boussemghoune, Ain Sefra, Figuig, Ich and Bechar, and they are known for the remains of fortified villages of presumed Medieval date. There are also foggaras known at all these sites except Ain Sefra.[26] What is particularly intriguing about these oasis clusters is that the route that connects them is a key pass through the Saharan Atlas, which, if projected north, passes close by the westernmost forts of the Roman frontier of Mauretania Caesariensis at Numerus Syrorum and Pomaria.[27] To the south-west, the route follows the Wadi Zousfana which skirts the north-western edge of the Great Eastern Erg to merge with the Wadi Gir and form the Wadi Saoura, carrying seasonal floodwater from the Atlas ranges deep into the desert.[28] The western side of the Wadi Saoura comprises a series of rocky escarpments, while the east side is defined by the limits of the sand sea. Remarkably, until the construction of the modern dam at Jorf Torba on the Gir, floods were regularly carried down this normally dry valley as far as the Tuwat oases (see below), a total distance of *c.*1,000 km. Ptolemy's description of the Gir states that it was one of two major rivers of the Sahara and that it united 'as it were, the Garamantian defile and the Usrgala mountains'.[29] If this was the Gir/Saoura, as seems entirely plausible, we might understand this comment as denoting a river valley running for a great distance south-east from the Atlas, in the general direction that the Romans knew the Garamantes lay, rather than absolutely to their door. Ptolemy also lists a settlement called Gira as a *metropolis* and numerous other *poleis* on the north (left) bank of the Gir, which would correspond well topographically with the *qsur* along

[26] Châtelain 1896; Heywood 1926, 94–100; Homo and Hugonot 1953; Remini *et al.* 2014.

[27] Laporte 2011 provides a useful overview of the western area of Mauretania Caesariensis, but does not consider the potential existence of oasis communities.

[28] Gautier 1970, 77–87. [29] Ptolemy, *Geography* 4.6; Stevenson 1991, 105–6.

the Souara in Tuwat. That some genuine information underlies Ptolemy's notion of rivers in the desert is confirmed by his references to rivers that disappeared at the surface, but which continued to run underground and to these desert rivers ending in seasonal lakes (chotts).

Even when surface flow is limited, the transference of sub-surface waters down this wadi is significant. Looking down the course of the Wadi Gir/ Saoura today, it is evident that numerous small oases have been developed along it. Some of these lie close to significant cemeteries of pre-Islamic burial monuments, some of exceptional scale or decorative features (as at Jorf Torba, see below). The irregular floodwaters were also augmented by the use of artificial means. Between Figuig and Adrar at the north of the Tuwat oases are a number of small oases that lie on the banks of the Wadi Saoura, many of which are foggara fed. Settlements and hillforts are visible on the escarpments overlooking Mazzer and Taghit which appear to encompass a range of periods. At Igli, where the Wadi Zousfana and Wadi Gir unite to form the Saoura, there is a low hillock, now much damaged, on which a settlement has stood. Another hillfort is visible opposite the oasis of Beni Abbas.

As noted already, the first Roman campaign in AD 41 crossed the Atlas and proceeded to a river valley called Ger, and this can surely be equated with the Wadi Gir.[30] The second campaign clearly went further, with the commander winning two major victories (presumably in two separate oasis areas), but also passing through hostile and waterless terrain. The headwaters of the Gir are in the High Atlas, close to the Algerian border of Morocco, but the Roman struggle to find water at a crucial point in the campaign suggests that this column marched a long way down the Gir/ Saoura towards Tuwat. The miracle of a rainstorm that allegedly came to the rescue of the second Roman army may well be a literary trope, but it might equally be an allusion to the sudden and astonishing appearance of a flood in a wadi deep in the Sahara.[31] The connectivity between the Atlas and the Tuwat oases along the Gir/Saoura is important because it would more or less guarantee that oasis technologies and crops were shared along this line once they were present at either of the ends.

An example of pre-Islamic connectivity comes from the distribution of burial monuments with 'funerary chapels' (*tombes à chapelles*) along the

[30] Dio, *Histories* 60.9; Pliny, *Natural History* 5.14–16; Ptolemy, *Geography* 4.6.

[31] A flood of this kind took place most recently after the rains in November 2014. The Saoura eventually branches, with part of its flow ending in a seasonal lake and a second branch running on south to the Tuwat (Gautier 1970, 80–82), perhaps a distant echo of Ptolemy's garbled account (*Geography* 4.6) of the tributary streams, lakes and marshes associated with the Gir.

Gir, in the Tafilalat and the Draa. This has rarely been considered in the context of sedentary oasis cultivators, yet equally, the default assumption that these were tombs of pastoralists is unproven and the monuments are clustered in areas that were suited to oasis development.[32] Of particular interest are a corpus of carved and painted stele that were found in association with a number of tombs at Jorf Torba on the upper Wadi Gir.[33] The images include many horses and horsemen (something also paralleled on two early-mid-first millennium AD settlement sites in the Wadi Draa), people associated with a Libyan inscription and most notably a scene with six people represented frontally, including a man and a boy armed with spears and four women, two bearing small 'crosses'.[34] All the figures evidently wore woven garments, some with geometric patterning. As we shall see, there is now a parallel for this sort of decoration in a tomb in the Draa in an area where we do seem to have evidence of pre-Islamic oasis development. An approximate dating would place these images somewhere in the late antique era.

Tafilalat (Erfoud and Sijilmasa)

The Tafilalat is the second most extensive oasis in Morocco, after the Wadi Draa (see below), with *c.*1,000,000 palms in the 1950s.[35] This area, centred on Erfoud, utilises both seasonal run-off waters from the mountains and some limited groundwater sources to support an extensive oasis zone.[36] Although there is no perennial flow from the Atlas into this basin, a broad extent of plain land is irrigated by a combination of a low volume flow in part of the year (at most 5–6 months), augmented by the exploitation of violent seasonal floods spilling out from the mountain front. There are two major seasonal rivers here, the Wadi Ziz (Sis) and the Wadi Rheris (Gheris), along with a number of smaller tributaries. Although sometimes

32 Bokbot 2019.

33 See Camps 1984, 208–12, especially figure 10; Lihoreau 1993; Reygasse 1950, 104–8, figures 158–161. Radiocarbon dating on three of these monuments place them in the late first millennium BC/early-mid-first millennium AD.

34 These crosses have conventionally been seen as possibly Christian crucifixes, Camps 1984, 209–11, but they could just as plausibly be something more prosaic such as an item of female equipment to match the arms of the males – could these be spindle whorls and distaffs depicted as they would be carried? See Lihoreau 1993, 109–15 for a detailed description of the painted slabs recovered from Tomb 5 within an extensive cemetery. The slabs seem to have been placed in the inner recess of a 'funerary chapel' attached to the east side of Tomb 5 (1993, 70–74). The other painted slabs are believed to derive from two further large '*tombes a chappelles*', nos 1 and 6 (1993, 24–25, 27–32).

35 El-Khoumsi *et al.* 2017, 46.

36 El-Khoumsi *et al.* 2017; Gaucher 1948; Ricard 1925, 377–80.

used in the more geographically limited sense of one of the sub-groups of oases in this plain, the Tafilalat also functions as the collective name for all the oases here. The Tafilalat oases exploit the wide alluvial deposits dumped in front of the mountains, into which the wadis have incised channels, making it more difficult to divert water out of the wadis onto the neighbouring plains.[37]

The upper courses of the two wadis contain a number of smaller oases, fed by more or less perennial flow and springs. In the Tafilalat proper, starting from the point where the wadis debouche from gorges into a wide plain, the hydrology becomes more complicated and difficult. The irrigation largely depends on control of the floods and the diversion of waters into canals and a large artificial channel (the 'Ziz filali'), which has effectively diverted the main flow of the Ziz into a man-made system. The Wadi Rheris eventually joins the Ziz in the southern Tafilalat, but the two wadis run in parallel a comparatively short distance apart (*c.*30 km average) for a considerable distance through the oasis belt. As the bed of the Ziz is 10–12 m higher than the Rheris, most of the irrigation water is taken from the Wadi Ziz. However, at one point the wadis come within 2.5 km of each other and given the strength of some of the peak flood incidents, there is a serious danger that the Rheris could at some point capture the Ziz much higher up, at a stroke depriving about 75 per cent of the oasis zone of its irrigation.[38] Foggaras have also been constructed at some point in time in considerable numbers in the Tafilalat to supplement the water in the wadis, with large numbers identified on the west side of the Wadi Rheris (see Fig. 1.4d), but others also to the east of the Ziz.[39]

The oasis comprises a number of distinct zones. Along the Wadi Ziz from north to south are the oasis districts of Medarhera, Reteb, Tizimi, Erfoud, Rissani/Tafilalat; along the Rheris are the palmeries of Goulmina, Tiliouine, Touroug, Fezna and Jorf. Beyond Tafilalat, the two wadis combine as the Wadi Daoura.[40] In the 1860s, Rohlfs listed 150 fortified villages spread across the various palmeries of the Tafilalat.[41] From Sijilmasa, routes ran south-west to the Draa at Zagora (*c.*200 km) and north up the gorge of Wadi Ziz to the Atlas passes of Tizi n'Talghemt and Tizi N'Zad, leading across the mountains to Fez.[42]

[37] Gaucher 1948; Jacques-Meunié 1982, 146–54 for a detailed explanation of the topography and hydrology of the Tafilalat.

[38] Jacques-Meunié 1982, 150–52. Much effort has been expended in modern times to try to avert this danger.

[39] Castellani 1999, 231–38.

[40] Rohlfs 2001, 59–61, 163–75, for descriptions of the Tafilalat in the mid-nineteenth century.

[41] Rohlfs 2001, 174. [42] Jacques-Meunié 1982, 400–1 (map).

Sijilmasa

Little is known about the earliest archaeology of the oasis, with most attention directed to the study of the celebrated Islamic site, Sijilmasa.[43] The legendary account of al-Bakri specifies that the town was founded in AD 757–758, by the Bani Midrar following up on a tip from one of a group of pastoralists who had allegedly hitherto only used the potential of the location for pasturing their flocks.[44] This traditional account of an Arab foundation of the oasis and canonical dating is still followed in much recent work, despite the fact that excavations and a series of radiocarbon dates suggest that the activity at the location of Sijilmasa prior to the mid-eighth century may have amounted to more than some seasonal pastoral visits.[45] Beneath the main mosque at the centre of Sijilmasa, there was an elite residence and beneath that a hard-packed floor and hearth which has been dated to calAD 138–527 (2-sigma). A further sample from beneath the mosque has a date of calAD 413–863 and excavations to the west of the mosque dated another fire pit to calAD 545–863.[46] The logic of the three dates is that Sijilmasa existed as a site prior to the mid-eighth century, though the character of its early occupation requires further investigation. There are certainly some substantial pre-Islamic cemeteries in this area and a number of hillfort sites in the periphery of the oasis again hint at pre-Islamic origins of sedentary settlement.[47] It is quite plausible that the Islamic foundation myth has served to misdirect us from recognising a pre-existing oasis farming community here.

Rock Art and Protohistoric Settlement

Recent studies by Yves and Christine Gauthier have mapped the location of chariot representations across the Saharan regions, with a particular cluster in southern Morocco.[48] The very densest concentration of chariot imagery

[43] For the history, cf. Jacques-Meunié 1982. For the archaeology, see Lightfoot and Miller 1996; Messier 1997; Messier and Miller 2015.

[44] Levtzion and Hopkins 2000, 65 for al-Bakri's classic account of the foundation and the state of the town in the mid-eighth century. See Capel, Chapter 16, this volume for a full description surrounding the founding of Sijilmasa.

[45] Messier and Fili 2011, 129 present the new dates, but stick with the orthodox interpretation. This probably needs revisiting in light of the information emerging from the Draa (see below). See also Messier 1997, 81–82.

[46] Messier and Fili 2011, 129.

[47] On the cemeteries, Bokbot 2005; 2019; on the hillforts, see Capel, Chapter 16, this volume.

[48] Gauthier and Gauthier 2011. Additional work, reported on in Gauthier and Gauthier 2015 (with map at 69), adds further weight to the Moroccan cluster and many of these discoveries are in the southernmost mountains, bordering the open desert and relatively close to the major Moroccan oases.

occurs at three closely linked sites about 30 km south of the Tafilalat on the Wadi Ziz at a place known as Taouz, a topographic control point for people moving towards the oasis from the south. The number of individual chariot images recorded here is an unprecedented 323 (22 per cent of the total of 1,424 scenes in their database for the entire Sahara).[49] The vast majority were carved on rocks alongside the defended southern side of a hillfort that controlled a bend in the Wadi and from where extensive views of people approaching could be had.[50] The other chariot engravings at Taouz were closely associated spatially with some very large pre-Islamic tombs.[51] While the contemporaneity of hillfort (with a mix of rectangular and sub-rectangular buildings) and the large tombs with the engravings is not certain, the geographical co-location is very suggestive as is the likelihood that the people here were at last partly sedentarised. Although there are no date palms here, there is some modern cultivation of the wadi alluvium, especially in the less volatile side channels. Overall, Taouz could be viewed as a portal from the desert into the main oasis zone to the north. There are certainly reasons to believe that spread of horses and chariots was closely linked with the establishment of oasis communities and trade networks.[52]

Wadi Draa

New information on the Draa valley *c.*200 km to the west of Tafilalat adds weight to the argument for Protohistoric origins. The Wadi Draa is one of the most extraordinary and largest of all Saharan oases, spread along a 900 km long valley, with an estimated 2,000,000 date palms.[53] The source of the wadi lies in the High Atlas above Ouarzazate and for a substantial part of its initial course, running broadly north-west to south-east, the wadi is a perennial river, though of highly variable flow across the year and between years.[54] In Roman times it allegedly (but plausibly) still had a population of crocodiles.[55] South of

[49] Gauthier and Gauthier 2015, 13–32.
[50] Gauthier and Gauthier 2015, 13 and 69 for maps and 14–18 for discussion of location.
[51] Gauthier and Gauthier 2015, 18–27.
[52] See further, Mattingly 2017, 22–24. This is the same site called Jabal Afilal and illustrated in Figures 16.4–16.6 by Capel, Chapter 16, this volume.
[53] Jacques-Meunié 1982, 142–46 (for a detailed explanation of the topography and hydrology of the Draa); Ricard 1925, 300–1 (brief and lacunous, reflecting poor state of knowledge at that date); Richet 1920 (covers the lower Draa only); Zaïnabi 2004, 30 (for the number of palms).
[54] Jacques-Meunié 1982, 145.
[55] Pliny, *Natural History* 5.9: 'flumen Darat in quo crocodilos gigni'; cf. Desanges 1980, 114–15, 117–18 for commentary. Crocodiles have been reported in the lower river Draa as recently as 1950 - Monteil 1951. See Brito *et al.* 2011 for a general discussion of Saharan crocodiles from the Holocene to the present.

Ouarzazate the river runs through a narrow defile before opening into a broad valley bordered by mountains on either side. This section of the valley (the Middle Draa) is divided into a series of oasis zones: from north-west to south-east these are Agdz/Mezguita (30 × 1.5 km and 16 × 0.5 km palmeries), Tinzouline (20 × 1.5 km), Ternata (20 × 5–10 km), Fezwata (30 km × 3 km), and Ktawa (20 × 6–8 km).[56] Only after making a turn to run east to west (the 'coude du Draa'), does the wadi finally disappear underground beyond the final major oasis zone of Mhamid (20 × 4 km). The dates of the Wadi Draa have a high reputation and the productive capacity is large.[57]

To the west, there are sporadic palm stands on the many tributaries (but not on the main channel) along its course to the Atlantic seaboard.[58] Only in the most exceptional flood conditions do the waters from the high Atlas get carried all the way down the Draa to the Atlantic.[59] More commonly, the conditions along the lower Draa are not conducive for sedentary settlement.[60]

The Agdz to Mhamid sector of the valley thus constitutes the Draa oasis proper, but it is by no means uniform. Year-round flow has tended to reach only as far as Zagora and then rather sluggishly. Irrigation in the Draa valley depends on diverting water from the river when the water is high into canals that feed garden areas laid out parallel to the wadi downstream of the diversion dam (Fig. 1.4a/b). The upper sections of the Middle Draa have thus traditionally been much better served by water than the region to the south-east of Zagora. In average years the main irrigation for Fezwata, Ktawa and Mhamid came from three or four extended flood incidents of 15–20 days duration, when a substantial flow was carried beyond Zagora. In poor years, when only one or two floods of a brief duration have occurred, this did little more than keep alive the palm groves and ruled out cultivation of cereals.[61] Irrigation has been supplemented by wells, but there are only limited traces of foggara systems in the Draa.

A singular aspect of the topography of the Middle Draa is provided by the steep escarpments of Jabal Bani, which from certain directions limited access into and out of the wadi. Jabal Bani runs west to east south of and parallel to the Anti-Atlas range, with two branches crossing the Draa valley and dividing it into distinct basins. On the east bank of the Draa the Jabal Bani turns and runs north-west. The presence of Jabal Bani thus accounts for the strange

[56] Rohlfs 2001, 53–59; Zaïnabi 2004, 17–24. [57] Rohlfs 2001, 55.

[58] Jacques-Meunié 1982, 143–44; cf. also Richet 1920; Riser 1996.

[59] Jacques-Meunié 1982, 144 records that this happened in two exceptional floods in 1949 and 1950.

[60] See Tayler 2003 for a revealing account of the rigours of journeying down the Draa from near Ouarzazate to the Atlantic, with the difficulties escalating significantly beyond Mhamid.

[61] Jacques-Meunié 1982, 146.

dog-leg course of the Wadi Draa – once it breaks through the southern branch of Jabal Bani at Foum Larjam, the wadi turns west along the south side of the range towards the Atlantic.[62] The principal routes out of the valley to the east run north-east from Zagora to Sijilmasa in the Tafilalat, north-west of Agdz across the mountains towards Ouarzazate and Marrakech across the High Atlas passes, south-east from Foum Larjam towards Tabalbala. At two points along its course, the valley narrows and the river flows through defiles or 'passages obligés' in the Jabal Bani, at the Imi n'Takat pass between the Fezwata and Ktawa, and at Tidri controlling the key pass between Ktawa and Mhamid. An additional significant topographic control point in the valley is marked by Jabal Zagora, an imposing mountain that dominates the valley at the division between the Ternata and Fezwata oases.

A huge area of the Middle Draa (where the flow is north-west to south-east) is irrigated by diverting water from the river into irrigation channels and gardens created along its course. There is an abundance of archaeology visible on satellite imagery in the wadi: hillforts, fortified settlements, extensive cemeteries of pre-Islamic tombs, and so on (Fig. 6.2). Since 2015, we have been conducting fieldwork along this section of the Draa, researching the abundant evidence of pre-Islamic cairn cemeteries and abandoned hillforts and villages. The areas of the oasis that are still cultivated are studded with hundreds of minor villages, mostly of the fortified *qasba* type and probably dating to the last few hundred years. The earliest settlements within the oasis belt itself are buried or masked by the later phases of settlement and cultivation, so our initial survey work has concentrated on structures that lie at or close to the fringes of the palm groves, often on the higher ground bordering the oasis.

We have obtained a number of radiocarbon dates that attest to sedentary settlement in the first half of the first millennium AD. Ten hillfort sites and one oasis site date to the first half of the first millennium AD, with evidence of numerous fragments of rotary quern stones and a distinctive cordoned pottery tradition (Fig. 6.3).[63] The sites are all associated with pre-Islamic burials (in three cases the cairns overlie the settlement) and in two instances also with horse-dominated rock art scenes. At three of the sites we have recovered wheat and barley grains that are dated to the same period.[64]

A classic example of a Protohistoric hillfort is TIN001, situated on top of the Foum Chenna cliff face that holds a dense concentration of rock art and

[62] Jacques-Meunié 1982, 116–17.

[63] Mattingly *et al.* 2017; 2018. The hillfort sites are LAR002, LAR005/6, TAK006, TAM001, TIN001, TIN015, TIR008, TIR013, TIS007 and TIS008, the oasis site is TAG014.

[64] Sites TIN015, TIR013 and LAR002.

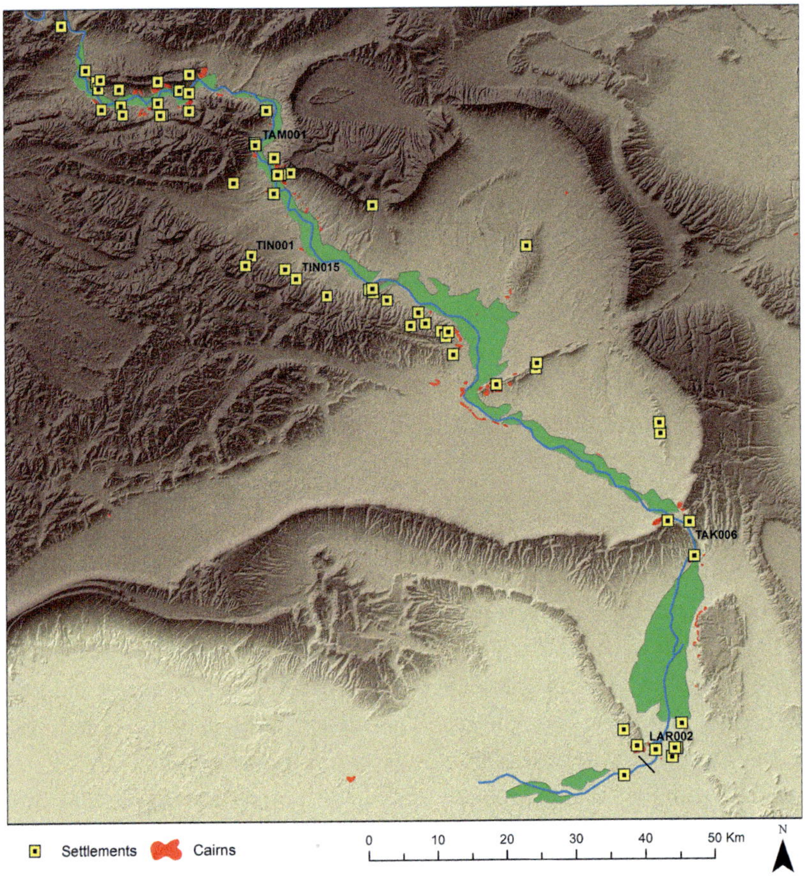

Figure 6.2. Protohistoric settlements and funerary zones in the Wadi Draa.

Libyan inscriptions (TIN012).[65] The hilltop site was protected by a series of substantial drystone walls, each with a single gateway. The walled core of the site comprises a series of enclosures and *c.*8–10 buildings leading off a central alley that led to the highest point of the hill, which was left empty apart from a cairn at the top. There are at least two phases of construction visible: the earliest consists of loosely coursed boulders and the second of drystone slab masonry. A number of horse engravings were found built into the structures of the settlement implying a close relation between the rock art and the people of this site. Another nearby site (TIN015) shares some similarities of layout, with a lower outer enclosure (that contained a few vestigial traces of structures), a middle zone entered through a gate in a second wall, where most of the habitation seems to have been concentrated. A central road led up through

[65] See Pichler 2000; Simoneau 1972a/b.

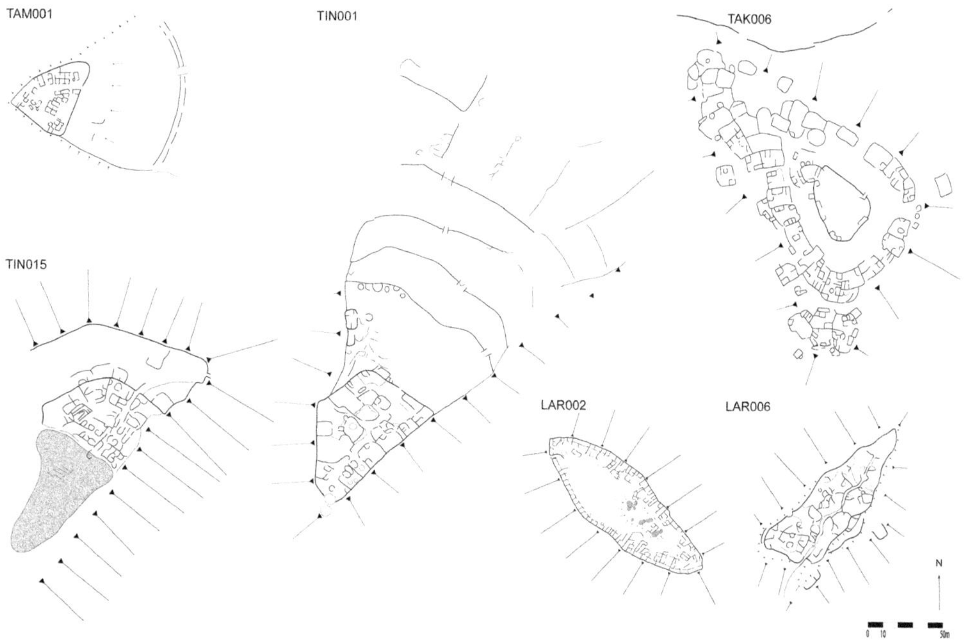

Figure 6.3. Comparative plans of protohistoric sites in the Wadi Draa.

the settlement to a third area on the highest part of the site that was empty of structures, but which was covered in rock art on natural rock surfaces and many boulders. The vast majority of the images relate to horses (or to crudely engraved quadrupeds which are thought likely to represent horses). Once again, horses (both riderless and with riders), were engraved on blocks built into the walls of dwellings as well as natural boulders and bare rock surfaces.

The highly structured placement of the rock art imagery in relation to both these settlements strongly supports the view that the two activities were at least in part contemporaneous. Both hillforts have produced pre-Islamic AMS dates (see below) and TIN015 has yielded both wheat and barley grains of fourth- to sixth-century AD date. The sites share a consistent handmade ceramic assemblage that is characterised by many cordon decorated jars and an absence of wheel-made or glazed material. Rotary querns are another conspicuous find on these sites. Overall the indications are of a society that was in part at least sedentarised and part of or closely linked to an incipient oasis community. Although no chariots have been noted here, the emphasis on warriors on horseback finds parallels with the Garamantian heartlands and a close association between the spread of oases and horses is probable.[66]

[66] For Garamantian horse (and chariot) imagery from key topographic locations, see Mattingly 2003, 287, 297, 314–17; 2007, 101–2, 146, 192–93.

Another interesting hillfort site (LAR002) lies in the region of Foum Larjam, just on the west side of the point where the Draa breaks through the final ridge of hills to enter the open desert and make its turn to the west. This site has so far yielded five dates that indicate occupation from at least the fifth to the eighth centuries.[67] To the south and south-west of this settlement on the opposite bank of the Draa there is a large area of abandoned gardens, irrigation canals and fortified settlements (*qsur*) built in mudbrick rather than the ubiquitous pisé of the early modern *qasabas*. Initial dating of these sites seems to indicate they were constructed in a major phase of expansion of the oasis in the eleventh to twelfth centuries AD. However, two dates from an area with clay-lined pits and building foundations (BOU054: calAD 646–765 and calAD 650–765)[68] are contemporary with barley cultivation at LAR002: calAD 612–679[69] while one of the *qsur* has a slightly later date of the eighth to tenth centuries.[70] On the same side of the wadi we have identified a group of large tumuli with painted funerary chapels, providing a very close parallel to those excavated at Jorf Torba, *c.*400 km to the north-east.[71] Radiocarbon dates from one of the painted tombs in the Draa suggests it was built in the fourth century AD or earlier.[72] These dates from the terrace on the south side of the wadi, where later oasis gardens were established, is a strong hint that there was also pre-Islamic farming activity on this land (whether proto-oasis cerealiculture or fully developed palm oasis we cannot say at this stage of research).

There are dozens of these Protohistoric settlements identifiable along the Middle Draa and the nature of the settlement is strikingly similar to early oasis farming sites, like Zinkekra in Fazzan, but evidently originating about 1,000 years later. There are large cemeteries of pre-Islamic drum cairns and corbelled cairns associated with Foum Larjam.[73] A fragment of

[67] OxA-33826, 1676±28 BP, calAD 260–422; OxA-33827, 1638±27 BP, calAD 339–534; OxA-33825, 1616±27 BP, calAD 389–536; OxA-33829, 1377±27 BP, calAD 612–679; OxA-33828, 1121±28 BP, 778–994.

[68] OxA-35367, 1338±28 BP, calAD 646–765; OxA-35366, 1318±27 BP, calAD 650–765.

[69] OxA-33829, 1377±27 BP, calAD 612–679. [70] OxA-33784, 1196±32 BP, calAD 713–945.

[71] Painted scenes had been previously photographed from inside one of the large tombs (Zaïnabi 2004, 40), but we were able to excavate a second funerary chapel in 2016. Many of the images are similar to the well-known scenes from the late antique tomb of Jorf Torba (above).

[72] Use of the painted tomb BOU057.T1 is dated to calAD 92–320 (OxA-35403, 1820±29 BP) and calAD 230–381 (OxA-35185, 1751±27 BP), contemporary with, or slightly earlier than the nearby hillforts and similar tombs from Jorf Torba (above).

[73] The cemeteries of Foum Larjam are also important because some tombs were excavated in the 1950s, (Jacques-Meunié 1958). The recent radiocarbon dates suggest that these pre-Islamic burial monuments were constructed from the early first millennium BC until late antiquity.

bone on the surface of one of the large tombs *c.*1 km south of LAR002 has produced an AMS date of 894–791 calBC, though for the moment this date is far earlier than other Protohistoric dates.[74] Two hillfort sites have yielded evidence of copper working, perhaps in the early centuries AD, and the mineral resources of the region are another important factor that may have underlain the Protohistoric settlement in the region.

While the literary evidence and the early burial mentioned above may hint at origins in the first millennium BC, the AMS dates from the Draa at present highlight a significant phase of development of settlement associated with oasis agriculture in the third–sixth centuries AD. One point to bear in mind, though, is that to this stage most of our investigation has taken place in the central and southern areas of the Middle Draa valley, whereas the part of the Draa that received the highest and most reliable water supply was the upper half of the valley closer to Agdz. That is perhaps the area where we may ultimately find the earliest oasis development in Morocco.[75]

There seems to have been subsequent and very significant growth in the oasis in the Medieval period, especially in the vicinity of the major control points along the valley, as at Zagora, which was a major town in the eleventh century. Other urban-scale settlements of Medieval date have been recorded at Imi n'Takat and Tidri and there are further areas of abandoned oasis close to both of these sites, with traces of gardens, irrigation canals and settlements. Certainly, this area (like the Tafilalat) has a long and complex Medieval history too, but the key conclusion of the new archaeological work here is that there were pre-Islamic origins for at least some parts of the oasis.[76]

Wadi Noun and Tamdult

The Wadi Noun is the southernmost perennial stream in north-west Africa, running east to west into the Atlantic beyond Guelmim. The area was surveyed by Bokbot *et al.* who identified a range of archaeological remains from Neolithic to present.[77] Many cairn cemeteries were identified, including Adrar Zerzem where three tombs were excavated and dated to calAD 565–660 and a number of examples of chariot rock art[78] The

[74] OxA-33338, 2649±28 BP, 894–791 calBC. A similar date was recovered from a tomb in the vicinity in the 1970s – Gif-2912, 2369±250 BP, 1082–129 calBC.

[75] A brief reconnaissance in January 2018 identified a number of Protohistoric and Medieval sites in this region.

[76] Bokbot 2019. [77] Bokbot *et al.* 2011; 2013a; 2013b.

[78] Bokbot 2019; Bokbot *et al.* 2008; El Graoui *et al.* 2010.

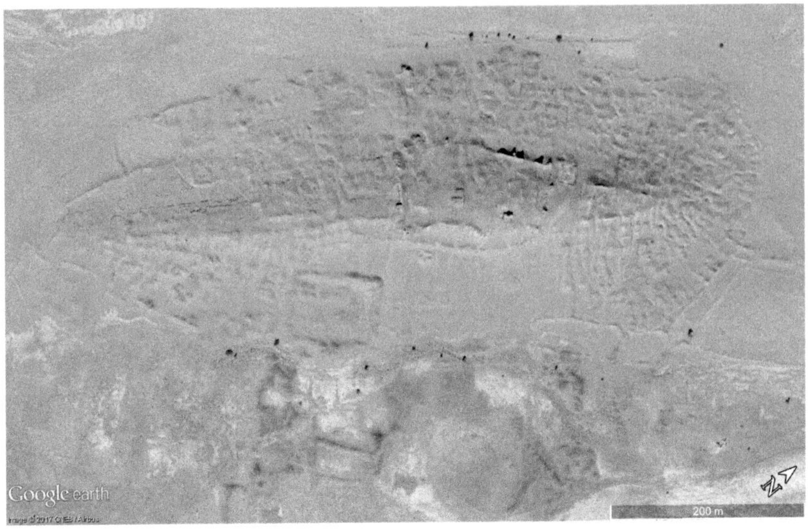

Figure 6.4. Satellite image of Tamdult (imagery: Google, DigitalGlobe).

palmeries are in small clusters, often at the junction of wadis. Many of these oasis areas have evidence of foggara cultivation and there are several important Medieval settlements, most prominent of which is the tenth–thirteenth century Agwidir fortress, potentially linked to Nul Lamta, the site of a gold mint in the Almoravid period.[79] Protohistoric settlement is less visible than in the Draa, but may underlie some of the Medieval hilltop sites. Along the Atlantic coast, just to the north of the Noun, there is evidence of Protohistoric purple dye production at Foum Asca.[80] Here deposits of shellfish including *stramonita haemastoma* shells (from a type of predatory sea snail), a key ingredient of purple production, have been uncovered that date to the first millennium BC to first centuries AD.[81]

In the area between the Noun and the Middle Draa (and bordered to the south by the lower Draa) there are many more small oases with small palmeries often located where a wadi moves through a pass in the mountains (thus concentrating the flow of water).[82] These oases have seen little exploration, but of particular interest is the early Medieval town of Tamdult, which survives as a tell of some 16 ha that is located 13 km to the south-west of Akka (Fig. 6.4).[83] The ninth-century geographer al-Yaqubi described it as dominated by a fort with deposits of gold and silver nearby.[84]

79 Bokbot *et al.* 2013a; 2013b. 80 Onrubia Pintado *et al.* 2016.

81 Beta-295799, 2880±40, 1207–931 calBC; Beta-295800, 1950±40, 41 calBC–calAD 129.

82 Richet 1920. 83 Rosenberger 1970. 84 Levtzion and Hopkins 2000, 22.

Oases of Western Algeria

Gourara, Tuwat and Tidikelt

The Gourara, Tuwat and Tidikelt oases (Fig. 6.5) are three closely related zones of dense oases and are among the best researched for their irrigation works (foggaras).[85] The northerly cluster is Gourara, a roughly triangular area of 200 km side centred on the oasis of Timimoun, set back about 50 km east of the lower course of the Wadi Saoura. The oases in the western part of Gourara are aligned along north-south valleys, but there is an east-west spread along the southern edge of the Great Western Erg. Tuwat comprises a north-south line of oases spread over *c.*140 km along the most southerly sector of the Wadi Saoura, now with the Chech sand sea extending to the west and the Tademaït plateau to the east. The Wadi Gir/Saoura finally peters out in the sabkha flanking the west side of the Tuwat oases, *c.*1,000 km from its source in the Atlas (see above, pp. 252–54). The Tidikelt is a plain running for about 300 km west to east from Reggane at the southern end of the Tuwat to In Salah. All three of these oases zones are notable locations to find foggara irrigation and numerous fortified villages (*qsur*).[86] Rohlfs recorded the names of more than 175 villages and fortified sites across the Gourara and Tuwat oases, recognising Timimoun and Tamentit as towns or principal markets.[87] In the 1880s, a French study of the Saharan frontier identified the western Algerian oases as a particular threat, listing 258 *qsur* (Gourara 164; Tuwat 60, Tidikelt 34).[88] The total palms spread across Gourara, Tuwat and Tidikelt in the late nineteenth century was recorded as 1,429,652,[89] and the population recorded by the French census around this time was *c.*50,000, with 20,000 in the Gourara, 18,000 in Tuwat and 12,000 in Tidikelt.[90] South of Reggane there is a long and difficult (but fairly straight) north-south route that eventually reaches the Niger at Gao. However, the better-watered and more travelled route in pre-modern times crossed the Tidikelt, then turned south-south-east from In Salah towards the Ahaggar.

[85] All three oases groups are covered in Gabriel 1984; Gautier 1905; Martin 1908; Rohlfs 2001, 189–245; see also Gourara: Bisson 1957; 1989; 1999; Capot-Rey 1956; Cornet 1952; Echallier 1972; 1973; Tuwat: Daumas 1845; Capot-Rey and Damade 1962; Tidikelt: Chaintron 1957/1958; Lehuraux 1943; Lô 1953/1954; Voinot 1909.

[86] Capot-Rey 1953, 324–26 (1,520 km of subterranean channels); Cornet 1952; Echallier 1972; Gabriel 1984; Lô 1953/1954.

[87] Rohlfs 2001, 216–19. [88] Rinn 1886, especially the fold-out map.

[89] Martin 1908, 301 (Gourara: 644,447 palms; Tuwat 453,490; Tidikelt: 331,715), but note that *c.*720,000 of the total palms were immature or in declining yield or fallen out of production.

[90] Gautier 1905, 18.

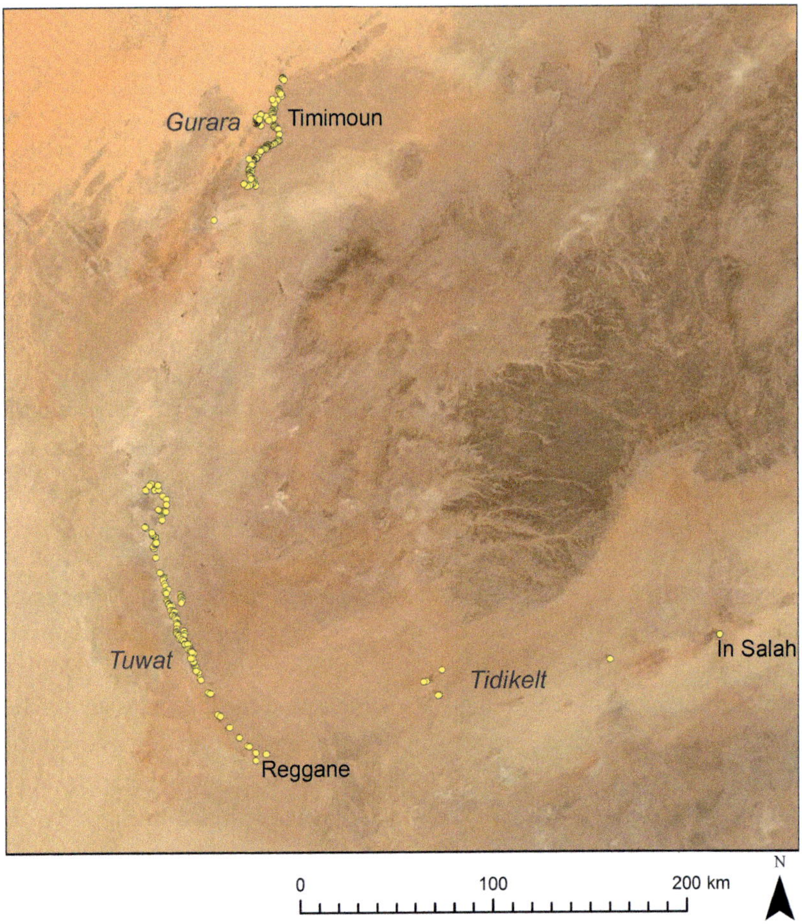

Figure 6.5. Distribution of fortified sites in the Gourara, Tuwat and Tidikelt oases.

The initial French investigations of the Gourara/Tuwat/Tidikelt area were quite open to the idea that some of the hundreds of abandoned villages and foggara-fed gardens might be pre-Islamic.[91] Martin correlated a number of toponyms in Ptolemy's *Geography* (associated with the Niger rather than the Gir) with the Tuwat.[92] However, a lack of recorded finds of Roman material culture and a failure to follow up some excellent work creating a typology of the older settlements with radiocarbon dating has left the chronology

[91] Echallier 1972, 51–59; Martin 1908, 25–55; Vallet in Nesson *et al.* 1973.

[92] Martin 1908, 30–31. cf. Ptolemy, *Geography* 4.6, but if the Souara was in fact Ptolemy's Gir rather than the Niger, the following sites were associated with it: Gira, Thycimath, Geva, Badiath, Ischeri, Turcumanda, Thuspa, Artagara, Rubune, Lynxama.

floating. Echallier preferred a date of *c.*AD 1000–1500, and two radiocarbon dates collected by Gabriel gave dates in this range.[93] Many specialists have preferred to accept the idea of Islamic-era origins. The first (certain) toponym to appear in the historical record is Buda which was visited by Ibn Battuta on his way from Takadda to Sijilmasa in 1353.[94] Similarly, the local traditions, preserved in written Arabic chronicles recorded by the French in the nineteenth century, seem to indicate a wave of village foundations from the tenth to thirteenth centuries.[95] However, there is also a strong tradition of 'Berber' and 'Jewish' foundation stories in this region.[96] Gautier suggested that the initial migration of Berbers and Jews pre-dated the Islamic conquest of the Maghrib, but that it related to the Vandal or Byzantine period, rather than earlier.[97] Many of the abandoned *qsur* and foggaras in the late nineteenth century had strong Jewish associations.[98] A Hebrew inscription from a tombstone found in the Buda region near Qasr Ghormali (north-east of Adrar) records a date of 5089 AM corresponding with AD 1329 and there is correspondence between the oases and rabbis in Algiers from the late fourteenth and early fifteenth century that mention seven 'wardens'.[99]

In terms of earlier evidence, the nearest pre-Islamic ceramic evidence is a fragment of a long-necked Byzantine lamp that was recovered from Fort Miribel 400 km to the east in the Tademaït.[100] However, Wilson has convincingly argued that the foggaras may predate the arrival of Arabs in the region.[101] Echallier has also noted that there is a strong correlation between finds of Libyan inscriptions and his Type II *qsur*, again hinting at a pre-Islamic date for some of the sites.[102] Given that the Fazzan work has now demonstrated that there are Garamantian antecedents and parallels for virtually all the architectural forms that Echallier recorded in Gourara and Tuwat, the lack of radiocarbon dates for these sites is critical. It is by no

93 Echallier 1972; Gabriel 1984, 104–7 – the dates are from two mudbrick sites between Tamentit and Adrar, Hv-9702, wood splinters from mud mortar, 600±55 BP, calAD 1286–1421 and Hv-9703, wood set in the masonry of a 'mosque', 470±65, calAD 1310–1632.

94 Levtzion and Hopkins 2000, 304.

95 Daumas 1845, 273–303; Echallier 1972, 51–52; Lehuraux 1943; Martin 1908, 49–59.

96 Gautier 1905, 24–28; Martin 1908, 37–47.

97 Gautier 1905, 30: 'il semble que les Berbères ont peuplé les oasis à une époque postérieuer à l'empire Romain . . . les souvenirs indigènes . . . placent la première migration au VI siècle à l'époque des Vandales et de Justinian'.

98 Gautier 1905, 24–25; Oliel 1994.

99 Gautier 1905, 25; Hirschberg 1963, 323.

100 Salama 1981, 514–15.

101 Wilson 2005, 232–33; 2006, 213–14; 2009, 30–32. See also, Wilson *et al.* forthcoming.

102 Echallier 1972, 56–58.

means implausible that systematic dating of these sites could backdate the origins of some at least to the mid-first millennium AD or earlier. At any event, the often assumed Islamic origin should not be considered as proven on the currently available evidence.

Other evidence for pre-Islamic occupation of the oases is thin apart from a number of Neolithic hearths.[103] The only notable occurrences of cairns from the region come from the rocky Tademaït plateau to the east of the main oasis belt. All examples are highly dispersed and may be very early in date. Rock art is similarly scarce despite large corpora known to the north-east at Figuig and south in the Ahaggar. Rohlfs noted an abandoned hillfort site midway between Karsas and Tsabit, associated with an area of foggaras, rock-cut chambers (tombs?) and a Libyan inscription but this has not been subsequently located.[104]

Tabalbala

Tabalbala is a small oasis some 240 km to the east of the southern tip of the Draa and 300 km to the west of the Tuwat. The study by Champault makes this one of the best recorded oases in the Sahara.[105] One of the languages spoken in the oasis is Korandjé, a form of Northern Songhay, a Sahelian language. Souag suggests that these Songhay speakers moved into the oasis from a sedentary community (perhaps located in the Azawagh valley, Niger) with a mixed economy *c.*AD 1200.[106] Like Tuwat there is also evidence of a Jewish population from a tombstone dated to AD 1322 = 5082 AM and a single dated Arabic tombstone AD 1422 = 825 AH.[107] To the east of the modern settlement there is a small hill that is covered in rectilinear buildings, but the most remarkable features here are the *c.*200 foggara channels that run from the sand sea towards the escarpment. Either these required regular replacement or the oasis sustained a substantially larger population than it does today (around 5,000). Champault also mentions a copper mine in Djebel Ben Tadjine, 50 km to the south-east of Tabalbala.[108]

Like the Tuwat, Tabalbala does not feature in Medieval sources until the thirteenth century at the point when both oases became more important stopping points between the Sahel and Morocco. Souag's thesis of the enforced movement of Songhay speakers (with expertise in irrigated agriculture and copper mining) in order to supply a crucial stopping point for

[103] Gabriel 1984. [104] Rohlfs 2001, 202. [105] Champault 1969. [106] Souag 2015.
[107] Souag 2015. [108] Champault 1969, 15.

mobile Berbers (engaged in Trans-Saharan trade) ties up many loose ends. However, the construction of the foggaras is no trivial matter and must relate to the much larger concentration in the Tuwat rather than a Sahelian connection. While these may be a later technological transfer, the possibility of earlier occupation cannot be ruled out.

Conclusion

At least some of the people of the desert zones surveyed in this chapter were described as Gaetuli and characterised as pastoralists in the Roman literary sources.[109] As we saw in the previous chapter, there is in fact a close correlation between people called Gaetuli and oasis zones and this may in fact help explain the widespread occurrence of people under this nomenclature – that is, the name is more related to a way of life (probably a mix of oasis cultivation and pastoralism) rather than an ethnicity. In Western Algeria and Morocco the evidence for Protohistoric origins of the oases is most compelling for those that lay closest to the Roman frontiers. The evidence from radiocarbon dating currently suggests this occurred (or at least accelerated greatly) in the first millennium AD – in other words at a somewhat later date than the examples presented from the Central Sahara and the Roman frontier lands further east. Nonetheless, we cannot rule out Protohistoric origins of the oases further out into the Sahara, such as Gourara, Tuwat and Tidikelt. As noted, the presence of foggaras and of fortified sites that bear comparison with those of Garamantian Fazzan should give us pause for thought until more extensive radiocarbon dating is undertaken.

The detailed work carried out in the Wadi Draa currently provides our best evidence of the process of sedentarisation and oasis formation in the Western Sahara in Protohistoric times. The survey in the Draa has mainly focused to this point on the sites visible on satellite imagery on the escarpments flanking the river, rather than investigating in detail the oasis zone of the lower wadi terraces. There are strong resemblances between the hillfort sites flanking the Wadi Draa and the Early Garamantian sites like Zinkekra. A key question is whether these fortified sites, often located an hour or more walk from the valley floor, were accompanied by lower lying sites like the ones that emerged

109 Pliny, *Natural History* 5.9–10; cf. Desanges 1980, sv Gaetuli.

in the Garamantian case. There are practical difficulties in undertaking fieldwork within the active oasis gardens and in and around still inhabited traditional villages – especially while the chronology of the handmade pottery is still being established. Nonetheless, our research in a few places where gardens have been abandoned has revealed traces of Protohistoric activity and our model for further testing is that there were oasis villages on the low-lying land within and adjacent to the cultivated garden zone. The abandonment of some hillforts and their conversion to funerary landscapes also echoes the pattern in Libyan Fazzan and strongly hints that there are important sites still to discover within the Draa oasis belt.

The development of the oasis in the Draa appears to have begun somewhat later than in Fazzan, with the current radiocarbon dates suggesting a significant upsurge in sites and activity towards the middle of the first millennium AD. Again that is a hypothesis that will require further testing through future excavations, which will also hopefully provide fuller detail of the agricultural package (and dates of appearance of key crops).

The key conclusion of this chapter, however, is that the Islamic era florescence of the Moroccan oases, the rise of urban centres and of the Western Saharan trade routes was not the result simply of a late first-millennium AD sedentarisation of the north-western desert. Rather, this needs to be understood in relation to prior Protohistoric developments that were built on spectacularly following the Islamic conquest of the Western Maghrib.

References

Bisson, J. 1957. *Le Gourara. Etude de geographie humaine.* Alger: Memoires de l'Institut de recherches sahariennes 3.

Bisson, J. 1989. The origin and evolution of foggara oases in the Algerian Sahara. In P. Beaumont, M. Bonine and K. McLachlan (eds), *Qanat, Kariz and Khattara: Traditional Water Systems in the Middle East and North Africa.* London and Wisbech: MENAS Press, 178–209.

Bisson, J. 1999. Gourara. *Encyclopédie berbère fasc* 21: 3188–98.

Bokbot Y., 2005. Hydrogéologie et protohistoire du Tafilalet, quelques aspects de la recherche archéologique en milieu présaharien. In *L'eau: Source de vie à travers les âges. Jardin des Hespérides.* Rabat: Bulletin semestriel de la société marocaine d'archéologie et de Patrimoine 1, novembre 2004 – avril 2005, 42–44.

Bokbot, Y. 2015. Protohistoire du Maroc. *Encyclopédie berbère fasc.* 39: 6543–61.

Bokbot Y. 2019. Protohistoric and pre-Islamic funerary archaeology in the Moroccan pre-Sahara. In Gatto *et al.* 2019, 315–40.

Bokbot, Y., Onrubia-Pintado, J., Rodriguez-Rodriguez, A., Rodriguez-Santana, C. G., Velasco-Vasquez, J. and Amarir, A. 2008. Le complexe funéraire et cultuel d'Adrar Zerzem (Anti-Atlas, Maroc): Résultats préliminaires. In *Etudes d'Antiquités Africaines. Lieux de cultes: Aires votives, temples, églises, mosquées, Actes du IXème Colloque international sur l'histoire et l'archéologie de l'Afrique du Nord antique et médiévale, Tripoli, 2005*. Paris: Èditions du CNRS, 23–33.

Bokbot, Y., Onrubia-Pintado, J. and Salih, A. 2011. Néolithique et protohistoire dans le bassin de l'Oued Noun (Maroc présaharien), quelques données préliminaires. In *Actes du 1er colloque de Préhistoire Maghrébine, Tamanrasset, 2007*. Alger: CNRPAH, 305–22.

Bokbot, Y., Cáceres Gutiérrez, Y., Cressier, P., González Marrero, M. del C., Izquierdo Benito, R., de Juan Ares, J., Mabrouk, S., Onrubia Pintado, J. and Salesse, F. 2013a. La ville natale de Sîdî Waggag: Nûl-Lamta et l'archéologie de l'oasis d'Asrir. In Naïmi. M. (ed.), *Sidi Waggag b. Zalluw al-Lamtî, aux origins du malékisme étatique nord-ouest africain*. Rabat: DTGSN, 21–64.

Bokbot, Y., Cáceres Gutiérrez, Y., Cressier, P., González Marrero, M. del C., Hervás Herrera, M.A., Onrubia Pintado, J. 2013b. Viviendas medievales al sur del Anti-Atlas (Marruecos). Problemas de studio y especificidades. In S. Gutiérrez Lloret and I. Grau Mira (eds), *De la estructura doméstica al espacio social. Lecturas arqueológicas del uso social del espacio*. Alicante: Publicaciones Universidad de Alicante, 279–98.

Brito, J.C., Martínez-Freiría, F., Sierra, P., Sillero, N. and Tarroso, P. 2011. Crocodiles in the Sahara desert: An update of distribution, habitats and population status for conservation planning in Mauritania. *PLoS ONE* 6.2: e14734. https://doi.org/10.1371/journal.pone.0014734 [last accessed 10 September 2019].

Camps, G. 1984. Rex gentium Maurorum et Romanorum. Recherches sur les royaumes de Maurétanie des VIe et VIIe siècles. *Antiquités africaines* 20: 183–218.

Capot-Rey, R. 1953. *Le Sahara Français* (L'Afrique Blanche Francaise II). Paris: Presses universitaires.

Capot-Rey 1956. Greniers domestiques et greniers fortifiés au Sahara. Le cas du Gourara. *Travaux de l'Institut de Recherches Sahariennes* 14: 139–58.

Capot-Rey, R. and Damade, W. 1962. Irrigation et structure agraire à Tamentit (Touat). *Travaux de l'Institut de Recherches Sahariennes* 21: 99–119.

Carcopino, J. 1943. *Le Maroc antique*. Paris: Gallimard.

Castellani, V. 1999. *Civiltà dell acqua. Archeologia del territorio da Roma arcaica alle antiche civiltà mediterrannee*. Rome: Editorial Service System.

Chaintron, J.F. 1957/1958. Aoulef. Problèmes économiques et sociaux d'une oasis à foggaras. *Travaux de l'Institut de Recherches Sahariennes* 16: 101–29; 17: 127–56.

Champault, D. 1969. *Une oasis du Sahara nord-occidental. Tabelbala*. Paris: CNRS.

Châtelain, L. 1944. *Le Maroc des romains. Etude sur les centres antiques de la Maurétanie occidentale*. Paris: de Boccard.

Châtelain, P. 1896. *En Algérie. La Kabylie et les oasis du sud*. Nevers: Imp. Cloix.

Cornet, A. 1952. Essai sur l'hydrogéologie du Grand Erg Oriental et des régions limitrophes (les foggaras). *Travaux de l'Institut de Recherches Sahariennes* 8: 71–122.

Daumas, E. 1845. *Le Sahara algerien. Etudes geographiques, statistiques et historiques sur la region au sud des etablissments francais en Algerie*. Paris: Langlois et Leclerc.

De la Chapelle, F. 1934. L'expedition de Suétonius Paulinus dans le sud-est du Maroc. *Hesperis* 19: 107–24.

Desanges, J. 1962. *Catalogue des tribus africaines de l'antiquité classique à l'ouest du Nil*. Dakar: University of Dakar.

Desanges, J. 1978. *Recherches sur l'activité des Méditerranéens aux confins de l'Afrique*. Rome: Coll. École française de Rome 38.

Desanges, J. 1980. *(Pline l'ancien) Histoire naturelle Livre V.1–46 (L'Afrique du nord)*. Paris: Collection Budé.

Despois, J. and Raynal, R. 1967. *Géographie de l'Afrique du Nord-Ouest*. Paris: Payot.

Dunn, R.E. 1977. *Resistance in the Desert*. London: Croom Helm.

Echallier, J.-C. 1972. *Villages désertés et structures agraires anciennes du Touat et du Gourara*. Paris: RMG.

Echallier, J.-C. 1973. Fortéresses berbères du Gourara. Problèmes et resultants des fouilles. *Libyca* 21: 293–302.

El Graoui, M., Bokbot, Y., Jungner, H. and Searight-Martinet, S. 2010. Datation radiocarbone sur des ossements mis au jour dans un tumulus à l'Adrar Zerzem, Oued Eç-çayad, région de Taghjijt (Sud marocain). *Sahara* 21: 77–80.

El-Khoumsi, W., Hammani, A., Kuper, M. and Boaziz, A. 2017. La durabilité du système oasien face à la détérioration des ressources en eaux souterraines: Cas de la palmeraie de Tafilalet. *Revue Marocaine des sciences agronomiques et vétérinaires* 5.1: 41–51.

Euzennat, M. 1989. *Le limes de Tingitane I, la frontiére méridionale*. Paris: CNRS.

Gabriel, B. 1984. Zur vorzeitlichen Besiedlung Südalgeriens (Tanezrouft, Tidikelt, Touat, Gourara). *Die Erde* 115: 93–109.

Gatto, M.C., Mattingly, D.J., Ray, N. and Sterry, M. (eds). 2019. *Burials, Migration and Identity in the Ancient Sahara and Beyond*. Trans-Saharan Archaeology Volume 2. Series editor D.J. Mattingly. Cambridge: Cambridge University Press.

Gaucher, G. 1948. Irrigation et mise en valeur du Tafilalet. *Travaux de l'Institut de Recherches Sahariennes* 5: 95–120.

Gauthier, Y. and Gauthier, C. 2011. Des chars et des Tifinagh: Étude aréale et corrélations. *Les Cahiers de l'AARS* 15: 91–118.

Gauthier, Y. and Gauthier, C. 2015. Nouvelles figurations de chars sahariens: Technicité et positionnement chronologique relativement au style de Tazina. *Les Cahiers de l'AARS* 18: 5–70.

Gautier, E.-F. 1905. *Les oasis sahariennes*. Algérie: Imp Fontana.

Gautier, E.-F. 1970. *Sahara. The Great Desert* (translated from the French by D.F. Mayhew). London: Octagon.

Hamdoune, C. 2018. *Ad fines Africae Romanae. Les mondes tribaux dans les provinces maurétaniennes*. Bordeaux: Scripta Antiqua.

Heywood, C. 1926. *Algeria and Tunisia*. Paris and London: Librarie Hachette.

Hirschberg, H.Z. 1963. The problem of the judaized Berbers. *Journal of African History* 4.3: 313–39.

Homo, J.P. and Hugonot, R. 1953. Ich, oasis de montagne. *Travaux de l'Institut de Recherches Sahariennes* 9: 99–124.

Jacques-Meunié, D. 1958. La nécropole de Foum le Rjam, tumuli du Maroc présaharien. *Hespéris* 1958 1–2: 95–142.

Jacques-Meunié, D. 1982. *Le Maroc saharien des origins à 1670*, 2 vols. Paris: Klincksieck.

Joly, F. 1948. Sur la repartition du palmier dattier en Maroc. *Travaux de l'Institut de Recherches Sahariennes* 5: 203–12.

Landau, R. 1969. *The Kasbahs of Southern Morocco*. London: Faber and Faber.

Laporte, J.-P. 2011. Particularités de la province de Maurétanie Césarienne (Algérie centrale et occidentale). In C. Briand-Ponsart and Y. Modéran (eds), *Provinces et identités provincials dans l'Afrique romaine*. Caen: CRAHM, 111–50.

Lehuraux, A. 1943. Les origins des oasis du Tidikelt et du Bas-Touat. *Travaux de l'Institut de Recherches Sahariennes* 2: 105–20.

Levtzion, N. and Hopkins, J.F.P. (eds). 2000. *Corpus of Early Arabic Sources for West African History*. Princeton: Markus Wiener Publishers.

Lightfoot, D.R. and Miller, J.A. 1996. Sijilmassa: The rise and fall of a walled oasis in Medieval Morocco. *Annals of the Association of American Geographers* 86.1: 78–101.

Lihoreau, M. 1993. *Djorf Torba, nécropole saharienne antéislamique*. Paris: Karthala.

Lô, Capitaine 1953/1954. Les foggaras du Tidikelt. *Travaux de l'Institut de Recherches Sahariennes* 10: 139–79; 11: 49–77.

Lugan, B. 2000. *Histoire du Maroc des origines à nos jours*. Paris: Perrin.

Lydon, G., 2009. *On Trans-Saharan Trails: Islamic Law, Trade Networks and Cross-cultural Exchange in Nineteenth-Century Western Africa*. Cambridge: Cambridge University Press.

MacDonald, K. 2011. A view from the south. Sub-Saharan evidence for contacts between North Africa, Mauritania and the Niger 1000 BC–AD 700. In A. Dowler and E. Galvin (eds), *Money, Trade and Trade Routes in Pre-Islamic North Africa*. London: British Museum, 72–82.

Martin, A.G.P. 1908. *Les oasis sahariennes (Gourara-Touat-Tidikelt)*. Alger: Imp. Algérienne.

Mattingly, D.J., (ed.). 2003. *The Archaeology of Fazzan. Volume 1, Synthesis*. London: Society for Libyan Studies.

Mattingly, D.J. (ed.). 2007. *The Archaeology of Fazzan. Volume 2, Site Gazetteer, Pottery and other Survey Finds.* London: Society for Libyan Studies.

Mattingly, D.J. 2017. The Garamantes and the origins of Saharan trade. State of the field and future agendas. In D.J. Mattingly, V. Leitch, C.N. Duckworth, A. Cuénod, M. Sterry and F. Cole (eds), *Early Saharan Trade: The Inorganic Evidence.* Cambridge: Cambridge University Press, 1–52.

Mattingly, D.J., Rushworth, A., Sterry, M. and Leitch, V. 2013. *The African Frontiers.* Frontiers of the Roman Empire series. Edinburgh: Hussar Books.

Mattingly, D.J., Bokbot Y., Sterry M., Cuénod A., Fenwick C., Gatto M., Ray N., Rayne L., Janin K., Lamb A., Mugnai N., and Nikolaus J. 2017. Long-term history in a Moroccan oasis zone: The Middle Draa Project 2015. *Journal of African Archaeology* 15: 141–72.

Mattingly, D.J., Sterry, M., al-Haddad, M. and Bokbot, Y. 2018. Beyond the Garamantes: The early development of Saharan oases. In L. Purdue, J. Charbonnier and L. Khalidi (eds), *Des refuges aux oasis: Vivre en milieu aride de la Préhistoire à aujourd'hui. XXXVIIIe rencontres internationales d'archéologie et d'histoire d'Antibes.* Antibes: Éditions APDCA, 205–28.

Mattingly, D.J., Gatto, M.C., Sterry, M. and Ray, N. 2019. Burials, migration and identity. The view from the Sahara. In Gatto *et al.* 2019, 1–50.

Mauny, R. 1978. Trans-Saharan contacts and the Iron Age in West Africa. In J. D. Fage (ed.), *The Cambridge History of Africa*, vol. 2. Cambridge: Cambridge University Press, 272–341.

Maxwell, G. 2004. *Lords of the Atlas. The Rise and Fall of the House of Glaoua 1893–1956.* London: Elland.

Messier, R.A. 1997. Sijilmasa. Five seasons of archaeological inquiry by a joint Moroccan-American Mission. *Archéologie Islamique* 7: 61–92.

Messier, R.A. and Fili, A. 2011. The earliest ceramics of Sijilmasa. In P. Cressier and E. Fentress (eds), *La céramique maghrébine du haut moyen âge, VIIIe-Xe siècle: état des recherches, problèmes et perspectives.* Paris: École française de Rome, 129–46.

Messier, R. and Miller, J. 2015. *The Last Civilized Place. Sijilmasa and Its Saharan Destiny.* Austin: University of Texas Press.

Monteil, V., 1951. *Contribution à l'étude de la faune du Sahara occidental.* Paris: Larose.

Nesson, C., Rouvillois-Brigol, M., and Vallet, J. 1973. *Oasis du sahara algérien.* Paris: Institut géographique national.

Oliel, J. 1994. *Les juifs au Sahara: Le Touat au moyen age.* Paris: CNRS.

Onrubia Pintado, J., Bokbot, Y., Hervás Herrera, M.A., García García, L.A., Marchante Ortega, A., Cáceres Gutíérrez, Y., González Marrero, M. del C., Juan Ares, J. de, Moreno García, M. and Rodríguez Santana, C.G. 2016. Arqueología de Fum Asaca (Sidi Ifni-Marruecos). De probable instalación purpuraría gétula a Torre Colonial hispano-canaria. Anuaria. *Anuario de Estudios Atlánticos* 62: 1–25.

Pichler, W. 2000. The Libyco-Berber inscriptions of Foum Chenna/Morocco, *Sahara* 12: 176–78.

Rebuffat, R. 1999. La frontière de la Tingitane. In C. Lepelley and X. Dupuis (eds), *Frontières et limites géographiques de l'Afrique du nord antique. Hommage à Pierre Salama.* Paris: Sorbonne, 265–93.

Remini, B. Rezoug, C. and Achour, B. 2014.The foggara of Kenadsa (Algeria). *Larhyss Journal* 18: 93–105.

Reygasse, M. 1950. *Monuments funéraires préislamiques de l'Afrique du Nord.* Paris: Arts et Métiers Graphiques.

Ricard, P. 1925. *Le Maroc.* Paris: Libraire Hachette.

Richet, E. 1920. *Oued Sous Oued Draa.* Paris: Figuiere.

Rinn, L. 1886. *Nos frontières sahariennes.* Alger: Adolphe Jourdan.

Riser, J. 1996. Dra. *Encyclopédie berbère* fasc 17: 2537–41.

Rohlfs, G. 2001. *Voyages et explorations au Sahara. Tome I, Draa - Tafilalet - sud oranais - Touat - Tidikelt - Rhadamès 1861–1864* (translated by J. Debetz). Paris: Karthala.

Rosenberger, B. 1970. Tamdult, cité minière et caravanière présaharienne, IXe–XIVe s. *Hespéris-Tamuda* 1970: 103–39.

Salama, P. 1981. The Sahara in classical antiquity. In G. Mokhtar (ed.), *UNESCO General History of Africa, II Ancient Civilisations of Africa.* Paris: UNESCO, 513–32.

Shaw, B.D. 1987. Autonomy and tribute: Mountain and plain in Mauretania Tingitana. *Revue de l'Occident Musulman et de la Méditerranée* 41–41: 66–89.

Simoneau, A. 1972a. Les prospections rupestres dans la région du Drâa (Extrême Sud marocain), avril 1971 - avril 1972. *Almogaren* 3: 15–31.

Simoneau, A. 1972b. Nouvelle gravures rupestres du haut-Atlas et du Drâa. *Bulletin d'Archéologie Marocaine* 8: 2–39.

Simoneau, A. 1977. *Catalogue des sites rupestres du sud Marocain.* Rabat: Ministère des Affaires Culturelles.

Souag, L. 2015. Explaining Korandjé: Language contact, plantations and the trans-Saharan trade. *Journal of Pidgin and Creole Linguistics* 30.2: 189–224.

Stevenson, E.L. 1991. *Claudius Ptolemy, The Geography.* New York: Dover.

Tayler, J. 2003. *Valley of the Casbahs. A Journey across the Moroccan Sahara.* London: Little, Brown.

Vanacker, C. 1973. Géographie économique de l'Afrique du nord selon les auteurs arabes du IXe siècle au milieu du XIIe siècle. *Annales ESC* 28.3: 659–80.

Voinot, L. 1909. *Le Tidikelt. Etude sur la géographie, l'histoire, les moeurs du pays.* Oran: Fouque.

Wilson, A.I. 2005. Foggara irrigation, early state formation and Saharan trade: The Garamantes of Fazzan. *Schriftenreihe der Frontinus-Gesellschaft* 26: 223–34.

Wilson, A.I. 2006. The spread of foggara-based irrigation in the ancient Sahara. In D.J. Mattingly, S. McLaren, E. Savage, Y. al-Fasatwi and K. Gadgood (eds), *The Libyan Desert. Natural Resources and Cultural Heritage.* London: Society for Libyan Studies, 205–16.

Wilson, A.I. 2009. Foggaras in ancient North Africa or how to marry a Berber princess. In *Contrôle et distribution de l'eau dans le Maghreb antique et medieval.* Rome: Coll. École française de Rome, 19–39.

Wilson, A.I., Mattingly, D.J. and Sterry, M. Forthcoming. The diffusion of irrigation technologies in the Sahara in antiquity: Settlement, trade and migration. In C. Duckworth, A. Cuénod and D. Mattingly (eds), *Mobile Technologies in the Ancient Sahara and Beyond.* Cambridge: Cambridge University Press.

Zaïnabi, A.T. (ed.). 2004. *Trésors et merveilles de la vallée du Drâa.* Zagora: Ed Marsam.

7 Pre-Islamic Oasis Settlements in the Southern Sahara

MARTIN STERRY AND DAVID J. MATTINGLY

Introduction

The southern oases of the Sahara can be split into two broad groups.[1] First, there are a series located in and around the Saharan mountain ranges. From east to west these are: Ennedi, Tibesti, Aïr, Tassili n'Ajjer, Ahaggar and Adrar des Ilforas. These massifs receive higher levels of rainfall than other parts of the Sahara, resulting in seasonal rivers that feed permanent bodies of water (small lakes or pools/gueltas) or that support a high water table beneath the wadi beds.[2] There are still populations of crocodiles living in Ennedi and nineteenth- and early-twentieth-century reports of them also in Ahaggar and Tibesti.[3] However, these areas have traditionally been primarily exploited by pastoralists and they have little suitable land for oasis agriculture and highly variable rainfall. The dynamic wadi systems may also be a factor in the poor preservation of archaeological remains with less sturdy or older constructions either swept away or buried under sediment.

The second group consists of oases in the intervening depressions, including Agadez, Kawar, Djado, Kufra, Borku and a number of smaller oases. Apart from Agadez these have almost no rainfall and are entirely reliant on springs or lifting water from a locally restricted but elevated water table. Further to the west, there are a number of oases in the Southern Sahara within striking distance of Sahelian West Africa which were historically important in the Medieval era. The final section of the chapter

[1] Despois and Raynal 1967, 474–508 for a geographical synthesis of the western part of the Sahara.

[2] Gautier 1970, 85–93 on the water sources of the mountainous enclaves. Cf. Capot-Rey 1953, 38–45 on the higher rainfall of the mountains compared to the surrounding basins, but with annual levels still well below 100 mm.

[3] Gautier 1970, 91.

provides only a brief overview of these sites, as they are discussed in further detail in the second half of this book. One of the interesting aspects of the more southerly oases is that they played an important part in the rise of Sub-Saharan polities (such as Kanim-Bornu, Ghana, Mali, Songhay, the Sultanate of Agadez) and their influence on the history of Saharan trade. The rise of the Almoravid and Almohad dynasties in the Maghrib was also founded on deep desert contacts. Once again, a key question is whether such Medieval actualities were prefigured by connections and developments in the Protohistoric period.

Another basic division in the material presented in this chapter concerns a fundamental linguistic and ethnic divide between two major groups: the Teda and the Tuareg. These peoples were instrumental players in the early modern caravan and slave trade and it is highly likely that their domination of particular routes and zones of the Sahara was of much greater antiquity. The Teda operated the main routes between Chad and Libya and Egypt, while the Tuareg were more engaged in the Niger Bend trade routes leading to Libya, Tunisia, Algeria and Morocco.

Research into the southern oases has been variable and has tended to focus either on the prehistory of the 'Green Sahara' (that is before 3,000 BC) or on the historical archaeology of current communities.[4] The area around Aïr and Agadez has seen the most work with a number of major projects, while research in Chad and Mali has lagged behind albeit with some notable and important exceptions. The Dhar Tichitt area in south-east Mauritania for the moment provides a remarkably precocious manifestation of nucleated settlement, whose relationship with later phases of sedentarisation remains unclear.

In this chapter, we draw together the published data and combine it with our direct observations of high resolution satellite imagery. It is evident that in many of the oasis locations there is a rich and as yet poorly explored and mostly undated archaeological heritage. For several of the regions pre-Islamic activity is certainly attested and, while the nature of this activity cannot be certainly linked to oasis development at this stage, it is a crucial question that is highlighted here for future research. As in other chapters, we have also compiled the available radiocarbon dates for the region in Table 7.1, though detailed information on context is less readily available for many of these.

[4] Haour 2003.

Table 7.1 *Protohistoric and historic radiocarbon dates from the Southern Sahara*

Region/Site	Context	Material	Reference	Date	Calibrated
Ennedi					
Mornou T05/88–2		Cattle skull	Poz-16595	2480±30 BP	774–434 calBC
Borku/Bahr-al-Ghazal					
Bahali I			Gif-2895	630±90 BP	calAD1224–1441
Bahali IV			Gif-4201	1540±90 BP	calAD 332–660
Bochiangra			Gif-2611	1500±100 BP	calAD 333–761
Bochiangra			Gif-2612	1500±100 BP	calAD 333–761
Bochiangra			G.D. Paris VI	935±80 BP	calAD 973–1260
Bochiangra, Koro-Toro		Bone	?	1500±100 BP	calAD 333–761
Bochiangra, Koro-Toro		Bone	?	1015±80 BP	calAD 778–1215
Bochiangra, Koro-Toro		Bone	?	730±90 BP	calAD 1049–1412
Bochiangra, Koro-Toro	Furnace		Hv-3804	1960±60 BP	108 calBC–calAD 214
Bochiangra, Koro-Toro	Furnace	Charcoal with slag	Hv-4694	1570±50 BP	calAD 395–595
Bochiangra, Koro-Toro	Furnace	Charcoal with slag	Hv-2751	1510±75 BP	calAD 401–655
Djourab			Hv-4694	1570±50 BP	calAD 395–595
Kebir Bosa			Gif-4202	2360±100 BP	774–205 calBC
Kebir Bosa			Gif-4193	1480±100 BP	calAD 348–765
Kerki Bougui (site 97)			Gif-4200	1250±90 BP	calAD 643–978
Kolle	Charcoal with human bones and pottery in lake deposits		Ny-83	1460±220 BP	calAD 85–1012
Koro Toro			Hv-2751	1510±75 BP	calAD 401–655
Koro Toro (Site 4)			G.D. Paris	1670±80 BP	calAD 143–561
Koro Toro (Site 4)			Gif-4194	1580±100 BP	calAD 252–649
Koro Toro (Site 4)			Gif-4195	1400±100 BP	calAD 421–867
Koro Toro (Site 4)			Gif-4198	1230±100 BP	calAD 642–995
Koro Toro (Site 4)			Gif-4199	1170±90 BP	calAD 678–1016

Table 7.1 (*cont.*)

Region/Site	Context	Material	Reference	Date	Calibrated
Krime			Gif-4197	1410±100 BP	calAD 413–863
Krime			Gif-4196	670±100 BP	calAD 1161–1440
Nemra III			Gif-2613	730±90 BP	calAD 1049–1412
Site 97			Gif-4200	1250±100 BP	calAD 621–988
Toungour			Hv-3804	1960±60 BP	108 calBC–calAD 214
Toungour			Hv-2898	1655±55 BP	calAD 253–539
Toungour-Salado			Gif-2896	1340±100 BP	calAD 434–948
Tibesti					
Bardague Araye			Hv-6926	4125±100 BP	2916–2463 calBC
Bardague Araye			Hv-6933	3385±60 BP	1877–1528 calBC
Bardague Araye 2			Hv-6931	3900±155 BP	2872–1978 calBC
Bardague Araye 2			Hv-6929	3790±300 BP	3086–1456 calBC
Bardai			Hv-4668	370±90 BP	calAD 1399– . . .
Enneri Dirennao			Hv-2260	2690±435 BP	2022 calBC–calAD 138
Enneri Oyoroum			Hv-3763	3755±335 BP	3310–1322 calBC
Enneri Oyoroum			Hv-3765	2350±410 BP	1495 calBC–calAD 530
Gabrong			Hv-3709	6130±90 BP	5297–4846 calBC
Gabrong			Gif-1316	1570±100 BP	calAD 254–653
Gabrong			Hv-2198	1440±150 BP	calAD 254–940
Mount Ayando			Hv-3775	690±75 BP	calAD 1192–1415
Serir Tibesti			Hv-2749	1840±60 BP	calAD 52–335
Serir Tibesti			Hv-2936	1780±60 BP	calAD 89–391
Yebbigue		Human bone	Hv-2774	2427±225 BP	1074 calBC–calAD 24
Zouar	Burial vault	Human bone	Gif-1183	3375±120 BP	2008–1417 calBC
Zouar	Cremation burial	Cremated bone	Gif-1181	1330±100 BP	calAD 477–967

Zouar		Gif-1318	750±100 BP	calAD 1043–1405
Zoui		Hv-3771	2130±40 BP	355–46 calBC
Zoui		Hv-4351	2080±55 BP	350 calBC–calAD 52
Zoui		Hv-4498	2065±320 BP	839 calBC–calAD 603
Zoui		Hv-3773	1095±110 BP	calAD 688–1155
Zoui		Hv-3176	1130±55 BP	calAD 772–1015
Zoui		Hv-3775	690±75 BP	calAD 1192–1415
Zoui		Hv-4352	455±75 BP	calAD 1316–1638
Zoui		Hv-3774	430±35 BP	calAD 1417–1619
Zoui		Hv-4667	420±55 BP	calAD 1412–1635
Djado				
Diabessa (Djado)		R-1266	420±50 BP	calAD 1415–1633
Djaba		Gif-3547	760±80 BP	calAD 1045–1395
Djado 1		Gif-4130	90±90 BP	calAD 1664– . . .
Djado 4		Gif-4131	270±90 BP	calAD 1445– . . .
Termit				
Do Dimmi		Pa-288	2500±70 BP	795–428 calBC
Do Dimmi		DaK-145	2628±120 BP	1031–409 calBC
Do Dimmi		UPS	2590±120 BP	978–404 calBC
Do Dimmi		Pa-296	2580±120 BP	976–402 calBC
Do Dimmi		Pa-504	2270±90 BP	736–56 calBC
Do Dimmi		UPS	2065±60 BP	348 calBC–calAD 66
Do Dimmi		DaK-148	1747±110 BP	calAD 32–543
Gara Tchia Bo 48 a		Pa-810	3260±100 BP	1861–1290 calBC
Gara Tchia Bo 48 b		Pa-811	3265±100 BP	1868–1294 calBC
Tchi Guiriba 127 B		Pa-669	2955±100 BP	1417–917 calBC
Tchire Ouma 146		Pa-510	3230±170 BP	1928–1055 calBC
Termit	Charcoal with slag	Dak-147	2924±120 BP	1414–844 calBC
Termit	Charcoal with slag	Dak-145	2628±120 BP	1031–409 calBC
Termit		Dak-148	1747±100 BP	calAD 67–536

Table 7.1 (*cont.*)

Region/Site	Context	Material	Reference	Date	Calibrated
Termit Ouest 8			Pa-668	2880±120 BP	1390–819 calBC
Termit ouest 95 B			Pa-481	3100±100 BP	1611–1060 calBC
Tenere Desert					
Tenere, No. 7	Burial at depth 1.5 m under stone blocks 18 N 10 E	Human bone	Gif-3639	3180±100 BP	1691–1135 calBC
Tin Keradet			C-2619	3310±160 BP	
Tassili n'Ajjer					
Tissoukai	Tassili		Gif-840	3650±130 BP	2456–1694 calBC
Tahabort			Gif-2900	2560±100 BP	895–409 calBC
Tahabort			Gif-3324	1110±100 BP	calAD 681–1152
Tahabort			Gif-2898	1050±100 BP	calAD 726–1207
Tahabort			Gif-3325	930±100 BP	calAD 898–1273
Tahabort			Gif-3258	570±90 BP	calAD 1259–1609
Tamanrasset	Neolithic, double burial		Gif-357	3330±250 BP	2335–1000 calBC
Tamanrasset II			Mc-487	3900±100 BP	2834–2041 calBC
Tamanrasset II			Gif-357	3330±250 BP	2335–1000 calBC
Ahaggar					
Tin Hinan	Chambered tomb		?	1480±130 BP	calAD 247–856
Aïr					
Aghroum Balkorene			Gif-?	200±80 BP	calAD 1516–..
Anisaman			Gif-3522	230±80 BP	calAD 1485– . . .
Arlit		Faunal bone	Gif-1797	2640±100 BP	1022–431 calBC
Assodé			0	635±40 BP	calAD 1283–1400
Assodé			0	565±40 BP	calAD 1300–1432
Assodé			R-1268	360±50 BP	calAD 1449–1639
Assodé			0	290±60 BP	calAD 1450– . . .
Assodé			0	250±90 BP	calAD 1455– . . .

Assodé		0	245±60 BP	calAD 1472– . . .
Assodé		0	260±40 BP	calAD 1492– . . .
Assodé		0	205±40 BP	calAD 1640– . . .
Graboun Mountain	Olive tree (in situ!)	UCLA-1655	180±60 BP	calAD 1643– . . .
Ifanghalene		Gif-2938	3410±100 BP	1966–1461 calBC
Iwelen		Pa-234	3595±100 BP	2275–1687 calBC
Iwelen		Pa-508	3425±120 BP	2033–1449 calBC
Iwelen		Pa-133	3410±200 BP	2291–1231 calBC
Iwelen		Pa-506	3160±100 BP	1664–1131 calBC
Iwelen		Pa-600	3360±200 BP	2206–1130 calBC
Iwelen		Pa-656	3320±200 BP	2195–1113 calBC
Iwelen		Pa-683	3290±200 BP	2131–1055 calBC
Iwelen		Pa-117	2935±70 BP	1381–931 calBC
Iwelen		Pa-121	2940±100 BP	1411–908 calBC
Iwelen		Pa-319	2930±100 BP	1408–902 calBC
Iwelen		Pa-141	2795±120 BP	1374–773 calBC
Iwelen		Hv-3256	2635±60 BP	926–552 calBC
Iwelen		Pa-580	2710±140 BP	1260–434 calBC
Iwelen		Pa-112	2510±60 BP	799–430 calBC
Iwelen		Pa-496	2520±80 BP	803–416 calBC
Iwelen		Pa-884	2600±100 BP	969–412 calBC
Iwelen		Pa-885	2585±110 BP	969–406 calBC
Iwelen		Pa-645	2540±100 BP	891–403 calBC
Iwelen		Pa-628	2530±100 BP	841–401 calBC
Iwelen		Pa-655	2520±100 BP	831–401 calBC
Iwelen		Pa-525	2675±200 BP	1388–386 calBC
Iwelen		Pa-888	2590±150 BP	1110–386 calBC
Iwelen		Pa-116	2410±80 BP	781–379 calBC
Iwelen		Pa-886	2480±110 BP	832–376 calBC
Iwelen		Pa-635	2415±110 BP	801–231 calBC

Table 7.1 (*cont.*)

Region/Site	Context	Material	Reference	Date	Calibrated
Iwelen			Pa-860	2980±400 BP	2293–209 calBC
Iwelen			Pa-847	2395±121 BP	800–205 calBC
Iwelen			Pa-634	2305±110 BP	766–113 calBC
Iwelen			Pa-146	2200±60 BP	395–107 calBC
Iwelen			Pa-400	2520±250 BP	1279–43 calBC
Iwelen			Pa-862	2415±200 BP	996–40 calBC
Iwelen	IW68	Clothes	0	1220±60 BP	calAD 669–961
Iwelen	IW68	Leather	0	1165±60 BP	calAD 694–991
Iwelen	IW68	Carbonate hydroxulapatie	0	1175±80 BP	calAD 678–995
Iwelen	IW68	Hairs	0	1145±60 BP	calAD 722–1016
Iwelen	IW68	Collagen	0	1160±90 BP	calAD 677–1020
Iwelen S1			0	2160±50 BP	363–57 calBC
Iwelen S2			0	2680±40 BP	908–797 calBC
Iwelen S3			0	2510±60 BP	799–430 calBC
Iwelen S4			0	2190±70 BP	394–57 calBC
Iwelen S5			0	2340±70 BP	752–206 calBC
Kori Ibine	From a room in the settlement	Charcoal	Dak-146	685±100 BP	calAD 1058–1439
Tadeini 1	Blast furnace	Charcoal	Gif-3523	250±80 BP	calAD 1455–present
Tadeini 2	Blast furnace	Charcoal	Gif-3524	350±80 BP	calAD 1417–1799
Tadeliza	30–40 cm depth		Gif-2594	720±90 BP	calAD 1051–1417
Tadeliza	Surface		Gif-2593	510±90 BP	calAD 1283–1631
Tezamak			Gif-3525	400±80 BP	calAD 1400–1660
Tezamak			Gif-3526	330±80 BP	calAD 1427– . . .
Wadi Mammanet			?	1280±60 BP	calAD 651–884
Wadi Mammanet			?	1270±65 BP	calAD 647–936

Azawagh			
Afunfun (site 162)	MC-2404	2800±90 BP	1207–806 calBC
Afunfun (site 162)	MC-2404	2800±90 BP	1207–806 calBC
Afunfun (site 162)	MC-2406	2740±90 BP	1188–774 calBC
Afunfun (site 162)	MC-2406	2740±90 BP	1188–774 calBC
Afunfun (site 162)	Gif-5541	2590±90 BP	911–429 calBC
Afunfun (site 162)	MC-2405	2540±90 BP	831–408 calBC
Afunfun (site 162)	MC-2405	2540±90 BP	831–408 calBC
Afunfun (site 162)	MC-2402	2520±90 BP	811–407 calBC
Afunfun (site 162)	MC-2403	2520±90 BP	811–407 calBC
Afunfun (site 162)	MC-2402	2520±90 BP	811–407 calBC
Afunfun (site 162)	MC-2403	2520±90 BP	811–407 calBC
Afunfun (site 175)	MC-2399	4140±90 BP	2902–2488 calBC
Afunfun (site 175)	MC-2399	4140±90 BP	2902–2488 calBC
Afunfun (site 175)	Gif-5175	3960±110 BP	2866–2145 calBC
Afunfun (site 175)	Gif-5176	3950±110 BP	2864–2140 calBC
Afunfun (site 175)	MC-2398	3920±90 BP	2835–2137 calBC
Afunfun (site 175)	MC-2398	3920±90 BP	2835–2137 calBC
Afunfun (site 175)	MC-2401	3800±90 BP	2477–1977 calBC
Afunfun (site 175)	MC-2401	3800±90 BP	2477–1977 calBC
Afunfun (site 175)	Gif-5174	3840±110 BP	2580–1966 calBC
Afunfun (site 175)	Gif-5172	3680±50 BP	2202–1931 calBC
Afunfun (site 175)	Gif-5172	3680±50 BP	2202–1931 calBC
Afunfun (site 175)	Gif-5177	3790±110 BP	2562–1930 calBC
Afunfun (site 175)	MC-2400	3600±90 BP	2204–1696 calBC
Afunfun (site 175)	MC-2400	3600±90 BP	2204–1696 calBC
Afunfun (site 175)	Gif-5173	3390±110 BP	1957–1436 calBC
Afunfun (site 178)	Gif-5179	2900±100 BP	1386–844 calBC
Afunfun (site 179)	Gif-5178	3030±100 BP	1501–1002 calBC
Aktaouzou (site 178)	Gif-5179	2900±110 BP	1391–839 calBC

Table 7.1 (*cont.*)

Region/Site	Context	Material	Reference	Date	Calibrated
Azelik			Gif-4175	2490±90 BP	798–407 calBC
Azelik			Gif-4330	2480±90 BP	795–406 calBC
Azelik			Gif-?	2400±90 BP	792–239 calBC
Azelik			Gif-2156	800±100 BP	calAD 1023–1390
Azelik			Gif-?	590±80 BP	calAD 1272–1445
Azelik			Gif-4174	520±80 BP	calAD 1282–1619
Azelik			Dak-9	353±114 BP	calAD 1320– . . .
Azelik			DaK-121	modern± BP	0
Azelik (site 210)			Gif-5546	2510±70 BP	799–430 calBC
Azelik (site 210)			Gif-4175	2490±90 BP	798–407 calBC
Azelik (site 210)			Gif-4330	2480±90 BP	795–406 calBC
Azelik (site 210)			Gif-?	2400±90 BP	792–239 calBC
Chin Wasararan (site 117)			MC-1700	3160±95 BP	1659–1134 calBC
Chin Wasararan (site 117)			MC-1702	2870±95 BP	1369–828 calBC
Chin Wasararan (site 117)			MC-1701	2795±105 BP	1257–795 calBC
Efey Washaran (site 149)			MC-1703	2875±105 BP	1377–826 calBC
Ekne Wan Ataran (site 119)			MC-2397	2440±90 BP	792–393 calBC
Fagochia			Gif-4178	390±90 BP	calAD 1324–1798
Guelele			Gif-4176	680±80 BP	calAD 1193–1423
In Taylalen II			Gif-4170	2210±90 BP	452 calBC–calAD 1
In Taylalen II			Gif-4171	2010±90 BP	351 calBC–calAD 219
In Teduq			Pa-0299	3485±165 BP	2285–1431 calBC
In Teduq			Pa-0231	2810±80 BP	1196–811 calBC
In Teduq			Pa-1418	1890±40 BP	calAD 28–230
In Tekebrin			Pa-0233	2600±80 BP	923–433 calBC
In Waggeur			N-2131	255±60 BP	calAD 1463– . . .
In Waggeur			N-2130	155±70 BP	calAD 1653– . . .
Inufan			Orsat	1595±80 BP	calAD 256–623

Janjari			N-2129	335±60 BP	calAD 1445–1659
Marandet			Gif-2595	1430±100 BP	calAD 392–801
Marandet			Gif-2599	1420±100 BP	calAD 400–860
Marandet			Gif-2158	1400±100 BP	calAD 421–867
Marandet			Gif-2596	1360±100 BP	calAD 430–891
Marandet			Gif-2157	1310±100 BP	calAD 551–968
Marandet			Gif-2597	1310±100 BP	calAD 551–968
Marandet			Gif-2598	1160±100 BP	calAD 661–1031
Marandet			Gif-1726	1050±95 BP	calAD 729–1189
Mentes			Pa-1624	2740±100 BP	1215–673 calBC
Mio Site 169			MC-2395	3170±90 BP	1658–1215 calBC
Orub			Gif-4173	3390±100 BP	1941–1452 calBC
Sekiret			Gif-3862	3310±100 BP	1881–1407 calBC
Sekiret			Gif-4177	2900±100 BP	1386–844 calBC
Sekiret			Gif-5543	2700±70 BP	1016–773 calBC
Sekiret Valley			Gif-5544	2470±100 BP	806–392 calBC
Takene Bawat			Pa-0444	2010±200 BP	727 calBC–calAD 428
Tamaya Mellet			Pa-1366	3435±100 BP	2016–1505 calBC
Tamaya Mellet			Pa-410	3060±90 BP	1505–1049 calBC
Tamaya Mellet			Pa-411	3060±140 BP	1621–931 calBC
Tegef n'Agar (site 74)			Gif-4172	2090±90 BP	363 calBC–calAD 69
Tuluk 211			Gif-5545	2360±70 BP	760–231 calBC
Tyeral Site 207			Gif-5542	2410±90 BP	794–265 calBC
Adrar des Ilforas					
Tadmakka	EKA 5	Seed (Triticum sp.)	OxA-16012	961±28 BP	calAD 1020–1155
Tadmakka	EKA 18	Seed (Ziziphus sp.)	OxA-16013	630±27 BP	calAD 1288–1398
Tadmakka	EKA 77	Seed (Gossypium sp.)	OxA-16014	959±27 BP	calAD 1021–1155
Tadmakka	EKA 85	Seed (Acacia sp.)	OxA-16015	960±28 BP	calAD 1021–1155
Tadmakka	EKA 113	Seed fragments	OxA-16016	1086±28 BP	calAD 894–1016
Tadmakka	EKA 118	Seed fragments	OxA-16017	1141±28 BP	calAD 777–980

Table 7.1 (*cont.*)

Region/Site	Context	Material	Reference	Date	Calibrated
Tadmakka	EKA 45	Pot sherd temper	OxA-16150	579±30 BP	calAD 1300–1419
Tadmakka	EKA 114	Pot sherd temper	OxA-16151	1238±30 BP	calAD 685–878
Tadmakka	EKB 2	Pot sherd temper	OxA-16152	1032±30 BP	calAD 901–1040
Tadmakka	EKA 3	Pot sherd temper	OxA-16768	602±26 BP	calAD 1299–1406
Tadmakka	EKA 87	Pot sherd temper	OxA-16769	1087±27 BP	calAD 894–1015
Tadmakka	EKC 4	Pot sherd temper	OxA-16770	650±27 BP	calAD 1281–1394
Tadmakka	EKA 77	Pot sherd temper	OxAx-2178 19	1339±36 BP	calAD 640–769
Tadmakka	EKA 116	Pot sherd temper	OxAx-2178 22	1245±34 BP	calAD 678–876
Tilemsi			Dak-3	3181±89 BP	1660–1227 calBC
Tilemsi AZ15			Gif-5306	2160±250 BP	808calBC–calAD 378
Middle Niger					
Gao Ancien			Gx-20623	1105±165 BP	calAD 643–1247
Gao Ancien			Gx-21656	1160±75 BP	calAD 690–1015
Gao Ancien			Gx-21657	1430±90 BP	calAD 418–770
Gao Ancien			Gx-22806	1005±75 BP	calAD 885–1212
Gao Saney	ACGS Level 2		Beta-261360	950±60 BP	calAD 990–1214
Gao Saney	ACGS Level 33		Beta-261361	1170±40 BP	calAD 730–972
Gao Saney	GS1 Level 2		Wk-12629	1083±42 BP	calAD 781–1027
Gao Saney	GS1 Level 7b		Wk-12630	1297±52 BP	calAD 647–869
Gao Saney	GS1 Level 14		Wk-12631	1227±42 BP	calAD 680–890
Gao Saney	GS3 Level 1		Wk-12632	1124±37 BP	calAD 777–994
Gao Saney	GS3 Level 5		Wk-12633	1189±54 BP	calAD 690–972
Gao Saney	GS3 Level 12		Wk-12634	1126±44 BP	calAD 775–995
Gao Saney	GS3 Level 16		Wk-12635	1246±37 BP	calAD 675–879
Gao Saney	Main mound	Charcoal	Pa-412	1000±70 BP	calAD 891–1204
In Sakane AZ20			Gif-5440	2850±100 BP	1283–811 calBC
Oued Amded			Gif-375	2160±150 BP	749 calBC–calAD 135
Tichet AZ25			Gif5230	2000±210 BP	727 calBC–calAD 533

Timbuktu			Gx-24763	170±40 BP	calAD 1655– . . .
Timbuktu			Gx-24764	240±40 BP	calAD 1520– . . .
Tombouze I			Beta-256795	Not given	cal430–640± BP
Tombouze I			Beta-256796	Not given	cal120–330± BP
Mauritanian Sahara					
Ma'den Ijafen			Dak-1	860±108 BP	calAD 971–1385
Ma'den Ijafen			I-2769	785±110 BP	calAD 1024–1396
Tumulus Mauny, Massif R'Kiz			Gif-3001	480±90 BP	
Atlantic Coast					
Amtal	64280 on bank of Sebkha	Shell	Gif-3259	2000±90 BP	347 calBC–calAD 226
Amtal	H1 Burial in midden (date considered too young)	Human Bone	Gif-3466	1780±100 BP	calAD 16–532
Bguent		Shell	Ly-444	2700±100 BP	1187–544 calBC
Cap Timiris		Shell	Ly-457	2640±120 BP	1051–411 calBC
Cap Timiris		Shell	Gd-4270	1760±60 BP	calAD 128–402
Chami (dune 1)		Bone	Gif-1763	2450±110 BP	817–258 calBC
Chami (dune 1)		Bone	Gif-1857	2380±220 BP	996 calBC–calAD 54
Chami (dune 1)		Bone	Gif-1859	1520±140 BP	calAD 145–774
Chami 3 km		Shell	Gif-2496	3220±110 BP	1756–1216 calBC
Chami (dune 7)		Bone	Gif-2165	6580±350 BP	6220–4780 calBC
Chami		Bone	Gif-2167	3310±240 BP	2281–1001 calBC
Chami		Pottery temper	Gif-1970	3150±140 BP	1744–1026 calBC
Chami		Bone	Gif-2166	2290±130 BP	766–55 calBC
Chami (Graret Zra 6)		Bone	Gif-2168	2450±130 BP	836–209 calBC
Chami (Graret Zra A)		Shell	Gif-1856	3950±80 BP	2838–2200 calBC
Chami (Graret Zra A)		Pottery temper	Gif-1970a	3650±140 BP	2459–1692 calBC
Chami (Graret Zra A)		Charcoal	Gif-2492	3500±120 BP	2141–1528 calBC
Chami (Graret Zra A)		Shell	Gif-2488	3450±110 BP	2112–1501 calBC
Chami (Graret Zra A)		Bone	Gif-1762	3100±120 BP	1625–1020 calBC

Table 7.1 (*cont.*)

Region/Site	Context	Material	Reference	Date	Calibrated
Chami (Graret Zra A)		Bone	Gif-2162	2500±100 BP	814–399 calBC
Chami (Graret Zra A)		Bone	Gif-2161	2170±100 BP	406 calBC–calAD 49
Chami (Graret Zra B)		Shell	Gif-2164	2360±100 BP	774–205 calBC
Chami (Graret Zra B)		Bone	Gif-2163	2100±180 BP	745 calBC–calAD 328
Chami (Graret Zra B)		Bone	Gif-2489	2090±120 BP	401 calBC–calAD 135
Chami (Graret Zra)		Bone	Gif-3060	3530±220 BP	2257–1320 calBC
Chami (Graret Zra)		Ostrich eggshell	Gif-2491	2960±110 BP	1437–902 calBC
Chami 10 km N Graret Zra		Bone	Gif-2333	4190±130 BP	3322–2457 calBC
Chami 8 km N Graret Zra		bone	Gif-2486	3850±120 BP	2831–1949 calBC
Chami 8 km N Graret Zra		Shell	Ly-346	3570±120 BP	2282–1621 calBC
Chami 8 km N Graret Zra		Shell	Gif-2487	3220±110 BP	1756–1216 calBC
Chami 9 km N Graret Zra		Bone	Gif-1765	2500±100 BP	814–399 calBC
Chami 9 km N Graret Zra		Pottery temper	Gif-2334	1870±240 BP	406 calBC–calAD 650
Chedd Allal			Ly-4397	2600±80 BP	923–433 calBC
Edjaila	H2 Burial in dune sand	Human bone	Gif-3461	3020±110 BP	1502–941 calBC
Edjaila	H3 Burial in dune sand	Human bone	Gif-3462	3310±120 BP	1911–1303 calBC
El Maharra		Charcoal	Dak-22	1869±115 BP	159 calBC–calAD 404
Laasailia	63293 Burial under large flat stones next to sebkha	Human bone	Gif-3269	3100±110 BP	1681–1265 calBC
Mahariat	H11 Burial within shell midden (date considered too young)	Human bone	Gif-3467	1080±100 BP	calAD 695–1160
Manate		Shell	KI-570	3200±85 BP	1681–1265 calBC
Manate		Shell	KI-572	3050±65 BP	1449–1114 calBC
Manate		Shell	KI-571	2720±85 BP	1120–767 calBC
Manate		Cardium	KI-593	2100±80 BP	361 calBC–calAD 53

Nouamghar		Shell	Gd-4268	3000±70 BP	1414–1031 calBC
Nouamghar		Ostrea	KI-565	2000±45 BP	158 calBC–calAD 85
Tenioubrar		Cardium	Ly-351	2660±110 BP	1111–485 calBC
Tijirit		Ostrich eggshell	Alger-110	1070±100 BP	calAD 695–1166
Tijirit		Ostrich eggshell	Alger-111	1060±100 BP	calAD 715–1202
Tijirit		Ostrich eggshell	Gif-8120	735±50 BP	calAD 1189–1389
Tijirit		Ostrich eggshell	Alger-112	475±100 BP	calAD 1297–1638
Tijirit		Ostrich eggshell	Alger-113	380±100 BP	calAD 1319–present
Tijirit	05	Ostrich eggshell	Alger-106	1580±90 BP	calAD 257–645
Tijirit	05	Ostrich eggshell	Gif-8122	1330±40 BP	calAD 643–770
Tijirit	10B	Ostrich eggshell	Alger-109	2170±190 BP	767 calBC–calAD 210
Tijirit	15	Ostrich eggshell	Gif-8121	3520±60 BP	2020–1692 calBC
Tijirit	15	Ostrich eggshell	Alger-108	3070±110 BP	1607–1011 calBC
Tijirit	24	Ostrich eggshell	Alger-107	2145±170 BP	749 calBC–calAD 227
Tijirit	73	Ostrich eggshell	Alger-105	1680±100 BP	calAD 127–581
Tijirit	78	Ostrich eggshell	Alger-104	1560±100 BP	calAD 256–657
Tijirit	D11	Ostrich eggshell	Alger-103	2450±140 BP	893–204 calBC
Tintan necropole		Roots	Gif-2505	6070±130 BP	5312–4704 calBC
Tintan necropole		Shell	Orsay-85	5670±300 BP	5302–3945 calBC
Tintan necropole		Shell	Gif-84	5520±100 BP	4584–4062 calBC
Tintan necropole		Shell	Orsay-86	5320±150 BP	4455–3799 calBC
Tintan necropole		Shell	Orsay-87	5020±160 BP	4235–3385 calBC
Tintan necropole		Shell	Orsay-88	4860±160 BP	4040–3125 calBC
Tintan necropole		Shell	Orsay-89	4600±200 BP	3903–2780 calBC
Tintan necropole		Shell	Orsay-90	4570±140 BP	3633–2926 calBC
Tintan necropole		Shell	Orsay-91	4445±160 BP	3630–2679 calBC
Tintan necropole		Shell	Ly-503	4270±100 BP	3324–2576 calBC
Tintan necropole		Shell	Orsay-92	3970±200 BP	3012–1926 calBC
Tintan necropole		Shell	Orsay-93	3960±100 BP	2864–2147 calBC
Tintan necropole		Pottery temper	Ly-459	3930±120 BP	2864–2046 calBC

Table 7.1 (*cont.*)

Region/Site	Context	Material	Reference	Date	Calibrated
Tintan necropole		Shell	Gif-2485	3930±80 BP	2832–2147 calBC
Tintan necropole		Shell	Orsay-94	3850±100 BP	2576–2027 calBC
Tintan necropole		Shell	Orsay-95	3805±80 BP	2471–2030 calBC
Tintan necropole		Shell	Orsay-96	3695±80 BP	2345–1881 calBC
Tintan necropole		Shell	Orsay-97	3570±160 BP	2436–1527 calBC
Tintan necropole		Shell	Orsay-98	3550±490 BP	3339–820 calBC
Tintan necropole		Shell	Ly-460	3530±130 BP	2267–1529 calBC
Tintan necropole		Bone	Gif-2484	3240±100 BP	1751–1266 calBC
Tintan necropole		Bone	Ly-505	2860±170 BP	1505–592 calBC
Tintan necropole		Bone	Gif-1761	2470±100 BP	806–392 calBC
Tintan necropole		Pottery temper	Gif-1884	2460±100 BP	804–388 calBC
Akjoujt					
Akjoujt		Charcoal	Dak-25	2776±126 BP	1378–592 calBC
Akjoujt		Charcoal	Dak-29	2522±123 BP	912–384 calBC
Akjoujt		Charcoal	Gif-1287	2430±110 BP	806–234 calBC
Akjoujt		Charcoal	Gif-1285	2400±110 BP	798–210 calBC
Akjoujt		Charcoal	Gif-1286	2360±110 BP	779–203 calBC
Akjoujt		Charcoal	Gif-1284	2350±110 BP	783–197 calBC
Akjoujt	Grotte aux Chauves-Souris	Charcoal	Gif-1823	2700±100 BP	1187–544 calBC
Akjoujt	Grotte aux Chauves-Souris	Charcoal	Gif-1824	2500±100 BP	814–399 calBC
Akjoujt	Grotte aux Chauves-Souris	Charcoal	Gif-1822	2460±100 BP	804–388 calBC
Akjoujt	Grotte aux Chauves-Souris	Charcoal	Gif-1825	2460±100 BP	804–388 calBC
Akjoujt	Grotte aux Chauves-Souris		Dak-112	1213±110 BP	calAD 639–1022
Akjoujt	Grotte aux Chauves-Souris		Dak-119	483±115 BP	calAD 1282–1646
Lemdena		Charcoal	Dak-120	1760±110 BP	calAD 28–537
Khatt Lemaiteg		Pottery temper	Ly-2501	3350±130 BP	2014–1316 calBC

Khatt Lemaiteg		Pottery temper	Ly-2502	3310±200 BP	2141–1088 calBC
Khatt Lemaiteg		Pottery temper	Ly-2974	3040±160 BP	1640–853 calBC
Khatt Lemaiteg		Pottery temper	Gif-6891	2830±60 BP	1192–837 calBC
Adrar					
Assabet el-Meddahia		Bone	Gif-5322	2590±100 BP	922–411 calBC
Assabet el-Meddahia		Bone	Gif-5323	2500±100 BP	814–399 calBC
Azugi		Charcoal	Gif-5338	1010±80 BP	calAD 779–1217
Azugi		Charcoal	Gif-5340	950±80 BP	calAD 903–1256
Azugi		Charcoal	Gif-5337	950±80 BP	calAD 903–1256
Azugi		Charcoal	Gif-5336	890±80 BP	calAD 1015–1272
Azugi		Charcoal	Gif-5339	880±80 BP	calAD 1020–1271
Draa Malichigdane		Human bone	Gif-2551	3120±110 BP	1629–1056 calBC
Draa Malichigdane		Pottery temper	Gif-2550	2030±100	358 calBC–calAD 210
Foum Tizigui		Pottery temper	Ly-4243	2970±130	1497–856 calBC
Oum Arouaba		Hippotamus bone	Dak-53	2107±117	399 calBC–calAD 124
Oum Arouaba		Human bone	Dak-59	1689±110	calAD 86–584
Tichitt					
Akreijit			?	3850±250 BP	3009–1638 calBC
Akreijit		Charcoal	Dak-32	3776±120	2565–1889 calBC
Akreijit		Bone	Mc-427	3490±50 BP	1939–1689 calBC
Akreijit		Charcoal	Dak-203	3122±120 BP	1660–1050 calBC
Akreijit		Charcoal	I-3565	3100±105 BP	1612–1058 calBC
Akreijit		Charcoal	Dak-187	2975±110 BP	1447–911 calBC
Akreijit		Charcoal	Dak-190	2760±160 BP	1394–521 calBC
Akreijit		?	Gif-6083	2430±80 BP	778–395 calBC
Akreijit		Charcoal	Dak-185	1663±113 BP	calAD 125–615
Akreijit	Aouker lake ashy layer	Bone	Gif-3406	730±90 BP	Aouker lake ashy layer
Baidla I		Charcoal	GX-1325	2780±140 BP	1390–555 calBC
Bledd Initi		Charcoal	GX-1326	2600±105 BP	971–411 calBC

Table 7.1 (*cont.*)

Region/Site	Context	Material	Reference	Date	Calibrated
El Rhimiya		Hippotamus bone	Gif-2884	3830±120 BP	2619–1938 calBC
Goungou	A2	Fish bone	GX-1421	3465±160 BP	2272–1421 calBC
Goungou	A2	Charcoal	I-3561	3350±110 BP	1921–1416 calBC
Goungou	A5	Charcoal	GX-1323	3205±95 BP	1731–1234 calBC
Goungou	B3	Bone	GX-1889	3425±130 BP	2121–1435 calBC
Goungou	B3	Charcoal	I-3563	2950±100 BP	1415–914 calBC
Goungou	B3	Charcoal	I-3563	2950±100 BP	1415–914 calBC
Niemilane		Charcoal	I-3819	2170±105 BP	411 calBC–calAD 61
Oued Chebbi		Pottery temper	Ly-3334	2740±160 BP	1381–484 calBC
Seyyid Ouinquil		Charcoal	I-3565	3100±105 BP	1612–1058 calBC
Taidart II		Charcoal	I-3566	2330±105 BP	770–177 calBC
Tichitt (site 17)			GX-1890	3700±130 BP	2468–1763 calBC
Tichitt (site 30)		Charcoal	GX-1324	2700±115 BP	1195–539 calBC
Tichitt (site 30)		Charcoal	GX-1888	2885±140 BP	1414–808 calBC
Tichitt (site 30)		Charcoal	I-3564	3205±105 BP	1741–1219 calBC
Tichitt (TIC 70)	Hearth	Fish bone	Gif-4110	2610±110 BP	992–412 calBC
Tichitt (TIC 75)	Necropolis of Tichitt village	Human bone	Gif-4111	1930±110 BP	201–345 calBC
Tichitt (TIC75)	Lacustrine deposit	Hippopotamus bone	Gil-4112	2290±110 BP	756–93 calBC
Tichitt		Bone	Mc427 c	1540±50 BP	calAD 410–615
Tichitt		Bone	Mc427b	1370±60 BP	calAD 565–770
Tichitt Village v.39			Pa-1300	3000±120 BP	1500–919 calBC
Tichitt Village v.39			Pa-1310	2800±120 BP	1374–778 calBC
Tichitt Village v.147			Pa-1290	3060±80 BP	1500–1059 calBC
Tichitt Village v.147			Pa-1328	3590±80 BP	2195–1700 calBC
Tichitt Village v.304			Pa-1292	3360±100 BP	1898–1434 calBC
Tichitt Village v.304			Pa-1294	3085±100 BP	1606–1049 calBC
Bou Khzama II	Midden feature S5	Charcoal	Pa-2153	3765±35 BP	2291–2042 calBC
Bou Khzama II			Pa-2437	3690±60 BP	2279–1916 calBC

Bou Khzama II			Pa-665	3330±38 BP	1730–1513 calBC
Bou Khzama II	Inhumation SK1	Human bone	Pa-2129	3300±100 BP	1879–1329 calBC
Bou Khzama II	surface	Pottery temper	Pa-2170	3250±100 BP	1766–1281 calBC
Bou Khzama II			Pa-653	3231±36 BP	1611–1431 calBC
Bou Khzama II	Surface	Pottery temper	Pa-2128	2840±80 BP	1222–827 calBC
Bou Khzama II	Furnace, context 1	Pottery temper	GX-30818 AMS	2440±40 BP	756–407 calBC
Bou Khzama II	Surface, sample 1	Pottery temper	GX-28137 AMS	2340±40 BP	723–236 calBC
Bou Khzama II			Pa-671	1643±34 BP	calAD 268–535
Bou Khzama II			Pa-666	1634±34 BP	calAD 340–536
Bou Khzama II	Feature S9	Charcoal	Pa-2160	1530±50 BP	calAD 417–625
Bou Khzama II	Surface	Pottery temper	Pa-2127	1415±120 BP	calAD 390–886
Bou Khzama II	Surface	Pottery temper	Pa-2174	1390±100 BP	calAD 426–870
Djiganayai	Context 6	Pottery temper	GX-29358 AMS	3550±40 BP	2016–1756 calBC
Djiganayai	Surface, sample 7	Pottery temper	GX-29359 AMS	3370±40 BP	1752–1533 calBC
Djiganayai	Surface, sample 9	Pottery temper	GX-28140 AMS	3260±40 BP	1624–1445 calBC
Djiganayai	Context 2	Bos sp. tooth	GX-28139 AMS	2780±30 BP	1004–844 calBC
Elb Lehnoucha			Pa-661	2080±35 BP	195–1 calBC
Ngadi			Pa-667	3222±42 BP	1611–1420 calBC
Ngadi			Pa-2428	3005±60 BP	1408–1056 calBC
Ngadi			Pa-668	1192±34 BP	calAD 713–952
Nouaoudar			Pa-2438	3350±60 BP	1869–1498 calBC
Nouaoudar			Pa-2436	3050±60 BP	1434–1126 calBC
Nouaoudar			Pa-2435	2985±75 BP	1411–1011 calBC
Chigettomi (rkiz)	Bones from under rock shelter (burial?)	Human bone	Gif-2769	1400±90 BP	calAD 340–536
Tagdaoust			Dak-46	3556±142 BP	2295–1530 calBC
Tagdaoust			Dak-47	2901±151 BP	1450–801 calBC
Tagdaoust			Dak-194	1851±100 BP	51 calBC–calAD 401
Tagdaoust		Charcoal	Dak-96	1261±121 BP	calAD 573–1016
Tagdaoust		Charcoal	Dak-63	1143±124 BP	calAD 654–1154

Table 7.1 (*cont.*)

Region/Site	Context	Material	Reference	Date	Calibrated
Tagdaoust		Charcoal	Dak-195	1170±100 BP	calAD 662–1024
Tagdaoust		Charcoal	UCLA-696	1150±80 BP	calAD 689–1020
Tagdaoust		Charcoal	Dak-94	1066±120 BP	calAD 690–1207
Tagdaoust		Charcoal	Dak-173	1031±100 BP	calAD 773–1213
Tagdaoust		Charcoal	Dak-97	1003±119 BP	calAD 774–1255
Tagdaoust		Charcoal	Dak-172	1017±100 BP	calAD 776–1217
Tagdaoust		Charcoal	Dak-93	881±118 BP	calAD 895–1383
Tagdaoust		Charcoal	Dak-95	831±117 BP	calAD 983–1394
Tagdaoust			Dak-98	765±122 BP	calAD 1026–1408
Tagdaoust			Dak-42	692±118 BP	calAD 1045–1442
Tagdaoust			Gif-265	650±120 BP	calAD 1047–1476
Tagdaoust			Dak-158	633±120 BP	calAD 1051–1616
Tagdaoust			Dak-43	595±105 BP	calAD 1211–1616
Tagdaoust			Dak-45	538±113 BP	calAD 1261–1635
Tagdaoust			Dak-118	483±119 BP	calAD 1276–1653
Tagdaoust			Dak-117	276±121 BP	calAD 1440– . . .
Tagdaoust			Sa-219	150±100 BP	calAD 1522– . . .
Tagdaoust			Gif-266	Modern	N/A
Tagdaoust			DaK-44	Modern	N/A
Tagdaoust			Dak-48	Modern	N/A
Kumbi Saleh			Ly-1610	1400±160 BP	calAD 262–982
Kumbi Saleh			Ly-1792	1280±150 BP	calAD 428–1026
Kumbi Saleh			Ly-1616	1290±130 BP	calAD 437–1018
Kumbi Saleh			Ly-1613	1210±140 BP	calAD 565–1151
Kumbi Saleh			Dak-157	1122±125 BP	calAD 665–1155
Kumbi Saleh			Ly-1341	1000±150 BP	calAD 695–1275
Kumbi Saleh			Ly-1526	860±210 BP	calAD 695–1438
Kumbi Saleh			Ly-1615	980±130 BP	calAD 774–1270

Kumbi Saleh	Dak-156	981±114 BP	calAD 777–1264
Kumbi Saleh	Ly-1612	940±120 BP	calAD 778–1285
Kumbi Saleh	Ly-1611	870±120 BP	calAD 897–1387
Kumbi Saleh	Ly-1524	550±230 BP	calAD 1018– . . .
Kumbi Saleh	Sa-77	740±120 BP	calAD 1035–1415
Kumbi Saleh	Ly-1520	590±120 BP	calAD 1185–1631
Kumbi Saleh	Ly-1525	440±180 BP	calAD 1252– . . .
Kumbi Saleh	Ly-1614	540±120 BP	calAD 1257–1641
Kumbi Saleh	Ly-1522	500±120 BP	calAD 1273–1647
Kumbi Saleh	Ly-1523	500±110 BP	calAD 1283–1637
Kumbi Saleh	Ly-1521	230±120 BP	calAD 1468– . . .
Kumbi Saleh tombs	P-1101	925±30 BP	calAD 1026–1182
Kumbi Saleh tombs	Muse-162	895±30 BP	calAD 1039–1215
Kumbi Saleh tombs	P-1102	890±30 BP	calAD 1041–1218
Kumbi Saleh tombs	Muse-160	875±30 BP	calAD 1043–1241
Kumbi Saleh tombs	P-1100	835±30 BP	calAD 1157–1264

The Teda Lands: Kufra, Ennedi, Borku, Tibesti and Kawar

The Tibesti mountains, the Kufra oases and the Kawar oases are the heartlands of the Tubu, a people also known as the Teda (Fig. 7.1).[5] The Teda were notoriously hardy, unwelcoming to incomers, but well-adapted to the harsh terrain of the Tibesti massif and the oases in the surrounding desert areas. Another related branch of the Tubu describe themselves as Dazas, comprising today mainly semi-nomads who range between Lake Chad and Borku on the south side of Tibesti.[6] The influence of the Tubu extended across a wide zone of desert and they controlled the key oases and the trade routes to and from Lake Chad and northwards. The far higher mortality rates recorded in the nineteenth century on the Tubu slave caravans compared to the Tuareg ones further to the west can be attributed to the limited water availability in this region, obliging the Tubu to force the pace in their marches.[7] The Teda/Tubu are linguistically distinct from other Saharan peoples, have been little impacted on by intermarriage with other groups (especially Arabs) and are thought to represent a long-established Saharan people.[8] They are perhaps to be equated with the troglodyte *Aethiopes* described by Herodotus.[9] Rock art from Tibesti depicts warriors, some mounted on camels and horses, wearing ostrich feather plumes and armed with large-headed metal spears, and figure of eight and sub-rectangular shields.[10]

The ancestors of the Teda were the immediate southern and eastern neighbours of the Garamantes and will have undoubtedly had profound contacts with them. The landscapes occupied by the Teda, both ancient and modern, are extremely harsh and challenging and a significant component of their population has tended to be mobile and pastoralists. But, as we shall see, the Teda territories also contain sporadic small oases and sedentary communities and we should not underestimate the significance of such groups in the past. The Classical sources speak of campaigns by the Garamantes against *Aethiopes*, including an expedition led by a king of the Garamantes that travelled south from Jarma for four months.[11] If

[5] Beltrami 2007; Chapelle 1957; Cline 1950; Nachtigal 1974; Rohlfs 2003, for studies of the Teda.

[6] Beltrami 2007, 113. [7] Wright 1998.

[8] On their distinctiveness from Berber speaking groups in the Sahara, see Blench 2019, 439–40; Ehret 2019, 487–93.

[9] Herodotus, *Histories* 4.183; Beltrami 2007, 107–131, 63–86.

[10] Beltrami 2007, 16–77 (this also includes useful listings for Borku, Ennedi as well as Tibesti); Capot-Rey 1961; Huard 1953.

[11] Ptolemy, *Geography* 1.8–11 discusses the famous expedition of Julius Maternus who accompanied the Garamantian king as far south as the rhinoceros country of Agisymba

Figure 7.1. Eastern Sahara, main regions and sites discussed in the text.

the Garamantes were engaged, as seems likely, in enslaving Africans from other parts of the Sahara and the Sub-Saharan regions, the Teda may well have come to play a crucial role in procuring and transporting slaves as they did in later eras. A hint of this is preserved in the early Arab sources. In the ninth century, al-Yaʿqubi described the people of Kawar as responsible for bringing in the slaves to Zuwila in Fazzan. Interestingly, Kawar was the ultimate target of Uqba ibn Nafi's great raid of AD 666–667.[12]

(probably Lake Chad). These 'Aethiopians' are distinguished in Ptolemy's account (1.8) from those who were directly subject to the Garamantes, which perhaps included some of the closer Teda groups.

[12] Levtzion and Hopkins 2000, 13, 22.

Kufra

There was been little research on the historic phases of the Kufra oasis and the traditional settlements of the region are now largely obliterated as a result of modern development relating to oil and water extraction.[13] Prior to a campaign by the Ottoman rulers of Tripolitania in the early nineteenth century, Kufra was considered a Teda oasis, but in more modern times the population has become more mixed. Although there are important water resources in the Kufra depression, the great distances and difficult near waterless terrain separating this oasis and those to the east (Dakhla 600 km), north (Awjila 575 km) and west (Tmissa 850 km) have enhanced Kufra's reputation as an isolated community.[14] Historically, there is some evidence that Kufra has gained in importance at times when the direct south-north route through Fazzan has been cut or threatened, with some traffic diverting from the Borku area (*c.*1,000 km to the south-west of Kufra).[15] The closest links culturally appear to have been between Kufra and the Tibesti/Ennedi area, as well as with the Teda of that area.[16] The Kufra group comprises a number of distinct oases, with Tazurbu an outlier to the north-west (250 km from Kufra itself). Some distinctive pre-Islamic burials have been recorded at Tazurbu, with the corpse in a seated position, as well as an ancient castle (no longer identifiable in the 1990s).[17] The main cluster of oases at Kufra are known as the 'crown' (al-Tadj), with further outlying small oases at Wadi Zighan, Bzema, Rabiana. Although modern studies are lacking there are indications from pre-Islamic tombs and abandoned *qsur* of a potentially long chronology here.[18]

Ennedi

The most easterly of the Saharan massifs is Ennedi. Archaeological research remains very low in this area of northern Chad, but again there are some strong indications of pre-Islamic activity in the form of rock art of the horse and camel phases, funerary monuments and stone monuments of various types.[19] Work by Bailloud and Keding *et al.* has created a sequence

[13] Aerial photographs taken in the 1930s as part of the Italian occupation of Libya provide an important record of the oases before modern development, but they do not show evidence of any archaeological remains.

[14] See Aroca 1942 (for Waw al-Kabir, an important staging post on the route to Fazzan); Desio 1935, Scarin 1937a; 1937b; Thiry 1995.

[15] Meerpohl 2013. [16] Beltrami 2007. [17] Beltrami 2007, 126. [18] Beltrami 2007, 126–29.

[19] Bailloud 1969; 1997; Dalloni and Monod 1948; Keding *et al.* 2007.

from ceramics, OSL and ^{14}C dates, particularly from the sites known as Shekitye T04/227, T04/234 and Mornou T05/501 and T05/88.[20] The last phase of the ceramic sequence ('Djoki') dates to the first millennium AD, following a hiatus in the first millennium BC (although there is a cattle skull from this period).[21] This period is associated with numerous stone structures and iron objects that are similar to those found in the Borku region. This period is associated with an increase in the number of smaller sites in the region which has been interpreted as evidence of a form of cattle-based transhumance between Ennedi and the Wadi Howar region and a more widespread occupation than today.

Whilst surveyed Iron Age sites still await publication, there are numerous archaeological remains visible on the rock outcrops around Fada including stone villages, enclosures and dense cairn cemeteries. Some are undoubtedly the Medieval precursors of the modern town, but the numbers and association with cairns, the proximity of water sources such as the Guelta d'Archei and the access to grazing in the highlands is suggestive of earlier oasis settlement.

South of Ennedi in the Wadai highlands lie the impressive remains of Wara, one-time capital of the Wadai Sultanate. The remains are considered to date to the mid-seventeenth century and consist of a large sub-circular wall (*c.*330 m in diameter) within which are a number of large enclosures, one of which contains the mosque, palace and outhouses of the ruler.[22] To the north and south-west are many more enclosures taking the total area of the urban-scale settlement to around 60–70 ha.

Borku

The desert region between the Ennedi and the Tibesti mountains is also extraordinarily tough, with relatively few oases.[23] The Borku region to the south of the Tibesti contains a few scattered and small oases, such as Faya and Fada, but crucially some important salt sources, such as Wadi Doum and Beda in Borku and Demi to the north of Ennedi.[24] The most extensive survey of the area is by Treinen-Claustre who surveyed 127 sites and excavated sondages at a small number of these, many of which had iron objects from the first millennium AD.[25] Archaeological remains of mud-

[20] Keding *et al.* 2007, 36–38. [21] Site T05/88-2: Poz-16595, 2480 ± 30 BP, 774–434 calBC.
[22] Lebeuf 1962.
[23] See Bruce-Lockhart and Wright 2000; Richardson 1853; Rohlfs 1874/1875 for some early accounts of the routes south of Fazzan through this region and further west towards Kawar.
[24] Capot-Rey 1957; 1958; 1959; 1961, 124–30; Schiffers 1957. [25] Treinen-Claustre 1982.

brick structures including enclosures, dwellings and a monumental palace are noted in passing by Lebeuf along the Bahr-al-Ghazal, Bornu and at Galaka in Borku, he attributes these to the fourteenth to seventeenth centuries or even more recent eras.[26] There are numerous stone-built enclosures and thousands of cairns across Borku, especially to the north of Galaka.[27]

At the northern end of Bahr-al-Ghazal is the Koro-Toro region which is rich in ironstone. Early iron-working sites consisting of stone structures, iron furnaces and mounds of iron slag are associated with domestic cattle.[28] Radiocarbon dates imply a broad temporal range – samples from the base of slag heaps tend to lie somewhere between the late fourth and early eighth centuries AD (or perhaps a little earlier in some cases) and the latest dates are in the tenth–fifteenth centuries AD.[29]

Tibesti

The fan-shaped Tibesti mountains rise to *c*.3,000 m and cover an area of *c*.100,000 km^2.[30] The ranges contain several volcanic craters and the north-eastern extremity was the main source of amazonite (a turquoise semi-precious stone) exploited by the Garamantes.[31] Settlements are sparse due to the main water resources being dependent on irregular rain, rather than springs. Some of the main settlements are located in the valley outlets from the massif, others in valleys well within the massif, as at Bardai where Nachtigal barely escaped with his life in 1850.[32] It seems probable that this has long been the pattern, to judge from the distribution of rock art.[33] There are considerable numbers of burial cairns in Tibesti, of very similar types to Garamantian Proto-Urban phase ones and again strongly hinting at sedentary activity in pre-Islamic times.[34] There are also a number of

[26] Lebeuf 1963, 597.

[27] Some of these cairns were visited by a team from the University of Siena – many are drum tombs similar to those in Fazzan and some of the rouletted pottery is also similar (Gatto 2006).

[28] Close 1980, 152. Despite the publication of coordinates there are no clear traces on satellite imagery of these features.

[29] Close 1980; Posnansky and McIntosh 1976, 193.

[30] On the Tibesti, see, *inter alia*, Beltrami 2007; Desio 1942; 1950; Nachtigal 1974.

[31] Beltrami 2007, 107–13; Mattingly 2003, 356–58.

[32] Nachtigal 1974, 286–318, see also 379–422 for his extended discussion of the Teda and their history.

[33] Beltrami 2007; Huard 1953.

[34] See Beltrami 2007, figure 2.3.1, with examples of tombs that are intrinsically similar to Garamantian corbelled cairns (Type 1b) and drum tombs (Type 3b) in the Fazzan typology, see Mattingly 2003, 196–200. For a full list of 13 major pre-Islamic cemeteries see Beltrami 2007, 78–92.

major enclosures and ritual monuments with curving lines of stones set on edge.[35] The densest concentrations of cairns and enclosures are found along those wadis with the most vegetation and in which settlement is concentrated today. Two groups of settlements have been identified by the work of Rønneseth, the earlier group with huts in the wadis and on the slopes dates to the late first millennium BC. The second group, higher up in the mountains dates to the eleventh–sixteenth centuries AD.[36] There are a few radiocarbon dates from Tibesti for the mid-late first millennium BC, most are from cairn burials, although one implying elephants in the first millennium BC is probably centuries earlier based on its recalibration (perhaps as early as *c.*2000 BC).[37]

Kawar and Other Oases In and Close to the Bilma Sand Sea

Kawar comprises a north-south line of small oases extending down *c.*80 km into the Bilma Erg from its northern edge. The most direct route from Lake Chad to Fazzan passes along this line and Bilma at the heart of Kawar was a crucial salt mine.[38] Djado and Seguedine are important oases on the north side of the Bilma sand sea, at the southern end of a very difficult desert passage south from the last oasis of Fazzan over the pass of Tumu.

Djado is a collective name that is used for a group of three oases: Djado, Djaba and Chirfa, that lies on the southern edge of a large plateau. At all three of these sites there are the remains of still upstanding *qasaba* villages made from salt-enriched mudlumps.[39] According to Chappelle, the inhabitants of these villages were Kanuri with Tubu having erected tents around the palm groves.[40] A pair of AMS samples from Djaba returned dates of calAD 1045–1395 and calAD 1301–1631 although it is not clear from where these samples were taken or even which village.[41] However, there are some possible signs of earlier settlement. Also at Djaba, there is what looks suspiciously like a mudbrick Garamantian-style *qasr* – a square

[35] Beltrami 2007, 79–83, for 23 other stone monuments in Tibesti and Ennedi.

[36] Close 1984, 10–11; Jäkel and Geyh 1982; Rønneseth 1982a; 1982b.

[37] For the burials see Gabriel 1977; 1981; for dated cairns found at Yebbigue and Zoui, Close 1984, 9–10; Posnansky and McIntosh 1976, 185 (HV-2260: 2690 ± 435, 2022 calBC–calAD 138).

[38] Lovejoy 1986; Retaillé 1986; Vikør 1999. See also Haour 2017; MacEachern 2019, 418–22, for reviews of the early evolution of Trans-Saharan trade in relation to Kawar and Lake Chad.

[39] Lange and Berthoud 1977, recorded a series of villages in the 1970s where they noted that *qasabah* structures were still in use as date stores.

[40] Chappelle 1957.

[41] Gif-3547 and VRI-810, another date from Djaba and two from Djado were calibrated to post-calAD 1443.

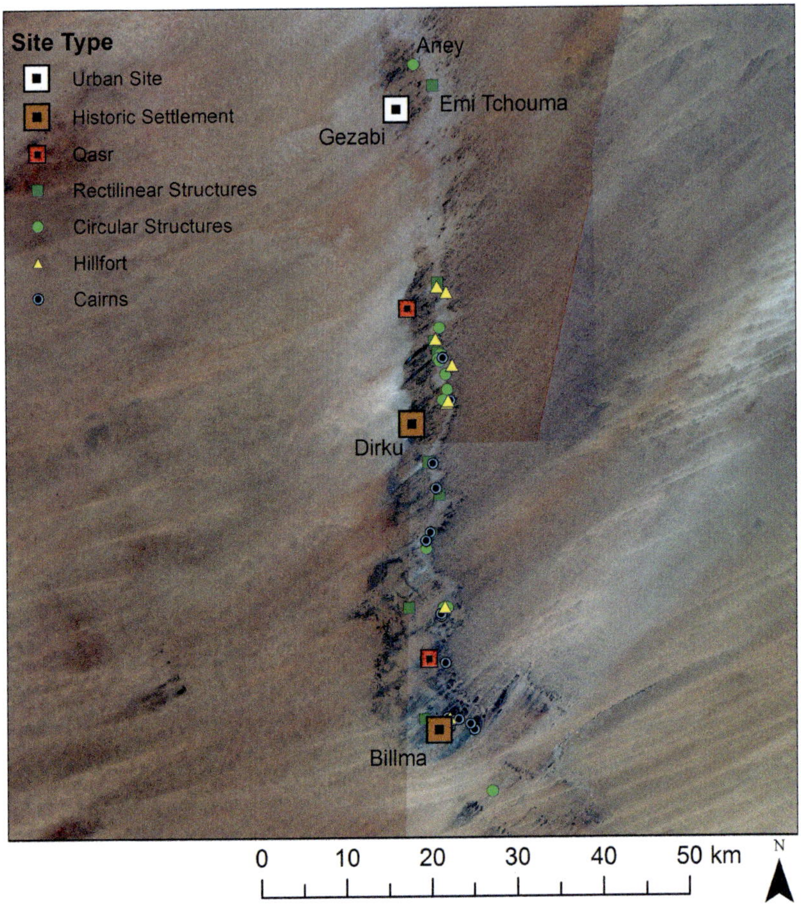

Figure 7.2. Sites in the Kawar Oasis.

building with square corner towers.[42] To the north and east of this structure are traces of a rectilinear field-system with central wells, again similar to Garamantian examples in eastern Fazzan. Likewise on the southern edge of Djado there is a square fortification with a small nucleated settlement that can be associated with an area of abandoned gardens.[43] Finally, 5–10 km to the north and east of Djado and Djaba there are several dense clusters of burial cairns on the rocky edge of the plateau.

Seguedine is a tiny oasis to the south-east of Djado and midway between Tajirhi and Kawar that is known for the quality of its salt. There does not appear to have ever been a large population here, but some 4 km to the west

[42] Lange and Berthoud 1977 were notified in Kawar of older ruins in this area specifically referencing a Qasr Maja.

[43] Again Lange and Berthoud 1977 note a Qasr Biri and to the south-west a Qasr Garem Djawin.

Figure 7.3. Satellite image of Gezabi (imagery: Google, DigitalGlobe).

of the modern settlement there is a large abandoned settlement with a central *qasaba*, this looks similar to the ones at Djado and is presumably of similar date. That the location has been much frequented in antiquity is indicated by the cairns that sit on nearly every rocky outcrop in the vicinity.

The Kawar oases stretch underneath an escarpment from Aney in the north to Bilma, some 80 km to the south (Fig. 7.2). By far the largest archaeological site lies 5 km to the south-east of Aney where there are the remains of the 20 ha Medieval town of Gezabi (Fig. 7.3). There are many well-preserved square houses up to about 25 × 25 m and a few more monumental buildings including a prominent mosque to the north-east of the town. Surrounding the settlement are the remains of an extensive area of oasis gardens (*c.*300 ha). Gezabi is considered by the inhabitants of Kawar to be the oldest settlement in the oasis. Mauny associated it with al-Qasaba (as in the capital) mentioned in al-Idrisi and a more certain reference to a Ghazbi comes from Ibn Furtu in the fourteenth century.[44]

[44] Levtzion and Hopkins 2000, 123; Mauny 1961, 141. Al-Idrisi also mentions a number of other towns in a line running south: Qasr Umm Isa, Ankalus (modern Kalala?), Abzar and Talamla. The latter two have somewhat variable geographies in other sources with Abzar (Abzan, Asben) associated with the Songhay name for Air (but see below) and Talamla (Tamalma, Lamlama) with Tibesti, see Levtzion and Hopkins, index entries. The relevant point is that the al-Idrisi recognised Kawar as consisting of a linear arrangement of large settlements (similar to Fazzan).

Agisymba in Ptolemy's *Geography* is another potential, but far less convincing reference.[45]

Just to the south of Aney there is a *c.*300 × 300 m settlement (Emi Tchouma) of more square houses with a mosque. This site lies to the south-west of a defended hilltop. The house forms are similar to those found at Gezabi and are also presumably of Medieval date. However, the hilltop settlement could be Protohistoric (similar ones in Libya date back to the first millennium BC or early first millennium AD).

Along the hills to the east of the oases are a number of archaeological sites.[46] There are a further 15 villages of stone-built houses. Typically these cluster around a promontory. There are two distinct groups based on house morphology: a rectilinear courtyard or blockhouse type and a type consisting of one to five circular or curved elements. There are nine villages that only have circular-type buildings and the remaining six have clusters of both types. In many cases it is clear that the rectilinear buildings have been built over the circular-type buildings; in others they may be on opposite slopes or the circular buildings are higher up than the rectilinear buildings. Five of the six clusters of rectilinear buildings contain a mosque (usually fairly small). At four of the sites there is also activity on the associated hilltop with features including walls cutting off promontories and clusters of small huts. There are a few other possible hilltop sites and enclosures, but these are generally poorly defined. Additionally there are a number of dense cairn cemeteries that suggest a permanent pre-Islamic presence in several parts of the oasis. Finally, to the north of Bilma (itself mentioned as the largest town of Kawar by Yaqut in the thirteenth century)[47] there is an undated Garamantian-style square *qasr* (27 × 20 m) with corner and intermediate towers and an entrance on the east side.

Fachi is a small but important oasis south-west of Bilma on the route through the Erg towards Agadez and the Aïr.[48] To the south-west of the main oasis there is a relict field-system close to a ruined village with large circular-type buildings. The village is walled, constructed of mudbricks and possibly divided into northern and southern halves. There is a sub-rectangular *qasr* with square towers on the north-east corner but this is likely Early Modern in date. There is also a large area of salt extraction

45 Ptolemy, *Geography* 1.8.

46 These were all noted as in ruins by 1823, Denham *et al.* 1985, 22–38.

47 Levtzion and Hopkins 2000, 171, 173; Yaqut also adds another town al-Bilas.

48 According to the map of Denham *et al.* 1985 Fachi should be associated with the town of Asben mentioned in Medieval Arabic sources.

*c.*7 km to the north but no visible settlement apart from the buildings around the digging.

Although all but abandoned, Agadem is the most southerly oasis before Lake Chad, lying *c.*200 km south of Bilma. In several places amongst the hills there are small villages of small circular huts, similar (but simpler) to those found in the Kawar and several cairn cemeteries that may be associated to the villages. Also notable is a walled hilltop site on a small plateau (undated) and a square enclosure (50 × 50 m).

Finally, in a remote area several hundred kilometres from the nearest oasis, the Termit massif has evidence of iron working and burial cairns along with copper and iron objects. A radiocarbon date placed the activity in the first to sixth centuries AD (further dates have given early dates of late second to early first millennium BC, but these have come under sustained critique).[49] There are no obvious signs of settlement or much else on the massif apart from a scattering of cairns (see also the map of Quéckon and Roset).

The Kawar oasis group (and its outliers) should be a critical focus for future research. It potentially holds the key to understanding the relationship between the Garamantes and the peoples of the Lake Chad basin to the south. The account of Ibn Abd al-Hakam of the mid-seventh-century raid of Uqba ibn Nafi has a ring of authenticity about its overall geographical context, even if the historical detail is disputed.[50] Uqba successively passed through and received the surrender of the oases of the Jufra (Waddan), Fazzan (Jarma, other 'castles' and Zuwila) and Kawar, following the main coordinates of the Tripoli-Lake Chad slave route of later times. The main *qasaba* of Kawar, evidently a hilltop site, initially held out against him, until captured by a ruse. His demand of hundreds of slaves from all the rulers who submitted to him could of course be an anachronism based on later developments, but it seems more plausible in light of what we now know of the Garamantes to view the raid as stimulated primarily by a desire to establish greater Arab control of a pre-existing and lucrative trade in slaves along this route. The Kawar oases, with their abundant salt sources, had a valuable resource with which to trade for people, but they were also both close enough to launch slaving expeditions and protected from pursuit by the intervening desert terrain. Garamantian trade goods are notably absent in the Lake Chad basin; if the wider Teda populations were responsible for much of the slave raiding, then the Kawar oasis is perhaps the place to look

[49] Poznasky and McIntosh 1976, 184; Quéckon and Roset 1974.
[50] Levtzion and Hopkins 2000, 11–13.

for evidence of Garamantian material culture (items such as carnelian and amazonite beads, glass beads, metals of distinctive alloys and textiles).[51]

The Tuareg Central Sahara: Tassili and Ahaggar

The Tassili n'Ajjer and Ahaggar are the two main mountain ranges in southern Algeria with highpoints of 2,158 m and 2,908 m respectively (Fig 7.4). Historically, both have been Tuareg territory with the Tassili facing the Tadrart Akakus across the north-south trench of Wadi Tanzzuft.[52] Again, the historical emergence of the Tuareg may well have overlapped with the Garamantian era, as their modern rangelands extend up to the western borderlands of Fazzan. It is interesting that the massifs of the central Sahara – Tadrart Akakus, Tassili, Immidir and Ahaggar (and Aïr to the south) contain a great number and density of images of chariots, especially the representations of the 'flying gallop' type. By way of comparison, representations of chariots in the Teda lands of Tibesti and other zones to the south and east of Fazzan are comparatively rare.[53] There was thus a distinctive cultural relationship between the western and south-western neighbours of the Garamantes and chariot imagery. Gauthier and Gauthier have demonstrated a strong association between the distribution of chariot imagery and early Libyan inscriptions in the Sahara.[54] Again the contrast with the Teda area is marked, suggesting that the modern cultural divide between Teda and Tuareg builds on something of considerable antiquity. The rock art, the written script and the funerary monuments of the mountain massifs to the west of Fazzan suggest that these areas had some cultural links with the Garamantes. Although these areas were perhaps best suited to support pastoral groups, who might have provided beasts of burden, desert guides and military muscle for the Garamantes, we should not neglect the possibility that some at least of the small oases of these areas also developed early.

Tassili n'Ajjer

Although famed for its rock art (a UNESCO World Heritage Site), there is little evidence to suggest that the Tassili ever had a substantial sedentary

[51] MacEachern 2019, 417–18. [52] See Mattingly *et al.*, Chapter 2, this volume.

[53] Gauthier and Gauthier 2011, 93–95. For five examples of chariots depicted in rock art from Teda lands, see Huard and Féval 1964, 85.

[54] Gauthier and Gauthier 2011, 105–14.

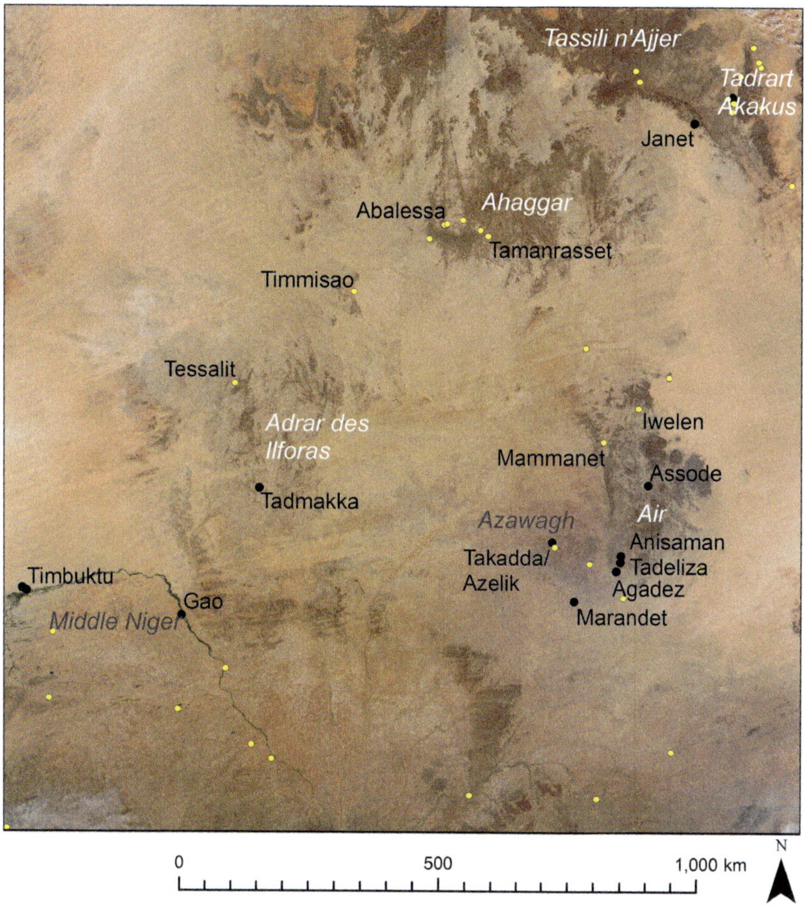

Figure 7.4. Mali and Niger, main regions and sites discussed in the text.

population.[55] The mountain valleys are rich in pasture and can still run with water after rain. The major oasis group is at Janet in the south-east which comprises three centres along the Wadi Egerew. In addition to rock art (which is of all major periods), finds from excavated burial cairns at Chaâba Arkouya include a bronze bracelet and Roman pottery from the second–third century AD and further tombs on the bank of the Wadi Tin Arilane (possibly the same site) suggest that these burials are similar in rite and material to those found in the Wadi Tanzzuft.[56] However, evidence of settlement is far scarcer with no oases mentioned in either Classical or Medieval sources, and the establishment of the modern oasis

[55] On the Tassili see Hachid 1998; 2000.

[56] Gast and Hachid 1995; Gatto *et al.* 2019, 108–33; Grébénart 1988; Lhote 1971 for a description of the Wadi Tanzzuft.

centres placed as late as the fifteenth or sixteenth centuries.[57] Analysis of satellite imagery across the Tassili shows a thin spread of small huts, enclosures, and other monuments across the mountain range which is consistent with a largely mobile population. On the western flank of the Wadi Egerew, adjacent to the oasis gardens are three small nucleated cemeteries with 20–50 probable drum tombs in each.[58] There is a fourth on the eastern flank although this has been damaged by modern developments which are encroaching up the slopes.

A smaller oasis group is found in the centre of the Tassili, in a bend of the Wadi Iherir, which contains a seasonal river running from October to April. Perret recorded three groups of ruins, one next to a village (Hiheras) which he considered to be three to four centuries old and two others with rectangular rooms which he considered likely to be Roman.[59] This attribution is dubious in the extreme, but his plan of Ikakaden shows three buildings, the most complete of which is 4.5 × 18 m, divided into five equal-sized rooms and made from cemented stone.[60] The third might still survive (Tadjart) although there is little about the plan to support an ancient date. As at Janet there are a few small nucleated cairn cemeteries visible on the satellite imagery. A slightly confusing addendum is the finding of fourth-century AD Roman coins and ceramics from Tadrart and Dider. Salama and Wilson placed this south of Ghat, but it seems more likely that these toponyms belong in the Wadi Iherir, giving further weight to a pre-Islamic presence around this oasis.[61] The proximity encourages comparison to the Wadi Tanzzuft and Wadi al-Ajal in Fazzan, but given the fluvial action of the wadi (around three days of floods a year were recorded in the mid-twentieth century),[62] oasis settlement such as is found at Fewet or Saniat Jibril is likely to have been buried or swept away.[63] However, given the limited number of burials this is perhaps unlikely to have amounted to more than a hamlet or two. The urban expansion of the oasis appears directly linked to economic and political developments in the Early Modern period. Lhote also mentioned a ruined enceinte with towers at the head of Wadi Aitou on the track from Iherir to Dider, though we have not been able to relocate this.[64]

[57] Duveyrier 1864, who provides the first written account of the oasis.

[58] One of these is likely the cemetery excavated by Lhote.

[59] Perret 1935; 1936; cf. also Lhote 1984, 117.

[60] The plan is not dissimilar to the buildings on the south-east flank of Zinkekra (ZIN003 – Mattingly 2010, 65–74), although the construction technique of mud-mortared stone is far more reminiscent of Medieval and Early Modern settlements in the Wadi al-Ajal.

[61] Salama 1981; Wilson 2012. [62] Gast and Hachid 1995.

[63] See Mattingly *et al.*, Chapter 2, this volume. [64] Lhote 1984.

Ahaggar Mountains

The Ahaggar mountains comprise one of the areas of the Sahara with the highest archaeological potential, but it has been long neglected.[65] The most famous discovery in this area is the tomb of Tin Hinan at Abalessa on the south-west fringe of the range.[66] The impression of a Roman coin, glassware, a lamp and some of the jewellery found with this burial indicates a society that was in contact with the Roman world. Tin Hinan is regularly described as relating to a pastoral group, but the burial site in fact lies adjacent to a major valley with evidence of past cultivation. Furthermore, baskets of dates and cereal grains were found with the burial.[67] The burial was actually placed within a room of a fortified building (*qasr*), which was later converted into a funerary structure. It is thus equally possible that the burial related to a leading member of an oasis/sedentary community in the Ahaggar. Even if the burial of Tin Hinan was a late antique insertion into a former dwelling by a pastoral group, the existence of the *qasr* surely implies an earlier sedentary component of the local population. Lhote mentions two other fortified sites (*qsur*) at Tit and Silet, though he suggested they might be of 'recent' origin.[68] There are numerous cairns throughout the mountains, many of substantial size, but these do not form clustered cemeteries. The pre-Islamic tombs of the Ahaggar include monuments that are very similar to those of Fazzan, with some drum cairns accompanied by proto-stelae.[69]

A multi-area site on a plateau has been excavated at Tahabort to the north-east of Tamanrasset with three dates ranging from the seventh to thirteenth centuries AD, one earlier, and one later.[70] Like the Tassili, the region is rich in rock art and has a strong prehistoric tradition. There is a notable concentration of horse period rock art here, including numerous chariot representations.[71] The region also has a distinctive form of foggara irrigation with channels running along wadis rather than into them.[72] Little is known of the history of this region before the nineteenth century.

On the route south-west from the Ahaggar to the Adrar des Ilforas and the Niger bend at Gao is the well of Timmissao, another suggestive site, where Roman coins have been reported in the past as well as a chariot rock

[65] Lhote 1984, 67–119 for a summary of the archaeology; Yacono 1968, for a detailed geographical study, which makes some reference to irrigation of the wadis within the massif (148).

[66] Camps 1997; Prorok 2001; Reygasse 1950, 88–106. [67] Reygasse 1950, 98.

[68] Lhote 1984, 117.

[69] Lhote 1984, 111 for a photo of a tomb that looks very similar to those of Garamantian Fazzan.

[70] Close 1984, 13; Maître 1976. [71] Gauthier and Gauthier 2011.

[72] Capot-Rey 1953, 327–29.

art scene, a possible Latin or Latino-Punic inscription and an Islamic inscription purportedly from the eighth century.[73] This again looks like a route that was developed from an early date, though there is no modern oasis development in the vicinity or evidence of permanent settlement in the past.[74]

The Tuareg Southern Sahara: Aïr and Adrar des Ilforas

There is substantial evidence of human activity in the southern part of the Tuareg range-lands. Multiple sites have been surveyed and funerary structures can be traced at least as far south as Tahoua (14°53' N) making them the most southerly group of cairns in the Sahara.

Aïr

The northern part of Aïr has lower rainfall than the south and has a very low population density, similar to the other Saharan mountain ranges. Burial cairns are widespread on and around the massif and are generally thought to date between the Late Neolithic and the first millennium AD.[75] Excavations at a number of sites have demonstrated the long chronology of this form of site and samples from burials at In Teduq, Mentes, Takene Bawat, Inufan, Tuluk, Iwelen, Mammanet and Agadez have been dated to the period 1000 BC–AD 1000.[76] In general though, the excavators have argued that these are the graves of nomads or semi-nomads.[77]

The site of Iwelen in the north-eastern part of the Aïr region is the most thoroughly investigated location and is notable for the recording of a settlement and major rock art scenes alongside several cemetery zones, from which more than 50 tombs have been excavated.[78] Many of the tombs have been radiocarbon dated and the funerary activity evidently spanned a long period from the second millennium BC to the late first millennium AD. On the other hand, the main use of the settlement

[73] Capot-Rey 1953, 187; Mauny 1956, 252; Salama 1981, 514–15. Pichler 1997 for a possible Latino-Punic inscription with Libyan undertones.

[74] There are also a very large collection of crescent cairns on the eastern side of the massif of presumably Neolithic date.

[75] Beltrami 1987. [76] Haour 2003; Paris 1996; Paris *et al.* 1986.

[77] Though note Dupuy 2010, argues that this was 'un pastoralisme peu mobile' on account of the emphasis on horses in the rock art, which are not suited to wide-ranging nomadism in the Sahara.

[78] Paris 1990; Roset 1988; 2007.

apparently fell in the mid-first millennium BC.[79] The settlement and rock art lies in a bend in the Wadi Iwelen, which is known for seasonal floods, with the cemeteries mainly on the rocky plateau above the Wadi. The settlement comprises an area with traces of stone footings, many saddle querns and abundant pottery. Although some lithics were found here, the site is also notable for the occurrence of copper alloy items, including spearheads. The rock art includes images of biconical human figures, associated with chariots and horses, wearing elaborate headdresses and carrying spears. The finds from the burials included leather shrouds, patterned textiles, copper alloy and bone bracelets, handmade pottery, saddle querns and grinding stones. Although Iwelen is located in a very forbidding environment today, with no sedentary settlement in the vicinity, the seasonal floods in the wadi could have supported some cultivation, especially if rainfall was marginally higher or more predictable in the past.

In the south of the massif, there are a number of investigated settlements of Medieval or more recent date. Agadez has been the primary urban centre in the Aïr region since the fifteenth century and part of a sequence of capitals (in order Assodé, Tadeliza, Tin Chamane, Agadez) culminating in the Tuareg Sultanate of Agadez. From Agadez, there are routes that run north towards Tamanrasset and the Ahaggar (*c.*650 km), east (with a difficult crossing of the Ténéré sand sea) to Bilma and the Kawar oases (*c.*750 km) and south-west towards Niamey and the Niger (600 km). Its foundation is normally placed in the eleventh or fifteenth century with the most reliable early description that of Leo Africanus who implied that it consisted of 'Barbary' (that is, Berber) houses. Little remains of the Medieval town apart from the mosque, the earliest phase of which is dated to the fifteenth century.[80] The most northerly of the capitals of Aïr is Assodé, the ruins of which encompass an area of 60 ha (although the large compound houses imply a much lower population density than towns in the northern Sahara). It is positioned high in a basin on the wetter, west side of the massif with a few satellite settlements of similar construction type nearby. Excavations in six locations have recovered material that dates no earlier than the late thirteenth/fourteenth century AD, although as elsewhere in the massif, cairns of 'Protohistoric' type are widespread. A little to the south, closer to the still inhabited Timia region, there are some small hilltop enclosures with possible huts within them and to the north-east there are many villages of stone-built structures

[79] Paris 1990, 67–71.

[80] Cressier and Bernus 1984. The site was recently added to the UNESCO World Heritage List which provides the most up-to-date survey of the old town.

of different types to those found at Assodé, some have nearby Islamic cemeteries. Together, these point to a more complex settlement history than has previously been put forward and raises the possibility of earlier agriculture in this region. On the southern edge of the Aïr massif are Anisamane and Tadeliza, 31 and 20 km north-west of Agadez respectively and as with Assodé, both are considered to be former capitals of the region. These have been examined by Lhote with Anisamane dated to the fifteenth century or later and the citadel of Tadeliza to the eleventh–fifteenth century.[81] A further Medieval settlement is known at Kori Ihine on the eastern edge of Aïr.[82] There are around 20 small rectangular houses (3–4 × 2.5 m) with thick stone walls and a high concentration of pottery and lithics (including a red-burnished pitcher with black painted designs). Satellite prospection in this area suggests a diffuse settlement with many sub-circular enclosures and many drum tombs in the surrounding hills.

Earlier settlements are somewhat harder to come by. The tail end of occupation at a number of Neolithic sites (for example, Arlit) has yielded a few first millennium BC radiocarbon dates, but these do not indicate anything more than seasonal occupations in the Aïr massif. Given the nature of habitation remains (or lack thereof) from Marandet it is difficult to draw hard conclusions about whether there was or was not permanent settlement in the first millennium BC/AD, but certainly there were suitable conditions.

The Azawagh Region

The Azawagh valley is a dry wadi system that runs from the Aïr mountains westwards towards the Niger river. Although a running river has not existed since the Neolithic, the lowlands have some vegetation – indicating sporadic run-off. To the west of Agadez is Azelik the assumed location of the mines and town of Takadda.[83] Here archaeological remains stretch over several kilometres including settlement agglomerations, copper mining and cemeteries. The most important part of the site is Azelik wan Birni where there is an urban-scale site of some tens of hectares surrounded by Islamic burials.[84] Excavations and radiocarbon dates suggest that the main period of occupation was the fourteenth to sixteenth

[81] Calvocoressi and David 1979, 20; Lhote 1973; Posnansky and McIntosh 1976, 183.

[82] Roset 1977. Dak-146, 685±100 BP, calAD 1058–1439.

[83] Bernus and Gouletquer 1976; Lhote 1972; see also Nixon, Chapter 17, this volume.

[84] See Bernus and Gouletquer 1976, 27–31; regrettably much of the site has been disturbed or damaged since its initial exploration.

centuries, but tumuli just to the south imply some earlier occupation of the area. A few kilometres to the west are the salt mines and adjoining settlement of Tegidda-n-tesemt, on the basis of ceramics this appears to be a successor to rather than contemporary with Azelik. Between Agadez and Azelik six Medieval settlements have been identified, with three phases of settlement that show variation in trade routes, copper mining and demography.[85] From Azelik to the area of Agadez there are a number of sites with evidence of copper metallurgy and whose dating is the subject of some argument. As this review is concerned with evidence for settlement, we shall not revisit this debate except to note that despite the many sites, there is little direct evidence of Protohistoric habitation or structures. They do however imply the presence of metalworking communities in the general region from at least the late first millennium BC and into the mid-second millennium AD.

Further west again, a sondage in the so-called 'western structure' in the small settlement of In Teduq produced two early dates of material (ninth to third century BC and seventh to tenth century AD) although it is difficult from the excavation to distinguish whether this related to an earlier settlement or the continual use of the place as a convenient stopping point.[86] The rocky outcrops to the south and west of the site have a dense covering of cairns of various types.

Marandet

In recent years there has been some important work at the site of Marandet, which lies at a convenient break in the topography to the south of Agadez. An area of *c.*60 ha is covered with scatters containing *c.*50,000 clay crucibles used for copper working.[87] Geophysical survey and excavation have shown that at least some of the crucibles are from pits whose primary use appears to have been for dumping domestic waste.[88] These pits have been radiocarbon dated between the sixth–ninth century AD and along with evidence for copper working they contained finds of imported pottery from North Africa, carnelian and amazonite beads, glass objects and date stones. These finds reopen the debate about pre-Islamic Saharan trade and by extension of settlements and oases in this region as well.[89] By the ninth century the site was appearing in Arabic sources as a key node between Gao and

[85] Bernus and Cressier 1991; 1999, 370; Haour 2003.

[86] Bernus and Cressier 1999, 288–90. 2450±150 and 1210±60.

[87] Grébénart 1985; Lhote 1972; Magnavita 2013; Mauny 1961. [88] Magnavita 2013.

[89] Magnavita 2013; 2017.

Zuwila. However, in the twelfth century al-Idrisi described it as populous, but with little merchandise or industry.[90] It is also helpful to note that similar pits in the modern village were dug for house construction and this may be the only archaeological remains of the structures of the settlement. These features are not visible from the surface and show the limits of what can be viewed from satellite imagery.

Adrar des Ilforas

The rock art of the Adrar des Ilforas range shares many similarities with the material from Aïr, including the presence of horses, chariots and metal weapons.[91] However, less is known of the contemporary cemeteries and there is a lack of certain settlement evidence. Recent research at the early Islamic town of Tadmakka has not recorded any evidence of pre-Islamic activity there.[92] There are no major oases in the Adrar des Ilforas, but the wadis flowing out of the massif do receive sporadic floodwaters after rains. As with all the massifs, cairns are widespread and do concentrate around those wadis with more vegetation, particularly on the western side of the massif. There are also occasional abandoned stone buildings of unknown date, but not too dissimilar to Tadmakka in form. The exception to this sparse evidence is the region immediately around Kidal. The hills here have many stone structures on them whose date and function is unknown.

Taghaza and Tawdenni

The salt mining centres of Taghaza and Tawdenni lie in the Western Sahara *c.*700 km north of Timbuktu and played a significant role in the Medieval trading networks of that region.[93] The former is dated from the thirteenth–sixteenth centuries, after which point it was replaced by the latter site, where mining still continues. At Taghaza there are two settlements on either side of the sabkha, possibly these are of different date, but both have remains of mosques.[94] At Tawdenni, to the north of the prison are the ruins of Ksar de Smida which covers around 2 ha and has large cemeteries to the south-east. As at Bilma, it would be interesting to investigate the possibility that salt extraction began earlier.

[90] Levtzion and Hopkins 2000, 46, 125. [91] Dupuy 2010.
[92] Nixon 2009; 2013; 2017; Chapter 17, this volume. [93] Lydon 2009, 89–90; McDougall 2006.
[94] Mauny 1961; Monod 1938.

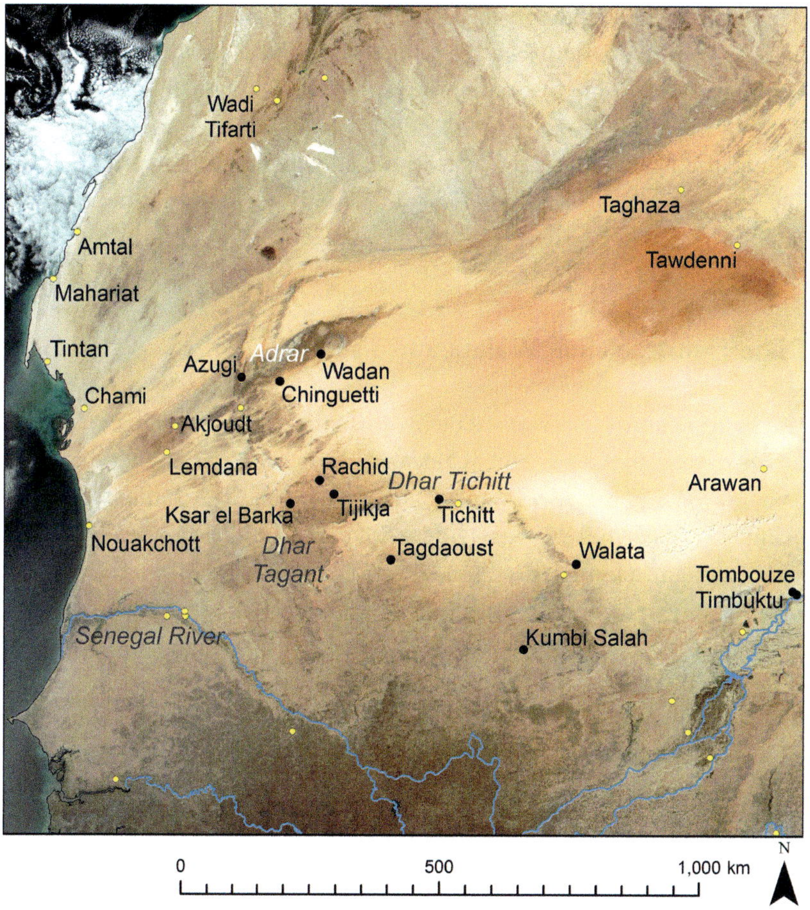

Figure 7.5. Mauritania sites discussed in the text.

A little further south on the route to the Niger is Arawan, there is little information about this site and today it consists of a handful of houses in between the sand dunes with a dozen or so palms. There are traces of some structures to the south, but it is unclear what the antiquity of this place is.

Middle Niger 'Oases'

The Niger Bend

This area is covered later in this volume by the chapters of McIntosh, MacDonald and Nixon. Occupation from the early Medieval period has been convincingly demonstrated by modern excavation at Timbuktu and

Gao.[95] However, it remains an open question whether there may be sites close to these important centres with earlier antecedents. In the case of Timbuktu, a plausible case can be advanced for Tombouze 1.[96] There was certainly no shortage of advanced pre-Islamic urban-scale settlements around the Niger Bend area as a whole and there are increasingly signs that some at least of these were in contact with the Mediterranean world, albeit probably indirectly.[97]

Dhar Tichitt, Nema, Walata and Tagant

The Tichitt culture is described by MacDonald elsewhere in this volume.[98] There are numerous settlements located along the escarpments that have seen several campaigns of survey and excavation. The settlements date mainly to *c.* 1600–400 BC with evidence of precocious cultivation of cereals, metallurgy and a four-tier settlement hierarchy. There are also many tombs and rock art of a Saharan tradition. The settlements are easily detectable from satellite imagery and a thorough survey of remains would likely identify hundreds of archaeological sites. Of particular interest is the area of the Tagant to the west where there is very varied morphology including both circular and rectilinear buildings that suggest multiple chronological phases (as in southern Morocco). Ould Khattar has identified a late phase of the Tichitt culture in this region and the presence of water (and crocodiles) in its wadis makes continuous occupation more likely, but not certain.[99] A tomb with a funerary chapel identified by Monod at Foum el Hadjar is potentially of first millennium AD date.[100]

Trading Centres in the South-West Sahara

In the South-western Sahara there are a number of major trading centres of Medieval date, contemporary with the towns of Sijilmasa, Zagora and Tamdult in Morocco (Fig. 7.5). The best known are Tagdaoust/Awdaghast and Kumbi Saleh both of which have had several campaigns

[95] Cissé 2010; 2017; Insoll 1996; 2000; Nixon 2009; 2013.
[96] MacDonald 2011; Chapter 13, this volume; Park 2010.
[97] McIntosh, Chapter 14, this volume.
[98] MacDonald, Chapter 13, this volume.
[99] Ould Khattar 1995.
[100] Chapelle and Monod 1937, 518 (one of a number of examples of 'tombes à chapelle' in Mauretania).

of excavations that date the early phases broadly to calAD 660–1020 and calAD 430–1020, respectively.[101] Azugi, Wadan, Chinguetti, Rachid, Tijkja, Kasr el Barka, Tichitt and Walata are other Mauritanian oases with substantial settlements of Islamic date in the Western Sahara that might all repay investigation for earlier antecedents – again if not at the known Islamic centres, then in the vicinity.[102]

Azugi

Although mentioned by both al-Bakri and al-Idrisi as a strategic stop on routes to the south, little is known of this site and it is not mentioned after the twelfth century.[103] It apparently existed as a town before falling under the control of the Almoravids in the eleventh century. It is located in the centre of the Adrar area of Mauritania, close to modern Atar. When the site was investigated in the 1950s there were remains of a fortress (100 × 70–80 m with 20 bastions) located to the south of the palmerie. Around 1 ha of ruined buildings were located 100 m to the north-west.[104] Excavations outside the fortress in the 1980s identified two phases of rectangular stone buildings with the earliest (at a depth of 5 m) producing dates of calAD 779–1217 and calAD 1020–1271 (similar dates also come from deposits under the walls of the fortress).[105] Three radiocarbon dates from the fortress walls themselves indicate that this was much later, probably constructed in the fifteenth–seventeenth centuries.[106] Around 7 km to the north-west of the main oasis there are the remains of a *c.*2 ha hilltop settlement of enclosures and small round huts of unknown date. A loose scatter of cairns and walls are also found on the escarpments to the east and west of the oasis.

Chinguetti

Moving to the east, Chinguetti is a much better preserved town with a famous dry-stone mosque and major Medieval manuscript libraries reflecting its history as a gathering place for pilgrims.[107] Little archaeological

[101] On Tagdaoust see Devisse 1983; Polet 1985; Robert *et al.* 1970; Robert-Chaleix 1989; Vanacker 1979. On Kumbi Saleh see Berthier 1997; Capel *et al.* 2015. For a full discussion of both see Nixon, Chapter 17, this volume.

[102] See Robert 1982 for a study of mosques from several of these sites.

[103] Levtzion and Hopkins 2000, 73, 127–28.

[104] Mauny 1955.

[105] Saison 1981; Gif-5337, Gif-5340, Gif-5336, Gif-5338 – 880 ± 80, Gif-5339 – 1010 ± 80.

[106] Gif-5331, Gif-5332, Gif-5333. Also Gif-5334 – 200 ± 80 BP.

[107] Mauny 1955; Ould Mohamed Yahya and Rebstock 1997; Stewart *et al.* 1990.

investigation has taken place at the site, but the town dates back to the twelfth to fifteenth centuries.

Wadan

The most easterly town in Adrar is Wadan. Like Chinguetti this is probably of Medieval origin, although the earliest references to the toponym are in Portuguese accounts from the fifteenth century.[108] A mosque of presumed Medieval date, part of an enceinte and many other buildings are preserved on the west side of the town.

There is potential for early settlement along the valleys of Adrar and indeed some cairn cemeteries to the north of Atar and along the south-eastern edge may be indicative of such activity north of Atar, but to date no habitation sites have been reported.

Ksar el Barka

Between Adrar and the Dhars, Ksar el Barka is a town of *c.*10 ha reputedly founded in 1690. The ruins today are partly obscured by windblown sand but were visited by Monod.

Walata

Walata is situated in the Dhars of southern Mauritania at a nodal point on the edge of the Sahara. The earliest settlement is of the Tichitt tradition (see above, p. 317) from *c.*1000–200 BC of similar type to that described by MacDonald.[109] From the thirteenth century AD a town started to develop with links to trade from the salt mines of northern Mali and the site's name was changed from Biru (Mande) to Iwalaten (Berber).[110] It appeared rather late in Arabic sources in the fourteenth century where it was described as the next stopping point south after Tabalbala (see above, p. 278) and was visited by Ibn Battuta.[111]

Other towns in the Dhars

Within the area of the Dhars are a number of towns that have seen little archaeological attention: Rachid, Tijika and Tichitt (at the foot of the

[108] Mauny 1955.
[109] Munson 1980; see MacDonald, Chapter 13, this volume for discussion of Tichitt.
[110] Cleaveland 2002. [111] Levtzion and Hopkins 2000, 276, 282–86.

escarpment of the eponymous Dhar). They all have stone-built rectilinear architecture in varying states of preservation and are most likely Medieval or later in date.[112]

Akjoujt

The area of Akjoujt is an area of relief *c.*200 km to the east of the Atlantic coast and at a latitude that has at points been at the border of the Sahel. There is minimal water today, although there is an aquifer at the town of Akjoujt. The region is well known for its mineral resources and there is evidence of copper mining and processing sites, the best-known of which is the Grotte aux Chauvres-souris which dates to the mid-first millennium BC.[113] Further evidence of copper working comes from the sites of Lemdana and Touizigt where metalworking slags have been found along with weapons, tools and objects of personal adornment. Although there is a large cemetery of drum-tombs in Akjoujt at Lembetet el Kbir, no contemporary settlements have been identified. There is also very little evidence of activity in this region between the late first millennium BC until the Medieval period when activity restarted in the Grotte aux Chauvres-souris. It has been suggested that this mining activity reflects the periods which were wetter and in which the edge of the Sahel lay further to the north.[114] Finally, there are a number of Roman finds from southern Mauritania, including coins from Resseremt (near Akjoujt) and Tamkartkart (near Tichitt) and a bronze fibula from Akjoujt.[115]

The Atlantic Coast

Between the Draa (in Morocco) and Adrar there are no major oases and few wells. However, there are some distinctive sites that suggest a degree of sedentarisation occurred here. Along the coast a number of sites have been identified that have their origins in the Neolithic, but continued to be used into the first millennium BC.[116] These have little or no significant architectural remains, but artefact scatters stretch over more than 1 ha in area. Shellfish, fish and marine mammals were of primary importance to the diet of these communities, particularly given the aridity of the region

[112] Monod 1948. [113] Lambert 1986; Vernet 1993.
[114] See McIntosh Chapter 14, this volume. [115] Mauny 1956; 1978; Salama 1981, 514–15.
[116] Close 1984.

(although shell middens do not occur until south of Nouackchott). Further south in Mauritania the sites are found along the edges of coastal lagoons. Cemeteries were part of, or close by many of these sites, and follow Saharan styles of burial including both earlier (for example, antenna tomb) and later (chapel and drum tomb) types.[117] Important sites include Tarfaya in Morocco; Amtal, Wadi Tifarti and Mahariat in Western Sahara; and Chami, Tintan and a cluster of sites around Nouakchott in Mauritania. Vernet has studied the Mauritanian coast in more detail and identified a later phase of shellfish harvesters: the Tin Mahham culture 400 BC–AD 300.[118]

Conclusions

The southern Sahara is a region of few major oases, though some of the salt-producing centres have been historically very important on account of that vital resource of Saharan trade. The relative paucity of water sources, apart from sporadic and unpredictable rainfall watering pasture lands in the wadis flowing out of the massifs, has favoured adventitious exploitation of these desert landscapes by pastoral groups. In recent times, the southern Sahara has been dominated by two major groups, the Teda in the Libyan Sahara and the Tuareg between Fazzan and the Niger. The archaeological evidence reviewed above suggests that this broad division is of long relevance. The burial of Tin Hinan was celebrated by the Ahaggar Tuareg as their founding princess long before Prorok dug her up in the 1920s. The proto-Teda and proto-Tuareg of the Garamantian era of the areas surveyed above were thus most likely predominantly pastoralists and occasionally bellicose. But the evidence of potential sedentary farming elements should be recognised and future research needs to investigate this possibility in the environmental niches where cultivation is possible.

A final point to make about the Tuareg (Berber) and Teda peoples of the southern Sahara is that they were clearly operating in the early Medieval period from centres within the desert north of the Sahelian communities of the Chad Basin and the Niger. The Kawar oases played a key role not only in supplying Chad with salt, but also were a gathering point for slaves to be traded north. It is possible that some of the centres that were established north of the Niger bend (Tadmakka is a case in point) served a similar

[117] Vernet 1993. There are a large number of radiocarbon dates from these cemeteries that similarly confirm their long chronology from the fourth–first millennium BC.

[118] Vernet and Tous 2004.

purpose in relation to developing trade there. Such sites were located far enough into the desert to be difficult to reach from the Sahelian lands, but close enough to facilitate exchanges and predation by slave-trading societies.

References

Aroca, A. 1942. *Ual el Chebir: L'oasi della redenzione*. Milano: Edizioni Alpe.

Bailloud, G. 1969. L'évolution des styles céramiques en Ennedi (République du Tchad). In *Mémoires I, Actes du Premier Colloque International d'Archéologie Africaine*. Fort Lamy: Institut National Tchadien pour les Sciences Humaines, 31–45.

Bailloud, G., 1997. *Art rupestre en Ennedi*. Saint-Maur: Éditions Sépia.

Beltrami, V. 1987. *Repertorio preistorico-archeologico del territorio dell'Aïr ed aree limitrofe*. Rome: Istituto Italo-Africano.

Beltrami, V. 2007. *Il Sahara Centro-Orientale Dalla Preistoria Ai Tempi Dei Nomadi Tubu: The Central-Oriental Sahara from Prehistory to the Times of the Nomadic Tubus*. Oxford: Archaeopress.

Bernus, E. and Cressier, P. 1991. *La région d'In Gall-Tegidda n Tesemt (Niger)-programme archéologique d'urgence, 1977–1981. Azelik-Takadda et l'implantation sédentaire médiévale*. Niamey: Institut de Recherches en Sciences Humaines.

Bernus, E. and Cressier, P. 1999. *In Teduq du moyen-âge à l'époque actuelle. (Vallée de l'Azawagh (Sahara du Niger)* vol 2). St Maur: Editions Sepia.

Bernus, S. and Gouletquer, P., 1976. Du cuivre au sel. Recherches ethno-archéologiques sur la région d'Azelik (campagnes 1973–1975). *Journal des africanistes* 46.1: 7–68.

Berthier, S., 1997. *Recherches archéologiques sur la capitale de l'empire de Ghana: Étude d'un secteur d'habitat à Koumbi Saleh, Mauritanie. Campagnes II-III-IV-V (1975–1976)-(1980–1981)* (Cambridge Monographs in African Archaeology 41/ BAR International Series 680). Oxford: Archaeopress.

Blench, R. 2019. The linguistic prehistory of the Sahara. In Gatto *et al.* 2019, 431–63.

Bruce-Lockhart, J. and Wright, J. 2000. *Difficult and Dangerous Roads. Hugh Clapperton's Travels in Sahara and Fezzan 1822–1825*. London: Sickle Moon Books.

Calvocoressi, D. and David, N. 1979. A new survey of radiocarbon and thermo-luminescence dates for West Africa. *Journal of African History* 20.1: 1–29.

Camps, G. 1997. Tin Hinan et sa légende. A propos du tumulus princier d'Abalessa (Ahaggar, Algérie). *Bulletin archéologique du comité des travaux historiques et scientifiques* ns 24: 173–95.

Capel, C., Zazzo, A., Saliège, J-F. and Polet, J. 2015. The end of a hundred-year-old archaeological riddle: First dating of the columns tomb of Kumbi Saleh (Mauritania). *Radiocarbon* 57.1: 65–75.

Capot-Rey, R. 1953. *Le Sahara Français* (L'Afrique Blanche Francaise II). Paris: Presses universitaires.

Capot-Rey, R. 1957. Introduction à une géographie humaine du Borkou. *Travaux de l'Institut de Recherches Sahariennes* 16: 41–72.

Capot-Rey, R. 1958. Decouvertes archeologiques au Borkou. *Travaux de l'Institut de Recherches Sahariennes* 17: 203–5.

Capot-Rey, R. 1959. Le sel et le commerce du sel au Borkou-Ennedi-Tibesti. *Travaux de l'Institut de Recherches Sahariennes* 18: 187–93.

Capot-Rey, R. 1961. *Borkou et Ounianya. Etude de géographie régionale*. Alger: IRS.

Chapelle, J. 1957. *Black Nomads of the Sahara* (translated by F. Schütze). Paris: Librairie Plon.

Chapelle, J. and Monod, T. 1937. Notes sur la grande sepulture d'El Mreïti. *Bulletin du Comité des études historiques de l'A.O.F.* 20: 507–21.

Cissé, M. 2010. *Archaeological Investigations of Early Trade and Urbanism at Gao Saney (Mali)*. Unpublished PhD thesis, Rice University.

Cissé, M. 2017. The Trans-Saharan trade connection with Gao during the first millennium AD. In D.J. Mattingly, V. Leitch, C.N. Duckworth, A. Cuénod, M. Sterry and F. Cole (eds), *Trade in the Ancient Sahara and Beyond*. Cambridge: Cambridge University Press, 101–130.

Cleaveland, T. 2002. *Becoming Walata: A History of Saharan Social Formation and Transformation*. Portsmouth, N.H.: Heinemann.

Cline, W. 1950. *The Teda of Tibesti, Borkou and Kawar*. Mwenasha: General Series in Anthropology.

Close, A.E. 1980. Current research and recent radiocarbon dates from northern Africa. *Journal of African History* 21.2: 145–67.

Close, A.E., 1984. Current research and recent radiocarbon dates from northern Africa, II. *Journal of African History* 25.1: 1–24.

Cressier, P. and Bernus, S. 1984. La grande mosquée d'Agadez. *Journal des africanistes* 54.1: 5–40.

Dalloni, M. and Monod, T. 1948. *Mission scientifique du Fezzan (1944–1945). VI Géologie et préhistoire (Fezzan méridionale, Kaouar et Tibesti)*. Alger: Impr. Imbert.

Denham, D., Clapperton, H. and Oudney, W. 1985. *Narratives of Travels and Discoveries in North and Central Africa in the years 1822, 1823, and 1824*. London: Darf Publishers (reprint).

Desio, A. 1935. *Missione scientifica della Reale Accademia d'Italia a Cufra (1931–32)*. Vols I–III. Rome: Reale Accademia d'Italia.

Desio, A. 1942. *Sahara Italiano. Il Tibesti nord-orientale*. Rome: università la Sapienza.

Desio, A. 1950. *Le vie della sete*. Milan: Hoepli.

Despois, J. and Raynal, R. 1967. *Géographie de l'Afrique du Nord-Ouest*. Paris: Payot.

Devisse, J. (ed.). 1983. *Tegdaoust III: Recherches sur Aoudaghost. Campagnes 1960/65, enquête generals.* Paris: Editions Recherches sur les Civilisation.

Dupuy, C. 2010. Les apports archéologiques des gravures rupestres de l'Aïr (Niger) et de l'Adrar des Iforas (Mali). *Les Nouvelles d'archéologie* 120–121: 29–37.

Duveyrier, H. 1864. *Les Touareg du nord. Exploration du Sahara.* Paris: Challamel.

Ehret, C. 2019. Berber peoples in the Sahara and North Africa. Liguistic historical proposals. In Gatto *et al.* 2019, 464–94.

Gabriel, B. 1977. Zum ökologischen Wandel im Neolithikum der östlichen Zentralsahara. *Berliner Geographische. Abhandlungen* 27: 1–94.

Gabriel, B. 1981. Die oestliche Sahara in Holozaen: Klima, Landschaft und Kulturen. In C. Roubet, H.L. Hugot and G. Souville (eds), *Mélanges offerts au Doyen Lionel Balout.* Paris: A.D.P.F., 195–211.

Gast, M. and Hachid, M. 1995. Djanet. *Encyclopédie berbère fasc* 16: 2379–90.

Gatto, M.C. 2006. The local pottery. In M. Liverani (ed.), *Aghram Nadarif. A Garamantian Citadel in the Wadi Tannezzuft.* Firenze: All'Insegna del Giglio, 201–40.

Gatto, M., Mattingly, D.J., Ray, N. and Sterry, M. (eds). 2019. *Burials, Migration and Identity in the Ancient Sahara and Beyond.* Trans-Saharan Archaeology Volume II. Series editor D.J. Mattingly. Cambridge: Cambridge University Press and The Society for Libyan Studies.

Gautier, E.-F. 1970. *Sahara. The Great Desert* (translated by D.F. Mayhew). London: Octagon.

Gauthier, Y. and Gauthier, C. 2011. Des chars et des Tifinagh: étude aréale et corrélations. *Cahiers de l'association des amis de l'art rupestre saharien* 15: 91–118.

Grébénart, D. 1985. *Le néolithique final et les débuts de la métallurgie.* Niamey: Inst. de recherches en sciences humaines.

Grébénart, D. 1988. *Les origines de la métallurgie en Afrique occidentale.* Paris: Errance.

Hachid, M. 1998. *Le Tassili des Ajjer. Aux sources de l'Afrique.* Paris: Ed Paris-Méditerranée.

Hachid, M. 2000. *Les premiers berbères. Entre Méditerannée, Tassili et Nil.* Aix-en-Provence: Edisud.

Haour, A.C. 2003. One hundred years of archaeology in Niger. *Journal of World Prehistory* 17.2: 181–234.

Haour, A.C. 2017. What made Islamic trade distinctive as compared to pre-Islamic trade? In Mattingly *et al.* 2017, 80–100.

Huard, P. 1953. Gravures rupestres de la lisiere nord-occidentale de Tibesti. *Travaux de l'Institut de Recherches Sahariennes* 10: 75–106.

Huard, P. and Féval, J.-C. 1964. Figurations rupestres des confins Algero-Niger-Tchadiens. *Travaux de l'Institut de Recherches Sahariennes* 23: 61–94.

Insoll, T. 1996. *Islam, Archaeology and History. Gao Region (Mali) Ca.AD 900–1250*. Cambridge Monographs in African Archaeology 39. BAR S647. Oxford: Tempus Reparatum.

Insoll, T. 2000. The origins of Timbuktu. *Antiquity* 74: 495–96.

Jäkel, D. and Geyh, M.A. 1982. 14C-Daten aus dem Gebiet der Sahara. *Berliner Geographische Abhandlungen* 32: 143–65.

Keding, B., Lenssen-Erz, T. and Pastoors, A. 2007. Pictures and pots from pastoralists. Investigations into the prehistory of the Ennedi highlands in NE Chad. *Sahara* 18; 23–46.

Lambert. N. 1986. Akjoujt (Axamuk). In *Encyclopédie berbère* 3, Ahaggar – Ali ben Ghaniya, 417–19.

Lange, D. and Berthoud, S. 1977. Al-Qasaba et d'autres villes de la route centrale du Sahara. *Paideuma* 23: 19–40.

Lebeuf, J.P. 1962. *Archéologie tchadienne: Les Sao de Cameroun et du Tchad*. Paris: Hermann.

Lebeuf, J.P. 1963. Prehistory, proto-history and history in Chad. *Journal of the Historical Society of Nigeria* 2.4: 593–601.

Levtzion, N. and Hopkins, J.F.P. (eds). 2000. *Corpus of Early Arabic Sources for West African History*. Princeton: Markus Wiener.

Lhote, H. 1971. Ronde-Bosse néolithique du Tassili représentant un Bovidé. *Objets et Mondes* 11.2: 227–35.

Lhote, H. 1972. Recherches sur Takedda, ville décrite par Ibn Battouta et située en Aïr. *Bulletin de l'Institut Français d'Afrique Noire* 34: 429–47.

Lhote, H. 1973. Découverte des ruines de Tadeliza: ancienne résidence des sultans de l'Aïr. *Notes africaines* 137: 9–16.

Lhote, H. 1984. *Le Hoggar. Espace et temps*. Paris: Armand Colin.

Lovejoy, P. 1986. *Salt of the Desert Sun. History of Salt Production and Trade in the Central Sudan*. Cambridge: Cambridge University Press.

Lydon, G. 2009. *On Trans-Saharan Trails: Islamic Law, Trade Networks and Cross-cultural Exchange in Nineteenth-century Western Africa*. Cambridge: Cambridge University Press.

MacDonald, K.C. 2011. A view from the south: Sub-Saharan evidence for contacts between North Africa, Mauritania and the Niger, 1000 BC – AD 700. In A. Dowler and E.R. Galvin (eds), *Money, Trade and Trade Routes in Pre-Islamic North Africa*. London: British Museum Press, 72–82.

MacEachern, S. 2019. Burial practices, settlement and regional connections around the southern Lake Chad basin 1500 BC–AD 1500. In Gatto *et al.* 2019, 399–428.

Magnavita, S. 2013. Initial encounters: Seeking traces of ancient trade connections between West Africa and the wider world. *Afriques: débats, méthodes et terrains d'histoire 04*. Available at: http://afriques.revues.org/1145 [last accessed 12 September 2019].

Magnavita, S. 2017. Track and trace. Archeometric approaches to the study of early Trans-Saharan trade. In Mattingly *et al.* 2017, 393–413.

Maître, J.-P. 1976. *Inventaire archéologique du sud-est nigérien*. Niamey: Institut de Recherches en Sciences Humaines.

Mattingly, D.J. (ed.). 2003. *The Archaeology of Fazzan. Volume 1, Synthesis*. London: Society for Libyan Studies, Department of Antiquities.

Mattingly, D.J. (ed.). 2010. *The Archaeology of Fazzan. Volume 3, Excavations Carried out by C. M. Daniels*. London: Society for Libyan Studies, Department of Antiquities.

Mattingly, D.J., Leitch, V., Duckworth, C.N., Cuénod, A., Sterry, M. and Cole, F. (eds). 2017. *Trade in the Ancient Sahara and Beyond*. Cambridge: Cambridge University Press.

Mauny, R. 1955. Notes d'histoire et d'archéologie sur Azougui, Chinguetti et Ouadane. *Bulletin de l'Institut Français d'Afrique Noire* (B) 17: 142–62.

Mauny, R. 1956. Monnaies antiques trouvées en Afrique au sud du limes romain. *Libyca* 4: 249–61.

Mauny, R. 1961. *Tableau géographique d'ouest africain au moyen âge*. Dakar: Mémoires de l'I.F.A.N.

Mauny, R. 1978. Trans-Saharan contacts and the Iron Age in West Africa. In J.D. Fage (ed.), *The Cambridge History of Africa, Volume 2*. Cambridge: Cambridge University Press, 272–341.

McDougall, E.A. 2006. Snapshots from the Sahara: Salt the essence of being. In D. Mattingly, S. McLaren, E. Savage, Y. al-Fasatwi and K. Gadgood (eds), *The Libyan Desert: Natural Resources and Cultural Heritage*. London: Society for Libyan Studies, 295–303.

Meerpohl, M. 2013. Footprints in the sand: Recent long distance camel trade in the Libyan Desert (north-east Chad/southeast Libya). In F. Förster and H. Reimer (eds), *Desert Road Archaeology in Ancient Egypt and Beyond*. Köln: H. Barth Inst., 167–91.

Monod, T. 1938. Teghaza, la ville en sel gemme (Sahara occidental). *La Nature* 3025: 289–96.

Monod, T. 1948. Sur quelques constructions anciennes du Sahara occidental. *Bulletin de la Société de Géographie et d'Archéologie d'Oran* 71: 1–30.

Munson, P.J. 1980. Archaeology and the prehistoric origins of the Ghana Empire. *Journal of African History* 21: 457–66.

Nachtigal, G. 1974. *Sahara and Sudan, vol I, Tripoli and Fezzan, Tibesti or Tu* (translated by A.G.B. and H.J. Fisher). London: C. Martin.

Nixon, S. 2009. Excavating Essouk-Tadmakka (Mali): New archaeological investigations of early Islamic trans-Saharan trade. *Azania: Archaeological Research in Africa* 44.2: 217–55.

Nixon, S. 2013. Tadmekka: Archéologie d'une ville caravanière des premiers temps du commerce transsaharien. *Afriques* 4. Available at: http://afriques.revues.org/1237 [last accessed 12 September 2019].

Nixon, S. (ed.). 2017. *Essouk-Tadmekka: An Early Islamic Trans-Saharan Market Town*. Leiden: Brill.

Ould Khattar, M. 1995. *La fin des temps préhistoriques dans le sud-est Mauritanien*. Unpublished PhD dissertation, Université de Paris-I, Pantheon-Sorbonne.

Ould Mohamed Yahya, A. and Rebstock, U. 1997. *Handlist of Manuscripts in Shinqit and Wadan*. London: Al-Furqan Islamic Heritage Foundation.

Park, D.P. 2010. Prehistoric Timbuktu and its hinterland. *Antiquity* 84: 1076–88.

Paris, F. 1990. Les sépultures monumentales d'Iwelen (Niger). *Journal des Africanistes* 60.1: 47–75.

Paris, F. 1996. *Les sépultures du Sahara nigérian, du Néoloithique à l'Islamisation*. Paris: ORSTOM.

Paris, F., Roset, J.-P. and Saliège, J.F. 1986. Une sépulture musulmane ancienne dans l'Aïr septentrional (Niger). *Comptes-Rendus de l'Académie des Sciences de Paris* 303 (Série III.12): 513–18.

Perret, R. 1935. Observations géographiques faites au cours d'un voyage au Tassili des Ajjers. *Bulletin de l'Association de géographes français* 12.89: 96–100.

Perret, R. 1936. Recherches archéologiques et ethnographiques au Tassili des Ajjers (Sahara central). Les gravures rupestres de l'Oued Djaret, la population et les ruines d'Iherir. *Journal de la Société des Africanistes* 6.1: 41–64.

Pichler, W. 1997. A Latin inscription at Ti-m Missaou (Algeria). *Sahara* 9: 150–51.

Polet, J. 1985. *Tegdaoust IV: Fouille d'un quartier de Tegdaoust*. Paris: Editions Recherche sur les Civilisations.

Posnansky, M. and McIntosh, R. 1976. New radiocarbon dates for northern and western Africa. *The Journal of African History* 17.2:161–95.

Prorok, B.K. de. 2001. *In Quest of Lost Worlds: Five Archaeological Expeditions 1925–1934*. Santa Barbara: Narrative Press (reprint of 1935 book).

Quéchon, G. and Roset, J.-P. 1974. Prospection archéologique du massif de Termit (Niger). *Cahiers ORSTOM, Série Sciences Humaines* 11.1: 85–104.

Retaillé, D. 1986. Le Kawar, problème géographique. *Cahiers géographiques de Rouen* 26: 37–60.

Reygasse, M. 1950. *Monuments funéraires préislamiques de l'Afrique du Nord*. Paris: Arts et Métiers Graphiques.

Richardson, J. 1853. *Narrative of a Mission to Central Africa*, 2 vols. London: Chapman and Hall.

Robert, D., Robert, S., Devisse, J. 1970. *Tegdaoust I: Recheches sur Aoudaghost*. Paris: Arts et Métiers Graphiques.

Robert, S. 1982. *Rapport sur les mosquées historiques des villes anciennes de Oualata, Tichitt et Chinguetti*. Nouakchott: IMRS.

Robert-Chaleix, D. 1989. *Tegdaoust V: Une concession médiévale à Tegdaoust: implantation, évolution d'une unité d'habitation*. Paris: Editions Recherche sur les Civilisations.

Rohlfs, G. 1874/1875. *Quer durch Afrika: Reise vom Mittelmeer nach dem Tschadsee und zum Golf von Guinea*, 2 vols. Leipzig: F.A. Brockhaus Verlag.

Rohlfs, G. 2003. *Voyages et explorations au Sahara. Tome V, Koufra – les oasis de Djofra et de Djalo 1878–1879* (translated by J. Debetz). Paris: Karthala.

Rønneseth, O. 1982a. Verlassene Siedlungen im Tibestigebirge. *Berliner Geographische Abhandlungen* 32: 27–62.

Rønneseth, O. 1982b. *Gräber im nordwestlichen Tibesti (Tschad)*. Munich: Zabern.

Roset, J.-P. 1977. Un site à céramique peinte dans l'Aïr oriental (Niger). *Cahiers Office de la Recherche Scientifique et Technique Outre-Mer, ser Sci Hum* 14: 337–46.

Roset, J.-P. 1988. Iwelen – an archaeological site of the chariot period in Northern Aïr, Niger. In *Libya Antiqua*. Paris: UNESCO, 13–46.

Roset, J.-P. 2007. La culture d'Iwelen et les débuts de la métallurgie du cuivre dans l'Aïr, au Niger. In J. Guilaine (ed.), *Le chalcolithique et la construction des inégalités. II, Proche et Moyen-Orient, Amérique, Afrique*. Paris: Errance, 107–36.

Saison, B. 1981. Azugi: Archéologie at historie en Adrar mauritanien. *Recherche, pédagogie et culture* 11.55: 66–74.

Salama, P. 1981. The Sahara in classical antiquity. In G. Mokhtar (ed.), *UNESCO General History of Africa, II Ancient Civilisations of Africa*. Paris: UNESCO, 513–32.

Scarin, E. 1937a. *Le oasi cirenaiche del 29° parallelo*. Firenze: Sansoni.

Scarin, E. 1937b. Descrizione delle oasi e gruppi di oasi. In *Il Sahara Italiano, I. Fezzan e oasi di Gat*. Rome: Società Italiana arto grafiche, 603–44.

Schiffers, H. 1957. Le Borkou et ses inhabitants. *Travaux de l'Institut de Recherches Sahariennes* 15: 65–88.

Stewart, C.C., Salim, S.A. and Yahya, A.O. 1990. Catalogue of Arabic manuscripts at the Institut Mauritanien de Recherche Scientifique. *Islam et sociétés au Sud du Sahara* 2.1: 179–84.

Thiry, J. 1995. *Le Sahara libyen dans l'Afrique du nord médiévale*. Leuven: Peeters.

Treinen-Claustre, F. 1982. *Sahara et Sahel à l'âge du fer. Borkou, Tchad*. Mémoires de la Société des Africanistes. Paris: Musée de l'Homme.

Vanacker, C. 1979. *Tegdaoust II. Recherches sur Aoudaghost. Fouille d'un Quartier Artisinal*. Nouakchott: Institut Mauritanien de la Recherche Scientifique.

Vernet, R. 1993. *Préhistoire de la Mauritanie*. Nouakchott: Centre Culturel Français A. de Saint Exupéry – Sépia.

Vernet, R. and Tous, P. 2004. Les amas coquilliers de Mauritanie occidentale et leur contexte paléoenvironnemental (VIIe–IIe millénaires BP). *Préhistoires méditerranéennes* 13: 55–69.

Vikør, K. 1999. *Oasis of Salt. History of Kawar: Saharan Centre of Salt Production*. Bergen: Centre for Middle Eastern and Islamic Studies.

Wilson, A.I. 2012. Saharan trade: Short-, medium- and long-distance trade networks in the Roman period. *Azania: Archaeological Research in Africa* 47.4: 409–49.

Wright, J. 1998. Murzuk and the Saharan slave trade in the 19th century. *Libyan Studies* 29: 89–96.

Yacono, D. 1968. L'Ahaggar. *Travaux de l'Institut de Recherches Sahariennes* 27, fasc. 1–2.

8 | Discussion

Sedentarisation and Urbanisation in the Sahara

MARTIN STERRY AND DAVID J. MATTINGLY

Introduction

This chapter is intended as an analytical counterpoint to the descriptive presentation of the evidence of pre-Islamic activity at Saharan oases and as an engagement with some of the more theoretical introduction to the volume.[1] Here we make the case for a dynamic Saharan history with frequent episodes of sedentarisation and urbanisation in the past. The related issue of state formation will be considered as the conclusion of the book, with a discussion of how we might define states and state formation in the Saharan milieu and the contribution that oasis centres have made to early desert states, like the Garamantes.[2] We do not seek to deny the importance of pastoral lifeways, or the social complexity of such mobile societies, but we argue that the pastoral and mobile dimension of the Trans-Saharan world has been over-emphasised to the neglect of its sedentary communities. Several factors play into the choices made by communities as to how to live: social and political circumstance, environmental affordances, regional dynamics and trade. The fact that pastoral groups have tended to be more dominant in later history does not exclude the possibility that in some earlier ages sedentary and oasis populations have had greater social and political weight. Trans-Saharan history we suggest has been characterised by a continually changing power balance between pastoralists and sedentarists (as is also evident at times in the recent past).

In this chapter we shall test two hypotheses, developed from the preceding chapters. These are that:

[1] See Chapter 1 and Chapters 2–7 above. [2] Sterry and Mattingly, Chapter 19, this volume.

- sedentary oasis communities were established much earlier and across much broader areas than has conventionally been recognised, totalling many hundreds of settlements, and following different chronological trajectories in different zones (broadly earlier in the Eastern Sahara compared to the Central and Western Sahara);[3]
- sites that we can recognise as urban in character, albeit with some distinctive Saharan aspects, existed by the late first millennium BC/ early first millennium AD in several Saharan regions, but always in small numbers in relation to the totality of oases;

Our discussion here will first explore these factors with regard to the Garamantes of Fazzan, as this is the oasis group with the largest concentration of evidence for the early spread of sedentary oasis cultivators. We present the factors that persuade us that this society was urban and set out some ideas about the characteristics of Saharan urbanisation, reflecting on how this may differ from Mediterranean or Sub-Saharan urbanism. We then broaden our analysis to consider the evidence from the wider Sahara.

At the outset, we should be clear that we do not view these elements in an evolutionary or strictly linear relationship with each other. However, it is clear from the archaeological evidence from Fazzan that Garamantian urban centres (and their putative state) only developed after oasis agriculture and several other new technologies were well established.[4] On this basis the first question we would pose is how and on what basis were the first permanent settlements associated with oasis cultivation formed? A related issue concerns the extent to which sedentary cultivators and semi-sedentarised pastoral groups were distinct from one another. To put it another way, was there also a process towards reduced mobility in pastoral communities?

Sedentarisation

Sedentarisation is a deceptive paradigm, as for many scholars, it is the successful end of an evolutionary process away from pastoralism and mobility. The fallacies of such a mind-set in the context of the Sahara are well established.[5] Faced with the environmental challenges thrown up by the desert climate and landscapes, it is far from certain that communities

[3] See in particular the discussion of chronology in Chapters 2, 3, 5 and 6 above.
[4] See Duckworth *et al.* forthcoming. [5] Scheele 2010; 2012; 2017.

would favour a life as sedentary agriculturalists over the dynamic possibilities of adaptive pastoral strategies. Pastoral groups often seem to have been more appropriately scaled for resilience, while the labour needs of oasis communities are disproportionately high.

In many oases, irrigation schemes depend on the maintenance of drastically unequal labour relations, involving slaves or other notionally free but highly dependent groups.[6] An interesting phenomenon of the early modern Sahara has been the leading role played by far-flung pastoral groups like the Tuareg in maintaining dependency relations over oasis cultivators. The historical depth of such relationships is uncertain and a further variable for future work to consider is how the balance of power between different types of pastoralist and different sedentary groups within the varied parts of the Sahara have developed and changed over time.

Sedentarisation is not a one way street and decline in water sources or diminished access to dependent labour could easily spark a move back to more pastoral-based lifestyles. While some oases have grown over time, many others have shrunk dramatically, especially impacted by changes to the groundwater availability. As we shall see, a recurrent theme of this volume is the cyclical nature of development and decline in Saharan oases, rather than a linear evolutionary trajectory.

The processes of sedentarisation and its end results were far from uniform across time and space within the Trans-Saharan zone. Equally it was not an either/or choice between pastoral and agricultural lifestyles. Mixed strategies are apparent at Early Garamantian sites like Zinkekra and the earliest cultivation in some areas may have reflected a shift to fixed base transhumance linked to locations where scratch cultivation could exploit seasonally available water. Cereal cultivation may have preceded the arrival of the date palm in some regions, with the spread of the latter being a much clearer marker of fully sedentary farming communities.[7] Sedentarisation also evidently took many different forms as is evident from a comparison between the run-off farming of the Libyan pre-desert and the oases of the Garamantes.[8] In this volume our focus is primarily on the emergence of intensive oasis agriculture, rather than on more extensive floodwater farming regimes. That is not to deny the importance of the latter, but rather

[6] For example, the population of the Tabalbala oasis, Sterry *et al.*, Chapter 6, this volume.

[7] It is interesting that thus far our fieldwork in Wadi Draa (southern Morocco) has identified Protohistoric cerealiculture, but no certain evidence for the date palm, though this may be an artefact of the small scale till now of our trial sondages at sites identified.

[8] Mattingly 2004.

to highlight the overall significance of oases in underpinning the Trans-Saharan networks that we suggest supported the development of urban centres and states. It is also apparent that sedentarisation was reversible (or not necessarily sustainable) and that in many areas of the Sahara, the balance has tipped back at some point towards pastoral exploitation of the landscape.

Chronology of Sedentarisation and Oasis Formation

A key aim of this volume is to review and reassess the chronology of oasis agriculture in the Sahara. There are signs that the processes described for Fazzan were replicated in other parts of the Sahara, but not in any uniform manner. However, there are hints in the available dating evidence of a progressive intensification of activity from east to west.

The earliest evidence of Saharan sedentarisation comes from opposite sides of the Sahara: in the Dakhla oasis of Egypt during the Old Kingdom (2649–2150 BC) and Second Intermediate Period (1650–1550 BC),[9] and in Mauritania with the Tichitt tradition of escarpment settlements and millet cultivation around the Dhars Tichitt, Walata and Nema dating to the mid-second millennium BC.[10]

As might be expected the first Saharan oases appear to have developed in the Western Desert of Egypt, an area strongly integrated into Nilotic socio-economic and political systems. However, although oasis agriculture and urban sites appeared from the third millennium BC, it was not until the Hellenistic and Roman periods that there was expansion into all parts of the Siwa, Bahariya, Farafra, Dakhla and Kharga oases.[11]

Among the oases of Tripolitania, southern Tunisia and eastern Algeria, we have little knowledge of the first millennium BC, although hilltop and escarpment sites are located in or near many of them. However, as we saw in Chapters 5 and 6, the Roman period saw the growth of urban centres around Roman forts (e.g. Bu Nijim, Negrine, Gemellae), in oasis groups such as the Nefzaoua and Jarid and the expansion of irrigation-based agriculture on the southern flank of the Aures mountains, as at Badias and in the Libyan pre-desert. Beyond the Roman frontier the settlements are essentially undated, though given the scale of oasis development in the frontier zone, we suggest our default assumption should now be that the

9 Boozer, Chapter 4, this volume.

10 MacDonald *et al.* 2009; MacDonald, Chapter 13, this volume.

11 As discussed by Mattingly *et al.*, Chapter 3, and Boozer, Chapter 4, this volume. See also Gill 2015.

major spring-fed oases just beyond the frontier (for example, Wadi Rihr and Tuggurt) were in all probability already active by this date.

Thus, despite a number of lacunae, and a particular lack of evidence for the second millennium BC, it is clear that by the late first millennium BC there had been a substantial change in oases of the Northern, Eastern and Central Sahara with a large growth in the numbers of settlements (oases in Fazzan, al-Jufra, Western Desert, Roman frontier zone in Algeria and Tunisia) that were largely sustained by oasis agriculture (that is, date palms, fruits, cereals, chickens and in some cases pigs). Technological transfers must have been key to facilitating this transition with the adoption of Near Eastern/Mediterranean crops, transport animals, irrigation technologies and iron-working affecting both the make-up and rhythms of communities, but also their connectivity with one other. Other factors may also have been prominent. Although the major drying of the Sahara took place millennia before sites such as Zinkekra, the evidence from the Tanzzuft implies that many surface water sources were still shrinking because of aridification until at least the first millennium AD.[12] This may have encouraged pastoral communities to develop more permanent (and better defended) sites at the locations with the most reliable water sources. The locations with the most reliable or easily accessible water sources will also have been those to which pioneer agriculturalists were drawn. Logically, either these oasis cultivators will have been in competition with pre-existing pastoral groups or they must have involved groups of the latter.

Sedentary Settlements

What were the earliest forms of sedentary settlements? In the Wadi al-Ajal there are 12 hilltop sites of varying morphology that seem to represent the earliest sedentary settlement in the region. Of these sites, only Zinkekra has seen any serious excavations, producing evidence of oasis agriculture and stone buildings in the tenth to seventh centuries BC (the first stages of the Early Garamantian phase).[13] A second site, Tinda (near Ubari), has also yielded evidence of oasis agriculture dated to the latter centuries BC.[14]

Similar sites have also been identified from satellite imagery in other Saharan oases (for example, al-Jufra, Kawar, Aïr) and in northern

[12] Cremaschi 2006. [13] Mattingly 2003, 136–42; 2010, 19–119.

[14] Mattingly 2007, 294–95 for AMS dates on barley, pearl millet and sorghum spanning 390 calBC–calAD 20. See also Mattingly 2010, 78–82 for radiocarbon dates from Zinkekra.

pre-desert areas such as the Libyan Valleys, the Aures Mountains in Algeria, the Anti-Atlas Mountains and the Draa Valley in Morocco.[15] However, it could be argued that such hillforts are not in themselves indicative of a shift to agriculture. Some Saharan communities appear to have constructed permanent or at least semi-permanent settlements whilst maintaining pastoralist lifeways.[16] With this in mind we might put Saharan settlements on a continuum, with sites such as Afunfun and Gobero at one end (semi-permanent),[17] Dakhlet el Atrous in the middle (some mobile pastoralism, some agriculture),[18] and Zinkekra at the other end (sedentary oasis agriculture alongside localised livestock raising, although this does not preclude the continuation of mobile parts of the population). What is most notable about the Zinkekra and Tinda evidence is that the development of agricultural lifeways preceded major architectural and cultural change at these sites. The initial buildings at Zinkekra were oval one- or two-room structures, associated with enclosures, with abundant traces of the presence of livestock alongside the clear signature of adoption of a developed package of agricultural crops (dates, wheat, barley, grapes, etc.). Although the later buildings at Zinkekra in the latter centuries BC had more complex and extensive rectangular layouts, at the Tinda escarpment settlement, the curvilinear architectural form seems to have persisted to the end of the site's occupation.[19] The material culture from Zinkekra (pottery and lithics) also suggests a strong continuity with pre-existing Pastoral communities of this part of the Sahara.[20]

This Early Garamantian phase of settlement in Fazzan appears to be characterised by the adoption of new lifeways, but overall these communities remained small, and may have been only a minority of the overall Saharan populations in the first millennium BC. However, in the last few centuries BC (the Proto-Urban Garamantian phase) mudbrick settlements started to appear in greater numbers in the centre of the oasis depressions.[21] Initially these may have remained fairly close to the fortified hilltop sites (some of which were still in use), but they gradually spread

[15] Fentress 1979, 30–39; Gsell 1972, 232–45; Mattingly 1995, 41–49. For the Libyan Valleys, Barker *et al.* 1996a, 116–18 and individual entries in 1996b; for the Draa, see now Mattingly *et al.* 2017b.

[16] Garcea 2013. [17] Garcea 2013. [18] MacDonald, Chapter 13, this volume.

[19] Mattingly 2010, 78–84 (Zinkekra) and 85–102 (Tinda).

[20] See especially the finds assemblages illustrated in Mattingly 2010, 27–62.

[21] A particularly clear example is the Taqallit area, where the pioneer phase of oasis cultivation, marked by the first valley-centre villages, the construction of foggara irrigation systems and the arrival in the region of sub-Saharan cereals like sorghum and pearl millet (that allowed more intensive summer cropping) can be comprehensively dated to the last centuries BC by multiple forms of evidence, see Mattingly *et al.* 2010.

more widely in the landscape supported by the digging of foggaras and wells. It is around this time that we start seeing the first material evidence of regular trade links across the Sahara, with Punic imports to Fazzan common by the second century BC. Sedentary populations continued to increase as evidenced by the greater numbers of settlements and the appearance of nucleated cairn cemeteries. However, the real boom appears to have taken place in the first–sixth centuries AD (the Classic and Late Garamantian phases – also the period in which ceramic imports to Fazzan peaked). During this time we see the intensification of the settlement system and its expansion into new areas with little evidence for prior occupation. The Murzuq region is the prime example with no certain settlement from the first millennium BC, but over one hundred substantial settlements supported by well and foggara irrigation by the fourth century AD.

A recent article by Fentress and Wilson has postulated a Late Antique period of Berber 'migration' in the Sahara and Maghrib.[22] How does this fit with the evidence presented in this volume? The overall picture for the development of mudbrick fortified structures within oasis villages highlights Late Antiquity as a time of significant change, with some oases exhibiting signs of declining populations, as in the Western Desert or the North African *limes*, but others showing an expansion in oasis settlements, as in the Murzuq area in the Central Sahara or the Wadi Draa in Morocco. The dating of the expansion of fortified oasis settlement across these regions is broadly consistent with the Fentress and Wilson model, but it is not clear if these phenomena are related or if the changes in settlement systems are exceptional or symptomatic of oasis living (where water resources are always finite).

The Implications of Garamantian Sedentarisation and Oasis Settlement

There are several important lessons to be learned from the recent work on the Garamantes. First, intensive ground survey work has revealed numerous Garamantian settlements to have existed in places where no evidence could be adduced previously. Absence of evidence in other areas of the Sahara is clearly not evidence of absence.[23] It is apparent that successive phases of oasis development and exploitation can obliterate

[22] Fentress and Wilson 2016; see also Fentress 2019 for a development of the argument based on linguistic evidence.

[23] Sterry and Mattingly 2011.

many of the physical traces of preceding sites, but intensive survey work is capable of detecting traces. For example, archaeological survey along a systematic grid of lines criss-crossing the Jarma oasis in advance of oil exploration seismic survey discovered pottery scatters and traces of mudbrick structures relating to numerous previously unsuspected Garamantian sites.[24] This is the most likely explanation for the paucity of Garamantian settlements recorded to date in the al-Barkat oasis, where Aghram Nadharif is the only securely identified settlement, closely adjacent to a cemetery on the east side of the oasis. There are a further 11 ancient cemeteries that surround the al-Barkat oasis on all sides and the existence of a similar number of separate settlements seems a logical conclusion.[25] The lesser visibility of unfortified sites in comparison to fortified sites should also give us pause for thought where our survey is based on remote sensing and major standing monuments. Settlement phases based on unfortified and dispersed sites may well be drastically underrepresented in the recorded archaeology.

Second, our AMS dating programme of recent years has completely overturned initial assumptions about the dating of sites based on their plan or state of preservation.[26] It is now clear that many of the classic settlement forms believed to characterise Medieval villages and fortified sites (*qsur*) in the Sahara can be closely paralleled in Garamantian Fazzan or the Protohistoric period of the Draa.[27] This does not mean that we can make a clear association between similar site types in the Murzuq area and the Tuwat oases – indeed it is clear that some of these forms have been very long lived. But neither is it any longer acceptable to assume a default Medieval date for all the sites in the Tuwat (and elsewhere), especially those that are not associated with mosques and Islamic cemeteries. As our survey above demonstrates, in many areas of the Sahara there are undated hillforts and castle-like fortified sites, sometimes close to funerary zones of pre-Islamic type burial monuments.[28] Each site needs to be assessed on its merits and there is an urgent need for an extension of scientific dating methods to these types of sites to establish more secure regional chronologies.

Third, it should also be recognised that the centres of power in Saharan oasis zones have moved around over time, rather than always remaining

[24] Lahr *et al.* 2009. [25] Liverani 2006, 2, 25–27.
[26] Sterry and Mattingly 2013; Sterry *et al.* 2012.
[27] See for example the work of Echallier 1972; 1973; Chekhab-Abudaya 2016 seems to start with the assumption that these types of site must be Medieval in date.
[28] For our parallel work on the burial monuments, see Gatto *et al.* 2019.

fixed on specific sites. Until more extensive work has been done at a range of sites, we should be wary of drawing definitive historical conclusions for an oasis group on the basis of excavation at only a single site.

The expansion of settlement in Saharan oases has regularly been considered to have gone hand-in-hand with Islamic-period Trans-Saharan trade, especially at oases such as Tuwat and Kawar. The connection between oasis settlement and trade is further explored below, but whilst trade may bring in investment and food security for supporting small settlement development, this may only have been at local rather than Trans-Saharan levels. The population at agricultural sites may have grown with the increasing food resources, but also, to the north and south of the Sahara, there were likely booming populations. We may therefore consider increased connectivity and migration as a factor. It is worth noting that our evidence would suggest that the earliest agricultural settlements pre-dated visible evidence of trade in commodities.[29] While we believe the existence of trade, or at least the possibility of trade, was an important factor in the investment in oasis development, there was no simple linear progression from establishing oases to creating flows of trade. The distribution of settlements in Fazzan and other large oasis chains cannot be seen as a string of trading posts. Rather, in each case they need to be evaluated firstly as local systems of settlement and only secondly as parts of interconnected networks. The development of oases was not some sort of diffusionist tidal wave that spread evenly and predictably across the Sahara. The substantial hydrological differences between many neighbouring locations in the Sahara have posed significant barriers to a neat and predictable diffusion of oasis farming technology (see Figs 1.4–1.5). The Medieval Trans-Saharan network certainly built on an embryonic network established earlier, but the particular historical circumstances in each phase emphasised different nodes and routes – sparking further investment and intensification of activity around these key sites and routes.

Factors Affecting Oasis Development

What were the mechanisms by which new settlements were created? The earliest development should have favoured the areas with the most

[29] Though we should be cautious here as much Saharan trade at all periods has been in 'invisible' commodities, see Mattingly *et al.* 2017a. Moreover, there is clear evidence for the transference of technologies along the Saharan trade routes from an early date, see Liverani, forthcoming.

abundant and most easily accessible water. For ease of exploitation we can distinguish between, on the one hand, oases fed by surficial waters (rivers like the Nile or Draa, flash floods in desert wadis, artesian and other natural springs) and, on the other, oases dependent on artificial means of accessing sub-surface water (foggaras, man-made artesian wells, other wells, palmeries tapping into a high water table).[30] These different scenarios have varied potential and problems for oasis farmers to overcome.[31] The naturally occurring water sources in the Sahara will have been the most obvious ones to find and potentially the easiest for population groups to start to exploit. These were locations that will have already been exploited by Saharan pastoral groups, so their development probably involved partnership between those people and incomers with knowledge of new agricultural technologies. The scale of exploitation of the naturally occurring water sources within the Sahara was always limited by and proportional to the volume of water available. The effective use of a spring could be improved by constructing efficient tanks at the spring head and canals to conduct the water to individual gardens, but there would always be a limit to the absolute area that can be irrigated with a given volume of water. Beyond a certain point the further expansion of oases can only be obtained by the introduction of additional technologies to augment the available water.

In accordance with this idea, many of the oasis locations surveyed in the earlier chapters appear to have embraced a range of different technologies for exploiting water. For example, the Wadi al-Ajal area may originally have benefitted from a number of perennial springs that encouraged agricultural development at a few select locations. However, the intensification of agriculture in the valley after 400 BC was almost certainly due to the introduction of foggara technology, allowing the dramatic augmentation of the supply of running water. At a later date the foggara irrigation was replaced by irrigation using only well technology – perhaps due to the exhaustion of the aquifer that had fed the foggara channels.

In some instances, it is possible that technological barriers inhibited the initial growth of some oasis areas. This is particularly the case with oases where the natural artesian springs were few or not productive enough to support a large population until augmented by additional man-made artesian wells – as seems to have been the case in the Wadi ash-Shati or Wadi Righ.

[30] For a fuller discussion of the importance of hydrology, see the chapter by Wilson *et al.* forthcoming.

[31] See also Sterry *et al.* 2019.

Another issue concerns the transference of oasis farming technology beyond an area where it became established. This was not always a case of the application of the same technical competencies at a neighbouring location. As we have seen, the earliest settlements tended to rely on knowledge of springs and other surface sources of water, whereas subsequent phases of expansion often involved the application of more labour-intensive methods of accessing ground water. Furthermore, the movement of sedentary oasis farming often took place over large distances and often into zones with different and more difficult hydrological conditions. This implies both prior knowledge and investment in order to develop successful settlements and their associated infrastructure (one wonders how many failed enterprises there were). In thinking about these, we should not be drawn to analogies of island-hopping ocean exploration, but instead reflect that there must have been a good societal knowledge of water sources among the Saharan pastoral groups that had used them for millennia.[32] The crucial aspect is to what extent this knowledge of springs, gueltas, wadis with vegetation supported by mountain run-off, lakes/playas, shallow groundwater and other hydrological sources could be used as a basis for irrigation schemes. Overall, there are significant indications of mobility and migration within the populations responsible for the first oases.

A number of important technological innovations were brought in developed form from outside the Sahara: a package of crops and some new domesticated animals from the direction of the Nile/Western Desert, balance wells and foggaras can both be found at earlier dates in the same area, several Sub-Saharan crops were added later.

The model put forward by Hardesty (itself derived from Kirch) is perhaps appropriate in this case.[33] In this model, the first colonisers bring with them standardised knowledge of the environment (where the water is), technology (how to reach it) and social relations (who they are and how to organise themselves). Once established we might then expect the diversification of these categories with a better understanding of the water sources, how to access it and changing social relations within and between groups. Finally in the third stage we might expect the proliferation of the most effective strategies.

[32] Rockman 2003 draws attention to the difference between landscape learning with and without resident populations. In the case of the Sahara, we should consider there to be resident populations although the degree to which pastoral and sedentary societies were integrated or friendly to one another is difficult to assess. The Roman and early Arabic sources seem to make little distinction between sedentary and mobile groups perhaps suggesting a high degree of integration, but they are far from conclusive.

[33] Hardesty 2003, 83; Kirch 1980.

We want to emphasise the point about technological choices being driven by pragmatic and empirical knowledge, not by evolutionary schema from simplest to most complex. Two different examples of ancient foggara irrigation at Ghadamis and Murzuq illustrate this point. At Ghadamis, the limitations of the main spring has for much of its history constrained the absolute development of the size of the oasis and its population. At various times (not closely dated) attempts have been made to create additional irrigated gardens around the periphery of the oasis through the labour-intensive construction of foggaras and wells. By contrast, in the Murzuq region the earliest dated settlements, comprising nucleated settlements similar to those in the Wadi al-Ajal, were located close to playas and used a form of foggara technology to irrigate a system of fields. But the relative unsuitability of this landscape for foggara irrigation constrained that development. By the fourth–fifth centuries AD, a wider range of settlement forms and sizes had been built, but the later settlements fell into two more easily defined categories – the *qasr* and the walled village each supported by their own system of well-based gardens. In this case, the more appropriate technology was actually the simplest form of balance well, facilitated by the existence of a high water table. On the other hand, it is equally apparent that the existence of technology (or knowledge of it) is not an adequate explanation for the spread of oases. The expansion of oasis agriculture in almost every scenario involves significant labour inputs and without the availability and investment of that human capital, the enterprise cannot advance.

To summarise our model for the development of oasis and sedentary settlement in the Sahara, we have suggested that the first settlements sat at one end of a spectrum of permanent bases used by pastoral groups. Once these appeared, and in conjunction with a number of converging technologies, intensive oasis agriculture could be developed (or imported), probably through social partnerships involving both established pastoral communities and some migrant groups. For fully fledged oases to emerge, external contacts were important for accessing crops and animals domesticated elsewhere and the supporting technologies. Finally, this accumulated knowledge then formed the basis for developing new areas and new oases in the Sahara.

In our descriptive chapters on early Saharan oasis development, we have identified a broad trend from precocious oasis agriculture and permanent settlements in the Nile Valley and the Western Desert in the third–second millennia BC, to the emergence of Central Saharan oases by the early first millennium BC, to increasing evidence for oases in the Northern Sahara

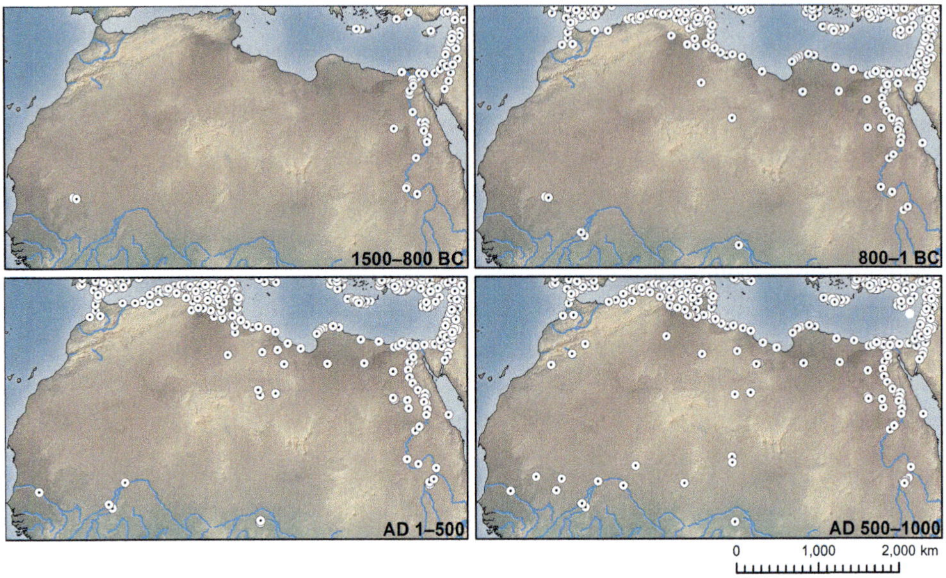

Figure 8.1. Spread of urbanisation across the Trans-Saharan region (circles indicate urban or other significant population agglomerations, smaller oases are not shown).

within and just outside the Roman frontier zone by the early centuries AD, to possible penetration of oasis settlements into most of the suitable hydrological niches of the Southern and Western Sahara by the mid-first millennium AD (Fig. 8.1). The dating schema is increasingly weak as one moves further from the Roman frontier zone and further west and south, where most of the investigated sites have been of Medieval date and in part influenced by the descriptions in the Arabic sources.

The implications of this new model for conventional understanding of the socio-economic status of the indigenous peoples of the Roman frontier zone and beyond (Gaetuli and Garamantes) are profound.[34] The conventional narrative has portrayed Roman military advances in the late first century BC and first century AD as essentially engaging with pastoral peoples (though with the Garamantes now recognised as a possible exception).[35] The orthodox interpretation has presented Roman

[34] Lassère 2015, 21–45, acknowledges the fact that not all indigenous peoples of the Maghrib were pastoralists on the eve of Roman conquest, but limits his recognition of sedentary living and proto-urban development to the areas far from the desert. Cf. Mattingly 2016, for a deconstruction of the commonly assumed Roman responsibility for the urban and agricultural boom of the early centuries AD.

[35] Even in recent summaries, where the old emphasis on 'nomads' is more nuanced, the presence and significance of sedentary oasis dwellers remains a bit elusive: Guédon 2018; Leveau 2018; Reddé 2014, 121–34.; cf. Mattingly *et al.* 2013a.

pacification of the pastoral peoples of the desert margins as the essential starting point for their sedentarisation in a progressive evolutionary model. The new evidence presented above changes the paradigm and our starting assumptions. For one thing, it is clear that the start-up date of many oases in the Eastern and Central Sahara preceded military contact with Rome and we have argued that it is more plausible that the Roman forts of the Roman frontier zone of Libya, southern Tunisia and Algeria were established alongside already existing oasis communities rather than the other way around. For instance, the interactions between Rome and the various peoples described as Gaetuli in the sources were thus more complex than containment of transhumance lifestyles; they also involved large sedentary oasis populations by the early first millennium AD. This is a new starting point for scholarly debate and it impacts the entire northern fringes of the Sahara from Egypt to Morocco. Oases were, of course, not restricted to the area of the Roman frontier and a priority in future research must be to investigate in greater detail the early history of oases in regions that remained well outside the Roman frontier zone.

Urbanisation

In the introduction to this volume, we reviewed theoretical debate on ancient urbanism, expressing doubts about the ready application of checklist models developed in relation to Near Eastern or Mediterranean societies to the African context. That is not to say that Saharan sites cannot conform to external models related to urban function or settlement hierarchies, but rather to acknowledge that the differences in application (and the relevant lack of excavation of the Saharan sites) can confound expectations. A key issue for us in thinking about Saharan towns is the need to look beyond traditional urban models of ancient Egypt, Mesopotamia or the Mediterranean. Although those well-known urban traditions may have had some influence on what emerged in the Sahara, through proximity and contacts, there are other possible explanations for the emergence of Saharan urban centres.[36] Given the evidence for Sub-Saharan urbanisation in the first millennium BC, we cannot exclude the possibility of influence from that direction.[37] More importantly, if oasis settlements became

[36] Mattingly and MacDonald 2013; Mattingly and Sterry 2013.

[37] MacDonald 2013; Sinclair 2013 – we might note that his survey of African urbanisation by region excludes the Sahara from consideration! Cf. Mattingly and MacDonald 2013, for an attempt to reintegrate the Sahara into such discussions.

widespread before towns and state formation occurred, we should expect a proto-urban phase of development reflecting internal characteristics of desert societies. In other words, the idea of the town and its physical manifestation in the Sahara may have reflected both the wider Trans-Saharan world and the particularities of oasis communities. A further point to consider with regard to Saharan urbanisation is the relationship between the overall spread of oasis settlements (as modelled in Fig. 8.1) and the eventual emergence of certain settlements with urban characteristics.

If we accept the proposition that Saharan towns may have had some distinctive characteristics that differentiate them from other contemporary urban forms, the next question is to ask what are the defining characteristics of desert urbanisation and what makes them stand out as something distinctive in the settlement system?

A useful starting test of 'Saharan towns' is the extent to which they meet the basic parameters of multiple models of towns. How far can we identify them as:

- centres or agglomerations of size and population density;[38]
- foci of distinctive functions and craft specialisations;[39]
- nodes of economic networks;[40]
- organising hubs of farming hinterlands or zones of raw material exploitation;[41]
- places of social complexity and authority;[42]
- transformational settlements reorganising town–country interactions?[43]

Within the overall picture of sedentary oasis settlements, a case can certainly be made for the special status of certain sites in terms of the bulleted characteristics, of which the Garamantian capital at Jarma is the prime example. Although small by Mediterranean standards at *c.*10 ha, it was at the larger end of Garamantian settlements, evidently with distinctive features and functions, its architecture reflecting unusual social complexity and authority, its material culture demonstrating the existence of atypical access to distant markets. For a defined period it was clearly a nodal point in Saharan trade, as well as a focal point in the exploitation of regional resources, including things like metals and semi-precious stones, as well as agricultural production and labour.

We have argued that it was in the Classic and Late Garamantian phases that the evidence for urban sites and a Garamantian polity is clearest. Our

[38] Marzano 2011. [39] McIntosh, R. 2005; 2015. [40] Wilson 2011. [41] Cowgill 2004.
[42] Smith, A.T. 2003; Smith, M. 2003; cf. McIntosh, S. 1999. [43] Yoffee 2005, 61–62.

excavations at the Garamantian capital at Jarma suggests that monumental stone buildings first appeared at the very end of the Proto-Urban phase in the first century BC, but that the most exceptional development at the site occurred in the first–fourth centuries AD.[44]

The modern debate about how to define towns, and the evidence thresholds laid down by different models, complicate things to some degree. Some modern theorists ignore the testimony of contemporary witnesses. While Greco-Roman sources were notoriously biased against 'barbarian' societies, often presenting them in stereotypical terms as underdeveloped, there are references that should give us pause for thought in seemingly pointing to higher development. For example, it is commonplace for these sources to refer to some significant settlements beyond the Roman frontiers as 'towns' (*oppidum, urbs, polis*). We should be cautious here as it is certainly conceivable that these terms for upper echelon settlements in the Mediterranean region were being inappropriately applied to non-urban sites in regions for which first-hand accounts were lacking or inadequately detailed. On the other hand, there are indications that distinctions were being reflected in the choice of vocabulary. In the section of Ptolemy's *Geography* relating to North Africa, he does discriminate between sites that he describes as 'towns' (*poleis*) and others he refers to as 'villages' (*komai*).[45] The description of sites in the Libyan interior, essentially the Sahara, contains reference to numerous 'towns' (*poleis*) and three sites that he highlights by the term *metropolis*, Garama, Nigira and Gira.[46] We can add to this the fact that a number of oasis settlements in Roman frontier zones were explicitly assigned urban rank by the Romans, with an administrative function (as is described below in more detail). This suggests that however Saharan towns may have deviated from Mediterranean norms, they were still recognisable as urban equivalents and adaptable within Roman administrative structures when required. In some cases these Saharan towns were explicitly identified as the principal place of a prominent people, such as the Garamantes. By the early first century AD the Romans were dealing with Garamantian 'kings' (another term not normally invoked for petty chieftains), implying the existence of not only an urban society but a genuine polity.[47] In the past our assumptions about the relatively unsophisticated nature of ancient Saharan societies and doubts about

[44] Mattingly 2013.

[45] See for instance, Ptolemy, *Geography* 4.5, where Awjila is indicated as a village, while Ammon (Siwa) is identified as a town.

[46] Ptolemy, *Geography* 4.6. [47] Sterry and Mattingly, Chapter 19, this volume.

the interconnectedness of the Roman provinces with the Saharan hinterland, led to a default reading of such source material as being ill-informed or fanciful. The archaeological evidence from the Garamantian case study in particular, but with support from the persuasive evidence for more widespread oasis development presented in this book, suggests that we need to recalibrate our starting assumptions. The implications are that within many of the areas of Protohistoric oasis settlement that we have postulated, one or more primate centres emerged with characteristics and functions that differentiated them from other settlements. Visitors from the Mediterranean world or the Sub-Saharan zone would have readily seen these centres as equivalents to urban sites outside the Sahara.

What Was Distinctive about Saharan Towns?

What our survey of Protohistoric Saharan oasis settlement demonstrates is that there were many villages, but relatively few sites of demonstrable urban scale and status. Nonetheless the urban sites we can identify (or postulate) played a significant role in these desert societies. Understanding the urbanisation process in the desert requires careful consideration of the particularities of these exceptional sites. If we start by reflecting on the main groups of towns identified on Figure 8.1, some regional specificities emerge or, to put it more bluntly, a distinct heterogeneity. The oases that were closest to the Mediterranean and Nile were much more likely to reflect some influences from the established civilisations of those regions. The towns in the oases of the Western Desert are distinctive as a group from those of the rest of the Sahara. In layout, architecture and cultural reference points they look towards the Nile Valley and Egypt and were organised following historical urban categories of Pharaonic, Hellenistic and Roman governance. Most of the oasis depressions contained at least one town, with externally recognised authority in local government: for Kharga, these are Hibis and Kysis; for Dakhla, Kellis, Mothis, and Trimithis; for Bahariya, al-Bawiti; for Siwa, Ammon. These main centres were marked out by their size, by monumental architecture and by the richness of associated cemeteries. Many of these Egyptian oases towns show a degree of planning around a major temple complex, as at Kellis and Trimithis in the Dakhla oasis.[48] In addition to these few urban centres, there were dozens of smaller villages.

[48] See Boozer, Chapter 4, this volume.

Within the province of Africa, a number of pre-Roman oasis centres were formally recognised as Roman towns – most notably Tacapae (Gabes) and Capsa (Gafsa), though there are strong reasons to suggest that these deviated in important respects from the towns of northern Tunisia. Some other pre-existing indigenous centres further out in the frontier zone appear to have been recognised or promoted to be *civitas* towns, *municipia* and even *coloniae*: in the Nefzaoua, Turris Tamalleni, in the Jarid, Thiges, Nepta, Thusuros. However, these appear to have been much smaller and less monumentalised than the cities in Northern Tunisia. In some cases, rather than a single coherent urban unit, as Mediterranean models might lead us to expect, it seems possible that they were in fact fragmented into multiple village-scale complexes within a single oasis, as in the Nefzaoua, Jarid and at Gabes.

The few oasis sites in the Roman frontier zone of Algeria and Tunisia that were accorded urban status under Rome have quite a varied morphology. Gemellae and Nigrenses Maiores are two examples that we know were promoted to *municipium* rank, but which seem essentially to have been walled garrison settlements around long-term Roman forts situated outside the oasis proper. There were quite a number of such sites along the African frontier and these are the locations where stone architecture appears to be most commonly encountered.

These oasis towns of the Western Desert and the Roman frontier zones were to some extent administrative towns of more distant political authorities – serving as centres for local tax collection, law and governance. Further out into the Sahara, towns were both rarer and more specialised.

The clearest indication that there were African or Saharan urban principles at play, alongside Punic or Roman ones, within the oases is the existence of settlements of urban character beyond the frontiers. The urban centres of the Garamantes appear to be rather different in form and scale to the towns of Egypt, with a prominent emphasis on fortified complexes at their core.[49]

Ancient oasis towns were in general characterised by a relatively small area and population, but with a significantly enhanced role for craft production and trade specialists when compared to other oasis settlements. They were served by a hinterland of intensive irrigated cultivation that needed to be large enough to support the settlement, but practical difficulties of walking far in Saharan summer heat favoured the development of satellite villages over expansion of the urban core. Trade rather than

[49] Mattingly and Sterry 2013; Mattingly *et al.* 2013b, 530–34.

agriculture created the additional surplus required to support the growth of the town, although water and agricultural supplies were needed to support caravans. Saharan oasis towns have thus attracted and facilitated trade and their wellbeing was intimately tied to the flow of commerce. Islamic Ghadamis, Ghat, Murzuq and Zuwila can be seen to have operated in this manner. When Trans-Saharan trade routes were disrupted, the cities stagnated and shrank in population.[50] Similarly, in the Tuwat oases, when French colonial forces stopped all movement of trade goods, shortages and malnutrition quickly followed.[51] Therefore some external stimulus was required for an oasis city to develop successfully.[52]

New capital investment could come from another already developed oasis city, but could also have been drawn from outside the desert region. In the Islamic era, for example, states to the north and south of Fazzan deliberately developed new urban centres, as at Traghan and Murzuq. Similarly, Roman period expansion of the Dakhla oasis has been attributed to direct imperial interest.[53] A key conclusion of this chapter is that the same socio-economic factors for urban growth and decline also applied to pre-Islamic Saharan society. It follows that the wellbeing of these desert towns could be just as profoundly affected by political and economic shifts as by environmental changes.

Yoffee has described cities as 'not things or essences but points of entry into . . . what changed in the urban revolution'.[54] Any examination of ancient urbanisation in the Sahara and its environs should thus investigate what changed. Another question that needs to be addressed is how isolated were the different urbanised zones from one another? We are certainly not advocating a return to diffusionist models of towns and states in relation to these entities in Saharan and Sub-Saharan Africa. However, we do think that towns and urban networks were an important element in the emergence of extensive patterns of Trans-Saharan connections and that this was happening across a wide space as early as the second half of the first millennium BC.

In the wider Saharan context, preliminary observations and reports suggest that there are remains of urban character in a number of other oasis zones, though by no means all.[55] The picture is not always clear;

[50] Eldblom 1968, 305–14; Mattingly *et al.* 2015. [51] Scheele 2010.

[52] Some operated at an agricultural deficit, as proposed for Tadmakka by Nixon 2009; 2017.

[53] Mills 1993, 194–95. [54] Yoffee 2009, 282.

[55] See Chapters 2–7, this volume. An example of an area that may not have developed towns until a later date, despite having a number of Garamantian era settlements is the Ghat oasis, see Liverani 2006, 457–62; Mori 2013. The presence of a notably richer cemetery by Ghat compared to the other known cemeteries is a possible indication that there was in fact a Garamantian-era antecedent to the Medieval and Early Modern town of Ghat.

excavations at Tadmakka and Timbuktu have suggested that there is little evidence at those locations of Trans-Saharan trade before the late first millennium AD. Yet as we have discussed, there is no reason to assume that Protohistoric centres would underlie those of Medieval date – centres in one period have frequently been replaced by new nodal sites in a succeeding era.[56] More research is urgently needed to investigate the possibility of pre-Islamic activity at oases further afield: Djado and Bilma in Niger, Tuwat and Tamanrasset in Algeria; Wadi Ziz and Wadi Draa in southern Morocco.[57]

In Fazzan, we have suggested that 4 ha (and perhaps *c.*400–800 inhabitants) represents the upper limit for a purely agricultural settlement that was reliant on wells or foggaras for irrigation. There are also centres of *c.*7.5–10 ha and above and we have argued that these belong to an urban element in the pre-modern settlement hierarchy.[58] These figures are significantly below what we encounter in many other parts of the world, but we must recognise that the harsh desert conditions constrain the emergence of larger nucleated centres. Fletcher provides a possible explanation when he links maximum settlement area with communication range and traffic capacity.[59] We suggest that hyper-intensive farming in gardens requiring hours of irrigation every day *increases* traffic (in Fletcher's terms), whilst the low availability of (and restricted access to) water and high summer temperatures effectively *lowers* communication range far below that seen in temperate agricultural regimes. It is no coincidence that many oases comprise multiple small villages spread through the palm groves, reducing travel distance between dwelling and gardens. As demonstrated in Chapter 5, some of the oases in the Tunisian Gabes, Jarid and Nefzaoua oases were recognised as 'proper' towns by Rome, but on the ground seem to have comprised a series of closely spaced villages, with no one element being significantly larger or more developed architecturally. Some oasis towns may thus be seen as distributed or composite centres, comprising multiple village-scale settlements. The scatter of centres at Waddan is a prime archaeological example. But sites in the Central Sahara like Jarma, Qasr ash-Sharraba, and Zuwila demonstrate that the alternative model of a single primate centre was also present.

56 Insoll 1998; Nixon 2009.

57 For other recent reviews of urbanisation in Africa, see MacDonald 2013; Mattingly and MacDonald 2013; McIntosh 2015; Sinclair 2013.

58 Mattingly and Sterry 2013.

59 Fletcher 1995, 84.

How to Build (and Sustain) a Saharan Town?

Urban settlements of Fazzan were not the consequence of the region having particularly high potential for its fertility or privileged access to natural water sources. There were lots of oases, but relatively few of them were spring-fed and many have historically been dependent on well irrigation.[60] The reality seems to be that substantial outside investment had to be made to create urban centres that had functions *beyond* farming. The most likely reason behind this investment is undoubtedly in securing trade routes or exercising political authority.

A paradox of Saharan oases is that they were vulnerable economically if they were solely dependent on irrigated agriculture. The capital-intensive costs of irrigated farming have constrained the self-sufficiency of most oases through time. Trade is a crucial adjunct to agriculture, even if it is mainly routed through a few nodal settlements, which have acquired higher economic and political status as a consequence.[61] It has been hypothesised that oasis societies are non-viable without parallel development of trade. We would add the additional argument that successful oasis agriculture coupled with long-range trade was also liable to result in urbanisation. It can equally be argued that towns were unlikely to have developed in the Sahara on the basis of oasis agriculture alone and their sustainability was closely linked to the vagaries of Saharan trade. The Trans-Saharan networks of interconnections changed over time, with new nodes emerging periodically, often at least in part as a result of external events and changes.[62] The fortunes of Jarma changed dramatically when trade routes shifted away from that town in the Islamic era.[63] Where we see evidence of intensive growth in oasis agriculture, it is likely that there would also be a related primate centre either in the oasis or closely connected to it. The Saharan town is thus another example of transformative urban forms.[64]

So far we have mainly focused on the possible identification of Protohistoric origins of some Saharan urban settlements, though noting also the importance of Islamic foundations later, especially in the Western and Southern Sahara. Several chapters in the next part of the book will assess in more detail the specific character of the caravan cities associated with Islamic era Trans-Saharan trade. A case could be made, perhaps, for Islamic innovation in the spread of Saharan urbanisation. However, at this point we would simply restate a key point of this section of the book: the existence of pre-Islamic origins of large-scale and atypical oasis settlements

[60] Scarin 1934. [61] See Scheele 2010, 284–88. [62] Lydon 2009.
[63] Mattingly *et al.* 2013b, 512–38. [64] Cf. Renfrew 2008.

at locations that went on to be Islamic era centres (for example, Jarma, Zuwila, Ghadamis, etc.) introduces a major difficulty for that argument. Even if the Medieval Saharan towns had some unique features, it is hard to deny the existence of pre-existing urban or proto-urban traditions. Though these remain ill-defined archaeologically in many cases, they need to be taken account of in relation to the Medieval developments.

References

Barker, G., Gilbertson, D., Jones, B. and Mattingly, D.J. 1996a. *Farming the Desert. The UNESCO Libyan Valleys Archaeological Survey. Volume 1, Synthesis.* (Principal editor, G. Barker). Paris/London: UNESCO, Society for Libyan Studies.

Barker, G., Gilbertson, D., Jones, B. and Mattingly, D.J. 1996b. *Farming the Desert. The UNESCO Libyan Valleys Archaeological Survey. Volume 2, Gazetteer and Pottery.* (Principal editor, D.J. Mattingly). Paris/London: UNESCO, Society for Libyan Studies.

Bowman, A. and Wilson, A. (eds). 2011. *Settlement, Urbanization, and Population.* Oxford: Oxford University Press.

Chekhab-Abudaya, M. 2016. *Le qṣar, type d'implantation humaine au Sahara: Architecture du Sud Algérien.* Oxford: Archaeopress.

Cowgill, G.L. 2004. Origins and development of urbanism: Archaeological perspectives. *Annual Review of Anthropology* 33: 525–49.

Cremaschi, M. 2006. The Barkat oasis in the changing landscape of Wadi Tannezzuft during the Holocene. In Liverani 2006, 13–24.

Duckworth, C., Cuénod, A., and Mattingly, D.J. (eds). Forthcoming. *Mobile Technologies in the Ancient Sahara and Beyond.* Trans-Saharan Archaeology Volume 4. Series editor D.J. Mattingly. Cambridge: Cambridge University Press and The Society for Libyan Studies.

Echallier, J.-C. 1972. *Villages désertés et structures agraires anciennes du Touat et du Gourara.* Paris: RMG.

Echallier, J.-C. 1973. Fortéresses berbères du Gourara. Problèmes et resultants des fouilles. *Libyca* 21: 293–302.

Eldblom, L. 1968. *Structure foncière, organisation et structure sociale. Une étude sur la vie socio-économique dans les trois oasis libyennes de Ghat, Mourzouk et particulièrement Ghadamès.* Lund: Uniskol.

Fentress, E.W.B. 1979. *Numidia and the Roman army. Social, military and economic aspects of the frontier zone.* Oxford: BAR S53.

Fentress, E. 2019. The archaeological and genetic correlates of Amazigh linguistics. In Gatto *et al.* 2019, 495–24.

Fentress, E. and Wilson, A. 2016. The Saharan Berber diaspora and the southern frontiers of Byzantine North Africa. In S.T. Stevens and J.P. Conant (eds), *North*

Africa under Byzantium and Early Islam, Dumbarton Oaks Byzantine Symposia and Colloquia 7. Washington, DC: Dumbarton Oaks Research Library and Collection, 41–63.

Fletcher, R. 1995. *The Limits of Settlement Growth. A Theoretical Outline*. Cambridge: Cambridge University Press.

Garcea, E.A.A. (ed.). 2013. *Gobero: The No-Return Frontier: Archaeology and Landscape at the Saharo-Sahelian Borderland*. Frankfurt: Africa Magna Verlag 9.

Gatto, M.C., Mattingly, D.J., Ray, N. and Sterry, M. (eds). 2019. *Burials, Migration and Identity in the Ancient Sahara and Beyond*. Trans-Saharan Archaeology Volume 2. Series editor D.J. Mattingly. Cambridge: Cambridge University Press.

Gill, J.C.R. 2015. *Dakhleh Oasis and the Western Desert in Egypt under the Ptolemies*. Oxford: Oxbow Books.

Gsell, S. 1972. *Histoire ancienne de l'Afrique du nord. Tome V Les royaume indigènes, orientation sociale, politique et économique*. Osnabrück: Otto Zeller Verlag.

Guédon, S. 2018. *La frontière romaine de l'Africa sous le Haut-Empire*. Madrid: Casa de Velazquez.

Hardesty, D.L. 2003. Mining rushes and landscape learning. In Rockman and Steele 2003, 81–95.

Insoll, T. 1998. Archaeological research in Timbuktu, Mali. *Antiquity* 72: 413–17.

Kirch, P.V. 1980. The archaeological study of adaptation: Theoretical and methodological issues. In M. Schiffer (ed.), *Advances in Archaeological Method and Theory* 3. New York: Academic Press, 101–56.

Lahr, M.M., Foley, R.F., Mattingly, D.J. and Le Quesne, C. 2009. *Area 131, Jarma, Fazzan: Archaeological Mitigation of Seismic Acquisition 2006-2008 – Final Report*. Unpublished Consultancy report for Occidental Libya Oil and Gas BV and Libyan Department of Antiquities.

Lassère, J.-M. 2015. *Africa, quasi Roma (256 av. J.C. – 711 apr. J.C.)*. Paris: CNRS editions.

Leveau, P. 2018. Climat, sociétés et environment aux marges sahariennes du Maghreb: Une approche historiographique. In S. Guédon (ed.), *La frontière méridionale du Maghreb. Approches croisées (Antiquité-Moyen Âge)*. Bordeaux: Ausonius, 19–106.

Liverani, M. (ed.). 2006. *Aghram Nadharif. The Barkat Oasis (Sha'abiya of Ghat, Libyan Sahara) in Garamantian Times*. Firenze: All'Insegna del Giglio.

Liverani, M. Forthcoming. Technological innovation transfer through the hyper-arid belt. In Duckworth *et al.*, Forthcoming.

Lydon, G. 2009. *On Trans-Saharan Trails: Islamic Law, Trade Networks and Cross-cultural Exchange in Nineteenth-Century Western Africa*. Cambridge: Cambridge University Press.

MacDonald, K. 2013. Complex societies, urbanism and trade in the western Sahel. In Mitchell and Lane 2013, 829–44.

MacDonald, K.C., Vernet, R., Martinon-Torres, M., and Fuller, D.Q. 2009. Dhar Nema: From early agriculture to metallurgy in southeastern Mauritania. *Azania: Archaeological Research in Africa* 44.2: 280.

McIntosh, R. 2005. *Ancient Middle Niger: Urbanism and the Self-Organizing Landscape*. Cambridge: Cambridge University Press.

McIntosh, R. 2015. Different cities: Jenne-jeno and African urbanism. In N. Yoffee (ed.), *The Cambridge World History: Volume 3, Early Cities in Comparative Perspective, 4000 BCE–1200 CE*. Cambridge: Cambridge University Press, 364–80.

McIntosh, S. 1999. *Beyond Chiefdoms: Pathways to Complexity in Africa*. Cambridge: Cambridge University Press.

Marcus, J. and Sabloff, J.A. (eds). 2008. *The Ancient City: New Perspectives on Urbanism in the Old and New World*. Santa Fe: School for Advanced Research Press.

Marzano, A. 2011. Rank-size analysis and the Roman cities of the Iberian Peninsula and Britain: Some considerations. In Bowman and Wilson 2011, 196–228.

Mattingly, D.J. 1995. *Tripolitania*. London: Batsford.

Mattingly, D.J. 2003. *The Archaeology of Fazzan, Volume 1 Synthesis*. London: Society for Libyan Studies.

Mattingly, D.J. 2004. Surveying the desert: From the Libyan Valleys to Saharan oases. In M. Iacovou (ed.), *Archaeological Field Survey in Cyprus. Past History, Future Potentials. Proceedings of a Conference Held at the University of Cyprus, 1–2 December 2000*. London: BSA monograph 11, 163–76.

Mattingly, D.J. 2007. *The Archaeology of Fazzan, Volume 2. Site Gazetteer, Pottery and Other Finds*. London: Society for Libyan Studies.

Mattingly, D.J. 2010. The *Archaeology of Fazzan. Volume 3, Excavations Carried out by C.M. Daniels*. London: Society for Libyan Studies.

Mattingly, D.J. 2013. *The Archaeology of Fazzan, Volume 4. Survey and Excavations at Old Jarma (Ancient Garama) Carried out by C.M. Daniels (1962–69) and the Fazzan Project* (1997–2001). London: Society for Libyan Studies.

Mattingly, D.J. 2016. Who shaped Africa? The origins of agriculture and urbanism in Maghreb and Sahara. In N. Mugnai, J. Nikolaus and N. Ray (eds), *De Africa Romaque. Merging Cultures across North Africa*. London: Society for Libyan Studies, 11–25.

Mattingly, D.J. and MacDonald, K. 2013. Early cities: Africa. In P. Clark (ed.), *The Oxford Handbook of Cities in World History*. Oxford: Oxford University Press, 66–82.

Mattingly, D.J. and Sterry, M. 2013. The first towns in the Central Sahara. *Antiquity* 87.366: 503–18.

Mattingly, D.J., al-Aghab, S., Ahmed, A., Moussa, F., Sterry, M and Wilson, A.I. 2010. DMP X: Survey and landscape conservation issues around the Taqallit headland. *Libyan Studies* 41: 105–32.

Mattingly, D.J., Rushworth, A., Sterry, M. and Leitch, V. 2013a. *The African Frontiers*. Frontiers of the Roman Empire series, general editor, D. Breeze. Edinburgh: Hussar.

Mattingly, D.J., Sterry, M. and Thomas, D. 2013b. Jarma in its Saharan context: An urban biography. In Mattingly 2013, 505–44.

Mattingly, D.J., Sterry, M. and Edwards, D.N. 2015. The origins and development of Zuwīla, Libyan Sahara: An archaeological and historical overview. *Azania: Archaeological Research in Africa* 50.1: 27–75.

Mattingly, D.J., Leitch, V., Duckworth, C.N., Cuénod, A., Sterry, M. and Cole, F. (eds). 2017a. *Trade in the Ancient Sahara and Beyond.* Trans-Saharan Archaeology Volume 1. Series editor D.J. Mattingly. Cambridge: Cambridge University Press and The Society for Libyan Studies.

Mattingly, D.J., Bokbot, Y., Sterry, M., Cuénod, A., Fenwick, C., Gatto, M.C., Ray, N., Rayne, L., Janin, K., Lamb, A., Mugnai, N. and Nikolaus, J. 2017b. Long-term history in a Moroccan oasis zone: The Middle Draa Project 2015. *Journal of African Archaeology* 15: 141–72.

Mills, A.J. 1993. The Dakhleh oasis colombarium farmhouse. *Bulletin de la Societé archéologique d'Alexandrie* 45: 192–8.

Mitchell, P. and Lane, P. (eds). 2013. *The Oxford Handbook of African Archaeology.* Oxford: Oxford University Press.

Mori, L. (ed.). 2013. *Life and Death of a Rural Village in Garamantian Times. The Archaeological Research in the Oasis of Fewet (Libyan Sahara)*, AZA Monographs 6. Firenze: All'Insegna del Giglio.

Nixon, S. 2009. Excavating Essouk-Tadmakka (Mali): New archaeological investigations of early Islamic trans-Saharan trade. *Azania: Archaeological Research in Africa* 44.2: 217–55.

Nixon, S. (ed.). 2017. *Essouk-Tadmekka: An Early Islamic Trans-Saharan Market Town.* Leiden: Brill.

Reddé, M. 2014. *Les frontières de l'empire romain (1er siècle avant J.C. – 5e siècle après J.C.).* Lacapelle-Marival: Archéologie Nouvelle.

Renfrew, C. 2008. The city through time and space. In Marcus and Sabloff 2008, 29–52.

Rockman, M. 2003. Knowledge and learning in the archaeology of colonization. In Rockman and Steele 2003, 3–24.

Rockman, M. and Steele, J. (eds). 2003. *Colonization of Unfamiliar Landscapes: The Archaeology of Adaptation.* London: Routledge.

Scarin, E. 1934. *Le oasi del Fezzan.* Bologna: Nicola Zanichelli.

Scheele, J. 2010. Traders, saints, and irrigation: Reflections on Saharan connectivity. *The Journal of African History* 51.3: 281–300.

Scheele, J. 2012. *Smugglers and Saints of the Sahara: Regional Connectivity in the Twentieth Century.* Cambridge: Cambridge University Press.

Scheele, J. 2017. The need for nomads: Camel-herding, raiding, Saharan trade and settlement. In Mattingly *et al.* 2017a, 55–79.

Sinclair, P. 2013. The archaeology of African urbanism. In Mitchell and Lane 2013, 689–702.

Smith, A.T. 2003. *The Political Landscape: Constellations of Authority in Early Complex Polities.* Los Angeles: University of California Press.

Smith, M. (ed.). 2003. *The Social Construction of Ancient Cities*. Washington, DC: Smithsonian Books.

Sterry, M. and Mattingly, D.J. 2011. DMP XIII: Reconnaissance survey of archaeological sites in the Murzuq area. *Libyan Studies* 42: 89–116.

Sterry, M., and Mattingly, D.J. 2013. Desert Migrations Project XVII: Further AMS dates for historic settlements from Fazzan, south-west Libya. *Libyan Studies* 44: 127–40.

Sterry, M., Mattingly, D.J. and Higham, T. 2012. Desert Migrations Project XVI: Radiocarbon dates from the Murzuq region, Southern Libya. *Libyan Studies* 43: 137–47.

Sterry, M., Mattingly, D.J. and Wilson, A.I. 2019. Foggaras and the Garamantes: Hydraulic landscapes in the Central Sahara. In S. Rost (ed.), *Irrigation in Early States: New Directions*. Chicago: The Oriental Institute of the University of Chicago.

Wilson, A.I. 2011. City sizes and urbanization in the Roman Empire. In Bowman and Wilson 2011, 161–95.

Wilson, A.I., Mattingly, D.J. and Sterry, M. Forthcoming. The diffusion of irrigation technologies in the Sahara in antiquity: Settlement, trade and migration. In Duckworth *et al.* Forthcoming.

Yoffee, N. 2005. *Myths of the Archaic State: Evolution of the Earliest Cities, States and Civilizations*. Cambridge: Cambridge University Press.

Yoffee, N. 2009. Making ancient cities plausible. *Reviews in Anthropology* 38: 264–89.

PART III

Neighbours and Comparanda

9 | Early States and Urban Forms in the Middle Nile

DAVID N. EDWARDS

Introduction

Studies of the political organisation of the Meroitic state (*c.*350 BC–AD 300) have often underlined the importance of an explicit recognition of its Sudanic context, and place within longer-term traditions of Sudanic political developments.[1] Its study may also benefit from a more explicit engagement with African political anthropology, along with a greater concern with political practices, as more recently envisaged by Smith.[2] In turn, it may also be argued that many features of early Sudanic polities of the Middle Nile (for example, Kerma) differ in some fundamental ways from their northern neighbours of the Egyptian Lower Nile, or indeed the Mediterranean. Meroe shares a number of distinctive characteristics of more recent Sudanic kingdoms; some are emphasised in this chapter. A number of challenges to rulership are readily identifiable in the Sahelian-Sudanic landscapes of the Middle Nile, and many of these may be familiar to those working in other contexts across the continent. It can be suggested, for example, that the ability of the Meroitic kings to directly control subsistence production was probably limited to a relatively small core region, while more diffuse forms of power could be exerted beyond, extending also to more mobile populations. Control of exchange systems and certain forms of production may have remained more royally focused; forms of ritual suzerainty may also have provided an important power source (potentially with a long history). It should be emphasised that urban settlements remained exceptional, as they have in the longer-term history of the region. As such their presence invites close scrutiny when and where it occurred. The extent to which urban forms were relevant to the

[1] Edwards 1996; 1998. [2] Smith 2011.

development of the Meroitic kingdom, or indeed other early states of the Middle Nile also merits further exploration. Considering other possible foci of early states in this region, the often fundamental differences from the Egyptian state in the Lower Nile may be reiterated, notwithstanding well-recognised cultural linkages. Looking in other directions, demonstrable links with the Ethiopian highlands remain limited. Over the long term, however, the distinctiveness of Ethiopian cultural trajectories must also be recognised.

In recent years much new archaeological data has been acquired relevant to state development in the Middle Nile, relating not just to the Meroitic state but its Napatan predecessor, which briefly ruled Egypt in the seventh century BC, as the Twenty-fifth Dynasty,[3] and indeed the Bronze Age Kerma kingdom, centred at old Kerma, of the third–second millennia BC.[4] Drawing on such material, this paper will revisit some general issues concerning our conceptualisation of the Meroitic kingdom, its sources of social and political power, and their material manifestations. Some suggestions will also be offered on some of the more noteworthy features of its settlement landscapes, and especially its 'urban' centres, which seem likely to be closely linked to the state and disappeared with it in the third–fourth centuries AD. Rather than considering these 'settlement patterns' as politically neutral elements it will be suggested that they should be understood as deeply imbued with political intent. How such sites were created and what purposes they may have served will be considered; not least as centres of production, and in turn central to the creation of a Meroitic imperial culture.[5] Comparisons can be made with examples from the Meroitic period of the features of later kingdoms such as the Sultanate of Sinnar.[6] There are also many points of comparison in some of the more recent state-generated landscapes of West African states,[7] suggesting that there may be much here for fruitful discussion of the features of states in and around the Sahara.

In the Middle Nile Basin, as across most of the continent,[8] the early history of urbanism remains poorly understood. Settlement has remained relatively dispersed, with a non-urban character into recent times,[9]

[3] Pope 2014. [4] Bonnet and Valbelle 2014.

[5] In view of the huge scale of the Meroitic state, its reach extending from the Gezira region south of Khartoum to the Egyptian frontier in the north (>1,500 km of the Nile valley and its hinterlands), its characterisation as 'imperial' is perhaps justified, not least in its likely incorporation of many and varied populations.

[6] Spaulding 1985. [7] For example, MacDonald and Camara 2012.

[8] For example, Anderson and Rathbone 2000. [9] Lebon 1965.

although with some possible early exceptions – potentially the earliest urban centres in Sub-Saharan Africa. Historically, while few in number and perhaps more enigmatic than we commonly allow, these are likely to have had a disproportionate significance as foci of political and economic activity. Archaeology has begun to explore a number of these, ranging from Bronze Age Kerma to the Medieval metropolises of Dongola and Soba, near the confluence of the Niles.[10] Such work has revealed parts of what may be quite extensive townscapes, and some of our most detailed information for early urban sites anywhere on the continent.

However, if there do seem to have been some remarkably early urban developments in the region, our understanding of their character remains uncertain. As recent research in West Africa has suggested,[11] urban developments may take many forms, although defining the 'urban' continues to present many challenges, beyond the formal definition of any large nucleated settlement as a 'town'. In the Middle Nile, what we call urban may well have been highly variable in both form and function(s). If we are indeed finding early urban forms here, or in other parts of Sub-Saharan (or Saharan) Africa, their particular interest would seem to lie in understanding the roles they served. Many may have been centres of religious and ritual power, albeit often closely linked to political authority. Others may have developed as centres of trade and economic activity. In historical times, as is also the case in West Africa, such trading towns may have been deliberately set apart from political centres. Their histories may be very sensitive to many external factors, not least those that may determine shifting caravan routes. Those that were political foci were commonly also centres of consumption and display, focused on royal palaces. Contemporary accounts, such as Nachtigal's of more recent royal centres (El-Fasher in north Darfur), may be instructive in highlighting the structuring principles underlying the creation of such urban centres.[12] Unlike some other parts of Sub-Saharan Africa,[13] fortified towns are not commonly encountered in the Middle Nile. As is also more widely encountered, towns and their inhabitants may have been, or have become culturally distinct from, their surrounding countryside. They may have been the homes of immigrants and traders, of elites speaking foreign languages, but also places of moral danger of many kinds, not least in the genesis of new kinds of urban populations, with new identities. In more recent histories of the Sudanese Middle Nile, the 'Sudani' identity is

[10] On Dongola – Jakobielski and Scholz 2001; Soba – Welsby 1998; Welsby and Daniels 1991.
[11] McIntosh and McIntosh 1993. [12] Nachtigal 1971, 259 and following.
[13] See for example Magnavita, Chapter 15, this volume.

strongly associated with urban living. In such terms urban centres have the potential to play formative roles in the creation of new identities, as well as being places of hardship and vulnerability.[14]

Their histories were also dynamic. In the Middle Nile, few of the early urban experiments established deep roots and most disappeared without trace; few modern Sudanese towns can claim an urban ancestry of more than a few centuries. Most originated in initiatives of the Turco-Egyptian government in the nineteenth century and the *zariba* (fortified camps) of traders and slavers,[15] which were further developed by the Anglo-Egyptian Condominium government of the twentieth century. The most prominent contribution was of course the foundation and development of Khartoum in the 1830s, which acquired a population of perhaps 30,000 by the mid-nineteenth century. This population was formed around, and to a considerable degree serviced the new government and a substantial military garrison – sometimes in the order of 10,000 troops. With many and varied contemporary accounts we may draw on, one persistent and recurrent theme which we might discuss concerns the very real challenges of densely populated urban living in tropical environments, with conditions being particularly difficult in the rainy season. At Khartoum, disease (typhus) outbreaks soon decimated the population in the 1860s; malaria was also a major and recurrent problem. Interesting insights can be gained in the early reports of the Wellcome Research Laboratories in Khartoum (1908) which were greatly concerned with sanitation and the threat of malaria, in attempts to 'improve' the Khartoum environment. While such issues need not be pursued here, we should not underestimate the challenges of sustaining urban populations.[16] With their many and varied functions, we may consider that our urban centres were 'consumers of people'. This raises interesting questions about the composition of their populations, which may return us to more fundamental questions concerning the sources and exercise of state power in the Meroitic world.

Notwithstanding the absence of many forms of data that we would wish to have, some of the more pertinent questions we might ask in the Middle Nile, and indeed elsewhere, might include: 'Why would one live in a town?' or indeed 'Would one choose to live in a town?' Whatever the perceived merits of *urbanitas* amongst some ancient populations in some parts of the Mediterranean, these were not necessarily self-evident and universal

[14] See Leonardi 2013, 156. [15] Lane and Johnson 2009.

[16] We seem, however, to remain poorly equipped to establish even the most basic demographic parameters for our research, building on early work in this field (for example, Fyfe and McMaster 1981).

truths. It need not be something that should be aspired to or, as we have been reminded in Mediterranean contexts, 'an accolade to be awarded'.[17] Within the broad geographical region we are dealing with there may have been strong reasons for *not* living in towns, while many of those who did live in towns might have been viewed as undesirable for varied reasons. In the Meroitic Middle Nile, it may not overstate the case that urban spaces were where the aspirations of an imperialistic state confronted the rather different values, desires, and indeed the objections of its subjects.[18]

Urban Forms before Meroe

Kerma

While this chapter will focus mainly on the Meroitic period of the later first millennium BC to the early first millennium AD, it may be useful to contextualise this to some extent in relation to earlier manifestations of possible urban forms in the Middle Nile. Much of this work has only been recently published. The site of Kerma is of some interest as, over more than a millennium, it developed as a major settlement agglomeration (Fig. 9.1), apparently associated with what grew to be a massive necropolis. This was set within a regional landscape of dispersed farmsteads and a rich environment of braided river channels that annually flooded a wide alluvial plain. Over the long term, such a site clearly has particular significance in potentially establishing a model for urban living in the Middle Nile. However, it has some curious features. For example, it can be noted that it did not necessarily originate as a specifically political centre. It would seem its centre, from an early date, was a temple, manifested in its latest forms as a massive mudbrick monument (Fig. 9.2).[19]

While it seems reasonably clear that by the mid-second millennium BC forms of kingship with a strong military capability had developed at Kerma, and indeed were to pose significant challenges to Pharaonic Egypt, it is far less certain that Kerma had necessarily been the seat of kings in earlier centuries. It was not obviously dominated by great palaces, while the rare external historical sources hint at the existence of a number

[17] Osborne 2005, 7.

[18] For example, Scott 1998. Such issues are not unrelated to current debates about African urbanisation and their perceived benefits, or otherwise (Potts 2012).

[19] Its survival across 4,000 years, until today, also makes it one of the most remarkable ancient monuments of Sub-Saharan Africa.

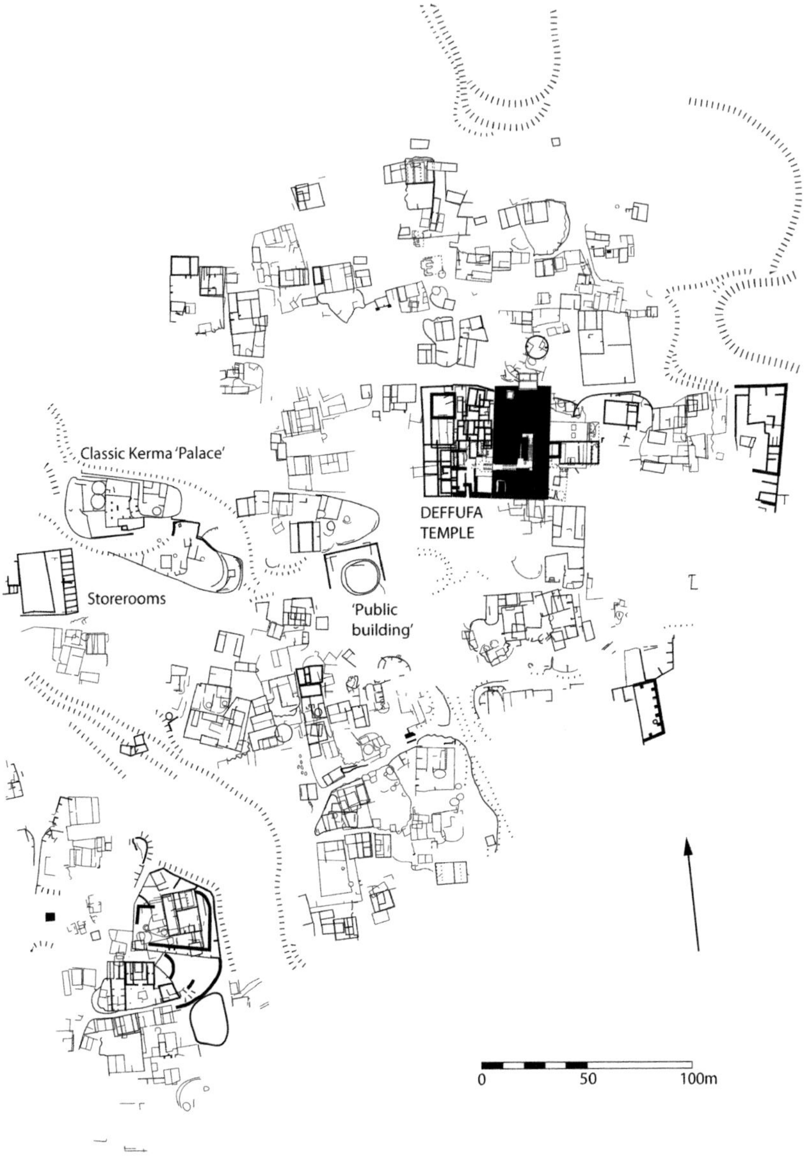

Figure 9.1. Plan of Kerma 'town' *c.*2300–1450 BC (after Bonnet and Valbelle 2014).

of Kushite polities in earlier centuries.[20] The manifestations of what we perceive as royal power in the late phases of the Classic Kerma period (*c.*1750–1450 BC), are also suggestive of quite novel forms of kingship

[20] Edwards 2004, 78–79.

Figure 9.2. Massive mudbrick temple, *c.*2000 BC – the 'Defuffa' – in the centre of Kerma.

developing in that period, associated with what may have been a new warrior elite.[21] On present evidence, the settlement at Kerma is also perhaps most remarkable for its uniqueness. If this was an early experiment in urban living, it did not catch on. However, in relation to African traditions of kingship in which ritual and the religious are often highly developed,[22] it may not be surprising to find such kingship – if such it was – developing at a religious centre. Its focal role may in turn provide a basis for the longer-term development of shared 'Kerma' cultural forms over large areas of what is now northern Sudan. It is worth bearing in mind that researchers have yet to move beyond potentially rather teleological approaches to the history of Kerma, or indeed to attempt to disentangle Kerma the place, the culture and potentially complex and dynamic political structures.

Temple-Towns of the New Kingdom Occupation

Following the conquest of Kerma *c.*1450 BC by the revived and expansive New Kingdom Egyptian state, the old townsite seems to have been destroyed. The locale seems however to have been maintained as a significant centre through the construction of a number of temples and associated buildings just to the north, on a site previously occupied by a series of Kerma/Kushite monuments. Research has focused mainly on the

[21] Hafsaas-Tsakos 2013. The most striking are perhaps the massive royal tumulus burials, which incorporated large numbers of human sacrifices, as well as numerous later secondary burials (O'Connor 2013).

[22] For example, Mair 1977, Chapter 2.

series of temples built by a succession of New Kingdom pharaohs. While these temples were apparently enclosed, whether there was ever an attempt to establish a more permanent Egyptian settlement at the site remains less certain.[23] Clearer manifestations of the Egyptian colonial presence and their own distinctive urban forms (commonly described as temple-towns) are found further north, beyond the Third Cataract. This may well have been the southern limit of Egyptian vice-regal administration during the New Kingdom occupation of Nubia (*c.*1450–1150 BC). Notwithstanding their urban label, it may be useful to draw attention to some of their specialised characteristics. In addition to housing a number of Egyptian officials, there is a growing body of evidence that they also had direct links to gold-mining enterprises in their vicinity. As such, it seems likely that they also housed the workforce for these enterprises, in regimented buildings, along with their workshops.[24] In the case of Sesibi (Fig. 9.3), the domestic (as opposed to temple) component extended to *c.*2 ha.[25] Amara West,[26] a new foundation established several generations later is also suggestive, with an initial formal layout including large magazines/storehouses, but which was then reconstructed with new residential layouts. It seems likely that these modifications reflect the agency of its inhabitants finding more appropriate ways of living in what may have been quite trying circumstances. Already by that period, climatic deterioration was probably becoming a significant factor, with increasingly mobile Saharan sands infiltrating and ultimately overwhelming the settlement.

The small scale of these temple-towns suggests they had relatively modest populations, but including both Egyptian and Nubian material elements, suggestive of potentially complex colonial interactions and entanglements. Their role as seats of colonial governance seem clear, while also having more specific productive functions, notably in the higher level management of Nubian gold extraction. What still remains uncertain is how they sat in the wider landscape, and the extent to which they interacted with or drew in surrounding populations. An enduring issue

[23] The status of other Egyptian temples, for example at Kawa some 55 km to the south, and at the sacred mountain of Jebel Barkal, also remains unclear. We see perhaps the appropriation of elements of sacred landscape (Barkal) as well as the imposition of an alien constructed landscape framed around Egyptian temples.

[24] Comparisons may perhaps be drawn with dense low-status housing in the Amarna 'workmen's village' – Kemp 1987.

[25] Such a size might be compared with a Roman auxiliary fort. The scale is suggestive of populations in the 100s rather than 1,000s.

[26] Spencer 2012, Spencer *et al.* 2012.

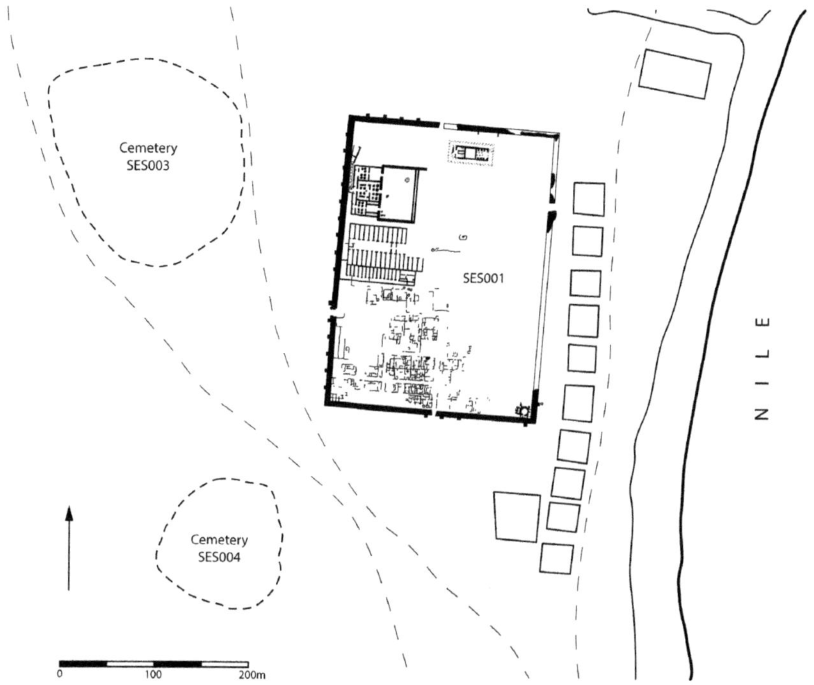

Figure 9.3. Plan of colonial Egyptian 'temple-town' of Sesibi, combining substantial temple complex and residential quarter.

of the New Kingdom colonial period in Nubia is the apparent decline of overall population levels over several centuries of Egyptian rule.[27] Since the Egyptian presence was focused on the (increasingly) arid northern parts of Nubia, this may not be unconnected with ongoing desiccation, as the rains retreated southwards.[28] The nature of the Egyptian colonial presence may also be a factor that contributed to this rural depopulation. For example, it seems likely that population dispersal rather than nucleation would offer better opportunities in such increasingly challenging environmental conditions. It may be noted that these northern regions only saw a significant revival of rural settlement during the first millennium AD, which was made possible by the introduction of the new irrigation technology of the *saqia* waterwheel (which represented an advance in the capability of water-lifting equipment over the balance well or Archimedes screw).

[27] Säve-Söderbergh and Troy 1991, 10–13.

[28] One result was a growing threat from increasingly mobile sand on the west bank of the Nile, known to have posed a significant threat in some areas. It may also be noted that it remains far from clear as to what extent date cultivation (an essential component of later Nubian farming communities) was established in this area during this period.

The Napatan Period

With the revival of a Kushite state in the early first millennium BC, new political and religious centres emerged in the Twenty-fifth Dynasty and Napatan period. Their urban components still remained poorly defined, although in the period of Egyptian rule, the Kushite kings would have been exposed to what may have been very different Egyptian forms of living. We may differentiate between royal centres such as Sanam (a palace-town?) and already ancient religious foci such as the Holy Mountain of Barkal, across the river, where a series of royal palaces were added to a temple complex. Recent work at Sanam has clarified the nature of its vast store-rooms (the 'Treasury', 267 × 68 m) and associated structures in what is presumed to have been the primary royal centre of the eighth–sixth centuries BC.[29] Extraordinary finds point to it serving as a major centre for the accumulation of raw materials, local and exotically rare, consumables such as imported wines, as well as the production of an array of prestigious as well as more mundane artefacts. The massive scale of this royal 'Treasury' cannot be over-emphasised. A religious dimension to this evidence of material accumulation and manufacture has recently been highlighted.[30] Pope's largely textual studies emphasise how Napatan governance remained focused on a series of six (?) palaces, each perhaps serving distinct territories.[31] As he also notes, there appears to be an absence of an obviously hierarchical articulation of major officials, which may in turn be suggestive of the character of royal claims on these territories. Ongoing excavations in and around the large settlement of this period at Kawa may throw further light on such centres. Here, hitherto unsuspected pyramid burials of an impressive size have been identified.[32] Kawa itself seems to have been an extended unenclosed linear river-bank site exploiting a hinterland that was watered by seasonally flooding braided river channels.

On current evidence, the urban centres we can identify in the earlier first millennium BC seem likely to have been based on a framework of palace centres, at that time still focused on the Dongola Reach. While some Napatan presence evidently extended much further south, it remains far from certain as to whether this was framed around major settlements. No Napatan towns seem to have been fortified, although a large fortress-like structure at Qala Abu Ahmed has recently been explored *c.*110 km from the Nile along the Wadi Howar, a major route running towards Darfur.[33]

[29] Vincentelli 2007; 2011. [30] Pope 2014. [31] Pope 2014, 150. [32] Welsby 2014.
[33] Fiedler and Jesse 2012; Jesse 2013.

Finds there of Greek *lekythoi* (a narrow jug used for storing oil) and glass vessels raise interesting new questions about the possible role of this site in trade between the Nile and the Darfur region during this period. North of the Dongola Reach, on the river route to Egypt, some more ancient sites seem to have been reoccupied as way-stations. That in this period the state was contending with substantial and mobile pastoral populations in the hinterlands away from the Nile should be envisaged. The presence of another fortified site (not dissimilar to that at Qala Abu Ahmed) at Fura Wells, a major water point in the central Baiyuda Desert, could perhaps be evidence for an early (Napatan) state presence reaching out into this hinterland. Control of permanent water supplies of course remains one key strategy for imposing state control over more mobile potential subjects.

The Meroitic Kingdom

The later centuries of the first millennium BC saw a major restructuring of the Kushite state, traditionally associated with a shift in royal cemeteries southwards to Meroe. This initiated a distinct Meroitic kingdom in the Middle Nile which persisted to the third–fourth centuries AD (Fig. 9.4). Notwithstanding longstanding debates about the significance of this perceived southwards shift, several features distinguish this period that bring into focus something of the structure of what became a massive kingdom (perhaps empire?) whose reach extended from the southern margins of Egypt to somewhere south of the confluence of the Niles. Within this huge region, territorial cores emerged and what are generally conceived of as Meroitic urban centres seem to have played a crucial role. These centres were focused on a relatively small region of the east Nile bank with a hinterland extending to the south-east, towards an area of greater rainfall and the grazing lands it supported. Bounded by the seasonal Atbara river on its north-east side, this may be envisaged as a core territory of perhaps 10,000–15,000 km^2, marked by the presence of a number of mudbrick and stone-built urban centres as well as other monuments. This may be contrasted with territories further north (the core territory of the Napatan state in the early part of the millennium) in which permanent settlements were confined to the river. The large hinterland of what is now the Baiyuda desert seems to have lacked a state presence beyond a handful of stations along the main routes traversing it and at water points. The almost continuous spreads of burial cairns along the west bank of the Nile

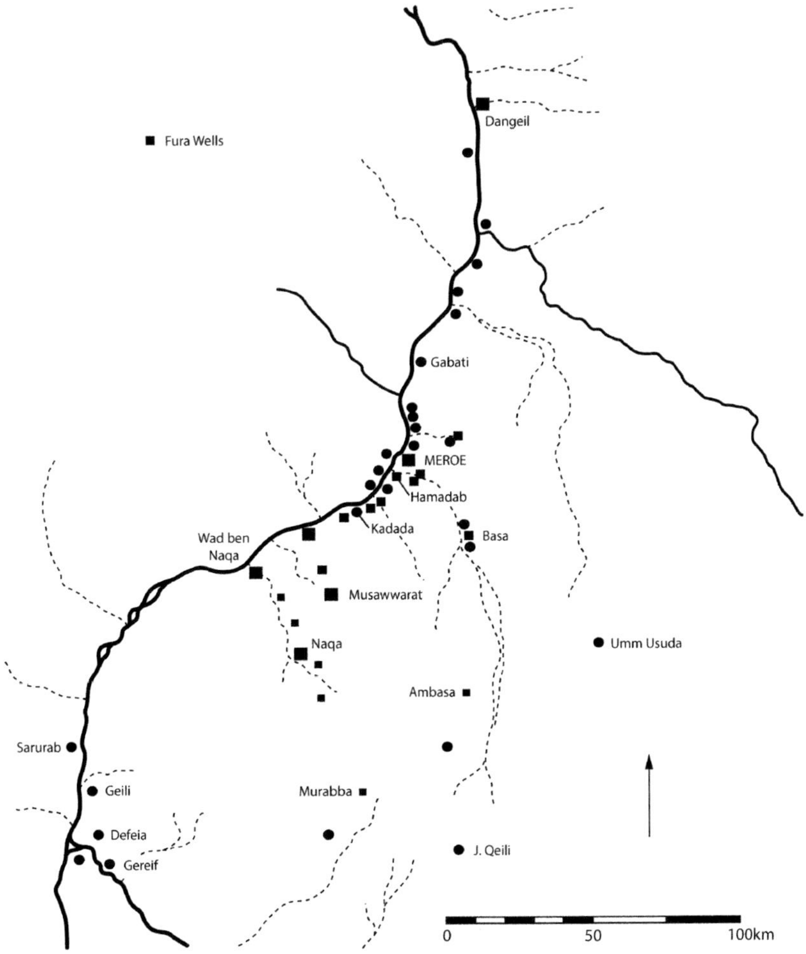

Figure 9.4. General map of central Meroitic territories.

would seem to relate to predominantly pastoral populations grounded in the Baiyuda, but whose relationship to the Meroitic state would seem to have been very different from those with populations of the Western Butana.

We have little hard evidence concerning the core Meroitic region prior to the fourth–third centuries BC. In the first millennium BC this region seems likely to have received significantly greater and more reliable rainfall than in more recent centuries. Under such circumstances the non-riverine areas will have had great potential both for rain-fed cultivation and collecting, as well as grazing. Notwithstanding the considerable potential for riverside farming, it would perhaps be premature to assume that this was necessarily the more preferable or productive form of exploitation. The risks inherent in the unpredictable Nile floods were not insignificant, while the relatively late development of domesticated tropical crops in the region may reflect deeper-seated pastoral preferences. However we might expect that populations choose to exploit both riverine areas as well as the interior. We can be reasonably sure that prior to the Meroitic period, such exploitation was not based around large nucleated settlements. Archaeological traces of earlier settlement in the region that was to become the Meroitic heartlands remain, to date, elusive, notwithstanding some recent detailed survey work close to Meroe.[34]

In this context, as in many other parts of the continent where we may also confidently assume relatively low population densities combined with relatively abundant productive land, it seems likely that the scarcity of people and a need to establish control of people, was of crucial importance to Meroitic state building. This was one of several ways in which state formation in the Middle Nile followed a quite different course from the Egyptian Lower Nile.[35] Here we might also emphasise the lack of environmental constraints which may circumscribe populations, a crucial and fundamental difference from both the Egyptian Lower Nile, and Saharan oases. As in other savannah regions 'wealth and power in men rather than acres' was crucial, while 'those who exercised authority were people-owners rather than landowners'.[36]

Such imperatives may in turn be related both to Meroitic perceptions of identity as well as throwing light on key aspects of rulership. Such perceptions may be traced back through external historical references to the 'Noba' (Nubians), though this term has traditionally been interpreted as an ethnic designation. However, recent work suggests that some rather different understandings of the 'Noba' are possible, which relate to fundamental principles of the Meroitic state. Briefly stated, the 'Nob' appear in Meroitic texts as defeated and subjugated peoples; they may be represented as bound prisoners (one, identified as 'a king of the Noba'), as well as in lists of slaughtered enemies.[37] However, rather than as a specific ethnic identifier, the term in fact seems to serve as a generic and pejorative identifier, identifying slaves. If we may seek a hypothetical etymology for Meroitic 'Nob' (slaves/Nubians) this may lie in a term meaning something like 'men of the land', suggesting a derogatory term for agriculturalists, who were in turn potential slaves. In this context, the significance of such an

[34] Wolf 2015. [35] Edwards 1996, 14–15. [36] Hopkins 1973, 26. [37] Rilly 2008, 216–17.

understanding is that the term is an effective reflection of practical power relations, rather than ethnic designations.[38]

If this was a reality of the Meroitic period, this sits well within the longer-term history of the region, where just such designations are a familiar presence within the traditions of later kingdoms of the Middle Nile, where the idioms of slavery and enslavement have remained central to the structuring of social and political relations.[39] The 'Nuba' of the medieval Arab texts, and indeed more recent usages maintain almost exactly these connotations of the Meroitic usage. The work of Spaulding and Kapteijns in particular,[40] has argued for the persistence of social structures 'composed almost exclusively of a landowning elite, called in later times the *hukkam* (those who rule)', and subject commoners. Communities of subjects might be obliged to 'buy peace from the government with precious goods, to seize neighbours as captives at tax times, or to endure government reprisals in the form of slave-collecting raids'.[41] When discussing notions of a 'Sudanic serfdom' we are reminded of the narrowness of the line dividing uncooperative subjects from slavery; the threat of enslavement remained the essential inducement to 'free' subjects to continue to serve their masters. Enslavement was the fate visited on whoever failed in their obligations to those who ruled; the terminology of slaves is in fact the natural idiom in which power relations would be expressed. I suggest that such a perspective can help us understand the relationship of the Meroitic state to all its subjects. Where this may be most obvious is in dealing with its more peripheral subjects and the familiar pattern of extracting resources from the peripheries. Such a relationship may also be relevant in its heartlands, where a direct state presence was established and constructed around a framework of urban centres.

Meroitic Urbanism?

Meroe

The origins of Meroe itself still remain obscure, although the location may have been occupied early in the first millennium BC, if not before.[42] It should be noted that there is no textual reference to a major centre at this site from the period of the Twenty-fifth Dynasty, though a Napatan

[38] Early in the first millennium BCE we find donations of 'landworkers' to temple establishments recorded in (Egyptian language) royal texts – Pope 2014, 120.

[39] Kopytoff and Miers 1977. [40] Kapteijns and Spaulding 2005; Spaulding and Kapteijns 2002.

[41] Spaulding 2006; Spaulding and Kapteijns 2002, 46–47.

[42] See Pope 2014 for a recent overview.

presence in the region is evident in the following centuries to the mid-first millennium BC.[43] Jeremy Pope has characterised this as 'a gradual annexation of the Meroe region'.[44] The process by which this region was integrated into the larger state may also be seen as fundamentally transformative. The urban centres would seem likely to have been fundamental to such transformations, creating new state-generated landscapes.[45]

At Meroe itself, the beginning of the Meroitic period (*c.*350 BC) does seem to have witnessed major building episodes. Perhaps the most prominent of these was the construction of a massive rectilinear enclosure, whose heavy masonry walls surrounded an area of *c.*8 ha (Fig. 9.5). Its construction seems to mark a new development in defining a nucleated core to the settlement. Traditionally referred to as the 'Royal City', it certainly included several palatial buildings, and notwithstanding the caution that must be exercised in assuming the existence of a single capital, Meroe would seem marked out as a centre with some unique qualities. Its construction may have taken place at about the same time as that of a major new Amun temple against its east side, which was extended over the next few centuries.[46] A series of smaller shrines were later built to the east of its entrance, facing on to a processional way, oriented like most temples on the winter solstice, replacing earlier domestic structures in that area.

The more general character of Meroe the town remains unclear. To the north-east of the enclosure was a large settlement mound covering *c.*10 ha, with a second large mound (3–4 ha) to the south. Outlying features include a temple complex (the 'Isis temple') to the north, as well as an area of pottery kilns and a large temple complex with a *hafir* (known to earlier generations as the 'Sun Temple') to the south-east of the town. Only small areas of the northern settlement have been excavated, revealing deep stratified deposits, up to 10 m thick; as noted above, these potentially date back to the early first millennium BC. In the absence of widespread open-area excavations, we as yet have very little idea about the character of such areas as only small parts of buildings have been exposed. It still remains to be demonstrated that the mounds represent the remains of nucleated domestic settlement that we would conventionally expect for an urban area. Parts of the north mound were certainly used for other industrial activities, as workshops were found there for smelting and

[43] Pope 2014, 27–31; Wolf 2015. [44] Pope 2014, 33.
[45] These were 'political landscapes', in the sense explored by Smith 2003. [46] Török 1997.

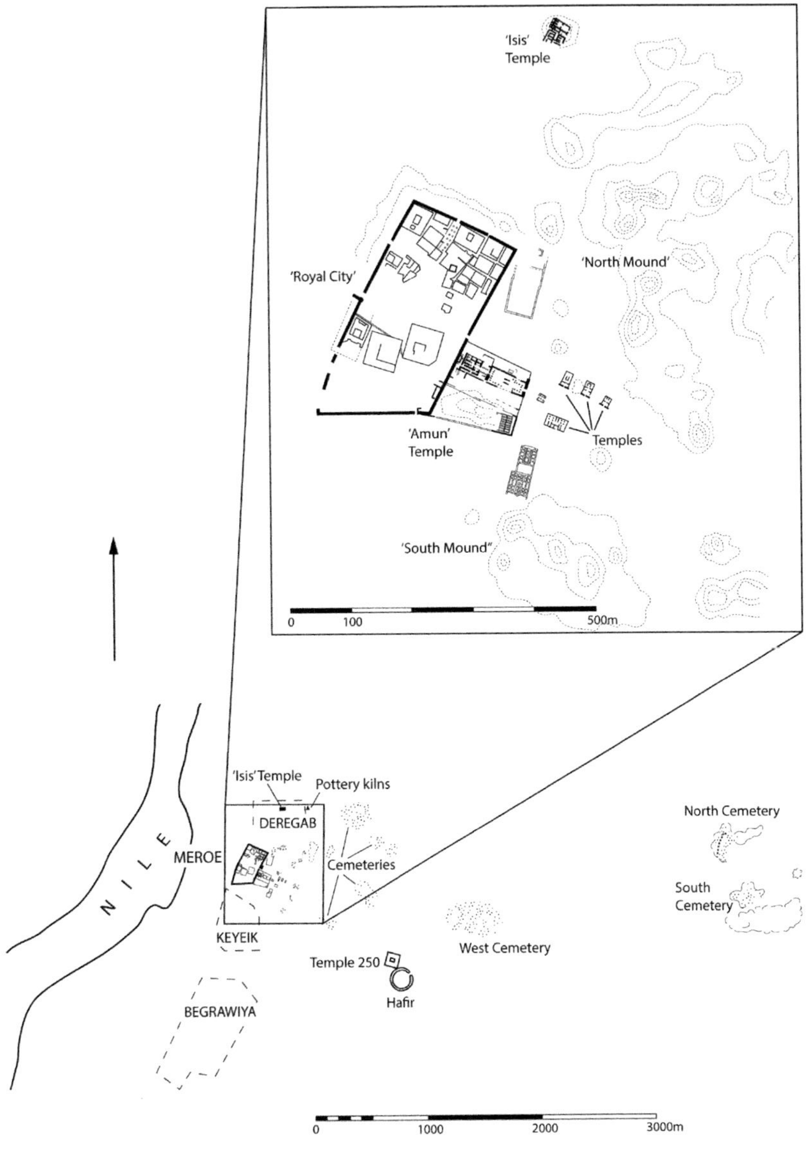

Figure 9.5. Meroe 'royal city' and environs.

forging iron. Cotton textile manufacture (evidenced in abundant spindle whorls) is also likely to have been important. Cloth is likely to have been a very significant manufacture, both as a status marker and perhaps a medium of exchange,[47] as in later periods.[48]

47 Edwards 2004, 170.

48 One of the identities of elites in later periods may be as the 'clothes-wearing people' – Spaulding 1985, 78–83.

Such productive activities also required considerable resource inputs. This must be considered as part of wider questions concerning how urban living/activities relate to a much wider hinterland and interlinking supply networks. Urban-rural linkages and interdependence are perhaps central to any model we can suggest for Meroe and other Meroitic urban centres. Meroitic ironworking is likely to be of particular importance here, requiring a range of key raw materials (for example, ores and charcoal), in turn requiring significant labour inputs. This iron industry has attracted considerable attention since the first excavations at Meroe,[49] and is now the subject of renewed interest.[50] The scale of production appears to have been considerable,[51] demanding significant inputs of various resources, with the supply of wood/charcoal in particular probably generating significant environmental impacts,[52] although recent work suggests that the volume of production may have been more modest than once supposed.[53]

Many uncertainties still surround the nature of the urban centre at Meroe. Was it primarily a religious centre, or a palace-city inhabited by royal households and their attendants? To what extent did it attract a broader population base with its own independent dynamics? The size of its population remains a matter of speculation, although it is worth bearing in mind that the total area of the site is rather less than that of the two modern villages (a few hundred households) which adjoin the archaeological site.

Other Meroitic Urban Centres

Meroe was clearly not an isolated phenomenon. Several similar large sites, often combining the presence of palatial structures with temples, are known to lie both to the south and north (Fig. 9.6).[54] Some of these are again of considerable size, covering *c.*10–15 ha, including both official, religious and domestic quarters. Most are known mainly from finds of architectural elements and none have as yet been investigated in any detail. However, survey and test-excavation at a number of these have in recent years begun to provide better definition of their character.

Wad ben Naqa is the southernmost yet identified, *c.*80 km upriver from Meroe. The main palace, measuring 61 m square, would seem to have been constructed by Queen Amanishakheto, currently dated to the late first

49 For example, Garstang *et al.* 1911, 55; Shinnie 1985; Shinnie and Kense 1982.
50 Humphris 2014; Rehren 2001. 51 Haaland 1985; Tylecote 1982. 52 Haaland 1985.
53 Humphris 2014, 128. 54 Baud 2011, 211–24; Lenoble 2008.

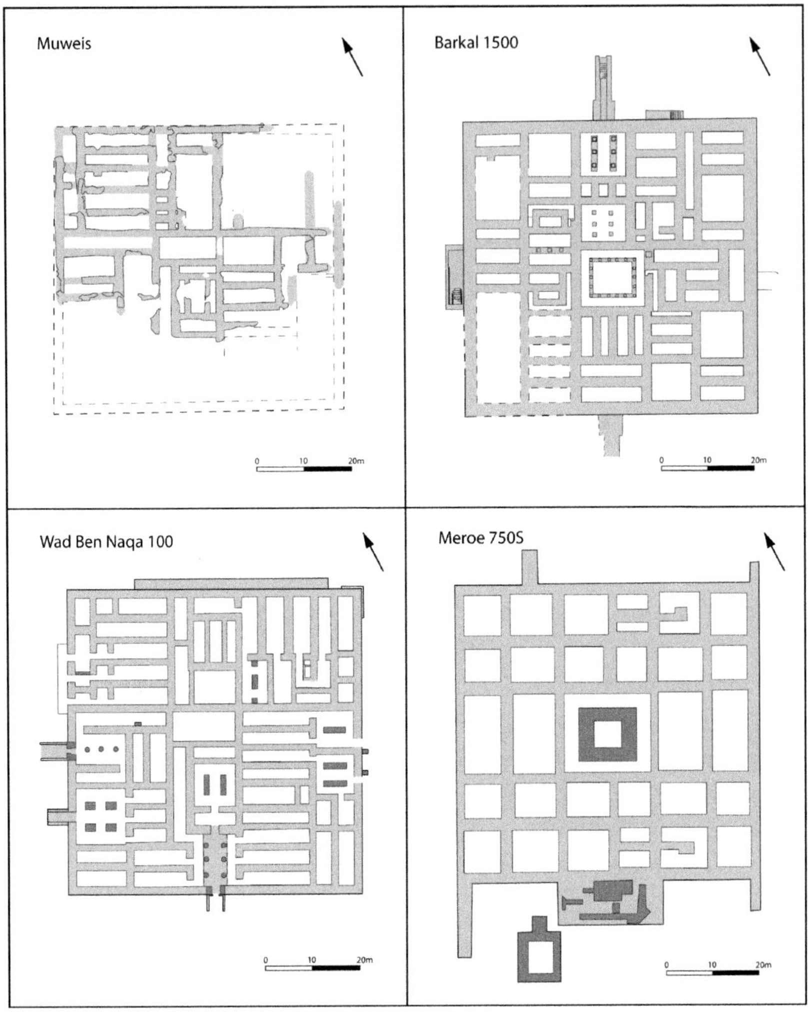

Figure 9.6. Examples of regularly designed 'palace' structures, with examples from Meroe, Muweis and Wad ben Naqa in the Meroitic riverine heartlands, as well as from the religious centre of Jebel Barkal (after Maillot 2014).

century BC, or early first century AD. Here, as in other examples, the surviving ground floor provided both storerooms and a casemate foundation for a raised upper storey, now lost apart from architectural fragments. How long this survived remains unclear but elements seem to have been reused in the construction of a temple and adjoining storerooms in the second–third centuries.[55] The purpose of a large and, to-date, unique

[55] Onderka and Vrtal 2014, 147.

circular brick building remains unknown. Early speculations suggested it might be a granary, but a religious function has also been suggested.[56] Indirect evidence for the role of this, and other urban sites, in the accumulation, storage and redistribution of goods is found in a range of mud-sealings. Comparisons may be drawn with other archaic administrative systems, operating without more complex written accounting systems,[57] albeit coexisting with some use of written accounts (preserved in ostraca). The context and character of such sealings may also support a case that it was palaces, rather than temples which played central roles in economic administration.[58]

Muweis, *c.*30 km from Wad ben Naqa had at its core another palatial building of very similar dimensions and plan to that at Wad ben Naqa, a temple complex, and two associated settlement areas, at least one with industrial areas.[59] While early results suggest a history spanning several centuries, major building episodes are identifiable at the start of the first century AD and abandonment of the palatial building by perhaps the mid-third century, soon followed by robbing for reuse of building materials.[60] Finds of mud-sealings again indicate some of the administrative features of the palace.[61] Another temple and palace complex at El Hassa-Damboya displays a similar combination of a substantial temple, with one or more palatial structures set within a substantially larger settlement.[62] Preliminary investigations here beyond the temple have raised the possibility of a rather larger settlement of more ephemeral post-built structures around the more formal brick buildings. This is, as yet, a still poorly documented aspect of Meroitic settlements.

While there are few smaller-scale settlements yet known, there are some sites with both temples and substantial brick-built architecture (although less impressive than palatial buildings described above). One such complex is located within 10 km of Meroe near the mouth of the Wadi Hawad drainage at Abu Erteila-Awlib. Initial excavations suggest the presence of a temple, 'official' structures and a *hafir* water reservoir.[63] This is very reminiscent of the arrangement of the so-called 'Sun Temple', 'Priest House' and *hafir* just south-east of Meroe. The locations of a number of other centres may be suggested, potentially as far north as Dangeil, the site of a large royal temple, although, as yet with no associated palace or urban centre.

[56] Onderka and Vrtal 2014, 153–55. [57] Vincentelli 1993, 41. [58] Edwards 1996, 26.
[59] Baud 2008; 2014; Maillot 2014; 2015; 2016. [60] Baud 2014, 771. [61] Baud 2011, 244–45.
[62] Lenoble and Rondot 2003. [63] Borkowski and Paner 2005.

Figure 9.7. Map of planned enclosed settlement and later 'suburbs' to the south, with pottery kilns and iron-working slag heaps (after Wolf *et al.* 2014, Fig.2).

Hamadab – A Planned Settlement

Another rather different kind of settlement is found closer to Meroe at Hamadab located only *c.*3 km south of the 'royal city' (Fig. 9.7). Some unusual features provide further suggestive data relating to its foundation. With a number of distinctive features, it is our most convincing example of an urban space. It was clearly planned and was enclosed (I will avoid the term fortified), *c.*110 m square, with a small temple on a central axis.[64] The provision of a small (20 m square) tower-house in the south-east corner of the site is also an otherwise unique feature, similar in construction to, but much less substantial than, the large palaces encountered elsewhere. The enclosed and planned settlement appears to date to the first century BC. In the early centuries AD this planned structure was substantially reshaped, however, with the abandonment (and robbing) of the enclosure wall and outward spread into substantial 'suburbs'. As such it may be differentiated on a number of counts from other known urban centres of the Meroitic heartlands, lacking both a large palace core, major temples, but also provided with a substantial, but soon superseded enclosure wall. Like other urban centres the site was engaged in ceramic and textile production, with direct archaeobotanical evidence for cotton as well as finds of spindle whorls and loomweights.[65] Long recognised as the site of major iron-working, recent work suggests that this may largely be a feature of the later, or indeed post-Meroitic period, raising a number of interesting issues concerning its relationship with Meroe and its iron-workers.[66] Its specific origins are perhaps suggested in two Meroitic stele of Queen Amanirenas and Akinidad associated with the central temple. Rilly's restudy of these notes explicit reference to 'Tameya prisoners' and may well relate to military campaigns, and indeed the acquisition of 'non-African' captives. While we must await a full presentation of these texts, many features of the site seem suggestive of an enclosed settlement (walls to keep people in as much as out?) including a range of royal craft-workers (see further discussion below).

The Western Butana

Unlike most of the centres spread along the Nile, two other major centres are known within the hinterland of Western Butana, an area that received considerable seasonal rainfall and that had good agricultural and grazing potential along major drainages. It is likely, as is the case in more recent periods, that these drainages were actively managed with forms of water-harvesting techniques. However, most Meroitic settlement within this region seemingly relied on more ephemeral and mobile architectural forms, appropriate to seasonal cultivation and grazing. Permanent centres with mudbrick and stone architecture are much rarer. The two main centres, Mussawarat and Naqa, take very different forms.

[64] Wolf *et al.* 2014a; 2014b. [65] Fuller 2014, 173. [66] Humphris 2014.

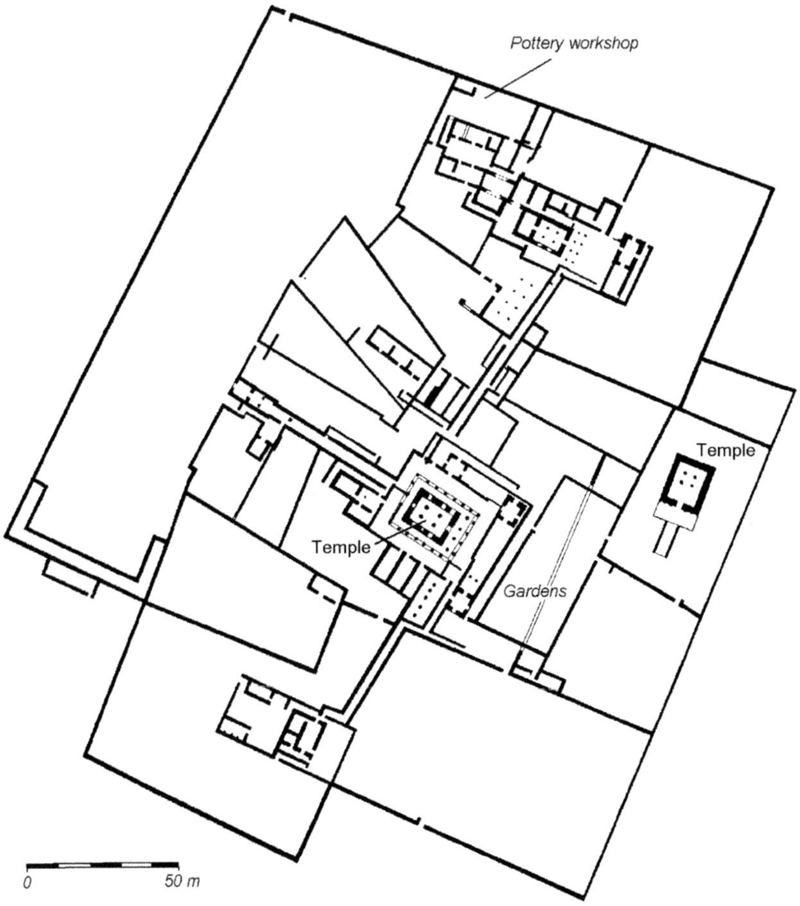

Figure 9.8. Musawwarat es Sofra – royal pilgrimage centre – a periodic royal centre?

Mussawarat, known to the Meroites as *Aborepe,* seems primarily to have served as a religious pilgrimage centre, notwithstanding a number of other, more or less imaginative, interpretations offered in the past (Fig. 9.8).[67] Within the 'Great Enclosure', there was a complex of interconnected temples, set in courtyards spread over 5.5 ha. At least some of the courtyards were irrigated gardens, laid out with trees, brought-in from the Nile; the pots of Nile silt in which they were planted were readily identifiable during excavation.[68] Indications of larger public spaces within the complex, the nature of its monuments,

[67] These include that the site might have been used for training elephants (Shinnie 1967) and that the complex may have been some form of 'animal garden' or hunting palace (Török 1997).

[68] Wolf 1999.

the many thousands of graffiti[69] and the large natural arena which surrounds the site would be consistent with its use as a periodic (pilgrimage?) centre. While the Meroitic monarchs were undoubtedly closely linked to the site, and may well have played a central role in whatever festivals or other events were enacted there, its very special status seems clear. A group of ancillary buildings, the 'Small Enclosure', had a more domestic character, with cooking and store-rooms, probably relating to the priests and other staff servicing the main complex.[70] A small pottery workshop was also located beside the north wall of the enclosure.[71]

By contrast, a quite substantial settlement grew up around a series of small temples located on a major wadi *c.*35 km from the Nile at Naqa, ancient *Tolkte* (Fig. 9.9). Occupying a very different savannah landscape than the riverine settlements, this site was located at the confluence of two large wadis. Best known for a series of temples, the larger settlement complex would seem to include several palatial structures and ancillary buildings. Naqa may also perhaps be the focus of a larger complex of smaller settlements, marked by a series of small temples; one such site lies *c.*5 km away on the west side of the wadi, at Nasb es Sami. It is set within large areas suitable for rain-fed agriculture, with managed grazing on its margins. This will in turn have required careful management of arable and pastoral exploitation, and of perennial water supplies, the latter likely to have been important in managing (and controlling) more mobile and pastoral parts of the population. Their reorientation towards arable production seems probable. The many wells and the *hafirs* (water reservoirs) in the region, some marked with Meroitic monuments will have formed part of this wider system of population management. Overall, within this region we might identify the larger productive hinterland which fed in to a series of regional urban centres on the Nile, including Meroe itself. Naqa appears unique as the largest settlement of the interior with major investment in brick and stone architecture.

The particular importance of the Western Butana hinterland would seem to lie in its role as a core productive territory, capable of supporting both arable and pastoral farming, on a larger scale, this may well be the only such area so directly controlled, and controllable, by the Meroitic state.[72] Only here is a state presence clearly manifested in the form of temples, often associated with *hafirs* and (a small

[69] MGA 2015. [70] Fitzenreiter *et al.* 1999. [71] Edwards 1999. [72] Edwards 1996, 25–26.

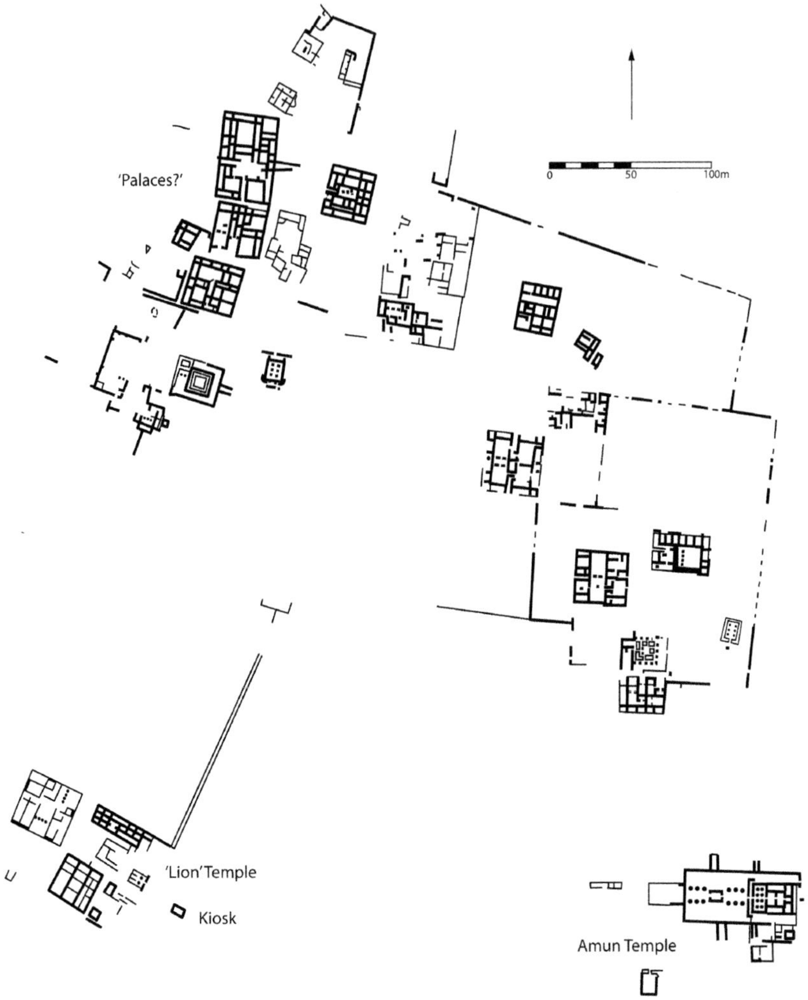

Figure 9.9. Hinterland settlement of Naqa – palace complexes and temples.

number) of more permanent settlements.[73] The investment in water supplies in turn seems likely to have also provided further opportunities for state controls, not least in the extraction of taxes/tribute.[74] The southern margins of this area may well be marked by the suggestive iconography of an otherwise unique Meroitic stele at Jebel Qeili, a point of transition beyond which lay the open plains of the Butana proper, which were perhaps beyond any direct state control (Fig. 9.10). Notwithstanding long-standing suggestions of an earlier Napatan

[73] Näser 2011. [74] Hinkel 1991.

Figure 9.10. Jebel Qeili inscription.

exploitation of the Western Butana, this state presence manifested in monumental structures (and perhaps a religious colonisation) may well be a phenomenon of the Meroitic period of the later first millennium BC.[75] That this reflects significant and fundamental changes in state organisation also seems likely. As in other contexts, the productions of territory are likely to have had profound practical implications for subject populations.[76]

The Roles of Meroitic Towns

While it has become usual to represent these temple-palace centres as towns it is already possible to recognise considerable variety in their

[75] Näser 2011. [76] Smith 2011, 423–24.

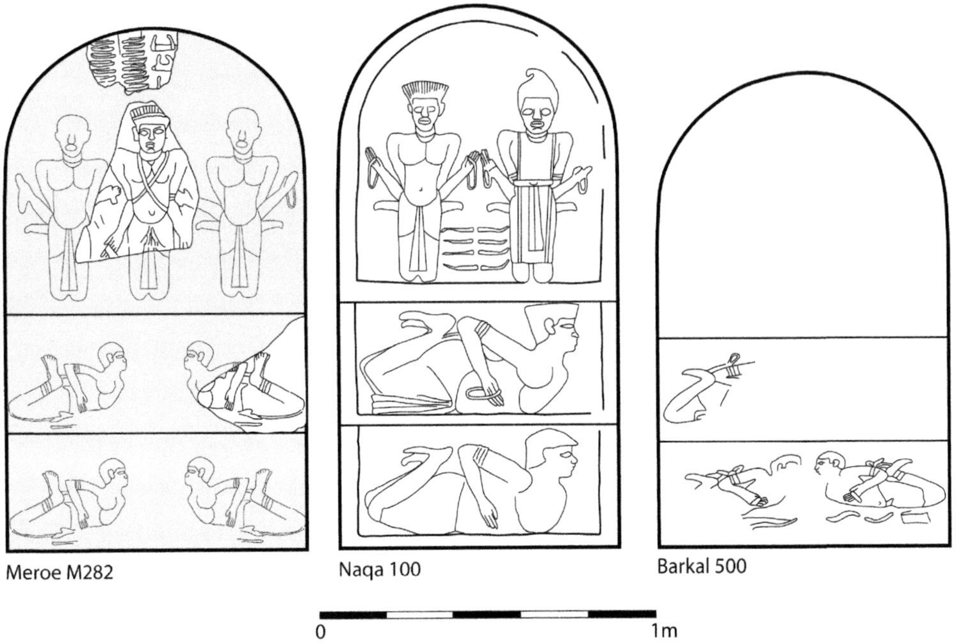

Figure 9.11. Examples of throne dais, emphasising subjugation – mainly fragmentary finds from Meroitic palace centres (based on Baud 2014).

forms and scale. The royal presence at many of these centres is emphasised in temple foundations of royal cults, as well as the larger palaces, although they are mostly associated with only a small number of particularly active monarchs in the later first century BC–first century AD. The royal presence is also very evident in other associated material such as throne daises (Fig. 9.11), which have been found at several of them. Representations of the subjugation of bound captives were a common feature of these royal thrones.[77] Such major riverine centres may be part of a wider network of nodal points of different kinds, including key watering points (wells, *hafirs*) and religious centres.

In general terms, what we currently characterise as urban centres seem likely to have performed crucial roles in the exercise of royal control of the heartlands of Meroe, forming its core productive territories. The nature of these centres, with their strong royal associations, emphasised in such displays of rulership, suggest they may be perceived very much as key nodes in a state-generated landscape, not dissimilar to examples known from elsewhere in Sub-Saharan Africa in more recent centuries.[78] Such

[77] Baud 2014, 775–78, figure 8. [78] For example, MacDonald and Camara 2012, 187.

comparisons might also suggest that we should consider the extent to which redeployments of population may have been required, and that the creation of these urban spaces may have involved coercion, to varying degrees. As we have seen, representations of the coercive reach of royal power are much in evidence and we should not discount that these may be expressing fundamental aspects of royal rule over local audiences (and not just external threats). While the Jebel Qeili stele may project Meroitic royal power outwards into the open grazing lands of the Butana, the royal thrones at each of the riverine urban centres provide more localised reminders of the obligations of subjects, and how they were originally imposed. The lavish decoration and scale of the palaces which lay at the heart of many of these centres also contributed to their role in 'aesthetics of awe'; an aspect of sovereignty encountered in other African contexts, and beyond.[79]

As has been suggested, these centres show strong associations with pottery and textile manufacture and ironworking and other related specialist skills (such as faience manufacture). Hamadab in its original enclosed form, dominated by a tower-house (at least as first conceived) and with its possible associations with captives, is particularly marked out. The ceramic workshops widely encountered at urban centres may also be linked to the requirements of managing and processing grain crops, not least in the form of grain beers, a likely dietary staple. One specific feature of the pottery workshops of the Meroitic heartlands is their production of distinctive and apparently quite standardised beer-jar forms. To date, their distribution also suggests their use/circulation within a quite circumscribed zone. Abundant on settlement sites these also became increasingly prominent in burial contexts through the early centuries AD. Interestingly, by the later Meroitic centuries large quantities of grain-beer were deployed in funerary contexts,[80] at least within the Meroitic 'core', marking a very major shift in practice, one which survives beyond the Meroitic period.[81] If related to status displays, this could in turn be linked to the control of agricultural resources.[82] Such a shift may well have been one outcome of the increased state-level management of the Western Butana. In such ways we are reminded that urban and rural histories cannot be studied independently.

The social significance of textiles and their production has already been suggested. Cotton growing and processing, spinning and weaving may be

[79] Monroe 2010; Smith 2011, 424–25. [80] Lenoble 1994. [81] Edwards 2011.
[82] See also Arthur 2003, 523.

linked to sites such as Hamadab, and other urban centres. Whether or not cotton growing developed as a specialised crop remains to be seen, but this is one possibility we might consider, brought on by societal changes wrought by the Meroitic state, of the kind envisaged by Brite and Marston.[83] In later periods, cotton-growers continued to have specific obligations to their lords.[84] The practical demands of cotton-growing also suggest some significant level of management was required, perhaps distinct from generalised grain-based agriculture practised along the wadis of the interior, or following the Nile flood.[85]

On current evidence a regional system of royal palace towns may have been sustained for at least a few centuries, but it may also have changed significantly within the Meroitic period. We may suppose that once these palaces were being quarried for building materials, the original system of control which had been constructed around these urban centres was already unravelling. If, as is suggested these palaces and their towns played central roles in economic administration, the decay and abandonment of the palaces may be very tangible demonstrations of both economic and political restructurings underway by the third century AD, if not before. It is possible that these urban sites may have persisted as nodal points in local economies, although control may already have been passing out of the hands of the central monarchy in the face of political fragmentation, presumed to be a central feature of the 'end of Meroe'. While our evidence remains slight, it seems likely that the changing fate of these urban centres had significant wider impacts.

Notwithstanding the conventional identification of Meroitic towns in more areas of Middle and Lower Nubia, on the route to Egypt, urban terminology may perhaps be misleading, at a number of levels. In terms of scale, few if any could match the substantial size of contemporary Egyptian villages.[86] In terms of function, most known settlements have features that mark them off from what we might expect of rural (agricultural) settlements, perhaps, suggesting more urban roles. However, when examined together at a landscape scale, it is apparent that if they were towns then they lacked any rural hinterlands.[87] That they were Meroitic 'colonies' may not be an inappropriate characterisation; their unusual features reflecting their origins and purpose. Where we can date Meroitic activity in the region, patterns emerge which are suggestive of phases of site foundation, as well as

[83] Brite and Marston 2013, 51; cf Griffith and Crowfoot 1934. [84] Spaulding 1985, 81.
[85] Fuller 2014. [86] See Boozer, Chapter 4, this volume.
[87] The fullest study of the known extent of Meroitic settlement in the north remains Edwards 1996.

abandonment and reoccupation. Wider cultural patterns are suggestive of the gradual emergence of a distinct regional culture within the Meroitic north, increasingly distinct from its Sudanic origins, also demonstrating developing cultural links with Roman Egypt.

The proximity and accessibility of Roman Egypt is manifest in many features of northern Meroitic culture, especially between the Second and First Cataracts. Notwithstanding the presence of long-established religious/pilgrimage centres such as Qasr Ibrim, it remains difficult to identify Meroitic urban centres that are distinct from the series of small nucleated settlements that traverse Middle and Lower Nubia. By the fourth century AD, with the gradual appearance of the *saqia* waterwheel, we may however begin to see the transformation of this northern form of settlement built around a new type of agricultural system, which was to later sustain the early medieval kingdom of Nobadia. In the same period, the accessibility of Egypt was similarly evidenced in many aspects of the political and religious transformation of northern Nubia.[88]

While we know a great deal about well-preserved Meroitic archaeology in the north, the Nubian 'corridor' across the Sahara is less studied. There is good reason to believe that Kushite settlements in the north through the first millennium BC and beyond were deliberately established to manage what were in effect Trans-Saharan communications.

Urban Centres and New Identities?

A final issue to explore concerns the wider role that Meroitic urban centres may have played in the creation of both the material world of the Meroitic state and new forms of social identities. That many of the most distinctive forms of Meroitic material culture were created in these urban centres seems increasingly likely. It is also probable that access to most forms of imported materials was controlled by such urban centres (with the exception of the northern frontier zone in Lower Nubia).

As new forms of living in these landscapes, these centres may also have had wider social impacts.[89] In addition to craftworkers, other elements of extended royal retinues and households may also have settled in new palace-centred settlements. The fundamental importance of such royal

[88] Edwards 2014b.

[89] As elsewhere in the continent urban centres may also have played other important roles, not least in language development (Coquery-Vidrovitch 2005, xxix); the development of written standardised Meroitic, and indeed in medieval 'Old Nubian' may perhaps be linked particularly with their urban centres.

dependents as a primary source of power should be reiterated; such 'wealth in people' still being central to more recent constructions of power in the region.[90] Whether or not the Meroitic royal households possessed a significant military component remains unknown, but this also seems likely. Bearing in mind the very long traditions of slave troops in the region,[91] it is possible that this was already an institutionalised practice in the Meroitic period, although this may again represent one extreme in a continuum of dependency amongst royal retinues. In later periods, slave troops were settled in garrison communities and engaged in cultivation to support themselves; within a more general pattern of settlement wherein the proportion of slaves/captives increased as a factor of proximity to the capital.[92] While 'slaughtering the men [and] enslaving the women' was a recurrent feature of Kushite royal activities,[93] enslavement was likely an important component of a range of strategies deployed to extend retinues.[94] It may also be suggested that these strategies provided the population base for the urban centres of the Meroitic core. Similar techniques of spatial production may be widely encountered, as for example suggested in Parker's study of Assyrian imperial construction.[95] This is perhaps a hypothesis that could be further explored in investigations of the socio-political character of the Meroitic urban settlements currently being excavated. It is a reasonable premise that these settlements did not arise organically as voluntary aggregations.

The afterlife and legacies of such urban communities also invite further investigation. Since not all these urban centres were necessarily the same (Hamadab, for example, being rather different on a number of counts), varied later histories should perhaps be expected in the aftermath of political changes. While some sites may well have been abandoned, others may have been more resilient, finding new purposes. One interesting outcome of recent work at Hamadab has been to demonstrate the persistence of ironworking at the site, apparently well into the post-Meroitic period. As suggested in some preliminary work this may well be linked with changes in the (royal) control of ironworking.[96] Such a persistence raises a number of interesting questions, not least concerning the nature of the community established in the enclosed settlement. It is clear that ironworkers had long-existed at Meroe, although their status relationship (free or servile) to the Meroitic crown remains unknown. But equally, like

[90] Leonardi 2013, 27; Simonse 1992, 233. [91] Johnson 1989. [92] Spaulding 1985, 208–9.
[93] Pope 2014, 98–108; Rilly and De Voogt 2012. [94] Simonse 1992. [95] Parker 2003.
[96] Humphris 2014.

potters, their crafts were transformed and developed during the Meroitic period.

In terms of the legacies of such Meroitic urban centres, one further outcome that may be suggested is that within communities such as Hamadab we might find one explanation for how craft-based castes take form. While very familiar in various forms across much of Sahelian-Sudanic Africa, how these might originate has remained a puzzle.[97] In the Meroitic case we might suggest the central role for the state in the generation of craft-based communities and also identities in such urban centres. Their likely central role in technological development may also be highlighted. In relation to ceramic manufacture, the first century BC seems to have been a period of significant transformations of already very long-established potting traditions, with the re-appearance of wheel-made mass-produced coarsewares. It is apparent that these were able to integrate both long-established craft practices and technologies with new ones, for example in new pottery kiln technologies, within an emerging new 'imperial' culture.[98] We might also consider that other craft groups may also have undergone similar transformations, within royally controlled contexts. Meroitic towns provided these contexts.

Like other forms of identity, these urban/craft identities would have been dynamic. A political collapse of Meroitic kingship would have opened up new trajectories for such groups, already distinct from other population elements. The extent to which urban centres created their own 'internal frontier zone' around them, as recently explored in Leonardi's work,[99] might be usefully explored in relation to these much earlier urban experiments. Equally, the implications of their disappearance must also be considered. While we have little hard evidence for the exact nature of the social transformations which accompanied the disintegration of the Meroitic state, it is possible that this was a period of pastoral resurgence that unpicked the structures which encouraged or supported more intensive agriculture in the Meroitic heartland. More specifically however we see an abandonment of the urban forms which had been such distinctive material manifestations of the state. Under such circumstances, the options open to groups with craft-based identities, the product of several centuries of enclosed, or at least controlled living, would seem to be very different. What did the post-Meroitic future hold for royal potters, or indeed royal ironworkers if they chose to or were required to 'go feral'? Possessed of valuable skills, but quite possibly also lacking claims to land or owning

[97] Haaland and Haaland 2008; Tamari 2012. [98] Edwards 2014a. [99] Leonardi 2013, 217.

herds, or indeed social ties to those who did, their possible futures may have been more constrained than many. However, their skills would continue to represent an important power source that was desirable to control.[100] Their subsequent histories doubtless developed and took on new forms in the new regional centres of power that emerged by the sixth century in what was to become Nubia.

Notwithstanding many significant gaps in our knowledge of Meroitic urbanism, the many-layered political implications of the very existence of these centres should not be overlooked. A consideration of the necessary conditions for their creation, persistence, and practical purposes takes us close to many of the fundamental bases of the Meroitic state and enforcement of its sovereignty. Echoing Smith, we may here recognise material manifestations of authority and subjection at many different scales.[101] Within political landscapes we encounter re-orderings of space and territory; while within urban spaces, the built environment may itself represent a technology of order and control.

References

Anderson, D. and Rathbone, R. (eds). 2000. *Africa's Urban Past.* Oxford: James Currey.

Anderson, J. and Welsby, D. (eds). 2014. *The Fourth Cataract and Beyond. Proceedings of the 12th International Conference for Nubian Studies.* Leuven: Peeters.

Arthur, J. 2003. Brewing beer: Status, wealth and ceramic use alteration among the Gamo of south-western Ethiopia. *World Archaeology* 34.3: 516–28.

Baud, M. 2008. The Meroitic royal city of Muweis: First steps into an urban settlement of riverine Upper Nubia. *Sudan & Nubia* 12: 52–63.

Baud, M. (ed.). 2011. *Meroe, un empire sur le Nil.* Paris: Louvre.

Baud, M. 2014. Downtown Muweis – a progress report (2007–2014). In Anderson and Welsby 2014, 763–82.

Bonnet, C. and Valbelle, D. 2014. *La ville de Kerma – Une capitale nubienne au sud de l'Egypte.* Lausanne: Favre.

Borkowski, Z. and Paner, H. 2005. The Awlib Temple Complex: Report on the 2001 and 2003 Excavation Seasons. *Gdansk Archaeological Museum African Reports* 3: 47–60.

Brite, E.B. and Marston, J.M. 2013. Environmental change, agricultural innovation, and the spread of cotton agriculture in the Old World. *Journal of Anthropological Archaeology* 32: 39–53.

[100] Compare Simonse 1992, 237–38. [101] Smith 2011, 423–26.

Coquery-Vidrovitch, C. 2005. African urban spaces. History and culture. In S. J. Salm and T. Falola (eds), *African Urban Spaces in Historical Perspective*. Rochester, N.Y.: University of Rochester Press, xv–xl.

Edwards, D.N. 1996. *The Archaeology of the Meroitic State: New Perspectives on Its Social and Political Organization*. Oxford: Archaeopress.

Edwards, D.N. 1998. Meroe and the Sudanic kingdoms. *Journal of African History* 39.2: 175–93.

Edwards, D.N. 1999. *A Meroitic Pottery Workshop at Musawwarat es Sufra*. (Meroitica 17.2). Wiesbaden: Harrassowitz.

Edwards, D.N. 2004. *The Nubian Past: An Archaeology of the Sudan*. London: Routledge.

Edwards, D.N. 2011. From Meroe to 'Nubia' – exploring culture change without the 'Noba'. In V. Rondot, F. Alpi and F. Villeneuve (eds), *La Pioche et La Plume (Hommages Archéologiques à Patrice Lenoble)*. Paris: PUPS, 501–14.

Edwards, D.N. 2014a. Early Meroitic pottery and the creation of an early imperial culture? In A. Lohwasser and P. Wolf (eds), *Ein Forscherleben zwischen den Welten. Zum 80. Geburtstag Steffen Wenig*, Berlin: SAG, 51–63.

Edwards, D.N. 2014b. Creating Christian Nubia: Processes and events on the Egyptian frontier. In J. Dijkstra and G. Fisher (eds), *Inside and Out. Interactions between Rome and the Peoples on the Arabian and Egyptian Frontiers* [Late Antique History and Religion 8]. Leuven: Peeters, 407–31.

Fiedler, M. and Jesse, F. 2012. Griechische Keramik aus der Festung Gala Abu Ahmed im Nordsudan. *Archäologischer Anzeiger* 2011–12: 67–80.

Fitzenreiter, M, Seiler, A. and Gerullat, I. 1999. *Musawwarat es Sufra III. Die Kleine Anlage*. Wiesbaden: Harrassowitz.

Fuller, D. 2014. Agricultural innovation and state collapse in Meroitic Nubia. The impact of the Savannah package. In C.J. Stevens, S. Nixon, M.A. Murray and D. Q. Fuller (eds), *The Archaeology of African Plant Use*. Walnut Creek: Left Coast Press, 165–77.

Fyfe, C. and McMaster, D. (eds). 1981. *African Historical Demography: Proceedings of a Seminar held in the Centre of African Studies, University of Edinburgh, 24th and 25th April 1981*. Vol. 2. Edinburgh: Centre of African Studies.

Garstang, J., Sayce, A.H. and Griffith, F.L. 1911. *Meroe. The City of the Ethiopians*. Oxford: Clarendon Press.

Griffith, F.L. and Crowfoot, G.M. 1934. On the early use of cotton in the Nile Valley. *Journal of Egyptian Archaeology* 20: 5–12.

Haaland, R. 1985. Iron producing, its socio-cultural context and ecological implications. In R. Haaland and P.L. Shinnie (eds), *African Iron Working – Ancient and Traditional*. Oslo: Norwegian University Press, 50–72.

Haaland, R. and Haaland, G. 2008. Craft specialization, caste identities and political centralization. The use of anthropological perspectives in reconstructing archaic forms of economic organization. In K. Chilidis, J. Lund and C. Prescott (eds), *Facets of Archaeology. Essays in Honour of Lotte Hedeager on her 60th Birthday*, Oslo Archaeological Series 10. Oslo: Unipub, 155–65.

Hinkel, M. 1991. Hafire im antiken Sudan. *Zeitschrift für Ägyptische Sprache* 118.1: 32–48.

Hafsaas-Tsakos, H. 2013. Edges of bronze and expressions of masculinity: The emergence of a warrior class at Kerma in Sudan. *Antiquity* 87: 79–91.

Hopkins, A.G. 1973. *An Economic History of West Africa*. London: Longman.

Humphris, J. 2014. Post-Meroitic iron production: Initial results and interpretations. *Sudan & Nubia* 18: 121–29.

Jakobielski, S. and Scholz, P. (eds). 2001. *Dongola-Studien*. Warsaw: ZAS.

Jesse, F. 2013. The Gala Abu Ahmed fortress in Lower Wadi Howar (Northern Sudan). In F. Jesse and C. Vogel (eds), *The Power of Walls – Fortifications in Ancient Northeastern Africa*. Cologne: Heinrich-Barth-Institut, 321–52.

Johnson, D.H. 1989. The structure of a legacy: Military slavery in Northeast Africa. *Ethnohistory* 36.1: 72–88.

Kapteijns, L. and Spaulding, J. 2005. The conceptualisation of land tenure in the precolonial Sudan: Evidence and interpretation. In D. Crummey (ed.), *Land, Literacy and the State in Sudanic Africa*. Trenton, N.J.: Red Sea Press, 21–41.

Kemp, B.J. 1987. The Amarna workmen's village in retrospect. *Journal of Egyptian Archaeology* 73: 21–50.

Kopytoff, I. and Miers, S. 1977. African 'slavery' as an institution of marginality. In S. Miers and I. Kopytoff (eds), *Slavery in Africa*. Madison: University of Wisconsin Press, 3–81.

Lane, P. and Johnson, D. 2009. The archaeology and history of slavery in South Sudan in the nineteenth century. In A. Peacock (ed.), *The Frontiers of the Ottoman World*. Oxford: British Academy, 509–37.

Lebon, J.H.B. 1965. *Landuse in Sudan*. Bude: Geographical Publications.

Lenoble, P. 1994. *Du Méroïtique au Postméroïtique dans la Région méridionale du Royaume de Méroé. Recherches sur la période de transition*. Unpublished PhD thesis, Paris: Sorbonne.

Lenoble, P. 2008. Une carte des derniers siècles de Méroé. Sites préchrétiens autour de l'ancienne capital entre Wad ben Naqa et Gabati. *Kush* 19: 59–65.

Lenoble, P. and Rondot, V. 2003. À la redécouverte d'El-Hassa. Temple à Amon, palais royal et ville de l'empire méroitique. *Cahiers de recherches de l'Institut de papyrologie et d'égyptologie de Lille* 23: 101–15.

Leonardi, C. 2013. *Dealing with Government in South Sudan*. Woodbridge: James Currey.

MacDonald, K. and Camara, S. 2012. Segou, slavery and *Sifinso*. In J.C. Monroe and A. Ogundiran (eds), *Power and Landscape in Atlantic West Africa: Archaeological Perspectives*. Cambridge: Cambridge University Press, 169–90.

McIntosh, S. and McIntosh, R. 1993. Cities without citadels: Understanding urban origins along the middle Niger. In T. Shaw, P. Sinclair, B. Andah and A. Okpoko (eds), *The Archaeology of Africa: Food, Metals and Towns*. London: Routledge, 622–41.

Maillot, M. 2014. The palace of Muweis in the Shendi Reach: A comparative approach. In Anderson and Welsby 2014, 783–95.

Maillot, M. 2015. The Meroitic palace and royal city. *Sudan & Nubia* 19: 80–87.

Maillot, M. 2016. *Palais et grandes demeures du royaume de Méroe*. Paris: PUPS.

Mair, L. 1977. *African Kingdoms*. Oxford: Oxford University Press.

Monroe, J.C. 2010. Power by design: Architecture and politics in precolonial Dahomey. *Journal of Social Archaeology* 10: 367–97.

MGA 2015. *Musawwarat Graffiti Archive. Exploring Pictures in Place*. Available at: http://musawwaratgraffiti.mpiwg-berlin.mpg.de/index_html [last accessed 12 September 2019].

Näser, C. 2011. Early Musawwarat. In Rondot *et al.* 2011, 317–38.

Nachtigal, G. 1971. *Sahara and Sudan* (translated by A.G.B. Fisher and H.J. Fisher). London: Hurst.

O'Connor, D. 2013. Kerma in Nubia, the last mystery: the political and social dynamics of an early Nilotic state. In R.B. Koehl (ed.), *Amilla: The Quest for Excellence. Studies Presented to Guenter Kopcke in Celebration of His 75th Birthday*. Philadelphia: INSTAP Academic Press, 189–205.

Onderka, P. and Vrtal, V. 2014. *Nubia. A Land on the Crossroads of Cultures. Wad Ben Naga 2014*. Prague: National Museum.

Osborne, R. 2005. Urban sprawl: What is urbanization and why does it matter? In R. Osborne and B. Cunliffe (eds), *Mediterranean Urbanization 800–600 BC*. Oxford: British Academy, 1–16.

Parker, B. 2003. Archaeological manifestations of empire: Assyria's imprint on southeastern Anatolia. *American Journal of Archaeology* 107: 525–57.

Pope, J.W. 2014. *The Double Kingdom Under Taharqo*. Leiden: Brill.

Potts, D. 2012. Challenging the myths of urban dynamics in Sub-Saharan Africa: The evidence from Nigeria. *World Development* 40.7: 1382–93.

Rehren, T. 2001. Meroe, iron and Africa. *Antike Sudan* 12: 102–9.

Rilly, C. 2008. Enemy brothers, kinship and relationship between Meroites and Nubians (Noba). In W. Godlewski and A. Lajtar (eds), *Between the Cataracts*. Warsaw: Warsaw University Press, 211–25.

Rilly, C. and DeVoogt, A. 2012. *The Meroitic Language and Writing System*. Cambridge: Cambridge University Press.

Rondot, V., Alpi, F. and Villeneuve, F. (eds). 2011. *La pioche et la plume: Autour du Soudan, du Liban et de la Jordanie: hommages archéologiques à Patrice Lenoble*. Paris: PUPS.

Säve-Söderbergh, T. and Troy, L. 1991. *New Kingdom Pharaonic Sites (The Finds and Sites (Volume 5:2)*. Uppsala: Scandinavian Joint Expedition to Sudanese Nubia.

Scott, J.C. 1998. *Seeing Like A State: How Certain Schemes to Improve the Human Condition Have Failed*. New Haven: Yale University Press.

Shinnie, P.L. 1967. *Meroe: A Civilization of the Sudan*. London: Thames and Hudson.

Shinnie, P.L. 1985. Iron working at Meroe. In R. Haaland and P.L. Shinnie (eds), *African Iron Working – Ancient and Traditional*. Oslo: Norwegian University Press, 28–35.

Shinnie, P.L. and Kense, F. 1982. Meroitic Iron Working. In N. Millet and A. L. Kelley (eds), *Meroitic Studies (Meroitica 6)*. Berlin: Akademie-Verlag, 17–28.

Simonse, S. 1992. *Kings of Disaster: Dualism, Centralism, and the Scapegoat King in Southeastern Sudan*. Leiden: Brill.

Smith, A.T. 2003. *The Political Landscape: Constellations of Authority in Early Complex Polities*. Berkeley: University of California Press.

Smith, A.T. 2011. Archaeologies of sovereignty. *Annual Review of Anthropology* 40: 415–32.

Spaulding, J. 1985. *The Heroic Age in Sinnār*. East Lansing: Michigan State University.

Spaulding, J. 2006. Pastoralism, slavery, commerce, culture and the fate of the Nubians of Northern and Central Kordofan under Dar Fur Rule, c.1750 – c.1850. *International Journal of African Historical Studies* 39.3: 393–412.

Spaulding, J. and Kapteijns, L. 2002. Land tenure and the state in the precolonial Sudan. *Northeast African Studies* 19.1: 33–66.

Spencer, N. 2012. Insights into life in occupied Kush during the New Kingdom: new research at Amara West. *Antike Sudan* 23: 21–28.

Spencer, N., Woodward, J. and Macklin, M. 2012. Re-assessing the abandonment of Amara West: the impact of a changing Nile? *Sudan & Nubia* 16: 37–43.

Tamari, T. 2012. De l'apparition et de l'expansion des groups de spécialistes endogames en Afrique: Essai d'explication. In C. Roboin-Brunner and B. Martinelli (eds), *Métallurgie du fer et Sociétés africaines*. Oxford: Archaeopress, 5–31.

Török, L. 1997. *The Kingdom of Kush*. Leiden, Brill.

Tylecote, R.F. 1982. Metal working at Meroe, Sudan. In N. Millet and A.L. Kelley (eds), *Meroitic Studies. (Meroitica 6)*. Berlin: Akademie-Verlag, 29–42.

Vincentelli, I. 1993. A discharge of clay sealings from the Natakamani palace. *Kush* 16: 116–41.

Vincentelli, I. 2007. Some clay sealings from Sanam Abu Dom. *Cahiers de recherches de l'Institut de papyrologie et d'égyptologie de Lille* 26: 371–78.

Vincentelli, I. 2011. The treasury and other buildings at Sanam. In Rondot *et al.* 2011, 269–82.

Welsby, D. 1998. *Soba II*. London: British Institute in Eastern Africa.

Welsby, D. 2014. The Qatar-Sudan Archaeological project in the Northern Dongola Reach. *Sudan & Nubia* 18: 47–68.

Welsby, D. and Daniels, C.M. 1991. *Soba: Archaeological Research at a Medieval Capital on the Blue Nile*. London: British Institute in Eastern Africa.

Wolf, P. 1999. Recent fieldwork at Musawwarat es Sufra, *Sudan & Nubia* 1: 20–9.

Wolf, P. 2015. The Qatar-Sudan Archaeological project – the Meroitic town of Hamadab and palaeo-environment in the Meroe region. *Sudan & Nubia* 19: 115–31.

Wolf, P., Nowotnik, U. and Hof, C. 2014a. The Meroitic urban town of Hamadab in 2010. In Anderson and Welsby 2014, 719–37.

Wolf, P., Nowotnik, U. and Woss, F. 2014b. Meroitic Hamadab – a century after its discovery. *Sudan & Nubia* 18: 104–20.

Wolf, P. 2015. The Qatar-Sudan Archaeological Project – The Meroitic town of Hamadab and the palaeo-environment of the Meroe region. *Sudan & Nubia* 19: 115–31.

10 Mediterranean Urbanisation in North Africa

Greek, Punic and Roman Models

ANDREW I. WILSON

Introduction and Historical Background

This chapter seeks to identify the distinctive characteristics of Greek, Punic and Roman urbanism in North Africa, and to explore similarities and differences between them. It presents an overview of urban morphology, infrastructure (streets, water supply), architectural characteristics (materials and aesthetics), and the common range of public buildings and types of domestic housing found in the various cultures; it also explores the extent to which we can reconstruct the use of public space and the character of urban life from inscriptions and the evidence of the statue habit in Roman towns. Questions of size and population, and economic roles, will also be considered. The main aim is to provide a succinct summary of fundamental information to enable comparison and contrast with other chapters in the collection which look at indigenous state formation and urbanism in the Maghrib and the Sahara.

The first cities along the North African coast were founded as Phoenician trading centres. The traditional date for the foundation of the earliest of these, Utica, equates to 1101 BC, although in fact no archaeological remains earlier than the eighth century BC have been discovered. Likewise, although Carthage was said to have been founded in 814 BC, the earliest archaeological material is about a hundred years later.

The Greek colonisation of Cyrenaica (Eastern Libya) began in the later seventh century BC, with the founding of Cyrene, traditionally in *c.*631 BC, by settlers from Thera under their leader Battos, who became the city's first king.[1] Its harbour, Apollonia, some 14 km distant, must have developed gradually in the wake of Cyrene's foundation. Barca (modern al-Marj),

[1] Herodotos, *Histories* 4, 150–59.

inland on the middle terrace of the Cyrenaican plateau, and the coastal city of Taucheira (Tocra), were founded after Cyrene in the later seventh century; the port of Barca was distant from it, and by the third century BC developed into a city in its own right, Ptolemais. Together with Euesperides (modern Benghazi), the last of the cities to be founded, perhaps in the early sixth century BC, these five cities formed the Cyrenaican Pentapolis.[2]

In the Archaic and Classical period down to *c.*440 BC, Cyrene was ruled by the Battiad dynasty, descendants of King Battos, alternately named Battos and Arkesilas. Dynastic struggles eventually undid them, and the last king, Arkesilas IV, was murdered at Euesperides. Thereafter Cyrene appears to have had a more democratic or republican form of government, but the end of royal control saw Cyrene pitted against shifting alliances of the other Cyrenaican cities, sometimes Cyrene with Euesperides against Barca and Taucheira; at other times Euesperides allied with Barca. A decree (late fourth- or possibly even early third-century BC) from Euesperides informs us that the city had at that period a *boule* (council), with *gerontes* (elders), and *ephors* (magistrates) involved in the city's governance.[3] But Cyrenaica was also affected by external factors, notably in the Late Classical and Hellenistic periods when the cities were subject at times to control by Persian and Ptolemaic rulers in Egypt.

Alexander's conquest of Egypt (332 BC) brought an end to Persian rule there and to Persian hegemony over Cyrenaica. Following his death, Cyrenaica came under Ptolemaic control, and it was in the reign of Ptolemy II that the port of Barca took the name Ptolemais, probably being laid out on an ambitious grid plan in this period, while Taucheira took the name Arsinoë after Ptolemy's wife.

In the Maghrib, inland from the coastal belt of Phoenician/Punic emporia, we hear in ancient authors principally of two cities in the second century BC, both called Cirta: Constantine in Algeria and El Kef in Tunisia, the latter more commonly known as Sicca Veneria. This for long encouraged the view that Numidian society knew little in the way of urban life; but more recent archaeological work is now changing that picture. Excavations at Althiburos in inland Tunisia show settled occupation, with an agricultural component, from the ninth century BC (see below).[4]

2 Though the subsequent further development of Apollonia and the foundation of a further city in the second century AD, Hadrianopolis, eventually meant the region supported seven major cities.

3 Fraser 1951.

4 See Sanmartí *et al.*, Chapter 11, this volume on Althiburos and Numidia more generally.

Rome acquired territory in North Africa progressively: in 146 BC following the final defeat of Carthage in the Third Punic War; Cyrenaica in 96 BC, Numidia in 46 BC, Mauretania in the AD 40s, with subsequent expansion into the desert margins. Under Roman rule, North Africa – at least from the Lesser Syrtes westward – became one of the most densely urbanised regions of the empire, comparable with Italy and coastal Asia Minor.[5] This was in part due to a development of the pre-Roman urban base along the littoral, but it is clear also that the dense network of Numidian settlements away from the coast were developed, expanded and monumentalised as cities.[6]

Punic Cities

Many early Phoenician emporia were founded on promontories or projecting capes which offered alternative anchorages either side, sheltered from different winds; many of these are identifiable by the common toponym Rus- ('cape', 'headland'): Rusicade, Rusaddir, Rusucurru, Rusazu, Rusguniae.

Carthage, which became the pre-eminent of these Punic cities, was founded on a broad promontory with marine inlets to the north and south, later supplemented by artificial harbour works.[7] Overlooking these, the Byrsa hill formed the nucleus and defended citadel. The ancient artificial harbour – the Cothon – is represented today by two lagoons north of the bay of el-Kram. The Punic harbour had two parts: an outer part (referred to as the rectangular harbour but actually originally a very elongated hexagon) for merchant shipping, and an interior, circular, basin with a central island, reserved for warships.

> The harbours had communication with each other, and a common entrance from the sea seventy feet wide, which could be closed with iron chains. The first port was for merchant vessels, and here were collected all kinds of ships' tackle. Within the second port was an island, and great quays were set at intervals round both the harbour and the island. These embankments were full of shipyards which had capacity for 220 vessels. In addition to them were magazines for their tackle and furniture. Two Ionic columns stood in front of each dock, giving the appearance of a continuous portico to both the harbour and the island. On the island was built the admiral's house, from which the trumpeter gave signals, the herald delivered orders, and the admiral himself oversaw everything.[8]

[5] See now Hanson 2016, for a study of the urban geography of the Roman world.
[6] Mattingly 2016. [7] For a history of Carthage, see Lancel 1995.
[8] Appian, *Punic Wars* 14.95 (Loeb translation).

Excavations have broadly confirmed Appian's description and show that the ports of Carthage were impressive technical achievements: *c.* 120,000 m^3 of earth were removed to dig the merchant harbour basin, and another 115,000 m^3 for the circular harbour.[9]

Well-appointed Punic houses of the fourth century BC were originally supplied with wells, but during the third century most, if not all, of the houses underwent a change in their water supply. This involved the construction of cisterns with capacities between 5.5 and 14.3 m^3, which collected rain run-off from roofs and courtyards by means of terracotta downspouts. They were of the classic Punic 'cigar-shaped' type – deep, long and narrow with rounded ends, their narrowness resulting from the use of stone slabs for the roof, which could not be made very long without cracking (Fig. 10.1). The construction of such cisterns within existing houses involved considerable disruption, necessitating the demolition of some walls to get the cover slabs in, and since ordinarily water from wells was preferable to water from cisterns, there must have been some compelling reason to make the switch.

Figure 10.1. Carthage – Punic houses on the Byrsa hill, destroyed in the Third Punic War, 146 BC. The houses are constructed in *opus africanum*, with large orthostats and smaller masonry infill between them. A cistern, long and narrow with rounded ends, is visible in the room in the right foreground where some of its massive cover slabs have been removed. The concrete rubble masonry to the right and in the background belongs to the foundations of Roman structures built over the ruins of the Punic city (Photo: A. Wilson).

9 Hurst 1993a; 1993b.

The change must have been a necessary response to changing conditions in water supply that rendered the wells unusable, either a lowering of the local water table due to declining rainfall, or to increased abstraction by a growing population, or perhaps a contamination of the water table by sewage and effluent.[10]

The Tophet to the south of Carthage and west of the harbours was an area where children (up to four years old) were sacrificed and buried. Sometimes animals would be substituted in place of children, but human sacrifice continued through to the end of the Punic Wars (if not beyond). Squat, gray funeral stelae marked the location of cinerary urns containing the ashes of infants, small children and animals. Some stelae are inscribed with texts saying that the burial is an offering to the gods; many are inscribed with the triangular symbol of the goddess Tanit. One third-century BC stone even bears a depiction of a priest carrying a small child. From this evidence, most (but not all) scholars conclude that the Tophet was a burial ground for infants sacrificed to the gods Tanit and Baal Hammon.[11]

The siege of Carthage in the third Punic War lasted more than three years – Scipio Aemilianus eventually took command and imposed a blockade on the port, aiming to starve the city into submission. Carthage finally fell to Scipio's forces in 146 BC – it took six days of urban fighting, house-to-house, for the Roman forces fully to take the city, which was sacked and burnt.

The Punic town whose archaeology is most completely known to us is the site of Kerkouane on Cap Bon, chiefly because it was destroyed in the mid-third century BC and not subsequently overbuilt. The site was occupied from the sixth century BC, and two major phases of destruction have been associated with the invasion of Agathocles in 310 BC, and the First Punic War in 253 BC. A rampart enclosed an area of about 8 ha with a perimeter street around the inside of the rampart, and within this the bulk of the site was laid out on an irregular grid plan, with large public spaces at some street intersections. A large courtyard building near the centre of the town has been identified as a sanctuary of Semitic type. The masonry houses were equipped with bathrooms with a hip bath, waterproofed with *cocciopesto* lining, and an open channel drain through the entrance corridor out to the street (Fig. 10.2). Evidence for the production of salted fish and murex dye shows the importance of marine resources to

[10] Wilson 1998. [11] Xella *et al.* 2013.

Figure 10.2. Kerkouane – interior of Punic house with basin and bath tub (Photo: A. Wilson).

the city's economy; glassmaking debris and a cluster of pottery kilns provide further evidence of craft activities.[12]

Meninx, on the island of Jerba, was in existence by 253 BC and was sacked by the Romans in 217 BC. The Punic site covered at least some 19 ha and was engaged in purple dye production. The other main town on Jerba, Burgu (probably ancient Thoar or Phoar), reached its maximum size (*c.*20 ha) in the second century BC; it is known largely as a surface scatter of pottery, with traces of structures possibly suggesting a centripetal arrangement of streets rather than an orthogonal grid, and a Punic tower tomb on its south-eastern edge. A steep scarp around the perimeter of the site may suggest that it was originally walled (in mudbrick?).[13]

Greek Colonies

Much of what is visible at many of the Cyrenaican cities belongs to the Roman and late Roman periods, but Cyrene, Tocra and Euesperides in particular provide good information about the Archaic, Classical and Hellenistic phases (Fig. 10.3).

[12] Fantar 1984–1986; 1998. [13] Fentress 2009.

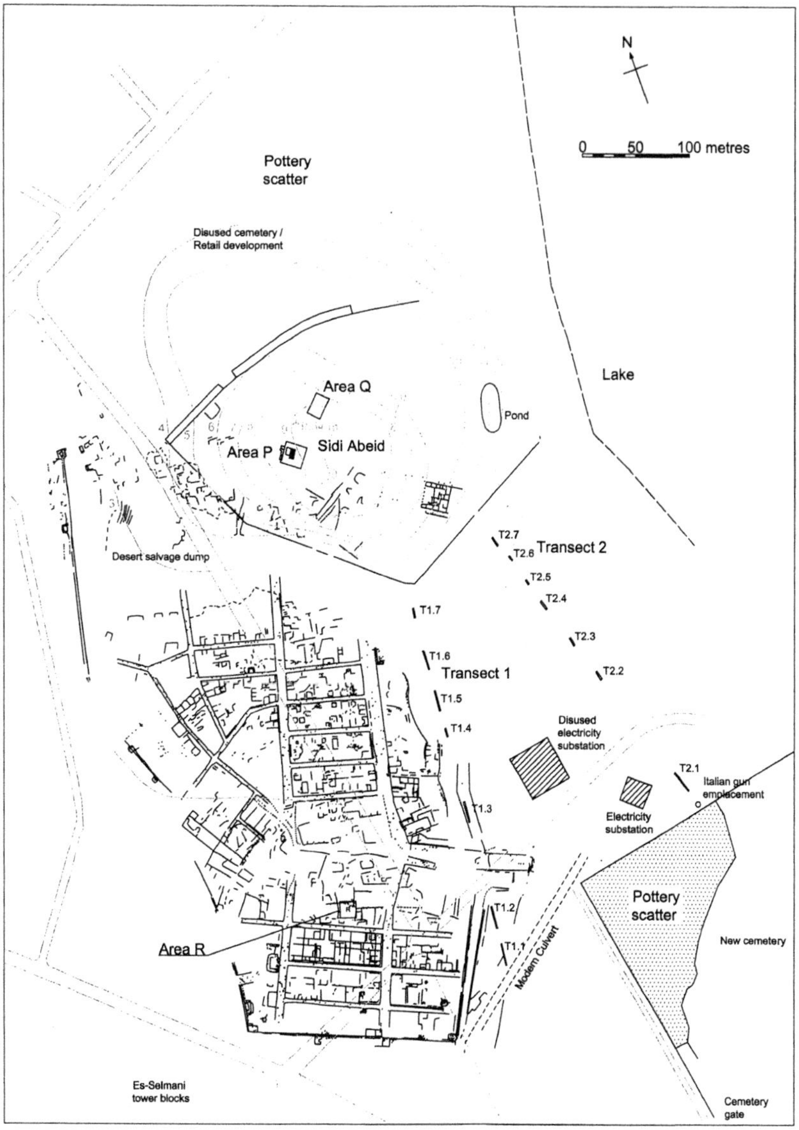

Figure 10.3. Plan of the Greek city of Euesperides (Benghazi). The original Archaic nucleus of the city was on the low mound occupied in the twentieth century by the cemetery of Sidi Abeid; in the Classical period (by the fourth century BC) the city had been extended considerably to the south, where the grid plan of rectangular city blocks, enclosed by a defensive wall, could be traced from air photographs. The extent of pottery scatters suggests that suburban activity extended beyond the limits of the wall circuit (A. Wilson).

Figure 10.4. Cyrene – Temple of Zeus (sixth century BC), built with massive columns in the Doric order (Photo: A. Wilson).

Cyrene was founded on the edge of the upper Cyrenaican terrace, where a copious spring, the Fountain of Apollo, emerges from the limestone karst. Next to this developed a sanctuary of Apollo, with a monumental temple in the Doric style that gradually accreted a number of smaller temples and shrines around it. Above the spring and overlooking the sanctuary of Apollo was a fortified citadel or acropolis; to the south, on flatter ground, lay the *agora* or main market place, and civic centre. A large temple of Zeus lay in the north-east part of the city (Fig. 10.4), and there was a third temple of the Archaic period, dedicated perhaps to Demeter, just outside the city walls to the south.[14] This temple lay within its own walled sanctuary area, which included a theatre for ritual dramatic performances, and a monumental *propylon*. A smaller sanctuary of Demeter with a set of shrines, excavated in the 1970s along the Wadi Belgadir immediately to the north,[15] is probably an outlier of the more recently discovered main sanctuary. The public architecture of Archaic and Classical Cyrene was built in monumental limestone ashlars, with colonnaded temples. Less is known about the domestic housing of the period, largely overbuilt by Roman phases, and in any case most excavation has concentrated on the monumental public structures. Outside the gates, the roads leading out of town were lined with necropoleis (it being forbidden to bury the dead within the city limits), and their expansion and development over time can

[14] Luni 2001; 2006; cf. Kane and White 2007. [15] White 1984; 1993.

clearly be traced: in the northern necropolis, rock-cut tombs of the Archaic period were carved into the rock face above the road leading to Apollonia and the coast just outside the sanctuary of Apollo, with later rock-cut tomb complexes and sarcophagi of the Classical period increasingly further out. In the southern necropolis, increasing competition in funerary display led to spectacularly ornamented columnar façade tombs in the Hellenistic period.[16]

The earliest phases of Cyrene's port, Apollonia, are largely buried below Roman and Byzantine layers, but parts of an Archaic/Classical sanctuary with statuettes and ritual offerings have been found on the highest point of the site. The harbour and ship-sheds go back to the Classical/Hellenistic periods.

Little is known of the archaeology of Barca, founded after 565 BC by the brothers of king Arkesilas II, but its port, Ptolemais (Tolmeita) has yielded Archaic pottery from the shore near the modern lighthouse, and the theatre, cut into the hillside overlooking the site, is probably of Classical date. A Hellenistic wall circuit can be traced, though largely dismantled in the late Roman period, the west gate towers surviving as a fortified blockhouse. The city was laid out on a regular grid plan with city blocks as elongated rectangles. In the western necropolis, situated in an area of quarries that provided building stone for the city, an imposing tower tomb, with several layers of *loculi*, must represent the mausoleum of one of the city's leading families in the Hellenistic period.

At Taucheira, on the coast further to the west, excavations in the 1960s found a deposit of Archaic pottery from the late seventh century BC, interpreted as a part of a deposit within a sanctuary, perhaps of Demeter. The pottery indicates trade links with Corinth and the East Greek islands and cities of the Asia Minor coast.[17] The approximate limits of the early city can be gauged from the traces of the city wall, of mudbrick on a stone rubble foundation, visible in the seaward cliff where it has been exposed by coastal erosion,[18] and the locations of some stone quarries which were originally extramural, later incorporated within the much expanded ashlar defensive wall circuit laid out in the Hellenistic period (though later rebuilt).[19]

At Euesperides, the most westerly of the cities of the Pentapolis, whose site now lies within the suburbs of Benghazi at Sidi Abeid, rather more of the Greek levels have been investigated because the city was abandoned in

[16] Cherstich 2008. [17] Boardman and Hayes 1966. [18] Bennett *et al.* 2004.
[19] Smith and Crow 1998.

the mid-third century BC and not rebuilt. The earliest phases belong to the early sixth century BC, *c.*580 BC, suggesting that Euesperides was founded after the other Cyrenaican colonies (its location, on the less fertile Benghazi plain, is consistent with this, the most favourable territory having been colonised first). The city was surrounded by a defensive wall of mudbrick on a rubble foundation, as at Taucheria, later widened and fronted with a facing of mudbrick; part of a projecting tower on ashlar foundations was also discovered. Outside the wall a quarry ditch provided extra defence, and into the sides of the quarry tombs were subsequently cut in the late fourth century BC.[20]

Within the walls, two phases of Archaic-period housing have been excavated in different parts of the site: the houses were of mudbrick on rubble dwarf wall foundations, with beaten earth floors; an amphora or jar in the corner of many rooms acted as a storage receptacle. The streets were unpaved and without drains or sewers; refuse was thrown out into the street, and trodden in; periodically they were resurfaced with a layer of clay to even out the worst potholes. Structures of the later fourth and third centuries BC are better preserved, and seem to show better built walls; by the third century BC some of the houses had floors in pebble mosaic, mixed pebble and tessera technique, or even some purely in tesserae. Most of the mosaic floors were fairly plain, but one had a wave-crest border, and some indications of figural compositions, including a pair of dolphins, have been inferred from very damaged fragments from a phase of the early third century BC. Water supply came mainly from wells, with some houses provided with rock-cut cisterns towards the end of the city's life.

The city appears to have suffered an earthquake between 262 and 250 BC, and though rebuilt thereafter, its final abandonment no later than 250 BC is shown by the abrupt cessation of coin finds. The deliberate filling of wells, abundant finds of slingshot, and a Hellenistic epigram by Callimachus apparently referring to a siege of the city by Queen Berenice, combine to suggest that the city was sacked during the civil wars in Cyrenaica that followed the death of King Magas in 250. The population was transferred to the Sidi Khrebish area of modern Benghazi where a new city was founded, called Berenice after the victor of these wars.[21]

Of the Cyrenaican cities, Cyrene and Barca in particular enjoyed access to a very fertile agricultural hinterland, abundant not only in grain, vines and olives (these latter two probably introduced to the region by the Greeks), but also, to the south, the medicinal and aphrodisiac plant

[20] Buzaian and Lloyd 1996; Lloyd *et al.* 1995; 1998. [21] Wilson 2005.

silphium, exported for very high prices. The excavations at Euesperides have also highlighted the role of the exploitation of marine resources in the economy of the coastal cities; at Euesperides large deposits of crushed *Murex trunculus* attest the production of purple dye, and imply that some kind of textile, probably wool, was dyed with it. This in turn hints at the raising of sheep on the thin soils, poorly suited to agriculture, of the Benghazi plain.[22]

Pottery from Cyrene and Tocra shows the expected trade connections with the Aegean in the Archaic and Classical periods, but only the fine pottery has been studied and published, and not in any quantified form. More detailed study and quantification of the material from Euesperides shows that in addition to the usual links with the Greek world (although there is no identified material from the Black Sea region), from the fourth century BC trading links with Punic North Africa begin to intensify, and that by the third century BC, 30 per cent of the cooking wares were imported from outside Cyrenaica, and half of these imports were Punic. Punic amphorae accounted for about 5 per cent of the total amphorae from the site.[23]

Numidian Urbanisation

As noted already, recent excavations have revealed permanent settlement at the inland site of Althiburos in Tunisia by the ninth century BC.[24] Certainly, one cannot assume that Althiburos was a town at this early date, and only a relatively small extent of these earliest levels has been excavated, but it is surely important that there was continuous occupation from the ninth century BC through the Roman period, and that what had by the Roman period become a town with a full complement of monumental architecture had developed out of a Numidian village. Although it may be difficult to state at what point Althiburos developed urban characteristics, comparative evidence from other sites shows that we should certainly not assume that it did not happen before the Roman period. The last three centuries BC saw an increasing Mediterranean influence of Numidian architecture: at Bulla Regia, for example, excavations below the Baths of Julia Memmia revealed ashlar foundations of a monumental stone building, dating to the late second or early first century BC,

22 Wilson 2005; 2013. 23 Göransson 2004; Swift 2006; Wilson 2005; 2013.

24 See Sanmartí *et al.*, Chapter 11 and Bokbot, Chapter 12 for further reflections on the contributions of indigenous North African populations to urbanism in the Maghrib.

suggesting public urban architecture already at this period.[25] At Chemtou there is a Numidian monument below the Roman forum, and an elaborate altar on the top of the hill above the marble quarries, showing strong Hellenistic influence in its carved motifs.

A major problem for our knowledge of Numidian urbanism is the fact that most if not all Numidian settlements continued to be occupied, and indeed were expanded and rebuilt, in the Roman period, and relatively little excavation has taken place below Roman levels in these towns. The physical evidence for the architecture, layout and appearance of these Numidian settlements is thus scant. But the fact that the vast majority of toponyms of Roman cities in North Africa have Berber roots is a clear indication that the massive urbanisation of the Roman period was not imposed on an empty landscape, but implanted in pre-existing settlements, which were expanded and (perhaps rather gradually) monumentalised. Mattingly has observed that many of these sites with Berber toponyms, Althiburos included, are sited on spurs with steep drops either side of a central ridge, and that this appears to have been a preferred situation.[26]

Sallust, in his account of the Jugurthine War (112–106 BC), refers to a handful of Numidian towns and sheds a little light on their nature. He mentions '. . . a town of the Numidians called Vaga, the most frequented emporium of the entire kingdom, where many men of Italic race traded and made their homes'.[27] He also calls Zama 'a large city' and mentions its walls,[28]and that it was 'situated in an open plain and fortified rather by art than by nature';[29] his reference also to the gates of Sicca shows that it too was a walled city.[30] Thala, too, is described as 'a large and wealthy town in which the greater part of his [Jugurtha's] treasure was kept, and his children were being brought up in grand style'.[31] It was clearly walled, and with a palace. Indeed, nearly all the cities Sallust mentions are said to be large and wealthy; this may be mere rhetoric, and in any case we have no way of knowing what that meant in absolute terms. But the presence of Roman traders at Vaga, and at Cirta in 113 BC (where their massacre by Jugurtha was a *casus belli* or a cause of war for Rome),[32] is important, as it shows these towns hosting Roman and Italian merchant communities engaged in trade, certainly in grain and apparently also in other goods, in the late second century BC.

[25] Broise and Thébert 1993, 204–5. [26] Mattingly 2016, 15. [27] Sallust, *Jugurthine War* 47.
[28] Sallust, *Jugurthine War* 56. [29] Sallust, *Jugurthine War* 57. [30] Sallust, *Jugurthine War* 56.
[31] Sallust, *Jugurthine War* 75–76. [32] Sallust, *Jugurthine War* 21.2, 26–27.

Roman Urbanism

Roman Carthage

Roman urbanisation in Africa consisted only in part of deliberate acts of colonial foundation, and most of those long after the territory first fell under Rome's control with the final defeat of Carthage in 146 BC. There was a short-lived and abortive attempt to re-found Carthage as a colony for settlers from Italy in 133 BC, as part of C. Gracchus's programme of land reforms, but it clearly did not prosper, and archaeological traces of it are scant.[33] Julius Caesar founded a series of veteran colonies around Cap Bon in Africa Proconsularis (modern Tunisia);[34] and Augustus founded additional colonies across a wider region of North Africa to settle more veterans after the end of the civil wars.[35] The successful refoundation of Carthage, as Colonia Concordia Iulia Karthago, belongs to this period; Caesar had certainly drawn up plans for a colony at Carthage, although it remains unclear whether it was actually begun before his assassination, or whether it was carried out after Caesar's death by Octavian/Augustus. The 3,000 colonists sent from Italy were too few to fill out the city's plan, and must have been supplemented by locals as well.

As refounded in the late first century BC, the city was laid out on a regular grid plan, rigidly imposed on the undulating topography so that where they ascended to the forum, on the summit of the Byrsa hill, the streets had to turn into flights of steps (Fig. 10.5). The main streets, the *cardo* and *decumanus maximus*, met at right angles in the forum, and the city blocks were laid out as rectangular *insulae* twice as long as they were wide. The city grid takes its alignment from the coastline between the Bordj Djedid hill and the harbours, following part of the Punic street plan, but diverges from other streets. The harbours were put back into service, and by the fourth century AD the island in the middle of the circular harbour housed a facility where shipments of olive oil received perhaps as tax in kind (the *canon olei*?) were weighed and checked for quality.[36] Most of the Roman houses excavated in Carthage are elite residences, peristyle houses with reception rooms lavishly decorated with mosaics.

33 Saumagne 1928.

34 Clupea (Kelibia), Curubis (Korbous), Carpi (Henchir Mraïssa), Neapolis (Nabeul).

35 Thuburbo Minus (Tebourba), Hippo Diarrhytus (Bizerte), Maxula (Rades), Caspis, Thuburnica (Tebournuc), Simitthus (Chemtou), Sicca Veneria (El Kef), and Assuras in what is now Tunisia; Igilgili (Jijel), Saldae (Bejaia), Rusucurru, Rusazu, Rusguniae, Aquae Calidae, Zuccabar, Gunugu and Cartenna in what is now Algeria.

36 Peña 1998.

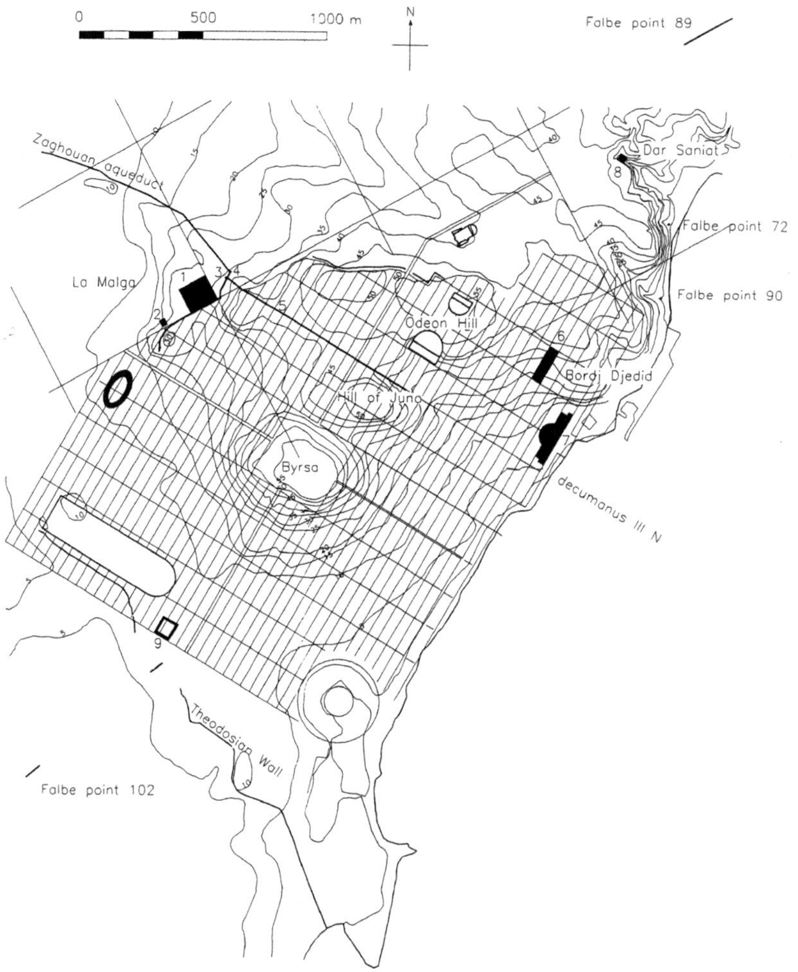

Figure 10.5. Plan of Roman Carthage showing the main public buildings and known elements of water-supply infrastructure. The theatre and odeon are on the Odeon Hill; the circus is towards the south-west edge of the city, and the amphitheatre is the oval structure between this and the La Malga cisterns. Numbered features: 1) Large La Malga cisterns. 2) Small La Malga cisterns. 3) Castellum excavated by Vernaz. 4) Castellum excavated by Ellis. 5) Aqueduct branch traced by Vernaz under decumanus III N. 6) Bordj Djedid cisterns. 7) Antonine Baths. 8) Dar Saniat cisterns. 9) Turris Aquaria (Wilson 1998, 66, Fig. 1).

Little is known of the buildings of Augustan Carthage, although the German excavations down by the seashore have documented the re-use of Punic domestic cisterns in houses of the Augustan period, and the employment of rubble from the Punic destruction layers. Most of the public architecture now surviving belongs to the first century AD or later, and in particular to a large-scale rebuilding of the urban centre in the Antonine period after a fire around AD 150.[37] The Byrsa hill was monumentalised to transform the former Punic citadel into a lavish forum complex, the top of the hill being levelled to create a massive platform extended out across the natural slope of the hill by a dumped terrace fill, to create a platform 30,000 m^2, three times the size of the Augustan forum at Rome. This was the commercial, religious and civic heart of the city, with a monumental paved forum plaza surrounded by a basilica, library and temples including a *Capitolium* (to Jupiter, Juno and Minerva). This latter is known only from inscriptions that mention it, and probably lies beneath the Cathedral of St Louis, built on the highest point of the site in the late nineteenth century AD.

Of the theatre only a part of the *cavea*, backed against the side of the 'Hill of Juno', to the north of the Byrsa, is still intact. The Augustan city probably had a theatre from its foundation (in book four of the *Aeneid*, Virgil has Dido building a theatre in a scene which has been taken to reflect Augustus's refoundation of the city at the time Virgil was writing), but the structure visible today is of the second century AD, badly reconstructed in the early twentieth century with the seating rake at the wrong angle.

The odeon at Carthage is one of the largest known from the Roman world, built in *c.*AD 200 over earlier houses; it has been suggested that its construction may have been an imperial initiative, linked with Septimius Severus granting permission to Carthage to hold the Pythian Games in 203.[38] The circus, too, is the longest known outside Rome, with a total length of 570–580 m, and an arena at least 496 m long; with 27 rows of seats, the total capacity is estimated at 60,000–63,000 spectators. The amphitheatre, whose capacity is estimated at 30,000, dates probably from the early first century AD with a rebuild and expansion in the mid-second century AD.[39] It was built of sandstone from Cap Bon for its annular and radial walls, with limestone used for the exterior façade, and the characteristically Italian technique of *opus reticulatum* used for facing the *cavea* vaults.

As in most Mediterranean towns in the ancient world, rainwater collection cisterns were a standard part of domestic water supply, and besides the reuse of some Punic cisterns, new cisterns were also constructed in concrete with barrel-vaulted roofs, a technological advance enabling the creation of larger domestic cisterns than had been possible in the Punic period. But in addition, several aqueducts were built; ultimately, Carthage came to have four or five of them. The earliest probably tapped the sources closest to the city, while the

[37] Thomas 2007, 146. [38] Wells 2005. [39] Bomgardner 1989, 145–46.

later ones came from further away. In the Julio-Claudian period, and possibly as early as the reign of Augustus, a massive set of reservoir cisterns on the north-western outskirts of the city was constructed, with 16 barrel-vaulted chambers holding a total of 50,000 m^3 of water. The complex was clearly aqueduct-fed, probably from a spring at Sidi Bou Said. In the mid-second century, probably under Hadrian, a long aqueduct was built from springs at Zaghouan, 98 km away, and this was extended under Septimius Severus to additional springs at Aïn Djouker, bringing the total length to 132 km. This lengthy and massive project was probably the last in the series of Carthage's aqueducts; other shorter systems, which probably fall between the Julio-Claudian period and Hadrian, include a subterranean aqueduct in the plain of La Soukra (serving at least in part for irrigation), an underground aqueduct near La Malga, and a channel feeding reservoir cisterns at Dar Saniat to the north of the city proper.[40] Recent excavations at La Malga have also exposed part of the arcade of another aqueduct running alongside the aqueduct from Zaghouan, at a slightly higher level and feeding reservoir cisterns and baths beside the modern Phoenix restaurant.

This multitude of aqueducts reflects the demands of a populous city in a hot climate, demands that were both essential and ornamental. The aqueducts supplemented domestic cisterns, and the richest houses were directly connected, via lead or terracotta pipes, to the aqueduct network. Yet these elite houses tended to use their piped water principally for display, feeding ornamental fountains in peristyle courtyards. On the other hand, the public fountains, while monumental and spectacular, decorated with coloured marble veneer and with bronze and marble statues, also served as an important source of water for those houses without piped water, and as the primary source for those without wells or cisterns; slaves would fetch water from the public fountains. The large reservoir cisterns at La Malga enabled regulation of the supply of at least one of the aqueducts, enabling for example night-time supply to be stored to augment the distribution through the network during the day.[41]

The aqueduct engineering projects also supported a typically Roman culture of public bathing, and the construction of the long aqueduct from Zaghouan enabled the subsequent development of the massive Antonine baths, a huge imperial bath complex built under Antoninus Pius (construction began in the late 140s or 150s and the building was dedicated in 161–162) on a site overlooking the sea.[42] The most extensive example of

[40] Wilson 1998. [41] Wilson 1998.
[42] For the date, *CIL* 8.12513 and *AE* 1949, 27; Wilson 1997, 242–43.

Roman baths in North Africa, they were once the largest in the Roman world, with a central pool the size of a present-day Olympic swimming pool; the whole complex was lavishly equipped with mosaics and imported marbles.

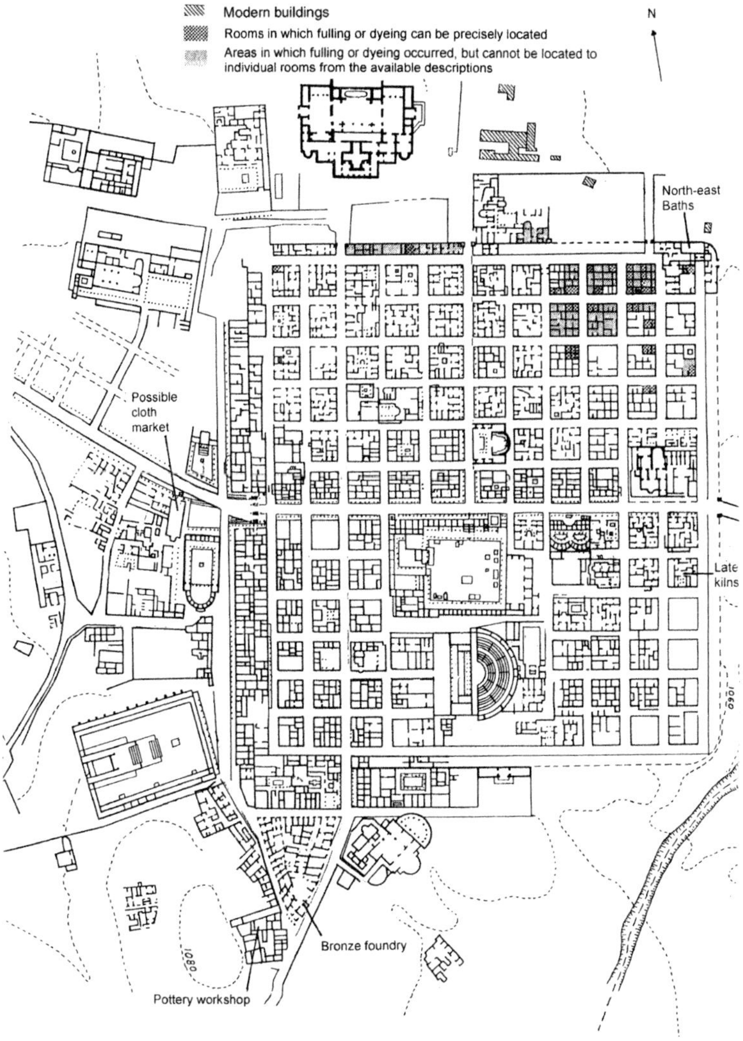

Figure 10.6. Plan of Roman Timgad, showing fulleries (shaded) and other workshops. The Trajanic core of the original city is clearly visible, with the forum near the centre and the theatre below this; the Capitolium is in the south-west, with the Market of Sertius and a possible cloth market above it. At the top centre are the large Northern Baths (Wilson 2001a, 279, Fig. 12.08).

City Planning

Like Carthage, those sites which were colonial foundations, or which saw the implantation of veteran colonies on pre-existing sites, tended to be planned on a grid layout. At Utica, an extensive grid plan layout has been traced from excavation, air photography, and recently geophysics, with rectangular *insulae* similar to Carthage, though without an evident *cardo maximus* and *decumanus maximus*; its date, however, remains to be established and a pre-Roman origin cannot yet be excluded.[43] The most celebrated example of a grid-planned town in North Africa is Timgad (ancient Thamugadi), founded as a colony under Trajan in AD 100, and laid out on a square grid with the forum at the centre at the junction of the *decumanus maximus* and *cardo maximus* (Fig. 10.6). Because the forum lies at the dead-centre of the plan, the southern part of the *cardo maximus* has to make a dog-leg around it. The plan is similar in many respects to that of legionary fortresses, with the forum in the place of the fort's headquarters building or *principia*. However, for all that Timgad is often taken as a textbook example of Roman town planning, such regularity is actually extremely rare. Indeed, even at Timgad, the subsequent development of the city, growing from its initial size of just under 10 ha to some 47.5 ha, lacks the order of the original foundation. The wall that originally surrounded the Trajanic colony was demolished in the later second century and the town expanded over it, the original gates marked by monumental arches (Fig. 10.7). These expansions chiefly took the form of ribbon development following the roads out of town, in stark contrast to the regularity of the original grid; and the third-century *Capitolium* temple complex is located outside the original colony, on a completely different alignment.

Timgad in fact shows the reverse of the much more common pattern of urban development in North Africa, which generally comprises an early nucleus (Punic or Numidian) of irregular streets, with later outgrowths of regularly planned expansion, as at Sabratha, where the early core around the forum contrasts with the regularly planned area (second century AD) to the north of the theatre, or Volubilis, where the north-east quarter is a more regular and spaciously planned later development. At Lepcis Magna, successive phases of expansion are traceable through different alignments of sections of the city plan.

Cuicul (modern Djemila), a Nervan colony founded in AD 96, shortly before Timgad, shows a nearly regular plan adapted slightly to the topography of the narrow ridge on which it sits, although here too later development along the ridge takes a less regular form, determined as much by the

[43] Ben Jerbania *et al.* 2015; Hay *et al.* 2010; Kallala *et al.* 2010; Lézine 1968.

Figure 10.7. Timgad – the view along the *decumanus maximus* towards the so-called 'Arch of Trajan', in fact a late second-century honorific arch built on the site of the original west gate when the wall circuit was torn down as the city expanded. The *decumanus maximus* (the main east-west street) and the *cardo maximus* (the main north-south street, seen departing to the left) are both colonnaded and paved in blue lias, while the minor streets (right) are paved in local limestone. Note how the paving slabs are set at 45 degrees to the line of the road so that the ruts caused by wheeled traffic do not enlarge the joints between them (Photo: A. Wilson).

constraints of topography as by the main street axis along the ridge. Cuicul, like Thamugadi, is a Berber toponym, suggesting a pre-Roman settlement here, and it is noteworthy that like so many of the other Berber settlements it occupies a site on a spur delimited by ravines either side.

The areas of Roman cities in North Africa range from a few hectares up to some 450+ ha for Lepcis Magna (Table 10.1). We have no direct evidence for the size of their population, which can only be roughly estimated from the areas, by applying approximate population densities. Evidence from sites where housing has been extensively excavated suggest that at Sabratha a range of 165–414 inhabitants/ha is plausible, giving a total population of between 5,730 and 14,330, while Trajanic Timgad seems to have had *c.*3,550 inhabitants in 9.96 ha at a density of *c.*357/ha; the city's later expansion may have taken the population up to perhaps between 8,000 and 14,000 but at a rather lower density per hectare.[44] But in addition to these better known, larger cities, there were numerous smaller cities, many developed from the

[44] Wilson 2011a, 175–76.

Table 10.1 *Areas of selected large and medium-sized cities in Roman North Africa, c.second century AD*

City	Area (ha)
Lepcis Magna	452
Iol Caesarea	318
Ptolemais	217
Thelepte	180
Hadrumetum	155
Cyrene	123
Uthina	120
Utica	95
Ammaedara	61
Hippo Regius	60
Theveste	56
Tipasa	55
Ksar el-Guellal	53
Thamugadi	50
Tocra	41
Volubilis	40
Thapsus	39
Sufetula	38
Leptiminus	38
Sabratha	35
Cillium	31
Bulla Regia	31
Thugga	25
Thuburbo Maius	25

Numidian villages. These number two or three hundred, and by the early third century AD had acquired some at least of the categories of public buildings discussed below, even if their populations were never more than a thousand or two. It is the near-ubiquity of these small but monumentally impressive settlements that is one of the most striking features of North African urbanism in the Roman period.

Architecture and Buildings

No two Roman cities are exactly alike, but they share a common architectural language and the same types of public buildings. Usually a rectangular space, the forum was the religious, political, and often also the commercial heart of the city. From the first century AD onwards fora were regularly paved, and in several towns (e.g. Lepcis Magna, Hippo Regius) bronze letters set into the paving record the generosity of the benefactor who paid for the work. One side of the forum was frequently bounded by a basilica or law court, and overlooked by one or more temples, dedicated to the protective deities of the city or to Roma and Augustus (indeed, the forum at Lepcis Magna has three temples to Roma and Augustus, to Hercules, and to Liber Pater), or to the Capitoline Triad of Jupiter, Juno and Minerva (e.g. Thuburbo Maius). Contrary to what is commonly assumed, however, *Capitolia* were not by any means a universal phenomenon, and even where they do exist many post-date the foundation or development of a city (for example, Cuicul, or Thugga). The *Capitolium* at Timgad was built well outside the original colony and far from its forum (Fig 10.6).[45] Temples to other deities might be found at other points throughout the city, or even on its outskirts: temples of Mercury Sobrius, for example, seem to have been located on the edge of town on major routes, and may have served also as the location of periodic markets or fairs.[46] Specialised market buildings or *macella* supplemented the commercial function of the forum; they took the form of a square, or more usually, rectangular enclosure with stalls around the edges and a circular or polygonal kiosk in the centre (the *macellum* at Lepcis is unusual in having two central kiosks). The permanent fixtures of the stalls consisted of little more than a stone counter between columns, and a space behind for the stall holder to stand. In addition, a *macellum* usually had a set of standard weights and measures for dry or liquid goods, set in a stone table called a *mensa ponderaria*, that enabled city magistrates to check trading standards. Roman-period inscriptions in Punic from Lepcis Magna record public amenities (such as benches) set up by magistrates from the fines imposed on market traders. *Macella* may have served in particular for the sale of meat or fish, although a stone engraved with standard length measurements from the *macellum* at Lepcis indicate that the goods sold included cloth, and one of the stalls in the *macellum* at Timgad was selling children's toys at the time of the city's destruction in the late fifth century AD. A noticeable characteristic of Roman city development in North Africa as elsewhere was the imbrication of shops and elite residences: many larger houses, and especially those on the most frequented thoroughfares, had shops built into their street frontages, which might be staffed by slaves, operated through freedmen, or rented to other individuals.

A distinguishing feature of Roman cities, in North Africa as elsewhere, was their dependence on long-distance aqueducts that tapped water

[45] Quinn and Wilson 2013. [46] Fentress 2007.

Figure 10.8. The Severan nymphaeum (monumental fountain) at Lepcis Magna. A two-storey columnar façade of coloured marble columns framed niches which originally housed statues of gods and the imperial family (Photo: A. Wilson).

sources at some distance from the city. There has been some debate over how necessary they really were, usually couched as a false opposition between aqueducts as a utility and aqueducts as a luxury.[47] In reality they were simultaneously both: they celebrated a lavish command of water resources through monumental fountains and in the *thermae* or baths, sumptuous palaces for public bathing, but at the same time these fountains (Fig. 10.8) provided the basic water supply for the majority of the urban population, and supplemented with better and fresher supplies the water stored in domestic cisterns. The fact that aqueducts, cisterns and wells, and occasionally local springs, coexisted within the same settlement is not an argument that aqueducts were redundant. The Romans were clearly alive to the different qualities of water provided by different sources, and how they might best be suited to different purposes. It is apparent that aqueducts both allowed a larger urban population to be sustained than would have been possible otherwise, and that they facilitated a peculiarly Roman lifestyle of public bathing and lavish public and private display of water in ornamental fountains.[48] In addition to the public baths, aqueducts enabled the construction of public latrines flushed by (usually continuous) running

[47] Leveau 1987; Leveau and Paillet 1976; 1983; Shaw 1984; 1991.
[48] Wilson 1997; 1998; 2001b; 2012.

water; toilets were often included in public bath complexes (although sometimes accessible directly from the street, without having to use the baths), or adjacent to the forum, as at Timgad.[49] Most Roman cities of any size acquired one or more aqueducts, often in the course of the second century AD; we have already seen that Carthage had several, as did for example Thysdrus (two),[50] Volubilis, Cirta, Timgad, and Berenice (three each), and Meninx (four). Towns without an aqueduct are rare, and perhaps the only certain example is Tiddis, a small settlement in Numidia perched on a hill to which it would have been well-nigh impossible to bring an aqueduct. Even here, substantial water supply works were undertaken in AD 251 to create a water-collecting area just below the summit of the hill that fed large reservoir cisterns supplying a small set of public baths, a rare example in the empire of such an amenity fed entirely by rainfall collection.

Entertainment buildings were usually (though not always) to be found towards the edges of towns where space was less at a premium than in the centre, although Timgad, with its theatre behind the forum, provides an exception. Of the main types of building dedicated to entertainment, theatres were much the most common, reflecting both their lesser construction cost compared to other entertainment buildings, and, perhaps more importantly, the lower cost of putting on theatrical performances compared with gladiatorial shows or circus games. Amphitheatres were less common than theatres, although the larger cities have them and over 38 are known from Africa Proconsularis alone.[51] They were used for displays of gladiatorial combat and for wild beast hunts, by professional troupes of animal-hunters such as the Telegenii, who are recorded on several inscriptions and mosaics.[52] Several amphitheatres had tunnels and cells below the arena from which animals could be winched up in cages and released through trapdoors into the arena.[53] Circuses were even less common, and (with one exception) restricted to the larger cities: Carthage, Iol Caesarea, Thysdrus, Lepcis Magna – and, oddly, Thugga, a small town of perhaps 5,000 inhabitants. In general, entertainment buildings broadly reflect a hierarchy of urban rank and significance, suggesting different catchment areas for the different categories of entertainment provided.

[49] Wilson 2000; 2011b.
[50] Cintas 1956, *pace* Shaw 1991, 81 who erroneously believed that it had none.
[51] Lachaux 1979, 16, 156–57.
[52] See, for example, the mosaic of Henchir Smirat: Beschaouch 1966.
[53] See, for example, Carthage, Thysdrus (El Jem).

Figure 10.9. Aerial view of Sabratha, looking west. The theatre is clearly visible on the left, with several blocks of housing excavated between it and the sea. The second major area of excavation, in the upper centre of the picture, includes the forum and several temple complexes, with the Seaward Baths by the shore, set off-axis to the main grid (Wilson 2001a, 108, Fig. 1).

Outside the cities of the living stretched the cities of the dead, necropoleis lining the main routes out of town, with tombs large and small jostling for the attention of the passer-by, in a competition of commemoration.

Roman cities in general exhibit an extraordinary high level of monumental overhead – a vast mass of imposing public buildings considering the level of population (Fig. 10.9).[54] These buildings projected messages about the fruits of empire, the stability and permanence of Roman rule, the scale of imperial power, and the wealth of the local elites who had paid for many of these construction projects. Cities in North Africa displayed all these features, and the impact of their buildings was enhanced by the abundance of local good quality stone, enabling many to be built in good limestone or sandstone ashlar, in contrast to many domestic houses whose superstructure was built in mudbrick or pisé (rammed earth). In particular, it is remarkable how relatively small places put up monumental arches,

[54] Wilson 2011a, 177.

structures with no practical utility, but which served to project an image of prosperity and of loyalty to the empire (something apparently especially frequent in the Severan period).[55] Sometimes this was part of a campaign to petition the emperor for an upgrade in civic status.

The monumentality of public buildings was further underscored by the Roman practice of inscribing them prominently with the names of their builders. Members of the local elite in many cases would promise to construct a particular building if they were elected to office, spending above and beyond the stipulated fee or *summa honoraria* that was levied on magistrates, priests and other holders of municipal office. The built landscape became an arena where competition between wealthy families was played out, with the building inscriptions often specifying the sums expended. This practice of public benefaction, or euergetism, had Hellenistic roots, but became especially widespread under Rome: it harnessed to useful ends the politically competitive instincts of local elites, who with incorporation into the Roman empire had become small fish in a very large pond, and at the same time it devolved the costs of urban development from the state onto rich local families.

Imperial involvement becomes more common in building projects of the second century AD. Phrases like *ex indulgentia* (as at Verecunda in Numidia, or occurring as the legend with the symbolic depiction of the Carthage aqueduct on a Severan coin issue) may imply state aid to a town, perhaps in the form of a remission of taxes. The words *ex auctoritate imperatoris* or *imperator . . . fieri iussit* ('by imperial authority' or 'the emperor commanded it be done') show that emperors, generally through the intermediaries of their procurators or legates, either approved construction or even commanded works to be carried out which were paid for by the towns.[56] The expense might be lightened by the use of military labour, as with the aqueduct of Saldae.[57] Cities financed many projects from public money (*pecunia publica*), and individual euergetism became very common, often in connection with the fees paid (*summa honoraria*) for holding public office, and more rarely as a testamentary benefaction. In return for their buildings, benefactors received the honour of a statue erected at civic expense in a prominent public space – often the forum, or the theatre – and this 'statue habit' caused cities progressively to accumulate a sculpted population of stone and bronze honorands.

[55] Wilson 2007b. [56] Jouffroy 1986, 233. [57] *ILS* 5795.

The Economies of Roman Cities

The wealth of Roman Africa came principally from agriculture, and especially from its fertile fields of grain and its olive groves; it exported grain and olive oil in large quantities, but there were also appreciable exports of wine; and of salted fish and derived products (*garum*, *liquamen*, and *allec*, fish sauces and paste). The wealth of the cities was founded on this rich productive base, and it is clear that North African agriculture was sufficiently productive to support a considerable population of city dwellers who were not engaged in primary agriculture. But the cities too produced goods and services: textiles, dyes, metalwork and craft goods. The coastal cities also frequently acted as the bottling points for the olive oil and wine exported from the interior of the province. This is not the place to reprise the lengthy debate over whether the ancient city was a consumer city or a producer city, a debate whose very terms are largely false because it assumes that a city plus its territory formed a cellular self-sufficient unit, ignoring the plentiful evidence for long-distance trade between cities. Some cities do indeed seem to have acted as agrovilles, residential and administrative centres a large part of whose population worked the surrounding land – Volubilis, Madauros and site KS 022 in the Kasserine Survey area seem to have played this role, on the evidence of the numerous oil presses they contain.[58] But the full extent, and indeed the nature, of urban production remains difficult to grasp, largely because of evidential problems connected with the size of production units, and the preservation (or lack of it) in the archaeological record of diagnostic traces of production, whether infrastructure or equipment, or the waste or residues from production processes.[59]

Most production units in the ancient world were relatively small, although in fact some large factories, and especially fish-salting factories, do indeed survive in urban contexts (e.g. Lixus in Morocco). Establishing that there was, or that there was not, significant production of a particular item, or even of urban production in general, requires the investigation of large swathes of an urban landscape in order to prove the existence – or the absence – of numerous small production units.[60] But in those cases where excavation has been carried out extensively across large areas of Roman cities – for example, Timgad between *c.*1880 and 1920, or Sabratha between 1923 and 1942 – the quality of excavation has been poor and finds recording very limited; in most cases the key evidence of production debris will have gone unnoticed or unrecorded. And yet in fact in both these cases

[58] Hitchner 1990. [59] Wilson 2002b. [60] Wilson 2002b.

plentiful evidence was uncovered (some of it not recognised at the time) of productive activities that required particular built infrastructure – probable fulleries at Timgad (Fig. 10.6), and fish-salting vats at Sabratha.[61] At Sabratha, too, the evidence of crushed murex shells re-used as aggregate in cement floors indicates the production of purple dye, and indeed the dyeing of some textile fibres (probably wool) with it, somewhere at the site. By contrast, modern excavation techniques usually cover too small an area to establish whether or not there are multiple production units – although with the aid of magnetometry and surface survey and pottery collection, for example, clusters of kilns have been found at some sites: coarseware kilns on the outskirts of Utica, and amphora and coarseware kilns at Leptiminus and at Sullecthum (Salakta).[62]

Geophysical survey and surface sherd collection have been employed at some sites to investigate the question of the extent and scale of some production industries – at least, those that leave readily detectable production waste. Besides the examples just cited, numerous kilns are indicated at Ptolemais in Cyrenaica by kiln wasters and overfired pottery scattered across parts of the site. Purple dye production is indicated by crushed murex shell reused as aggregate in structural mortars at Lepcis Magna, and large spreads of crushed murex shell at Berenice (Benghazi) and, most spectacularly, at Meninx on Jerba, where a dump of crushed murex at least 500 × 300 m, and over 2.5 m deep, can still be seen, attesting the production of purple dye on a massive scale and over a long period of time.[63] Many of the amphora sherds associated with the dump are from first- to third-century AD forms, but the mention of an imperial dyeworks at the site in the *Notitia Dignitata*, shows that production continued into the late Roman period.[64] While such non-invasive surface investigation techniques potentially allow city-wide examination of the question of urban production, they provide very little information on chronology, and of course are limited to those activities which produce either clear geophysical signals, or durable and recognisable production waste. Nonetheless, they do show a mixture of activities at those sites at which they have been conducted: pottery production and fish-salting at Utica; fish-salting, metalworking (of imported iron ore), coarseware and amphora production (for fish

[61] Timgad: Wilson 2001a. Sabratha: Wilson 1999; 2007a.

[62] Utica: Ben Jerbania *et al.* 2015; Fentress *et al.* 2013. Leptiminus: Mattingly *et al.* 2011, 224–52. Sullecthum: Peacock *et al.* 1989, 192–94.

[63] Wilson 2002a; 2002b.

[64] *Notitia Dignitata, occidentis* 11.70; Wilson 2002a. Excavation of parts of two buildings with evidence for murex dye production shows that this activity continued into the fourth and fifth centuries: Aït Kaci *et al.* 2009, 9–20, 215–16.

products, wine and olive oil) at Leptiminus, fish-salting and amphora production at Sullecthum; fish-salting, olive oil production and glassworking at Sabratha.[65]

Urban Systems and Networks

Cities controlled an area of territory around them, from which they drew rents on land and farms owned directly by the city, and levied local taxes. The territory of self-governing cities might include smaller dependent towns without self-governing status. Control of territory was important: Oea (Tripoli) and Lepcis Magna went to war with each other in AD 68–69 over a boundary dispute. The Roman road system networked cities to their nearest neighbours and through them to larger and more important towns, and ultimately the large administrative centres like Carthage.

The juridical statuses of Roman urban settlements, in North Africa as elsewhere, do not map neatly onto differences in size or even in monumentality.[66] While the provincial capital (Carthage for Africa Proconsularis, Sitifis for Mauretania Sitifensis, Iol Caesarea for Mauretania Caesariensis, Tingis for Mauretania Tingitana; and, later, Cirta for Numidia) was usually one of the largest cities of its province, *coloniae* were not always larger than *municipia*, and some *vici* (small towns) rivalled towns with a higher status. Political links can be traced upwards from small towns to the provincial capital and even to Rome, as at Dougga, some of whose magistrates also held political office at Carthage, and one was adlected into the jury courts at Rome. Similarly, one of the richest councillors at Timgad, Sertius, was a priest of the cult of the city of Rome. Entertainers, theatrical players, gladiatorial troupes and *venatores* (professional animal hunters for amphitheatre shows) will have travelled their own circuits between towns to give performances; and just as the catchment areas for different kinds of entertainment varied according to which towns had circuses, amphitheatres, or theatres, so too would the entertainment circuits travelled by these performers.

Many of the most prosperous and largest cities appear to have been coastal ports. More systematic research would be needed to prove this as a rule, but it is a strong impression. Their role as export points connected to a wider Mediterranean network of markets was apparently a source of their wealth. Amphora production at many of the large coastal cities shows that they served as bottling points for olive oil and even wine, which was

[65] Wilson 1999. [66] Cf. Hanson 2016, 81–87.

produced inland and then exported through these cities together with the salted fish products from seasonal catches of migratory species caught off their coasts. Cooking wares produced at these coastal sites seem to have piggy-backed on the export flows of amphora-borne products to reach a wide distribution of overseas coastal markets around the western Mediterranean, and to a lesser extent the eastern Mediterranean too.

The cities with their fora, *macella*, and streets lined with fixed shops or *tabernae* forming a cluster of fixed retail outlets constituted permanent, not merely periodic, markets. As such they must have had a different relationship with their surrounding villages than had been the case in a world of periodic markets; although there were in addition some periodic markets (or *nundinae*) at towns – or on their outskirts – and at rural sites too.[67]

Inland cities served as local markets for a rural economy based on agriculture and livestock with a smaller radius of action. Sites in the Tunisian Tell and Sahel within some 200 km of the coast seem to have exported their oil and grain to coastal sites. Along with the agricultural products went the shiny red table pottery (African Red Slip Ware), which was exported around the Mediterranean from AD 90 onwards. By contrast, cooking wares produced at sites away from the coast were not exported and had only a limited distribution. Further west and further away from the coast (in what is modern Algeria), the inland Numidian table pottery industries had only a limited distribution, over a radius of up to *c*.35 km.[68]

As with the Numidian period, the larger towns of the interior were in the major grain-growing plains.[69] Using the example of Sétif, an inland town in Numidia, Fentress identifies two economies: a regionally self-sufficient economy in which the town played the part of a regional market for surplus crops, largely wheat, and for locally made goods in leather, pottery and cloth; and a second economy based on the surrounding imperial estates and the grain market. Tax grain collected by the State and the rent in kind from tenants (*coloni*) on imperial estates were collected in *horrea* (granaries) and transported to coastal ports from where it was exported to Rome. It was not until the fourth century that the two economies merged, when the military response to Moorish raids and incursions saw a growing body of administrative and military personnel stationed in the town, with cash income for the city derived both from these administrative salaries and the opportunities for profiting from supplying the army.[70]

67 Fentress 2007; Shaw 1981. 68 Fentress 2013, 332.
69 Fentress 2006, 21, speaking of the Numidian towns in the fourth–second centuries BC.
70 Fentress 1990.

For the cities in the immediate vicinity of large troop concentrations the supply of the army will have been an important feature of their economy. The small town of Diana Veteranorum was no doubt involved in the supply of the legionary fortress at Lambaesis until the *legio III Augusta* was disbanded in the mid-third century; thereafter, Fentress suggests that it supplied units stationed south of the Aurès mountain range.[71] Timgad was presumably engaged in supplying the legionary base at Lambaesis, 19 km to the west, with food over and above the local market. A large number of fulleries (22) and a cloth market (mid-fourth century) suggest that by the late Roman period the town had become a major centre for textile production, playing a coordinating role in turning the wool from the livestock economy of the surrounding countryside into textiles. Thelepte in the Tunisian steppe may have played a similar role, as Hitchner suggests that enclosures on its outskirts may have been yards for livestock.[72]

Unsurprisingly, the density of cities decreases towards the southern margins of the Roman African provinces, as more arid environments make it harder (though not impossible) to support large nucleated populations. As Chapter 5 above has demonstrated, in the frontier zone, the major settlements were at oasis centres, and these often became the sites of frontier forts.[73] But while we tend to think of these as oasis forts, with military *vici* (settlements) around them, in all probability some kind of oasis settlement existed before the forts (this was certainly the case at Cidamus/ Ghadamis). The case of al-Qurayyat al-Gharbia, where the Severan fort built in the early third century was abandoned *c.*275–280 and reoccupied in the fourth and early fifth centuries, but with occupation continuing until *c.*540 possibly under a Libyan chieftain, and also at times (whether continuous or not) during the Medieval period, shows that the viability of the site was not entirely dependent on the presence of a Roman military unit.[74] Rather, the oasis marked the northern end of the longest waterless stretch on the Saharan route down to Fazzan. Little is known in any detail of the nature and morphology of these oasis settlements, although the 18-ha settlement around the fort of Bu Nijim shows that some could be sizeable (Fig. 10.10). The *vici* at Bu Nijim and al-Qurayyat al-Gharbia had temples and shrines, and a bathhouse, although no other kinds of public buildings are known. Ostraca from the fort of Bu Nijim suggest that here the oasis centre acted as a major terminus for camel caravans coming up from the Sahara via the Jufra oasis group further south.[75]

[71] Fentress 2013. [72] Hitchner 1994, 39–40. [73] Mattingly *et al.*, Chapter 5, this volume.
[74] Mackensen 2012; Mackensen *et al.* 2010, 379–85. [75] Marichal 1992.

Figure 10.10. Satellite image of the Roman fort of Bu Nijim and its surrounding vicus or settlement, before encroachment by modern intensive olive culture between 2006 and 2012 (imagery: Google, DigitalGlobe, 24 March 2006).

Late Antique Urbanism

Late antiquity, and especially the Vandal and Byzantine periods in North Africa, saw profound transformations in the appearance and roles of cities.[76] From the mid-third century onwards there was a marked decline in euergetism and the construction of public buildings. A resurgence of activity in the 360s and 370s, especially in Numidia, is to a considerable extent accounted for by repairs (although there was new construction too), but whether this was prompted by a period of intense seismic activity or reflects a bout of fourth-century prosperity remains an open question. New construction effort was indeed channelled into churches, but it is hard to see this before the fifth century, and even then this activity was on a much smaller aggregate scale than the building activity of the second century. The argument that by the third century most cities had all the public buildings they needed is not wholly persuasive (more temples, to other deities, could always be built), and does not explain the decay or change in use of some buildings that already existed. In cities with more than one set of large public baths we find that in

[76] See in particular Leone 2007. Sears 2007 places the accent on continuity rather than decline, and argues that cities were 'thriving' into the fifth century, a view achieved largely by ignoring contrary evidence.

Figure 10.11. Sufetula (Sbeïtla): Late antique building with two oil presses, attached to the church of Saints Gervasius and Tryphon (out of the picture, to the right), built across and entirely blocking a Roman street (Photo: A. Wilson).

late antiquity (by the later fourth century) these had been renamed 'Summer Baths' and 'Winter Baths', the 'Winter Baths' always being the smaller and easier to heat.[77] Civic finances no longer ran to heating two sets of baths, and the second-century urban lifestyle could no longer be funded. Conversely, though, we see some of the richer private houses enlarging in the third and fourth centuries, sometimes with lavish apsidal or tri-apsidal reception halls.

The reasons for these changes were multiple and not entirely evident, but clearly involved fiscal pressure. They included: the military and economic crises of the mid- to late third century, whose effect on the imperial finances had repercussions on local taxation; reduced autonomy of town councils and a consequent reluctance of local elites to undertake the euergetic burdens of municipal office, preferring to expend their wealth on their own dwellings; depopulation caused by the 'Plague of Cyprian' (AD 251–270),[78] and later, the Justinianic Plague of the 540s; and changing religious practices. In the space left by the retreat of town councils, the church increasingly insinuated itself into the expanding administrative vacuum. At Lepcis Magna a fifth-century church and baptistery were built

[77] For example, at Madauros, Sufetula, and Thuburbo Maius: Nielsen 1992, 138–40. This phenomenon is also seen in the Eastern Mediterranean, as for example at Aphrodisias: Wilson 2016, 193.

[78] Harper 2015.

Figure 10.12. Sabratha – late antique graves (in the foreground) in a street by the church to the north of the theatre (Photo: A. Wilson).

in the forum, and civil basilicas or lawcourts were turned into churches at Sabratha and, after the Justinianic conquest, at Lepcis Magna. The growing power of the church in controlling civic space is suggested, for example, by the double oil-press building attached to the church of Saints Gervasius and Tryphon at Sufetula, built across and entirely blocking a street (Fig. 10.11).

The new dominance of Christianity saw a marked change in the location of cemeteries: martyrs' shrines, then churches, grew up around the graves of martyrs in cemeteries, and increasingly people wanted to be buried *ad sanctos*, next to the holy martyrs.[79] As churches became spatially associated with graves, the taboo on intramural burial broke down and we find burials around churches in city centres, for example around the former civic basilica-turned-church at Sabratha (Fig. 10.12), or in the forum at Lepcis Magna.

In the course of the fourth century there were repeated attempts to close the pagan temples (repeated because initially unsuccessful in many regions). In North Africa the chronology of this process remains unclear, but it must have been largely complete by the end of the century. We find inscriptions recording the transfer of statues *ex squalidis locis*, from dilapidated buildings (literally, 'from filthy places') to more public areas, and these may in

[79] Yasin 2009, Chapter 2.

some cases relate to the salvage of statuary from temples, although not, presumably, the unacceptable cult images. At Thuburbo Maius, at some undefined time in late antiquity, an olive press was installed in the basement of the *Capitolium* – reflecting a more widespread phenomenon by which agricultural processing equipment, already prominent in some cities in the mid-Roman period (Volubilis, Madauros), was installed in formerly public spaces in late antiquity (for example, Lepcis Magna, where a late antique oil press is found in the gymnasium adjoining the Hadrianic Baths).

The end of the Roman aqueducts came later, although again the timing is uncertain. Numerous fourth-century inscriptions commemorate the repair of aqueducts,[80] and even the construction of new ones.[81] Many aqueducts may have functioned until the Arab conquest: Carthage's aqueduct was still functioning until it was cut in the siege of 682, which saw Carthage finally fall to the Arabs. At Leptiminus, further south along the Tunisian coast, the eastern aqueduct was still functioning normally until the 640s, when it was blocked immediately downstream of the reservoir cisterns for the eastern baths, which thus received the entire flow of the aqueduct. The baths themselves, however, were no longer serving their original purpose: a group of amphora kilns had been built in them, and the water was presumably therefore used for pottery production.[82]

Demographic decline is apparent, in North Africa as in much of the rest of the Western Roman empire after the third century, from the shrinking areas of cities. Lepcis Magna contracted progressively in late antiquity. The early imperial defensive perimeter that had enclosed *c.*452 ha in the first and second centuries AD was abandoned, perhaps in the fourth century, and replaced by a defensive wall built of *spolia* and incorporating the arch of Marcus Aurelius as a gateway, enclosing a total of 143 ha. In the sixth century AD the city had further shrunk: the Byzantine fortifications enclosed just 16.9 ha, defending the harbour, the Old Forum, and the Severan Forum.[83] A similar process of contraction happened at Sabratha, where the Byzantine walls enclose an area around the forum and the harbour, leaving most of the Roman city outside them. How far this demographic contraction may have been exacerbated by the Justinianic Plague remains an open question, as we have little direct evidence for its

[80] For example, *ILAlg.* 1.296 Calama; *CIL* 8.27818 Sidi Achmed el Hachemi; *ILTun* 622 Henchir Haouli, AD 339/350; *CIL* 8.18700 = 4766 Ksour el-Ahmar, AD 305; *AE* 1899, 216 Mascula, AD 367/375.

[81] Cirta: *ILAlg.* 2.619 = *ILS* 5789 = *CIL* 8.7034, and *AE* 1902, 166, both dating to AD 388/392; Henchir el-Left: *AE* 1949, 49 = *BAC* 1947, 376, AD 321/324.

[82] Stirling *et al.* 2001.

[83] Mattingly 1995, 117, figure 6.1; Wilson 2011a, 167.

Figure 10.13. Sullecthum (Salakta) – late defensive enclosure, belonging probably to the Vandal period (late fifth or early sixth century AD) (Photo: A. Wilson).

effect on North Africa, although it is hard to believe that the region escaped its impact.

Increased fortification is an especially striking feature of these late antique towns. While some Roman towns had had wall circuits – Timgad at its foundation, although the wall circuit had already been demolished by the Severan period – and Tipasa in the second century, most towns were unfortified in the second and even third centuries AD under the *pax Romana*. But – at a still largely undetermined date – fortifications were increasingly deemed necessary in late antiquity. Carthage was fortified with a rampart under Theodosius, *c*.425, presumably in response to the Vandal threat.[84] But even before the Vandal conquest, and increasingly after it, raids by Saharan tribesmen prompted the construction of fortifications at cities in the south of Roman Africa.[85] At Sullecthum, a crude defensive wall is probably to be identified with the fortification wall mentioned by Procopius that was built between houses on the edge of the city to defend the town against Berber raids before the Byzantine reconquest in AD 533 (Fig. 10.13). A similar style of fortification has been identified at Leptiminus.[86] Blockhouses, of unknown date, within the former urban zone are found at towns in southern Tunisia and also in Cyrenaica. At

[84] Wells 1980. [85] For these Moorish raids, see Fentress and Wilson 2016.
[86] Fentress and Wilson 2016, 43–44. Leptiminus: Wilson *et al.* 2011, 536–38.

Sufetula we find blockhouse construction in the outlying parts of the town, with a fortified wall around the forum, while at Ptolemais the 3-km long Hellenistic wall circuit was actually torn down, presumably because there were insufficient forces to man it properly, and a number of small forts built within the city area. These are in addition to the so-called 'Fortress of the Dux', a Byzantine fort built certainly no later than the reign of Anastasius (491–518) and possibly already by the early fifth century AD.[87]

During the century between the Byzantine reconquest and the first Arab incursions of the AD 640s, forts were constructed at nearly every town in Byzantine Africa.[88] These ranged from small blockhouse-type affairs incorporating Roman honorific arches, for example at Diana Veteranorum or Ammaedara, to large forts, with projecting corner towers, that protected water sources, as at Timgad or Ksar Lemsa (Limisa). The distribution of Byzantine fortifications across the former Roman territory throughout what is now Tunisia and eastern Algeria makes it meaningless to talk of a Byzantine *limes* – it was evidently expected that raids might penetrate deep into Byzantine territory, and that the best way of holding out against them was to retreat into fortified blockhouses, or reduced wall circuits, until the immediate threat had passed.

Conclusions

The Roman period stands out as a phase of extraordinary urbanisation across the Maghrib, during which levels of urban population were achieved that were not equalled again until the late nineteenth or early twentieth century. It is now evident that this urbanisation built on a local tradition of Numidian villages and early towns, in addition to the much better known Punic colonies of the coast. Africa's famous agricultural prosperity is clearly reflected in the monumental grandeur of the Roman public buildings and the confident infrastructure of the aqueducts, striding across a pacified landscape – a water supply technology suited to the *pax Romana*, but vulnerable to disruption in the more turbulent centuries following the Vandal conquest. Urban life declined under Vandal rule, and even further in the later sixth and the seventh centuries; and after the Arab conquest of the seventh century, the Medieval Maghrib developed an urban system organised around new centres – either developed out of minor Roman

[87] Reynolds 1976, 248–49. [88] Pringle 1981.

towns like Tunis, or entirely new foundations like the holy city of Kairouan, founded by the Umayyads *c.*AD 670.

References

Aït Kaci, A., Drine, A., Fentress, E.W.B., Morton, T.J., Rabinowitz, A. and Wilson, A.I. 2009. The excavations. In E. Fentress, A. Drine and R. Holod (eds), *An Island through Time: Jerba Studies 1. The Punic and Roman Periods.* Portsmouth, Rhode Island: Journal of Roman Archaeology Supplement 71, 212–40.

Ben Jerbania, I., Fentress, E., Ghozzi, F., Wilson, A.I., Carpentiero, G., Dhibi, C., Dufton, J.A., Hay, S., Jendoubi, K., Mariotti, E., Morley, G., Oueslati, T., Sheldrick, N. and Zocchi, A. 2015. *Excavations at Utica by the Tunisian-British Utica Project 2014.* Unpublished Field Report: University of Oxford.

Bennett, P., Wilson, A.I., Buzaian, A.M. and Kattenberg, A. 2004. The effects of recent storms on the exposed coastline of Tocra. *Libyan Studies* 35: 113–22.

Beschaouch, A. 1966. La mosaïque de la chasse à l'amphithéâtre découverte à Smirat en Tunisie. *Comptes rendus de l'Académie des inscriptions et belles-lettres* 1966: 134–57.

Boardman, J. and Hayes, J. 1966. *Excavations at Tocra 1963–1965. The Archaic Deposits*, vol. 1. London: British School of Archaeology at Athens.

Bomgardner, D.L. 1989. The Carthage amphitheater: A reappraisal. *American Journal of Archaeology* 93.1: 85–103.

Broise, H. and Thébert, Y. 1993. *Recherches archéologiques franco-tunisiennes à Bulla Regia. II, Les architectures.* Rome: Collection de l'École française de Rome, 28.2.

Buzaian, A.M. and Lloyd, J.A. 1996. Early urbanism in Cyrenaica: New evidence from Euesperides (Benghazi). *Libyan Studies* 27: 129–52.

Cherstich, L. 2008. From looted tombs to ancient society: A survey of the Southern Necropolis of Cyrene. *Libyan Studies* 39: 73–93.

Cintas, J. 1956. L'alimentation en eau de Thysdrus dans l'antiquité. *Karthago. Revue d'archéologie africaine* 7: 179–87.

Fantar, M. 1984–1986. *Kerkouane. Cité punique de Cap Bon (Tunisie).* 3 vols. Tunis: Persée.

Fantar, M. 1998. *Kerkouane: A Punic Town in the Berber Region of Tamezrat : VIth to IIIrd Century BC.* Translated by J. McGuinness. Tunis: Alif.

Fentress, E.W.B. 1990. The economy of an inland city: Sétif. In *L'Afrique dans l'occident romain Ier siècle av. J.-C. – IVe siècle ap. J.C. Actes du colloque organisé par l'École française de Rome sous la patronage de l'Institut national d'archéologie et d'art de Tunis (Rome 3–5 décembre 1987).* Rome: Collection de l'École française de Rome 134, 117–28.

Fentress, E.W.B. 2006. Romanizing the Berbers. *Past and Present* 190: 3–33.

Fentress, E.W.B. 2007. Where were North African *nundinae* held? In C. Gosden, H. Hamerow, P. de Jersey and G. Lock (eds), *Communities and Connections: Essays in Honour of Barry Cunliffe*. Oxford: Oxford University Press, 125–41.

Fentress, E.W.B. 2009. The Punic and Libyan towns of Jerba. In S. Helas and D. Marzoli (eds), *Phönizisches und punisches Städtewesen*. Mainz: Iberia Archaeologica 13, 203–19.

Fentress, E.W.B. 2013. Diana Veteranorum and the dynamics of an inland economy. *Late Antique Archaeology* 10.1: 315–42. doi:http://dx.doi.org/10.1163/22134522-12340035 [last accessed 13 September, 2019].

Fentress, E.W.B., Ghozzi, F., Quinn, J., Wilson, A., Anastasi, M., Hobson, M., Leitch, V., Morley, G., Ray, N. and Rice, C. 2013. *Excavations at Utica by the Tunisian-British Utica Project 2012*. Unpublished Field Report: University of Oxford.

Fentress, E.W.B. and Wilson, A.I. 2016. The Saharan Berber diaspora and the southern frontiers of Byzantine North Africa. In S.T. Stevens and J.P. Conant (eds), *North Africa under Byzantium and Early Islam*, Washington, D.C.: Dumbarton Oaks Byzantine Symposia and Colloquia 7, 41–63.

Fraser, P.M. 1951. An inscription from Euesperides. *Bulletin de la Société royale d'Archéologie d'Alexandrie* 39: 132–43.

Göransson, K. 2004. Transport amphorae from Euesperides (Benghazi), Libya. A presentation of preliminary results. In J. Eiring and J. Lund (eds), *Transport Amphorae and Trade in the Eastern Mediterranean*. Athens: Monographs of the Danish Institute at Athens, 137–42.

Hanson, J.W. 2016. *An Urban Geography of the Roman World, 100 BC to AD 300*. Oxford: Archaeopress Roman Archaeology, 18.

Harper, K. 2015. Pandemics and passages to late antiquity: Rethinking the plague of c.249–270 described by Cyprian. *Journal of Roman Archaeology* 28: 223–60. doi:10.1017/S1047759415002470.

Hay, S., Fentress, E.W.B., Kallala, N., Quinn, J. and Wilson, A.I. 2010. Archaeological fieldwork reports: Utica. *Papers of the British School at Rome* 78: 325–29.

Hitchner, R.B. 1990. The Kasserine archaeological Survey. 1986 [Institut national d'archéologie et d'art de Tunisie-University of Virginia, USA]. *Antiquités africaines* 26.1: 231–59.

Hitchner, R.B. 1994. Image and reality: The changing face of pastoralism in the Tunisian High Steppe. In J. Carlsen, P. Ørsted and J.E. Skydsgaard (eds), *Landuse in the Roman Empire*. Rome: Analecta romana Instituti danici Supplement, 27–43.

Hurst, H.R. 1993a. Excavations in the southern part of the Carthage harbours, 1992–1993. *CEDAC Carthage Bulletin* 13: 10–19.

Hurst, H.R. 1993b. Le port militaire de Carthage. *Histoire et archéologie. Les dossiers [Paris]* 183: 42–51.

Jouffroy, H. 1986. *La construction publique en Italie et dans l'Afrique: Études et Travaux*. Strasbourg: Association pour l'étude de la civilisation romaine.

Kallala, N., Fentress, E.W.B., Quinn, J., Wilson, A.I., Ben Slimane, W., Booms, D., Friedman, H., Ghozzi, F., Hay, S. and Jerray, E. 2010. *Survey and Excavation at Utica 2010*. Unpublished Field Report: University of Oxford.

Kane, S. and White, D. 2007. Recent developments in Cyrene's chora south of the Wadi bel Gadir. *Libyan Studies* 38: 39–52. doi:10.1017/S0263718900004234.

Lachaux, J.C. 1979. *Théatres et amphithéatres d'Afrique Proconsulaire*. Aix-en-Provence: Edisud.

Lancel, S. 1995. *Carthage: A History*. Oxford: Blackwell.

Leone, A. 2007. *Changing Townscapes in North Africa from Late Antiquity to the Arab Conquest*. Bari: Edipuglia.

Leveau, P. 1987. A quoi servaient les aqueducts romains? *L'Histoire* 105: 96–104.

Leveau, P. and Paillet, J.L. 1976. *L'alimentation en eau de Caesarea de Maurétanie et l'aqueduc de Cherchell*. Paris: Éditions l'Harmattan.

Leveau, P. and Paillet, J.L. 1983. Alimentation en eau et développement urbain à Caesarea de Maurétanie. In J.P. Boucher (ed.), *Journées d'études sur les aqueducs romains. Tagung über römische Wasserversorgungsanlagen, Lyons, 26–28 mai, 1977*. Paris: Société d'édition 'Les Belles Lettres', 231–34.

Lézine, A. 1968. *Carthage. Utique. Études d'architecture et d'urbanisme*. Paris: CNRS.

Lloyd, J.A., Buzaian, A.M. and Coulton, J.J. 1995. Excavations at Euesperides (Benghazi), 1995. *Libyan Studies* 26: 97–100.

Lloyd, J.A., Bennett, P., Buttrey, T.V., Buzaian, A., El Amin, H., Fell, V., Kashbar, G., Morgan, G., Ben Nasser, Y., Roberts, P.C., Wilson, A.I. and Zimi, E. 1998. Excavations at Euesperides (Benghazi): An interim report on the 1998 season. *Libyan Studies* 29: 145–68.

Luni, M. 2001. Le temple dorique hexastyle dans le sanctuaire découvert hors de la porte sud à Cyrène. *Comptes rendus de l'Académie des inscriptions et belles-lettres* 2001: 1533–52.

Luni, M. 2006. Un demi-siècle de recherches archéologiques à Cyrène. *Comptes rendus de l'Académie des Inscriptions et Belles-Lettres* 2006: 2173–201.

Mackensen, M. 2012. New fieldwork at the Severan fort of Myd (. . .)/Gheriat el-Garbia on the limes Tripolitanus. *Libyan Studies* 43: 41–60. doi:10.1017/S0263718900000054.

Mackensen, M., Schimmer, F., Schmid, S., Seren, S., Stephani, M. and Weber, M. 2010. Das severische Vexillationskastell Myd (–)/Gheriat el-Garbia am *limes Tripolitanus* (Libyen). Bericht über die Kampagne 2009. *Mitteilungen des Deutschen Archäologischen Instituts, Römische Mitteilungen* 116: 363–458.

Marichal, R. 1992. *Les ostraca de Bu Njem*. Tripoli: Department of Antiquities, Suppléments de Libya Antiqua 7.

Mattingly, D.J. 1995. *Tripolitania*. London: Batsford.

Mattingly, D.J. 2016. Who shaped Africa? The origins of urbanism and agriculture in Maghreb and Sahara. In N. Mugnai, N. Ray and J. Nikolaus (eds), *De Africa Romaque: Merging Cultures Across North Africa*. London: Society for Libyan Studies, 11–25.

Mattingly, D.J., Stone, D.L., Stirling, L.M., Moore, J.P., Wilson, A.I., Dore, J.N. and Ben Lazreg, N. 2011. Economy. In Stone *et al.* 2011, 205–71.

Nielsen, I. 1992. *Thermae et Balnea. The Architecture and Cultural History of Roman Public Baths*, 2 vols. 2nd ed. Aarhus: Aarhus University Press.

Peacock, D.P.S., Bejaoui, F. and Belazreg, N. 1989. Roman amphora production in the Sahel region of Tunisia. In M. Lenoir, D. Manacorda and C. Panella (eds), *Amphores romaines et histoire économique. Dix ans de recherche. Actes du colloque de Sienne (22–24 mai 1986)*. Rome: Collection École française de Rome, 179–222.

Peña, J.T. 1998. The mobilization of state olive oil in Roman Africa: The evidence of late 4th-c. *ostraca* from Carthage. In *Carthage Papers: The Early Colony's Economy, Water Supply, a Private Bath, and the Mobilization of State Olive Oil*. Portsmouth, Rhode Island: Journal of Roman Archaeology Supplementary Series, 117–238.

Pringle, D. 1981. *The Defence of Byzantine Africa from Justinian to the Arab Conquest*, 2 vols. Oxford: BAR International Series.

Quinn, J. and Wilson, A.I. 2013. Capitolia. *Journal of Roman Studies* 103: 117–73.

Reynolds, J.M. (ed.). 1976. *Libyan Studies. Select Papers by R. G. Goodchild*. London: Elek.

Saumagne, C. 1928. Notes de topographie carthaginoise: I, La «Turris Aquaria» (d'après les fouilles de 1926); II, Les vestiges de la colonie de C. Gracchus à Carthage. *Bulletin achéologique du Comité des Travaux Historiques et Scientifiques* 1928: 629–64.

Sears, G. 2007. *Late Roman African Urbanism: Continuity and Transformation in the City*. Oxford: BAR International Series 1693.

Shaw, B.D. 1981. Rural markets in North Africa and the political economy of the Roman Empire. *Antiquités africaines* 17: 37–83.

Shaw, B.D. 1984. Water and society in the ancient Maghrib: Technology, property and development. *Antiquités africaines* 20: 121–73.

Shaw, B.D. 1991. The noblest monuments and the smallest things: Wells, walls and aqueducts in the making of Roman Africa. In A.T. Hodge (ed.), *Future Currents in Aqueduct Studies*. Leeds: Francis Cairns, 63–91.

Smith, D.J. and Crow, J. 1998. The Hellenistic and Byzantine defences of Tocra (Taucheira). *Libyan Studies* 29: 35–82.

Stirling, L., Mattingly, D.J. and Ben Lazreg, N. 2001. The East Baths and their industrial re-use in late antiquity: 1992 excavations. In L.M. Stirling, D.J. Mattingly and N. Ben Lazreg (eds), *Leptiminus (Lamta): A Roman Port City in Tunisia. Report no. 2*. Ann Arbor: Journal of Roman Archaeology Supplementary series 41, 29–74.

Stone, D.L., Mattingly, D.J. and Ben Lazreg, N. (eds). 2011. *Leptiminus (Lamta), Report no. 3: The Field Survey*, vol. 3. Portsmouth, Rhode Island: JRA Supplementary Series 87.

Swift, K. 2006. *Classical and Hellenistic Coarse Pottery from Euesperides (Benghazi, Libya): Archaeological and Petrological Approaches to Production and Inter-Regional Distribution.* Unpublished DPhil thesis, School of Archaeology, University of Oxford.

Thomas, E. 2007. *Monumentality and the Roman Empire: Architecture in the Antonine Age.* Oxford: School of Archaeology Monograph.

Wells, C.M. 1980. Carthage. The Late Roman defences. In W. Hanson and L. Keppie (eds), *Roman Frontier Studies 1979.* Oxford: BAR International series, 999–1004.

Wells, C.M. 2005 A cuckoo in the nest: The Roman Odeon at Carthage in its urban context. *American Journal of Ancient History* ns 3–4 [2007]: 131–42.

White, D. 1984. *The Extramural Sanctuary of Demeter and Persephone at Cyrene, Libya. Final Reports*, vol. 1. Philadelphia: University Museum monographs.

White, D. 1993. *The Extramural Sanctuary of Demeter and Persephone at Cyrene, Libya. Final Reports*, vol. 5. Philadelphia: University Museum monographs.

Wilson, A.I. 1997. *Water Management and Usage in Roman North Africa: A Social and Technological Study.* Unpublished DPhil thesis, University of Oxford.

Wilson, A.I. 1998. Water supply in ancient Carthage. In *Carthage Papers: The Early Colony's Economy, Water Supply, a Private Bath, and the Mobilization of State Olive Oil.* Portsmouth, Rhode Island: Journal of Roman Archaeology Supplement, 65–102.

Wilson, A.I. 1999. Commerce and industry in Roman Sabratha. *Libyan Studies* 30: 29–52.

Wilson, A.I. 2000. Incurring the wrath of Mars: Sanitation and hygiene in Roman North Africa. In G.C.M. Jansen (ed.), *Cura Aquarum in Sicilia. Proceedings of the Tenth International Congress on the History of Water Management and Hydraulic Engineering in the Mediterranean Region. Syracuse, May 16–22,* 1998. Leuven: Peeters, 307–12.

Wilson, A.I. 2001a. Timgad and textile production. In D.J. Mattingly and J. Salmon (eds), *Economies beyond Agriculture in the Classical World.* London: Routledge, 271–96.

Wilson, A.I. 2001b. Urban water storage, distribution and usage in Roman North Africa. In A.O. Koloski-Ostrow (ed.), *Water Use and Hydraulics in the Roman City.* Boston, MA: Archaeological Institute of America Colloquia and Conference Papers, New series, 83–96.

Wilson, A.I. 2002a. Marine resource exploitation in the cities of coastal Tripolitania. *Africa Romana* 14: 429–36.

Wilson, A.I. 2002b. Urban production in the Roman world: the view from North Africa. *Papers of the British School at Rome* 70: 231–73.

Wilson, A.I. 2005. Une cité grecque de Libye: Fouilles d'Euhésperidès (Benghazi). *Comptes rendus de l'Académie des inscriptions et belles-lettres* 2003: 1648–75.

Wilson, A.I. 2007a. Fish-salting workshops in Sabratha. In L. Lagóstena, D. Bernal and A. Arévalo (eds), *Cetariae* 2005. *Salsas y Salazones de Pescado en Occidente durante la Antigüedad. Actas del Congreso Internacional (Cádiz, 7–9 de noviembre de 2005).* Oxford: BAR International Series 1686, 173–81.

Wilson, A.I. 2007b. Urban development in the Severan Empire. In S.C.R. Swain, S. J. Harrison and J. Elsner (eds), *Severan Culture.* Cambridge: Cambridge University Press, 290–326.

Wilson, A.I. 2011a. City sizes and urbanization in the Roman Empire. In A. Bowman and A.I. Wilson (eds), *Settlement, Urbanization, and Population.* Oxford: Oxford University Press, 161–95.

Wilson, A.I. 2011b. Urination and defecation Roman-style. In G.C.M. Jansen, A. O. Koloski-Ostrow and E.M. Moormann (eds), *Roman Toilets: Their Archaeology and Cultural History.* Leuven: BABesch Supplement 18, 95–111.

Wilson, A.I. 2012. Water, power and culture in the Roman and Byzantine worlds: An introduction. *Water History* 4.1: 1–9. doi:10.1007/s12685-012-0050-2.

Wilson, A.I. 2013. Trading across the Syrtes: Euesperides and the Punic world. In J. Quinn and J. Prag (eds), *The Hellenistic West: Rethinking the Ancient Mediterranean.* Cambridge: Cambridge University Press, 120–56.

Wilson, A.I. 2016. The Olympian (Hadrianic) baths at Aphrodisias: Layout, operation, and financing. In R.R.R. Smith, J. Lenaghan, A. Sokolicek and K. Welch (eds), *Aphrodisias Papers 5: Excavation and Research at Aphrodisias, 2006–2012.* Portsmouth, Rhode Island: Journal of Roman Archaeology Supplementary Series 103, 168–94.

Wilson, A.I., Mattingly, D.J., Stone, D.L., Stirling, L.M., Dodge, H. and Ben Lazreg, N. 2011. Gazetteer of sites in the urban survey. In Stone *et al.* 2011, 495–628.

Xella, P., Quinn, J., Melchiorri, V. and van Dommelen, P. 2013. Cemetery or sacrifice? Infant burials at the Carthage Tophet: Phoenician bones of contention. *Antiquity* 87.338: 1199–207.

Yasin, A.M. 2009. *Saints and Church Spaces in the Late Antique Mediterranean. Architecture, Cult, and Community.* Cambridge: Cambridge University Press.

11 Numidian State Formation in the Tunisian High Tell

JOAN SANMARTÍ, NABIL KALLALA, MARIA CARME BELARTE, JOAN RAMON, FRANCISCO JOSÉ CANTERO, DANI LÓPEZ, MARTA PORTILLO AND SÍLVIA VALENZUELA

Introduction

> Il faudrait donc, en collaboration avec les archéologues et les préhistoriens, nous interroger sur les processus qui ont fait naître sur la surface du globe des hiérarchies nouvelles de statuts et de pouvoirs entre des groupes sociaux qui entretenaient toujours des rapports de parenté au sein d'une même unité sociale globale.[1]

For many archaeologists this quote from Godelier encapsulates one of the main goals of our discipline. The formation of states and cities (one of the elements normally accompanying this form of societal organisation) cannot therefore be limited to the study of individual cases. Whatever the specific differences, these cases may, when interpreted under the light of well-founded hypothetical models, constitute a fundamental part in understanding the intercultural processes in the creation of new hierarchies. However, there is not widespread agreement on how this may take place. For some of our colleagues, the notion of 'state' (and perhaps the notion of 'city' as well?) is just a 'Western' construction, which does not have any significance in many other parts of the world. According to this constructivist point of view, the state simply did not exist in these areas. Consequently, this notion should be eliminated from our discourse, which should focus on the analysis of local and regional realities from a strictly emic perspective (if we may use a term so heavily connoted by modernist thought). For us, however, reality is *not* constituted (but just designated) by words or texts, nor is it the particular vision of those who live it, either in the past or in the present. On the contrary, we understand that it has a completely independent existence, which can be analysed and

[1] Godelier 1980, 662.

can be objectively known (with limitations), whenever appropriate tools and procedures are used. States, consequently, may theoretically exist anywhere. That being said, it is true that the lack of a clear definition about what a state actually is among historians, archaeologists and anthropologists inevitably hinders any debate that is focused on this concept. For Lull and Risch, for example, evidence of private property and elite control over the means of production is in itself sufficient to assert the existence of a state, regardless of the society's territorial or demographic size.[2] Johnson and Earle, by contrast, think that a state is characterised by a multi-ethnic and large population that runs into the hundreds of thousands of people.[3] For them, administrative and institutional complexity and organisation, as implied by large settlement sizes, are critical indicators of a state. Crumley, however, believes that non-centralised heterarchic structures that she has argued existed in Iron Age Europe, must be regarded as states.[4] The real issue, then, is not the term in itself, or whether it is applicable worldwide, but rather, what is meant by its use in specific circumstances.

Others within this volume express their scepticism about the validity of evolutionary models to explain social change, arguing that they reduce human diversity to a single trajectory, which, moreover, has been formulated from a European model.[5] Therefore such a model would supposedly be at once a Eurocentric and a dehumanising theory, one that would ignore both human agency and history. As argued below, we believe that this view of evolutionary theory does not take into account the development that social evolutionism has experienced since the mid-twentieth century. For the moment, let us just remember Harris's lucid observations on this issue:

> . . . if the causal processes of history result in predictable or retrodictable patterns of thought and behaviour, it is not because a mysterious teleological supra-individual force or system has imposed its will on individuals. Rather it is because individuals who are confronted with similar constraints and opportunities tend to make similar choices regarding their self-interest.[6]

His stance boils down to a profoundly humanistic idea of human psychic unity.

If we accept that the notion of 'the state' is operative and that there are objective causes and mechanisms that may explain its rise, the study of the pre-Roman Maghrib has an obvious interest, due to the peculiar nature of the complex autochthonous polities that developed in the region. However,

[2] Lull and Risch 1995, 97–101. [3] Johnson and Earle 2000, 35, 305. [4] Crumley 1995.
[5] See, for example, Scheele, Chapter 16, this volume. [6] Harris 1995, 77.

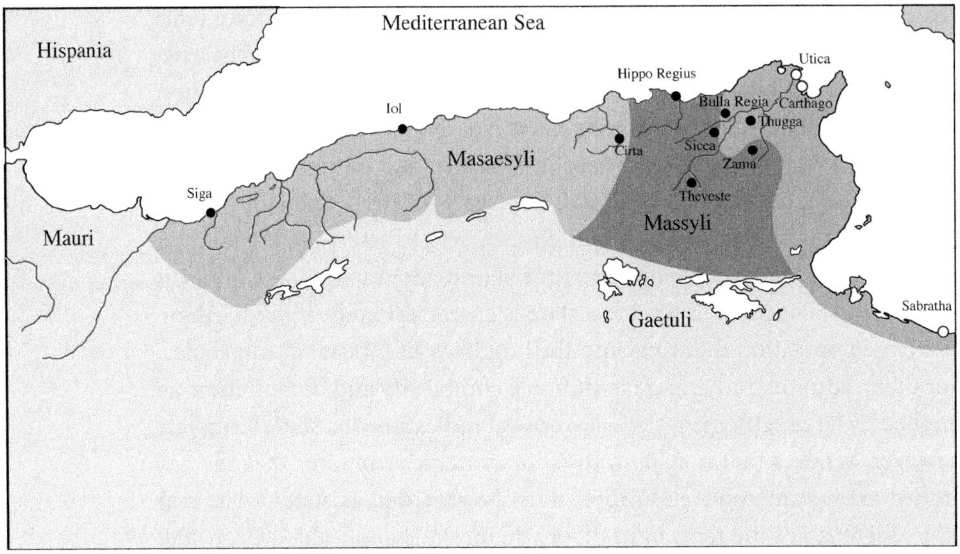

Figure 11.1. Map of the late third-century BC polities in the Central and Eastern Maghrib.

it is hindered, as we shall see below, by the lack of solid data regarding their formation and early development. Indeed, it is only from the third century BC onwards that historical sources and some scarce but significant archaeological data (mainly consisting of large mausolea and commemorative monuments related to monarchs and elites) shed some light on these polities. By that time, the autochthonous states were already very large. Leaving aside the area of Carthage's territory, the whole of the Maghrib was divided into only three political entities, each one apparently corresponding to a specific ethnic group (Mauri, Masaesyli Numidians and Massyli Numidians, see Fig. 11.1). At its peak, just before the Second Punic War, the Masaesylian state covered an area of about 150,000 km^2, comparable to modern England (130,000 km^2), while the Massylian polity stretched over some 80,000 km^2. These are very large figures; in fact, they are closer to the primary or pristine states attested in America and in the Old World (Mexico valley, Oaxaca valley, pre-dynastic Egypt, Uruk Mesopotamia) than to the early states that emerged in later stages in the Mediterranean area: both in the east (Canaanite city-states, Minoan and Mycenaean states, succeeded by the *poleis* of the Archaic and Classical periods) and in the west (in Etruria and the eastern coast of the Iberian peninsula, etc.). All these were comparatively small in size, often quite close to the theoretical average extension 1,500 km^2 proposed by Colin Renfrew for the 'early state module'.[7] Quite interestingly, another exceptional example is the Saharan Garamantian state of the Classic phase (AD 1–400), which stretched over an area of about 250,000 km^2.[8] Consequently, the Maghribian (and Saharan) states appear as a special case of Iron Age state formation in the Western Mediterranean context, and one that should be studied and explained. The closest parallels are probably the Macedonian and Epirote states, but their formation processes are not particularly well known either.

Some Theoretical Issues

Research on state formation and the origin of cities remains one of the central themes of archaeological investigation, as demonstrated by the intense contemplation that, over the last decades, has refined the models from mid-twentieth-century neo-evolutionist North-American anthropology. On the one hand, in the fields of both sociology and anthropology the very notion of 'evolution' has been claimed as a useful, even essential tool for the understanding of historical processes. It has also been confronted by the often exacerbated criticism of post-modern theorists and post-processualists.[9] The latter have rightly remarked on the deficiencies of mid-twentieth-century neo-evolutionism (to which one should add the most dogmatic Marxist evolutionary trajectories),[10] but they have ignored that it was not a fully developed theory, with little empirical testing by archaeologists.[11] Among sociologists who have proclaimed the validity of evolutionary thinking, E.O. Wright has clarified that the essential nature of a social evolutionary theory does not include the criteria, or flaws, that are criticised by contemporary anti-evolutionism.[12] More specifically, he clearly states that they do not necessarily involve functionalist approaches based on the 'needs' of society or on teleologically based trends, neither do they necessarily define a rigid and unilinear sequence of stages. Instead, they allow for the possibility of regression, make no claim that all societies must evolve, and, finally, they do not postulate the existence of only one mechanism to explain the transition from one social type to another. Thus, each case

[7] Renfrew 1986; Sanmartí 2009.

[8] Mattingly *et al.* 2003, 351. See also Mattingly *et al.*, Chapter 2, this volume.

[9] 'In particular, we intend to urge that any notion of social evolution is theoretically flawed and almost always embodies unwarranted ethnocentric evaluations. We suggest that evolutionary theories, *of whatever kind*, need to be abandoned in favour of a theoretical framework that can adequately cope with the indelibly social texture of change within a framework avoiding both reductionism and essentialism.' Shanks and Tilley 1987, 138 (emphasis added).

[10] Klejn 1993, 22–24; Trigger 1989, 222–26; 1998, 93–95. [11] Marcus 2008. [12] Wright 1983.

can and should be historically explained. From the field of anthropology, Godelier remarked that history is also evolution, 'car tout n'est pas possible à tout moment pour toute société ... il y a des étapes à franchir' and 'si des sociétés peuvent éviter de passer par certaines étapes c'est parce que d'autres y sont passées'.[13]

From the other side of the Atlantic, Johnson and Earle have attempted to reformulate the evolutionary sequence generated by neo-evolutionary anthropologists.[14] What is more, drawing on cultural materialism, but also on structural Marxism and other theoretical sources, they have proposed a coherent model of the mechanisms of change. In this model, a crucial role is played by the solution to the problems created in the subsistence economy by population increase or, as happened in Fazzan during the Pastoral period, by a decrease of subsistence resources due to increasing aridity.[15] For these authors, indeed, the solution to these problems was the growth of political economy, that is, the creation of more complex institutions related with the administration of economic activities. These institutions may improve the management of subsistence resources by means of the intensification of production or by improving storage. Alternatively, they may obtain extra resources through trade or aggression and protect them from external attacks.

The management of these institutions, in turn, makes possible the consolidation of hierarchical social relationships and the constitution of elites that, at least at a first stage, must appear as beneficial or benign to the rest of the population. Beyond the terminological differences, this approach is essentially the same as one proposed by Godelier from structuralist Marxism, when he states that consent more than violence is necessarily at the base of social differentiation processes (though violence, and, it goes without saying, the legitimising ideology of inequality is also implicated).[16] Without consent, it would be impossible to understand why the dominated sectors of society accept the supremacy of the dominant. In short, some specific historical conditions are necessary so that processes of social differentiation occur. For Johnson and Earle, these conditions are linked to the relationship between population size and the carrying capacity of a territory, in specific conditions of technological development.[17] The basic premise, with which we agree, is that the acceptance of an

[13] Godelier 1980, 19. This is equivalent to reasserting the fundamental role of diffusion without necessarily opposing it to evolution.
[14] Johnson and Earle 2000.
[15] Mattingly *et al.* 2003, 339–42. See also Mattingly *et al.*, Chapter 2, this volume.
[16] Godelier 1980, 657–63; 1999, 27. [17] Johnson and Earle 2000.

institutionalised regime of social inequality that accompanies the development of the state is only possible if common people perceive there to be objective benefits in it. Therefore, immediate real or perceived benefit is crucial in the initial stages of the process, given that access to wealth may have been theoretically equal until then. It does not follow that commoners are not aware, to some extent, of the charges involved, neither that they easily or uncritically accept them. Put another way, the crucial point is the perception that the benefits of participating in the political economy and delivering a part of the product of their work to the elites outweigh the disadvantages of having to sustain them. Needless to say, the benefits lie in the solution to the subsistence problems, which, under some particular historical circumstances, may ultimately cause new population growth.

In the long term, this growth is bound to provoke a new situation of stress, which can only be resolved through a further growth of political economy. The formation of states is but the culmination of these cycles of growth, when increased population size and territorial extent create the need of an administrative and institutional system of this kind. From the archaeological point of view, therefore, the analysis of these processes should focus on long-term study of the exploitation of the environment, on the analysis of demographic oscillations and on the technological changes that may increase the carrying capacity of the territory, along with indicators of social differentiation. This involves a large amount of data that must be obtained from surveys of relatively large territories and excavations coupling the uncovering of large areas with the analysis of long temporal sequences.

Another important contribution of the last twenty years has to do with a better understanding of the dynamics of archaic states, both in their formation and in their development, and relates to the introduction of the notion of heterarchy.[18] This states that certain complex societies may have had decentralised forms of social organisation that do not fit with the idea that centralisation is a necessary or inevitable condition for the formation of archaic states.[19] Moreover, some authors have been able to demonstrate that both the formation process and the development of these states often have saw-toothed trajectories, where stages of centralisation alternate with others characterised by the sharing of power between different actors.[20]

One final aspect worth commenting on is the renewed interest by some researchers in the formation processes of secondary states, namely those

[18] Crumley 1995. [19] Bondarenko *et al.* 2002.

[20] For formation see Brun 2015; Rodríguez *et al.* 2010; on development, Blanton 1998; Marcus 1998.

that arose after the appearance of pristine states and in contact with them. In this respect, the recent work of Parkinson and Galaty should be mentioned.[21] They propose, for the specific context of the Aegean Bronze Age, different trajectories that are explained by both the structure of pre-state societies existing at the origins of the Minoan and Mycenaean states and by the nature of the interactions with the first generation states of this region.

All these developments constitute an important advance on the evolutionary theory of societies, and must be considered in any case study. However, it should be noted that they in no way contradict the need for specific historical conditions that made it possible for a given society to accept the transition to institutionalised inequality. Put another way, the structures of kinship and neighbourhood, for example, can decisively determine the development of archaic states, favouring, for instance, the formation of more or less centralised structures.[22] Similarly, the integration of the regional exchange systems of earlier states can accelerate the formation of further archaic states or condition to some extent their structures. We believe, however, that this does not invalidate the assumption according to which states are formed through the consent to an inequality that is perceived as beneficial. This is necessary, regardless of the specific forms and rhythms of development, or the particular structure that a state finally adopts. Any study on the formation of the state should start, therefore, by proving the existence, or at least the probable existence, of the conditions that made possible the process of politogenesis. This inevitably leads us to the study of the subsistence economy, that is, the relationship between population size and the carrying capacity of the territory. It should continue by searching for evidence of the existence of institutional complexity and social segregation. We will come back to these issues, for the specific case of Numidia, after briefly reviewing the history of research and the state of the art in this particular area.

History of Research and State of the Art

As mentioned above, the study of state formation in Numidia (comprising north-eastern Algeria and western Tunisia) has severe limitations due to the absence or, at best, poor quality of available archaeological data for the first millennium BC. Regarding settlement sites, there is almost no archaeological evidence for the period prior to the second century BC (leaving

[21] Parkinson and Galaty 2007. [22] Bondarenko *et al.* 2002, 65.

aside our contribution at Althiburos).[23] In the final stages of the Numidian period (fourth to second/first century BC), it is limited to fragmentary information that is often difficult to interpret. At Cirta there is a sector of supposedly Punic type houses,[24] at Thugga, a house of the second century BC excavated a few years ago which is preserved in a quite fragmentary state,[25] – and at Bulla Regia, hints of an orthogonal urban layout.[26] We can also add the second to first century BC layers of the sanctuary of Hathor Miskar at Mactaris, and especially the large Ionic temple recently excavated at Zama Regia, which remains unpublished. A special case is Simitthus, where archaeological remains that could date back to the fourth century BC have been found, but these too remain almost completely unpublished.[27] One consequence arising from this state of affairs is the total absence of environmental archaeological studies and the lack of information regarding the technology applied to agricultural production. The evidence, in short, is very poor, which is explained by two factors: on the one hand, the difficulty for excavators to reach the lower layers in archaeological sites that were very often occupied until at least Late Antiquity; on the other hand, and most especially, the almost total absence of this issue in the agenda of archaeological research. This absence has various causes, which we have discussed in previous works.[28]

The difficulties involved in the study of funerary remains are of a different kind. Leaving aside the great monuments we have already mentioned, the funerary record is extremely rich and easily accessible. As a matter of fact, it constitutes a characteristic element of the landscape in many regions of the Eastern Maghrib due to the very large number of tombs and their visibility.[29] Hundreds were excavated, the vast majority during the colonial period, from the mid-nineteenth to mid-twentieth century. However, the scientific value of these works is largely limited by the combination of four factors: firstly, the methodological shortcomings of most of them (with some significant exceptions);[30] secondly, the previous plundering of many structures (in particular the *haouanet*, but also,

23 See also Bokbot, Chapter 12 and Wilson, Chapter 10, this volume.

24 Only sketchily published in Berthier 1980. 25 Khanoussi *et al.* 2005. 26 Thébert 1992.

27 Excepting a general overview derived from the extremely welcome restart of the activity at this site; see Khanousi and Von Rummel 2012.

28 Kallala 2002; Sanmartí *et al.* 2012, 23–24. See also Bokbot, Chapter 12, this volume, about the widespread but poorly grounded assumption by many researchers working in the Western Maghrib that any site where wheel-thrown pre-Roman pottery has been found must necessarily be considered as Phoenician. This has probably biased the image about the nature of the autochthonous populations' economy and social organisation.

29 Camps 1961a; 1995.

30 Exceptions include the work of Camps and Camps-Fabrer (1964) at Djebel Mazela.

very often, the dolmens); thirdly, the fact that the funerary offerings are frequently materially poor and do not, in general, include diagnostic imported materials that can be tightly dated; finally, the small number of research projects conducted in the last 50 years, when the improvement of excavation techniques and the use of radiocarbon dating could have replaced the limitations of dating based on artefacts. We still need to add, in the case of the large megalithic necropoleis, that their huge dimensions (frequently hundreds or thousands of graves spread over several square kilometres) makes it very difficult to document them accurately, and, therefore, to understand their possible internal structure. In short, as in the case of settlements, the enormous potential of the funerary sites has hardly been exploited.[31]

Under these conditions, studies of the formation of the Numidian states have been almost exclusively based on indirect evidence provided by ancient texts and epigraphic sources of the Roman imperial period. These documents suggest that in the historical period of the Numidian kingdoms (third to first century BC) there were also important tribal structures that dated back, with more or less changes, to the period before the formation of these monarchies. Drawing implicitly on this idea and explicitly on the historically known cases of the Medieval Maghrib, Stéphane Gsell hypothesised that the formation of the Numidian kingdoms should be explained by the violent action of powerful tribal chiefs who had imposed their power over other tribes.[32] He also believed that the introduction of the horse, and especially of iron metallurgy (which he placed around 1000 BC) had played an important role in ensuring the military supremacy of groups possessing them. More than 30 years later, another great historian of the Berber world, Gabriel Camps, made Gsell's hypothesis his own, and even in the early eighties Elisabeth Smadja advocated essentially the same.[33] This model, however, has little explanatory value. Territorial expansion in a tribal framework does not provide by itself a clear understanding of the development of the institutional complexity that is typical of states. In fact, Gsell himself understood, or at least suspected, this interpretative weakness, although this did not lead him to modify or further develop his model.[34]

A different model was proposed by Tadeusz Kotula, following the line of thought initiated by Herbert Spencer in the nineteenth century (and subsequently developed by other authors, in particular Carneiro). He believed

[31] See now Gatto *et al.* 2019, for the parallel Trans-Saharan Archaeology overview volume on funerary traditions of the Maghrib and Sahara.

[32] Gsell 1927, 77–82. [33] Camps 1961b, 161; Smadja 1983, 686. [34] Gsell 1927, 80–81.

that the territorial expansionism of Carthage during the fifth century BC was the main cause of the formation of the Numidian states, since it was likely to have promoted the centralisation of power among local populations in order to deal with this threat more effectively.[35]

Finally, we have to mention the Marxist inspired techno-determinist model of Pierre Lévêque. For this scholar, the crucial triggering factor was the development of iron metallurgy, which he believed was introduced by the Phoenicians. This technological shift would have encouraged the extension and intensification of agricultural production; simultaneously, the demand of commodities by the Phoenicians would have intensified production and trade relations. As a consequence of improved technology, population would have increased, which in turn would have made possible the formation of urban centres and caused the rise of intertribal violence. The final outcome would be the emergence of more powerful tribal chiefs, who, Lévêque believed, tended to form a rural and commercial aristocracy, while peasants were reduced to a situation of dependency.[36]

All these hypotheses are plausible to some extent, or at least we can assume that they must contain some elements of truth, but the available data are too scarce to verify them. In any case, as we said above, we believe that, whatever the endogenous process, and whatever the weight of contact with the Phoenicians, the acceptance of institutionalised inequality and population pressure were fundamental to the development of Numidian states. As a matter of fact, this assumption underlies most of the abovementioned hypotheses. In the case of Kotula's model, it can be argued that, whatever the military pressure of Carthage, native states could not have been constituted without a sufficient population size. As for Lévêque's model, we must take into account that technological innovations are not necessarily beneficial to all members and groups of a given society. They involve risks and uncertainties that often tend to slow down their adoption until they are imposed by elites, in order to increase their power and wealth,[37] a situation that may be favoured by population pressure on resources. The expansion of iron metallurgy, therefore, could be the consequence rather than the cause of the formation of elites. However, it is true that the consequent increase of techno-environmental efficiency must have resulted in a further population growth that was presumably decisive in the long term for the development of early states.

[35] Kotula 1976, cited by Lassère 2001, 149, note 2. [36] Lévêque 1986; 1999. [37] Kim 2001.

The Project of the Institut National du Patrimoine and the University of Barcelona at Althiburos

This project was specifically designed for obtaining relevant data on state formation in an area that, according to historical sources, was occupied by the Massyli Numidians.[38] In addition, a neo-Punic inscription found in the nineteenth century proved the existence at Althiburos (Fig. 11.2), at least in the last centuries BC, of municipal institutions, and therefore of a pre-Roman city.[39]

The research strategy adopted was based on Johnson's and Earle's aforementioned model of socio-cultural change. Consequently, it was primarily conceived to retrieve data on population growth, technological

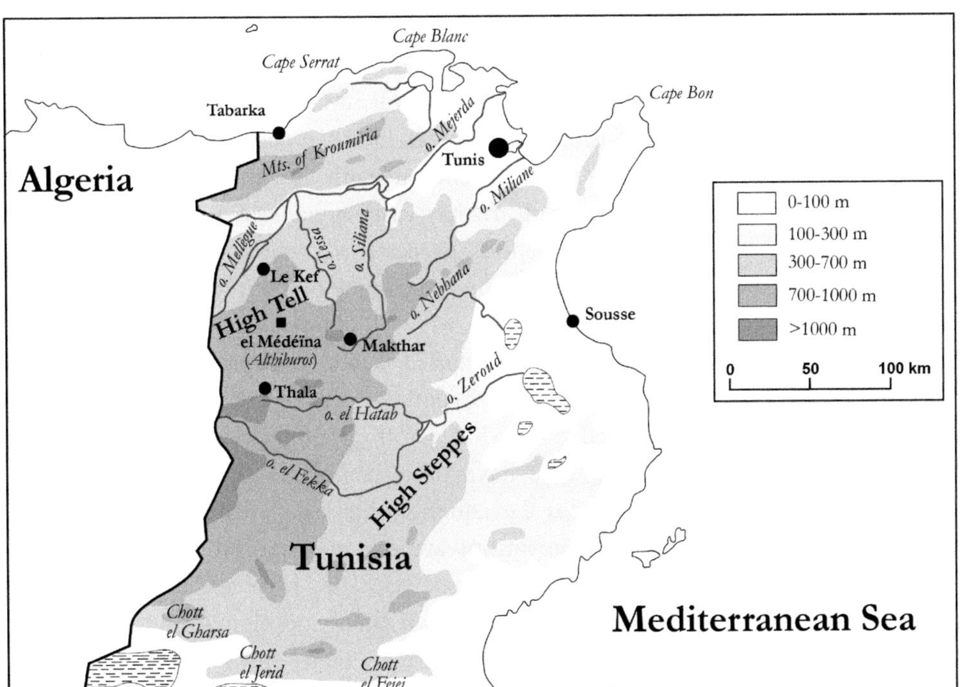

Figure 11.2. Northern Tunisia and the location of Althiburos.

[38] The project involved the Tunisian Institut National du Patrimoine and the University of Barcelona, with the collaboration of the Catalan Institute of Classical Archaeology.

[39] More specifically, it indicates the existence of a religious position (BLL 'the sacrificer') and a college of three *suffetes* (Ennaïfer 1976, 27). The existence at Althiburos and Mactaris (Makthar) of colleges of three *suffetes* (as opposed to the two that are typical of the Punic tradition) indicates the specific nature of this local institution, Belhakia and Di Vita-Évrard 1995, 262.

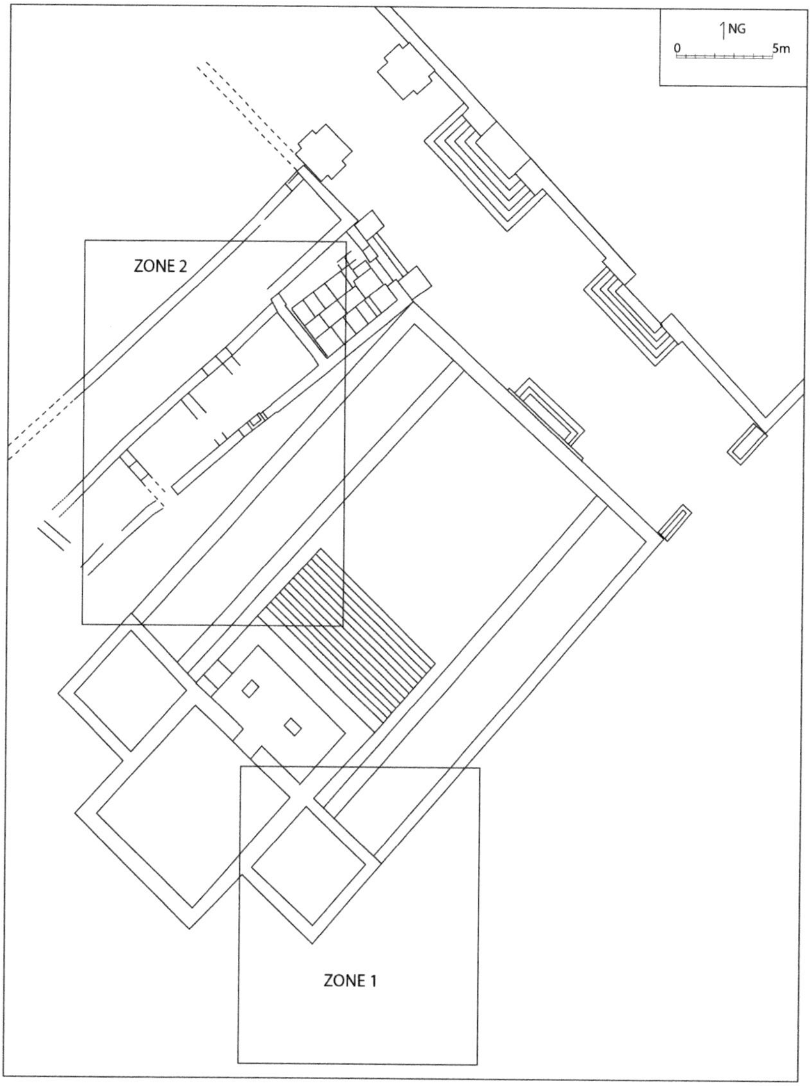

Figure 11.3. Schematic plan of the capitol area and location of the excavation zones.

change and hints about urbanisation. Also, given the historical context, it considered the city's relations with the Phoenician world. Regarding the first of these goals, demography, it was expected to retrieve significant information from the survey of the city itself and its closer territory, on the assumption that ground survey would provide datable materials. Another expected source of information was the environmental data obtained from the excavation of the site of Althiburos, presuming that population growth implies agricultural intensification, and that the latter should be recognisable in the archaeozoological and archaeobotanical record. It was also assumed that the excavation of this site could provide more or less strong evidence on the urbanisation process (the nature of domestic architecture, public buildings, urban planning, defensive walls, etc.), on the contact with Phoenician-Punic civilisation and on technological changes. Of particular interest was the introduction of iron metallurgy and its potential application to agricultural production. The correlation of these aspects could provide relevant information about the specific historical conditions, in terms of the subsistence economy and the contact with other societies, in which the formation and development of the Numidian state took place.

Although it was not initially planned, the progress of the project also led us to analyse the funerary record, particularly the great megalithic necropolis located on the El Ksour massif, which was probably related to Numidian Althiburos. From its study it is expected to obtain data related to demography, insofar as we are able to refine the dates of the tombs, and to social structure. The latter can be interpreted from the spatial organisation of the necropolis (for example, by studying the differential distribution of distinct tomb types, or their relative proximity to Althiburos) and, from the variability of structure, size and contents of the different graves. The study of the necropolis has provided some interesting results.[40]

We present below a brief overview of the results obtained in each of these aspects, followed by a synthesis focusing on state formation and urbanisation at Althiburos.

The Results of the Survey and the Excavation at the Capitol Area

The results of the survey have been interesting, but scarcely explicit to the topic at hand because of difficulties of dating. These are due to the virtual absence in collected assemblages of well characterised Greek, Punic and Italic imported pottery and the highly fragmented nature of the Numidian ceramics, which can only be dated when a significant part of the profile is preserved.

Despite these limitations, it is worth noting that the survey within the city of Althiburos led to the collection of Numidian pottery in the entire area between the two wadis that define its core, that is, in a space of about

[40] It could not be otherwise considering its enormity: over a thousand structures have been recorded so far, stretching over an area of 30 km^2, and only four of them have been excavated. See Kallala *et al.* 2014; 2018; Sanmartí *et al.* 2015; 2019.

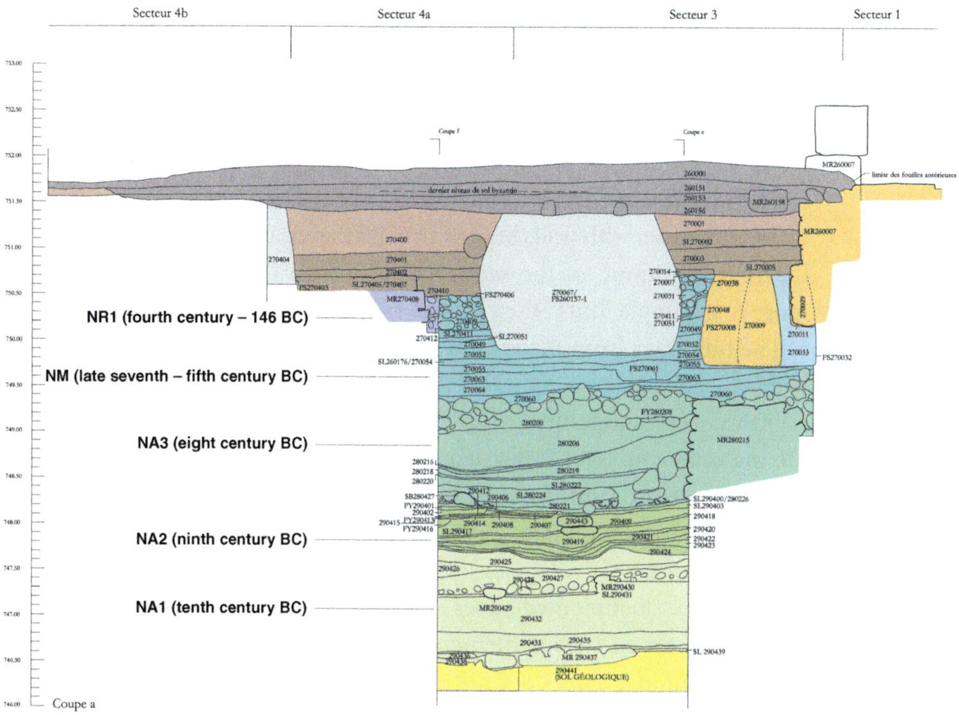

Figure 11.4. Section of sectors 3–4a in excavation zone 2 showing the stratigraphic sequence of the Numidian period.

7 ha.[41] However, this only proves that the Numidian settlement *could* have stretched over this area at some time in its history. This is likely the case in the final centuries of the first millennium, but nothing can be said, for the time being, for the previous stages. As indicated by Mattingly, the topography of Althiburos, an elongated ridge delimited by steep drops, is typical of Numidian towns.[42]

The excavation of the Capitol area (Fig. 11.3) has provided some relevant data regarding the subject we are dealing with.[43] Firstly, it has allowed us to document a virtually uninterrupted sequence of occupation and material culture dating back to the tenth century calBC (Fig. 11.4).[44] Secondly, for

[41] Regarding the topography of Althiburos, see Kallala and Sanmartí 2011, 10 and figures 1.11–1.14; Sanmartí *et al.* 2012, 28–30, figures 3–5.

[42] Mattingly 2016, 15. See also Wilson, Chapter 10, this volume.

[43] On this dig, see Belarte 2011, and Ramon Torres and Maraoui Telmini 2011. For more detail on the Numidian architecture, see Belarte and Ramon in Kallala *et al.* 2016.

[44] It is worth noting that, at the opposite end of the Maghrib, Bokbot, Chapter 12, this volume, proposes an early dating, in the first centuries of the first millennium BC, for the autochthonous occupation of several habitation sites, such as Lixus, Mogador, Kach Kouch, Sidi Driss, Les Andalouses and Rachgoun, most of which have been traditionally considered as Phoenician sites.

the first time it sheds some light on the structure of a Numidian settlement and the building techniques employed. The data recovered, however, are still very limited, as the very nature of this deep stratification, with a history of over 2,000 years, imposes restraints on the excavated areas of the earliest levels and hinders the understanding of structural remains. Nevertheless, it can be said that the area excavated around the Capitol was mainly devoted to domestic use, with walls built with solid materials (stone and earth) from the very beginning of the sequence. Although these were plainly much more than simple 'huts', their overall plan cannot be clearly defined as yet.

The buildings from the earliest phases, tenth–early seventh century BC, had little consistency: the walls, though sometimes very thick, were often slightly curved and built in a series of juxtaposed sections (Fig. 11.5). Often the material employed consisted of large river stones. The nature of this first settlement cannot be ascertained, since we do not know its total size and the structural remains discovered so far are few. It could be either a small hamlet or a village of larger dimensions. In any case, the type of architecture documented does not seem the most appropriate for a properly urban-type settlement, organised following a more or less regular planning. This does not mean that there could not be a sizeable population, maybe distributed in different villages. One of these could have been located at the northern end of the Roman city, at the confluence of the wadis, others could have been the scattered sites that are described later in this section.

From the end of the seventh century BC, after an apparent hiatus of several decades whose causes are unknown, there was a reorganisation of the settlement in terms of architecture and layout, although the necessary data to recognise the total area of occupation are still lacking. Due to the confined space of the excavation, it remains impossible to reconstruct the urban layout or to reconstitute the complete plan of any house, but the available evidence hints at a more regular architecture, with rectilinear walls clearly and solidly built (though not as wide as some dated to the previous phase). The reasons for this change are not easy to state. Beside the internal dynamics of the Numidian society we could take into account an intensification of the contacts with the Phoenician world, revealed by a slight increase in the volume of imported ceramics (which, however, are still very rare: 1 per cent of the total ceramics) and, more clearly, by a biapsidal cistern (CT290111) that indicates close familiarity with Punic hydraulic technology (Fig. 11.6). To this should be added the existence of pavements and wall coverings made with lime mortar, as well as the use of mudbricks (but this could have already started in the eighth century BC).

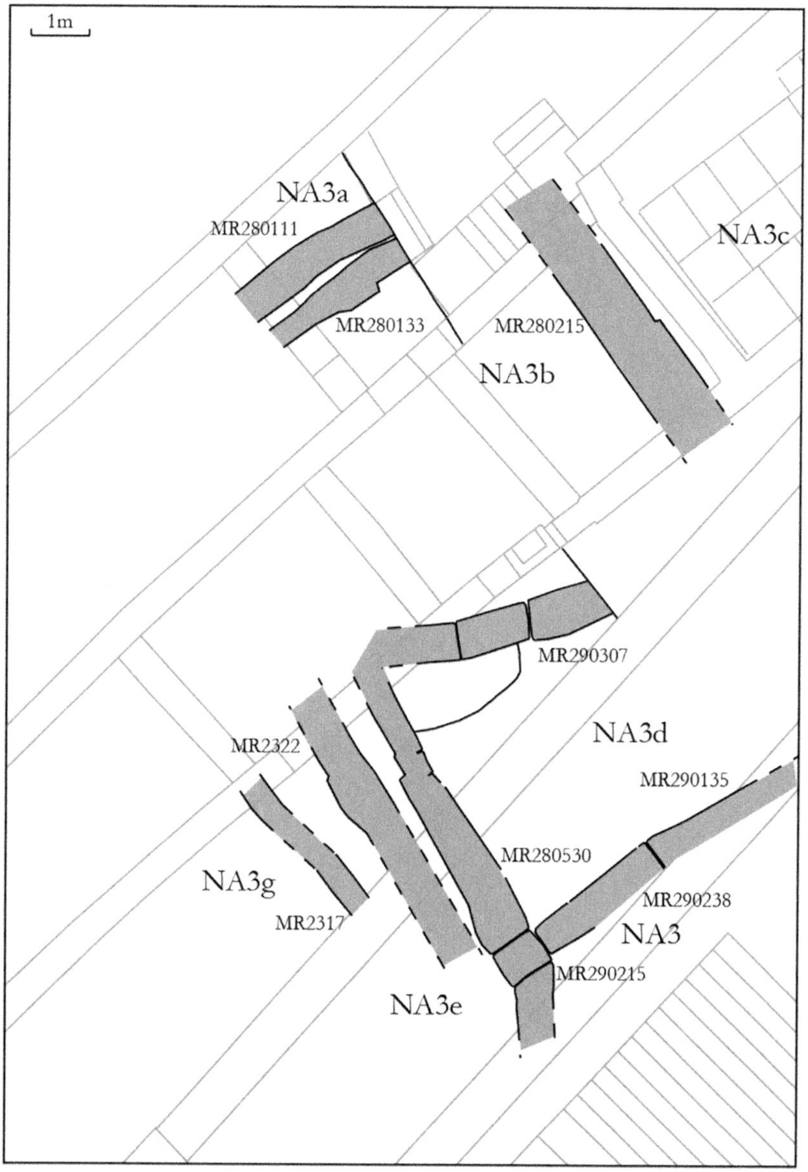

Figure 11.5. Schematic Early Numidian 3 constructions in excavation zone 2.

That being said, we should also note the profoundly autochthonous character of the mid-first-millennium BC settlement in all the spheres of life, such as cooking and the forms of food consumption, as well as most of the architectural features, not to mention the funerary world, which will be discussed later. The most powerful indicator of the likely urban nature of Althiburos before the second century BC is a thick wall, probably with

Figure 11.6. Punic-type cistern of the Middle Numidian period in excavation zone 2.

Figure 11.7. Defensive wall seen from the south-west.

defensive function, which was erected in the fourth century BC. Its remains are located in the area immediately to the south of the Capitol (Fig. 11.7).

With regard to the peri-urban area, in the same Althiburos valley, five more settlements, of much smaller dimensions (as compared to the total area of Althiburos) have been located, which have also provided Numidian potsherds of imprecise dating, and that continued to be inhabited at least until late antiquity. It is possible that these sites were created as a result of population growth and sedentarisation during the first millennium BC, but the available data do not allow precision about when this occurred. It seems likely, in any case, that all of them were occupied in the final stage of the Numidian period.

In summary, the recovered data seem to indicate a significant increase in the population during the first millennium BC, particularly during its second half, and an early contact with the Phoenician settlements of the coastal areas, which intensified greatly from the fourth century BC. This is proved not only by the acquisition of table-ware and other kinds of pottery (including amphoras), but also by the adoption of Punic hydraulic techniques already in the sixth century BC. The erection of the defensive wall in the fourth century BC may also indicate instability, which could have been caused by internal troubles or related to Carthage's expansionist policy. In any case, the huge effort required for its construction confirms the existence of a sizeable community at Althiburos.

The Environmental Data

Althiburos has provided a large amount of palaeoenvironmental data, thanks to the development of high-resolution integrated sampling strategies within the site. However, palynological research conducted in different parts of the region has not given usable results. We present in this section the conclusions reached from the archaeozoological and archaeobotanical studies in the area of the Capitol, in order to recognise signs of economic intensification that could be the result of a significant population increase; that is to say, to verify one of the predictions of the model. We are aware that the absence of palynological data represents a serious limitation for delineating vegetation change at the regional level. Nevertheless we believe that the available data are sufficiently significant to propose well-grounded hypotheses.

Anthracological data provide some (albeit incomplete) information on the changing characteristics of surrounding woodlands.[45] From the earliest excavated phase (NA1), at the beginning of the first millennium BC, the charcoal mainly came from pines rather than holm-oak woodlands, which are native to this region, with a considerable presence of wild (maybe also domestic?) olive-trees. The replacement of oak woods by Aleppo pine suggests the existence of a dry Mediterranean forest, as a consequence of an important anthropic action. It is possible, therefore, that during the second millennium BC the area had already been intensively exploited and the native woodland modified. This is consistent with the results of palynological studies carried out in the region of Aïn Draham, in north-western Tunisia, that indicate a decline in deciduous oak forest due to a combination of anthropic activities (clearance) and climatic changes (a peak in aridity) that can be recognised as early as *c.*2000 BC.[46] Given this situation, it is particularly striking that, in the present state of research,

[45] Cantero and Piqué 2016. [46] Stambouli-Essassi *et al.* 2007.

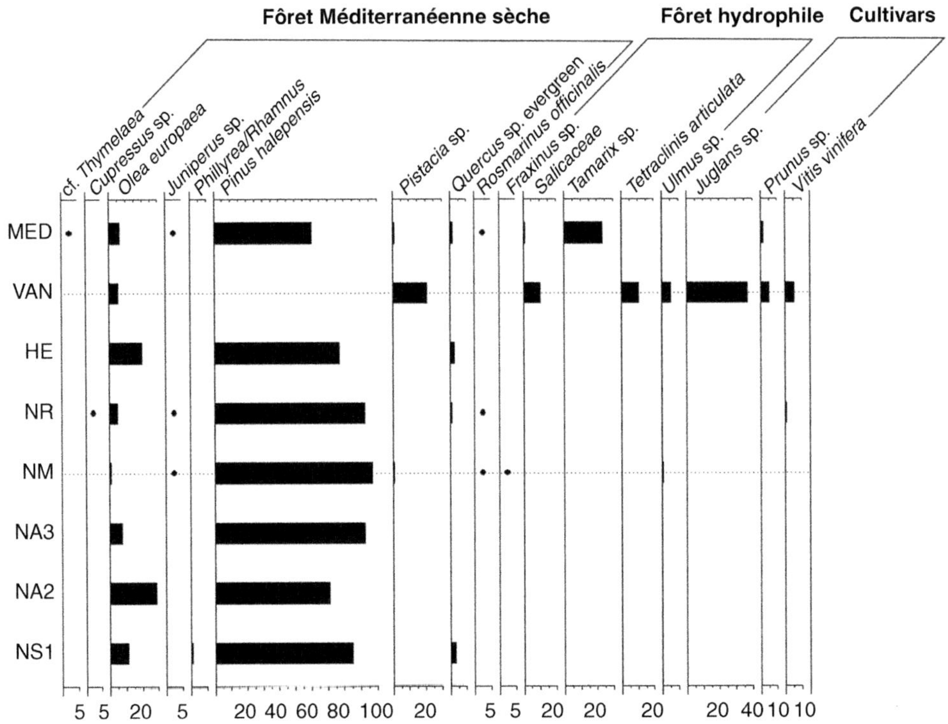

Figure 11.8. Percentage of charcoal taxa per phase, from a diachronic perspective (Early Numidian to Medieval times).

there are virtually no archaeological remains datable to the second millennium BC across the Eastern Maghrib.[47]

The results of the wood charcoal analyses are consistent with paleocarpological data (Figs 11.8–11.9).[48] They indicate the preponderance of cultivated species during the tenth century calBC (82.1 per cent of the remains) and, among these, of cereals (92.3 per cent), mainly barley (*Hordeum vulgare*) and free-threshing wheat (*Triticum aestivum/durum*). There is also a considerable presence of cultivated grape seeds (*Vitis vinifera*). This is not surprising by any means, since the cultivated vine is attested in Fazzan in the early first millennium BC.[49] Vines are a delayed-yield crop, whose cultivation demands a considerable initial effort.

[47] Only two recently discovered tombs at Thugga; see Khanoussi *et al.* 2005. It is also worth noting that the Bronze Age is relatively well attested in western Algeria and Morocco (Camps 1960; see also Bokbot, Chapter 12, this volume).

[48] López Reyes and Cantero 2016.

[49] Mattingly *et al.* 2003, 342; van der Veen and Westley 2010, 507, 509.

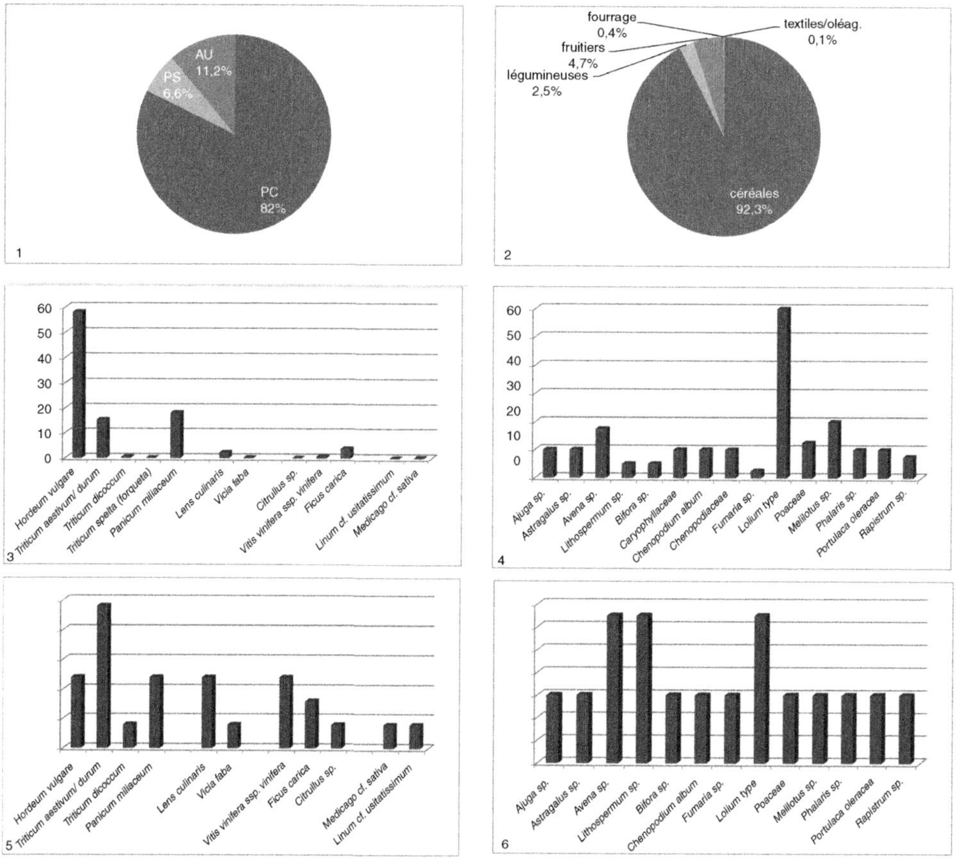

Figure 11.9. 1) Percentage of cultivated plants (PC), wild plants (PS) and other types (AU) over the total of the remains (1,294 individuals and fragments); 2) Percentage of different types of cultures over the total number of individuals (836); 3) and 4) Percentage of the total number of cultivated and wild plants; and 5) and 6) estimation of the distribution of frequencies (25 and 16 mentions respectively).

Although it does not produce fruits for five or six years, once mature, it can subsequently be exploited for a long period of time. The logical consequence is that the population who cultivated it had to be fully sedentary. From the perspective of socio-cultural evolution, these data suggest that in the early first millennium BC, if not before (maybe long before?), the population had grown beyond the limits within which a semi-sedentary lifestyle is feasible. Extensive swidden agriculture and widespread exploitation of wild resources, both animal and vegetable would have become impossible as the territory became completely occupied and exploited, leading to a fully sedentary way of life. Additional evidence comes from the study of microfossil livestock dung assemblages.[50] From the tenth century calBC onwards, these remains contain significant concentrations of calcitic dung spherulites and grass phytoliths, mostly of leaves and stems, probably from Pooid domestic varieties. This may suggest that fodder was obtained from agricultural by-products (such as wheat and barley, chaff and straw). This grass-rich diet for livestock may be linked to the expansion of cereal crop production. Yet, the study of faunal remains of the tenth–ninth centuries BC indicates a large supply of bovines, whose slaughter age pattern suggests a focus on meat production and rapid herd renewal.[51] This, in turn, implies that despite the human pressure on the environment, these herds were viable. Grazing was probably available either on fallow crop fields or grasslands (their use is still ethnographically documented in the area), although the possibility that cattle were brought in from somewhere else cannot be excluded.

The eighth century BC marks a major turning point. At this time, the relative frequency of bovines decreases significantly, while the number of cattle over four years old slaughtered increases (Fig. 11.10). This may be

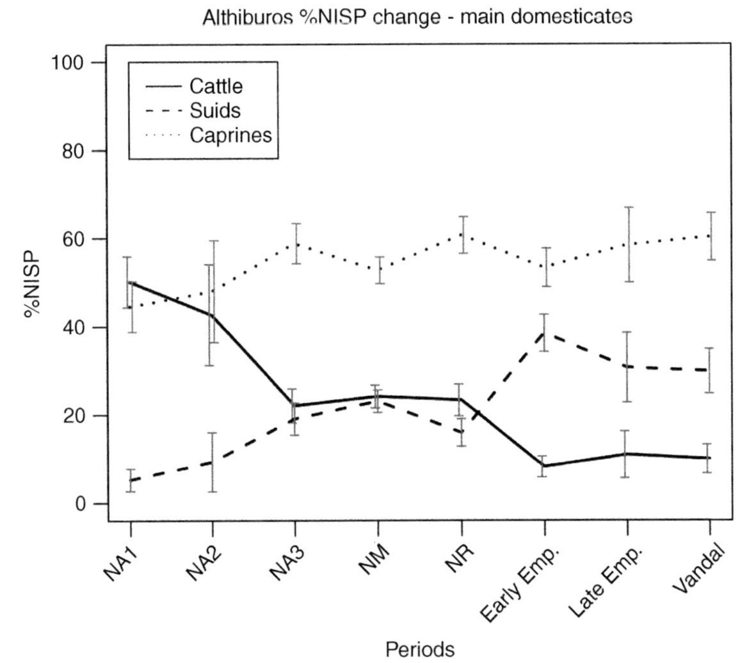

Figure 11.10. Relative frequency of the three main faunal taxa all over the occupation. The vertical lines indicate twice the standard deviation (confidence level of 95 per cent).

[50] Portillo and Albert 2011; 2016; Portillo *et al.* 2012. [51] Valenzuela-Lamas 2016.

due to the need to employ them for a longer period working in the fields, maybe as a result of agricultural intensification. This trend increased even further during the sixth–fifth centuries, when animals slaughtered at over six years' of age predominated, while the presence of calves severely decreased. From the eighth century BC, and most particularly from the sixth century BC, meat supply also became largely dependent on sheep, goats and, especially pigs. These are species that are better adapted to low quality pastures, typical of dry environments, or in the case of pigs, can be fed with scraps of human food and, therefore, away from agricultural land. This is an important indicator of intensification that is confirmed to some extent by the archaeobotanical data. Indeed, the anthracological remains indicate, for the sixth century BC and onwards, an increase in the number of species and the exploitation of new ecological niches. In particular, the presence for the first time of *Ulmus* sp., *Salix*/*Populus* and *Fraxinus* sp., three hydrophilic trees, may indicate that pine, olive and other trees that grow in dry environments were no longer enough. Perhaps this was because there were more people exploiting them, perhaps because increasing agricultural activity had reduced the extent of the forest (unless some climatic shift may account for this). The same could be indicated by the presence of *Juniperus* sp., a shrub/tree that grows within the forests of Aleppo pine. This may suggest that pine woods were more open, due to more intensive exploitation. Likewise, grapevines are documented for the first time as a fuel source. In short, there is evidence to suggest an extension of the catchment areas for wood, and that those sources that were previously used were more intensively exploited. Finally, the carpological data indicate the presence of new plants that may be used as fodder, particularly clover during the eighth century BC, and during the sixth century BC alfalfa, *Coronilla*, horseshoe vetch, *Astragalus*, *Melilotus*, etc. This supports the idea of a landscape with less grasslands and large areas of crops.

In summary, the environmental data seem to support the idea of a considerable economic intensification from the eighth century BC onwards, and that this might have been the consequence of sustained population increase. Given that there is reason to assume that the area was already well populated by the end of the second millennium BC, it is plausible to suppose that this further growth entailed high pressure on the environment. This in turn urged the development of political economy and thereby opened the way to the formation of state-like polities. Obviously, one cannot exclude that this process was influenced by a demand for farming products by the Phoenicians, but even in this case we would conclude the existence of a sizeable population and a pressure on the environment that would have led to an increase in social and institutional complexity. Interestingly enough, botanical remains prove that a similar pattern of agricultural intensification occurred in Fazzan in the early first millennium BC, in the form of irrigated cultivation, with comparable social impact.[52]

Technological Change

The oldest iron fragment excavated from the site is dated to the late ninth century calBC, but is unfortunately shapeless. Since it could be an extremely early Phoenician import, it cannot definitely prove the existence of local iron production at that time, though the latter possibility is altogether likely. Two further small undiagnostic fragments of iron slag can be dated to the eighth century BC; for the moment we cannot state whether they were produced by smelting or smithing. Therefore, this material does not prove that there was local iron production, though in our opinion this is quite probable.

From these data we may infer the possibility that iron instruments were used for agricultural work from the eighth century BC onwards. This technology would have facilitated an increase in the territory's carrying capacity. Indeed, iron tools would have made possible the expansion of cultivation into areas that were difficult to exploit with wood or stone instruments. It could also have led to the progressive implementation of a Eurasian grain-farming model, based on permanent fields and rotating fallow.[53] Given that in a dry area such as the Althiburos region, the fallow lands must be ploughed and the natural vegetation removed to facilitate the accumulation of water, the use of iron tools is necessary for an efficient permanent use of the fields.

It is logical to assume that, as in Europe, agricultural iron tools were widely used during the first millennium BC, and that they constituted one of the key elements of the economic and demographic potential of the Numidian kingdoms. While we do not have direct evidence of iron agricultural implements, nor is it possible, *a fortiori*, to know when they began to be used on a large scale, in any case, the data recovered at Althiburos indicate that iron production could have started in the eighth century BC (if not before). However, we have to keep in mind that knowledge of a particular technology does not necessarily mean its immediate

[52] See Mattingly *et al.*, Chapter 2, this volume; Mattingly and Sterry, Chapter 19, this volume.
[53] Wolf 1966, 30–32.

application to production as has been observed in several case studies.[54] Application is usually linked to the interests of elites, among who the needs of the domestic economy may be included. A better understanding of the spread of this technology as applied to agriculture is therefore highly desirable to facilitate our understanding of the formation processes of cities and states.

Figure 11.11. View of monument 53 during the excavation.

The Funerary Data

The development of the Althiburos project has led to the study of a large megalithic necropolis located to the south of the city and stretching over much of the El Ksour massif.[55] This complex, multi-site, funerary landscape, which had not previously been recorded as such, has been intensively surveyed in the western and central zones of the massif, and more

[54] Kim 2001. [55] Kallala *et al.* 2014; 2018; Sanmartí *et al.* 2019.

Figure 11.12. Chamber of monument 53.

rapidly explored in the remaining areas. To date 1,035 structures have been recorded, most of which relate to the type of monuments that Camps designated as 'dolmens sur socle et dolmens à manchon', which are typical of the interior areas of the Eastern Maghrib.[56] We prefer to call them 'zenithal access dolmens'. As mentioned above, in spite of the fact that many examples of these structures were excavated between 1850 and 1960, the available information about them is very scarce, particularly with regard to their dating. For this reason, and also to try to understand the apparent variability existing among them, three zenithal access dolmens of the El Ksour necropolis (monuments 42, 53 and 647) have been excavated. The ^{14}C dating for the latter (Beta-333228) has provided a chronology in the Hallstatt plateau, with a strong likelihood for the fifth century BC, whilst that of monument 53 (Beta-283142), also in the Hallstatt plateau, corresponds to the eighth to mid-fifth century BC.[57] This dating is consistent with the associated Numidian pottery, whose chronology begins to be known following our excavations at Althiburos. As for monument 42, the few pottery sherds recovered from the layer on which it was built indicate a construction date in the second half of the first millennium BC. The parallels with well-dated ceramics from Althiburos allow a proposed dating between the eighth and the fifth century BC for at

[56] Camps 1961a, 130–36.

[57] Conventional radiocarbon age: 2480±40 BP. 2 Sigma calibrated result: (95 per cent probability) 775–430 calBC (Beta-283142).

least five more tombs excavated in the 1950s by G. Camps and H. Camps-Fabrer in the necropolis of Djebel Mazela (Bou Nouara, Algeria).[58] The rest of the tombs excavated at Djebel Mazela cannot be precisely dated from parallels at Althiburos, but it is worth indicating that the ceramic shapes typical of the fourth–first century BC on our site are completely absent there. This may suggest that they were erected no later than the fifth century BC. To this we should add the dating of two dolmens of the necropolis of Henchir Mided, at least one of which belongs to a different type from those at El Ksour and Djebel Mazela, as it is a free-standing dolmen (that is, with no tumulus surrounding it). The ^{14}C dating for the latter also corresponds to the Hallstatt plateau,[59] while the other one contained an Attic cup of *Vicup* type, whose production is dated to the second quarter of the fifth century BC.[60] To sum up, in spite of the very low number of (to some extent) well-dated monuments, it seems to us remarkable that all of them belong to a period spanning from the eighth to the fifth century BC. This could also be a clue, though certainly still very tenuous, of population increase in the central centuries of the first millennium BC.

A second aspect regarding the three excavated monuments concerns their variability in size, construction quality, number of depositions and other matters related to the funerary ritual. Indeed, one of the three excavated tombs (number 53) stands out for its remarkable size (diameter *c.*13 m, with a burial chamber measuring 1.40 × 1.20 m) (Figs 11.11–11.12), whilst monuments 42 and 647 are much smaller: diameters respectively 5.50 m and 5 m; dimensions of the chambers are 0.97 × 1.12 m and 0.85 × 0.60–0.70 m respectively (Figs 11.13–11.15). The latter figures are among the most common in the whole necropolis. Indeed, 77 per cent of these monuments measure between 4 and 7.9 m diameter, and the modal peak is 5 to 5.9 m (30 per cent). Only 2 per cent measure more than 12 m in diameter. Monument 53 is also remarkable due to the careful construction of the chamber which was built from large, relatively well-cut blocks that were superimposed in several courses. Conversely, monument 647 was composed of vertical slabs and monument 42 a combination of both systems. Added to this is the fact that in monument 53 the circular wall delimiting the tumulus was double-faced and rather carefully built, while in the other two cases it was made up of only one row of slabs or blocks. Another noticeable feature is the existence in monument 53 of two 'antennas' or 'arms', that is, projecting rectilinear walls (Fig. 11.16), whose significance remains obscure, but that lead us to suspect a high degree of ritual

[58] Kallala *et al.* 2014, 55. [59] Marras *et al.* 2009, 188. [60] Ferjaoui 2010, 344.

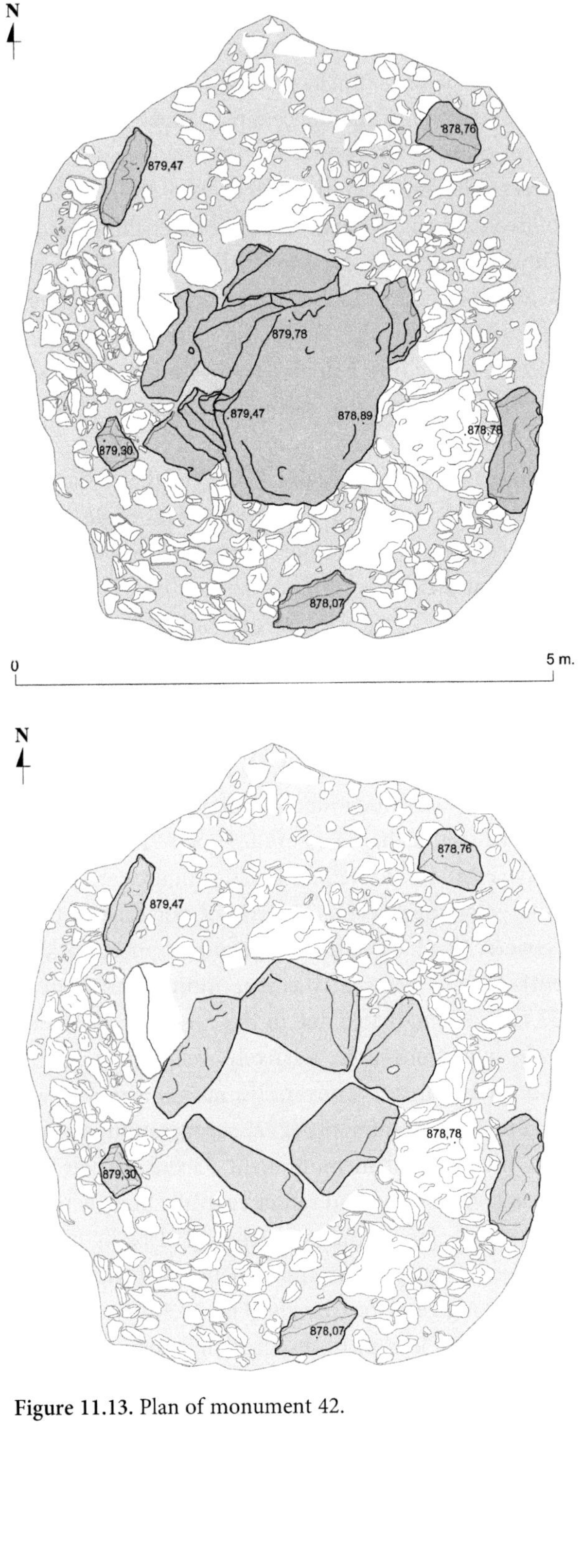

Figure 11.13. Plan of monument 42.

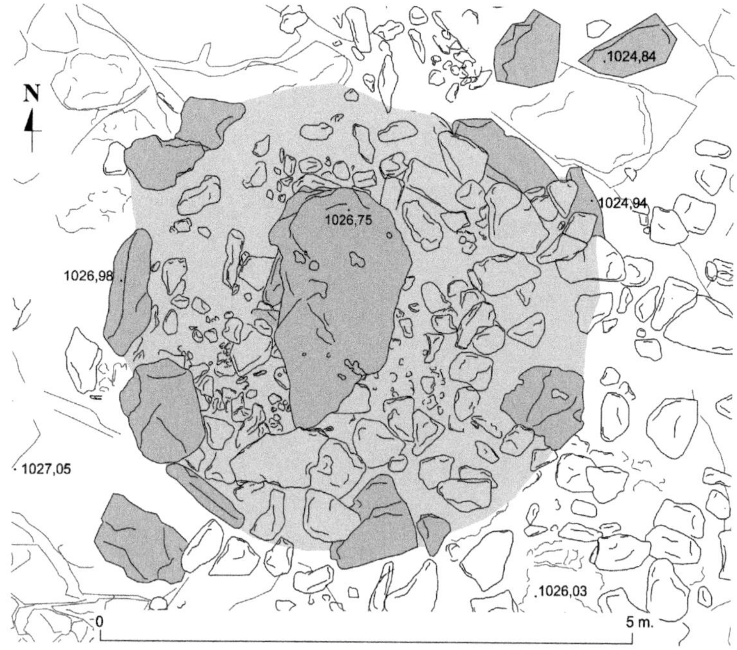

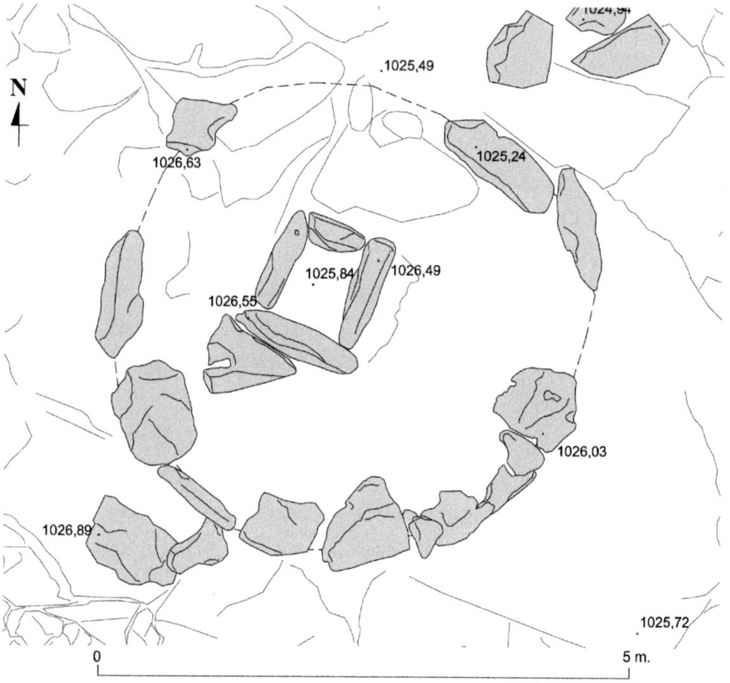

Figure 11.14. Plan of monument 647.

Figure 11.15. Chamber of monument 647.

complexity; stronger, at any rate, than in the other two monuments. A further important difference lies in the fact that, while the burial chamber of monument 647 contained the remains of a single individual (an adult), monument 53 has produced the remains of at least six bodies of different ages,[61] three of them infants (the chamber of monument 42 was completely plundered). Finally, it is very important to note that a relatively large quantity of pottery vessels, mainly tableware, was recovered in the space between the chamber and the wall that delimitated monument 53. They suggest a remarkable ritual activity, of which there is no sign in the other tombs we have excavated.

It goes without saying that the small number of data points makes interpretation very delicate. However, considering that the three monuments are roughly contemporary, it is a logical assumption that the observed variability reflects the appearance of a hierarchical structure of Numidian society by the mid-first millennium BC. More specifically,

[61] In every case, human remains are few, due to previous excarnation of the bodies (Kallala *et al.* 2014, 29, 30, 56). This practice had already been clearly attested by Camps and Camps-Fabrer at Djebel Mazela (Camps and Camps-Fabrer 1964, 75–79; see also Camps 1961a, 481–501 for a general discussion on this issue).

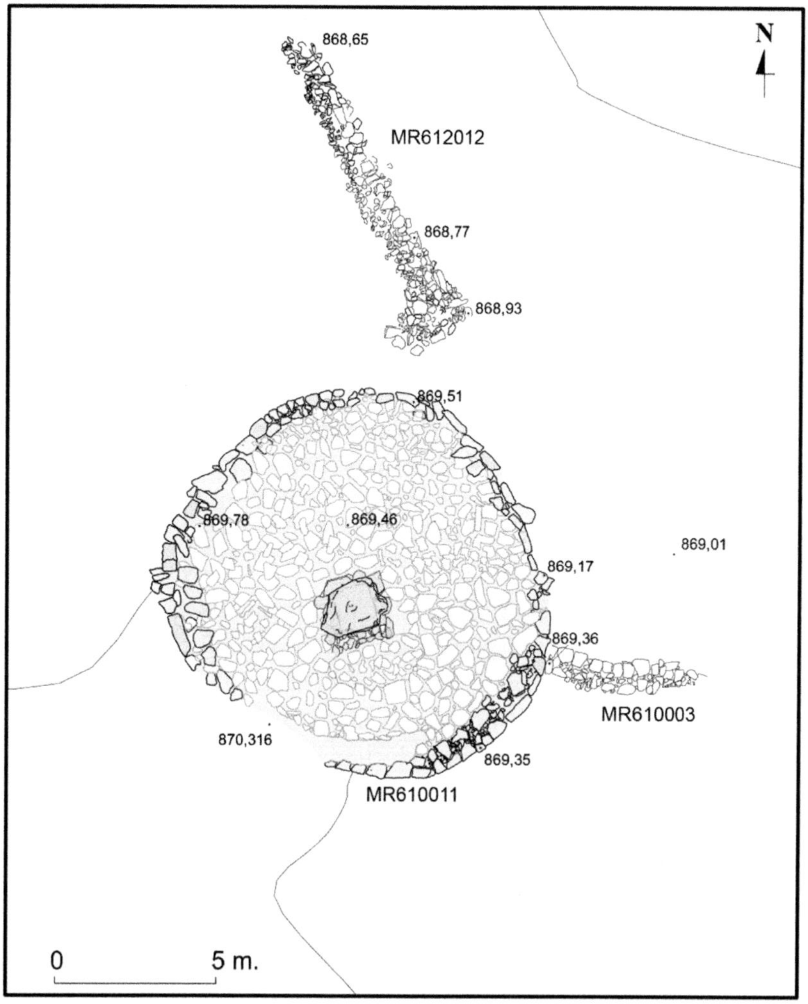

Figure 11.16. Plan of the first phase of monument 53 with the two 'antennas' or 'arms'.

monument 53 seemingly contained the remains of the members of a high status family or even of a larger kinship group.

Conclusions

To summarise, we can say, firstly, that the environmental data are apparently consistent with the predictions of our model that urbanisation and state formation were contingent on the emergence of hierarchy, population growth and an intensification of land-use leading to the development of the political economy. The evidence presented indicates, from the eighth century BC, a pressure on the environment that can be reasonably attributed to population increase. Unfortunately, the lack of palynological data makes it impossible to analyse the situation at a regional or even micro-regional scale, but it is reasonable to assume that this trend was not strictly limited to Althiburos and its immediate surroundings. This is also consistent with available information on the funerary world, as the few more or less well-dated tombs all belong to the central centuries of the first millennium BC. However, this may be purely accidental, since we are dealing with only seven tombs among the hundreds of thousands that comprise the megalithic necropoleis of Numidia. This possible population increase, if it really resulted in food shortages and difficulties for the domestic economy, could have caused a growth of political economy. In the sense of Johnson and Earle's model, a higher institutional complexity resulted and, in the end, the consolidation of social hierarchies. The most obvious evidence to support this is the observed variability between the three tombs excavated in the El Ksour necropolis, since monument 53 evidently stands out with respect to the other two (and, at least for its size, in relation to the vast majority of tombs identified through the survey). Finally, evidence on the restructuring of the settlement of Althiburos in the sixth century BC, as well as the introduction of some elements of technical sophistication, specifically the Punic-type cistern, suggest that the urbanisation process was already underway by the sixth century BC. This is chronologically consistent with what has been said about economic intensification and the signs of social differentiation in the megalithic necropolis. The existence of a powerful defensive wall from the fourth century BC can also be an indication of the importance and possible urban category of Althiburos.

The final conclusion to be drawn bringing together, in the most prudent way, all these pieces of information, is that the formation of the Numidian city of Althiburos, and likely of the archaic state to which it belonged, began by the mid-first millennium BC. This was probably the final result of a long process of population growth and consequent pressure on the environment, decisively accentuated in the eighth century BC. This process, however, must certainly have started in the course of the second millennium BC, prior to the arrival of the first Phoenician settlers along the North African coast. Research on this earlier period, completely unknown at present in the Eastern Maghrib, is long overdue. But it is a crucial topic if we are to paint the great picture of North African Protohistory.

It is also clear that Althiburos did not stand alone in the first millennium BC, but must in some sense be illustrative of 'Numidian' developments more generally. Nor was this the only autochthonous transitioning to urbanisation and statehood. State formation in Fazzan seemingly followed a similar pathway, with increasing demographic pressure on the environment as the key element that may explain the formation of the vast Garamantian kingdom.[62]

It goes without saying that, in the present state of research, little can be stated about the specific ways in which state formation developed. To do so, it would be necessary to gather more extensive information on the nature and internal organisation of the settlements, as well as on the spatial structure of the necropoleis, which would hopefully provide information about the specific forms of social organisation. As a matter of fact, all we can say in this regard is that the classical texts and epigraphic documents of the Roman period attest the persistence of powerful tribal structures at the end of the Numidian period, and even in the Roman Imperial period.[63] It is possible, or even likely, that these tribal chiefdoms constituted, at some moment in the mid-first millennium BC, polities of an intermediate stage between the local group (which we think was still dominant by the early first millennium BC) and the monarchic states attested by the Greco-Roman written sources. The latter were strongly constituted in the third century BC, but their origins must certainly date back at least to the fourth century.[64] This view is consistent with Justin's indication that the kingdom of the Mauri already existed by the mid-fourth century BC.[65] The same probably holds true for the Massyle kingdom, since Massinissa's father, Gaia, was the heir of a dynasty. It is likely that one of his ancestors was Aylimas, the 'Libyan king' mentioned by Diodorus as an ally of Agathocles.[66] The precise moment when these kingdoms were constituted is obviously unknown, but it is not unreasonable to think that, as proposed by Kotula many years ago, it was related to the territorial Carthaginian expansion from the fifth century BC. Maybe this is the *differentia specifica* that may explain the particular pathway followed by the North African states as opposed to the much smaller polities that developed on the north shores of the western Mediterranean.

62 Mattingly *et al.* 2003. See now, Mattingly and Sterry, Chapter 19, this volume.

63 Fentress 2006; Gsell 1927; Lassère 2001.

64 A similar dating is proposed by Bokbot, Chapter 12, this volume for the rise in the Western Maghrib of mighty tribal confederations, or even kingdoms.

65 Justin, *Epitome* 18.6.

66 Diodorus Siculus, *Bibliotheca Historica* 20.17.

May we assume that the contact with the Phoenicians had other effects on urbanisation and state formation processes? Maybe the aspect where it could have been the most decisive is the diffusion of iron metallurgy. However, as noted above, the data recovered at Althiburos suggest the possibility of a local development of this technology. Another aspect where it could have been important, is in the introduction of prestige goods that could have been given a high status and could have been used as dowries in matrimonial exchanges, as well as in the creation of social debts, particularly through feasting.[67] This could have caused a rise of the price of dowries among certain lineages that had easier access to imported products, and thus promoted the creation of closed circuits of marriage exchange of superior status. However, even in this situation we should be able to explain the reasons why the society would have accepted the consolidation of these hierarchies and institutionalised inequality, which leads us back to the role of elites in solving the problems of the subsistence economy.

On the other hand, and returning to the specific material data, the hypothesis of Phoenician imports used in the context of a prestige goods economy can be perfectly consistent with their extremely small number (no more than 1 per cent of ceramic materials at Althiburos) until the fourth century BC, by which period hereditary inequality must have been well established. However, it seems difficult to understand their absence (although there may exist ideological reasons to explain it) among the tableware found in the tumulus of a seemingly elite grave such as monument 53, which, as already mentioned, has delivered exclusively locally hand-made vessels. It is also worth recalling that one dolmen at Henchir Mided has produced a fifth century BC Attic black-glazed cup.

Despite the contribution of the Althiburos project, the state formation process in pre-Roman North Africa is still, at the beginning of the twenty-first century, the most poorly understood in the whole western Mediterranean area. Our work has provided some information that may be useful to its understanding, but it is only a small glimmer on an area of hundreds of thousands of square kilometres that remain in absolute darkness. To turn this glimmer into a powerful spotlight will require the continuation of this project for many years. The next steps are to better understand the structure and chronology of the city and the megalithic necropolis, and to contextualise this information by digging some of the

[67] Regarding the model of prestige-goods economy and its application to an archaeological case study, see Frankenstein and Rowlands 1978.

periurban settlements. But even if this desideratum were accomplished (which is, at present, very uncertain), the information recovered would still have a purely local character, and could hardly be considered as representative of the process of state formation on the whole of the territory occupied by the Numidian kingdoms. Other projects, and probably other insights, are, therefore, necessary (preferably within the framework of an international well-coordinated programme) in order to bring to light the evidence that may clarify the emergence of pre-Roman states in both the Maghrib and Sahara.[68]

References

Belarte, M.C. 2011. Les sondages dans la zone 1. In Kallala and Sanmartí 2011, 45–110.

Belkahia, S. and Di Vita-Évrard, C. 1995. Magistratures autochtones dans les cités pérégrines de l'Afrique romaine. In P. Trousset, P. (ed.), *Monuments funéraires, institutions autochtones en Afrique du Nord antique et médiévale, VIe colloque international sur l'histoire et l'archéologie de l'Afrique du Nord.* Paris: Editions du CTHS, 255–74.

Berthier, A. 1980. Un habitat punique à Constantine. *Antiquités africaines* 16: 13–26.

Blanton, R.E. 1998. Beyond centralization. Steps toward a theory of egalitarian behaviour in archaic states. In Feinman and Marcus 1998, 135–72.

Bondarenko, D.M., Grinin, L.E. and Korotayev, A.V. 2002. Alternative pathways of social evolution. *Social Evolution & History* 1.1: 54–79.

Brun, P. 2015. L'évolution en dents de scie des formes d'expression du pouvoir durant l'âge du Fer en Europe tempérée. In C. Belarte, D. Garcia and J. Sanmartí (eds), *Les estructures socials protohistòriques a la Gàllia i Ibèria (Homenatge a Aurora Martín i Enriqueta Pons), VII Reunió Internacional d'Arqueologia de Calafell (Calafell, del 7 al 9 de març de 2013).* Barcelona: Institut Català d'Arqueologia Clàssica, 49–59.

Camps, G. 1960. Les traces d'un Âge du Bronze en Afrique du Nord. *Revue africaine* 104: 31–55.

Camps, G. 1961a. *Monuments et rites funéraires protohistoriques: Aux origines de la Berbérie.* Paris: Arts et Métiers Graphiques.

Camps, G. 1961b. *Aux origines de la Berbérie. Massinissa ou les débuts de l'histoire.* (*Libyca* 8). Algiers: Service des Antiquités.

Camps, G. 1995. Les nécropoles mégalithiques de l'Afrique du Nord. In P. Trousset (ed.), *Monuments funéraires, institutions autochtones en Afrique du Nord*

[68] This research has been funded by the Spanish Ministry of Economy and Competitiveness (projects HAR2012-39189-C02-01 and HAR2012-39189-C02-02).

antique et médiévale, VIe colloque international sur l'histoire et l'archéologie de l'Afrique du Nord. Paris: Editions du CTHS, 17–31.

Camps, G. and Camps-Fabrer, H. 1964. *La nécropole mégalithique du Djebel Mazela à Bou Nouara*. Mémoires du Centre de recherches anthropologiques, préhistoriques et ethnographiques, III. Paris: Arts et métiers graphiques.

Cantero, F.J. and Piqué, R. 2016. Ressources forestières à partir de l'étude des charbons de bois. In Kallala *et al.* 2016, 491–515.

Crumley, C. 1995. Building an historical ecology of Gaulish polities. In B. Arnold and D.B. Gibson (eds), *Celtic Chiefdom, Celtic State. The Evolution of Complex Social Systems in Prehistoric Europe*. Cambridge: Cambridge University Press, 26–33.

Ennaïfer, M. 1976. *La cité d'Althiburos et l'ëdifice des Asclëpieia*. Bibliothèque Archéologique, vol. I. Tunis: lnstitut National d'Archéologie et d'Art.

Feinman, G.M. and Marcus, J. (eds). 1998. *Archaic States*. Santa Fe: School of American Research Press.

Fentress, E. 2006. Romanizing the Berbers. *Past and Present* 190: 3–32.

Ferjaoui, A. 2010. Les relations entre Carthage et l'intérieur de l'Afrique. Le cas de Zama Regia et sa région. In A. Ferjaoui (ed.), *Carthage et les autochtones de son empire du temps de Zama. Hommage à Mhamed Hassine Fantar*. Tunis: Institut National du Patrimoine, 341–52.

Frankenstein, S. and Rowlands, M.J. 1978. The internal structure and regional context of Early Iron Age society in south-western, Germany. *Bulletin of the Institute of Archaeology* 16: 73–112.

Gatto, M.C., Mattingly, D.J., Ray, N. and Sterry, M. (eds). 2019. *Burials, Migration and Identity in the Ancient Sahara and Beyond*. Trans-Saharan Archaeology, vol. 2. Series editor D.J. Mattingly. Cambridge: Cambridge University Press.

Godelier, M. 1980. L'État: Les processus de sa formation, la diversité de ses formes et de ses bases. *Revue internationale des sciences sociales* 32.44: 657–71.

Godelier, M. 1999. Chefferies et États, une approche anthropologique. In Ruby 1999, 19–30.

Gsell, S. 1927. *Histoire ancienne de l'Afrique du Nord, t. V. Les royaumes indigènes. Organisation sociale, politique et économique*. Paris: Librairie Hachette.

Harris, M. 1995. Anthropology and postmodernism. In M.F. Murphy and M. L. Margolis (eds), *Science, Materialism and the Study of Culture*. Gainesville: University Press of Florida, 62–77.

Johnson, A.W. and Earle, T. 2000. *The Evolution of Human Societies from Foraging Group to Agrarian State*. Second Edition. Stanford, California: Stanford University Press.

Kallala, N. 2002. Archéologie romaine et colonisation en Afrique: Enjeux et pratiques. (L'exemple du Kef (Sicca Veneria) et de sa région, dans le nord-ouest de la Tunisie). *Africa* 19: 57–81.

Kallala, N. and Sanmartí, J. (eds). 2011. *Althiburos I. La fouille dans l'aire du capitole et dans la nécopole méridionale* (Documenta 18). Tarragona: Institut Català d'Arqueologia Clàssica.

Kallala, N., Sanmartí, J., Jornet, R., Belarte, M.C., Canela, J., Chérif, S., Campillo, J., Montanero, D., Miniaoui, S., Bermúdez, X., Fadrique, T., Revilla, V., Ramon, J. and Ben Moussa, M. 2014. La nécropole mégalithique de la région d'Athiburos, dans le massif du Ksour (Gouvernorat du Kef, Tunisie). Fouille de trois monuments. *Antiquités africaines* 50: 15–52.

Kallala, N., Sanmartí, J. and Belarte, M.C. (eds). 2016. *Althiburos II. L'aire du capitole et la nécropole méridionale: Etudes* (Documenta 18). Tarragona: Institut Català d'Arqueologia Clàssica.

Kallala, J., Sanmartí, J. and Belarte, M.C. (eds). 2018. *Althiburos III. La nécropole protohistorique de Althiburos (massif du Ksour)*. Tarragona: Institut Català d'Arqueologia Clàssica.

Khanoussi, M. and Von Rummel, P. 2012. Simitthus (Chimtou, Tunesien). Vorbericht über die Aktivitäten 2009–2012. *Mitteilungen des deutschen archäologischen Instituts, römische Abteilung* 118: 179–222.

Khanoussi, M., Ritter, S. and Von Rummel, P. 2005. The German-Tunisian Project at Dougga: First results of the excavations south of the Maison du Trifolium. *Antiquités africaines* 40–41: 43–66.

Kim, J. 2001. Elite strategies and the spread of technological innovation: The spread of iron in the Bronze Age societies of Denmark and Southern Korea. *Journal of Anthropological Archaeology* 20.4: 442–78.

Klejn, L. 1993. *La Arqueología soviética: Historia y teoría de una escuela desconocida*. Barcelona: Crítica.

Kotula, T. 1976. *Masynissa*. Warsaw: PIW.

Lassère, J.-M. 2001. La tribu et le monarche. *Antiquités africaines* 37: 140–55.

Lévêque, P. 1986, L'émergence des pouvoirs structurés dans l'Afrique mineure de l'Age du Fer. In *Gli interscambi culturali e socio-economici fra l'Africa settentrionale e l'Europa mediterranea, Atti del Congresso Internazionale di Amalfi (5–8 dicembre 1983)*. Naples: Istituto Universitario Orientale, 637–51.

Lévêque, P. 1999. Avant et après les Princes. L'Afrique mineure de l'Age du fer. In Ruby 1999, 153–64.

López Reyes, D. and Cantero, F.J. 2016. Agriculture et alimentation à partir de l'étude des restes de graines et des fruits. In Kallala *et al.* 2016, 449–90.

Lull, V. and Risch, R. 1995. El estado argárico. *Verdolay* 7: 97–109.

Marcus, J. 1998. The peaks and valleys of ancient states: an extension of the dynamic model. In Feinman, and Marcus 1998, 59–94.

Marcus, J. 2008. The archaeological evidence for social evolution. *Annual Review of Anthropology* 37: 251–66.

Marras G., Doro L., Floris R. and Zedda M. 2009. Il dolmen 102. Nota preliminare. In G. Tanda, M. Ghaki and R. Marras (eds), *Storia dei paesaggi preistorici e protostorici nell'Alto Tell tunisino. Missioni 2002–2003*. Cagliari: Università degli Studi di Cagliari and Ministère de la Culture et de la Sauvegarde du Patrimoine (Tunisia), 179–200.

Mattingly, D.J. 2016. Who shaped Africa? The origins of urbanism and agriculture in Maghreb and Sahara. In N. Mugnai, N. Ray, and J. Nikolaus (eds), *De Africa Romaque: Merging Cultures across North Africa.* London: Society for Libyan Studies, 11–25.

Mattingly, D.J., Reynolds, T. and Dore, J. 2003. Synthesis of human activities in Fazzan. In D.J. Mattingly (ed.), *The Archaeology of Fazzan, vol. 1, Synthesis.* London: Society for Libyan Studies, 327–73.

Parkinson, W.A. and Galaty, M.L. 2007. Secondary states in perspective: an integrated approach to state formation in the prehistoric Aegean. *American Anthropologist* 109.1: 113–29.

Portillo, M. and Albert, R.M. 2011. Husbandry practices and livestock dung at the Numidian site of Althiburos (el Médéina, Kef Governorate, northern Tunisia): the phytolith and spherulite evidence. *Journal of Archaeological Science* 38.12: 3224–33.

Portillo, M. and Albert, R.M. 2016. Les activités domestiques de la période numide à travers l'étude des micro-restes végétaux et fécaux: phytolithes et sphérolithes. In Kallala *et al.* 2016, 517–27.

Portillo, M., Valenzuela, S., and Albert, R.M. 2012. Domestic patterns in the Numidian site of Althiburos (northern Tunisia): The results from a combined study of animal bones, dung and plant remains. *Quaternary International* 275: 84–96.

Ramon Torres, J. and Maraoui Telmini, B. 2011. Les sondages dans la zone 2. In Kallala and Sanmartí 2011, 153–262.

Renfrew, C. 1986. Peer polity interaction and social change. In C. Renfrew and J.F. Cherry (eds), *Peer Polity Interaction and Social Change.* Cambridge: Cambridge University Press, 1–18.

Rodríguez, A., Pavón, I. and Duque, D. 2010. Población, poblamiento y modelos sociales de la Primera Edad del Hierro en las cuencas extremeñas del Guadiana y Tajo. *Arqueología Espacial* 28: 41–64.

Ruby, P. (ed.). 1999. *Les princes de la protohistoire et l'émergence de l'État. Actes de la table ronde internationale de Naples.* Naples/Rome: Collection du Centre Jean Bérad 17/Collection de l'École Française de Rome, 252.

Sanmartí, J. 2009. From the archaic states to romanization: A historical and evolutionary perspective on the Iberians. *Catalan Historical Review* 2: 9–32.

Sanmartí, J., Kallala, N., Belarte, M.C., Ramón, J., Maraoui, B., Jornet, R. and Miniaoui, S. 2012. Filling gaps in the Eastern Maghreb's Protohistory: The Althiburos archaeological Project (el Kef, Tunisia). *Journal of African Archaeology* 10.1: 21–44.

Sanmartí, J., Kallala, N., Jornet, R., Belarte, M.C., Canela, J., Chérif, S., Campillo, J., Montanero, D., Bermúdez, X., Fadrique, T., Revilla, V., Ramon, J., Ben Moussa, M. 2015. Roman Dolmens? The Megalithic necropolises of Eastern Maghreb revisited. In M. Díaz-Guardamino, L. García Sanjuán and D. Wheatley

(eds), *The Lives of Prehistoric Monuments in Iron Age, Roman, and Medieval Europe*. Oxford: Oxford University Press, 287–304.
Sanmartí, J., Cruz Folch, I., Campillo, J. and Montanero, D. 2019. Numidian burial practices. In Gatto *et al.* 2019, 249–80.
Shanks, M. and Tilley, C. 1987. *Social Theory and Archaeology*. Cambridge: Polity Press.
Smadja, E. 1983. Modes de contact, sociétés indigènes et formation de l'Etat numide au second siècle avant notre ère. In *Modes de contacts el processus de transformations dans les sociétés anciennes, Actes du Colloque de Crotone (1981)*. Pisa/Rome: Scuola normale superiore di Pisa/École française de Rome, 685–702.
Stambouli-Essassi, S., Roche, E. and Bouzid, S. 2007. Evolution of vegetation and climatic changes in North-Western Tunisia during the last 40 millennia. *Geo-Eco-Trop* 31: 171–214.
Thébert, Y. 1992. Bulla Regia, *Encyclopédie Berbère* 11, 1647–53.
Trigger, B. 1989. *A History of Archaeological Thought*. Cambridge: Cambridge University Press.
Trigger, B. 1998. *Sociocultural Evolution: Calculation and Contingency*. Oxford: Blackwell Press.
Valenzuela-Lamas, S. 2016. Alimentation et élevage à Althiburos à partir des restes fauniques. In Kallala *et al.* 2016, 421–48.
Van der Veen, M. and Westley, B. 2010. Palaeoeconomic studies. In D.J. Mattingly (ed.), *The Archaeology of Fazzan. Volume 3, Excavations Carried out by C.M. Daniels*. London: Society for Libyan Studies, 488–522.
Wolf, E.R. 1966. *Peasants*. Englewood Cliffs, New Jersey: Prentice-Hall, Inc.
Wright, E.O. 1983. Giddens's critique of Marxism. *New Left Review* 138: 11–35.

12 The Origins of Urbanisation and Structured Political Power in Morocco

Indigenous Phenomenon or Foreign Colonisation?

YOUSSEF BOKBOT

Introduction

This chapter reviews the evidence for the emergence of urbanisation in Morocco and evaluates the contributions of Phoenician settlers and of local communities to this process. In line with the new evidence from Tunisia, the previously emphatic emphasis on the role of outsiders in introducing urbanism and sparking the initial steps towards state formation now seems less convincing, with a much more significant role for local actors.[1]

After first reviewing the ancient source evidence and the history of archaeological research, I shall present the latest archaeological findings based on my personal experience of a number of key settlements, as well as some impressive funerary monuments that illustrate the emergence of hierarchy within early Berber (Imazighen) society (Fig. 12.1).

The rarity of identified Iron Age settlements in North Africa has led historians and archaeologists to suggest that a nomadic pastoral economy predominated in the Protohistoric period, despite hints that the sedentary agrarian society began as early as the Neolithic period.[2] Both ancient and modern authors alike have not hesitated to paint a dark picture of the populations of the Maghrib, who they characterise as barbarians, still limited to producing tools from flint, condemned to a state of stagnation and isolation that only the arrival of the Phoenicians and Romans could interrupt.

Some classical authors presented the populations of the Maghrib as eternal wanderers who ignored agricultural activity and sedentary life. Strabo, Valerius Maximus, Appian and Polybius all claimed that Numidia

[1] See Sanmartí *et al.*, Chapter 11, this volume. [2] Martínez-Sánchez *et al.* 2018.

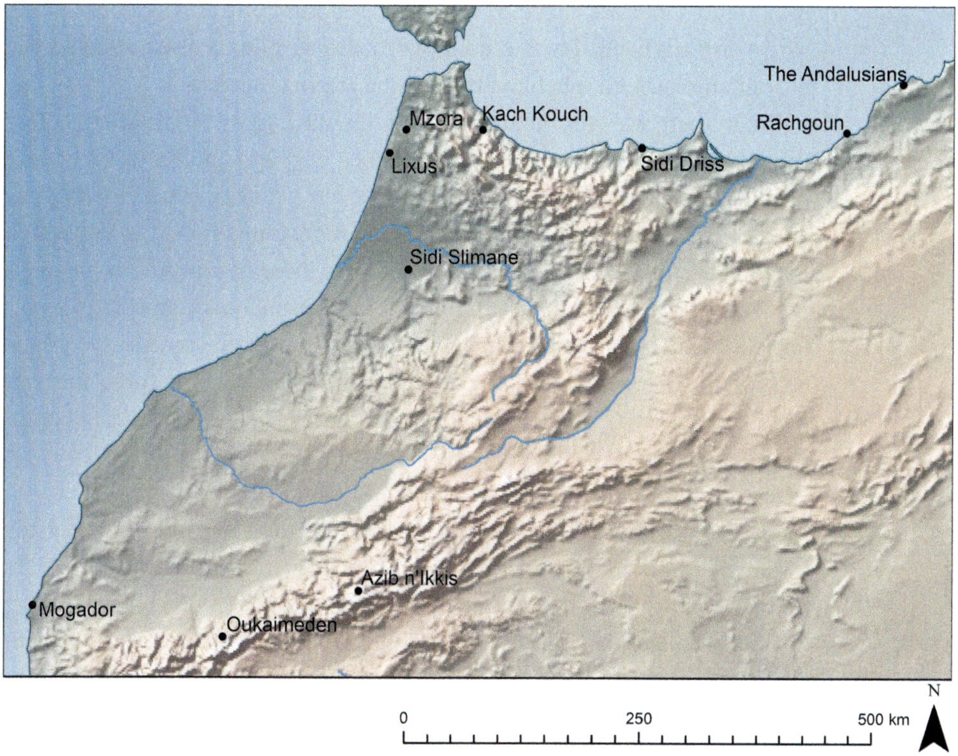

Figure 12.1. Map of sites mentioned in this chapter.

was valueless before Massinissa and incapable of agricultural production.[3] According to Strabo, Massinissa rendered the Numidians sociable and made them into farmers.[4] Similarly, Appian wrote that divine favour allowed him to develop a vast country where previously the Numidians ate only grass because they did not cultivate the land themselves.[5]

Such attitudes were readily embraced by colonial-era scholarship, which was naturally inclined to the view that innovations were brought to Africa by outsiders.[6] According to this discourse, the ancestors of the Imazighen were condemned to a completely passive role. They are presented as having received a ready-formed civilisation from the East that was transported by a handful of Phoenician seafarers from the Levant.

Herodotus, on the other hand, specified that 'at the river Triton, [the Gulf of Gabes in the south-east of Tunisia], there are Libyan farmers ... They

[3] Gsell 1927, 169–212, especially 186–90. [4] Strabo, *Geography* 17.3.15.
[5] Appian, *Historia Romana* 106; Gsell 1927, 187.
[6] See Mattingly 2011, 43–72; 2016 for a full discussion of the impact of the colonialist discourse.

have houses and are called Maxyes'.[7] Herodotus contrasted eastern Libya, where nomads lived, to western Libya, which was mountainous, wooded, full of wild animals and inhabited by sedentary agriculturalists.

What then was the actual state of the Imazighen civilisation before the arrival of the Phoenicians? Evidence for agricultural activity and pre-Phoenician settlements is well established. With the development of archaeological research, it has now been demonstrated that at the arrival of the Phoenicians, the Imazighen were not uncivilised or primitive barbarians. Rock art discovered in the Central High Atlas dating back to the Bronze Age depicts scenes of agricultural activities. A ploughing scene is engraved on the cliffs of the Yaggour at Azib n'Ikkis, and Jean Malhomme interprets the bent lines present at Oukaïmedden as representing sickles.[8]Archaeobotanical evidence for the introduction and cultivation of cereals in Morocco dates as early as the Neolithic as recent finds demonstrate.[9] Cereals were an established resource already in the eighth century BC, suggested by the frequent representation of iron sickles among the funerary offerings in indigenous burials in the hinterland of Tangier at that time.[10]

Data from archaeological excavations thus often contradict the ancient sources and raise several questions. Can one speak of Phoenician trading posts everywhere? Were there only Phoenician trading posts on the coast? What was the nature of these settlements? What differentiated them from other indigenous settlements?

The existence of Phoenician trading posts is well attested in texts. In particular, the Greek geographer Pseudo-Scylax enumerates a series of relevant points, towns and trading posts on the coasts of the Maghrib.[11] When Pseudo-Scylax wrote about Phoenician trade with the Atlantic regions of Morocco, he drew a detailed, and very different, picture from that described by Herodotus. The Phoenicians no longer had dealings with primitive and fearful natives who fled all contact with civilised peoples. The Ethiopians (a term used to describe the Imazighen) lived in a city and imported a variety of goods, indicating a relatively developed and complex society.[12] This passage from Pseudo-Scylax may relate to trade with the ancient city of Lixus, especially since, in another passage, the same author indicates that the Ethiopians also had a great city where Phoenician merchant ships went to trade.[13]

[7] Herodotus, *Histories* 4.191; Gsell 1916, 29.
[8] Malhomme 1953, figure 1, 384; de Torres and Ruiz-Gálvez 2014.
[9] Martínez-Sánchez *et al.* 2018. [10] Ponsich 1967; 1969; 1970.
[11] Gsell 1927, 160; Shipley 2012. [12] Psuedo-Skylax, *Periplous* 112; Villard 1960, 21.
[13] Gsell 1927, 113.

Therefore, we have strong reasons to believe that these trading posts were not founded by the Phoenicians alone, but rather were established alongside existing indigenous settlements. However, much of the research in the last century, instead of relying on physical evidence revealed by archaeological excavations, continued to deny any urban character to the paleo-Amazigh world. In perpetuating this narrative, some local and foreign researchers continue to describe any ancient settlements where imported material is discovered as Phoenician, Punic or Roman.[14]

Unfortunately, the excavations carried out at Moroccan sites during the first half of the twentieth century did not produce any valid data able to refute these arguments. During this period, the emphasis was placed on monumental archaeology, rather than stratigraphic excavations. The archaeological syntheses produced during this period were too greatly influenced by the writings of the Greek and Latin authors. Pierre Cintas, one of the great scholars of Phoenician/Punic culture has drawn a contentious conclusion. According to him, the excavations confirm the existence of Phoenician trading posts discussed in the texts: 'an excellent mooring in the centre of an island, cape or estuary could not have escaped the eye of the Phoenician sailors'.[15] Everything is described as if these coastal areas, overrun by the Phoenicians, were completely unoccupied and these foreigners from the Lebanese coast settled where they wanted without worrying about the resistance of local populations.

In recent years the development of archaeological research in Morocco and western Algeria has sparked new questions concerning the origins of some cities and trading posts, usually considered as Phoenician or Punic foundations. In the second half of the twentieth century, archaeological excavations had already begun to reveal occupation levels beneath the Punic and Roman layers belonging to an indigenous culture possessing agriculture knowledge, a sedentary lifestyle and even early urbanisation.[16] In order to reach a more objective and complete reconstruction of the history of these coastal sites we must put the ancient texts to the test using archaeological data, studying them in their entirety, from an emic perspective, limiting bias and influence from outside sources such as ancient texts. This chapter will focus on a selection of sites (Lixus, Mogador, Kach Kouch, Sidi Driss, Mzora and Sidi Slimane), but it needs stating at the

[14] See Mattingly *et al.* 2017 for discussion of imported material in the Maghrib and Sahara more generally.

[15] Cintas 1954. [16] Camps 1961a, 49.

outset that knowledge of the Protohistoric development of a number of other sites is also advancing in important ways (Rirha, Volubilis, Sala, Thamusida, Tingi, Tamada, Ceuta, Melila).[17]

The Ancient City of Lixus

The earliest traditions refer to Lixus as being among the oldest cities in the western Mediterranean basin. The ancient texts trace its foundation to the same period as that of Gades in the eleventh century BC. These sources are contradicted, however, by the evidence from archaeological excavations. Surveys carried out by Miguel Tarradell in the ancient city of Lixus have provided a basic stratigraphy: a level of occupation characterised by an abundance of hand-made ceramic material, which he described as belonging to a 'Neolithic tradition'.[18] Excavations undertaken at the same site by Michel Ponsich confirmed the existence of this distinct archaeological layer.[19] The pottery recovered in this layer was hand-made, generally smooth or polished and its surface was rarely decorated, although sometimes a decorative horizontal band appears surrounding the top of the vessel. When present, this band was either embossed using fingers, or decorated with an alignment of impressed patterns.

The most determinative piece of evidence for a pre-Phoenician phase, however, is the discovery of a new type of pottery, labelled 'graffito' (Fig. 12.2, 1–2), previously unknown in North Africa, and for which analogies are found in pre-Phoenician ceramic traditions of the southern Iberian Peninsula.[20] As a whole, the forms and patterns of the pottery from the lower levels of Lixus are almost identical to those of the Bronze Age levels of the Ghar Cahal and Khaf Taht el Ghar caves (Figs 12.2, 3–11).[21] Similar examples of 'grafitto' style pottery were also discovered during the recent excavations undertaken by the joint Moroccan and Spanish team, INSAP-Universidad de Valencia (Figs 12.2, 12–13). This discovery further demonstrates the relative abundance of this pottery type in the pre-Phoenician levels of Lixus.

This archaeological material did not exist in isolation, but was rather found in association with relatively archaic domestic structures. Michel

[17] Callegarin *et al.* 2016; Papi 2019; Papi and Akerraz 2008. [18] Tarradell 1954, 790.
[19] Ponsich 1981, 131. [20] Bokbot 1991, 198, 321. [21] Bokbot and Onrubia-Pintado 1992, 20.

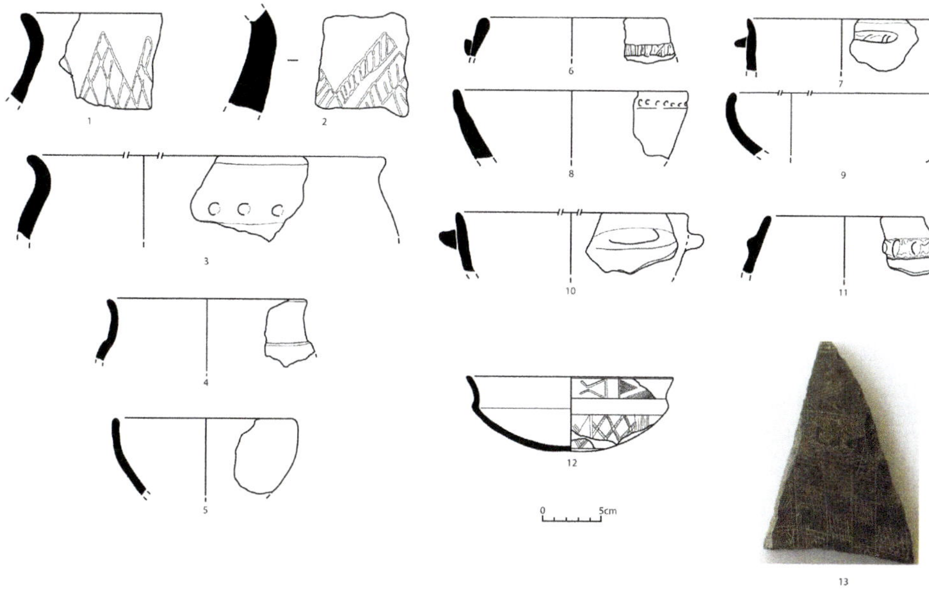

Figure 12.2. Ceramics from Lixus: 1)–2)'Graffito' pottery from Lixus (Ponsich Survey); 3)–5) Pre-Phoenician pottery from Lixus; 6)–11) Bronze Age pottery, Ghar Cahal and Kahf Taht el Ghar caves; 12) Vase with incised decoration applied after firing, Lixus (recent survey); 13) Lixus (recent survey) sherd with graffito.

Ponsich pointed out that certain wall construction techniques and certain pre-Roman walls at Lixus do not correspond with those found in the Phoenician east. Furthermore, Ponsich pointed out that the city opened onto the countryside through a megalithic door preceding the Punic gate, which led to a road lined with ancient tombs.[22]

The presence of these settlement structures with megalithic characteristics, as well as the hand-made ceramics, make it possible to envisage the prospect of a pre-Phoenician settlement at Lixus. The assertion of early local occupation is sustainable, especially since the site of Lixus and its immediate surroundings produced metallic objects attributable to the Bronze Age. At the Second Pan-African Congress on Prehistory, Bernardo Sáez Martín announced the discovery of a bronze sword at the mouth of the Loukkos (Fig. 12.3).[23] Although then lost, this was subsequently re-located, some 30 years later, in the Museum for Pre- and Early History, Berlin. This sword is generally described as a 'Ballintober' type, which dates

[22] Ponsich 1988, 86. [23] Sáez Martín 1955, 659.

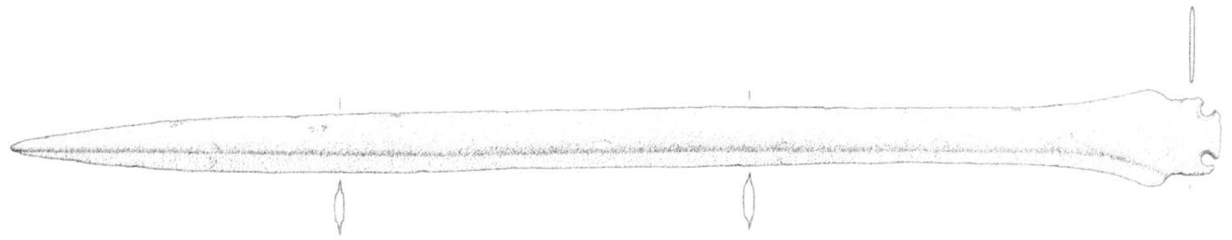

Figure 12.3. Sword from the Loukkos, used with permission (Brandherm 2007).

to the Atlantic Late Bronze Age *c.*1300–1150.[24] Georges Souville argues instead that it can only be compared to examples coming from the deposition of the Ria de Huelva and is more akin to the 'Ballintober' type. In addition, Enrique Gozalbes-Gravioto reported the presence of a flat bronze axe in the collections of the Tetuan Museum, the source of which may be the site of Lixus.[25]

It is likely that these metal objects are directly related to the funerary megaliths from the site of Lixus and its surroundings. Paul Pallary recorded the presence of so many dolmens between the town of Larache and the ruins of Lixus that it led him to conclude that dolmen burials were indigenous to Lixus.[26] Tarradell reported two burials composed of large blocks of stone at Lixus and according to his description, one of them could potentially coincide with the extramural tomb discovered in the nineteenth century by the French diplomat Charles Tissot and cleared by Henri De la Martinière.[27] It consists of a megalithic tomb composed of a corridor made from large vertically placed slabs and covered by five transverse juxtaposed tiles.[28] Locally named 'al-Quantara' (Fig. 12.4), this monument, which corresponds typologically to an 'allée couverte', remains a unique excavated specimen in Morocco. However, on the hillock where it stands, I noticed several large slabs of similar type which raises the possibility that the al-Quantara 'allée couverte' monument is one of a group of megalithic tombs.

The Pre-Roman Settlement on the Island of Mogador

Pierre Cintas reported the recovery of hand-made ceramic material in the oldest layers of the site of Mogador and concluded that it was locally

[24] It was originally described as a 'Rosnoën' blade by Ruiz-Gálvez 1983, 64. Souville 1995, 248 argued in favour of the 'Ballintober' classification. The most up-to-date publication of the sword is Brandherm 2007, 34, 134 – A 1.

[25] Gozalbes-Gravioto 1975, 14. [26] Pallary 1907, 308; 1915, 195. [27] Tarradell 1960, 167.

[28] Bokbot 1991, 181.

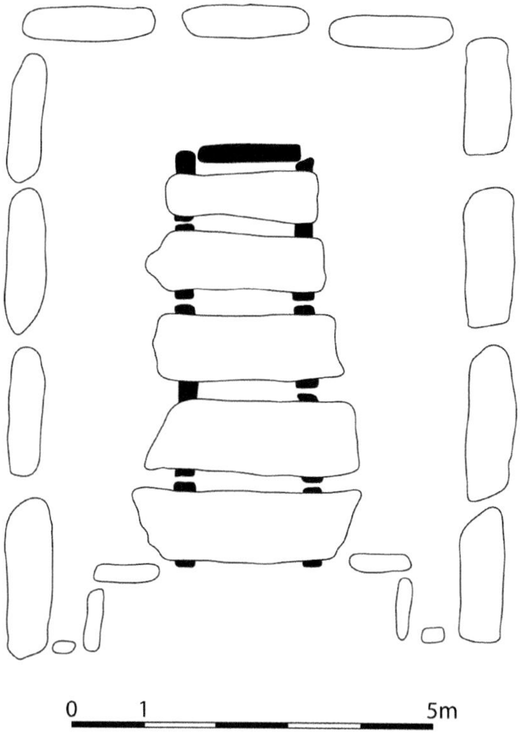

Figure 12.4. The 'allée couverte' tomb of al Quantara.

produced and preceded the Punic trading posts (Fig. 12.5a).[29] The pottery usually has a smooth or polished surface and little variation in form – mainly large vases with a flat bottom with applied cords decorated either digitally or incised with a nail. These cords were placed horizontally around the neck and serpentiform on the body. The vessels have similar characteristics to those found in the Bronze Age levels of the El-Khill, Ghar Cahal, Khaf Taht el Ghar and Dar es Soltane caves,[30] as well as those found in the lower layers of Lixus.[31] André Jodin has drawn attention to the resemblance of this pottery type to those of the European Bronze Age.[32] Excavations recently carried out at the site of Mogador by the Moroccan-German mission (INSAP-DAI Madrid) confirmed the presence of this type of pottery (Fig. 12.5b). Although the stratigraphic position of their provenance is not entirely clear, it seems probable that they came from the deepest levels.

[29] Cintas 1954, 41. [30] Jodin 1966, 166. [31] Bokbot 1991. [32] Jodin 1957, 37.

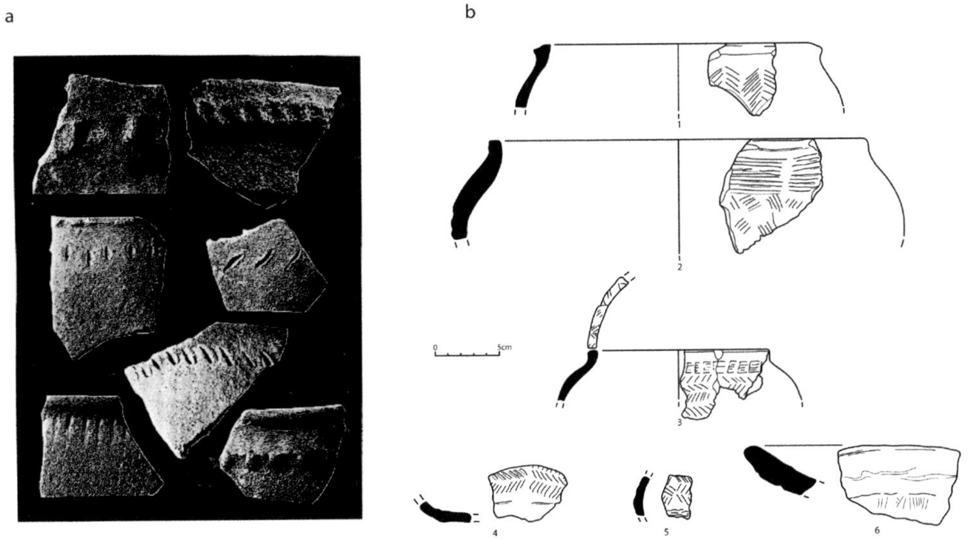

Figure 12.5. a) Mogador: hand-made pottery with decoration applied with fingers; b) Mogador (recent survey): hand-made pottery.

Excavations have also uncovered the remains of furnaces, nozzles and iron slag, representing the oldest testimonies of metallurgical activities related to iron in Morocco. According to recent surveys, the iron ore originated from sites approximately 10 km north of Essaouira.[33] Moreover, geomorphological studies carried out by a Moroccan–German team have yielded important results concerning changes in the configuration of coastal shores from the early Neolithic to the present. During the period of Phoenician expansion, Mogador was not an island, but rather a peninsula contiguous with the continent. This new piece of information has opened the debate on the geographical nature of the location of Phoenician trading posts on the Moroccan coast and on the nature of relations between colonial and indigenous populations.

The Hilltop Settlement at Kach Kouch

The summit of the hill of Kach Kouch, also known as Dhar el-Moudden, consists of a series of calcareous outcrops, partly blocked by sediment, which terminate in steep slopes. These outcrops delimit a roughly circular

[33] El Khayari 2007, 57.

Figure 12.6. Kach Kouch plateau, overlooking the lower Oued Laou valley.

area, with a diameter of approximately 40 m and provide the site with natural fortifications. The hill of Kach Kouch is located on the right bank of the Oued Laou, at the beginning of the meander indicating the approach of the mouth. Located about 70 m above sea level, the hill dominates the great alluvial plain of the lower valley of Oued Laou towards the north-east (Fig. 12.6).

The first investigations carried out on the site in 1988 produced surface finds, notably fragments of indigenous hand-made ceramic traditions, mixed with rare fragments of amphorae produced in the Phoenician tradition, which led to the conclusion that there was a broad phase of Protohistoric occupation. The subsequent archaeological surveys in 1992 were carried out with the intention of determining the presence of archaeological structures dating to that period, as well as to ascertain if the sedimentary fill showed signs of stratified anthropogenic deposits. Four trenches were dug perpendicular to the axis of a recent threshing floor that occupied the centre of the hill. Only two of the trenches produced evidence of structures and allowed for observations on the stratigraphy.[34] The stratigraphic profiles of test trenches B and D are as follows:

[34] Bokbot and Onrubia-Pintado 1995.

- Level 1: A disturbed upper deposit of agricultural soil comprising a fine brown sediment and redeposited archaeological material from deeper deposits.
- Level 2: A middle layer created distinguishable in part by the accumulation of thick fragments of orange-coloured daub, composed of reddish clay mixed with stems of herbaceous plants and retaining the imprints of the wooden rods on which it was applied.
- Level 3. An occupation level, slightly offset from the line of the steep slopes, composed of earthy brown to greyish compacted local sediments resting directly on the limestone substrate. This bedrock, which has many cracks, has been artificially modified by the installation of structures, and the digging of pits and funerary trenches.

The structures revealed in the trenches can be grouped into three distinct categories: combustion features (hearths), semi-cylindrical pits, possibly for storage, and burial trenches. The hearths were characterised by two small paving stones, roughly circular in form and reddened by thermal action. The semi-cylindrical storage pits, which were on average 0.4 m in diameter and 0.3 m in depth, appeared in both trenches (Fig. 12.7a). Eight of these pits were located in trench D and three in trench B. The six burial trenches, on the other hand, were exclusively found in trench B, across its entire surface (Fig. 12.7b). These burial trenches were

Figure 12.7. a) Kach Kouch: storage structures; b) Kach Kouch: archaeological structures revealed during excavation.

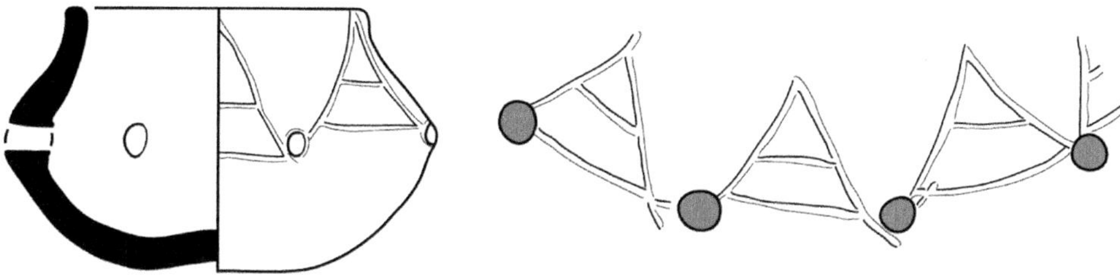

Figure 12.8. Kach Kouch, vase decorated with 'graffito'.

elongated and shallow and were carved into the bedrock. They contained the remains of three adults and three children buried in extended right lateral position. The burials were all oriented north-south, heads turned towards the east and hands resting on the pelvis.

Among the ceramic repertory, indigenous hand-made types coexist with Phoenician wheel-thrown pottery. The hand-made pottery is represented by a series of fairly open flat-bottomed storage jars, often decorated at the shoulder with incisions or impressions made either directly on the wall of the vessel or on an applied cord. Some vessels were equipped with gripping elements in the form of an inverted crescent. A small bowl decorated in 'graffito', similar to those from Lixus, was also found. It has a concave font and its thin walls were carefully polished (Fig. 12.8).[35] In the absence of absolute dates, the ceramics allow this Protohistoric settlement to be dated within a chronological range of the ninth to the sixth century BC.

The Protohistoric Settlement of Sidi Driss

The site of Sidi Driss is located on the Mediterranean coast, halfway between Al-Hoceima and Nador. It occupies the last hill on the left bank of the Oued Amekrane, overlooking the mouth of the river.[36] Sidi Driss was a coastal settlement contemporary with the Phoenician expansion, overlaid by the current village of Sidi Driss. The archaeological surface material collected makes it possible to attribute the oldest occupation to the eighth and seventh centuries BC. Amphorae types from Sidi Driss are possibly related to the Rachgoun 1 and 4 types, their closest typological parallel being those from Mersa Madakh on the neighbouring Orense coast.[37] This imported material coexists with indigenous hand-made

[35] Bokbot and Onrubia-Pintado 1995, 223. [36] Kbiri-Alaoui *et al.* 2004.
[37] Vuillemot 1965, 27–28.

pottery decorated with finger impressions, analogous to those found in the Bronze Age levels of the caves of north-west Morocco.[38]

Other Sites in Northern Morocco and Western Algeria

If we extend our geographical scope to the nearby regions along the north-eastern coast of Morocco, we find the site of The Andalusians, west of Oran, which occupies the edge of a steep cliff at the bottom of a wide bay and consists of a settlement and a necropolis partially excavated by G. Vuillemot. One of the investigations carried out on the settlement revealed that the oldest level, representing a settlement characterised by hearths and hand-made pottery, rests on the sandstone substrate of the cliff. Above this level, ceramic material dated to the fifth century BC was found. Vuillemot concludes that the first level seems to reveal a self-enclosed world.[39] Several circular tumuli, which seem to always contain a cremation burial, have been excavated on the slopes of the plateau that closes the bay of the Andalusians towards the west.

Further to the west of Oran, 2 km from the coast opposite the mouth of the Oued Tafna, is the small island of Rachgoun (*c.*15 ha). Theoretically, the position is ideal for a Phoenician/Punic site, however the archaeological data reflects the reality of occupation. The oldest unproblematic datable ceramic fragments come from an Attic amphora from the second half of the seventh century BC. However, the excavation reports mention the presence of local ceramics contemporary to, and even prior to, the Attic amphora.

Vuillemot called these sites Punic, under heavy influence of the theories of his mentor Pierre Cintas, for whom no coastal point favourable for defense must have slipped the attentive eye of the Phoenicians. He did make a very significant remark, however, when he stated that certain essential aspects of the inhabitants of the island of Rachgoun were not consistent with those expected of a Phoenician population.[40] The funeral rites of the groups that occupied these trading posts do not correspond to those of the Phoenicians, but are rather evidence of Protohistoric Amazigh sepulchral practices.

[38] Bokbot 1991; Kbiri-Alaoui *et al.* 2004, 596–97. [39] Vuillemot 1965, 42.
[40] Vuillemot 1965, 93.

Discussion

Indigenous and Phoenician Urbanisation in the Western Mediterranean

If we broaden our scope to the northern shore of the western Mediterranean where similar problems arise, we will find the answers to our questions. Archaeological work in Spain and France has demonstrated the complexity of the phenomenon of Hellenisation of the littoral zone and its hinterland. There were certainly colonies and trading posts, but, equally certainly, there were also numerous indigenous settlements where trade was carried out and where an original civilisation evolved through varied contact with the Greek and Punic world.

At the coastal sites of the Maghrib, whenever Punic or Phoenician imported ceramics are found, the majority of excavators automatically think of these sites as being occupied by eastern seafarers. We must pay tribute to Gabriel Camps, who aggressively opposed this interpretation of the archaeological data when he stated 'That coastal villages received Mediterranean productions from their origins is so normal that it cannot be presented as a scientifically valid argument about their own origins'.[41]

Paul Albert Février questioned whether all the trading posts or small settlements had actually been founded by Phoenicians or whether, instead, they should be regarded as indigenous. For him there was no doubt that indigenous villages existed long before the creation of trading posts, which could very well have been newly established, but alongside older settlements previously founded by indigenous populations.[42]

Pseudo-Scylax distinguished between two cities on the Loukkos, one Phoenician and the other populated by Libyans.[43] This statement more accurately reflects, in my view, the ancient reality. In order to trade their products, the Phoenicians would logically have chosen to settle where there was already a fairly large human occupation. Moreover, Pseudo-Scylax, discussing Phoenician trade with the Atlantic regions of Morocco, may have been referring to trade with the city of Lixus, since the author mentions in another passage that the Ethiopians made a great deal of wine from their vines, which the Phoenicians exported.[44]

[41] Camps 1979, 48. [42] Février 1967, 108. [43] Carcopino 1949, 89. [44] Villard 1960, 22.

François Villard concluded that the cities of the North African coast labelled as Phoenician may have had an earlier origin. He also noted that the birth of urbanism in Morocco appears not to have been, properly speaking, the result of colonisation.[45] Maurice Euzennat, for his part, drew attention to the fact that it is inappropriate to make the Punic influence play too important a role.[46]

Similarly, Gabriel Camps observed that many pre-Roman cities in North Africa had megalithic necropolises at the gates of the ancient centre, corresponding to funerary rites that were foreign to those of the Romans and Phoenicians.[47] These burials were the work of the Amazigh populations who inhabited these cities before any contact or foreign occupation. This observation probably applies to the ancient city of Lixus as well.

For François Villard, the process of urbanisation in Morocco, which he placed during the sixth century BC, was the result of the intensification of commercial contacts with the Phoenicians of Gades, the Carthaginians and the Greeks, but was not the result of colonisation.[48] According to Villard, when ancient tradition describes a city as Phoenician, it only means that its inhabitants had adopted the language and manners of the Phoenicians, but does not necessarily imply that it was founded by them.[49]

This Protohistoric occupation at sites that have previously been characterised as primarily Phoenician or Punic leaves open the question of the date of origin of Palaeo-Amazigh villages of proto-urban character, for which we currently lack a precise chronology. It is tempting to link this emergence to the development of metallurgy, which enabled increased cultivation and productivity and which in turn offered the potential for the population growth that was necessary for any increase in the socio-economic complexity of these communities. Openness to Mediterranean trade must also be taken into consideration, even if such trade is still ill-defined.[50]

The necropoleis of the Tangier hinterland contribute to a clearer vision of the populations of the Late Bronze Age. They indicate a presence, as early as the sixth century BC, of indigenous rural settlements, still characterised by Bronze Age traditions.[51] In these same necropoleis, appearing alongside the megalithic cists of the Middle and Final Bronze Age, burials

45 Villard 1960. 46 Euzennat 1965, 261.

47 Camps 1993; cf. Sanmartí *et al.*, Chapter 11, this volume. 48 Villard 1960, 22.

49 Villard 1960, 23.

50 There are striking similarities of evidence and interpretation with the situation of the Eastern Maghrib laid out by Sanmartí *et al.*, Chapter 11, this volume.

51 Ponsich 1988, 87.

with somewhat different architecture and funerary rites are also found. This evidence for the coexistence, without a transition, of the Libyan civilisation of the Late Bronze Age and the 'phoenicianised' Libyans of the eighth and seventh centuries BC provides an image that best corresponds to the protohistoric settlements of Kach Kouch and Sidi Driss, and to the oldest phases of occupation at Lixus and Mogador.

Figure 12.9. Aerial view of the Mzora tumulus (Camps 1961, pl. I.2).

Monumental Tombs and Social Hierarchy

Mzora is one of the best-known Moroccan megalithic monuments attributable to the Protohistoric period. This large burial mound, surrounded by a ring of stone monoliths, is currently the only known example of its kind in North Africa (Fig. 12.9). Because of the lack of an excavation report, however, its dating poses a real problem. The tumulus of Mzora is distinguished from the other burial mounds in north-west Morocco by the larger dimensions of the monoliths of its enclosure. Gabriel Camps noted that although this characteristic was not typically African, it represents the development, in a vertical dimension, of annular arrangements of stones around the base of other North African tumuli.[52]

The megalithic nature, which was used as a criterion for linking Mzora to Iberian megalithic tradition, is not unknown in the funerary monuments of north-west Morocco. Other large tumuli have been reported in

[52] Camps 1961b, 76–78.

northern Morocco: the tumulus of Sidi Khelili, which is 90 m long, 30 m wide and 8 m high; the tumulus of Nouillat Kebira measuring 41 m in diameter and 8 m in height; and finally, the large tumulus identified by Danilo Grébénart in the region of Taza measuring 100 m in diameter at the base and 15 m in height.[53] The Mzora monument also displays evidence of Atlantic influences. The location of the two large monoliths seems to suggest an orientation towards the west. Such an orientation is rare, if not totally absent, in the Protohistoric funerary monuments of Morocco since burials were oriented either east or south-east. Miguel Tarradell and Gabriel Camps considered the tumulus of Mzora as an indigenous monument presumably built in pre-Roman times for a regional chief or Moorish king. This raises the question of social hierarchy in north-west Africa.[54]

At Sidi Slimane of Gharb, the removal of a tumulus, located in the centre of a weekly market (*souk*), revealed a funerary monument in the form of a dwelling (Fig. 12.10). This atypical house had a corridor, a courtyard and a funerary chamber covered with cedar logs. Two bodies rested in the chamber, and two others in the corridor and in the court, these were doubtless servants buried after immolation to guard the burial of the chiefs.[55] Finds included pieces of ivory that must have originally been part of a box. Nearby, a Libyan inscription refers to the burial of two individuals, a father and his son. Using the amphorae present in the tomb, a date for the monument can be assumed to be between the fourth and third centuries BC.

If it is true that two servants were sacrificed to accompany their masters to the afterlife, these human sacrifices may represent an essential rite of power in emerging class societies. The question of the emergence of the Mauritanian kingdoms is therefore probably related to these great tombs, which have tended to be associated with princely societies.[56] Their importance should to be taken into account because they imply an authority powerful enough to control considerable surplus labour, but also because they denote a legitimisation of the tribal chiefs in the process of becoming kings.

Do the several large burials of this type in north-west Morocco demonstrate an intermediate stage where powerful leaders of tribal confederations were engaged in displays of power? In any case, it is clear that these chiefs benefited from a marked increase in productive forces, probably connected

[53] Grébénart 1967. [54] Camps 1961b, 78; Tarradell 1952, 233. [55] Camps 1961b, 196–99.
[56] For developed argument along these lines, see further, Papi 2019.

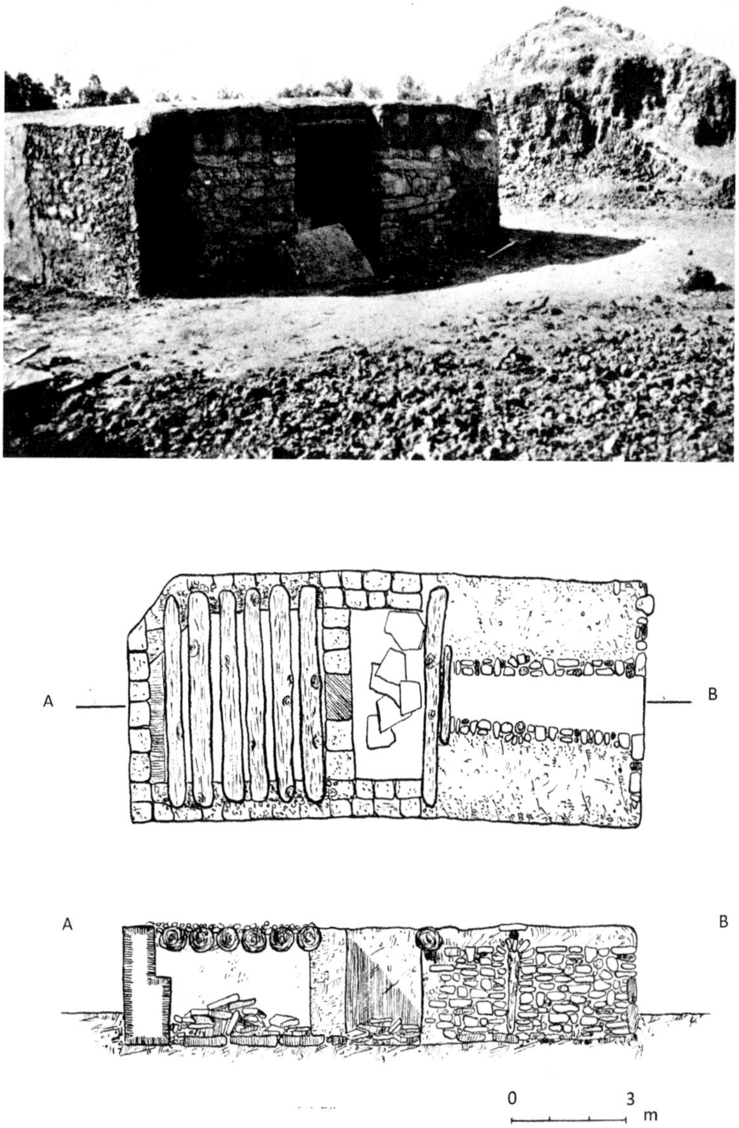

Figure 12.10. Monument in the form of a dwelling under the mound of Sidi Slimane: a) general view; b) plan and cross-section (Camps 1961, pl. X.3 and Fig. 81).

with the use of a plough, however archaic, which led to considerable development in production and significant demographic growth. The organisation of agricultural labour and the distribution of social products required greater authority and the ability to exercise their power and influence over wider territories.

Everything suggests that powerful confederations, if not kingdoms, were formed in Morocco in the fourth century BC. The origins of the Mauritanian dynasties remain mysterious, but this is hardly surprising. Their power, which eventually spread to cover immense territories, was, in fact, derived from that of tribal leaders who succeeded in widening their field of action and influence.

We can therefore imagine the urgency for Moroccan and Maghribian archaeology in general to consider more excavations extending into the pre-Roman and pre-Phoenician levels of ancient cities and trade posts. These excavations are indispensable to the development of knowledge about the Protohistoric civilisations of the Maghrib.

References

Aranegui-Gasco, C. 2001. *Lixus: Colonia fenicia y ciudad punico-mauritana.* Valencia: SAGVNTVM, Papeles del Laboratorio de Arqueologia de Valencia. Extra 4.

Brandherm, D. 2007. *Las espadas del Bronce Final en la Península Ibérica y Baleares.* Prähistorische Bronzefunde, vol. IV. Stuttgart: Franz Steiner, 16.

Bokbot, Y. 1991. *Habitats et monuments funéraires du Maroc protohistorique.* Thèse de Doctorat, Université de Provence.

Bokbot, Y. 1998. Une céramique à graffito à Lixus. *Bulletin d'Archéologie Marocaine* 18: 321–23.

Bokbot, Y. and Onrubia-Pintado, J. 1992. La basse vallée de l'Oued Loukkos à la fin des temps préhistoriques. In *Actes du Colloque International: la ville antique de Lixus. Larache 8–11 Novembre 1989.* Rome: Collection de l'Ecole Française de Rome 166, 17–26.

Bokbot, Y. and Onrubia-Pintado, J. 1995. Substrat autochtone et colonisation phénicienne au Maroc. Nouvelles recherches protohistoriques dans la péninsule tingitane. In *Actes du 118 Congrès National des Sociétés Historiques et Scientifiques.* Paris: CNRS, 219–31.

Callegarin, L., Kbiri Alaoui, M., Ichkhakh, A. and Roux, J.C. (eds). 2016. Rirha: Site antique et medieval du Maroc. II. Période Maurétanienne (Ve siècle av. J.-C. – 40 ap. J.-C.). Madrid: Casa de Velázquez.

Camps, G. 1961a. Aux origines de la Berbérie. Massinissa ou les débuts de l'histoire. *Libyca* 8. Algiers: Service des Antiquités.

Camps, G. 1961b. *Monuments et rites funéraires protohistoriques: Aux origines de la Berbérie.* Paris: Arts et Métiers Graphiques.

Camps, G. 1979. Les Numides et la civilisation punique. *Antiquités africaines* 14: 43–53.

Camps, G. 1993. Réflexions sur l'origine protohistorique des cités en Afrique du Nord. In L. Serra (ed.), *La città mediterranea: Eredita antica e apporto arabo-islamico sulle rive del Mediterraneo occidentale e in particolare nel Maghreb: atti del Congresso internazionale di Bari, 4–7 maggio 1988*. Napoli: Istituto universitario orientale, 73–81.

Carcopino, J. 1949. *Le Maroc antique*. Paris: Gallimard.

Cintas, P. 1954. *Contribution à l'étude de l'expansion carthaginoise au Maroc*. Paris: Publication de l'Institut. des Hautes Etudes Marocaine 56.

Chifman, C. 1963. *Naissance de la puissance carthaginoise*. Moscow.

de Torres, J. and Ruiz-Gálvez, M., 2014. Unravelling patterns in Oukaïmeden rock art. *Complutum* 25.2: 167–87.

El Khayari, A. 2007. La présence phénicienne au Maroc. *Les Dossiers d'Archéologie* (Hors Série 13, La Méditerranée des Phéniciens): 56–59.

Euzennat, M. 1965. Héritage punique et influences gréco-romaines au Maroc à la veille de la conquête romaine. In *Le rayonnement des civilisations grecque et latine sur les cultures périphériques. VIIIème Congrès International d'Archéologie Classique*. Paris: de Boccard, 265–66.

Février, P-A. 1967. Origine de l'habitat urbain en Maurétanie césarienne. *Journal des Savants* 2: 107–23.

Gozalbes-Gravioto, E. 1975. Las edades del cobre y bronce en el N-O de Marruecos. *Cuadernos de la biblioteca espanola de Tetuan* 12: 7–32.

Grébénart, D. 1967. Prospection archélogique dans la region de Taza (Maroc), préhistoire et protohistoire. *Libyca* 15: 147–55.

Grillo W.F. 2003. *Recherches archéologiques maroco-italiennes 2002–2003*. Rome: Edizioni Quasar, Istituto Italiano di Cultura.

Gsell, S. 1916. *Hérodote*. Textes relatifs à l'Histoire ancienne de l'Afrique du Nord. Algiers and Paris: Ernest Leroux.

Gsell, S. 1927. *Histoire ancienne de l'Afrique du Nord, vol V*. Paris: Librairie Hachette.

Jodin, A. 1957. Note préliminaire sur l'établissement préromain de Mogador. *Bulletin d'Archéologie Marocain* 2: 9–40.

Jodin, A. 1966. *Mogador: Comptoir Phénicien du Maroc atlantique*. Rabat: Etudes et Travaux d'Archéologie Marocaine 2.

Kbiri-Alaoui, M., Siraj, A. and Vismara, C. 2004. Recherches archéologiques maroco-italiennes dans le Rif. *L'Africa romana* 15: 567–604.

Malhomme, J. 1953. Les représentations anthropomorphes du Grand Atlas. *Libyca anthropologie-préhistoire-ethnographie* 1: 373–85.

Martínez-Sánchez, R.M., Vera-Rodríguez, J.C., Pérez-Jordà, G., Peña-Chocarro, L. and Bokbot, Y. 2018. The beginning of the Neolithic in northwestern Morocco. *Quaternary International* 470 B: 485–96.

Marzoli, D. and El Khayari, A. 2010. Vorbericht Mogador (Marokko) 2008. *Deutsches Archäologisches Institut, Abteilung Madrid* 51: 61–108.

Mattingly, D.J. 2011. *Imperialism, Power and Identity. Experiencing the Roman Empire*. Princeton: Princeton University Press.

Mattingly, D.J. 2016. Who shaped Africa? The origins of agriculture and urbanism in Maghreb and Sahara. In N. Mugnai, J. Nikolaus and N. Ray (eds). *De Africa Romaque. Merging Cultures across North Africa*. London: Society for Libyan Studies, 11–25.

Mattingly, D.J., Leitch, V., Duckworth, C.N., Cuénod, A., Sterry, M. and Cole, F. (eds). 2017. *Trade in the Ancient Sahara and Beyond*. Trans-Saharan Archaeology Volume 1. Series editor D.J. Mattingly. Cambridge: Cambridge University Press and The Society for Libyan Studies.

Pallary, P. 1907. Recherches palethnologiques sur le littoral du Maroc en 1906. *L'Anthropologie* 18: 301–14.

Pallary, P. 1915. Recherches préhistoriques effectuées au Maroc (1912–1913). *L'Anthropologie* 26: 193–217.

Papi, E. and Akerraz, A. (eds). 2008. *Sidi Ali Ben Ahmed – Thamusida 1. I contesti*. Rome: Quasar.

Papi, E. 2019. Revisiting first millennium BC graves in north-west Morocco. In M. C Gatto, D.J. Mattingly, N. Ray and M. Sterry (eds), *Burials, Migration and Identity in the Ancient Sahara and Beyond*. Cambridge: Cambridge University Press, 281–312.

Ponsich, M. 1967. *Nécropoles phéniciennes de la région de Tanger*. Rabat: Etudes et Travaux d'Archéologie Marocaine 3.

Ponsich, M. 1969. Influences phéniciennes sur les populations rurales de la région de Tanger. In *Tartessos y sus problemas. V Symposium Internacional de Prehistoria Peninsular*. Barcelona: Universidad de Barcelona, 173–84.

Ponsich, M. 1970. *Recherches archéologique à Tanger et dans sa région*. Paris: CNRS.

Ponsich, M. 1981. *Lixus: Le quartier des temples*. Rabat: Etudes et Travaux d'Archéologie Marocaine 9.

Ponsich, M. 1988. Implantation rurale du Maroc phénicien. *Dossiers Histoire et Archéologie* 132: 84–87.

Ruiz-Gálvez Priego, M. 1983. Espada procédante de la ria de Larache en el Museo de Berlin Oeste. In *Homenaje al Prof Martin Almagro-Basch*. Madrid: Ministerio de Cultura, vol. 2, 63–68.

Sáez Martín, B. 1955. Sobre la supuesta existencia de una edad del bronce en Africa menor. In *IIe Congrès Panafricain de Préhistoire, Alger 1952*. Paris: Arts et Métiers Graphiques, 659–62.

Shipley, G. 2012. *Pseudo-Skylax's Periplous: The Circumnavigation of the Inhabited World. Text, Translation and Commentary*. Exeter: Bristol University Press.

Souville, G. 1995. Pénétrations atlantiques des influences ibériques au Maroc protohistorique. In *IIe Congreso Internacional: El Estrecho de Gibraltar, Ceuta Novembre 1990*. Madrid: Universidad Nacional de Educación a Distancia, vol. 2, 245–92.

Tarradell, M. 1952. El tumulo de Mezora (Marruecos). *Archivo de Prehistoria Levantina* 3: 229–39.
Tarradell, M. 1954. Las excavaciones de Lixus. In *IV congreso internacional de ciencias prehistóricas y protohistóricas*. Zaragoza: La Académica, 789–96.
Tarradell, M. 1960. *Historia de Marruecos: Marruecos Punico*. Tetuan: Cremades.
Villard, F. 1960. Céramique grecque du Maroc. *Bulletin d'Archéologie Marocaine* 4: 1–26.
Vuillemot, G. 1965. *Reconnaissances aux échelles puniques d'Oranie*. Autun: Musée Rolin.

13 Architecture and Settlement Growth on the Southern Edge of the Sahara

Timing and Possible Implications for Interactions with the North

KEVIN C. MACDONALD

Introduction

Since the 1970s, there has been a significant increase in regional data sets relating to tell sites in the West African Sahel. Previous colonial notions that Trans-Saharan commerce in the Islamic era created the first Sub-Saharan towns and polities have now been largely abandoned; it is all too apparent that complex settlement systems were widespread in the south long before the eighth century.[1] Yet questions of Trans-Saharan interactions with the Berber world in preceding centuries have not been so effectively addressed. In this chapter, I examine archaeological evidence for architectural development and settlement growth within the Hodh and Middle Niger basins: the Tichitt, Walata, Tagant and Néma escarpments, the Méma, the Inland Niger Delta, the Lakes Region, the area of Timbuktu and the Gourma (Fig. 13.1). The advent of different types of dry stone, coursed earth or mudbrick structures and the regional timing of settlement growth will be the primary factors under consideration. This analysis will focus on data between 1600 BC and AD 800 and propose multiple points of change during this timeframe. It is intended that this micro-synthesis will provide a means for the systematic comparison of Sahelian developments with early Berber settlements in the Sahara.

In this text, concepts of urbanism and statehood are intentionally not invoked as defined categories. This is for two reasons:

1) Definitions of urbanism go beyond mere size of settlement (although typically one does not even think of urbanism in sites of less than 20 ha). Yet there is a paucity of adequate temporally defined data for most regions concerning factors such as occupational specialism, public

[1] See McIntosh and McIntosh 1988.

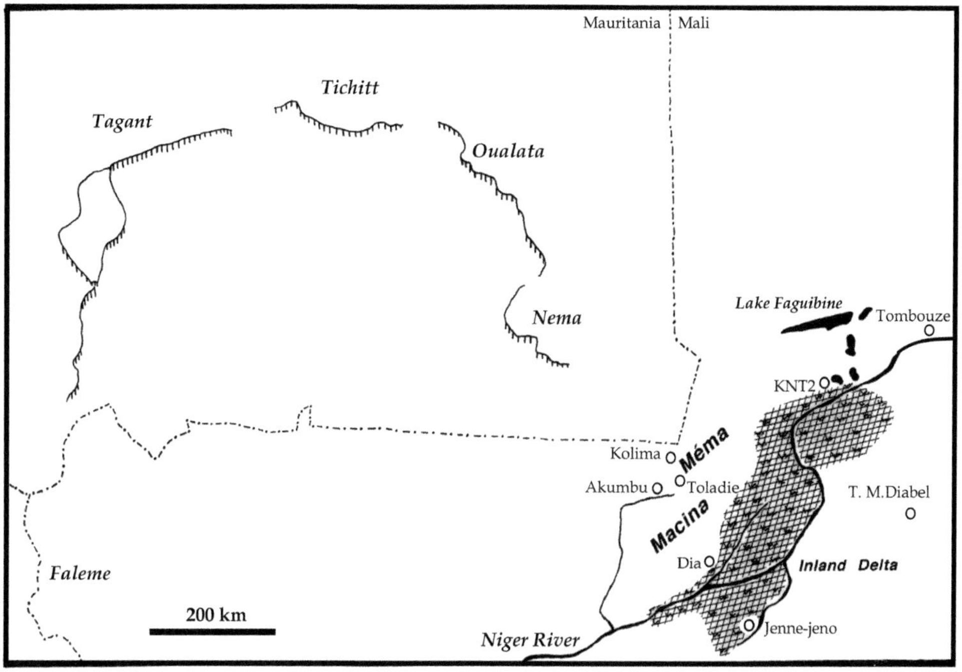

Figure 13.1. Map of regions and key sites discussed in this chapter.

works and trade networks, which makes qualitative assessment of urbanisation difficult. Jenné-jeno is an important exception to this caveat.[2] More recently, tentative cases have been advanced for still earlier urbanism at Dia and Tombouze.[3] With more data, cases for urban status should eventually be made for many localities in the first-millennium AD Middle Niger, in some places potentially even earlier. However to argue about these cases in advance of suitable data is unwise.

2) The definition of statehood is a contentious issue and largely depends on how, and if, one buys into existing social evolutionary frameworks. Tichitt – for example – has been described in the literature as a 'Chiefdom' or as a 'Complex Chiefdom',[4] conceptual frameworks borrowed from historic Polynesia and of doubtful direct applicability to Africa.[5] It is therefore better to discuss polities in more qualitative and individual terms rather than in exteriorly derived and arbitrary categories. There is insufficient space to do so here. The case of Ghana/Wagadu alone, given its connections to both Arabic and

[2] McIntosh 1995. [3] Dia: Bedaux *et al.* 2001; 2005; Tombouze: Park 2010.
[4] Holl 1985; Munson 1971. [5] See Pauketat 2007.

oral literature and other data sets, could easily consume a chapter in its own right. Thus, I have limited my concerns to changes in built environment and periods of settlement growth.

Architectural Development

The potential influence of pre-Islamic North African architectural forms on the Sahel has had a long currency. Prussin, for example, asserts a Roman origin for the Berber 'courtyard house' or fortified farms, seen as leading to subsequent allied Islamic forms in the Sahel.[6] However she also claims an ill-defined syncretic aspect for the 'internal courtyard house', with an 'indigenous prototype being known from southern Mauritania by the mid-second millennium BC' (that is Tichitt and Tagant). Indeed, were it not for the ample and early architecture of the Tichitt Tradition an argument could have been advanced for a primarily North African role in the creation of the West African compound. Instead, when Tichitt is taken into account, we are left with a much more nuanced and complex sequence of architectural change and accommodation in the Trans-Saharan region.

The Tichitt Architectural Sequence

Tichitt and its neighbouring settled escarpment ranges in southern Mauritania remains one of African archaeologies greatest enigmas. It is one of the continent's earliest agricultural landscapes and first polities – potentially a pristine one. It also possesses a four-tier hierarchy of stone-built settlements interspersed over 200,000 km^2 and has strong material connections to the foundation of key first-millennium BC Middle Niger settlements.[7] As such, Tichitt could be viewed as the western counterpart of Kerma, but it remains much less celebrated and discussed in world archaeology. The reasons for this obscurity might be explained by its very remoteness, the small number of (largely Francophone) researchers who have worked at these sites, and the reluctance of some scholars to place confidence in the ceramics-based sequences constructed for its deflated and sometimes unstratified settlements. Critically, its mortuary archaeology, while manifestly abundant and at times monumental, has gone almost entirely unexcavated.[8]

6 Prussin 1986, 105–8. 7 Holl 1993; MacDonald 2011a.
8 Amblard-Pison 2006; Vernet 1993.

Although the massive architectural sites of the Tichitt Tradition have undergone a range of different field enquiries, Munson's original work in the Tichitt region remains the only one that attempts to trace the temporal evolution of its architecture.[9] When considered via recent re-evaluations of the Tichitt ceramic sequence, ^{14}C dates and associated phasing of sites, it is possible to consider two broad architectural periods: Classic (1600–1000 BC) and Late (1000–400 BC).[10] To these can be added a Terminal phase from the Tagant, where the building of smaller, if more internally complex sites, continued over the period of 400 BC to AD 350.[11]

From the outset of the Classic Tichitt phase (1600–1000 BC), defensive considerations played an important part in settlement design: high (*c.*2 m) and robust (*c.*1–1.5 m thick) stone walls surrounded major settlements, with means of access including gateways capped with lintel stones.[12] The internal space of sites was divided into tens, sometimes hundreds, of irregularly shaped curvilinear compounds defined by relatively low (*c.*1 m high) stone walls. The interior dimensions of these compounds ranged widely, falling anywhere between 70 and 4,050 m^2.[13] The reason for this wide variation is likely because some of these enclosures were domestic while others served as livestock pens or cultivation areas. A remarkable aspect of Classic Tichitt phase sites is the relative scarcity of signs of internal dwellings within these compounds. Most common are so-called 'pillar' or nine-stelae structures which are variously interpreted. These groupings of stone pillars (of *c.*1–2 m in height) may have served as granary bases or the frames for shelters covered in mats or hides.[14] While both uses appear possible, the dimensions of most would be in line with traditional granary styles still extant amongst the Soninke and Bamana of Mali.[15] Much rarer during this initial phase are circular stone structures. Munson perceived these as being stone-capped 'igloo' – or 'beehive' – shaped dwellings or granaries chinked with mud.[16] Amblard-Pison prefers to compare them to circular hybrid stone-thatch dwellings, chinked with mud and dung on their interiors only, a tradition still known from eastern Senegal.[17] The comparatively small numbers of such enclosed dwelling places in Classic Tichitt sites may argue for either relatively low population density on sites or the extensive use of more mobile and less durable

[9] Amblard Pison 2006; Holl 1986; Munson 1971; Ould-Khattar 1995; Vernet 1993.
[10] MacDonald 2011a; 2015. [11] Ould-Khattar 1995. [12] Munson 1971, II, 334–35.
[13] Holl 1993, Table 16. [14] Amblard-Pison 2006, 79–90; Munson 1971, II, 338.
[15] MacDonald *et al.* 2009. [16] Munson 1971, II, 340.
[17] Amblard-Pison 2006, 78–79; compare Dujarric 1981.

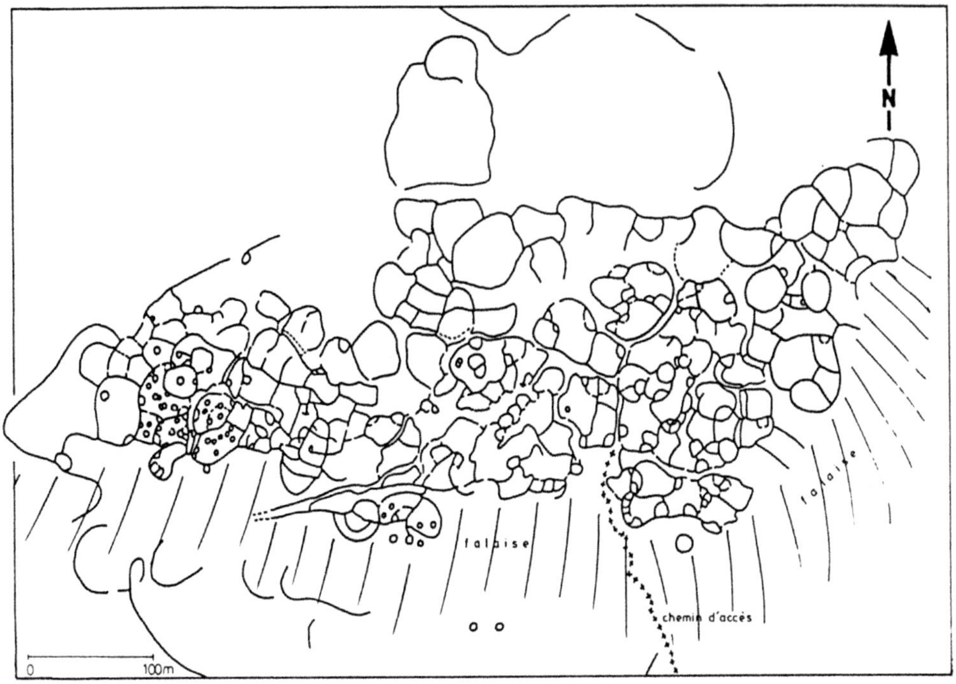

Figure 13.2. Plan of Tichitt 'Village 72' (Akreijit) (after Vernet 1993, 274).

supplementary structures of thatch, mat and pole, such as those built by recent historic Tuareg or Fulani.[18]

The best studied of Classic Tichitt sites is Akreijit, also known as Village 72 and Seyyid Ouinquil (Fig. 13.2). It stands as a good example of a medium-sized (15 ha) Tichitt settlement and is well-dated to *c.*1500–900 BC.[19] The site, oblong in shape, is situated atop an escarpment and composed of 177 compounds (including notional livestock pens), themselves grouped into 12 contiguous clusters.[20] Domestic stone structures (not including the nine-stelae granary type, which is almost ubiquitous) occur in only 60 of these compounds. These 146 single-room stone houses are of three sub-types: circular isolated structures of 9 to 10 m^2 (51), semi-circular structures built into the corner of a concession of 9 to 12.5 m^2 (48), and oblong structures backing onto the long wall of a compound of up to 16 m^2 (47).[21] Rarely, those backing onto compound walls could form up to three contiguous structures,

[18] David 1971; Nicolaisen and Nicolaisen 1997, I, 413–35.

[19] Amblard-Pison 2006, Figure 11. The largest known Tichitt settlement is that of Dakhlet el Atrouss I, with a remarkable 540 compounds and walled livestock pens, as well as extensive tumuli, covering a surface of 80.5 ha, see Holl 1993.

[20] Holl 1993, 116–17. [21] Ambard Pison 2006, 75–77.

but most were isolated. Thus, the clustering of modular room blocks so common in traditional West African courtyard compounds was only marginally extant, while the overall tendency of wall-lines was curvilinear rather than rectilinear.

The Late Tichitt phase (1000–400 BC) saw the increase of individual stone 'dwellings' within compounds. Munson notes that average compounds were at this time 30 to 40 m in diameter with surrounding dry-stone walls *c.*1.5 m in height.[22] Internal stone structures now numbered between one and ten per compound and were equally divided in number between 'stelae' structures and so-called 'rubble-circle houses'. Settlements in this phase tend to have been placed higher on escarpments in positions of less visibility and greater natural defensibility. In the Terminal Tichitt phase (400 BC–AD 350), known only from the Tagant, there was increasing occurrence of internal stone dwellings within compounds. A well-dated and thoroughly studied example is site T150 (*c.*150 BC–AD 70).[23] The site comprises approximately 200 compound enclosures formed of dressed stone usually attaining 1 m in height, though the evident subsequent robbing-out of many of these walls makes estimating their true height rather difficult. Two forms of smaller (one room) stone domestic structures are apparent, circular and rectangular, with the former being more common and at least equal in number to the compound enclosures. The rarer rectangular structures were quite substantial, measuring between 6 and 12 m in length. Both types of internal structure occurred in approximately half the compounds, the rest were seemingly empty. The circular dwellings clustered in twos and threes and frequently abutted rectangular structures (Fig. 13.3). Stelae structures were not present. It is notable that sites such as T150 in the Tagant, like those of the Late Tichitt phase in the Néma, exhibit evidence of both iron-working and iron objects.[24]

In summary, post-1000 BC Tichitt sites have clearer architectural evidence of compounds serving extended family units, with multiple granaries and multiple single room dwellings within each. The classic Sahelian curvilinear compound form now seems fully developed. The appearance of rectangular dwellings by 150 BC–AD 70 in the Tagant is a particularly interesting development and the earliest yet documented in Sub-Saharan Africa. It may represent evidence for the advent of a Trans-Saharan sphere

[22] Munson 1971, II, 340–41. [23] Ould-Khattar 1995, 241–51, figure 12.
[24] MacDonald *et al.* 2009.

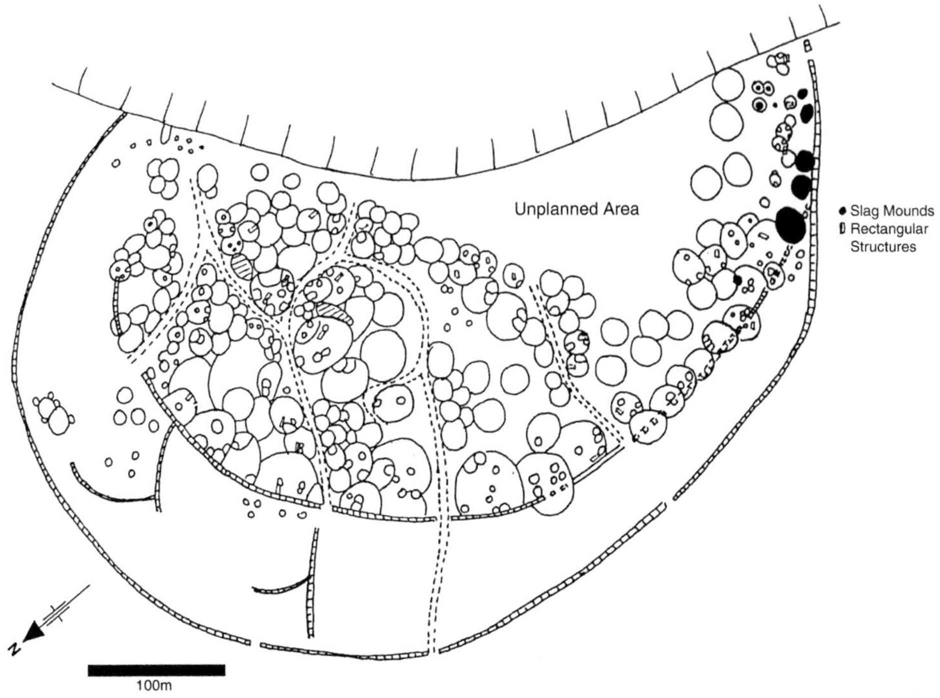

Figure 13.3. Plan of the Tagant site T150 (after Ould-Khattar 1995, figure 12).

of interaction, given the appearance of comparable rectilinear structures at Fewet and elsewhere in southern Libya in this same era.[25] Further temporal indicators for such connections will be considered below.

Pre-Islamic Architecture in the Middle Niger

The lack of raw materials suitable for stone construction over most of the Middle Niger's floodplain means that despite the material culture association of many 'founder' sites with the Tichitt Tradition one is obligated to search for traces of earthen architecture.[26] Generally speaking such structures were made of either layers of coursed earth (termed variously 'banco', 'bogoton', 'sana', etc. according to local usage) or out of mudbrick (usually loaf-shaped in early periods, but also cylindrical).

Only two examples of earthen architecture are known from the first millennium BC Middle Niger, both incompletely published. The earlier of the two is the site of Kolima Sud-Est, a low 10-ha tell in the multi-period

[25] Mattingly *et al.*, Chapter 2, this volume; Mori 2013. [26] MacDonald 1996; 2011a; 2015.

Kolima cluster at the centre of Mali's Méma region. The site was first surveyed and surface collected by Téréba Togola and the author in 1990. We recorded the traces of several eroding curvilinear 'tauf' wall lines at the site, notable by their colour and heavy clay composition, being of the dimensions of both compound and individual round house walls. Although these walls were mentioned in my doctoral dissertation,[27] and remain better described in my notes, they were not recorded when the site was test excavated by Takezawa and Cissé in 2000. The deposits, featuring late Tichitt Tradition pottery and evidence of cattle and fonio agriculture, were dated by three ^{14}C dates across a range from 910 to 540 BC.[28] Unfortunately, the Méma has been a region of high insecurity since the 1990s, access is risky and no further field research has been completed there since 2000.

Just to the south, in the Macina region, further traces of early earthen architecture were found and dated at the site of Dia-Shoma by a multinational 1998–2003 excavation team.[29] The earliest layers of this vast 50-ha tell were heavily eroded – perhaps by intermittent inundation – and such traces of building as there were often took the form of hardened or burned floors of indeterminate shape with occasional postholes. However burned loaf-shaped brick fragments were recovered from the lowest layer of exposure A/B. A single charcoal date from the conflagration which burned them gave the result of 9 calBC–calAD 67.[30] If these were indeed burned mudbricks, instead of broken fragments of a burned coursed earth wall, they would be amongst the oldest in Sub-Saharan Africa.

After these early manifestations, patchy evidence shows considerable variation in the material and form of earthen architecture across the Middle Niger. Back in the Méma, the next dated area of earthen construction comes from Mound B of the Akumbu complex (unit AK3) where a wall constructed with 'irregular mudbrick' was dated by an associated hearth to calAD 342–442.[31] Subsequent documented constructions at Akumbu were all of roughly rectangular, loaf-shaped, mudbrick with structures themselves being both round and rectangular in outline.

Curvilinear earthen walls (of both coursed earth and mudbrick) were frequently recorded during the 1989 Méma survey at sites attributed to the 'Early Period' (AD 200–600) via their ceramics.[32] Thus, very provisionally, it appears that curvilinear built forms were dominant in the Méma from

[27] MacDonald 1994, 92. [28] MacDonald 2011a; Takezawa and Cissé 2004.
[29] Bedaux *et al.* 2005. [30] Bedaux *et al.* 2005, 130–31. [31] Togola 2008, 34.
[32] MacDonald 1994, 92; Togola 2008.

the first millennium BC through to the mid-first millennium AD when rectilinear structures appeared.

Relatively early mudbricks are also documented from the Malian Lakes Region at the tell site of Mouyssam II (aka KNT 2).[33] A curvilinear wall of irregular loaf-shaped mudbricks was excavated at a depth of 7.59–7.79 m comprising a structure exceeding 6 m in diameter – more likely a segment of a compound wall than a domestic structure. This feature lies stratigraphically between two ^{14}C samples of calAD 340–540 and calAD 570–690.

On the opposite side of the Inland Delta and east of the Lakes Region there is the urban or proto-urban settlement mound complex of Tombouze, near historic Timbuktu. The 2008 excavations at the mound of TBZ1 revealed curvilinear 'banco' (coursed earth) structures at the margin of 'Phase 1' and 'Phase 2' layers, the nearest associable ^{14}C date being calAD 120–330.[34] More extensive excavations at TBZ2 in the following years have revealed compound clusters of such round 'banco' dwellings dating from the mid-first millennium AD.[35] No mudbrick or rectilinear structures were encountered in any of the Tombouze excavations, which overall cover a period of AD 100–1000.[36]

Directly south of Timbuktu there is the well-preserved architectural sequence of Tongo Maaré Diabel, situated between the Bandiagara and Dyoundé escarpments at the western limit of the Inland Delta floodplain. As yet incompletely published,[37] intermittent excavations at the site between 1993 and 2010 by Togola, MacDonald and Gestrich have exposed a detailed multi-phase architectural sequence.[38] The earliest occupational horizon at the site (AD 500–650) featured circular coursed earth structures very similar in size and layout to those of Tombouze (Fig. 13.4). However there was a sudden shift in the next horizon (AD 650–750) to rectilinear structures built in both coursed earth *and* loaf-shaped mudbrick. Since there is no corresponding material culture change between these two occupations otherwise, and because coursed earth forms then co-existed with mudbrick structures at the site until its abandonment (*c.*AD 1150), this appears to represent continuity in the face of new architectural ideas.[39]

It should be noted that the loaf-shaped mudbricks of Tongo Maaré Diabel, despite being hand-formed, were remarkably regular in their size

[33] Raimbault and Sanogo 1991, 301–23. [34] Park 2010. [35] Park *et al.* 2010.

[36] Park, personal communication.

[37] MacDonald 1998; Walicka Zeh and MacDonald 2004. See now Gestrich and MacDonald 2018.

[38] Gestrich 2013. [39] Gestrich and MacDonald 2018.

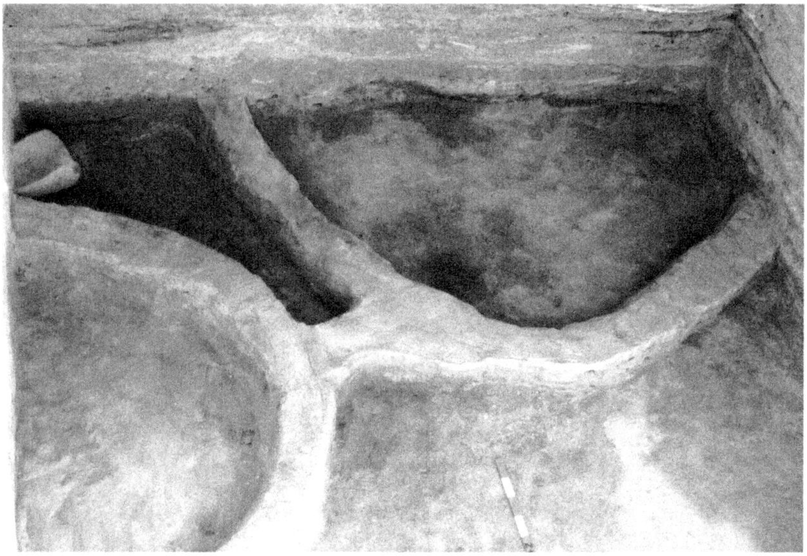

Figure 13.4. Linked round structures with coursed earth walls from Tongo Maaré Diabel, Horizon I, Unit B, AD 500–650 (photo: K. MacDonald).

Figure 13.5. Loaf-shaped mudbrick from Tongo Maaré Diabel, Horizon II, AD 650–750 (scale marked at 10 cm intervals) (photo: K. MacDonald).

and shape, being 300–400 mm in length, 170–200 mm in width and 60–80 mm in thickness (with a tendency towards the smaller end of this range in earlier periods). Their upper surfaces were invariably convex and their lower surfaces mildly concave to facilitate stacking (Figs 13.5 and 13.6). Interestingly, they are comparable in length and width, although thicker, to the mould-formed bricks at Gao-Saney that date to *c.*AD 1000.[40]

From the foregoing paragraphs it should be apparent that earthen architecture was widespread in the Middle Niger from the early first

[40] See Cissé *et al.* 2013; McIntosh, Chapter 14, this volume.

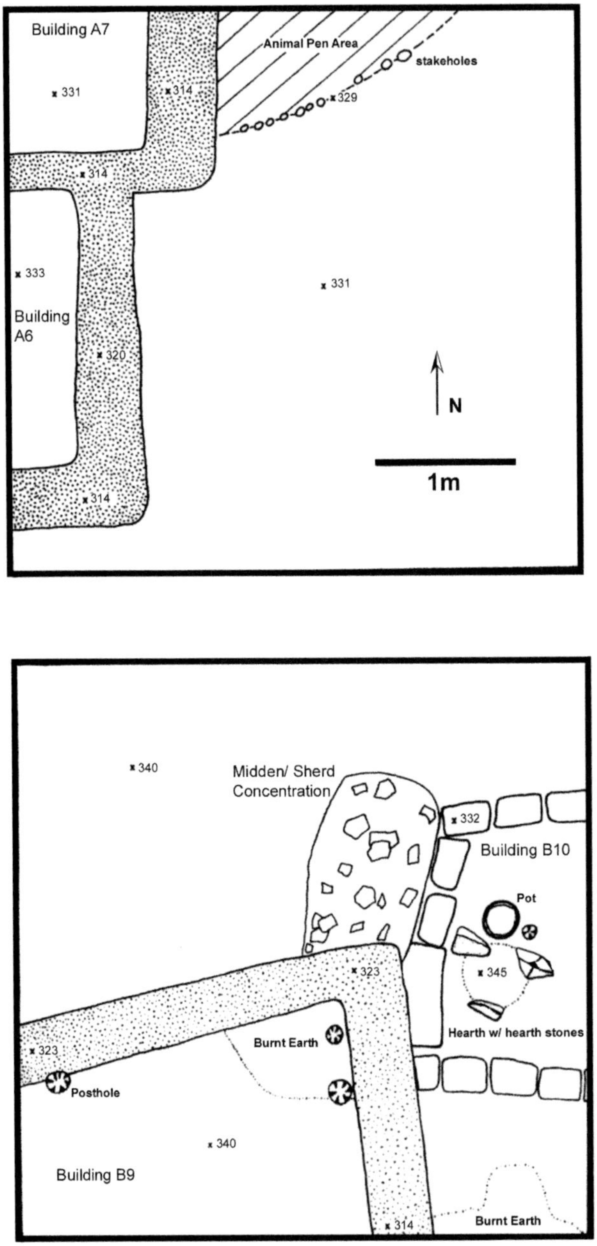

Figure 13.6. Plan of excavations at Unit(s) A-B-C, Tongo Maaré Diabel, Horizon II, AD 650–750. Note combination of coursed-earth and mudbrick structures.

millennium AD. The key urban tell complex of Jenné-jeno is therefore curious for its relatively tardy and idiosyncratic architectural sequence, perhaps due to local ecological and cultural factors. Simple mat and pole structures daubed with clay seem to have prevailed in the site's initial occupation phases (250 BC–AD 400). Curvilinear 'tauf' (coursed earth) structures only appear in Phase III (AD 400–850), with mudbrick (of a locally distinctive cylindrical variety) beginning in round structures after AD 850.[41] Indeed, rectilinear structures, also built using cylindrical brick, began only after AD 1200.

At first glance, from the results of 45 years of Middle Niger archaeology, it is difficult to perceive a neat pattern in the spread of coursed earth, mudbrick, round and rectilinear structures. There is good reason to believe that coursed-earth walled compounds with multiple circular interior structures were ubiquitous along the margins of the Inland Delta in the first few centuries AD. The fact that the only early first millennium BC settlement with such structures yet known is a derivative of the Tichitt Tradition (Kolima Sud-Est), suggests that the development of such earthen structures stemmed from the need to find a local substitute for sandstone. The spread of such modular, round, coursed earth compounds may also have been part of the wider Tichitt diaspora and its knock-on influence. Even well to the south, in central Burkina Faso, such structures appear by *c.*AD 100 (the Kirikongo complex in the Mohoun Bend).[42]

If curvilinear coursed earth structures may be taken as the Sahelian status quo for the period of AD 100–900, we are left with a puzzling series of local architectural changes over the second half of that period, with the advent of both rectilinear forms and mudbrick. Mudbrick is an important innovation in building technology facilitating both greater planning and more monumental construction. Formerly, Sahelian architectural specialists like Labelle Prussin were satisfied, via supposition and historical linguistic linkages, that 'the most persuasive argument for the introduction of masonry techniques into the African savannah by Islamic agency lies in the building technologies associated with them'.[43] In other words, mudbrick was evidence of Islamic intervention in the South. Yet even if we put aside the questionable early mudbricks of Dia, our evidence for this innovation in building technology appears to go in a clockwise direction around the pre-Islamic periphery of the Middle Niger: the Méma *c.*AD 400, the Lakes Region *c.*AD 550, and the Gourma *c.*AD 650. Still farther east, loaf-shaped mudbricks are present in the earliest layers of Gao-Saney *c.*AD 700.[44] However sparse this pattern might be, it disassociates Islamic trade from the first appearances of early Sahelian (loaf-shaped) mudbrick and is suggestive of the gradual spread of a fashion coming from the north and

[41] McIntosh 1995, 64–66. [42] Dueppen 2012, 277. [43] Prussin 1986, 38.
[44] Cissé *et al.* 2013; McIntosh, Chapter 14, this volume.

west towards the south and east between AD 400 and 700 – whether driven by the innovations of a nascent empire (Ghana) and/or via the Trans-Saharan sphere of interaction.[45]

Early Settlement in the Sub-Sahara: Perceiving Its Historic Amplitude

It is clear from the archaeological record of the West African Sahel that there has not been a simple, gradual growth in regional settlement, but rather peaks and troughs in settlement size and density. For the pre-Islamic period we witness a peak in Tichitt-Walata settlement size and density between *c.*1200–1000 BC together with the Tichitt tradition's spread into the Tagant, Néma and Méma regions.[46] After an apparent scattering of populations in the Western Sahel during the first millennium BC, published sequences from the Middle Niger show substantial settlement growth in the mid-first millennium AD: Jenné-jeno from AD 450, Dia from AD 500, the Méma from AD 500, or for the area of Timbuktu beginning sometime between AD 200 and 600.[47] The consequence has therefore been a notion of post-Tichitt decline and obscurity in the first millennium BC, followed by gradual re-emergence of small settlements in the early first millennium AD succeeded by a rapid reflorescence from AD 500. But is this really so?

One of the primary difficulties in estimating settlement dynamics in the Middle Niger is the nature of earthen-settlement-mound archaeology. Naturally what we see and record on the surface of sites are *abandonment* assemblages – so, in fact, moments of crisis. Additionally, our temporal estimates for surface survey are based upon association with pottery phases, with a best resolution of 400 to 600 year time periods. Site sizes and distributions so recorded are not only not punctual, they do not speak

[45] It should be noted that the curious cylindrical mudbricks of Jenné-jeno and its successor city, Djenné (known as *Djenné-ferey* or *Djenné-wéré*) are as yet archaeologically unrecorded in Mali outside of the central Inland Niger Delta, however they are also known in second-millennium AD Kano and contemporary Hausa urban architecture in Northern Nigeria (where they are termed *tubali*; Dmochowski 1990). While outside the time range of this volume, this suggests some connection between castes of masons across the Northern Sahel during the Islamic period. Mould-formed rectangular mudbricks (today called *toubobou-fery* – the foreigner's brick) are rarely documented in the Sahel until recent historic times (specifically, the nineteenth century), but see McIntosh, Chapter 14, this volume, who notes the presence of mould-made bricks in the more recent (*c.*AD 1000) layers of Gao-Saney.

[46] Holl 1985; 1993; MacDonald 1996; 2011a; 2015.

[47] Bedaux *et al.* 2005; McIntosh 1995; Park 2010; Togola 2008, 23.

to periods of prosperity, when there may have been few abandonments. These highpoints in the life of settlements lie buried beneath abandonment layers. In other words, our methodology is likely to be biased towards recording abundant settlement only at times of collapse, periods *after* those of initial settlement growth.

A secondary difficulty is how one quantifies the surface area of tell clusters. Do we quantify the area of sites on the basis of individual mounds (often separated by no more than 10 m of 'cordon sanitaire') or the total area of a mound cluster? This has a role in how we evaluate the growth of site hierarchy but could also be largely illusory. Historically we know that large singular tells can come about through the gradual joining of many distinct quarters.[48] The appearance of tell clusters may merely be the artefact of the stage of site formation at the moment of abandonment, and not necessarily a representation of the cognition of connectedness in the minds of the ancient inhabitants. In other words, would there really be a qualitative difference, in terms of urbanisation, between a single 25-ha settlement mound and ten 2.5-ha settlement mounds no more than 100 m apart from one another?

Let us take as a case in point the Méma region as surveyed by Téréba Togola and the author in 1989–1990. If we were to merely innumerate individual mounds from the Early (AD 200–600) Middle (AD 600–1400) and Late (AD 1600–1800) Periods (Fig. 13.7) we can see that 'Early' sites are most numerous, but usually quite small. If, however, site areas are grouped and summed by their clusters we see much more concentrated Early settlement, with traces of size hierarchy (Fig. 13.8). If 'dead space' in between mounds is included, the size of early clusters increases by at least a third. The real question, however, is how much Early settlement lies *beneath* Middle Period abandonment deposits and thus un-detected and un-counted? One notable proof of this is the principal mound of Toladié – at 76 ha and with 15-m depth of stratigraphy the largest single occupation mound yet recorded in Mali. A ^{14}C sample taken from midway down an erosion gully at the site produced a date of 1465 ± 60 BP (calAD 429–663) broadly within the Early Period.[49] If such major sites abandoned during the Middle Period were indeed widely occupied in the Early Period, settlement dynamics extrapolated from mound abandonment surfaces would clearly be highly misleading.

Likewise, one of the Akumbu settlement mounds (Mound B) excavated by Togola and myself had Early Period ceramics with a calAD 342–442 ^{14}C

[48] Walicka Zeh 2000. [49] Togola and Raimbault 1991; T. Togola, personal communication.

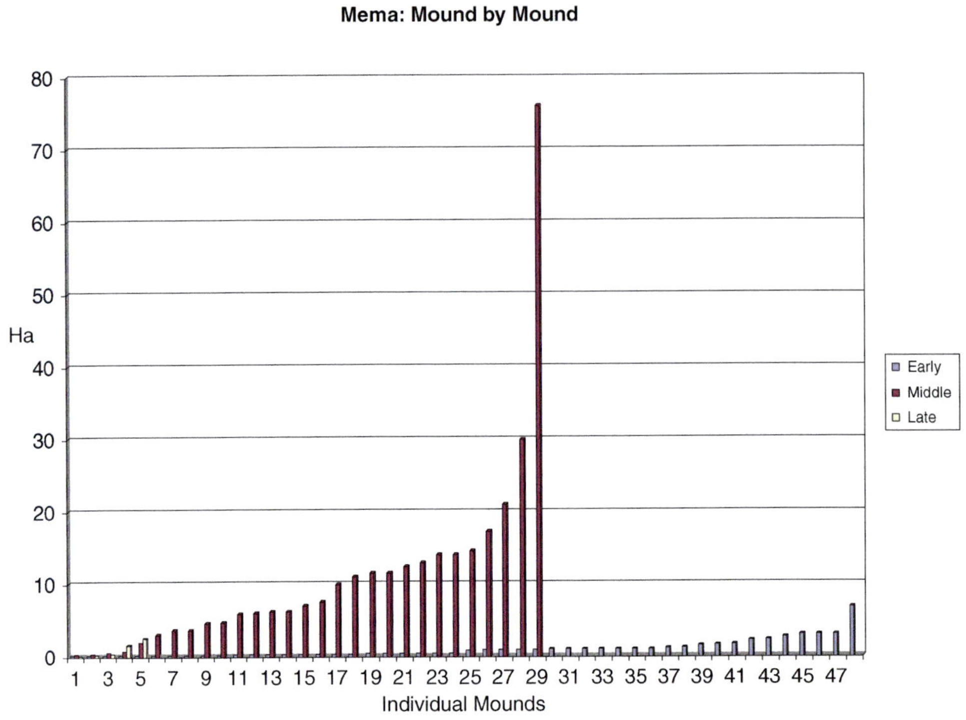

Figure 13.7. Chart showing the size distribution (ha) of individual settlement mounds surveyed in the Méma by Togola and MacDonald in 1989–1990.

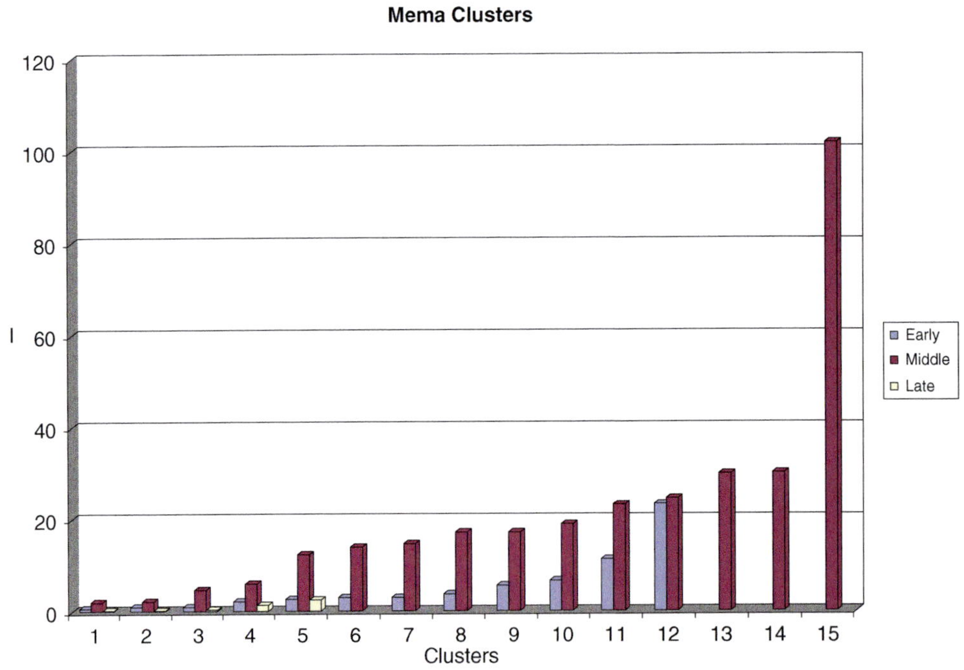

Figure 13.8. Chart showing the size distribution (ha) by aggregated settlement mound clusters – each mound's dimension summed by the cluster to which they belong – surveyed in the Méma by Togola and MacDonald in 1989–1990.

date and first millennium BC Faita facies ceramics in the next strata below. Additionally, eroding from flanks of other mounds at the site were these same first millennium BC Faita facies ceramics.[50] As Togola noted, 'We believe that many of these deeply stratified Early Assemblage sites rest upon Terminal LSA [first millennium BC] deposits.'[51] Thus, sites like Kolima Sud-Est (10 ha between *c.* 900–500 BC) rather than being the top examples of early settlement in the Méma, may instead be the unsuccessful sites of that period – those which did not get deeply buried beneath subsequent centuries of continuing settlement. So, in summary, important settlement growth may in fact have begun in the Méma during the first millennium BC, and it is very likely to have begun by AD 400.

To this same end we can re-examine the growth of settlement at Dia one of Mali's great 'Medieval' cities. The site monograph places the initial Horizon I occupation (800–1 BC) of the site as comprising two habitation zones – one of 19 ha and the other of 3 ha.[52] However sampling coverage is far from complete and main occupation area could be easily redrawn as 22 ha (an addition of 3 ha). Likewise, if one assesses occupation on the basis of the spread of Horizon I diagnostic material collected by systematic field walking, they occur in 11 of 16 transects, and are indicative of an early occupation covering 50 per cent or more of the mound's 50-ha surface.[53] Additionally, surrounding the site there are at least nine satellite mounds of 0.4 to 3 ha surface, abandoned in Horizon I.[54] Once again, substantial first millennium BC occupation seems a greater prospect at Dia than has thus far been asserted.

The Dia sequence is also of interest because of the area's almost complete abandonment (notionally due to a period of drought) between AD 1–500. Likewise, the western Gourma seems to have experienced a period of abandonment at this time until settlement growth recommenced in the fifth century, perhaps for similar ecological reasons. Proliferation of settlement at the eastern edge of the IND and Lakes Region, around Timbuktu, seems only to have taken place in the pre-Islamic period between AD 200 and 600.[55]

In summary, we can tentatively advance three periods of settlement growth for our study regions: 1200–1000 BC in the area of Tichitt-Walata and its margins, 800–1 BC in the Méma and Macina regions of the old IND and the Mauritanian Tagant, and a settlement transformation with abandonment, growth and nucleation around AD 400 across most of our zone.

[50] MacDonald 2011a; MacDonald and Schmidt 2004; Togola 2008. [51] Togola 2008, 83.
[52] Bedaux *et al.* 2005, 446. [53] See Wilson and Schmidt 2005, 35–41, Figure 3.I.3.
[54] Schmidt 2005, Table 10.1.2. [55] Park 2010.

Assessing Parallels with the Trans-Saharan World

What might all of this mean for the Sahel's relationship with its northern neighbours? At a broad, synthetic level, I prefer to see the Trans-Saharan region as a sphere of interaction in trade and ideas – much like the Mediterranean. These ideas go both ways. It is to our advantage to investigate both potential syncretisms in architecture and relationships in settlement dynamics. It is possible to make a number of preliminary observations concerning both local innovations and connections within our sphere of interaction.

1) The flourishing of Tichitt appears to long pre-date any comparable proto-urban, proto-state development on the northern margins of the Sahara. True, there remain relatively un-prospected and poorly dated areas in southern Morocco and Algeria, but at 1200–1000 BC Tichitt and Walata still remain without peer. As such Tichitt represents that great rarity – a pristine complex society – making its relative lack of global status within archaeology all the more remarkable.
2) The peak of Classic Garamantian civilization in southern Libya was between the first century BC and the fourth century AD, with related social forms dating back to the early first millennium BC.[56] The outset of this period corresponds with the decline and dissolution of settlement around Tichitt-Walata and the end of this period falls shortly before the greatest flowering of early urbanism in the Middle Niger.[57] Conflict with Berber populations, made manifest in fortified sites and rock art, has been claimed as one of the reasons for the decline of Tichitt.[58] Others have also put forward a case for some element of syncretism between incoming Berber populations and local populations during the Late Tichitt Phase (1000–400 BC).[59] During the earliest Garamantian heyday (100 BC), Sahelian settlement is only known to have been vibrant in the Tagant, Méma, Macina and the Inland Niger Delta. Between 100 BC to AD 300 one can only point to the Jenné-jeno and the Tombouze cluster near Timbuktu as areas experiencing documented settlement growth. That Tombouze, in a more proximate zone, may have to some extent been stimulated by Trans-Saharan interactions is not outside the realm of possibility, but it appears to lack any raw material indices of such

[56] Liverani 2003; Mattingly 2011; Mori 2013.
[57] Though the late antique expansion of Garamantian fortified settlements noted by Mattingly *et al.*, Chapter 2, this volume overlaps.
[58] Munson 1980. [59] MacDonald *et al.* 2009.

interaction.[60] Likewise, the initial floruit of urban settlement in Gao appears to be much later – in the seventh century AD.[61] Thus, one is left with a surprising lack of linkages between Classic Garamantian age Fazzan and sites at the Sahelian margins – areas where correspondence should have been at its strongest.

3) Architecturally there is no reason to see an external hand behind the round compounds and structural forms of Classic Tichitt. Likewise there is no reason to view the transformation of this stone block and shingle built technology to similar forms in coursed earth as anything but a localised development. However it is interesting to note the advent of rectangular built forms in the Tagant (*c.*150 BC–AD 350) and much later in the Gourma (*c.*AD 600). It is tempting to view these developments as syncretic phenomena tied to long-distance interactions with the wider 'Berber' world. Parallels between the rectilinear coursed earth structures of Aghram Nadharif (Liverani 2006) and those of Tongo Maaré Diabel are very interesting in this regard. Similarly, there is the question of the advent of Sahelian mudbrick (AD 400–600), which may either be part of the exchange of ideas at the Saharan margin or a local development linked to the local (Sahelian) growth of settlement during this period.
4) It is apparent that the first millennium BC is not the obscure period of low settlement it was once thought to be. There appears to have been concentrated settlement growth and individual sites exceeding 10 ha in three portions of the wider Sahel: the Méma (Kolima, Akumbu, etc.), the Macina (the Dia-Shoma cluster) and, much further to the east, the southern margins of Lake Chad (the Zilum cluster).[62] With such dates as we have, growth seems to fall closer to the middle of the millennium (*c.*600–400 BC) than to either end. Such developments pre-date comparable nucleated settlements in south-west Fazzan around Ghat, but overlaps with occupation at Zinkekra in the Garamantian heartlands.[63] At the current state of evidence I would agree with Magnavita *et al.* that in these areas we are witnessing the 'first steps towards urbanism' with growing site hierarchies and densities, evidence for specialists and (at least in the case of Zilum) defences.[64] I would also agree that 'increasing

60 Park, personal communication. 61 Cissé *et al.* 2013.
62 Kolima, Akumbu, etc.: MacDonald 2011b; Togola 2008; the Dia-Shoma cluster: Bedaux *et al.* 2005; MacDonald 2011b; and the Zilum cluster: Magnavita *et al.* 2006.
63 For the Ghat area, see Mori 2013 (Fewet) and Liverani 2006 (Aghram Nadharif). For the Garamantian heartlands, see Mattingly 2003, 136–42; Mattingly 2010, 19–119.
64 Magnavita *et al.* 2006, 168.

social complexity evolved in Sub-Saharan Africa at an early date from a fully indigenous cultural background'.[65]

5) Liverani speculates that Garamantian Trans-Saharan trade routes might extend back as far as the sixth century BC, even if supporting evidence for this assertion is fairly thin on the ground.[66] As I have written elsewhere, there is persistent, scattered evidence for down-the-line trade in Saharan stone beads (especially carnelian and amazonite) since the second millennium BC, but there is no physical evidence at southern sites for an acceleration of such interaction until the fourth century AD.[67] From AD 300 to AD 700 indices of long distance exchange increase in variety and ubiquity, if not in quantity: copper and chickens at Jenné-jeno, glass beads at Dia and chickens at Tongo Maare Diabel; glass and carnelian beads and wool cloth at Kissi, and so forth.[68] The timing of this greater flow of materials may align with the advent of the Trans-Saharan gold trade, as posited by Garrard,[69] but it is most likely that such trade grew in partnership with emergent Sub-Saharan urban or proto-urban networks. In sum, it is difficult to engage with long-distance trading partners who are not already adept at assembling goods from their own regional networks.

From the foregoing it should be apparent that there is no dramatic or straight-forward parallel between the Classical Garamantean era and the growth of settlement in the West African Sahel. However, there are many disparate elements which indicate a Trans-Saharan network of communication (exchanges of ideas) since at least the first millennium BC, intensifying post AD 300. The largest missing pieces in our puzzle – which covers the coalescing Trans-Saharan zone in the first millennia BC/AD – lie in other areas of the Saharan rim, particularly southern Algeria. We must envy the future generations to whom that terrain will be open.

References

Amblard-Pison, S. 2006. *Communautés villageoises néolithiques des Dhars Tichitt et Oulata (Mauritanie)*. Oxford: Archaeopress.

[65] Magnavita *et al.* 2006, 168. [66] Liverani 2003. [67] MacDonald 2011b.
[68] MacDonald 2011b; Magnavita 2017; McIntosh 1995.
[69] Garrard 1982; Phillipson 2017; cf. Nixon 2017.

Bedaux, R., MacDonald, K.C., Person, A., Polet, J., Sanogo, K., Schmidt, A. and Sidibé, S. 2001. The Dia Archaeological Project: Rescuing cultural heritage in the Inland Niger Delta (Mali). *Antiquity* 75: 837–48.

Bedaux, R., Polet, J., Sanogo, K. and Schmidt, A. (eds). 2005. *Recherches archéologiques à Dia dans le Delta Intérieur du Niger (Mali): Bilan des saisons de fouilles 1998–2003*. Leiden: CNWS Publications.

Cissé, M., McIntosh, S.K., Dussubieux, L., Fenn, T., Gallagher, D. and Chipps Smith, A. 2013. Excavations at Gao Saney: New evidence for settlement growth, trade and interaction on the Niger Bend in the first millennium CE. *Journal of African Archaeology* 11: 9–37.

David, N. 1971. The Fulani compound and the archaeologist. *World Archaeology* 3: 111–31.

Dmochowski, Z.R. 1990. *An Introduction to Nigerian Traditional Architecture, Volume I: Northern Nigeria*. London: Ethnographica.

Dowler, A. and Galvin, E.R. (eds). 2011. *Money, Trade and Trade Routes in Pre-Islamic North Africa*. London: British Museum Press.

Dueppen, S.A. 2012. *Egalitarian Revolution in the Savanna: The Origins of a West African Political System*. Sheffield: Equinox.

Dujarric, P. 1981. L'architecture traditionnelle au Sénégal oriental. *Objets et Mondes* 21: 141–48.

Garrard, T. 1982. Myth and metrology: The early Trans-Saharan gold trade. *Journal of African History* 23: 443–61.

Gestrich, N. 2013. *The Archaeology of Social Organisation at Tongo Maaré Diabel*. Unpublished PhD Dissertation, University College London.

Gestrich, N. and MacDonald, K.C. 2018. On the margins of Ghana and KawKaw: Four seasons of excavation at Tongo Maaré Diabal (AD 500–1150), Mali. *Journal of African Archaeology* 16.1: 1–30.

Holl, A. 1985. Background to the Ghana Empire: Archaeological investigations on the transition to statehood in the Dhar Tichitt region (Mauritania). *Journal of Anthropological Archaeology* 4: 73–115.

Holl, A. 1986. *Economie et société néolithique du Dhar Tichitt (Mauritanie)*. Paris: Editions Recherche sur les Civilisations.

Holl, A. 1993. Late Neolithic cultural landscape in southeastern Mauritania: an essay in spatiometrics. In A.F.C. Holl and T.E. Levy (eds), *Spatial Boundaries and Social Dynamics: Case Studies from Food-Producing Societies*. Ann Arbor: International Monographs in Prehistory, 95–133.

Liverani, M. 2003. Aghram Nadharif and the southern border of the Garamantian kingdom. In M. Liverani (ed.), *Arid Lands in Roman Times: Papers from the International Conference (Rome, July 9th–10th* 2001), Arid Zone Archaeology Monograph no.4. Firenze: All'insegna del Giglio, 23–36.

Liverani, M. 2006. *Aghram Nadharif. The Barkat Oasis (Sha'abiya of Ghat, Libyan Sahara) in Garamantian Times*. Arid Zone Archaeology Monographs no.5. Firenze: All'insegna del Giglio.

MacDonald, K.C. 1994. *Socio-Economic Diversity and the Origins of Cultural Complexity along the Middle Niger (2000 BC to AD 300)*. Unpublished PhD dissertation, University of Cambridge.

MacDonald, K.C. 1996. Tichitt-Walata and the Middle Niger: Evidence for cultural contact in the second millennium BC. In G. Pwiti and R. Soper (eds), *Aspects of African Archaeology: Papers from the 10th Congress of the Pan-African Association for Prehistory and Related Studies*. Harare: University of Zimbabwe Publications, 429–40.

MacDonald, K.C. 1998. More forgotten tells of Mali: An archaeologist's journey from here to Timbuktu. *Archaeology International* 1: 40–42.

MacDonald, K.C. 2011a. Betwixt Tichitt and the IND: The pottery of the Faïta facies, Tichitt tradition. In *Identity Fashion and Exchange: Pottery in West Africa (special issue edited by A. Haour and K. Manning) = Azania: Archaeological Research in Africa* 46.1: 49–69.

MacDonald, K.C. 2011b. A view from the south: Sub-Saharan evidence for contacts between North Africa, Mauritania and the Niger, 1000 BC–AD 700. In Dowler and Galvin 2011, 72–82.

MacDonald, K.C. 2015. The Tichitt tradition in the West African Sahel. In G. Barker and C. Goucher (eds), *The Cambridge World History, Volume II: A World with Agriculture 12000 BCE – 500 CE*. Cambridge: Cambridge University Press, 499–513.

MacDonald, K.C. and Schmidt, A. 2004. The Faïta facies and the 'obscure millennium' of the Middle Niger. In Sanogo and Togola 2004, 222–29.

MacDonald, K.C., Vernet, R., Martinon-Torres, M. and Fuller, D.Q. 2009. Dhar Néma: From early agriculture to metallurgy in southeastern Mauritania. *Azania: Archaeological Research in Africa* 44: 3–48.

Magnavita, C., Breunig, P., Ameje, J. and Posselt, M. 2006. Zilum: A mid-first millennium BC fortified settlement near Lake Chad. *Journal of African Archaeology* 4: 153–69.

Magnavita, S, 2017. Track and trace. Archaeometric approaches to the study of early Trans-Saharan trade. In Mattingly *et al.* 2017, 393–413.

Mattingly, D.J. 2003. *The Archaeology of Fazzan, Volume 1 Synthesis*. London: Society for Libyan Studies.

Mattingly, D.J. 2010. The *Archaeology of Fazzan, Volume 3, Excavations Carried out by C.M. Daniels*. London: Society for Libyan Studies.

Mattingly, D. 2011. The Garamantes of Fazzan: An early Libyan state with trans-Saharan connections. In Dowler and Galvin 2011, 49–60.

Mattingly, D.J., Leitch, V., Duckworth, C.N., Cuénod, A., Sterry, M. and Cole, F. (eds). 2017. *Trade in the Ancient Sahara and Beyond*. Trans-Saharan Archaeology Volume 1. Series editor D.J. Mattingly. Cambridge: Cambridge University Press and The Society for Libyan Studies.

McIntosh, R.J. and McIntosh, S.K. 1988. From 'siècles obscurs' to revolutionary centuries on the Middle Niger. *World Archaeology* 20: 141–65.

McIntosh, S.K. and McIntosh, R.J. 1980. *Prehistoric Investigations in the Region of Jenné, Mali: Part I.* Oxford: British Archaeological Reports.

McIntosh, S.K. (ed.). 1995. *Excavations at Jenné-Jeno, Hambarketolo, and Kaniana (Inland Niger Delta, Mali), the 1981 Season.* Berkeley: University of California Press.

Mori, L. (ed.). 2013. *Life and Death of a Rural Village in Garamantian Times: Archaeological Investigations in the Oasis of Fewet (Libyan Sahara).* Arid Zone Archaeology Monographs no. 6. Firenze: All'insegna del Giglio.

Munson, P.J. 1971. *The Tichitt Tradition: A Late Prehistoric Occupation of the Southwestern Sahara.* Unpublished PhD dissertation, University of Illinois at Urbana-Champaign.

Munson, P.J. 1980. Archaeology and the prehistoric origins of the Ghana Empire. *Journal of African History* 21: 457–66.

Nicolaisen, J. and Nicolaisen, I. 1997. *The Pastoral Tuareg: Ecology, Culture and Society.* 2 vols. London: Thames and Hudson.

Nixon, S. 2017. Trans-Saharan gold trade in pre-modern times: Available evidence and research agendas. In Mattingly *et al.* 2017, 156–88.

Ould-Khattar, M. 1995. *La fin des temps préhistoriques dans le sud-est Mauritanien.* Unpublished PhD dissertation, Université de Paris-I, Pantheon-Sorbonne.

Park, D.P. 2010. Prehistoric Timbuktu and its hinterland. *Antiquity* 84: 1076–88.

Park, D.P., Coutros, P., Mahmoud Abdallahi, M. and Ould Sidi A. 2010. *La campagne de recherche archéologique dans la région de Tombouctou et la région des lacs: Rapport sur la troisième campagne de recherche à Tombouctou préhistorique.* Report to the DNPC (Mali), La Mission Culturelle de Tombouctou, and Yale University. Available online at: www.academia.edu/1497424/_3 [last accessed 13 September, 2019].

Pauketat, T.R. 2007. *Chiefdoms and Other Archaeological Delusions.* Lanham: Alta Mira.

Phillipson, D.W. 2017. Trans-Saharan gold trade and Byzantine coinage. *The Antiquaries Journal* 97: 145–69.

Prussin, L. 1986. *Hatumere: Islamic Design in West Africa.* Berkeley: University of California Press.

Raimbault, M., and Sanogo, K. (eds). 1991. *Recherches archéologiques au Mali: Les sites protohistoriques de la zone lacustre.* Paris: ACCT-Karthala.

Sanogo, K. and Togola, T. (eds). 2004. *Acts of the XIth Congress of the Pan-African Association Prehistory and Related Fields, Bamako, February 7–12, 2001.* Bamako: Soro Print Color.

Schmidt, A. 2005. Prospection régionale autour de Dia. In Bedaux *et al.* 2005, 401–22.

Takezawa, S. and Cissé, M. 2004. Domestication des cereales au Méma, Mali. In Sanogo and Togola 2004, 105–21.

Togola, T. 2008. *Archaeological investigations of Iron Age sites in the Méma Region, Mali (West Africa).* Oxford: British Archaeological Reports.

Togola, T. and Raimbault, M. 1991. Les missions d'inventaire dans le Méma, Karéri et Farimaké (1984–1985). In Raimbault and Sanogo 1991, 81–98.
Vernet, R. 1993. *Préhistoire de la Mauritanie*. Nouakchott: Centre Culturel Français A. de Saint Exupéry, Sépia.
Walicka Zeh, R. 2000. *Building Practice and Cultural Space amongst the Bamana, Senufo and Bozo of Mali: An Ethnoarchaeological Study*. Unpublished PhD Dissertation, University College London.
Walicka Zeh, R. and MacDonald, K.C. 2004. An ethnoarchaeological study of architectural remains and spatial organization, an example from the site of Tongo Maaré Diabal, Mali. In Sanogo and Togola 2004, 353–64.
Wilson, J. and Schmidt, A. 2005. La prospection de Dia-Shoma. In Bedaux *et al.* 2005, 35–41.

14 Long-Distance Exchange and Urban Trajectories in the First Millennium AD

Case Studies from the Middle Niger and Middle Senegal River Valleys

SUSAN KEECH MCINTOSH

Introduction

It has been 40 years since the first publication of results of archaeological investigations at the massive settlement mound of Jenné-jeno challenged traditional historiography concerning towns and trade in West Africa. Prior assumptions that Arab-initiated Trans-Saharan trade provided the impetus for town growth along the Middle Niger have yielded to an explanatory model grounded in the local development of regional, inter-regional and long-distance exchange and interaction by the mid-first millennium AD.[1] These findings coincided with an active political and scholarly agenda to decolonise Africa's past, which provided an incentive for archaeologists to seek additional instances of early trade and town growth along the Middle Niger (Méma, Dia, Timbuktu, Gao, Bentia) and the Middle Senegal (Fig. 14.1).[2]

The deployment of comparable research methodologies by many of these projects has made possible the construction of preliminary, evidence-based frameworks for discussing trade and exchange, interaction, and town growth in different areas, although data density remains notably low and patchy. Central to these discussions are definitions of towns, urbanism, and trade. Back in the 1980s, Rod McIntosh and I grappled with the question of urbanism in the context of Jenné-jeno's unexpected pattern of early settlement growth and close clustering of other, contemporaneous settlement mounds, at which we found no evidence for public

[1] McIntosh S. and McIntosh R. 1980; McIntosh, R. and McIntosh, S. 1981.

[2] Méma: McIntosh S. 2017; Togola 1996; 2008; Dia: Bedaux *et al.* 2005; Haskell *et al.* 1988; McIntosh, R. and McIntosh, S. 1987; Timbuktu: Insoll 2000a; McIntosh, S. and McIntosh, R. 1986; Park 2010; 2011; Gao: Cissé *et al.* 2013; Insoll 1996; 2000b; Bentia: Arazi 1999; Middle Senegal: McIntosh, S. *et al.* 1992; McIntosh, R. *et al.* 2016; McIntosh and Bocoum 2000.

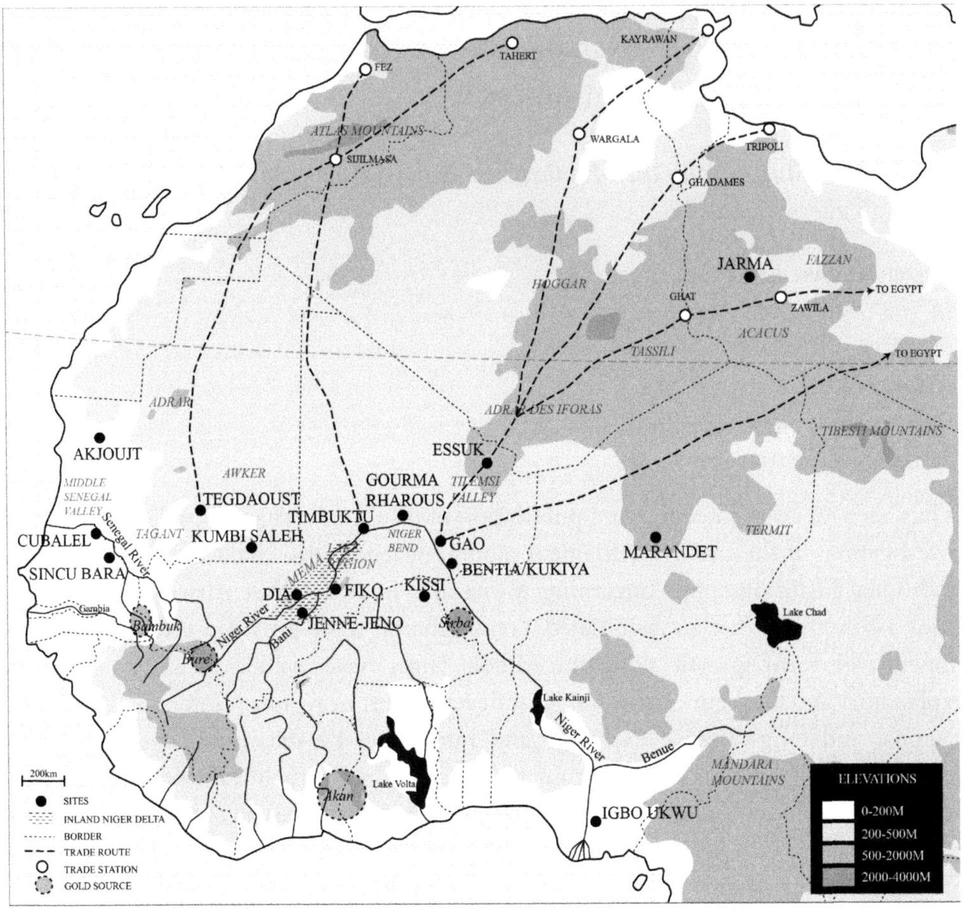

Figure 14.1. Map of sites, regions and major trade routes from the tenth century.

architecture or detectable ranking or stratification during the first millennium of occupation. We proposed expanding the definition of urban beyond the then-dominant classical, evolutionary models in order to include 'cities without citadels'.[3] Key elements in our definition of urbanism were site size, population density and heterogeneity, and functional specialisation, in line with Trigger's definition of a city as providing specialised services to a broader hinterland.[4] As our thinking developed, we theorised that both site clustering and absence of monumental architecture or clear social ranking at Jenné-jeno could be related to an effective resistance to the monopolisation of power. The result would be power relations that were counterpoised and horizontally distributed (that is,

[3] McIntosh, S. and McIntosh, R. 1993. [4] Trigger 1972.

heterarchy), rather than effectively consolidated vertically in a hierarchy of elites.[5] The debate surrounding urban definitions continues, with archaeologists forging new frameworks for understanding population aggregation on a substantial scale in other areas of the world where it was likewise not visibly accompanied by one or more of the classical markers of urbanism.[6] Africanist archaeology continues to provide important inputs to this debate.[7]

Definitions of trade and exchange figure importantly in the discussions in this chapter and in this volume. Analytic programmes focused on identifying source areas of non-local raw and manufactured materials at African sites have increased significantly over the past two decades. Consequently, we have some insight, albeit preliminary, into the networks along which certain categories of goods – especially glass, copper-based metals, and some kinds of stone – moved in West Africa and their chronology. Reports on foreign goods have been an important component of the recent Africanist literature,[8] reflecting archaeology's recent global turn. Ironically, this has occurred as theorising about trade in the broader archaeological literature has waned. Bauer and Agbe-Davies provide a useful overview of the shifting position of trade studies in archaeology.[9] As they point out, most of the influential archaeological literature on trade, exchange and interaction appeared in the 1970s and 1980s. The subsequent decline in trade-oriented theoretical studies probably reflects the influence of post-processual concerns and the association of trade with the positivist programme of processualism. In twenty-first-century Africanist archaeology, however, trade has remained a strong theme, emphasising the role of African agency in trade relationships ranging from the Roman period to the Atlantic trade and the mapping of global intersections both within and beyond these historically-documented systems.

In the Africanist literature, 'trade' is frequently invoked to account for exotics present in an archaeological site, without specifying what the term encompasses. As Renfrew pointed out 40 years ago, goods can move over distances by many different modalities with very different levels of organisation, from hand-to-hand, down-the-line reciprocal exchange, to central place redistribution, to market-based trade.[10] His proposition that the

[5] Crumley 1995; McIntosh, S. 1999b.
[6] For example, Birch 2013; Chapman *et al.* 2014; Creekmore and Fisher 2014; Fletcher 2009; Lekson 2018.
[7] For example, Haour 2005; Kusimba 2008; Manyanga *et al.* 2010; McIntosh, R. 2015; Wynne-Jones and Fleisher 2014. See also, Magnavita, Chapter 15, this volume.
[8] For recent summaries see Dowler and Galvin 2011; Magnavita 2013; Mattingly *et al.* 2017.
[9] Bauer and Agbe-Davies 2010, 28–47.
[10] Renfrew 1975.

patterned distribution and scale of exotics would permit identification of specific modalities ultimately proved unrealistic. It not only required a very high density of reliably representative data from a large number of sites, but it also could not resolve the problem of equifinality – that different processes could result in similar patterns. In West Africa, the exceptionally sparse, patchy nature of the data on exotics is a challenge for anyone who wishes to investigate the changing landscape of interaction and exchange in the centuries preceding historical documentation of market-dominated Trans-Saharan trade. Central to such studies is an understanding that material exchange is embedded in larger webs of communication that facilitate the exchange of ideas, values, and information along any or all directions of the network.[11] Here, I am using exchange in the sense of interaction, as outlined by Oka and Kusimba.[12] It is a key point because it implies that even if material evidence of foreign goods or raw materials is lacking, other clues to exchange relationships and interactions may be present. We must be attentive to evidence for changes in style and taste, technological practice, symbolic systems, and social organisation, in addition to the presence of exotics. In the absence of all of these, it is difficult to make a case for interaction, let alone trade.

In this chapter, I follow Bauer and Agbe-Davies' definitions for exchange and trade:

> Exchange refers to the transfer of goods through a wide range of mechanisms, from ritualised gift exchange to the negotiated transactions of barter and markets and the one-way exchange of coercion and piracy. Trade is a more specific category of activity in which the exchange is more formalised and market based, both in the individual interaction and on a systemic scale. Trade is thus one type of exchange relationship in which each interaction is usually 'closed', or completed in a single moment of exchange of x for y, and which often occurs across otherwise powerful social and geographic boundaries.[13]

This definition of trade corresponds to our understanding of the historic Trans-Saharan trade, in which commodities (gold, slaves, salt, cloth, copper) were exchanged at entrepôts and market towns. The trade was supported by broader networks linking traders and towns into webs of interaction that involved many different kinds of exchange.

The case studies in this chapter outline the evidence for exchange at different scales and its temporal relation to settlement growth. At Gao on the eastern Niger Bend, a surge in the scale and intensity of long-distance

[11] Bauer and Agbe-Davies 2010, 19. [12] Oka and Kusimba 2008, 340.
[13] Bauer and Agbe-Davies 2010.

exchange after the seventh century AD was accompanied by rapid settlement expansion. In the western middle Niger at Jenné-jeno, settlement growth is associated with regional exchange systems that are present from initial colonisation. Networks expanded to include the Southern Sahara by AD 500. Only after AD 900 is there material evidence of interactions that extend across the Sahara, by which time, the settlement mound had reached its maximum extent of over 30 ha. In the Middle Senegal, exchange interactions and agropastoral mobility linked the river with mobile populations as far north as the Mauritanian Adrar during the later first millennium BC, as attested by the distribution of Mauritanian copper and related pottery styles. These interactions appear to have largely ceased *c.*100 BC and did not reappear for almost a millennium. Evidence for long-distance exchange and interaction reappears after *c.*AD 800, including copper and glass working, new building technologies, and pottery styles, along with newly founded Saharan entrepôts. Arabic sources identify the existence of the Takrur polity along the Middle Senegal by the eleventh to twelfth centuries; unexpectedly, we found no evidence of urban centres within our study region.

Before continuing on to the case studies, I would emphasise the critical role of paleoclimate. Shifting patterns of rainfall, wind and evaporation, groundwater recharge, and river regimes fundamentally affect food security and exchange in the marginal lands of the Sahel and neighbouring Sahara.[14] Movement in the desert is dependent on aquifer and water table recharge to supply wells and oases. The limits of agricultural and pastoral production fluctuate within different regions depending on local rainfall, which varies both interannually and at longer scales of decades and centuries. During the last 3,000 years, the Sahel-desert boundary has shifted 200 km or more north of its present latitude on several occasions, most recently, in the seventeenth century, as documented by Webb (Fig. 14.2).[15] Conversely, intense arid episodes analogous to the Sahelian drought of the 1970s and 1980s have occurred multiple times in the past 3,000 years. At these times, the Senegal and Niger river valleys attracted diverse populations from surrounding areas, creating significant interaction zones.

The colonisation of the Middle Niger and Middle Senegal floodplains by cultivators and agropastoralists in the early first millennium BC was linked to an arid period in an already dry Sahara. Early farming/herding/fishing communities were established on the northern margins of the Niger and

[14] Maley and Vernet 2015. [15] Webb 1995.

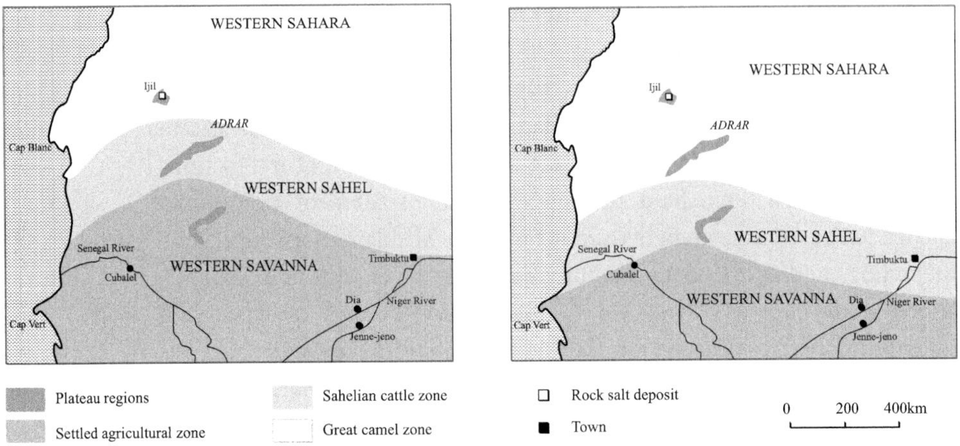

Figure 14.2. Change in land use zones from 1600 (left) to 1850 (right) as reconstructed from historical documents by Webb (1995, 6, 10).

Senegal middle valleys at this time.[16] Subsequently, a wetter period between 800–400 BC in Mauritania appears to correspond to the extension of cattle herding activities northward towards the Adrar. Copper ores at Akjoujt were processed and widely exchanged among these pastoral/agro-pastoral groups. This may have been a period in which movement over long distances both north-south and east-west was facilitated. Evidence for exchange between the Middle Senegal valley and the Northern Sahel/ Southern Sahara disappears sometime between 100 BC and AD 100. This possibly coincided with a dramatic arid episode in the course of an erratic, erosive phase that lasted until AD 300–400. During this period, river flood regimes and rainfall would have been very unpredictable. Until *c.*AD 600, rainfall in the Sahel was very low, even as the rainfall further south was high and 'out of phase' with the Sahel,[17] supplying generous floods to the Middle Senegal and Niger floodplains. Higher rainfall and lower evaporation returned to the Sahel and Southern Sahara in the seventh century AD, coincident with the appearance of glass and copper on a significant scale along the eastern Niger Bend and further east in Niger at Marandet.[18]

The current state of our knowledge about the three areas discussed here – the upper Inland Niger Delta around Jenné-jeno, the eastern Bend of the Niger at Gao Saney and Gao Ancien, and the Middle Senegal Valley at Cubalel and Sincu Bara – is lamentably partial. However, the sequences

[16] Bedaux *et al.* 2005; Deme and McIntosh 2006; MacDonald, Chapter 13, this volume.
[17] Maley and Vernet 2015, 191.
[18] Grébénart 1985, 354–79; Magnavita 2013; Magnavita *et al.* 2007.

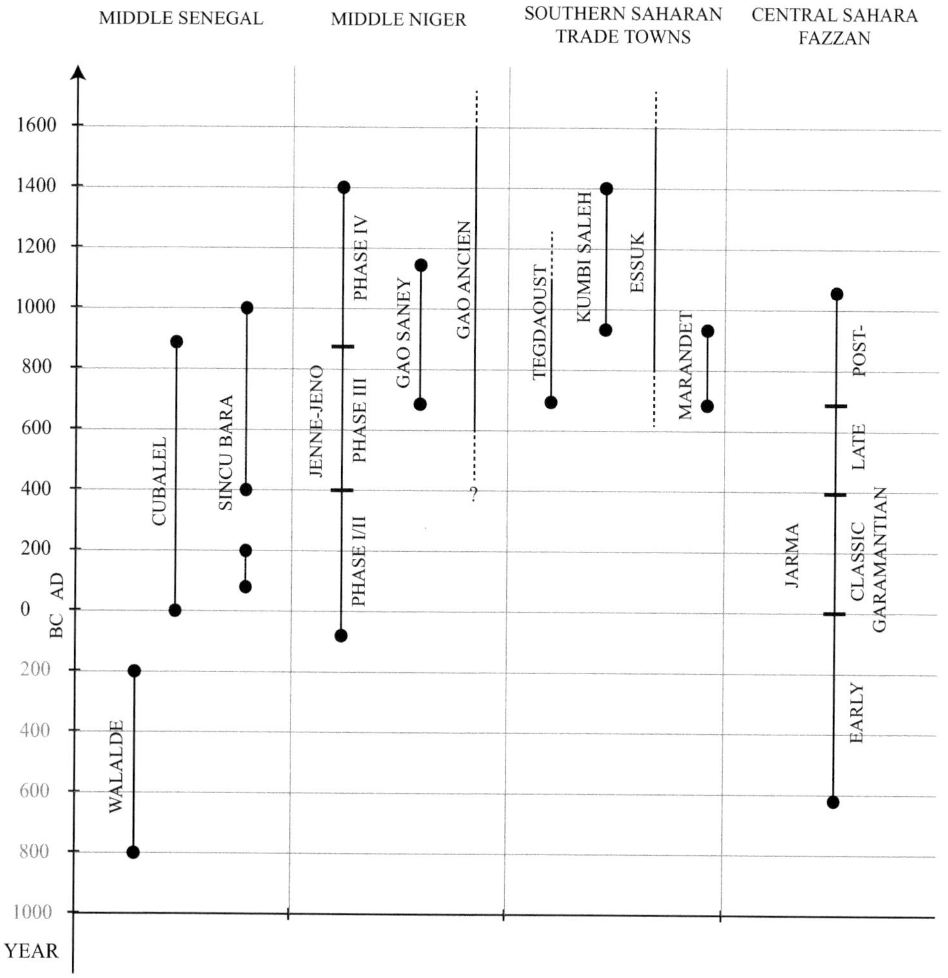

Figure 14.3. Timeline showing excavation sequences discussed in the text.

excavated thus far provide a preliminary framework for evaluating the case for multi-scalar interaction, exchange, and settlement growth at each (Fig. 14.3).

Jenné-jeno: An Early Town Centre for Regional Exchange in the Inland Niger Delta

Jenné-jeno shares with its descendant settlement, Djenné, a location on the Inland Niger Delta (IND) floodplain that is optimal for numerous subsistence pursuits, including flood cultivation of African rice, dry season pasturage for livestock, rain-fed cultivation of millet on non-inundated lands, and fishing, plus nearby access to the Bani River for transport and trade. Beginning in 1977 and continuing in 1980–1981, 1994, 1997–1998, 2008, and 2010, the occupation mounds in the vicinity of the town of Djenné have been investigated through multiple phases of excavation, coring, and surface survey, with a primary focus on the 30 ha mound of Jenné-jeno.[19] Eighteen units of sizes up to 10 × 6 m have been excavated down to sterile earth on Jenné-jeno (maximum depth, 6 m) with ten additional units excavated on neighbouring mounds. A robust material culture sequence has been established and confirmed by analysing the material culture in each excavated unit separately to test the proposed time-sensitive attributes and diagnostic pottery types for the four occupation phases we defined.[20] Excavation proceeded according to identifiable deposition contexts, seeking to maintain maximal stratigraphic integrity. Excavated contexts included houses, workshops, burials, refuse pits, mud wall melt accumulations, and abandonment surfaces. A series of 29 radiocarbon dates anchors the sequence in time, beginning with initial occupation at 112 calBC–calAD 65,[21] and continuing until final abandonment by 1400. From initial settlement, the subsistence economy included domestic cattle and ovicaprids, fish, wild bovids, domestic rice, millet, and wild cereals, with little evidence for major change in emphasis over time.

Exploration of urbanism at Jenné-jeno has focused on the evidence for rapid settlement mound expansion in the first millennium AD accompanied by the development of numerous other mounds in a distinctive, tightly clustered pattern. The absence of evidence for large public buildings or monuments, or wealthy elites, and the settlement's participation in widening networks of exchange and interaction have been of particular interest. The major architectural feature at the site is a 3.7 m wide

[19] Initial instrument survey in 1977 indicated an area of 33 ha. The reduction to 30 ha according to instrument survey in 2008 by D. Park reflects significant erosion, especially on the western side of the site, in addition to differences in defining site boundaries on the descending slope of the mound. The excavations at Jenné-jeno and regional surveys have been published in two volumes, McIntosh, S. and McIntosh, R. 1980; McIntosh, S. 1995.

[20] A typological approach to identifying and recording pottery was, however, avoided, see McIntosh, S. and McIntosh, R. 1980; McIntosh, S. 1995, 130–32. Rather than organising pottery recording on the basis of pre-established types or wares, feature sherds (rims, bases) were processed individually, with 15 formal variables recorded for each sherd, in the interest of preserving potentially significant data on variability, both intra-site and inter-site.

[21] McIntosh, S. 1995, 60; McIntosh, S. and McIntosh, R. 1980, 93, 195–97. A new AMS ^{14}C date of 2018±36 (AA94432) for the initial occupation deposit in Unit LX-N narrows the date range previously available from low precision standard radiocarbon dates.

mudbrick wall that encircled the northern three quarters of the site.[22] Unlike Takrur and Gao, Djenné was not mentioned in any written trade itinerary or account until the fifteenth century. Located on an internal waterway, it apparently existed outside the reach of Arab and Berber traders who plied Saharan trade.

Several aspects of the Jenné-jeno data have been the focus of our interpretive efforts.

Rapid Settlement Growth

The presence of the earliest, Phase I pottery types at the bottom of six excavation units (ALS, LXN, LXS, M1, M2, CTR, DT) in the central and south-eastern sectors of the site suggests that the site was quite large by AD 400 although we cannot be sure that occupation was continuous across the *c.*10 ha expanse these units encompass (Fig. 14.4). Models of site growth have included the possibility of two or more small mounds accreting over time.[23] Furthermore, all excavated units, including neighbouring Hambarketolo, have painted polychrome pottery that is diagnostic for Phase III, dated to AD 400–900. We interpret this as indicating that Jenné-jeno had reached its maximum expanse by the end of this phase. The massive city wall was built at this time, enclosing 3,000 or more inhabitants.[24] By the end of Phase IV, *c.*AD 1400, Jenné-jeno was abandoned for reasons about which it is possible only to speculate.

Exchange and Interaction

The presence of iron and stone beads and grindstones from the beginning of occupation indicates probable exchange relationships, as these materials are not present in the floodplain. Copper appeared *c.*AD 500 and gold was present at the end of the first millennium AD. Lead isotope analysis by T. Fenn (personal communication) indicates that the Phase IV (AD 900–1400)

[22] Although the existence of the Jenné-jeno city wall has been called into question by Schmidt *et al.* 2005, 124, the wall has been mapped several times since 1977 and, as a result of accelerating erosion, is now elevated 10 cm or more above the surface at multiple points around the circumference of the site.

[23] McIntosh, S. 1995, 23.

[24] Estimates of population size are fraught with pitfalls, see McIntosh, S. and McIntosh, R. 1993, 633 and McIntosh, S. 1999b, 71–73 for discussion of methods. Our early estimates, based on average population densities at occupied mounds in the Inland Delta historically, were undoubtedly too high, since Jenné-jeno lacked the two-storey buildings that characterise settlements today and have been revised.

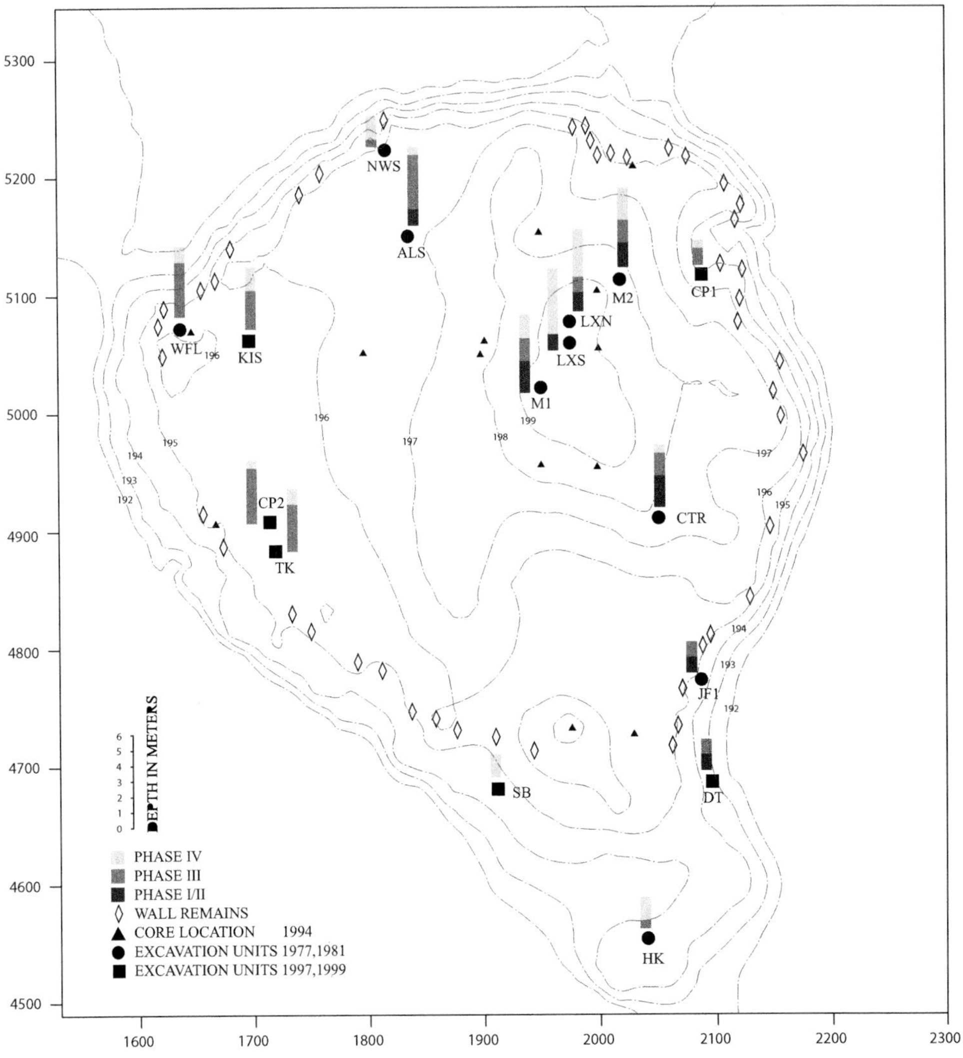

Figure 14.4. Excavation and augur coring locations on Jenné-jeno, showing the depth of deposits and phase chronology for the excavation units.

copper alloy artifacts are all from a Moroccan source. The earliest, unalloyed copper artifact (sample 1460), on the other hand, appears to derive from an unknown West African source. While luxury exotics (glass, copper, stone beads) were rare throughout the sequence (Table 14.1), imports of stone grinders number in the hundreds, and iron slag is nearly ubiquitous in the deposits, suggesting regional movement of iron blooms on a significant scale or, less likely, the import of ore for smelting. The beginnings of large-scale

Table 14.1 *Imported materials excavated from Jenné-jeno in 1977 and 1981*

Period	Iron Objects	Copper-Based Objects	Gold	Glass Beads	Stone Beads	Sandstone Unit LX-N (43 Kg)
I/II						
100 BC -AD 400	1125 g			3	7	83 pieces
III						
AD 400–900	1654 g	10 (12 g)	1 (3.9 g)	2	2	83 pieces
IV						
AD 900–1400	1739 g	23 (73 g)		8	5	67 pieces

regional iron smelting have been dated to the seventh century at Fiko, 100 km downriver near Mopti.[25]

Based on the historical role of Djenné in provisioning drier areas downriver to the north with surplus staple goods such as rice and dried fish,[26] we have speculated that Jenné-jeno in the first millennium similarly engaged in exchange at multiple scales that included regions downriver and outside the floodplain, as well as long-distance exchange for salt and copper.[27] We propose that exchange is implicated in the rapid growth of the settlement, and note that evidence of North African cultural influences (rectilinear house plans, technology transfer (spinning, weaving, cotton seeds), and imported brass) all post-date AD 900. The date at which Jenné-jeno's networks became effectively linked to Trans-Saharan trade is not definitively known. Interaction with the Lakes Region and the town of Kumbi Saleh is suggested by the presence of distinctive white-on-red geometric pottery, which dates to AD 800–1000 at Jenné-jeno (Fig. 14.5).

The earliest painted pottery at Jenné-jeno (100 BC–AD 200) used cross-hatched red paint on a burnished, unslipped surface.[28] Around AD 200 polychrome pottery (white and black paint on red slip) appeared contemporaneously with polychrome in both the Lakes Region and at Tombouze near Timbuktu.[29] The inspiration for this new decorative style is not

[25] Robion-Brunner 2010.

[26] Transport of these goods by large canoes to Timbuktu was reported by Leo Africanus in the sixteenth century and René Caillié in the nineteenth century.

[27] McIntosh, S. 1995; 2018; McIntosh, S. and McIntosh, R. 1993.

[28] Rare finds of similarly decorated sherds in the Garamantian sphere have been proposed as evidence of interaction between the Garamantes and Jenné-jeno in the early first millennium AD by Gatto 2006 and Liverani 2006, 446. Chemical analysis confirmed that tested sherds were not trade items – Artioli *et al.* 2006. With regard to both vessel forms and fabrication technique, I find the Garamantian pottery assemblage to be fundamentally unlike Phase I Jenné-jeno pottery.

[29] Raimbault and Sanogo 1991; Park 2011.

Figure 14.5. White-on-red geometric pottery links the Lakes Region (left), Jenné-jeno (centre), and Kumbi Saleh (right; in IFAN, Dakar collection) (photographs by S. McIntosh).

known.[30] The chronologies are not firm enough to determine whether it appeared earlier along the Niger Bend or in the Inland Niger Delta. Yet its distribution along 500 km of the Middle Niger indicates a robust interaction zone.

Absence of Monumental Architecture or Evidence of Elites

Of the 34 burials excavated, none has provided more than an iron finger ring by way of grave goods, regardless of burial context (funerary urn or simple inhumation). This is not to conclude that ranking or inequality were not present and potentially materialised in non-durables such as salt or livestock, textiles, or pirogues for fishing or river transport. Rather, it simply points out that the frequently used archaeological scale of differential grave goods cannot be applied. Nor has differential access to prestige goods been detected in residential contexts. In addition, no possible public or religious buildings have been identified. We have repeatedly emphasised that this may be a sampling artifact, given the minute area of Jenné-jeno that we have excavated, yet the more we dig and uncover the same pattern, the more deserving of serious consideration it appears to be. Grave goods have been reported from urn burials of Jenné-jeno type at other mound sites, including one recently excavated by A.C. Stone.[31] Is the absence of grave goods at Jenné-jeno a sampling artifact or perhaps an indication that material distinctions in death ritual were consciously minimised at Jenné-jeno in particular?

[30] There is no obvious Garamantian connection. Contemporaneous painted pottery from Jarma uses red paint over a white painted base or slip, see Mattingly 2013. Black geometric and cross-hatched paint is documented on terminal Late Stone Age pottery of 'wasa' type from Niger, dated *c.*1000 BC, Grébénart 1985, 88–98.

[31] Stone 2015.

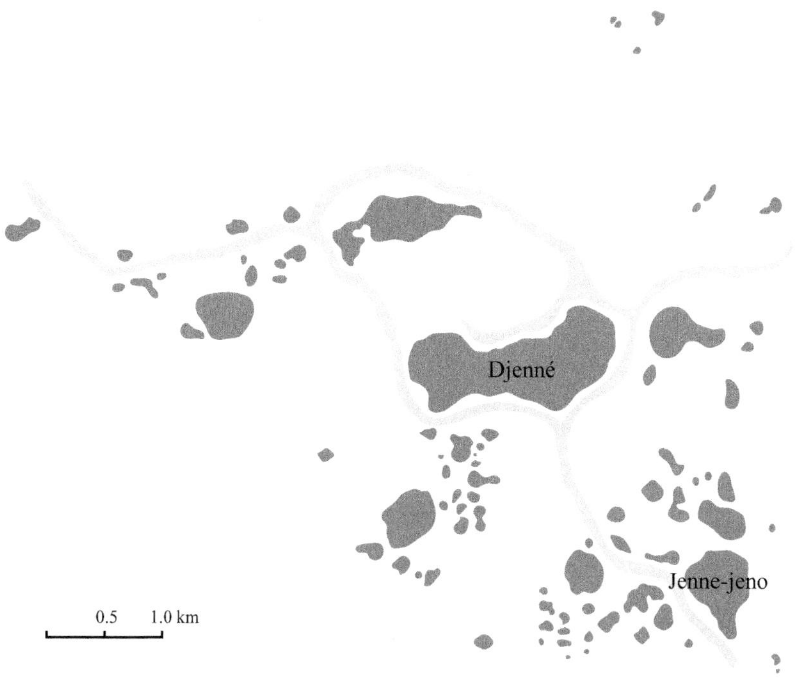

Figure 14.6. Clustered mounds around Jenné-jeno and Djenné.

Unusual Settlement Pattern of Clustered Mounds

In the immediate vicinity (within 4 km) of Djenné, there are 65 occupation mounds, creating a distinctive and predominantly anthropogenic landscape (Fig. 14.6). Surface survey at 32 of these mounds showed that three-quarters had Phase IV (AD 900–1400) surface pottery, but nothing more recent, suggesting abandonment during that period. Since many mounds have more than 2 m of deposits, we proposed that their occupation spanned several centuries.[32] This was confirmed by the presence at many sites, including the largest mounds near Jenné-jeno, of Phase III surface pottery as well, from which we infer that population in the area reached peak density during Phase III and IV, before a major settlement pattern shift occurred, concentrating population in single, non-clustered sites, such as the modern town of Djenné.[33] Basal levels at Djenné have recently been radiocarbon dated to calAD 1297–1409,[34] indicating very little overlap between the two occupation sequences. The area sampled by excavation

[32] McIntosh, S. 1995; McIntosh, S. and McIntosh, R. vol. 2, 1980.

[33] However, over the past two decades, new housing has increasingly spread beyond Djenné onto long-abandoned mounds.

[34] Beta 416884, 600±30 BP.

is extremely small, however. The presence of Phase III and IV deposits at satellite mounds has been confirmed by 17 radiocarbon dates on surface and sub-surface features at six of these mounds.[35] The inhabitants of Djenné consider that all these mounds were, in the past, an integral part of the town. Given these various elements, we have proposed that the contemporaneously occupied mounds in Phase III and IV functioned as part of a single, urban complex.

An Urban Landscape Reconsidered

Both R. McIntosh and I have argued that Jenné-jeno grew as a centre for river-based exchange in foodstuffs for iron, stone, and very plausibly salt, with copper and gold as rare markers of expanding interaction networks. R. McIntosh has proposed that individual sites in the mound clusters around Jenné-jeno were occupied by a proliferating set of subsistence and craft specialists, forming an urban network of specialised parts integrated into a generalised economy.[36] In its latest iteration, this process of proliferation has become the basis of a hypothesised series of transformations that trace the emergence of a self-organising urban landscape, beginning with expansion of subsistence specialists and continuing with craft specialists.[37] The clustered form of the town was instrumental in resisting monopolisation of power by any one group. The total population settled on the mounds within 1 km for Jenné-jeno is estimated at between 6,000 and 13,000.[38] Evidence for population heterogeneity has recently emerged from Stone's isotopic studies on human teeth from burials on Jenné-jeno, which indicate a variety of non-local origins, in contrast to individuals buried on small, rural settlements who show a local isotopic signature.[39]

The original hypothesis of functional interdependence among mounds relied heavily on surface features and artifacts that were argued to be markers for particular specialisations. These included brick ring features interpreted as granary bases (= farmers), furnace bases (= blacksmiths), netweights (= fishers), loomweights (= weavers).[40] Mary Clark's outstanding doctoral dissertation reported on her surface survey of all 67 mounds in the Urban Cluster. It included a closer examination of intersite feature and artifact variability attributed to differences in site function. She also

[35] Clark 2003, 136–39. [36] McIntosh, R. 1991; 1993; 1998. [37] McIntosh, R. 2005.
[38] McIntosh, S. 1999b, 73. [39] Stone 2015. [40] McIntosh, R. 1991; 1993; 1998; 2005; 2015.

excavated 35 surface features in order to ascertain chronology and investigate function. Several of her findings are particularly relevant:

- Certain features and artifacts used in the model are ambiguous with regard to function. The brick ring features identified as granaries may instead be fish-drying platforms and netweights and loomweights proved to be difficult to differentiate unambiguously.[41]
- Surface features produced a wide variety of dates between AD 400 and 1400, forcing reconsideration of any assumption that all surface elements are relatively contemporaneous. Differential erosion is likely implicated.
- Some features originally thought to be forges turned out to have walls of dried clay or clay fired at low temperatures, and are thus not metallurgical.[42] Others were confirmed to be hearths used for melting copper or forging iron. At three sites, these forges occur in linear alignments suggestive of smithing precincts.

Additionally, Clark noted that five mounds inventoried in 1977 had disappeared, likely due to fluvial erosion, and five new mounds of <1 ha had been formed by floodwaters carving up mounds into smaller pieces.[43] Given the amount of erosion that has occurred in recent decades at the 41 ha site of Kaniana to the north of Jenné-jeno, she predicts that it will soon be divided into a cluster of mounds. The highest mounds, including Jenné-jeno and Hambarketolo, are being remodelled by erosion, but are less threatened by dissection. This serves as an important reminder that the surface and margins of sites are constantly being reshaped by dynamic processes. Because we began our research at Jenné-jeno at the height of the Sahelian drought, we did not witness the power of rainwater and floods on the mounds until the 1990s, and it was a considerable shock to see how much change could take place in a very short time.[44]

While the functional interdependence hypothesis for clustering around Jenné-jeno remains open for investigation and 'good to think with', Clark's findings underscore the need for excavation at multiple sites in the cluster in order to evaluate the model appropriately. Regardless of potential post-depositional partitioning of lower elevation mounds, the existence of closely spaced settlement mounds in greater or lesser numbers is a phenomenon that demands explanation. Clark's ^{14}C dates confirm active deposition at the same time that

[41] Clark 2003, 82, 108. [42] Killick 2003. [43] Clark 2003, 190–91.

[44] We inaugurated an erosion monitoring programme on Jenné-jeno in 2008, and re-surveyed the mound again in 2011, but have not been able to return to continue the project.

Jenné-jeno was occupied. Why were people creating occupation mounds in places that limited proximity to their rice fields? The functional interdependence hypothesis is an excellent starting point for investigating this question, but we have barely scratched the surface in terms of the work required to evaluate it.

The organic nature of the urban cluster is thus less clear than previously thought. In the absence of obvious power differentials, centralisation, or specialisation by site, what bound the mounds of the cluster together? Functional interdependence remains a strong candidate for the principle integrating the mounds, but spatial separation of occupational specialists may not have been fundamental to its operation. How did the inhabitants resolve disputes over access to agricultural land and grazing rights or any of the myriad disagreements that inevitably arise in large populations? Where did effective power reside? The question has been raised as to the relevance of historical Mande (Bamana) concepts of occult power and the landscape, as discussed by R. McIntosh, for our understanding of Jenné-jeno's urban landscape in the first millennium AD.[45] Yet how can their degree of relevance ever be determined? A more appropriate question is whether they serve as a useful heuristic for transcending entrenched Western assumptions about the nature of power.[46] I think they do. The concept of heterarchy gives us some insight,[47] but a deeper understanding of the details will require considerable additional research.

Gao/Gawgaw: Elite and Commercial Centre on the Niger River

Located at the intersection of the Niger River and Tilemsi valley, which extends north to the Adrar des Ilforas, Gao commands a strategic point for trade (Fig. 14.7). In contrast to Djenné/Jenné-jeno, Gawgaw appears early in historical sources. In the ninth century, al-Yaqubi describes it as 'the greatest of the realms of the Sudan'. Al-Muhallabi a few decades later provides details of dual towns: the market town, Sarnah, and the royal town, residence of the 'king', whose treasure was salt.[48] Archaeological research at the badly looted, 32 ha mound of Gao Saney has established a preliminary framework for the history of occupation, from AD

[45] McIntosh, R. 2005; Smith 2006. [46] Fleisher and Wynne-Jones 2010.
[47] McIntosh, S. 1999b. [48] Levtzion and Hopkins 1981.

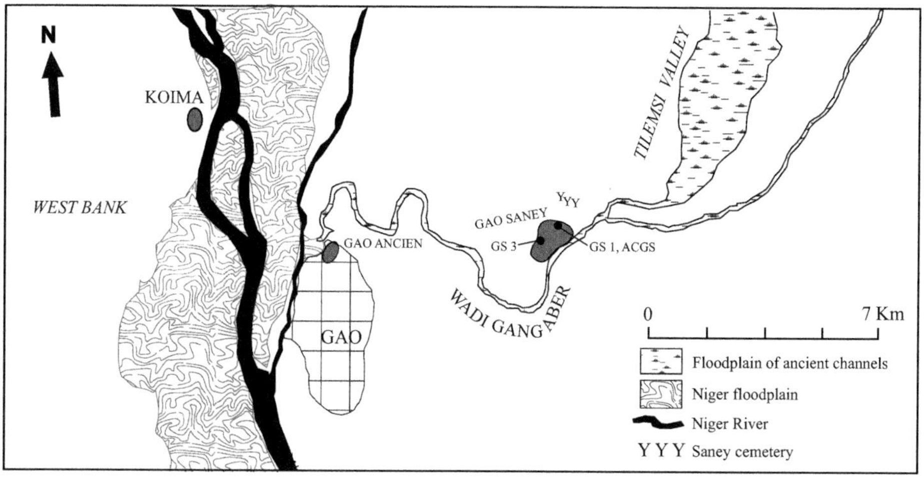

Figure 14.7. The location of Gao Ancien and Gao Saney.

700–1100,[49] revealing craft activity on a scale that supports its identification as Sarnah.[50] Again in contrast to Jenné-jeno, imports of glass and copper were reaching Gao-Saney in considerable quantities from the earliest period of documented occupation. While the data in hand are absolutely inadequate for the task of reconstructing the history of this massive mound, they do suggest that the initial occupation was extensive. Hunwick proposed that Sarnah originated as a settlement of North African Muslim merchants,[51] but the archaeological evidence suggests a considerable Berber influence with perhaps a certain hybridisation of ceramic influences with local Songhay groups. Hunwick's argument, that the Songhay Za dynasty (in the *Ta'rikh al-Sudan*) relocated from Kukiya to Gao in the ninth century to provision (and control) North African merchants trading through Tadmakka, aligns fairly closely with the evidence for North African, Berber, and Songhay interaction at Gao-Saney.[52]

The initial settlement of Gao Saney coincides with a period of reduced aridity in the Sahel. This may have produced increased rainfall in the Adrar des Ilforas, raising the water table in the Tilemsi Valley and facilitating long-distance movement along it. The Wadi Gangaber, on which Gao Saney is located, may have flowed seasonally during this period, but we have no evidence regarding this.

[49] The surface is likely to be significantly deflated; Insoll 1996 found imported and local ceramics on the surface that likely date somewhat later.

[50] Cissé *et al.* 2013. [51] Hunwick 1999, xxxiv. [52] Hunwick 1994, note 21; 1999.

The excavations at Gao-Saney have recently been published, so only a brief summary is presented here.[53] Three excavation units in stable, unlooted areas of the mound revealed 7 m of deposit representing occupation between the eighth and twelfth centuries, with unfired mudbrick architecture throughout the sequence. The lower deposits have large, loaf-shaped bricks of a type known earlier in the Niger Bend, along with walls of irregularly shaped banco lumps that recall construction technology elsewhere on the Niger Bend and at Jarma.[54] Architectural features in later deposits have standardised mould-formed rectangular bricks (400 × 200 × 45 mm). The inhabitants were involved in the secondary processing of both glass beads and copper. Excavations recovered hundreds of glass bead wasters from the earliest deposits and over 400 copper crescent fragments from the upper 3 m of deposits, along with 150 copper crucibles. Lead isotope analysis of several of the copper-alloy artefacts indicates, tentatively, a Tunisian source. Similar material also reached other Sub-Saharan sites, including Kissi, Marandet, Essouk-Tadmakka, and Igbo Ukwu along what increasingly appears to be an early Trans-Saharan route from Ibadite centres, such as Tahert in North Africa.[55] Other copper objects appear to derive from different sources, possibly located in Morocco.[56] The glass beads at Gao Saney include both plant ash glass manufactured east of the Euphrates and natron glass from Syro-Palestinian sources.[57]

The entire Saney sequence is dominated by distinctive, polychrome, funnel-neck jars and a smaller number of red slipped, burnished and comb-impressed bowls. A virtually identical assemblage appears in the Tombouze sequence near Timbuktu in the seventh/eighth century AD.[58] The origin of this distinctive assemblage is of considerable interest, as it appears to combine vessel forms and channelled decoration documented at earlier sites in north-eastern Burkina Faso with polychrome decoration that appeared in the third century in other excavated sequences along the Middle Niger.[59]

The same funnel-neck jar assemblage was excavated at Gao Ancien in association with a pillared structure that was constructed in dressed

53 Cissé 2017; Cissé *et al.* 2013.

54 At several sites in the Méma and Lakes Region, discussed by MacDonald, Chapter 13, this volume. For Jarma, see Mattingly 2013, 141, though note that the mud lump construction is a later Medieval development there, postdating mudbrick.

55 Fenn 2011; Fenn *et al.* 2009; Nixon 2009. 56 Fenn 2011. 57 Dussubieux 2011.

58 Park 2011.

59 Czerniewicz 2004; Magnavita, personal communication. See also, Jenné-jeno: McIntosh, S. 1995; occupation mounds in the Lakes Region: Raimbault and Sanogo 1991; and Tombouze: Park 2011.

stone in the tenth century.[60] From inside the structure, fragments of gold and over 6,000 glass beads were recovered. The nature of this building is a puzzle, but the pillars are a distinctly North African architectural feature and are evocative of religious structures, such as mosques and tombs.[61] More recent excavations in adjacent areas have revealed other stone walls in the immediate vicinity, one with a pillar visible in the section, plus a basin lined with fired brick, and a toilet and washing area. Radiocarbon dates indicate that they were all built between calAD 880 and 1020.[62] Because of the extent of wall robbing and later construction, it will take considerable ingenuity to reconstruct how all these stone walls related to one another. Were they part of a complex of structures, or part of a single structure? At the moment, we do not know. But it is clear that a singularly important building or building complex was constructed in a North African style in the tenth century. These excavations add considerable detail on this period, which was initially documented by Insoll's work in the same sector of Gao Ancien.[63] Several aspects of the Gao Saney evidence merit particular emphasis here.

Rapid Settlement Growth

The earliest occupation at Gao Saney appears to have been extensive, with functional differentiation between residential areas (unit GS3) and workshops (units GS1, ACGS).

Trade and Interaction

The data from Gao-Saney powerfully situate the site within much more extensive networks of trade and interaction. Funnel-necked, polychrome pots accompanied by red burnished comb-impressed bowls are widespread along the Niger during the period AD 700–1100; they are present near Timbuktu, Gourma Rharous, and Bentia in addition to Gao, clearly indicating river-based cultural interaction.[64] However, the Saney pottery is very unlike Late Garamantian pottery or the contemporaneous, presumably Berber pottery in the early deposits at Essouk-Tadmakka (Essuk on Fig. 14.1).[65] Overland trade networks extending

[60] Loaf-shaped banco bricks underlie this structure but earlier levels were not excavated.
[61] Cissé 2017; Cissé *et al.* 2013, 14. [62] M. Cissé, personal communication.
[63] Insoll 1996; 2000b. [64] Arazi 1999; McIntosh, S. and McIntosh, R. 1986; Park 2011.
[65] Mattingly 2013; Nixon 2008; 2017.

north-south and east-west are certain and historically documented by the ninth century. The introduction of mould-formed bricks in the ninth–tenth century in unit GS3 may indicate the presence of North African merchants or styles, a hypothesis supported by the presence of oil lamps (albeit of unusual form), which have almost never been found in Middle Niger archaeological sites. Their domed form is unusual and matched by an example recovered at Sijilmasa.[66] A number of sherds of glazed, wheel-made pottery were also recovered.[67]

For earlier periods, the evidence is more tenuous. Polychrome wares earlier than the seventh century have not yet been documented at Gao; the levels under the massive stone architecture complex at Gao Ancien remain unexcavated, so we may find some relevant information there. However, across the river at Koima, an assemblage of short everted rims and ogival rims, often embellished with paint (predominantly black) resembles the Middle Assemblage (AD 100–650) at Tombouze.[68] Neither glass nor copper has been documented in excavations at Niger Bend sites prior to the seventh century, unlike at Kissi (Burkina Faso) where both were present between the second and sixth centuries AD.[69] In the western Niger Bend, at Tongo Maaré Diabel, copper and glass appear only in the late first millennium AD, but the presence of chicken from the fifth century AD and mudbrick building technology provide evidence of wider interaction earlier in time.[70]

Gao-Saney joins the growing ranks of archaeological sites that document an expansive increase during the first millennium AD in the movement of exotics, both interregionally, between the Sahara and the Sahel, and across the Sahara. Locally, the relationship between Gao Saney and Gao Ancien corresponds closely to the Arab accounts of the dual towns of Gawgaw, despite conflicting details on locations with regard to the river.[71] The construction of

[66] Fauvelle-Aymar 2016. [67] Cissé 2011.

[68] Based on Koima pottery collected by S. McIntosh, see Park 2011 for the assemblage from Tombouze.

[69] The copper and beads from burials at Kissi have been abundantly published: Magnavita 2003; 2013; 2015; Robertshaw *et al.* 2009. For the Niger Bend, Park 2010 reported large amounts of carnelian and glass beads in an early first millennium AD context from Tombouze 1 Unit 6. However, the full excavation report indicates that these materials came from a different excavation unit (Unit 5) in which the sequence begins no earlier than the seventh century – Park 2011. In that unit, ten carnelian beads, eight glass beads and 103 bone beads were recovered near a burial with two copper bracelets and a copper ring – Park 2011, 397–98. No glass beads or carnelian were recovered from any of the levels in Unit 6 – Park 2011, 403–15.

[70] Gestrich 2013; MacDonald, Chapter 13, this volume. [71] Discussed in Hunwick 1994.

the dressed stone pillar structure complex falls strikingly close in time to the conversion of the ruler of Gawgaw to Islam by the second half of the tenth century.[72]

Gao: Summary

The archaeological evidence thus far excavated from Gao Saney and Gao Ancien corresponds remarkably well to historical descriptions and reconstructions based on the *Ta'rikh al-Sudan* and Songhay oral traditions. These two sites have identical ceramic assemblages in the late first millennium AD, but evidence of very different functions, as Insoll first proposed: elite consumption and architecture occurs at Gao Ancien and craft and manufacture at Gao Saney.[73] Although both sites might appear superficially to conform to an Arab-led-trade model stimulating town growth, the earliest material culture suggests a Songhay-Berber, rather than an Arab presence, reflecting interaction along the Niger Bend from Bentia to Tombouze. The well-developed glass processing industry in the earliest levels raises questions about possible antecedents to the glass and copper trade at Gao Saney, perhaps extending back two or more centuries and linked to the transit of the copper and glass in dated mid-first millennium burials at Kissi, as well as Sirba gold.[74] Luckily, the levels under the massive stone architecture complex at Gao Ancien remain unexcavated, so we may find some relevant information there.

Takrur: A Riverside Trade Town/Polity in the Middle Senegal River Valley

The Senegal River has for centuries been a vital artery for the transport of gold from the Bambuk source area along the Faleme River, which flows into the Senegal south of Bakel. The French established forts at the Faleme confluence in the late seventeenth century to control the gold trade and transport downriver to their fort at St. Louis on the Atlantic Ocean. But prior to the establishment of the Atlantic trade, gold was traded to towns in the Middle Senegal Valley for transport north by caravan across the desert.

[72] Hunwick 1980. [73] Insoll 1996.
[74] This eastern Niger route has been proposed by Insoll and Shaw 1997 and Nixon 2017, 268–69.

In the twelfth century, Takrur was the preeminent trade town and polity on the Senegal River for the export of gold and slaves.[75] A century earlier, Silla held that distinction. Despite al-Bakri's description of Silla as the capital of a 'vast kingdom' led by a ruler almost as grand as Ghana's,[76] archaeological interest in identifying and illuminating the history of either Silla or Takrur has been dwarfed by the attention focused on Ghana. This disparity may be attributed to several factors: the earlier historical prominence of Ghana as a source of gold, the detail provided by al-Bakri on Ghana and its trade networks, and the visible and monumental nature of archaeological sites such as Tagdaoust (Tegdaoust) and Kumbi Saleh that are identified with these trade networks.[77] Whatever the reasons, little systematic research had been conducted to locate Takrur and Silla and to document their development and interaction networks over time.

Throughout the 1990s, the Middle Senegal Valley Archaeological Project undertook a series of investigations in the region thought to be the traditional heartland of Takrur. I will review the evidence these projects provide on exchange, trade, and town growth. Most of the relevant data comes from excavation and survey in a 460 km^2 study area between the towns of Walaldé and Saldé and upriver at Sincu Bara.[78] The occupation sequences documented by the project at more than a dozen different sites date to the period 800 BC–AD 1200. To this database, we can add other excavated and dated occupation first millennium sequences at Tulel Fobo (AD 700–1000),[79] Ogo (AD 900–1200)[80] and, further upriver near the confluence of the Senegal and Faleme rivers, Arondo (AD 500–1000)[81] (Fig. 14.8). These sequences document two periods of interaction with regions to the north of the Middle Senegal Valley: 600–300 BC, and post-AD 800. In marked contrast to Middle Niger sites, there is no evidence of first millennium AD exchange and interaction with regions to the north or west earlier than AD 800, and the quantity of imports prior to AD 1000 is extremely limited. This is unexpected in an area of the river that has historically been important to Saharan trade, not only as a conduit for the gold trade, but also as a grain-producing area that provisioned Saharan trade towns. This suggests a different trajectory than either of our earlier town case studies. In

[75] Al-Idrisi, in Levtzion and Hopkins 1981, 107.
[76] Al-Bakri in Levtzion and Hopkins 1981, 77–78.
[77] Nixon, Chapter 17, this volume, discusses the archaeology of Tagdaoust, presumed site of historical Awdaghust, and Kumbi Saleh.
[78] Deme 2003; Deme and McIntosh 2006; McIntosh, R. *et al.* 2016; McIntosh and Bocoum 2000.
[79] Bocoum 2000. [80] Chavane 1985. [81] Thiaw 1999.

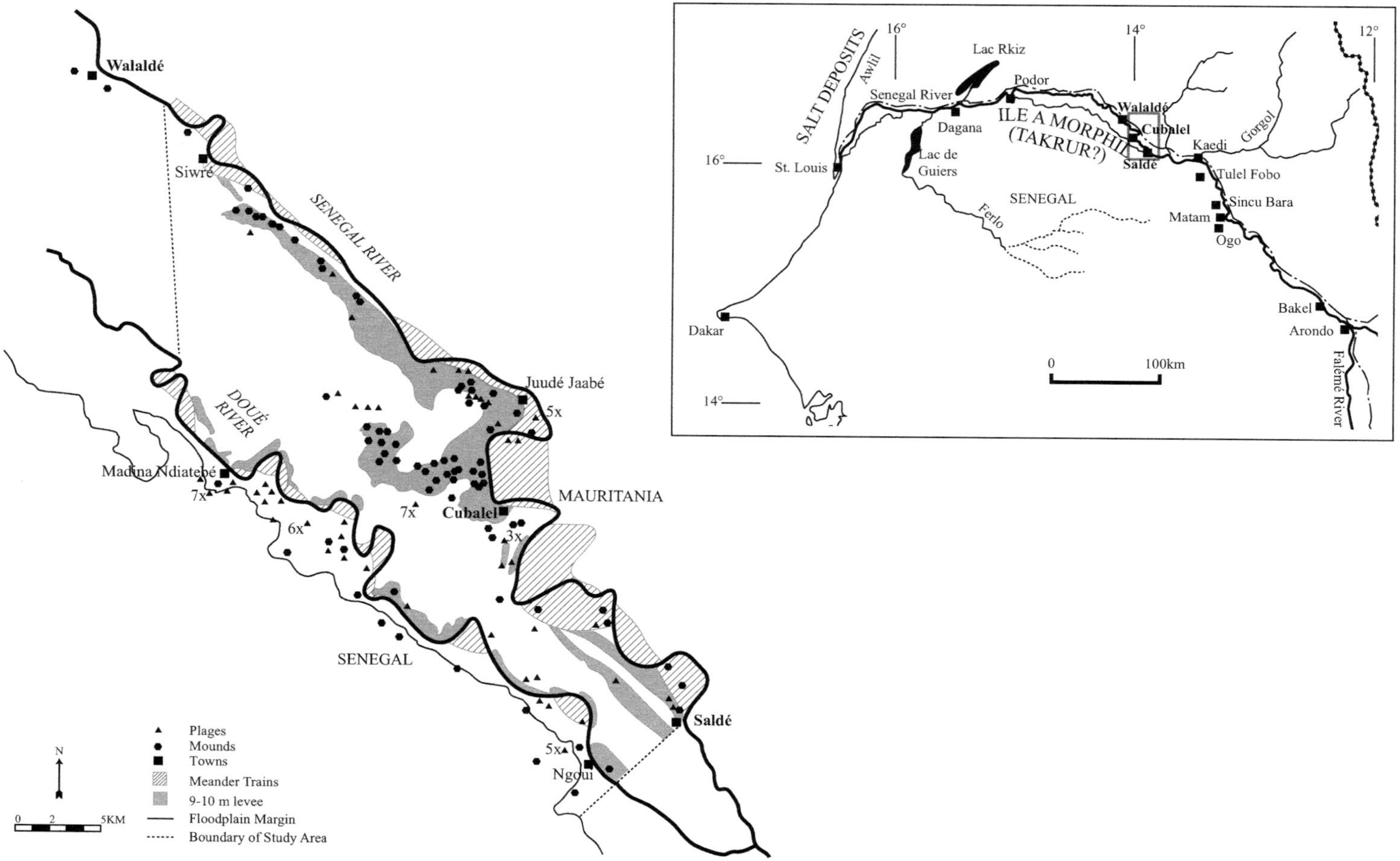

Figure 14.8. Middle Senegal study area with inventoried sites and geomorphological features. Inset shows other sites mentioned in the text.

addition, evidence is sparse for town growth in the first millennium AD until copper and brass, spinning and weaving, glass, and other exotics appeared in the region, along with sorghum.

Overview of the Middle Senegal Valley Archaeological Project and Results

The middle sector of the Senegal Valley is 20–30 km wide in the area called the Ile à Morphil, where the river bifurcates into a southern branch, the Doué. Historically, this sector has been the most populous because of the concentration of clay basins suitable for recession cultivation of sorghum.[82] This region today is dominated by *Hal-pulaar'en* (Pulaar speakers), a broad grouping that includes fishers (*subalbe*), sedentary Tukolor,[83] and pastoral Fulbe. All three groups cultivate rain-fed millet, but the Tukolor also practice recession cultivation of sorghum. Due to high interannual variability in flood and rainfall, the extent of the area flooded may vary from year to year by a factor of five or more.[84]

In our study area within the Ile à Morphil, there are two broad categories of archaeological site: mound sites 2–6 m high located on the high levees (9–10+ m above mean sea level), and surface scatters known as 'plages' with negligible (<1 m) above-ground accumulation (Fig. 14.8). Most of these plages have scatters of sherds and fired earth or ash. Our excavations focused on 11 mound sites in the vicinity of the villages of Cubalel, Siwré and Walaldé. The bulk of the excavated deposits date to the period 500 BC–AD 1000. All of the excavated mounds revealed a quite consistent picture of episodic agropastoralist occupation of variable but generally low intensity, punctuated by periods of abandonment lengthy enough for the development of recognisable erosion surfaces in a number of cases. The most common features encountered in all units were pits and fired earth of various kinds associated with domestic structures or wall melt from such structures, and domestic debris. Most of the structures appeared to be circular pole-and-daub houses 3–4 m in diameter. Mound area is generally less than 3 ha, but some sites exceed that, reaching up to 12 ha. Subsistence economy was relatively generalised, with a primary emphasis on ovicaprids, cattle, and dog (apparently a regular food item), pearl millet and fonio, plus small amounts of fish and wild bovids. Sorghum, so important

[82] Boutillier 1962.

[83] Tukolor, a French transcription of the Arabic Takrur or Takruri (Bâ 2002, 62) originally referred to 'people of Takrur'.

[84] Michel 1973, 135.

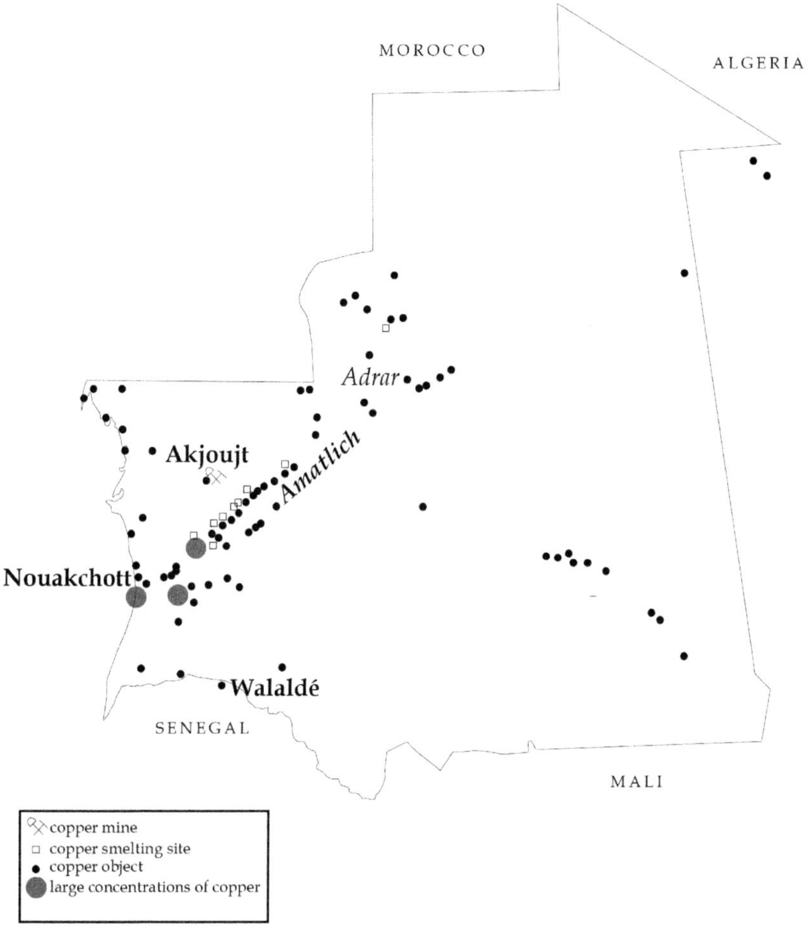

Figure 14.9. Distribution of first-millennium BC copper in Mauritania extending to Walaldé (after Vernet 2012, 112).

to the Middle Senegal Valley economy historically, is absent for most of the first millennium AD in all units within the study area, at Sincu Bara and at Arondo. This absence is significant, because a systematic flotation protocol that sampled every context was followed at all these sites.

The earliest evidence of floodplain settlement dates to 800–500 calBC at the 5 ha mound of Walaldé, which was occupied by agropastoralists with herds dominated by cattle.[85] This coincides with a very dry episode signalled by a sharp spike in dust accumulation off the Mauritanian coast and an inferred southward retraction of the cattle zone.[86] During the wetter

[85] Deme and McIntosh 2006. [86] Hanebuth and Henrich 2009.

period *c.*500–300 BC, copper from the ore source at Akjoujt was present at Walaldé and throughout much of central and western Mauritania (Fig. 14.9).[87] We have suggested that copper moved with and among pastoralists/agropastoralists in their seasonal migrations.[88]

Interactions, likely indirect, between Mauritanian sites, Walaldé, and North Africa are indicated by Phoenician-style copper earrings at Walaldé and around Akjoujt similar to those found in Moroccan graves of the eighth to sixth centuries BC.[89] In addition, perforated *A. senilis* shells at Walaldé indicate possible interaction with coastal areas.

We thus have concrete evidence of linkages between the Mediterranean and the Senegal River in the first millennium BC, but little compelling reason to think in terms of regular Trans-Saharan exchange or trade relations. The only identifiable northern import reported from Mauritania is a Punic-style bronze fibula with an iron pin discovered near Akjoujt.[90] Other finds of bronze are extremely rare, and brass artifacts, also rare, are of more recent date.[91]

The end of occupation at Walaldé *c.*200 BC appears to coincide with the onset of an unstable arid episode with sporadic flash flooding.[92] Settlement at Cubalel at the turn of the first millennium AD marks the next documented occupation. The settlement pattern during Cubalel Phase I (AD 1–200) of small (<3 ha), regularly spaced settlements on the high (10+ m) levees indicates that population density was low. However, an unknown number of unexcavated mounds may have Phase I deposits at their base, and we have no data regarding seasonal influxes of pastoralists and their herds.

At some point during this arid period, an exceptionally arid episode of unknown duration occurred, and seawater flowed into the Ferlo valley (normally a tributary of the Senegal River) for 350 km.[93] Its duration was sufficiently prolonged (from decades to a century or more) to support saltwater shellfish all along the valley. A ^{14}C date on the shell deposits indicates a date between 100 calBC and calAD 300. Possible contributing factors include prolonged reduction in rainfall, increased evaporation,

[87] Vernet 2012.

[88] Deme and McIntosh 2006; Vernet 1993. Horses may have been among the livestock herded in these pasturelands; rock art depicting horses occurs in the Adrar, conventionally attributed to invading 'Libyco-Berbers'. The high number of copper spears and arrows is certainly suggestive of violent confrontations; alternatively, these may have been used in hunting.

[89] Compare Deme and McIntosh 2006, 335; Jodin 1966, 71; Ponsich 1967, 34, 91, 196; Vernet 1993, 347.

[90] Lambert 1972. [91] Lambert 1983. [92] Bouimetarhan *et al.* 2009; Nizou *et al.* 2010.

[93] Monteillet *et al.* 1981.

and/or a drop in the water table. This raises the question of a possible connection between the apparent cessation of Akjoujt copper exploitation by the end of the first millennium and this exceptional arid episode.[94] If this episode produced an emphatic southward movement of the cattle pastoralism zone, the Akjoujt copper mines could have become remote and inaccessible. A climate episode of such severity could have been devastating for cattle herds in the Sahel, resulting in huge losses and wholesale abandonment of formerly occupied areas, entirely disrupting prior interaction networks.

It may be at just this time that Berber groups began developing and/or expanding camel herds into the southern desert, ultimately reaching the Senegal River at Siwré. A single camel bone was recovered there from deposits dating to AD 200–400.[95] Without speculating on the linguistic affinity of the Siwré occupants, it may be noted that their material culture was quite different from that of Phase I at Cubalel. They had highly decorated pottery that shares certain distinctive features (pastilles, linear appliqués, high frequency of slip) with the pottery several centuries later at Tagdaoust.[96]

Occupation throughout the first millennium is well represented in our excavations. Survey shows that occupation on small mounds (0.5–3 ha in area) located on the highest levees (10+ m) was common. If goods were moving between the river and the desert in the early first millennium AD, no evidence for it has yet turned up. Indeed, it is noteworthy that no evidence of copper, glass or any other northern import has been found in first millennium deposits prior to *c.*AD 800 at any excavated site in the Middle or Upper Senegal Valley.[97] Also absent are any signs of contact with the coast, such as *A. senilis* beads. In contrast with the Middle Niger, where domestic chicken appears between the fifth and seventh centuries AD,

[94] Dating is regrettably imprecise; Lambert 1983 records a single date of calAD 28–537 (1760 ± 110 BP) on a smelting furnace at Lemdena that may indicate exploitation in the first millennium AD. The argument that the surface finds of copper in Mauritania all date to the first millennium BC is based on typological criteria linked to the date range for the operation of the Grotte aux Chauves Souris mine at Akjoujt and several copper smelting furnaces – Lambert 1971; 1975; 1983; Vernet 2012. Recovery of copper artifacts from closed and dated contexts is needed to confirm this chronology.

[95] MacDonald and MacDonald 2016. [96] For example, Robert-Chaleix 1989, 227–32.

[97] The claim by Hatté *et al.* 2010 that Sincu Bara pottery was slipped or otherwise surface-treated with bitumen imported from the Dead Sea, Egypt, or Nigeria from AD 400 onward cannot be evaluated until the surface slip is analysed by gas chromatograph–mass spectroscopy to confirm the presence of bitumen. ^{14}C dates of over 10,000 BP for the slip on two potsherds prompted the search for possible sources of old carbon. These results certainly demand deeper investigation; the case for bitumen is not yet established.

there is no chicken in the first millennium AD assemblages.[98] Because so little is known of first millennium AD material culture north of the Senegal River and downstream to the coast, it is unfortunately impossible to assess any other potential evidence for interaction during this period.[99]

Interaction along the river expanded by AD 600 to establish a common material culture with distinctive collared pottery over much of the middle valley, from Cubalel to Matam, with variants found in the Falémé at Arondo.[100] In the Cubalel study area, copper appears after AD 800 in association with this collared ware assemblage. Only three pieces of copper were recovered from excavations at Cubalel sites; all were pure copper, in levels dating between AD 800 and 950.[101] Upriver, at Sincu Bara and Arondo, copper and brass appear at approximately the same date.[102] Also at this time, there is the first evidence of new architectural technologies, including banco and unfired mudbrick, supplementing the earlier wattle-and-daub technology. Shortly thereafter, cordoned pottery in a distinctive style documented at Tagdaoust and Kumbi Saleh appears at sites in the Cubalel study region, at Sincu Bara, and at Arondo (Fig. 14.10).

These developments inaugurated a period of intense interaction with Saharan trade towns and North Africa. Cordoned pottery at Sincu Bara and Ogo developed a uniquely exuberant style of raised geometric motifs on the body, including oculi, ovals, lozenges, chevrons, and hearts that may mimic patterns on ninth- and tenth-century Fatimid glassware, several examples of which were recovered at Tagdaoust.[103] The forms include new vessel types, such as footed goblets.[104] This very distinctive pottery dates to between AD 1000–1200 at Ogo and is associated with disturbed deposits at Sincu Bara that appear to date to this same time period.[105] Also recovered from the disturbed deposits was a fragment of green glazed ware from North Africa, 150 pendants and beads made on marine shell (*A. senilis*, *Conus*), plus eleven cowries (*Cypraea moneta*).[106] No marine shell was found in the earlier, undisturbed deposits. Glass beads or vessel glass have not yet been recovered in any significant numbers from excavations at any site of any date on the Senegal River.

After analysing copper-based metals from a variety of Senegal Valley sites, Garenne-Marot concluded that there was a trade circuit involving Tagdaoust and the Middle Senegal sites of Sincu Bara and Saré-Coffi (Podor) beginning in

[98] MacDonald and MacDonald 2016. [99] Vernet 2004. [100] Thiaw 1999.
[101] Fenn and Killick 2016. [102] Bocoum and McIntosh 2002, 82; Thiaw 1999.
[103] Chavane 1985, 127; Vanacker 1979, 163–66. [104] Thilmans and Ravisé 1980, 49–51.
[105] Chavane 1985; Bocoum and McIntosh 2002 refer to this pottery as assemblage IVb.
[106] Thilmans and Ravisé 1980, 66, 70–75.

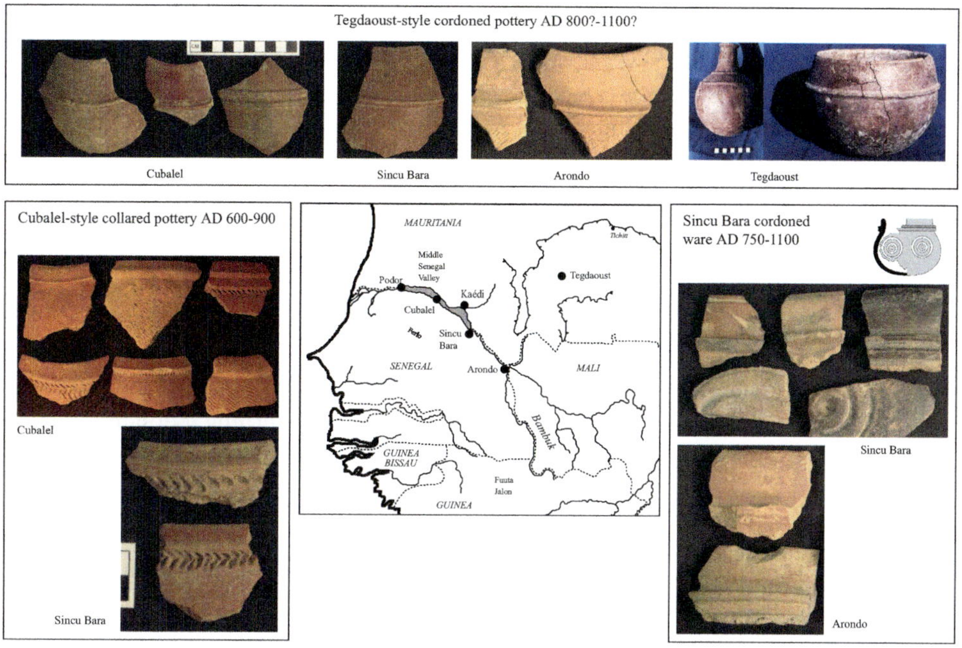

Figure 14.10. Ceramic styles on the Middle Senegal from AD 600 to 1100. The known distribution areas are: Cubalel collared ware – Cubalel to Sincu Bara; Sincu Bara cordoned ware – Kaédi to Arondo; Tagdaoust-style cordoned ware – Podor to Arondo.

the ninth century and gaining in intensity towards the eleventh and twelfth centuries.[107] Similarities are particularly marked in the brass *clochettes* (small bells), trefoils, and bar links that may have been decorative and harness elements for horses.[108] These suggest the presence of an elite culture associated with horses and horse riding. Copper and brass bracelets found at Saré-Coffi and Sincu Bara have engraved geometric decoration that resembles Fulbe motifs historically.[109] A number of these were created using lost-wax casting.

Cotton, absent from the hundreds of first millennium AD flotation samples from Cubalel sites, has been identified in the early second millennium deposits at Ogo; spindle whorls co-occur.[110] In the Middle Senegal Valley study zone, 42 spindle whorls were recovered from survey, primarily at second-millennium sites. The three spindle whorls from excavated contexts all post-date the ninth century.

[107] Garenne-Marot 1993; Garenne-Marot *et al.* 1994
[108] Chavane 1976, 63, 67; Thilmans and Ravisé 1980, 30–38.
[109] Chavane 1976; Thilmans 1977; Thilmans and Ravisé 1980, 22.
[110] Chavane 1985, 111–12, 150; Murray n.d..

The available evidence for exotics, spinning and weaving technology, lost-wax casting, and interaction with Saharan trade towns indicates that they first appeared all along the river around or shortly after AD 800. This correlates with climate amelioration between AD 700/800 and 1100/1200 due to a 'longer rainy and cloudy period during the year and decreased evaporation'.[111] The result would have been northward displacement of ecological zones, consistent with the report by al-Bakri that Awdaghust (arguably the site of Tagdaoust) in the eleventh century abounded with date palms, henna trees, many cattle and sheep, and good well-water.[112]

It goes without saying that our limited excavation sample from the Senegal Valley does not permit any firm conclusions regarding the scale and distribution of imports over time. The patterning of durable goods recovered thus far is suggestive, but hardly definitive.

Towns and Polities: Where and When Did Takrur and Silla Emerge?

The absence of evidence for trade or exchange with the north along the Middle Senegal for most of the first millennium is broadly consistent with historical accounts. Ibn Hawqal in the eleventh century mentions the coastal salt source, Awlil,[113] and links it directly with Awdaghust without any intermediary stops along the Senegal River.[114] He does not mention either Takrur or Silla. Both first appear historically in the eleventh century. Al-Bakri discusses Takrur mainly in reference to its leader, Warjabi b. Rabis, who converted to Islam in the early eleventh century, then effected the conversion of the inhabitants of both Takrur and Silla, and allied Takrur with the Almoravids in a battle against the Gudala Berbers in the Mauritanian Adrar.[115] No specific role in trade is mentioned, nor is Takrur linked to any trade network or itinerary. The main trade town in al-Bakri's time appears to have been Silla, which he links to Ghana. He notes that its inhabitants use sorghum, salt, copper rings, and lengths of cotton manufactured in nearby TRNQH for money.[116] The *viroles* recovered in vast quantities from Sincu Bara may correspond to the copper rings he mentions.

[111] Maley 2010, 250; Maley and Vernet 2015. [112] Levtzion and Hopkins 1981, 68.

[113] Awlil is thought to be located in the sebkhas of the Aftout es Saheli in southern Mauritania – MacDougall 1990; Robert-Chaleix 1991.

[114] Levtzion and Hopkins 1981, 46. [115] Levtzion and Hopkins 1981, 73.

[116] Levtzion and Hopkins 1981, 77–78.

A century later, al-Idrisi provided significant new information.[117] He places the town of Takrur upriver from Silla on the main river route for the salt trade from Awlil, and describes it as the capital of a powerful trading polity to which Silla was now subject. Its rise was likely related to its alliance with the Almoravids and control of the coastal salt deposit at Awlil. The salt was transported down the coast to the Senegal River and then by boat to Silla, Takrur, Barisa and other towns. While Silla was still 'a meeting place for the Sudan and a good market', Takrur was the larger town and had more trade. 'The people of the Maghreb al-Aqsa go there with wool, copper, and beads, and they export from there gold and slaves.'[118] This is the first mention of gold trade in connection with the Middle Senegal. The itineraries link Takrur, Silla, and Awlil with Sijilmasa via the Almoravid stronghold in the Adrar.[119]

Since our undisturbed excavation sequences largely end at the beginning of the second millennium AD, archaeology provides only limited insights into the processes of town growth and polity formation referenced by the historical sources. The largest site excavated, Sincu Bara, has surface material covering an area of 67 ha, most of it dating to AD 900–1200, according to the pottery sequence developed for the site.[120] From the quantity and quality of copper-alloy artifacts recovered by Thilmans and Ravisé it is clear that Sincu Bara was an important regional centre with extensive trade connections.[121] Our excavations there encountered mainly first millennium deposits that provided no evidence for earlier exchange, or for agricultural intensification,[122] but the sample is small. An elephant tusk was recovered from the excavated deposits, suggesting at least one possible item traded north. How Sincu Bara was positioned strategically for trade is unclear. A great deal more research at the site and its region is required in order to understand Sincu Bara's development and its involvement in trade.

Within the Cubalel study area, population aggregation appears to have increased in the second millennium, based on surface surveys. Several sites exceed 10 ha in area, in contrast to the period between AD 1 and 900,[123] in which occupation mounds ranged in size from 0.5 to 3 ha.[124] There is at present no evidence for an urban network extending back into the past as far as the fourth century, specifically in regard to Takrur, as proposed by

117 Levtzion and Hopkins 1981, 106–7. 118 Levtzion and Hopkins 1981, sv al-Idrisi, 107.
119 Devisse 1988. 120 Bocoum and McIntosh 2002. 121 Thilmans and Ravisé 1980.
122 Murray 2008. 123 Ceramic phases I, II, and III – McIntosh, S. 2016.
124 The 12 ha mound at Siwré is a possible exception, but the upper deposits are second millennium AD in date and we do not know the extent of the early first-millennium deposits.

Becker and Bocoum.[125] It must be recalled, however, that the largest sites in the Middle Senegal Valley have historically been on the *jeejegol*, the lands bordering the floodplain that are transitional to the dryland *jeeri*. While we surveyed the *jeejegol* in the study region, the Mauritanian side of the river was not open to us for survey. We are undoubtedly missing a significant component of the settlement pattern of the populations that lived and interacted along this stretch of the river. Understanding the full dimensions of human settlement in the Middle Senegal Valley at any period requires additional in-depth investigation of the *jeeri* and *jeejegol* on both sides of the Ile à Morphil, as well as the floodplain sites studied intensively during the Middle Senegal Valley Archaeological Project. Subsurface geoarchaeology could well reveal settlements under the sands or alluvium that are unsuspected from surface traces. Our current conclusions about trade are based on the expectation that floodplain sites should reflect larger regional integration in the exchange networks that sustained the towns on either side of the river, even if we have not yet located those towns.

A final piece of evidence for the emergence of new social, economic, and political configurations in the early second millennium is the production of iron on an industrial scale within the study region and immediately across the river. At the site of Juude Jaabe just north-west of Cubalel, we inventoried 150 melting furnaces arranged in sinusoidal alignments. Dates on excavated furnaces suggest two periods of use: AD 1000–1200 and 1200–1400.[126] Immediately across the river, Robert-Chaleix and Sognane inventoried more than 40,000 furnaces in alignments that occur close to laterite ore outcroppings. Dates on two furnaces also fall in the early second millennium.[127] The emergence of specialised smelting precincts at this time appears to be a new pattern that contrasts with the preceding two millennia, in which iron smelting furnaces occur on habitation sites and iron slag is ubiquitous in the occupation deposits at all sites except Siwré. Without comparable second millennium occupation sequences, we cannot say whether domestic production of iron ceased when smelting precincts appeared. As polities such as Takrur emerged, it would have been advantageous to control the production of iron for weapons. However, outcrops of laterite occur frequently enough along the Mauritanian side of the river that it is unlikely that a monopoly on production could be maintained.

Oral histories link the origins of political power in the Senegal Valley with the Jaa-Ogo, who legendarily introduced metallurgy to the Senegal

[125] Becker and Bocoum 1998. [126] Killick 2016.
[127] Robert-Chaleix 1994; Robert-Chaleix and Sognane 1983.

Valley. According to one account of the Jaa-Ogo (and there are many),[128] the ability of the Jaa-Ogo to smelt iron established their spiritual authority, which permitted them ultimately to reserve the right to mine and smelt ore. Bâ links Takrur and the Jaa-Ogo in an 'Etat-forgéron' in which the emergence of craft specialisation provided the functional interdependence necessary for the formation of the state.[129]

In this unfolding scenario of towns, trade, and craft specialisation, the appearance of sorghum in the late first millennium AD plays a critical role. Without sorghum as a recession crop, agricultural production was dependent on rain-fed cultivation of millet and fonio. The potential for producing surpluses was greatly increased when a second annual cultivation cycle was adopted that exploited the clay-rich depressions in the floodplain where millet cannot be grown but sorghum thrives. Agricultural scheduling then occupied the entire year, resulting in an increase in sedentarism by a previously agropastoral sector. This group took on the historical identity of Tukolor. Tochoror and Felle both appear on Angelino Dulcert's 1339 map of western North Africa. I suggest that the adoption of sorghum agriculture underwrote the expansion of specialisations of all types – smithing, weaving, trading – that were in existence by the time of al-Bakri's account. If the evidence we have for the Ile à Morphil in the first millennium AD is correct, then an agropastoral system with low agricultural productivity was substantially transformed between the ninth and eleventh centuries, concomitant with the historical emergence of Takrur and Silla. This involved incorporation into the Trans-Saharan trading sphere after a period of almost a millennium with negligible evidence for desert-side exchange or interaction.

Conclusions

The three archaeological case studies outlined here focus on areas of the Senegal and Niger rivers that have historically been nodes for trade and interaction networks linking regions along the rivers with the desert, the savanna, and beyond. Attempts to establish the time depth and shifting configurations of these networks are hampered by the patchiness of our current database. Where exotics are present, we can often identify source areas, but can only speculate on the routes or modes of their transport. Where exotics are absent, changes in style, technology, or spatial and social

[128] Summarised in Thilmans and Ravisé 1980, 176–78. [129] Bâ 2002, 91–93.

organisation might be the material manifestations of interaction, exchange, and trade that are otherwise invisible. The difficulty is that we often lack archaeological data from neighboring regions in the desert and savanna with which to compare our river valley sequences. In that case, the inferences we can draw about networks that predate historical documentation of trade beginning in the ninth century AD are quite tentative.

For the first millennium BC, the best-documented interaction zone extends from the Mauritanian Adrar to the Middle Senegal Valley at Walaldé. The distribution of copper artifacts with the distinctive chemical signature of the Akjoujt ores as well as related pottery styles throughout central and southern Mauritania describes an area within which ideas and goods circulated between *c.*500–200 BC. Evidence that networks extended to Punic settlements in North Africa is slim, however, and suggests mainly stylistic borrowings of jewellery fashions by mobile Berber groups. Evidence for movement of copper from Akjoujt or shells from the coast ends by *c.*100 BC, and, despite the presence of camels by AD 400, no further exotics are encountered in Middle Senegal Valley excavated sites before *c.*AD 800–900. At that time, new building technologies appear (mudbrick and banco). River-based interaction between Sincu Bara and Arondo is attested by the presence of a distinctive style of cordoned pottery; subsequently, another style of cordoned ware associated with Tagdaoust becomes widespread along the river from Cubalel to Arondo. This coincides with the appearance of brass, glass, cotton, and spindle whorls, at approximately the same time that Arab sources first mention Takrur in relation to trade. Reliable evidence for village or town settlements exceeding 10 ha also dates to this period.

Along the Middle Niger valley, regional and interregional exchange in stone and iron were essential to settlements in the Inland Niger Delta, such as Jenné-jeno. A trickle of exotics from much greater distances included several glass beads, one in Hellenistic style and one with a chemical signature best known from south-east Asia.[130] Both came from deposits dated between 100 BC and AD 200. Taken in conjunction with the appearance after AD 100 of polychrome pottery at Jenné-jeno and the Lakes Region, the glass beads seem to be associated with increased interaction along the river, but their mode of transport and exchange cannot be determined. For this reason, I have not identified the glass beads as a sign of Trans-Saharan trade. There are few, if any, signs of interaction with desert regions at this time, and none suggesting Fazzan–Jenné-jeno contacts.

[130] Brill 1995; a Phoenician/Punic glass eye bead has recently been identified in a first-millennium BC context east of the Bandiagara plateau, Giachet *et al.* 2019.

More extensive Niger River networks from the fourth to seventh centuries are indicated by the presence of copper at Jenné-jeno in addition to the continuing presence of glass beads, matched by evidence for copper, brass, glass beads and wool textiles at Kissi in Burkina Faso. These elements are absent in deposits of this period at Tombouze, near Timbuktu, and there is likewise no evidence for exotics in the pre-AD 750 deposits at Tadmakka. A novel faunal element, domestic chicken, appears at Jenné-jeno, Tongo Maaré Diabel and Kirikongo, Burkina Faso.[131] Along the Middle Niger, new building technologies appear, including mudbrick and banco. At Jenné-jeno, basal deposits with pottery dating from 100 BC to AD 400 occur over an area 500 m in extent, suggesting robust settlement growth.

From the eighth century onward, Middle Niger sequences provide much richer evidence of interaction and trade. The region from Timbuktu to Bentia appears to be an expansive interaction zone, with common pottery types and a proliferation of imported glass and copper, especially at Gao. Other North African elements at Gao include building technologies in mould-formed mudbrick and dressed stone, imported glazed pottery, and oil lamps. Gold is present at Gao, Jenné-jeno, and Tadmakka after AD 850. The large mound site of Gao Saney grew very rapidly after initial settlement in the eighth century, reaching over 30 ha before abandonment around AD 1100–1200. Jenné-jeno reached its maximum extent (33 ha) by AD 900, when its interaction networks included the Lakes Region and Kumbi Saleh, as indicated by the distribution of white-on-red painted pottery. The notable increase in the scale and intensity of interaction, especially after AD 900, is consistent with historical accounts of the establishment of regular Trans-Saharan trade after AD 700.

References

Arazi, N. 1999. An archaeological survey in the Songhay heartland of Mali. *Nyame Akuma* 52: 25–43.

Artioli, G., Laddaga, L. and Dapiaggi, M. 2006. Archaeometry of pottery: Mineralogical and chemical analyses. In Liverani 2006, 249–57.

Bâ, A. 2002. *Le Takrur: Des origines à la conquête par le Mali (VIe–XIIIe siècles).* Dakar: IFAN/Université Cheikh Anta Diop; Nouakchatt: CRIAA, Université de Nouakchott.

[131] Dueppen 2011.

Bauer, A.A. and Agbe-Davies, A.S. 2010. Trade and Interaction in Archaeology. In A.A. Bauer and A.S. Agbe-Davies (eds), *Social Archaeologies of Trade and Exchange*. Walnut Creek: Left Coast Press, 29–47.

Becker, C. and Bocoum, H. 1998. Manifestations of urbanism in Senegambia. In B. W. Andah, M.A. Sowunmi, A.I. Okpoko and C.A. Folorunso (eds), *Africa: The Challenge of Archaeology*. Ibadan: Heinemann Educational Books, 149–70.

Bedaux, R., Polet, J., Sanogo, K. and Schmidt, A. (eds). 2005. *Recherches archéologiques à Dia dans le Delta intérieure du Niger (Mali): Bilan des saisons de fouilles 1998–2003*. Leiden: CNWS Publications.

Birch, J. (ed.). 2013. *From Prehistoric Villages to Cities: Settlement Aggregation and Community Transformation*. London: Routledge.

Bocoum, H. 2000. *L'age du fer au Sénégal: Histoire et archéologie*. Dakar: IFAN/ Université Cheikh Anta Diop; Nouakchatt: CRIAA.

Bocoum, H. and McIntosh, S. 2002. *Fouilles à Sincu Bara, un site de l'age de fer dans la moyenne vallée du Sénégal*. Dakar: IFAN/Université Cheikh Anta Diop; Nouakchott: CRIAA.

Bouimetarhan, I., Dupont, L., Schefuss, E., Mollenhauer, G., Mulitza, S. and Zonneveld, K. 2009. Palynological evidence for climatic and oceanic variability of NW Africa during the late Holocene. *Quaternary Research* 72.2: 188–97.

Boutillier, J.-L. 1962. *La moyenne vallée du Sénégal: Étude socio-économique*. Paris: INSEE Servicé de Coopération; Presses Universitaires de France.

Brill, R. 1995. Chemical analysis of some glasses from Jenné-Jeno. In McIntosh 1995, 252–56.

Chapman, J., Videiko, M., Gayadarska, B., Burdo, N., Hale, D., Villis, R., Swann, N., Thomas, N., Edwards, P., Blair, A., Hayes, A., Nebbia, M. and Rud, V. 2014. The planning of the earliest European proto-towns: A new geophysical plan of the Trypillia mega-site of Nebelivka, Kirovograd Domain, Ukraine. *Antiquity* 88, Project Gallery.

Chavane, B.A. 1976. *Le site protohistorique de Saré-Thioffi (Podor, Sénégal)*. Unpublished mémoire de maîtrise. Université Cheikh Anta Diop, Dakar.

Chavane, B.A. 1985. *Villages de l'ancien Tekrour*. Paris: Editions Karthala.

Cissé, M. 2011. *Archaeological Investigations of Early Trade and Urbanism at Gao Saney (Mali)*. Unpublished PhD thesis, Rice University.

Cissé, M. 2017. The Trans-Saharan trade connection with Gao (Mali) during the first millennium. In Mattingly *et al.* 2017, 101–30.

Cissé, M., McIntosh, S., Dussubieux, L., Fenn, T., Gallagher, D. and Smith, A. 2013. Excavations at Gao-Saney. *Journal of African Archaeology* 11: 9–37.

Clark, M.E. 2003. *Archaeological Investigations at the Jenné-jeno Settlement Complex, Inland Niger Delta, Mali, West Africa*. Unpublished PhD thesis, Southern Methodist University.

Creekmore, A. and Fisher, K.D. (eds). 2014. *Making Ancient Cities: Space and Place in Early Urban Societies*. Cambridge: Cambridge University Press.

Crumley, C.L. 1995. Heterarchy and the analysis of complex societies. In R.M. Ehrenreich, C.L. Crumley and J.E. Levy (eds), *Heterarchy and the Analysis of Complex Societies*. Archaeological Papers of the American Anthropological Association 6.1: 1–6.

Czerniewicz, M. von. 2004. L'évolution de la décoration et de la forme des céramiques pendant l'Age du Fer au Nord du Burkina Faso. *Préhistoire Anthropologie Méditerranéennes* 13: 127–32.

Deme, A. 2003. *Archaeological Investigation of Settlement Evolution and Emerging Complexity in the Middle Senegal Valley*. Unpublished PhD thesis, Rice University.

Deme, A. and McIntosh, S. 2006. Excavations at Walaldé: New light on the settlement of the Middle Senegal Valley by iron-using peoples. *Journal of African Archaeology* 4.2: 317–47.

Devisse, J. 1988. Trade and trade routes in West Africa. In *UNESCO General History of Africa III: Africa from the Seventh to the Eleventh Century*. Oxford: Heinemann, 367–435.

Dowler, A. and Galvin, E.R. (eds). 2011. *Money, Trade and Trade Routes in Pre-Islamic North Africa*. London: British Museum Press.

Dueppen, S. 2011. Early evidence for chickens at Iron Age Kirikongo, Burkina Faso. *Antiquity* 85: 142–57.

Dussubieux, L. 2011. LA-ICP-MS Analysis of glass beads from Gao-Saney. In Cissé 2011, Appendix III.1.

Fauvelle-Aymar, F.-X. 2016. Why and how did most African Islamic sites disappear in the 15th century? Paper presented at the workshop 'Did the Plague impact sub-Saharan Africa before 1899?' 22 April 2016, College of William and Mary.

Fenn, T. 2011. Preliminary report: lead istopic ratio analysis of copper objects excavated from Gao Saney. In Cissé 2011, 334–49

Fenn, T. and Killick, D. 2003. Metallurgical report on Walaldé copper. In Deme 2003, Appendix C3.

Fenn, T. and Killick, D. 2016. Copper alloys. In McIntosh, R. *et al.* 2016, 281–98.

Fenn, T., Killick, D., Chesley, J. and Ruiz, J. 2009. Contact between West Africa and Roman North Africa: Archaeometallurgical results from Kissi, northeastern Burkina Faso. In Magnavita *et al.* 2009, 119–46.

Fleisher, J. and Wynne-Jones, S. 2010. Authorisation and the process of power: The view from African archaeology. *Journal of World Prehistory* 23.4: 177–93.

Fletcher, R. 2009. Low-density, agrarian-based urbanism: A comparative view. *Insights (University of Durham)* 2.4: 2–19.

Garenne-Marot, L. 1993. *Archéologie d'un métal: Le cuivre en Sénégambie (Afrique de l'Ouest) entre le Xe et le XIVe siècle* [thèse nouveau régime, Paris 1], 2 vols. Paris: Université de Paris I Pantheon-Sorbonne, UER d'Histoire.

Garenne-Marot, L., Wayman, M. and Piggott, V. 1994. Early copper and brass in Senegal. In S. Terry Childs (ed.), *Society, Culture, and Technology in Africa*,

MASCA Research Papers in Science and Archaeology. Philadelphia: University of Pennsylvania Museum of Archaeology and Anthropology, 45–62.
Gatto, M.C. 2006. The local pottery. In Liverani 2006, 201–40.
Gestrich, N. 2013. *The Archaeology of Social Organisation at Tongo Maaré Diabal.* Unpublished PhD thesis, University College London, Institute of Archaeology.
Giachet, M.T., Gratuze, B., Ozainne, S., Mayor, A. and Huysecom, E. 2019. A Phoenician glass eye bead from 7th–5th c. cal BCE Nin-Béré 3, Mali: Compositional characterisation by LA–ICP–MS. *Journal of Archaeological Science: Reports* 24: 748–58.
Grébénart, D. 1985. *Le néolithique final et les débuts de la métallurgie. La région d'In Gall – Tegidda N Tesemt (Niger).* Etudes Nigeriennes no. 49. Niamey: Institut de Recherches en Sciences Humaines.
Hanebuth, T. and Henrich, R. 2009. Recurrent decadal-scale dust events over Holocene western Africa and their control on canyon turbidite activity (Mauritania). *Quaternary Science Reviews* 28: 261–70.
Haour, A. 2005. Power and permanence in precolonial Africa: A case study from the central Sahel. *World Archaeology* 37.4: 552–65.
Haskell, H., McIntosh, R.J. and McIntosh, S.K. 1988. *Archaeological Reconnaissance in the Region of Dia, Mali.* Final report to the National Geographic Society, Washington DC.
Hatté, C., Saliège, J.-F., Senasson, D. and Bocoum, H. 2010. Cultural and trade practices in Sincu Bara (Senegal): A multi-proxy investigation. *Journal of Archaeological Science* 37: 561–68.
Hunwick, J.O. 1980. Gao and the Almoravids: A hypothesis. In B. Swartz and R. Dumett (eds), *West African Cultural Dynamics: Archaeological and Historical Perspectives.* The Hague: Mouton, 413–30.
Hunwick, J.O. 1994. Gao and the Almoravids revisited: Ethnicity, political change and the limits of interpretation. *Journal of African History* 35.2: 251–73.
Hunwick, J.O. 1999. *Timbuktu and the Songhay Empire: Al-Sa'di's Tarikh al-Sudan down to 1613 and other Contemporary Documents.* Leiden: Brill.
Insoll, T. 2000a. The origins of Timbuktu. *Antiquity* 74: 483–84.
Insoll, T. 2000b. *Urbanism, Archaeology and Trade: Further Observations on the Gao Region (Mali), the 1996 Field Season Results.* Oxford: British Archaeological Reports Ltd.
Insoll, T. 1996. *Islam, Archaeology and History: Gao Region (Mali) ca. AD 900–1250.* Oxford: Tempus Reparatum.
Insoll, T. and Shaw, C.T. 1997. Gao and Igbo-Ukwu: Beads, interregional trade, and beyond. *African Archaeological Review* 14.1: 9–24.
Jodin, A. 1966. Bijoux et amulettes du Maroc Punique. *Bulletin d'Archéologie Marocaine* 6: 55–90.
Killick, D. 2016. Iron working in the Middle Senegal Valley. In McIntosh, R. *et al.* 2016, 191–280.

Killick, D. 2003. Examination of archaeological samples from Djenné, Mali. In Clark 2003, 415–25.

Kusimba, C. 2008. Early African cities: Their role in the shaping of urban and rural interaction spheres. In J. Marcus and J. Sabloff (eds), *The Ancient City: New Perspectives on Urbanism in the Old and the New World.* Santa Fe: School for Advanced Research Press, 229–46.

Lambert, N. 1971. Les industries sur cuivre dans l'ouest Saharien. *West African Journal of Archaeology* 1: 9–21.

Lambert, N. 1972. Objets en cuivre et néolithique de Mauritanie occidentale. In H.J. Hugot (ed.), *Actes de 6e session congrès panafricain de préhistoire, Dakar 1967. Pan-African Congress on Prehistory and Quaternary Studies, 1967, Dakar, Senegal.* Chambéry: Les Imprimeries Réunies de Chambéry, 159–74.

Lambert, N. 1975. Mines et métallurgie antiques dans la région d'Akjoujt. *Annales de l'Institut Mauritanien de Recherche Scientifique* 1: 6–24.

Lambert, N. 1983. Nouvelle contribution à l'étude du Chalcolithique de Mauritanie. In N. Echard (ed.), *Métallurgies africaines: Nouvelles contributions.* Paris: Mémoires de la Société des Africanistes 9, 63–87.

Lekson, S. 2018. *A Study of Southwestern Archaeology.* Salt Lake City: The University of Utah Press.

Levtzion, N. and Hopkins, J.F.P. 1981. *Corpus of Early Arabic Sources for West African History.* Cambridge: Cambridge University Press.

Liverani, M. 2000. Looking for the southern frontier of the Garamantes. *Sahara* 12: 31–44.

Liverani, M. (ed.). 2006. *Aghram Nadharif: The Barkat Oasis (Sha'abiya of Ghat, Libyan Sahara) in Garamantian Times*, Arid Zone Archaeology Monographs 5. Florence: All'Insegna del Giglio.

MacDonald, K.C. 1998. More forgotten tells of Mali. *Archaeology International* 1: 40–42.

MacDonald, K.C. and MacDonald, R.H. 2016. Mammalian, avian and reptilian remains. In McIntosh, R. *et al.* 2016, 311–34.

Magnavita, S. 2003. The beads of Kissi, Burkina Faso. *Journal of African Archaeology* 1.1: 127–38.

Magnavita, S. 2013. Initial encounters: Seeking traces of ancient trade connections between West Africa and the wider world. *Afriques: débats, methods, et terrains d'histoire* 4. Available at: http://afriques.revues.org/1145 [last accessed 15 September, 2015].

Magnavita, S. 2015. *1500 Jahre am Mare de Kissi: Eine Fallstudie zur Besiedlungsgeschichte des Sahel von Burkina Faso.* Frankfurt: Africa Magna Verlag.

Magnavita, S., Maga, A., Magnavita, C. and Idé, O.A. 2007. New studies on Marandet (central Niger) and its trade connections: An interim report. *Zeitschrift für Archäologie Außereuropäischer Kulturen* 2: 147–65.

Magnavita, S., Kolé, L., Breunig, P. and Idé, O.A. (eds.). 2009. *Crossroads Carrrefour/ Sahel. Cultural and Technological Developments in the First Millennium BC/AD West Africa*. Frankfurt: Africa Magna Verlag.

Maley, J. 2010. Climate and palaeoenvironment evolution in north tropical Africa from the end of the Tertiary to the Upper Quaternary. *Palaeoecology of Africa* 30: 227–78.

Maley, J. and Vernet, R. 2015. Populations and climatic evolution in north tropical Africa from the end of the Neolithic to the dawn of the modern era. *African Archaeological Review* 32.2: 179–232.

Manyanga, M., Pikirayi, I. and Chirikure, S. 2010. Conceptualising the urban mind in pre-European Southern Africa: Rethinking Mapungubwe and Great Zimbabwe. In P.J. Sinclair, G. Nordquist, F. Herschend and C. Isendahl (eds), *The Urban Mind: Cultural and Environmental Dynamics*. Uppsala Studies in Global Archaeology 15. Uppsala: Uppsala University, 573–90.

Mattingly, D.J. (ed.). 2003. *Archaeology of Fazzan, Volume 1, Synthesis*. London: Society for Libyan Studies.

Mattingly, D.J. (ed.). 2013. *Archaeology of Fazzan, Volume 4, Survey and Excavations at Old Jarma*. London: Society for Libyan Studies.

Mattingly, D.J., Leitch, V., Duckworth, C.N., Cuénod, A., Sterry, M. and Cole, F. (eds). 2017. *Trade in the Ancient Sahara and Beyond*. Trans-Saharan Archaeology Volume I. Series editor D.J. Mattingly. Cambridge: Cambridge University Press and The Society for Libyan Studies.

McDougall, E.A. 1990. Salts of the Western Sahara: Myths, mysteries, and historical significance. *International Journal of African Historical Studies* 23.2: 231–57.

McIntosh, R.J. 1991. Early urban clusters in China and Africa: The arbitration of social ambiguity. *Journal of Field Archaeology* 18: 199–212.

McIntosh, R.J. 1993. The pulse model: Genesis and accommodation of specialization in the Middle Niger. *The Journal of African History* 34.2: 181–220.

McIntosh, R.J. 1998. *The Peoples of the Middle Niger: Island of Gold*. Oxford: Blackwell.

McIntosh, R.J. 2005. *Ancient Middle Niger: Urbanism and the Self-Organizing Landscape*. Cambridge: Cambridge University Press.

McIntosh, R.J. 2015. Different cities: Jenne-jeno and African urbanism. In *The Cambridge World History: Volume 3, Early Cities in Comparative Perspective, 4000 BCE–1200 CE*. Cambridge: Cambridge University Press, 364–80.

McIntosh, R.J. and McIntosh, S.K. 1981. The Inland Niger Delta before the Empire of Mali: Evidence from Jenne-jeno. *Journal of African History* 22: 1–22.

McIntosh, R.J. and McIntosh, S.K. 1987. Prospection archéologique aux alentours de Dia, Mali 1986–1987. *Nyame Akuma* 29: 42–45.

McIntosh, R.J., McIntosh, S.K. and Bocoum, H. (eds). 2016. *The Search for Takrur: Archaeological Excavations and Reconnaissance along the Middle Senegal Valley*. New Haven: Yale University Publications in Anthropology.

McIntosh, S.K. (ed.). 1995. *Excavations at Jenne-jeno, Hambarketolo and Kaniana (Inland Niger Delta, Mali): The 1981 Season*. University of California Monographs in Anthropology. Berkeley: University of California Press.

McIntosh, S.K. 1999a. *Beyond Chiefdoms: Pathways to Complexity in Africa*. Cambridge: Cambridge University Press.

McIntosh, S.K 1999b. Modeling political organization in large-scale settlement clusters: A case study from the Inland Niger Delta. In McIntosh 1999a, 66–79.

McIntosh, S.K. 2016. The Cubalel and Siwré pottery assemblages. In McIntosh, R. *et al*. 2016, 117–73.

McIntosh, S.K. 2017. The Akumbu mound complex (Méma, Republic of Mali): Ceramics, change, and continuity in the first millennium AD. In N. Rupp, C. Beck, G. Franke, and K.P. Wendt (eds), *Winds of Change: Festschrift for Peter Breunig*. Frankfurt am Main: Afrika Magna Verlag, 193–204.

McIntosh, S.K. 2018. Surplus and complexity in the inland Niger Delta, Mali: The invisibility conundrum. In H. Meller, and R. Risch (eds), *Surplus without the State: Political Forms in Prehistory*. Halle: Tagungen des Landesmuseums für Vorgeschichte Halle Band 18, 373–86.

McIntosh, S.K. and Bocoum, H. 2000. New perspectives on Sincu Bara, a first millennium site in the Senegal Valley. *African Archaeological Review* 77.1: 124–78.

McIntosh, S.K. and McIntosh, R.J. 1980. *Prehistoric Investigations in the Region of Jenne, Mali: A Study in the Development of Urbanism in the Sahel*. Cambridge Monographs in African Archaeology 2, 2 vols. Oxford: British Archaeological Reports.

McIntosh, S.K. and McIntosh, R.J. 1986. Archaeological reconnaissance in the region of Timbuktu, Mali. *National Geographic Research* 2: 302–19.

McIntosh, S.K. and McIntosh, R.J. 1993. Cities without citadels: Understanding urban origins along the middle Niger. In T. Shaw, P. Sinclair, B. Andah, and A. Okpoku (eds), *The Archaeology of Africa: Food, Metals and Towns*. London: Routledge, 622–41.

McIntosh, S.K., McIntosh R.J. and Bocoum, H. 1992. The Middle Senegal Valley Project: Preliminary results from the 1990–91 field season. *Nyame Akuma* 38: 47–61.

Michel, P. 1973. *Les basins des fleuves Sénégal et Gambie: Étude géomorphologique*. Paris: Mémoire de l'ORSTOM, 63.

Monteillet, J., Faure, H., Pirazzoli, P. and Ravisé, A. 1981. L'invasion saline du Ferlo (Sénégal) à l'Holocène supérieure (1900 B.P.). In J.A. Coetzee and E.M. van Zinderen Bakker (eds), *Palaeoecology of Africa and the Surrounding Islands*, Volume 13. Rotterdam: A.A. Balkema, 205–15.

Murray, S.S. 2008. A report on charred botanical remains from Sincu Bara, a mid-first millennium AD Middle Senegal Valley site. *Nyame Akuma* 69: 56–63.

Murray, S.S. n.d. *Report on Charred Botanical Remains from Cubalel Sites and Siwré*. Unpublished report, Rice University Department of Anthropology.

Nixon, S. 2008. *The Archaeology of Early Islamic Cross-Saharan Trading Towns in West Africa: A Comparative View and Progressive Methodology from the Entrepot of Essouk-Tadmekka*. Unpublished PhD Thesis, University College London.

Nixon, S. 2009. Excavating Es-Souk–Tadmakka (Mali): New archaeological investigations of early Islamic trans-Saharan trade. *Azania: Archaeological Research in Africa* 44.2: 217–55.

Nixon, S. (ed.). 2017. *Essouk-Tadmekka: An Early Islamic Trans-Saharan Market Town*. Leiden: Brill.

Nizou, J., Hanebuth, T.J., Heslop, D., Schwenk, T., Palamenghi, L., Stuut, J.-B. and Henrich, R. 2010. Senegal river mud belt: A high-resolution archive of paleoclimatic change and coastal evolution. *Marine Geology* 278.1-4: 150–64.

Oka, R. and Kusimba, C. 2008. The archaeology of trading systems, part I: Towards a new trading synthesis. *Journal of Archaeological Research* 16.4: 339–95.

Park, D.P. 2010. Prehistoric Timbuktu and its hinterland. *Antiquity* 84: 1076–88.

Park, D.P. 2011. *Climate Change, Human Response and the Origins of Urbanism at Timbuktu*. Unpublished PhD thesis, Yale University.

Ponsich, M. 1967. *Nécropoles phéniciennes de la région de Tanger*. Tanger: Editions Marocaines.

Raimbault, M. and Sanogo, K., 1991. *Recherches archéologiques au Mali*. Paris: Editions Karthala.

Renfrew, C. 1975. Trade as action at a distance: Questions of integration and communication. In J.A. Sabloff and C.C. Lamberg-Karlovsky (eds), *Ancient Civilization and Trade*. Albuquerque: University of New Mexico Press, 3–59.

Robert-Chaleix, D. 1989. *Une concession médiévale à Tegdaoust: Implantation, evolution d'une unité d'habitation*. Paris: Editions Recherche sur les Civilisations.

Robert-Chaleix, D. 1991. Sel, coquillages et jarosite: À propos de la saline médiévale d'Awlil. *Journal des Africanistes* 61.2: 169–85.

Robert-Chaleix, D. 1994. Métallurgie du fer dans la Moyenne Vallée du Sénégal: Les bas fourneaux de Silla. *Journal des Africanistes* 64.2: 113–27.

Robert-Chaleix, D. and Sognane, M. 1983. Une industrie métallurgique ancienne sur la rive mauritanienne du Fleuve Sénégal. *In Métallurgies Africaines: Nouvelles contributions*. Paris: Mémoires de la Société des Africainistes 9: 45–62.

Robertshaw, P., Magnavita, S., Wood, M., Melchiorre, E., Popelka-Filcoff, R.S. and Glascock, M.D. 2009. Glass beads from Kissi (Burkina Faso): Chemical analysis and archaeological interpretation. In Magnavita *et al.* 2009, 105–18.

Robion-Brunner, C. 2010. *Forgerons et sidérurgie en pays dogon. Vers une histoire de la production du fer sur le plateau de Bandiagara (Mali) durant les empires précoloniaux*. Frankfurt: Africa Magna Verlag.

Schmidt, A., Sanogo, K. and Keita, D. 2005. Les fortifications. In Bedaux *et al.* 2005, 117–24.

Smith, M. 2006. Review of R.J. McIntosh, 'Ancient Middle Niger: the Self-Organizing Landscape'. *Journal of African Archaeology* 4.2: 357–59.

Stone, A.C. 2015. *Urban Herders: An Archaeological and Isotopic Investigation into the Roles of Mobility and Subsistence Specialization in an Iron Age Urban Center in Mali.* Unpublished PhD thesis, Washington University, Department of Anthropology.

Thiaw, I. 1999. *Archaeological Investigation of Long-Term Culture Change in the Lower Falemme (Upper Senegal Region): A.D. 500–1900.* Unpublished PhD thesis, Rice University.

Thilmans, G. 1977. Sur les objets de parure trouvés à Podor (Sénégal) en 1958. *Bulletin de l'Institut Fondamental d'Afrique Noire (BIFAN)* Series B 39.4: 669–94.

Thilmans, G. and Ravisé, A. 1980. *Protohistoire du Sénégal: Recherches archéologiques. Vol. 2, Sinthiou-Bara et les sites du fleuve.* Mémoires de l'Institut Fondamental d'Afrique Noire 91. Dakar: IFAN.

Togola, T. 1996. Iron Age occupation in the Méma region, Mali. *African Archaeological Review* 13.2: 91–110.

Togola, T. 2008. *Archaeological Investigations of Iron Age Sites in the Meme Region, Mali (West Africa).* Cambridge Monographs in African Archaeology no. 73. Oxford: B.A.R.

Trigger, B. 1972. Determinants of urban growth in pre-industrial societies. In P.J. Ucko, R. Tringham and G.W. Dimbleby (eds), *Man, Settlement and Urbanism.* London: Duckworth, 575–99.

Vanacker, C. 1979. *Tegdaoust II: Recherches sur Aoudaghost. Fouille d'un quartier artisinale.* Paris: ADPF.

Vernet, R. 1993. *Préhistoire de la Mauritanie.* Nouakchott: Centre culturel français A. de Saint-Exupéry, Sepia.

Vernet, R. 2000. Un habitat de l'âge du cuivre (2500 BP) de la région de Nouakchott (Mauritanie occidentale: Imbich-Est). *Sahara* 12: 83–90.

Vernet, R. 2004. L'archéologie sur la rive mauritanienne du fleuve Sénégal: Un chantier à ouvrir. *MASADIR: Cahiers des Sources de l'Histoire de la Mauritanie* 4: 21–31.

Vernet, R. 2012. Le Chalcolithique de Mauritanie (3000–2500 cal BP): État de la question. *Sahara* 23: 7–28.

Webb, J.L. 1995. *Desert Frontier: Ecological and Economic Change along the Western Sahel 1600–1850.* Madison: University of Wisconsin Press.

Wynne-Jones, S. and Fleisher, J.B. 2014. Swahili urban spaces of the eastern African coast. In Creekmore and Fisher, 2014: 111–44.

15 First Millennia BC/AD Fortified Settlements at Lake Chad

Implications for the Origins of Urbanisation and State Formation in Sub-Saharan Africa

CARLOS MAGNAVITA

Introduction

Between 2004 and 2009, a programme of ground-based geophysical surveying revealed a number of large ancient fortified settlements at the south-western margins of Lake Chad.[1] Dating to the first millennia BC/AD, these archaeological sites are amongst the oldest evidence for communal-level protection in Sub-Saharan Africa. On the one hand, settlement defences and dense populations, estimated in the low thousands, clearly indicate that security must have been a major concern for people living in the area at that time. On the other, these sites raise a series of questions that are fundamental for understanding the emergence of urban centres and state-level societies in the Lake Chad area and in Sub-Saharan Africa. This chapter introduces the archaeological evidence pertaining to those settlements and discusses their implications for the current debate on the origins of urbanisation and state formation in Sub-Saharan Africa.

The scholarly interest in the ancient city as an object of analysis mainly goes back to the early twentieth century.[2] In archaeology, the growing interest in the city as a unit of analysis came after V. Gordon Childe (in 1934) coined the term 'urban revolution' for highlighting what he regarded as one of the major socioeconomic turning-points in human history.[3] Beyond Childe's ideas, theory-backed systematic archaeological investigations of early urban settlements and the landscapes in which they are embedded are a relatively recent phenomenon rooted in the Processual

[1] The central goal of this chapter is to present and discuss archaeological data collected over a period of six years (2004–2009) in the scope of an archaeological research programme based at the Goethe-University Frankfurt and generously funded by the German Research Council (DFG).

[2] Most famously through Weber 1958. [3] Trigger 1989, 253–54.

Archaeology (New Archaeology) of the 1960s to 1970s.[4] Though much criticised from the 1980s onwards due to the often inflexible and one-dimensional neo-evolutionary approach used by many processualist researchers, the practical results of the archaeological work conducted on urban sites in the scope of that school of thought was of great scientific value. For the first time, there was indeed a major effort in revealing and understanding the origins and the function that cities played within a given archaeological landscape.[5]

Embracing a processual and landscape-wide archaeological research agenda, the origins and function of urban settlements likewise became central themes of archaeological research on Sub-Saharan African urbanisation in the late 1970s and early 1980s.[6] In fact, that research approach developed into a major paradigm change in the historiography of Sub-Saharan Africa. Departing from the traditional, document-based view that evoked a strong role for white North Africans and Near Eastern immigrants in the foundation of cities and states south of the Sahara, archaeological research in the 1980s began to show that at least the roots of Sub-Saharan urban life were much older and much more closely linked to local and regional socio-economic and political developments than earlier thought.[7] Likewise, rigid and universal definitions of what the ancient city *is* or what it must have looked like gave way to a more flexible definition that emphasised what a city *does*, that is, what do they provide in terms of specialised production and services for its hinterland.[8] In West Africa, the best studied archaeological instance demonstrating a gradual and indigenous process of settlement growth culminating in an ancient urban landscape comes from the hierarchical cluster of sites around Jenné-jeno in Mali.[9] However, there are at least three other, older, archaeological regional occurrences in West Africa that lend support to the indigenous roots and long-term development of urbanisation within Sub-Saharan Africa. The first is the hierarchical cluster of settlements at Dhar Tichitt (1600–1000 BC) in southern Mauritania.[10] The second is the hierarchical cluster of settlements in the Macina region of Mali, dated to *c.*900–400 BC.[11] The third is a number of, in part hierarchically organised, fortified settlement sites

4 See, for example, Sabloff 1994 for the Mayan case.
5 Compare Creekmore and Fisher 2014, 3.
6 McIntosh and McIntosh 1984.
7 See McIntosh, S., Chapter 14, this volume; McIntosh, S. and McIntosh R. 1984; 1993.
8 Cowgill 2004, 527; McIntosh, S. and McIntosh, R. 1993, 625; Trigger 1972, 577.
9 See McIntosh, S., Chapter 14, this volume; McIntosh, S. and McIntosh, R. 1993.
10 Holl 1993; MacDonald 2003; Munson 1980; see also MacDonald, Chapter 13, this volume.
11 Bedaux *et al.* 2001; 2005.

near Lake Chad in Nigeria, dated to the first millennia BC/AD.[12] This paper presents and discusses the archaeological evidence recovered at the latter sites and considers their implications for understanding the rise of urbanisation and state-level societies in the Lake Chad Basin and in Sub-Saharan Africa.

The Origins of Food Production and Settled Life in the Chad Basin: The Gajiganna Complex

The deepest foundations of urbanisation are clearly linked to food production. Urbanisation occurred as part of long-term processes set in train by the initial domestication of plants, but dependent also on the human capacity for developing techniques to intensify and diversify the production of food for a growing number of people. In the Lake Chad Basin, approximately 2,500 years elapsed between the beginnings of food production and the appearance of historically known urban communities in the southern margins of Lake Chad. Since the 1960s, the growing commitment to archaeological research around the Chad Basin has greatly expanded our knowledge of the cultural developments in the region. It is true that the archaeological data so far recovered are only mere snap-shots of those developments, and details about the processes leading from one point to the other are broadly unknown. Nevertheless, it can be acknowledged that we are now better informed about the cultural trajectories of the human groups that inhabited the Chad Basin in pre-historical times than we were 20 years ago.

In our present state of knowledge, the first food-producing communities that appeared in the Lake Chad region occupied the lake's south-western margins at the onset of the second millennium BC.[13] Archaeologically, those groups of people came to be known as the Gajiganna Complex (*c.*1800–400 BC) in view of their shared material culture, settlement patterns and other aspects.[14] At the beginning of this period, those groups seem to have been relatively mobile, since their archaeological remains are characterised by mere scatters of potsherds over some few square metres. At that stage (Gajiganna Phase I) their economy was mainly based on livestock-keeping but a minor contribution of (domesticated) plants cannot yet be ruled out. From *c.*1500 BC there are the first clues for a growing reliance on domesticated vegetal food compared to livestock farming. This change was gradually accompanied by a more settled way of life in hamlets

[12] Magnavita, C. *et al.* 2006; 2009. [13] Breunig and Neumann 2002. [14] Breunig *et al.* 1996.

and village-like communities with clay houses, the long-standing locations of which resulted in the formation of the first Gajiganna settlement mounds (Gajiganna Phase IIa/b). This settled way of life can be traced back until about 1000 BC. After that, and for about 400 years, the archaeological evidence merely suggests the presence of small Gajiganna human groups temporarily living in the area (Gajiganna Phase IIc). The reason(s) for the abandonment of their permanently settled living spots in the previous millennium is unclear, but there is the suspicion that environmental factors may have played the major role in this development. In fact, it is known that a vast, formerly year-round flooded area south of Lake Chad must have become seasonally dry from this time on, thus allowing the beginning of a possibly cyclic and, later on, permanent occupation by settled farmers.[15] This event may indicate a major change of rainfall patterns that led to an extensive period of drought in the Chad Basin and elsewhere. In view of the absence of climatic proxy data for the region, the explanation of a drastically changed environment remains tentative. Alternatives for understanding the abandonment of the Gajiganna settlement mounds have been offered recently,[16] but hard data that might support them has yet to be found.

However, the archaeological evidence reveals a revival of the settled way of life of Gajiganna groups in the area some centuries later, in the middle of the first millennium BC (Gajiganna Phase III, *c.*600–400 BC). Local faunal data indicates that this phase of occupation might coincide with a short humid period in the south-western Lake Chad region, which possibly explains the return to a fully settled way of life in the area.[17] Chronologically, this evidence correlates with an occupation hiatus recorded in the stratigraphies of a number of settlement mounds in the southern fringes of Lake Chad.[18] Characterised by a succession of sterile clay bands that formed within a period of 110–350 ^{14}C-years, this site abandonment event was originally thought to have resulted from a major transgression of Lake Chad with water levels rising to 290 m asl, that is, 3 m above *c.*1000 BC levels.[19] Though such a large lake oscillation is now regarded as improbable,[20] there are at least some indications that Gajiganna Phase III settlements might have emerged in an environmentally comparatively favourable phase in the middle of the first millennium BC.

15 Brunk and Gronenborn 2004, 108–9. 16 Breunig 2013, 562. 17 Breunig *et al.* 2006.
18 Gronenborn 1998, 250. 19 Brunk and Gronenborn 2004, 109; Gronenborn 1998, 250.
20 Brunk and Gronenborn 2004, 108–9.

Current regional proxy data indicate major millennial and centennial environmental trends for the Lake Chad Basin during the period discussed in this paper. For the time between *c.*1600 and 100 calBC, the data available point to a relatively drier environment compared to previous centuries and millennia.[21] Conversely, a trend to wetter conditions is attested for the period 100 calBC–calAD 500/700.[22] Though I recognise that those major environmental trends may have been a major factor in shaping the long-term dynamics of settlement foundation and abandonment at the Lake Chad margins, as referred to above, shorter-term environmental changes not detected by those studies also seem to have played a non-negligible role in those developments. Since regional environmental studies generally lack specific, reliable and finer-grained evidence of actual local environmental conditions, I will abstain from making any serious attempts at correlating particular cultural developments attested archaeologically with the environmental data available on a regional scale.

The following narrative is necessarily focused on three settlements, as they are presently the only substantial source of information related to the archaeological themes, time period and region discussed. Where it appears meaningful, other archaeological sites in the Chad Basin and elsewhere are mentioned for the sake of comparison.

First Millennium BC Fortified Settlements at Lake Chad

Altogether 14 Gajiganna Phase III sites are so far known at the southwestern margins of Lake Chad.[23] They all consist of flat sites with no, or just a minimal, succession of cultural deposits. This implies a relatively short period of occupation of each site that probably did not exceed two or three generations. The estimated and confirmed site sizes vary widely from 1 ha to about 12–14 ha (Fig. 15.1). Particularly interesting is the fact that the small to mid-sized sites are located as satellites of the two largest settlements known, Galgalkura A (12–14 ha) and Zilum (12–13 ha). In fact, the clustering indicates some kind of interrelation between settlements of different sizes. Though the Gajiganna Phase III sites are smaller than their counterparts in second-millennium BC Mauritania and first-millennium BC Mali, like those they display the very first regional evidence for a sort of trait that seems deeply connected with the rise of

[21] Holmes *et al.* 1997, 317. [22] Holmes *et al.* 1997, 317. [23] Magnavita, C. *et al.* 2006.

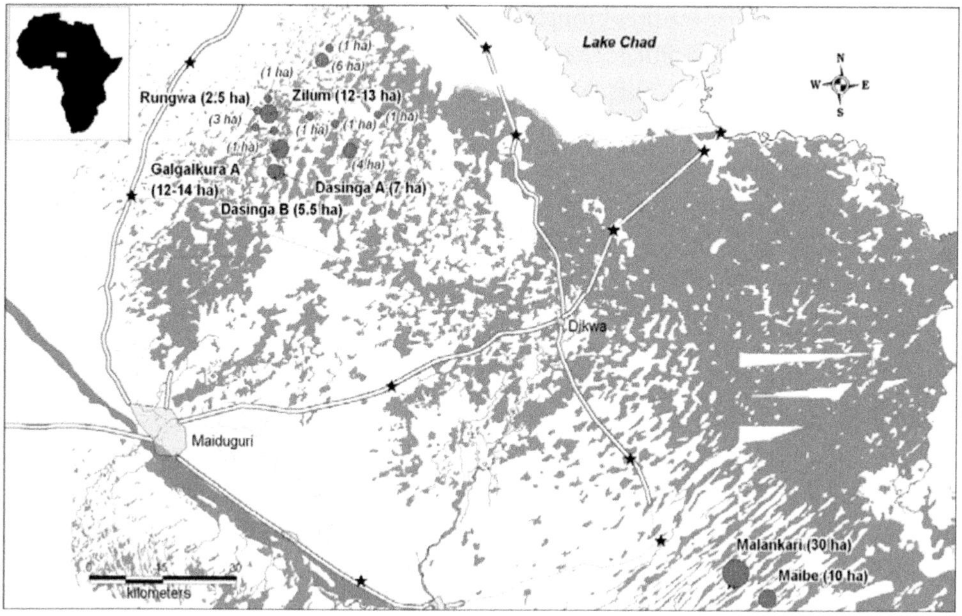

Figure 15.1. Map showing the location of sites discussed in the text.

West African urbanisation: site-size hierarchy or hierarchical settlement clustering (see discussion below).

In a sub-continental scale, the specific reasons and processes leading to the formation of early hierarchical settlement clusters may have greatly varied. In most cases, however, the developments were related to the deliberate foundation of smaller settlements near previously established larger ones, either by people from within the larger communities or by outsiders. At least in the particular case of the first millennium BC Gajiganna III sites, there is strong evidence suggesting that site-size hierarchy was triggered, or at least catalysed, by an increased need of security.

Zilum

Of the 14 Gajiganna Phase III sites known, the best yet investigated and published is Zilum. Research at that location comprised a geophysical survey, mapping and excavation programme carried out over three field seasons. Geophysical work was conducted using fluxgate gradiometry (magnetometry) and resulted in the mapping of the site's entire subsurface extent;[24] topographic surveys and plotting of specific find types and

[24] Magnavita, C. *et al.* 2006.

particular features brought about an idea of the distribution of craft-related tools and facilities. Excavations produced detailed insights into archaeological features that were related to the occupation at the site. Beyond confirming the total site area that had been previously identified by test pitting,[25] geophysical survey provided fundamental information that contributed to understanding the nature of Zilum. A large part of the flat site had its upper archaeological deposits reduced by erosion, thus exposing numerous finds' concentrations and archaeological features at the surface; geophysical survey was also able to detect and locate subsurface features that were not immediately discernible.[26]

Figure 15.2, the magnetometry plot of Zilum, shows the shape and extent of the site as well as the location of the numerous subsurface features (magnetic anomalies) detected and related to past human activity at the settlement. The most frequent kind of magnetic anomaly is dot-like in shape. They mainly represent the location of pits sunk into the ground during the time the settlement was occupied and are scattered all over the site extent. Their relatively high density and distribution across the site indicates both the area of the site which was settled in the past and, likewise, how nucleated Zilum was, since virtually no vacant space existed within the settlement. Other features visible from the magnetogram are areas within the settlement that were once enclosed by fences or earthen walls, thus implying the former existence of residential compounds. This interpretation is supported by the find of a series of anomaly-free circular spaces with diameters of up to 5 m and surrounded by pits; this strongly suggests that these were the location of former round houses (Fig. 15.2). Though excavations carried out at the site did not locate a single post hole, finds of burnt daub with impressions of wattle indicate the main construction technique of residential structures.[27] Perhaps the most surprising and, likewise, most revealing subsurface feature detected by geophysical work at Zilum was a number of peripheral ditches that once enclosed large portions of the site. Though magnetometry was able to detect long segments of those features, some sectors remain barely discernible (Fig. 15.2). However, there is little doubt that the segments are parts of continuous ditch features that once surrounded the site at different times. At least three phases of construction and expansion of the surrounding ditch are discernible at Zilum, which hints at an increase of the settlement size over time. While direct evidence of a superstructure in the form of an earthen rampart or wall is no longer visible, there is strong geophysical support for the former existence

[25] Magnavita, C. 2008, 49. [26] Magnavita, C. *et al.* 2006. [27] Magnavita, C. 2008, 32.

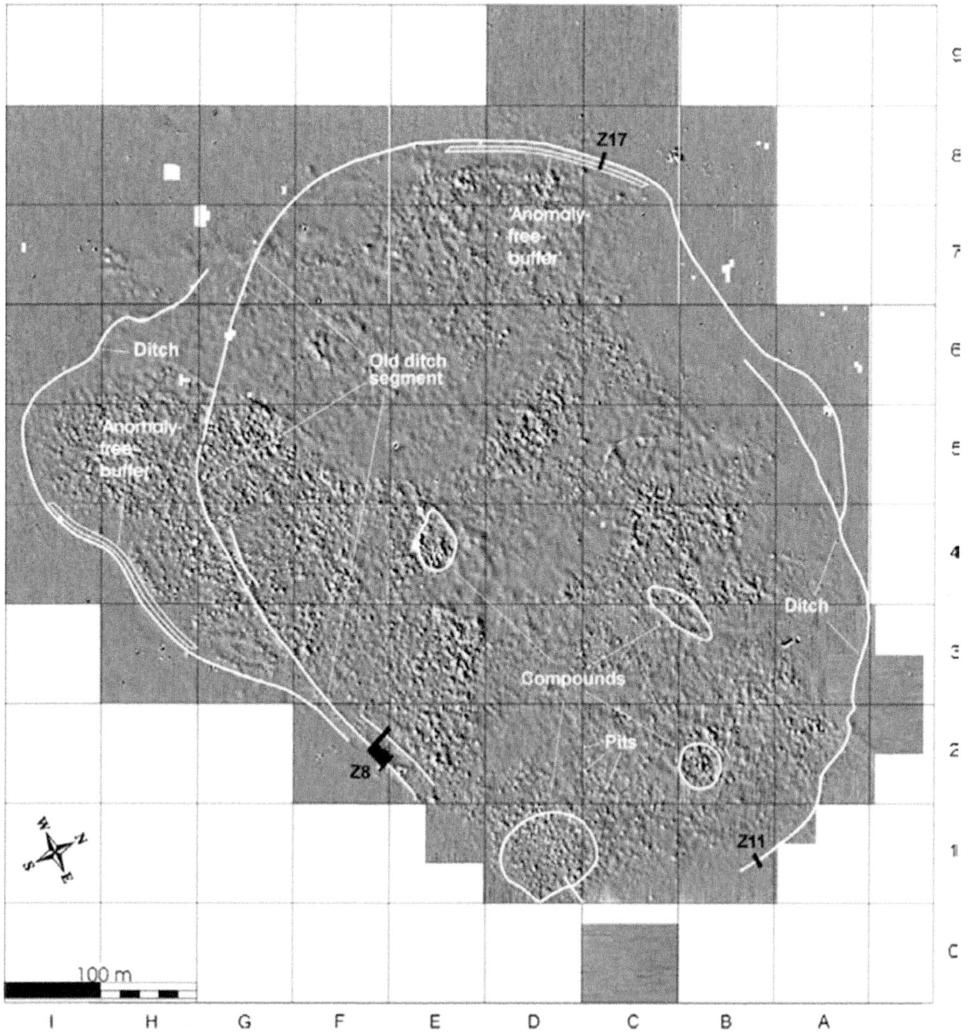

Figure 15.2. Magnetogram of Zilum, with indication of features discussed.

of such a construction. Evidence for this is the presence of elongated anomaly-free areas adjacent to some ditch segments (Fig. 15.2) that hints at the location of such a structure. Excavations of the enclosing ditch conducted at three different sectors of the site, reveal that its shape and dimensions were not uniform throughout.[28] With a U-shape and a volume of only about 3 m^3/1 m section, the ditch was smaller in the south sector than at the east and north sectors, where it had a V-profile and volumes of *c.*7 m^3 and 8–10 m^3/1 m section. Altogether, the evidence collected at

[28] Magnavita, C. *et al.* 2006.

Zilum suggests the construction of a sizeable earthen rampart or wall behind the ditch. In tandem, the ditch and rampart/wall must have worked as a real obstacle that protected the settlement and its inhabitants from external threat, whether robbery or armed attacks. Meanwhile, the existence of former ditch-wall systems are attested at each of the five Gajiganna Phase III settlements investigated by geophysical prospection in the past years. In at least one further case, anomaly-free areas along an enclosing ditch support the existence of now decayed earthen walls. The results of that work are about to be published, but they fully agree with the view that at least some of the food-producing communities living at Lake Chad in the first millennium BC did seek protection by erecting earthen walls.

Beyond walls, another strategy for coping with insecurity (felt or real) caused by external threat was nucleation and aggregation. The results of geophysical surveys at Zilum demonstrate how frequent the settlement ground was transformed by repeated digging activities, ultimately demonstrating the nucleated nature of the settlement. They also provide evidence that can be used to calculate the number of people living in Zilum at the time the settlement achieved its maximum size. Based on the area and number of houses within a particular residential compound in the south-eastern part of Zilum, it was estimated that the whole settlement once had between about 1,750 and 2,500 inhabitants or *c.* 140–210 people/hectare.[29] Since large human groups are, due to their sheer size, relatively stronger than smaller ones and in a better position to defend themselves, it is not surprising to see a trend towards large and relatively dense populated settlements as in the case of Zilum. In the same line of reasoning, the need of security also explains why smaller settlements tended to aggregate near larger ones, thus producing the familiar picture of a hierarchical settlement system.

In addition to the benefits of security, a secondary effect of nucleation and aggregation of human groups at Zilum pertains to an apparent change in socio-economic relations within and, potentially, between communities. To judge from the lack of evidence, neither metal tools nor any form of metallurgy was known by the inhabitants of Zilum. Whilst they were mainly farmers growing pearl millet and cowpeas, raising cattle, sheep and goats, they also did some hunting and fishing.[30] There is archaeological evidence for craft production on the site that hints at some occupational differentiation. The mapping of craft-related artefacts and features at

[29] Magnavita, C. 2004, 87. [30] Linseele 2007; Magnavita, C. *et al.* 2004.

Zilum resulted in the discovery that pottery (at least certain forms such as large storage vessels), stone beads or bone points and, possibly, leather were produced in distinct parts of the site by different people.[31] Given the relatively large residential population of the settlement, it seems indeed probable that at least some items (whose production required enhanced skills or special knowledge) became the domains of (part-time) specialists. In view of Zilum's relatively large population and, therefore, the relatively high demand for certain products, it is reasonable to think at least of a seasonal (dry-season) occupational differentiation of people. Inevitably, demand for certain products from nearby settlements may have formed the basis for economic relations beyond an exchange of natural produce. Although inter-community exchange remains archaeologically elusive, the archaeological evidence of nucleation and aggregation around Zilum may be seen as an instance of how the initial stages of socio-economic and occupational differentiation took place in Sub-Saharan Africa.

Apart from the regional procurement of stones for domestic use in the Mandara Mountains and Biu Plateau,[32] very little evidence from Zilum and contemporary sites hints at long-distance contacts. In fact, the only finds that might have any significance in this regard are two polished lip-plugs made of amazonite, one of them fragmented.[33] The origin of the rocks used in their manufacture is unknown, but regional (potentially, the Mandara Mountains *c.*140 km away or the Biu Plateau *c.*190 km away) or Saharan sources (Air Mountains *c.*900 km away, Tibesti *c.*1600 km away) are conceivable options.

Zilum and adjacent sites are the earliest walled settlements currently known in the Chad Basin. Whilst similarly large or even larger settlements (10–30 ha) are known to have existed *c.*120 km further south (Maibe and Malankari), they consist of rather dispersed non-walled locations.[34] Along with Zilum, only two other West African fortified sites are dated to the last two millennia BC: Akrejit in Mauretania and In Begouen in Mali, are known to have been enclosed by, respectively, stone walling and wooden palisades.[35] Instead, most of the archaeologically known enclosed settlements in Sub-Saharan Africa date from the last thousand years,[36] but a number of them such as Jenné-jeno in Mali and Namudu in Sudan as well as Zubo and Dorota, both in Nigeria, date to the first millennium AD.[37] As is shown by the fieldwork at Zilum and

[31] Magnavita, C. 2004; 2008, 121–25; Magnavita, C. *et al.* 2006. [32] Rupp 2005.
[33] Magnavita, C. and Breunig 2008. [34] Breunig 2009, 18.
[35] Gaussen and Gaussen 1988, 202; Holl 1993, 111. [36] Connah 2000, 21.
[37] McIntosh, S. and McIntosh, R. 1984, 91; Mohammed 1986, 185–86.

the other archaeological sites described below, it can be supposed that the comparatively low number of as yet known first millennia BC/AD Sub-Saharan enclosed settlements is probably the result of the poor archaeological visibility of enclosures rather than their general absence.

First Millennium AD Fortified Settlements at Lake Chad

Following the abandonment of the fortified Gajiganna III sites (*c.*600–400 BC), no archaeological evidence hinting at a settled way of life is known at the south-western margins of Lake Chad for the next four to five centuries. Whilst permanent community life is attested in the southern margins of Lake Chad (in Nigeria, Cameroon and Chad) by the rise of settlement mounds in the second half of the first millennium BC,[38] the former Gajiganna area appears to have been virtually deserted. Environmental constraints may explain the abandonment of the area for several centuries, but there is as yet no (climatic) proxy data that might support such a claim. This situation changed dramatically around the beginning of the first millennium AD when people with a pottery tradition distinct from that of the former Gajiganna population enter the stage. It is unknown from whence they originated, but some decorative elements of their pots are not dissimilar to ceramics from the southern margins of Lake Chad.[39]

Several dozens of sites connected to the novel pottery tradition are known from the former Gajiganna area (Fig. 15.3). Their sizes range from 1 ha to almost 50 ha and, unlike Gajiganna III sites, they all consist of low settlement mounds. Preliminary test excavations and analysis of the archaeological remains recovered from four of those sites provided first insights into their chronology and the economy practised by the former residents. Nine radiocarbon dates place their rise and development into the time between the first and the early seventh centuries AD.[40] As in the case of Gajiganna Phase III settlements, the inhabitants of the sites were mainly farmers who grew pearl millet and cowpeas, but a new sort of cultivar is also attested in the period: sorghum.[41] Domestic animals were by far the most important source of protein, with hunting and fishing playing secondary roles in the economy.[42] Compared to Gajiganna III settlements, however, ovicaprines grew in

[38] Connah 1981; Gronenborn 1998; Holl 2002. [39] Magnavita, C. *et al.* 2009.
[40] Magnavita, C. *et al.* 2009, table 1. [41] Magnavita, C. 2002; Magnavita, C. *et al.* 2009.
[42] Linseele 2007, 97 and figures 35–36.

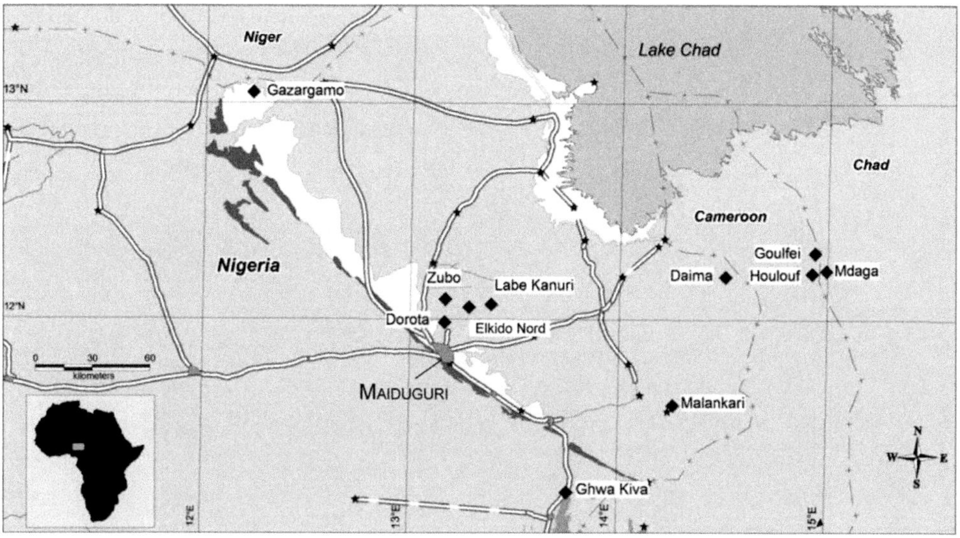

Figure 15.3. Map showing the location of Iron Age sites in the Gajiganna area.

economic importance relative to cattle, a fact thought to be a strategic adaptation to a drier environment during the first millennium AD.[43] Unlike at Zilum, the inhabitants of the first-millennium AD sites used and produced iron artefacts in or near their settlements, although the required iron in the form of blooms, bars or objects must have been brought from somewhere else. The nearest source of iron ore is the plains around the Mandara Mountains (*c.*100 km away), where evidence from iron working dates to as early as the mid-first millennium BC.[44] The Mandara Mountains are also the main rock source for the grinding stones used in the settlements of the period.[45]

Zubo and Dorota

The two largest sites known in the area (Zubo and Dorota) were the focus of intensive geophysical survey and subsequent archaeological work by the author between 2007 and 2009. The younger of the two sites, Dorota, dated to the second to sixth centuries AD, is the best investigated. It is located *c.*40 km south-west of Zilum. The outcome of topographical and geophysical mapping (employing fluxgate gradiometry) indicates that the settlement had a maximum size of *c.*33.5 ha.[46] The geophysical plan of the site (Fig. 15.4) displays a myriad of magnetic anomalies within the settlement

[43] Linseele 2007, 147, table 14, figure 49. [44] MacEachern 1996. [45] Rupp 2005.
[46] Magnavita, C. *et al.* 2009.

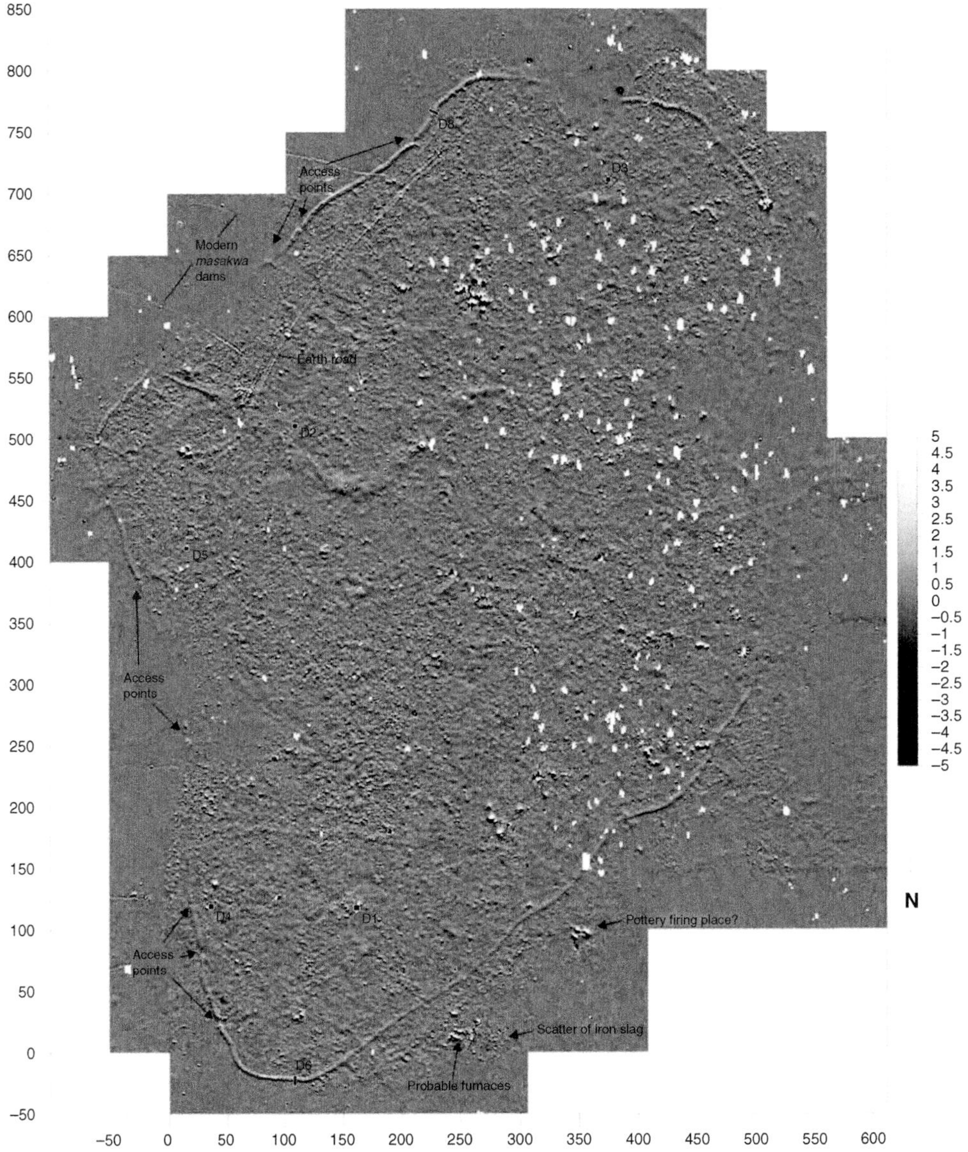

Figure 15.4. Geophysical survey of Dorota.

area, revealing both intensive digging activities and the presence of major subsurface archaeological features. The most obvious of these is an elongated magnetic anomaly situated along the edges of the mound. As in the case of Zilum and other Gajiganna Phase III sites, the elongated anomaly is interpreted as being a peripheral ditch, potentially associated with a now decayed earthen wall or rampart. With a total length of about 2,200 m, it marks the limits of the main settlement area. While the anomaly is discernible for several hundred metres along the site's fringes, the magnetic contrast between the feature and the surrounding sediment is in places so low that the ditch seems to be non-existent. This, however, is not the case. A closer look at the image shows that it is an almost continuous feature, only interrupted by a series of anomaly-free passages that were probably access points to the settlement (Fig. 15.4). Two archaeological sondages that sectioned the ditch at different locations provided information on its dimensions and shape. The first sondage (D6), set at the northernmost margin of the site, revealed that the ditch was a V-shaped feature with a maximum width of about 4 m and a depth of at least 1.9 m. The second sondage (D8) at the south-eastern limits of the site showed that the ditch was likewise V-shaped, but a bit smaller than at sondage D6, being about 3 m wide and 1.4–1.6 m deep. Altogether, a volume of earth *c.*2.1–3.8 m^3/1 m section was once quarried from Dorota's ditch. These figures are somewhat smaller than those calculated for Zilum and Zubo (see below). Though it is suggested that a substantial earthen rampart or wall was once associated with the ditch in the past, there is no clear geophysical evidence for its presence at Dorota. As Figure 15.4 shows, there are no anomaly-free areas along the interior border of the ditch, which should be the area where such a structure once stood. A probable explanation for this relates to the chronology of the ditch digging. Extensive zones at the edges of the site, especially at the northern, western and southern portions, have the same pattern of magnetic anomalies as those visible within the enclosure. The location of those anomalies suggests that the settlement once comprised areas beyond the ditch, which appears to be a secondary construction. In this respect, a closer look at the magnetic plan reveals that the ditch was quarried after the pits in the vicinity of the ditch were dug. This strongly suggests that the ditch was only built some years after the settlement attained its maximum extent.

Apart from their chronological implications, the enormous number and density of the dot-like anomalies that are interpreted as pits within the settlement area demonstrate the intensive use of Dorota's inner space for activities possibly related to food storage, building and other human actions such as burying the dead and disposing of domestic refuse. Their distribution likewise points to the nucleated character of the settlement. In fact, virtually no open space is left within the area enclosed by the ditch, suggesting that people must have lived closely together within the settlement. Unlike at Zilum, the longer occupation and the repeated digging of

Dorota's cultural deposits hinder the identification of the location of former houses and living areas in the magnetic plan. This in turn precludes calculating the size of Dorota's population directly from on-site evidence. If, however, the population density of first-millennium BC Zilum (140–210 persons per ha) is taken as a measure for estimating the number of people living at Dorota,[47] a figure of 4,700–7,000 people seems a realistic approximation, especially if compared with those for historically known settlements with similar physical characteristics (see discussion below).

The analysis of the magnetic plan and an inspection of the terrain suggest that some craft activities like iron working and the firing of pottery may have taken place outside the area confined by the ditch (see Fig. 15.4). Unlike at Zilum, no evidence of occupational differentiation could be discerned in the few excavations carried out at Dorota, but it is hardly imaginable that a settlement with a population numbering in the low thousands would lack people working as specialists, at least in a part-time or seasonal manner.

The second settlement, Zubo, is dated to the first to third century AD. Located *c.*10 km north of Dorota, the site consists of a sizeable, low mound widely surrounded by clay depressions. Research at Zubo involved extensive geophysical and topographical surveys and a test-excavation. The geophysical survey encompassed a total area of 41.5 ha and provided information on the location of the major archaeological features as well as the size and shape of the settlement, though *c.*12.5 ha at its centre remains unexplored. The geophysical plan (Fig. 15.5) shows an overview of the site's subsurface extent. As at Dorota, the most conspicuous magnetic anomaly is a long subsurface archaeological feature that roughly marked the site's limits. Identified as a ditch, this feature has a total length of around 2,600 m and enclosed an area of about 46 ha. It is interrupted by a small number of breaches, probably access points, particularly at the settlement's south-eastern limits. Another similar anomaly, with an estimated length of 1,300 m, is visible in the north-western central part of Zubo. Encompassing a smaller area of the site (approximately 18 ha), it partly runs parallel to the peripheral feature, joining the latter at two distinct points along the settlement's western and northern sides. The smaller ditch was obviously constructed sometime after the larger one, and as in the case of Dorota, both ditches seem to have been dug after a large part of the settlement had reached its

[47] Magnavita, C. *et al.* 2009, 51.

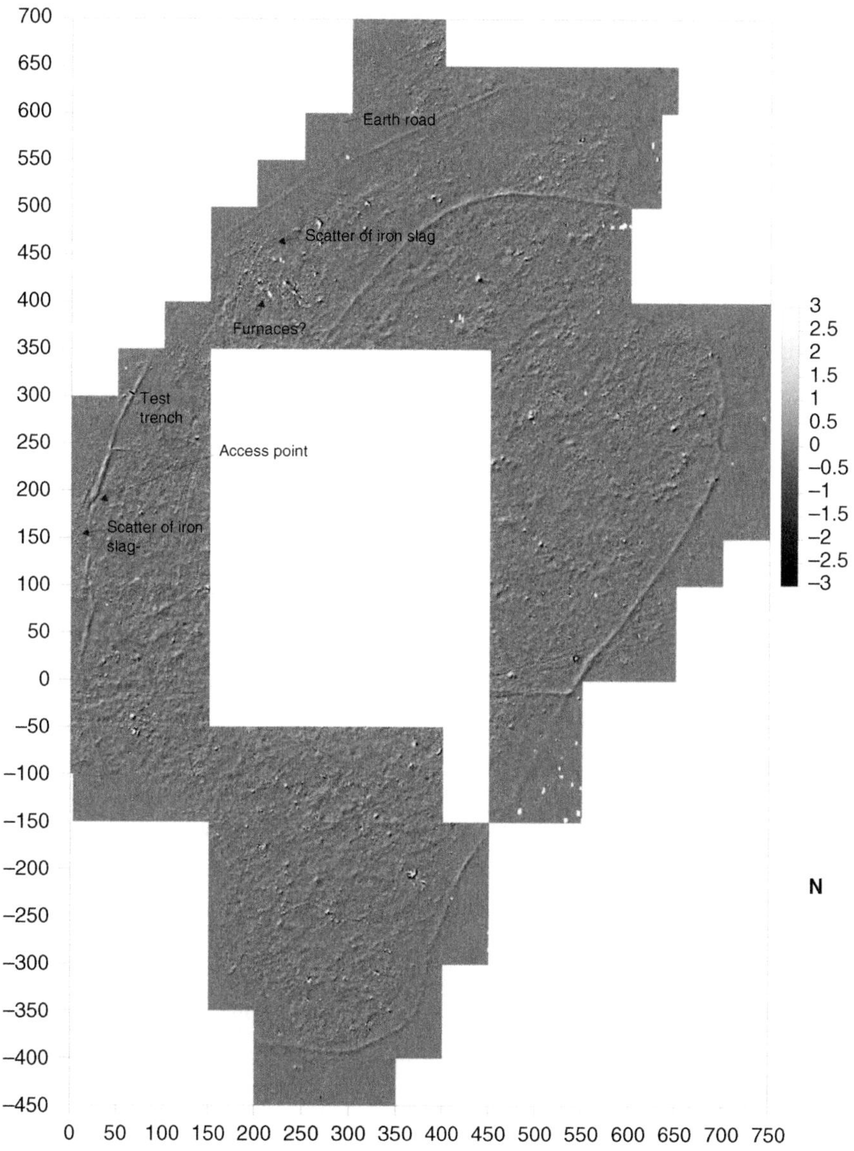

Figure 15.5. Magnetogram of Zubo showing the location of features discussed.

maximum extent. This is indicated by continuous scatters of dot-like anomalies, which in several places are apparently cut by the ditches. However, a few locations such as the southern and northern extremities of the settlement seem to display some anomaly-free areas along the interior border of the ditch. Contrary to former assertions,[48] the

[48] Magnavita, C. *et al.* 2009, 55.

anomaly-free sectors at Zubo can be taken as evidence that its ditches were once accompanied by now decayed earthen walls/ramparts. A test-cutting made at the south-eastern sector of Zubo's peripheral ditch revealed a massive V-shaped feature with a width of 4.5 m and a depth of about 2.3 m. Those figures indicate that a total soil volume of about 5 m^3/1 m section was once quarried, suggesting the construction of a sizeable structure associated with the ditch.

As at Dorota, both features enclose numerous dot-like magnetic anomalies that most likely indicate the location of former pits, the functions of which certainly encompassed activities such as grain storage, clay extraction for building purposes, refuse disposal and interments. Similarly to Zilum and Dorota, their large number and density express the intensive use of space and the nucleated character of the settlement. As with Dorota, no houses or living spaces can be unmistakably identified from the geophysical plot available, hence, there is no direct archaeological evidence that can be used for estimating the resident population of Zubo. Based on the population density (*c.*140–210 persons/ha) calculated for the *c.*500 years older fortified settlement of Zilum, however, we can suggest that the number of people living in the settlement may have ranged from about 6,500–9,700 individuals.

The only evidence for craft activities performed at Zubo relates to iron working. The eastern periphery of the site is characterised by a wide scatter of iron slag fragments, indicating that iron was being worked in that area (Fig. 15.5). Another extensive scatter of iron slag, visible both on the magnetic plan and on the surface, is likewise located inside the outer ditch in the southern sector of the site. This area is furthermore related to large, strong magnetic anomalies that possibly indicate the presence of buried iron-working hearths or forges. Considering the large resident population, it is again reasonable to suppose the existence of at least seasonal occupational differentiation among the inhabitants of the settlement. In particular, crafts that required expertise, such as the production of large storage vessels, might conceivably have been performed by skilled (or at least part-time) specialists. However, as at Dorota, direct archaeological evidence remains elusive.

An interesting point to be made relating to Zubo and Dorota is that, unlike at Zilum, field surveys were unable to locate small- or medium-sized satellite sites in their immediate surroundings. Provisionally, the lack of satellite settlements around Zubo and Dorota could be considered a matter of visibility and as an artefact of the surveys carried out around the sites. Future fieldwork in the area may certainly change this initial impression.

The significance of this and other facets of the archaeology of the first millennia AD/BC fortified settlement at Lake Chad are discussed below within the scope of explanations of the origin of urbanisation and the state in the Lake Chad region and in Sub-Saharan Africa.

Origins of Urbanisation in the Lake Chad Region and Sub-Saharan Africa

Other than livestock-keeping, the cultivation of plants was, in many parts of the world, the critical step that enabled a sustained process towards the development of urbanisation. The archaeological sequences now available for the Dhar Tichitt region of Mauritania, the Macina region of Mali and the Chad Basin demonstrate that only about 500 to 1,000 years elapsed between the initial emergence of plant cultivation locally and the first appearance of a fundamental social feature associated with later West African urbanisation: hierarchically organised settlement clusters.[49] The archaeological record also shows that other social and economic traits later linked to mature urbanisation made their initial appearance at a relatively early date in West Africa (*c.*1600–500 BC). These include the relatively large size of central settlements, comparatively large resident populations and (at least seasonal) occupational differentiation of some persons. Most of those traits, while occurring early in Mauritanian, Malian and Chad Basin communities, did of course not materialise on the scale and complexity that later was commonplace in and around late first-millennium AD Jenné-jeno: the earliest and best researched archaeological instance of a fully urban settlement and its hinterland in West Africa.[50]

The hierarchical settlement clusters of Dhar Tichitt (Mauritania), Macina (Mali) and the Chad Basin may not be labelled by most researchers as urban, as there is indeed no convincing evidence yet that their central settlements were, by definition, providing specialised services and goods for its hinterland.[51] However, in keeping with the questions debated in this volume, the issue over where the threshold lies between non-urban and urban settlement clusters is open to debate. Or, to put it more precisely, what is the scale and how diverse must be the services and goods provided

[49] MacDonald 2013; Magnavita, C. *et al.* 2006; McIntosh, S. and McIntosh, R. 1993.

[50] See McIntosh, Chapter 14, this volume. [51] McIntosh, S. and McIntosh, R. 1993, 625.

by a central settlement to its hinterland for prehistoric settlement clusters to be recognised as urban?

Despite inherent problems with the practical use of definitions in archaeology in general, what can be indisputably stated is that the early archaeological instances mentioned above add to the increasing awareness that some of the fundamental characteristics of late urbanisation in Sub-Saharan Africa appeared very early in the West African archaeological record. In fact, those instances remind us that the rise of the fully urban settlements of late first- and second-millennia AD West Africa were preceded by centuries of social, economic and political processes that eventually led to the emergence of what might be seen as the forerunners or even the earliest stages of urbanisation in Sub-Saharan Africa.[52] Whether the early hierarchical settlement clusters from the three regions mentioned are regarded as such or not, two major conclusions can be drawn. The first relates to the cause or causes leading to the rise of those hierarchical settlement clusters. The other is linked to their autochthonous versus allochthonous nature and, by extension, the autochthonous versus allochthonous nature of Sub-Saharan Africa urbanisation in general.

Whilst the reason(s) for hierarchical settlement clustering in the Mauritanian–Malian borderland remains contentious,[53] the cause of similar aggregations in the Chad Basin seems related to a greater concern with security. Considering the fact that each of the settlements investigated was once surrounded by ditches and, probably earthen walls or ramparts, protection seems to have been a major factor in the emergence of Zilum's site clustering. In this sense, both nucleation and site aggregation must be seen as human responses or strategies for coping with imminent or latent threats. It is much more probable that local, rather than long-distance factors,[54] were the major contributor in instigating the mixture of nucleation, fortification and site clustering detected in the Gajiganna area. Possible triggers for that are disputes for land between settled farmers, conflicts for resources between nomadic cattle keepers and settled farmers or banditry and raids.[55]

For decades, the emergence of urban life in Sub-Saharan Africa was explained as resulting from the direct or indirect influence exercised by Arab-driven long-distance Trans-Saharan trade on Sub-Saharan peoples. Since the 1980s and 1990s at least, when archaeological research was

[52] McIntosh, S. and McIntosh, R. 1984, 89–90.

[53] See discussion in MacDonald, Chapter 13, this volume.

[54] Magnavita, C. and Breunig 2008.

[55] Magnavita, C. and Breunig 2008, 77.

conducted by Susan and Roderick McIntosh at Jenné-jeno and its surroundings in the Inland Niger Delta of Mali, it became clear that that was not the case. Instead, the picture that emerged was one of a gradual development of urbanisation that pre-dated Arabic Trans-Saharan trade and possibly derived from, amongst other factors, increasing local and regional interaction and commerce along the Niger River. The evidence of developments leading to the emergence of hierarchical settlement clusters in three different West African regions (Mauritania, Mali, Chad Basin) preceding the events around Jenné-jeno by several centuries clearly underlines the view that Sub-Saharan Africa urbanisation resulted from local and regional processes rather than from long-distance (North African) influences. This notion is further supported by the virtual paucity of archaeological finds from extraneous (North African or Nile Valley) origin in those and other Sub-Saharan Africa sites until the mid-to late first millennium AD and, locally, perhaps even much later.[56]

Origins of the State: A Hypothesis for the Lake Chad Region

Just as with urbanisation, the foundation of the earliest West African states and empires were for a long time accredited to foreigners or to their direct or indirect influence.[57] In attempting to detect 'the early state' or 'the process of state formation' from archaeological remains, archaeologists face the problem that the identification of political institutions and decision-making individuals from material evidence is rarely straightforward. For instance, in the absence of highly visible signs of status differences assigned to state-level societies, trying to infer the level of socio-political integration of non-literate human groups from other kinds of archaeological data – such as the presence/absence or scale of site hierarchies – is regarded as both conceptually and methodologically problematic.[58] Similarly, the almost obsessive attempts of researchers to fit prehistoric societies into simplistic neo-evolutionary 'categories of human progress' (band, tribe, chiefdom and state) have been highly criticised for their correctness and questionable value for archaeology as a whole.[59] Instead of over-emphasising classification, it has been advocated that archaeologists would be better off doing what they do best: evidencing diachronic

[56] Gronenborn 2001a; MacEachern *et al.* 2001; Magnavita, C. and Breunig 2008; see also Connah 1981.

[57] Compare the discussion in Munson 1980, 458–59. [58] Cowgill 2004, 543.

[59] McIntosh, S. 1999; Yoffee 2005, 31–32.

changes in the archaeological record over lengthy time spans and trying to explain those changes in terms of local and regional economic, social and political trajectories.[60]

Notwithstanding whether (and which) labels are used to describe pre-colonial human groups, the fact is that highly hierarchical and stratified (state-level) societies were a historical reality in the Chad Basin and West Africa in the late first to second millennium AD.[61] It is also certain that the latter undoubtedly developed out of societies that were relatively undifferentiated socio-economically and were politically structured primarily by kin-relations. Following the above mentioned methodological and theoretical principles, the ultimate goal of archaeologists and historians interested in understanding the emergence of stratified (state-level) societies is, therefore, to reveal the specific developmental trajectories of the latter. In the Chad Basin, this can be done by considering the socio-political developments of the late first and second millennia AD, when stratified societies demonstrably emerged. That glimpse can serve as a basis for achieving an understanding of the forces that may explain both the origins of early state societies in the Chad Basin and the emergence of first millennium BC/AD sites such as Zilum, Zubo and Dorota, described above.

Written and oral historical sources suggest that at least two types of states emerged in the Lake Chad region at the end of the first and the beginning of the second millennium AD. The first and older of these appears to be Kanim-Borno (from around the eighth century AD), a regional expansionist state whose core area was first situated at the north-eastern and, later, at the north-western margins of Lake Chad.[62] There is strong evidence that Kanim-Borno's early economic and political success is tightly linked to the early Arabic Trans-Saharan trade, but its socio-political roots may predate those large-scale commercial linkages.[63] The archaeology of early Kanim-Borno remains elusive as its early administrative centres do not seem to have been densely populated cities.[64] Only later, from the fifteenth century onwards, did its putative capitals (the contemporaneous sites of Birni Gazargamo and Garumele) develop into large fortified urban centres displaying monumental architecture.[65] The second and later state-level society is represented by the series of small independent Kotoko (or Makeri) principalities or city-states on the southern margins of Lake Chad.[66] Dated by oral traditions, king lists and archaeology as emerging in the

[60] Yoffee 2005, 5. [61] Forkl 1983; Hunwick 1985; Lange 1977; Levtzion 1973.
[62] Barkindo 1985. [63] Lange 1977, 141–43. [64] Gronenborn 2001b: 103–4.
[65] Haour and Gado 2009. [66] Forkl 1983.

Figure 15.6. Aerial view of Goulfei.

time between the twelfth and the fourteenth century AD, each of those polities was characterised by a single fortified town (Fig. 15.6 for the example of Goulfei) and a territory of one to several hundred km^2.[67] Alongside their perimeter walls, architectural evidence for the existence of a central government comes in the form of a palace. Just as the extent of the territory (and villages) controlled by each town provides evidence of the ruler's power, so do the size of the town and its population. In this context, the walled town of the Houlouf principality (twelfth–sixteenth century AD) and those of Goulfei and Logone-Birni attained sizes of about 16, 20 and 57 ha, respectively.[68] The population size of Houlouf at its political climax in the early sixteenth century AD is unknown, but Goulfei's and Logone-Birni's populations were estimated to have respectively amounted to about 8,000 and 15,000 individuals in the second half of the nineteenth century.[69]

Unlike the case of the regional state of Kanim-Borno which appears to have been non-urbanised in its early days, the Kotoko principalities seem to have been essentially urban from their beginning, thus justifying the

[67] Lebeuf 1981, 213. [68] Griaule and Lebeuf 1951, 1; Holl 2002, 139; Lebeuf 1969, figure 8.
[69] H. Barth and G. Nachtigal in Lebeuf 1969, 30.

label city-state for the latter polities. The question that has to be posed in this context is why did early Kanim-Borno not develop urban centres, while the Kotoko did? Ninth-century and later Arabic written sources describing the involvement of Kanim-Borno in the Trans-Saharan trade suggest that the main commodity given by that state in exchange for products imported from North Africa was slaves.[70] While in the ninth–tenth century AD the supply of slaves may have been guaranteed by raids carried out in or around the territories under the state's dominions,[71] it appears that such targeted attacks extended later into independent regions. Thus, the areas of the southern margins of Lake Chad appear to have been attacked for such purpose at the latest from around the eleventh–twelfth centuries AD onward.[72] In the thirteenth century several expeditions are also said to have been carried out against areas around Lake Chad and between the thirteenth and fourteenth century the western margins of Lake Chad (Borno) appear to have been under Kanim-Borno authority.[73] The available evidence thus largely suggests that political pressure exerted by Kanim-Borno on southern Lake Chad populations alongside intercommunity conflicts were probably main factors in the emergence of the urbanised Kotoko principalities historically known from the twelfth century on.[74]

It is today largely acknowledged that the large majority of the earliest state-level societies worldwide were not large and expansionist territorial states. Instead, they consisted of comparatively small polities centred on single urban settlements, which, greatly differing in size, complexity and wealth, were variously called city-states, town-states, petty states, micro-states or statelets.[75] A major factor leading to the emergence of the earliest city-states is regarded as something called 'defensive coalescence', that is, the convergence of people to a central settlement to seek protection against raids from neighbouring polities.[76] In fact, city-states did not rise in isolation, but in clusters from a few to several dozens and hundreds. The analysis of several archaeological cases suggests that their emergence was intimately linked both to competition and hostility among nascent peer-polities,[77] but also by alliances among some of them. It is within such a scenario of external threat that the southern Lake Chad Kotoko city-states emerged around the twelfth century AD.

70 Al-Yaqubi in Levtzion and Hopkins 1981, 22.
71 Al-Yaqubi and Yaqut in Levtzion and Hopkins 1981, 22, 171. 72 Barkindo 1985, 235.
73 Barkindo 1985, 238–39; Lange 1993, 270–72. 74 Gronenborn 1998, 246–47; Holl 2002, 213.
75 Cowgill 2004, 542; Gat 2002, 125; Yoffee 2005, 44. 76 Gat 2002, 125. 77 Gat 2002, 129.

As in the case of Zilum, the first millennium AD fortified settlements of Dorota and Zubo may be, by definition, hardly labelled as urban, the more so as we do not know if they even had satellite settlements. Similarly, the question of the kind of political organisation of their inhabitants cannot be fully answered, as reliable archaeological evidence for that is as yet lacking. However, Zilum as well as Dorota and Zubo display a number of physical traits (fortifications, dimensions and population sizes) that are strikingly similar to those of the Kotoko central settlements. The rise and development of the second millennium AD Kotoko settlements are, of course, chronologically and culturally unrelated to those of first-millennia BC/AD Zilum, Dorota and Zubo. Nevertheless, the archaeological evidence recorded at these fortified settlements attests that the human groups that inhabited the region must have experienced comparable levels of socio-political pressure generated by external threats to those suggested as triggering the rise of the Kotoko city-states. Whether people sought protection due to warfare among peer-polities, due to attacks of an expansionist state or merely due to the insecurity caused by marauding bands, the now available archaeological evidence points out that real or latent violence was for centuries and millennia a central feature of social life and politics in the Chad Basin. The first millennia BC/AD archaeological settlements discussed do not yet show evidence of the kind of political organisation (consensus-based decision within groups or formalised central authority) that had to face and manage the consequences of external threat. Nevertheless, their existence demonstrates that the first historically known state-level societies in the Lake Chad region – both eighth century AD Kanim-Borno and the twelfth century AD Kotoko principalities – postdate centuries of social, economic and politic 'experimentation' that produced densely populated physical and social spaces that were intriguingly similar to the central settlements of second millennium AD Kotoko city-states.

These parallels allow us to draw three major conclusions. First, far-reaching economic and socio-political developments (the foundation of the densely populated fortified settlements of Zilum, Zubo and Dorota) that, in favourable circumstances, might have paved the way towards the rise of state-level societies appear to have been recurrent events from the middle of the first millennium BC to at least the middle of the first millennium AD. Second, those early economic and socio-political developments occurred several centuries before Trans-Saharan contacts and trade might have had any significant influence on Lake Chad Basin human groups, thus strongly indicating that they were entirely autochthonous developments. Third, and perhaps most important, the origins of early urban centres in the Chad Basin appears to be strongly linked to the rise of state-level societies, namely those labelled by some as city-states. Regarding the latter, it can be hypothesised that the political structure of the Kotoko states and their possibly less complex ancestral counterparts, may have developed years or decades after the formation of their walled towns. That would mean that state-like political structures and its symbols arose in the wake of the process of nucleation or 'defensive coalescence' devised in the archaeological and historical record of the Chad Basin in the course of the last 2,500 years.

Summary and Conclusions

Looking back at the relevant archaeological and historical evidence now available for the Lake Chad region in the course of the last 2,500 years, it seems that a first hypothesis or local trajectory that might account for the origins of urbanisation and the state in the Lake Chad Basin can be put forward.

The most recent archaeological data demonstrate that the emergence of relatively large, densely populated (nucleated) and fortified settlements were a conspicuous feature in the economic, social and political trajectory of Lake Chad societies. Though smaller sites did exist, some even figuring as satellites of the larger ones, the largest sites in particular and their fortifications tell a story that may explain their own rise. That story highlights that, in the first millennia BC/AD and for reasons that we do not fully understand, human groups inhabiting the south-western Lake Chad margins were under recurring threat. This threat, be it real or merely perceived, led them to gather together in large settlements around which they built protective ditches and earthen ramparts/walls. Altogether, their relatively large areas, fortifications and population estimates in the low thousands bear a strong resemblance to the walled central settlements of the Kotoko principalities or city-states of the early second millennium AD. Those polities are the earliest urbanised state-level societies presently known in the Lake Chad region. Though it is clear that, chronologically and culturally, the Kotoko city-states are unrelated to the fortified settlements of the first millennia BC/AD, the physical similarities (fortification, dimensions and population size) of those central social spaces are so remarkable that at least a common factor might be seen as having triggered their emergence. Local historical and oral sources, the analysis of the circumstances leading to the appearance of city-states in other regions of the world as well as the results of more recent archaeological and geophysical research presented in this paper reveals that that common factor was various forms of local and regional threats and conflicts, either real or latent.

Just as historically attested regional or local conflicts were able to trigger the appearance of the Kotoko city-states, so it is justifiable to suggest that, by analogy, the economic and socio-political developments around the foundation of the densely populated fortified settlements of Zilum, Zubo and Dorota might also have led, under propitious circumstances, to the rise of state-like polities. Though there is no archaeological evidence that hints at the kind of political organisation of their past inhabitants, the sheer size of those settlements, their early dates and the paucity of archaeological finds that demonstrate external influences largely support the suggestion that they resulted from local economic, social and political processes. Finally and again based on the archaeological evidence, it can be suggested that the emergence of the first urban centres in the Lake Chad region occurred almost in tandem with the rise of state-level societies, with state structures possibly appearing just years or decades after settlement growth.

While the archaeological evidence appears to suggest that this trajectory might have led to the formation of the first urban centres and, in fact, the first urbanised states in the Lake Chad Basin, it is also plausible that similar conflict driven trajectories may have led to the emergence of comparatively compact central and defended settlements elsewhere in Africa. This hypothesis adds to the growing awareness among prehistorians[78] that the processes and trajectories linked to the origins and development of Sub-Saharan Africa urbanisation may have been more diverse than hitherto thought.

References

Ajayi, J.F.A. and Crowder, M. (eds). 1985. *History of West Africa*. Vol.1. Harlow: Longman.

Barkindo, B. 1985. The early states of the Central Sudan: Kanem, Borno and some of their neighbours to c.1500 AD. In Ajayi and Crowder 1985, 225–54.

[78] See MacDonald and Camara 2012, 186–88.

Bedaux, R., MacDonald, K.C., Person, A., Polet, J., Sanogo, K., Schmidt, A. and Sidibe, S. 2001. The Dia archaeological project: Rescuing cultural heritage in the Inland Niger Delta (Mali). *Antiquity* 75: 837–48.

Bedaux, R., Polet, J., Sanogo, K. and Schmidt, A. (eds). 2005. *Recherches archéologiques à Dia dans le Delta intérieur du Niger (Mali): bilan des saisons de fouilles 1998–2003*. Leiden: CNWA Publications.

Breunig, P. 2009. Cultural change in the first millennium BC: Evidence from Nigeria, West Africa. In Magnavita, S. *et al.* 2009, 15–26.

Breunig, P. 2013. Pathways to food production in the Sahel. In Mitchell and Lane 2013, 555–70.

Breunig, P. and Neumann, K. 2002. From hunters and gatherers to food producers: New archaeological and archaeobotanical evidence from the West African Sahel. In F.A. Hassan (ed.), *Droughts, Food and Culture: Ecological Change and Food Security in Africa's Later Prehistory*. New York: Kluwer, 123–55.

Breunig, P., Neumann, K. and Van Neer, W. 1996. New research on the Holocene settlement and environment of the Chad Basin in Nigeria. *African Archaeological Review* 13.2: 111–45.

Breunig, P., Eichhorn, B., Kahlheber, S., Linseele, V., Magnavita, C., Neumann, K., Posselt, M. and Rupp, N. 2006. G(l)anz ohne Eisen: Große Siedlungen aus der Mitte des ersten Jahrtausends BC im Tschadbecken von Nordost-Nigeria. In H.-P. Wotzka (ed.), *Grundlegungen. Beiträge zur europäischen und afrikanischen Archäologie für Manfred K.H. Eggert*. Tübingen: Narr Francke Attempto Verlag GmbH & Co. KG, 255–70.

Brunk, K. and Gronenborn, D. 2004. Floods, drought and migrations: The effects of Late Holocene lake level oscillations and climate fluctuations on the settlement and political history in the Chad Basin. In Krings and Platte 2004, 101–32.

Connah, G. 1981. *Three Thousand Years in Africa: Man and His Environment in the Lake Chad Region of Nigeria*. Cambridge: Cambridge University Press.

Connah, G., 2000. African city walls. A neglected source? In D.M. Anderson and R. Rathbone (eds), *Africa's Urban Past*. Oxford: James Currey, 36–51.

Cowgill, G.L. 2004. Origins and development of urbanism: Archaeological perspectives. *Annual Review of Anthropology* 33: 525–49.

Creekmore, A.T. and Fisher, K.D. (eds). 2014. *Making Ancient Cities: Space and Place in Early Urban Societies*. Cambridge: Cambridge University Press.

Forkl, H. 1983. *Die Beziehungen der zentralsudanischen Reiche Bornu, Mandara und Bagirmi sowie der Kotoko-Staaten zu ihren südlichen Nachbarn unter besonderer Berücksichtigung des Sao-Problems*. Münchner ethnologische Abhandlungen 3. München: Minerva Publikation.

Gat, A. 2002. Why city-states existed? Riddles and clues of urbanization and fortifications. In M.H. Hansen (ed.), *A Comparative Study of Six City-State Cultures*. Copenhagen: Reitzels Forlag, 125–39.

Gaussen, J. and Gaussen, M. 1988. *Le Tilemsi prehistorique et ses abords. Sahara et Sahel Malien*. Paris: Éditions du CNRS.

Griaule, M. and Lebeuf, J.P. 1951. Fouilles dans la region du Tchad (III). *Journal de la Société des Africanistes* 21.1: 1–95.

Gronenborn, D. 1998. Archaeological and ethnohistorical investigations along the southern fringes of Lake Chad, 1993–1996. *African Archaeological Review* 15.4: 225–59.

Gronenborn, D. 2001a. Beads and the emergence of the Islamic slave trade in the southern Chad Basin (Nigeria). *The Bead Forum* 38: 4–11.

Gronenborn, D. 2001b. Kanem-Borno: A brief summary of the history and archaeology of an empire of the central bilad-al-sudan. In C. DeCorse (ed.), *West Africa during the Atlantic Slave Trade: Archaeological Perspectives*. Leicester: Leicester University Press, 101–30.

Haour, A. and Gado, B. 2009. Garumele, ville médiévale du Kanem-Bornu? Une contribution archéologique. *Journal of African History* 50: 1–21.

Holl. A.F.C. 1993. Late Neolithic cultural landscape in southeastern Mauritania: An essay in spatiometrics. In A.F.C. Holl and T.E. Levy (eds), *Spatial Boundaries and Social Dynamics: Case Studies from Food-Producing Societies*. Ann Arbor: International Monographs in Prehistory, 95–133.

Holl, A.F.C. 2002. *The Land of Houlouf. Genesis of a Chadic Polity, 1900 BC–AD 1800*. Ann Arbor: The Museum of Anthropology.

Holmes, J.A., Street-Perrott, F.A., Allen, M.J., Fothergill, P.A., Harkness, D.D., Kroon, D. and Perrott, R.A. 1997. Holocene palaeolimnology of Kajemarum Oasis, Northern Nigeria: An isotopic study of ostracodes, bulk carbonate and organic carbon. *Journal of the Geological Society* 154: 311–19.

Hunwick, J.O. 1985. Songhay, Borno and the Hausa states 1450–1600. In Ajayi and Crowder 1985, 323–65.

Krings, M. and Platte, E. (eds). 2004. *Living with the Lake: Perspectives on Culture, Economy and History of Lake Chad*. Köln: Köppe.

Lange, D. 1977. *Le diwan des sultans du (Kanem-)Bornu: Chronologie et histoire d'un royaume africain (de la fin du Xe siècle jusqu'à 1808)*. Wiesbaden: Franz Steiner Verlag.

Lange, D. 1993. Ethnogenesis from within the Chadic state: Some thoughts on the history of Kanem-Borno. *Paideuma* 39: 261–77.

Lebeuf, A.M.D. 1969. *Les principautés Kotoko. Essai sur le caractère sacre de l'autorité*. Paris: CNRS.

Lebeuf, A.M.D. 1981. L'origine et la constitution des principautés Kotoko (Cameroun septentrional). In C. Tardits (ed.), *Contribution de la recherche ethnologique à l'histoire des civilisations du Cameroun*. Paris: CNRS, 209–18.

Levtzion, N. 1973. *Ancient Ghana and Mali*. London: Methuen.

Levtzion, N. and Hopkins, J.F.P. 1981. *Corpus of Early Arabic Sources for West African History*. Cambridge: Cambridge University Press.

Linseele, V. 2007. *Domestic Livestock, Subsistence Strategies and Environmental Changes in Sahelian West Africa during the Past 4000 years: Evidence from Archaeofaunal Remains*. Oxford: BAR, Archaeopress.

MacDonald, K. 2003. New light on the Tichitt tradition: A preliminary report on survey and excavation at Dhar Néma. In P.J. Mitchell, A. Haour and J. Hobart (eds), *Researching Africa's Past: New Contributions from British Archaeologists.* Oxford: Oxford University School of Archaeology, 73–80.

MacDonald, K. 2013. Complex societies, urbanism and trade in the western Sahel. In Mitchell and Lane 2013, 829–44.

MacDonald, K. and Camara, S. 2012. Segou, slavery and Sifinso. In J.C. Monroe and A. Ogundiran (eds), *Power and Landscape in Atlantic West Africa: Archaeological Perspectives.* Cambridge: Cambridge University Press, 169–90.

MacEachern, S. 1996. Iron Age beginnings north of the Mandara Mountains, Cameroon and Nigeria. In G. Pwiti, and R. Soper (eds), *Aspects of African Archaeology.* Harare: University of Zimbabwe Press, 489–96.

MacEachern, S., Bourges, C. and Reeves, M. 2001. Early horse remains from northern Cameroon. *Antiquity* 75: 62–67.

McIntosh, S.K. 1999. *Beyond Chiefdoms: Pathways to Complexity in Africa.* Cambridge: Cambridge University Press.

McIntosh, S.K. and McIntosh, R.J. 1984. The early city in West Africa: Towards an understanding. *The African Archaeological Review* 2: 73–98.

McIntosh, S.K. and McIntosh, R.J. 1993. Cities without citadels: Understanding urban origins along the middle Niger. In T. Shaw, P. Sinclair, B. Andah and A. Okpoko (eds), *The Archaeology of Africa. Food, Metals and Towns.* London: Routledge, 623–41.

Magnavita, C. 2002. Recent archaeological finds of domesticated Sorghum bicolor in the Lake Chad region. *Nyame Akuma* 57: 14–20.

Magnavita, C. 2004. Zilum – towards the emergence of socio-political complexity in the Lake Chad region. In Krings and Platte 2004, 73–100.

Magnavita, C. 2008. *Studien zur endsteinzeitlichen und früheisenzeitlichen Besiedlung im südwestlichen Tschadbecken (1300 BC – 700 AD).* Unpublished PhD thesis, Goethe-University Frankfurt.

Magnavita, C. and Breunig, P. 2008. Facts and speculations: A reply to D. Lange's The emergence of social complexity in the southern Chad Basin towards 500 BC: archaeological and other evidence. *Borno Museum Society Newsletter* 74–75: 71–83.

Magnavita, C., Kahlheber, S. and Eichhorn, B. 2004. The rise of organisational complexity in mid-first millennium BC Chad Basin. *Antiquity* 78: 1–17.

Magnavita, C., Breunig, P., Ameje, J. and Posselt, M. 2006. Zilum: A mid-first millennium BC fortified settlement near Lake Chad. *Journal of African Archaeology* 4.1: 153–69.

Magnavita, C., Breunig, P., Ishaya, D. and Adebayo, O. 2009. Iron Age beginnings at the south-western margins of Lake Chad. In Magnavita, S. *et al.* 2009, 27–58.

Magnavita, S., Koté, L., Breunig, P. and Idé, O.A. (eds). 2009. *Crossroads/Carrefour Sahel: Cultural and Technological Developments in First Millennium BC/AD*

West Africa. Journal of African Archaeology Monograph Series 2. Frankfurt: Africa Magna Verlag.
Mitchell, P. and Lane, P. (eds). 2013. *The Oxford Handbook of African Archaeology*. Oxford: Oxford University Press.
Mohammed, I.M. 1986. *The Archaeology of Central Darfur (Sudan) in the 1st Millennium AD*. Oxford: BAR S285.
Munson, P.J. 1980. Archaeology and the prehistoric origins of the Ghana Empire. *The Journal of African History* 21.4: 457–66.
Rupp, N. 2005. *Land ohne Steine: die Rohmaterialversorgung in Nordost-Nigeria von der Steinzeit bis zur Eisenzeit*. Unpublished PhD thesis, Goethe-University Frankfurt.
Sabloff, J.A. 1994. *The New Archaeology and the Ancient Maya*. New York: Scientific American Library.
Trigger, B. 1972. Determinants of urban growth in pre-industrial societies. In P.J. Ucko, R. Tringham and G.W. Dimbleby (eds), *Man, Settlement and Urbanism*. London: Duckworth, 575–99.
Trigger, B.G. 1989. *A History of Archaeological Thought*. Cambridge: Cambridge University Press.
Weber, M. 1958. *The City*. Translated by D. Martindale and G. Neuwirth. New York: The Free Press.
Yoffee, N. 2005. *Myths of the Archaic State: Evolution of the Earliest Cities, States and Civilizations*. Cambridge: Cambridge University Press.

16 | At the Dawn of Sijilmasa

New Historical Focus on the Process of Emergence of a Saharan State and a Caravan City

CHLOÉ CAPEL

Preamble: On the Origins of the State?

The French sociologist Pierre Bourdieu taught us in the early 1990s that to question the 'genesis of the state' is one of the most arduous tasks for the historian.[1] Indeed, in essence, the state defines itself when it is already accepted and firmly installed. Then it produces instruments of recognition and domination, including symbolic ones, to confirm the social norm, the social order that it supervises or even imposes, and to validate this 'fundamental consensus on the social world' of which it is the guarantor.[2] For instance, it is customary for historians to define a state by the establishment of taxation, which at first sight would be preliminary in any policy construction. However, Bourdieu, and Weber before him, pointed out that for this step to occur, it is necessary that the taxing authority has already been recognised by the social body and that the legitimacy of such an initiative has already been accepted by society.[3] The collection of taxes is a result of the formation of the state, not its founding and like other means of conceptualising and structuring political power, it always occurs after the strengthening and the recognition of that power. This is why the production of these bureaucratic instruments can take place after, or even much later than, the birth of the state, whether they are texts (constitution, legal powers and rules, received religious texts, historical accounts) or have a material scope (currency issue, monumental architecture, territorial and environmental markers). Therefore, there are no contemporary records of the emergence of the state produced by itself. This is enough to explain the difficulties of studying such a historical moment. But, archaeologists and historians who wish to study the birth of the state

[1] Bourdieu 2012. [2] Genêt 2014, 101; Lenoir 2013, 134. [3] Genêt 2014, 100.

precisely use these kinds of data and documents – the ones that the state produces to legitimate its position once firmly established – to build their arguments. As a consequence, they are continuously prisoners of what Bourdieu calls 'the thought of the state'.[4] These mental and cognitive structures, promoted by the state because they strengthen its authority, are necessarily anachronistic compared to the society in which this power emerged.[5] In order to study the birth of political authority or the birth of the state, one should reconstitute the social space in which this conceptual changeover was made possible. Comparing sources from different origins, including external sources that escape the shackles of the thought of the state, at least partially, may be a way. But because of the current state of these sources, this approach is still a challenge and this is why it is so complex to theorise the birth of states, especially for ancient periods, for which documents are so scarce.

Introduction: Reconsidering the Foundation of Sijilmasa

Studying the emergence of urban societies in the Medieval Sahara does not escape the epistemological obstacles raised by Bourdieu. When the historian is for instance interested in the development of Sijilmasa,[6] the most famous of these northern cities, the only historical sources concerning the birth of the city are Arabic texts. All of them were written far from the city, mostly by authors who had never been there and who had no idea of environmental, social and political conditions of this remote Saharan place. Above all, they were, consciously or not, part of a political system of thought centred on Mediterranean Islamised societies and involved in a state-controlled (re)construction of the history of the city. The only external data, produced outside of the Islamic scholarly circles, which could illustrate the state of society on the eve of the birth of Sijilmasa are archaeological in nature. But to this day, they remain poorly studied and underappreciated. Studies on the development of the state and the city of Sijilmasa have therefore not made much progress over the last 30 years,

[4] Bourdieu 2012. [5] Lenoir 2013, 132–33.

[6] To conform with the volume style, a simplified transliteration of Arabic is used for proper names (e.g., al-Bakri). Only words commonly used in English comply with fully westernised spelling (e.g., Sijilmasa, Cordoba). Anglicised nouns and adjectives stemmed from Arabic or Berber terms do not respect the transliteration rules either (filalian). On the etymology of Sijilmasa, see Mezzine 1984.

since the work of Charles Pellat in 1960, Isma'il Mahmud 'Abd al-Raziq in 1985 and Mohamed Mellouki in the same year.[7]

These three studies were predictably and almost exclusively based on the review of al-Bakri's text, which is the main reference for understanding the early periods of the city. Writing in Cordoba, al-Bakri completed his *Kitab al-Masalik wa'l-Mamalik* around 460 AH/AD 1068. But in the note he devoted to the city of Sijilmasa, his main source of information was the work of the much earlier Andalusian al-Warraq. This writer was born in North Africa in 292 AH/AD 904 and probably visited Sijilmasa in his youth.[8] His text, which is now lost but largely revived by al-Bakri, offers a unique historical depth. It is from al-Warraq that al-Bakri took the majority of his information about the dynastic power of the first centuries of Sijilmasa. Indeed, his sovereign list stops in the third quarter of the tenth century, precisely when al-Warraq was writing his work. The text of al-Bakri presents several versions to the founding story of the city, which, as a scrupulous historian, he listed successively (though he declared one version more likely than others). Al Bakri's favoured version was the one of a foundation precisely occurring in 140 AH/AD 757 and being the act of a nomadic shepherd of the Miknasa tribe. This man, as he was traversing the area now called Tafilalt (or Tafilalat) managed to unite a number of Miknasa companions in converting to Islam and to the belief in *khariji* faith. From this human and spiritual gathering arose a political authority and a city. Another version was that Sijilmasa was founded in the aftermath of the revolt of the suburbs of Cordoba in 202 AH/AD 818, by a Miknasi man, settled in al-Andalus, but driven out from his city at the end of the Cordoba rebellion. He brought with him into the Maghrib the art of blacksmithing and, after settling in Tafilalt, he won the trust and respect of the Berber shepherds grazing in the area, selling them weapons and tools of his own production and was recognised as their leader. The city and the state of Sijilmasa arose shortly afterwards. In both versions, the founders established a dynastic political system wherein Sijilmasa acquired the status of an autonomous state, being governed by an hereditary prince. In both cases, al-Bakri also reported that nomadic people were grazing in Tafilalt (though he does not name the region in this way) before the foundation of Sijilmasa. He also described an annual gathering of people, based on a market fair, this being the same one where the blacksmith used to sell his production. This gathering would have represented the population base

[7] 'Abd al-Raziq 1985, 109–43, 210–29; Mellouki 1985, 51–98, 109–58; Pellat 1960.

[8] Gilliot 2002.

from which Sijilmâsa was built. To this double myth, other indications from al-Bakri must be added, complicating this hitherto fairly linear frame. First, the Miknasi shepherd, founder of the city in the 140s AH, was evidently the grandfather of the Andalusian blacksmith, also known as the founder of the city 60 years later. In another variant, the first of the two founders for a period transferred authority over his community to a third character. The reign of 15 years of this latter, very likely not a member of the Miknasa tribe, did not prevent the return to power of the founder of the dynasty. This first dynasty is often known as the Midrarids (or Banu Midrar), named after the Andalusian blacksmith Midrar. Arabic literature also sometimes refers to this family as the Banu Wasul, named after the first character, Abu al-Qasim Samgu ibn Wasul, the shepherd and grandfather of Midrar.[9]

In this complex history, with multiple sides, most historians adopt al-Bakri's position where the story of Samgu, the shepherd and *khariji* preacher, seems the most plausible version of the foundation of Sijilmasa. Midrar's version is generally excluded mainly for chronological reasons: this myth would place the development of the city too late as it is mentioned in Arabic cosmogonies written in the Abbasid court of Baghdad at precisely the same time.[10] With these references it is customary to consider that the reputation of the Saharan city, located at the other end of Dar al-Islam, took quite a long time to reach the Caliphate Iraqi court and that it was not simultaneous with its founding. Furthermore, the version of Midrar is also dismissed because al-Bakri provides many indications about Sijilmasa in connection to the period before the time of the revolt of the suburbs of Cordoba. It does not make sense to invalidate this information and consider it as a complete fabrication on the grounds that the city was supposedly founded later. Among this information, topographic clues, about the wall and the great mosque for instance, are valuable for the study of the city and thus incline historians to definitively rule out the later dating of the foundation of Sijilmasa.

The warning of Pierre Bourdieu about the terms of the study of the birth of states suggests that we need to look into these foundation myths once more. Even if they may not report actual historical events, they carry clues about the societies and the powers that produced these texts. For this reason, all versions of the Sijilmasa foundation must be taken into account because they certainly contain many elements clarifying the social space in

9 Al-Bakri 1911, 148–52, 167; 1913, 282–90, 315–16.

10 Al-Masʿudî 1865, IV.39, working in the mid-tenth century but stemming his information from *Kitab al-zij* of al-Fazari, who wrote in the first quarter of the ninth century.

which the city emerged. This is why a new reflection on the birth of Sijilmasa is required. Firstly, al-Bakri must be reconsidered beyond the simple examination of the historical facts he relates in order to detect social or cultural elements in connection with primeval times. Secondly, the fact that al-Bakri got most of his historical information from a writer who was active in al-Andalus a century before him must be kept in mind. Finally, original archaeological data have to be included into this new reflection. These archaeological data represent new information about Sijilmasa: they are the results of surveys carried out between 2011 and 2013.[11] This considerable renewal of sources of information, in association with the written sources previously exploited, allows a leap forward in understanding the emergence of the city.

Sijilmasa: Paragon of Triumphant Kharijism in the Maghrib and Construction of a Proselyte State

Modern historians of Sijilmasa adopt al-Bakri's point of view explaining the emergence of the city in terms of sufri proselytism having found in pastoral lands of the southern Maghrib a fertile ground for its preaching. The Miknasi Abu al-Qasim Samgu, bearing the *khariji* fire, managed to unite around him some nomadic shepherds in Tafilalt. These companions, freshly converted to the egalitarianism of *khariji* faith, rapidly formed a model state, where only the best Muslims are worthy of community responsibility. Forty men formed the first circle which, in the sufri system, elected as a leader the wisest of them: ʿIsa ibn Mazid, who was black, a characteristic sufficiently exceptional for al-Bakri to mention it. This pigmentary detail emphasises that human qualities and piety were the only requirements to weigh in the balance of power, without any interference of social, economic, tribal or ethnic issues. The Sijilmasian state was thus based on *khariji* doctrinal exemplarity. But after 15 years of governance, ʿIsa ibn Mazid, severely criticised for irresponsible management of common affairs and whose skin colour is again highlighted, but now as an aggravating element of his faults, was violently manoeuvred out of power. Then, Samgu was called to lead in turn but, breaking with the *khariji* ideal,

[11] My doctoral thesis (2016) fell within a framework of Saharan archaeology initiated in 2009 at the University Paris 1 Panthéon-Sorbonne under the supervision of Professor Jean Polet. This doctoral work is also based on the exploitation of the archives of the Moroccan American Project at Sijilmasa (MAPS), conducted between 1988 and 1998 under the supervision of Ronald Messier (MTSU). For some initial results, see Capel 2016; 2018; Capel and Fili 2018.

he started a hereditary dynastic cycle of Miknasi princes, which ruled until it was finally deposed in 366 AH/AD 976 by Maghrawa, allies of the Umayyads of Cordoba.

Twentieth-century studies emphasise that the growth of this sufri hub south of the Atlas can only be understood in the light of the religious situation affecting the whole Maghrib at the same time. The mid-eighth century was actually a period of considerable development of kharijism, whether it is Sufri or Ibadi, against the caliphal Kairouanese power. Several major events followed within the space of a generation: the uprising of Maysara in 122 AH/AD 739–740 in Tangier, followed by the victory of Khalid over the Kairouanese forces during the 'Battle of the Nobles'; then, after a time of setbacks, such as the storming of Kairouan in 140 AH/AD 757 by Warfajjuma people, invoking sufrism, and the same year the proclamation of the Ibadi imamate in Tripolitania, which began the conquest of the region under the authority of Abu al-Khattab and then, strengthened by a new wave of proselytism, took the Ifriqiyan capital.[12] Thus, kharijism not only emerged as a dogmatic branch of Islam in North Africa but also as a powerful armed movement and a real political force confronting the Umayyad and then Abbasid entity of Kairouan. The foundation of Sijilmasa precisely occurred in this context. But by balancing this point of view, our work has already pointed out that if this intellectual and conquering environment was partly responsible for the birth of the Sijilmasian state, this is probably as much the result of successes of the movement as defeats or setbacks. These latter could have caused migration waves of *khariji* people to distant and protected lands south of the Atlas, as in Tafilalt, where people, as fighters enduring reprisals following the assassination of Maysara by his own allies or even Warfajjuma expelled from Kairouan by the confrontation with the Ibadi, could have found refuge.[13] Thus, Sijilmasa was equally built on a local development of religion and an influx of population, which contextualises the presence of Miknasa in this remote region, considered as peripheral to their main areas of development, which were primarily in the Atlas moutains.

The Myth of Samgu: Hypothesis of a Strong Political Structure in Tafilalt before Sijilmasa

Without questioning al-Bakri's text, Tafilalt, the preaching area of Samgu, is usually considered as a land abandoned to pastoralism in pre-Islamic

[12] 'Abd al-Raziq 1985, 48–49, 62, 70, 77; Mellouki 1985, 55–59, 110. [13] Capel and Fili 2018.

times. It is portrayed as a region that is relatively hostile and devoid of natural resources, outside of any state-controlled or authority framework and with a low and limited population density.[14] The foundation of the Sijilmasian state, though certainly idealised as most historians recognise it, marks the opening of the region to Islamic social structuring and to an economic and political expansion era. Without compromising the historical frame which was recently built about the *khariji* process in Tafilalt, a careful reading of al-Bakri's text and its comparison to archaeological sources invite a complementary approach to the question of the birth of power in Sijilmasa.

Historians have questioned the name of the first ruler of Sijilmasa 'Isa ibn Mazid, called 'the black', stressing that it suggested that political egalitarianism had led to the emergence of the city.[15] But no one has dwelt upon the name of the preacher Abu al-Qasim Samgu ibn Wasul, whose ancestry appears predominantly Arab, but also contains a Berber term: Samgu which also can be spelt Samghû. The SMX root of this name means in modern Berber 'slave', or even 'black slave' in a pejorative sense.[16] This name perhaps throws light on the history of Tafilalt on the eve of the emergence of Sijilmasa. The success of kharijism in the Maghrib is usually attributed to the defense of religious egalitarianism that allowed Berber people as well as Arab conquerors to claim supreme religious and community responsibilities. Perhaps one should combine with this reason the possibility for men to access the highest responsibility whatever their social status, prince of noble blood or simple slave. It is through the prism of this possibility of social emancipation, and not just through ethnolinguistic matters, that we should read the zeal of Samgu, slave or freedman in Tafilalt. Appropriating Islam and its new intellectual and dogmatic universe allowed low social classes, Samgu among them, to reverse the logic of the 'natural' authority structuring the social body in the region. Thus, the name of Samgu is certainly a window on filalian society (of Tafilalt) and its forms of power at the time of emergence of Sijilmasa.

Therefore, the origins of 'Isa, the first governor of the city, coupled with the assumption of the servility of Samgu can be reconsidered on a new grid of analysis. If 'Isa 'the Black' was elected at the head of the young sufri community, if the authority was ultimately entrusted to him to the detriment of Samgu the spiritual figure, maybe it is not so much for purely ethical or religious reasons (to the credit of *khariji* egalitarianism). Instead,

[14] 'Abd al-Raziq 1985, 113; Mellouki 1985, 55–59.
[15] 'Abd al-Raziq 1985, 116; Mellouki 1985, 111. [16] Amanis 2009, 493.

it was much more for strategic and pragmatic aims, in order to respect a local social order, which was firmly rooted and where Samgu, the slave of subordinate condition, could not aspire to any upper position or social power in this society. By installing ʿIsa at the head of the community, the new circle of believers led by Samgu would only have respected and have submitted to a power structure effective in Tafilalt before the establishment of kharijism. This authority, embodied by ʿIsa, was possibly exercised not by Berber people, but by another sociolinguistic group and was based, at least partly, on a pastoral economy that included servile schemes. The prevalence of this authority in the region was certainly so important that a new social system, based on *khariji* faith, could not overcome it easily. Although the filalian society, or at least a part of it, may have been won over kharijism and Islam, it preserved its old political system, at least for a time. Consequently, the social and economic context in which Samgu asserted himself was probably not as poor as historians suggested it and the presence of a hierarchical society with a strong political authority established in pre-Islamic Tafilalt should be reconsidered. It is often argued that Samgu was from a more northerly region, which would explain his hypothetical involvement in the uprising of Maysara in 122 AH/AD 740, as proposed by historians, and his intellectual formation in Kairouan with the famous preacher ʿIkrima, a figure of oriental kharijism, as al-Bakri relates. We already emphasised the historical weakness of such a biography and underlined the logic of such an intellectual parentage towards the requirements of power and recognition of the Midrarid authority.[17] These biographical elements illustrate the structuring instruments that the state creates *a posteriori* as Bourdieu analysed them. To push further our arguments, we propose to see Samgu as a filali, that is a person from Tafilalt, fully integrated into the social structure of his region, but taking part in a considerable change in the established order by the introduction, or at least the spread, of kharijism south of the Atlas. Samgu was not preaching alone in the desert but he was instead part of a strong human settlement with a powerful political organisation, whatever the nature of this organisation was. It was this community that had to accept the changes of the 'social consensus'. This struggle required a minority group to respect the well-established structure in order to gradually instill new religious and political aspirations without overthrowing the established order. This would have been considered as an affront and would have represented a potential source of violent response. Maintaining an already recognised

[17] Capel and Fili 2018.

local leader at the head of the state was part of this strategy, it ensured social peace but did not prohibit progressive lifestyle changes or even a more radical overthrow of the system at a later date. By stepping aside in favour of ʻIsa, Abu al-Qasim Samgu only respected the authority ʻIsa already enjoyed within the society. The final fall of ʻIsa, which occurred 15 years later, probably resulted to a shift in the local power balance due to the progressive arrival of *khariji* immigrants from the north, following the setbacks of their leaders in major battles of the 140s AH. It probably provoked a deep swing in attitudes and social habits. Therefore, Sijilmasa was probably not born *ex nihilo* by structuring isolated and unattached shepherd communities, but by the gradual transformation of a local authority.

The Myth of Midrar: Rereading the Parable of the Blacksmith in Light of the Filalian Context

The second version of the founding of Sijilmasa, involving the rebels from Cordoba in the birth of the city, has been ruled out of the debate until now because of its improbability. But rereading this text actually provides information of major importance and would enlighten the history of the city. To this day, this text has never been read in the light of its context of production, though this probably represents the key to its interpretation. Al-Bakri gets this myth, like the majority of his information about Sijilmasa, from al-Warraq. But al-Warraq, who died in 363 AH/AD 973 in Cordoba, exercised his talent at the court of the Umayyads of al-Andalus, which would not have been without any effect on his work. He composed his own *Kitab al-Masalik wa-l-mamalik* at the end of his life on behalf of the caliph al-Hakam.[18] This intellectual and political context alone would justify the omnipresence of Cordoba, and the real or imagined involvement of Cordoba, in many historical events in the Islamic West, as presented by al-Warraq. But in more concrete terms, it should be noted that it is precisely during the reigns of al-Hakam and his father ʻAbd al-Rahman, that the Umayyads significantly extended their authority in the Maghrib, to the detriment of the Fatimids, their biggest political rivals. They first took Fez and then Sijilmasa in 366 AH/AD 976, in both cases through Maghrawa clans, opposed to the Fatimids, but loyal supporters of the caliphs of Cordoba. In Sijilmasa, Maghrawa armies overthrew the founding Midrarid dynasty. This Cordoban control on Sijilmasa and the

[18] Gilliot 2002.

will to fully integrate the Saharan site in the caliphate could justify the production of a new foundation myth giving Cordoba a significant responsibility, even if it was indirect, in the development of the city. One should notice that Sijilmasa was not the only city to attach an important role to Cordoba in its founding myths. For instance, the same process was adopted in Fez, where the name of an Andalusian district was explicitly linked to the migration which occurred in the aftermath of the revolt of the suburbs of Cordoba. Although the first mention of this *fassi* (Fez) myth is quite late (fourteenth century), the district's name dates from the Umayyad period at least.[19] However, neither al-Warraq nor al-Bakri after him, reported the Maghrawa conquest of Sijilmasa in their chronicles, simply because the first of these Andalusian authors was already dead at this time. It thus follows that the invention of the myth of the Andalusian foundation of Sijilmasa post-dated the effective conquest of the city. Yet this does not invalidate its origin since the expansionist policy of the Umayyads, and their justifications, date back to the early days of the caliphate. Historical and genealogical references to Corboda and al-Andalus are numerous in literature from the western Islamic world, whatever the period. The practice goes beyond the case of Sijilmasa and therefore the passage from al-Bakri's text must not be retained for itself. But it must not be ruled out either because if it does not actually inform on the period of the city's emergence, it is nonetheless a valuable document for understanding its history in the tenth century.

If we leave aside the origin of this founding myth and its doubtful chronology, it is the theme of the blacksmith that is of interest. The myth of the blacksmith founder was considered unlikely by al-Bakri. He related the story for documentary rigour, but then dismissed its historicity. Historical literature of the twentieth century has followed his lead and considered it to be an unclear anecdote, devoid of any real historical substance.[20] For one thing, the social function of the blacksmith was not so innocuous as a trader or a peasant. It was a despised activity in Medieval Islamic culture, especially in the Middle East, where it was associated with impurity and dishonesty, relegating the blacksmiths to the bottom of the social scale. Considering a blacksmith to be the founder of a dynasty tarnished the prestige of a power seeking for political recognition.[21]

However, blacksmithing did not have the same connotations on the African continent, especially in the Saharo-Sahelian area. Here, even if the

[19] Lévi-Provençal 1938. [20] ʿAbd al-Raziq 1985, 114; Mellouki 1985, 70; Pellat 1960.
[21] Chelhod 1978.

smithy is usually synonymous with some social constraints and social isolation, the blacksmith could be esteemed for his know-how and his technical superiority that allowed him to be closely associated with the symbolic world in many Sahelian societies. This form of power gave him the position of a well-advised and shrewd man whose social position could be related to a privileged caste or an intellectual activity.[22] Thus, the blacksmith parentage has been invoked repeatedly in the genealogies of major African dynasties, especially among Mandé populations, including the case of the Soso Kingdom in the twelfth century.[23] From this new perspective, the association of the founder of Sijilmasa with a blacksmith is understandable if the emergence of this political structure was in an African, not an Arabic, cultural environment. This is an altogether logical situation in the eighth century south of the Atlas. Al-Bakri related an historical version that was obviously totally incomprehensible for an Arabised author like himself. This text reinforces the hypothesis of a 'black' power at the beginnings of Sijilmasa, strongly rooted in local social stratification and indigenous political references, and not so much on the eastern ideology of kharijism that was still little known in the region. A historical detail about al-Warraq is also meaninful. Al-Warraq was born in North Africa and travelled in the Maghrib in his youth, perhaps even to Sijilmasa, which was the main topic of a monographic text he wrote in al-Andalus (but which is now lost).[24] Al-Warraq could have collected and understood such a mythical tale in Tafilalt. Thus, the theme of the blacksmith certainly has a genuine ideological and social foundation and perhaps it reveals a lot about the real context of the emergence of the filalian state, in this non-orientalised social body, which was probably not even Islamised.

Environmental Survey: The Hypothesis of a 'Salt Cure' in Tafilalt before Sijilmasa

As mentioned above, Medieval authors and contemporary historiography have not considered the area where Sijilmasa emerged as having any pre-existing form of political power, let alone being a proto-state, before the foundation of the city. Tafilalt, in the account of al-Bakri, was described as a vast plain with favourable pastures for nomadic activities, but hostile and lacking any permanent settlement and territorial development. However,

[22] Heusch 1956, 62. [23] Dieterlen 1964, 13; Levtzion 1973, 51. [24] Gilliot 2002.

in the light of the previous arguments, the hypothesis of a well-established and structured political power in Tafilalt before the foundation of Sijilmasa must not be ruled out. Nor can we exclude the idea of the presence of a significant, or even dense, population in the region. Several archaeological arguments tend to support this option. Indeed, the large number of pre-Islamic monuments known in the Tafilalt is a very visible sign of human occupation before the rise of Sijilmasa.[25] All around the current oasis occupying the heart of the Tafilalt plain where stand the ruins of Sijilmasa, are thousands of funeral structures, mostly pre-Islamic tumuli. The area of Erfoud, about 20 km north of the archaeological tell of Sijilmasa, is the only place where they have been studied archaeologically, but there are many other spots with funeral monuments standing within short distances of the Medieval site.[26] Unfortunately, these graves are not dated, but Jean Margat believes that many of them only slightly preceded the emergence of Sijilmasa. He even proposes the possibility that such funeral rites survived the early days of the introduction of Islam.[27] Populations were necessarily associated with these burial practices and thus were established in the region, at least seasonally.

This human concentration in Tafilalt can find several explanations. First, although it is a desert region, it is favourable to life because of exceptional hydrological conditions. Indeed, Tafilalt forms a vast depression of about 50 km in diameter, located between the foothills of the Atlas mountains and the Algerian hamadas, into which many wadis naturally drained (Fig. 16.1). The two most important of these wadis, the Ziz and the Gheris, flow from north to south, cross the plain before drying up a short distance beyond the main depression. These two rivers have exceptional flow and are active for a substantial part of the year, but especially in spring time when they are swollen up by snowmelt.[28] The recurring humidity of the depression, added to a rainy season in the autumn, promotes the development of pastures. Furthermore, Tafilalt has a loamy soil that is highly favourable to the development of pastures compared to the sterile rocky floor of the surrounding hamadas. This would have encouraged the seasonal arrival of pastoral people as evoked by al-Bakri and is why Samgu was one among numerous sheperds in Tafilalt before the foundation of Sijilmasa. But this does not fully explain the record of the annual trade gathering as related by al-Bakri in his explanation of the emergence of Sijilmasa. The foundation myths in connection with sufrism or with the blacksmith are superimposed in al-Bakri's text onto his account of

[25] See Sterry *et al.*, Chapter 6, this volume.

[26] Margat and Camus 1959; Ruhlmann 1939. See now, Bokbot 2019, 317–24 for a useful summary.

[27] Margat and Camus 1959, 370. [28] Margat *et al.* 1962, 32.

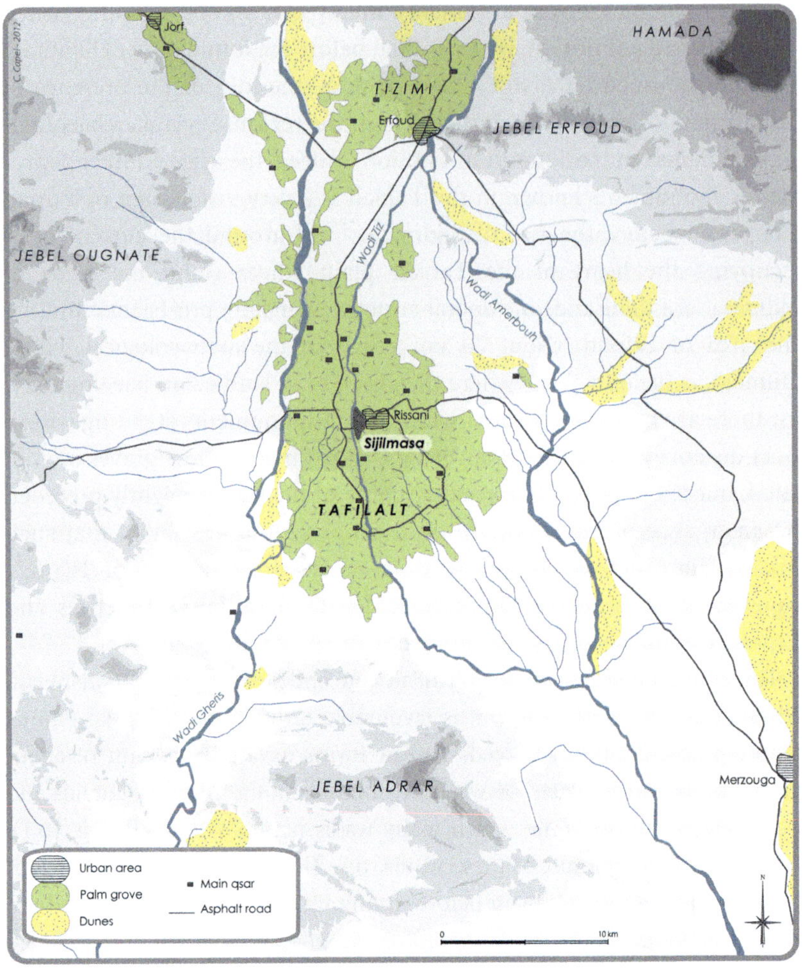

Figure 16.1. Map of Tafilalt today (C. Capel).

this gathering. The hypothesis of a seasonal fair in Tafilalt, with (commercial) exchanges, where Midrar was supposed to have sold/exchanged his tools, must be discussed in relation to the *khariji* rise and the pre-Islamic political structure of the region. These three assumptions are not mutually exclusive. Rather, it could be that pastoralists, who regularly frequented the place, already knew Tafilalt as a stable and famous regional place of exchanges and perhaps the location of a settlement before the rise of Islam. But if a favourable climate and environment were the reason for nomads to gather in Tafilalt, it is not the only place with such natural conditions south of the Atlas Mountains and it is probably necessary to consider other arguments of why Tafilalt was a place of preferential attraction.

Certainly, the annual gathering of nomadic people was justified by economic necessities, as al-Bakri related. As some nomads still proceed nowadays, one could also invoke tribal, social and marriage requirements to justify such fairs in order to maintain bonds between communities that were isolated from one another for the rest of the year. But the reason why it would have taken place precisely in Tafilalt could be because of its salt deposit. The (re)discovery of a sabkha in the immediate neighbourhood of Sijilmasa, which presents clues of human exploitation, brings a decisive argument in the choice of populations to gather and even settle in Tafilalt.[29] It also sheds a new light on the way the region could have developed economically. The commercial fair that al-Bakri describes could have been primarily motivated by the completion of a 'cure salée' (salt cure) among shepherds, even if the antiquity of this activity cannot be estimated. This salt deposit is certainly a key element in understanding the seasonal aggregation phenomena in pre-Islamic times in Tafilalt, but also the development of sedentary lifestyles at the time of emergence of Sijilmasa. The metabolism of domestic ungulates in desert environments requires nutritional supplements, particularly in terms of minerals; this may be facilitated by organising stays in areas with brackish water and/or salty pastures. The geomorphology of the Tafilalt plain is of a closed hydrological basin from which groundwater cannot escape underground, but only by evaporation. Consequently, the loamy soil of the plain has a significant salt content, especially in the southern part of the basin, along the Ziz river, where the waters are concentrated and blocked against the surrounding mountains.[30] From Cordoba, al-Bakri himself heard about this information since he mentions it in his description of the vicinity of Sijilmasa. On the south-eastern side of Sijilmasa, about 15 km from the main archaeological mound, lies a wide area of salty land called the Tamezguida sabkha. Moreover, at the end of the rainy season, a large salty pond forms in the immediate vicinity of the sabkha. The brackish water of this Daya Tamesguida makes it a valued watering point for wild and domestic animals. Thus Tafilalt provides ideal and rare conditions for a salt cure, either by brackish surface water, by salty pastures or by the direct consumption of natural salty efflorescences forming at the surface of the sabkha. This is a good reason for why pastoralists would have gathered annually in Tafilalt.

[29] The existence of this sabkha is not a real discovery as it is mentioned on old topographic maps, especially the one produced in the 1930s (but not on the versions of the 1970s).

[30] Margat *et al.* 1962, 120–28.

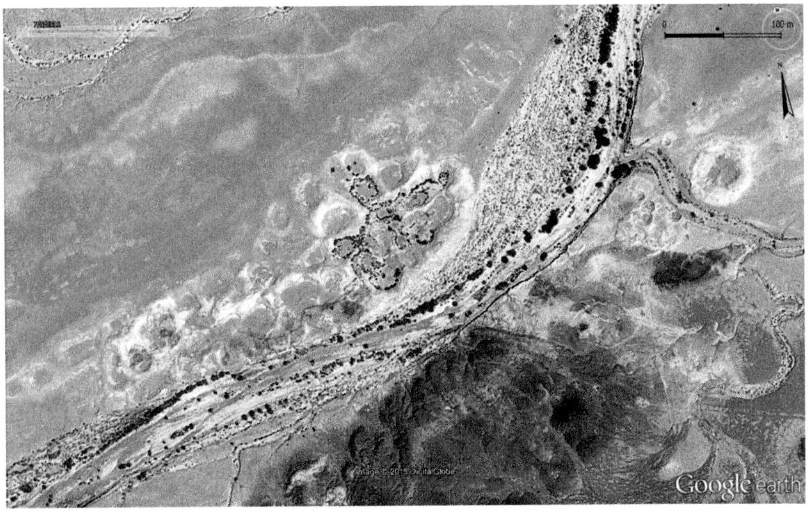

Figure 16.2. Aerial view of a salt extraction site along Wadi Ziz at the place called Tamellaht. This spot is not dated and may be modern but does not go back before the ninth century AD (image: Google, DigitalGlobe).

The salt deposit of Tafilalt is a new aspect for understanding the economic development of the region and its position on the caravan routes, regardless of any Trans-Saharan economy prior to the appearance of Sijilmasa. The salt, which was certaintly exploited in Tafilalt between the twelfth and the eighteenth century (and later for a period of ten years),[31] may have been mined much earlier.[32] It is possible that salt exploitation dates back as far as the pre-Islamic period when pastoralists would have collected salt in Tafilalt for the needs of their animals and society, either freely and informally, or according to community regulations. Furthermore, salt may have been more than an informal resource for pastoralists, but exploited for its economic potential with a 'mining' management earlier than the twelfth century. Clues of salt extraction in the sabkha of Sijilmasa (Fig. 16.2) do not reach the scale and the density of those in the salt deposits of Taghaza and Tawdenni, well known for their intensive exploitation and traded at a continental scale. But even if the saltwork of Sijilmasa was of a smaller scale to these Saharan deposits, its role in the local economy could have been considerable and it may have

[31] Unpublished personal doctoral research. The exploitation of salt in Tafilalt is made by leaching and not by mine working.

[32] Unfortunately, archaeological evidence of salt extraction in Tafilalt cannot be dated at the moment. Historical sources confirm this activity since at least the twelfth century, but the practice could be older.

had important repercussions for the structuring for the state of Sijilmasa. Indeed, the salt would have become a capitalised property of the state on which it could have imposed control and therefore legitimated part of its authority. This mineral resource may be key to explaining the basis of the Sijilmasian authority, beyond the justification of the spirituality of *khariji* teaching. Sijilmasa might also have created an economic monopoly on salt, although to this day it remains impossible to establish its effectiveness or to define its terms. If an ancient salt exploitation in Tafilalt is now proven, the way this operation took place and the date of its beginnings remain unknown.

Archaeological Survey: The Hypothesis of Dense Settlements in Tafilalt before Sijilmasa

Could the annual gathering in Tafilalt have led to some people adopting a sedentary lifestyle here even before the rise of Sijilmasa? The environmental optimum of the Tafilalt plain may at first sight have favoured permanent settlements and not just seasonal dwellings as in the context of pastoral activities. As this volume makes clear, this phenomenon was observed elsewhere in the Sahara, especially during episodes of climatic downturn in the Neolithic period. On these occasions, people gathered in areas of privileged environment and developed a light agriculture based on the exploitation of ponds or springs by means of a moderate irrigation.[33] As a matter of fact, the Western Maghrib in general and the Tafilalt plain in particular may have faced an episode of sharp climatic deterioration between the seventh and ninth centuries, compared to a much wetter early millennium.[34]

This significant change in environmental conditions, unfavourable to pastoral activity, may have forced population settlement and the development of agriculture, although the environmental realities prohibit any dry farming in the region. But in Tafilalt, whether these climatic variations happened or not, if environmental conditions are ideal for pastoral lifestyle, they seem to be less appropriate for agriculture. Indeed, without irrigation, there is no means to develop long-term agriculture here. The Wadis Ziz and the Gheris provide surface water during most of the year, but are not well adapted to irrigation because of the deep downcutting of their channels in the substratum of the plain – except in the downstream

[33] Amblard-Pison 2011.

[34] Publications on recent climate history in the Maghrib are scarce and this prohibits any definitive statement. However, it seems that the rise of Sijilmasa more or less coincided with a period of desiccation of the environment, Capel, forthcoming; cf. Schneider 2017.

Figure 16.3. Bed and riverbanks of Wadi Ziz on the northern side of Tafilalt plain (C. Capel). The power of floods has cut the riverbed into the level of bedrock and continuously erodes the banks, which makes cultivation along the Ziz difficult. Agriculture is most feasible downstream, where the riverbed is not so deep, in the south of Tafilalt plain, or close to seasonal ponds.

area, south of the basin. Other factors that constrain irrigation include the great instability of the river banks and the violence of the flow during the flood season (Fig. 16.3). But cultivation was nonetheless certainly possible on small short-lived plots, established in the beds of the rivers – especially just after the flood season – and around seasonal water ponds left by the rains, like the (large) Daya Tamesguida. Therefore, prior to the foundation of Sijilmasa, Tafilalt may have not only been a focus for seasonal nomadic people but also sedentary agricultural populations practicing a strategy of itinerant exploitation along the main wadis of the plain. Margat and Jacques-Meunié, with different arguments, both put forward the thesis of sedentary and rural settlement in Tafilalt before the Islamic era.[35] This type of practice enables crops which require little water and have a short growth cycle (less than 120 days). Cereals are the most suitable species (durum wheat and barley especially), but the culture of a number of hardy species of legumes (peas, beans, lentils, alfalfa), many of which are forage plants, can also be made possible.[36] The date of introduction of palm trees in Tafilalt, and in the Maghrib in general, is not known and we must not rule

[35] Jacques-Meunié 1982, 195–96; Margat and Camus 1959, 370.
[36] Chiche 1984, 151; Pascon 1984, 17.

out a pre-Islamic presence as date palm cultivation has been identified in Kharga oasis (Egypt) as early as the fifth century BC and even earlier in Fazzan.[37] But the date palm cultivation requires a lot of water and, without irrigation all the year long, it can only be possible in the immediate vicinity of wadis, which seems unlikely in Tafilalt without a system of dykes and canals being developed to mitigate the violence of the floods. Consequently, the introduction of the date palm in Tafilalt seems relatively late and could be contemporary with the huge irrigation system that was dug contemporaneously with the beginning of Sijilmasa (see below).

Under these conditions, it would be possible to argue for the existence of a pre-Islamic dense sedentary society in Tafilalt associated with agriculture. Did not al-Bakri tell us that the city of Ziz gradually emptied of its inhabitants for the ultimate benefit of Sijilmasa?[38] The city of Ziz has never been located, but following a proposal by Daniel Eustache in 1971, most authors agree to place it far upstream from the Tafilalt, in the area of the High Atlas plateau.[39] A careful reading of the Arabic sources mentioning the city of Ziz leads me to reconsider the location of this city. There is no evidence in textual sources that Ziz would be within the Atlas Mountains and it appeared that this suggested location is based on an incorrect, or truncated, translation by Mohammed Hadj Sadok published in 1949.[40] Contrary to what has been usually asserted since Eustache, Ziz cannot be located in the Atlas Mountains because according to Ibn Khurradadhbih, who is the only author to mention the city at the same period of its activity, it was located south of Der'a, in the same direction as 'the land of Habasha', that is the *Bilad al-Sudan*, 'the land of the Blacks'.[41] This topographical clue requires us to locate Ziz south of the Atlas and because the wadi had already taken its name by the late ninth century,[42] this suggests that this city was located not far from its banks. The crosschecking of this information makes Tafilalt one of the best candidates for the location of the city of Ziz as it is situated both south of the Atlas and along the river of the same name. In addition, as discussed above, it enjoys a very favourable environment in this desert landscape where a light cultivation could be possible. Moreover, if Sijilmasa had such an impact on the demography and the economy of Ziz, by depopulating it as al-Bakri said, then Ziz should have been located in the area of direct influence of the new city of Sijilmasa, and

[37] Tenberg 2012, 146; Van der Veen 2010, 514; see also Mattingly *et al.*, Chapter 2, this volume.
[38] Al-Bakri 1911, 148; Al-Bakri 1913, 282. [39] Eustache 1971, 142.
[40] Hadj-Sadok 1949, 32–33. [41] Ibn Khurradadhbih 1865, 209; 1889, 88.7.
[42] Al-Ya'qubi 1892, 358–60; 1937, 225–26.

probably much closer than the High Atlas plateau, which is geographically, economically and socially distinct of the Saharan oasis system.

Archaeology, if it does not bring (yet) decisive arguments in this debate, provides evidence that urban-scale settlements were possible in Tafilalt before the rise of Sijilmasa. The site of Sijilmasa has remained quite poorly documented until now from a strictly archaeological point of view. Nevertheless, three major excavation programmes have taken place there and a fourth one is currently underway. Due to a combination of political and nationalistic reasons, since Tafilalt is the cradle of the dynasty reigning over Morocco today, Sijilmasa became a major archaeological focus in the early 1970s. The Moroccan authorities appealed to an Italian team to start a programme of research in Sijilmasa in 1971 and 1972. These two campaigns led to a short publication of limited archaeological interest, but with valuable information about oral traditions.[43] At the end of this programme, scientific and political disputes led the Moroccan authorities to ban any foreign teams from new excavations in Sijilmasa. A second Moroccan project made a short campaign in 1974, but without any follow-up or publication. It was ultimately in the 1980s that Morocco consolidated its archaeological institutional basis – with the creation of an archaeological department at the Ministry of Culture and the opening of a national institute for training in archeology and heritage (INSAP). INSAP was then able to reconsider Sijilmasa within the framework of an ambitious archaeological programme. In partnership with the ceramics laboratory of Lyon (France), Morocco organised a survey and surface collections at Sijilmasa, which resulted in a major article about trade connections between Tafilalt and Awdaghust (Tagdaoust) but which told little about Sijilmasa itself.[44] This Moroccan–French project had no follow-up, but the renewed interest was beneficial to the team of Ronald Messier (Middle Tennessee State University) that was finally allowed to open new excavations, as the Moroccan–American Project at Sijilmasa (MAPS) in cooperation with INSAP. MAPS started a work of greater magnitude with six successive campaigns between 1988 and 1998, mostly focused on the main archaeological mound of the site. The MAPS programme is today the main source of archaeological information about Sijilmasa which has been published between 1993 and 2015 in a series of 20 articles and a recent monograph. Despite some archaeological weaknesses, these documents are of paramount interest since they are the first to offer a fairly accurate view of the archaeological reality of the site.

[43] Rachewiltz 1973. [44] El-Hraiki *et al.* 1986.

Since 2011, a new Moroccan–French programme, led from Toulouse, has taken over the site of Sijilmasa. The first publications are expected soon. Meanwhile, my doctoral research, initiated in 2009, built on the remarkable but still under-exploited work of MAPS. Furthermore I conducted extensive and fruitful survey of the Tafilalt plain between 2011 and 2013, in order to gain a broader historical view and a finer understanding of the context of development of the city.

Two interesting sites are located in the vicinity of the Medieval city. Both consist of the ruins of several dozen buildings or enclosures, constructed in a stone architecture. Both sites are located on rocky hilltops (Jabal Afilal and Jabal Oulad Zohra) directly overlooking the course of Wadi Ziz, being enclosed by an enceinte, defining a perimeter of 7 and 3.5 ha respectively. Respectively located 46 and 12 km from the archaeological tell of Sijilmasa, they were previously reported in the archaeological literature, but have never been studied.[45] Surveys on these two sites, as part of my work in Tafilalt, revealed that they were likely permanent dwellings (although with less certainty for the second site which has more enclosures), each one containing several structures of unusual design and dimensions which can be identified as collective places or monuments of power (Figs 16.4–16.6).

Figure 16.4. Jabal Afilal and its pre-Islamic settlement on the top of a hill, view from north-east (C. Capel).

[45] Allain and Meunié 1956; Margat and Camus 1959. Jabal Afilal is the site described in Sterry *et al.*, Chapter 6, this volume, as Taouz 1, from which engravings of >200 chariots have been recorded.

Figure 16.5. Aerial view of Jabal Afilal, surrounded by cliffs and overlooking Wadi Ziz (south-eastern corner). About 50 houses are enclosed in a wall with a separate 'citadel' (west side) where some unusual buildings (by size and plan) are concentrated, opposite the site's eastern gate (imagery: Google, DigitalGlobe).

Figure 16.6. The northern wall of the Jabal Afilal settlement. In the background, the Wadi Ziz runs through the southern part of Tafilalt plain, where the riverbed is not deep and where agriculture is feasible along its banks (C. Capel).

The closeness of these sites to Wadi Ziz would have allowed some agricultural cultivation of the river bed. Consequently, all these elements could allow us to identify these sites as villages, or as urban or proto-urban areas.

The main issue remains the question of their dating. Without any excavation, it is of course difficult to accurately identify and date these sites. The surface collection provided very few artefacts, mainly ceramics which were badly abraded and with almost no diagnostic shapes. Despite this, it seems assured that these sherds are not Medieval or modern because their fabric, with a lot of vegetal temper, has nothing in common with the ceramics from Sijilmasa. All other Medieval or modern sites discovered in the Tafilalt plain during my survey campaigns, even far from Sijilmasa, revealed thin or domestic ceramics of the type found in the MAPS excavations of the city. The ceramic artefacts collected on both sites can plausibly be suggested to indicate a pre-Islamic dating.[46]

Conclusion: From the Emergence of the Filalian State to the Building of the City of Sijilmasa

In Tafilalt, as elsewhere in the world, the emergence of a new political authority, of a new power, does not necessarily mean the birth of a city and the rise of an urban society, as Judith Scheele emphasises.[47] The process leading to the birth of a city and the close match between the state and its capital city derives from another scheme, from a complementary development. Social constraints, but also economic and technological factors are involved in this separate process. However, the special case of Sijilmasa could apparently reflect Bourdieu's model of the birth of the state, although this model was conceived for and from modern industrialised and capitalist societies. In Bourdieu's model, the final stage completing the structuring of a power is the production of arguments of its own legitimacy. Once the state starts to think about itself in order to definitively establish its authority, it gives birth to a wide range of instruments which not only justify the existence of this power, but in turn, fully contribute to build and develop it further. This initiates a vicious circle where the foundations of power and its means of action are the same.[48] It is during this final step that the instruments and productions of the state appear and multiply, as issues of currency or writing of historical vulgates, as creation of legal and legislative rules or production of state symbols, as physical materialisation of domination through architectural programmes or the exercise of this

[46] Mattingly *et al.* 2017 discuss comparable hilltop sites in the Draa valley to the west of Tafilalt, which have similar ceramics and have been radiocarbon dated to the pre-Islamic period. See also Sterry *et al.*, Chapter 6, this volume.

[47] Scheele, Chapter 18, this volume. [48] Lenoir 2013, 148.

domination by the management of collective rules of life. All these elements ultimately define the state and its essence but, as mentioned in the introduction to this chapter, they *follow* the birth of the state.

In the case of Sijilmasa, all these structural elements may indeed gradually have appeared after the emergence of a political power and a state in Tafilalt. In the intellectual and symbolic field for example, the creation of an Eastern descent for the Midraride dynasty, with references to the preacher ʿIkrima, was part of this legitimacy step.[49] We propose to connect the founding of the city of Sijilmasa to this precise step. It then follows that the emergence of the new power in Tafilalt was in a temporality that would not be exactly superimposed. Indeed, we propose to date the foundation of Sijilmasa, as the city documented by the vast archaeological site located west of the modern town of Risani in the heart of Tafilalt, from around 200 AH/AD 815, that is to say about half a century after the social and political changes that occurred according to al-Bakri in Tafilalt in the middle of the eighth century. My work, in the process of being published,[50] has developed many historical, archaeological and environmental arguments, leading me to propose a new conclusion. Under the reign of the fourth *khariji* king of Tafilalt, Abu al-Muntasir al-Yasaʿ, the second son of Samgu and father of Midrar, who ascended the throne in 174 AH/AD 790–791, a royal city was built on the initiative of the prince at some distance from the original nucleus of sedentary filalian population. The prince would have moved his headquarters and residence there after the completion of a vast architectural and land improvement programme. One of the aims, but not the only one, was an ambitious assertion of his power, justified by the contemporaneous threat of a growing Idrisid hegemony over the Maghrib and the will to strengthen his own supremacy towards his own allies and people. The symbolic value of such an initiative would be decisive. The construction of this city was also coupled with a vast programme of agricultural development in Tafilalt in order to support the population growth of this new sedentary nucleus and the involvement of the city in Trans-Saharan trade. It meant the establishment of intensive agriculture, that is to say irrigated agriculture, thanks to the construction of a huge artificial hydraulic system. This was probably constructed by a decision of the state rather than a collective societal decision. It is this new city that subsequently became the urban heart of Tafilalt and was named Sijilmasa. This new city was therefore a relatively late foundation in connection with the constitution of the filalian state. This mirrors the delay between

[49] Capel and Fili 2018. [50] Capel 2016; 2018.

assuming power and starting new architectural programmes by other Islamic dynasties such as the Umayyads of Damascus (who built the Dome of the Rock, for instance, 30 years after taking power) and the Abbasids (who built Baghdad as their capital 12 years after they overthrew the Umayyad caliphs). Hence, the Midrarids of Tafilalt visually imposed their authority on the filalian landscape one to two generations after their effective political rise in the region. Finally, the date we propose for the founding of Sijilmasa, based on historical, archaeological and environmental arguments, roughly coincides with the uprising of Cordoba. It is thus very likely that the Cordoban foundation myth of Sijilmasa is actually the expression of the remembrance of the founding of this new city and one that linked it to the discourse of the Umayyad caliphs.

The analysis of the process of emergence of Sijilmasa, first as a social and political authority and then as a city, emphasises that Tafilalt was probably a major meeting place and perhaps had several small rural settlements, with quite strong political organisation, a long time before the rise of Trans-Saharan trade. As David Mattingly and Martin Sterry remind us in this volume, this pattern shows similarities with the history of Fazzan which was a regular stop on Islamic-era trade routes across the Sahara because it had previously developed an autonomous economic and political system. The case of Tafilalt would underpin the assumption that Islamic trade routes that formed across the Sahara from the eighth century, were determined according to sites which were previously occupied and were not an *ex nihilo* creation. This does not mean that all these sites were necessarily already involved in a continental-scale exchange system, which remains essentially an Islamic project. Some areas, such as Fazzan, were already maintaining long-distance trade routes with the Mediterranean coast, but some others, like Tafilalt, were merely local centres. Unlike Fazzan, the political and economic achievement of Tafilalt was in the development of Islamic era Trans-Saharan trade. Without it, and without the movement of gold with which it is closely associated, Tafilalt would probably have only remained a major place of nomadic gathering, a modest oasis zone, but not the huge city and the powerful state it became in the Medieval period.

References

ʿAbd al-Raziq, M.I. 1985. *Al-khawârij fî bilâd al-Maghrib hattâ muntasaf al-qarn al-râbi'al-Hijrî*. Casablanca: Maktabat al-Hurrîyah al-Hadîthah.

Allain, J. and Meunié, J. 1956. Quelques gravures et monuments funéraires de l'extrême sud-marocain. *Hespéris* 43: 51–86.

Amanis, S.A. 2009. *Dictionnaire Tamazight-Français (Parlers du Maroc central)*. Paris: Harmattan.

Amblard-Pison, S. 2011. Villages et territoires villageois néolithiques d'une zone refuge au Sahara méridional. In G. Kourtessi-Philippakis and R. Treuil (eds), *Archéologie du territoire, de l'Égée au Sahara*. Paris: Publications de la Sorbonne, 169–79.

Al-Bakri, 1911. *Kitâb al-masâlik wa-'l-mamâlik*. 2nd edition (1st edition 1857). Edited by W. Mac Guckin de Slane. Algiers: A. Jourdan.

Al-Bakri, 1913. *Description de l'Afrique septentrionale*, 2nd edition (1st edition 1859). Translated by W. Mac Guckin de Slane. Algiers: A. Jourdan.

Bokbot, Y. 2019. Protohistoric and pre-Islamic funerary archaeology in the Moroccan pre-Sahara. In M. Gatto, D.J. Mattingly, N. Ray and M. Sterry (eds), *Burials, Migration and Identity in the Ancient Sahara and Beyond*. Cambridge: Cambridge University Press and The Society for Libyan Studies, 315–40.

Bouderbala, N., Chiche, J., Herzenni, A. and Pascon, P. (eds). 1984. *La question hydraulique. 1. Petite et moyenne hydraulique au Maroc*. Rabat: Institut Agronomique Hassan II.

Bourdieu, P. 2012. *Sur l'Etat: Cours au Collège de France (1989–1992)*. Paris: Points.

Capel, C. 2016. Une grande hydraulique saharienne à l'époque médiévale: L'oued Ziz et Sijilmassa (Maroc). *Mélanges de la Mélanges de la Casa de Velàzquez*. 46.1: 139–65.

Capel, C. 2018. Sijilmasa in the footsteps of the Aghlabids: The hypothesis of a ninth century new royal city in Tafilalt Plain (Morocco). In G. Anderson, C. Fenwick and M. Rosser-Owen (eds), *The Aghlabids and their Neighbours: Art and Material Culture in the 9th-century North Africa*. Leiden: Brill, 531–50.

Capel, C. Forthcoming. The impact of climate modulations on the economic, social and political reorganisation of Maghreb al-Aqsa in the 8th-9th centuries. *Al-Masaq* 32.

Capel, C. and Fili, A. 2018. Sijilmâsa au temps des Midrârides: Nouvelles approches historiques et premier bilan archéologique. In C. Aillet (ed.), *L'ibadisme dans les sociétés de l'Islam médiéval. Modèles et interactions*. Berlin/Boston: De Gruyter, 137–67.

Chelhod, J. 1978. Qayn. *Encyclopedia of Islam*, 2nd edition. Leiden: Brill, 2: 819.

Chiche, J. 1984. Description de l'hydraulique traditionnelle. In Bouderbala *et al.* 1984, 119–319.

Dieterlen, G. 1964. Contribution à l'étude des forgerons en Afrique occidentale. *Annuaire 1965–1966 de l'École Pratique des Hautes Etudes, Section des sciences religieuses* 73: 3–28.

El-Hraiki, R., Picon, M. and Robert, D. 1986. Ateliers et commerce transsaharien à l'époque médiévale. In *La ceramica medievale nel Mediterraneo occidentale. Siena, Faenza, 8–13 ottobre 1984*. Firenze: Edizioni all'Insegna del Giglio, 51–54.
Eustache, D. 1971. *Corpus des dihrmas idrisites et contemporains: Collection de la Banque du Maroc et autres collections mondiales, publiques et privies.* Rabat: Banque du Maroc.
Genêt, J.P. 2014. A propos de Pierre Bourdieu et de la genèse de l'Etat moderne. *Actes de la recherche en sciences sociales* 201–202: 98–105.
Gilliot, C. 2002. Al-Warrâq. *Encyclopedia of Islam*, 2nd edition. Leiden: Brill, 11: 151.
Hadj-Sadok, M. 1949. *Description du Maghreb et de l'Europe au iiie/ixe siècle: extraits du Kitâb al-masâlik wa'l-mamâlik, du Kitâb al-buldân et du Kitâb al-a'lâq an-nafîsa.* Alger: Jules Carbonel.
Heusch, L. 1956. Le symbolisme du forgeron en Afrique. *Reflets du monde* 10: 57–70.
Ibn Khurradadhbih. 1865. *Le livre des routes et des provinces.* French translation by C. Barbier de Meynard. Paris: Imprimerie Impériale.
Ibn Khurradadhbih 1889. *Kitâb al-masâlik wa-'l-mamâlik.* Edition M.J. de Goeje. Leiden: Brill.
Jacques-Meunié, D. 1982. *Le Maroc saharien des origines à 1670.* Paris: Klincksieck.
Lenoir, R. 2013. L'état selon Pierre Bourdieu. *Sociétés contemporaines* 87 (2012–2013): 123–54.
Lévi-Provençal, E. 1938. La fondation de Fès. *Annales de l'Institut d'études orientales* 4: 23–53.
Levtzion, N. 1973. *Ancient Ghana and Mali.* London: Methuen.
Margat, J., Destombes, J. and Hollard, H. 1962. *Mémoire explicatif de la carte hydrogéologique au 1:50000 de la plaine du Tafilalt, Notes et Mémoire du Service Géologique.* 150 bis. Rabat: Éditions du Service Géologique du Maroc.
Margat, J. and Camus, A. 1959. La nécropole de Bouïa au Tafilalt. *Bulletin d'Archéologie Marocaine* 3: 63–74.
Al-Mas'udî 1865. *Murûj al-dhahab wa-ma'âdin al-jawhar.* Edition and French translation, C. Barbier de Meynard and A. Pavet de Courteille, volume IV. Paris: Imprimerie Nationale.
Mattingly, D.J., Bokbot, Y., Sterry, M., Cuénod, A., Fenwick, C., Gatto, M., Ray, N., Rayne, L., Janin, K., Lamb, A., Mugnai, N. and Nikolaus, J. 2017. Long-term history in a Moroccan oasis zone: The Middle Draa Project 2015. *Journal of African Archaeology* 15: 141–72.
Mellouki, M. 1985. *Contribution à l'histoire des villes médiévales du Maroc: Sijilmâsa des origines à 668/1269.* Unpublished PhD dissertation, Université Aix-Marseille.
Mezzine, L. 1984. Sur l'étymologie du toponyme Sijilmasa. *Hespéris* 22: 19–25.
Pascon, P. 1984. La petite et moyenne hydraulique. In Bouderbala *et al.* 1984, 7–44.

Pellat, C. 1960. Les Banû Midrâr. *Encyclopedia of Islam*, 2nd edition, vol. 1. Leiden: Brill.

Rachewiltz, B. de. 1973. Missione etno archeologica nel Sahara Maghrebino. *Quaderni delle rivisa Africa* 2: 519–68.

Ruhlmann, A. 1939. *Recherches de préhistoire dans l'extrême sud marocain, 5.* Rabat: Publications du Service des Antiquités du Maroc.

Schneider, A.W. 2017. The Medieval Climate Anomaly as a factor in the history of Sijilmasa, southeastern Morocco. *The Journal of North African Studies* 1: 132–52.

Tenberg, M. 2012. Beginnings and early history of date palm garden cultivation in the Middle East. *Journal of Arid Environments* 86: 139–47.

Van der Veen, M. 2010. Plant remains from Zinkekra. Early evidence for oasis agriculture. In D.J. Mattingly (ed.), *The Archaeology of Fazzan. Volume 3, Excavations of C.M. Daniels.* London: The Society of Libyan Studies, 489–519.

Al-Ya'qubi 1892. *Kitâb al-buldân.* Edition, M.J. De Goeje. Leiden: Brill.

Al-Ya'qubi 1937. *Les Pays*, French translation by G. Wiet. Cairo: Institut Français d'Archéologie Orientale.

17 The Early Islamic Trans-Saharan Market Towns of West Africa

SAM NIXON

Introduction

In the early Islamic period, trade across the Sahara escalated to new levels as the rich resources of West African gold, slaves and ivory were imported on camel caravans to the markets of North Africa and the wider Islamic world trade system, these goods being exchanged for products from North Africa such as copper, textiles and glasswares.[1] The immediate destinations for Trans-Saharan camel caravans coming from North Africa were the market towns which developed on the southern fringes of the Sahara, in the most arid zones of the Sahel (*Sahel* meaning 'shore' in Arabic; see Fig. 17.1). These centres became the principal locations for the Trans-Saharan commercial exchange, meeting points between traders from North Africa and the Sahara and those coming from further south in West Africa. Certain trading centres directly involved in the Trans-Saharan exchange also grew up slightly further south in the Sahel, close to the centres of the West African states controlling the gold, slaves, and ivory resources (see Fig. 17.1). In the earliest period of study of Trans-Saharan commerce, these various market centres were understood largely as transplantations of Islamic urban culture.[2] This was a somewhat simplistic model centred around the concept that Muslim traders from North Africa and elsewhere in the Islamic world imported wholesale models of town planning and architectural design to create towns resembling those north of the Sahara and catering to expatriate Muslims. With the increasing awareness of the pre-Islamic origins of urbanism in West

1 See Austen 2010; Devisse 1988; Mitchell 2005, Chapter 5; Nixon 2017b. Cf. also Mattingly *et al.* 2017a.

2 For example, Bovill 1958; Lhote 1951; and for discussion McIntosh, R. 1999.

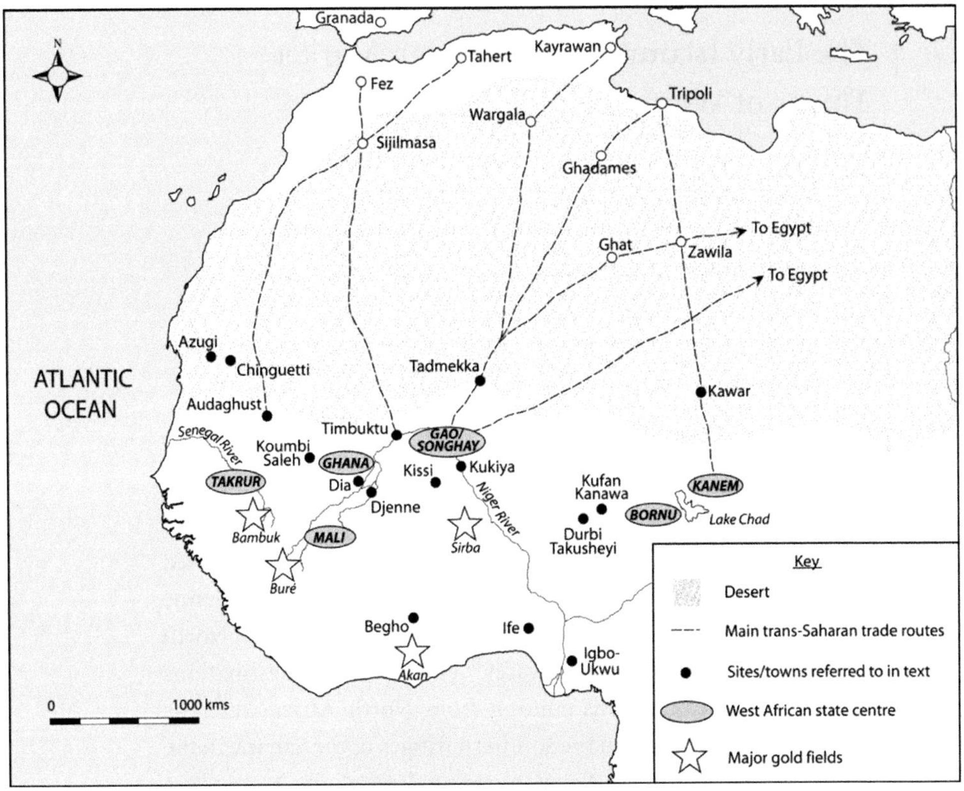

Figure 17.1. Map showing Trans-Saharan trade routes to West Africa and localities referred to in the text.

Africa[3] – and indeed the existence of pre-Islamic urban models from the Sahara itself[4] – as well as a greater recognition of the cultural diversity of early merchant populations,[5] a more nuanced approach has been developed in relation to these towns. This has also been significantly informed by more in-depth archaeological studies of several key sites.

Despite this reassessment, the earliest market towns at the southern fringes of the Sahara – from Mauritania to Niger – and the early trading enclaves established further south are still often commonly discussed together as a distinctive urban phenomenon.[6] This is due to the belief in them having a broadly similar function, based on the following criteria:

1. Being clearly identifiable urban nodes directly associated with the function of Trans-Saharan exchange in the early stages of this commerce;

[3] See McIntosh, S. 1995; Chapter 14, this volume; McIntosh, S. and McIntosh, R. 1993.
[4] See Mattingly and Sterry 2013; Chapter 19, this volume. [5] See Moraes Farias 2003.
[6] For example, Devisse 1988; Insoll 2003, Chapter 5; Kea 2004; Monroe 2017.

2. Their identification as centres with elevated levels of contact with the central Islamic world and associated influence from those regions;
3. The presence there of significant immigrant communities of long distance traders, many of whom were Muslim.

In line with previous scholars, this chapter maintains the utility of considering these towns side by side as a distinctive urban phenomenon whose discussion can help us illuminate wider patterns of urban development in West Africa.

Three localities are identifiable within the Arabic records as key early Islamic centres of exchange at the immediate southern edge of the Sahara. These are Awdaghust, Tadmakka (or Tadmekka) and Kawar,[7] situated on three different routes across the Sahara. In addition to being the earliest entrepôts, these centres also continued to hold this role for centuries after their foundation. All three centres can be associated with archaeological sites, though only Awdaghust and Tadmakka have seen in depth investigation. The Arabic records also provide clear descriptions of the trading centres located slightly further south in the Sahel, in close proximity to the West African state centres. The most significant of these more southerly trading centres – celebrated both by the early Arabic historians and by modern scholars – is that described as located close to the capital of the Empire of Ghana (see below for historical descriptions). The town as described in the Arabic records has never been unequivocally identified with an archaeological site. The archaeological ruins of Kumbi Saleh,[8] which is broadly within the zone of Ghana and its successor states, potentially relates to a chronologically later entrepôt within the orbit of late-period Ghana or its successors. The significance of this site and the relatively extensive investigation undertaken there has established it as an important site for considering the evolution of early merchant centres in West Africa. The other important market centre described by the sources further south in the Sahel lies in close proximity to the royal city of Gao, on the Niger Bend. This is clearly identifiable within the archaeological complex around and under the modern settlement of Gao. Despite the presence of the modern town, the archaeological remains have seen quite significant investigation.[9]

Together this grouping of market centres – Awdaghust, Tadmakka, Gao and Ghana/Kumbi Saleh – forms the core set of historical and archaeological data to allow the exploration of the nature of early Islamic urban

[7] See respectively, Devisse 1983; Nixon 2017a; and Lange and Berthoud 1977.
[8] Berthier 1997. [9] Cissé 2017; Cissé *et al.* 2013.

centres of Trans-Saharan commerce in West Africa, as well as the evolution of these centres with the growth of this commercial system. As a distinctive grouping widely considered to be fundamental for understanding the development of urbanism in the Trans-Saharan network, it is not surprising that various syntheses have been undertaken, both in terms of the wider study of the archaeology of Islam in Sub-Saharan Africa,[10] as well as studies of West African urbanism.[11] This chapter seeks to introduce these urban centres through focused summary accounts of the Arabic historical descriptions of them and the archaeological investigations which have taken place, and within the context of this volume to provide a broad discussion that can direct further debate and investigation of the Trans-Saharan centres. While the review will focus principally on these key market centres, this study will also provide a brief overview of some of the other early market towns that we know of from Arabic texts and archaeology, in order to collate the current body of knowledge relating to them, and to address four key aspects within the broad debate that form the latter part of this chapter:

- Pre-Islamic occupations at the sites of early Trans-Saharan market towns;
- Relationships between the early Islamic Trans-Saharan market towns and surrounding settlements;
- Urban landscapes and settlement planning at the early Islamic Trans-Saharan market towns;
- Architectural construction and building types.

The Trans-Saharan Market Towns: Historical and Archaeological Overview

Awdaghust/Tagdaoust

On the far western Trans-Saharan route running from Morocco through Mauritania the first major settlement south of the Sahara recorded within Arabic records was Awdaghust. This location is first mentioned in AD 872/3 by al-Yaqubi who described it as 'a town called "Ghust", an inhabited valley with dwellings . . . It is the residence of their king who has no religion or law'.[12] Within al-Yaqubi's text the description of Awdaghust clearly

[10] Insoll 2003, Chapter 5. [11] For example, Kea 2004; Monroe 2017.
[12] Levtzion and Hopkins 2000, 22.

shows it to be the first significant location after the desert on the way to the kingdom of Ghana, though the description of its ruler appears to indicate he was not Muslim. At the end of the tenth century (*c.*AD 967–988) the town of Awdaghust was again singled out by Ibn Hawqal as the pre-eminent settlement at the southern fringes of the Sahara on this western route, the writer describing Awdaghust as 'a pleasant town, and of all God's lands it most resembles Mecca . . . ' – this description is clearly designed to identify this as a locality with a strong Muslim presence and recognisable features of an Islamic town.[13] Ibn Hawqal's description also provides a compelling account of the high value of trade conducted at Awdaghust, indicating this to be a flourishing market location:

> I saw at Awdaghust a warrant in which was the statement of a debt owed to one of them [the people of Sijilmasa] by one of the merchants of Awdaghust, who was [himself] one of the people of Sijilmasa, in the sum of 42,000 dinars. I have never heard anything comparable to this story in the East [i.e. in Asia].[14]

Seemingly confirming Awdaghust's status at this period as the major town in this region and a place of flourishing trade, al-Muhallabi (*c.*AD 990), quoted in Yaqut (*c.*AD 1229), stated that:

> The king of Awdaghust maintains relations with the ruler of Ghana . . . there are excellent markets in Awdaghust, and it is one of the most important metropolises, and there is a continuous flow of traffic towards it from every land.[15]

In addition to indicating its commercial importance, al-Muhallabi also seems to identify it as an important Islamic centre: 'its people are Muslims, who recite the Koran, study Islamic jurisprudence and possess mosques and oratories'.[16] Further references appear to indicate certain cultural practices imported from further north, including the cultivation of wheat.[17] In the mid-eleventh century the documents indicate that Awdaghust was attacked by the Almoravids, an Islamic reform movement that developed in the western regions of the Sahara.[18] They went on to subdue certain other urban centres in the Saharan network,[19] before going on to conquer and found a dynasty in the western Maghrib and southern Spain. During this episode, many of the inhabitants of the town were reportedly massacred and the town was said to have been sacked.[20] Reports of Awdaghust after this eleventh-century destruction are less easy

[13] Levtzion and Hopkins 2000, 46. [14] Levtzion and Hopkins 2000, 47.
[15] Levtzion and Hopkins 2000, 168. [16] Levtzion and Hopkins 2000, 168.
[17] Lewicki 1974, 22–26. [18] See Sterry *et al.*, Chapter 6, this volume.
[19] See also Capel, Chapter 16, this volume. [20] Levtzion and Hopkins 2000, 73–74.

to interpret, it being unclear from the reports whether it revived again or lost its status.[21] It is difficult to distinguish in fourteenth-century references whether the name was being used in connection with a permanent settlement or simply in relation to a pastoral locality.[22] This is the last documentary reference to Awdaghust.

From these descriptions it is quite clear that by the ninth century Awdaghust was a permanently inhabited centre, and by the end of the tenth century a location of flourishing commerce with an (at least partly) Islamic population.

The site of Tagdaoust (Tegdaoust) in central Mauritania has been identified with the early Islamic centre of Awdaghust described in the Arabic records (see Fig. 17.2).[23] The equation of Tagdaoust with Awdaghust rests in part on locational information within the early Arabic documents that placed it south of the Tagant in Mauritania.[24] The identification of Tagdaoust as a potential site of Awdaghust's ruins was made initially due to the fact that the site was larger than other sites in the region – though it should be pointed out there are indeed a number of other sites in the surrounding region – something which appeared to correspond with Awdaghust's major early Islamic role in this zone of the Sahel.[25] Another factor which suggested Tagdaoust and Awdaghust were one and the same place was that the specific geographical description of Awdaghust appeared to show strong correspondences with the contemporary environs of Tagdaoust.[26] Although the linguistic correspondence between 'Tagdaoust' and 'Awdaghust' can be seen to be negligible,[27] the contemporary groups possessing the name 'Tagdaoust' have oral traditions which correspond well with the known written history of the town of Awdaghust.[28] When these factors are combined with the findings of archaeology the initial identification is given considerable further weight,[29] so much so that I am not aware of any scholars who contest the assertion that Tagdaoust and Awdaghust are one and the same.

The site of Tagdaoust is situated in a very arid part of the northern Sahel, yet the immediate locality still retains a certain sparse vegetation cover. The site comprises a central tell of *c.*10 ha over which stone architectural ruins of the terminal occupation of the site can be clearly defined. The majority

[21] See Robert *et al.* 1970, 15–27. [22] Levtzion and Hopkins 2000, 274.
[23] Devisse 1983, 5–29. [24] Robert *et al.* 1970, 33–38.
[25] Devisse 1983, 5–29; Robert *et al.* 1970, 39–67. [26] Devisse 1983, 539–49.
[27] Robert *et al.* 1970, 29–30. [28] Robert *et al.* 1970, 97–107. [29] Devisse 1983, 5–29.

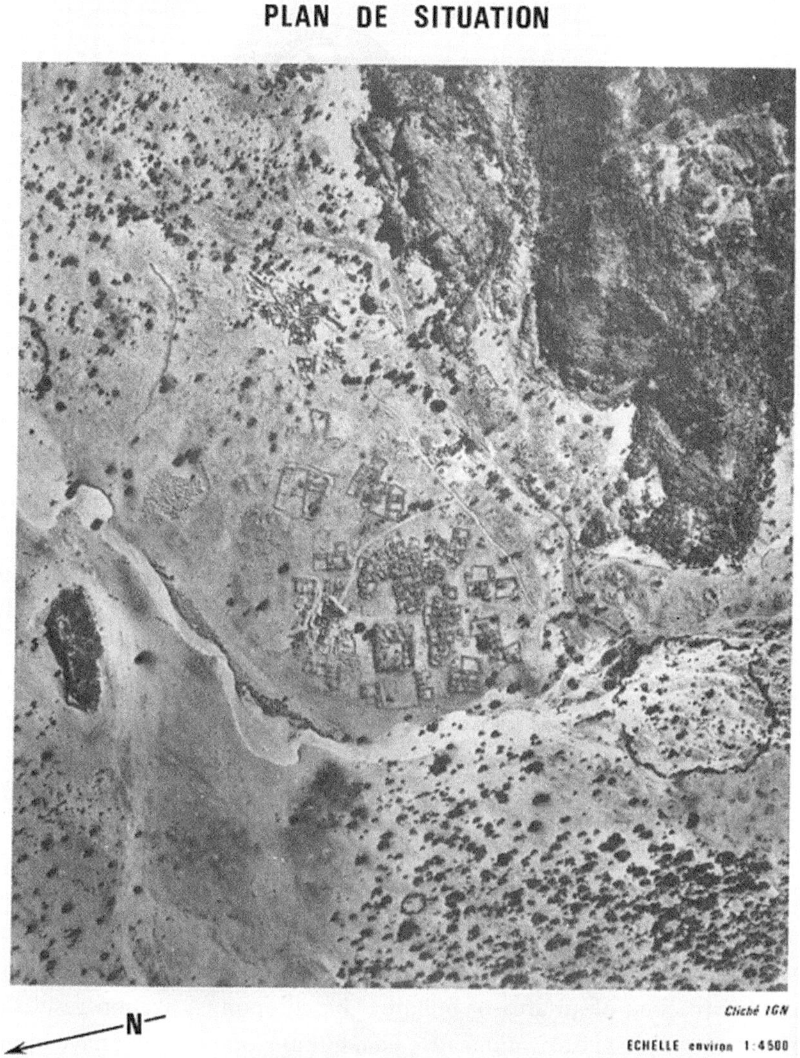

Figure 17.2. Aerial photograph of the site of Tagdaoust (from Vanacker 1979, 2).

of buildings appear to be compounds constructed on a broadly rectilinear plan in dry stone architecture, having rooms arranged around a central courtyard (see Fig. 17.2). There is no evidence that the urban area was defined by a surrounding wall or that it featured other elements of fortification. Amongst the building remains seen on the surface at least one mosque was discovered. In addition to the central tell, there were a number of associated structures surrounding the site – including a *musalla* (open

Figure 17.3. Plan of the excavated area at Tagdaoust, Mauritania, Building Phase 6 (after Holl 2006, fig. 13).

prayer ground) as well as a large cemetery.[30] Fieldwork at Tagdaoust was conducted between 1960 and 1965 by a team of French archaeologists. During this period all zones of the site saw sub-surface investigation and the area which was designated as the principal Medieval tell saw numerous large-exposure excavations (see Fig. 17.2 where extensive excavations can be identified in the northern section of the ruins; see also Fig. 17.3 for a reconstruction of an area of buildings based upon excavation results). The results of these excavations formed a number of theses and have been published in four separate volumes.[31]

The results of the Tagdaoust excavations provided a good stratified occupational and material culture sequence for the site that was dated both by radiocarbon samples and trade goods of known age.[32] The earliest levels of Tagdaoust were dated to the eighth/ninth century AD. These levels were not associated with clear evidence for a full-scale urban settlement, but they did show significant occupation and evidence of mudbrick

[30] For a more detailed description of the site see Devisse 1983, 5–29.
[31] Devisse 1983; Polet 1985; Robert-Chaleix 1989; Vanacker 1979.
[32] See Devisse 1983; Polet 1985, 231–43; Robert-Chaleix 1989.

architecture. No significant quantities of material culture imports from North Africa were found in the very earliest deposits and, indeed, significant quantities of these are not seen until the tenth century. The tenth century deposits of Tagdaoust appear to provide good evidence for major settlement expansion and a change in architectural construction. Following the early experimentation with mudbrick architecture, there was a shift to mostly stone-built construction, although still combined with mud, in the form of bricks and *banco* coating.[33] Building and urban planning appear to have followed a model which has strong parallels with Islamic architectural construction and town planning. Specifically, we see structures with an enclosure wall containing rooms arranged around a courtyard (see, for example, Fig. 17.3), a prevalent type throughout North Africa during this period,[34] as well as in the Central and Northern Sahara.[35] At Tagdaoust this building type is identified as one of the important markers of the arrival of North African trading communities.[36] Extensive excavations have enabled the reconstruction of entire urban quarters from this period, the period incidentally when Tagdaoust was described as a flourishing location in the Arabic records.

Coinciding with this tenth century expansion and redevelopment, there was also a large increase in evidence for imported, North-African material culture, such as vessel glass, glazed ceramics, and glass beads.[37] The next significant shift in the occupation sequence took place in the eleventh century when the site appears to have suffered a major setback associated with destruction,[38] including the industrial quarter on the perimeter of the town.[39] This closely corresponds with the date of the Almoravid destruction recorded by the Arabic texts. The rebuilding following this rupture was more limited, with certain areas of the site abandoned and never re-occupied. However, some of the rebuilt buildings are of a noticeably high quality – one feature of these is the use of red ochre plaster, a feature only encountered in the late phase occupations.[40] Following this rebuilding phase, North African imports were less evident and local metallurgy (which previously had been important) seems to have disappeared.[41] In the thirteenth century the site declined further in size and in the fourteenth century it was abandoned.[42]

[33] Polet 1985, 233–34. [34] Fentress 1987; Insoll 1999, Chapter 3.
[35] Mattingly 2013, Chapter 12. [36] Polet 1985. [37] Devisse 1983; 1988.
[38] Devisse 1983; Polet 1985. [39] Vanacker 1979.
[40] Polet 1985, 239; Robert-Chaleix 1989, 182. [41] Vanacker 1979.
[42] Devisse 1983; Polet 1985.

The Merchant Town of 'Ghana'/Kumbi Saleh

For traders travelling south of Awdaghust, the next major trading centre on the far western route was the Empire of Ghana itself. While 'Ghana' is first referred to in Arabic documentary sources in the first half of the ninth century,[43] it was not until the eleventh century that a distinct 'merchant town' of Ghana is described. This description is as follows:

> The city of Ghana consists of two towns situated on a plain. One of these towns, which is inhabited by Muslims, is large and possesses twelve mosques, in one of which they assemble for the Friday prayer. There are salaried imams and muezzins, as well as jurists and scholars . . . . The king's town is six miles distant from this one and bears the name al-Ghaba. Between these two towns there are continuous habitations.[44]

Shortly after this description was written, Ghana like Awdaghust came under the influence of the Almoravids and 'turned Muslim' (that is, converted to orthodox Islam) in the late eleventh century.[45] The texts are not clear as to the consequences of this for Ghana and its merchant town. Part of the difficulty of interpreting Ghana's history after the development of relations with the Almoravids stems from the potential for the name 'Ghana' to have been used to describe multiple different states or centres across the region.[46] Our understanding of the 'entrepôt of Ghana' from the sources therefore focuses essentially on the eleventh-century report of al-Bakri. The origins of this eleventh-century town and its subsequent role are unclear. Additionally, we cannot clearly gauge the possible histories and natures of other potential merchant towns of Ghana.

Central to discussions of the merchant town of Ghana has been the site of Kumbi Saleh, situated in the south of Mauritania close to the Malian border. At one time the equation between the site of Kumbi Saleh and the capital of the empire of Ghana was generally accepted, but in more recent years there has been increasing scepticism.[47] To begin with, the historical description of Ghana located the stone-built merchant town with mosques some six miles from the royal town. The failure to find the royal town, or any other major settlements in a wide radius from the site, makes the identification of Kumbi Saleh with the merchant town of al-Bakri somewhat problematic. More importantly, the fact that Kumbi Saleh is an isolated centre without a hinterland presents further difficulties; it is

[43] See Levtzion and Hopkins 2000, 5–10. [44] Al-Bakri in Levtzion and Hopkins 2000, 79–80.
[45] Levtzion and Hopkins 2000, 99. [46] Cf. Masonen 2000; McIntosh, R. 1998.
[47] See Lange 1996; Masonen 2000; McIntosh, R. 1998, 256–58.

more than 100 km from the hundreds of major, contemporary and earlier Middle Niger urban centres in the Méma, Middle Niger, and Lakes Region.[48] Finally, the publication of excavation results from the site has revealed once and for all that Kumbi Saleh did not exist as an urban site until the eleventh century – virtually the end of the historical polity of Ghana of the Arabic sources, which notionally dates from sometime before the eighth century to the late eleventh century AD.[49] Based upon the various evidence at our disposal, the most widely held opinion now is that the archaeological site of Kumbi Saleh was a major entrepôt of the final period of Ghana, and perhaps even served as its ultimate capital, continuing as a trade entrepôt through the time of the Malian Empire.

Kumbi Saleh is truly vast, the central tell covering an area of some 100 ha (Fig. 17.4). In addition, there are multiple necropoleis surrounding it. From the surface of the main site, it is evident that at its abandonment Kumbi Saleh was a well-defined urban complex, with large blocks of stone architecture and carefully laid out streets. The town does not appear to have had a surrounding wall or other elements of fortification. Various fieldwork projects have been carried out at Kumbi Saleh in the last 100 years.[50] However, in terms of publication the site has been poorly represented, with only one substantive monograph, that of Berthier,[51] emerging from 12 seasons of excavation – the 1975–1981 excavations of Serge and Denise Robert being almost entirely unpublished. In more recent years renewed work has been attempted, but due to insecurity this has not progressed. Archival work on the Kumbi Saleh material has produced some important results, including the work of Capel *et al.* on the human remains found at the site, and a recent study of the pottery.[52]

Through the combination of Berthier's study and the more limited publications produced by others it is possible to build a fairly good idea of the sub-surface deposits of Kumbi Saleh.[53] The sector of the site excavated by Berthier (see Fig. 17.5) was first occupied at the end of the ninth century, with the first evidence for an urban structure and permanent architecture dateable to the eleventh century, seemingly just prior to the advent of the Almoravid movement.[54] The apogee of the site began in the twelfth century and continued through the fourteenth

48 Lange 1994; 1996; Togola 1996; and MacDonald, personal communication.
49 Berthier 1997; Levtzion 1980.
50 Berthier 1997; Bonnel de Mézières 1923; Thomassey and Mauny 1951; 1956.
51 Berthier 1997. 52 Capel *et al.* 2015; Van Doosselaere 2014. 53 Berthier 1997.
54 See Berthier 1997, 103.

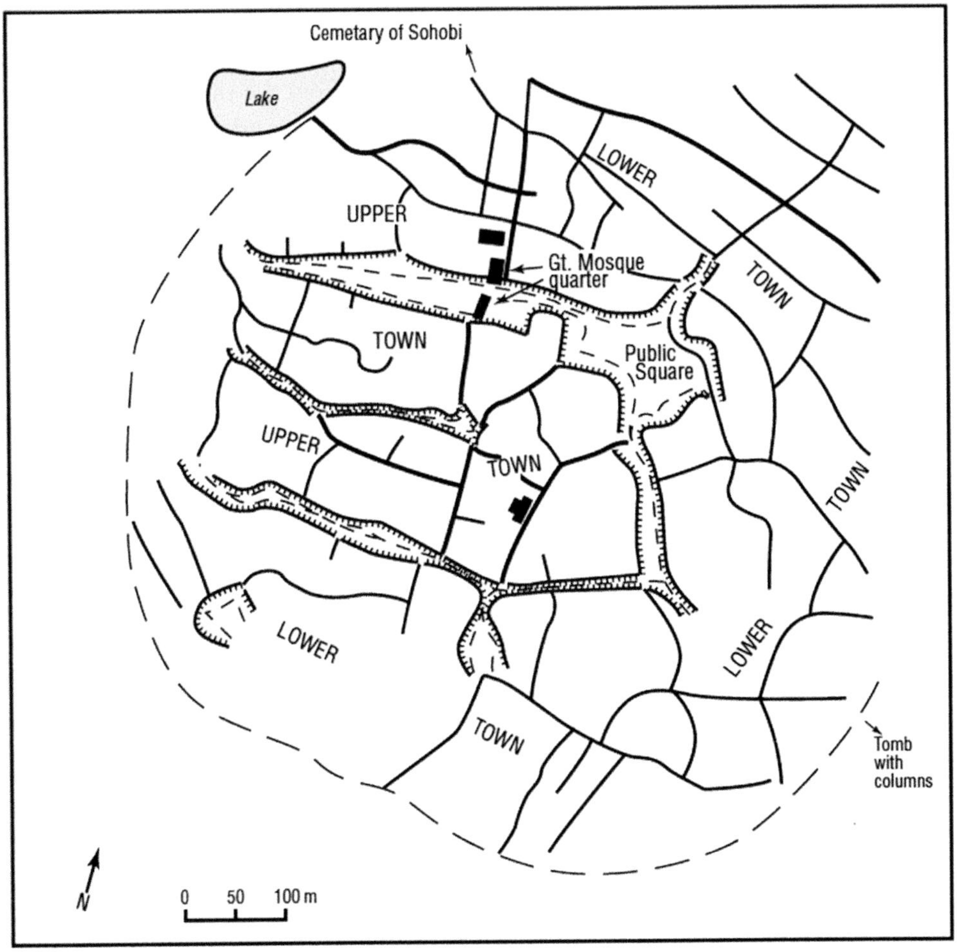

Figure 17.4. Plan of the central area of the urban ruins of Kumbi Saleh (after Berthier 1997; from Monroe 2017).

century. In the twelfth century a monumental columned mosque was constructed at the site,[55] coupled with well-made stone domestic structures. These structures consistently follow a rectilinear format and can be broadly grouped into a Berber or Arabo-Berber tradition. The site reached its largest extent by the thirteenth century. The end of the fourteenth century through the fifteenth centuries saw a dramatic decline in the portions of the site being occupied, with ultimate abandonment sometime in the fifteenth century. In addition to the main tell

[55] See Nixon 2014 for reproduction of B. Nantet image of the mosque under excavation.

Figure 17.5. Excavated buildings at Kumbi Saleh (Berthier 1997, 127).

site, there were also two large necropoleis to the west and east of the site,[56] the western necropolis featuring a monumental 'columned tomb'.[57]

Trans-Saharan trade goods and other material culture indicators of a Trans-Saharan trade function are noticeably limited at Kumbi Saleh, especially in view of the large-scale excavations which have taken place there. For example, Berthier's extensive excavations found only 125 glass beads, scattered relatively evenly across the entire sequence, with a minor quantitative peak in the twelfth century.[58] Glass gold-weights (seven in all) – a rare but excellent indicator of commerce – were also recovered from twelfth- and fourteenth-century contexts.

Tadmakka/Essouk

On the central Trans-Saharan route, leading from the region of Tiaret in Algeria in the direction of Gao on the Niger Bend, the first major centre

[56] See Capel *et al.* 2015, including Figure 1. [57] See Capel *et al.* 2015 for extensive discussion.
[58] Berthier 1997.

recorded in Arabic records south of the Sahara is Tadmakka (or Tadmekka). For the tenth century Ibn Hawqal provided a description of some form of cultural centre at Tadmakka, describing an ethnically and culturally mixed Berber/black population whose rulers were apparently Muslim:

> The supreme kings of Tadmakka in our time are Fusahr b. Alfara and Inaw b. Sabanzak. They are the rulers, who combine leadership with learning, jurisprudence, and political skill, as well as some knowledge of biographies and they are versed in traditions and history. They are Banu Tanamak.[59]

While crucially Ibn Hawqal's report does not specifically describe a permanent settlement at Tadmakka, certain oral traditions recounting tenth-century events at Tadmakka, but recorded in the eleventh/twelfth century, suggest there was at that time a place of thriving commerce with 'treasure houses', implying therefore a permanent settlement:

> Three shaykhs, Abu 'Amr ['Uthman b. Khalifa al-Sufi], Abu Nuh [Salih b. Ibrahim b. Yusuf al-Mazati] and Abu 'l-Rabi [Sulayman b. 'Abd al-Salam al-Wisyani] (may God have mercy upon them), recount that a man of the B. Wisyan named Tamli was mean (*muqill*) in his early years . . . He belonged to the people of the Qusur . . . He began to travel to Tadmakkat where he attained great wealth . . . He began to send from Tadmakkat every year 16 bags, each bag containing 500 dinars. These bags were of cowhide and on each of them was written 'This is God's property'. The shaykh returned. He used to recount of his treasure houses: 'I saw there marked bags which I can only liken to puppies piled one on another, as full of gold. On each bag was written: This is God's property. Praise be to God the Lord of the Worlds'.[60]

These oral traditions recounted above related to Ibadi Muslims, a minority Islamic group who were however of great importance within early Trans-Saharan trade,[61] seemingly indicating the importance of this group at early Tadmakka. Likewise, Yaqut, writing in the early thirteenth century but considered to be borrowing from the tenth-century text of al-Muhallabi, refers to the 'Kingdom of Tadmak' and its capital 'Zakram',[62] Lewicki maintaining this latter name relates to the Berber meaning of 'town' or 'built up locality'.

Following the tenth century, the next mention we have of Tadmakka is al-Bakri's description of 1068, where it was described as a thriving large town with a strong market component and merchants, and a burgeoning

[59] Levtzion and Hopkins 2000, 50–51. [60] Levtzion and Hopkins 2000, 90–91.
[61] See for example, Savage 1992; Van Berchem 1960; see also Capel, Chapter 16, this volume.
[62] Lewicki 1981, 441–42.

gold trade, the latter described as supported by a locally produced 'coinage'. Like Awdaghust, the town was also described as 'resembling Mecca', but in the case of Tadmakka (as al-Bakri states) its name can actually be translated as 'the Mecca like':

> From Bughrat you go to Tiraqqa and from there across the desert plain to Tadmakka, which of all the towns in the world is the one that resembles Mecca the most. Its name means 'the Mecca like'. It is a large town amidst mountains and ravines and is better built than Ghana or Kawkaw. The inhabitants of Tadmakka are Muslim Berbers who veil themselves as the Berbers of the desert do. They live on meat and milk as well as on a grain which the earth produces without being tilled. Sorghum and other grains are imported for them from the land of the Sudan. They wear clothes of cotton, nuli, and other robes dyed red. Their king wears a red turban, yellow shirt, and blue trousers. Their dinars are called 'bald' because they are of pure gold without any stamp. Their women are of perfect beauty, unequalled among people of any other country, but adultery is allowed among them.[63]

Another important aspect of this description is that the inhabitants of the town appear to have had a culture based on strong relationships to the nomadic pastoralists of the surrounding region. While al-Bakri's text dates from just after the mid-eleventh century, in fact his account is widely seen to have drawn on the tenth-century work of al-Waraq – it is quite possible therefore that this description of Tadmakka dated from that time, copied from this earlier text.[64]

Towards the end of the eleventh century Tadmakka, like Awdaghust and Ghana, came into contact with the Almoravid movement and is said to have 'turned Muslim' (converted to Sunni Malikism) under Almoravid influence.[65] Whereas Tadmakka was not specifically referred to as having been sacked like Awdaghust (see above), the reference to it as having 'turned Muslim' does appear to be associated with some form of conflict. Due to the vagueness of the source which refers to Tadmakka's involvement with the Almoravids we cannot gain a clear sense of the effects this might have had on the town, either in a socio-cultural or physical sense. However, there is no clear description of the town being sacked, as is the case with Awdaghust. The sources for Tadmakka from the late-eleventh century up until the early-fourteenth century are generally either very sparse or obviously copies of earlier sources, and the significance of the few new references to Tadmakka during this period is unclear. In the early fourteenth century however, there is another clear reference to Tadmakka,

[63] Levtzion and Hopkins 2000, 85. [64] See Levtzion and Hopkins 2000, 62 for explanation.
[65] Levtzion and Hopkins 2000, 99.

by al-Umari, it being described as associated with a nomadic cultural group who can clearly be related to ancestral Tuareg groups.[66] There is no specific reference to Tadmakka as a market centre nor as a permanent settlement and therefore it is difficult to judge whether we are seeing a reference to a flourishing trade centre or some other form of cultural centre, perhaps not even urban. After this fairly detailed early-fourteenth-century description there are no clear records of Tadmakka, with the last reference in the early fifteenth century being just to the name of Tadmakka as a locality, potentially even a copying of earlier sources.[67]

The ruins of Tadmakka, today called Essouk (Figs 17.6–17.8), are situated in the mountains of the semi-autonomous Tuareg region of north-east Mali, at the most arid extremes of the Sahel.[68] Specifically, they are located 45 km north-west of Kidal at a point where the Wadi Essouk runs through a dense range of cliffs. Essouk consists of *c.*50 ha of stone structural remains in the central town area, within a valley defined by the surrounding rocky cliffs. Beyond the cliffs, the town is surrounded by six Islamic cemeteries bearing Arabic epigraphy from the eleventh to fourteenth centuries.[69] A wadi, which experiences flooding in the summer months, runs through the middle of the site. The ruins of Essouk are the most extensive in the wider region where the Arabic records place Tadmakka, and oral traditions also clearly identify these ruins as those of Tadmakka.[70] Additionally, in the 1980s the epigrapher Paulo Moraes Farias discovered an Arabic inscription at the ruins reading 'and there shall remain a market in conformity to (or with a longing for) Mecca (or Bakka)',[71] providing confirmation of the site's identification with Tadmakka, fitting as this does with the translation of Tadmakka's name quoted by al-Bakri ('resemblance to Mecca'). This is one of a series of Arabic and Tifinagh (indigenous Berber script) inscriptions carved in the cliffs overlooking the town. These Arabic cliff inscriptions also include the earliest known internally dated writing in West Africa, from the early eleventh century AD.[72] On the Essouk cliffs there are also petroglyphs of animals, people and objects, some clearly pre-Islamic in age.[73] While the wider landscape around Essouk is devoid of other known settlement evidence, at a distance of *c.*40 km is the much smaller site of Junhan, which also features some early Islamic Arabic inscribed gravemarkers.[74]

[66] Levtzion and Hopkins 2000, 274. [67] See Levtzion and Hopkins 2000, 354.
[68] See Nixon 2017a, Chapters 3–4. [69] Moraes Farias 2003; 2017.
[70] See Nixon 2017a, Chapter 2. [71] Moraes Farias 2003; 2017.
[72] Moraes Farias 2003, 87–89. [73] Dupuy 1999. [74] Moraes Farias 2003, 151–52.

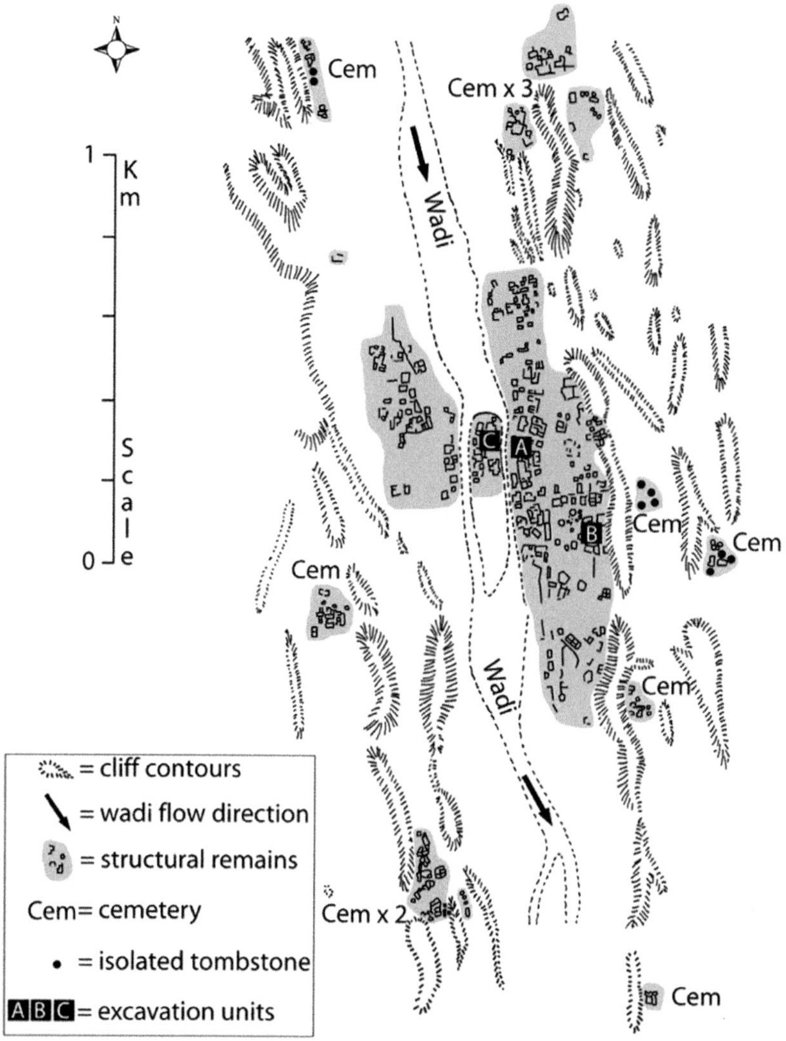

Figure 17.6. Map showing the Essouk-Tadmakka ruins in relation to the Wadi Essouk and surrounding cliffs, and also illustrating excavation locations (adapted from Mauny 1961; Moraes Farias 2003).

The central town ruins of Essouk comprise *c.*50 ha covered with stone structures, and the excellent preservation means that these can be easily traced both on the ground and with aerial photography.[75] The various districts of the ruins are composed of clusters of buildings with streets and alleyways weaving around and through these, with no clear overall governing structure to layout. The level of preservation and visibility of surface

[75] Nixon 2017a.

Figure 17.7. East-west view across a portion of the central Essouk-Tadmakka ruins showing the various stone structural remains distributed across the surface (the wadi and the island within it are seen in the middle-distance).

remains allows one to trace individual roadways and alleyways, the dimensions of individual buildings, and even individual room spaces. The majority of structures were rectilinear buildings having an enclosure wall and a courtyard with rooms arranged around it, most likely commercial or residential buildings. There were two mosques, one a pillared building *c.*25 m long with attached courtyard, principally constructed of stone, but also having some preserved traces of mud construction. The other mosque was a single room structure (un-pillared) *c.*8.5 m in length, again constructed of stone. In the south-eastern area of the ruins there was also a series of large open spaces defined by low walls, possibly for the corralling of animals. There is no evidence of a surrounding wall for the town (though a long wall is traceable on the west side of the ruins, seemingly to prevent flooding from the wadi). Beyond the area of the central town and cemeteries several isolated structures can be observed, most importantly a *musalla* (open prayer ground) to the north of the town.

In 2005 excavations were undertaken by the author and colleagues to achieve a better understanding of this previously unexcavated town and its trade.[76] Three areas of the site were excavated (see Fig. 17.6). The excavations recorded and radiometrically dated a 5-m occupation

[76] Nixon 2009; 2017a.

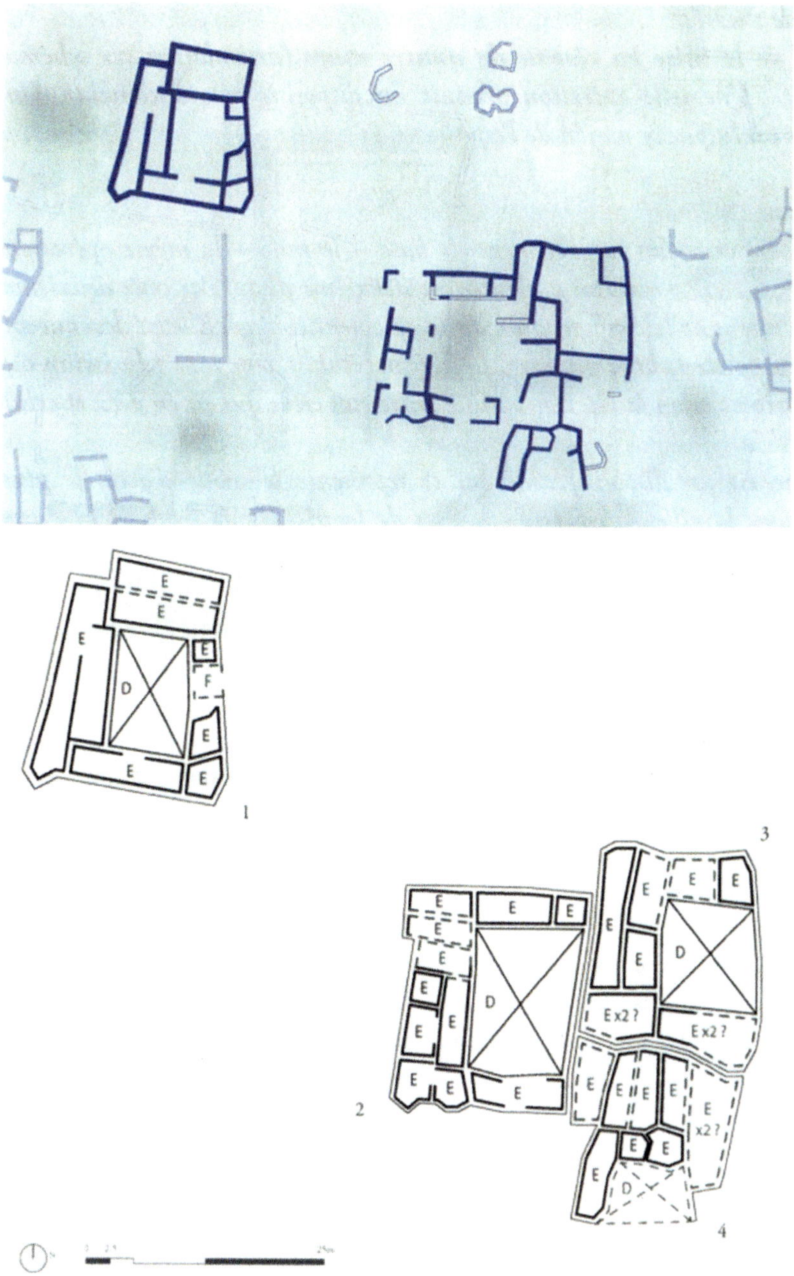

Figure 17.8. Plan of selected structures present on the surface of Essouk-Tadmakka, providing representative examples of the nature of the buildings seen across the surface at the site (developed by Benoit Suzanne from EOM aerial photos taken by Raymond Mauny). For full site plan, see Nixon 2017a.

Figure 17.9. Essouk-Tadmakka: looking down into excavation unit Ek-A from the surface – the image shows digging at depth of *c*.5 m, the depth of the earliest walls revealed within the unit (note: stone structural remains seen in this image represent a palimpsest of different building constructions built one on top of the other, using previous walls as the foundations for new constructions).

sequence associated with permanent architecture, dated *c*.AD 900–1400, and a further 1.5 m of undated cultural deposits below this. Essouk's occupation was seemingly uninterrupted, despite major rebuilding phases. In the earliest levels (those below the first walls recorded) post-holes were recorded within relatively rich deposits, probably indicating semi-permanent structures. No Trans-Saharan or other long-distance trade evidence was found in association with these. The earliest architecture recorded, dated to *c*.AD 900 and at *c*.5 m below the site surface, is a well-built structure in a combination of dry-stone and rammed earth (Fig. 17.9). Throughout the sequence, varying combinations of dry stone and mud-architecture existed. The later phases of construction saw more rudimentary dry-stone construction, though associated also with the use of red ochre plaster. From the survey results it can be seen that the majority of the structures on the surface dated to the fourteenth century – thereby covering the earlier buildings – though certain sectors of the ruins were abandoned in the eleventh century.

Evidence for long-distance trade is seen throughout the sequence, though significant North African imports were not present until *c*.AD

1000. Before evidence for North African imports there is a significant marker for the gold trade, in the form of gold-coin moulds.[77] The portion of the sequence *c.*AD 1000–1100 saw the richest evidence of North African imports, in the form of glass, glass beads, and glazed ceramics. Amongst the botanical remains we also recorded wheat grains, providing a strong parallel with the Arabic references to wheat cultivation at Awdaghust.

Gao

For traders continuing south of Tadmakka the next major market centre was that of Gao, *c.*300 km distant. While Gao (Kawkaw) was first mentioned by name in the ninth century,[78] it was not until the end of the tenth century that there was reference to a merchant town of Gao. This is the record of al-Muhallabi, supposedly dating to the tenth century, but recounted in the twelfth century by Yaqut:

> Their king pretends before his subjects to be a Muslim and most of them pretend to be Muslims too. He has a town on the Nile [i.e. the Niger], on the eastern bank, which is called Sarnah, where there are markets and trading houses and to which there is continuous traffic from all parts. He has another town to the west of the Nile where he and his men and those who have his confidence live.[79]

This text therefore describes a market town as one element of a larger settlement, and seemingly separated from the indigenous royal town by the Niger river, though this is complicated by the statement that the ruler himself purported to be Muslim and to also be associated with the market town.

Al-Bakri also recorded the presence of two settlements at Gao/Kawkaw.[80] One of the towns was evidently inhabited by Muslims and the king of the Sudanic polity of Gao was also described by al-Bakri as being Muslim. In the twelfth century al-Idrisi referred to Gao as a major town, but there is no reference to a separate merchant centre.[81] The twelfth-century documents do provide an account of the merchants of Gao, though they do not obviously describe North African merchants, and more likely referred to local merchants who inhabited the Tuareg/Songhay world between and including Tadmakka and Gao:

[77] Nixon *et al.* 2011.
[78] On the identification with 'Kawkaw', see Levtzion and Hopkins 2000, 7.
[79] Levtzion and Hopkins 2000, 174. [80] Levtzion and Hopkins 2000, 87.
[81] Levtzion and Hopkins 2000, 113, 186–87.

> Their merchants wear chemises and mantles, and woollen bands rolled around their heads. Their ornaments are of gold. The nobles and eminent persons among them wear waist-wrappers. They mix with the merchants, sit in their company, and take shares in their wares [participating in the profit] by way of *muqarada.*[82]

From the thirteenth century onwards we do not have particularly clear descriptions of the merchant centre of Gao but, it is assumed on the basis of the Arabic sources that the Sudanic polity of Gao as a whole continued to thrive in terms of commerce.[83] Indeed, one can only assume that a strong commercial function was retained in the town right up to the end of the early Islamic era, since it continued to be a major centre and in the fifteenth century became the capital of the Songhay empire.

It can be seen therefore that we can gain useful ideas of Gao and its merchant population from the sources regarding its earlier period especially, and the key motif relates to some form of division between the merchant town and the royal town at that time. It is unclear what we should make of the lack of new references to this merchant settlement in the twelfth century and the documents after that point are not terribly clear on the nature of merchant activities at Gao nor on the nature of the urban complex as a whole.

Modern Gao is situated at the Niger Bend in Mali, on the left bank (or northern side) of the river. In and around it there are archaeological components of varying ages, including Gao Ancien, Gao-Saney, and the Gao-Saney cemetery (see Fig. 14.7).[84] Gao Ancien has been identified with the Sudanic capital of Arabic records, and Gao-Saney with the merchant centre. Due to the relationship between the names of the site of Saney and the reference in the historical records to the merchant site of 'Sarnah' (see above) this seems a reasonable identification and this appears further confirmed by the epigraphy at Gao-Saney cemetery, which contains within it references to the name 'Saney'.[85] It is important to point out, however, that these two settlements are not separated by the Niger River but rather by a small river which runs into the Niger (see Fig. 14.7).

The site of Gao Ancien is difficult to access as the modern city of Gao rests atop it. This 'urban archaeology' was first seriously investigated by Insoll who opened a small exposure in an open square in the city's old quarter at the northern end of the town.[86] There he found a sequence of occupation that, on the basis of dateable trade goods rather than ^{14}C

[82] Al-Idrisi in Levtzion and Hopkins 2000, 113.
[83] See index entries in Levtzion and Hopkins 2000.
[84] Cissé 2017; Cissé *et al.* 2013; Insoll 1996; 1997; 2000.
[85] Moraes Farias 2003.
[86] Insoll 1996; 1997; 2000.

determinations, started in the ninth century. However, structural remains do not appear to be present until the late ninth or early tenth century when mud architecture began. In eleventh-century deposits Insoll found a substantial cache of hippopotamus ivory, no doubt destined for the Trans-Saharan trade.[87] Directly overlying this cache was more mudbrick architecture, which Insoll believed to date to the eleventh/twelfth centuries. It was in these deposits that Insoll found the bulk of his Trans-Saharan trade goods (glass beads, glass fragments, and glazed pottery). Overlying this horizon was a very substantial structure made of fired brick, with fired tile floors (Figs 17.10–17.11). This structure was seized upon by the Malian media as a portion of the ruins of the Mosque of Mansa (Kankou) Moussa, rumoured to have existed in the vicinity of these excavations. The name has stuck to the site, although it is now known with certainty that Insoll's structure pre-dates the fourteenth century reign of this illustrious Malian monarch. Insoll believed the structure to date to the twelfth or thirteenth century on the basis of associated trade items. However, much more extensive excavations of this area from 2003 to 2005 by Téréba Togola, the late director of the Malian Direction National du Patriomoine Culturelle,[88] and subsequently Mamadou Cissé's continued work at Gao have shed significant further light on the structures here. The dating of these buildings now looks to favour the eleventh century, including a large monumental pillared building made of schist and with extensive evidence for trade goods, dating most probably to the eleventh century (Fig. 17.10).[89] The more recent deposits at Gao Ancien are much disturbed and do not present a sequence of any great certainty.

The tell and cemetery of Gao-Saney have seen a number of investigations over the years, but have also suffered from heavy looting – largely to get at the quantities of valuable glass trade beads which occur in the tell, or to remove epigraphic stone stele from the cemetery.[90] The site was investigated, but never fully published, by Flight in the 1970s.[91] Moraes Farias undertook an extensive investigation of the Arabic inscriptions from the cemetery,[92] recording a number of very important inscriptions, dating from *c.*AD 1100 onwards, including a number that refer to royal connections at the site. Certain of these were marble stelae imported from southern Spain. Some of the inscriptions refer to individuals with Berber names and point to a population with mixed Berber-Songhay ancestry. The royal presence at the supposed merchant site of Gao-Saney raises questions as to

[87] Insoll 1995. [88] Sanogo *et al.* 2006. [89] Cissé 2017; Cissé *et al.* 2013. [90] Cf. Insoll 1993.
[91] Flight 1975. [92] Moraes Farias 2003.

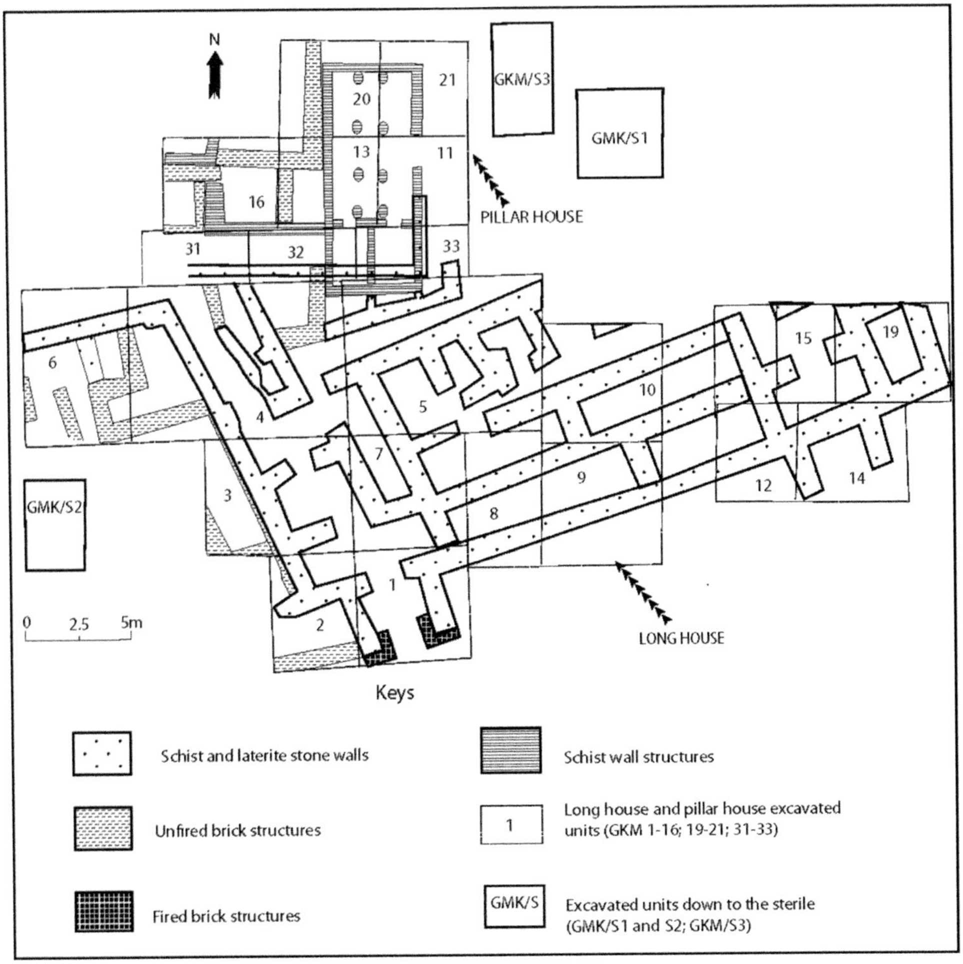

Figure 17.10. Structural remains detected during large-scale exposure at Gao Ancien, including pillared schist building (after Cissé *et al.* 2013).

the clear division between an indigenous royal site at Gao Ancien and a merchant site at Gao-Saney, a question in fact already indeed raised by a careful reading of the Arabic descriptions themselves. A single radiocarbon date for the tell 1000 ± 70 BP (calAD 891–1204) was obtained by Raimbault and Sanogo as part of the Malian national site inventory programme in the 1980s.[93] Flight suggested that the site was abandoned in the thirteenth century, as there are no dated inscriptions from after that time. However, Insoll has suggested that occupation may have continued until much more recent times, given the date of a seventeenth-century AD

[93] Raimbault and Sanogo 1991, 520.

Figure 17.11. Close-up of example of architectural construction in early Islamic Gao Ancien – this illustrates the use of multiple building materials in this structure, including fired brick, stone, and air dried mud brick (image courtesy of Timothy Insoll) – this is part of the larger complex illustrated within Figure 17.10.

Chinese ceramic fragment found on the surface of the site.[94] New investigations are required on this heavily damaged site before the nature of its sequence of occupation can be fully understood.

Other Early Islamic Market Centres in West Africa and Their Archaeology

While the localities reviewed above are the most prominently referred to in discussions of early Islamic entrepôts at the Southern Saharan fringes in West Africa, it is important to clarify that there were a range of other trading localities closely associated with the Trans-Saharan trade networks in West Africa. I am here referring to sites potentially identifiable as primarily centres of Trans-Saharan commerce – rather than other centres of trade further south in the Sahel such as Jenné-jeno and Dia, as well as other Medieval sites, including those associated with the capitals of the kingdom of Mali.[95]

[94] Insoll 1996, 12. [95] Bedaux *et al.* 2005; MacDonald *et al.* 2011; McIntosh, S. 1995.

Working my way west to east across the Sahel, firstly, there is a group of sites within the wider sub-region around Tagdaoust. Located to the desert to the north of Awdaghust, Azugi has been identified as an important early centre of the Almoravids (Fig. 17.1).[96] Aerial photography has provided a useful record of the stone-built ruins found on the surface, and limited excavation enabled a sample of these to be dated to the Almoravid era. Not far from Azugi is Chinguetti (see Fig. 17.1), a locality which became very important for caravan routes from at least the fifteenth century, and was particularly associated with the Hajj journeys across the Sahara – there is though strong potential its trading history precedes this period and the lack of archaeological research there needs to be rectified.[97] Located just south of Tagdaoust is the town of Walata, clearly an important part of the Trans-Saharan system by the mid-fourteenth century, and specifically recorded as a trading centre associated with the Empire of Mali.[98] Walata is another centre which has seen no archaeological research.

The Niger Bend is the next area where a series of further trade localities are located where future research has great potential. Excavations close to Timbuktu, at the site of Tombouze, have revealed a settlement dating back to the mid-first millennium AD, and whose finds include long distance trade goods, with the site seemingly abandoned by the tenth century.[99] Given its proximity to Timbuktu this site has generated great interest and highlights the need to explore the earlier levels of the city of Timbuktu itself. Timbuktu is referred to in the Arabic sources from the mid-fourteenth century.[100] Excavations at Timbuktu have been attempted, but did not manage to reach Medieval levels due to the great depths of more recent deposits.[101]

Located between Timbuktu and Gao the early Arabic records refer to the market centre of Tireqqa, at a point on the River Niger where merchants from Ghana and Tadmakka met.[102] Bonnel de Mézières claimed to have identified this site 35 km east of Timbuktu,[103] though this identification has been much disputed and a clear resolution or further investigation is still awaited. Downriver of the Niger Bend is the complex of Bentyia-Kukiya (see Fig. 17.1), a place which was part of the same Songhay culture sphere as Gao, and which also features cemeteries with significant quantities of early Arabic inscriptions.[104] The exact nature of this site and its trading population is unclear, but given the significant presence of Arabic

[96] Saison 1981. [97] Nixon 2013; Norris 1962. [98] Levtzion and Hopkins 2000, 284–86.
[99] Park 2010. [100] Levtzion and Hopkins 2000, 287. [101] Insoll 2002.
[102] Al-Bakri, eleventh century AD – see Levtzion and Hopkins 2000, 84–85.
[103] Bonnel de Mézières 1914. [104] Arazi 1999.

inscriptions (and the rarity of these in West Africa) this is an important place to flag up in this debate.

Further to the east, in Niger, is the site of Azelik-Takadda, related to the town of Takadda, an important trade centre referred to in the Arabic sources from the mid-fourteenth century.[105] There have been some important studies of the stone ruins here, albeit mainly restricted to surface studies.[106] To the south of the modern city of Agadez in Niger is the site of Marandet, a locality which has presented some of the earliest Trans-Saharan trade evidence, though it appears to have been principally associated with copper production, rather than being an entrepôt centre as such.[107]

The most crucial missing 'piece of the puzzle' of the southern end of Trans-Saharan trade is perhaps the Kawar oases sites.[108] This complex is a series of mud-built fortified villages on the route from Fazzan to the West African state of Kanim, broadly relating to the forts of Kawar first referred to in ninth-century accounts of the raid of Uqba bin Nafi.[109] While sustained archaeological investigations have not taken place here, a series of sites identified by satellite remote sensing appear to provide some support for a pre-Islamic permanent occupation at these sites.[110]

Discussion

Pre-Islamic Occupations at the Sites of Early Trans-Saharan Market Towns

Since the beginning of research into early Trans-Saharan trade, a crucial question has been whether the localities mentioned in the early Islamic sources had pre-Islamic levels, and if so what was their nature. In particular, there has naturally been a desire to discover whether or not the early Islamic urban centres overlay pre-Islamic urban sites, especially given the failure to find any obvious pre-Islamic Trans-Saharan entrepôt sites elsewhere in the western Sahel. There is then a great importance in understanding any pre-Islamic levels below the early Islamic sites, both in order to contextualise the evolution of the specific Trans-Saharan market towns,

105 Levtzion and Hopkins 2000, 301–3. 106 Bernus and Cressier 1991.
107 Magnavita *et al.* 2007. 108 Lange and Berthoud 1977; Vikør 1987.
109 Levtzion and Hopkins 2000, 13.
110 See Sterry and Mattingly, Chapter 7, this volume; whether this hypothesised permanent settlement can be associated with Trans-Saharan trade evidence would be the next crucial question if and when the early dating can be confirmed.

and also what this might tell us more widely about the interface between early Islamic and pre-Islamic trade and settlement.

Looking firstly at the settlements of Awdaghust/Tagdaoust and Tadmakka/Essouk – the best explored Trans-Saharan market towns in the far northern Sahel – there is little positive evidence for substantial pre-Islamic permanent settlement, either below or adjacent to these sites. The extensive excavations at Tagdaoust produced an earliest date for permanent occupation around the eighth/ninth century,[111] while at Essouk the earliest evidence recorded was dated to *c.*AD 900.[112] These dates would appear to correlate very well with the nascent Islamic trade described in the early Arabic sources at these two locations. While clearly there is still potential for recovering evidence of a pre-Islamic urban centre at Essouk, this does seem unlikely. In addition to the absence of evidence from these sites, there is also no clear evidence for pre-Islamic permanent settlement in the wider catchment areas around these sites. Aside from the archaeological evidence, it is important to highlight the early Arabic historical evidence discussed by Lewicki for the name of the capital of Tadmakka, 'Zakram' ('town' or 'built up locality'), suggesting permanent settlement was a concept that had only recently arrived in the region.[113]

While there is no compelling evidence for pre-Islamic urban settlements at either Tagdaoust or Essouk, the evidence from these sites does indicate some form of cultural activity at these locations prior to the urban settlements, likely relating at least in part to the pre-Islamic period. At Essouk for instance the *c.*1.5 m of deposits associated with multiple levels of postholes below the earliest recorded permanent architecture would appear to indicate some form of semi-permanent settlement of tented or mat-and-pole structures.[114] In addition there is the extensive rock art at the site testifying to Essouk's long-term role as an important point in the landscape, and the obvious significance that all locations with good water sources like Essouk and Tagdaoust would have had as meeting places before the Islamic era. The existence of some form of pre-Islamic Trans-Saharan trade network before the early Islamic era is unquestionable – based upon such finds as those from Kissi in Burkina Faso – and the nature of Tagdaoust or Essouk as obvious nodal points close to the southern edge of the desert plausibly links them into these networks in some form.[115] Accordingly, it does suggest the Islamic occupation at both of these sites

[111] Devisse 1983; Polet 1985, 231–43; Robert-Chaleix 1989. [112] Nixon 2017a.
[113] Lewicki 1981. [114] Nixon 2017a. [115] Fenn *et al.* 2009; Magnavita 2009; 2013.

was grafted onto pre-existing settlements of some form, rather than starting on 'virgin' ground.

We move next to discuss the trading settlements that lay south of Awdaghust/Tagdaoust and Tadmakka/Essouk, in the realms of the states of Ghana and Gao. The Arabic sources give the impression these West African states were already in existence at the beginning of the Islamic era (see above), therefore raising the distinct possibility that the early Islamic Trans-Saharan market centres were built at pre-existing settlement complexes. There is though as yet little compelling evidence from the archaeology for a true urban centre preceding the Islamic era at Ghana[116] or Gao.[117] At the same time, it also has to be said that the absence of evidence so far should not necessarily be taken as evidence of absence. At Gao the sequence is not entirely clear, due to much of Gao Ancien being obscured by the modern town and Gao-Saney being a hugely problematic site due to the extensive looting that has taken place there. Likewise, the uncertainty over the location of early 'Ghana'[118] has made the nature of this pre-Islamic state and its settlement network an even more problematic question. The site of Kumbi Saleh does not really illuminate the debate here as the site was a later establishment to the 'Ghana' of the earliest Arabic sources. While it is clear that urban settlements existed in the Sahel in the pre-Islamic period,[119] we are still a long way from defining the urban component of Ghana and Gao at the start of early Islamic Trans-Saharan trade. This includes not being sure of the exact nature of the 'royal towns' described in relation to these two polities by the early Arabic sources – one must indeed keep open the idea that these were settlements created for trade at the beginning of the early Islamic era, rather than the capitals of the states themselves.

In addition to the four key localities discussed above, two other locations are particularly crucial to this debate. Firstly, the site of Tombouze,[120] immediately next to Timbuktu, which appears to show a pre-Islamic settlement of some form connected with long-distance trade, and one that then also continued into the earliest period of the Islamic era. While this was clearly an important site, crucially we do not know if it was a dedicated Trans-Saharan centre as such, and there exists no Arabic records or solid archaeological proof to indicate the presence of an Islamic trading population there.

116 Berthier 1997; Bonnel de Mézières 1923; Thomassey and Mauny 1951; 1956.
117 Cissé 2017; Cissé *et al.* 2013; Insoll 1996; 1997; 2000.
118 Lange 1996; Masonen 2000; McIntosh, R. 1998, 256–58.
119 McIntosh, S. 1995; Chapter 14, this volume; McIntosh, S. and McIntosh, R. 1993.
120 Park 2010.

Away from the trading routes leading to Ghana and Gao and the western Sahel, the route through Kawar to Kanim presents another key element to this debate. The 'urban' nature of this is still highly debatable and clear identification of a pre-Islamic urban presence here must await excavation of this important site complex. The possibility that the Kawar oases were plugged into Trans-Saharan trade networks at so early a date is also unsubstantiated.

Trans-Saharan Settlement in the Early Islamic Era: Local and Regional Dynamics

The broad model for understanding the development of the earliest formation of Islamic entrepôts in West Africa is of a settlement patterning related to two cultural and environmental zones, associated with two stages of the trade routes at the western end of the Trans-Saharan exchange network.[121] Awdaghust and Tadmakka represent entrepôts established at the most northerly habitable point of the Sahel, where the Berber world of the Sahara has its most southerly extension. Situated in a precarious arid environment, these towns represented isolated permanent centres in a wider nomadic world, along the lines of desert oases. Further south, there were then the merchant towns of Ghana and Gao, established in proximity to the centres of the most powerful Sudanic states supplying the key commodities of gold, slaves, and ivory. These centres were situated in a relatively less arid environment and more easily able to support wider networks of permanent settlement. Here I explore this broad model – examining how the market towns were positioned in relation to contemporaneous settlements in their immediate environment, and the wider landscape of settlement in their wider catchment area – as well as highlighting a number of other questions in relation to local and regional settlement dynamics.

I first look at the desert edge towns of Awdaghust/Tagdaoust and Tadmakka/Essouk.[122] Exploration of the immediate periphery of these settlements appears to confirm that they were isolated urban establishments in a wider settlement landscape. However, we do need to consider the question of temporary or semi-permanent occupations in the immediate environs of these sites that have left less obvious archaeological traces. Given the functioning of these sites as exchange centres for at times extremely large camel caravans – early Arabic authors referring in some

[121] See Insoll 2003, Chapter 5. [122] Devisse 1983; Nixon 2017a.

cases to up to 12,000 camels in a single caravan[123] – it is quite possible that a series of semi-permanent settlements of some size might have existed on their peripheries. While no systematic archaeological soundings were made of the peripheries of these sites, one possibly indicator of activity in their immediate vicinity are the *musalla* which are found *c.*1 km outside both Tagdaoust and Essouk, religious structures that would have served the short-term needs of visiting camel caravans.

Another question relates to the occupation of the wider area around these sites by desert nomads, groups who were clearly the political powers of the regions within which the market towns were located. An early Arabic reference to Ibn Battuta's visit to the trading town of Takadda (in modern Niger) recounted the meeting at which he paid his respects to the nomadic leader under whose authority Takadda fell. This took place at a location one day distant from the town.[124] Importantly, Ibn Battuta referred to the existence of 'houses' at this location, though it does not appear that this leader himself lived in a house. Almost certainly the same dynamic would have existed at Awdaghust and Tadmakka. While archaeologically there is not a huge visibility of nomadic or semi-permanent settlements in the wider region, we should not ignore the well-defined interaction networks and political relationships that would have existed between these desert edge urban centres and nomadic groups in the surrounding region.

On a regional level, also, we need to be aware of the existence of other permanent settlements contemporaneous to these major desert-edge centres. The existence of a range of smaller permanent settlements in the wider region around Tagdaoust is seldom commented on.[125] Likewise, the existence of the permanent settlement of Junhan in the wider region around Essouk seldom features in relation to discussion of this town.[126] There needs to be further consideration of how such smaller permanent centres functioned within the orbit of the larger Trans-Saharan towns, including the possibility that they fulfilled a function as semi-permanent centres of the 'nomadic' political authorities of the region.

While Awdaghust and Tadmakka evidently continued for some time as important centres in the region, it appears that their roles changed, potentially following the rise to power of the Almoravids in the mid-eleventh century. Certainly, by the fourteenth century they were no longer the major locations, with Timbuktu, Walata, and Takadda described as of importance.[127] Effectively then the urban legacy of the two principal

[123] Levtzion and Hopkins 2000, 336–38. [124] Levtzion and Hopkins 2000, 302–3.
[125] Robert *et al.* 1970. [126] Moraes Farias 2003.
[127] See index entries in Levtzion and Hopkins 2000.

early Trans-Saharan market centres in the Sahel/Sahara borderlands was taken up by these other localities. While considering these large-scale regional shifts within the urban network of Trans-Saharan trade in the relatively abstract terms of larger economic, geographical and political shifts in the networks, we must also recognise the role of population transfers between these centres. For example, in the immediate post-Almoravid period at Awdaghust it seems very likely that merchants and skilled craftspeople were either forcibly moved to new localities within the Almoravid network – potentially even Kumbi Saleh for instance – or that they migrated of their own will to new centres. In the case of Tadmakka, the oral historical accounts and the archaeology demonstrate a transfer in the fourteenth century of the population of Tadmakka towards the region of Azelik-Takadda and the new urban centres which grew up there.[128] These strands of movement and influence between urban centres are difficult to explore, but they nonetheless form an important element of the story of these urban centres in the Sahel/Sahara borderlands.

Further south, the market towns of Ghana and Gao are most commonly understood in terms of their positioning within a 'dual town' relationship, in proximity to an indigenous 'royal town' (even though the pre-Islamic background to settlement in the areas of these polities is unclear). Due to the confusion concerning the identification of archaeological sites in relation to Ghana, we are unfortunately unable to make a clear assessment of the statement in the Arabic sources that the market town of Ghana was located six miles distant from the royal town.[129] However, we do have unequivocal archaeological evidence for the dual town complex described by the Arabic sources at Gao.[130] The existence of two distinct early Islamic settlements at a distance of *c.*2 km, and the clear correspondence between the name 'Sarnah' given for the market town in the Arabic sources and the name 'Saney' within the epigraphy of the cemetery of the site known as Gao-Saney, allows us complete confidence in the existence of such a dual early town.[131]

While accepting the existence of this 'dual town' paradigm, the Arabic historical records and archaeology provide important data to help nuance this model. The Arabic historical records describe the attempt by the ruler of Gao to negotiate a dual identity in relation to both the royal and the merchant town, appearing alternately as both non-Muslim and Muslim respectively in the royal and the merchant town. Unsurprisingly, these

[128] See Nixon 2017a, Chapter 12. [129] Levtzion and Hopkins 2000, 79–80.
[130] Cissé 2017; Cisse *et al.* 2013; Insoll 1996; 1997; 2000; Levtzion and Hopkins 2000, 174.
[131] Moraes Farias 2003.

records describe not only cultural exchange, but a culturally mixed merchant population, seemingly linked to and merged with the indigenous population. The archaeology provides concrete evidence of such a culturally mixed and complex picture, in the form of the Arabic inscriptions bearing royal titles in the merchant town.[132]

Given that Gao-Saney is an abandoned settlement with no apparent modern-era occupation, while Gao Ancien is still occupied, it seems clear that at some point the 'dual town' model was abandoned, though the archaeology is not clear enough for us to know exactly when and why. One assumes this was at a point when the increasing Muslim population within the indigenous town made the existence of separate royal/indigenous and merchant/Muslim settlements no longer necessary or desirable. Perhaps this might have been as early as the twelfth century, as by that time there is no mention of a 'dual town' in the Arabic records and the archaeology could accord with this too.[133] While it remains at the level of pure hypothesis, one can also imagine that a similar process of abandonment of a 'dual town' model took place in late period Ghana or with its successors in the region.

Given the very limited nature of the archaeology conducted on the Kawar-Kanem Trans-Saharan route it would be pure speculation to examine such questions in that region. The regional patterning of a significant series of settlements in the Kawar oases area may suggest a different regional dynamic to that occurring in relation to the settlements further west.[134]

Urban Structure and Urban Features

When we speak of Trans-Saharan market towns, we need to establish crucially what these looked like, how they were structured and what features they possessed. These data allow us to gain a sense not only of their physical appearance, but also what facilities and services they provided as urban centres. In approaching this question obviously one must be clear that these towns were not single-phase constructions, but had significant occupations evolving over periods of 500 years plus, with phases of destruction and rebuilding, and with urban stratigraphies of up to 5 m depth. The complexity of understanding these urban forms is obviously rendered more difficult for the earlier occupations, most of which are covered by later occupations. This said, the combination of surface ruins

[132] Moraes Farias 2003. [133] Levtzion and Hopkins 2000, 113.
[134] Lange and Berthoud 1977; Sterry and Mattingly, Chapter 7, this volume; Vikør 1987.

and excavated deposits enables us to build up a good picture of the urban structure and features of the desert-edge entrepôts, as well as to make certain statements about other towns. The Arabic sources also provide important additional information. I shall explore how these towns might have looked during the period of their initial urban structures and the apparent period of their apogee, as well as trying to examine their nature in their later phases, examining first the more easily approachable desert edge towns of Awdaghust/Tagdaoust and Tadmakka/Essouk, followed by a brief consideration of the available evidence for other towns.

The desert edge towns of Awdaghust/Tagdaoust and Tadmakka/Essouk with their stone ruins, excellent preservation, and lack of overlying modern structures enable us to understand a significant amount about the nature of these key urban complexes, including their overall settlement distribution and their individual attributes. Firstly, neither of these towns appears to have been fortified, nor have contemporaneous refuge sites been identified nearby, in the manner of Sedrata or Sijilmasa.[135] Essouk lay within a relatively protected valley with good lookout positions, and the terrain around Tagdaoust likewise provides a good outlook. However, both places relied for their security largely on being embedded within powerful nomadic confederations whose people occupied the surrounding landscape. Both sites also had a symbolic definition as places of Islam. Most obviously at both sites this is communicated by the presence of Muslim cemeteries on the periphery of the town. In the case of Essouk practically every entry point into the town passed a cemetery. The use of Arabic epigraphy at one of the crucial entry-points into Essouk defined it as a place of Islam by stating its identity as 'a market resembling Mecca'.[136] While there is no concrete evidence of settlements in the immediate periphery of these sites, these urban spaces surely existed within a surrounding semi-permanent landscape of mobile settlement, associated both with visiting caravans and with groups offering services to the town, including craft production. It is also interesting that both towns possessed a *musalla*, positioned to the north of the settlement in the direction of the Trans-Saharan routes. These were no doubt used by large caravans arriving and departing the town, as well as for larger communal prayer on feast days, for example. The final thing we need to consider in terms of the periphery of the town is the potential for market places to have existed there, in the same manner as is hypothesised for Sijilmasa.[137] Clearly the urban infrastructures of these

135 Aillet *et al.* 2017; Capel, Chapter 16, this volume; Messier and Miller 2015; Van Berchem 1960.
136 Moraes Farias 2003. 137 Messier and Miller 2015.

towns were not designed to support the influx of very large caravans and it would have made sense to have certain market functions take place outside the town.

In terms of the internal structure of the urban centres of Awdaghust/Tagdaoust and Tadmakka/Essouk the combined textual and archaeological evidence enables us to build up a reasonable picture. In the earliest period, both Tagdaoust and Essouk possessed multiple complex buildings across different areas of the site. From the Tagdaoust evidence this seems somewhat random and unplanned, something which would make sense within the initial phase of settlement. With the arrival of diverse merchant groups, different family, cultural, and religious units, it is likely that occupation took place at several locations within the valley,[138] rather than a planned urban centre developing outwards from a central core. The findings from Tagdaoust however indicate that after this initial phase of occupation a more clearly planned settlement developed from around the tenth century, and the excavations of various wards from this period clearly show a very solid structure of linked building compounds and associated lanes weaving between them (see Fig. 17.3). The surface traces and excavated buildings at Essouk suggest a comparable situation. Corresponding with the dated urban deposits, epigraphy from Essouk clearly shows that at least three of the six cemeteries were in use by the early eleventh century. This gives us a sense of the scale of the town already by this point, as well as potentially indicating the division of the town into wards relating to different groups. Crucially, one of the cemeteries at Essouk features no inscriptions, and it has been suggested that this might accordingly relate to an early Ibadi group. One assumes this division seen in death would also have been represented in the urban structure by a putative Ibadi population enclave as well.

In terms of specific features of the urban environment which these towns possessed, the Arabic records make mention of the following: markets (though without specifying whether inside or outside the town), mosques, 'oratories', and 'treasure houses'. The archaeological evidence for structures appears to indicate unsurprisingly the presence of a range of domestic and commercial buildings. Amongst these are simple large structures with walls enclosing a large courtyard space, featuring only a few rooms. There is a strong chance that these were either the 'treasure houses' noted in relation to Tadmakka,[139] or potentially something

138 As is the case at the modern settlement developing near to Essouk, observed by the author during fieldwork.

139 Note also the recording of what appears to be a door-key at Essouk-Tadmekka: Nixon 2017a.

approaching a rudimentary caravanserai. Some further structures may also potentially equate to caravanserai, while the layout of other buildings appears to resemble a market-type street. Early mosques have been identified at both these town sites, at Tagdaoust a larger 'Friday' mosque and at Essouk what appears to be a single-roomed mosque, potentially relating to the Ibadi faith.[140] A further important feature to note is the presence of industrial areas and workshops. At Tagdaoust a developed industrial area was located on the perimeter of the town,[141] while at Essouk evidence across the town indicates that metal working and other crafts took place within the urban fabric.[142] One important further feature of the towns was the presence of possible patch gardens – wheat is referred to as being grown at Awdaghust and it is also present in the excavated material at Tadmakka.

Consideration must also be given to features that appear to be absent. There is nothing distinguishable from other clusters of buildings that can be clearly equated with a palace, and likewise certain key features of Islamic towns have not been recorded, including hammams (bathhouses).

Nonetheless, the evidence we have available clearly shows the development of towns that to the eyes of arriving merchants coming from North Africa would have appeared as recognisably Muslim towns – regardless of the 'non-Muslim' actions of some of the residents, as commented on for example by al-Bakri. Accordingly, it is not surprising that al-Bakri and others compared these towns to Mecca, as well as alluding to Tadmakka as being 'better built than Ghana or Kawkaw',[143] thereby identifying it as a recognisable Islamic town. We must however be careful not to over-characterise these places as classic Islamic 'urban' centres of trade. Again, returning to al-Bakri, we should note his description of the inhabitants of Tadmakka living like the Berbers of the desert. This would also surely have been reflected in their 'urban practice'. The contemporary practice of erecting a tent within the courtyard of buildings in Kidal is perhaps such a desert-dwelling practice that might have occurred in these towns.[144]

Following the early period of both Awdaghust/Tagdaoust and Tadmakka/Essouk many aspects of the urban structure of these towns continued through to their decline in the fourteenth century. A measure of continuity can be seen in the practice at Essouk of using earlier house structures as the foundations for new buildings throughout the entire sequence (see Fig. 17.9). However, there were clearly significant changes within the

[140] Elizabeth Fentress, personal communication; the pillared mosque seen on the surface at Essouk relates to the terminal occupation of the site.

[141] Vanacker 1979. [142] Nixon 2017a. [143] Levtzion and Hopkins 2000, 85.

[144] As noted by the author.

urban structure. The abandonment of whole areas of both towns half-way through the sequence is striking, clearly showing that for long portions of their occupations these towns had ruins in some sectors. The entire industrial area at Tagdaoust was abandoned from the eleventh century. One can obviously over-dramatise this period of decline and both centres retained key features of Islamic towns. For example, Essouk's Muslim cemeteries continued into the fourteenth century and there was a fourteenth-century pillared mosque built, with attached courtyard. The final phase structures of both sites provide a clear picture of a complex urban establishment, with multiple wards and a variety of built features. The lack of compelling accounts of these towns by the Arab authors at this time has, however, been seen as a sign of their declining status as Muslim urban centres.

Compared to Awdaghust and Tadmakka, we have far less evidence of the urban structure and features of the merchant towns of Ghana and Gao. The Arabic records for Ghana paint a picture of a flourishing town, mentioning numerous mosques, as well as the religious, judicial, and scholarly authorities of the town.[145] The inability to link the Ghana of the Arabic histories to an archaeological site prevents us saying more. For Gao, the Arabic records are less informative about the merchant town as a physical space. Archaeology has provided evidence of Muslim cemeteries associated with the merchant town, but little else besides. The large, complex series of structures from Gao Ancien does at least provide us with evidence of some clear urban features from the Gao archaeological complex, including what is potentially a pillared mosque.[146]

While Kumbi Saleh is obviously a later phenomenon, it does however provide us with a good example of an urban locality in the semi-arid Sahel which was built in the eleventh century. Given the limited publications on this site, it is difficult to say much about its possible planned character. What one can say is that certain features recorded from the town indicate a developed urban formation. The complex domestic or commercial structures that have been recorded over multiple periods (see Fig. 17.5), were accompanied by a very significant pillared mosque, as well as an intriguing pillared tomb within the cemetery.[147]

While again we cannot speak with any certainty about early Islamic occupation in the Kawar oases, one fundamental difference can be posited. The archaeological sites in the Kawar oases complex appear to have been strikingly different from those further west, principally in relation to

[145] Levtzion and Hopkins 2000, 79–80. [146] Cissé 2017; Cissé *et al.* 2013.
[147] Capel *et al.* 2015.

having a fortified aspect to them, far more in keeping with the Central Sahara and North African pre-desert settlements.

Architecture: Materials, Construction Techniques, and Form

The nature and evolution of architecture in West Africa has been a crucial area of discussion for both historians and archaeologists, including in debates on construction materials, form, and techniques.[148] Beyond the physical appearance of these Trans-Saharan centres, because of the important role they played in bringing new ideas and cultural influences to West Africa, these localities also provide insight into an important area of experimentation and expression within the 'arts' of pre-modern West Africa. Of particular interest is the extent of transfer of architectural style from Islamic traditions in North Africa,[149] as well as the background to the evolution of regional styles.

In terms of materials, a key feature of the discussion of these towns relates to the relative use of stone and mud. Stone has come to be identified with the merchant towns – the surface remains of the key towns of Tagdaoust and Essouk are of stone, the merchant town of Ghana was described as built of stone, and likewise the ruins of Kumbi Saleh are of stone. Only Gao amongst the earliest merchant towns in the western Sahel appears not to strongly feature stone. However, this strong identification between the merchant towns and stone is deceptive, given the sub-surface deposits of Tagdaoust and Essouk. At Tagdaoust the initial occupation featured primarily mud-architecture; and the later move away from solely mud-architecture may have reflected its unsuitability in an environment where it was subject to rapid water erosion. In the second phase of the site, building construction tended to use both stone and mud to create more durable structures. At Essouk likewise, the sub-surface deposits reveal far more in the way of mud-architecture than is displayed by the surface ruins. This includes a mixed stone/mud construction in the earliest building excavated. The desire to build in mud was certainly influenced by cultural factors; many of the towns like Sijilmasa or Sedrata, where merchants were coming from, made extensive use of mudbrick and rammed earth (pisé). Also, the load-bearing and insulating properties of mud made it an ideal building material. However, the plentifully available local stone was also turned to as an expedient measure.

148 Aradeon 1989; Insoll 1996; 1999; Prussin 1986; and see Nixon 2014 for a brief summary.
149 Cf. Aradeon 1989.

The mud-architecture at Tadmakka was mainly rammed-earth, although some mudbrick is also seen. At Tagdaoust mudbrick appears to have been far more plentifully used. Whether this was just a cultural preference is unclear, but rammed-earth does have different load bearing potential, and this may have contributed to the differences of construction between the two localities. The earliest building recorded at Tadmakka features either a massive pillar, or a staircase to a roof.[150] Regardless of which of these techniques was being applied, they are evidence for the presence of skilled artisans in mud-architecture in these desert-edge locations. While there are only a few excavated or visible archaeological structures from Gao, there is clear evidence of the use of mudbrick at the site of Gao Ancien.[151] Given the difficulty of defining buildings in excavations at Gao-Saney and elsewhere at Gao, it is most likely that much of the construction was in the piled or rammed earth technique. Indeed, the mudbrick building recorded at Gao Ancien appears to be an exceptional structure.

One particularly important technique to point out is the extensive use of mud-plaster, covering up stone wall cores, used both at Tagdaoust and Essouk. The use of mud plaster both within and on the outside of buildings clearly related to an aesthetic choice, and this appears to have been connected to the relatively rough finish provided by the stone in this region (see below). Accordingly, even where we see extensive stone building in the sequence, the outer appearance of these buildings would have been one related to mud-architecture. In this respect it is interesting to observe that none of the early Arabic commentators refer to Awdaghust or Tadmakka as 'stone towns', even though the market town of Ghana is described exactly in this way (see below for further discussion of Ghana). One particularly distinctive aspect of the mud plastering to note is the use of thick red ochre plaster in the final phase at both Essouk and Tagdaoust (where white paint was also used in association with this) - clearly these are early examples of the ochre and white painted plaster techniques that became a strong aesthetic tradition in the Southern Sahara.[152]

There are a number of important observations to make concerning the nature of the stone used in the Trans-Saharan market towns. At both Tagdaoust and Essouk, though the locally available stone made for easy if rudimentary constructions, it required great skill to create refined stonework (only one example of this is seen at Essouk). As inferred above, the difficulty of dressing this stone probably led to it often being coated with mud plaster

[150] See Nixon 2017a. [151] Cissé *et al.* 2013.

[152] Prussin 1986, including for example in the modern town of Walata.

to create a more aesthetic finish. While these two towns have not produced much good quality stonework, regular stonework was more prominent at Kumbi Saleh, indeed being the dominant feature of the architecture. Unlike the stone found around the other two towns discussed here, the geology of Kumbi Saleh features a particular type of stone that enables the easy creation of thin, flat, almost slate-like blocks. These were used to build a very refined style of stone architecture. Clearly this stone finish became a feature to be displayed, including in the creation of triangular niches which are a feature of the site.[153] This refined stonework is also seen in the large mosque excavated at the site. The fact that Ghana's merchant town is referred to as 'of stone' within the early Arabic documents is important, suggesting that stone was not just a core material to be covered with mud, but was the visible aesthetic of the town. This tradition of refined stone construction is seen more widely in the region, including for example at Chinguetti. One final type of stone to comment on is the schist seen in the pillared building at Gao Ancien[154] and in the pillared tomb at Kumbi Saleh[155] – the restriction of this evidence to what one might term exceptional or elite structures so far does suggest this was a highly restricted use.

There are two further specific materials and techniques to discuss. Firstly, one of the most distinctive architectural traditions in the early Islamic towns at the northern fringes of the Sahara is highly distinctive decorative carved plaster work, for example seen at the Ibadi site of Sedrata in Algeria.[156] Given the supposed very strong early Ibadi influence at Tadmakka and other West African trading sites one might perhaps expect to see an experimentation with such styles – it is possible though that the social and material technology for such a transfer did not exist. Secondly, there is some evidence of the technology of fired-brick work, as at Gao within a *mihrab* and portions of the large and complex structure uncovered at Gao Ancien.[157] While one sees this at North African towns linked to the Trans-Saharan networks, including Aghmat and the Medieval site at Zagora,[158] no evidence of this has been discovered at either Tagdaoust or Essouk. Other places where fired-brick has been found in significant quantities in West Africa include the Kanim-Bornu zone (as at Garu Kime). Potentially then, fired brick was restricted to elite structures and away from the Southern Saharan edge towns.

In terms of the form of building seen in the Trans-Saharan trading towns, the key type to highlight, and the most common seen at the sites of

[153] Berthier 1997. [154] Cissé *et al.* 2013. [155] Capel *et al.* 2015.
[156] Aillet *et al.* 2017; Van Berchem 1960. [157] Cissé *et al.* 2013; Insoll 1996.
[158] Fili *et al.* 2013; 2014; Mattingly *et al.* 2017b.

Tagdaoust and Essouk, features an enclosure wall containing rooms arranged around a courtyard. This relates to a very common tradition in the Islamic world that would have been the prevalent type throughout North Africa during this period,[159] as well as in the Central and Northern Sahara.[160] At Tagdaoust this building type is identified as one of the important markers of the arrival of North African trading communities.[161] One important thing to note is that in addition to the private internal rooms, the courtyard also provides a self-contained space to undertake a range of domestic activities removed from the public world of the town; something which is often discussed as one of the classic hallmarks of Islamic architecture.[162] This differs greatly for instance from the small structures built today at the settlement near Essouk-Tadmakka which lack a courtyard and where consequently a greater amount of activities take place in the public areas outside the structure.

The other key building types to highlight are the mosques. The recorded mosques from the Trans-Saharan trading towns provide a useful illustration of the wider development of Southern Saharan mosque design. At Tadmakka the earliest mosque recovered was a simple single-cell structure, likely a ward mosque. When the Arabic geographers described the Southern Saharan towns as having multiple mosques and 'oratories' they were most likely referring to this sort of building. The grander form of 'Friday mosques' would appear to post-date the eleventh century. That from Kumbi Saleh, dated seemingly to around the twelfth century, has already been noted as providing a very good example of a highly developed mosque form in well-worked stone. The largest mosque observable amongst the ruins at Tadmakka (measuring 23.5 × 15.5 m) dates most likely to the late fourteenth century in the form we see it. This mosque had five aisles parallel to the *qibla*, identifiable by the remains of pillars. Study by Cressier indicated that it had no minaret or moveable minbar,[163] this being standard within the Southern Saharan mosque traditions. Cressier has already highlighted the potential regional importance of this mosque in terms of influencing later mosque design in the wider region,[164] and certainly we should consider this important religious building within the context of Tadmakka's acknowledged role as an origin point for Islamic religious movements in Niger in the late Medieval and early modern era.[165]

[159] Fentress 1987; Insoll 1999, Chapter 3. [160] Mattingly 2013, Chapter 12. [161] Polet 1985.
[162] Insoll 1999, Chapter 3. [163] Cressier 1992. [164] Cressier 1992.
[165] Cressier 1992; Moraes Farias 2003; Norris 1975.

References

Aillet, C., Cressier, P. and Gilotte, S. (ed.). 2017. *Sedrata. Histoire et archéologie d'un carrefour du Sahara médiéval à la lumière des archives inédites de Marguerite van Berchem*. Madrid: Casa de Velázquez.

Aradeon, S. 1989. Al-Saheli. The historian's myth of architectural technology transfer from West Africa. *Journal des Africanistes* 59: 99–131.

Arazi, N. 1999. An archaeological survey in the Songhay heartland of Mali. *Nyame Akuma* 52: 25–43.

Austen, R. 2010. *Trans-Saharan Africa in World History*. New York: Oxford University Press.

Bedaux, R., Polet, J., Sanogo, K. and Schmidt, A. 2005. *Recherches archéologiques à Dia dans le Delta intérieur du Niger, Mali: Bilan des saisons de fouilles 1998–2002*. Leiden: CNWS.

Bernus, S. and Cressier, P. 1991. *La région d'in Gall – Tegidda N Tesemt (Niger). Programme archéologique d'urgence 1977–1981. Azelik-Takadda et l'implantation sédentaire médiévale (Études Nigériennes No.51)*. Niamey: Institut de Recherches en Sciences Humaines.

Berthier, S. 1997. *Recherches archéologiques sur la capitale de l'empire de Ghana: Etude d'un secteur d'habitat à Koumbi Saleh, Mauritanie. Campagnes II–III–IV–V (1975–1976)-(1980–1981)*. (Cambridge Monographs in African Archaeology 41/BAR International Series 680). Oxford: Archaeopress.

Bonnel de Mézières, A. 1914. Découverte de l'emplacement de Tirekka. *Bulletin du Comite des travaux historiques et scientifiques de l'Afrique occidentale française* 29: 132–35.

Bonnel de Mézières, A. 1923. Recherche de l'emplacement de Ghana (fouilles à Koumbi et Settah). *Mémoires présentés par divers savants à l'Académie de Inscriptions et Belles Lettres* 13.1: 227–64.

Bovill, E. 1958. *The Golden Trade of the Moors*. London: Oxford University Press.

Capel, C., Zazzo, A., Saliège, J-F. and Polet, J. 2015. The end of a hundred-year-old archaeological riddle: First dating of the columns tomb of Kumbi Saleh (Mauritania). *Radiocarbon* 57.1: 65–75.

Cissé, M. 2017. The Trans-Saharan trade connection with Gao (Mali) during the first millennium. In Mattingly *et al.* 2017a, 101–30.

Cissé, M., McIntosh, S.K., Dussubieux, L., Fenn, T., Gallager, D. and Smith, A.C. 2013. Excavations at Gao Saney: New evidence for settlement growth, trade, and interaction on the Niger Bend in the first millennium CE. *Journal of African Archaeology* 11.1: 9–37.

Cressier, P. 1992. Archéologie de la devotion soufi. *Journal des africanistes* 62.2: 69–90.

Devisse, J. (ed.). 1983. *Tegdaoust III. Recherches sur Aoudaghost (campagnes 1960–1965, enquêtes générales)*. Paris: Éditions Recherche sur les Civilisations (ADPF).

Devisse, J. 1988. Trade and trade routes in West Africa. In M. El Fasi (ed.), *General History of Africa, Volume 3: Africa from the Seventh to the Eleventh Century.* Berkeley: University of California Press, 367–435.

Dupuy, C. 1999. L'art rupestre à gravures naturalistes de l'Adrar des Iforas (Mali). *Sahara* 11: 69–86.

Fenn, T., Killick, D., Chesley, J., Magnavita, S. and Ruiz, J. 2009. Contacts between West Africa and Roman North Africa: archaeometallurgical results from Kissi, northeastern Burkina Faso. In Magnavita *et al.* 2009, 119–46.

Fentress, E. 1987. The house of the prophet: North African Islamic housing. *Archeologia Medievale* 14: 47–68.

Fili, A., Messier, R., Capel, C., Naji, S. and Fili, L. 2013. *Archaeology, Conservation, Development. Progress and Prospects of the Moroccan-American Project.* Casablanca: Aghmat Foundation.

Fili, A., Messier, R., Capel, C. and Héritier-Salama, V. 2014. Les palais mérinides dévoilés: le cas d'Aghmat. In Y. Lintz, C. Déléry and B. Tuil Leonetti (eds), *Maroc Médiéval. Un empire de l'Afrique à l'Espagne.* Paris: Hazan, 446–50.

Flight, C. 1975. Excavations at Gao (Republic of Mali) in 1974. *Nyame Akuma* 7: 28–9.

Holl, A. 2006. *West African Early Towns: Archaeology of Households in Urban Landscapes.* Ann Arbor, MI: Museum of Anthropology, University of Michigan.

Insoll, T. 1993. Looting the antiquities of Mali: The story continues at Gao. *Antiquity* 67: 628–32.

Insoll, T. 1995. A cache of hippopotamus ivory at Gao, Mali and a hypothesis of its use. *Antiquity* 69: 327–36.

Insoll, T. 1996. *Islam, Archaeology and History. Gao Region (Mali) ca. AD 900–1250.* (Cambridge Monographs in African Archaeology 39/BAR International Series 647.) Oxford: Tempus Reparatum.

Insoll, T. 1997. Iron Age Gao: An archaeological contribution. *Journal of African History* 38: 1–30.

Insoll, T. 1999. *The Archaeology of Islam.* Oxford: Blackwell.

Insoll. T. 2000. *Urbanism, Archaeology and Trade: Further Observations on the Gao Region (Mali) – The 1996 Fieldseason Results (BAR International Series 829).* Oxford: BAR.

Insoll, T. 2002. The archaeology of post-Medieval Timbuktu. *Sahara* 13: 7–22.

Insoll, T. 2003. *The Archaeology of Islam in Sub-Saharan Africa.* Cambridge: Cambridge University Press.

Kea, R. 2004. Expansions and contractions: World-historical change and the western Sudan World-System (1200/1000 B.C. – 1200/1250 AD). *Journal of World-Systems Research* 10.3: 723–816.

Lange, D. 1994. From Mande to Songhay: Towards a political and ethnic history of Medieval Gao. *Journal of African History* 35: 275–301.

Lange, D. 1996. The Almoravid expansion and the downfall of Ghana. *Der Islam* 73: 122–59.

Lange, D. and Berthoud, S. 1977. Al-Qasaba et d'autres villes de la route centrale du Sahara. *Paideuma* 23: 19–40.

Levtzion, N. 1980. *Ancient Ghana and Mali (Revised Edition)*. New York: Africana.

Levtzion, N. and Hopkins, J.F.P. (eds). 2000. *Corpus of Early Arabic Sources for West African History*. Princeton: Markus Wiener Publishers.

Lewicki, T. 1974. *West African Food in the Middle Ages According to Arabic Sources*. Cambridge: Cambridge University Press.

Lewicki, T. 1981. Les origines et l'islamization de la ville de Tadmakka d'aprés les sources arabes. In J. Devisse, C.H. Perrot, Y. Person and J.P. Chrétien (eds), *Le sol, la parole et l'écrit. Mélanges en hommage à Raymond Mauny, vol.1*. Paris: Societé française d'histoire d'outremer, 439–44.

Lhote, H. 1951. Sur l'emplacement de la ville de Tademekka, antique capitale des berbères soudanais. *Notes Africaines* 51: 65–69.

McIntosh, R. 1998. *The Peoples of the Middle Niger*. Malden, MA: Blackwell Publishers.

McIntosh, R. 1999. Western representations of urbanism and invisible African towns. In S.K. McIntosh (ed.), *Beyond Chiefdoms: Pathways to Complexity in Africa*. Cambridge: Cambridge University Press, 56–65.

McIntosh, S. 1995. *Excavations at Jenne-Jeno, Hambarketolo and Kaniana (Inland Niger Delta, Mali), the 1981 Season*. Berkeley and Los Angeles: University of California Press.

McIntosh, S. and McIntosh, R. 1993. Cities without citadels: Understanding urban origins along the middle Niger. In T. Shaw, P. Sinclair, B. Andah and A. Okpoko (eds), *The Archaeology of Africa: Food, Metals and Towns*. London: Routledge, 622–41.

MacDonald, K., Camara, S., Canós, S., Gestrich, N. and Keita, D. 2011. Sorotomo: A forgotten Malian capital? *Archaeology International* 13: 52–64.

Magnavita, S. 2009. Sahelian crossroads: Some aspects on the Iron Age sites of Kissi, Burkina Faso. In Magnavita *et al.* 2009, 79–104.

Magnavita, S. 2013. Initial encounters: Seeking traces of ancient trade connections between West Africa and the wider world. *Afriques* 4 [online only]. Available at: http://afriques.revues.org/1145 [last accessed 16 September, 2019].

Magnavita, S., Maga, A., Magnavita, C. and Idé, O. 2007. New studies on Marandet (central Niger) and its trade connections: an interim report. *Die Zeitschrift für Archäologie außereuropäischer Kulturen* 2: 147–65.

Magnavita, S. Koté, L. Breunig, P. and Idé, O. (eds). 2009. *Crossroads: Cultural and Technological Developments in First Millennium BC/AD West Africa*. Frankfurt am Main: Africa Magna Verlag.

Masonen, P. 2000. *The Negroland Revisited: Discovery and Invention of the Sudanese Middle Ages*. Helsinki: The Finnish Academy of Science and Letters.

Mattingly, D.J. (ed.). 2013. *The Archaeology of Fazzan. Volume 4, Survey and Excavations at Old Jarma (Ancient Garama) Carried out by C.M. Daniels (1962–69) and the Fazzan Project (1997–2001)*. London: Society of Libyan Studies.

Mattingly, D.J. and Sterry, M. 2013. The first towns in the Central Sahara. *Antiquity* 87.366: 503–18.

Mattingly, D.J., Leitch, V., Duckworth, C., Cuénod, A., Sterry, M. and Cole, F. (eds). 2017a. *Trade in the Ancient Sahara and Beyond.* Cambridge: Cambridge University Press and The Society for Libyan Studies.

Mattingly, D.J., Bokbot, Y., Sterry, M., Cuénod, A., Fenwick, C., Gatto, M., Ray, N., Rayne, L., Janin, K., Lamb, A., Mugnai, N. and Nikolaus, J. 2017b. Long-term history in a Moroccan oasis zone: The Middle Draa Project 2015. *Journal of African Archaeology* 15: 141–72.

Mauny, R. 1961. *Tableau géographique de l'Ouest Africain au Moyen Âge d'après les sources écrites, la tradition et l'archéologie.* Dakar: IFAN.

Messier, R. and Miller, J. 2015. *The Last Civilized Place. Sijilmasa and Its Saharan Destiny.* Austin: University of Texas Press.

Mitchell, P. 2005. *African Connections. Archaeological Perspectives on Africa and the Wider World.* Walnut Creek: Altamira.

Monroe, J.C. 2017. 'Elephants for want of towns': Archaeological perspectives on West African cities and their hinterlands. *Journal of Archaeological Research.* Doi:10.1007/s10814-017-9114-2.

Moraes Farias, P.F. de. 2003. *Arabic Medieval Inscriptions from the Republic of Mali. Epigraphy, Chronicles and Songhay-Tuāreg History.* Oxford: Oxford University Press (British Academy).

Moraes Farias, P.F. de. 2017. Arabic and Tifinagh inscriptions. In Nixon 2017a, 41–51.

Nixon, S. 2009. Excavating Essouk-Tadmakka (Mali): New archaeological investigations of early Islamic trans-Saharan trade. *Azania: Archaeological Research in Africa* 44: 217–55.

Nixon, S. 2013. 'A longing for Mecca': The trans-Saharan Hajj and the caravan towns of West Africa. In V. Porter and L. Saif (eds), *Hajj: Collected Essays.* London: British Museum Press, 65–73.

Nixon, S. 2014. West Africa: Islamic archaeology. In C. Smith (ed.), *Encyclopedia of Global Archaeology.* New York: Springer, 7720–33.

Nixon, S. (ed.). 2017a. *Essouk-Tadmekka: An Early Islamic Trans-Saharan Market Town.* Leiden: Brill.

Nixon, S. 2017b. Trans-Saharan gold trade in pre-modern times: Available evidence and research agendas. In Mattingly *et al.* 2017a, 156–88.

Nixon, S., Filomena Guerra, M. and Rehren, T. 2011. New light on the early Islamic West African gold trade: Coin moulds from Tadmekka, Mali. *Antiquity* 85: 1353–68.

Norris, H. 1962. The history of Shinqit according to the Idaw 'Ali tradition. *Bulletin de l'institut fondamental d'Afrique noire* 24: 39–413.

Norris, H. 1975. *The Tuaregs: Their Islamic Legacy and its Diffusion in the Sahel.* Warminster: Aris and Philips.

Park, D.P. 2010. Prehistoric Timbuktu and its hinterland. *Antiquity* 84: 1076–88.

Polet, J. 1985. *Tegdaoust IV, Fouille d'un quartier de Tegdaoust (Mauritanie Orientale): Urbanisation, architecture, utilisation de l'espace construit.* Paris: Éditions Recherche sur les Civilisations (ADPF).

Prussin, L. 1986. *Hatumere: Islamic Design in West Africa.* Berkeley: University of California Press.

Raimbault, M. and Sanogo, K. (eds). 1991. *Recherches archéologiques au Mali.* Paris: Éditions Karthala.

Robert, D., Robert, S.D. and Devisse, J. 1970. *Tegdaoust I: Recherches sur Aoudaghost.* Paris: Arts et Métiers Graphiques.

Robert-Chaleix, D. 1989. *Tegdaoust V, Une concession médiévale à Tegdaoust: Implantation, évolution d'une unité d'habitation.* Paris: Éditions Recherche sur les Civilisations (ADPF).

Saison, B. 1981. Azugi; Archéologie et histoire en Adlar mauritanien. *Recherche, pedagogie et culture* 5: 66–74.

Sanogo, K., Cissé, M. and Fane, Y. 2006. *Site de la mosquée Kankou Moussa à Gao: Homage au docteur Téréba Togola.* Bamako: Ministère de la Culture/ Direction Nationale du Patrimoine Culturel.

Savage, E. 1992. Berbers and blacks: Ibadi slave traffic in eighth-century North-Africa. *Journal of African History* 33.3: 351–68.

Thomassey, P. and Mauny, R. 1951. Campagne de fouilles à Koumbi Saleh. *Bulletin de l'Institut Français [later Fondamental] d'Afrique Noire (Dakar)* 13: 438–62.

Thomassey, P. and Mauny, R. 1956. Campagne de fouilles de 1950 à Koumbi Saleh (Ghana?). *Bulletin de l'Institut Français [later Fondamental] d'Afrique Noire (Dakar)* 18: 117–40.

Togola, T. 1996. Iron Age occupation in the Méma region, Mali. *African Archaeological Review* 13.2: 91–110.

Vanacker, C. 1979. *Tegdaoust II, Fouille d'un quartier artisanal.* Paris: Memoire de l'I.M.R.S.

Van Berchem, M. 1960. Sedrata et les anciennes villes berbères du Sahara dans les récits des explorateurs du XIXe siècle. *Bulletin d'Institut Français d'Archéologie Orientale* 59: 289–308.

Van Doosselaere, B. 2014. *Le roi et le potier. Etude technologique de l'assemblage céramique de Koumbi Saleh, Mauritanie (5e/6e–17e siècles).* Frankfurt: Africa Magna Verlag.

Vikør, K. 1987. The early history of the Kawar oasis: A southern border of the Maghrib or a northern border of the Sudan? *The Maghreb Review* 12.3–4: 78–83.

18 | Urbanisation, Inequality and Political Authority in the Sahara

JUDITH SCHEELE

Introduction

Recent archaeological research has shown that Garamantian civilisation was much more extensive than previously thought, allowing for surprisingly high population density, agricultural exploitation and urbanisation. This, then, poses the question of how to make sense of the available material, and how to best describe the Garamantian polity and its evolution. Several aspects of the archaeological and historical record are at issue here: the nature of settlements and their interrelation, their connections with the surrounding political and economic landscape, their ecology and economic base, and the nature and organisation of their polity. Most recent publications have interpreted these features as necessary components of one coherent political complex, conveniently labelled as an 'early state'. Thus, Wilson describes the Garamantes as a 'substantial agriculturally-based trading state'.[1] For Mattingly and Sterry, Garamantian settlements 'give clear evidence of state-level activity in the north-eastern Sahara'; Mattingly postulates the 'existence of an incipient state in Fazzan from the first millennium BC'; and Mattingly, Sterry and Thomas speak of a 'literate, state-level society'.[2] By the early centuries AD, Mattingly claims elsewhere, this was moreover a territorial state, 'covering c. 250,000 km^2 of the Libyan Sahara'.[3] For Liverani, the matter leaves even less room for doubt:

> We can confidently postulate the existence of a Garamantian complex chiefdom in mid-first millennium BC; while a true or proper Garamantian state or kingdom (well attested in Roman times) could have begun slightly later, with the first urbanization in Germa.[4]

[1] Wilson 2012, 409.
[2] Mattingly 2003, 355; Mattingly and Sterry 2013, 517; Mattingly *et al.* 2013a, 517.
[3] Mattingly and MacDonald 2013, 72. [4] Liverani 2000, 511.

Elsewhere, and perhaps more cautiously, the term 'Garamantian kingdom' is used, with references to classical authors that speak of a 'Garamantian king'. In all these cases, the development of the Garamantian polity is mapped on an evolutionary scale: 'the rise of the Garamantes bears on a long-term process involving the transformation of pastoral communities of the central Sahara into increasingly unequal and territorial agricultural societies, eventually coalescing as a slave-using kingdom'.[5]

This paper attempts to unpick the knot here implied, of urbanisation, sedentarism, socio-economic inequality, labour exploitation, territoriality, and central state power, with reference to more recent and hence better documented Saharan history and ethnography. Such evidence cannot of course describe social and economic developments in the Fazzan of two millennia ago, and the aim of this chapter is in no way to suggest stasis, or even structural continuity. More recent evidence can, however, alert us to our own, forcibly parochial assumptions, and to problematic shortcuts that link phenomena that are *a priori* separate and independent – such as the existence of social inequality and urbanisation, and the development of territorial states – by showing how these, in the Sahara at least, did not always necessarily imply each other. Much of this might simply be a question of the terminology chosen ('state', versus 'complex polity', for instance), but words matter, inasmuch as they bear assumptions that in turn might shut off potentially fruitful avenues of inquiry, pre-empting important questions and preventing others from being asked.

Urbanisation

The archaeological evidence leaves no doubt that ancient Garama is best understood as a town:

> Garama was a site of unusual size and complexity within the Garamantian kingdom, and much of its monumental architecture is unique at present. There are ample indications that this was a place of high political and religious authority and an unusually well-connected economic focus. Garama seems urban by these criteria, though Saharan urbanism clearly differed in important respects from Mediterranean (or indeed sub-Saharan) urbanism.[6]

For Mattingly and Sterry, this degree of urbanisation and traces of complex settlement hierarchies provide 'key evidence of . . . complexity':

[5] Mattingly *et al.* 2013a, 510. [6] Mattingly *et al.* 2013b, 290.

> The large urban centres of Fazzan were not the consequence of particular fertile locales, but places where substantial outside investment had been made to create a centre that had functions *beyond* farming. The most likely reasons behind this investment are undoubtedly control of trade routes or exercising of political authority.[7]

This impression is furthered by the existence of 'public buildings' and 'the large-scale erection of forts and urban defences'.[8] Indeed, according to archaeological markers – the existence of a town wall, a *qasaba*, two mosques, and several saints' tombs – Jarma continued to be 'urban' until the end of the seventeenth century.[9] But can we conclude from this that Garama was also necessarily the centre of a state, or indeed that it functioned within a settlement hierarchy that would pull its hinterland together in a hierarchical fashion?

In Fazzan as in the Sahara more generally, the existence of urban centres can only be justified through functions and sources of income that go beyond local resources: trade and 'the exercise of political authority' are indeed obvious candidates here. Yet while there is ample evidence for the existence of trade, and indeed for the decline of Garama/Jarma after trade-routes shifted,[10] the notion of 'political authority' is more difficult to capture. As much as we can assume that a town like Garama, distinctive from everything that surrounded it, exerted some kind of dominance over its 'hinterland', and might have been constructed with external, state-based models in mind, the term 'political authority' can cover many realities apart from centralised state administration. And indeed, factors that are usually seen to indicate the presence of states – records of taxes, administration, or coined money – are conspicuously absent from the findings at Garama, although the necessary techniques and raw materials were locally available.[11] Similar caution is warranted when analysing the existence of monumental 'public' buildings in Garama. These indeed seem to have been impressive; but too little is known of their function and use to be able to say with certainty that these were really 'public', rather than privately constructed temples. Indeed, Mattingly *et al.* themselves use the term 'public' in inverted commas, and note that 'we need to keep an open mind about domestic/public attribution of our fragmentary remains'.[12] And although the notion of the state necessarily implies some idea of a public sphere or good, the converse is not true: 'public' buildings can be erected and

[7] Mattingly and Sterry 2013, 506, 515; see also Mattingly *et al.*, Chapter 2, this volume.
[8] Mattingly *et al.* 2013b, 292; Mattingly and MacDonald 2013, 73.
[9] Mattingly *et al.* 2013a, 523. [10] Mattingly *et al.* 2013a, 522.
[11] Mattingly *et al.* 2013a, 515, 517. [12] Mattingly *et al.* 2013b, 295.

maintained by other forms of collective authority, such as local councils, or they can be provided by leading families or individuals. Susan McIntosh thus calls for caution in the interpretation of the archaeological record:

> In societies where political action and coordination is achieved through assemblies, councils, and other forms of horizontally arrayed or democratic structures, and not through conspicuous vertical control hierarchies, we have relatively little idea of how we might recognise the material manifestations of such an organisation.[13]

In the Sahara of written history, meanwhile, there are many more examples of municipal councils and local initiatives than of state projects. Despois noted that most *qsur* in the Fazzan were built by individual families whose names were still known in the 1940s.[14] Local archival records and French colonial sources attest the importance of municipal self-government throughout the area, in the eighteenth and nineteenth centuries at least.[15] Before then, *jama'at* (local assemblies or tribal councils) were seen as a defining feature of the *bilad al-siba*, the country beyond the reach of central government – which covered all of the contemporary Sahara and much of the Maghrib.[16] These councils were routinely in charge of the construction and maintenance of complex irrigation systems, fortresses and defensive walls, markets, mosques and shrines.[17] Lest these settlements are seen as too small to qualify as 'urban', there are plenty of examples elsewhere in the Sahara of longstanding trading towns that, at a later date, grew to impressive size and clearly deserved to be qualified as 'towns', and that prospered in the absence or margins of states, such as, for instance, Timbuktu, Walata, Ghadamis, or the cities of the Mzab.[18] For the fourteenth century, Nixon thus speaks of urban centres that were strongly associated not with states but with 'strong nomadic groups'.[19] These urban centres were usually based on independent internal forms of government, through councils or large dominant families, with little internal taxation, a clear preoccupation with trade and mobility, little territorial appetite, and no independent state institutions.[20] In the Sahara perhaps

[13] McIntosh 1999, 22. [14] Despois 1946, 101. [15] Scheele 2010.

[16] Touati 1993, 98; Voguet 2009.

[17] Irrigation: Bédoucha 1987; Grandguillaume 1978; Powers 2002, 95–140; fortresses: Montagne 1930; Nehlil 1916; markets: Aspinion 1954; mosques and shrines: Scheele 2012, 48.

[18] See Cleaveland 2002; Eldblom 1968; Masqueray 1886; Milliot and Giacobetti 1930; Saad 1983.

[19] Nixon, Chapter 17, this volume.

[20] These towns can perhaps be described as 'city-states', but they show little in the way of a public sphere or independent institutions, and indeed leave one to wonder what might be gained by such a label, apart from a (possibly mistaken) impression of familiarity.

even more than elsewhere, the development of cities and that of states hence needs to be treated separately.[21]

Settlement Hierarchies

Arguments derived from settlement hierarchies pose similar problems. Mattingly *et al.* identify a number of distinct supporting settlements near ancient Garama, in 'areas of higher potential for exploiting agriculture and perhaps more importantly trade', that would have provided supplies for Garama, and in turn received services, perhaps of an administrative kind.[22] In the Sahara, however, classic models of settlement hierarchies need to be qualified. Oases, of whatever size and even those that relied on a similar technological infrastructure as the Garamantian Fazzan, rarely produced a reliable surplus of any kind, and barely managed to reproduce a labour force sufficient to maintain their existence. Indeed, an argument can be made for their inherent outside dependency, whatever their size (as the cost of irrigation does not diminish proportionally) – a point that Mattingly and Sterry fully recognise elsewhere.[23] Such fundamental subsistence problems cannot simply be solved through political fiat or increased exploitation of local populations or neighbouring villages, as surplus can only be produced through imports – of labour and goods – mostly from areas beyond the Sahara proper, or that rely on different forms of production (such as neighbouring pastoral economies).[24] Saharan economies thus never evolved within a closed system, making regional settlement hierarchies necessarily porous on all levels, and shifting problems of political control from internal exploitation to external relations, mobility and transport. Concepts of 'dispersed hinterlands', developed by Horden and Purcell might thus be more apposite here.[25]

In the Sahara of recorded history, production for export was thus crucial, but limited in kind. It mostly consisted in dates, while some

[21] Compare also Cowgill 2004, 526; McIntosh, R. 2005. [22] Mattingly *et al.* 2013a, 533.

[23] Mattingly and Sterry 2013, 516; and Chapter 8, this volume.

[24] This makes the Sahara fundamentally different from the model of state inception proposed by Sanmartí *et al.*, Chapter 11, this volume (drawing on Godelier 1980 and Johnson and Earle 2000), who explain the development of hierarchies through the need for increased productivity and technological change.

[25] 'If the term hinterland is to be retained, then the presumption should be that what is in question is fragmented, not a compact domain that can be mathematically modelled and limned on a map . . . The *dispersed*, changeable, hinterland has, we suggest, been the Mediterranean norm' (Horden and Purcell 2000, 112, also 115–22).

oases could draw on nearby salt-mines (salt-mines that had no agricultural base near them were mostly worked by anybody who could organise transport).[26] This means that there was little incentive to develop exchange between neighbouring *qsur*. Most *qsur* had no markets: this was as true of the early twentieth-century Fazzan as of southern Algeria:

> There is no market in the Tidikelt, nor is there a special site [for trade]. Business is conducted at the arrival of caravans who are offered hospitality in different *qsur* and carry out their exchanges while staying with their hosts. ... Exchanges are carried out behind locked doors. Rich *qasr*-dwellers receive caravaneers into their homes, lodge them and are in charge of selling their goods.[27]

Trade thus connected places far afield, not neighbouring settlements; and until colonial times, it seems that most Saharan oases groups had no 'central place', neither in economic nor in political terms. Economic regional integration was not a matter of exchange or hierarchical supply towards an 'urban' centre, as even the smallest *qsur* were not self-sufficient in all they needed and hence relied on exchange (and therefore had in a sense 'urban' economies).[28] Rather, it was a matter of overlapping property rights. Individual owners invested in several *qsur*, neighbouring and distant, mostly, it seems to have spread risk.[29]

As a result, hierarchies, or relations of mutual dependency, tended to be established with places much further afield, within the Sahara or on its boundaries. Hence, in 1919, the Tuwat as a whole had close economic relations with 'the Doui Menia and Ouled Djérid (today near the border with Morocco), with the Ahaggar Tuareg (in the far south) and caravaneers from El Goléa and the Hauts Plateaux (in north and central Algeria)'.[30] Similarly, the 'hinterland' of the oases of Fazzan in the early twentieth century included not only the pastures of northern Arabic-speaking pastoralists, but also the Ajjer mountains, whose inhabitants 'absolutely needed' Fazzani grain and dates, while themselves being indispensable to Fazzani trade and thus survival.[31] Indeed, the droughts that hit the Sahel in the 1970s and 1980s were catastrophic not because of their unusual severity, but because southern Saharan economies had been cut off from their usual Sahelian or even Sudanese outlets.[32]

[26] See for example, Clauzel 1960; Gouletquer and Kleinmann 1975; Vikør 1982.

[27] Lethielleux 1948, 70; and 'Rapports annuels, annexe du Tidikelt', 1908 and 1911, Archives nationales d'outre mer (ANOM), box 23H102.

[28] The French geographer Capot-Rey (1953, 239) thus remained uncertain whether *qsur* are best qualified as villages or towns, 'since their rural and urban characteristics are so closely mixed'.

[29] Scheele 2012, 42–43.

[30] 'Rapport annuel, annexe du Touat', 1919, ANOM 22H50.

[31] Despois 1946, 191.

[32] Baier and Lovejoy 1975.

As a result perhaps, internal Saharan classifications of settlements tend not to speak in terms of ranks, with villages, towns and cities, but rather in terms of different kinds of settlement, some used primarily by nomadic populations, others by agriculturalists, some which allow for permanent settlement and production, and others acting as storehouses or defensive structures in times of need.[33] As Mattingly and Sterry observe, traces of settlement do not necessarily imply a fully sedentary lifestyle, but should rather be understood to lie on a continuum of practices.[34] In the western and central Sahara, the most common term used to refer to oases is thus '*qasr*' (plural *qsur*) or 'fortress', indicating an emphasis on safe storage and defence corresponding to regional rather than local economic strategies.[35] In southern Morocco, collective storehouses (*hisn*, *agadir* or *tighremt*) count among the oldest settlements, and have given rise to a lively municipal and customary law tradition.[36] These had few permanent residents, and clearly relied on a widely dispersed nomadic hinterland, which could shift over time, as access to *agadir* was mediated through property rights rather than membership in social groups. Despois noted the architectural similarities between the *qsur* in Fazzan that he visited in the 1940s, and the Moroccan collective storehouses – a similarity that was, decades later, endorsed by Thiry, who warned that 'the beauty of the Moroccan *tighremt* should not make us forget the similar plan, and apparently also the similar use, that they share with the castles (*qsur*) in the Fazzan'.[37]

Settlement hierarchies as they appear in the archaeological record might thus not just rank more or less complex manifestations of the same thing, but rather describe different kinds of constructions. As Fenwick notes, drawing on the much better documented example of Umayyad North Africa, the function of towns cannot merely be understood through their location or appearance. They need to be seen as part of larger networks and connections: archaeologically, a town might still look the same although structurally, it has fundamentally changed, say from an agro-town on the apex of its own regional hierarchy (with a classic productive 'hinterland') to a relay-post in a much larger network.[38] This structural diversity that might not be apparent in the physical appearance of towns makes the use of the

[33] For a description of the early-twentieth-century Fazzan in these terms, see Despois 1946, 101.
[34] Mattingly and Sterry, Chapters 1 and 8, this volume.
[35] Hence, Ibn Khaldun describing Berber pastoralists in the fourteenth century says that 'in their homelands [among which he cites the Algerian Tuwat] they have built *qsur* and strongholds and have made gardens of palms and grapes and other fruits' (in Hopkins and Levtzion 1981, 339); five centuries later, Auguste Geoffroy (1887) writes of the *qasr* of Aïn Madhi as built by and for nomads: 'settlement was only developed with regards to the seasonal needs of the nomads'.
[36] See for example, Montagne 1930. [37] Despois 1946, 60; Thiry 1995, 92.
[38] Fenwick 2013, 15; forthcoming.

term 'settlement hierarchy' potentially difficult, especially in an environment that is as ecologically fragile and complex as the Sahara: as Taylor *et al.* note, 'to show the existence of a hierarchy, power relations between levels must be demonstrated'.[39]

Spiritual Centres

Other types of centrality can be identified in Saharan contexts. From the eleventh century onwards, the most visible and perhaps also the most common in the Sahara is that established by religious settlements, or *zawaya* (singular *zawiya*). These are settlements founded by saints, connected genealogically and spiritually to the wider Islamic world. They tend to be centred on the founding saint's tomb, which continues to be a pole of *baraka* and an attraction for pilgrims (and thus of outside goods, funds and labour), and often but not always administered by his descendents, spiritual or otherwise. Some of these *zawaya* belong to larger Sufi *turuq*, and some set up colonies further afield, often in areas where the original *zawiya* has economic interests; many doubled up as more or less temporary markets or fairs, under the saint's protection. The more successful among them accumulated considerable property holdings, again situated in a widely dispersed hinterland. They thereby bound various sedentary and nomadic populations together in complex networks of overlapping ownership, protection and donations, providing initial funding for agricultural and commercial projects, and redistributing surplus. The Awlad Sidi Shaykh, for instance, originally from north-west Algeria, invested in houses and storage places in the Gourara and Tuwat in southern Algeria; several *zawaya* had long been set up in their name throughout the greater Tuwat, owning large gardens as *ahbas* (endowments) and worked by slaves or *haratin* (freed slaves) given to the *zawiya*. These *zawaya* acted as markets and travel lodges, and sent their revenues back to the mother *zawiya* in Abiodh Sidi Cheikh, their original fief.[40] In southern Morocco, the *zawiya* of Tamgrout described by Abdullah Hammoudi and David Gutelius owned 10 per cent of all irrigated land in the Draa valley, as well as 35,000 palm trees throughout the area; meanwhile, the *zawiya* of Iligh, also in southern Morocco, invested heavily in irrigation in its immediate vicinity and beyond, as well as controlling and financing regional and trans-regional trade.[41] Further east, the Sanusiyya spread from central and

[39] Taylor *et al.* 2010, 2806.

[40] Simon, 'Notices sur le Tidikelt', 20 June, 1900, ANOM 22H50; see also Scheele 2012, 45–46, 62–70.

[41] Gutelius 2002; Hammoudi 1980; Pascon 1980.

southern Libya south, setting up agricultural colonies in north-eastern Niger and northern Chad, and providing eastern Trans-Saharan trade routes with a much needed infrastructure.[42]

The flow of goods – tribute, rents or gifts – from colonies and clients to the 'mother-*zawaya*' described its own kind of regional hierarchy. Yet these *zawaya* were usually established far afield, and no compact hinterland emerged; moreover, *zawaya* were inherently colonies, inverting images of settlement hierarchies constructed from the bottom up. Secondary places were established from the core outwards: a *zawiya* did not earn its prestige from the sway it held over its daughter establishments, but rather, the latter prospered owing to the former's *baraka* (and founder's investment, and ability to centralise funds and labour). Hierarchy more generally was imagined on a family model: saints established original settlements, while their 'sons' travelled on and set up dependencies, thereby diffusing their father's *baraka* throughout the region. As segmentary imaginings more widely, such patterns were limited in range, and eventually lead to fission: no independent state apparatus ever emerged. Classic political anthropology of the Maghrib postulates that *zawaya* were essentially set up in the interstices of tribal structures, acting as mediators and arbitrators, and deriving their influence from their lack of political power which was vested in the surrounding, acephalous tribes.[43] This is historically inaccurate, as *zawaya* accumulated independent influence, as economic agents, repositories and arbitrators of Islamic legality, but also as mediators with coastal states.[44] Nonetheless, *zawaya* never developed into states themselves, and indeed lost their influence if they became too closely associated with state endeavours.[45] Economic and spiritual power, in other words, was not converted into political dominance, but rather used to play the locally influential off against each other. Saints acted as arbitrators and mediators, not as territorial sovereigns.[46]

Hence, the Sanusiyya, although it was commonly decried as a rival 'colonial state' by French military officers,[47] seems to have had some success in northern Chad precisely because it did not act as a state in the

[42] Triaud 1995. [43] See for example, Evans-Pritchard 1949; Gellner 1969.

[44] Hammoudi 1974; 1980. [45] Ennaji and Pascon 1988, 17.

[46] Edwards, Chapter 9, this volume, similarly stresses the importance of spiritual authority in the development of cities in early Meroe; see also Crone 1986.

[47] Hence, according to the French colonial officer Boujol in 1939, in Chad, the Sanusiyya acted like a 'genuine state, I would even say a colonial state . . . [Their] *zawaya* were almost exactly like colonial outposts, around which local populations crystalised. Through a regular courier service, they constantly kept in touch with their capital at Kufra, and the *muqaddamin* who managed them were genuine administrators. Taxes were paid to them, forced labour carried out, agriculture and trade developed, and caravans found in them safe relay posts and protection against plunderers' (Boujol, 'La Senoussya au Tchad', 7 June, 1939, ANOM 10 APOM 401).

European sense, aiming at territorial sovereignty. Rather, it attempted to control strategic points, by setting up trade relays and agricultural colonies with labour they had brought with them. Their focus was on control of (some) people, rather than territory, arbitration rather than force, a reliance on gifts rather than taxes, and flexibility instead of centralised control.[48] Its internal administrative structure was loose, based primarily on family and spiritual ties, with different *zawaya* vying for resources, and little control at all exerted over their nomadic auxiliaries.[49] This was so because the Sanusiyya intrinsically relied on existing infrastructures and alliances, without which they could not have survived; and they adopted and partially restructured existing regional relations. Instead of superimposing an alien political construct on local resources that could not finance it, the Sanusiyya infiltrated existing patterns and structures, temporarily pulling them together into a larger whole. Hence, perhaps, their visible fragility (they were easily defeated by the French, and ostensibly left few traces when they collapsed), coupled with an underlying long-term resistance (the patterns of ownership they established in northern Chad for instance are still visible, as are the trade networks they established or rather co-opted and expanded). The *zawiya* of Iligh in southern Morocco similarly

> attempted to play, among the tribes, the role of a state, but without a state's prerogatives or legitimacy. It seems that Iligh never raised taxes ... nor did it intervene militarily among the tribes in other cases than those that immediately concerned it. Iligh carried out reconciliations, acted as guarantors for securities and received fines for breach of tribal peace agreements ... without getting involved in relations among tribes as long as these did not threaten them.[50]

A different type of internal Saharan colonisation is exemplified by a more regionally and historically specific type of Saharan settlement, the *zariba* (plural *zara'ib*). Most contemporary towns in the eastern Sahara and Sahel originated as *zara'ib* – that is, temporary camps set up by slave raiders on their way south.[51] Many of these turned into more permanent settlements, through the agricultural settlement of slaves around them.[52]

[48] As Evans-Pritchard (1945, 187) noted: 'Within this vast theocratic empire there was little centralised planning or control. New lodges were founded often by the initiative of influential families and the head of the order might even not hear of a new foundation till after it had been completed. In the more distant parts the lodges were autonomous or came under the control of a local mother lodge.'

[49] Djian 1996 [1915–1916], 123. [50] Ennaji and Pascon 1988, 27–28.

[51] Johnson 1989, 80; see also O'Fahey 1973, 34. [52] Johnson 1989, 78.

These slave raiders were initially either sent by the Egyptian state, or by private companies that supplied the Egyptian armies with slave soldiers, but they sparked imitations through the eastern and central Sahel, often by slave soldiers themselves.[53] They thus constituted another form of Saharan settlement, again bound up with external logics of trade, production and conquest that were closely connected to state aspirations, but that never aimed at establishing state control in the region itself.[54] Although they might thus look at first sight similar to the slave towns identified by MacDonald and Camara in Segou, they were clearly peripheral to the state, and often constructed at great distance from areas under state control – as they could effectively only function beyond the state's boundaries.[55] Indeed, Douglas Johnson claims that one of the reasons why the British conquest of Sudan was so slow was because the British needed a periphery beyond their direct control, ideally a periphery torn apart by warfare, whence they could draw supplies for their own slave army (which they had taken over directly from the Egyptians).[56] Similar arguments for the maintenance of a necessary slaving frontier could be made for regions further west, although here this has not resulted in the development of permanent settlements of the *zariba*-type.[57]

There can, then, be no doubt about the outside dependency of Saharan settlements, or indeed the fact that they were often bound up with projects of regional control. But these projects of regional control might be spiritual and commercial, or based on the hunting and gathering of slaves, as much as on stable institutionalised political rule by a state apparatus independent of local social structures (which, again, taking into account the limited resources of the Sahara proper, would have been difficult to sustain). Nor did they necessarily aim at a monopoly of force, but rather inscribed themselves into a polycentric political world – a world they attempted to manipulate, not to dominate. In a sense, they developed a particular form of centrality, parasitic on economic developments elsewhere, beyond the boundaries of the Sahara proper, and that favoured extraversion over territorial consolidation.[58]

[53] Cordell 2003, 34; Johnson 1989, 73.

[54] Note, however, possible parallels here with the garrison towns, identified by Fenwick forthcoming, in Umayyad North Africa.

[55] MacDonald and Camara 2012, 178. [56] Johnson 1989, 81. [57] Testart 1998, 61.

[58] On extraversion, see Bayart 2000; on the utility of the concept in archaeological research, see Edwards 2004; Mattingly *et al.* 2015, 58; Stahl 2014.

Inequality, Slavery and the Exploitation of Labour

In much of the literature, the stark inequality that characterised Garamantian society – as is apparent from evidence both for the use of slave labour and for internal socio-economic distinctions – is seen as an additional proof of the existence of a centralised state. Hence, Mattingly concludes that monumental burials, expressing status distinctions, indicate social hierarchies of a kind generally associated with a state.[59] Mattingly and MacDonald, meanwhile, cite as one of the main proofs for the existence of a centralised Garamantian state 'the simple consideration of the amount of work required just to construct the irrigation systems'.[60] This, however, assumes that inequality, labour exploitation and especially slavery are necessarily related to the existence of states.[61] Conversely, the absence of traces of state centralisation would indicate equality, or 'heterarchy', and presumably the absence of slave labour.[62] Saharan history belies both assumptions.[63] While states are rare (although not unheard of) in the Saharan historical record, slavery has long been at the heart of Saharan modes of production, and has probably preceded and certainly outlasted particular political formations. Again, beyond the historical evidence, a structural argument can be made for this: if the only way in which Saharan oases can be made to yield a surplus is by starving its workforce, the regular importation of slaves appears a fundamental necessity.[64] At a much later period, the French colonial sources leave no doubt that oasis populations were unable to reproduce themselves, and chronic demographic decline – only offset by mostly forced immigration –

[59] Mattingly 2003, 87; but see McIntosh 1999, 14 for a different possible explanation.

[60] Mattingly and MacDonald 2013, 75; see also Mattingly *et al.* 2013a, 510.

[61] In a similar vein, MacDonald and Camara (2012, 171, 174) link the observation of a generally recognised need for labour with the close connection established in Segou (and other Sahelian states) between states, warfare and slave-raiding: for a similar argument, see Azevado 1998; Reyna 1990; Roberts 1987. All of these latter cases, however, inscribe themselves into a particular historical context: that is, Sahelian and Sudanic Africa while it was rapidly exposed to international slave trade, and suffering from a high degree of internal warfare. See also Sanmartí *et al.*, Chapter 11, this volume, who state that the formation of states 'normally accompanies' hierarchical organisation of human societies.

[62] McIntosh, R. 2005; McIntosh, S. 1999.

[63] More generally, there is no reason to assume that slavery – or any other form of labour exploitation – was ever the monopoly of states: 'Slavery is a wild card whose use depends on social strategies, defined elsewhere. The existence of slavery does not define a type of society, but particular societies define types of slavery' (Testart 1998, 41).

[64] As Meillassoux (1986) famously argued, slavery is a means of obtaining labour without having to meet the cost of the biological and social reproduction of people; it can thus operate at a permanent disequilibrium.

is a recurrent theme in historical descriptions of virtually all settled Saharan societies.[65] As Edwards notes in the very different context of early Meroe, cities were often 'consumers of people', at a scale that we now find difficult to imagine.[66] They were also unpleasant places, and people did not necessarily choose to live there unless coerced.

However they were structured politically, Saharan societies historically relied heavily on servile and slave labour, for herding, guarding the flocks, and salt mining, but even more so for irrigated horticulture, religious settlement, and, especially in the eastern Sahara, military endeavours.[67] Slaves were also crucial to local and regional reproductive strategies, leading to complex gradations of hierarchy and status within families.[68] In the Sahara as elsewhere, slaves were first and foremost strangers who could claim no prior ties with their captors or buyers; their servile status was defined by their lack of connectivity, and hence mobility.[69] This means that once a slave was put to work in an oasis and deprived of independent means of transport, no state apparatus was needed to keep him or her there; connections made between low status and immobility were self-fulfilling.[70] Conversely, enslavement was not only a way of incorporating much needed outside labour into Saharan economies, but also a guarantee of internal flexibility, crucial in an environment where crises are always to be expected: status hierarchy 'functioned primarily to assure first access to resources in times of scarcity'.[71] Slaves and clients could be set free to fend for themselves when resources were scarce: it is thus not the state-like aspect of the system, but rather its unbounded and decentralised nature, coupled with structural uncertainty and the need for risk management, that explains the persistence of slave labour and other forms of dependency.[72]

[65] Faced with demographic catastrophe after the abolition of the slave trade, the French colonial administration thus proposed to forcibly settle French West African soldiers in the Saharan oases, with little success: see 'Note sur la question noire en Algérie'; 'Lettre du Gouverneur Général de l'Algérie au Général commandant le 19e corps de l'Armée', 23 April 1913; and 'Rapport du Capitaine Vincent, chef d'annexe de Beni Abbès, sur l'installation des troupes noires en Algérie', 3 March 1919, all ANOM 3H13.

[66] Edwards, Chapter 9, this volume.

[67] See Bonte 1998; Gutelius 2002; Johnson 1989; Lovejoy 1986; and McDougall 1986, respectively.

[68] McDougall 1998. [69] Meillassoux 1986; Rossi 2009; Testart 1998.

[70] This makes the Saharan case very different from regions with more abundant natural resources: see for example, Cooper (1980) on the great difficulties experienced by British colonial officers in setting former slaves to work on plantations, as the latter tended to run off into the forest where they could easily appropriate land to grow their own food, far from any form of coercion. In the Sahara, this was just not a possibility.

[71] Baier and Lovejoy 1975, 561. [72] Baier and Lovejoy 1977.

Slavery, moreover, only describes the bottom rung of a complex system of gradation that admits no centre and no boundaries. The classic account of such hierarchies is given by Stewart on Mauritania, who provides a description of a complex system of gradations between full slavery and 'nobility', on the one hand, and Islamic excellence on the other, with tribute-paying free men and freedman somewhere in between.[73] Although the distribution of wealth did not necessarily follow such status-distinctions – as those at the 'top' were defined by their boundless generosity, but also by their unlimited access to other people's property – real differences in socio-economic position were clearly very much part of Saharan life for most of its history, in 'tribal' as much as in urban settings.[74] An early twentieth-century manuscript from Timbuktu gives us an internal view of these distinctions: all people of the Sahara and the Sahel are ranked here according to their genealogical excellence, which can be mapped into Islamic history; these differences matter, inasmuch as they describe relations of tribute-paying and protection, many of which still persist today (and explain, for instance, political alignments in the current northern Malian civil war).[75] This allows for much internal differentiation; meanwhile, centrality and value here is not given by the existence of a state-apparatus, but rather by the Islamic revelation that reasons in terms of spiritual rather than political power.[76] Indeed, contemporary states and their armies are often seen by those on the bottom of a scale as a way of breaking out of such status hierarchies; and we can surmise that this was also the case of historic states, in those cases where they had a direct impact on Saharan realities.[77] Social complexity, in other words, much as exploitation, might thrive in the margins of states as much as at their core.[78]

Although there can be no doubt that these Saharan status hierarchies did not derive from state influence, they at times led to the formation of state-like structures, in particular on the edges of the Sahara. Hence, Pierre Bonte describes the emergence of the Mauritanian emirates from the seventeenth

73 Stewart 1973.

74 There is a tendency, in much of the literature, to associate tribal systems with equality; this only holds true if we believe local ideologies, and discount all those – in many cases a majority – who cannot pretend to full tribal status, and hence 'drop out' of such reckonings altogether. For an account of the longevity of Saharan inequalities in one such setting, see Hall 2011.

75 Muḥammad Maḥmūd wuld Shaykh, Kitab al-turjaman fī ta'rīkh al-sahara wa al-sudan wa bilad tinbuktu wa shinjit wa Arawan wa nubadh fi ta'rikh al-zaman fi jami'a al-buldan, further discussed in Scheele 2012, 139–42.

76 Corresponding status categories can be found among Tuareg, see e.g. Casajus 1990; Clauzel 1962; and, in a somewhat attenuated form, among Tubu-speakers, Brandily 1988.

77 Klein 2005, 832; Schmitz 2009.

78 For a different period, Fenwick 2013, 18 similarly notes clear indications of socio-economic inequalities within North African tribal societies.

century as a result of internal stratification among the 'nobles' brought about by marriage strategies.[79] Yet the 'states' thus developed had certainly no territorial reality, nor much administrative power (or indeed aspiration): the *amirs* received tribute, and acted as supreme arbiters, but they never developed anything that resembled an administrative state apparatus that could become independent of the regional tribal structure: 'the Moorish emirate reveal themselves as original tribal political formations'.[80] They are not tribes turned into states, but rather 'tribal states' (or rather state-like constructs) that were momentarily superimposed on a tribal structure without profoundly altering it.[81] Elsewhere in the Sahara, 'sovereigns' similarly turn out to be primarily arbitrators – as is the case of the 'sultan' of Agadez, who famously had to be of slave descent.[82] The scope of political action of the Tuareg *amenokal* was similarly limited, unless he acted in times of conflict.[83] Such 'sultans' might look the part to outsiders, and even act it in external relations, but they had in fact little influence on the ground, and certainly did not develop an independent centralised state administration, or even territorial ambitions beyond the control of strategic trade routes and settlements.[84]

Centralisation and Territoriality

The notion of pre-colonial African states is a contested one, to the point where some say that we should stop using the term altogether.[85] Hence, Skalník warns us that 'what students of the African past labelled as 'state' has, on the whole, little to do with the state as it developed both as a concept and as a social reality within the orbit of western civilisation'. Worse,

> by labelling e.g. a certain kind of African political organisation a 'state' one does disservice to African history and the Africans themselves because not only is African originality forced into a Eurocentric straight-jacket but worst of all this

[79] Bonte 2008. [80] Bonte 2008, 519.

[81] 'A tribal state is a state superimposed on a society that is designed to cope without it and which may accordingly revert to statelessness at any time. It is only when the autonomous and self-sufficient nature of the building blocks has been undermined that we have a state as opposed to a tribe' (Crone 1986).

[82] Claudot-Hawad 1998, 23; Urvoy 1934. [83] Claudot-Hawad 1990; Keenan 1977.

[84] As Fentress 2006, 13 notes for the North African coast and its immediate hinterland, Berber Hellenistic princes or kings might have looked such to their 'civilised' neighbours and overbearing allies, while back home, they acted like rotating chieftains within a segmentary world (see also Brett and Fentress 1996, 33).

[85] Lonsdale 1981, 139.

bias denies the possibility that, in Africa, viable alternatives to the state, as it evolved in the West, may have been developed.[86]

Instead, as Lonsdale notes, 'the most distinctively African contribution to human history could be said to have been precisely the civilised art of living fairly peaceably together *not* in states'.[87] But even those scholars who are less sceptical mostly agree that it is difficult to apply Western European territorial models of statehood to Sub-Saharan Africa. Most of Sub-Saharan Africa has historically been marked by an abundance of land and a shortage of labour, which means that notions of power, wealth and influence were mediated through people rather than land, while agricultural surplus was exceptional and in any case difficult to transport and store.[88] As a result, Sub-Saharan polities, however coercive they might have been, rarely had defined boundaries, but rather a core and an ill-defined periphery. This also means that historically, much of Sub-Saharan Africa was best characterised as a 'frontier society', making it possible for people to try their luck elsewhere, and thereby limiting state coercion, or alternatively, basing it on continual violence.[89] As a result, state revenue was generally derived less from taxation than the control of trade and booty, in other words, raids in the state's peripheries.[90]

Similar features seem to emerge from the archaeological record in Fazzan, where Mattingly and MacDonald point to 'the disparity of material culture between the core and the periphery of Garamantian territory'.[91] Yet in the Sahara, where permanent agriculture is limited to a few nodal points, and most land is used extensively by inherently mobile people (whether pastoralists or farmers), notions of territory, let alone of territorial states, have to be treated with even more caution.[92] Political formations were inherently mobile, to the point where Grémont, in his study of the historically dominant Tuareg group north of the Niger Bend, the Iwellimiden,

86 Skalník 1983, 25, 26. 87 Lonsdale 1981, 139. 88 Coquery-Vidrovitch 1975.

89 Kopytoff 1987.

90 Edwards 1998; Edwards, Chapter 9, this volume, applied these arguments to his analysis of Meroe on the Upper Nile. Citing historical and contemporary Sudanic examples, he concludes that in Meroe also, 'the control of land did not form a primary power base. The major determinant of production remained the availability of labour rather than land, and political power associated with it was derived from the control of people rather than territory'. As a result, 'the most important state revenues were derived elsewhere, from non-agricultural exotic resources' (Edwards 1998, 178, 183).

91 Mattingly and MacDonald 2013, 73.

92 In any case, in light of the increased evidence for early urbanisation and perhaps even state formation in Sub-Saharan Africa, there is no good reason to assume that northern political models would have had more impact on the Garamantes than southern ones. As MacDonald notes in this volume, 'at a broad, syncretic level, I prefer to see the Trans-Sahara as a sphere of interaction in trade and ideas – much like the Mediterranean. These ideas go both ways'.

quickly gave up all attempts to describe their political structure in terms of territory, as such questions simply made no sense to his interlocutors.[93] This high degree of mobility was also true of earlier dominant polities in the area.[94] More generally, although there is no shortage in Saharan history of the emergence and decline of dominant groups, these generally did not attempt to establish territorial states, but rather vied with each other for the control over people, routes and strategic way-points: they established 'network territories', as Pliez writes of the Sanusiyya.[95] In the Sahara, local production mostly did not even allow for self-sufficiency, making the extraction of regular taxes difficult, while distances were such that any practical continued projection of power was severely limited.[96] Tribute, raiding and sporadic taxation of mobility thus appear as the dominant forms of 'governance'; 'power lies in movement', as Retaillé summarises, and internal hierarchies are perhaps best expressed as gradations of mobility and immobility.[97] The inherent mobility of dominant political groups was exacerbated by the fact that strategically important points were themselves rarely fixed: in the Sahara, 'connections produce places, and not vice versa; places that matter are crossroads. Centrality moves across the desert according to the flow of social networks'.[98]

This corresponds to Saharan ethnography and history more widely: historically, there simply has been no point in attempting to control vast stretches of desert, nor has it ever been profitable. What mattered were routes and crossroads, and certain groups of people, and these were best controlled – or rather, taxed – either sporadically, or through proxy.[99] From the internal point of view, questions of power and coercion were relegated to the domestic sphere of slavery and tribute extraction, whereas 'politics' was generally couched in terms of opposition, arbitration, hospitality and protection.[100] As Fenwick notes, even in contexts where the existence of a central state cannot be doubted, such as Umayyad and post-Umayyad North Africa, we need to be careful not to impose our own

93 Grémont 2012, 133; see also Grémont 2010.
94 See, for example, McIntosh 2008, 360; Retaillé and Walther 2013, 607.
95 Pliez 2006, 692.
96 Witness, for instance, the repeated failure of nineteenth- and twentieth-century imperial powers to 'govern' the Sahara in any meaningful way, until they could rely on motorised transport and aviation; and witness also contemporary difficulties to militarily control most of the Sahara, despite foreign intervention.
97 Retaillé 1998, 77; Rossi 2009; and see the discussion of slavery above.
98 Retaillé and Walther 2013, 608.
99 For notions of 'wealth in people' expressed in qualitative rather than quantitative terms, see Guyer 1993, 246.
100 As Bonte 1998, 124 notes with regards to the Mauritanian Adrar, status conflicts were mostly fought out in the economic rather than the political sphere.

contemporary assumptions of the purpose and functioning of states. She hence describes the Umayyad empire as a 'low-cost imperial endeavour' leading to a 'node-and-corridor' strategy that meant that many areas remained beyond state control.[101] This, of course, only becomes a 'problem' if we assume a territorial approach, whose historical validity is often questionable.[102]

Although we cannot know at this point whether similar reflections applied to the Garamantes, the limited narrative historical evidence for the existence of a Garamantian state tends to emphasise control over trade routes and mobility rather than territory. The Garamantian 'kings' of Greco-Roman writers were never portrayed as sedentary governors of a territorial state, but rather as inherently mobile: setting out on a raid, in Ptolemy, or coming in aid of the 'brigand' Tacfarinas, in Tacitus.[103] This, of course, reflects a Mediterranean sedentary perspective, describing a potentially dangerous 'other', whose mobility was a military problem, but also a necessary asset for trade; and clearly it cannot, on its own, sum up Garamantian civilisation.[104] Yet we should not dismiss the reference to mobility and raiding altogether: not only does it fit with a 'nodes-and-corridor' model, or with the idea of a 'network-territory', but the predatory rather than territorial nature of many pre-colonial states, in particular in Sub-Saharan Africa, should be kept in mind.[105] In the Sahara as much as in the Sahel, raiding was not an accidental attribute of states, but rather at the core of their development, a means of 'importing' crucial resources, in a context where state raids in the periphery were probably more productive than taxation in core areas.[106] As Edwards puts it, with regards to one of the examples that Mattingly and Sterry cite as a potential inspiration to Garamantian state formation, 'the ability of Meroitic kings to directly control subsistence production was likely to be limited to a relatively small core region, while more diffuse forms of power could be exerted over often more mobile populations'.[107] Control of mobility and exchange

[101] Fenwick 2013, 33; Forthcoming.

[102] Compare, Retaillé 1993; Trousset 1984. This might also go some way towards solving the puzzle posed by Sanmartí *et al.*, Chapter 11, this volume, of the huge territorial extension of what they label early North African states, and their resulting oddity within the Mediterranean context.

[103] Ptolemy, *Geography* 1.8.4, and Tacitus, *Annals* 4.23.

[104] Mattingly 2003, 86.

[105] Azevedo 1998; Diamond 1996; MacDonald and Camara 2012; Reyna 1990; Roberts 1987. The argument for the inherently predatory nature of early states was first made by Tilly 1985; for contemporary analyses that link warfare, crime and state formation, see for example, Charlton and May 1989.

[106] Compare Edwards 1998, 181.

[107] Edwards, Chapter 9, this volume; Sterry and Mattingly, Chapter 8, this volume.

systems remained thus key to state power, while territorial concerns were secondary. Whether such political formations are best described as 'states' or not is a separate question, but we certainly need to take the label 'state' as a starting rather than the end-point of analysis.

Conclusion

Although the 'Garamantian state' has by now become a convenient shorthand for the complex polity that developed in Fazzan from the fifth century BC onwards, we have to be wary of terms that assume both too much – that is, in this case, an independent state administration, centralisation and territoriality – and too little, by potentially masking local and regional originality. Whatever the Garamantian 'kings' of the Greco-Roman writers were, and however they interacted with the Garamantian 'tribes' attested in the same sources, it is important not to stop at outside descriptions, but to attempt to understand how Garamantian civilisation was held together, whether this implied any kind of political centralisation, and what this meant on the ground. Similarly, while Garamantian towns might have exercised political authority in one form or another, and while labour exploitation clearly was at the heart of Garamantian – as of all Saharan – settlement, it is more difficult to grasp the nature of this authority. In order to do this, we need to keep in mind the rarity of historically attested state formations in the Sahara, the inherent difficulty of territorial control in desert areas, and the longevity of other political traditions. Also, the Saharan context provides ecological givens that, far from determining political structure or even social organisation, nonetheless indicate the limits of what could be done, even by the most ambitious of leaders. Assertions of vast territorial control exercised by a Garamantian 'kingdom' hence have to be taken with a pinch of salt, as this control was forcibly very different in kind and degree from what our current assumptions and experiences might lead us to believe. Similarly, questions of urban status and of socio-economic inequality and labour exploitation should be analytically divorced from assumptions about statehood, unless there is clear proof that they really were related. Exploitation can take many forms, and central territorial state administration is only one of them, and not necessarily historically the most common – or, indeed, the most efficient. The problem with labelling the Garamantian polity a 'state' is thus not so much that it might be wrong, but rather that it stops us from asking certain types of questions, by creating a false impression of recognition.

References

Aspinion, R. 1954. Un llouh du Sous: règlement coutumier du Souq el Jemaa des Ida ou Gnidif. *Hespéris* 41.3–4: 395–409.

Azevedo, M. 1998. *Roots of Violence: A History of War in Chad*. Amsterdam: Horden and Breach.

Baier, S. and Lovejoy, P. 1975. The desert-side economy of the Central Sudan. *International Journal of African Historical Studies* 8.4: 551–81.

Baier, S. and Lovejoy, P. 1977. The Tuareg of the Central Sudan: Gradations in servility at the desert's edge (Niger and Nigeria). In I. Kopytoff and S. Miers (eds), *Slavery in Africa: Historical and Anthropological Perspectives*. Madison: University of Wisconsin Press, 291–311.

Bayart, J.-F. 2000. Africa in the world: A history of extraversion. *African Affairs* 99: 217–67.

Bédoucha, G. 1987. *L'eau, l'amie du puissant. Une communauté oasienne du sud tunisien*. Paris: Éditions des archives contemporaines.

Bonte, P. 1998. Esclaves ou cousins. Évolution du statut servile dans la société mauritanienne. In B. Schlemmer (ed.), *Terrains et engagements de Claude Meillassoux*. Paris: Karthala, 157–82.

Bonte, P. 2008. *L'émirat de l'Adrar mauritanien: Harīm, compétition et protection dans une société tribale saharienne*. Paris: Karthala.

Brett, M. and Fentress, E. 1996. *The Berbers*. Oxford: Blackwell.

Brandily, M. 1988. Les inégalités dans la société du Tibesti. In C. Baroin (ed.), *Gens du roc et du sable. Les Toubous. Hommage à Charles et Marguerite Le Cœur*. Paris: Éditions du CNRS, 37–72.

Capot-Rey, R. 1953. *Le Sahara français*. Paris: Presses universitaires de France.

Casajus, D. 1990. Islam et noblesse chez les Touaregs. *L'Homme* 115: 7–30.

Charlton, R. and May, R. 1989. Warlords and militarism in Chad. *Review of African Political Economy* 16.45–46: 12–25.

Claudot-Hawad, H. 1990. Honneur et politique: Les choix stratégiques des Touaregs pendant la colonisation française. *Revue du monde musulman et de la Méditerranée* 57: 11–47.

Claudot-Hawad, H. 1998. La hiérarchie des savoirs et des pouvoirs dans la société touarègue précoloniale et la recomposition des rôles socio-politiques pendant la guerre anti-coloniale et après la défaite. *Nomadic Peoples* 2.1–2: 17–38.

Clauzel, J. 1960. *L'exploitation des salines de Taoudeni*. Algiers: Institut des recherches sahariennes.

Clauzel, J. 1962. Les hiérarchies sociales en pays touareg. *Travaux de l'institut de recherches sahariennes* 31: 120–75.

Cleaveland, T. 2002. *Becoming Walata: A History of Saharan Social Formation and Transformation*. Portsmouth: Heinemann.

Cooper, F. 1980. *From Slaves to Squatters: Plantation Agriculture in Zanzibar and Coastal Kenya*. New Haven: Yale University Press.

Coquery-Vidrovitch, C. 1975. Research on an African mode of production. *Critique of Anthropology* 2.4–5: 38–71.

Cordell, D. 2003. The myth of inevitability and invincibility: Resistance to slavers and the slave trade in Central Africa, 1850–1910. In S.A. Diouf (ed.), *Fighting the Slave Trade. West African Strategies*. Athens: Ohio University Press, 31–49.

Cowgill, G.L. 2004. Origins and development of urbanism: Archaeological perspectives. *Annual Review of Anthropology* 33: 525–49.

Crone, P. 1986. The tribe and the state. In J.A. Hall (ed.), *States in History*. Oxford: Blackwell, 48–77.

Despois, J.J. 1946. *Mission scientifique au Fezzân (1944–1945). Tome 3: Géographie humaine*. Algiers: Institut de recherches sahariennes.

Diamond, S. 1996. Dahomey: The development of a proto-state. *Dialectical Anthropology* 21.2: 121–216.

Djian, G. 1996. *Le Tchad et sa conquête, 1900–1914* (reprint of 1915–1916 edition). Paris: L'Harmattan.

Edwards, D. 1998. Meroe and the Sudanic kingdoms. *Journal of African History* 39.2: 175–93.

Edwards, D. 2004. *The Nubian Past: An Archaeology of the Sudan*. London: Routledge.

Eldblom, L. 1968. *Structure foncière, organisation et structure sociale. Une étude sur la vie socio-économique dans les trois oasis libyennes de Ghat, Mourzouk et particulièrement Ghadamès*. Lund: Uniskol.

Ennaji, M. and Pascon, P. 1988. *Le makhzen and the Sous al-aqsa: La correspondance politique de la maison d'Illigh (1821–1894)*. Paris: Éditions du CNRS.

Evans-Pritchard, E.E. 1945. The distribution of Sanusi lodges. *Africa* 15.4: 183–87.

Evans-Pritchard, E.E. 1949. *The Sanusi of Cyrenaica*. Oxford: Clarendon Press.

Fentress, E. 2006. Romanizing the Berbers. *Past and Present* 190: 3–34.

Fenwick, C. 2013. From Africa to Ifrîqiya: Settlement and society in early medieval North Africa (650–800). *Al-Masaq* 25: 9–33.

Fenwick, C. Forthcoming. Archaeology, empire and the Arab conquest of North Africa. *Past and Present*.

Gellner, E. 1969. *Saints of the Atlas*. London: Weidenfeld and Nicolson.

Geoffroy, A. 1887. Arabes pasteurs nomades de la tribu des Larbas. *Les Ouvriers des deux mondes* 1.8: 409–64.

Godelier, M. 1980. L'État: Les processus de sa formation, la diversité de ses formes et de ses bases. *Revue internationale des sciences sociales* 32.4: 657–71.

Gouletquer, P.L. and Kleinmann, D. 1975. Structure sociale et commerce du sel dans l'économie touarègue. *Revue de l'occident musulman et de la Méditerranée* 22: 131–39.

Grandguillaume, G. 1978. De la coutume à la loi: Droit de l'eau et statut des communautés locales dans le Touat précolonial. *Peuples méditerranéens* 2: 119–33.

Grémont, C. 2010. *Les Touaregs Iwellemmedan (1647–1896). Un ensemble politique de la boucle du Niger.* Paris: Karthala.

Grémont, C. 2012. Villages and crossroads: Changing territorialities among the Tuareg of Northern Mali in the twentieth century. In J. McDougall and J. Scheele (eds), *Saharan Frontiers: Space and Mobility in Northwest Africa.* Bloomington: Indiana University Press, 131–45.

Gutelius, D. 2002. 'The path is easy and the benefits large': The Nasiriyya, social networks and economic change in Morocco, 1640–1830. *Journal of African History* 43: 27–49.

Guyer, J. 1993. Wealth in people and self-realization in equatorial Africa. *Man* (n. s.) 28.2: 243–65.

Hall, B. 2011. *A History of Race in Muslim West Africa, 1600–1960.* Cambridge: Cambridge University Press.

Hammoudi, A. 1974. Segmentarité, stratification sociale, pouvoir politique et sainteté. *Hespéris – Tamuda* 16: 147–80.

Hammoudi, A. 1980. Sainteté, pouvoir et société: Tamgrout aux XVIIe et XVIIIe siècles. *Annales Économies, Sociétés, Civilisations* 35.3–4: 615–41.

Hopkins, J.F.P. and Levtzion, N. 1981. *Corpus of Early Arabic Sources for West African History.* Cambridge: Cambridge University Press.

Horden, P. and Purcell, N. 2000. *The Corrupting Sea.* Oxford: Blackwell.

Johnson, A.W. and Earle, T. 2000. *The Evolution of Human Societies From Foraging Group to Agrarian State.* Stanford: Stanford University Press.

Johnson, D. 1989. The structure of a legacy: Military slavery in northeast Africa. *Ethnohistory* 36.1: 72–88.

Keenan, J. 1977. Power and wealth are cousins: Descent, class and marital strategies among the Kel Ahaggar (Tuareg – Sahara). Part 1. *Africa* 47.3: 242–52.

Klein, M. 2005. The concept of honour and the persistence of servility in the Western Sudan. *Cahiers d'études africaines* 45.179–80: 831–51.

Kopytoff, I. 1987. The internal African frontier: The making of African political culture. In I. Kopytoff (ed.), *The African Frontier: The Reproduction of Traditional African Societies.* Bloomington: Indiana University Press, 3–84.

Lethielleux, J. 1948. *Le Fezzan, ses jardins, ses palmiers: notes d'ethnographie et d'histoire.* Tunis: Imprimerie Bascone et Muscat.

Liverani, M. 2000. The Libyan caravan road in Herodotus IV.181–185. *Journal of the Economic and Social History of the Orient* 43.4: 496–520.

Lonsdale, J. 1981. States and social processes in Africa: A historiographical survey. *African Studies Review* 24.2–3: 139–225.

Lovejoy, P. 1986. *Salt of the Desert Sun: A History of Salt Production and Trade in Central Sudan.* Cambridge: Cambridge University Press.

MacDonald, K. and Camara, S. 2012. Segou, slavery and Sifinso. In J. Cameron Monroe and A. Ogundiram (eds), *Power and Landscape in Atlantic West Africa*. Cambridge: Cambridge University Press, 169–90.

McDougall, E.A. 1986. The economies of Islam in the Southern Sahara: The rise of the Kunta clan. *Asian and African Studies* 20: 45–60.

McDougall, E.A. 1998. A sense of self: The life of Fatma Barka. *Canadian Journal of African Studies* 32.2: 285–315.

McIntosh, R.J. 2005. *Ancient Middle Niger. Urbanism and Self-Organising Landscape*. Cambridge: Cambridge University Press.

McIntosh, S. 1999. Pathways to complexity: An African perspective. In S. McIntosh (ed.), *Beyond Chiefdoms: Pathways to Complexity in Africa*. Cambridge: Cambridge University Press, 1–30.

McIntosh, S. 2008. Reconceptualizing early Ghana. *Canadian Journal of African Studies* 42.2–3: 347–73.

Masqueray, E. 1886. *Formation des cités chez les populations sédentaires de l'Algérie: Kabyles du Djurdjura, Chaouïa de l'Aourâs, Beni Mezâb*. Paris: E. Leroux.

Mattingly, D. (ed.). 2003. *The Archaeology of Fazzan. Volume 1*. London: The Society for Libyan Studies.

Mattingly, D. (ed.). 2013. *The Archaeology of Fazzan. Volume 4*. London: The Society for Libyan Studies.

Mattingly, D. and MacDonald, K. 2013. Africa. In P. Clark (ed.), *The Oxford Handbook of Cities in World History*. Oxford: Oxford University Press, 66–82.

Mattingly, D. and Sterry, M. 2013. The first towns in the central Sahara. *Antiquity* 87: 503–18.

Mattingly, D., Sterry, M. and Edwards, D.N. 2015. The origins and development of Zuwîla, Libyan Sahara: An archaeological and historical overview of an ancient oasis town and caravan centre. *Azania: Archaeological Research in Africa* 50.1: 27–75.

Mattingly, D., Sterry, M. and Thomas, D.C. 2013a. Jarma in its Saharan context: An urban biography. In Mattingly 2013, 505–44.

Mattingly, D., Thomas, D.C., Sterry, M. and Preston, J. 2013b. Public and domestic architecture of Garama. In Mattingly 2013, 287–98.

Meillassoux, C. 1986. *Anthropologie de l'esclavage. Le ventre de fer et d'argent*. Paris: Presses universitaires de France.

Milliot, L. and Giacobetti, A. 1930. Recueil des délibérations des djema'a du Mzab. *Revue des études islamiques* 4: 171–230.

Montagne, R. 1930. *Un magasin collectif de l'Anti-Atlas, l'agadir des Ikounka*. Paris: Larose.

Nehlil. 1916. L'azref des tribus et qsour berbères du Haut Guir. *Archives Berbères* 1.1: 77–89; 2: 88–103, 109–34.

O'Fahey, R. 1973. Slavery and the slave trade in Dâr Fûr. *Journal of African History* 14.1: 29–43.

Pascon, P. 1980. Le commerce de la maison d'Ilîgh d'après le register comptable de Husayn b. Hachem. *Annales Économies, Sociétés, Civilisations* 35: 700–29.

Pliez, O. 2006. Nomades d'hier, nomades d'aujourd'hui. Les migrants africains réactivent-ils les territoires nomades au Sahara? *Annales de Géographie* 652: 688–707.

Powers, D. 2002. *Law, Society and Culture in the Maghrib: 1300–1500*. Cambridge: Cambridge University Press.

Retaillé, D. 1993. Afrique: Le besoin de parler autrement qu'en surface. *Espaces Temps* 51–2: 52–62.

Retaillé, D. 1998. L'espace nomade. *Revue de géographie de Lyon* 73.1: 71–81.

Retaillé, D. and O. Walther. 2013. L'actualité sahélo-saharienne au Mali: Une invitation à penser l'espace mobile. *Annales de Géographie* 694: 595–618.

Reyna, S.P. 1990. *Wars without End. The Political Economy of a Precolonial State*. Hanover: University Press of New England.

Roberts, R.L. 1987. *Warriors, Merchants and Slaves: The State and the Economy in the Middle Niger Valley, 1700–1914*. Stanford: Stanford University Press.

Rossi, B. (ed.). 2009. *Reconfiguring Slavery: West African Trajectories*. Liverpool: Liverpool University Press.

Rossi, B. 2009. Slavery and migration: social and physical mobility in Ader (Niger). In Rossi 2009, 182–203.

Saad, E. 1983. *Social History of Timbuktu: The Role of Muslim Scholars and Notables 1400–1900*. Cambridge: Cambridge University Press.

Scheele, J. 2010. Councils without customs, qadis without states: Property and community in the Algerian Touat. *Islamic Law and Society* 17.3: 350–74.

Scheele, J. 2012. *Smugglers and Saints of the Sahara: Regional Connectivity in the Twentieth Century*. Cambridge: Cambridge University Press.

Schmitz, J. 2009. Islamic patronage and republican emancipation: The slaves of the Almaami in the Senegal River Valley. In Rossi 2009, 85–115.

Skalník, P. 1983. Questioning the concept of the state in indigenous Africa. *Social Dynamics* 9: 11–28.

Stahl, A.B. 2014. Africa in the world: (Re)centering African history through archaeology. *Journal of Anthropological Research* 70: 5–33.

Stewart, C. 1973. *Islam and Social Order in Mauritania*. Oxford: Clarendon Press.

Taylor, P., Hoyler, M. and Verbruggen, R. 2010. External urban relational process: Introducing central flow theory to central place theory. *Urban Studies* 47.13: 2803–18.

Testart, A. 1998. L'esclavage comme institution. *L'Homme* 38.145: 31–69.

Thiry, J. 1995. *Le Sahara libyen dans l'Afrique du nord médiévale*. Leuven: Peeters Press.

Tilly, Charles. 1985. War making and state making as organized crime. In P.B. Evans, D. Rueschemeyer and T. Skocpol (eds), *Bringing the State Back In*. Cambridge: Cambridge University Press, 169–91.

Touati, H. 1993. La loi et l'écriture. Fiqh, 'urf et société au Maghreb d'après les Ajwiba d'Ibn Nâsir (m. 1085/1674). *Annales islamologiques* 27: 93–108.

Triaud, J.-L. 1995. *La légende noire de la Sanûsiyya. Une confrérie musulmane saharienne sous le regard français (1840–1930).* Paris: MSH.

Trousset, P. 1984. L'idée de la frontière au Sahara et les données archéologiques. In P.-R. Baduel (ed.), *Enjeux sahariens.* Paris: Éditions du CNRS, 47–78.

Urvoy, Y. 1934. Chroniques d'Agadez. *Journal de la société des africanistes* 4.2: 145–77.

Vikør, K. 1982. The desert-side salt trade of Kawar. *African Economic History* 11: 115–44.

Voguet, E. 2009. Islamisation de 'l'intérieur du Maghreb': Les *fuqahâ'* et les communautés rurales. *Revue du monde musulman et de la Méditerranée* 126: 141–52.

Wilson, A. 2012. Saharan trade in the Roman period: Short-, medium- and long-distance trade networks. *Azania: Archaeological Research in Africa* 47.4: 409–49.

PART IV

Concluding Discussion

19 State Formation in the Sahara and Beyond

DAVID J. MATTINGLY AND MARTIN STERRY

Introduction

In this concluding chapter we focus on debates about state formation and to what extent it is possible to recognise historical instances of this key process among Saharan societies. Here we make the case for a dynamic Saharan history with frequent episodes of urbanisation and state formation in the past. However, we also emphasise the ephemeral nature of these polities, which challenges more evolutionary models of the rise of towns and states. Towns and states have existed among a range of forms of organisation utilised by Saharan societies, with the balance of power swinging back and forth between sedentary and more mobile lifestyles.

Our exploration of these factors commences with general questions about the definitions and types of towns and states that are detectable in the Trans-Saharan world, coupled with a discussion of the sorts of models that can explain their rise and fall.

A crucial debate, and one of the reasons why the material presented in this volume is important, concerns the identification and interpretation of pre-colonial states in Africa.[1] As Monroe observes, for much of the twentieth century the emphasis on external factors and influences was perniciously pervasive, ignoring endogenous pathways to complexity.[2] As part of post-colonial theoretical backlash, there has sometimes been a tendency for external contacts to be entirely airbrushed out of the discussion. This volume emphasises the central importance of local actors, who in articulating 'both local and exotic sources of power . . . shaped the political contours of early states in Africa'.[3] While the existence of early states has been recognised for many areas bordering the Sahara, hitherto there has been

[1] Monroe 2013, 703–5. [2] On African pathways to complexity, see *inter alia* McIntosh, S. 1999.
[3] Monroe 2013, 703.

a reluctance to accord similar status to Saharan societal developments.[4] If we are correct in identifying the existence of Saharan polities and early interconnectedness of the Trans-Saharan world, this creates a new paradigm and opens the possibility of parallel development in Trans-Saharan regions that were most likely already in contact with each other in the pre-Islamic era.[5]

History reveals a great flaw in evolutionary models – social change is not unilinear and states have often proved unstable and ephemeral. 'Social progress' may in some cases be rejected and communities revert to less centralised forms of organisation. Nonetheless, it is also the case that knowledge of states has been a powerful source of information that cannot be uninvented within connected networks. Pristine states and empires will almost invariably have significant impact and influence on their neighbours, who cannot remain ignorant of their innovative socio-political organisation for long.[6]

Such approaches call into question traditional and simple evolutionary models of social change, which emphasise progressive steps from primitive to civilised, from tribe to chiefdom to state.[7] Nonetheless, as the recent work of Flannery and Marcus reminds us, there are common characteristics of early states across space and time and one of their key arguments is that rising levels of social inequality was fundamental in the emergence of states.[8]

We conclude the chapter with a final review of our work on the Garamantes of Fazzan, as this is the ancient people and the oasis region with the largest concentration of evidence. In Chapters 2 and 8 above, we presented the factors that persuade us that Garamantian society was urban and set out some ideas about the characteristics of Saharan urbanisation, reflecting on how this differed from Mediterranean or Sub-Saharan urbanism. In this final discussion, we broaden our analysis to consider the evidence from the wider Trans-Saharan zone, in relation to the vexed issue of how we might define state formation in a Saharan milieu. Given the Saharan focus of this volume, a key issue concerns the viability of oasis states. From another perspective if we are correct to identity the Garamantes as a polity, we also need to ask what was the contribution made by oasis centres to the evolution and governance of such a desert state?

[4] See Gronenborn 2013 (Lake Chad basin); MacDonald 2013 (Western Sahel); Moussa 2013 (Maghrib); Phillipson 2013 (Aksum); Shaw 2013 (Pharaonic Egypt); Welsby 2013 (Kerma and Meroe).

[5] The analysis offered here and in other books in this series demands a repudiation of a conventional narrative that is outdated and outmoded in terms of a lack of engagement with recent archaeological and theoretical advances, see for example Fauvelle 2018.

[6] Flannery and Marcus 2012, 503–44 on how new empires learn from old. See also Whitehead 1992.

[7] Trigger 2003; Yoffee 2005.

[8] Flannery and Marcus 2012, especially 341–544 on the rise of kingdoms and empires.

There are several questions to consider relating to semantics, ancient and modern. We have tended to use the terms 'state' and 'polity' interchangeably, recognising that there is considerable variance in what this may have meant even in relation to a single case study traced across several centuries. Some of the other authors in this collection seem to discriminate between states and polities, but without it being clear where the dividing line is to be drawn. There is also a question of the extent to which states were part of broader cultural groupings, as opposed to independent civilisations. It may be a characteristic of more mature state formations that they reshape material culture and behaviours in ways that make the society synonymous with the political entity. We would argue that the Garamantes were not merely a state, but a civilisation, in Trigger's terms.[9] Although we are not advocating a checklist approach, the Garamantes meet the key criteria of civilisation as defined by ancient Mediterranean societies: being based around agriculture[10] and urbanisation,[11] having a writing system,[12] using monumental architecture,[13] employing advanced technologies of production (metallurgy, textiles, etc.),[14] possessing a pronounced social hierarchy (including the practice of slavery),[15] and the development of wide trading relations.[16] Garama was also an important centre of religion, with a substantial stone-footed temple building and freestanding statuary.[17] Some of the elements of Garamantian culture appear to be shared with other early Saharan societies and may be considered formative components of oasis societies more generally. However, there are distinctive aspects of the Garamantian material record, certainly as regards sites like Jarma at the centre of Garamantian power, that seem to diverge markedly from other settlements that lay more at the periphery, like Aghram Nadharif and Fewet.

What Type of Towns?

Throughout this volume there has been an underlying tension as to what constitutes an urban centre and what constitutes a state. Scholarly definitions of urbanism are highly varied, as discussed in Chapters 1 and 8 above.[18] Our starting point in this final discussion is that there are distinctive

[9] Trigger 2003, 43–48. [10] Pelling 2013a; 2013b. [11] Mattingly and Sterry 2013.
[12] Mattingly 2013a, 517–18. [13] Mattingly 2013a, 73–125, 291–93.
[14] Duckworth *et al.* forthcoming; Mattingly 2013a, 462–63; Schrüfer-Kolb 2007.
[15] See arguments in Fentress 2011; Mattingly 2013a, 508.
[16] Mattingly 2013b; Mattingly *et al.* 2017; Wilson 2012. [17] Mattingly 2013a, 289–93.
[18] See Fernández-Götz and Krausse 2017.

and contingent aspects of Saharan urbanism that make it difficult to apply in a neat way models developed for other regions or time periods in a checklist approach.[19] A similar stance that seeks to differentiate Late Iron Age central European urbanism from Mediterranean models has proved equally helpful in developing new paradigms.[20]

The previous chapters have presented examples of ancient towns and states from across the Trans-Saharan zone. A starting point in defining urbanism in a Saharan context is to suggest that towns were different to other settlements – whether in scale, architecture and monumentality, function and occupation of their population. It is also worth considering that, regardless of modern definitions, a number of Saharan sites were explicitly recognised as urban by Roman and Arabic sources. The Garamantian capital at Jarma was specifically referred to by Greco-Roman sources in the late first and second century AD as a *clarissimum oppidum* (top-level centre) and a *metropolis* – marking it out as something out of the ordinary for the Central Sahara.[21] Archaeology fully supports this judgement with the evidence of monumental stone architecture, deploying Classical elements, and abundant Roman material culture consumed there. While the site reveals some influences from external sources (a Roman style bath was built there), many other aspects are not so easily recognisable from Mediterranean models of urbanism.

The Roman towns described by Wilson with their monumental centres, aqueducts and water amenities and conspicuous elite competition fit a classical, Mediterranean view of the ancient city.[22] Yet, these cities are peculiar to a relatively small, if populous, part of Africa and existed in this idealised form for only a few centuries. Though they had an important role to play in the Mediterranean, their influence on forms of urbanism in other Trans-Saharan regions seems slight. In Roman Egypt, the towns of the Western Desert follow some Mediterranean precedents, with densely-packed urban areas of mixed usage (houses and workshops alongside each other), but the main civic buildings were temples and these could be argued to follow pre-Roman traditions.[23] The significant aspect of the

[19] Smith 2017. [20] See Fernández-Götz and Krausse 2013.

[21] Pliny, *Natural History* 5.35; Ptolemy, *Geography* 4.6.12. Ptolemy records two other sites as 'metropolis' in inland Africa, Nigira (near the Nigir river – not certainly the Niger in this context) and Gira (associated with the Gir river). This might be a clue to the existence of at least two other state-level societies recognised by Rome. For some discussion on Pliny's African knowledge, see Desanges 1980; for Ptolemy's world view, see Berggren and Jones 2000.

[22] Wilson, Chapter 10, this volume. For a range of views on the Classical Mediterranean city, see Bowman and Wilson 2011; Clark 2013; Marcus and Sabloff 2008; Osborne and Cunliffe 2005.

[23] Boozer, Chapter 4, this volume.

Roman period sites in the Egyptian oases is the relative size of the largest of these desert towns, with Trimithis estimated by Boozer to have had a population of 10–15,000 and an occupied area of perhaps 40–60 ha.[24] As we have seen, that is much larger than other pre-Islamic oasis towns of the Central and Western Sahara.

Roman urbanism in North Africa followed a model based on agricultural hinterlands, monumentality and institutionalised inequality. These are commonly assumed to have originated due to external influences on North African society. However, Sanmartí *et al.* and Bokbot identify pre-Roman origins of these characteristics in the Numidian and Mauretanian centres of modern-day Tunisia and Morocco.[25] That suggests an earlier and more active engagement with urbanism in African societies and that this may have contributed to the precise form of towns that emerged. There are indeed traces of this – for instance, in the evidence of Roman towns built over Numidian fortified promontory sites like Althiburos and Cuicul.[26] The oft remarked successes of urbanisation and agriculture in Roman Africa have rarely been associated with endogenous factors, but contrary to the myth of 'wandering pastoralists' we now know that North Africa in the first millennium BC was a landscape already punctuated by numerous nucleated sedentary farming settlements. The Roman 'urban success' story and 'agricultural boom' built on these pre-existing conditions.[27]

Although urbanism was central to society and economy to the north of the Sahara, Edwards suggests that the early urban centres of Nubia and Meroe in the Middle and Upper Nile were parasitic.[28] Like Roman towns of the north, they were centres of craft production, but these were linked to militaristic royal households that drew their wealth from the exploitation of external environments rather than productive hinterlands. The relationship to surrounding lands was quite different, with seemingly few social ties between groups of craftspeople (who held no land rights) and groups of agriculturalists and pastoralists. For Edwards, these early towns were negative places in which the population had to be compelled to live. Leaving aside the chronological difference, there is to some extent a parallel between these towns and the oasis forts of the Roman frontier – where there was also a large concentration of military power, but little direct connection to surrounding lands or flocks other than the extraction of tax and tribute.[29]

[24] Cf. Mattingly and Sterry 2013. [25] Chapters 11 and 12, this volume.
[26] Mattingly 2016, 15–16. [27] Mattingly 2016, 21–22; Hobson 2015.
[28] Edwards, Chapter 9, this volume; Welsby 2013.
[29] Mattingly *et al.*, Chapter 5, this volume; Wilson, Chapter 10, this volume.

The otherness of the urban is also seen in the construction of complexes such as the dual towns of Gao, Ghana and Zuwila in which some urban zones were mercantile and some were royal.[30] This zoning within urban environments can also be seen in the accounts of Takadda where the town had trading and manufacturing functions, but the ruler was located some distance away.

For West Africa a dominant trend in the last decades has been the argument that many early urban sites in the Middle Niger region arose out of heterachical rather than hierarchical societies, being 'self-generated' and not dependent on states.[31] However, as Kevin MacDonald has observed, even in Mali there may have been distinctive types of early urban sites present alongside one another. He distinguishes between *Fadugu* (settlements of state power) and *Markadugu* (towns of commercial/spiritual function).[32] A crucial distinction is that the former were often ephemeral settlements due to the transitory nature of the power behind them and the latter much longer lasting.

Craft specialisation plays an important role in many of the case studies of this volume. In the Middle Niger and Senegal regions it reached an industrial scale in the large mound accretions that form the urban landscape. While the evidence is sparser in the walled enclosures around Lake Chad, metalworking appears to have been particularly prominent at these sites. Edwards considers the towns of Nubia and Meroe to be essentially craft centres and Wilson stresses the importance of urban production in his chapter. Saharan towns echo this pattern, as is evident at Jarma, the Garamantian capital.[33] At Sijilmasa, Capel identifies salt production as a factor in the siting of the town, while copper and silver mining were associated with the three early Medieval towns of southern Morocco – Tamdult, Dar'a (Zagora) and Sijilmasa.[34] Other Saharan centres such as Tadmakka and Zuwila may not have nearby natural resources, but both were involved in processing the goods that passed through them, notably gold. An important but less archaeologically visible aspect of oasis manufacturing across history has been textile and garment production. These goods have also been staples of trade in all periods within the Trans-Saharan zone and again are much under-estimated in many archaeologically focused accounts.[35]

[30] Mattingly *et al.* 2015; Chapter 2, this volume; McIntosh, Chapter 13, this volume; Nixon, Chapter 17, this volume.

[31] McIntosh, R. 2005; 2015.

[32] MacDonald 2013, 837; Mattingly and MacDonald 2013.

[33] Mattingly 2013a, 511–17.

[34] Capel, Chapter 16, this volume; Sterry *et al.*, Chapter 6, this volume.

[35] Mattingly *et al.* 2017, especially 211–30.

Caravan towns have played an important part in the history of the Sahara, though beyond the surviving literary sources, the detail is surprisingly meagre. This is more a result of absence of archaeological evidence, rather than evidence of absence. The case studies of Sijilmasa, Awdaghust, Kumbi Saleh, Gao and Tadmakka are complemented by sites like Jarma, Marandet and Ghadamis. Sam Nixon's chapter in particular stresses the different Islamic traditions of urbanisation that need to be recognised in the Medieval trading entrepôts.[36] Nonetheless, a key contribution of this book is the observation that those Islamic trading towns were not entirely externally produced, since, in some places at least, they can be shown to have built on existing Saharan traditions of oasis centres and commercial networks.

Fortification and defence are recurring themes for many, but not all centres. The defining and enduring feature of the Lake Chad settlements were the walls that protected the population and perhaps also livestock.[37] In Fazzan, and large parts of the Sahara in historic times, fortifications have been the norm for a wide range of settlements. However, there is much variation. At Sijilmasa and Ghadamis, the walls enclosed not only the core settlement area, but the oasis palmery; at the other end of the spectrum, the towns of Zuwila and Qasr ash-Sharraba possessed walled citadels rather than walls protecting the whole settlement and Tadmakka had no defences at all.

There is thus a good deal of variation in the physical appearance of towns in the Trans-Saharan zone. Whereas in the past most study has focused on the Islamic-era context of urbanisation, it is now apparent that there were also pre-Islamic initiatives and examples that may have influenced later developments. Some desert towns have been extraordinarily long-lived, like Ghadamis, but a recurrent pattern in the case studies reviewed in this volume is that desert towns have often been quite ephemeral and sensitive to broader shifts in political power, which have periodically re-routed trade across different parts of the Saharan network. In Fazzan, we can trace the successive shifts of the main capital from Jarma, to Zuwila, to Traghan, to Murzuq and finally to Sabha.[38] Each of those relocations can be linked to the emergence of a new polity or over-riding political change. It is to the connection between towns and incipient states that we now turn.

[36] Nixon, Chapter 17, this volume. [37] Magnavita, Chapter 15, this volume.
[38] Mattingly 2013a, 530–44.

What Type of States?

Scheele has made important points in Chapter 18 about the unsuitability of Saharan societies for developing into recognisable states. In responding to her arguments, we would first agree that any model of Saharan state formation must take account of the peculiar geographical and social conditions of the region, which since the first oases were created have always interlinked the lives of sedentary communities and pastoral groups. However, we diverge from her perspective in asserting that we believe that state formation has been achieved a number of times in the Sahara and that by and large it has been more commonly associated with the major oasis clusters, where large sedentary populations lived alongside pastoral groups, rather than in areas of the Sahara where pastoral groups have been more dominant and oasis communities fewer and more thinly spread.

There has been considerable recent debate about the relationship between urbanisation and state formation, with many commentators questioning evolutionary assumptions about progressive levels of social complexity.[39] There is a strong consensus among contributors to this volume that simplistic progressive assumptions about rising levels of social complexity from tribe, to chiefdom, to state are unhelpful in exploring state formation in the Trans-Saharan world. The ephemeral nature of many polities clearly indicates that states are not a natural high-end social outcome in this sort of environment. Periods of state level organisation have often been followed by periods of non-state structures.

The extent to which towns were a necessary precondition for the emergence of states has also been questioned and indeed Jennings and Earle have suggested that the initial development of towns may actually 'have served as a brake rather than an accelerant to central power'.[40] There is nonetheless a strong correlation between early towns and precocious state formation, especially once hierarchy started to emerge among the nucleated settlement agglomerations.[41] This was also often accompanied by a restructuring of the rural landscape – what Yoffee terms 'an equally important counterpart: "ruralisation" . . . the creation of the countryside'.[42]

While there are dangers of imposing western notions about state formation in a region and social milieu they are ill adapted for, we think there

[39] See Yoffee 2005 for a sustained challenge to neo-evolutionary interpretation.

[40] Jennings and Earle 2016, 475. But note also the critical responses to their paper, 485–89.

[41] Flannery and Marcus 2012, 457–60 on the rise of Uruk, with the emergence of four levels of urban/village settlements.

[42] Yoffee 2005, 60.

is also a serious danger of anachronism in retrojecting across all of time the political structures and patterns of power recorded in early modern and contemporary times in the Sahara. There have been significant changes across the last three millennia – the intensification of camel raising and what that meant for the size, range and importance of pastoral groups, a gradual decline in water availability in some oasis groups (like Fazzan), conquests and migrations in the Medieval period, etc. It is arguable that these have 'rewired' the Saharan networks in new ways.

Some aspects of the Saharan milieu have tended to influence the way that state power has operated there. Distances between places can be vast, crossing terrain with limited potential for settled occupation. Conventional notions of territorial states are thus potentially misplaced and territorial control will have become increasingly difficult to exercise over distance. But the Garamantes suggest that the territorial ambition of Saharan polities could be considerable – bearing in mind the documented ability of Garamantian kings to engage in active warfare between the Mediterranean coast and the Lake Chad region *c.*3,000 km to the south.[43] The core territory of the Garamantes has been estimated as *c.*250,000 km^2, though plainly it would be absurd to assert they exercised direct control of most of this landscape. Control of the network of water sources and the main oasis clusters within this was the key for the Garamantes and this may have been achieved by working through intermediaries in the main oasis settlements in the different regions. We would argue that the Garamantes were a state to the extent that they appear to have maintained dominance over a network of distinct oasis farming communities from their principal heartlands in Wadi al-Ajal. It also follows from the widespread zone of Garamantian activity that power over people and control of trade must have involved pastoral groups in the connective spaces between the oasis centres. We shall return later to the question of whether pastoralists or sedentary groups were predominant in Garamantian society.

Other types of Saharan state may also be envisaged, notably the city state and the slaving state. City states represent one of the earliest and smallest forms of polity across large parts of the world. That is not to say that Saharan city states, like Ghadamis or Wargla, are exactly akin to the early Near Eastern autonomous settlements, the *poleis* of ancient Greece, or the small-scale states of Medieval Italy.[44] Given the relative isolation of oasis groups one from the next it is not surprising to see that a level of local

[43] For source evidence to this wide-range of Garamantian activity, see Ptolemy, *Geography* 1.8–11; Tacitus, *Histories* 4.50 and Mattingly 2003, 76–86.

[44] Hansen 2000; 2002; Yoffee 2005, 44–62.

autonomy and self-defence capability developed in many oases. In many periods of history we can identify a pre-eminent centre in most of the main oasis clusters for which we have good archaeological or historical data. These sites tended to be significant nodal points in the caravan trade as well as productive oases. Indeed in the Saharan context, the trade connections and wider networks of oasis towns might be suggested as a characteristic of the Saharan city state. Shifts in the caravan routes and geo-political changes played a part in the resilience of such towns and the continuance of their city-state status. From the intensive evidence for Jarma being a centre of trade, a case could be advanced for their society having expanded out from a city state basis.

The slaving state has become most visible in relatively recent times, where documentary records are more abundant, as in the well-documented case of West African Dahomey.[45] Such states have developed in scale and wealth not through local production, but through long-range slave raiding and trading. Typical characteristics are the development of significant mobile armed forces and a well defended frontier region. Given the probable long-term significance of slaves in Trans-Saharan commerce, the possibility of pre-Islamic slave states needs to be carefully considered and the Garamantes are also potential contenders for such a role.[46]

Finally, leaving the Garamantes to one side for the moment, it seems simply wrong to infer that states have not existed in the Medieval and early modern period within the Sahara. Just as in the pre-Islamic era, the geographical and political context in which they occurred was quite particular. On the one hand, Ghadamis is an example of a long-lived mercantile city state. But territorial states have also existed. Fazzan, the heartlands of the Garamantes kingdom, was later the centre of a series of states and when external powers have attempted to control the Central Sahara, they have regularly focused on this region, often taking over the power structures of the Saharan states they supplanted. Thus the Ibadi regime of the Banu Khattab at Zuwila could be viewed as an attempt to reinvent the Garamantian kingdom of Fazzan and after it was reduced to the status of a province of the kingdom of Kanim for a while, the dynasty of the Awlad Muhamid functioned as a state, with a number of interludes when the Ottoman and Qaramanli powers from Tripoli again annexed the kingdom as a province.[47] A number of other prominent Medieval Saharan centres were established or flourished as the power bases of Khajarite/Ibadi persuasion (for example, Sedrata by Wargla). In southern Morocco, the main oasis

[45] Law 1992. [46] Fentress 2011. [47] Mattingly 2003, 90–106; Mattingly *et al.* 2015.

zones may have rarely been independent, but they were important in the rise of a number of new dynasties that took over wider territories. The densest oasis clusters were thus by no means unfamiliar with state structures and state functions. Nonetheless, there are interesting questions to address concerning why the idea of the state was not more widely diffused within the Sahara and whether we may be confronted by different models of the state. City states, territorial states, pastoral or slaving states all seem options to consider, as well as why some parts of the Sahara seem to have managed perfectly well without state structures. The processual paradigm linking inequality, urbanism and statehood is apparent in the Sanmartí *et al.* chapter on the origins of the Numidian state.[48] For them, the territorial states that covered much of the Maghrib in the last centuries BC were the apogée of a long process from intensification, agglomeration and an increasingly rigid hierarchy. Sanmartí *et al.* recognise that as much as this makes sense of the evidence, Althiburos must always have been entwined in networks of other agglomerations and other communities.

The role of outside influences is poorly understood – would the Numidian or Mauretanian states have occurred in the way they did without the presence of Carthage and the Phoenicians? For McIntosh, outsiders played a greatly reduced role (if any at all) in the development of the earliest states in West Africa.[49] Contacts from across the Sahara were present, but only at a later date, initially through the introduction of technologies of construction (mudbrick), animal husbandry (camels, horses, chickens) and later still through forms of religion (Islam), trade and governance. Nixon's view of a particular brand of urban site associated with the emergence of Islamic trade networks needs to be balanced against this.[50]

But let us step aside from the discussion of the development of the first states, for no-one would claim that these should lie within the Sahara. Any and all states within the Sahara must be seen as secondary states, states created within a world in which power was already held and articulated by neighbouring polities.[51] The earliest forays by states into the Sahara appear to be in Egypt's Western Desert. This had the form of a colonial project, an expansion of the Nilotic kingdom. The evidence is somewhat slight, but it would appear that the oasis settlements of Dakhla and Kharga were not independent, but instead linked to pulses of power from the Nile – the New Kingdom, the Persians, the Ptolemies and the Romans. Similar imperial expansions of power can be seen in the string of Roman forts in the

[48] Sanmartí *et al.*, Chapter 11, this volume. [49] McIntosh, Chapter 14, this volume.
[50] Nixon, Chapter 17, this volume.
[51] Emberling 2015; Parkinson and Galaty 2007; Price 1978.

northern Sahara from Bu Nijim in Libya to Castellum Dimmidi in Algeria – a large investment in people, agriculture and power in regions that were populated, but with little evidence for states. In the south, territorial states of Mali, Kanim and Songhay also expanded to include parts of the Sahara. Here there is a different mechanism (although with the caveat that our source material is largely from the 'outsider' Arab sources rather than 'insiders') whereby the Sahelian states made little investment, but undertook campaigns against key nodes of Saharan trade. Small independent cities such as Awdaghust, Tadmakka, Takadda and Agadez appear to have been the main targets along with the salt mines of northern Mali and Kawar. The control of Fazzan by the Kanimi kingdom in the thirteenth and fourteenth century is the most extreme and unusual example due to the 2,000 km distance. Control over these oases on the southern edge of the Sahara was precarious (as with all oases) and typically lasted only a century or two at most. Threats elsewhere might lead to their abandonment or they might be sources of rebellion themselves as with the Laguatan or the Kharajites, or the Tuareg in the south. Of the territorial empires, the Almoravids were unusual in seeking to control a Pan-Saharan territory, rather than just its edge. This reflects their origins, emerging from the Sanhaja of the Western Sahara. The Almoravid movement thus had strong Saharan roots and many of its initial targets were against Saharan entrepôts – Dar'a, Sijilmasa and Awdaghust. However, as the Almoravids extended themselves into Morocco, they split, with the northern Maghribian part separated from the Sahara. The Saharan faction led by Abu Bakr is not well-documented, but does not appear to have survived long after his death in 1087 (although it may have conquered Ghana in the interim).[52]

There are many historical examples of Saharan polities beyond the Almoravids (Table 19.1). Regrettably, we know little about most of these beyond a couple of fleeting references, but in aggregate we can build a picture suggesting some common characteristics. As with Saharan cities, Saharan polities were uniformly small in terms of territory, population and power. Most occupied only a single oasis, with one major trading town – Sijilmasa is the clearest example, but we may note also Ghadamis, Waddan, Wargla, Marandet, Tadmakka, Takkada and Awdaghust.

A second group occupied a string of neighbouring oases, for example the Lawata Berber state in the Egyptian oases, the dominant group within the oases of Kawar or the range of different polities that are mentioned as holding

[52] On the Almoravids, see Lugan 2000, 63–86.

Table 19.1 *States and proto-states in the Sahara*

Where	Capital	Who	When	Comments
Kharga, Dakhla, Farafra and Bahriya[53]	Al-Kalamun Al-kasr	Lawata Berber – Abd al-Malik ibn Marwan	<941–942>	Mixed population and religions Several thousand horsemen
Al-Jufra oases[54]	Waddan	King	7th century	Account is somewhat problematic
Sanhadja (zenaga) (also Anbiya)	Tribal Azugi after 11th century	Led by Lamtuna (list of kings in Ibn Khaldun)	7th–11th century?	
Kawar[55]	Shifts, starts at al-Qasaba (Gezabi?)	Majority Berber	7th/9th century? Not beyond 1220	Mixed Tubu, Berber, Arab
Sijilmasa[56]			8th century	
Air Maranda	Marandet	Tuareg	9th century	Under sway of kingdom of Gao
Air Al-Hazban[57]	Marquart identifies with Air	Tuareg	9th century	Under sway of kingdom of Gao
Air Tikarkarin	Somewhere between Agadez and Tahua	Tuareg	9th century	Under sway of kingdom of Gao
Fazzan (ash-Sharqiyat)[58]	Zuwila	Banu Khattab	10th–13th century	
Tadmakka	Zakran	Banu Tanmak Saghmara Berber	10th century	Sanhadja, Zenata, muslim and non-muslim
Wargla	Sedrata	Ibadi, Zenata Berber	10th–12th centuries	Mixed religion, some Lawata, some Christian Collection of towns in the oasis
Awdaghust	Awdaghust[59]	Sanhadja	10–11th century?	Mixed Arabs, Berbers
Wadi Draa	Dar'a/Tiymetin (Monteil thinks in region of Tagounite)	Banu Massufa	10–11th century?	Fleeting reference only

[53] Lewicki 1988, 281. [54] See Mattingly *et al.*, Chapter 5, this volume.
[55] See Sterry and Mattingly, Chapter 7, this volume. [56] See Capel, Chapter 16, this volume.
[57] Marquart 1913, lxxviii, cix–cxvi. [58] Mattingly *et al.* 2015.
[59] See Nixon, Chapter 17, this volume.

Table 19.1 (*cont.*)

Where	Capital	Who	When	Comments
Jarid and Jabal Nafusa (and parts outside the Sahara inc. Balearics)	Gabes, Jarid	Banu Ghaniya Offshoot of the Almoravids	Late 12th– early 13th century	Dynasty trying to establish stability in the eastern Maghrib
Air	Agadez	Tuareg?	14th century	
DMWShH (awdaghust?)	Awdaghust?	?	14th century	
Tadmakka	Tadmakka[60]	Ibadi	14th century	
Takadda	Takadda[61]	Tuareg?	14th century	
Karkari	Kahir			
Gobir	Marandet (and moving south)	Hausa	15th century	
Air	Agadez (1495)[62]	Tuareg	15th century onwards	Chronicle of Agadez
Timbuktu	Timbuktu		16th century	
Awlad Muhammad	Murzuq	Fazzani	16th century	
Ader	Tahoua area		17th century	

sway over the Aïr massif. The Fazzani states of the Banu Khattab (at Zuwila) and the Awlad Muhammad (at Murzuq) sit in between these models, both appear to have tried to exert control over the entirety of Fazzan, but the strength of this control seems to have been somewhat variable.

A third group comprises those polities that are described as more mobile – the Tuareg polities of Aïr, the Sanhadja of the Western Sahara (but particularly Adrar) although these may still have made use of towns. With populations likely to have been in the 10,000s rather than 100,000s or higher, the claims to statehood of all three groups is perhaps questionable to some readers. But these forms of polity appear to have been recurrent in the Sahara.

Nomads and Other Non-State Entities

There are two risks in focusing upon cities and states. First that we equate one with the other without critique; second, that we exclude all other types of

[60] See Nixon, Chapter 17, this volume. [61] See Nixon, Chapter 17, this volume.
[62] See Nixon, Chapter 17, this volume; Scheele, Chapter 18, this volume.

community and social organisation from debate. Hence we turn next to consider these other groups (and by inference, what was distinctive about Saharan states). Scheele demonstrates in her chapter how other types of network have existed across the Sahara such as the religious connections of the Senussi of the Eastern Sahara or the *zawiya* of Morocco.[63] In many ways these religious communities had much in common with what we might regard as states, but they lacked the formal bureaucracies or the territorial ambitions. Trading families provide a second major form of network. Letters and accounts preserved from the last centuries provide a particularly rich account of merchant families from Ghadamis in Libya, Timbuktu in Mali or Ighil in Morocco. Finally, nomads have always been a key characteristic of the Sahara, whether in the past or in more modern times able to build alliances and confederacies, but often without a permanent base.

Honeychurch has outlined four ways in which mobile pastoralists have coalesced into states:[64] by constructing their own complex political system, primarily involving nomadic populations as their constituents;[65] by integrating urban centres and trade into their networks and movements; by conquering sedentary polities; or by being subsumed by an expanding non-pastoralist state. He specifically suggests the Garamantes as an example of the second category of state formation.[66] While we can observe examples of all four within and around the Sahara, it is the first of these that is the least explored in the Sahara.

To identify such an entity we need to demonstrate the existence of a polity that was internally complex. The archaeological evidence for a wholly nomadic state is thin (although this is arguably due to a lack of exploration than necessarily a lack of evidence *per se*). Although the burial record of the Sahara points to a degree of hierarchy since *c*.3000 BC with the construction of a wide array of complex monuments and commemorations, these can hardly be taken to be the evidence of states. The ethnographies of the Tuareg indicate a great degree of social and political complexity, with slave owning, land and water rights and so forth, but there is again little evidence of more integrated political action. What might define them as a polity, according to Honeychurch, was their capacity to transform productive mobility into power and the control of space along with their involvement in long-distance trade.[67] We might conclude that,

[63] Scheele, Chapter 18, this volume. [64] Honeychurch 2014, especially 292–99.
[65] Cf. Emberling 2015 who proposes that Kush was a pastoral state – a state with significant mobility of population and for which herd animals were a source of wealth and symbolic capital. See also, Edwards, Chapter 9, this volume.
[66] Honeychurch 2014, 292–93. [67] Honeychurch 2014, 296–97.

though there was a capacity among such groups for statehood, this has only rarely occurred. The list of kings of the Sanhadja that appear to denote a polity is perhaps the only compelling example.

The polities based in Air and the Azawagh are more convincing as states. Here although there was a demonstrable urban centre for the different states, they differed from more traditional city states in that the political authority remained with a community that went to great lengths to express their nomadic heritage and practices. It is in this sense that the meeting of the Sultan of Takadda with Ibn Battuta should be viewed or the chronicles of Agadez. This drawing on nomadic values is not unique to the Sahara but can be found in many of the Medieval North African states in origin myths, as at Sijilmasa, or dynasties – Almoravids, Marinids. This latter category follows a pattern of a network of nomadic Berber groups becoming a military force, then conquering a swath of the Maghrib before settling and founding a new capital. It is striking that in the Medieval period the elite emphasised their nomadic roots in direct contrast with the elites of the classical period who focused upon farming and sedentism.[68]

In the opposite sense, though, a problem with the fixation on the reality of the nomad state is that it also ignores the contribution of sedentary communities in regions like the Sahara. The archaeological evidence from the Sahara suggests that sedentary oasis communities co-existed with the pastoral groups and that there were strong mutual interests in exchange and trade development to promote patterns of symbiotic co-existence and coalition, rather than continual competition and confrontation. Although the mobile pastoral groups are commonly considered to have been the more dominant militarily, this has not necessarily been the case throughout history.

Abandonment Versus Resilience

We have noted already that a characteristic of some of the Saharan urban centres has been their ephemeral nature. Although there are a few centres that have been proved resilient and long-lived (such as Ghadamis in western Libya), much more numerous are the instances where Saharan towns have flourished for a few generations (or at most a few centuries) and then been abandoned or shrunk back to a smaller size and functionally

[68] Groupe de recherches sur l'Afrique antique 1993, on the funerary monument of the Flavii at Kasserine, with its emphasis on the establishment of estates and viticulture close to the town.

less diverse status. The reasons for the seeming lack of resilience of many desert towns are varied, but readily comprehensible when their geographical, environmental and historical contexts are explored. Factors contributing to the abandonment of Saharan towns include:

- Collapse of political regime;
- Climate change or environmental deterioration (including hydrological difficulties);
- Changing trade routes;
- Conquest by external group;
- Religious change.

The same factors that contributed to the lack of resilience of Saharan towns have also impacted on early states in the region.

It also needs emphasizing that the different types of Saharan oasis and their varied hydrological resources and supports, as highlighted in the first section of this book, contributed to their different historical trajectories. At the simplest level, those with the most abundant and readily exploitable water sources had the potential to develop large populations. But equally, difficult and precarious water reserves could constrain development and precipitate decline. Even the existence of water did not guarantee success; trajectories of urbanisation and state formation were also impacted by factors like connectedness and trade.

What of the Garamantes?

Finally then, we return to the Garamantes. In a previous paper we suggested that Saharan cities should not be measured up against cities of the Mediterranean, Mesopotamia or Mesoamerica, but rather they should be seen primarily in comparison to other settlements within the Sahara.[69] Although these Saharan cities had a small population they were an order of magnitude larger than other villages and fortified farms around them, they contained craft specialists and had a particular economy and forms of authority related to conducting and supporting long-distance trade. A similar kind of argument could be made for Saharan states – these tended to be territorially small, mostly equivalent to city states dominating individual oasis groups, though sometimes with greater reach along networks of routes. Typically, they exhibit evidence of craft production and trade

[69] Mattingly and Sterry 2013.

connections, the organisation of labour and the promotion of individuals as rulers. But the question we wish to end on is whether the Garamantes fit into the different modes that we and our contributors have explored above and throughout this volume or if they are a different kind of entity altogether?

Political Complexity

The Roman sources provide some indications that the Garamantes were ruled by kings, not by chieftains.[70] This is important as the Roman writers tended not to overinflate the status of neighbouring rulers. When the term *rex* is used, it is generally reserved for rulers of polities or for individuals with a formal status of client king.[71] There is no reason to dismiss these references to kings as fanciful or meaningless. The conclusion is supported by the archaeological evidence from Jarma, where there are tombs that were an order of magnitude grander and more richly furnished than others in the area. The conclusion that these are burials of a small high elite group, perhaps focused on a royal dynasty or dynasties, is highly plausible.[72] Ptolemy indicates that the Garamantian kings on occasion campaigned far to the south of their core territory and that Ethiopian people were subject to their authority.[73] After supporting the ultimately unsuccessful Tacfarinan revolt against Rome in the reign of Tiberius, the Garamantes sent a deputation to Rome to plead their cause with the emperor and embassies were also sent in the reign of Augustus.[74] This shows not just a Garamantian self-evaluation of their importance, but also Roman recognition of the proper way to receive royal emissaries.

In terms of political complexity the Garamantes certainly have strong evidence of hierarchy, reflected in things like funeral monuments and of material consumption, but this inequality is also reflected in the differences between the capital Jarma, its hinterland, more distant parts of the Wadi al-Ajal and other parts of the Fazzan. Trade and conspicuous consumption of imported goods was evidently highly centralised as was the experimentation in building and funerary forms. Indeed this diversity in forms also seems to reflect a diversity of people in and around Jarma itself. In this sense Jarma appears very similar to many of the later Medieval trading towns of the Sahara – structurally locked into long distance trade networks and highly diverse.

[70] Historical references: Pliny, *Natural History* 8.142; Ptolemy, *Geography* 1.8; 1.11; Tacitus, *Annals* 4.23–26; Lucian *Dipsades* 2; Isidorus of Seville 9.11.125. Poetic: Virgil, *Aeneid* 4.198; Silius Italicus, *Punica* 2.58. For similar analytical conclusions, see also Liverani 2006a, 434; 2006b; 2007.

[71] See Braund 1984 on client kings.

[72] Ayoub 1967a; 1967b; Mattingly 2007, 140–44; 2010, 359–69; Mattingly *et al.* 2011.

[73] Ptolemy, *Geography* 1.8.

[74] Tacitus, *Annals* 4.26; Aurelius Victor, *de Caesaribus* 1.7.

Scale of Population

Roman sources describe the Garamantes as a great and numerous people (though the picture is partly obscured by the existence of strong stereotypical tropes in the ancient sources' depiction of the 'barbarian other').[75] Although individual settlements were quite small (typically 1–4 ha), this largely reflects the limiting factors of water availability and ease of access to land in excessive summer heat. In aggregate, Garamantian society appears large when modelled on the basis of hundreds of thousands of tombs or hundreds of settlements of village or larger scale. The extent of Garamantian settlement across Fazzan is extraordinary. Conservative estimates put the population of Fazzan in the region of 100–150,000 people in *c.*AD 1–300 compared to the *c.*25,000–35,000 people in the 1850s–1950s (just after the end of the Awlad Muhammad state and during the Ottoman and Italian colonial regimes).[76]

Territorial Scale of Kingdom

The large extent of Garamantian territory and hegemony is indicated by a number of factors. Tacitus records in the first century that Garamantian authority extended far to the north and they intervened in the civil discord between two of the coastal cities in AD 69, 1,000 km from Jarma.[77] A Roman visitor to Fazzan in the late first century AD accompanied a Garamantian king on a four-month journey (again arguably far in excess of 2,000 km) to the south of Fazzan, to a region of 'Aethiopia' where the rhinoceros was to be found.[78] We may also note the intensive development within Garamantian territory of hundreds of substantial settlements of intrinsically similar layout and appearance and investment in a labour-intensive irrigation regime.[79] The import of raw carnelian and amazonite for primary processing at Jarma from quarry sources located several hundred kilometres away is another factor indicating wide territorial control.[80]

[75] Herodotus, *Histories* 4.183; Dionysius Periegetes, *Description of the Known World* 217; Iulius Honorius, *Cosmographia* 47, 53, A48, 54 – all imply that Garamantes were one of major peoples of inland Africa. Liverani 2006a, 431–34; Mattingly 2011, 34–36 for discussion of the *topos* of the barbarian other.

[76] See Mattingly 2013a, 538–42, for the population modelling from archaeological data; Mattingly *et al.* 2015, for detailed summary relating to Zuwila.

[77] Tacitus, *Histories* 4.50 (Garamantes attacked lands and the city of Lepcis Magna).

[78] Ptolemy, *Geography* 1.8. [79] Mattingly 2013a, 530–34; Mattingly and Sterry 2013.

[80] Mattingly 2013a, 456–60.

Contrast between Jarma and Peripheral Settlements

The discussion in this volume highlights significant differences between the archaeology of the Garamantian heartlands and the peripheral zone near Ghat where Mario Liverani, Lucia Mori and the Italian mission have worked.[81] If Jarma has the look of a primate centre evoking a strong sense of social hierarchy, Fewet or Aghram Nadharif are much more standardised and homogenous settlements with little differentiation also in the burial monuments and grave good assemblages associated with them.[82] This seems to suggest the existence in the Tanzzuft of much more egalitarian communities. The difference between the Jarma area and what may well have been a peripheral territory allied to or subject to the Garamantian kingdom requires an explanation and for the moment the state model really does this best. As has been stated already, sedentary oasis settlement was more widely spread in the Sahara, but if we had more archaeological data for the pre-Islamic period we suspect that the picture would look more like the Tanzzuft than the Wadi al-Ajal. Again, we return to the exceptionality of the Garamantes and this needs further discussion.

Territorial State or City-State?

By the standards of the Nile Valley or the northern Maghrib, the achievements of the Garamantes may seem relatively minor. But thinking about this in emic terms highlights the extraordinary nature of their society in its Saharan context at this early date. Certainly this was a complex society, a polity or a state depending on the preferred nomenclature. But was it an early form of the type of polities that would subsequently form in the Medieval period? This question rests on the degree of integration across Fazzan. Historical parallels from other parts of the Sahara such as the Azawagh or the Wadi Righ would suggest that the urban centres of Jarma, Qasr ash-Sharraba and Zuwila most likely competed for trade, making Jarma the leading town at the time of Roman contact. In this model the territorial control of kings ruling from Jarma may have been quite weak, perhaps with more of a role as an arbitrator than a despot. Complexity would be as much horizontal – in the different familial and tribal networks linking groups of fortified oasis settlements and pastoral groups together – rather than hierarchical. If we follow this line of reasoning we

[81] Liverani 2006a; Mori 2013.

[82] The monumental grave of In Aghelachem is some 30 km distant and post-dates the main occupation of these settlements.

can see Jarma in a long line of trading towns with Sijilmassa, Tadmakka, Tagdaoust, Marandet, etc. However, we have also seen how the Medieval states of North Africa were structurally different to the Classical states. The scale of settlement and population in Fazzan outstrips anything seen anywhere in the Sahara, apart from the Egyptian Western Desert, until the modern period (at which point Fazzan was constituted as a province). The rugged geography and limited water sources of Fazzan have historically made territorial control difficult, but perhaps a larger mass of population helped to overcome these barriers. This would make the Garamantes a unique form of state in the history of the Sahara, but in archaeological terms they stand out dramatically. The evidence of trade goods is not the few imported vessel fragments found at Medieval trading towns, but that of thousands of amphora carried in by camel every year. In this model the closest parallel is the manner in which the oases of the Western Desert operated between the Persian and Roman periods. But instead of being a provincial expansion of a larger state beyond the Sahara, the Garamantes existed independently of any major empire.

A recurrent question throughout this chapter has been whether the Garamantes were a pastoralist dominated state – in the manner that oases have often been subservient to nomadic groups like the Tuareg in later times. The focus of wealth, power and material consumption at the Garamantian oasis centres is a strong argument in favour of the significance and autonomy of these sedentary populations. The widespread erection of fortified buildings at the heart of oasis settlements suggests a continued capacity for self-defence (but also perhaps a growing threat from pastoral groups). But the strict dichotomy between oasis dwellers and nomadic pastoralists may be misleading here. A key argument emerging from our work is that the Garamantes were a close amalgam of sedentary and pastoral groups, with their mutual interests sufficiently aligned to promote oasis development, trade and raiding across a broad expanse of the Central Sahara. Returning to Honeychurch's four models of nomadic state, this looks more akin to his third case of synthesis of pastoral and non-nomadic systems 'with long histories of integrated nomadic and sedentary sectors', rather than, as he argued, seeing the Garamantes as aligned with his secondary model of state structures emerging in a pastoral society through trade networks.[83]

[83] Honeychurch 2014, 292–93.

Changes in Urbanisation and State Formation

We conclude that there are several different types of state that have existed within and around the Sahara. Although there are many differences between these in terms of political complexity (and the degree of heterarchy or hierarchy), territoriality, demographic size, power and stability, we can identify recurring themes.

Firstly, the environment, the Sahara itself, played a major role in the establishment of states and their sustainability. At its most hostile it could spell the end of a state as aquifers dried up, rains failed or groundwater levels dropped to unreachable depths. But, we should be careful of thinking that these dramatic environmental events were the major drivers of change. Of the many different states discussed, it is notable how the same places appear again and again – the Fazzan, the Azawagh, southern Morocco, the Niger bend. It is the more subtle changes in the environment then that have characterised its effects, the increase in rains that brings a trading town within reach of a Sahelian state, the gradual drying up of a well far from any major oasis that limits the numbers of caravans that can pass in any year. In this sense, the Sahara desert is a dynamic player, always in flux, changing the terms on which each state is built from year to year. At all times, the states that we have been examining were both affected by and in turn affected their environment. Equilibrium is a characteristic that has generally been absent from the states of the Sahara.

Resilience is the second major theme, or its lack thereof. Few of the states that engaged with the Sahara were long-lived, many had a powerful leader who established the state followed by a dynasty that desperately tried to hang on to power as circumstances changed outside their control. The most resilient states were often the most flexible and the smallest – city states such as the Banu Khattab of Zuwila. But there were far more resilient systems in the Sahara than state networks or even urban networks. The mercantile ties of Ghadamis endured for centuries linking places as far flung as Timbuktu, Bornu and Tripoli and resisting the imperial ambitions of territorial states until the nineteenth century. In so doing, the Ghadamensi remained flexible enough to reconfigure their networks so that the city remained a key node in Trans-Saharan trade even as other states grew and fell, while also managing their delicate but essential relationship with their Tuareg partners, so as to maintain the independence of the sedentary population from would-be nomadic overlords.

The third theme revolves around trade and networks. The continuing success of a state relied on the success of states around it. A disruption in one part of the network could have far-reaching consequences elsewhere in the network. The notion of the western, central and eastern north–south routes across the Sahara can cloud the complexities and interconnectedness across the Sahara.

A fourth theme of the volume has been the inter-relationships between sedentary and pastoral populations. A key contribution of this volume has been to open up debate on the extent of pre-Islamic sedentarism, urbanisation and state formation in the Saharan region. We hope to have demonstrated impressive evidence of the spread of oasis cultivation and the growth of agglomerated settlement, with the most spectacular instance represented by the Garamantes meriting recognition as a precocious territorial state. Pastoral groups undoubtedly played an important role in Garamantian military and trading success, but what is most striking about the archaeological record of this kingdom is the extent to which its wealth seems to have been founded on and invested in and around oasis communities. In later times, it is more difficult to perceive sedentary communities having the whip hand in the 'symbiotic' relations with mobile groups. The camel may have been a key element in redefining the relationships and the relative balance of power between sedentary communities and pastoralists in the Sahara. Camels had already been around for several centuries, when its importance started to increase in Late Antiquity. However, the enlargement of the long-range networks of routes into the Western Sahara and the falling water table beneath much of the Sahara meant that longer stages between major water points became more common, making the camel increasingly indispensable, thus strengthening the hand of pastoral elements within Saharan communities.[84]

Finally, we want to highlight the chronological complexity that is emerging from recent studies. The radiocarbon date lists we have assembled demonstrate the potential to assemble more detailed historical models. The methods for dating mudbrick and *pisé* architecture advocated in this book have been shown to be effective and remarkably consistent in the chronological indications. The challenge now will be to augment the date list in a systematic manner, to include more of the key, but as yet undated cities of the Sahara. There is also a clear need for more stratified excavations that penetrate to the natural subsoil beneath oasis towns, to assess the ultimate origins of such sites. This may look

[84] Mattingly *et al.* forthcoming.

a forlorn prospect in the current political situation, with most of the Sahara archaeologically off-limits for foreign missions and also difficult to access for local archaeologists. We hope that the long-term legacy of this book will be an expansion of work on Saharan historical settlement and society whenever conditions allow.

References

Ayoub, M.S. 1967a. *Excavations in Germa Between 1962 and 1966.* Tripoli: Ministry of Education.

Ayoub, M.S. 1967b. The Royal cemetery at Germa. A preliminary report. *Libya Antiqua* 3–4: 213–19.

Berggren, J.A. and Jones, A. 2000. *Ptolemy's Geography. An Annotated Translation of the Theoretical Chapters.* Princeton: Princeton University Press.

Bowman, A. and Wilson, A. (eds). 2011. *Settlement, Urbanization, and Population.* Oxford: Oxford University Press.

Braund, D. 1984. *Rome and the Friendly King.* London: Duckworth.

Clark, P. (ed.). 2013. *The Oxford Handbook of Cities in World History.* Oxford: Oxford University Press.

Desanges, J. 1980. *(Pline l'ancien) Histoire naturelle Livre V.1–46 (L'Afrique du nord).* Paris: Persée.

Duckworth, C., Cuénod, A., and Mattingly, D.J. (eds). Forthcoming. *Mobile Technologies in the Ancient Sahara and Beyond.* Trans-Saharan Archaeology Volume IV. Series editor D.J. Mattingly. Cambridge: Cambridge University Press and The Society for Libyan Studies.

Emberling, G. 2015. Pastoral states: Toward a comparative archaeology of early Kush. *Origini XXXVI: Preistoria e protostoria delle civiltà antiche/Prehistory and Protohistory of Ancient Civilizations*: Rome: Sapienza Università di Roma, 125–56.

Fauvelle, F.-X. 2018. *The Golden Rhinoceros. Histories of the African Middle Ages.* Princeton: Princeton University Press.

Fentress, E. 2011. Slavers on chariots. In A. Dowler and E.R. Galvin (eds), *Money, Trade and Trade Routes in Pre-Islamic North Africa.* London: British Museum Press, 64–71.

Ferguson, N. and Whitehead, N. (eds). 1992. *War in the Tribal Zone: Expanding States and Indigenous Warfare.* Santa Fe: School for American Research.

Fernández-Götz, M. and Krausse, D. 2013. Rethinking early Iron Age urbanisation in Central Europe: The Heuneberg site and its archaeological environment. *Antiquity* 87.336: 473–87.

Fernández-Götz, M. and Krausse, D. 2017. *Eurasia at the Dawn of History. Urbanization and Social Change.* Cambridge: Cambridge University Press.

Flannery, K. and Marcus, J. 2012. *The Creation of Inequality. How Our Prehistoric Ancestors Set the Stage for Monarchy, Slavery and Empire*. Cambridge, MA: Harvard University Press.

Gronenborn, D. 2013. States and trade in the Central Sahel. In Mitchell and Lane 2013, 845–58.

Groupe de recherches sur l'Afrique antique. 1993. *Les Flavii de Cillium. Étude architecturale, épigraphique, historique et littéraire du mausolée de Kasserine (CIL VIII, 211–216)*. Rome: Collection de l'École Française de Rome, 169.

Hansen, M. (ed.). 2000. *A Comparative Study of Thirty City-State Cultures*. Copenhagen: Reitzels.

Hansen, M. 2002. *A Comparative Study of Six City-State Cultures*. Copenhagen: Reitzels.

Hobson, M. 2015. *The North African Boom: Evaluating Economic Growth in the Roman Province of Africa Proconsularis*. Portsmouth, Rhode Island: Journal of Roman Archaeology Supplementary.

Honeychurch, W. 2014. Alternative complexities: The archaeology of pastoral nomadic states. *Journal of Archaeological Research* 22.4: 277–326.

Jennings, J. and Earle, T. 2016. Urbanization, state formation and co-operation. A reappraisal. *Current Anthropology* 57.4: 474–93.

Law, R. 1992. Warfare on the West African Slave Coast 1650–1850. In Ferguson and Whitehead 1992, 103–26.

Lewicki, T. 1988. The role of the Sahara and Saharians in relationships between north and south. In M. El Fasi (ed.), *General History of Africa III: Africa from the Seventh to the Eleventh Century*. London: James Currey/UNESCO, 146–62.

Liverani, M. (ed.). 2006a. *Aghram Nadharif. The Barkat Oasis (Sha'abiya of Ghat, Libyan Sahara) in Garamantian Times*. Firenze: All'Insegna del Giglio.

Liverani, M. 2006b. Imperialismo, colonizzazione e progresso technico: Il caso del Sahara libico in eta romana. *Studi Storici* 4: 1003–57.

Liverani, M. 2007. La struttura sociale dei Garamanti in base alle recenti scoperte archaelogiche. *Rendiconti dell'Accademia Nazionale dei Lincei* Ser 9.18: 155–204.

Lugan, B. 2000. *Histoire du Maroc des origenes à nos jours*. Saint-Amand-Montrond: Perrin.

MacDonald, K. 2013. Complex societies, urbanism and trade in the western Sahel. In Mitchell and Lane 2013, 829–44.

McIntosh, R. 2005. *Ancient Middle Niger: Urbanism and the Self-Organizing Landscape*. Cambridge: Cambridge University Press.

McIntosh, R. 2015. Different cities: Jenné-jeno and African urbanism. In *The Cambridge World History: Volume 3, Early Cities in Comparative Perspective, 4000 BCE–1200 CE*. Cambridge: Cambridge University Press, 364–80.

McIntosh, S. 1999. *Beyond Chiefdoms: Pathways to Complexity in Africa*. Cambridge: Cambridge University Press.

Marcus, J. and Sabloff, J.A. (eds). 2008. *The Ancient City: New Perspectives on Urbanism in the Old and New World*. Santa Fe: School for Advanced Research Press.

Marquart, M. 1913. *Die Benin-Sammlung des Reichsmuseums für Völkerkunde in Leiden*. Leiden: Brill.

Mattingly, D.J. 2003. *The Archaeology of Fazzan, Volume 1, Synthesis*. London: The Society for Libyan Studies.

Mattingly, D.J. 2007. *The Archaeology of Fazzan, Volume 2. Site Gazetteer, Pottery and Other Finds*. London: The Society for Libyan Studies.

Mattingly, D.J. 2010. The *Archaeology of Fazzan. Volume 3, Excavations Carried out by C.M. Daniels*. London: The Society for Libyan Studies.

Mattingly, D.J. 2011. *Imperialism, Power and Identity. Experiencing the Roman Empire*. Princeton: Princeton University Press.

Mattingly, D.J. 2013a. *The Archaeology of Fazzan, Volume 4. Survey and Excavations at Old Jarma (Ancient Garama) Carried out by C.M. Daniels (1962–69) and the Fazzan Project (1997–2001)*. London: The Society for Libyan Studies.

Mattingly, D.J. 2013b. To south and north: Saharan trade in antiquity. In H. Eckardt and S. Rippon (eds), *Living and Working in the Roman World*. Portsmouth, RI: JRA Supplementary, 169–90.

Mattingly, D.J. 2016. Who shaped Africa? The origins of agriculture and urbanism in Maghreb and Sahara. In N. Mugnai, J. Nikolaus and N. Ray (eds), *De Africa Romaque. Merging Cultures across North Africa*. London: The Society for Libyan Studies, 11–25.

Mattingly, D.J. and MacDonald, K. 2013. Early cities: Africa. In Clark 2013, 66–82.

Mattingly, D.J. and Sterry, M. 2013. The first towns in the Central Sahara. *Antiquity* 87.366: 503–18.

Mattingly, D.J., Abduli, H., Ahmed, M., Cole, F., Fenwick, C., Fothergill, B.T., Gonzalez Rodriguez, M., Hobson, M., Khalaf, N., Lahr, M., Moussa, F., Nikita, E., Nikolaus, J., Radini, A., Ray, N., Savage, T., Sterry, M. and Wilson, A. I. 2011. DMP XII: excavations and survey of the so-called Garamantian Royal Cemetery (GSC030–031). *Libyan Studies* 42: 89–102.

Mattingly, D.J., Sterry, M. and Edwards, D. 2015. The origins and development of Zuwīla, Libyan Sahara: an archaeological and historical overview. *Azania* 50.1: 27–75.

Mattingly, D.J., Leitch, V., Duckworth, C.N., Cuénod, A., Sterry, M. and Cole, F. (eds). 2017. *Trade in the Ancient Sahara and Beyond*. Trans-Saharan Archaeology Volume I. Series editor D.J. Mattingly. Cambridge: Cambridge University Press.

Mattingly, D.J., Sterry, M. and Fothergill, B.T. Forthcoming. Animal traffic in the Sahara. In V. Blanc-Bijon (ed.), *XIe Colloque international Histoire et Archéologie de l'Afrique du Nord*. Marseille: Presses universitaires de Provence.

Mitchell, P. and Lane, P. 2013. *The Oxford Handbook of African Archaeology*. Oxford: Oxford University Press.

Monroe, J.C. 2013. The archaeology of the precolonial state in Africa. In Mitchell and Lane 2013, 702–22.

Mori L. (ed.). 2013. *Life and Death of a Rural Village in Garamantian Times. The Archaeological Research in the Oasis of Fewet (Libyan Sahara)*, AZA Monographs 6. Firenze:All'Insegna del Giglio.

Moussa, F.K. 2013. Berber, Phoenicio-Punic and Greek North Africa. In Mitchell and Lane 2013, 765–76.

Osborne, R. and Cunliffe, B. (eds). 2005. *Mediterranean Urbanization 800–600 BC*. Oxford: Oxford University Press.

Parkinson, W.A. and Galaty, M.L., 2007. Secondary states in perspective: An integrated approach to state formation in the prehistoric Aegean. *American Anthropologist* 109.1: 113–29.

Pelling, R. 2013a. The archaeobotanical remains. In Mattingly 2013a, 473–94.

Pelling, R. 2013b. Botanical data appendices. In Mattingly 2013a, 841–52.

Phillipson, D.W. 2013. Complex societies of the Eritrean/Ethiopian highlands and their neighbours. In Mitchell and Lane 2013, 799–815.

Price, B.J. 1978. Secondary state formation: an explanatory model. In R. Cohen and E. Service (eds), *Origins of the State: The Anthropology of Political Evolution*. Philadelphia: Institute for the Study of Human Issues, 161–86.

Schrüfer-Kolb, I. 2007. Metallurgical and non-metallurgical industrial activities. In Mattingly 2007, 448–62.

Shaw, I. 2013. Pharaonic Egypt. In Mitchell and Lane 2013, 737–50.

Smith, M.E. 2017. How can archaeologists identify early cities: definitions, types, and attributes. In Fernández-Götz and Krausse 2017, 153–68.

Trigger, B. 2003. *Understanding Early Civilizations: A Comparative Study*. Cambridge: Cambridge University Press.

Welsby, D. 2013. Kerma and Kush and their neighbours. In Mitchell and Lane 2013, 751–64.

Whitehead, N. 1992. Tribes make states and states make tribes: Warfare and the creation of colonial tribes and states in northeastern South America. In Ferguson and Whitehead 1992, 127–50.

Wilson, A.I. 2012. Saharan trade: Short-, medium- and long-distance trade networks in the Roman period. *Azania: Archaeological Research in Africa* 47.4: 409–49.

Yoffee, N. 2005. *Myths of the Archaic State: Evolution of the Earliest Cities, States and Civilizations*. Cambridge: Cambridge University Press.

Index

[Page numbers in italics are figures; with 't' are tables; with 'n' are notes.]